Saudi Arabia Capital Markets Law

edited by

Michael O'Kane

ANDALUS PUBLISHING

Andalus Publishing 2022

Saudi Arabia Capital Markets Law

ISBN: 978-1-945979-21-7
ePub: 978-1-945979-22-4

Contents

Introduction 3

1 Glossary of Defined Terms 5

2 AMENDED SECURITIES BUSINESS REGULATIONS 27
2.1 PART 1: GENERAL PROVISIONS . . . 27
2.1.1 Article 1: Definitions . . . 27
2.2 PART 2: THE SECURITIES BUSINESS . . . 27
2.2.1 Chapter One: Carrying on Securities Business . . . 27
2.2.2 Chapter Two: Exclusions from Authorization . . . 28
2.3 PART 3: SECURITIES ADVERTISEMENTS . . . 29
2.4 PART 4: PUBLICATION AND ENTRY INTO FORCE . . . 29
2.5 ANNEX 1: EXEMPT PERSONS . . . 29

3 ANTI-MONEY LAUNDERING AND COUNTER-TERRORIST FINANCING RULES 31
3.1 PART 1 GENERAL PROVISIONS . . . 31
3.2 PART 2 GENERAL APPLICATION OF AML/CTF REQUIREMENTS . . . 32
3.3 PART 3 CUSTOMER DUE DILIGENCE . . . 33
3.4 PART 4 RECORD KEEPING . . . 36
3.5 PART 5 SUSPICIOUS TRANSACTION REPORT . . . 37
3.6 PART 6 INTERNAL POLICIES, PROCEDURES AND CONTROLSnternal Policies, Procedures and Controls . . . 38
3.7 PART 7 CLOSING PROVISIONS . . . 39
3.8 Annex 1 Securities Business Indicators for Money Laundering or Terrorist Financing . . . 39

4 AUTHORIZED PERSONS REGULATIONS 41
4.1 PART 1: GENERAL PROVISIONS . . . 42
4.2 PART 2: THE PRINCIPLES FOR AUTHORIZED PERSONS . . . 42
4.3 PART 3: AUTHORIZATION . . . 43
4.3.1 Chapter One – Applications for Authorization . . . 43
4.3.2 Chapter Two – Maintenance of Authorization . . . 44
4.4 ANNEX 3.1 INFORMATION AND DOCUMENTS REQUIRED FOR AUTHORIZATION . . . 46
4.5 ANNEX 3.2 NOTIFICATION REQUIREMENTS . . . 47
4.6 PART 4: REGISTERED PERSONS . . . 48
4.6.1 Chapter One - Background and scope . . . 48
4.6.2 Chapter Two - Registration . . . 49
4.6.3 Chapter Three - General Provisions . . . 49
4.7 PART 5: CONDUCT OF BUSINESS . . . 50
4.7.1 Chapter One: General Provisions . . . 50
4.7.2 Chapter Two - Securities Advertisements . . . 50
4.7.3 Chapter Three - Accepting Clients . . . 51
4.7.4 Chapter Four - Client Relations . . . 51
4.7.5 Chapter Five - Reporting to Clients . . . 53
4.7.6 Chapter Six – Miscellaneous . . . 53
4.8 ANNEX 5.1 CONTENTS REQUIREMENTS FOR SECURITIES ADVERTISEMENTS . . . 54
4.9 ANNEX 5.2 TERMS OF BUSINESS REQUIREMENTS . . . 55
4.10 ANNEX 5.3 KNOW YOUR CUSTOMER FORM . . . 56
4.11 ANNEX 5.4 FIDUCIARY DUTIES . . . 57
4.12 ANNEX 5.5 REQUIRED CONTENTS OF CONTRACT NOTES . . . 58
4.13 ANNEX 5.6 REQUIRED CONTENTS OF PERIODIC VALUATION STATEMENTS FOR CLIENT PORTFOLIOS 58
4.14 ANNEX 5.7 PERSONAL ACCOUNT DEALING . . . 59
4.15 MODEL UNDERTAKING . . . 60
4.16 PART 6: SYSTEMS AND CONTROLS . . . 60
4.16.1 Chapter One – Scope of Application . . . 60
4.16.2 Chapter Two – Management Arrangements . . . 60
4.17 Part 7: Client Money and Assets . . . 62
4.17.1 Chapter One – General Provisions . . . 62
4.17.2 Chapter Two – Client Money Rules . . . 62
4.17.3 Chapter Three – Client Asset Rules . . . 64
4.17.4 Chapter Four – Collateral and Money and Assets Passed to Third Parties . . . 66

4.18 PART 8: INSOLVENCY PROVISIONS . . . 67
4.19 PART 9: PUBLICATION AND ENTRY INTO FORCE . . . 67

5 CAPITAL MARKET INSTITUTIONS REGULATIONS 69
5.1 PART 1: GENERAL PROVISIONS . . . 70
5.2 PART 2: PRINCIPLES FOR CAPITAL MARKET INSTITUTIONS . . . 70
5.3 PART 3: AUTHORIZATION . . . 71
5.3.1 Chapter One Applications for Authorization . . . 71
5.3.2 Chapter Two – Maintenance of Authorization . . . 72
5.4 ANNEX 3.1 Information and Documents Required for Authorization and Commencement of Business . . . 74
5.5 ANNEX 3.2 Notification Requirements . . . 75
5.6 PART 4: REGISTERED PERSONS . . . 76
5.6.1 Chapter One - Background and Scope . . . 76
5.6.2 Chapter Two – Registration . . . 77
5.6.3 Chapter Three – General Provisions . . . 78
5.7 PART 5: CONDUCT OF BUSINESS . . . 78
5.7.1 Chapter One: General Provisions . . . 78
5.7.2 Chapter Two – Securities Advertisements . . . 79
5.7.3 Chapter Three – Accepting Clients . . . 80
5.7.4 Chapter Four - Client Relations . . . 80
5.7.5 Chapter Five - Reporting to Clients . . . 83
5.7.6 Chapter Six - Miscellaneous . . . 83
5.8 ANNEX 5.1 CONTENTS REQUIREMENTS FOR SECURITIES ADVERTISEMENTS . . . 84
5.9 ANNEX 5.2 TERMS OF BUSINESS REQUIREMENTS . . . 85
5.10 ANNEX 5.3 (A) KNOW YOUR CLIENT FORM . . . 86
5.11 ANNEX 5.3 (B) INVESTMENT INFORMATION FORM . . . 87
5.12 ANNEX 5.4 FIDUCIARY DUTIES . . . 88
5.13 ANNEX 5.5 REQUIRED CONTENTS OF CONTRACT NOTES . . . 88
5.14 ANNEX 5.6 REQUIRED CONTENTS OF PERIODIC VALUATION STATEMENTS FOR CLIENT PORTFOLIOS 88
5.15 ANNEX 5.7 PERSONAL ACCOUNT DEALING . . . 89
5.16 PART 6: SYSTEMS AND CONTROLS . . . 90
5.16.1 Chapter One – Scope of Application . . . 90
5.16.2 Chapter Two – Management Arrangements . . . 90
5.16.3 Chapter Three – Systems and Controls . . . 91
5.17 ANNEX 6.1 – REQUIRED CONTENTS OF THE BOARD OF DIRECTORS' REPORT . . . 93
5.18 Part 7: Client Money and Assets . . . 94
5.18.1 Chapter One – General Provisions . . . 94
5.18.2 Chapter Two – Client Money Rules . . . 94
5.18.3 Chapter Three – Client Asset Rules . . . 96
5.18.4 Chapter Four – Collateral and Money and Assets Passed to Third Parties . . . 98
5.19 PART 8: INSOLVENCY PROVISIONS . . . 99
5.20 PART 9: PUBLICATION AND ENTRY INTO FORCE . . . 100

6 Capital Markets Law 101
6.0.1 Chapter 1: Definitions . . . 101
6.0.2 Chapter 2: The Capital Market Authority . . . 101
6.0.3 Chapter Three – The Stock Exchange . . . 104
6.0.4 Chapter Four – The Securities Depositary Center . . . 105
6.0.5 Chapter Five – Brokers Regulation . . . 106
6.0.6 Chapter Six: Investment Funds and Collective Investment Schemes . . . 107
6.0.7 Chapter Seven – Disclosure [Prospectus] . . . 107
6.0.8 Chapter Eight Manipulation and Insider Trading . . . 109
6.0.9 Chapter Nine – Regulation of Proxy Solicitations, Restricted Purchase and Restricted Offer for Shares . . 109
6.0.10 Chapter Ten – Sanctions and Penalties for Violations . . . 110

7 Corporate Governance Regulations 113
7.1 PART 1: PRELIMINARY PROVISIONS . . . 114
7.2 Part 2: RIGHTS OF SHAREHOLDERS . . . 115
7.2.1 Chapter 1: General Rights . . . 115
7.2.2 Chapter 2: Rights Related to the Meeting of the General Assembly . . . 116
7.3 PART 3: BOARD OF DIRECTORS . . . 118
7.3.1 Chapter 1: Formation of the Board . . . 118
7.3.2 Chapter 2: Responsibilities and Competencies of the Board . . . 119
7.3.3 Chapter 3: Competencies of the Chairman and the Board Members . . . 121
7.3.4 Chapter 4: Board Meeting Procedures . . . 123
7.3.5 Chapter 5: Training, Support and Assessment . . . 124

7.3.6 Chapter 6: Conflicts of Interest . . . 124
7.4 PART 4: COMPANY COMMITTEES . . . 126
7.4.1 Chapter 1: General Provisions . . . 126
7.4.2 Chapter 2: The Audit Committee . . . 126
7.4.3 Chapter 3: Remuneration Committee . . . 127
7.4.4 Chapter 4: Nomination Committee . . . 128
7.4.5 Chapter 5: Risk Management Committee . . . 129
7.5 PART 5: INTERNAL CONTROL . . . 129
7.6 PART 6: COMPANY AUDITOR . . . 130
7.7 PART 7: STAKEHOLDERS . . . 130
7.8 PART 8: PROFESSIONAL AND ETHICAL STANDARDSrofessional and Ethical . . . 131
7.9 PART 9: DISCLOSURE AND TRANSPARENCY . . . 131
7.10 Part 10: IMPLEMENTATION . . . 134
7.11 Part 11: DOCUMENT RETENTION . . . 134
7.12 Part 12: CLOSING PROVISIONS . . . 134
7.13 APPENDIX 1: Remuneration Schedule . . . 134
7.14 APPENDIX 2: Committee Members Remuneration . . . 135

8 CREDIT RATING AGENCIES REGULATIONS 137
8.1 PART 1: PURPOSE AND SCOPE . . . 137
8.2 PART 2: AUTHORIZATION AND MAINTENANCE OF AUTHORIZATION . . . 138
8.3 PART 3: CONDUCT OF BUSINESS REQUIREMENTS . . . 139
8.4 PART 4: SYSTEM AND CONTROLS . . . 142
8.5 PART 5: REGISTERED PERSONS . . . 146
8.6 PART 6: CLOSING PROVISIONS . . . 148
8.7 ANNEX 1: INFORMATION AND DOCUMENTS REQUIRED FOR AUTHORIZATION APPLICATION . . . 148
8.8 ANNEX 2: STANDARD FORM CREDIT RATING DISCLOSURE . . . 149

9 Depository Centre Procedures 151
9.1 Section 1: Preliminary Provisions . . . 151
9.1.1 1. Provisions and Definition . . . 151
9.1.2 2. Conditions for Depository Centre Membership . . . 151
9.1.3 3. Membership approval and Activation . . . 151
9.1.4 4. Fees, Payment and Invoice . . . 151
9.1.5 5. Notices . . . 152
9.2 Section 2: Accounts Structure and Types . . . 152
9.2.1 6. Depository Centre Accounts . . . 152
9.2.2 7. Special Accounts . . . 152
9.2.3 8. Account Attributes . . . 152
9.3 Section 3: Investors . . . 153
9.3.1 9. Investors Identification . . . 153
9.3.2 10.Investor Types and Identification Mechanism . . . 153
9.4 Section 4: Cash Payments and Cash Accounts . . . 153
9.4.1 11.Cash Payment . . . 153
9.4.2 12.Cash Accounts . . . 153
9.4.3 13.Settlement agreements and Cash Settlement Headroom . . . 154
9.4.4 14.Cash Settlement . . . 154
9.5 Section 5: Settlement Instructions . . . 154
9.5.1 15.Settlement Instructions . . . 154
9.5.2 16.Holding Settlement . . . 156
9.5.3 17.Releasing Settlement . . . 156
9.5.4 18.Request to Cancel . . . 156
9.5.5 19.Settlement Instructions Cancellation by The Depository Centre . . . 156
9.5.6 20.Settlement Instructions Amendments . . . 156
9.5.7 21.Priority of Settlement Instructions . . . 156
9.5.8 22.Partial Settlement . . . 156
9.6 Section 6: Settlement . . . 157
9.6.1 23.Settlement . . . 157
9.6.2 24.Free of Payment (FoP) Settlement . . . 157
9.6.3 25.Delivery versus Payment Settlement . . . 157
9.7 Section 7: CCP Settlement . . . 157
9.7.1 26.Settlement related to CCP . . . 157
9.8 Section 8: Securities Transfers . . . 157
9.8.1 27.Transfer of Securities . . . 157
9.8.2 28.Murabaha . . . 157
9.8.3 29.Collateral transfers . . . 157

9.8.4 30.Unlisted Securities Transfers . . . 157
9.8.5 31.Transfer of Foreign Securities . . . 157
9.9 Section 9: Pledge . . . 158
9.9.1 32. Pledge . . . 158
9.10 Section 10: Restrictions . . . 158
9.10.1 33. Restrictions . . . 158
9.11 Section 11: Corporate actions . . . 158
9.11.1 34.Corporate action Activities and Dates . . . 158
9.11.2 35.Corporate Action Event and Entitlement . . . 158
9.11.3 36.Aggregation of Fractions . . . 158
9.11.4 37.Capital Reductions . . . 158
9.11.5 38.Bonus Shares Issuance and Capital Reductions . . . 158
9.11.6 39.Tradable Rights . . . 158
9.11.7 40.Claims . . . 158
9.11.8 41.Transformation of settlement instructions . . . 158
9.11.9 42. SBL Agreement . . . 159
9.11.10 43.Corporate Actions Activities on Foreign Securities Listed on The Exchange . . . 159
9.12 Section 12: Securities Borrowing and Lending (SBL) . . . 159
9.12.1 44. SBL Registration . . . 159
9.12.2 45.Collateral . . . 159
9.12.3 46.Loan Return . . . 159
9.13 Section 13: Reconciliation . . . 159
9.13.1 47.Reporting and Reconciliation . . . 159

10 Depositary Receipts 161
10.1 Part 1: Preliminary . . . 161
10.2 Part 2: Definitions . . . 161
10.3 Part 3: Waivers . . . 161
10.4 Part 4: General Provisions . . . 161
10.5 Part 5: Authority's Approval for Issuing Depositary Receipts out of the Kingdom . . . 162
10.6 Part 6: Issuer's Obligations . . . 162
10.7 Part 7: Depositary Bank's Obligations . . . 162
10.8 Part 8: Capital Market Institution's Obligations . . . 163
10.9 Part 9: Investment Limits . . . 163
10.10 Part 10: Authority's Powers in Relation to the Depositary Bank . . . 163
10.11 Part 11: Publication and Entry into Force . . . 163
10.12 Annex: Required Information and Documents to Apply for the Authority's Approval for Issuing Depositary Receipts out of the Kingdom . . . 164

11 Direct Financing Investment Funds 165

12 Fintech 167
12.1 PART A OVERVIEW . . . 167
12.2 PART B: FINTECH REQUIREMENTS . . . 168
12.3 APPENDIX A: APPLICATION PROCESS . . . 169
12.4 APPENDIX B: APPLICATION TEMPLATE . . . 169

13 Foreign Strategic Ownership 173
13.1 Part 1: Preliminary . . . 173
13.2 Part 2: Definitions . . . 173
13.3 Part 3: Waivers . . . 173
13.4 Part 4: Right to Appeal . . . 173
13.5 Part 5: Requirements for the Foreign Strategic Investor Ownership of Strategic Shareholdings . . . 173
13.6 Part 6: Investment Limits . . . 174
13.7 Part 7: Publication and Entry into Force . . . 174

14 Foreign Depositary Receipts 175
14.1 ANNEX: DEPOSITARY RECEIPTS REQUIREMENTS . . . 177

15 Companies Announcements 179
15.1 Introduction . . . 180
15.2 General Instructions . . . 181
15.3 Financial Results Announcements . . . 182
15.4 Announcement Form for the Interim and Annual Financial Result . . . 183
15.4.1 (1) Announcement Form for Annual Financial Results for Companies except Banks and Insurance Companies 183
15.4.2 (2) Announcement Form for Interim Financial Results for Companies except Banks and Insurance Companies 183
15.4.3 (3) Announcement Form for Annual Financial Results for Banks . . . 184

15.4.4 (4) Announcement Form for Interim Financial Results for Banks 184
15.4.5 (5) Announcement Form for Annual Financial Results for Insurance Companies 185
15.4.6 (6) Announcement Form for Interim Financial Results for Insurance Companies 185
15.5 Administrative Changes 186
15.5.1 (1) Announcement Form for the Nomination for Board of Directors Membership 186
15.5.2 (2) Announcement Form for the Resignation of a Board Member 187
15.5.3 (3) Announcement Form for the Appointment of a New Board Member 187
15.5.4 (4) Announcement Form for the Resignation of a Board Member and the Appointment of a New Board Member 187
15.5.5 (5) Announcement Form for the Resignation of the Chief Executive Officer of the Company 187
15.5.6 (6) Announcement Form for the Appointment of a New Chief Executive Officer for the Company 187
15.5.7 (7) Announcement Form for the Resignation of the Chief Executive Officer and the Appointment\Delegation of a New Chief Executive Officer for the Company 187
15.5.8 (8) Announcement Form for the Resignation of an Audit Committee Member 188
15.5.9 (9) Announcement Form for the Appointment of an Audit Committee Member 188
15.6 Instructions for Companies Announcements Regarding Capital Alternation 188
15.6.1 (1) Offering Rights Issue Shares 188
15.6.2 (1) Announcement Form for Board's Recommendation for Capital Increase by Offering Rights Issue 188
15.6.3 (2) Announcement Form for the Appointment of a Financial Advisor to Manage the Subscription in the Rights Issue 188
15.6.4 (3) Announcement Form for Submitting an Application File for Capital Increase by Offering Rights Issue to the Capital Market Authority for Approval 188
15.6.5 (4) Announcement Form for Material Developments Regarding the Application File for Capital Increase by Offering Rights IssueSubmitted to the Capital Market Authority. 189
15.6.6 (5) Announcement Form for Determining the Period for Rights Issue Trading and Subscriptions in the New Shares. 189
15.6.7 (6) Reminder Announcement Form for the Start of the Period for Rights Issue Trading and Subscriptions in the New Shares. 189
15.6.8 (7) Reminder Announcement Form for the Last Day for Trading Rights Issue and the Last Day for Subscriptions in the New Shares 189
15.6.9 (8) Announcement Form for the Process Details of the Sale of the Un-Subscribed Shares and the Start of the Offering Stage, in Addition to the Results of Trading Rights Issue and Subscription in the New Shares. 190
15.6.10 (9) Announcement Form for Rump Offering Results and the Allocation of the Rights Issue shares. 190
15.6.11 (10) Announcement Form for the Distribution of Compensations (if any) among Rights Issue Holders Who Did Not Exercise Their Right of Subscribing in the New Shares 190
15.6.12 (11) Announcement Form for the Deviation of 5% or more between the Actual Usage of the Proceeds of Issuing Rights Issue than What Has Been Disclosed in the Prospectus 190
15.6.13 Second: Bonus Shares (1) Announcement Form for Board's Recommendation for Capital Increase by way of Issuing Bonus Shares 190
15.6.14 (2) Announcement Form for the Completion of Shares Fractions Sale (if any) and Distribution of the Sale Proceeds among Eligible Shareholders 191
15.6.15 (3) Announcement Form for the Non-Completion of Shares Fractions Sale (if any) and Distribution of the Sales Proceeds Amount among Eligible Shareholders within the Specified Period 191
15.6.16 Third: Capital Reduction. (1) Announcement Form for the Board's Recommendations of Any Suggested Company's Capital Reduction 191
15.6.17 (2) Announcement Form for the Appointment of a Financial Advisor for Capital Reduction 191
15.6.18 (3) Announcement Form for Submitting an Application File for Capital Reduction to the Authority to Obtain Its Approval 191
15.6.19 (4) Announcement Form for Material Developments on the Application File for Capital Reduction Submitted to the Authority. 192
15.6.20 SAMA's (Saudi Arabian Monetary Authority) Approval on Insurance Products 197
15.6.21 Addendum and Corrective Announcement (1) Addendum Announcement Form 197
15.6.22 (2) Corrective Announcement Form 197
15.6.23 Instruction for Companies' Announcement Regarding Signing a Memorandum of Understanding (1) . . . 197
15.6.24 Instructions for Companies' Announcement Regarding their Projects 197
15.6.25 Instructions for Companies' Announcements for Transactions of Sale, Purchase, Mortgage or Leasing of an Asset 198
15.6.26 Instructions for Companies' Announcements for Obtaining Financing 198
15.6.27 Instructions for Companies' Announcements Related to Debt Instruments 198
15.6.28 (4) Announcement Form for the Redemption of Issued Debts Instruments 199
15.6.29 Instructions for Companies' Announcements Regarding the Company's Shares Buy-Back and Sale 199
15.6.30 First: Instructions for Companies' Announcements Regarding the Buy-Back of its shares 199
15.6.31 Second: Instructions for Companies' Announcements Regarding a Company's Sale of its Shares. 199
15.6.32 Instruction for Companies' Announcements Regarding the Company Pledge of Its Shares 199
15.6.33 Instructions for Companies' Announcement Regarding Lawsuits Announcement Form for Lawsuits: 200
15.6.34 Instructions for Companies' Announcement of Previously Announced Developments Announcement Form for Previously Announced Developments. 200

15.6.35 Instructions for Companies' Announcements for Companies with Accumulated Losses Reaching 20% or More of Their Share Capital . . . 200
15.6.36 (1) Announcement Form for Accumulated Losses Reaching 20% or More and Less Than 35% of Share Capital. 200
15.6.37 (2) Announcement Form for the Reduction of the Accumulated Losses Below 20% of Share Capital 201
15.6.38 Second: Companies with Accumulated Losses Reaching 35% or More and Less Than 50% of Share Capital (1) Announcement Form for Accumulated Losses Reaching 35% or More and Less Than 50% of Share Capital 201
15.6.39 (2) Announcement Form for the Reduction of the Accumulated Losses Below 35% of Share Capital. 201
15.6.40 Third: Companies with Accumulated Losses Reaching 50% or More of Share Capital . . . 201
15.6.41 Accumulated Losses . . . 202
15.6.42 Instructions for Companies' Announcement Pursuant to the Requirements of Article (150) of the Companies Law . . . 202
15.6.43 (2) Announcement Form for the Deadline for Convening the Extraordinary General Assembly Meeting to Address the Accumulated Losses after the Company's Announcement for the call for the Extraordinary General Assembly Meeting . . . 202
15.6.44 (3) Reminder Announcement Form for the Deadline for Convening the Extraordinary General Assembly Meeting to Address the Accumulated Losses Two Days Prior to Convening the Extraordinary General Assembly Meeting to Address the Accumulated Losses. . . . 203

16 INVESTMENT ACCOUNTS INSTRUCTIONS 205
16.1 PART 1: GENERAL PROVISIONS . . . 205
16.2 PART 2: INSTRUCTIONS FOR OPENING INVESTMENT ACCOUNTS . . . 206
16.3 PART 3: INSTRUCTIONS FOR OPERATING INVESTMENT ACCOUNTS . . . 209
16.4 PART 4: REGULATORY AND SUPERVISORY INSTRUCTIONS . . . 210
16.5 PART 5: PUBLICATION AND ENTRY INTO FORCE . . . 211
16.6 Annex 1: Guidance List of Documents for Opening an Investment Account for Saudi Companies or Companies from GCC Member States . . . 211
16.7 Annex 2: Guidance List of Documents for Opening an Investment Account for Qualified Foreign Investors 212
16.8 Annex 3: Guidance List of Documents for Opening an Investment Account for Investment Funds Established in the Kingdom or GCC Member States . . . 212
16.9 Annex 4: Required Information in the Investment Account Statement . . . 212

17 Investment Funds Announcements 213
17.1 General Instructions: . . . 213

18 INVESTMENT FUNDS REGULATIONS 221
18.1 PART 1: GENERAL PROVISIONS . . . 222
18.2 PART 2: FUNDS MANAGEMENT . . . 223
18.3 PART 3: CUSTODY . . . 227
18.4 PART 4: PUBLIC FUNDS . . . 229
18.5 PART 5: PRIVATE FUNDS . . . 244
18.6 PART 6: FOREIGN FUNDS . . . 248
18.7 PART 7: MERGER OF INVESTMENT FUNDS . . . 250
18.8 PART 8: INVESTMENT FUNDS THAT TAKE THE FORM OF A SPECIAL PURPOSES ENTITY . . . 250
18.9 PART 9: PUBLICATION AND ENTRY INTO FORCE . . . 251
18.10 ANNEX 1: REQUIREMENTS OF THE FUND'S TERMS AND CONDITIONS . . . 251
18.11 ANNEX 2: CONTENTS OF THE APPLICATION FOR OFFERING OF A PUBLIC FUND'S UNITS . . . 255
18.12 ANNEX 3: CONTENTS OF FUND'S REPORTS . . . 257
18.13 ANNEX 4: CONTENTS OF QUARTERLY STATEMENTS . . . 258
18.14 ANNEX 5: VALUATION METHODOLOGIES FOR PUBLIC FUNDS . . . 259
18.15 ANNEX 6: PRIVATE PLACEMENT NOTIFICATION TO THE AUTHORITY - PRIVATE FUNDS AND FOREIGN FUNDS . . . 259
18.16 ANNEX 7: FUND'S DECLARATION TO THE AUTHORITY - PRIVATE FUND . . . 260
18.17 ANNEX 8: FUND'S DECLARATION TO THE AUTHORITY - FOREIGN FUND . . . 260
18.18 ANNEX 9: STATEMENT TO BE INCLUDED IN THE PRIVATE PLACEMENT OFFERING DOCUMENTS . . . 260
18.19 ANNEX 10: APPROVAL AND NOTIFICATION REQUESTS PROVIDED TO THE AUTHORITY . . . 260
18.20 ANNEX 11: REQUIREMENTS OF THE PRIVATE FUND'S TERMS AND CONDITIONS . . . 261
18.21 ANNEX 12: LEGAL ADVISOR LETTER FORM . . . 264
18.22 ANNEX 13: FUND MANAGER LETTER FORM . . . 264
18.23 ANNEX 14: FUND TERMINATION REPORT . . . 264

19 Instructions for Book Building Process and Allocation Method in Initial Public Offerings (IPOs) 267
19.1 Part 1: Preamble . . . 267
19.2 Part 2: Definitions . . . 267
19.3 Part 3: General Provisions . . . 268
19.4 Part 4: Requirements for Book building and Changing the Price Range . . . 268
19.5 Part 5: Participating Parties . . . 268

19.6 Part 6: Subscription Price . . . 269
19.7 Part 7: Shares Allocation for Participating Entities after Completing the Book building . . . 269
19.8 Part 8: Offering for Retail Subscribers . . . 269
19.9 Part 9: Publication and Entry into Force . . . 269

20 IPO Price Stabilization Mechanism 271
20.1 Part 1: Preliminary . . . 271
20.2 Part 2: Definitions . . . 271
20.3 Part 3: General Provisions . . . 271
20.4 Part 4: Obligations of the Price Stabilization Manager . . . 271
20.5 Part 5: Exemptions . . . 272
20.6 Part 6: Records for the Price Stabilization Transactions . . . 272
20.7 Part 7: Publication and Entry Into Force . . . 272

21 Regulatory Rules and Procedures issued pursuant to the Companies Law relating to Listed Joint Stock Companies273
21.1 INTRODUCTION . . . 273
21.2 PART 1: PRELIMINARY PROVISIONS . . . 273
21.3 PART 2: REMUNERATION OF BOARD MEMBERS: . . . 274
21.4 PART 3: CONVENING GENERAL AND SPECIAL ASSEMBLY SHAREHOLDER MEETINGS AND CONTEMPORARY TECHNOLOGY . . . 275
21.5 PART 4: BUY-BACK, SALE, PLEDGE OF SHARES . . . 276
21.5.1 CHAPTER 1: Share Buy-back Rules RULES: . . . 276
21.5.2 CHAPTER 2: Effect of Buy-Back Transaction . . . 277
21.5.3 CHAPTER 3: Rules for Sale and Pledge of Treasury Shares . . . 278
21.5.4 CHAPTER 4: Employee Shares . . . 278
21.6 PART 5: PLEDGE OF SHARES . . . 279
21.6.1 CHAPTER 1: SHARE PLEDGE RULES . . . 279
21.6.2 CHAPTER 2: Pledge Agreements and Registration . . . 279
21.6.3 CHAPTER 3: Foreclosure of Pledged Shares . . . 279
21.6.4 CHAPTER 4: General Provisions . . . 279
21.7 PART 6: ISSUANCE, BUY-BACK AND CONVERSION OF PREFERRED SHARES BY THE COMPANY: . . . 279
21.8 PART 7: DIVIDEND DISTRIBUTION TO SHAREHOLDERS OF THE COMPANY . . . 280
21.8.1 CHAPTER 1: Dividend Payment Timing . . . 280
21.9 PART 8: ISSUANCE AND SALE OF PRE-EMPTIVE RIGHTS RESULTING FROM CAPITAL INCREASE . . . 281
21.9.1 CHAPTER 1: Definition of Pre-Emptive Rights . . . 281
21.9.2 CHAPTER 2: Trading of Pre-Emptive Rights . . . 283
21.9.3 CHAPTER 3: Options Available to Registered Shareholders and New Investors . . . 283
21.9.4 CHAPTER 4: Pre-emptive Rights Indicative Value . . . 283
21.10PART 9: PROXY PROCEDURES FOR ATTENDING GENERAL AND SPECIAL ASSEMBLIES . . . 283
21.11PART 10: RULES OF AUTHORIZATION FOR BUSINESSES AND CONTRACTS THAT ARE EXECUTED FOR THE COMPANY'S ACCOUNT, IN WHICH A BOARD MEMBER HAS DIRECT OR INDIRECT INTEREST . . . 285
21.12PART 11: PUBLICATION AND ENTRY INTO FORCE . . . 286
21.13Annex 1: Proxy Form . . . 286

22 MARKET CONDUCT REGULATIONS 287
22.1 PART 1: PRELIMINARY PROVISIONS . . . 287
22.2 PART 2: PROHIBITION OF MARKET MANIPULATION . . . 287
22.3 PART 3: INSIDER TRADING . . . 288
22.4 PART 4: UNTRUE STATEMENTS . . . 289
22.5 PART 5: CAPITAL MARKET INSTITUTIONS CONDUCT . . . 289
22.6 PART 6: LIABILITY FOR ACTS OF OTHERS . . . 290
22.7 PART 7: PUBLICATION AND ENTRY INTO FORCE . . . 290

23 Mergers & Acquisitions 291
23.1 PART 1: GENERAL PROVISIONS . . . 291
23.2 PART 2: ACQUISITIONS . . . 293
23.2.1 Chapter 1: Private Transactions Rules . . . 293
23.3 PART 3: MERGER . . . 307
23.4 PART 4: PUBLICATION AND ENTRY INTO FORCE . . . 307

24 Parallel Market 309
24.1 Part 1: The Objective of the Guidance Note . . . 309
24.2 Part 2: Categories of Non-resident Foreigners who are Allowed to Invest in the Parallel Market . . . 309
24.3 Part 3: Investment Restrictions . . . 309
24.4 Part 4: Requirements for Opening an Investment Account . . . 309
24.5 Part 5: Reliance on Third Parties for CDD . . . 310

24.6 Part 6: Continuing Obligations . . . 310

25 OFFER OF SECURITIES 311
25.1 PART 1: GENERAL PROVISIONS . . . 312
25.2 PART 2: EXEMPT OFFER . . . 313
25.3 PART 3: PRIVATE PLACEMENT OFFER . . . 314
25.4 PART 4: PUBLIC OFFER . . . 315
25.4.1 Chapter 1: General Provisions . . . 315
25.4.2 Chapter 2: Advisors to the Issuer . . . 316
25.4.3 Chapter 3: Conditions for a Public Offer . . . 317
25.4.4 Chapter 4: Application for Registration and Offer . . . 318
25.5 PART 5: FINANCING TRANSACTIONS FOR SPECIAL PURPOSE ENTITY . . . 322
25.5.1 Chapter 1: New Financing Transactions For Special Purposes Entity . . . 322
25.5.2 Chapter 2: Financing Transactions Conditions for Special Purposes Entity . . . 323
25.6 PART 6: CAPITAL ALTERATION . . . 324
25.6.1 Chapter 1: Capital Increase for Issuers of Listed Shares . . . 324
25.6.2 Chapter 2: Capital Reduction for Issuers of Listed Shares . . . 325
25.7 PART 7: CONTINUING OBLIGATIONS . . . 326
25.7.1 Chapter 1: Disclosures . . . 326
25.7.2 Chapter 2: Restrictions on Dealings . . . 329
25.8 PART 8: OFFER OR REGISTRATION IN PARALLEL MARKET . . . 329
25.9 Part 9: PROVISIONS FOR REVERSE TAKEOVER AND DEMERGER . . . 334
25.10 PART 10: Publication and Entry into Force . . . 336
25.11 PART 11: ANNEXES . . . 336
25.12 ANNEX 1: CONTENTS OF A PRIVATE PLACEMENT NOTIFICATION IN RESPECT OF SHARES AND OTHER SECURITIES . . . 336
25.13 ANNEX 2: CONTENTS OF A PRIVATE PLACEMENT NOTIFICATION IN RESPECT OF DEBT INSTRUMENTS 336
25.14 ANNEX 3: OFFEROR DECLARATION . . . 337
25.15 ANNEX 3A: SPONSOR'S DECLARATION . . . 337
25.16 ANNEX 4: CAPITAL MARKET INSTITUTION'S DECLARATION . . . 338
25.17 ANNEX 5: STATEMENT TO BE INCLUDED IN THE PRIVATE PLACEMENT OFFERING DOCUMENTS . . . 338
25.18 ANNEX 6: CONTENTS OF APPLICATION . . . 338
25.19 ANNEX 7: ISSUER'S DECLARATION . . . 339
25.20 ANNEX 7A: SPONSOR'S DECLARATION . . . 339
25.21 ANNEX 7B: ISSUER'S DECLARATION TO REQUEST THE REGISTRATION OF IT'S SHARES IN THE PARALLEL MARKET . . . 340
25.22 ANNEX 8: DIRECTOR'S DECLARATION . . . 341
25.23 ANNEX 8(A): DIRECTOR'S DECLARATION IN A STRUCTURE WITH RIGHT TO RECOURSE . . . 342
25.24 ANNEX 9: CONTENTS OF A PROSPECTUS FOR SHARES . . . 342
25.25 ANNEX 10: CONTENTS OF A PROSPECTUS FOR A RIGHTS ISSUE . . . 347
25.26 ANNEX 11: CONTENT OF A PROSPECTUS FOR DEBT INSTRUMENTS FOR AN ISSUER WITHOUT SECURITIES LISTED ON THE EXCHANGE . . . 351
25.27 ANNEX 11(A): CONTENTS OF A PROSPECTUS FOR DEBT-BASED RECOURSE DEBT INSTRUMENTS . . . 355
25.28 ANNEX 11(B); CONTENTS OF A PROSPECTUS FOR ASSET-LINKED RECOURSE DEBT INSTRUMENTS . 360
25.29 ANNEX 12: CONTENT OF A PROSPECTUS FOR DEBT INSTRUMENTS FOR AN ISSUER THAT HAS SHARES CURRENTLY LISTED ON THE EXCHANGE . . . 367
25.30 ANNEX 13: CONTENTS OF A SHAREHOLDERS' CIRCULAR FOR A CAPITAL INCREASE BY DEBT CONVERSION . . . 370
25.31 ANNEX 14: CONTENTS OF A CIRCULAR FOR A CAPITAL INCREASE TO ACQUIRE A COMPANY OR PURCHASE AN ASSET . . . 373
25.32 ANNEX 15 EXTERNAL AUDITOR'S REPORT . . . 375
25.33 ANNEX 16: FORM OF A FINANCIAL ADVISOR'S LETTER . . . 376
25.34 ANNEX 16(A): FORM OF A FINANCIAL ADVISOR'S LETTER . . . 377
25.35 ANNEX 17: FORM OF A LEGAL ADVISOR'S LETTER . . . 377
25.36 ANNEX 17(A): FORM OF A LEGAL ADVISOR'S LETTER FOR A SPECIAL PURPOSES ENTITY . . . 377
25.37 ANNEX 18: FORM OF LETTER REQUIRED FOR A CAPITALIZATION ISSUE . . . 378
25.38 ANNEX 19: CONTENT OF LETTER REQUIRED FOR CAPITAL REDUCTION . . . 378
25.39 ANNEX 20: CONTENT OF A PROSPECTUS FOR PARALLEL MARKET OFFERS . . . 378
25.40 ANNEX 20A: CONTENT OF A REGISTRATION DOCUMENT . . . 381
25.41 ANNEX 21: FORM OF FINANCIAL ADVISOR'S LETTER WITH REGARDS TO AN APPLICATION FOR REGISTRATION AND OFFER ON THE PARALLEL MARKET OR AN APPLICATION FOR REGISTRATION IN THE PARALLEL MARKET . . . 383
25.42 ANNEX 22: CONTENTS OF SHAREHOLDERS' CIRCULAR FOR A CAPITAL INCREASE OF A COMPANY THE SHARES OF WHICH ARE LISTED ON THE PARALLEL MARKET BY DEBT CONVERSION . . . 384

25.43 ANNEX 23: CONTENTS OF SHAREHOLDERS'S CIRCULAR FOR A CAPITAL INCREASE OF A COMPANY WHICH SHARES ARE LISTED ON THE PARALLEL MARKET TO ACQUIRE A COMPANY OR PURCHASE AN ASSET . . . 384
25.44 ANNEX 24: CLASS TEST . . . 385

26 Listed Companies with Losses 387
26.1 PART ONE: PRELIMINARY PROVISIONS . . . 387
26.1.1 Article One: Definitions . . . 387
26.1.2 Article Two: Scope and Application . . . 387
26.1.3 Article Three: When Accumulated Losses of a company reach 20% or more and less than 35% of its Share Capital . . . 387
26.1.4 Article Four: When Accumulated Losses reach 35% or more and less than 50% of the Share Capital . . . 388
26.1.5 Article Five: When Accumulated Losses reach 50% or more of the Share Capital . . . 388
26.2 PART THREE: DELISTING . . . 388
26.2.1 Article Six: Delisting . . . 388

27 Prudential Rules 389
27.1 Part 1: INTRODUCTION . . . 390
27.1.1 Chapter 1: Scope, Purpose and Definitions . . . 390
27.2 Part 2: CAPITAL BASE . . . 391
27.2.1 Chapter 2:The Capital Base Requirement . . . 391
27.3 Part 3: PILLAR I - MINIMUM CAPITAL REQUIREMENTS . . . 391
27.3.1 Chapter 4: General Provisions for the Trading Book . . . 391
27.3.2 Chapter 5: Management Requirements for the Trading Book . . . 392
27.3.3 Chapter 6: General provisions for Non-trading Activities . . . 392
27.3.4 Chapter 7: Calculating a Risk-Weighted Exposure Amount for non-Trading Activities . . . 392
27.3.5 Chapter 8: Use of Credit Ratings . . . 393
27.3.6 Chapter 9: General Provisions Regarding Operational Risks . . . 394
27.3.7 Chapter 10:The Basic Indicator Approach for Operational Risk . . . 394
27.3.8 Chapter 11:The Standardized Approach for Operational Risk . . . 394
27.3.9 Chapter 12: Expenditure-Based Approach for Operational Risk . . . 395
27.3.10 Chapter 13: General Provisions Regarding Foreign Exchange Rate Risk . . . 395
27.3.11 Chapter 14: Valuation and Conversion to Local Currency . . . 395
27.3.12 Chapter 15: Calculating the Capital Requirement for Foreign Exchange Rate Risk . . . 395
27.3.13 Chapter 16: General Provisions Regarding Commodities Risk . . . 395
27.4 Part 4: LARGE AND EXCESS EXPOSURES . . . 396
27.4.1 Chapter 17: General Provisions for Large and Excess Exposures . . . 396
27.5 Part 5 MINIMUM LIQUIDITY REQUIREMENTS . . . 396
27.5.1 Chapter 18: General Provisions Regarding Liquidity Requirements . . . 396
27.5.2 Chapter 19 ORGANIZATIONAL REQUIREMENTS . . . 396
27.6 Part 6 PILLAR II - ASSESSMENT OF ALL RISKS . . . 397
27.6.1 Chapter 20: Internal Capital Adequacy Assessment Process (ICAAP) . . . 397
27.7 PART 7 PILLAR III - DISCLOSURE AND REPORTING . . . 397
27.7.1 Chapter 21: Disclosure . . . 397
27.7.2 Chapter 22: Reporting . . . 397
27.8 PART 8 FINANCIAL GROUPS . . . 398
27.8.1 Chapter 23: General Provisions Regarding Financial Groups . . . 398
27.8.2 Chapter 24: Consolidated Accounts . . . 398
27.8.3 Chapter 25: Foreign Undertakings . . . 399
27.8.4 Chapter 26: Systems and Controls . . . 399
27.9 PART 9 CLOSING PROVISIONS . . . 399
27.9.1 Chapter 27: Publication and Entry into Force . . . 399
27.10 Annex 1: Capital Base . . . 399
27.10.1 Chapter 1:Tier-1 Capital . . . 399
27.10.2 Chapter 2: Tier-2 Capital . . . 400
27.10.3 Chapter 3: Deductions from Capital . . . 402
27.11 ANNEX 2: Trading Book . . . 403
27.11.1 Chapter 1: Interest Rate Risks . . . 403
27.11.2 Chapter 2: Equity Price Risks . . . 409
27.11.3 Chapter 3: Risks Related to Investment Funds . . . 411
27.11.4 Chapter 4: Underwriting . . . 412
27.11.5 Chapter 5: Excess Exposure . . . 412
27.12 ANNEX 3: Non-Trading Activities . . . 414
27.12.1 Chapter 1: Exposure Classes and Risk Weights . . . 414
27.12.2 Chapter 3: Calculating the non-Trading Book Exposure Amount for Derivatives . . . 416
27.12.3 Chapter 5: Guarantees and Credit Derivatives . . . 419

27.12.4 Chapter 7: Netting Agreements . . . 424
27.12.5 Chapter 8: Other Credit Protection . . . 426
27.13 ANNEX 4: Operational Risk . . . 427
27.13.1 Chapter 1:The Basic Indicator Approach . . . 427
27.13.2 Chapter 2:The standardized Approach . . . 427
27.14 ANNEX 5: Foreign Exchange Rate Risk . . . 428
27.14.1 Chapter 1:The Two-Step Method . . . 428
27.14.2 Chapter 2: Calculating the Capital Requirement . . . 428
27.14.3 Chapter 3: Options . . . 428
27.14.4 Chapter 4: Investment Funds . . . 429
27.14.5 Chapter 5: Composite Currencies . . . 429
27.14.6 Chapter 6: Collateral in a Third Country's Currency . . . 429
27.14.7 Chapter 7: Exceptions . . . 429
27.15 ANNEX 6: Commodities Risk . . . 429
27.15.1 Chapter 2: The Maturity-Based Method . . . 430
27.15.2 Chapter 3: The Simple Method . . . 431
27.16 Annex 7: Large Exposures . . . 431
27.16.1 Chapter 1: Management Requirements . . . 431
27.17 Annex 8: Liquidity Risk . . . 432
27.17.1 Chapter 1: Identification and Measurement of Liquidity Risk . . . 432
27.17.2 Chapter 2: Liquidity Risk Management . . . 433
27.18 ANNEX 9: INTERNAL CAPITAL ASSESSMENT . . . 434
27.18.1 Chapter 1: Internal Capital Adequacy Assessment Process (ICAAP) . . . 434
27.18.2 Chapter 2: Strategies on How to Reach and Maintain Capital Targets . . . 435
27.18.3 Chapter 3: Self-Assessment and Stress Testing . . . 435
27.19 ANNEX 10: Disclosure . . . 435
27.19.1 Chapter 1: Disclosure Regarding Authorized Person And Financial Group . . . 435
27.19.2 Chapter 2: Disclosure regarding Capital Base . . . 435
27.19.3 Chapter 4: Disclosure Regarding non-Trading Activities . . . 436
27.19.4 Chapter 5: Disclosure Regarding Liquidity Risk . . . 437
27.19.5 Chapter 6: Disclosure Regarding Counterparty Risk . . . 437
27.19.6 Chapter 7: Disclosure Regarding Operational Risk . . . 437
27.19.7 Chapter 8: Periodic Disclosure . . . 437

28 PUBLIC CONSULTATION 439
28.1 PART 1: GENERAL PROVISIONS . . . 439
28.1.1 Article 1: Preliminary Provisions . . . 439
28.1.2 Article 2: Definitions . . . 439
28.2 PART 2: PUBLIC CONSULTATION . . . 439
28.2.1 Article 3: Public Consultation . . . 439
28.2.2 Article 4: Public Consultation Methods . . . 439
28.2.3 Article 5: Public Consultation Period . . . 440
28.2.4 Article 6: Receiving Public Comments . . . 440
28.3 Part 3: PUBLISHING PUBLIC COMMENTS . . . 440
28.3.1 Article 7: Publishing Public Comments . . . 440
28.3.2 Article 8: Participants' Names and Information Confidentiality . . . 440
28.4 PART 4: ENTRY INTO FORCE . . . 440
28.4.1 Article 9: Entry Into Force . . . 440

29 Qualified Foreign Financial Institutions 441
29.1 PART 1: GENERAL PROVISIONS . . . 441
29.2 PART 2: APPLICATIONS FOR QUALIFICATION . . . 442
29.2.1 Chapter One: Qualification conditions . . . 442
29.2.2 Chapter Two: Qualification procedures . . . 443
29.2.3 Chapter Three: Determination of Applications . . . 443
29.2.4 Chapter Four: Further Requirements Following Qualification . . . 443
29.3 ANNEX 2.1 Information and Documents for Qualification . . . 443
29.4 PART 3: CONTINUING OBLIGATIONS . . . 444
29.5 ANNEX 3.1: Information and documents to be disclosed by QFIs to Assessing Authorized Persons . . . 445
29.6 PART 4: AUTHORIZED PERSONS OBLIGATIONS . . . 445
29.7 PART 5: POWERS OF THE AUTHORITY IN RELATION TO QFIs . . . 445
29.8 PART 6: CLOSING PROVISIONS . . . 446

30 QFI FAQ 447
30.1 Introductory Questions . . . 447
30.2 PART A: Introductory Questions . . . 447

30.3 PART B: Qualification Conditions for QFIs . . . 448
30.4 PART C: Qualification Process . . . 450
30.5 PART D: Trading . . . 451
30.6 PART E: Investment Limit(s) . . . 452
30.7 PART F: Ongoing Obligations . . . 453
30.8 PART G: Other Questions . . . 454

31 Real Estate Investment Funds 457
31.1 PART 1: GENERAL PROVISIONS . . . 458
31.2 PART] 2: AUTHORIZATION . . . 458
31.3 OPERATION OF FUNDS . . . 459
31.3.1 Chapter 1: Fund's Organizational Structure . . . 459
31.3.2 Chapter 2: Fund Management . . . 460
31.3.3 Chapter 3: Disclosure . . . 464
31.3.4 Chapter 4: Fundamental and Non-Fundamental Changes . . . 464
31.3.5 Chapter 5: Fund Assets Requirements, Custody of its Assets and Operation Rules . . . 465
31.4 PART 4: REAL ESTATE INVESTMENT TRADED FUND . . . 470
31.5 SPECIAL PURPOSE ENTITIES . . . 474
31.6 PART 6: PUBLICATION AND ENTRY INTO FORCE . . . 475
31.7 Requirements . . . 475
31.8 REIF Requirements . . . 478
31.9 Application Contents . . . 481
31.10 Application Form . . . 481
31.11 Annual Reports . . . 483
31.12 Semi-Annual Statement . . . 483
31.13 Quarterly Statement . . . 483
31.14 Form of Letter . . . 484
31.15 REITF Manager's Letter . . . 484
31.16 Fund Manager's Declaration . . . 485
31.17 REITF Fund Manager's Declaration . . . 486
31.18 Legal Advisor's Letter . . . 487
31.19 Notifications and Requests . . . 487
31.20 Annex 13: Fund Termination Report . . . 487
31.21 Supplementary Annex . . . 488

32 Registration of Auditors 491
32.1 PART 1: GENERAL PROVISIONS . . . 491
32.1.1 Article 1 : Preliminary . . . 491
32.1.2 Article 2 : Definitions . . . 491
32.1.3 Article 3: Waivers . . . 492
32.1.4 Article 4: Right to Appeal . . . 492
32.2 PART 2: REGISTRATION . . . 492
32.2.1 Article 5: Registration Required . . . 492
32.2.2 Article 6 : Registration Procedures . . . 492
32.2.3 Article 7: Accounting Firm Registration Conditions . . . 492
32.2.4 Article 8: CPA Registration Conditions . . . 492
32.2.5 Article 9: Procedures and Powers of the Authority in relation to an Application for Registration . . . 493
32.2.6 Article 10: Fees . . . 493
32.3 PART 3: CONTINUING OBLIGATIONS . . . 493
32.3.1 Article 11: Conditions for Maintenance of Registration . . . 493
32.3.2 Article 12: Notification Requirements . . . 493
32.3.3 Article 13: Transparency Report . . . 493
32.3.4 Article 14: Periodic Information . . . 493
32.3.5 Article 15: Compliance with the Rules . . . 493
32.3.6 Article 16: Participation of the Registered CPA . . . 494
32.4 PART 4: ISSUES AFFECTING REGISTRATION . . . 494
32.4.1 Article 17: Registration Cancelation and Suspension . . . 494
32.4.2 Article 18: Ceasing to Carry on Audit Engagements . . . 494
32.5 PART 5: FINAL PROVISIONS . . . 494
32.5.1 Article 19: Publication and Entry into Force . . . 494
32.6 ANNEX 1: Information Required in the Transparency Report . . . 494

33 Reporting Violations 497
33.1 Article 1: Preamble . . . 497
33.2 Article 3: Exemptions . . . 497
33.3 Article 4: Right of Appeal . . . 497

33.4 Article 5: Reporting Channels . . . 497
33.5 Article 6: Requirements when Reporting . . . 497
33.6 Article 8: Reward Amount Determination . . . 498
33.7 Article 9: Legal Support . . . 498
33.8 Article Ten: Protection Policy for Reporting Individuals . . . 498
33.9 Article 11: Confidentiality . . . 498
33.10 Article 12: Violator Reporting . . . 498
33.11 Article 13: False Reporting . . . 498
33.12 Article 14: Entry into Force . . . 498

34 Securities Borrowing and Lending 499
34.1 PART 1 PRELIMINARY PROVISIONS . . . 499
34.1.1 Article 1: Preliminary . . . 499
34.1.2 Article 2: Definitions . . . 499
34.1.3 Article 3: SBL Transactions . . . 499
34.1.4 Article 4: Eligible Participants . . . 499
34.1.5 Article 5: Eligible Listed Securities . . . 500
34.1.6 Article 6: Minimum Collateral . . . 500
34.1.7 Article 7: SBL Agreement . . . 500
34.1.8 Article 8: Return of Borrowed Securities and Collateral . . . 500
34.2 PART 3 LENDING AGENT . . . 500
34.2.1 Article 9: Lending Agent . . . 500
34.2.2 Article 10: Powers of the Authority and the Depository Centre . . . 500
34.3 PART 5: REPORTING AND RECORD KEEPING REQUIREMENTS . . . 500
34.3.1 Article 11: Copy of the SBL Agreement . . . 500
34.3.2 Article 12: Reporting of SBL Transactions . . . 500
34.3.3 Article 13: Public Disclosure of Information . . . 501
34.3.4 Article 14: Record Keeping . . . 501
34.4 PART 6: GENERAL PROVISIONS . . . 501
34.4.1 Article 15: Limit of Liability . . . 501
34.4.2 Article 16: Waivers . . . 501
34.4.3 Article 17: Publication and Entry into Force . . . 501
34.5 ANNEX 1: MATTERS TO BE INCLUDED IN SBL AGREEMENTS . . . 501

35 Securities Disputes 503
35.1 PART 1: PRELIMINARY PROVISIONS . . . 504
35.2 PART 2: FILING THE SUIT AND PLACING IT IN THE COMMITTEE'S DOCKET . . . 504
35.3 PART 4: COMMITTEE HEARINGS . . . 505
35.4 PART 5: APPEARENCE AND ABSENCE OF SUIT'S PARTIES . . . 505
35.5 PART 6: EVIDENCE . . . 505
35.6 PART 7: EXPERTS . . . 505
35.7 PART 9: APPEAL . . . 507
35.8 PART 10: FINALITY AND ENFORCEMENT OF DECISIONS . . . 507
35.9 PART 11: Class Action Suits . . . 508

36 Short Selling Regulations 513
36.1 PART 1: PRELIMINARY PROVISIONS . . . 513
36.1.1 PART 2: SHORT SELLING . . . 513
36.2 PART 3: POWERS OF THE AUTHORITY . . . 513
36.3 PART 4: REPORTING AND RECORD KEEPING REQUIREMENTS . . . 514
36.4 PART 5: GENERAL PROVISIONS . . . 514

37 Securities Counterparties 515
37.1 PART 1: GENERAL PROVISIONS . . . 516
37.2 PART 2: AUTHORIZATION . . . 517
37.3 PART 3: CLEARING . . . 520
37.4 PART 4: CAPITAL BASE . . . 521
37.5 PART 5: CLEARING MEMBERS . . . 521
37.6 PART 6: COLLATERAL . . . 522
37.7 PART 7: CUSTODY AND INVESTMENT RISKS . . . 524
37.8 PART 8: MARGIN . . . 524
37.9 PART 9: CREDIT RISK . . . 525
37.10 PART 10: LIQUIDITY RISK . . . 526
37.11 PART 11: SETTLEMENT FINALITY . . . 527
37.12 PART 12: SEGREGATION AND PORTABILITY . . . 528
37.13 PART 13: CLEARING MEMBER DEFAULT MANAGEMENT . . . 529

37.14PART 14: CCP RECOVERY . . . 530
37.15PART 15: OTHER CCP OBLIGATIONS . . . 530
37.16PART 16: OPERATIONAL RISK . . . 531
37.17PART 17: LINKS BETWEEN CCPS . . . 532
37.18PART 18: QUALIFYING CENTRAL COUNTERPARTY . . . 533
37.19PART 19: PUBLICATION AND ENTRY INTO FORCE . . . 533

38 Special Purpose Entities 535
38.1 PART 1: GENERAL PROVISIONS . . . 536
38.2 PART 2: SPECIAL PURPOSES ENTITIES ISSUING OR INTEND TO ISSUE DEBT INSTRUMENTS . . . 536
38.2.1 CHAPTER 1: GENERAL PROVISIONS . . . 536
38.2.2 CHAPTER 3: BY-LAWS . . . 536
38.3 CHAPTER 4: SPONSOR . . . 537
38.3.1 CHAPTER 5: TRUSTEE OF A SPECIAL PURPOSES ENTITY . . . 537
38.3.2 CHAPTER 6: BOARD OF DIRECTORS . . . 538
38.3.3 CHAPTER 7: CUSTODIAN . . . 539
38.3.4 CHAPTER 8: ACCOUNTS AND AUDIT . . . 540
38.3.5 CHAPTER 9: RECORD KEEPING . . . 541
38.3.6 CHAPTER 10: MERGER AND CONVERSION . . . 541
38.4 PART 3: INVESTMENT FUNDS THAT TAKE THE FORM OF SPECIAL PURPOSES ENTITIES . . . 541
38.4.1 Chapter 1: PRELIMINARY PROVISIONS . . . 541
38.4.2 Chapter 2: AUTHORIZATION . . . 541
38.4.3 CHAPTER 3: BY LAWS . . . 541
38.4.4 Chapter 4: MONITORING PROCEDURES AND SYSTEMS . . . 542
38.5 PART 4: GENERAL PROVISIONS . . . 542
38.5.1 CHAPTER 1: PROCEDURES AND POWERS OF THE AUTHORITY IN RELATION TO THE AUTHORISATION APPLICATION . . . 542
38.5.2 CHAPTER 2: LIABILITY TOWARDS PRE-AUTHORIZATION CONTRACTS . . . 542
38.5.3 CHAPTER 3: THIRD PARTY RELIANCE . . . 542
38.5.4 CHAPTER 4: SETTLEMENT AND INSOLVENCY PROCEEDINGS . . . 542
38.5.5 CHAPTER 5: FEES . . . 542
38.5.6 CHAPTER 6: AUTHORITY REGISTERS . . . 543
38.5.7 CHAPTER 7: TERMINATION OF A SPECIAL PURPOSES ENTITY . . . 543
38.6 PART 5: PUBLICATION AND ENTRY INTO FORCE . . . 543
38.7 Annex 1: Notification Requirements . . . 543

39 Swap Agreements Framework 545

Introduction

Not long ago, a bank in Chicago learned that it was acting as custodian for a Saudi securities broker. A junior lawyer in the legal department downloaded a copy of the Saudi Capital Markets Law from the website of the Saudi regulator, the Capital Markets Authority (CMA). It was clear, the junior lawyer reasoned, that by acting as custodian for the Saudi broker the bank was engaging in the securities business in Saudi Arabia.

A quick review of the legislation revealed that the bank was subject to criminal and civil penalties. The criminal penalties were the worst part, so the junior lawyer informed his boss and after a brief discussion, both were convinced that the bank had a problem.

Their solution was to self-report their crime and hope the CMA would be lenient. After all, they had a licensed subsidiary in the Kingdom, though this subsidiary did not have the proper license to provide custody services. That could be remedied easily enough; the problem was that the bank had been providing unlicensed services for more than a decade. Surely the CMA would impose fines, if for no other reason than to set an example for others.

Before going to the CMA, the general counsel contacted me. Did I reach the same conclusion? Was the bank really in trouble?

Using an earlier version of this tool, I quickly turned up different regulations which provided for the use of foreign custodians. The threat of criminal prosecution disappeared and the rush to self-report was halted at the last minute.

The CMA has published thirty-seven principle securities laws, regulations, rules and even a FAQ. For those who need to read relevant CMA rules, until now there has been no easy way to quickly find them. Google will not help; some of the rules are published as image pdf files and are not indexed. Even those who are familiar with CMA legislation may not remember whether a particular rule is to be found in the Offers of Securities Regulations; the Securities Business Regulations, the Capital Markets Institutions Regulations or elsewhere.

With roughly 2000 pages to wade through, finding the relevant law is a needle in the haystack exercise. With this book, I hope to end all that. With all relevant CMA laws in a single volume, a desktop search will quickly find *all* of the CMA's guidance concerning a single topic.

While the price may seem high in comparison to other securities manuals, before this tool existed it was necessary to hire a lawyer–and sometimes more than one–to comb through all the laws in the hopes of finding a relevant article. Compared to paying a lawyer hourly rates, this book is a bargain.

About the text: the book contains an in-depth table of contents, which in itself is a useful finding tool. The CMA does not always name articles in laws it passes; all articles have been given a name for convenience in finding relevant provisions. Definitions found in CMA rules have been added to and so expanded the Glossary of Defined Terms and marked accordingly.

A copy of this book, I am told, is on the general counsel's laptop in Chicago. He reports that he has used it on more than one occasion whenever a Saudi securities issue presents itself.

Michael O'Kane
Riyadh, 2022

1 Glossary of Defined Terms Used in the Regulations and Rules of the Capital Market Authority

Issued by the Board of the Capital Market Authority pursuant to its Resolution Number 4-11-2004 Dated 20/8/1425 H.(4/10/2004 G.), based on the Capital Market Law issued by Royal Decree No. M/30 dated 2/6/1424 H., as amended by Resolution of the Board of the Capital Market Authority Number 2-22-2021 dated 12/7/1442 H. (24/2/2021 G.)

Important Notice: The current version of this Glossary, as may be amended, can be found at the Authority's website: www.cma.org.sa

Unless the context indicates otherwise, the words and expressions in this Glossary shall have the meaning herein specified:

A

- **Accounting Firm**: The entity which carries on audit engagements in accordance with the provisions of the Law of Certified Public Accountants, whether it is an individual or professional firm.[Art.2(c), Registration of Auditors]

- **Accounts**: are to be read to include any business relationships between Authorized Person and its client. [Art 2, AML Regulations]

- **Accredited Valuer**: A legal or natural person licensed to carry out the valuation profession in accordance with the Accredited Valuers Law issued by Royal Decree no.(M/43) dated 9/7/1433H. and its implementing regulation (Real-Estate Valuation Sector).

- **Accumulated Losses**: The company's results for the current period added to the company's accumulated results from prior periods, which in aggregate represent a loss, and appear as a separate item under shareholder's equity on the balance sheet.[Art. 1, Procedures for Listed Companies with Losses]

- **Acting in Concert**: means, at the sole discretion of the Authority, actively co-operating, pursuant to an agreement (whether binding or non-binding) or an understanding (whether formal or informal) between persons, to be controllers (whether directly or indirectly, excluding indirect ownership of shares through swap agreements or through an investment fund whose unit owner have no discretion in its investment decisions) of a company, through the acquisition by any of them (through direct or indirect ownership) of voting shares in that company. Moreover, "concert parties" shall be construed accordingly. Without prejudice to the general application of this definition, the following persons, shall be presumed to be acting in concert with other persons of the same class unless the contrary is established, including but not be limited to:

1) Members of the same group;

2) a person's relatives;

3) Person(s) who provided financial assistance to the offeror or offeree or members of the group with such person (other than a bank in the ordinary course of business) in order to purchase shares that carry voting rights or convertible debt instruments.

- **Acting in Concert**: means in the *Rules on the Offer of Securities and Continuing Obligations*, actively co-operating, pursuant to an agreement or understanding (whether formal or informal) between persons, to acquire interest in or exercise voting right in the shares or in the convertible debt instruments of the issuer.

- **Administrative Team**: A group of individuals who make strategic decisions of the person. The Board is the Company's Administrative Team.[Art 1, Corporate Governance Regulations]

- **Advising**: advising a person in relation to a security, including advising on the merits of dealing in it, exercising any right to deal conferred by it or financial planning and wealth management in it.

- **Affiliate**: a person who controls another person or is controlled by that other person, or who is under common control with that person by a third person. In any of the preceding, control could be direct or indirect.

- **Anti-Money Laundering Law**: the Anti-Money Laundering Law issued by Royal Decree No. M/20 dated 5/2/1439 H.

- **Applicant**: a foreign investor that submits an application for qualification to an Assessing Authorized Person. [Art. 2(c), Qualified Foreign Financial Institutions Regulations]

- **Application for Listing**: means in the *Rules on the Offer of Securities and Continuing Obligations*, any application submitted to the Exchange to list securities of any type.

- **Application for Registration and Offer**: the registration of securities with the Authority, or where the context permits, the application to the Authority for registration and offer of securities.

- **Appeal Panel**: the appeal panel formed pursuant to paragraph (g) of Article 25 of the Capital Markets Law.[Art. 1, Securities Disputes Proceedings Regulations]

- **Appropriate Close-out Period**: the time period to close all open positions of the defaulting Clearing Member which starts from the last collateral provided by the defaulted clearing member until the closing of his positions. [Article 2, Securities Central Counterparts Regulations]

- **Arranging**: introducing parties in relation to offering of securities, arrangement of its underwriting, or advising on corporate finance business.

- **Assessing Authorized Person**: an Authorized Person who has agreed with an applicant to assess its application for registration as a QFI, or an Authorized Person who has executed a QFI assessment agreement with a QFI. Art. 2(c), Qualified Foreign Financial Institutions Regulations.

- **Asset-Backed Debt Instrument**: means a debt instrument issued by a special purposes entity under whose terms: (a) the entitlement of holders of the debt instrument to a return is wholly dependent on the returns generated by the special purposes entity's assets; and (b) the sponsor is not obliged to the holders of the debt instrument (whether by guarantee or otherwise) to pay any amounts due on the debt instrument.

- **Asset-Linked Recourse Debt Instrument**: means a debt instrument issued by a special purposes entity under whose terms: (a) the entitlement of holders of the debt instrument to a return is defined by a percentage of the returns generated by the special purposes entity's assets; and (b) the sponsor is obliged to the holders of the debt instrument (whether by guarantee or otherwise) to pay all amounts due on the debt instrument.

- **Associate**:

  1) in relation to the senior executives or a director or to a substantial shareholder who is an individual any of the following:

    (a) that individual's spouse or minor children (together "the individual's family"); and

    (b) any company in whose equity shares the individual or any member or members (taken together) of the individual's family or the individual and any such member or members (taken together) are directly or indirectly interested so that they are able:

      (i) to exercise or control the exercise of 30% or more of the votes at the general meeting on all, or substantially all, matters; or

      (ii) to appoint or remove directors holding a majority of voting rights at board meetings on all, or substantially all, matters; and

  2) in relation to a substantial shareholder which is a company:

    (a) any other company which is its subsidiary or parent or fellow subsidiary of the parent;

    (b) any company whose directors are accustomed to act in accordance with the substantial shareholder's directions or instructions; and

    (c) any company in the capital of which the substantial shareholder, and any other company under (a) or (b) taken together, are directly or indirectly interested so that they are able:

      (i) to exercise or control the exercise of 30% or more of the votes at the general meeting on all, or substantially all, matters; or

      (ii) to appoint or remove directors holding a majority of voting rights at board meetings on all, or substantially all, matters.

- **Attachment**: shall mean the provisional ban on transferring, exchanging, disposing with or moving funds and proceeds or attaching same pursuant to an order by a court or a competent authority.[Art.2, AML Regs.]

- **Audit Engagements**: Audit of financial statements, prepared by an entity, in accordance with the auditing standards adopted by the Saudi Organization for Certified Public Accountants for the purpose of expressing an opinion as to whether such financial statements present fairly the financial position of the entity at a specific date, and the results of its operations for a specific financial period, or review of the interim financial statements, prepared by the entity, to determine if significant amendments are needed for the interim financial statements to be in agreement with the accounting standards adopted by the Saudi Organization for Certified Public Accountants. [Art.2(c), Registration of Auditors]

- **Authorized Credit Rating Agency**: a legal person which is incorporated, and authorized, in the Kingdom to carry out rating activities in accordance with the Credit Rating Agencies Regulations or an authorized foreign credit rating agency.

- **Authorization Requirement**: the authorization requirement [as] stated in Article (5) of the Securities Business Regulations. [i.e., {a} person must not carry on securities business in the Kingdom unless he is a Capital Market Institution authorized by the Authority; [Art. 2(c), Qualified Foreign Financial Institutions Regulations]

- **Authorized Foreign Credit Rating Agency**: a foreign credit rating agency authorized to carry out rating activities in the Kingdom in accordance with the Credit Rating Agencies Regulations.

- **Authorized Person**: means a Capital Market Institution.

- **Authorized Persons Regulations**: means the *Capital Market Institutions Regulations* issued by the Board of the Capital Market Authority.

- **Authority**: the Capital Market Authority, including where the context permits any committee, sub-committee, employee or agent to whom any function of the Authority may be delegated.

B

- **Backtesting**: an ex-post comparison of observed outcomes with expected outcomes derived from the use of margin models. [Article 2, Securities Central Counterparts Regulations]

- **Bank**: a financial institution that has a legal personality which engages in banking business. [Art. 2(c), Qualified Foreign Financial Institutions Regulations]

- **Bankruptcy Regulations**: the *Bankruptcy Law* issued by Royal Decree No. M/50 dated 28/5/1439H. or any applicable provisions relating to insolvency or bankruptcy under the Companies Regulations, or any other legislation dealing with bankruptcy issues in the Kingdom.

- **Beneficiary**: for the purposes of the Rules for the Special Purposes Entities, means; the person for which the special purposes entity is established to provide such a person with the necessary financing by issuing debt instruments, in accordance with the provisions of the Rules for the Special Purposes Entities. [the beneficiary of the financing. Art. 2(d), Direct Financing Investment Funds Instructions]

- **Beneficial Owner**: refers to the natural person(s) who ultimately own(s) or control(s) the funds of the clients or on whose behalf a transaction or activity is being conducted. It also incorporates those persons who exercise ultimate effective control over a legal person or arrangement.[Art.2, AML, see, "Ultimate beneficiary."]

- **Bidding Application (Appended)**: The application submitted to the financial advisor of the issuer when the price range is changed, in accordance with paragraph (b) of Part (4) of these Instructions, in time no later than the last day of the Book building period, and submitted by participating parties in order to participate in the book building or by the participating entities for the purpose of changing their requests concerning the price range.[Art. 2(c), IPO Book Building]

- **Book Building**: The process by which a financial advisor registers bids from participating entities in order to determine the offering price.[Art. 2(c), IPO Book Building]

- **Book building Period**: A period determined by the financial advisor, after obtaining the consent of the issuer, without prejudice to paragraph (d) of Part (3) of [the law]. It starts from the first day of the financial advisor offering the issuer's shares to the participating entities in accordance with paragraph (a) of Part

(3) of the [Book Building Instructions.] [Art. 2(c), IPO Book Building]

- **Bidding Participation Application**: The application submitted by the participating entities to the financial advisor of the issuer in order to participate in the book building process, and submitted to the financial advisor in time no later than the last day of the book building period.[Art. 2(c), IPO Book Building]

- **Brokerage and Securities Firm**: a financial institution that has a legal personality which engages in securities business, including portfolio managers. [Art. 2(c), Qualified Foreign Financial Institutions Regulations]

- **Brokerage Professional**: an employee of a Capital Market Institution who performs the activity of dealing on behalf of a Capital Market Institution.

- **Business Relationship**: means professional or commercial relationship between an Authorized Person and a client. A relationship need not involve the Authorized Person in an actual transaction; giving advice shall also constitute establishing a business relationship. [Art. 2, AML Regs.]

- **Buys or Buying**: includes buying a security or commodity for consideration.

C

- **Calendar Day**: any day, whether or not such day is a business day.

- **Capital Base**: comprised of Tier-1 capital and Tier-2 capital.[Art. 1(f), Prudential Rules]

- **Capital Market Institution**: a person authorized by the Authority to carry out securities business.

- **Capital Market Institutions Regulations**: the Capital Market Institutions Regulations issued by the Board of the Capital Market Authority.

- **Capital Market Law**: the Capital Market Law issued by Royal Decree No. M/30 dated 2/6/1424H.

- **Capital Protected Fund**: an investment fund whose primary investment objective is to protect and return the capital invested by unitholders at a pre-determined date in the future.

- **Capitalization Issue**: an offer of further shares to existing shareholders, fully paid up out of the issuer's reserves, in proportion to existing shareholders holdings.

- **Carve Out**: is a type of Demerger transaction where the Listed Company sells off a portion of its assets, business or a subsidiary by transferring them as a whole, to one or several existing entities (acquiring legal entities) or to be newly formed, or to the public in return for cash or shares in the acquiring legal entity being granted to the Listed Company.

- **CCP**: a central counterparty authorized in carrying out securities clearing activities in the Kingdom in accordance with the *Capital Market Law* and the *Securities Central Counterparties Regulations.*

- **CCP Rules**: the regulations, rules, procedures and instructions proposed by the Board of Directors of the CCP and approved by the Board of the Authority.

- **CDD**: an acronym for "Customer Due Diligence."

- **Center or Depository Center**: the Securities Depositary Center to be established in accordance with Article 26 of the Capital Market Law. Pending the establishment of the Depositary Center, any reference to the Depositary Center shall be construed as a reference to the Tadawul Depositary System at Tadawul.

- **Central Bank**: the Saudi Central Bank.

- **CEO**: the chief executive officer, being any individual who heads the operations of any person and includes the managing director, the chief executive, the president of the company or equivalent.

- **Certificates**: certificates or other instruments which confer contractual or property rights:

  1) in respect of any shares, debt instruments, warrants, being a security held by a person (other than the person on whom the rights are conferred by the certificate or instrument); and
  2) the transfer of which may be effected without the consent of that person; but excluding any certificates or instruments which confer contractual or ownership rights of the type of the options, futures or the contracts for differences, and excluding any certificate or instrument which confers rights in respect of two or more securities issued by different persons.

- **Certified Public Accountant** (CPA): The natural person who carries on and is responsible for audit engagements, its performance, and signing of audit reports issued by the accounting firm in accordance with the provisions of the Law of Certified Public Accountants. [Art.2(c), Registration of Auditors]

- **CFO**: any natural person who manages the financial affairs of any person, whether under the name of chief financial officer or finance manager or equivalent.

- **Charged Person**: a person who is charged with violation of any provision related to the public right of the provisions of the Law, its implementing regulations, and the regulations, rules and instructions issued by the Authority and the Exchange.[Art. 1, *Securities Disputes Proceedings Regulations.*]

- **Chinese Wall Arrangements** means written policies and procedures established by a Capital Market Institution to secure confidential or inside information obtained by the Capital Market Institution in the course of carrying out securities business that are designed to ensure that the information is known only to employees of the capital market institution who are authorized to receive it, and to ensure that the information is not disclosed to any other persons.

- **Citizens of the Cooperation Council for the Arab States of the Gulf**: natural persons who hold citizenship of one of the Cooperation Council for the Arab States of the Gulf countries , or legal persons that (i) the capital of which is majority owned by citizens or governments of the Cooperation Council for the Arab states of the Gulf; and (ii) are holding the citizenship of one of the Cooperation Council for the Arab states of the Gulf countries ,in accordance with the definition set out in the resolution of the Supreme Council of the Cooperation Council for the Arab States of the Gulf in its 15th session approved by the Council of Ministers Resolution Number (16) dated 20/1/1418H. [Part 2(a), Foreign Strategic Ownership in Listed Companies; see "GCC Citizens" and "GCC Companies.]

- **Class Action Suit**: a suit filed by a group of plaintiffs against one or more defendants, where the group of plaintiffs' suit share the same legal bases, merits and the subject matter of the requests. Any decision made on the case shall affect all of its parties.[Art. 1, Securities Disputes Proceedings Regulations]

- **Class Action Suits Docket**: a docket created by the Committee for Class Action Suits. [Art. 1, Securities Disputes Proceedings Regulations]

- **Class Tests**: the tests set out in Annex 24 of the Rules on the Offer of Securities and Continuing Obligations, which are used to determine whether a transaction constitutes a Demerger requiring shareholders' approval.

- **Clearing**: the process of establishing each party's rights and obligations arising from securities trading, including the calculation of net obligations, and ensuring that financial instruments or cash are available to secure the exposures arising from such obligations. [Article 2, Securities Central Counterparts Regulations]

- **Clearing Member**: a Direct Clearing Member or a General Clearing Member. [Article 2, Securities Central Counterparts Regulations]

- **Client**: a person for whom a Capital Market Institution executes securities transactions.

- **Client**: refers to a customer, execution-only customer either natural or legal person and counterparty for whom an Authorized Person executes securities business. [Art. 2, AML Regs.] Also, "a natural or legal person which: 1) is not a Clearing Member; and 2) has a contractual relationship with a Clearing Member which enables that person to clear its transactions with the CCP." [Article 2, Securities Central Counterparts Regulations]

- **Client Account**: an account at a local bank which is in the name of a Capital Market Institution and fulfills the conditions required by the Client Money Rules.

- **Client Assets**: assets treated as client assets as specified in Part 7 of the Capital Market Institution Regulations.

- **Client Asset Rules**: the rules relating to client assets contained in Part 7 of the Capital Market Institutions Regulations.

- **Client Money**: money treated as client money as specified in Part 7 of the Capital Market Institutions Regulations.

- **Client Money Rules**: the rules relating to client money contained in Part 7 of the Capital Market Institutions Regulations.

- **Close Links**: in the *Capital Market Institutions Regulations*, the *Credit Rating Agencies Regulations* and the *Securities Central Counterparties Regulations*, means the relationship between a person (who is an applicant for authorization, a Capital Market Institution, an authorized credit rating agency or a CCP) and any of the following persons:

1) a controller of that person;
2) a company controlled by that person;
3) a company controlled by a controller of that person; or
4) a company controlled by any combination of the persons described in (1), (2) or (3) above.

- **Closed-Ended Investment Fund**: any investment fund which is not an open-ended investment fund.

- **Closed-Ended Investment Traded Fund**: a closed-ended investment fund, the units of which are traded on the Main Market or the Parallel Market.

- **Collateral**: for the purposes of the Client Money Rules and Client Asset Rules, means money or an asset which has been paid for in full by a client and which is held by the Capital Market Institution or under its charge, either for its own account or under the terms of a deposit, pledge or other pledge arrangement.

- **Combating-Terrorism Crimes and its Financing Law**: The Combating-Terrorism Crimes and its Financing Law issued by the Royal Decree No. M/21 dated 12/2/1439H.

- **Commercial Paper**: a debt instrument creating or acknowledging indebtedness that has a maturity of less than one year from the date of issue.

- **Committee (The)**: the Committee for the Resolution of Securities Disputes. [Art. 25, *Capital Markets Law*]; Art. 1, *Securities Disputes Proceedings Regulations.*

- **Commodities**: food, metal, natural resources or other fixed physical substances in which contracts for future delivery are presently or in the future dealt in.[Art.1(f), Prudential Rules]

- **Companies Law**: the Companies Law issued by Royal Decree No. (M/3) dated 28/1/1437H.

- **Competition Law**: The Competition Law issued by Royal Decree No. M/75 dated 29/6/1440H.

- **Complaint and the Suit**: without prejudice to these term's meanings in the [Capital Markets] Law, each term shall, in relation to the application of these Regulations, bear the following meaning: Complaint: filing a claim (against decisions and actions taken by the authority or the exchange), a right's request or defending a right with the authority.[Art. 1, Securities Disputes Proceedings Regulations, see "Suit."]

- **Compliance Committee**: the committee that is set up by a Capital Market Institution to monitor the securities business that it carries on.

- **Compliance Officer**: the compliance officer of the Capital Market Institution appointed in accordance with paragraph (a) of Article 57 of the Capital Market Institutions Regulations, or the compliance officer of the external party delegated by the Capital Market Institution to function as a compliance officer, appointed in accordance with paragraph (e) of Article (20) of the Capital Market Institutions Regulations.

- **Conflict of Interest**: Refers to the conflict of interest between the issuer and any of the participating entities involved in the book building process, including but not limited to the following circumstances:

a) A director or an executive of any of the participating entities is a substantial shareholder in the issuer or any company that controls the issuer or any of the issuer's subsidiaries or vice versa.
b) A participating entity is a substantial shareholder in the issuer or any of the issuer's subsidiaries or vice versa.
c) Any of the persons, referred to in paragraph (a) and (b) above, is a director of the issuer or any of the issuer's subsidiaries. [Art. 2(c), IPO Book Building]

- **Connected Advisor**: means in the *Merger & Acquisition Regulations*:

1) an advisor that is advising the offeror or the offeree company in relation to an acquisition (whether through a private transaction or an offer);
2) a Capital Market Institution acting for the benefit of the offeror or the offeree company; and
3) an advisor that is advising a person who is acting in concert with the offeror or the offeree company in relation to an offer or in relation to the matter which is the reason for that person being a member of the relevant concert party.

- **Connected Fund Manager**: a fund manager of an investment fund who normally is connected with the offeror or the offeree company, as the case may be, if it is controlled by, controls or is under the same control as:

1) an offeror or any person acting in concert with it;
2) the offeree company or any person acting in concert with it; or
3) any connected advisor to any person above mentioned in (1) or (2).

- **Connected Person**: the managing director, a director, the senior executives, any shareholder who owns a substantial percentage of shares of a company with listed securities, or any associate of any such persons to whom this definition applies.

- **Constructionally Developed Real Estate**: real estate that is developed and ready for use and which fulfills the regulatory requirements, including residential, commercial, industrial, agricultural real estates and other types of real estates.

- **Contingent Liability Security**: a derivative under the terms of which the client will or may be liable to make further payments when the instrument expires or the position is closed out.

- **Contingent Liability Transaction**: a transaction in a contingent liability security.

- **Contract for Differences** (Derivatives): any contract for differences or any other contracts the purpose or pretended purpose of which is to secure a profit or avoid a loss by reference to fluctuations in:

1) the value or price of property of any description; or
2) an index or other factor designated for that purpose in the contract;

but excluding:

1) rights under a contract if the parties intend that the profit is to be secured or the loss avoided by one or more of the parties taking delivery of any property to which the contract relates;
2) rights under a contract under which money is received by way of deposit on terms that any return to be paid on the sum deposited will be calculated by reference to a specific index or other factor; and
3) rights under a contract of insurance.

- **Contractually Based Security**: any of the following:

1) options;
2) futures;
3) contracts for differences;
4) long term insurance contracts;
5) any right to or interest in anything which is specified by any of the previous sub-paragraphs.

- **Control**: the ability to influence the actions or decisions of another person through, whether directly or indirectly, alone or with a relative or affiliate (a) holding 30% or more of the voting rights in a company, or (b) having the right to appoint 30% or more of the members of the governing body; "controller" shall be construed accordingly.

- **Controlling Interest**: The ability to influence actions or decisions of another person directly, indirectly, individually or collectively with a relative or an affiliate through:

(A) owning %30 or more of the voting rights in a company,
(B) having the right to appoint %30 or more of the administrative team members.

[Art. 1, *Corporate Governance Regulations*]; [Art.1, *Regulatory Rules and Procedures issued pursuant to the Companies Law relating to Listed Joint Stock Companies*]

- **Convertible Currency**: a currency that can be bought or sold without restrictions imposed by any governmental authority in the Kingdom or in the jurisdiction which has issued the currency. [Article 2, Securities Central Counterparts Regulations]

- **Corporate Actions**: actions taken by an issuer which lead to increasing or decreasing the number of its securities or changing its nominal value including, for example, increasing or decreasing its capital.

- **Corporate Finance Business**: securities business carried on by a Capital Market Institution connection with:

1) the offer, issue, underwriting, repurchase, exchange or redemption of, or the variation of the terms of, those securities, or any related matter;
2) the manner in which, or the terms on which, or the persons by whom, any business activity is to be financed, structured, managed, controlled, regulated or reported upon;
3) an actual or proposed takeover or related operations; or
4) a merger, de-merger or reorganization.

- **Corporate Finance Professional**: an employee of a Capital Market Institution who engages in corporate finance business.

- **Corporate Governance**: rules to lead and guide the Company that includes mechanisms to regulate the various relationships between the Board, Executive Directors, shareholders and Stakeholders, by establishing rules and procedures to facilitate the decision making process and add transparency and credibility to it with the objective of protecting the rights of shareholders and Stakeholders and achieving fairness, competitiveness and transparency on the Exchange and the business environment.

- **Corporate Governance Regulations**: Corporate Governance Regulations issued by the Board of the Authority.

- **Council of Competition Protection**: the Council of Competition Protection as constituted under the Competition Law.

- **Counterparty**: a client who is an Authorized Person, an exempt person, an institution or a non-Saudi financial services firm. [Art.2, AML Regs.];

- **Counterparty**: means in the Capital Market Institutions Regulations and in the definition of the term "institutional client" stipulated in the Glossary, any of the following:

1) SAMA;
2) The Exchange, or any other exchange recognized by the Authority;
3) The Depository Center;
4) The CCP;
5) A Capital Market Institution;
6) A Local Bank;
7) A local insurance company;
8) A qualified foreign investor; and
9) A non-Saudi financial services firm.

and otherwise, counterparty means a counterparty to a transaction.

- **Credit Rating**: an opinion regarding the creditworthiness of an entity, or the creditworthiness of a security expressed in symbols, letters, numbers or any other form.

- **Credit Rating Agencies Regulations**: the Credit Rating Agencies Regulations issued by the Board of the Capital Market Authority.

- **Credit Risks**: risk of loss resulting from fluctuations in the credit standing of issuers of securities, counterparties and any debtors to which Authorized Persons are exposed.[Art. 1(f), Prudential Rules. See, Market Risk]

- **Cumulative Voting**: a method of voting for electing Board members that gives each shareholder a voting capacity equivalent to the number of shares he/she owns , and by which the shareholder is entitled to either exercise all of his/her votes towards one nominee or to divide his/her votes towards several nominees without any duplication of such votes. [Art.1, Corporate Governance Regulations]

- **Custodian**: a person who is authorized under the Capital Market Institutions Regulations to conduct the securities activity of custody.

- **Custody**: safeguarding assets belonging to another person which include securities, or arranging for another person to do so, and custody includes taking the necessary administrative measures.

- **Customer**: in the Authorized Persons Regulations, means a client who is not a counterparty, whether it is an individual or a juristic person.

D

- **Day**: a business day in the Kingdom in accordance with the official working days of the Authority. [Under the Corporate Governance Regulations, "Day" means a calendar day whether a business day or not. Art. 1, Corporate Governance Regulations.][Under the Securities Dispute Regulations, "Day" means: "the calendar day including official vacation days for the country. In relation to the dates mentioned in the {Securities Dispute} Regulations, if the last day is an official vacation then the date will be extended to the first business day thereafter."[Art. 1, Securities Disputes Proceedings Regulations]

- **Deal**: to buy, sell, subscribe for or underwrite a security.

- **Dealing**: to deal in a security, whether as principal or agent, and dealing includes the sale, purchase, manage the subscription or underwrite securities.

- **Dealing Day**: any day on which the units of an investment fund may be subscribed for and redeemed.

- **Debt Instrument**: tradable instrument creating or acknowledging indebtedness issued by companies, the government, public institutions or public organizations, but excluding:

  1) an instrument creating or acknowledging indebtedness for the consideration payable under a contract for the supply of goods or services, or for money borrowed to defray the consideration payable under a contract for the supply of goods or services;
  2) a cheque, a bill of exchange, a banker's draft or a letter of credit;
  3) a banknote, a statement showing a balance on a bank account, or a lease contract or any other evidence of disposition of property; and
  4) a contract of insurance.

- **Debt-Based Recourse Debt Instrument**: means a debt instrument issued by a special purposes entity under whose terms:

  (a) the entitlement of holders of the debt instrument to a return is not based on the returns generated by the special purposes entity's assets;
  (b) the sponsor is obliged to the holders of the debt instrument (whether by guarantee or otherwise) to pay all amounts due on the debt instrument; and
  (c) repayment of the nominal value of the debt instrument is to be made to the holders of the debt instrument at or before the maturity of such debt instrument.

- **Demerged Entity**: the entity that is the subject of a Demerger transaction resulting in it being Spun-Off, Split-Off or Carved Out from the Listed Company.

- **Demerger**: a transaction where a Listed Company wishes to effect the separation or divesture of a subsidiary, an asset or a business wholly or partly within its existing group whether through a separate listing of such subsidiary, asset or business on the Exchange or without listing. A Demerger could take the form of a Spin-Off, a Split-Off or a Carve Out.

- **Depository Bank**: a financial institution of legal personality authorized to issue and cancel Depository Receipts out of the Kingdom, appointed by the Issuer in accordance with the provisions of the [Instructions on Issuing Depositary Receipts Out of the Kingdom. Art. 2(c), Instructions on Issuing Depositary Receipts out of the Kingdom]

- **Depository Receipts**: Financial instruments listed and traded in a Foreign Market, issued by the Depository Bank for shares issued in the Kingdom and listed in the Exchange, or for shares issued in the Kingdom and its Issuer has made the necessary arrangements for listing them in the Exchange. [Art. 2(c), Instructions on Issuing Depositary Receipts Outside of the Kingdom]

- **Derivative**: a contract for differences, a future or an option.

- **Designated Securities**: Securities in respect of which the CCP has issued a notice designating such Securities as not benefitting from the Clearing service. [Article 2, Securities Central Counterparts Regulations]

- **Developer**: a person nominated by the fund manager to be responsible for executing the technical aspects to achieve the fund's purposes.

- **Direct Clearing Member**: has the meaning specified in paragraph (a) of Article 21 of the [Securities Central Counterparts] Regulations. [Article 2, Securities Central Counterparts Regulations]

- **Director**: in relation to a joint stock company, includes a member of the board of directors and in relation to any other company includes any manager or other senior executive who makes and implements the company's strategic decisions.

- **Direct Financing Fund**: An investment fund established for the purpose of carrying out the activity of direct financing for legal persons and investment funds.[Art 2(d), Direct Financing Investment Funds Instructions]

- **Discretionary Account**: means in the Merger and Acquisition Regulations, an account with a Capital Market Institution who is authorized to carry on managing activities, with the power to make investment decisions without prior reference to the holder of the account.

- **Distributor**: for the purposes of the Investment Funds Regulations and the Real Estate Investment Funds Regulations, means; a person who offers units of an investment fund in the Kingdom.

- **Dual Unit Price**: A settlement of the unit price calculated, in accordance with the financial statements, to which the expected credit losses are registered in the financial statements of the fund, against the unit price calculated for dealing purposes.

E

- **Edaa**: the Securities Depository Centre Company

- **Employee**: in relation to a person, includes a director or manager of a company, a partner in a partnership or any other individual who is employed under a contract of service or contract for service and whose services are placed at the disposal of and under the control of that person.

- **Employees' Shares**: Treasury Shares which are allocated by the Company to its employees. [Art.1, Regulatory Rules and Procedures issued pursuant to the Companies Law relating to Listed Joint Stock Companies]

- **Entities Subject to the Authority's Supervision (ESAS)**: for the purposes of these Rules, it shall mean the following:

 1) The Exchange.
 2) The Depository Center.
 3) Authorized persons licensed to carry on securities business, except Authorized Persons licensed to carry on arranging or advising activities.
 4) Investment Funds.
 5) Listed Companies. [Art.2(c), Registration of Auditors]

- **Excess Exposures**: large exposures in the trading book that exceed 25% of the Authorized Person's capital base.[Art.1(f), Prudential Rules]

- **Exchange**: the Saudi Stock Exchange Company ("Tadawul") or the Saudi Stock Exchange including where the context permits any committee, sub-committee, employee, officer, affiliate or agent to whom any function of the Exchange may for the time being be delegated, and "on Exchange" means any activity taking place through or by the facilities provided by the Exchange.

- **Exchange Rules**: the regulations, rules, procedures and instructions proposed by the Board of Directors of the Exchange and approved by the Board of the Authority.

- **Exchange Traded Fund**: an index fund that the units in which are traded on the Main Market or the Parallel Market.

- **Executive Director** (of a company): a member of the Board who is a full time member of the executive management team of the Company and participates in its daily activities. Non-Executive Director: a member of the Board who is not a full-time member of the management team of the Company and does not participate in its daily activities. [Art. 1, Corporate Governance Regulations];

- **Execution-Only Customer**: a customer for whom the Authorized Person only deals as agent in accordance with instructions provided by the customer and whom an Authorized Person does not advise.

- **Executive Board Member**: means in the Capital Market Institutions Regulations, a member of the board of directors who is full-time in the executive management of the Capital Market Institution and participates in its daily activities.

- **Executive Management** or Senior Executive: persons responsible for managing the daily operations of the Company, and proposing and executing strategic decisions, such as the Chief Executive Officer (CEO) and his/her delegates and the Chief Financial Officer (CFO). [Art 1, Corporate Governance Regulations]

- **Exposures**: items reported as assets in the balance sheet, derivatives reported as liabilities or off-balance sheet commitments.[Art.1(f), Prudential Rules (see Excess Exposures, Large Exposures)]

- **Exempt Offer**: where:

 1) securities are issued by the government of the Kingdom;
 2) offers of contractually based securities, provided that the offer of unlisted contractually based securities shall be limited to any of the following cases:

  a. Where all offerees are investors under the categories of Institutional and Qualified Clients.

  b. Where all offerees are employees of the issuer or of any of its affiliates.

 3) where an issuer whose shares are not listed on the Exchange increases its capital by offering new shares to existing shareholders;
 4) where the offeree is an affiliate of the issuer unless it is an offer of a class of shares that is listed on the Exchange;
 5) where all of the offerees are employees of the issuer or of any of its affiliates unless it is an offer of a class of shares that is listed on the Exchange; or
 6) offers in an insolvency situation where shares are offered to creditors.
 7) where an issuer whose shares are not listed on the Exchange increases its capital by way of debt conversion.
 8) where the subscription in total value for the securities being offered is less than 10 million SR or an equivalent amount, in accordance to the following conditions:

  a. The offer shall be not made more than one time during the twelve months after the completion of the offer.

  b. Subscription in the offered securities shall be limited to (50) offerees or less (excluding investors under the categories of Institutional and Qualified Clients) provided that the amount payable per offeree (excluding investors under the categories of Institutional and Qualified Clients) shall not exceed (200,000) two hundred thousand SR or an equivalent amount.

- **Exempt Person**: any of the persons specified in Annex 1 to the Securities Business Regulations.

F

- **FATF**: Financial Action Task Force on money laundering and terrorist financing. [Art. 2, AML Regs.]

- **Feeder Fund**: an investment fund whose primary investment objective is to invest all of its assets in another investment fund.

- **Finance Company**: a company licensed to engage in finance activities in accordance with the Laws of the Kingdom.

- **Financial Group**: Comprises an Authorized Person and: 1) The Authorized Person's local and foreign subsidiaries that are regulated by these Rules or by similar rules; 2) Companies with which the Authorized Person has a joint, or essentially joint, management or exercises a significant influence over ; 3) Private equity investments in which the Authorized Person owns a majority of the voting rights.(Art. 1(f), Prudential Rules]

- **Financial Resources**: in relation to a Capital Market Institution are the sum of the following:

 1) shares other than cumulative preferences shares;

2) any sums standing to the credit of a share premium account;
3) audited reserves; and
4) revaluation reserves;

less:

1) intangible assets;
2) current year losses;
3) holdings of shares in other Capital Market Institutions, banks or non-Saudi financial service firms unless held for trading purposes only; and
4) illiquid assets.

- **Financial Sector Entities**: any of the following:

1) banks;
2) Capital Market Institutions;
3) legal persons engaged in the business of extending credit;
4) insurance companies;
5) finance companies;
6) affiliates of any of the above; or
7) any other entity which the Authority determines should be included or treated as a financial sector entity.

- **Financing Transaction**: means the transaction under which a special purposes entity raises finance by the issue of debt instruments, including the acquisition, transfer or other use of assets required to generate amounts due under the terms of those debt instruments, and the issue of the debt instruments itself.

-**FIU**: refers to the Financial Intelligence Unit of the Ministry of Interior. [Art.2, AML Regs.]

- **Fixed-term Subordinated Loans**: the subordinated loans with a fixed term. These also include fixed term promissory notes.[Art.1(f), Prudential Rules. See, "Subordinated Loans' *infra*.']

- **Foreign Credit Rating Agency**: a credit rating agency incorporated in a jurisdiction other than the Kingdom and authorized or registered (as applicable) to conduct rating activities outside the Kingdom.

- **Foreign Fund**: an investment fund, which is established in a jurisdiction outside the Kingdom.

- **Foreign Fund Manager**: a person operating outside the Kingdom and working as a manager of a foreign fund.

- **Foreign Market**: A regulated market for the trade of securities out of the Kingdom. [Art. 2(c), Instructions on Issuing Depositary Receipts out of the Kingdom]

- **Foreign Portfolio Manager**: a foreign financial institution that has a legal personality which manages the assets of clients, that meets the requirements stated in sub paragraph (a/2) of Article (6) of these Rules, which engages or intend to engage with the QFI or the applicant for the purpose of investing on its behalf in listed securities. [Art. 2(c), Qualified Foreign Financial Institutions Regulations]

- **Foreign Regulator**: in relation to a foreign credit rating agency, its principal regulator in the jurisdiction of its incorporation and/or establishment.

- **Foreign Strategic Investor**: a foreign legal entity that aims to own a Strategic Shareholding in listed companies.[Part 2(a), Foreign Strategic Ownership in Listed Companies]

- **Freezing the Investment Account**: The temporary block on all money transfers from the investment account, the utilization of its balance, and the transfer or pledge of securities in the investment portfolios linked to it. The freezing of the investment account shall not prevent the client from selling securities and receiving its proceeds or profits on the investment account or transferring funds from his bank account to his investment account. [Art. 2(c), Investment Accounts Instructions]

- **Fund Board**: the fund directors appointed by the fund manager in accordance with the Investment Funds Regulations and the Real Estate Investment Funds Regulations, to oversee and supervise the relevant fund manager's conduct.

- **Fund Director**: a natural person appointed as a member of a fund board of an investment fund in accordance with the Investment Funds Regulations and the Real Estate Investment Funds Regulations.

- **Fund Management Fee**: the remuneration, expenses and fees in relation to advisory services paid to the fund manager.

- **Fund Manager**: the Capital Market Institution that carries out the management of the assets of an investment fund or a real estate investment fund, and the management of its business and offering of its units in accordance with the Investment Funds Regulations, the Real Estate Investment Funds Regulations and the Rules for Special Purposes Entities.

- **Fund of Funds**: an investment fund the main objective of which is to invest all of its assets in other investment funds.

- **Fund's Net Assets Value**: for the purposes of the Investment Funds Regulations and the Real Estate Investment Funds Regulations, means; the Fund's Total Assets Value minus its liabilities.

- **Fund's Net Profit**: for the purposes of the Real Estate Investment Funds Regulations, means the total revenues of the real estate investment fund after deducting the total expenses and fees incurred by the fund, except for the items of the other comprehensive income.

- **Fund Operator**: the fund manager licensed to carry out the activity of managing investments and operating funds or the capital market institution appointed in accordance with paragraph (b) of Article 8 of the Investment Funds Regulations; to operate investment funds.

- **Fund Size**: It means the Fund's Total Assets Value plus any capital pledged to be paid by the unitholders. [Art. 2(d), Direct Financing Investment Funds Instructions]

- **Fund's Total Assets Value**: for the purposes of the Investment Funds Regulations and the Real Estate Investment Funds Regulations it means; the fund's assets value that are valued based on the method of assets valuation stipulated in the Fund's Terms and Conditions.

- **Fund Sub-Custodian**: A third party contracted by the custodian to perform some or all of the custodian's functions in relation to an investment fund.

- **Fund Sub-Manager**: a third party contracted by a fund manager, under a contract, in accordance with the Investment Funds Regulations and the Real Estate Investment Funds Regulations, and takes on the fund manager's behalf all or part of the investment decisions for an investment fund managed by the fund manager.

- **Funds**: means assets or properties of whatever type, material or intangible, movable or immovable, along with the legal documents and deeds proving the ownership of the assets or any right pertaining thereto. [Art.2, AML Regs.]

- **Future**: rights under contracts for the sale of a commodity or property of any other description under which delivery is to be made at a prospective date and at a price agreed on when the contract is made, but excluding rights under any contract which is made for commercial and not investment purposes.

G

- **GCC**: The Cooperation Council for the Arab States of the Gulf. [Art. 2(c), Investment Accounts Instructions]

- **GCC Citizens**: Natural persons who have the nationality of one of the GCC countries, and legal persons that the majority of their capital is owned by citizens of GCC countries or governments and has the nationality of one of the GCC countries. [Art. 2(c), IPO Book Building]

- **GCC Companies**: Companies that have the nationality of one of the GCC countries, and are incorporated according to the Companies Law of such country, and which the majority of their capital is owned by citizens of the GCC countries or their governments. [Art. 2(c), IPO Book Building]

- **GCC Funds**: The investment funds which have legal personality that are established in one of the GCC countries, the units of which are publicly or privately offered to investors in these countries according to the applicable laws in these countries, and which the majority of their capital is owned by citizens of the GCC countries or their governments.[Art. 2(c), IPO Book Building]

- **GCC Legal Persons**: A legal person whose capital is majority owned by citizens or governments of the GCC member states and holds the nationality of one of the GCC member states.[Art. 2(c), Investment Accounts Instructions]

- **Geared Security**: any of the following:

  1) a contingent liability security; or
  2) a vehicle which provides a return (or purports to provide a return) by gearing, whether by borrowing or by investing in contractually based securities.

- **General Assembly**: the general assembly held with the attendance of the shareholders of the Company pursuant to the provisions of the Company's bylaws and the Companies Law.[Art.1, Regulatory Rules and Procedures issued pursuant to the Companies Law relating to Listed Joint Stock Companies]

- **General Business Risk**: the risks and potential losses arising from the CCP's operation as a business, but excluding risks and losses related to a Clearing Member default. General Business Risk includes any potential impairment of the CCP's financial position as a consequence of a decline in its revenues or an increase in its expenses. [Article 2, Securities Central Counterparts Regulations]

- **General Clearing Member**: has the meaning specified in paragraph (a) of Article 21 of the [Securities Central Counterparts] Regulations. [Article 2, Securities Central Counterparts Regulations]

- **Glossary**: *Glossary of Defined Terms used in the Regulations and Rules of the Authority* issued by the Board of the Authority.

- **Government Entities**: Refers to any of the following: a) Entities which the Custodian of The Two Holy Mosques or the Council of Ministers are their point of reference for their financial and administrative affairs, including Ministries, Departments, Authorities, General Agencies, Government Funds or Funds managed by government entities. b) Legal persons affiliated to one of the GCC countries.[Art. 2(c), IPO Book Building]

- **Government-owned Companies**: Companies fully owned by the government or any government entity. [Art. 2(c), IPO Book Building]

- **Government-related entities**: central banks, and investment funds – including sovereign funds and funds which take the form of pension and endowments funds – fully owned (directly or indirectly) by a government entity. [Art. 2(c), Qualified Foreign Financial Institutions Regulations]

- **Group**: in relation to a person, means that person and each affiliate of it. [When referring to a person, means the person and his affiliates. Art.1, Corporate Governance Regulations]

- **Group of Connected Counterparties**: two or more natural or legal persons who, unless otherwise shown, constitute a single risk because: 1) One of them, directly or indirectly, has control over the other or others in the group; or 2) they are so interconnected in a way that if one of them were to experience financial problems, the other or all of the others would be likely to encounter repayment difficulties.[Art. 1(f), Prudential Rules]

- **Governing Body**: the body of individuals which makes a person's strategic decisions, and the board of directors of a joint-stock company, or the board of managers of a limited liability company is considered its governing body.

H

- **Holding Company**: a Joint Stock Company or Limited Liability Company aims to control other Joint Stock Companies or Limited Liability Companies called affiliates by owning more than half of those companies' share capitals or by controlling the composition of their management. Art. 1, Corporate Governance Regulations.

I

- **ICAAP**: an acronym for "Internal Capital Adequacy Assessment Process." Prudential Rules, Chapter 20.

- **Identification Document**: The valid identification document issued by the competent authorities and accepted for opening an investment account for the client in accordance with the [Investment Accounts Instructions. Art. 2(c), Investment Accounts Instructions]

- **Illiquid Assets**: means any of the following:

  1) fixed assets;
  2) financial resources which are not readily realizable; or
  3) deposits not available for withdrawal within three months or less.

- **Implementing Regulations**: any regulations, rules, instructions, procedures and orders issued by the Authority relating to the implementation of the Capital Market Law.

- **Independent Board Member**: means in the Capital Market Institutions Regulations, a non-executive member of the board of directors who enjoys full independence in his position and decisions, and none of the negation of independence issues stipulated in paragraph (c) of Article 53 of the Capital Market Institutions Regulations, applies to him.

- **Independent Director**: a non-executive member of the Board who enjoys complete independence in his/her position and decisions and none of the independence affecting issues stipulated in Article 20 of the [Corporate Governance] Regulations apply to him/her. [Art. 1, Corporate Governance Regulations.]

- **Independent Financial Advisor**: means in the Merger & Acquisition Regulations, a financial advisor who is authorized by the Authority and is independent of its appointor (whether it is the offeror, offeree company or any other person obligated to appoint an independent financial advisor in accordance with the Merger & Acquisition Regulations). Circumstances under which the financial advisor shall not be considered independent of its appointor include, but are not limited to the following:

1) the financial advisor or any of its subsidiaries is a substantial shareholder in the appointor or any of its subsidiaries;
2) the financial advisor or any of its subsidiaries is a substantial shareholder in a controller of the appointer or any of its subsidiaries;
3) an employee of the financial advisor who is involved in the provision of financial advice to the person, is a substantial shareholder in the appointor or any of its subsidiaries;
4) any of the financial advisor's substantial shareholders or board member or in any of its subsidiaries is a substantial shareholders or board member with the appointer or in any of its subsidiaries;
5) any of the appointer's shareholders or board member or in any of its subsidiaries is a substantial shareholders or board member with the financial advisor or in any of its subsidiaries;
6) the appointor or any of its subsidiaries is a substantial shareholder in the financial advisor or any of its subsidiaries; or
7) the appointer or any of its subsidiaries is a substantial shareholder in a controller of the financial advisor or any of its subsidiaries.

- **Independent Fund Director**: an independent fund director who enjoys complete independence by way of example, the following shall constitute an infringement of such independence:

1) he is an employee of the fund manager or any of its affiliates, or any sub-manager or custodian for a fund or have a material business, or contractual relationship with the fund manager or any sub-manager or custodian for such fund.
2) he, during the preceding two years, has been a senior executive of the fund manager or any of its affiliates.
3) he is a first-degree relative of any board member or any senior executives of the fund manager or of any its affiliates.
4) he is a controlling shareholder of the fund manager or any of its affiliates, during the preceding two years.

- **Independent Investment Advisor**: the Capital Market Institution authorized to carry out advising business that holds itself out as an independent investment advisor in accordance with paragraph (f) of Article 41 of the Capital Market Institutions Regulations.

- **Independent Legal Advisor**: means in the Merger & Acquisition Regulations, a legal advisor who is licensed to practice law in Saudi Arabia and is independent of its appointor (whether the offeror, offeree company or any other person obligated to appoint an independent legal advisor in accordance with the merger & acquisition regulations) and independent of the appointor's financial advisor. circumstances under which the legal advisor shall not be considered independent of its appointor include, but are not limited to the following:

1) the legal advisor or any of its subsidiaries is a substantial shareholder or board member in the appointor or in the financial advisor or any of their subsidiaries;
2) a partner of the legal advisor is a substantial shareholder or board member in a controller of the appointor or in the financial advisor or any of their subsidiaries;
3) an employee of the legal advisor, who is involved in the provision of legal advice and service to the person, is a substantial shareholder or board member in the appointor or in the financial advisor or any of their subsidiaries;
4) any partner or board member of the legal advisor or any of its subsidiaries is a substantial shareholder or board member in the appointor or in the financial advisor or any of their subsidiaries;
5) any of the appointer's substantial shareholders or board member or in any of its subsidiaries is a substantial shareholders or board member in the legal advisor or any of its subsidiaries;
6) the appointer of the legal or financial advisor or any of their subsidiaries is a substantial shareholders or board member in the legal advisor or any of its subsidiaries; or
7) the appointer or any of its subsidiaries is a substantial shareholder in a controller of the legal advisor or any of its subsidiaries;

- **Independent Member**: a non-executive member of the board who enjoys complete independence in his position and decisions, including having no business, family or other relationship that raises a conflict of interests regarding the CCP, its management or its Clearing Members, and who has had no such relationship during the five years preceding his membership of the board. [Article 2, Securities Central Counterparts Regulations]

- **Index Fund**: an investment fund whose primary investment objective is to track the performance of a specified index.

- **Initial Margin**: margin that is collected to cover the potential future exposure resulting from potential changes in the value of the Clearing Member's position over the appropriate close-out period in the event that Clearing Member defaults. [Article 2, Securities Central Counterparts Regulations]

- **Inside Information**: has the meaning specified at Article 4(c) of the Market Conduct Regulations: "inside information shall mean any security whose price or value would be materially affected if the information was disclosed or made available to the general public." Also see Art. 50, Capital Markets Law: "Insider information means information obtained by the insider and which is not available to the general public, has not been disclosed, and such information is of the type that a normal person would realize that in view of the nature and content of this information, its release and availability would have a material effect on the price or value of a Security related to such information, and the insider knows that such information is not generally available and that, if it were available, it would have a material effect on the price or value of such Security."

- **Insider**: has the meaning specified at Article 4(b) of the Market Conduct Regulations.

- **Insolvency**: actual insolvency, or the commencement of any proceedings in respect of insolvency, liquidation or a voluntary arrangement under the Bankruptcy Regulations, or the commencement of any equivalent procedures in the Kingdom or in any other jurisdiction outside the Kingdom.

- **Insolvent**: a person to whom an insolvency event has occurred.

- **Inspection**: Analyzing periodic data and information provided by the accounting firm and inspecting and assessing the quality control system and the degree of compliance with it. [Art.2(c), Registration of Auditors]

- **Institution**: (means)

  1) any company which owns, or which is a member of a group which owns, net assets of not less than 10 million Saudi Riyals;
  2) any unincorporated body, partnership or other organization which has net assets of not less than 10 million Saudi Riyals;
  3) a person acting in the capacity of director, officer or employee of a legal person and responsible for its securities activity, where that legal person falls within the definition of paragraphs (1) or (2).

- **Institutional Client**: means any of the following:

  a. the Government of the Kingdom or any supranational authority recognized by the Authority.
  b. companies fully owned by the government or any government entity, either directly or through a portfolio managed by a Capital Market Institution authorized to carry on managing business.
  c. any legal person acting for its own account and be any of the following:

    1) a company which owns, or is a member of a group which owns, net assets of more than 50 million Saudi Riyals;

    2) an unincorporated body, partnership company or other organization which has net assets of more than 50 million Saudi riyals.

    3) a person acting in the capacity of director, officer or employee of a legal person and responsible for its securities activity, where that legal person falls within the definition of paragraph (c/1) or (c/2).

  d. a company fully owned by a legal person who meets the criteria of paragraph (b) or (c).
  e. an investment fund.
  f. a counterparty.

- **Instruction**: any instruction, election, acceptance or any other message of any kind sent or received by way of the Tadawul Trading System or the Tadawul Depositary System.

- **Insurance Company**: an insurance company which is regulated by SAMA. [also, "a financial institution that has a legal personality which engages in insurance business." Art. 2(c), Qualified Foreign Financial Institutions Regulations]

- **Intangible Assets**: non-cash assets, without physical substance, capable of providing the firm with services or benefits in the future, and in which the firm has acquired the right as a result of events that have occurred or operations that have been completed in the past. Intangible assets could be separately identifiable (could be separated from other assets), such as formation costs, trademarks, copyrights, industrial samples and designs, franchises and licenses. Intangible assets could also be unidentifiable in a separate manner such as goodwill, management skills and qualifications, and other factors which constitute the reputation.

- **Intermediate Broker**: a person through whom a Capital Market Institution undertakes a margined transaction for a client.

- **Internal Regulations**: the regulations issued by the Authority in relation to the Authority's administrative and financial affairs and its personnel and staff affairs. [Art. 1, Capital Markets Law]

- **Interoperability Arrangement**: an arrangement between two or more CCPs that involves a cross system execution of transactions. [Article 2, Securities Central Counterparts Regulations]

- **Investment Account**: An accounting record created by the Authorized Person for the client's money deposited in a client account opened by the Authorized Person to fund the client's transactions in securities and reflects all the details of the transactions in respect of that account.[Art. 2(c), Investment Accounts Instructions]

- **Investment Advisor**: an employee of a Capital Market Institution who performs the activity of advising on behalf of a Capital Market Institution with or for a client. [an adviser who provides, offers or agrees to provide, advice to others in their capacity as investors or potential investors, in relation to purchasing, selling, subscribing or underwriting a security, or exercising any right conferred by a security to acquire, dispose of, underwrite or convert a security. Art. 1, Capital Markets Law]

- **Investment Fund**: a collective investment scheme aimed at providing investors therein with an opportunity to participate collectively in the profits of the scheme which is managed by a fund manager for specified fees. [Also, means any of the following legal persons:

  1) a pension fund in which its main objective is to collect fees or periodic contributions from participants or for their interest, for the purpose of compensating them according to a specific mechanism.
  2) Endowment fund with a principal purpose of making grants to organizations, institutions, or individuals for scientific, educational, cultural purposes, including university endowments fund.
  3) a collective investment scheme aimed at providing investors therein with an opportunity to participate collectively in the profits of the scheme. Art. 2(c), Qualified Foreign Financial Institutions Regulations]

- **Investment Funds Regulations**: the *Investment Funds Regulations* issued by the Board of the Authority.

- **Investment Grade**: for the purposes of the Investment Funds Regulations, means; the rating category associated with relatively low default risks granted by recognized credit rating agencies.

- **Investment Portfolio**: An account linked to the investment account that reflects the client's assets received by the Authorized Person in the course of carrying out securities business as per the Client Asset Rules stipulated in the Authorized Persons Regulations and reflects all the details of the transactions in respect of that account.[Art. 2(c), Investment Accounts Instructions]

- **In Writing**: or other similar term, wherever it appears, in relation to a communication, notice, approval, agreement or other document, means in legible form and capable of being reproduced on paper, irrespective of the medium used.

- **Issuance Program**: a program under which a single prospectus under the *Rules on the Offer of Securities and Continuing Obligations* is produced pursuant to which a number of debt instruments or convertible debt instruments may be issued in the future, as stated in the prospectus.

- **Issuer**: a person issuing or intending to issue securities.

J,K

- **Joint Enterprise**: an arrangement between two or more persons for commercial purposes related to a business which they carry on or are to carry on jointly.

- **Kingdom**: the Kingdom of Saudi Arabia.

L

- **Large Exposures**: an exposure to a counterparty or group of connected counterparties that exceeds 10% of the Authorized Person's capital base.[Art.1(f), Prudential Rules]

- **Lead Plaintiff**: A person who represents Members of the Group of Plaintiffs in the proceedings before the Committees for the Resolution of Securities Disputes in connection with a Class Action Suit, and is appointed in accordance with the provisions of paragraph (b) of Article 56 of the [Securities Disputes] Regulations.[Art. 1, Securities Disputes Proceedings Regulations]

- **Lead Rating Analyst**: a rating analyst with primary responsibility for elaborating a credit rating or for communicating with the rated entity or the issuer of the security which is rated or to be rated.

- **Liability**: any liability, loss, damage, claim or expense of any kind or nature, whether direct, indirect, consequential or otherwise.

- **Limited Offer**: has the meaning specified in Article 9 of the Rules on Offers of Securities and Continuing Obligations.

- **Limited Offer**: An offer of securities is a limited offer if at the subscription is limited to no more than 100 offerees (excluding investors under the categories of Institutional and Qualified Clients) and the amount payable per offeree does not exceed 200,000 (two hundred thousand SR) or an equivalent amount. [Limited to one such offer per 12 month period.]

- **Liquidation of the Fund**: means wherever mentioned in the Investment Funds Regulations and the Real Estate Investment Funds Regulations, a maximum period of 6 months from the next day of the date for the Termination of the Fund, during which the assets of fund must be fully liquidated in accordance with the provisions of the Investment Funds Regulations and the Real Estate Investment Funds Regulations.

- **Liquid Net Assets**: assets funded by equity (common stock, disclosed reserves or other retained earnings) which are not otherwise encumbered and freely available to cover General Business Risk. [Article 2, Securities Central Counterparts Regulations]

- **Listed**: in relation to any type of securities, means the securities admitted to listing on the Exchange.

- **Listed Company**: any company with securities of any kind listed on the Exchange.

- **Listing**: listing securities on the Exchange either on the Main Market or on the Parallel Market, or, where the context permits, the application for listing.

- **Listing Rules**: the Listing Rules proposed by the Board of the Exchange and approved by the Board of the Authority.

- **Local Bank**: an institution that has received a license to engage in banking business in accordance with the Laws of the Kingdom.

- **Long Term Insurance Contract**: any long term insurance contract specified by the Authority.

M

- **Main Market**: the market of Exchange where securities, that have been registered and offered pursuant to Part 4 of the Rules on the Offer of Securities and Continuing Obligations, are traded.

- **Managing**: managing securities belonging to another person in circumstances involving the exercise of discretion, or operating investment funds.

- **Managing Investments**: making investment decisions for non-real-estate investment funds and clients' portfolios in circumstances involving the exercise of discretion.

- **Managing Investments and Operating Funds**: making investment decisions for investment funds and clients' portfolios in circumstances involving the exercise of discretion, and operating investment funds.

- **Margin**: a Variation Margin or an Initial Margin. [Article 2, Securities Central Counterparts Regulations]

- **Margin Transaction**: a transaction where a Capital Market Institution makes a loan to a client of a portion of the cost of the transaction.

- **Market Conduct Regulations**: the *Market Conduct Regulations* issued by the Board of the Capital Market Authority.

- **Market Maker**: means in the Investment Funds Regulations, a capital market institution that is authorizedto carry out dealing business where it enters continuous orders, during the trading hours, of buying and selling for the purpose of providing liquidity to the traded units of the exchange traded fund.

- **Market Risk**: risk of loss resulting from fluctuations in the level and in the volatility of market prices of assets, liabilities and financial instruments.[Art. 1(f), Prudential Rules. See, Credit Risks]

- **Member**: a member of the committee appointed by its establishment resolution and any member added to the committee or appointed as a substitute of a former member. This term includes the committee's chairman unless the contrary intention appears.[Art. 1, Securities Disputes Proceedings Regulations]

- **Members of the Group of Plaintiffs**: A group of persons who participate in filing a Class Action Suit.[Art. 1, Securities Disputes Proceedings Regulations]

- **Merger**: a transaction, however its nature, involving an offeree company listed on the exchange and resulting in any of the following:

  1) the absorption of that offeree company by another company listed on the exchange.
  2) the absorption of that offeree company by a company that is not listed on the exchange.
  3) the formation of a new legal entity by merging two companies or more (including the offeree company).

- **Merger and Acquisition Regulations**: the *Merger and Acquisition Regulations* issued by the Board of the Capital Market Authority.

- **Minimum Authorization Requirements**: means in the Credit Rating Agency Regulations, the authorization requirements specified in Article 8, Article 9 and Article 10 (as applicable in the Credit Rating Agencies Regulations).

- **MLRO**: the Money Laundering and Terrorism Financing Reporting Officer of the Capital Market Institution, appointed in accordance with Article 64 of the Capital Market Institutions Regulations, or the Money Laundering and Terrorism Financing Reporting Officer of the external party delegated by the Capital Market Institution to function as a Money Laundering and Terrorism Financing Reporting Officer, appointed in accordance with paragraph (e) of Article (20) of the Capital Market Institutions Regulations.

- **Money Laundering**: refers to committing or attempting to commit any act for the purpose of concealing or disguising the true origin of funds acquired by means contrary to Shari'ah or law, thus making the funds appear as if they had come from a legitimate source. [Art.2, AML Regs.]

- **Money Market Fund**: an investment fund the sole objective of which is to invest in short- term securities and money market transactions in accordance with the Investment Funds Regulations.

- **Money Market Transactions**: means short-term deposits and trade finance contracts.

N

- **Net Assets Value**: for the purposes of the Investment Funds Regulations and the Real Estate Investment Funds Regulations, means; the Fund's Net Assets Value divided by the number of units outstanding.

- **Non-Executive Board Member**: means in the Capital Market Institutions Regulations, a member of the board of directors who is not full-time managing the Capital Market Institution and does not participate in its daily activities.

- **Non-Executive Director**: a member of the Board who is not a full-time member of the management team of the Company and does not participate in its daily activities. [Art. 1, Corporate Governance Regulations];

- **Non-profit Organizations Entities**: refers to a legal person who is an entity or an organization that primarily engages in raising/collecting donations and/or disbursing funds for non-profit purposes. [Art 2, AML Regs.]; [any legal entity licensed to engage in collecting, receiving, or paying money for charitable, religious, cultural, educational, social, or solidarity purposes or other charitable activities. Art. 2(c), Investment Accounts Instructions]

- **Non-Saudi Financial Services Firm**: a person who engages in securities business in the course of his profession or trade outside the Kingdom.

- **Non-Trading Activities**: the positions that are held for non-trading purposes. [Art. 1(f), Prudential Rules]

- **Novation**: a process whereby the original contract between one party and another party is discharged and replaced with two new contracts, one between the CCP and the first party and the other between the CCP and the second party. [Article 2, Securities Central Counterparts Regulations]

O

- **Offer**: means in the Merger & Acquisition Regulations, a general tender offer, other than the offers provided by the offeree company itself, that is subject to the Merger & Acquisition Regulations, made to all holders of the shares carrying voting rights in the offeree company for any of the following purposes:

  1) purchase shares carrying Voting Rights in the offeree company or
  2) to effect a merger of the offeree company.

Any reference in the Merger & Acquisition Regulations to the term "offer" or "potential offer" shall be construed as the following:

  1) a merger or potential merger;
  2) an offer or partial offer for takeover, or a potential offer or partial offer for takeover; or
  3) partial offer or potential partial offer, not intended for takeover.

- **Offer Document**: the offer document that the offeror is required to prepare and publish in relation to an offer, in accordance with Article 38 of the Merger & Acquisition Regulations.

- **Offeree Company**: means in the Merger and Acquisition Regulations, a company listed on the Exchange (or unlisted company in the case of reversed takeover) in respect of which a takeover offer has been made.

- **Offering of Securities**: [See, Placement or Offering of Securities]

- **Offeror**: means in the *Rules on the Offer of Securities and Continuing Obligations*, a person who makes an offer or invites a person to make an offer which, if accepted, would give rise to the issue or sale of securities by him or by another person with whom he has made arrangements for the issue or sale of the securities; and in the Merger and Acquisition Regulations, a person who makes or intends to make a takeover offer that is subject to the Merger and Acquisition Regulations.

- **Offeror**: a person who makes or intends to make an Offer. The term also includes (where found in the *Merger & Acquisition Regulations*) any person(s) whom the offeror is acting in concert with. Moreover, "potential offeror" shall be construed accordingly.

- **Offer Period**: the period from announcing a confirmed intention to provide an offer until the offer becomes unconditional as to acceptance, or until the extraordinary general assembly issues a decision to the offeror, as the case may be, and the offeree company in case of acquisition by an offer to exchange securities against the total shares of the offeree company.

- **Open-Ended Investment Fund**: an investment fund with changing capital, the units of which would increase with the issuance of new units, and decrease with redemption by unitholders of some or all of their units. Unitholders are entitled to redeem the value of their units at their net asset value on dealing days set in the Fund's Terms And Conditions in accordance with the Investment Funds Regulations.

- **Open Offer**: a process whereby the CCP extends an open offer to act as a counterparty to market participants and is immediately interposed as counterparty in a transaction where the two parties agree on the terms when the pre-agreed conditions of the CCP are satisfied. [Article 2, Securities Central Counterparts Regulations]

- **Operating Investment Funds**: performing operations related to investment funds, including the calculation of its net assets value and the management of subscription and redemption for its units.

- **Option**: any option to acquire or dispose of any of the following:

  1) a security;
  2) currency;

3) oil, silver, gold, platinum and palladium; or
4) an option to acquire or dispose of an option specified by this sub-paragraph by virtue of (1), (2) or (3).

- **Order**: in relation to an order from a client:

1) an order to a Capital Market Institution from a client to execute a transaction as agent; or
2) any other order to a Capital Market Institution from a client to execute a transaction in circumstances giving rise to similar duties as those arising from an order to execute a transaction as agent. "Order" shall include any decision by a Capital Market Institution to execute a transaction in exercise of discretion for a client, an investment fund that it manages or for the purpose of aggregating orders for its clients in accordance with the Market Conduct Regulations. The definition of order shall not include any requests for purchasing a new securities issue.

- **Ordinary Course of Business**: a usual activity that is normal to the day to day operations of the business. Occasional or infrequent activities do not constitute an ordinary course of business.

- **Ordinary Fund Resolution**: means a resolution requiring an affirmative vote of the unitholders of more than 50% of the units in the investment fund present or represented by proxy at a meeting of unitholders or by modern means of technology.

- **Over-Allotment**: A process upon which a number of additional shares is allocated to the shares offered for subscription. Such shares are borrowed from the lending-shareholders and sold to the public during the initial public offering at the subscription price, in accordance with the over-allotment agreement.[Part 2, IPO Price Stabilization Mechanism]

- **Overseas Custodian**: any of the following:

1) a bank that provides custody services and that is licensed as a commercial bank in a jurisdiction recognized by the Authority;
2) a securities depository licensed as such by an authority outside the Kingdom recognized by the Authority; or
3) an investment firm that is licensed to provide custody services and that is a member of a securities or futures exchange that is recognized by the Authority.

P

- **Parallel Market**: the market of Exchange where shares, that have been registered and offered pursuant to Part 8 of the Rules on the Offer of Securities and Continuing Obligations, are traded.

- **Partial Offer**: an offer (except for offers made by the same offeree company) subject to the Merger & Acquisition Regulations, made to all holders of the shares carrying voting rights in the offeree company to purchase a certain percentage of shares in the offeree company.

- **Participating Entities**: Entities involved in the Book building process from the specified parties in Part (5) of the [IPO Book Building] Instructions.[Art. 2(c), IPO Book Building]

- **Participating Parties**: Those whom are entitled to participate in the Book building process as specified in Part (5) of the [IPO Book Building Instructions. [Art. 2(c), IPO Book Building]

- **Pass Through Service**: a service offered by the CCP in respect of Designated Securities to facilitate their settlement without providing Clearing services. [Article 2, Securities Central Counterparts Regulations]

- **Percentage Ratio**: in relation to a transaction, the figure, expressed as a percentage, that results from applying a calculation under a Class Test to the transaction.

- **Permitted Business Profile**: the permitted business profile of a Capital Market Institution.

- **Perpetual Subordinated Loans**: the subordinated loans with no fixed term.[Art. 1(f), Prudential Rules. See, "Subordinated Loans."]

- **Person**: any natural or legal person recognized as such under the laws of the Kingdom.

- **Placement or Offering of Securities**: issuing securities, inviting the public to subscribe therefor or the direct or indirect marketing thereof; or any statement, announcement or communication that has the effect of selling, issuing or offering securities, but does not include preliminary negotiations or contracts entered into with or among underwriters. [Art. 1, Capital Markets Law]

- **Pledge**: any form of a security interest recognized under the laws of the Kingdom capable of taking effect in relation to a security.

- **Politically Exposed Person** (PEP): is any individual who occupies, has recently occupied, is actively seeking or is being considered for, a senior civil position in a government of a country, state or municipality or any department including the military, any agency, government -owned company. The definition of PEP includes members of immediate family and close associates, collectively known as Related Individuals. Immediate family is typically defined as any known individual who is a member of the PEP's immediate family (i.e. spouse, parent, sibling or child). Close associate is defined as any individual who is a senior advisor closely associated with or an agent of the PEP.

[Amendment: "Politically Exposed Persons (PEPs)-PEPs refers to any of the following categories:

Individuals who are or have been entrusted with prominent public functions domestically or in a foreign country, for example Heads of State or of government, senior politicians, senior government, judicial or military officials, senior executives of state owned corporations, and important political party officials.

Persons who are or have been entrusted with a prominent function by a regional or international organization as members of senior management, including directors, deputy directors and members of the board or equivalent functions.

The PEPs definition covers the family members or relatives of the individuals, and does not cover the middle ranking or more junior individuals in the foregoing categories."]

(Amendment issued 02/10/2017)

- **Portfolio Manager**: an employee of a Capital Market Institution who performs the activity of managing on behalf of a Capital Market Institution with or for a client.

- **Position**: the Authorized Person's own market position and market position that derive from its activities on behalf of clients or as a market maker.[Art. 1(f), Prudential Rules]

- **Positions Held With Trading Intent**: the positions that are held intentionally for short-term resale and/or with the intent of benefiting from actual or expected short-term price movements or to lock in arbitrage profits.[Art. 1(f), Prudential Rules]

- **Prepared Securities Advertisements**: has the meaning given to it in the Capital Market Institutions Regulations.

- **Price Stabilization Mechanism**: A mechanism that contribute to the price stabilization of the newly listed shares on the Exchange, by means of Over- Allotment, and where all or any of the following transactions are conducted:

a) Borrowing a number of shares from lending-shareholders prior to the initial public offering, in an amount not exceeding the number resulted from the maximum limit allowed for Over-Allotment.
b) The short selling of shares during the offer period.
c) The Over-Allotment of shares not exceeding the limit set out in paragraph (a) of Part 3 of these Instructions.
d) Purchasing of shares from the Exchange during the Price Stabilization Period or by a Purchase Option in order to close any position under paragraph (a) above.[Part 2, IPO Price Stabilization Mechanism]

- **Price Stabilization Period**: A period of time for the Price Stabilization Mechanism that is agreed upon between the price stabilization manager and the issuer, provided that such period shall not exceed (30) calendar days from the first day of listing the shares on the Exchange.[Part 2, IPO Price Stabilization Mechanism]

- **Pricing Supplement**: a document which contains the final terms of each debt instruments or convertible debt instruments issue which is intended to be listed.

- **Principles**: the principles specified in Part 2 of the Capital Market Institutions Regulations.

- **Principles for Financial Market Infrastructures**: the international standards for financial market infrastructures issued by the Committee on Payment and Market Infrastructures (CPMI) and the Technical Committee of the International Organization of Securities Commissions (IOSCO). [Article 2, Securities Central Counterparts Regulations]

- **Private Fund**: an investment fund which is established in the Kingdom and which is not a public fund, and the units in which may be offered by the fund manager, in accordance with Part Five of the Investment Funds Regulations, to investors in the Kingdom.

- **Private Placement**: for the purpose of the Rules on the Offer of Securities and Continuing Obligations, means an offer of securities which falls within one of the categories of offers listed in Article 8 of the Rules on the Offer of Securities and Continuing Obligations; and for the purposes of the Investment Funds Regulations, means:

1) for private funds, the offer of units in accordance with paragraph (a) of Article 80 of the Investment Funds Regulations; and
2) for foreign funds, the offer of securities in accordance with paragraph (a) of Article 98 of the Investment Funds Regulations.

- **Private Placement Notification**: the notification required to be made to the Authority under sub-paragraph (2) of paragraph (a) of Article 10 of the Rules on the Offer of Securities and Continuing Obligations. For the purposes of the Investment funds regulations, means the notification required to be made to the Authority under sub-paragraphs (1,2 and 3) of paragraph (a) of Article 81 of the Investment Funds Regulations in relation to private funds or under sub-paragraphs (1,2 and 3) of paragraph (a) of Article 99 of the Investment Funds Regulation in relation to foreign funds.

- **Private Placement**: An offer of securities is a private placement where it is not an exempt offer, public offer or a Parallel Market Offer and falls under any of the following cases:

1) the subscription is restricted to investors under the categories of Institutional and Qualified clients; or
2) the offer is a limited offer. See, *Limited Offer* herein.

- **Private Real Estate Fund**: a private fund the objective of which is to invest in real estate, and it does not include funds that invest all of its assets outside the Kingdom.

- **Private Transaction**: transaction involving the purchase and/or sale of shares carrying Voting Rights in any company listed on the Exchange, negotiated between the Offeror and selling shareholder(s) of the Offeree Company without making an Offer or involving the other shareholders or directors of the Offeree Company.

- **Procyclical**: the changes in risk-management requirements or practices that are positively correlated with business or credit cycle fluctuations and that may cause or exacerbate financial instability. [Article 2, Securities Central Counterparts Regulations]

- **Professional Investor**: any natural person who fulfills at least one of the following criteria:

1) has carried out at least 10 transactions per quarter over the last 12 months of a minimum total amount of 40 million Saudi Riyals on securities markets;
2) his net assets is not less than 5 million Saudi Riyals;
3) works or has worked for at least three years in the financial sector in a professional position which requires knowledge of securities investment;
4) holds professional certificate that is related to securities business and accredited by an internationally recognized entity; or
5) holds the General Securities Qualification Certificate that is recognized by the Authority, and has an annual income that is not less than 600,000 Saudi Riyals in the two most recent years.

- **Professional Standards**: Accounting and auditing standards, the professional code of ethics and other standards and pronouncements adopted by the Saudi Organization for Certified Public Accountants. [Art.2(c), Registration of Auditors]

- **Prospectus**: the document required to offer securities in the Main Market or in the Parallel Market in accordance with the Capital Market Law and the Rules on the Offer of Securities and Continuing Obligations.

- **Public**: means in the Rules on the Offer of Securities and Continuing Obligations, the Instructions on the Price Stabilization Mechanism In Initial Public Offerings and the Instructions on Issuing Depositary Receipts Out of the Kingdom, persons other than the following:

1) affiliates of the issuer;
2) substantial shareholders of the issuer;
3) directors and senior executives of the issuer;
4) directors and senior executives of affiliates of the issuer;
5) directors and senior executives of substantial shareholders of the issuer;
6) any relative of persons described at (1), (2), (3), (4) or (5) above;
7) any company controlled by any persons described at (1), (2), (3), (4), (5) or (6) above; or

8) persons acting in concert, with a collective shareholding of (5%) or more of the class of shares to be listed. [For purposes of the Regulatory Rules and Procedures issued pursuant to the Companies Law relating to Listed Joint Stock Companies, the shares retained by the Company do not count as a part of the ownership of the public. Art.1, Regulatory Rules and Procedures issued pursuant to the Companies Law relating to Listed Joint Stock Companies]

- **Public Consultation**: A request for public comments on an implementing regulations project. [Art. 2(c), Public Consultations on Implementing Regulations]

- **Public Fund**: an investment fund which is established in the Kingdom and the units in which may be offered by the fund manager, in accordance with Part Four of the Investment Funds Regulations, to investors in the Kingdom otherwise than by way of a private placement.

- **Public Unitholders**: means in the Investment Funds Regulations and the Real Estate Investment Funds Regulations, any unitholder who own a unit or units in the closed-ended investment traded fund or the real estate investment traded fund other than the following:

  1) Substantial Unitholder;
  2) the fund manager and its affiliates; or
  3) the fund's board of directors' members.

- **Purchase Option**: A contractual option whereby the price stabilization manager is granted the right to buy an amount of shares not exceeding the amount of the shares included in the Over-Allotment at the subscription price in the initial offer period, during the price stabilization period or after its end.[Part 2, IPO Price Stabilization Mechanism]

- **Purchased Shares**: shares bought back by the Company pursuant to Article 112 of the Companies Law. [Art.1, Regulatory Rules and Procedures issued pursuant to the Companies Law relating to Listed Joint Stock Companies]

Q

- **QFI**: Qualified Foreign Investor. A QFI is a Qualified foreign investor to invest in securities listed in the Saudi Stock Exchange, in accordance with the Rules. [Part A.1, Qualified Foreign Institutions FAQs]

- **Quality Control System**: Policies and procedures approved by the accounting firm in order to reasonably verify the compliance of the firm's employees with the professional standards and related laws governing their performance in carrying on audit engagement, including the professional code of ethics approved by the Saudi Organization for Certified Public Accountants. [Art.2(c), Registration of Auditors]

- **Qualified Foreign Investor**: a qualified foreign investor in accordance with these Rules to invest in listed securities.[Art. 2(c), Qualified Foreign Financial Institutions Regulations]

- **QFI Assessment Agreement**: an agreement between the Assessing Authorized Person and the QFI meeting the requirements set out in Article (10) of the [Qualified Foreign Financial Institutions Regulations. Art. 2(c), Qualified Foreign Financial Institutions Regulations]

- **Qualified Client**: means any of the following:

  A) a natural person who meets at least one of the following criteria:

  1) has carried out at least 10 transactions per quarter over the last 12 months of a minimum total amount of 40 million Saudi Riyals on securities markets;

  2) his net assets is not less than 5 million Saudi Riyals.

  3) Works or has worked for at least three years in the financial sector in a professional position related to investment in securities.

  4) holds a professional certificate in securities business and accredited by an internationally recognized entity.

  5) holds the General Securities Qualification Certificate that is recognized by the Authority, and has an annual income that is not less than 600,000 Saudi Riyals in the last two years.

  6) being a client of a Capital Market Institution authorized by the Authority to conduct managing activities, provided that the following is fulfilled: a. the offer shall be made to the Capital Market Institution, and that all related communications be made by it. b. the Capital Market Institution has been appointed on terms which enable it to make investment decisions on the client's behalf without obtaining prior approval from the client.

  7) registered persons of a Capital Market Institution if the offer is carried out by the Capital Market Institution itself.

  B) a legal person, which meets at least one of the following criteria:

  1) any legal person acting for its own account and be any of the following:

  a. a company which owns, or which is a member of a group which owns, net assets of not less than 10 million Saudi Riyals and not more than 50 million Saudi Riyals.

  b. any unincorporated body, partnership company or other organization which has net assets of not less than 10 million Saudi Riyals and not more than 50 million Saudi riyals.

  c. a person acting in the capacity of director, officer or employee of a legal person and responsible for its securities activity, where that legal person falls within the definition of paragraph (1/a) or (1/b).

  2) clients of a Capital Market Institution authorized by the Authority to conduct managing activities, provided that the following is fulfilled:

  a. the offer shall be made to the Capital Market Institution, and that all related communications be made by it; and

  b. the Capital Market Institution has been appointed on terms which enable it to make investment decisions on the client's behalf without obtaining prior approval from the client.

  C) a company fully owned by a natural person who meets one of the criteria mentioned in paragraph (A) or a legal person who meets one of the criteria mentioned in paragraph (B).

- **Qualified Investor**: means in Part 8 of the Rules on the Offer of Securities and Continuing Obligations, Articles 46 and 47 of the Investment Funds Regulations and Article 45 of the Real Estate Investment Funds Regulations, any of the following:

  1) Capital Market Institutions acting for their own account.

2) Clients of a Capital Market Institution by the Authority to conduct managing activities provided that this Capital Market Institution has been appointed as an investment manager on terms which enable it to make decisions concerning the acceptance of an offer and investment in the Parallel Market on the client's behalf without obtaining prior approval from the client.
3) The Government of the Kingdom, any government body, any supranational authority recognized by the Authority or the Exchange, and any other stock exchange recognized by the Authority or the Securities Depository Center.
4) Government-owned companies, either directly or through a portfolio managed by a Capital Market Institution authorizedto carry out managing activities.
5) Companies and funds established in a member state of the Cooperation Council for the Arab States of the Gulf.
6) Investment Funds.
7) Non-resident foreigners permitted to invest in the parallel market and who meet the requirements stipulated in the Guidance Note for the investment of Non-Resident Foreigners in the Parallel Market.
8) Qualified foreign financial institutions.
9) Any other legal persons allowed to open an investment account in the Kingdom and an account at the Depositary Center.
10) Natural persons allowed to open an investment account in the Kingdom and an account at the Depositary Center, and fulfill any of the following criteria:

a. Has conducted transactions in security markets of not less than 40 million Saudi riyals in total, and not less than ten transactions in each quarter during the last twelve months

b. His net assets is not less than 5 million Saudi Riyals.

c. works or has worked for at least three years in the financial sector.

d. Holds the General Securities Qualification Certificate which is recognized by the Authority.

e. holds a professional certificate that is related to securities business and accredited by an internationally recognized entity.

11) Any other persons prescribed by the Authority.

- **Qualifying Central Counterparty**: a CCP that has demonstrated that it is established and operating consistently with the Principles for Financial Market Infrastructures. [Article 2, Securities Central Counterparts Regulations]

R

- **Rated Entity**: a legal person whose creditworthiness is explicitly or implicitly rated in the credit rating (including the issuer of the security to be rated), whether or not it has solicited that credit rating and whether or not it has provided information for that credit rating.

- **Rating Activities**: any of the following activities: data and information analysis with a view to a credit rating; and the evaluation and approval and issue and review of a credit rating.

- **Rating Analyst**: a person who performs analytical functions in connection with rating activities.

- **Rating Category**: a rating symbol, such as a letter or numerical symbol which might be accompanied by appending identifying characters, used in a credit rating to provide a relative measure of risk to distinguish the different risk characteristics of the types of rated entities, securities or other assets.

- **Ratio of Fund Costs** to the Fund's Total Assets Value: the ratio of total fund costs to the most recent Fund's Total Assets Value during the relevant half or quarter. Fund costs shall mean; all the expenses incurred by the fund, including fixed and variable expenses, beside the expenses associated with specific events.

- **Ratio of Shares to Depositary Receipts**: The number of Depositary Receipts for each of the Issuer's issued shares in the Kingdom.[Art. 2(c), Instructions on Issuing Depositary Receipts Outside of the Kingdom]

- **Real Estate Investment Fund**: a collective real estate investment scheme aimed at providing investors therein with an opportunity to participate collectively in the profits of the scheme which is managed by a fund manager for specified fees.

- **Real Estate Investment Traded Fund (REIT)**: a real estate investment fund, the units of which are traded on the Main Market or the Parallel Market, and whose primary investment objective is to invest in constructionally developed real estates, able to generate periodic and rental income, and distribute a specified percentage of the fund's net profit in cash to the unitholders in such fund during its operation period, at least annually.

- **Real Estate Investment Funds Regulations**: the *Real Estate Investment Funds Regulations* issued by the Board of the Authority.

- **Registration**: Registration of the accounting firm or the CPA to carry on audit engagements for ESAS in accordance with the provisions of the [Registration of Auditors] Rules. [Art.2(c), Registration of Auditors]

- **Reconciliation**: the identification and explanation of individual items of difference between two sets of records, but does not include the processing of necessary adjustments.

- **Registered Person**: a person who is registered with the Authority to perform a registrable function.

- **Registered Shareholders**: the shareholders registered in the Shareholders Register at the end of the day on which the Extraordinary General Assembly's meeting is held to approve the increase of the Company's share capital and issuance of related new shares or at the end of the day specified by the ordinary General Assembly or by the Board on which shareholders become entitled to dividends as to dividends distribution.[Art.1, Regulatory Rules and Procedures issued pursuant to the Companies Law relating to Listed Joint Stock Companies]

- **Registrable Functions**: any of the functions that the Authority specifies must be performed by a person registered with the Authority.

- **Registration Document:** the document required for the registration of shares with the Authority for direct listing on the Parallel Market pursuant to the Rules on the Offer of Securities and Continuing Obligations.

- **Regulatory Authority**: the Authority, SAMA or any other authority in the Kingdom or overseas which regulates or supervises the conduct of securities, banking, financial, insurance or investment business including any self-regulating organization.

- **Regulatory Information Service Provider**: means the Exchange or an alternative communication channel or platform recognized by the Authority that replaces the Exchange in cases when it's not possible for persons to make public announcements through the exchange.

- **Related Parties**: mean, in the *Investment Funds Regulations* and the *Real Estate Investment Funds Regulations*, the following:

1) Fund manager and fund sub-manager.
2) Custodian and sub-custodian.
3) The developer and engineering office.
4) The property manager (where applicable).
5) The accredited valuer.
6) The auditor.
7) fund's board of directors.
8) Members of the board of directors, any of the executive managers or any employees of one of the above mentioned parties.
9) Any unitholder who owns more than (5%) of the fund's net assets.
10) Any person who controls or who is an affiliate of any of the above mentioned parties.

- **Related Parties**: [for the purposes of the *Corporate Governance Regulations* means]:

A. Substantial Shareholders of the company.
B. Board members of the Company or any of its affiliates and their relatives.
C. Senior Executives of the Company or any of its affiliates and their relatives.
D. Board members and Senior Executives of Substantial Shareholders of the company.
E. Entities, other than companies, owned by a Board member or any Senior Executive or their relatives.
F. Companies in which a Board member or a Senior Executive or any of their relatives is a partner.
G. Companies in which a Board member or a Senior Executive or any of their relatives is a member of its Board of directors or is one of its Senior Executives.
H. Joint stock companies in which a member of the Board or a Senior Executive or any of their relatives owns (5%) or more, subject to the provisions of paragraph (D) of this definition.
I. Companies in which a Board member or a Senior Executive or any of their relatives has influence on their decisions even if only by giving advice or guidance.
J. Any person whose advice or guidance influence the decisions of the Company, the Board and the Senior Executives.
K. Holding companies or affiliates. [Art.1, Corporate Governance Regulations, but Advice or guidance that is provided on a professional basis by a person licensed to provide such advice shall be excluded from the provisions of paragraphs (I) and (J) of this definition]

- **Related Party**: in the *Rules on the Offer of Securities and Continuing Obligations*, means:

1) affiliates of the issuer;
2) substantial shareholders of the issuer;
3) directors and senior executives of the issuer;
4) directors and senior executives of affiliates of the issuer;
5) directors and senior executives of substantial shareholders of the issuer;
6) any relatives of persons described at (1), (2), (3), (4) or (5) above;
7) any company controlled by any person described at (1), (2), (3), (4), (5) or (6) above.

- **Related Party**: in the *Merger and Acquisition Regulations*, means a person who, in relation to each of the offeror (or any of its affiliates) and the offeree company (or any of its affiliates), satisfies one or more of the following conditions:

1) any person who has provided financial assistance (other than a bank in the ordinary course of business) to the offeror or the offeree company;
2) the board members of the offeror or the offeree company (or any of their subsidiaries);
3) a person owning 20% of the offeror and the offeree (whether individually or by acting in concert with other(s))
4) a substantial shareholder with the offeror who in the same time is a board member in offeree company, or vice versa.

- **Relative**: means in the *Capital Market Institutions Regulations*, parents, husband, wife, and children.

- **Relative**: husband, wife and minor children.

- **Relative**: means in the *Merger and Acquisition Regulations*: husband, wife, children and parents.

- **Relatives**:

- -Fathers, mothers, grandfathers and grandmothers (and their ancestors).
- children and grandchildren and their descendants.
- siblings, maternal and paternal half-siblings.
- Husbands and wives.

[Art. 1, *Corporate Governance Regulations*]; and "includes the husband, wife, children and parents."[Art. 2(c), *Reporting of Violations of the Capital Market Law*]

- **Remuneration (and Compensation)**: means in the *Capital Market Institutions Regulations*, amounts, allowances, profits and the like, periodic or annual bonuses linked to performance, long or short-term incentive plans and any other in-kind benefits, except for the actual reasonable expenses and fees incurred by the company to enable a board member to perform his duties. [in the Capital Governance Regulations, means: amounts, allowances, dividends and the like, periodic or annual bonuses linked to performance, long or short term incentive plans and any other in-kind benefits except the actual reasonable expenses and fees incurred by the company to enable the Board member to perform his duties. Art. 1, Corporate Governance Regulations]; [amounts, allowances, profits and their equivalent, periodic and annual performance-related bonuses, short and long term incentive plans, in addition to any other in- kind benefits, except for reasonable costs and expenses actually incurred by the Company on behalf of a Board member in performing his work. Art.1,*Regulatory Rules and Procedures issued pursuant to the Companies Law relating to Listed Joint Stock Companies*]

- **Remuneration Committee**: a committee formed pursuant to the provisions of the Corporate Governance Regulations. [Art.1, Regulatory Rules and Procedures issued pursuant to the Companies Law relating to Listed Joint Stock Companies]

- **Report**: means information provided to the Authority – through channels to be determined by the Authority – in relation to any acts or practices that constitute a violation of any provisions of the Law or its implementing regulations, or of the regulations of the Exchange, the Depository Center, or the Clearing Center.[Art. 2(c), Reporting of Violations of Capital Market Law]

- **Reported Individual**: means a person against whom a report to the Authority was made in relation to any acts or practices that constitute a violation of any provisions of the Law or its implementing regulations, or of the regulations of the Exchange, the Depository Center, or the Clearing Center.[Art. 2(c), Reporting of Violations of Capital Market Law]

- **Reporting Individual**: means a person who reports to the Authority any acts or practices that constitute a violation of any provisions of the Law or its implementing regulations, or of the regulations of the Exchange, the Depository Center, or the Clearing Center. [Art. 2(c), Reporting of Violations of Capital Market Law]

- **Restructuring**: a material merger or reorganization, including a material restructuring as described in paragraph (6) of Article 23 of the Rules on the Offer of Securities and Continuing Obligations.

- **Retail Client**: Any client who is not a qualified client or an institutional client.

- **Revaluation Reserve**: a reserve account considered as a part of an Authorized Person's Tier-2 capital, that records the surplus created when a revaluation finds that the current value of an asset is higher than its recorded historical cost. The revaluation surplus may be reduced where a subsequent revaluation finds that the current value of an asset has decreased. [Art. 1(f), Prudential Rules]

- **Reverse Takeover**: an arrangement where a listed company makes an offer of new shares in itself to the shareholders of an unlisted company in exchange for their shares and theses new shares will represent more than 50% of the listed company voting shares after the acquisition.

- **Reward**: means a monetary amount determined based on the amount of the fines and financial penalties collected as a result of the Report.[Art. 2(c), Reporting of Violations of Capital Market Law]

- **Risk-Weight**: a percentage that describes a risk level of an exposure under the non-trading activities. [Art. 1(f), Prudential Rules]

- **Rights Issue**: an offer of additional shares to existing shareholders which enables those shareholders to subscribe in proportion to their existing holdings.

- **Rules for Special Purposes Entities**: the Rules for Special Purposes Entities issued by the Board of the Authority.

- **Rules on the Offer of Securities and Continuing Obligations**: the Rules on the Offer of Securities and Continuing Obligations issued by the Board of the Authority.

S

- **Sales Professional**: an employee of a Capital Market Institution who performs the activities of dealing or arranging on behalf of a capital market institution with or for a client.

- **SAMA**: the Saudi Central Bank.

- **SBL** (Securities Borrowing and Lending) Transaction: a privately negotiated trade settled in Depository Center accounts. (Securities Borrowing and Lending Regulations, Art. 2)

- **Securities**: means any of the following:

1) shares;
2) debt instruments;
3) warrants;
4) certificates;
5) units;
6) options;
7) futures;
8) contracts for differences;
9) long term insurance contracts; and
10) any right to or interest in anything which is specified by any of the paragraphs (1) through (9) above.

- **Secretariat**: the secretariat of the Committees for the Resolution of Securities Disputes. [Art. 1, Securities Disputes Proceedings Regulations]

- **Secretary**: the secretary of the Committees for the Resolution of Securities Disputes.[Art. 1, Securities Disputes Proceedings Regulations]

- **Securities Activity**: has the meaning specified at Article 2 of the Securities Business Regulations.

- **Securities Business**: has the meaning specified at Article 3 of the Securities Business Regulations. [Securities business shall mean engaging in any of the securities activities specified in Article 2 of these Regulations by any person acting by way of business unless any of the exclusions specified in Chapter 2 of this Part apply.]

- **Securities Business Regulations**: the Securities Business Regulations issued by the Board of the Capital Market Authority.

- **Sells or Selling**: in relation to a security, includes selling the security for consideration, surrendering, assigning or converting rights under a security or assuming a corresponding liability.

- **Senior Executives**: any natural person to whom the governing body of the firm, or a member of the governing body of the firm, has given responsibility, either alone or jointly with others, for management and supervision and either reports to:

1) the governing body directly;
2) a member of the governing body; or
3) the CEO.

- **Senior Executive** [see Executive Management]

- **Settlement Agent**: a person with or through whom a capital market institution effects settlement of a transaction.

- **Settlement Risk**: the risk that the debt instrument or convertible debt instrument will be issued but will not be paid for by the subscriber of the instrument.

- **Share**: share of any company wherever incorporated. The definition of "share" includes every instrument having the characteristics of equity. [shares of listed joint stock companies. Art.1, Regulatory Rules and Procedures issued pursuant to the Companies Law relating to Listed Joint Stock Companies]

- **Shareholder Circular**: means in the Rules on the Offer of Securities and Continuing Obligations the document required in the context of certain capital alterations of an issuer to enable the shareholders to make an informed vote at the relevant general assembly.

- **Shareholders Register**: a register of shareholders prepared and maintained by the Depository Centre which includes names of shareholders, their nationality, place of residence, Shares numbers in which all relevant dealings related to the Shares issued by the Company are recorded.[Art.1, Regulatory Rules and Procedures issued pursuant to the Companies Law relating to Listed Joint Stock Companies]

- **Shares or Convertible Debt Instruments Exchange Offer**: means an offer in which the exchange includes shares or convertible debt instruments of the offeror.

- **Share Capital**: The balance which appears as a separate item under shareholders' equity on the balance sheet.[Art. 1, Procedures for Listed Companies with Losses]

- **Short Selling Transactions**: A short selling transaction means any sale of a borrowed listed security in accordance with the Securities Business Law Regulations.[Art.3, Short Selling Regulations]

- **Sophisticated Investor**: for the purposes of the *Rules on the Offer of Securities and Continuing Obligations*, has the meaning specified in Article 9; and for the purposes of the *Investment Funds Regulations* and the *Capital Market Institutions Regulations*, has the meaning specified in paragraph (b) of Article 74 of the *Investment Funds Regulations.*

- **Special Assembly**: the special assembly held with the attendance of holders of preferred shares of the same class in accordance with the Companies law, Company's bylaws and these rules and procedures.[Art.1, *Regulatory Rules and Procedures issued pursuant to the Companies Law relating to Listed Joint Stock Companies*]

- **Special Fund Resolution**: means a resolution requiring an affirmative vote of the unitholders of 75% or more of the units in the investment fund present or represented by proxy at a meeting of unitholders or by modern means of technology.

- **Special Purposes Entity**: means an entity established and licensed under the Rules for Special Purposes Entities.

- **Specialized Public Fund**: has the meaning specified in Article 53 of the *Investment Funds Regulations.*

- **Spin-Off**: a type of Demerger where all or a portion of the shares in the spun-off entity/new entity to be formed to hold the asset, are distributed on a pro-rata basis to the Listed Company's shareholders as dividend, resulting in a full separation of the two entities in a single transaction. In a Spin-Off transaction a portion of the shares of the spun-off entity/new entity to be formed to hold the asset, may be offered to the public through a public offering and listing on the Exchange.

- **Split-Off**: a type of Demerger transaction where the Listed Company makes an offer to its shareholders to exchange their parent shares which will be acquired by the Listed Company as treasury shares, in exchange for all or a portion of the shares of the spun-off entity/ new entity to be formed to hold the asset.

- **Sponsor**: The person responsible for sponsoring the special purposes entity in accordance with the provisions of the Rules for Special Purposes Entities.

- **Stakeholder**: any person who has an interest in the Company, including employees, creditors, customers, suppliers and the community. [Art. 1, Corporate Governance Regulations]

- **Strategic Shareholding**: the direct ownership percentage in the listed company's shares, and through which the aim is to contribute in promoting the financial or operational performance of the listed company.[Part 2(a), Foreign Strategic Ownership in Listed Companies]

- **Stress Testing**: For the purposes of the Investment Funds Regulations it means, preparing stress tests models and methods for analyzing hypothetical cases of the risks facing the fund, and the fund manager's policy to address them. In addition to analyzing the level of sensitivity to measure the level of fluctuation in the prices of investment funds units for the variables that affect them. Including, but not limited to, the fund manager carrying out a hypothetical simulation of the liquidity risks and the policy it will follow to address such risks, and the results of this hypothetical simulation, to assess the policy it followed in this regards and determine methods for its development.

- **Structured Product**: a security or other asset resulting from a securitization transaction or scheme or similar structure.

- **Subsidiary**: in relation to a company, another company which it controls.

- **Subordinated Loans**: the loans with conditions stating that in the event of liquidation or bankruptcy, the principal of the loans and its interest, shall not be paid until all other creditors have been paid in full.[Art. 1(f), Prudential Rules]

- **Substantial Shareholder**: a person holding (5%) or more of the class of shares of the issuer [or voting rights therein. Art 1., Corporate Governance Regulations]

- **Substantial Unitholder**: means in the Investment Funds Regulations and the Real Estate Investment Funds Regulations, a person who owns 5% or more of the units of the closed- ended investment traded fund or the real estate investment traded fund.

- **Suit**: the complaint filed with the Committee starting from submitting it in a written Statement of Claim according to the [Securities Dispute] regulations until the suit is closed by a final decision.[Art. 1, Securities Disputes Proceedings Regulations]

- **Suitability Report**: The report prepared in accordance with the requirements of paragraph (c) of Article 43 of the Capital Market Institutions Regulations.

- **Swap Agreements**: an agreement for the benefit of a foreign counterparts to transfer the economic benefits of securities listed on the Exchange to those foreign investors through swap transactions. [Art.1, Circular 5/2132]

T

- **Tadawul**: the automated system for trading of Saudi shares (See *Exchange, supra.*

- **Takeover**: the acquisition of control of a company listed on the Exchange.

- **Takeover Offer**: an offer (other than by the offeree company itself) made to the holders of the securities of the offeree company which has as its objective the acquisition of control of the offeree company.

- **Target**: the subject of a Reverse Takeover, consisting of either businesses, assets or an unlisted company.

- **Termination of the Fund**: means wherever mentioned in the *Investment Funds Regulations* and the *Real Estate Investment Funds Regulations*, the date on which the fund expires, as per its term end or the occurrence of the event determined on the fund's terms and conditions, including the stage of sale of assets and the distribution of the unitholders' dues among them.

- **Terms and Conditions (Fund's)**: the contracts containing those disclosures and provisions required under the Investment Funds Regulations and the Real Estate Investment Funds Regulations, signed between the fund manager and the unitholder.

- **Terms of Business**: a written statement, provided to a client, of the terms on which a Capital Market Institution will conduct securities business with or for the client.

- **Terrorist Financing**: refers to the financing of terrorist acts, terrorists and terrorist organizations. [Art. 2, AML Regs.]

- **Tick Size**: The minimum price increment and decrement allowed for share price as applied by the Saudi Stock Exchange Company (Tadawul).[Art. 2(c), IPO Book Building]

- **Tier-1 Capital**: the most loss-absorbing form of capital, which includes (i) paid- up capital, (ii) audited retained earnings, (iii) share premium, (iv) reserves (other than revaluation reserves), and (v) Tier-1 capital contributions. Tier-1 capital is the net figure after applicable deductions.[Art.1(f) *Prudential Rules*; *see* "Capital Base."]

- **Tier-2 Capital**: a less loss-absorbing form of capital compared to Tier-1 capital. Tier-2 capital is the net figure after applicable deductions. [Art.1(f) *Prudential Rules*; *see*, "Capital Base."]

- **Traded**: traded on the Exchange.

- **Traded Fund**: an investment fund the units of which are traded on the Main Market or the Parallel Market.

- **Traded Security**: a security traded on the Exchange.

- **Trading Book**: the accounting book for the positions held with trading intent.[Art.1(f) *Prudential Rules*]

- **Trading Halt**: the temporary suspension of trading in the securities during the trading period

- **Treasury Shares**: Purchased Shares which are retained by the Company, including Employees' Shares which are retained by the Company.[Art.1, Regulatory Rules and Procedures issued pursuant to the Companies Law relating to Listed Joint Stock Companies]

- **Treasury Units**: units bought-back which the fund manager keeps in accordance with the Investment Funds Regulations and the Real Estate Investment Funds Regulations.

- **Trustee of the Special Purposes Entity**: the person under the name of which the shares of a special purposes entity that issues debt instruments are registered, and it shall not be considered an owner of such, in accordance with the provisions of the Rules for Special Purposes Entities.

U

- **Ultimate beneficiary**: a non-resident foreign investor that receives the economic benefits of the securities listed on the Saudi Stock Exchange through swap transactions executed under the Swap Agreements [Question 63, QFI FAQ]

- **Unconditional as to Acceptances**: means in the *Merger and Acquisition Regulations*, that the offer is no longer conditional upon receipt by the offeror of acceptances from the shareholders of the offeree company.

- **Underwriter**: a person who buys securities from the issuer or an affiliate of the issuer for the purpose of offering, placing and marketing such securities to the public, or a person who sells securities on behalf of the issuer or an affiliate of the issuer for the purpose of making a public offering and placement of such securities. Relatives: husband, wife and minor children. [Art. 1, *Capital Markets Law*]

- **Unit**: the share of any owner in any fund consisting of units or a part of it. Each unit shall be treated as a common share in the net assets of the Fund.

- **Unitholder**: a person who owns units in an investment fund or a real estate investment fund, which represents a common share in the net assets of the Fund.

V

- **Variation Margin**: margin that is collected to cover the current exposure resulting from actual changes in market prices which affects the value of the Clearing Member's position.

- **Voting Rights**: all the voting rights attributable to the shares of a company which are exercisable at a general meeting.

W X Y Z

- **Warrant**: warrants and other instruments entitling the holder to subscribe for any shares or debt instruments.

- **Wrong-Way Risk**: the risk arising from exposure to a counterparty when the collateral provided by that counterparty is highly correlated with the credit quality of that counterparty.[Article 2, *Securities Central Counterparts Regulations*]

2 AMENDED SECURITIES BUSINESS REGULATIONS

Issued by the Board of the Capital Market Authority pursuant to its Resolution Number 2-83-2005 Dated 21/5/1426 H (28/6/2005 G) based on the Capital Market Law Issued by Royal Decree No M/30 dated 2/6/1424H, amended by Resolution of the Board of the Capital Market Authority Number 2-75-2020 dated 22/12/1441H (12/8/2020G.0

Important Notice: The current version of these Regulations, as may be amended, can be found on the Authority'a website: www.cma.org.sa

TABLE OF CONTENTS

PART 1: GENERAL PROVISIONS
Article 1: Definitions
PART 2: THE SECURITIES BUSINESS
Chapter One: Carrying on Security Business
Article 2: Securities Activity
Article 3: Securities Business Defined
Article 4: Carrying on Securities Business in the Kingdom
Article 5: authorization
Article 6: Contravention
Chapter Two: Exclusions from authorization
Article 7: Scope
Article 8: Activities within Groups and Joint Enterprises
Article 9: Activities Carried out in the Course of a Non-Securities Business
Article 10: Sales of Goods and Supply of Services
Article 11: Execution of Wills
Article 12: Activities in Connection with the Sale of a Company
Article 13: Exclusions from Dealing as Principal
Article 14: Exclusions from Arranging
Article 15: Exclusion from Advising
PART 3: SECURITIES ADVERTISEMENTS
Article 16: Preliminary
Article 17: Securities Advertisements
Article 18: Contravention
Article 19: Advertising in the Kingdom
Article 20: Exclusions
PART 4: PUBLICATION AND ENTRY INTO FORCE
Article 21: Publication and Entry into Force
ANNEX 1: EXEMPT PERSONS

2.1 PART 1: GENERAL PROVISIONS

2.1.1 Article 1: Definitions

(a) Any reference to the "Capital Market Law" in these Regulations shall mean the Capital Market Law issued by Royal Decree No. M/30 dated 2/6/1424H.

(b) Expressions and terms in these Regulations have the meaning, which they bear, in the Capital Market Law and in the Glossary of defined terms used in the Regulations and Rules of the Capital Market Authority, unless the context indicates otherwise.

2.2 PART 2: THE SECURITIES BUSINESS

2.2.1 Chapter One: Carrying on Securities Business

Article 2: Securities Activities A securities activity shall mean any of the following activities:

1) Dealing: a person deals in a security as principal or as agent, and dealing includes to sell, buy, manage the subscription or underwrite securities;

2) Arranging: a person introduces parties in relation to offering of securities or arrangement of its underwriting, or advises on corporate finance business;

3) Managing: a person manages a security belonging to another person in circumstances involving the exercise of discretion, or operates investment funds;

4) Advising: a person advises another person in relation to a security, which includes advising on the merits of that person dealing in it, exercising any right to deal conferred by it or financial planning and wealth management in it; or

5) Custody: a person safeguards assets belonging to another person which include a security, or arranges for another person to do so, and custody includes taking the necessary administrative measures.

(In accordance with the Board of Authority Resolution No. (2-75-2020) dated 22/12/1441H corresponding to 12/8/2020G, Article 2 of these Regulations shall become effective as of 28/5/1443H corresponding to 1/1/2022G, provided that Article 2 of the Securities Business Regulations issued by the Board of the Authority Resolution No. (2-83-2005) dated 21/05/1426H corresponding to 28/06/2005G shall continue to be effective until the effectiveness date of Article 2 of these Regulations.)

Article 3: Securities Business Defined Securities business shall mean engaging in any of the securities activities specified in Article 2 of these Regulations by any person acting by way of business unless any of the exclusions specified in Chapter 2 of this Part apply.

Article 4: Carrying on Securities Business in the Kingdom A person carries out securities business in the Kingdom if:

(a) he engages in securities activity from a permanent place of business in the Kingdom;

(b) he is presumed to carry on a securities activity from a permanent place of business in the Kingdom in any of the following situations:

1) he engages in the relevant activity, or in securities business generally, in the Kingdom; or

2) he engages in the relevant activity with or for a person in the Kingdom.

Article 5: Authorization A person must not carry on securities business in the Kingdom unless he is:

1) a Capital Market Institution authorized by the Authority; or

2) an exempt person as specified in Annex 1 to these Regulations.

Article 6: Contravention Contravention of Article 5 of these Regulations is an offense in accordance with Article 60 of the Capital Market Law.

2.2.2 Chapter Two: Exclusions from Authorization

Article 7: Scope Securities activities that are excluded by this Chapter do not require authorization by the Authority.

Article 8: Activities within Groups and Joint Enterprises (a) A transaction between two persons who act as principal is excluded from dealing if the two persons:

1) are members of the same group; or

2) are, or propose to be, participants in a joint enterprise (provided that the transaction is for the purpose of the joint enterprise).

(b) Each of arranging, managing, advising and custody by a person are excluded where:

1) the person is a member of a group and the services in question are provided for a member of the same group; or

2) the person is, or proposes to become, a participator in a joint enterprise and the services in question are provided for a participant in the joint enterprise (provided that the services are provided for the purpose of the joint enterprise).

Article 9: Activities Carried out in the Course of a non-Securities Business (a) A securities activity is excluded if it:

1) is carried out in the course of carrying on any profession or business which does not otherwise consist of carrying on securities business in the Kingdom;

2) may reasonably be regarded as a necessary part of other services provided in the course of that profession or business; and

3) is not remunerated separately from the other services.

(b) Arranging or advising carried out by a law firm or accountancy firm registered in the Kingdom is presumed to fall within paragraph (a) of this Article if:

1) the arranging or advising is provided in the ordinary course of the business of the firm; and

2) the firm does not hold itself out as carrying on, and does not carry on, securities business.

Article 10: Sale of Goods and Supply of Services (a) A securities activity between a supplier and a customer is excluded if it is carried out for the purposes of, and is reasonably necessary for or ancillary to, the sale or supply of goods or services.

(b) For the purpose of the application of paragraph (a) of this Article:

1) supplier: means a person whose main business is to sell goods or supply services and not to carry on securities business; and

2) customer: means a person, other than an individual, to whom a supplier sells goods or supplies services, or agrees to do so.

Article 11: Execution of Wills A securities activity carried out by an executor of a will is excluded if:

1) it is undertaken in his capacity as an executor;

2) the executor does not hold himself out as carrying on, and does not carry on, securities business; and

3) the executor is not remunerated for the activity separately from the other services.

Article 12: Activities in Connection with the Sale of a Company Entering into a transaction is excluded from dealing if the purpose of the transaction is to acquire or dispose of 50 percent or more of the voting shares in a company whose shares are not listed on the Exchange.

Article 13: Exclusions from Dealing as Principal (a) Dealing by a person as principal in a security that is not a contractually based security is excluded unless:

1) the person holds himself out as engaging in the business of dealing in securities; or

2) the person regularly solicits members of the public to deal in securities.

(b) In paragraph (a) of this Article, "members of the public" excludes Capital Market Institutions and exempt persons.

(c) Dealing by a person in a contractually based security as principal is excluded if a Capital Market Institution or an exempt person deals or advises in relation to the transaction.

(d) Dealing by a person as principal is excluded if the dealing is the acceptance of an instrument creating or acknowledging indebtedness in respect of any loan, credit, guarantee or other similar financial accommodation or assurance which he has made, granted or provided.

(e) The issuance by a person of its own shares, debt instruments or warrants is excluded from dealing.

(f) A Capital Market Institution investing its money in securities is excluded from dealing as principal.

Article 14: Exclusions from Arranging The following activities are excluded from arranging:

1) Arranging by a person of a transaction to which it is a party.

2) Arrangements under which a person accepts or is to accept (as principal or agent) an instrument creating or acknowledging indebtedness in respect of any loan, credit, guarantee or other similar financial accommodation or assurance which he has made, granted or provided.

3) Arranging by a person of the issuance of its own shares, debt instruments or warrants.

4) Arranging introductions of persons to a Capital Market Institution or an exempt person for the provision of custody services.

Article 15: Exclusion from Advising Advising is excluded if the following two conditions are fulfilled:

1) the advice is either:

(i) in writing and contained in a newspaper, journal, magazine, or other periodical publication, or given by way of a service comprising regularly updated news or information; or

(ii) contained in a broadcast or transmission of a television or radio programme; and

2) its principal purpose is neither to advise nor to induce persons to deal.

2.3 PART 3: SECURITIES ADVERTISEMENTS

Article 16: Preliminary (a) A securities advertisement means any form of verbal, electronic, written or otherwise communication in relation to securities or securities activity made in the course of business for the purpose of inviting or inducing a person to engage in securities activity.

(b) References to making or communicating a securities advertisement in this Part include causing a securities advertisement to be made or communicated but do not include acting as a mere conduit for information with no editorial control over its content.

Article 17: Securities Advertisements A person must not make or communicate any securities advertisement to a person in the Kingdom unless:

1) the person making the advertisement is a Capital Market Institution; or

2) the contents of the securities advertisement have been approved for the purpose of this Part by a Capital Market Institution.

Article 18: Contravention Contravention of Article 17 of these Regulations is an offense under Article 60 of the Capital Market Law.

Article 19: Advertising in the Kingdom (a) Subject to paragraph (b) of this Article, a securities advertisement is made or communicated to a person in the Kingdom if it is available to persons in the Kingdom, including advertisements made via the internet.

(b) A securities advertisement is not made or communicated to a person in the Kingdom if it is directed only at persons outside the Kingdom.

(c) It is a question of fact based on the circumstances, including those relating to the communication of the securities advertisement and its contents, whether a securities advertisement is directed only at persons outside the Kingdom.

Article 20: Exclusions A securities advertisement is excluded from the prohibition in Article 17 of these Regulations if it:

1) relates to securities activity that is excluded from securities business under these Regulations;
2) is made to a Capital Market Institution or an exempt person by a person seeking to obtain information about, or to receive, securities business services;
3) is made by an exempt person and relates to that person's exempt activities;
4) is directed only at Capital Market Institutions or exempt persons;
5) is made by a member of a group to another member of the same group;
6) is made by a participant in a joint enterprise to another participant (or potential participant) for a purpose relating to the joint enterprise;
7) is made by a journalist acting in that capacity;
8) is required to be made under the law of the Kingdom, including the Implementing Regulations; or
9) is directed at persons who own, or are entitled to obtain, securities issued by the person making the advertisement, or creditors of that person.

2.4 PART 4: PUBLICATION AND ENTRY INTO FORCE

Article 21: Publication and Entry into Force These Regulations shall become effective upon their publication.

2.5 ANNEX 1: EXEMPT PERSONS

(a) The following persons are exempt in relation to securities business activities undertaken by them:

1. the Government of the Kingdom;
2. SAMA;
3. the Exchange and any other stock exchange approved by the Authority;
4. the Depositary Centre;
5. CCP; and
6. a supranational authority recognized by the Authority.

(b) An insolvency practitioner is exempted in relation to his activities undertaken in his capacity as such.

(c) An insurance company is exempted in relation to its insurance activities regulated by SAMA. (d) The Authority may exempt other persons.

3 ANTI-MONEY LAUNDERING AND COUNTER-TERRORIST FINANCING RULES

Issued by the Board of the Capital Market Authority pursuant to Resolution Number 1-39-2008 dated 3/12/1429 H (1/12/2008). Based on the Capital Market Law issued by Royal Decree No. M/30 dated 2/6/1424H, amended by Resolution No. 5-53-2016 dated 25/7/1437H (2/5/2016).

The current version of these Regulations, as may be amended, can be found at the CMA website: www.cma.org.sa.

Table of Contents

PART 1 General Provisions
Article 1: Preliminary
Article 2: Definitions
PART 2 General Application of AML/CTF requirements
Article 3: General principles
Article 4: Application of policies and procedures to overseas branches and subsidiaries
Article 5: Cash Payments
PART 3 CUSTOMER DUE DILIGENCE
Article 6: Know Your Customer
Article 7: Client Acceptance
Article 8 Customer Due Diligence (CDD)-- General
Article 9: Risk-based approach -- Reduced and Enhanced costumer Due Diligence
Article 10: Politically exposed Persons (PEP)
Article 11: Non-profit Organizations & Entities
Article 12: When Authorized Person must perform CDD
Article 13: Investment Funds
Article 14: Reliance on other Third Parties for CDD
Article 15: Acquisition
Article 16: Non-Face-to-Face Business Relationships
Article 17: Ongoing CDD and Unusual Transactions
Article 18: Review and updating of records
PART 4 Record Keeping
Article 19: Record Keeping Requirements
PART 5 Suspicious Transaction Report
Article 20 Suspicious Transaction Report
Article 21: Tipping Off
Article 22: Designated Persons -- UNSCR Resolutions
PART 6 Internal Policies, Procedures and Control
Article 23: Internal Policies and Compliance
Article 24: Internal Audit
Article 25: Education and Training
PART 7 Closing Provisions
Article 26: Sanctions
Article 27: Publication and Entry into Force
Annex 1 Securities Business Indicators for Money Laundering or Terrorist Financing

3.1 PART 1 GENERAL PROVISIONS

Article 1: Preliminary The objectives of these Rules

The objectives of these Rules are that all Authorized and registered persons must comply fully with the controls and procedures issued by the Capital Market Authority to ensure that:

(a) fully apply the Anti-Money Laundering Law issued by Royal Decree No. M/39 dated 25/06/1424 H and its implementing Regulation, and apply the requirements of the FATF's 40 Recommendations and 9 Special Recommendations dealing with anti -money laundering and combating the financing of terrorism, the International Convention for Suppression and Financing of Terrorism (New York 1999), the United Nations Convention on Illicit Traffic in Narcotic Drugs and Psychotropic Substances (Vienna 1988) and the United Nations Convention (against transnational) on Organized Crime (Palermo 2000) and UN Security Council Resolutions 1267 and 1373 and successor resolutions relating to combating terrorist financing.

(b) the credibility, integrity and reputation of the capital market is maintained.

(c) Authorized Persons and their clients are protected from illegal transactions involving money laundering, terrorist financing or other criminal activity.

Article 2: Definitions 1. For the purpose of implementing these Rules, the following expressions and terms shall have the meaning they bear as follows unless the contrary intention appears:

Accounts: are to be read to include any business relationships between Authorized Person and its client.

Beneficial owner: refers to the natural person(s) who ultimately own(s) or control(s) the funds of the clients or on whose behalf a transaction or activity is being conducted. It also incorporates those persons who exercise ultimate effective control over a legal person or arrangement.

Business relationship: means professional or commercial relationship between an Authorized Person and a client. A relationship need not involve the Authorized Person in an actual transaction; giving advice shall also constitute establishing a business relationship.

Client: refers to a customer, execution -only customer either natural or legal person and counterparty for whom an Authorized Person executes securities business.

Counterparty: a client who is an Authorized Person, an exempt person, an institution or a non-Saudi financial services firm.

FIU: refers to the Financial Intelligence Unit of the Ministry of Interior.

Funds: means assets or properties of whatever type, material or intangible, movable or immovable, along with the legal documents and deeds proving the ownership of the assets or any right pertaining thereto.

Money Laundering: refers to committing or attempting to commit any act for the purpose of concealing or disguising the true origin of funds acquired by means contrary to Shari'ah or law, thus making the funds appear as if they had come from a legitimate source.

Non-profit Organizations Entities: refers to a legal person who is an entity or an organization that primarily engages in raising/collecting donations and/or disbursing funds for nonprofit purposes.

Politically Exposed Person (PEP): is any individual who occupies, has recently occupied, is actively seeking or is being considered for, a senior civil position in a government of a country, state or municipality or any department including the military, any agency, government -owned company. The definition of PEP includes members of immediate family and close associates, collectively known as Related Individuals. Immediate family is typically defined as any known individual who is a member of the PEP's immediate family (i.e. spouse, parent, sibling or child). Close associate is defined as any individual who is a senior advisor closely associated with or an agent of the PEP.

Amendment: Politically Exposed Persons (PEPs)-PEPs refers to any of the following categories:

Individuals who are or have been entrusted with prominent public functions domestically or in a foreign country, for example Heads of State or of government, senior politicians, senior government, judicial or military officials, senior executives of state owned corporations, and important political party officials.

Persons who are or have been entrusted with a prominent function by a regional or international organization as members of senior management, including directors, deputy directors and members of the board or equivalent functions.

The PEPs definition covers the family members or relatives of the individuals, and does not cover the middle ranking or more junior individuals in the foregoing categories."

(Amendment issued 02/10/2017)

Terrorist financing: refers to the financing of terrorist acts, terrorists and terrorist organizations.

FATF: Financial Action Task Force on money laundering and terrorist financing.

Attachment: shall mean the provisional ban on transferring, exchanging, disposing with or moving funds and proceeds or attaching same pursuant to an order by a court or a competent authority.

2 - Without prejudice to paragraph (1) of this article, expressions and terms in these Rules have the meanings which they bear in the Capital Market Law and in the Glossary of defined terms used in the Regulations and Rules of the Capital Market Authority.

3.2 PART 2 GENERAL APPLICATION OF AML/CTF REQUIREMENTS

Article 3: General principles 1. Authorized Person must, in establishing policies and procedures to prevent money laundering and terrorist financing, consider carefully the specific nature of its business, organizational structure, type of client and transaction, and shall ensure that the measures taken by it are adequate and appropriate to meet the requirements and general objectives set out in these Rules.

2. Saudi Arabia has ratified and implemented the United Nations Convention on Illicit Traffic in Narcotic Drugs and Psychotropic Substances (Vienna 1988), the United Nations Convention on Organized Crime (Palermo 2000) and the International Convention for Suppression and financing of Terrorism (New York 1999). These Conventions require to establish systems, controls and procedures aimed at preventing money laundering and terrorist financing, including procedures for reporting suspected money laundering or terrorist financing transactions. Senior management of Authorized Person is responsible for effectively managing the risks facing the business, including the risks of money laundering and terrorist financing. Senior management must therefore be fully committed to establishing appropriate and effective policies and procedures for the prevention of money laundering and terrorist financing and to ensuring compliance with those policies and with all relevant legal and regulatory requirements. To ensure this, senior management must appoint a director or senior manager with direct responsibility for over -sighting compliance with the AML/CFT policies and procedures and relevant legal and regulatory requirements.

3. Authorized Person is required to:

(a) issue an effective statement of policies and procedures aimed at preventing money laundering and terrorist financing, and ensuring compliance with current legal and regulatory requirements including the maintenance of records; and co-operation with the FIU and relevant law enforcement authorities in accordance with the relevant regulations and rules, including the timely disclosure of information;

(b) ensure that the content of these Rules is understood by all officers and employees, and that they are aware of the requirements and vigilant in guarding against money laundering and terrorist financing;

(c) regularly review the policies and procedures on prevention of money laundering and terrorist financing to ensure their effectiveness. For example, reviews performed by the internal audit or compliance officer to ensure compliance with policies, procedures and controls relating to prevention of money laundering and terrorist financing (areas of review shall include:

(i) an assessment of the system for detecting suspected money laundering and terrorist financing transactions;

(ii) evaluation and checking of the adequacy of reports generated on large and / or irregular transactions;

(iii) review of the quality of reporting of suspicious transactions; and (iv) an assessment of the level of awareness of front line staff regarding their responsibilities); and

(d) adopt client acceptance policies and procedures, and undertake required Customer Due Diligence ("CDD ") measures, as set out in Part (3), including taking into account the risk of money laundering and terrorist financing depending on the type of client, business relationship or transaction.

Article 4: Application of policies and procedures to overseas branches and subsidiaries 1. Authorized Person must ensure that its overseas branches and majority-owned subsidiaries ("subsidiaries") comply with the laws and regulations of Saudi Arabia concerning money laundering and terrorist financing, and the FATF Recommendations, to the extent that the laws and regulations applicable in the host country permit.

2. Authorized Person shall pay particular attention to the application of paragraph (1) of this article in its branches and subsidiaries which are located in countries that do not or insufficiently implement the FATF's Recommendations including jurisdictions designated as such by the FATF.

3. Where the minimum AML/CFT requirements of Saudi Arabia and host countries differ, branches and subsidiaries in host countries shall apply the higher standard, to the extent that host

country laws and regulations permit. Where the law of the host country conflicts with Saudi Arabian law or regulations such that the overseas branch or subsidiary is unable to fully observe the higher standard, the Authorized Person's head office shall report this to the Authority and comply with such further directions as may be given by it.

4. Where an overseas branch or subsidiary is unable to observe group standards because this is prohibited by host country laws, regulations or other measures, the Authorized Person shall inform the Authority immediately.

Article 5: Cash Payments At no time, whether at the commencement of or during a business relationship shall an Authorized Person accept cash from a client, whether for investment purposes or as payment for services provided by the Authorized Person.

3.3 PART 3 CUSTOMER DUE DILIGENCE

Article 6: {Know Your Customer} For the purposes of these rules and before accepting any client, the Authorized Person must prepare a "Know Your Customer" form containing the information required by Annex (5-3) of the Authorized Persons regulations and the other information required by these rules.

Article 7: Client Acceptance 1. Authorized Person must develop client acceptance policies and procedures that aim to identify the types of clients that are likely to pose a higher risk of money laundering and terrorist financing.A more extensive customer due diligence process must be adopted for higher risk clients, and this must include clear internal policies on the approval of a business relationship with such clients.

2. In determining whether a particular client or type of clients may be higher risk, Authorized Person must take into account factors such as the following:

(a) the background or profile of the client;

(b) the nature of the client's business, and the degree of money laundering or terrorist financing risk;

(c) the place of establishment of the client's business and location of the counterparties with which the client does business, such as countries designated by the FATF or those known to the Authorized Person to lack proper standards in the prevention of money laundering or terrorist financing;

(d) unduly complex structure of ownership for no good reason;

(e) means of payment as well as type of payment (third party cheque the drawer of which has no apparent connection with the prospective client may be a cause for increased scrutiny);

(f) any other information that may suggest that the client is of higher risk (e.g. knowledge that the client has been refused a business relationship by another financial institution).

3. Authorized Person must reconsider the risk categorization of a client if, following acceptance of the client, the pattern of account activity of the client does not fit in with the Authorized Person's knowledge of the client. Authorized Person must also consider making a Suspicious Transaction Report (STR).

4. Authorized Person must not accept any client or open an account for a client without meeting the client directly face -to -face, except where article (14) of these Rules applies.

Article 8 Customer Due Diligence (CDD)-- General 1. Authorized Person must take all steps necessary to be able to establish the true and full identity of each client, and of each client's financial situation and investment objectives. Authorized Person must not open anonymous accounts, accounts using false or fictitious names, or accounts for prohibited persons notified by the Authority.

2. CDD must be carried out on all clients, and CDD requires Authorized Person to take the following steps:

(a) Identify the client and verify their identity using the original documents prescribed in the AML Law and its implementing Regulation and paragraph (4) of this Article. This also applies to all persons with signatory authority over the account;

(b) identify and verify beneficial ownership and control using the original documents prescribed in the AML Law and its implementing Regulation and paragraph (4) of this article.

(c) obtain information on the purpose and intended nature of the business relationship -- depending on the type of client, business relationship or transaction, Authorized Person must obtain sufficient information such that ongoing due diligence on the client can be appropriately conducted; and

(d) Ensure applying ongoing due diligence and scrutiny, i.e. perform ongoing scrutiny of the transactions and account throughout the course of the business relationship to ensure that the transactions being conducted are consistent with the Authorized Person's knowledge of the client, the client's profile, taking into account, where necessary, the client's source of funds.

Authorized Person must apply the specific requirements CDD of Article 13 dealing with investment funds.

Authorized Person shall verify the identity of clients and any beneficial owners by checking the valid original documents as follows:

(a) Natural Persons:

-Saudi nationals:

- The client's National Identification Card or family record.
- The client's residential address & place of work and work address.

- Individual expatriates:

- A residence permits (iqama) or a five-year special residence permit or a passport for Gulf Cooperation Council (GCC) nationals or a diplomatic identification card for diplomats.
- The client's residential address & place of work and work address.

(b) Legal persons:
For all clients that are legal persons, Authorized Person must obtain sufficient information about the nature of the business and its ownership and control structure so that it can identify the individual(s) that ultimately own(s) or control(s) the client. Specimen signatures shall be obtained for all account signatories.

-Companies:

a) A copy of Commercial register issued by the competent authority.
b) A copy of the Articles of association, or the memorandum of association and their annexes, and any amendments
c) A copy of the identification card of the manager in charge.

d) A copy of the issued resolution forming the Board of Directors.
e) A copy of the Board resolution evidencing the approval of the opening of the account and conferring Authorization on the signatories;
f) A List of the persons Authorized who are qualified to deal with the accounts, pursuant to what is provided for in the commercial register, and a copy of the identification card of each.
g) A List of all company's owners whose names are included in the Articles of Association and a copy of identification card of each.
h) If the company has activities that require license from another government authority, a copy of that license is required.

- Non profit Organizations & Entities:

a) A copy of the license issued by the relevant government authority.
b) A copy of the Board resolution evidencing the approval of the opening of the account.
c) A copy of the articles of association.
d) Authorization from the board of directors for the persons who would open & deal with & operate the accounts and a copy of the identification card of each.
e) A copy of the Authority's approval of accepting the client open account for.

-Government entities:

a) A copy of all required documents in accordance with its Law and organization regulatory.
b) A copy of the authority approval of accepting the client & open account for.

If a client is a type of legal person other than one of the types set out in paragraph (4/b) of this article, the Authorized Person must obtain the approval of the Authority.

5. For all clients, except where the Authorized Person is relying on a third party in accordance with Article (14) of these Rules, the identity of a prospective client shall be verified face to face at an Authorized Person before an account is opened or a business relationship is commenced..

6. If there is doubt or difficulty in determining whether the document obtained to verify identity is genuine, Authorized Persons must not open the account, and shall consider whether they need to make a suspicious transaction report.

7. Authorized Person must retain copies of all documents used to verify the identity of the client pursuant to Part (4) from these rules.

8. For the purpose of assisting an Authorized Person to identify the beneficial owner of an account, the Authorized Person must, when establishing a business relationship, ask whether the client is acting for his or its own account or for the account of another party or parties.

9. An Authorized Person must understand the purpose and intended nature of the business relationship or transaction, but additional information might also need to be obtained, and this could include some or all of the following information:

- record of changes of address;
- the expected source and origin of the funds to be used in the relationship;
- initial and ongoing source(s) of wealth or income;
- copies of the financial statements;
- the various relationships between signatories with underlying beneficial owners;
- The anticipated level and nature of the activity that is to be undertaken through the relationship.

Article 9: Risk-based approach -- reduced and enhanced costumer Due Diligence 1. The general rule is that clients shall be subject to the full range of CDD measures. The only exception to this rule is, that on the basis of the lower risk, and the fact that information on the identity of the client and beneficial owners is publicly available, Authorized Person may perform reduced CDD measures on a client that is a company listed on the stock exchange of a country sufficiently implement the FATF's Recommendations, or is a subsidiary of such a listed company. In such a case, only the requirements of article 8(2)(a),(c) and (d) need be carried out. However, where such a listed company is closely held i.e. subject to the beneficial ownership/control of an individual or a small group of individuals, an Authorized Person shall carefully review the AML/CFT risks and consider whether it is necessary to verify the identity of such individual(s).

2. Authorized Person must adopt an enhanced CDD process referred to Part 3 of these rules, for higher risk type of clients, business relationships or transactions. The relevant enhanced CDD process may vary from case to case depending on clients' background, transaction types and specific circumstances. Authorized Person must exercise its own judgment and adopt a flexible approach when applying the specific enhanced CDD measures to clients of particular high risk types.

3. Authorized Person must establish clearly in its client acceptance policies the risk factors for determining what types of clients and activities are to be considered as high risk, while recognizing that no policy can be exhaustive in setting out all risk factors that must be considered in every possible situation, such risk factors must include client risk, country, geographic risk and product/service risk.

4. In assessing whether or not a country sufficiently applies the FATF standards in combating money laundering and terrorist financing, Authorized Person must:

(a) carry out an assessment of the standards of prevention of money laundering and terrorist financing. This could be based on Authorized Person's knowledge and experience of the country concerned or be acquired from relevant authority. The higher the risk, the greater the due diligence measures that must be applied when undertaking business with a client from the country concerned;

(b) pay particular attention to assessments of compliance with the FATF Recommendations that have been undertaken by the FATF, FATF -style regional bodies, or the International Monetary Fund (IMF) and the World Bank; and

(c) maintain an appropriate degree of ongoing vigilance concerning money laundering and terrorist financing risks and to take into account information that is available to Authorized Persons about the standards of AML/CFT systems and controls that operate in the country with which any of their clients are associated.

5. Apart from the risk factors set out in paragraph (3) of this article for determining a client's risk profile, the following are some examples of high risk types of clients:

(a) complex legal arrangements that have no apparent legal or economic purpose;

(b) persons (including companies and other financial institutions) from or in countries which do not or insufficiently apply the FATF's Recommendations

e.g. countries designated as such by the FATF; and

(c) PEPs.

6. Authorized Persons must perform enhanced due diligence on higher risk clients. In higher risk cases. The Authorized Person must consider applying other additional measures such as:

(a) Obtaining declarations in writing from the beneficial owners about the identity of, and the relationship with the directors and substantial shareholders;

(b) obtaining comprehensive client profile information; e.g. extra information on the purpose and reasons for opening the account, business or employment background, source of funds and anticipated account activity;

(c) assigning designated staff to serve the client and those staff must conduct CDD and more frequent ongoing monitoring, in order to ensure that any unusual or suspicious transactions are identified on a timely basis; and

(d) Conducting face -to -face meetings with senior management of the client on a regular basis throughout the business relationship;

(e) obtaining the approval of senior management of the Authorized Person when opening an account.

Article 10: Politically exposed persons (PEP) 1. Authorized Person shall have risk management systems in place to identify whether a client or potential client, or a beneficial owner, is a PEP. Any accounts identified as being held by such persons shall be considered higher risk and Authorized Person shall conduct enhanced ongoing monitoring of such accounts.

2. The opening or continued operation of an account for a PEP must be approved by senior management of the Authorized Person pursuant to these article.

3. Authorized Person shall take measures to establish the source of wealth and source of funds of PEPs that are clients or beneficial owners.

Article 11: Non-profit Organizations & Entities Authorized Person shall have in place policies, procedures and controls to comply with the Authority's requirements regarding the opening and handling of accounts and transactions for non-profit organizations & entities. The following requirements shall be observed when dealing with accounts of any such organizations:

(1) Non -profit organizations entities must have an official registration/license issued by the relevant government authority, specifying the purposes and activities of the organization.

(2) Authorized Person shall classify non -profit organizations entities as high risk, and shall apply enhanced due diligence when dealing with such clients.

Article 12: When Authorized Person must perform CDD 1. An Authorized Person must carry out CDD measures when it:

(a) opens an account or establishes a business relationship;

(b) suspects money laundering or terrorist financing; or

(c) doubts the veracity of documents, data or information previously obtained for the purpose of identification or verification.

2. In general, an Authorized Person must verify the identity of the client or potential client and beneficial owner before or during the course of establishing the business relationship. When the Authorized Person is unable to perform the CDD process satisfactorily at the account opening stage, it must terminate the business relationship and not perform any transaction, and must consider whether a Suspicious Transaction Report (STR) must be made.

Article 13: Investment Funds 1. Where Authorized Person act for a client who is investing in an investment fund or a real estate investment fund, Authorized Person must carry out CDD on the client and shall comply with the other requirements of these Rules, except that where the client is a counterparty, the Authorized Person need not identify and verify the identity of the beneficial owners that are investing through the counterparty, provided that the requirements of paragraph (2) of this article are met.

2. The Authorized Person must ensure that the counterparty:

(a) is regulated, and licensed by the relevant government authority;

(b) is based in a jurisdiction that adequately applies the FATF Recommendations;

(c) is applying, as a minimum, requirements for AML/CFT (including measures or CDD and identification of beneficial owners) that are consistent with the requirements of these Rules and of the FATF Recommendations and

(d) has entered into an agreement with the Authorized Person agreeing, that upon the request of the Authorized Person or the Authority, the counterparty will provide any information requested regarding the beneficial owners.

Article 14: Reliance on other third parties for CDD 1. This Article refers to a third party that introduces clients to an Authorized Person and performs the client identification and verification. For the purposes of this article, a third party must either be a commercial bank or financial institution that engages in securities activities.

2. The Authorized Person may rely on the third party to perform elements in subparagraph (a) to (c) of the CDD measures in paragraph (2) article (8) of these Rules provided that the criteria set out below are met. However, the ultimate responsibility of client identification and verification always remains with the Authorized Person and not with the third party.

3. Authorized Person can only rely on third parties to perform the CDD if the client is located in a country other than Saudi Arabia.;

4. Prior to reliance, Authorized Person must satisfy itself that it is reasonable to rely on a third party to apply the CDD and that the CDD measures are as rigorous as those which the Authorized

Person would have conducted itself for the client. Authorized Persons must establish clear policies in order to determine whether the third party in question possesses an acceptable level of reliability.

5. Authorized Person relying upon a third party must:

(a) obtain copies of the CDD documentation and information, as required by paragraphs (2/a) to (2/c) of Article (8) of these Rules, including other information referred in article (6) of these rules;

(b) take adequate steps to satisfy itself that copies of relevant documentation relating to the CDD requirements will be made available from the third party upon request without delay, such as establishing their respective responsibilities in writing, including reaching an agreement with the third party that copies of other relevant documentation relating to the CDD requirements will be made available from the third party upon request without delay and the Authorized Person will be permitted to verify the CDD undertaken by the third party at any stage; and

(c) ensure the third party is regulated and supervised by a competent authority, and has measures in place to comply with CDD and record keeping requirements in line with these rules and the FATF recommendations.

6. Authorized Persons must conduct periodic reviews to ensure that a third party upon which it relies, continues to conform to the criteria set out above. This may involve review of the relevant policies and procedures and sample checks of the due diligence conducted.

7. Authorized Persons must not rely on third parties based in country considered as high risk, such as countries that have no or inadequate AML/CFT systems.

Article 15: Acquisition When an Authorized Person acquires, either in whole or in part, a financial institution in a foreign country, the Authorized Person shall ensure that the acquired financial institution has or will perform CDD measures consistent with the requirements in these Rules at the time of acquisition unless:

(a) the subsidiary it acquired holds the CDD records for all clients (including all relevant client identification information) and the Authorized Person has no doubt or concerns about the veracity or adequacy of the information so acquired, and

(b) the Authorized Person has conducted due diligence enquiries that have not raised any doubt on its part of as to the adequacy of AML/CFT procedures and controls previously adopted by the other financial institution.

Article 16: Non-Face-to-Face Business Relationships 1. An Authorized Person shall consider money laundering and terrorist financing threats that may arise from the misuse of new or developing technologies, and must formulate its policies, procedures and controls, to prevent such threats.

2. An Authorized Person must formulate its policies, procedures and controls in a way that addresses the specific risks associated with non -face to face business relationships and transactions. The specific risks associated with non -face to face business relationships must be addressed by specific and effective measures, both at the time the business relationship is established and as part of ongoing CDD.

Article 17: Ongoing CDD and Unusual Transactions 1. An Authorized Person must monitor on an ongoing basis the business relationships it has with clients. It must during the course of such relationships, monitor the conduct of the client's account and scrutinize transactions undertaken to ensure that the transactions are consistent with the Authorized Person's knowledge of the client, its business and risk profile and the source of funds.

2. Authorized Person must pay attention to all complex, large transactions and all unusual patterns of transactions which have no apparent economic or visible lawful purpose.

3. Authorized Person shall pay special attention to business relationships and transactions with clients or financial institutions from countries which do not or insufficiently apply the FATF's Recommendations. Where the Authority advises Authorized Person that such countries continue to not or insufficiently apply the FATF's Recommendations, Authorized Person shall treat all business relationships and transactions as higher risk and shall apply the measures set out in paragraph (6) of article (9) of these Rules.

4. The background and purpose of all such transactions, including transactions that have no economic or visible legal purpose, must be examined, the findings established in writing and those findings must be retained for at least 10 years and be made available to the Authority, and internal and external auditors if requested.

Article 18: Review and updating of records Identification data collected under the CDD process must be kept up to date, accurate and relevant. Authorized Person must undertake annual or ad hoc reviews of existing records, particularly for higher risk categories of clients or business relationships, when appropriate trigger events occur. Examples of trigger events that might prompt an Authorized Person to seek appropriate updated information include:

- an existing client applying to open a new account or establish a new relationship, or significantly alter the nature of an existing relationship;
- when there is a transaction that is unusual or not in line with the client's normal trading pattern based on the Authorized Person's knowledge of the client; or
- when the Authorized Person is not satisfied that it has sufficient information about the client or has doubts about the veracity or adequacy of previously obtained identification data.

3.4 PART 4 RECORD KEEPING

Article 19: Record Keeping Requirements 1. Authorized Person shall ensure to comply with the record keeping requirements contained in the relevant rules & regulations of the Authority and the company Saudi Stock Exchange (Tadawul), and must keep a record of all client identification data and other information and documents obtained as part of the CDD process, account files and business correspondence, as well as all transaction records.

2. Authorized Person shall maintain sufficient records to permit reconstruction of individual transactions (including the amounts and types of currencies involved) so as to provide, if necessary, evidence for prosecution of criminal activity.

3. Authorized Person shall keep the type of information regarding the accounts of its clients in particular the following:

(a) details of the client and beneficial owner(s) (if any) of the account, and any other CDD information required;

(b) account details, including the volume of the funds moving through the account; and

(c) for transactions: the origin of the funds, the form in which the funds were provided or withdrawn, such as, cheques, transfer, the identity of the person undertaking the transaction, the destination of the funds, and the form of instruction and authorization.

4. Authorized Person shall ensure that all client and transaction records and information are available on a timely basis to the Authority.

5. All records on transactions, both domestic and international, shall be maintained by Authorized Person for at least ten years after the date of the transaction.

6. All CDD records, account files and business correspondence shall be kept by Authorized Person for at least ten years after the account is closed.

7. In situations where the records relate to on-going investigations or where records relate to transactions which have been the subject of a suspicious transaction report, they shall be retained until it is confirmed that the case has been closed even if this is still ongoing after 10 years.

8. Authorized Person may retain documents as originals or copies, in paper or electronic form, provided that they are admissible as evidence in a court of law.

3.5 PART 5 SUSPICIOUS TRANSACTION REPORT

Article 20 Suspicious Transaction Report 1. Consistent with the obligations set out in the AML Law and its implementing Regulations, Authorized Person must immediately report to the FIU any complex, huge or unusual transaction or raises doubt and suspicion concerning its nature and purpose, or is related to money laundering, financing of terrorism, terrorist acts, or terrorist organizations.

2. Within 10 days the Authorized Person must submit a detailed report setting out all available data and information about the suspicious transactions and parties involved to the FIU. At a minimum the report shall include the following details:

- Account statements for a period of six (6) months
- Copies of all account opening documents
- Any data related to the nature of the reported transactions
- The indications and justifications for the suspicion, along with all supporting documents

3. Suspicious transactions must be reported regardless of whether they are also thought to involve other matters. The fact that a report may have already been filed with the FIU in relation to previous transactions of the client in question must not necessarily preclude the making of a fresh report (without delay) if new suspicions are aroused.

4. Authorized Person shall appoint an appropriately senior employee within the Authorized Person to whom all staff are instructed to promptly refer all complex, huge or unusual transaction or raises doubt and suspicion concerning its nature and purpose, or is related to money laundering, financing of terrorism, terrorist acts, or terrorist organizations, for possible referral to the FIU as an STR. The senior officer (referred hereafter as the Money Laundering Reporting Officer (MLRO)). must be a registered person, and have sufficient academic, scientific and practical experience in AML/CFT.

5. The MLRO shall act as a central reference point within the Authorized Person to facilitate onward reporting to the FIU. The MLRO must play an active role in the identification and reporting of suspicious transactions, and shall review reports of large or irregular transactions generated by the Authorized Person's internal systems on a regular basis as well as of ad hoc reports made by any employee of the Authorized Person.

6. Where Authorized Person employee brings a transaction to the attention of the MLRO, the circumstances of the case shall be reviewed at that level to determine whether the suspicion is justified. If a decision is made to not report the transaction to the FIU, the reasons for this shall be fully documented by the MLRO.

7. Authorized Person must keep records of all transactions referred to the MLRO, together with all internal findings and analysis done in relation to them. A register must be maintained of all STR made to the FIU as well as of all reports made by employees to the MLRO, including those where a decision is made by the MLRO not to report to the FIU.

8. Authorized Person shall use the standard form prescribed by the FIU for reporting, and must report by fax, email or any other means agreed by the FIU to ensure that the FIU receives the report promptly. If reports are initially made by telephone, the STR must be confirmed in writing within 24 hours.

9. The Authorized Person must verify that it has received an acknowledgement of receipt from The FIU.

10. Authorized Person must continue to monitor the account and the client, and must send a further STR if appropriate in the case where a response is not received from the FIU regarding an STR

11. A list of indicators of types of potentially unusual or suspicious transactions or activities that could be a cause for further scrutiny is set out in Annex 1 of these Rules. The list is not exhaustive and Authorized Person must remain vigilant to their obligation to report any unusual or suspicious transactions or activity, whether these are of a type set out in Annex 1 of these Rules or not. The existence of one or more of the factors described in the list warrants some form of increased scrutiny of the transaction, but by itself does not necessarily mean that a transaction is suspicious.

12. In relation to terrorist financing, the FATF issued a paper in April 2002 on guidance for financial institutions in detecting terrorist financing, and a further report on terrorist financing typologies in March 2008. Authorized Persons shall ensure that their staff are familiar with these documents.

13. Where the FIU requires further information from an Authorized Person to follow up on an STR, the Authority will act as a conduit for the request and shall ask the Authorized Person to provide the information requested by the FIU.

14. In accordance with the AML Law article 25 Authorized Persons and their directors, officers and employees (permanent and

temporary) are protected by law from both criminal and civil liability for breach of any restriction on disclosure of information imposed by contract or by any legislative, regulatory or administrative provision, if they report unusual or suspicious transactions or activity in good faith to the FIU. This protection is available even if they did not know precisely what the underlying criminal activity was, and regardless of whether illegal activity actually occurred.

Article 21: Tipping Off 1. In all circumstances, Authorized Person, its directors, officers and employees must ensure that clients or related parties are not alerted to the fact that they have made or are considering making an STR or providing documents or information linked to an STR to the FIU. An Authorized Person shall at all times keep its reporting of suspicious transactions highly confidential, and reports of suspicious transactions or reports that are to be reviewed by the MLRO for possible reporting shall be accessible only by specifically Authorized staff of the Authorized Person.

2. Where an STR has been made to the FIU and it becomes necessary to make further enquiries of the client, great care must be taken to ensure that the client does not become aware that the STR has been made. The Authorized Person shall continue its business dealing with the reported clients as usual, it must not warn its clients or other relevant parties of the suspicious transactions, and it shall await further instructions from the Authority.

Article 22: Designated persons -- UNSCR Resolutions 1. Authorized Person must have in place effective procedures to promptly identify any clients or potential clients (including beneficial owners) that have been designated "designated persons " by the United Nations Committee under UNSCR 1267(1999) "the 1267 Committee"; and successor resolutions.

2. If an Authorized Person identifies a client or potential client as a designated person or a transaction where one of its parties is a designated persons, it must immediately send an STR to the FIU and in accordance with the AML Law and its implementing Regulation, must freeze any property that it holds for a designated person. Once an STR is made, the Authorized Person shall continue freezing the account and transactions of the client until receive instructions from the Authority.

3. Prior to opening any new account, Authorized Person must check the potential client's name against the lists of designated persons. Authorized Persons must, on a daily basis, check the names of all existing clients against the lists of names of designated persons by reviewing the UN website.

4. Where a person is listed by the competent authority in Saudi Arabia under UNSCR 1373 (or a successor resolution), the Authority will notify all Authorized Persons of that listing and they must immediately freeze the property of such persons.

5. Where funds that have been frozen, are unfrozen because the designated person has been delisted, or because the person whose assets were frozen was incorrectly thought to be a designated person, or because authorization was made by the competent authority to release funds for legal or living expenses, then the Authority will notify the Authorized Person.

3.6 PART 6 INTERNAL POLICIES, PROCEDURES AND CONTROLSnternal Policies, Procedures and Controls

Article 23: Internal Policies and Compliance 1. Authorized Person shall develop and implement internal policies, procedures and controls to help prevent money laundering and terrorist financing and must communicate these to its employees. The compliance officer shall also ensure compliance with the AML/CFT policies, procedures and controls.

2. The policies, procedures and controls must include, amongst other things, CDD measures, record retention, the detection of unusual and/or suspicious transactions and the obligation to make an STR.

3. An Authorized Person shall ensure that the MLRO and any of its staff (performing compliance function) have timely access to all client and transaction records and other relevant information which they require to discharge their functions.

4. The MLRO shall undertake the following duties:

- Develop, update and implement the Authorized Person's system, procedures and controls on AML/CFT.
- Keep pace with developments in AML/CFT laws and regulations, trends, techniques, and update indicators of money laundering or terrorist financing.
- Ensure that the Authorized Person complies with its policies and procedures.
- Receiving directly from staff any reports of suspicious transactions or activity And analyze those reports and then decide whether to file an STR with the FIU.
- Prepare a report annually to the Board of the Authorized Person setting out all actions that have been taken to implement the internal policies, procedures and controls and proposals for increasing the effectiveness and efficiency of the procedures. Thereafter, the report shall be submitted to the Authority.
- Ensure that staff of the Authorized Person maintains all necessary records.
- Organize ongoing training for all staff of the Authorized Person.

Article 24: Internal Audit 1. The internal audit in the Authorized Person shall regularly assess the effectiveness of the Authorized Person's internal AML/CFT policies, procedures and controls and the Authorized Person's compliance with these Rules.

Article 25: Education and Training 1. Authorized Person must take all appropriate steps to ensure that their staffs (group-wide) receive regular training on:

(a) AML/CFTlaws and regulations, and in particular, CDD measures, detecting and reporting of suspicious transactions;

(b) prevailing techniques, methods and trends in money laundering and terrorist financing; and

(c) the Authorized Person's internal policies, procedures and controls on AML/CFT and the roles and responsibilities of staff in combating money laundering and terrorist financing.

2. Authorized Persons must have educational programmes in place for training all new employees. Refresher training must also be provided at regular intervals to ensure that staff, in particular those who deal with the public directly and help clients open new accounts.

3.7 PART 7 CLOSING PROVISIONS

Article 26: Sanctions Without prejudice to the sanctions imposed under AML Law, Authorized Person or any director, manager or employee of an Authorized Person that fails to comply with any article of these Rules shall be subject to the sanctions set out in Articles 59 and 62 of the Capital Market Law.

Article 27: Publication and Entry into Force These Rules shall become effective upon their publication.

3.8 Annex 1 Securities Business Indicators for Money Laundering or Terrorist Financing

Examples of possible indicators that a transaction or activity may be linked to money laundering or terrorist financing are as follows:

1. The client exhibits unusual concern regarding the firm's compliance with AML/CTF requirements, particularly with respect to his identity and type of business.
2. Client refuses to identify himself or to indicate legitimate sources for his funds and other assets.
3. The client wishes to engage in transactions that have no apparent legal or economic purpose or are inconsistent with the declared investment strategy.
4. The client tries to provide the Authorized Person with incorrect or misleading information regarding his identity and/or source of funds.
5. The Authorized Person knows that the client was involved in money laundering or terrorist financing activities, or in other criminal offenses or regulatory violations.
6. The client exhibits a lack of concern regarding risks, commissions, or other transaction costs.
7. An Authorized Person suspects that the client appears to be acting as an agent on behalf of an undisclosed principal, but declines or is reluctant, without legitimate commercial reasons, to provide information about that person or entity.
8. The client has difficulty describing the nature of his business or lacks general knowledge of his activities.
9. The client holds multiple accounts under a single name or multiple names, with a large number of inter-account or third-party transfers with no apparent reason for that activity.
10. The client makes multiple of wire transfers to his investment account followed by an immediate request that the money be wired out to a third party without any apparent business purpose.
11. The client makes a long -term investment followed shortly thereafter by a request to liquidate the position and transfers the proceeds out of the account.
12. The client's activities vary substantially from normal practices.
13. A client refuses to provide the Authorized Person with basic information for a mutual fund to verify the client's identity.
14. The client requests that the Authorized Person uses wire transfers in such a manner that originator information is not transferred from the sending to the receiving destination.
15. A client seeks to change or cancel a transaction after being informed of the information verification or record keeping requirements by the Authorized Person.
16. The client requests that a transaction be processed in such a manner to avoid more documentation.
17. The client 's account shows an unexplained high level of wire transfers with very low levels of securities transactions.
18. The Authorized Person knows that funds or property is proceeds that come from illegal sources.
19. Change source of funds constantly.

4 AUTHORIZED PERSONS REGULATIONS

Issued by the Board of the Capital Market Authority Pursuant to its Resolution Number 1-83-2005 dated 21/05/1426H (28/06/2005G) based on the Capital Market Law issued by Royal Decree No. M/30 dated 2/6/1424H, amended by Resolution of the Board of the Capital Market Authority Number 3-85-2017 dated 27/12/1438H (18/9/2017G).

[Practice Note: these regulations have in large part been replaced by the Capital Market Institutions Regulations. Note however, that several provisions of the Authorized Persons Regulations remain in effect as mentioned in the Capital Market Institutions Regulations.]

TABLE OF CONTENTS

PART 1: GENERAL PROVISIONS
Article 1: Preliminary
Article 2: Definitions
Article 3: Compliance with the Regulations and Rules
Article 4: Waivers
PART 2: THE PRINCIPLES FOR authorized PERSONS
Article 5: The Principles
PART 3: authorization
Chapter One: Applications for authorization
Article 6: Requirements for authorization
Article 7: Procedure and powers of Authority in relation to an application
Article 8: Right of appeal
Chapter Two: Maintenance of authorization
Article 9: Fit and Proper
Article 10: Scope of Business
Article 11: Variation or amendment
Article 12: Authorized Person withdrawal and cancelling of authorization
Article 13: Controllers
Article 14: Close links
Article 15: Notification requirements and powers of Authority
Article 16: Record-keeping
Article 17: Fees
ANNEX 3.1 INFORMATION AND DOCUMENTS REQUIRED FOR authorization
ANNEX 3.2 NOTIFICATION REQUIREMENTS
PART 4: REGISTERED PERSONS
Chapter One: Background and scope
Article 18: Scope of application
Article 19: Registrable functions
Article 20: Performance of registrable functions
Chapter Two: Registration
Article 21: Requirements for application for registration
Article 22: Procedure and powers of the Authority
Article 23: Right of appeal
Chapter Three: General provisions
Article 24: Responsibilities of registered persons
Article 25: Cancellation of registration
PART 5: CONDUCT OF BUSINESS
Chapter One: General Provisions
Article 26: Preliminary provisions
Article 27: Inducements
Article 28: Special commission arrangements
Article 29: Confidentiality
Article 30: Chinese walls arrangements
Article 31: Exclusions of liability
Chapter Two: Securities advertisements
Article 32: Scope of Application
Article 33: Prepared securities advertisements
Article 34: Direct communications
Article 35: Non-retail investment funds and derivatives
Chapter Three: Accepting clients
Article 36: Client classification
Article 37: Money laundering and terrorism financing
Article 38: Terms of business with clients
Article 39: Know your customer
Chapter Four: Clients relations
Article 40: Fiduciary duties
Article 41: Conflicts of interest
Article 42: Understanding risk
Article 43: Suitability
Article 44: Customer borrowing
Article 45: Margin Requirements
Article 46: Fees and commissions
Chapter Five: Reporting to clients
Article 47: Contract notes
Article 48: Periodic reporting
Chapter Six: Miscellaneous
Article 49: Client records
Article 50: Employee's personal dealings
Article 51: Recording telephone calls
ANNEX 5.1 CONTENTS REQUIREMENTS FOR SECURITIES ADVERTISEMENTS
ANNEX 5.2 TERMS OF BUSINESS REQUIREMENTS
ANNEX 5.3 KNOW YOUR CUSTOMER FORM
ANNEX 5.4 FIDUCIARY DUTIES
ANNEX 5.5 REQUIRED CONTENTS OF CONTRACT NOTES
ANNEX 5.6 REQUIRED CONTENTS OF PERIODIC VALUATIONS STATEMENTS FOR CLIENT PORTFOLIOS
ANNEX 5.7 PERSONAL ACCOUNT DEALING
PART 6: SYSTEM AND CONTROLS
Chapter One: Scope of application
Article 52: Scope of application
Chapter Two: Management arrangements
Article 53: Division of responsibilities
Article 54: Establishment and maintenance of systems and controls
Chapter Three: Systems and controls
Article 55: General Provisions
Article 56: Review by the governing body
Article 57: Compliance
Article 58: Compliance committee
Article 59: Outsourcing
Article 60: Audit committee
Article 61: Internal audit
Article 62: Audit and inspection
Article 63: Resolution of complaints
Article 64: Money laundering and terrorism financing
Article 65: Employees
Article 66: Business continuity
Article 67: Record retrieval
Article 68: Mandate over an account in the client's name
PART 7: CLIENT MONEY AND ASSETS

Chapter One: General Provisions
Article 69: Purpose and Scope
Article 70: Effect of Segregation
Chapter Two: Client Money Rules
Article 71: Money received by an Authorized Person
Article 72: Money which is not client money
Article 73: Money to be held with a bank
Article 74: Acknowledgement by a bank
Article 75: Client accounts
Article 76: Money ceasing to be client money
Article 77: Commission
Article 78: Records and auditor's report
Article 79: Amounts to be held in client money bank accounts
Article 80: Reconciliations
Article 81: Client money reporting requirement
Chapter Three: Client Asset Rules
Article 82: Assets received by an Authorized Person
Article 83: Assets which are not client assets
Article 84: Segregation
Article 85: Holding and registration of client assets
Article 86: Lending of client securities
Article 87: Assessment of custodian
Article 88: Client agreements
Article 89: Custodian agreement
Article 90: Reconciliations
Article 91: Client statements
Chapter Four: Collateral and money and assets passed to third parties
Article 92: Scope of Application
Article 93: Collateral subject to the Client Money Rules or the Client Asset Rules
Article 94: Other collateral
PART 8: INSOLVENCY PROVISIONS
Article 95: Supervision of insolvency proceedings
Article 96: Rights of clients on insolvency of an Authorized Person holding client money and assets
Article 97: Settlement Proceedings
Article 98: Liquidation Proceedings
PART 9: PUBLICATION AND ENTRY INTO FORCE
Article 99: Publication and entry into force

Article 1: Preliminary

4.1 PART 1: GENERAL PROVISIONS

The purpose of these Regulations is to regulate Authorized Persons and registered persons and to specify the procedures and conditions for obtaining a license, as well as the conditions for the maintenance of the license or the registration, to provide for the rules of conduct that Authorized Persons must comply with when conducting their business, as well as the rules and provisions governing the conduct of business, and to set the systems and controls as well as the provisions relating to client money and assets.

Article 2: Definitions

a. Any reference to the "Capital Market Law" in these Regulations shall mean the Capital Market Law issued by Royal Decree No. M/30 dated 2/6/1424H.

b. Expressions and terms in these Regulations have the meaning which they bear in the Capital Market Law and in the Glossary of defined terms used in the Regulations and Rules of the Capital Market Authority, unless the contrary intention appears.

Article 3: Compliance with the Regulations and Rules

a. An Authorized Person and a registered person must comply with the Regulations and Rules applicable to them and must provide to the Authority without delay any information, records or documents that the Authority may require for the purpose of administration of the Capital Market Law and its Implementing Regulations.

b. The governing body and employees of an Authorized Person and a registered person, must comply with any requirement issued by the Authority to appear to explain any matter or to assist in any enquiry relating to the administration of the Capital Market Law and its Implementing Regulations.

Article 4: Waivers

a. The Authority may waive a provision of these Regulations in whole or in part as it applies to an applicant or an Authorized Person either on an application from the applicant or the Authorized Person or on its own initiative.

b. The Authority will make an announcement of the waiver of any provisions where it believes that:

1) the waiver of the provision may be of application to more than one type of Authorized Persons; and

2) the publication of the waiver will not materially prejudice the Authorized Persons.

This is to achieve the policy of the Authority to promote competition, including retaining a level playing field between Authorized Persons.

4.2 PART 2: THE PRINCIPLES FOR AUTHORIZED PERSONS

Article 5: The principles

a. The Principles provided for in this Part are a general statement of the fundamental obligations of Authorized Persons. They are intended to form a universal statement of the standards of conduct expected of Authorized Persons under these Regulations.

b. An Authorized Person must comply with the following principles:

1) Integrity, by conducting its business with integrity.

2) Skill, care and diligence, by conducting its business with due skill, care and diligence.

3) Efficiency of management and control, by taking reasonable care to organize its affairs responsibly and effectively, with adequate risk management policies and systems.

4) Financial prudence, by maintaining adequate financial resources in accordance with the Rules issued by the Authority.

5) Proper market conduct, by observing proper standards of market conduct.

6) Protection of Clients' assets, by arranging for adequate protection of its clients' assets.

7) Co-operation with regulators, including disclosing to the Authority any material event or change in the Authorized Person's business operations or organization.

8) Communications with clients, by communicating information to them in a way which is clear, fair and not misleading.

9) Paying due regard to customers' interests, by treating them fairly and paying due regard to their interests.

10) No conflicts of interest, by managing conflicts of interest fairly, both between itself and its customers and between a customer and another client.

11) Customers' suitability, by taking reasonable care to ensure the suitability of its advice and discretionary managing decisions for any customer to whom it provides those services.

4.3 PART 3: AUTHORIZATION

4.3.1 Chapter One – Applications for Authorization

Article 6: Requirements for Authorization

a. For the purposes of these Regulations, an applicant for authorization means the person that is applying for authorization to carry on securities business. An applicant for authorization becomes subject to these Regulations from the date of submission of his application.
b. An application for authorization may be submitted by the founders or controlling shareholders of an applicant if the applicant is not yet established. The founders or controlling shareholders become subject to the provisions that apply to an applicant from the date of submission of the application.
c. An application for authorization must be made on the application form prescribed by the Authority and be accompanied by the information and documents required in Annex 3.1.
d. The form and contents of the application and all information and documents filed with it must be as prescribed by the Authority.
e. An applicant must demonstrate to the Authority that:

1) it is fit and proper to carry on securities business of the kind and scale for which it seeks authorization in accordance with the rules prescribed by the Authority;

2) it has adequate expertise and resources for the kind of securities business that it proposes to carry on in accordance with the rules prescribed by the Authority;

3) it has managerial expertise, financial systems, risk management policies and systems, technological resources, and operational procedures and systems that are sufficient to fulfill its business and regulatory obligations and to conduct the kind of securities business that it proposes to carry on; and

4) its directors, officers, employees and agents who will be involved in the applicant's securities business have the necessary qualifications, skills, experience and integrity to carry on the kind of securities business that it proposes to carry on.

f. In order to engage in dealing, custody and managing business, an applicant must be established in the Kingdom and must be:

1) a subsidiary of a local bank;

2) a joint stock company;

3) a subsidiary of a Saudi joint stock company that is engaged in financial services business; or

4) a subsidiary of a foreign financial institution that is licensed under the Banking Control Law issued by Royal Decree No. M/5 dated 22/2/1386H.

The applicant may be of any legal form established in the Kingdom to apply for a license to conduct arranging or advising.
g. The paid up capital of the applicant must not be less than the following:

1) dealing and custody: SR 50 million;

2) managing: SR 20 million for managing investment funds and client portfolios; and SR 5 million for managing private non-real-estate investment funds and sophisticated investor portfolios;

3) arranging: SR 2 million; and

4) advising: SR 400,000.

h. An applicant must have its management and head office in the Kingdom.
i. If the applicant has close links with another person, the Authority must be satisfied with the integrity, regulatory status, business record and financial soundness of any such person, and that such close links will not impair the effective supervision of the applicant, or its operations and compliance with these Regulations.
j. The applicant for authorization must pay such fees as may be prescribed by the Authority.

Article 7: Procedure and powers of the Authority in relation to an application

a. In considering an application, the Authority may:

1) carry out any enquiries that it considers appropriate;

2) require the applicant, or his representative, to attend before the Authority to answer questions and explain any matter the Authority considers relevant to the application;

3) require the applicant to provide such additional information as the Authority considers appropriate within 30 days of the request; and

4) verify any information furnished by the applicant.

b. The Authority may refuse to consider the application for authorization where an applicant has failed to provide information requested from it, or has failed to provide information requested from it within the time requested.

c. The Authority shall, upon receipt of all information and documents required, notify the applicant in writing of the same, and shall take any of the following decisions within a maximum period of 30 days from the date of the notice:

1) approve the application in whole or in part;

2) approve the application subject to such conditions and limitations as it considers appropriate;

3) refuse the application, giving reasons.

d. If the Authority resolves to authorize the applicant, it will inform the applicant of this in writing and of its permitted business profile including any limitations that the Authority may consider appropriate.

e. If the Authority resolves to refuse the application, it will notify the applicant in writing.

f. An applicant must not carry on, or hold itself out as carrying on, securities business prior to receiving the Authority's decision referred to at paragraph (d) of this Article.

Article 8: Right of Appeal The applicant may appeal to the Committee in respect of any decision or action that the Authority takes under this Part.

4.3.2 Chapter Two – Maintenance of Authorization

Article 9: Fit and Proper

a. As a condition for the maintenance of authorization, an authorized person must continue to be fit and proper to carry out the securities business which it is authorized to carry out at all times.
b. The skills, experience, competence and integrity of an authorized person's or applicant's employees, officers or agents is an important factor in assessing whether it is fit and proper. The skills, experience, competence and integrity of the employees, officers or agents will be assessed against the following criteria:

1) they must possess adequate qualifications and professional experience to carry out their responsibilities, including appropriate technical knowledge and skills;

2) they must have probity and soundness of judgement commensurate with their positions;

3) they must fulfill their responsibilities with diligence and to protect clients' interests in accordance with the Implementing Regulations;

4) they must not have committed an offense involving fraud or dishonesty; and

5) they must not have contravened or broken any laws or regulations governing securities business or aimed at protecting investors.

Article 10: Scope of Business

a. An Authorized Person must not carry on, or hold itself out as carrying on, securities business unless that business is within its permitted business profile.

b. An Authorized Person must comply with the rules applicable to it and with any limitation, condition or other requirement that the Authority specifies.

c. Client money must be held with a local bank.

d. The value of assets under management by an Authorized Person shall not exceed SR (one) billion if his activity is limited to managing private non-real-estate investment funds or managing sophisticated investor portfolios, and he shall have a continuous control mechanism to ensure the value does not exceed the maximum limit stated in this paragraph. If the limit was exceeded, the Authorized Person must take the following steps:

1) Notify the Authority at occurrence immediately; and

2) submit a corrective plan to the Authority within a maximum period of one month from occurrence date, and refrain from receiving any additional funds or assets from clients from occurrence date until the situation is corrected.

Article 11: Variation or Amendment

a. An Authorized Person must apply to the Authority for approval of any proposed variation or amendment to its permitted business profile.

b. The Authority has all the powers set out in Article 7 of these Regulations to consider a proposed variation or amendment, and may also require some or all of the information or documents referred to in Article 6 of these Regulations to be updated.

c. The Authority will aim to process an application to vary or amend an Authorized Person's permitted business profile within 30 days from receiving all information that it considers necessary.

d. After considering an application to vary or amend an authorized person's permitted business profile, the Authority may:

1) approve the application for variation or amendment in whole or in part;

2) approve the application subject to such conditions and limitations as it considers appropriate;

3) defer making a decision for such period as it may consider necessary to carry out further study or examination or to allow for the provision of additional information; or

4) refuse the application, giving reasons.

e. If the Authority resolves to approve an application for a change in a permitted business profile, it will inform the Authorized Person of this in writing and of its new permitted business profile, including any limitations that the Authority may consider appropriate.

f. The Authorized Person must not carry on (or hold itself out as carrying on) the kind of securities business concerned before receiving the Authority's notification under paragraph (e) of this Article.

g. If the Authority resolves to refuse the application for variation or amendment, it will notify the Authorized Person in writing.

h. The Authorized Person may appeal to the Committee in respect of any decision or action that the Authority takes under this Article.

Article 12: Withdrawal from business and cancellation of authorization

a. An Authorized Person that proposes to cease to carry on securities business must notify the Authority in writing of the date on which it intends to cease to carry securities business and the reasons for the decision:

1) at least 45 days in advance of that date; or

2) if such advance notice is not possible because cessation of business is caused by an external event of which the Authorized Person was not aware, immediately on making a decision to cease to carry on securities business.

b. Where an Authorized Person decides to cease providing securities business to clients, it must ensure that any such business that is outstanding is properly completed or is transferred to another Authorized Person and that it provides reasonable notice to its clients of the cessation of business.

c. An Authorized Person may request the cancellation of its authorization, and must in this case submit a written request to the Authority not less than three months prior to the proposed date of the cancellation.

d. A request to cancel an authorization must include sufficient information concerning the circumstances of the cancellation to enable the Authority to determine whether to accept the cancellation, to postpone the date of the cancellation, or to require other measures that it considers necessary for the protection of clients of the authorized person.

e. The Authority may refuse a request to cancel an authorization if it considers that the maintenance of the authorization is necessary to investigate any matter affecting the Authorized Person, to protect the interests of the Authorized Person's clients, or to impose a prohibition or requirements on such Authorized Person under the Capital Market Law or its Implementing Regulations.

f. The Authority may suspend the Authorized Person's authorization on its own initiative if the Authorized Person does not carry on any securities business for a period of 12 months, or 6 months following the date on which an Authorized Person has ceased to carry on securities business after notification to the Authority in accordance with paragraph (a) of this Article.

g. An Authorized Person continues to be subject to the jurisdiction of the Authority in respect of any act or omission that occurred before the cancellation of its authorization and for two years thereafter. If at any time during this period the Authority commences any enforcement investigation or proceedings, the Authorized Person shall continue to be subject to the jurisdiction of the Authority until the end of the enforcement investigation or proceedings.

Article 13: Controllers

a. An Authorized Person must notify the Authority, in such form as the Authority may prescribe, that a person is intending to become, or cease to be, a controller of the Authorized Person:

1) at least 30 days in advance of the proposed effective date; or

2) if such advance notice is not possible, immediately on the authorized person becoming aware of such intention.

b. An Authorized Person must not permit any person to become or act as a controller unless the Authority has approved the controller in writing.

c. A person who intends to become a controller of an Authorized Person must notify the Authority of such intention at least 30 days in advance of the proposed effective date, and must provide the Authority with such information as the Authority requires to satisfy itself of its identity, integrity, regulatory status, business record and financial soundness.

d. Before approving a controller the Authority must be satisfied that the person's control of the Authorized Person will not impair the effective supervision of the Authorized Person or its operations and compliance with the Capital Market Law and the Implementing Regulations.

e. In considering any application submitted under this Article, the Authority has all of the powers set out in Article 7 of these Regulations.

Article 14: Close Links

a. An Authorized Person must notify the Authority, in such form as the Authority may prescribe, that a person is intending to establish close links with the Authorized Person:

1) at least 30 days in advance of the proposed effective date; or
2) if such advance notice is not possible, immediately on the authorized person becoming aware of any change in close links.

The notice must include such information as the Authority requires to satisfy itself of the identity of the person with whom the authorized person proposes to establish close links, its integrity, regulatory status, business record and financial soundness.

b. An Authorized Person must not establish close links with another person unless the Authority has approved the close links in writing.

c. Before approving any close links, the Authority must be satisfied that such links will not impair the effective supervision of the Authorized Person or its operations and compliance with the Capital Market Law and the Implementing Regulations.

d. In considering any application to establish close links, the Authority has all of the powers set out in Article 7 of these Regulations.

Article 15: Notification requirements and Powers of Authority

a. An Authorized Person must comply with the notification requirements set out in Annex 3.2.

b. On receiving a notice under paragraph (a) of this Article, the Authority may:

1) require the Authorized Person to provide any additional information that it considers necessary to properly assess the matter; and
2) impose any conditions, restrictions or additional requirements on an Authorized Person, including limitations on its permitted business profile, that it reasonably considers to be necessary to address a regulatory concern raised by any matter that it is notified of under this Article.

Article 16: Record-keeping

a. An Authorized Person must record and retain sufficient information about its securities business to demonstrate compliance with these Regulations.

b. Records required to be maintained by these Regulations must be retained for a period of ten years unless the Authority specifies otherwise.

c. The Authority may inspect the records directly or through a person it appoints for that purpose.

d. Records made by an Authorized Person may be recorded in any form, but must be capable of reproduction in hard printed form.

e. When a client or a former client requests any records kept during the regulatory record-keeping period, the Authorized Person must make available, within a reasonable period, any of the following:

1) any written material or records which relate to that client and which the Authorized Person has sent, or is required to send, to that client under Part 5 of these Regulations; and

2) copies of any correspondence received from or sent to that client relating to securities business.

Article 17: Fees An Authorized Person must pay such fees as the Authority may prescribe for the maintenance of the license.

4.4 ANNEX 3.1 INFORMATION AND DOCUMENTS REQUIRED FOR AUTHORIZATION

These authorization requirements set out below apply to all types of securities business and the application of each requirement will differ depending on the nature, scope and complexity of the activities. Applicants whom the type of their activities will be limited to managing private non-real estate investment funds, managing sophisticated investor portfolios, arranging and advising will be excluded from submitting the information and documents stated in the sub-paragraphs (1), (3), (4) and (5) of paragraph (8) and the paragraphs (9), (10), (11), (12), (13), (16) and (17) of this Annex, provided that the applicant undertakes to obtain the documents and information contained in sub-paragraphs (1), (3), (4) and (5) of paragraph (8) and paragraphs (10), (13), (16) And (17) of this Annex before commencing his activity.

1. Controllers – An applicant must submit a list of all controllers of the applicant, and provide details of the identity, ownership (if applicable), integrity, regulatory status, business record and financial position of each proposed controller.

2. Close Links – An applicant must submit a list of all persons that have, or are proposed to have, close links with the applicant, and provide details of the identity, ownership (if applicable), integrity, regulatory status, business record and financial position of each such person.

3. Governing Body Resolution – An applicant must submit to the Authority a resolution of its governing body in the form prescribed by the Authority approving the application and its contents, and certifying the accuracy and completeness of the accompanying information and documents.

4. Business Profile – An applicant must submit a proposed business profile including full details of all securities and all services for which the applicant proposes to provide for each securities activity that it is applying to carry on. A schedule must be attached in the following form:

- Securities Business
- Types of Activity
- Details of Securities
- Details of Services
- Categories of clients
- Dealing
- Dealer (as principal or agent)
- Underwriter
- Custody
- Securities custody services
- Managing
- Manage investment funds
- Manage client portfolios
- Manage private non-real-estate investment funds
- Manage sophisticated investor portfolios

Arranging:

Financial advisor / corporate finance advisor:

Advising:

Investment Advisor:

5. Business Plan – An applicant must submit a business plan, setting out:

1) a detailed description of the securities business activities that the applicant proposes to undertake during, at least, the first 12 months after authorization, including:

- the products and services that it intends to provide to clients;
- the classes and types of securities that it intends to provide services in; and
- all exchanges and markets that it intends to trade in;

2) a description of the nature of the proposed clients of the applicant;
3) a list of any exchanges, clearing houses or depositaries of which the applicant is or intends to become a member.

6. Financial Statements – An applicant must submit financial statements prepared and accredited by the applicant's auditors in accordance with the standards issued by SOCPA and presented in the format prescribed by the Authority, and must:

1) show the applicant's current and projected financial position, including its capital, financial resources, revenues and expenses as at the date of the financial statements, the proposed commencement of business, and the financial position 12 months after the date of commencement of business;
2) provide supporting evidence of the capitalization and resources of the applicant and the presumptions on which the statements have been provided.

7. Registered Persons – An applicant must submit a list of each person who is to be a registered person and an application form for registration for each such person in the format prescribed by the Authority, including details of their qualifications and experience.

8. Systems and Controls – An applicant must, in accordance with Part 6 of these Regulations, submit the following systems and controls documentation:

1) risk management policies and systems;
2) anti-money laundering and anti-terrorism financing procedures;
3) compliance manual;
4) compliance monitoring programme; and
5) code of conduct.

9. Operations Manual – An applicant must submit an operational procedures manual detailing the procedures and systems to be employed in relation to all material business and administrative operations, including the following:

1) opening and processing of client accounts;
2) processing and recording of orders, and the execution, settlement and confirmation of trades;
3) the provision of prudent and suitable advice and services to clients;
4) handling and custody of client money and client assets;
5) reporting to clients; and
6) complying with all record-keeping requirements.

10. Terms of Business – An applicant must submit a copy of proposed terms of business (in accordance with Part 5 of these Regulations), and of the proposed forms.

11. Fees – An applicant must submit a list of proposed fees, commissions, charges and other expenses payable by clients.

12. Contracts – An applicant must submit agreements, arrangements and understandings with third parties to provide any material services or operations, including:

1) Execution, clearing and settlement of trades;
2) Custody of client money or client assets;
3) Arrangements to offer products or services provided by, sponsored by, or associated with a third party;
4) Arrangements to introduce clients;
5) Information technology, databases and computer systems;
6) Record-keeping;
7) Compliance services;
8) Audit services.

13. Insurance – An applicant must submit details of professional indemnity insurance policies in accordance with the requirements prescribed by the Authority.

14. Incorporation Documents – If the applicant is a company, it must submit a copy of its articles of association or by-laws.

15. Structure – If an applicant is a company, it must submit an ownership structure chart showing the group of which the applicant forms part, including each controller and each person with whom the applicant has close links.

16. Organization Chart – An applicant must submit an organization chart identifying the applicant's governing body, the CEO and senior management, the compliance officer and MLRO. The chart must outline the reporting lines of each department within the business in accordance with Part 6 of these Regulations.

17. Business Continuity – An applicant must submit a copy of the applicant's business continuity plan.

4.5 ANNEX 3.2 NOTIFICATION REQUIREMENTS

I. An Authorized Person must notify the Authority in writing not less than 30 days before any change in:

1. the name of the Authorized Person or, where the Authorized Person is a company, its registered name;
2. any business name under which the Authorized Person carries on securities business in the Kingdom; or
3. the address of the head office of the Authorized Person, or, if different, the address of the place for service of notices or documents.

II. An Authorized Person must notify the Authority in writing within 7 days of the occurrence of:

1. any change in the material information provided to the Authority on the form of application for registration relating to a registered person's name, good reputation or character. A registered person must give immediate notice to the compliance officer of his Authorized Person of any such changes;
2. if the Authorized Person is a company, the formation, acquisition, disposal or dissolution of a subsidiary specifying the subsidiary's name and its principal business;
3. if the Authorized Person is not a company, when it acquires or disposes of a holding of more than half in nominal value of the capital of a company or equivalent holding of an unincorporated body, specifying the name of the company or unincorporated body and its principal business; or
4. any changes in the information originally submitted under the following headings:
   - branch offices in the Kingdom from which the Authorized Person carries on securities business;
   - insurance arrangements;
   - the countries outside the Kingdom in which the Authorized Person carries on securities business indicating whether this is done through a branch office, a subsidiary or otherwise; and
   - the contracts or arrangements to clear and settle transactions or for custody of client money or client assets.

III. An Authorized Person must notify the Authority in writing immediately on the occurrence of:

1. the presentation of a petition for the winding up of the authorized person or of a company which is a subsidiary or controller of the Authorized Person or the summoning of any meeting to consider a resolution to wind up an Authorized Person or a company which is a subsidiary or controller of the Authorized Person;
2. any insolvency event;
3. the imposition of disciplinary measures or disciplinary sanctions on the Authorized Person in relation to its securities business by any regulatory authority;
4. the conviction of the Authorized Person for any offense under legislation relating to banking or other financial services, companies, insolvency, or for any offense involving fraud or any act involving a lack of integrity or dishonesty, or the imposition of any penalties for deliberate zakat or tax evasion;
5. a general partner in an Authorized Person becoming a limited partner;
6. the granting or refusal of any application for, or revocation of, authorization to carry on securities, banking or insurance business in any country or territory outside the Kingdom;
7. the withdrawal or refusal of an application for, or revocation of, membership of an exchange or clearing house;
8. the appointment of inspectors by an official or regulatory authority to investigate the affairs of the Authorized Person;
9. a significant act of misconduct by the Authorized Person or any of its registered persons;
10. the resignation or dismissal of any of the following persons:

1) CEO or Managing Director;
2) finance officer;
3) director or partner;
4) senior officer or manager;
5) compliance officer;
6) MLRO.

In cases of dismissal, full details of reasons for dismissal must be provided.

11. any matter which would be material to the requirements of the Authorized Person, any of its controllers, or any of its registered persons to remain fit and proper in accordance with the requirements under these Regulations;

12. any other matter which would be material to the Authority's supervision of the Authorized Person or any of its registered persons; or

13. any material changes to the information previously provided by the Authorized Person in any application for registration for one of its employees or prospective employees.

The duty to notify in connection with the matters set out in paragraphs 11, 12 and 13 arises immediately when the Authorized Person knows, or has reasonable grounds for believing, that any of these changes has occurred or will occur.

IV. An Authorized Person must inform the Authority immediately in writing of any material event or change in its business or operations.

V. An Authorized Person must give the Authority prior written notice, or where the event has occurred, written notice as soon as it becomes aware, of:

1. a proposed reorganization or business expansion or other change that could have a material impact on the Authorized Person's business, risk profile or resources, including, but not limited to, the following:
   - setting up a new business within an Authorized Person's group, or establishing a new branch;
   - commencing the provision of cross border services into a new territory;
   - commencing the provision of a new type of product or service;
   - sale or transfer of any material assets or parts of its business; or
   - ceasing to undertake a securities business activity, or significantly reducing the scope of any activity;
2. entering into, or significantly changing, a material outsourcing arrangement of a function of an Authorized Person of sufficient importance that failure of the function would jeopardize the authorized person's ability to comply with these Regulations;
3. any significant failure in the Authorized Person's systems or controls, including those reported to the Authorized Person by the Authorized Person's auditor; or
4. any event related to the Authorized Person that results in a material change in its capital adequacy, including:
   - any action that would result in a material change in the authorized person's financial resources or financial resources requirements under these Regulations;
   - the payment of a special or unusual dividend or the repayment of share capital or a subordinated loan;
   - for Authorized Persons which are subject to the rules on consolidated financial supervision, any proposal under which a member of the Authorized Person's group may be considering an action such as the actions mentioned above; or any significant losses, whether recognized or unrecognized.

4.6 PART 4: REGISTERED PERSONS

4.6.1 Chapter One - Background and scope

Article 18: Scope of Application

This Part applies to Authorized Persons, registered persons, applicants for individual registration and persons performing registrable functions.

Article 19: Registrable functions

a. The Authority shall prescribe the registrable functions.

b. The following functions are considered functions that must be performed by registered persons:

1) CEO or Managing Director;
2) finance manager;
3) a director or partner;
4) senior officers or managers;
5) compliance officer;
6) MLRO;
7) client functions, including sales representatives, investment advisors, portfolio managers and corporate finance professionals as defined by the Authority.

Article 20: Performance of Registrable functions

a. No person other than a registered person may perform a registrable function without the Authority's prior written consent.

b. Every Authorized Person must at all times have a person who is registered for each of the following functions:

1) CEO or Managing Director;
2) finance manager;
3) compliance officer; and
4) MLRO.

c. The Authority will not take action against an Authorized Person for failure to comply with paragraph (b) of this Article where there is a temporary gap in the performance of the registrable functions, provided that the Authorized Person actively seeks an appropriate substitute and notifies the Authority of another registered person who will temporarily take responsibility for that registrable function.

d. A person may perform more than one registrable function for an Authorized Person, except that:

1) the CEO, finance manager and compliance officer must be separate persons unless the Authority specifically approves another arrangement; and
2) the compliance officer should not perform a client function.

e. Except as provided in paragraph (a) of this Article, and without prejudice to the provisions of Article (59) of this regulations, an Authorized Person whose activity is limited to managing private non-real estate investment funds or managing sophisticated investor portfolios, arranging or advising may delegate the function of finance officer, compliance officer or MLRO to an external party, if the following conditions are met:

1) The external party responsible for the function of finance officer shall be a certified accounting firm licensed by the Saudi Organization for Certified Public Accountants, where one of its employee is assigned as finance officer for the Authorized Person;
2) the external party responsible for the function of compliance officer or the MLRO shall be an Authorized Person, a certified accounting firm licensed by the Saudi Organization for Certified Public Accountants or a law firm authorized to practice law in Saudi Arabia, where one of its employee is assigned as compliance officer or MLRO for the authorized person;
3) the employees assigned by the delegated third parties, aforementioned in paragraph (1) and (2), must pass the qualification examinations required by the Authority, or secure

an exemption from the Authority from such requirement; and
4) any other conditions that the Authority specifies.

f. Paragraph (b) of this Article does not apply where an authorized person activities are limited to managing private non-real-estate investment funds, managing sophisticated investor portfolios, arranging and advising, provided that he has two persons registered at all times one of which performs the functions of the Chief Executive Officer, and without prejudice to the provisions of paragraph (c) of this Article if one of their positions became vacant.

4.6.2 Chapter Two - Registration

Article 21: Requirements for application for registration

a. An Authorized Person must not apply for registration of a person to perform a registrable function without the consent of the relevant person.

b. The application for registration must be made on the form prescribed by the Authority.

c. An applicant for registration becomes subject to these Regulations from submission of the application.

d. An applicant for registration must have passed the qualification examinations required by the Authority, or secured an exemption from the Authority from such requirement.

e. The Authority will specify the examination requirements associated with the registrable functions, together with guidance on eligible qualifications and criteria for an exemption from the required examination.

f. The Authorized Person must pay such fees as may be determined by the Authority.

Article 22: Procedures and Powers of the Authority

a. In considering an application for registration, the Authority may take any of the following actions:

1) carry out any enquiries which it considers appropriate;
2) require the Authorized Person or the applicant for registration to appear before the Authority to answer any questions and explain any matter it considers relevant to the application;
3) require that additional information be provided;
4) verify the accuracy of any information furnished by the applicant for registration;

b. The Authority will aim to process an application for registration within 30 days of receiving all information and documents that it considers pertinent.

c. The Authority may, after considering the application, take any of the following actions:

1) approve the application for registration;
2) approve the application for registration subject to such conditions as it considers appropriate;
3) defer making a decision for such period as may be necessary to carry out further investigation or to allow for the provision of additional information; or
4) refuse the application for registration, giving reasons.

d. If the Authority resolves to register the applicant for registration, the Authority will add the applicant's name to the register of registered persons that the Authority shall maintain for this purpose and so inform the Authorized Person.

e. If the Authority resolves to reject the application, the Authority shall notify the applicant for registration and the Authorized Person named in the application in writing.

f. An applicant for registration must not perform the registrable function until he has been registered by the Authority.

Article 23: Right of appeal

An applicant for registration or the Authorized Person named in the application may appeal to the Committee in respect of any decision or action that the Authority takes under this Part.

4.6.3 Chapter Three - General Provisions

Article 24: Responsibilities of Registered Persons

a. A registered person must comply with the Principles stated in Part 2 of these Regulations, as applicable.

b. A registered person must be resident in the Kingdom unless the Authority exempts him from this requirement.

c. This Article applies to any person performing a registrable function who is not registered.

Article 25: Cancellation of registration

a. If a registered person's registration is cancelled, the authorized person must ensure that the person immediately ceases to perform a registrable function.

b. Within seven days of a registered person ceasing to carry on a registrable function or ceasing to be employed or associated with an Authorized Person, the Authorized Person must notify the Authority of that fact on the appropriate form. Upon receipt of the notice, the registration will be suspended, and the suspension shall remain in force until the Authority resolves any of the following:

1) agrees to the termination of the registration;
2) consent to the person becoming employed by an Authorized Person in a similar capacity; or
3) removes the person from the register of registered persons.

c. A registered person who is removed from the register by the Authority has a right of appeal to the Committee.

d. A registered person continues to be subject to the jurisdiction of the Authority in respect of any act or omission that occurred before the cancellation of his registration and for two years thereafter. If at any time during this period the Authority commences any enforcement investigation or proceedings, the registered person shall continue to be subject to the jurisdiction of the Authority until the end of the enforcement investigation or proceedings.

e. The Authority shall have the power to cancel the registration of a registered person if the registered person violates any provision of the Capital Market Law or its Implementing Regulations.

4.7 PART 5: CONDUCT OF BUSINESS

4.7.1 Chapter One: General Provisions

Article 26: Preliminary Provisions

a. This Part applies to all securities business carried on by an Authorized Person in the Kingdom or outside the Kingdom with or for a client who is in the Kingdom.

b. An Authorized Person must clearly state that it has obtained a license from the Authority on all communications, advertisements and notices that are issued to the public that are used by its employees and agents, whether in physical or electronic form.

Article 27: Inducements

a. An Authorized Person must not:

1) induce a client to engage in any transaction by offering or giving gifts or inducements; or
2) accept gifts or inducements if doing so would conflict to a material extent with any duty which it owes to a client.

b. The Authority will regard any gift or inducement given or received by an affiliate of an Authorized Person or by a third party at the direction of an Authorized Person as being given or received by the Authorized Person itself for the purposes of paragraph (a) of this Article.

c. An Authorized Person must not participate or offer to participate in any losses suffered by a client.

Article 28: Special commission arrangements

a. Special commission arrangement means an arrangement where an Authorized Person receives goods or services in addition to trade execution services from an intermediary in return for the commission paid on transactions directed through that intermediary.

b. An Authorized Person may enter into a special commission arrangement if the following conditions are met:

1) the person responsible for executing the transaction provides best execution to the Authorized Person;
2) the goods or services received by the Authorized Person may reasonably be regarded as being for the benefit of the authorized person's clients;
3) the Authorized Person has disclosed in its terms of business with clients that it may receive special commission; and
4) the amount of any fees or commission paid to the provider of the goods or services is reasonable in the circumstances.

Article 29: Confidentiality An Authorized Person must keep information obtained from clients confidential, except where:

1) its disclosure is required by the Capital Market Law or its Implementing Regulations or the applicable laws of the Kingdom;
2) the client has consented to its disclosure;
3) its disclosure is reasonably necessary to perform a particular service for the client; or
4) the information is no longer confidential.

Article 30: Chinese Walls Arrangements

a. "Chinese wall arrangements" means written policies and procedures established by an Authorized Person to secure confidential or inside information obtained by the Authorized Person in the course of carrying on securities business that are designed to ensure that the information is known only to employees of the Authorized Person who are authorized to receive it, and to ensure that the information is not disclosed to any other persons.

b. An Authorized Person that provides corporate finance services and also provides other types of dealing, advising or managing services must establish Chinese wall arrangements.

c. An Authorized Person or an employee acting on behalf of an Authorized Person is not in violation of the provisions of articles 5 or 6 of the Market Conduct Regulations if the Authorized Person deals or advises in a security related to inside information while another department of the Authorized Person is in possession of inside information, if the following conditions are met:

1) the Authorized Person has established appropriate Chinese wall arrangements in view of the nature and size of its securities business;
2) the Authorized Person has effectively implemented and maintained its Chinese wall arrangements; and
3) none of the individuals involved in the dealing or advising activity has knowledge of the inside information or has received advice on the dealing or advising activity from an individual who has knowledge of the inside information.

Article 31: Exclusions of liability

Any condition providing for the exclusion or restriction of the liability of an Authorized Person, whether under terms of business or otherwise, shall be void if the exclusion or restriction contravenes the Authorized Person's obligations under the Capital Market Law or the Implementing Regulations.

4.7.2 Chapter Two - Securities Advertisements

Article 32: Scope of Application

This Chapter applies to all securities advertisements made by an Authorized Person in the Kingdom, or approved by an Authorized Person for communication by another person. This Chapter does not apply to an advertisement that is excluded under the Securities Business Regulations.

Article 33: Prepared securities advertisements

a. A prepared securities advertisement means any securities advertisement that is prepared in advance and is communicated in writing, electronically or otherwise to one or more persons.

b. Before communicating a prepared securities advertisement, or approving one to be communicated by another person, an Authorized Person must ensure that:

1) the advertisement complies with the requirements of this Part after it is approved by a designated officer of the Authorized Person; and
2) the advertisement is clear, fair and not misleading.

c. A prepared securities advertisement must comply with the content requirements set out in Annex 5.1.

d. If the prepared securities advertisement relates to specific securities then it must contain sufficient information to enable a person to make an informed assessment of the securities or securities activity to which it relates.

e. If an Authorized Person becomes aware that a prepared securities advertisement does not comply with the requirements of this Part, it must withdraw the advertisement as soon as possible.

f. An Authorized Person must maintain a complete record of each prepared securities advertisement that it has approved and confirmed compliance for.

Article 34: Direct Communications

a. Direct communications means any securities advertisement that is not a prepared securities advertisement, including a meeting with a customer or potential customer, a telephone call, a presentation or any direct interaction with one or more persons.

b. Before making any direct communication an Authorized Person must ensure that:

1) the recipient has consented to receiving the securities advertisement; or
2) the recipient has an existing customer relationship with the Authorized Person and contemplates pursuant to such relationship that such securities advertisements will be made.

c. An Authorized Person must ensure that an individual who makes a direct communication on the Authorized Person's behalf, including any registered person or other employee:

1) does so in a way which is clear, fair and not misleading;
2) does not make any false or misleading statements;
3) makes clear the purpose of the securities advertisement at the initial point of communication, and identifies himself and the Authorized Person who he represents; and
4) does not communicate with a person outside of business hours, unless the person has previously agreed to such a communication.

d. An Authorized Person must have a Code of Conduct that require individuals seeking to obtain business on behalf of the authorized person to avoid using any undue pressure or making any misleading or deceptive statements, and to make clear their purpose and identity to customers or potential customers.

Article 35: Non-retail investment funds and derivatives

An Authorized Person must not communicate a securities advertisement to a customer relating to a non-retail investment fund or to derivatives securities unless it has determined that the securities are suitable for the customer.

4.7.3 Chapter Three - Accepting Clients

Article 36: Client classification

a. Before conducting securities business with or for any client, an Authorized Person must classify the client as one of the following:

1) a customer;
2) an execution-only customer;
3) a counterparty.

b. An Authorized Person must not classify a client in more than one of the categories set out in paragraph (a) of this Article.

c. An Authorized Person's dealing with its client classified as an execution-only customer must be restricted to dealing as his agent in accordance with the instructions that it receives from him, and the Authorized Person must not advise such client.

d. An Authorized Person must make a record of the classification established for each client under this Article, including sufficient information to support that classification.

Article 37: Money laundering and terrorism financing

Before conducting securities business with or for any client, an Authorized Person must ensure that it complies with all obligations under the Anti-Money Laundering Law and the rules and regulations on anti-money laundering and terrorism financing as in force in the Kingdom.

Article 38: Terms of business with clients

a. An Authorized Person must provide a client with terms of business setting out the basis on which securities business is to be conducted with or for the client. Such terms must be provided before conducting any securities business with or for the client.

b. The terms of business with a client must take the form of an agreement which takes effect once an executed copy of the terms of business has been provided by the client.

c. An Authorized Person must ensure that its terms of business set out in adequate detail the basis on which securities business is to be conducted.

d. An Authorized Person must ensure that its terms of business with its customers conform to the terms of business requirements set out in Annex 5.2.

e. An Authorized Person must retain a record of the terms of business it provides to a client, and any amendment to them.

Article 39: Know your customer

a. Before an Authorized Person deals, advises, or manages for a customer, it must obtain information from the customer concerning the customer's financial situation, investment experience and investment objectives relevant to the services to be provided. Such information must be obtained as a precondition to providing such services.

b. The information required under paragraph (a) of this Article must at a minimum include the information required by Annex 5.3.

c. The Authorized Person must request an update of such information from each customer at least once every three years.

d. If the customer refuses to provide the information required under this Article, the Authorized Person may not deal, advise or manage for him.

e. An Authorized Person must retain a record of all information obtained from the customer pursuant to this Article.

4.7.4 Chapter Four - Client Relations

Article 40: Fiduciary duties An Authorized Person owes the statutory fiduciary duties set out in Annex 5.4 to its customers.

Article 41: Conflicts of interest

a. An Authorized Person must ensure that it safeguards at all times the interests of its customer, and that no conflict of interest between its interest and the interest of it customer affects the transactions or the services that the Authorized Person carries out for its customer.

b. Where an Authorized Person who acts for a customer has an actual or a potential conflict of interest in relation to a transaction it shall disclose that conflict of interest to the customer in writing.

c. An Authorized Person is not required to disclose a conflict of interest if this information would constitute provision of inside information. In that instance an Authorized Person shall take reasonable steps to ensure fair treatment for the customer.

d. If there is a conflict between an interest of an Authorized Person and an interest of the customer in any transaction, the authorized person must pay to the customer the value of any loss incurred by the customer as a result of the conflict unless:

1) the Authorized Person has disclosed the conflict of interest to the customer in accordance with paragraph (b) of this Article; and
2) the customer has agreed in writing that the Authorized Person can proceed notwithstanding the conflict.

e. An Authorized Person must in all cases comply with Article 14 of the Market Conduct Regulations in any dealing as principal with a customer.

Article 42: Understanding risk

a. An Authorized Person must not deal, advise or manage for a customer, or take collateral for its own account from a customer, unless it has taken reasonable steps to enable the customer to understand the nature of the risks involved in the type of transaction in which the customer would be engaging.

b. An Authorized Person must not deal, advise, or manage for a customer:

1) in derivatives securities, contingent liability securities or non-retail investment funds, unless it has informed the customer of the nature and extent of the risks involved in such securities; or
2) in illiquid or speculative securities, unless it has informed the customer of the nature and extent of the risks involved in such securities, including any difficulties in determining their value.

Article 43: Suitability

a. An Authorized Person must not deal, advise or manage for a customer or take collateral for its own account from a customer, unless the advice or transaction is suitable for that customer having regard to the facts disclosed by that customer and other relevant facts about that customer of which the Authorized Person is, or reasonably should be, aware.

b. In reviewing the suitability of advice or a transaction for a customer, an Authorized Person must have regard to:

1) the customer's knowledge and understanding of the relevant securities and markets, and of the risks involved;
2) the customer's financial standing, including an assessment of his net worth or of the value of his portfolio based on the information disclosed by that customer;
3) the length of time the customer has been active in the relevant markets, the frequency of business and the extent to which he relies on the advice of the Authorized Person;
4) the size and nature of transactions that have been undertaken for the customer in the relevant markets; and
5) the customer's investment objectives.

c. Notwithstanding paragraph (a) of this Article, if an Authorized Person has advised a customer that a transaction is not suitable for him and the customer decides to proceed with the transaction, an Authorized Person may accept an order to buy or sell the security from the customer, provided that a record of the advice provided to the customer is retained.

d. This Article does not apply to dealing for an execution-only customer.

Article 44: Customer borrowing

a. An Authorized Person shall not, in relation to securities business, knowingly lend money or extend credit to a customer and must not arrange for any other person to do so, unless:

1) the Authorized Person has made and recorded an assessment of the customer's financial standing, based on information disclosed by that customer, and is satisfied that the amount and the arrangements for the loan or credit are suitable for the customer; and
2) the customer has given his prior written consent to the lending or credit facility, specifying the maximum amount of the loan or credit together with details of the amount and of any charges to be levied.

b. Paragraph (a) of this Article does not apply where an authorized person:

1) settles a transaction in the event of a default or late payment by the customer; or
2) pays an amount to cover a margin call made for a customer for a period no longer than five days.

Article 45: Margin Requirements

a. An Authorized Person may not effect a margined transaction with or for a client unless the client has entered into terms of business specifying the following:

1) the circumstances under which the client may be required to provide margin;
2) particulars of the form in which the margin may be provided;
3) particulars of the steps which the Authorized Person may be entitled to take if the client fails to provide the required margin, including the communication method(s) by which the margin call will be made on the client;
4) that failure by the client to meet a margin call may lead to the Authorized Person closing out the client's position after a time limit specified by the Authorized Person, and that the Authorized Person is entitled to close out the position in any event after a period of five days from such failure; and
5) any circumstances, other than failure to provide margin, which may lead to the client's position being closed without prior reference to him.

b. An Authorized Person may make a secured or unsecured loan or grant credit to a client for a period of more than five days for the purpose of making a deposit of margin or required margin payment if:

1) a credit assessment is made of the client by an employee of the Authorized Person who is independent of the trading or marketing functions; and
2) the client has given his prior written consent to the lending or credit facility, and such consent specifies the maximum amount of the loan or credit together with details of the amount and of any charges to be levied.

c. An Authorized Person who effects a margin transaction with or for a client must:

1) require the client to provide a minimum margin of 25 per cent of the value of the transaction prior to effecting the transaction;
2) take reasonable steps to satisfy itself that the client is aware of the risks of margin transactions; and
3) monitor the margin provided by the client daily, and ensure that the margin is maintained at a minimum level of 25 per cent of the current value of each applicable security position.

d. The Authority may prescribe a higher rate of margin to be provided for transactions in any security or category of securities, and the Authorized Person must require a client to provide any such prescribed rate of margin.

e. The Authority may prohibit margined transactions in relation to any security or category of securities.

f. Margin payable by a client in respect of a margin transaction on a regulated exchange or market must be of an amount or value at least equal to the margin requirements of the relevant exchange, market or clearing house.

g. Margin must be in the form of cash, fully-paid security positions or other acceptable collateral.

Article 46: Fees and commissions Fees and commission charged by an Authorized Person to its clients must be fully disclosed in advance of providing any services.

4.7.5 Chapter Five - Reporting to Clients

Article 47: Contract notes

a. An Authorized Person who effects a sale or purchase of a security with or for a client must send the client a contract note forthwith.

b. A contract note does not have to be sent where the Authorized Person is acting as manager and the client has confirmed that he will not require such contracts notes to be provided in writing.

c. Contract notes must provide the information required in Annex 5.5.

Article 48: Periodic reporting

a. An Authorized Person who acts as manager for a client must send a valuation report at least every three months in respect of securities or securities-related cash balances contained in the client's account.

b. Valuation reports must provide the information required in Annex 5.6.

4.7.6 Chapter Six – Miscellaneous

Article 49: Client records

a. An Authorized Person must keep and maintain proper records of each transaction it effects. Such records must be current at all times and be sufficient to demonstrate compliance with these Regulations.

b. An Authorized Person must keep and maintain proper records of client accounts. Such records must:

1) accurately record at all times the assets and liabilities of each client and of all clients collectively;
2) contain such information as is necessary to enable the authorized person to prepare a statement of each client's assets and liabilities, and details of transactions effected for the client; and
3) identify all client money and client assets that the authorized person, or its custodian, are responsible for.

c. The records of the Authorized Person must contain:

1) details of all orders in a security entered by a client;
2) details of all purchases and sales of a security made by the Authorized Person for a client, or by the Authorized Person for its own account;
3) a record of all income and expenses for each client, explaining their nature;
4) details of all receipts and payments of client money and client assets;
5) a record of the cash and securities held in each client account; and
6) a record of client money and client assets.

Article 50: Employees' personal dealings

a. An employee of an Authorized Person must not knowingly:

1) be a party to any transaction in a security where a client of the Authorized Person is a party; or
2) establish a trading account at another Authorized Person, except where the employee's Authorized Person does not offer the same service.

b. An employee of an Authorized Person must disclose to the compliance officer all transactions in securities transacted at an authorized person other than his/her own.

c. The compliance officer must establish procedures to monitor employees' personal dealings in securities to ensure compliance with the Capital Market Law and the Implementing Regulations.

d. An Authorized Person must implement personal account dealing procedures consistent with the provisions of Annex 5.7.

Article 51: Recording telephone calls

a. An Authorized Person must not make or accept telephone communications from clients or prospective clients in relation to securities business unless the Authorized Person records the telephone communications.

b. An Authorized Person must disclose to its clients or prospective clients that telephone communications in relation to securities business will be recorded.

c. An Authorized Person must retain the records of telephone communications in relation to securities business for a period of three years following the date of the telephone communication. In the event a telephone communication is relevant to a dispute with a client or a regulatory enquiry, the record must be retained until the dispute is fully resolved or the enquiry completed.

4.8 ANNEX 5.1 CONTENTS REQUIREMENTS FOR SECURITIES ADVERTISEMENTS

I. GENERAL CONTENTS REQUIREMENTS FOR ALL SECURITIES ADVERTISEMENTS

1 Clarity of Purpose

The purpose of the advertisement must be clear.

2 Clarity of subject

The nature or type of securities business and the type of securities being advertised must be clear.

3 Statements, promises or forecasts

Any statement, promise or forecast must be fair and not misleading in the form and context in which it appears. If any promise or forecast is based on assumptions, the assumptions must be stated. An advertisement must not forecast the possible future price of securities.

4 No false or misleading statements

The advertisement must not include false or misleading statements relating to the securities business, size or resources of the authorized person or any type of securities.

5 Name, address and regulatory status

The advertisement (or the person making the advertisement) must state the name and address of the Authorized Person, and that the authorized person is authorized by the Authority.

II. CONTENTS REQUIRED FOR PREPARED SECURITIES ADVERTISEMENTS PROMOTING A SPECIFIC SECURITY OR SECURITIES OR A SPECIFIC SECURITIES SERVICE

6 Guarantees

The advertisement must not describe a security as guaranteed unless there is a legally enforceable arrangement with a third party who undertakes to meet in full an investor's claim under the guarantee. If so, the advertisement must give details about both the guarantor and the guarantee sufficient for an investor to make a fair assessment about the value of the guarantee.

7 Comparisons

Advertisements that compare different securities or services must:

1. be based either on facts verified by the Authorized Person or on assumptions stated within the advertisement;

2. be presented in a fair and balanced way; and

3. not omit anything material to the comparison.

8 Material interest

An Authorized Person must include a statement acknowledging circumstances where the Authorized Person knows that it or its affiliates:

1. has or may have a position or holding in the securities concerned or in related securities; or

2. is providing or has provided within the previous 12 months significant advice or securities business services to the issuer of the securities concerned or of a related security.

9. Past performance

Any information about the past performance of securities or of an Authorized Person that is included in an advertisement must:

1. be a fair representation of the past performance of the securities or Authorized Person;

2. not be selected so as to exaggerate the performance of the securities or Authorized Person;

3. state the source of the information;

4. be based on verifiable information; and

5. warn that past performance is not necessarily a guide to future performance.

10 Zakat and Taxation

If the advertisement contains any reference to the impact of zakat or taxation, it must:

1. state the assumed rate of zakat or taxation and any relief; and

2. state that such rates and relief may change over time.

11 Cancellation rights

Any advertisement for securities to which cancellation rights apply must contain details of such rights, including the period within which they may be exercised.

III. RISK WARNINGS FOR PREPARED ADVERTISEMENTS OF SPECIFIC SECURITIES

12 Fluctuations in value

Where the securities can fluctuate in price or value, a statement must be made that prices, values or income may fall and, if applicable, a warning that the investor may get back less than he invested.

13 Suitability

Where the advertisement contains or refers to a recommendation about a specific security or securities service, a statement must be made warning that it may not be suitable for all recipients of the advertisement and a recommendation that, if they have any doubts, they should seek advice from their investment adviser.

14 Volatile securities

Where the advertisement relates to a security which is a geared security or a contingent liability security, it must state, if it is the case:

1. that the security may be subject to sudden and large falls in value which could cause a loss equal to the amount invested; and

2. that the investor's loss may not be limited to the amount originally invested or deposited, but may have to pay more.

15 Investment income

Where a security is described as being suitable for an investor particularly seeking income from his security, the investor must be warned, if it is the case, that:

1. income from the security may fluctuate; and

2. part of the capital invested may be used to pay that income.

16 Foreign currency denominated securities

Where a security is denominated in a foreign currency, the investor must be warned that changes in currency rates may have an adverse effect on the value, price or income of the security.

17 Illiquid Securities

An advertisement for an illiquid security must state that it may be difficult:

1. for the investor to sell or realize the security; and

2. to obtain reliable information about its value or the extent of the risks to which it is exposed.

18 Sales charges and fees

1. If an advertisement relates to a security on which deductions for charges and expenses are made at the time of the initial investment or on the sale of the investment, a warning that such charges apply must be included.

2. If an advertisement relates to a security on which performance fees are charged, a warning that such charges apply must be included.

4.9 ANNEX 5.2 TERMS OF BUSINESS REQUIREMENTS

An Authorized Person's terms of business to be entered into with or for a customer should, where relevant, provide for the following:

1. Commencement

The date on which the terms of business come into force.

2. Name, address and regulator

The name and address of the Authorized Person and a statement that the Authorized Person is regulated by the Authority.

3.Investment objectives

The customer's investment objectives.

4. Restrictions

Any restrictions on:

the types of securities in which the customer wishes to invest; and

the markets on which the customer wishes transactions to be executed.

5. Services

The services which the Authorized Person will provide.

6. Payments for services

Details of any payment for services payable by the customer to the Authorized Person, including the following:

1. structure and methods of the payments;

2. how it is to be paid and collected;

3. how frequently it is to be paid, and

4. any other payment that is receivable by the Authorized Person (or by any of its affiliates) in connection with any transaction executed by the Authorized Person, with or for the customer, in addition to or in lieu of any fees.

7. Investment manager

If the Authorized Person is to act as manager, the terms of business must include the following:

1. the arrangements for giving instructions to the Authorized Person and acknowledging those instructions;

2. the initial value of the managed portfolio;

3. the initial composition of the managed portfolio;

4. the period of account for which statements of the portfolio are to be provided;

5. the extent of the discretion to be exercised by the authorized person, including any restrictions on investments;

6. how performance will be measured;

7. how valuations will be made.

8. Accounting

The arrangements for accounting to the customer for any transaction executed on his behalf.

9. Cancellation rights

A description of any cancellation right to which the customer may be entitled.

10. Acting as a principal

That the Authorized Person may act as principal in a transaction with the customer, if applicable.

11. Risk warning

Any risk warning required under Part 5 of these Regulations.

12. Security lending

Whether the Authorized Person may undertake security lending activity with or for the customer.

13. Termination method

How the terms of business may be terminated.

14. Complaints

How to complain to the Authorized Person.

15. Right to realize customer's assets

A description of any right of the Authorized Person to realize the assets of the customer (including any collaterals) or to close out or liquidate positions on a default.

16. Contingent liability securities

A statement of the basis on which the customer will incur any contingent liability, including margin requirements, and the maximum limits placed on such funding.

17. Authority to borrow

Details of any authority to borrow or raise money on the customer's behalf, or enter into transactions which will involve the customer having to borrow or raise money and the maximum borrowing limit must be clarified.

18. Special commission arrangements

A statement explaining the Authorized Person's policy regarding special commission arrangements.

19. Custody Arrangements for:

1. registration of client assets if these will not be registered in the customer's name;

2. claiming and receiving dividends, commission payments and other entitlements accruing to the customer;

3. exercising conversion and subscription rights;

4. dealing with takeovers, other offers or capital re-organizations;

5. exercising voting rights;

6. the Authorized Person's liability in the event of a default by an eligible custodian;

7. the giving and receiving of instructions by or on behalf of the client or other person accredited by the client, and any restrictions to that authority; and

8. any agreement to lien or pledge interests over the client asset taken by the Authorized Person or an eligible custodian except in respect of charges relating to the administration or custody of the client assets.

20. Pooling

An Authorized Person must notify a customer where it intends to pool his client asset with that of one or more other clients and explain the meaning of pooling and warn the customer that:

1. customer assets or entitlements may not be separately identifiable by certificates, other physical documents of title or electronic record; and

2. customers may participate pro rata in any irreconcilable shortfall resulting from the default of a custodian.

21. Client assets held overseas

Where an Authorized Person in accordance with these Regulations arranges for client assets to be held overseas, it must notify a client in writing that there may be different settlement, legal and regulatory requirements in overseas jurisdictions from those applying in the Kingdom.

22. Client money

An Authorized Person must notify a customer in writing of the arrangements for holding client money.

4.10 ANNEX 5.3 KNOW YOUR CUSTOMER FORM

Customers must provide the information required by this Annex.

FILL THE FOLLOWING IF:

CUSTOMER IS AN INDIVIDUAL

PERSONAL INFORMATION

Name:

Date of birth:

ID Number/passport No.:

Marital Status:

Number of dependents:

Citizenship:

Address for Correspondence:

Home Phone:

Mobile Number:

Approximate annual income (in SAR)?

25,000 or less

25,001 to 50,000

50,001 to 100,000

100,001 to 250,000

250,001 to 500,000

500,001 to 1,000,000

Over 1,000,000

Approximate net worth (excluding residence) (in SAR)?

25,000 or less

25,001 to 100,000

100,001 to 500,000

500,001 to 1,000,000

1,000,001 to 5,000,000

Over 5,000,000

EMPLOYER INFORMATION

Employer's Name:

Employer's Address:

Employer's Phone Number:

Position / Title:

How long employed:

BANK INFORMATION

Bank's Name:

Branch:

Main Account Number

GENERAL INFORMATION

Is the customer a director or officer of a publicly listed company? YES / NO

Any other financial information on the customer's financial situation?

FILL THE FOLLOWING IF:

CUSTOMER IS A SOLE PROPRIETORSHIP OR A COMPANY

GENERAL INFORMATION

Name:

Commercial Registration No:

Registered Address:

Country of Registration:

Date of incorporation or start of business:

Business Phone:

Business Fax:

Number of employees:

Paid-up capital:

Annual Turnover:

COMPANY CONTACT

Name of Contact:

Address for Correspondence:

Business Phone:

Business Fax:

Mobile Number:

BANK INFORMATION

Bank's Name:

Branch:

Main Account Number

OTHER INFORMATION

Any other financial information on the customer's financial situation?

CUSTODIAN DETAILS

Name

Address for correspondence

Account name

Account number

Indicate where the following should be forwarded

The customer

The custodian

Other:

Specify all details as instructed by client

1) Certificates

2) Dividends/other income

3) Sale proceeds

INVESTMENT INFORMATION

Breakdown of Current Investment Portfolio

Shares

Debt instruments

Foreign exchange

Deposits

Trade finance

Investment funds

Commodities

Contracts for difference and options

Real-estate

Amount

Total

Investment knowledge and experience

Limited

Good

Extensive

INVESTMENT PROFILE

Customer's appetite for risk

High Medium Low

General investment objectives?

protection of capital

income

balanced

growth of capital

What are the customer's preferred investment assets (tick as many as required):

denominated in Saudi Riyals?

denominated in other foreign currencies?

State the foreign currencies:

FILL THE FOLLOWING IF:

THE APPLICANT IS AN INDIVIDUAL

Customer's ideal investment portfolio profile:

low risk (short-dated debt instruments main- stream investment funds)

medium risk (long-dated debt instruments; large companies)

high risk (small and single product companies; leveraged and high- yield products)

Shares % Debt instruments % Investment funds % Trade finance % Commodities % Options %

Ensure that the sum of all percentages above equal 100%

4.11 ANNEX 5.4 FIDUCIARY DUTIES

1. Loyalty

An Authorized Person must act in all cases in good faith and in the interests of the customer.

2. Conflict of interest

An Authorized Person must comply with principle 10 provided for at paragraph (b) of

Article 5 and with the provisions of Article 41 of these Regulations.

3. No secret profits

An Authorized Person must not use the customer's property, information or opportunities for its own or anyone else's benefit unless the Authorized Person makes full disclosure of such usage to the customer and obtains his consent.

4. Care, skill and diligence

An Authorized Person owes the customer a duty to exercise the care, skill and diligence which would be exercised in the same circumstance by a person having both:

a. the knowledge and experience that may reasonably be expected of a person in the same position as the Authorized Person; and

b. the knowledge and experience which the Authorized Person has

4.12 ANNEX 5.5 REQUIRED CONTENTS OF CONTRACT NOTES

Particulars

1. The Authorized Person's name and a statement that it is authorized by the Authority.

2. The trade date and time.

3. The client's name, account number, address or other identifier.

4. The security concerned, the size involved and the type of the transaction (sale or purchase), and:

1. the maturity and delivery or expiry date if the security is a contractually based security;

2. if the security is an option that has been exercised:

the strike price of the option; and

whether the exercise of the option creates a sale or purchase in the underlying asset.

5. The per security price at which the transaction was executed, or averaged and the total consideration due from or to the client, and a statement if applicable, that the price is an averaged price.

6. The settlement date where agreed.

7. The Authorized Person's charges to the client in connection with the transaction.

8. The amount of any front-end loading if the transaction is a purchase of a unit in an investment fund.

9. Whether the Authorized Person executed the transaction as principal, or with or through an affiliate.

10. Where any commission or other return which has accrued or will accrue on the relevant securities is accounted for separately from the transaction price, the amount of the commission or other return which the purchaser will receive or the number of days for which he will receive commission must be clarified.

11. A statement, if this is the case, that any dividend, bonus or other right which has been declared, but which has not been paid, allotted or otherwise become effective in respect of the relevant security, will not pass to the purchaser under the transaction.

12. The amount of any costs including transaction taxes which are incidental to the transaction and which will not be paid by the Authorized Person out of the charges mentioned in 7 above.

13. If the transaction involved or will involve the purchase of one currency with another, the currency conversion rate involved or a statement that the rate will be supplied on request.

14. If the security to which the contract note relates closes out an open position in a derivatives contract, the contract note must set out:

1. each derivatives contract that forms part of the open position;

2. each derivatives contract that forms part of the closing of the position; and

3. the net profit or loss made by the client on closing out the position.

4.13 ANNEX 5.6 REQUIRED CONTENTS OF PERIODIC VALUATION STATEMENTS FOR CLIENT PORTFOLIOS

1. Contents and value of Portfolio

1. Description of each security held in the portfolio, the number of shares, units or contracts held, and the current value of each security position;

2. Amount of cash balances;

3. Total value of the portfolio on the valuation date; and

4. Change in the value of the portfolio since the last valuation statement.

2. Basis of valuation

1. A statement of the basis on which the value of each security has been determined and an explanation of any change in the basis for valuing any securities since the previous valuation report.

2. Where any securities are valued in a currency other than the currency used to value the portfolio, the relevant currency conversion rates as of the valuation date must be shown.

3. Transactions and changes in portfolio

1. Particulars of each transaction entered into for the portfolio during the period;

2. Total amount of money transferred into and paid out of the portfolio during the period;

3. Details of any securities transferred into or out of the portfolio during the period; and

4. Total amount of commissions, dividends and other returns received by the Authorized Person for the portfolio during the period.

4. Charges and remuneration

1. Total amount of fees, charges and taxes paid out of the portfolio for purchases and sales of securities during the period;

2. Total amount of fees and charges for managing the portfolio and any other services provided by the Authorized Person during the period; and

3. Details of any remuneration received by the Authorized Person from a third party in respect of transactions entered into for the portfolio, or a statement that the basis or amount of any such remuneration has been separately disclosed in writing to the client.

5. Securities pledged or charged

1. Particulars of any securities that have been pledged as collateral for or charged to secure borrowings on behalf of the portfolio, and the identity of the person the securities are pledged to; and

2. Total amount of any commission or other payments made in respect of such borrowings during the period.

6. Derivatives positions

1. Profit or loss on each transaction to close out a derivatives position during the period

(including any commissions or other fees payable for the transaction); and

2. Details of each open derivatives position on the valuation date, including:

- the underlying securities, commodity, index or any other asset;
- the trade price and date of the opening transaction;
- the current market price of the derivatives contract;
- the current unrealized profit or loss on the position; and
- the exercise price and expiry date of the contract.

4.14 ANNEX 5.7 PERSONAL ACCOUNT DEALING

An Authorized Person must provide every employee with a written notice (the personal dealing notice) which must contain statements as prescribed by this Annex. Employees must undertake that they will observe the requirements of the personal dealing notice by signing a copy of it and returning it to the Authorized Person.

This Annex sets out a model personal dealing notice. An authorized person is free to impose more stringent requirements than those required by this Annex.

Model Personal Dealing Notice

So as to comply with the requirements for personal dealing transactions, it is required to comply with the provisions of this notice.

1. Permission to deal

It is permitted to buy and sell securities in these categories:

An Authorized Person should insert here types of securities or transactions in which the employee can deal. An Authorized Person will also need to clarify its procedure for restricting or withdrawing its consent in relation to particular securities in special conflict of interest circumstances.

An employee may not buy or sell any other securities without having obtained consent from the compliance officer or his deputy.

Note that where a general or specific consent is given for a transaction, the other requirements set out in this notice (e.g. reporting) still need to be complied with.

2. Rights issues, takeovers

The restrictions in this notice extend to making any formal or informal offer to buy or sell, taking up rights on a rights issue and exercising conversion or subscription rights and exercising an option.

The restrictions also extend to buying or selling securities under any offer, including a takeover or tender offer, which is made to the public or all (or substantially all) the holders of the security concerned.

3. Executors and agents

The restrictions extend to dealings by the employee:

a. as an executor of a will in which the employee or a relative of the employee has a significant interest;

b. as an executor of any other will, unless the employee is relying entirely on the advice of another person (such as another broker or lawyer); or

c. for another person, unless the employee is dealing as an employee of the Authorized Person.

4. General Exemptions

The restrictions do not extend to any transaction in a managed or discretionary account if the transaction is entered into without consultation with the employee.

5. Selling to or buying from a client

The employee may not sell to or buy from any client of the authorized person for his own account.

6. Reporting of transactions

The employee must immediately report to the Authorized Person in writing any purchase or sale of a security which the employee enters into otherwise than through [•] name of the Authorized Person or name of another group company that is an Authorized Person, including those transactions falling within 1 above. If, however, the employee has made arrangements for the Authorized Person promptly to receive a copy of the contract note (or similar report) in respect of the transaction, the employee does not have to report it to the Authorized Person.

7. Dealing ahead of a research recommendation

This restriction applies when the employee knows that the authorized person intends to publish a research recommendation and the employee knows, or should know, that the recommendation is likely to cause a price change in the security to which it relates. In that situation, the employee must not deal until the recommendation has been published and the clients for whom it was principally intended have had a reasonable opportunity to react to it. Dealing before the research recommendation has become public may also breach insider trading rules.

8. Dealing contrary to a client's interest

The employee must not deal in a security where he knows that such dealing is likely to have a direct adverse effect on the particular interests of one of the Authorized Person's clients.

9. Personal benefits

If the employee's functions involve giving securities advice, including the preparation of research material, or entering into transactions in securities for the Authorized Person's own account or the account of those for whom it deals, the employee must not accept any benefit or inducement which is likely to conflict with the employee's duties to the Authorized Person or any of the Authorized Person's clients.

"Benefit or inducement" means credit or any other financial advantages, money, property or gift; any services, facilities, or any opportunity to make, receive or increase a gain or revenue or to avoid or reduce a loss or expense.

If in any doubt the employee should consult with the compliance officer or his deputy.

10. Counseling and procuring

If the employee is precluded by the above provisions from entering into any transaction, the employee cannot advise or cause another person to enter into such a transaction or communicate any information or opinion to any other person if the employee knows, or has reason to believe, that that other person will as a result enter into such a transaction or cause or advise someone else to do so.

This does not apply to actions which the employee takes in the course of his employment with the Authorized Person.

11. Summary of insider trading rules

The employee may not act contrary to the provisions of the Capital Market Law, its Implementing Regulations, especially insider trading rules. A broad guide to the insider trading rules now follows:

Inside information is information that is not generally available, but would be price sensitive if it were generally available. An insider is a person who obtains inside information from a family, business or contractual relationship. The employee is likely to be an insider as a result of the employment, as is anyone to whom the employee passes the inside information. An insider may not trade in any security related to the inside information or communicate it to another person for him to trade in the security. Another person may not trade in a security after receiving inside information relating to it.

If the employee breaches these rules, the employee may face compensation claims, fines or prison.

4.15 MODEL UNDERTAKING

To: (Name of the Authorized Person)

a. I undertake to observe the provisions of the Capital Market Law and of the Market Conduct Regulations in relation to insider trading as they may be amended or replaced in future, and the requirements regarding personal dealing transactions that are set out in the foregoing notice.

b. I agree that this undertaking extends to any amended or replacement requirements that (name of the Authorized Person) set out in any written notice which you subsequently give to me.

c. I further agree that this undertaking shall form part of the contract of employment (or contract for services) with you and that any breach of this undertaking will entitle you, among other things, to terminate that contract without notice.

(print name)

Signed:

Date:

4.16 PART 6: SYSTEMS AND CONTROLS

4.16.1 Chapter One – Scope of Application

Article 52: Scope of application This Part applies to all the activities carried on by the Authorized Person.

4.16.2 Chapter Two – Management Arrangements

Article 53: Division of responsibilities

a. An Authorized Person must take appropriate measures to maintain a clear and appropriate division of the principal responsibilities among its directors or partners and senior management (if any) so that:

1) it is clear who is responsible for each function; and

2) the business and affairs of the Authorized Person are adequately monitored and overseen by the directors or partners, relevant senior managers and governing body of the Authorized Person.

b. The CEO is responsible for arranging the division of responsibilities under paragraph (a) of this Article, and overseeing the establishment and implementation of the Authorized Person's systems and controls.

Article 54: Establishment and maintenance of systems and controls

a. An Authorized Person must establish and maintain systems and controls that are appropriate to its business. The systems and controls must conform to the requirements of Chapter 3 of this Part and be sufficient to enable the Authorized Person to comply with the Capital Market Law and its Implementing Regulations.

b. The Authorized Person's governing body is primarily responsible for compliance with the Capital Market Law and its Implementing Regulations and all other regulatory requirements applicable to the authorized person. The governing body must make appropriate arrangements to ensure that the activities detailed in Chapter 3 of this Part are carried out.

Chapter Three – Systems and Controls

Article 55: General Provisions

a. The Authorized Person must establish systems and controls under this Part taking into account the following:

1) the nature, scale and complexity of its business;
2) the diversity of its operations;
3) the number and value of its transactions; and
4) the degree of risk associated with each area of its operation.

b. An Authorized Person must establish systems and controls to cover at a minimum:

1) the division of responsibilities and reporting lines in accordance with Article 53 of these Regulations;
2) risk management policies and systems;
3) anti-money laundering and terrorism financing procedures;
4) a compliance manual;
5) a compliance monitoring programme;
6) a code of conduct;
7) an operational procedures manual; and
8) continuity of business manuals and plans.

c. An Authorized Person must document its systems and controls appropriately and keep such documentation up to date.

d. The documentation described in this Article must be retained for ten years after it ceases to be used or is amended.

Article 56: Review by the governing body

a. An Authorized Person's governing body must carry out a regular review of the division of responsibilities and its systems and controls, including the documents referred to in Article 55(c) of these Regulations, at least annually.

b. An Authorized Person's governing body must expeditiously monitor the actions arising as a result of the review.

c. Each review conducted in accordance with paragraph (a) of this Article should be minuted and minutes of such reviews must be maintained for ten years.

Article 57: Compliance a. An Authorized Person must appoint a senior officer as compliance officer.

b. The governing body of the Authorized Person is responsible for supervising the following:

1) ensuring that appropriate policies and procedures are in place to enable the Authorized Person to comply with the Capital Market Law, the Implementing Regulations and all other applicable regulatory requirements;
2) ensuring that the compliance officer and his department are appropriately resourced and have access to all of the authorized person's records;
3) the establishment, implementation, enforcement and maintenance of the compliance manual and the compliance monitoring programme;
4) the establishment of and ensuring compliance with the code of conduct;
5) the preparation of reports and notifications to be filed with the Authority; and
1. 6) the procedures for reporting to the governing body on compliance matters.

c. The Authority may review the appropriateness of an authorized person's compliance arrangements at any time.

Article 58: Compliance committee
a. Depending on the nature, scale and complexity of its business, an Authorized Person may establish a compliance committee to monitor its securities business and its compliance program.

b. The Authority may require an Authorized Person to appoint a compliance committee if it considers one to be necessary based on the nature, scale and complexity of the business.

c. When a compliance committee is established, its members should include, but are not limited to, the CEO, the compliance officer, the MLRO and a senior officer from internal audit (if any).

d. The compliance committee must meet at least quarterly. Meetings must be minuted and the minutes must be retained for ten years.

Article 59: Outsourcing
a. An Authorized Person may delegate specific compliance or other functions to an external party, provided that appropriate safeguards are put in place, including:

1) an assessment of whether the delegate is suitable to carry out the delegated function or task, taking into account the degree of responsibility involved;
2) clear documentation of the extent and limits of any delegation;
3) suitable arrangements to supervise the delegation, and to monitor the discharge of the delegate's functions or tasks; and
4) appropriate remedial action if any concern arises about the performance of the delegate's functions or tasks.

b. An Authorized Person must exercise due diligence in the selection of an external party to perform specific functions.

c. The outsourcing of any function by the Authorized Person will not derogate from the Authorized Person's, compliance officer's or the compliance committee's regulatory obligations.

Article 60: Audit committee
a. Depending on the nature, scale and complexity of its business, an Authorized Person may appoint an audit committee.

b. The Authority may require an Authorized Person to appoint an audit committee if it considers one to be necessary based on the nature, scale and complexity of the business.

c. The audit committee must meet at least quarterly.

d. Meetings of the audit committee must be minuted and the minutes retained for ten years.

Article 61: Internal audit
a. Depending on the nature, scale and complexity of its business, an Authorized Person may delegate part of the task of monitoring the appropriateness and effectiveness of its systems and safeguards to an internal audit function.

b. An internal audit function should have clear responsibilities and reporting lines to the audit committee or appropriate senior manager, be adequately resourced and staffed by competent individuals, be independent of the day-to-day activities of the Authorized Person and have appropriate access to an Authorized Person's records.

c. Meetings of the internal audit function must be minuted and the minutes retained for a period of ten years.

Article 62: Audit and inspections
a. An Authorized Person's internal and external auditors must review books, accounts and other records related to securities business at least annually.

b. All accounts, records, terms of business and other agreements to which an Authorized Person is party must be retained for the period specified in Part 3 of these Regulations and must be made available to the internal and external auditors.

Article 63: Resolution of complaints
a. An Authorized Person must have written procedures to ensure:

1) timely and proper handling of complaints from clients;
2) that appropriate remedial action in respect of complaints is promptly taken; and
3) where a complaint arises from the conduct of a third party employed or recommended by an Authorized Person, an Authorized Person shall intercede on behalf of the client, making best efforts to resolve the complaint.

b. The Authorized Person must design the procedures to resolve complaints to ensure that:

1) each employee working with clients is aware of them;
2) a complaint is investigated promptly and fully by an officer of the Authorized Person who was not originally involved in the matter giving rise to the complaint; and
3) records of the written complaints are made and any action taken documented.

Article 64: Money laundering and Terrorism Financing An Authorized Person must appoint a senior employees as MLRO. The MLRO is responsible for ensuring compliance with the requirements of the Anti-Money Laundering Law and its Implementing Regulation and reporting to the governing body on matters relating to money laundering and terrorism financing.

Article 65: Employees
a. An Authorized Person must establish adequate procedures for the recruitment, training, supervision and discipline of employees.

b. An Authorized Person must establish recruitment procedures to ensure that it recruits employees who are appropriately qualified for the role and honest.

c. An Authorized Person must establish a programme to ensure that employees are trained appropriately (including passing any examinations required under Part 4 of these Regulations).

d. An Authorized Person must maintain records of the names of any employee disciplined by an Authorized Person in connection with any breach of the Capital Market Law or its Implementing Regulations or any other conduct which may affect the conduct of the Authorized Person's securities business. The records must also include particulars of:

1) the breach or conduct for which the employee was disciplined; and
2) the steps taken to discipline the employee.

e. An Authorized Person must train its employees periodically and such training must cover updates to the Capital Market Law, its Implementing Regulations and any other laws relevant to the business of the Authorized Person. Such training should occur at least annually.

f. An Authorized Person must retain appropriate records relating to its employees in connection with their recruitment procedure, experience and qualifications for a period of ten years from the date on which the Authorized Person recruited the employee.

Article 66: Business continuity
a. An Authorized Person should have in place appropriate arrangements, having regard to the nature, scale and complexity of its business, to ensure that it can continue to operate and meet its regulatory obligations in the event of an unforeseen interruption to its activities. These arrangements should be documented and regularly updated and tested to ensure their effectiveness.

b. Appropriate records relating to the arrangements in connection with business continuity must be retained for a period of ten years after it ceases to be used or is amended.

Article 67: Record retrieval All records required to be maintained by an Authorized Person under the Capital Market Law or its Implementing Regulations must be available for inspection by the Authority.

Article 68: Mandate over an account in the client's name An Authorized Person must establish and maintain adequate records and internal controls in respect of a mandate it has over an account in the client's own name. An Authorized Person must in particular ensure that all transactions entered into pursuant to a mandate are within the scope of the authority conferred by the mandate and establish procedures for the giving and receiving of instructions under the mandate.

4.17 Part 7: Client Money and Assets

4.17.1 Chapter One – General Provisions

Article 69: Purpose and Scope
a. The provisions in this Part implement Principle 6 which is provided for at paragraph (b) of Article 5 of these Regulations.

b. An Authorized Person must segregate its own money and assets from client money and client assets, and client money and client assets must only be used for the benefit of an Authorized Person's clients.

Article 70: Effect of Segregation
a. Client money and client assets which are segregated are deemed to be held for the Authorized Person's clients and are not deemed to be assets of the Authorized Person.

b. Creditors of an Authorized Person do not have any claim or entitlement to segregated money or assets.

4.17.2 Chapter Two – Client Money Rules

Article 71: Money received by an Authorized Person
a. Subject to Article 72 of these Regulations, all money that an Authorized Person receives from or on behalf of a client in the course of carrying on securities business is client money.

b. Client money must be segregated and held in a client account, separately from the assets of an Authorized Person, except where otherwise provided in this Part.

c. All money paid into a client account by an Authorized Person will be treated as client money.

d. Only client money should be held in a client account unless it is required to open or keep open the account or it is temporarily in the account.

e. An Authorized Person may transfer client money to another person for the purpose of settling a securities transaction with or through that other person or to provide collateral for a client.

Article 72: Money which is not client money Money is not client money if it is immediately due and payable to the Authorized Person for its own account (including, fees and commissions which are lawfully due to the Authorized Person).

Article 73: Money to be held with a bank
a. An Authorized Person must hold client money in a client account with a local bank.

b. An Authorized Person must assess the risk of a local bank prior to opening a client account and consider whether it is necessary to open client accounts with more than one bank.

c. An Authorized Person may open a client account with a local bank in its own group, provided it notifies its client of its intention and the client has not objected.

d. Client money may be held with an overseas bank but only if this is necessary for the settlement of a transaction in securities outside the Kingdom. Dividends or other income received outside the Kingdom for an Authorized Person's client may be paid into an account with an overseas bank in the Authorized Person's name, provided that the funds in question are either transferred to a client account or paid to the client no later than three days after notification of receipt. An Authorized Person must notify its client of its intention to hold client money with a bank outside the Kingdom.

e. The requirements specified in paragraphs (b) and (c) of this Article and the requirements in Article 74 of these Regulations apply equally to an account with an overseas bank.

Article 74: Acknowledgement by the bank
a. An Authorized Person must within 20 days of opening a client account obtain a written acknowledgement from the local bank with which a client account has been opened that:

1) the client account will hold client money and not money belonging to the Authorized Person; and
2) the local bank will not enforce any right or claim that it has against the Authorized Person against funds held in the client account and will not combine the client account with any other account.

b. If an Authorized Person does not receive the acknowledgement referred to in paragraph (a) of this Article within the 20 day period, it must withdraw all money in the account and pay it into another client account with another local bank.

Article 75: Client accounts
a. Except as otherwise provided in this Part 7 an Authorized Person must, where it receives client money, either:

1) pay the money into a client account no later than the next day after receipt; or
2) pay the money out in accordance with Article 76 of these Regulations.

b. If a remittance comprises part client money and part other money it must be paid in full into a client account. The part of the remittance that is not client money should be transferred out of the client account as soon as possible.

c. Client money may be held in a client account in a different currency from that of receipt. In such a case an Authorized Person must daily ensure that the amount held in the different currency is at least equal to the amount of the original currency and must adjust the amount held in the different currency accordingly (if necessary by making up any deficit). In carrying out the currency conversion the Authorized Person should use the closing spot currency conversion rate on the business day preceding the day on which the conversion calculation is carried out.

Article 76: Money ceasing to be client money Money ceases to be client money for which the Authorized Person is responsible if it is paid:

1) to the client;
2) to a third party on the instructions of the client;
3) into a bank account in the name of the client (not being an account which is also in the name of the Authorized Person); or
4) to an Authorized Person itself, where it is lawfully due and payable to the Authorized Person.

Article 77: Commission No commission is payable to a client in respect of client money held in a client account.

Article 78: Records and auditor's report
a. An Authorized Person must keep records which are sufficient to demonstrate compliance with the Client Money Rules.

b. An Authorized Person's auditors shall annually review the authorized person's compliance with the Client Money Rules and shall report on this review as part of its audit of the Authorized Person.

Article 79: Amounts to be held in client money bank accounts
a. An Authorized Person must:

1) daily confirm that the aggregate balance on all of its client accounts as at the close of the preceding business day was at least equal to the "client money requirement" calculated in the manner prescribed by the Authority; and
2) ensure that any shortfall is paid into a client account by the close of business on the day the calculation is performed, and any excess is withdrawn within the same time period.

b. For the purposes of paragraph (a) of this Article, an authorized person should use the values contained in its accounting records, such as its cash book, rather than values contained on statements received from banks. Fees and commissions may be excluded from the calculation.

c. So as to satisfy paragraph (a) of this Article, an Authorized Person may be required to pay money into a client account. Such money will be client money.

d. An Authorized Person must notify the Authority immediately if it is unable to perform the calculation required by this Article.

Article 80: Reconciliations
a. An Authorized Person must, at least once in every 7 days, reconcile:

1) the balance on each client account as recorded by the authorized person with the balance on that account as set out on the statement or other form of confirmation issued by the local bank;
2) the balance on each client transaction account with exchanges, clearing houses, intermediate brokers, settlement agents and counterparties as recorded by the Authorized Person with the balance on that account as set out in the statement or other form of confirmation issued by the person with whom the account is held; and
3) its records of collateral received from clients with the statement of collateral or other form of confirmation issued by the person with whom that collateral is located.

b. An Authorized Person must perform the reconciliations in paragraph (a) of this Article within 10 days of the date to which the reconciliation relates.

c. Where any difference arises on any of the reconciliations in paragraph (a) of this Article, the Authorized Person must correct it as soon as possible and in any event within 3 days.

d. An Authorized Person must notify the Authority as soon as possible where it is unable to perform any of the reconciliations required by the provisions in this Chapter.

e. Where an Authorized Person is unable to resolve a difference arising from a reconciliation, but the records examined by the Authorized Person during its reconciliation indicate that there might need to be a greater amount of money in the relevant client accounts or collateral than is in fact the case, the Authorized

Person must assume, until the matter is finally resolved, that those records are accurate and pay the difference from its own money into a client account and the amount paid will be client money.

Article 81: Client money reporting requirement An Authorized Person who holds client money must submit to the Authority such accounts as it requests.

4.17.3 Chapter Three – Client Asset Rules

Article 82: Assets received by an Authorized Person
a. An Authorized Person must not hold client assets unless it is authorized to provide custody services.

b. All assets which include, or may include, securities that are received by the Authorized Person in the course of carrying on securities business shall be treated as client assets unless they consist of cash or collateral, to which Article 83(b) of these Regulations applies.

c. An Authorized Person must segregate the client assets that it holds from its own assets.

d. An Authorized Person must not use client assets for its own account or the account of another client unless it has obtained the prior consent of the client to whom the assets belong.

Article 83: Assets which are not client assets
a. Client assets shall include collateral taken by way of pledge to satisfy an obligation arising from that pledge until applied to satisfy that obligation.

b. Collateral retained by an Authorized Person as Other Collateral (as defined at paragraph (a) of Article 94 of these Regulations) for its own account is not a client asset, provided that the Authorized Person has complied with the requirements of paragraph (b) of that Article.

Article 84: Segregation
a. If a client asset is recorded in an account with an authorized person, the Authorized Person must ensure that the title to the account makes it clear that such assets belong to the client and are segregated from the Authorized Person's assets.

b. An Authorized Person must require that where a client asset is recorded in an account with a custodian or with an overseas custodian, the custodian or overseas custodian makes it clear in the title of the account that the client asset belongs to one or more clients of the Authorized Person and that the assets are segregated.

Article 85: Holding and registration of client assets
a. Securities that are eligible for the Depositary Centre must be held in an account in the relevant client's name with the Depositary Centre.

b. An Authorized Person must hold a document of title to a client asset in its physical possession, or with a custodian in an account designated for client assets.

c. Where an Authorized Person registers or records title to a client asset it must ensure that it is registered or recorded in the name of the client, unless the client is an Authorized Person acting on behalf of its own client, in which case the asset must be registered in the name of that client.

d. Where the asset concerned is a security acquired overseas, title to the asset may be registered or recorded in the name of an overseas custodian or in the name of the Authorized Person, provided that the Authorized Person has satisfied itself that is not feasible for the asset to be registered or recorded in the client's name. An Authorized Person must obtain the prior written agreement of a client to the client's assets being recorded or registered in the name of an overseas custodian or in the name of the Authorized Person and must notify the client in writing of any adverse consequences of the assets being registered or recorded other than in its name. An Authorized Person must in particular:

1) before holding or arranging for an overseas custodian to hold client assets outside the Kingdom, notify the client in writing that there may be different settlement, legal and regulatory requirements in the relevant jurisdiction to those which apply in the Kingdom, in particular in relation to the segregation of client assets;
2) obtain the clients prior agreement to registering or recording legal title to their assets in the name of the Authorized Person and to the fact that the client assets may not be segregated from the authorized person's own assets and may be subject to claims from the authorized persons creditors in the event of its failure.

Article 86: Lending of client securities
a. An Authorized Person must not lend securities belonging to a client or engage in such lending activities with a client except after obtaining the client's express consent to this in writing.

b. Any securities lending activity must be subject to appropriate terms and conditions, including, as relevant, those specified by Annex 5.2 to these Regulations.

c. An Authorized Person must at all times during the period of a securities transaction:

1) ensure that the borrower provides collateral to cover the realizable value of the securities being lent;
2) daily monitor whether the amount of the collateral is sufficient to cover the realizable value of the securities; and
3) if the amount of the collateral is not sufficient to cover the realizable value of the securities, make up the level of collateral, unless otherwise agreed in writing with the client.

d. Securities, which are registered or otherwise held together for more than one client must not be used for the purpose of a securities lending transaction unless all of the clients to whom the securities belong consent in writing and, if only some of the clients consent, the Authorized Person must ensure and demonstrate that only securities belonging to clients who have given their consent are used for this purpose.

e. An Authorized Person must ensure that all securities lending transactions are appropriately documented.

Article 87: Assessment of custodian
a. An Authorized Person owes a duty of care to a client in deciding or recommending where to hold the client assets.

b. An Authorized Person must undertake a risk assessment prior to recommending or deciding to hold client assets with a custodian to ensure that the custodian has in place adequate arrangements to safeguard the assets, and is subject to appropriate standards of regulatory oversight. An Authorized Person must conduct a risk assessment of custodians holding client assets as frequently as required to be satisfied of the above matters on a continuing basis.

c. An Authorized Person must notify its client before holding that client's assets with a custodian in the Authorized Person's group and must not hold the relevant client's assets with a custodian in its group if the client objects.

d. An Authorized Person must not hold client assets with or recommend an overseas custodian to a client unless the proposed arrangements with the overseas custodian are necessary for the purpose of the acquisition or holding of securities outside the Kingdom.

e. The requirements set out in paragraphs (a) to (c) of this Article apply in relation to overseas custodians. In carrying out a risk assessment in relation to an overseas custodian, an Authorized Person must take into account the extent to which the overseas custodian is subject to regulatory obligations at least equivalent to those imposed on custodians under the Capital Market Law and the Implementing Regulations.

Article 88: Clients agreements

a. Before an Authorized Person provides custody services to a customer, it must agree in writing with that customer appropriate terms of business which must cover the matters set out in paragraph (b) of this Article. Before an Authorized Person provides custody services to a counterparty, it must send a written notice to the counterparty which must cover the matters set out in paragraph (b) of this Article.

b. The agreement or the notice referred to in paragraph (a) of this Article must cover the following matters:

1) the manner in which the client assets will be registered;
2) arrangements for the receiving and giving of instructions by the client in respect of custody services;
3) the Authorized Person's liability to the client;
4) any lien or security interest taken over the client assets by the Authorized Person or other party;
5) the circumstances in which the Authorized Person may realize client assets which are held as collateral, to meet the client's liabilities;
6) how the Authorized Person will deal with the claiming and receipt of dividends, commissions and other income and entitlements accruing to the client;
7) how the Authorized Person will deal with corporate actions, such as the voting of shares, capital reorganizations and take-overs;
8) the information to be provided to the client in respect of client assets that the Authorized Person holds;
9) the provision of statements to the client;
10) the fees and charges to the client in respect of the custody services; and
11) an explanation of whether the client's assets will be pooled with the assets of other clients and an explanation of the effect of that pooling.

Article 89: Custodian Agreement

a. Before an Authorized Person holds client assets with a custodian, it must agree in writing with the custodian appropriate terms of business, which must cover the following:

1) that the title of the account in which any client assets will be held indicates that the assets credited to the account do not belong to the Authorized Person;
2) that the custodian is not to permit withdrawal of any client assets from the account other than to the Authorized Person or to another person as the custodian may be instructed by the Authorized Person;
3) that the custodian will hold or record a client asset belonging to the Authorized Person's client separate from any securities or other assets of the custodian, and that it will treat the assets in the account as client assets;
4) that the custodian will deliver to the Authorized Person a statement as at a date or dates specified by the Authorized Person which details the description and amounts of all the securities credited to the account and the statement must be delivered to the Authorized Person within 7 days of the date of the statement;
5) that the custodian will not claim any lien, right of retention or sale, over the securities standing to the credit of any account designated in accordance with sub-paragraph (a)(1) of this Article,

except:

where the clients whose assets are held in the account have consented; or
in respect of any charges relating to the administration or custody of the client asset.

b. The requirements of paragraph (a) apply if client assets are lodged in an account with an overseas custodian.

Article 90: Reconciliations

a. An Authorized Person must as often as necessary, but at least every 7 days, reconcile its record of client assets which it does not physically hold, with statements obtained from the Depositary Centre, custodians or overseas custodians and, in the case of dematerialized securities not held with the Depositary Centre or through a custodian or overseas custodian, statements obtained from the person who maintains the record of entitlement.

b. An Authorized Person must as often as necessary, but at least every six months, carry out:

1) a count of all client assets physically held by it, and reconcile the results of that count to its record in this regard; and

2) a reconciliation between the Authorized Person's record of client holdings, and its record of the location of client assets.

c. The count and reconciliation in paragraph (b) of this Article must cover all of the Authorized Person's books and records, and must be performed by counting and reconciling all securities and other client assets as at the same date.

d. An Authorized Person must perform the reconciliations within 10 days of the date to which the reconciliation relates.

e. An Authorized Person must within 3 days correct any discrepancy which is revealed by any reconciliation that it has carried out. If the Authorized Person discovers any discrepancy which amounts to a shortfall, it must within 3 days make good any shortfall and if the discrepancy is not resolved within 7 days, report the matter to the Authority.

Article 91: Client statements

a. An Authorized Person must, as often as necessary, but not less frequently than annually, provide each client in writing with a statement prepared in accordance with paragraph (d) of this Article.

b. An Authorized Person is required to provide a statement in paragraph (a) of this Article to a client for whom a client asset, collateral or other asset has been held at any time during the Authorized Person's financial year even when there are no holdings at the statement date. However, there is no requirement to provide a statement where the client's account with the Authorized Person has been closed, and the Authorized Person has sent the client a closing statement which demonstrates that the Authorized Person no longer holds a client asset, collateral or other asset for the client.

c. Statements may be sent electronically with the client's prior written consent where the Authorized Person is capable of reproducing the statement and keeping a record of its despatch.

d. All statements produced by or on behalf of an Authorized Person in accordance with paragraph (a) of this Article must list all client assets, collateral and other assets owned by the client for which the Authorized Person is accountable and:

1) identify any securities registered in the client's name, separately from those registered in another name;
2) identify those securities and assets which are being used as collateral, or have been pledged to third parties, separately from any other securities and asset;
3) show the market value of any collateral held, as at the date of the statement; and
4) be based on information as of trade date or settlement date, and the basis must be notified to the client.

4.17.4 Chapter Four – Collateral and Money and Assets Passed to Third Parties

Article 92: Scope of Application

a. This Chapter applies to Authorized Persons which hold collateral or provide collateral to third parties, or which pass client money or client assets to settlement agents.

b. Article 93 of these Regulations applies to:

1) collateral that is subject to the Client Money Rules or the Client Asset Rules; and
2) client money and client assets passed to settlement agents.

c. Article 94 of these Regulations applies to collateral that is not subject to the Client Money Rules or the Client Asset Rules.

Article 93: Collateral subject to the Client Money Rules or the Client Asset Rules

a. An Authorized Person must take reasonable steps to ensure that collateral is properly safeguarded. Where the Authorized Person has reasonable grounds to believe that the collateral will not be properly utilized or safeguarded by a third party, then it must withdraw the collateral from the third party unless the client has indicated otherwise in writing.

b. Collateral held by the Authorized Person must be separately identifiable from assets of the Authorized Person. The Authorized Person must be able to identify at all times the client providing the collateral.

c. Where an Authorized Person passes collateral of a customer which is client money or client assets to a counterparty in the Kingdom, it must:

1) take reasonable steps to ensure that the counterparty treats the collateral as client money or client assets; or
2) have obtained the consent of the customer in the terms of business not to treat the money or assets as client money or client assets.

d. An Authorized Person must not undertake a transaction for a client that involves client money or client assets being passed either as collateral to a counterparty or to a settlement agent outside the Kingdom before formally notifying the client that:

1) his money or assets may be passed to such person;
2) the regulatory regime applying to such persons is different from that of the Kingdom; and
3) it has taken reasonable steps to ensure that the counterparty or settlement agent will effectively segregate the collateral from its own assets under the law of the country in which the counterparty or settlement agent is located.

e. An Authorized Person who transfers clients' collateral to an exchange or clearing house must:

1) notify the exchange or clearing house that the collateral is client money or client assets, and that the Authorized Person is under an obligation to keep clients' collateral separate from the authorized person's collateral; and
2) instruct the exchange or clearing house to:
   a) credit the value of that collateral passed by the Authorized Person to the Authorized Person's client transaction account with the exchange or clearing house; and
   b) treat the sale proceeds of that collateral in accordance with the requirements of that exchange or clearing house.

f. Before an Authorized Person deposits a client asset as collateral with, mortgages, pledges, charges or grants another encumbrance over any client asset to, a third party, it must:

1) properly consider the credit risk to its clients;
2) notify the client that the collateral will not be registered in the client's name; and
3) obtain the client's prior written consent whether in the terms of business or otherwise.

g. The Authorized Person must have prior written consent from its client if it proposes to return to the client collateral other than the original collateral, or original type of collateral, or money.

h. An Authorized Person must:

1) notify the Authority as soon as it is aware of the insolvency of a person to whom it has passed collateral; and
2) notify the Authority as soon as reasonably practicable, of its intentions regarding making good any shortfall in client money or client assets that has arisen or may arise, stating the amounts involved.

Article 94: Other collateral

a. Other collateral is collateral that an Authorized Person is entitled to treat as its own provided the Authorized Person is obliged to return equivalent assets to the client upon conclusion of a transaction or satisfaction of an obligation.

b. An Authorized Person must not receive or hold other collateral under this Article in the case of collateral of a customer before it has:

1) determined in accordance with Article 43 of these Regulations that the taking of collateral is suitable for the customer;

2) taken reasonable steps to ensure that the customer understands the nature of the risks involved in his providing other collateral to the Authorized Person;
3) disclosed to the customer in the terms of business that his collateral will not be subject to the protections under the Client Asset Rules and as a consequence, his collateral will not be separated from the assets of the Authorized Person and will be used by the authorized person in the course of the Authorized Person's business, and he will therefore rank as a general creditor of the Authorized Person; and
4) ensured that it maintains adequate records to enable it to meet any prospective obligations including the return of equivalent assets to the customer.

4.18 PART 8: INSOLVENCY PROVISIONS

Article 95: Supervision of insolvency proceedings The Authority shall supervise the compulsory and voluntary liquidation of Authorized Persons and shall have the power to take any of the steps set out in this Part, which it considers appropriate to ensure the proper protection of the rights of clients of the Authorized Person.

Article 96: Rights of clients on insolvency of an Authorized Person holding client money and assets
a. If, on an insolvency event of an Authorized Person holding client money or client assets, the Authorized Person has or may have insufficient client assets or client money to satisfy its obligations to return such money and assets to its clients, then the claims of clients in respect of any shortfall in client assets and client money rank ahead of all other creditors.

b. The Authority may represent the interests of all clients who may be entitled to the return of client money or client assets, or who may have any other claim relating to their account, in insolvency, liquidation or settlement proceedings of Authorized Persons.

Article 97: Settlement Proceedings
a. If an Authorized Person proposes to submit a petition to request a settlement under the Bankruptcy Regulations, the Authorized Person must:

1) notify the Authority of the proposed petition at least 14 days prior to its submission;
2) provide the Authority with any documentation it requests; and
3) cooperate with the Authority prior to initiating settlement proceedings in order to ensure that client money, client assets and all other claims of clients relating to their accounts are resolved.

b. The Authority may attend and be heard at any proceedings relating to the insolvency or bankruptcy of the Authorized Person, including:

1) any meeting of members or creditors of the Authorized Person; or
2) any application for conciliation with creditors or settlement to prevent bankruptcy under the Bankruptcy Regulations.

c. No settlement proceedings in respect of an Authorized Person may be granted unless the Authority consents to it.

d. From the initiation of settlement proceedings to the end of such proceedings, the Authorized Person may not, without the prior consent of the Authority, undertake any of the following actions:

1) accept further client money or client assets;
2) dispose of client money or client assets; or
3) compromise, effect a mortgage, charge or pledge, give a guarantee, donate any part of its assets or effect a transfer of ownership in relation to any of its assets.

e. The Authority is an interested party for the purposes of any proceedings relating to an Authorized Person under the Bankruptcy Regulations.

Article 98: Liquidation Proceedings
a. If an Authorized Person enters into the stage of liquidation under the Bankruptcy Regulations, the Authorized Person must:

1) notify the Authority of the liquidation and of the proposed date of any meeting of members or creditors relating to the liquidation;
2) provide the Authority with any documentation it requests in relation to the liquidation proceedings; and
3) cooperate with the Authority prior to initiating settlement proceedings in order to ensure that client money, client assets and all other claims of clients relating to their accounts are resolved.

b. No appointment of a liquidator in respect of an Authorized Person will be effective unless the Authority consents to it.

c. The Authority may attend and be heard at any proceedings relating to the insolvency or bankruptcy of the Authorized Person, including:

1) any meeting of members or creditors of the Authorized Person;
2) any liquidation proceedings under the Bankruptcy Regulations.

d. From the initiation of liquidation under the Bankruptcy Regulations, the Authorized Person may not, without the prior consent of the Authority, undertake any of the following actions:

1) accept further client money or client assets; or
2) dispose of client money or client assets; or
3) compromise, effect a mortgage, charge or pledge, give a guarantee, donate any part of its assets or effect a transfer of ownership in relation to its assets.

e. The Authority may direct the liquidator to take such steps as the Authority considers fit to establish the entitlements of clients of the Authorized Person at any time, or to appoint a third party to take such steps.

4.19 PART 9: PUBLICATION AND ENTRY INTO FORCE

Article 99: Publication and entry into force These Regulations shall become effective upon their publication.

5 CAPITAL MARKET INSTITUTIONS REGULATIONS

Issued by the Board of the Capital Market Authority pursuant to its Resolution Number 1-83-2005 dated 21/05/1426H (28/06/2005G) based on the Capital Market Law issued by Royal Decree No. M/30 dated 2/6/1424H, amended by Resolution of the Board of the Capital Market Authority Number 2-75-2020 dated 22/12/1441H (12/8/2020G)

Important Notice: The current version of these Rules, as may be amended, can be found at the Authority website: www.cma.org.sa

TABLE OF CONTENTS

PART 1: GENERAL PROVISIONS
Article 1: Preamble
Article 2: Definitions
Article 3: Compliance with the Regulations and Rules
Article 4: Waivers
PART 2: THE PRINCIPLES FOR CAPITAL MARKET INSTITUTIONS
Article 5: The Principles
PART 3: Authorization
Chapter One: Applications for authorization
Article 6: Requirements for authorization
Article 7: Procedure and Powers of Authority in Relation to an Application
Article 8: Right of Appeal
Chapter Two: Maintenance of Authorization
Article 9: Fit and Proper
Article 10: Scope of Business
Article 11: Variation or Amendment
Article 12: Capital Market Institution Withdrawal and Cancelling of authorization
Article 13: Controllers
Article 14: Close Links
Article 15: Notification Requirements and Powers of Authority
Article 16: Record-Keeping
Article 17: Fees
ANNEX 3.1 INFORMATION AND DOCUMENTS REQUIRED FOR authorization
ANNEX 3.2 NOTIFICATION REQUIREMENTS
PART 4: REGISTERED PERSONS
Chapter One: Background and Scope
Article 18: Scope of Application
Article 19: Registrable Functions
Article 20: Performance of Registrable Functions
Chapter Two: Registration
Article 21: Requirements for Application for Registration
Article 22: Procedure and Powers of the Authority
Article 23: Right of Appeal
Chapter Three: General provisions
Article 24: Responsibilities of Registered Persons
Article 25: Cancellation of Registration
PART 5: CONDUCT OF BUSINESS
Chapter One: General Provisions
Article 26: Preliminary Provisions
Article 27: Inducements
Article 28: Special Commission Arrangements
Article 29: Confidentiality
Article 30: Chinese Walls Arrangements
Article 31: The Liability of Capital Market Institution
Chapter Two: Securities advertisements
Article 32: Scope of Application
Article 33: Prepared Securities Advertisements
Article 34: Direct Communications
Article 35: Non-Retail Clients' Investment Funds and Derivatives
Chapter Three: Accepting clients
Article 36: Client Classification
Article 37: Anti-Money Laundering and Combating the Financing of Terrorism
Article 38: Terms of Business with Clients
Article 39: Know Your Client
Chapter Four: Clients Relations
Article 40: Fiduciary Duties
Article 41: Conflicts of Interest
Article 42: Understanding Risk
Article 43: Suitability
Article 44: Client Borrowing
Article 45: Margin Requirements
Article 46: Fees and Commissions
Chapter Five: Reporting to Clients
Article 47: Contract Notes
Article 48: Periodic Reporting
Chapter Six: Miscellaneous
Article 49: Client Records
Article 50: Employee's Personal Dealings
Article 51: Recording Telephone Calls
ANNEX 5.1 CONTENTS REQUIREMENTS FOR SECURITIES ADVERTISEMENTS
ANNEX 5.2 TERMS OF BUSINESS REQUIREMENTS
ANNEX 5.3 (A) KNOW YOUR CLIENT FORM
ANNEX 5.3 (B) INVESTMENT INFORMATION FORM
ANNEX 5.4 FIDUCIARY DUTIES
ANNEX 5.5 REQUIRED CONTENTS OF CONTRACT NOTES
ANNEX 5.6 REQUIRED CONTENTS OF PERIODIC VALUATIONS STATEMENTS FOR CLIENT PORTFOLIOS
ANNEX 5.7 PERSONAL ACCOUNT DEALING
PART 6: SYSTEM AND CONTROLS
Chapter One: Scope of Application
Article 52: Scope of Application Chapter Two: Management Arrangements
Article 53: Division of Responsibilities
Article 54: Establishment and Maintenance of Systems and Controls
Chapter Three: Systems and Controls
Article 55: General Provisions
Article 56: Review by the Governing Body
Article 57: Compliance
Article 58: Risks Committee and Compliance Committee
Article 59: Outsourcing
Article 60: Audit Committee
Article 61: Internal Audit
Article 62: Audit and Inspection
Article 63: Resolution of Complaints
Article 64: Anti-Money Laundering and Combating the Financing of Terrorism
Article 65: Employees
Article 66: Business Continuity

Article 67: Record Retrieval
Article 68: Mandate Over an Account in the Client's Name
ANNEX 6.1: REQUIRED CONTENTS OF THE BOARD OF DIRECTORS' REPORT
PART 7: CLIENT MONEY AND ASSETS
Chapter One: General Provisions
Article 69: Purpose and Scope
Article 70: Effect of Segregation
Chapter Two: Client Money Rules
Article 71: Money Received by a Capital Market Institution
Article 72: Money Which is Not Client Money
Article 73: Money to be Held With a Bank
Article 74: Acknowledgement by a Bank
Article 75: Client Accounts
Article 76: Money Ceasing to be Client Money
Article 77: Returns
Article 78: Records and Auditor's Report
Article 79: Amounts to be Held in Client Money Bank Accounts
Article 80: Reconciliations
Article 81: Client Money Reporting Requirement
Chapter Three: Client Asset Rules
Article 82: Assets Received by a Capital Market Institution
Article 83: Assets Which are Not Client Assets
Article 84: Segregation
Article 85: Holding and Registration of Client Assets
Article 86: Lending of Client Securities
Article 87: Assessment of Custodian
Article 88: Client Agreements
Article 89: Custodian Agreement
Article 90: Reconciliations
Article 91: Client Statements
Chapter Four: Collateral and Money and Assets Passed to Third Parties
Article 92: Scope of Application
Article 93: Collateral Subject to the Client Money Rules or the Client Asset Rules
Article 94: Other Collateral
PART 8: INSOLVENCY PROVISIONS
Article 95: Supervision of Insolvency Proceedings
Article 96: Rights of Clients on Insolvency of a Capital Market Institution Holding Client Money and Assets
Article 97: Settlement Proceedings Article 98: Liquidation Proceedings
PART 9: PUBLICATION AND ENTRY INTO FORCE
Article 99: Publication and Entry into Force

5.1 PART 1: GENERAL PROVISIONS

Article 1: Preliminary The purpose of these Regulations is to regulate capital market institutions and registered persons and to specify the procedures and conditions for obtaining a license, as well as the conditions for the maintenance of the license or the registration, to provide for the rules of conduct that Capital Market Institutions must comply with when conducting their business, as well as the rules and provisions governing the conduct of business, and to set the systems and controls as well as the provisions relating to client money and assets.

Article 2: Definitions

a. Any reference to the "Capital Market Law" in these Regulations shall mean the Capital Market Law issued by Royal Decree No. M/30 dated 2/6/1424H.

b. Expressions and terms in these Regulations have the meaning, which they bear in the Capital Market Law and in the Glossary of defined terms used in the Regulations and Rules of the Capital Market Authority, unless the context indicates otherwise.

Article 3: Compliance with the Regulations and Rules

a. A Capital Market Institution and a registered person must comply with the Regulations and Rules applicable to them and must provide to the Authority without delay any information, records or documents that the Authority may require for the purpose of administration of the Capital Market Law and its Implementing Regulations.

b. The governing body and employees of a Capital Market Institution and a registered person, must comply with any requirement issued by the Authority to appear to explain any matter or to assist in any enquiry relating to the administration of the Capital Market Law and its Implementing Regulations.

Article 4: Exemption

a. The Authority may exempt a provision of these Regulations in whole or in part as it applies to an applicant or a Capital Market Institution either on an application from the applicant or the capital market institution or on its own initiative.

b. The Authority will make an announcement of the exemption of any provisions where it believes that:

1) the exemption of the provision may be of application to more than one type of Capital Market Institutions; and
2) the publication of the exemption will not materially prejudice the Capital Market Institutions.

This is to achieve the policy of the Authority to promote competition, including retaining a level playing field between capital market institutions.

5.2 PART 2: PRINCIPLES FOR CAPITAL MARKET INSTITUTIONS

Article 5: The Principles

a. The Principles provided for in this Part are a general statement of the fundamental obligations of Capital Market Institutions. They are intended to form a universal statement of the standards of conduct expected of Capital Market Institutions under these Regulations.

b. A Capital Market Institution must comply with the following principles:

1) integrity, by conducting its business with integrity;
2) skill, care and diligence, by conducting its business with due skill, care and diligence;
3) efficiency of management and control, by taking reasonable care to organize its affairs responsibly and effectively, with adequate risk management policies and systems;
4) financial prudence, by maintaining adequate financial resources in accordance with the rules issued by the authority;
5) proper market conduct, by observing proper standards of market conduct;
6) protection of clients' assets, by arranging for adequate protection of its clients' assets;

7) co-operation with regulators, including disclosing to the authority any material event or change in the Capital Market Institution's business operations or organization;
8) communications with clients, by communicating information to them in a way, which is clear, fair and not misleading;
9) paying due regard to client's interests, by treating them fairly and paying due regard to their interests;
10) resolve the conflicts of interest, by dealing with the conflicts of interest cases fairly, both between itself and its clients and between a client and another client; and
11) clients' suitability, by taking reasonable care to ensure the suitability of its advice and discretionary managing decisions for any client to whom it provides those services.

5.3 PART 3: AUTHORIZATION

5.3.1 Chapter One Applications for Authorization

Article 6: Requirements for Authorization

a. For the purposes of these Regulations, an applicant for authorization means the person that is applying for authorization to carry out securities business. An applicant for authorization becomes subject to these Regulations from the date of submission of his application.

b. An application for authorization may be submitted by the founders or controlling shareholders of an applicant if the applicant is not yet established. The founders or controlling shareholders become subject to the provisions that apply to an applicant from the date of submission of the application.

c. An application for authorization must be made on the application form prescribed by the Authority and be accompanied by the information and documents required in Annex 3.1.

d. The form and contents of the application and all information and documents filed with it must be as prescribed by the Authority.

e. An applicant must demonstrate to the Authority that:

1) it is fit and proper to carry out securities business of the kind and scale for which it seeks authorization in accordance with the rules prescribed by the authority;
2) it has adequate expertise and resources for the kind of securities business that it proposes to carry out in accordance with the rules prescribed by the authority;
3) it has managerial expertise, financial systems, risk management policies and systems, technological resources, and operational procedures and systems that are sufficient to fulfill its business and regulatory obligations and to conduct the kind of securities business that it proposes to carry out; and
4) its board of directors' members, officers, employees and agents who will be involved in the applicant's securities business have the necessary qualifications, skills, experience and integrity to carry out the kind of securities business that it proposes to carry out.

f. In order to engage in dealing, custody and managing business, an applicant must be established in the Kingdom and must be:

1) a subsidiary of a local bank;
2) a joint stock company;
3) a subsidiary of a Saudi joint stock company that is engaged in financial services business; or
4) a subsidiary of a foreign financial institution that is licensed under the Banking Control Law issued by Royal Decree No. M/5 dated 22/2/1386H. The applicant may be of any legal form established in the Kingdom to apply for a license to conduct arranging or advising.

g. The paid up capital of the applicant must not be less than the following:

1) dealing and custody: SR 50 million;
2) managing: SR 20 million for managing investments and operating funds; and a capital that covers the expected expenses for a year for managing investments;
3) arranging and advising: a capital that covers the expected expenses for a year.

h. A Capital Market Institution must have its management and head office in the Kingdom.

i. If the applicant has close links with another person, the Authority must be satisfied with the integrity, regulatory status, business record and financial soundness of any such person, and that such close links will not impair the effective supervision of the applicant, or its operations and compliance with these Regulations.

j. The applicant for authorization must pay such fees as may be prescribed by the Authority.

Article 7: Procedure and Powers of the Authority in Relation to an Application

a. In considering an application, the Authority may:

1) carry out any enquiries that it considers appropriate;
2) require the applicant, or his representative, to attend before the Authority to answer questions and explain any matter the Authority considers relevant to the application;
3) require the applicant to provide such additional information as the Authority considers appropriate within 30 days of the request; and
4) verify any information furnished by the applicant.

b. The Authority may refuse to consider the application for authorization where an applicant has failed to provide information requested from it, or has failed to provide information requested from it within the time requested.

c. The Authority shall, upon receipt of all information and documents required, notify the applicant in writing of the same, and shall take any of the following decisions within a maximum period of 30 days from the date of the notice:

1) approve the application in whole or in part;
2) approve the application subject to such conditions and limitations as it considers appropriate;
3) refuse the application, giving reasons.

d. If the Authority resolves to authorize the applicant, it will inform the applicant of this in writing and of its permitted business profile including any limitations that the Authority may consider appropriate. The capital market institution must satisfy the requirements for commencement of business stipulated in Annex 3.1 of these Regulations before commencing its business.

e. If the Authority resolves to refuse the application, it will notify the applicant in writing.

f. An applicant must not carry out, or hold itself out as carrying out, securities business prior to receiving the Authority's decision referred to at paragraph (d) of this Article.

g. The duration of the authorization granted in accordance with the provisions of the Capital Market Law and these Regulations shall be ten years, automatically renewable for same periods when the capital market institution continues to fulfill the following conditions and criteria:

1) fit and proper requirements;
2) prudential requirements;
3) minimum capital requirements; and
4) payment of the fees determined by the Authority on an annual basis.

Article 8: Right of Appeal The applicant may appeal to the Committee in respect of any decision or action that the Authority takes under this Part.

5.3.2 Chapter Two – Maintenance of Authorization

Article 9: Fit and Proper

a. As a condition for the maintenance of authorization, a capital market institution must continue to be fit and proper to carry out the securities business, which it is authorized to carry out at all times.

b. The following criteria are an important factor in assessing whether a Capital Market Institution or an applicant is fit and proper:

1) the skills, experience, competence and integrity of the employees, officers and agents of a Capital Market Institution or an applicant, which shall be assessed against the following criteria:
   a) they must possess adequate qualifications and professional experience to carry out their responsibilities, including appropriate technical knowledge and skills;
   b) they must have probity and soundness of judgement commensurate with their positions;
   c) they must fulfill their responsibilities with diligence and to protect clients' interests in accordance with the Implementing Regulations;
   d) they must not have committed an offense involving fraud or dishonesty; and
   e) they must not have contravened or broken any laws or regulations governing securities business or aimed at protecting investors.
2) the founders of the Capital Market Institution or the applicant, its controlling shareholders or registered employees, shall not have been deemed bankrupt during the past ten years, prior to submit the application for authorization, change in the controlling shareholders or registration.

c. The Capital Market Institution must obtain the Authority's approval before the alteration of its capital.

Article 10: Scope of Business

a. A Capital Market Institution must not carry out, or hold itself out as carrying out, securities business unless that business is within its permitted business profile.

b. A Capital Market Institution must comply with the rules applicable to it and with any limitation, condition or other requirement that the Authority specifies.

c. A Capital Market Institution may carry out activities associated with the securities business upon satisfying the following:

1) carrying out such activities does not require obtaining authorization from other regulatory or supervisory bodies;
2) carrying out such activities will not affect the ability of the Capital Market Institution to comply with the principles set out in article 5 of these regulations; and
3) the Capital Market Institution must fulfill the prudential requirements at all times.

d. The Authority may impose any conditions or restrictions on the Capital Market Institution in conducting activities associated with the securities business, request to provide any information about such activities, or instruct the Capital Market Institution to cease conducting them.

e. A Capital Market Institution authorized to carry out advising business may provide advising in financial planning and in wealth management.

Article 11: Variation or Amendment

a. A Capital Market Institution must apply to the Authority for approval of any proposed variation or amendment to its permitted business profile.

b. The Authority has all the powers set out in Article 7 of these Regulations to consider a proposed variation or amendment, and may also require some or all of the information or documents referred to in Article 6 of these Regulations to be updated.

c. The Authority will aim to process an application to vary or amend a Capital Market Institution's permitted business profile within 30 days from receiving all information that it considers necessary.

d. After considering an application to vary or amend a capital market institution's permitted business profile, the Authority may:

1) approve the application for variation or amendment in whole or in part;
2) approve the application subject to such conditions and limitations as it considers appropriate;
3) defer making a decision for such period as it may consider necessary to carry out further study or examination or to allow for the provision of additional information; or
4) refuse the application, giving reasons.

e. If the Authority resolves to approve an application for a change in a permitted business profile, it will inform the Capital Market Institution of this in writing and of its new permitted business profile, including any limitations that the Authority may consider appropriate.

f. The Capital Market Institution must not carry out (or hold itself out as carrying out) the kind of securities business concerned before receiving the Authority's notification under paragraph (e) of this Article.

g. If the Authority resolves to refuse the application for variation or amendment, it will notify the Capital Market Institution in writing.

h. The Capital Market Institution may appeal to the Committee in respect of any decision or action that the Authority takes under this Article.

Article 12: Withdrawal from Business and Cancellation of Authorization

a. A Capital Market Institution that proposes temporarily cease to carry out securities business must notify the Authority in writing of the date on which it intends to temporarily cease to carry out securities business and the reasons for the decision:

1) at least 45 days in advance of that date; or
2) if such advance notice is not possible because the temporary cessation of business is caused by an external event of which the Capital Market Institution was not aware, immediately on making a decision to temporary cease to carry out securities business.

b. The notice referred to in paragraph (a) of this Article must contain the following:

1) the date on which the Capital Market Institution intends to temporary cease to carry out securities business;
2) reasons for the decision of temporary cessation;
3) the period of temporary cessation;
4) potential impacts on clients, and the actions that the capital market institution intends to take to address them, including the actions that it intends to take in relation to clients' money and assets; and
5) the status of registered persons during the temporary cessation.

c. The Capital Market Institution may not cease to carry out securities business for a period exceeding 12 months.

d. Where a Capital Market Institution decides to cease providing securities business to clients, it must ensure that any such business that is outstanding is properly completed or is transferred to another Capital Market Institution and that it provides reasonable notice to its clients of the cessation of business.

e. A Capital Market Institution may request the cancellation of its authorization, and must in this case submit a written request to the Authority not less than three months prior to the proposed date of the cancellation. A Capital Market Institution must notify its clients immediately upon submitting the request for cancellation of its authorization, and shall ensure that the outstanding business are properly completed or transferred to another Capital Market Institution. It shall also take the necessary measures to transfer the clients' money and assets and protect their rights.

f. A request to cancel an authorization must include sufficient information concerning the circumstances of the cancellation to enable the Authority to determine whether to accept the cancellation, to postpone the date of the cancellation, or to require other measures that it considers necessary for the protection of clients of the capital market institution.

g. The Authority may refuse a request to cancel an authorization if it considers that the maintenance of the authorization is necessary to investigate any matter affecting the Capital Market Institution, to protect the interests of the Capital Market Institution's clients, or to impose a prohibition or requirements on such Capital Market Institution under the Capital Market Law or its Implementing Regulations.

h. The Authority may suspend the Capital Market Institution's authorization on its own initiative if the Capital Market Institution does not carry out any securities business for a period of 12 months, or 6 months following the date on which a Capital Market Institution has ceased to carry out securities business after notification to the Authority in accordance with paragraph (a) of this Article.

i. A Capital Market Institution continues to be subject to the jurisdiction of the Authority in respect of any act or omission that occurred before the cancellation of its authorization and for two years thereafter. If at any time during this period the Authority commences any enforcement investigation or proceedings, the capital market institution shall continue to be subject to the jurisdiction of the Authority until the end of the enforcement investigation or proceedings.

Article 13: Controllers

a. A Capital Market Institution must notify the Authority, in such form as the Authority may prescribe, that a person is intending to become, or cease to be, a controller of the Capital Market Institution at least 30 days in advance of the proposed effective date; or if such advance notice is not possible, immediately on the Capital Market Institution becoming aware of such intention.

b. A Capital Market Institution must not permit any person to become or act as a controller unless the Authority has approved the controller in writing.

c. A person who intends to become a controller of a capital market institution must notify the Authority of such intention at least 30 days in advance of the proposed effective date, and must provide the Authority with such information as the Authority requires to satisfy itself of its identity, integrity, regulatory status, business record and financial soundness.

d. Before approving a controller the Authority must be satisfied that, the person's control of the Capital Market Institution will not impair the effective supervision of the Capital Market Institution or its operations and compliance with the Capital Market Law and the Implementing Regulations.

e. In considering, any application submitted under this Article, the Authority has all of the powers set out in Article 7 of these Regulations.

Article 14: Close Links

a. A Capital Market Institution must notify the Authority, in such form as the Authority may prescribe, that a person is intending to establish close links with the Capital Market Institution at least 30 days in advance of the proposed effective date, or if such advance notice is not possible, immediately on the Capital Market Institution becoming aware of any change in close links. The notice must include such information as the Authority requires to satisfy itself of the identity of the person with whom the Capital Market Institution proposes to establish close links, its integrity, regulatory status, business record and financial soundness.

b. The Authority may impose any conditions or restrictions it considers appropriate to ensure that the Capital Market Institution establishing close links with any person will not impair the effective supervision over the Capital Market Institution or over its operations, or the capital market intuition's compliance with the Capital Market Law and the Implementing Regulations.

Article 15: Notification Requirements and Powers of Authority

a. A Capital Market Institution must comply with the notification requirements set out in Annex 3.2.

b. On receiving a notice under paragraph (a) of this Article, the Authority may:

1) require the Capital Market Institution to provide any additional information that it considers necessary to properly assess the matter; and
2) impose any conditions, restrictions or additional requirements on a Capital Market Institution, including limitations on its permitted business profile, that it reasonably considers to be necessary to address a regulatory concern raised by any matter that it is notified of under this Article.

Article 16: Record-Keeping
a. A Capital Market Institution must record and retain sufficient information about its securities business to demonstrate compliance with these Regulations.

b. Records required to be maintained by these Regulations must be retained for a period of ten years unless the Authority specifies otherwise.

c. The Authority may inspect the records directly or through a person it appoints for that purpose.

d. Records made by a Capital Market Institution may be maintained in any form, but must be maintained in an organized manner and capable of reproduction in hard printed form.

e. When a client or a former client requests any records kept during the regulatory record- keeping period, the Capital Market Institution must make available, within a reasonable period, any of the following:

1) any written material or records which relate to that client and which the Capital Market Institution has sent, or is required to send, to that client under Part 5 of these Regulations; and
2) copies of any correspondence received from or sent to that client relating to securities business.

Article 17: Fees A Capital Market Institution must pay such fees as the Authority may prescribe for the maintenance of the license.

5.4 ANNEX 3.1 Information and Documents Required for Authorization and Commencement of Business

These authorization and commencement of business requirements set out below apply to all types of securities business and the application of each requirement will differ depending on the nature, scope and complexity of the business. Applicants whom the type of their activities will be limited to managing investments, arranging or advising will be excluded from submitting the information and documents stated in the paragraphs (8) and (11) of the information and documents required for authorization set out in this Annex, and the information and documents stated in sub-paragraphs (1), (3), (4), and (5) of paragraph (1) and paragraphs (2), (3) and (4) of the information and documents required for the commencement of business set out in this Annex.

(I) First: Information and Documents Required for Authorization

1. Controllers – An applicant must submit a list of all controllers of the applicant, and provide details of the identity, ownership (if applicable), integrity, regulatory status, business record and financial position of each proposed controller.

2. Close Links – An applicant must submit a list of all persons that have, or are proposed to have, close links with the applicant, and provide details of the identity, ownership (if applicable), integrity, regulatory status, business record and financial position of each such person.

3. Governing Body Resolution – An applicant must submit to the Authority a resolution of its governing body in the form prescribed by the Authority approving the application and its contents, and certifying the accuracy and completeness of the accompanying information and documents.

4. Business Profile – An applicant must submit a proposed business profile including full details of all securities and all services for which the applicant proposes to provide for each securities activity that it is applying to carry out. A schedule must be attached in the following form: Securities

Business Types of Activity Details of [•]

Securities Details of [•]

Services Categories of clients Dealing Dealing Custody Securities custody services Managing Managing investments and operating funds Managing investments Arranging Financial advisor / corporate finance advisor Advising Investment Advisor

5. Business Plan – An applicant must submit a business plan, setting out:

1) A detailed description of the securities business activities that the applicant proposes to undertake during, at least, the first 12 months after authorization, including:
- the products and services that it intends to provide to clients;
- the classes and types of securities that it intends to provide services in; and
- all exchanges and markets that it intends to trade in.

2) a description of the nature of the proposed clients of the applicant; and
3) a list of any exchanges, clearing centers or depositaries of which the applicant is or intends to become a member.

6. Financial Statements – An applicant must submit financial statements accredited by the applicant's auditors in accordance with the standards issued by SOCPA and presented in the format prescribed by the Authority, and must:

1) show the applicant's current and projected financial position, including its capital, financial resources, revenues and expenses as at the date of the financial statements; and
2) provide supporting evidence of the capitalization and resources of the applicant and the presumptions on which the statements have been provided.
(3) submit projected financial statements that state the expected financial position after 12 months after the proposed date of commencement.

7. Registered Persons – An applicant must submit a list of each person who is to be a registered person and an application form for registration for each such person in the format prescribed by the Authority, including details of their qualifications and experience.

8. Terms of Business – An applicant must submit a copy of proposed terms of business (in accordance with Part 5 of these Regulations), and the proposed forms.

9. Incorporation Documents – If the applicant is a company, it must submit a copy of its articles of association or by-laws.

10. Ownership Structure – If an applicant is a company, it must submit an ownership structure chart showing the group of which the applicant is a part, including each controller and each person with whom the applicant has close links.

11. Organization Chart – An applicant must submit an organization chart identifying the applicant's governing body, CEO, senior management, the compliance officer and MLRO. The chart must outline the reporting lines of each department within the business in accordance with Part 6 of these Regulations.

12. The applicant must submit any other requirements under the authorization application form determined by the Authority.

(II) Second: Information and Documents Required For the Commencement of Business

1. Systems and Controls – The Capital Market Institution must notify the Authority in writing of the availability of the following systems and controls documentation, in accordance with Part 6 of these Regulations:

1) risk management policies and systems;
2) anti-money laundering and combating the financing of terrorism procedures;
3) compliance manual;
4) compliance monitoring programme; and
5) code of conduct.

2. Operations Manual – The Capital Market Institution must notify the Authority in writing of the availability of an operational procedures manual detailing the procedures and systems to be employed in relation to all material business and administrative operations, including the following:

1) opening and operating clients' accounts;
2) processing and recording of orders, the execution, settlement, clearing, and contract notes of transactions;
3) the provision of prudent and suitable advice and services to clients;
4) handling and custody of client money and client assets;
5) reporting to clients; and
6) complying with all record-keeping requirements.

3. Contracts – The Capital Market Institution must submit to the Authority the agreements, arrangements and understandings with third parties to provide any material services or operations, including:

1) execution, clearing and settlement of trades;
2) custody of client money or client assets;
3) arrangements to offer products or services provided by, sponsored by, or associated with a third party;
4) arrangements to introduce clients;
5) information technology, databases and computer systems;
6) record-keeping;
7) compliance services;
8) audit services.

4. Business Continuity – The Capital Market Institution must submit a copy of its business continuity plan to the Authority.

5. Insurance – The Capital Market Institution must submit details of professional indemnity insurance policies to the Authority in accordance with the requirements stipulated in paragraph (b) of Article 31 of these Regulations.

6. Final Incorporation Documents – The Capital Market Institution must submit to the Authority copies of the final incorporation documents, including its articles of association and by-laws, the commercial registry, and the authorization issued by the Ministry of Investment (where applicable).

7. Technical Systems – The Capital Market Institution must notify the Authority in writing of the availability of appropriate technical systems.

8. Work Facilities – The Capital Market Institution must notify the Authority in writing of the availability of appropriate work facilities, including offices and support services.

9. Registered Persons – The Capital Market Institution must notify the Authority in writing of meeting the minimum registration requirements for registered persons.

10. Website – The Capital Market Institution must have a website in Arabic language - at a minimum - through which it discloses any information determined by the Authority.

11. The Capital Market Institution must comply with any other conditions or requirements determined by the Authority.

5.5 ANNEX 3.2 Notification Requirements

I. A Capital Market Institution must notify the Authority in writing not less than 30 days before any change in:

1. the name of the Capital Market Institution or, where the capital market institution is a company, its registered name;
2. any business name under which the Capital Market Institution carries out securities business in the Kingdom; or
3. the address of the head office of the Capital Market Institution, or, if different, the address of the place for service of notices or documents.

II. A Capital Market Institution must notify the Authority in writing within 7 days of the occurrence of:

1. any change in the material information provided to the Authority on the form of application for registration relating to a registered person's name, good reputation or character. A registered person must give immediate notice to the compliance officer of the capital market institution of any such changes;
2. if the Capital Market Institution is a company, the formation, acquisition, disposal or dissolution of a subsidiary specifying the subsidiary's name and its principal business;
3. if the Capital Market Institution is not a company, when it acquires or disposes of a holding of more than half in nominal value of the capital of a company or equivalent holding of an unincorporated body, specifying the name of the company or unincorporated body and its principal business; or
4. any changes in the information originally submitted under the following headings:
   - - branch offices in the Kingdom through which the capital market institution carries out securities business;
   - - insurance arrangements;
   - - the countries outside the Kingdom in which the capital market institution carries out securities business indicating whether this is done through a branch office, a subsidiary or otherwise; and
   - - the contracts or arrangements to clear and settle transactions or for custody of client money or client assets.

III. A Capital Market Institution must notify the Authority in writing immediately on the occurrence of:

1. the presentation of a petition for the winding up of the capital market institution or of a company which is a subsidiary or controller of the Capital Market Institution or the summoning of any meeting to consider a resolution to wind up a Capital Market Institution or a company which is a subsidiary or controller of the capital market institution;

2. any insolvency event;

3. the imposition of disciplinary measures or disciplinary sanctions on the Capital Market Institution in relation to its securities business by any regulatory authority;

4. the conviction of the Capital Market Institution for any offense under legislation relating to banking or other financial services, companies, insolvency, or for any offense involving fraud or any act involving a lack of integrity or dishonesty, or the imposition of any penalties for deliberate zakat or tax evasion;

5. a general partner in a Capital Market Institution becoming a limited partner;

6. the granting or refusal of any application for, or revocation of, authorization to carry out securities, banking or insurance business in any country or territory outside the Kingdom;

7. the withdrawal or refusal of an application for, or revocation of, membership of an exchange or clearing center;

8. the appointment of inspectors by an official or regulatory authority to investigate the affairs of the Capital Market Institution;

9. a significant act of misconduct by the Capital Market Institution or any of its registered persons;

10. any procedural error at the Capital Market Institution that may negatively affect any of its clients' interests;

11. any matter which would be material to the requirements of the Capital Market Institution, any of its controllers, or any of its registered persons to remain fit and proper in accordance with the requirements under these Regulations;

12. any other matter which would be material to the Authority's supervision of the Capital Market Institution or any of its registered persons; or

13. any material changes to the information previously provided by the Capital Market Institution in any application for registration for one of its employees or prospective employees.

The duty to notify in connection with the matters set out in paragraphs 11, 12 and 13 arises immediately when the Capital Market Institution knows, or has reasonable grounds for believing, that any of these changes has occurred or will occur.

IV. A Capital Market Institution must inform the Authority immediately in writing of any material event or change in its business or operations.

V. A Capital Market Institution must give the Authority prior written notice, or where the event has occurred, written notice as soon as it becomes aware, of:

1. a proposed reorganization or business expansion or other change that could have a material impact on the Capital Market Institution's business, risk profile or resources, including, but not limited to, the following:

- setting up a new business within a Capital Market Institution's group, or establishing a new branch;
- commencing the provision of cross border services into a new territory;
- commencing the provision of a new type of product or service; sale or transfer of any material assets or parts of its business; or ceasing to undertake a securities business activity, or significantly reducing the scope of any activity.

2. any significant failure in the Capital Market Institution's systems or controls, including those reported to the Capital Market Institution by the auditor; or

3. any event related to the Capital Market Institution that results in a material change in its capital adequacy, including:

- any action that would result in a material change in the capital market institution's financial resources or financial resources requirements under these Regulations;
- the payment of a special or unusual dividend or the repayment of share capital or a subordinated loan;
- any proposal under which a member of the Capital Market Institution's group may be considering an action such as the actions mentioned above; or
- any significant losses, whether recognized or unrecognized.

VI. A Capital Market Institution must notify the Authority within 2 days of the date of the resignation or dismissal of any of the following persons:

1) CEO or Managing member of the board of directors;
2) CFO;
3) member of the board of directors or partner;
4) senior executives and departments managers; directly related to securities business;
5) compliance officer; and
6) MLRO. In the event of dismissal, the full details of the reasons for the dismissal must be provided.

VII. A Capital Market Institution must notify the Authority 30 days prior to entering into, or materially changing, outsourcing arrangement of a function of a Capital Market Institution of sufficient importance that failure of the function would jeopardize the capital market institution's ability to comply with these Regulations.

5.6 PART 4: REGISTERED PERSONS

5.6.1 Chapter One - Background and Scope

Article 18: Scope of Application This Part applies to Capital Market Institutions, registered persons, applicants for individual registration and persons performing registrable functions.

Article 19: Registrable Functions

a. The Authority shall prescribe the registrable functions.

b. The following functions are considered functions that must be performed by registered persons:

1) CEO or Managing member of the board of directors;
2) CFO;
3) a member of the board of directors or partner;
4) senior executives and departments managers; directly related to securities business;
5) compliance officer;
6) MLRO; and

7) the employees providing clients with securities business activities including sales representatives, investment advisors, clients' or funds' portfolios managers, corporate finance professionals and brokerage professionals as defined by the Authority.

Article 20: Performance of Registrable Functions

a. No person other than a registered person may perform a registrable function without the Authority's prior written consent.

b. Every Capital Market Institution must at all times have a person who is registered for each of the following functions:

1) CEO or Managing member of the board of directors;
2) CFO;
3) compliance officer; and
4) MLRO.

c. The Authority will not take action against a capital market institution for failure to comply with paragraph (b) of this Article where there is a temporary gap in the performance of the registrable functions, provided that the Capital Market Institution actively seeks an appropriate substitute and notifies the Authority of another registered person who will temporarily take responsibility for that registrable function.

d. A person may perform more than one registrable function for a capital market institution, except that:

1) the CEO, CFO and compliance officer must be separate persons unless the Authority specifically approves another arrangement; and
2) the compliance officer should not perform a client function.

e. As an exception from paragraph (a) of this Article, and without prejudice to the provisions of Article (59) of these regulations, a Capital Market Institution whose activity is limited to managing investment, arranging or advising may delegate the function of CFO, compliance officer or MLRO to an external party, if the following conditions are met:

1) the external party responsible for the function of CFO shall be a certified accounting firm licensed by the Saudi Organization for Certified Public Accountants, where one of its employees is assigned as CFO for the Capital Market Institution;
2) the external party responsible for the function of compliance officer or the MLRO shall be a Capital Market Institution, a certified accounting firm licensed by the Saudi Organization for Certified Public Accountants or a law firm authorized to practice law in Saudi Arabia, where one of its employees is assigned as compliance officer or MLRO for the Capital Market Institution;
3) the employees assigned by the delegated third parties, aforementioned in paragraph (1) and (2), must pass the qualification examinations required by the Authority, or secure an exemption from the Authority from such requirement; and
4) any other conditions that the Authority specifies.

f. As an exception from the provisions of paragraph (b) of this Article, the Capital Market Institution must have –at minimum- two persons registered at all times one of which performs the functions of the Chief Executive Officer in case that its activity is limited to managing investments or arranging, and one person registered at all times performs the functions of the Chief Executive Officer in case its activity is limited to advising, without prejudice to the provisions of paragraph (c) of this Article, in the event that any of these functions become vacant, and provided that third parties are assigned to perform the rest of the registrable functions under paragraph (b) of this Article.

g. With regards to paragraph (d) of this Article, the number of persons registered to perform the function of the clients' or funds' portfolio manager in the Capital Market Institution authorized to carry out investment management business or investment management and operation of funds business must not be less than two persons at all times.

5.6.2 Chapter Two – Registration

Article 21: Requirements for Application for Registration

a. A Capital Market Institution must not apply for registration of a person to perform a registrable function without the consent of the relevant person.

b. The application for registration must be made on the form prescribed by the Authority.

c. An applicant for registration becomes subject to these Regulations from submission of the application.

d. An applicant for registration must have passed the qualification examinations required by the Authority, or secured an exemption from the Authority from such requirement.

e. The Authority will specify the examination requirements associated with the registrable functions, together with guidance on eligible qualifications and criteria for an exemption from the required examination.

f. The Capital Market Institution must pay such fees as may be determined by the Authority.

Article 22: Procedure and Powers of the Authority

a. In considering an application for registration, the Authority may take any of the following actions:

1) carry out any enquiries which it considers appropriate;
2) require the Capital Market Institution or the applicant for registration to appear before the Authority to answer any questions and explain any matter it considers relevant to the application;
3) require that additional information be provided; and
4) verify the accuracy of any information furnished by the applicant for registration.

b. The Authority will aim to process an application for registration within 30 days of receiving all information and documents that it considers pertinent.

c. The Authority may, after considering the application, take any of the following actions:

1) approve the application for registration;
2) approve the application for registration subject to such conditions as it considers appropriate;
3) defer making a decision for such period as may be necessary to carry out further investigation or to allow for the provision of additional information; or
4) refuse the application for registration, giving reasons.

d. If the Authority resolves to register the applicant for registration, the Authority will add the applicant's name to the register of registered persons that the Authority shall maintain for this purpose and so inform the Capital Market Institution.

e. If the Authority resolves to reject the application, the Authority shall notify the applicant for registration and the capital market institution named in the application in writing.

f. An applicant for registration must not perform the registrable function until he has been registered by the Authority.

g. The Capital Market Institution must obtain the Authority's approval before changing the job title of the registered person.

Article 23: Right of Appeal An applicant for registration or the Capital Market Institution named in the application may appeal to the Committee in respect of any decision or action that the Authority takes under this Part.

5.6.3 Chapter Three – General Provisions

Article 24: Responsibilities of Registered Persons
a. A registered person must comply with the Principles stated in Part 2 of these Regulations, as applicable.

b. A registered person must be resident in the Kingdom unless the Authority exempts him from this requirement.

c. This Article applies to any person performing a registrable function who is not registered.

Article 25: Cancellation of Registration
a. If a registered person's registration is cancelled, the capital market institution must ensure that the person immediately ceases to perform a registrable function.

b. Within seven days of a registered person ceasing to carry out a registrable function or ceasing to be employed or associated with a Capital Market Institution, the Capital Market Institution must notify the Authority of that fact on the appropriate form. Upon receipt of the notice, the registration will be suspended, and the suspension shall remain in force until the Authority resolves any of the following:

1) agrees to the termination of the registration;
2) consent to the person becoming employed by a capital market institution in a similar capacity; or
3) removes the person from the register of registered persons.

c. A registered person who is removed from the register by the Authority has a right of appeal to the Committee.

d. A registered person continues to be subject to the jurisdiction of the Authority in respect of any act or omission that occurred before the cancellation of his registration and for two years thereafter. If at any time during this period the Authority commences any enforcement investigation or proceedings, the registered person shall continue to be subject to the jurisdiction of the Authority until the end of the enforcement investigation or proceedings.

e. The Authority shall have the power to cancel the registration of a registered person if the registered person violates any provision of the Capital Market Law or its Implementing Regulations.

5.7 PART 5: CONDUCT OF BUSINESS

5.7.1 Chapter One: General Provisions

Article 26: Preliminary Provisions
a. This Part applies to all securities business carried on by a capital market institution in the Kingdom or outside the Kingdom with or for a client who is in the Kingdom.

b. A Capital Market Institution must clearly state that it has obtained a license from the Authority on all communications, advertisements and notices that are issued to the public that are used by its employees and agents, whether in physical or electronic form.

Article 27: Inducements
a. A Capital Market Institution must not:

1) induce a client to engage in any transaction by offering or giving gifts or inducements; or
2) accept gifts or inducements if doing so would conflict to a material extent with any duty which it owes to a client.

b. For the purposes of paragraph (a) of this Article, the Authority will regard any gift or inducement given or received by an affiliate of a Capital Market Institution or by a third party at the direction of a Capital Market Institution as being given or received by the capital market institution itself.

c. A Capital Market Institution must not participate or offer to participate in any losses suffered by a client.

Article 28: Special Commission Arrangements
a. Special commission arrangement means an arrangement where a capital market institution receives goods or services in addition to trade execution services from an intermediary in return for the commission paid on transactions directed through that intermediary.

b. A Capital Market Institution may enter into a special commission arrangement if the following conditions are met:

1) the person responsible for executing the transaction provides best execution to the Capital Market Institution;
2) the goods or services received by the Capital Market Institution may reasonably be regarded as being for the benefit of the capital market institution's clients;
3) the Capital Market Institution has disclosed in its terms of business with clients that it may receive special commission; and
4) the amount of any fees or commission paid to the provider of the goods or services is reasonable in the circumstances.

Article 29: Confidentiality A Capital Market Institution must keep information obtained from clients confidential, and may not disclose such information except where:

1) its disclosure is based on the Authority's or the Committees for Resolution of Securities Disputes' request under the Capital Market Law, its Implementing Regulations or the related laws, or based on the General Administration of Financial Investigations' request in accordance with the provisions of Anti- money Laundering Law and Combating-Terrorism Crimes and its Financing Law and their Implementing Regulations;

2) the client has explicitly consented to its disclosure;

3) its disclosure is reasonably necessary to perform a particular service for the client; or

4) the information is no longer confidential.

Article 30: Chinese Walls Arrangements
a. "Chinese Wall Arrangements" means written policies and procedures established by a Capital Market Institution to secure confidential or inside information obtained by the Capital Market Institution in the course of carrying out securities business that are designed to ensure that the information is known only to employees of the capital market institution who are authorized to receive it, and to ensure that the information is not disclosed to any other persons.

b. A Capital Market Institution that carries out arranging business and also carries out dealing as an agent or principal, advising or managing business must establish proper Chinese wall arrangements based on the nature, scale and complexity of its business.

c. A Capital Market Institution or an employee acting on behalf of a Capital Market Institution is not in violation of the provisions of articles 5 or 6 of the Market Conduct Regulations if the capital market institution deals or advises in a security related to inside information while another department of the Capital Market Institution is in possession of inside information, if the following conditions are met:

1) the Capital Market Institution has established appropriate Chinese wall arrangements in view of the nature and size of its securities business;
2) the Capital Market Institution has effectively implemented and maintained its Chinese wall arrangements; and
3) none of the individuals involved in the dealing or advising activity has knowledge of the inside information or has received advice on the dealing or advising activity from an individual who has knowledge of the inside information.

Article 31: The Liability of Capital Market Institution
a. Any condition providing for the exclusion or restriction of the liability of a Capital Market Institution, whether under terms of business or otherwise, shall be void if the exclusion or restriction contravenes the Capital Market Institution's obligations under the Capital Market Law or the Implementing Regulations.

b. The Capital Market Institution must have adequate indemnity insurance for the risks of professional failures, based on the nature, scale and complexity of its business.

5.7.2 Chapter Two – Securities Advertisements

Article 32: Scope of Application This Chapter applies to all securities advertisements made by a Capital Market Institution in the Kingdom, or approved by a Capital Market Institution for communication by another person. This Chapter does not apply to an advertisement that is excluded under the Securities Business Regulations.

(In accordance with the Board of the Authority Resolution No. (2-75-2020) dated 22/12/1441H corresponding to 12/8/2020G, Article 31 of these Regulations shall become effective as of 28/5/1443H corresponding to 1/1/2022G, provided that Article 31 of the Authorized Persons Regulations issued by the Board of the Authority Resolution No. (1-83-2005) dated 21/5/1426 H corresponding to 28/6/2005G and amended by the Board of the Authority Resolution No. (3-85-2017) dated 27/12/1438H corresponding to 9/18/2017G shall continue to be effective until the effectiveness date of Article 31 of these Regulations.)

Article 33: Prepared Securities Advertisements
a. A prepared securities advertisement means any advertisement for securities or securities activity, prepared in advance, for the purpose of inviting or inducing a person to engage in securities activity and communicated in writing, electronically or, otherwise to one or more persons.

b. Before communicating a prepared securities advertisement, or approving its contents to be communicated by another person, a capital market institution must ensure that:

1) the advertisement complies with the requirements of this Part after it is approved by a designated officer of the capital market institution;
2) the advertisement is clear, fair and not misleading; and
3) that the approved advertisement contents to be communicated by another person, include a clear, fair and not misleading disclosure that such person has received or will receive benefits in exchange for communicating that advertisement.

c. A prepared securities advertisement must comply with the content requirements set out in Annex 5.1.

d. If the prepared securities advertisement relates to specific securities then it must contain sufficient information to enable a person to make an informed assessment of the securities or securities activity to which it relates.

e. If a Capital Market Institution becomes aware that a prepared securities advertisement does not comply with the requirements of this Part, or when it receives instructions from the Authority in this regard, it must withdraw the advertisement as soon as possible.

f. A Capital Market Institution must maintain a complete record of each prepared securities advertisement that it has approved and confirmed compliance for.

Article 34: Direct Communications
a. Direct communications means any securities advertisement that is not a prepared securities advertisement, including a meeting with a client or potential client, a telephone call, a presentation or any direct interaction with one or more persons.

b. Before making any direct communication a Capital Market Institution must ensure that:

1) the recipient has consented to receiving the securities advertisement; or
2) the recipient has an existing client relationship with the capital market institution and contemplates pursuant to such relationship that such securities advertisements will be made.

c. A Capital Market Institution must ensure that an individual who makes a direct communication on the Capital Market Institution's behalf, including any registered person or other employee:

1) does so in a way which is clear, fair and not misleading;
2) does not make any false or misleading statements;

3) makes clear the purpose of the securities advertisement at the initial point of communication, and identifies himself and the capital market institution who he represents; and
4) does not communicate with a person outside of business hours, unless the person has previously agreed to such a communication.

d. A Capital Market Institution must have a Code of Conduct that requires individuals seeking to obtain business on behalf of the capital market institution to avoid using any undue pressure or making any misleading statements, and to make clear their purpose and identity to clients or potential clients.

Article 35: Non-Retail Client's Investment Funds and Derivatives A Capital Market Institution must not communicate securities advertisement to a retail client related to non-retail clients' investment funds or to derivatives securities, unless it has determined that the securities are suitable for such client.

5.7.3 Chapter Three – Accepting Clients

Article 36: Client Classification
a. Before conducting securities business with or for any client, a Capital Market Institution must classify the client as one of the following:

1) a retail client;
2) a qualified client; and
3) an institutional client.

b. A Capital Market Institution must not classify a client in more than one of the categories set out in paragraph (a) of this Article.

c. A Capital Market Institution must make a record of the classification established for each client under this Article, including sufficient information to support that classification.

(In accordance with the Board of the Authority Resolution No. (2-75-2020) dated 22/12/1441H corresponding to 12/8/2020G, Article 36 of these Regulations shall become effective as of 28/5/1443H corresponding to 1/1/2022G, provided that Article 36 of the Authorized Persons Regulations issued by the Board of the Authority Resolution No. (1-83-2005) dated 21/5/1426 H corresponding to 28/6/2005G and amended by the Board of the Authority Resolution No. (3-85-2017) dated 27/12/1438H corresponding to 9/18/2017G shall continue to be effective until the effectiveness date of Article 36 of these Regulations.)

Article 37: Anti-Money Laundering and Combating the Financing of Terrorism Before conducting securities business with or for any client, a capital market institution must ensure that it complies with all obligations under the Anti-Money Laundering Law and its implementing regulations and the Combating-Terrorism Crimes and its Financing Law and its implementing regulations.

Article 38: Terms of Business with Clients
a. A Capital Market Institution must provide a client with terms of business setting out the basis on which securities business is to be carried out with or for the client. Such terms must be provided before conducting any securities business with or for the client.

b. The terms of business with a client must take the form of an agreement which takes effect once an executed copy of the terms of business has been provided by the client.

c. A Capital Market Institution must ensure that its terms of business set out in adequate detail the basis on which securities business is to be conducted.

d. A Capital Market Institution must ensure that its terms of business with its retail client conform to the terms of business requirements set out in Annex 5.2.

e. A Capital Market Institution must retain a record of the terms of business it provides to a client, and any amendment to them.

(In accordance with the Board of the Authority Resolution No. (2-75-2020) dated 22/12/1441H corresponding to 12/8/2020G, Article 38 of these Regulations shall become effective as of 28/5/1443H corresponding to 1/1/2022G, provided that Article 38 of the Authorized Persons Regulations issued by the Board of the Authority Resolution No. (1-83-2005) dated 21/5/1426 H corresponding to 28/6/2005G and amended by the Board of the Authority Resolution No. (3-85-2017) dated 27/12/1438H corresponding to 9/18/2017G shall continue to be effective until the effectiveness date of Article 38 of these Regulations.)

Article 39: Know Your Client
a. Before a Capital Market Institution carries out any securities business for a client or for its account, it must obtain information from the client concerning the client's financial situation, investment experience and investment objectives relevant to the services to be provided. Such information must be obtained as a precondition to providing such services.

b. The information required under paragraph (a) of this Article must include, at a minimum, the information required by Annex 5.3(A) and a capital market Institution may be guided by the information stipulated in Annex 5.3(B).

c. The Capital Market Institution must request an update of such information from each client under these Regulations, when there is any change to them, or at least once every three years, and the capital market institution shall establish permanent procedures and policies to achieve this.

d. If the client refuses to provide the information required under paragraph (a) of this Article, the Capital Market Institution may not conduct any securities business for him.

e. A Capital Market Institution must retain a record of all information obtained from the client pursuant to this Article.

(In accordance with the Board of the Authority Resolution No. (2-75-2020) dated 22/12/1441H corresponding to 12/8/2020G, Article 39 of these Regulations shall become effective as of 28/5/1443H corresponding to 1/1/2022G, provided that Article 39 of the Authorized Persons Regulations issued by the Board of the Authority Resolution No. (1-83-2005) dated 21/5/1426 H corresponding to 28/6/2005G and amended by the Board of the Authority Resolution No. (3-85-2017) dated 27/12/1438H corresponding to 9/18/2017G shall continue to be effective until the effectiveness date of Article 39 of these Regulations.)

5.7.4 Chapter Four - Client Relations

Article 40: Fiduciary Duties A Capital Market Institution owes the statutory fiduciary duties set out in Annex 5.4 to its clients.

Article 41: Conflicts of Interest

a. A Capital Market Institution must ensure that it safeguards at all times the interests of its client, and that no conflict of interest between its interest and the interest of it client affects the transactions or the services that the Capital Market Institution carries out for its client.

b. Where a Capital Market Institution who acts for, or provides advice to a client has an actual or a potential conflict of interest in relation to a transaction or advising a Capital Market Institution shall disclose that conflict of interest to the client in writing, and obtain a written acknowledgment from the client that he understands and is fully aware g of the actual or potential conflict of interest between the interests of the Capital Market Institution and his interests.

c. A Capital Market Institution is not required to disclose a conflict of interest if this information would constitute provision of inside information. In that instance a Capital Market Institution shall take reasonable steps to ensure fair treatment for the client.

d. If there is a conflict between an interest of a capital market institution and an interest of the client in any transaction, the Capital Market Institution must pay to the client the value of any loss incurred by the client as a result of the conflict unless:

1) the Capital Market Institution has disclosed the conflict of interest to the client in accordance with paragraph (b) of this Article; and
2) the client has agreed in writing that the Capital Market Institution can proceed notwithstanding the conflict.

e. A Capital Market Institution must in all cases comply with Article 14 of the Market Conduct Regulations in any dealing as principal with a client.

f. A Capital Market Institution authorized to carry out advising business may present itself as an independent investment advisor unless in the event of an actual or a potential conflict of interests between its interests and the interests of the person to whom advice is given.

g. The Capital Market Institution must establish a special record for each type of securities business to document all actual or potential conflicts of interest and the measures taken in their regard.

Article 42: Understanding Risk

a. A Capital Market Institution must not deal, advise, offer a security, distribute investment funds units, manage for a client or take collateral for its own account from a client, unless it has taken reasonable steps to enable the client to understand the nature of the risks involved in the type of transaction in which the client would be engaging, and to enable such client to understand the nature of the risks involved, the Capital Market Institution must have regard to:

1) The educational and knowledge level of the client (where applicable);
2) The client's field of work; and
3) The client's experience in the capital markets, its duration, and its nature;

b. This Article does not apply to the Capital Market Institution's carrying out any securities business with or for an institutional client as a counterparty.

(In accordance with the Board of the Authority Resolution No. (2-75-2020) dated 22/12/1441H corresponding to 12/8/2020G, Article 42 of these Regulations shall become effective as of 28/5/1443H corresponding to 1/1/2022G, provided that Article 42 of the Authorized Persons Regulations issued by the Board of the Authority Resolution No. (1-83-2005) dated 21/5/1426 H corresponding to 28/6/2005G and amended by the Board of the Authority Resolution No. (3-85-2017) dated 27/12/1438H corresponding to 9/18/2017G shall continue to be effective until the effectiveness date of Article 42 of these Regulations.)

Article 43: Suitability

a. A capital market Institution must not deal, advise, offer a security, distribute investment funds units or manage for a client or take collateral for its own account from a client, unless the advice or transaction is suitable for that client having regard to the facts disclosed by that client and other relevant facts about that client of which the capital market Institution is, or reasonably should be aware.

b. In considering the suitability of advice or a transaction for a client, a Capital Market Institution must have regard to:

1) The educational and knowledge level of the client (where applicable);
2) Client's field of work;
3) the client's knowledge and understanding of the relevant securities and markets, and of the risks involved, and its ability to withstand them;
4) the client's financial standing, including an assessment of his net worth or of the value of his portfolio based on the information disclosed by that client, the type of assets owned by the client, how long the client maintained them, and what the proposed transaction represents in all the assets of the client;
5) the length of time the client has been active in the relevant markets, the frequency of business and the extent to which he relies on the advice of the Capital Market Institution;
6) the size and nature of transactions that have been undertaken for the client in the relevant markets;
7) the client's investment objectives; and
8) the period during which the client expects to cash out his invested money.

c. A Capital Market Institution before advising the client or effecting the transaction must submit to the client a report on the suitability of that advice or transaction, provided that the report includes, at a minimum, the following:

1) The client's investment objectives and the client's risk tolerance;
2) Disadvantages and risks of advice or potential transaction; and
3) Justifications for concluding that the advice or potential transaction is suitable or not for the client, in light of the facts disclosed by that client.

d. As an exception from the provisions of paragraph (c) of this Article, the Capital Market Institution who acts as manager of the client's account must prepare a suitability report for that client at the beginning of the contractual relationship, upon updating its terms and upon renewing it.

e. As an exception from the provisions of paragraph (a) of this Article, if a Capital Market Institution has advised a client that a transaction is not suitable for him as per the suitability report and the client insisted on proceeding with the transaction after viewing the suitability report, a Capital Market Institution may accept an order to buy or sell the security from the client after informing him that the execution of the transaction is not consistent with the suitability report, and obtain an acknowledgment from the client of understanding that, provided that the suitability report records and the acknowledgment of the client are retained.

f. The client's acknowledgment referred to in Paragraph (e) of this Article must be prepared in a clear, fair and non-misleading manner, and shall include the client's acknowledgment of the following:

1) The client has reviewed the suitability report for the transaction it is insisting on executing;
2) The client is aware of all the details of the transaction it is insisting on executing, and understand its risks; and
3) The client understands that execution of the transaction is inconsistent with the suitability report.

g. The client's notice referred to in paragraph (e) of this Article must be reviewed and certified by a registered person independent of the person who prepared the suitability report.

h. A Capital Market Institution must not use pressure methods or give any misleading statements to the client that may lead the client to provide false, inaccurate, or incomplete information for the purposes of studying the suitability of the advice or transaction for the client.

i. A Capital Market Institution may rely on the information provided by the client for the purposes of studying the suitability of the advice or transaction for the client, unless it knows or must reasonably know that the information provided is false, inaccurate or incomplete.

j. This Article does not apply in the following cases:

1) Where the Capital Market Institution deals with a client as agent in accordance to the instructions it receives from the client without providing advice to the client, and the transactions will be executed in the listed debt instruments market, the main market or its equivalent securities markets outside the Kingdom;
2) Where the Capital Market Institution offers shares or publically offered debt instrument, or offers or distributes open public low risk investment funds units.
3) Where the Capital Market Institution deals with an institutional client as agent only in accordance with the instructions it receives from the client without providing advice to the client or managing for him, except for the counterparty; or
4) Where the Capital Market Institution deals with an institutional client as a counterparty.

k. The Capital Market Institution, after obtaining the Authority's approval, may rely on means of modern technologies to consider the suitability of the advice or transaction for the client, provided that the Capital Market Institution establishes permanent procedures and policies to verify the correctness and accuracy of the considering results and that they meet the requirements of this article.

(In accordance with the Board of the Authority Resolution No. (2-75-2020) dated 22/12/1441H corresponding to 12/8/2020G, Article 43 of these Regulations shall become effective as of 28/5/1443H corresponding to 1/1/2022G, provided that Article 43 of the Authorized Persons Regulations issued by the Board of the Authority Resolution No. (1-83-2005) dated 21/5/1426 H corresponding to 28/6/2005G and amended by the Board of the Authority Resolution No. (3-85-2017) dated 27/12/1438H corresponding to 9/18/2017G shall continue to be effective until the effectiveness date of Article 43 of these Regulations.)

Article 44: Client Borrowing

a. A Capital Market Institution shall not, in relation to securities business, knowingly lend money or extend credit to a client and must not arrange for any other person to do so, unless:

1) the Capital Market Institution has made and recorded an assessment of the client's financial standing, based on information disclosed by that client, and is satisfied that the amount and the arrangements for the loan or credit are suitable for the client; and
2) the client has given his prior written consent to the lending or credit facility, specifying the maximum amount of the loan or credit together with details of the amount and of any charges to be levied.
3) the lending of money or extension of credit facilities to the client shall not be linked to derivative contracts.

b. Paragraph (a) of this Article does not apply where a capital market institution:

1) settles a transaction in the event of a default or late payment by the client; or
2) pays an amount to cover a margin call made for a client for a period no longer than five days.
3) effects margined transactions.

Article 45: Margin Requirements

a. A Capital Market Institution may not effect a margined transaction with or for a client unless the client has entered into terms of business specifying the following:

1) the circumstances under which the client may be required to provide margin;
2) particulars of the form in which the margin may be provided;
3) particulars of the steps which the Capital Market Institution may be entitled to take if the client fails to provide the required margin, including the communication method(s) by which the margin call will be made on the client;
4) that failure by the client to meet a margin call may lead to the Capital Market Institution closing out the client's position after a time limit specified by the Capital Market Institution, and that the Capital Market Institution is entitled to close out the position in any event after a period of five days from such failure; and
5) any circumstances, other than failure to provide margin, which may lead to the client's position being closed without prior reference to him.

b. A Capital Market Institution may make a secured or unsecured loan or grant credit to a client for a period of more than five days for the purpose of making a deposit of margin or required margin payment if the following two conditions are met:

1) a credit assessment is made of the client by an employee of the Capital Market Institution who is independent of the trading or marketing functions; and
2) the client has given his prior written consent to the lending or credit facility, and such consent specifies the maximum amount of the loan or credit together with details of the amount and of any charges to be levied.

c. A Capital Market Institution that effects a margin transaction with or for a client must perform the following:

1) take reasonable steps to ensure that the client is aware of the risks of margin transactions;

2) in relation to effecting a margin transaction on shares of companies listed on the exchange, require the client to provide a minimum margin not less than 50% of the transaction value prior to effecting the transaction; and
3) in relation to effecting a margin transaction on shares of companies listed on the exchange, monitor the margin provided by the client daily, and ensure that the margin is not less than 25% of the current value of each applicable security position.

d. The Authority may prescribe a higher rate of margin to be provided for transactions in any security or category of securities, and the Capital Market Institution must require a client to provide any such prescribed rate of margin.

e. The Authority may prohibit margined transactions in relation to any security or category of securities.

f. Without prejudice to the provisions of paragraph (j) of this Article, margin payable by a client in respect of a margin transaction on a regulated exchange or market must be of an amount or value at least equal to the margin requirements of the relevant exchange, market or clearing centre.

g. Margin must be in the form of cash, fully-paid security positions or other acceptable collateral by the Capital Market Institution.

h. The Capital Market Institution must periodically determine the securities on which margin transaction can be affected with the client in accordance with specific standards and controls approved by its board of directors.

i. A Capital Market Institution may not effect a margin transaction on shares of listed companies whose accumulated loss reaches 50% or more of its capital, according to the disclosures issued by the listed companies.

j. A Capital Market Institution may not effect a margin transaction with a client or for his account on a derivative contract.

(In accordance with the Board of the Authority Resolution No. (2-75-2020) dated 22/12/1441H corresponding to 12/8/2020G, Article 45 of these Regulations shall become effective as of 28/5/1443H corresponding to 1/1/2022G, provided that Article 45 of the Authorized Persons Regulations issued by the Board of the Authority Resolution No. (1-83-2005) dated 21/5/1426 H corresponding to 28/6/2005G and amended by the Board of the Authority Resolution No. (3-85-2017) dated 27/12/1438H corresponding to 9/18/2017G shall continue to be effective until the effectiveness date of Article 45 of these Regulations.)

Article 46: Fees and Commissions Fees and commission charged by a Capital Market Institution to its clients must be fully disclosed in advance of providing any services.

5.7.5 Chapter Five - Reporting to Clients

Article 47: Contract Notes

a. A Capital Market Institution who effects a sale or purchase of a security with or for a client must send the client a contract note forthwith.

b. A contract note does not have to be sent where the capital market institution is acting as manager and the client has confirmed that he will not require such contracts notes to be provided in writing.

c. Contract notes must provide the information required in Annex 5.5.

Article 48: Periodic Reporting

a. A Capital Market Institution who acts as manager for a client must send a valuation report at least every three months in respect of securities or securities-related cash balances contained in the client's account.

b. Valuation reports must provide the information required in Annex 5.6.

5.7.6 Chapter Six - Miscellaneous

Article 49: Client Records

a. A Capital Market Institution must keep and maintain proper records of each transaction it effects. Such records must be current at all times and be sufficient to demonstrate compliance with these Regulations.

b. A Capital Market Institution must keep and maintain proper records of client accounts. Such records must:

1) accurately record at all times the assets and liabilities of each client and of all clients collectively;
2) contain such information as is necessary to enable the capital market institution to prepare a statement of each client's assets and liabilities, and details of transactions effected for the client; and
3) identify all client money and client assets that the capital market institution, or its custodian, are responsible for.

c. The records of the Capital Market Institution must contain:

1) details of all orders in a security entered by a client;
2) details of all purchases and sales of a security made by the capital market institution for a client, or by the Capital Market Institution for its own account;
3) a record of all income and expenses for each client, explaining their nature;
4) details of all receipts and payments of client money and client assets;
5) a record of the cash and securities held in each client account; and
6) a record of client money and client assets.

Article 50: Employees' Personal Dealings

a. An employee of a Capital Market Institution must not knowingly:

1) be a party to any transaction in a security where a client of the Capital Market Institution is a party; or
2) Opening an investment account at another Capital Market Institution, unless he has obtained the prior consent of the Capital Market Institution which he works for.

b. An employee of a Capital Market Institution must disclose to the compliance officer all transactions in securities that he executes for his account or any other account for which he is authorized, unless he was acting as an employee of a Capital Market Institution, within 7 days from the date of execution.

c. The compliance officer must establish procedures to monitor employees' personal dealings in securities to ensure compliance with the Capital Market Law and the Implementing Regulations.

d. A Capital Market Institution must implement personal account dealing procedures consistent with the provisions of Annex 5.7.

(In accordance with the Board of the Authority Resolution No. (2-75-2020) dated 22/12/1441H corresponding to 12/8/2020G, Article 50 of these Regulations shall become effective as of 28/5/1443H corresponding to 1/1/2022G, provided that Article 50 of the Authorized Persons Regulations issued by the Board of the Authority Resolution No. (1-83-2005) dated 21/5/1426 H corresponding to 28/6/2005G and amended by the Board of the Authority Resolution No. (3-85-2017) dated 27/12/1438H corresponding to 9/18/2017G shall continue to be effective until the effectiveness date of Article 50 of these Regulations.)

Article 51: Recording Telephone Calls

a. A Capital Market Institution must not make or accept telephone communications from clients or prospective clients in relation to securities business unless the Capital Market Institution records the telephone communications.

b. A Capital Market Institution must disclose to its clients or prospective clients that telephone communications in relation to securities business will be recorded.

c. A Capital Market Institution must retain the records of telephone communications in relation to securities business for a period of ten years following the date of the telephone communication. In the event a telephone communication is relevant to a dispute with a client or a regulatory enquiry, the record must be retained until the dispute is fully resolved or the enquiry completed.

(In accordance with the Board of the Authority Resolution No. (2-75-2020) dated 22/12/1441H corresponding to 12/8/2020G, Article 51 of these Regulations shall become effective as of 28/5/1443H corresponding to 1/1/2022G, provided that Article 51 of the Authorized Persons Regulations issued by the Board of the Authority Resolution No. (1-83-2005) dated 21/5/1426 H corresponding to 28/6/2005G and amended by the Board of the Authority Resolution No. (3-85-2017) dated 27/12/1438H corresponding to 9/18/2017G shall continue to be effective until the effectiveness date of Article 51 of these Regulations.)

5.8 ANNEX 5.1 CONTENTS REQUIREMENTS FOR SECURITIES ADVERTISEMENTS

I. GENERAL CONTENTS REQUIREMENTS FOR ALL SECURITIES ADVERTISEMENTS

1 Clarity of Purpose

The purpose of the advertisement must be clear.

2 Clarity of Subject

The nature or type of securities business and the type of securities being advertised must be clear.

3 Statements, Promises or Forecasts

Any statement, promise or forecast must be fair and not misleading in the form and context in which it appears. If any promise or forecast is based on assumptions, the assumptions must be stated. An advertisement must not forecast the possible future price of securities.

4 No False or Misleading Statements

The advertisement must not include false or misleading statements relating to the securities business, size or resources of the capital market institution or any type of securities.

5 Name, Address and Regulatory Status

The advertisement (or the person making the advertisement) must state the name and address of the Capital Market Institution, and that the Capital Market Institution is authorized by the Authority.

II. CONTENTS REQUIRED FOR PREPARED SECURITIES ADVERTISEMENTS PROMOTING A SPECIFIC SECURITY OR SECURITIES OR A SPECIFIC SECURITIES SERVICE

6. Guarantees

The advertisement must not describe a security as guaranteed unless there is a legally enforceable arrangement with a third party who undertakes to meet in full an investor's claim under the guarantee. If so, the advertisement must give details about both the guarantor and the guarantee sufficient for an investor to make a fair assessment about the value of the guarantee.

7. Comparisons

Advertisements that compare different securities or services must:

1. be based either on facts verified by the Capital Market Institution or on assumptions stated within the advertisement;
2. be presented in a fair and balanced way; and
3. not omit anything material to the comparison.

8. Material Interest

A Capital Market Institution must include a statement acknowledging circumstances where the Capital Market Institution knows that it or its affiliates:

1. has or may have a position or holding in the securities concerned or in related securities; or
2. is providing or has provided within the previous 12 months significant advice or securities business services to the issuer of the securities concerned or of a related security.

9 Past Performance

Any information about the past performance of securities or of a capital market institution that is included in an advertisement must:

1. be a fair representation of the past performance of the securities or Capital Market Institution;
2. not be selected so as to exaggerate the performance of the securities or Capital Market Institution;
3. state the source of the information;
4. be based on verifiable information; and
5. warn that past performance is not necessarily a guide to future performance.

10 Zakat and Taxation

If the advertisement contains any reference to the impact of zakat or taxation, it must:

1. state the assumed rate of zakat or taxation and any relief; and
2. state that such rates and relief may change over time.

11 Cancellation Rights

Any advertisement for securities to which cancellation rights apply must contain details of such rights, including the period within which they may be exercised.

12 Advertiser Benefits

If the contents of the advertisement are approved by the capital market institution to be communicated by another person, the capital market institution must include the advertisement with a statement disclosing clearly, fairly and not misleadingly that such person has received or will receive benefits in return for communicating that advertisement.

III. RISK WARNINGS FOR PREPARED ADVERTISEMENTS OF SPECIFIC SECURITIES

13 Fluctuations in Value

Where the securities can fluctuate in price or value, a statement must be made that prices, values or income may fall and, if applicable, a warning that the investor may get back less than he invested.

14 Suitability

Where the advertisement contains or refers to a recommendation about a specific security or securities service, a statement must be made warning that it may not be suitable for all recipients of the advertisement and a recommendation that, if they have any doubts, they should seek advice from their investment advisor.

15 Volatile securities

Where the advertisement relates to a security which is a geared security or a contingent liability security, it must state, if it is the case:

1. that the security may be subject to sudden and large falls in value which could cause a loss equal to the amount invested; and
2. that the investor's loss may not be limited to the amount originally invested or deposited, but may have to pay more.

16 Investment income

Where a security is described as being suitable for an investor particularly seeking income from his security, the investor must be warned, if it is the case, that:

1. income from the security may fluctuate; and
2. part of the capital invested may be used to pay that income.

17 Foreign Currency Denominated Securities

Where a security is denominated in a foreign currency, the investor must be warned that changes in currency rates may have an adverse effect on the value, price or income of the security.

18 Illiquid Securities

An advertisement for an illiquid security must state that it may be difficult:

1. for the investor to sell or realize the security; and
2. to obtain reliable information about its value or the extent of the risks to which it is exposed.

19 Sales Charges and Fees

1. If an advertisement relates to a security on which deductions for charges and expenses are made at the time of the initial investment or on the sale of the investment, a warning that such charges apply must be included.
2. If an advertisement relates to a security on which performance fees are charged, a warning that such charges apply must be included.

5.9 ANNEX 5.2 TERMS OF BUSINESS REQUIREMENTS

(In accordance with the Board of the Authority Resolution No. (2-75-2020) dated 22/12/1441H corresponding to 12/8/2020G, Annex 5.2 of these Regulations shall become effective as of 28/5/1443H corresponding to 1/1/2022G, provided that Annex 5.2 of the Authorized Persons Regulations issued by the Board of the Authority Resolution No. (1-83-2005) dated 21/5/1426 H corresponding to 28/6/2005G and amended by the Board of the Authority Resolution No. (3-85-2017) dated 27/12/1438H corresponding to 9/18/2017G shall continue to be effective until the effectiveness date of Annex 5.2 of these Regulations.)

A Capital Market Institution's terms of business to be entered into with or for a retail client should, where relevant, provide for the following:

1. Commencement: The date on which the terms of business come into force.

2. Name, Address and Regulator: The name and address of the capital market institution and a statement that the Capital Market Institution is subjected to the Authority's supervision and control.

3. Investment Objectives: The retail client's investment objectives.

4. Restrictions: Any restrictions on: the types of securities in which the retail client wishes to invest; and the markets on which the retail client wishes transactions to be executed.

5. Services: The services which the Capital Market Institution will provide.

6. Payments for Services: Details of any payment for services payable by the retail client to the Capital Market Institution, including the following:

1. structure and methods of the payments;
2. how it is to be paid and collected;
3. how frequently it is to be paid, and
4. any other payment that is receivable by the capital market institution (or by any of its affiliates) in connection with any transaction executed by the Capital Market Institution, with or for the retail client, in addition to or in lieu of any fees.

7. Investment Manager: If the Capital Market Institution is to act as manager, the terms of business must include the following:

1. the arrangements for giving instructions to the capital market institution and acknowledging those instructions;
2. the initial value of the managed portfolio;
3. the initial composition of the managed portfolio;
4.. the period of account for which statements of the portfolio are to be provided;
5. the extent of the discretion to be exercised by the capital market institution, including any restrictions on investments;
6. how performance will be measured;
7. how valuations will be made.

8. Accounting: the arrangements for accounting to the retail client for any transaction executed on his behalf.

9. Cancellation Rights: a description of any cancellation right to which the retail client may be entitled.

10. Acting as Principal: that the Capital Market Institution may act as principal in a transaction with the retail client, if applicable.

11. Risk Warning: any risk warning required under Part 5 of these Regulations.

12. Security Lending: whether the Capital Market Institution may undertake security lending activity with or for the retail client.

13. Termination Method: how the terms of business may be terminated.

14. Complaints: how to complain to the Capital Market Institution.

15. Right to Realize Retail Client's Assets: a description of any right of the Capital Market Institution to realize the assets of the retail client (including any collaterals) or to close out or liquidate positions on a default.

16. Contingent Liability Securities: a statement of the basis on which the retail client will incur any contingent liability, including margin requirements, and the maximum limits placed on such funding.

17. Authority to Borrow: details of any authority to borrow or raise money on the retail client's behalf, or enter into transactions which will involve the retail client having to borrow or raise money and the maximum borrowing limit must be clarified.

18. Special Commission Arrangements: a statement explaining the Capital Market Institution's policy regarding special commission arrangements.

19. Custody Arrangements for:

1. registration of client assets if these will not be registered in the retail client's name;
2. claiming and receiving dividends, commission payments and other entitlements accruing to the retail client;
3. exercising conversion and subscription rights;
4. dealing with takeovers, other offers or capital reorganizations;
5. exercising voting rights;
6. the Capital Market Institution's liability in the event of a default by an eligible custodian;
7. the giving and receiving of instructions by or on behalf of the client or other person accredited by the client, and any restrictions to that authority; and
8. any agreement to lien or pledge interests over the client asset taken by the Capital Market Institution or an eligible custodian except in respect of charges relating to the administration or custody of the client assets.

20. Pooling: a Capital Market Institution must notify a retail client where it intends to pool his client asset with that of one or more other clients and explain the meaning of pooling and warn the retail client that:

1. client assets or entitlements may not be separately identifiable by certificates, other physical documents of title or electronic record; and
2. retail clients may participate pro rata in any irreconcilable shortfall resulting from the default of a custodian.

21. Client Assets Held Overseas: where a Capital Market Institution in accordance with these Regulations arranges for client assets to be held overseas, it must notify a client in writing that there may be different settlement, legal and regulatory requirements in overseas jurisdictions from those applying in the Kingdom.

22. Client Money: A Capital Market Institution must notify a retail client in writing of the arrangements for holding client money.

5.10 ANNEX 5.3 (A) KNOW YOUR CLIENT FORM

(In accordance with the Board of the Authority Resolution No. (2-75-2020) dated 22/12/1441H corresponding to 12/8/2020G, Annex 5.3 (A) of these Regulations shall become effective as of 28/5/1443H corresponding to 1/1/2022G, provided that Annex 5.3 of the Authorized Persons Regulations issued by the Board of the Authority Resolution No. (1-83-2005) dated 21/5/1426 H corresponding to 28/6/2005G and amended by the Board of the Authority Resolution No. (3-85-2017) dated 27/12/1438H corresponding to 9/18/2017G shall continue to be effective until the effectiveness date of Annex 5.3 (A) of these Regulations.)

Client must provide the information required by this Annex.

FILL THE FOLLOWING IF:

CLIENT IS AN INDIVIDUAL

PERSONAL INFORMATION Full Name:(in accordance with identification document):

Date of birth:
ID Number/passport No.:
Marital Status:
Number of dependents:
Educational level: Primary / Intermediate /
High school / Diploma / Bachelor/ Postgraduate)
Citizenship:
Address for Correspondence (national address if the client is resident of the Kingdom)
Mobile Phone:
Another phone:
Approximate annual income (in SAR)?
100,000 or less
100,001-300,000
300,001-600,000
600,001 -1,500,000
1,500,001 -5,000,000
5,000,001 – 10,000,000
10,000,001 – 50,000,000
Over 50,000,000
Approximate net worth (excluding residence) (in SAR)?
100,000 or less
100,001-300,000
300,001-600,000
600,001 -1,500,000
1,500,001 -5,000,000
5,000,001 – 10,000,000
10,000,001 – 50,000,000
Over 50,000,000

EMPLOYER INFORMATION Employer's Name:

Employer's Address:
Employer's Phone Number:
Position / Title:

Duration of Employment:

BANK INFORMATION

Bank's Name:

Branch:

Main Account Number:

CLIENT'S PROFESSIONAL EXPERIENCES IN THE FINANCIAL SECTOR

Has the client worked in the financial sector during the past five years? Yes/ No

(This includes, for example: working for Capital Market Institutions, banks, finance companies, insurance companies) Does the client have any other practical experience related to the financial sector? Yes/ No

GENERAL INFORMATION Is the client a board of directors member, an audit committee member or a senior executive in a listed company? Yes/ No

Does the client have a close association with a board of directors member, an audit committee member or a senior executive in a listed company? Yes /No

Is the client entrusted with prominent public functions in the Kingdom or a foreign country, senior management positions, or a position in an international organization? Yes/ No

Does the client have a relationship (by blood or marriage up to the second degree), or have an association with a person entrusted with a prominent public function in the Kingdom or a foreign country, senior management positions, or a position in an international organization? Yes/ No Is the client the beneficial owner of the account or business relationship? Yes/ No The identity of the beneficial owner of the account or business relationship (if the answer to above question is No) Any other financial information on the client's financial situation?

FILL THE FOLLOWING IF: CLIENT IS A LEGAL PERSON

GENERAL INFORMATION Name:
Commercial Registration No. or its equivalent:
Registered Address:
Country of Registration:
Main business:
Date of incorporation or start of business:
Country of practicing business:
Names of natural persons who own or control 25% or more of the shares:
Names of all directors and senior executives:
Business Phone:
Number of employees:
Paid-up capital:
Annual Turnover:
CONTACT Name of Contact:
Address for Correspondence:
Business Phone:
Mobile Number:
Email address:
BANK INFORMATION Bank's Name:
Branch:
Main Account Number
OTHER INFORMATION Any other financial information on the client's financial situation?
CUSTODIAN DETAILS Name:
Address for correspondence:
Account name:
Account number:

5.11 ANNEX 5.3 (B) INVESTMENT INFORMATION FORM

A Capital Market Institution may use this guidance annex.

INVESTMENT INFORMATION

Investment knowledge and experience
Low
Medium
High
Number of years of investment in securities
Products previously invested in
Professional certificates (if the client is a natural person)
Loan to invested money ratio
Margin transactions over the past five years
Securities transactions outside the Kingdom over the past five years
If securities transactions were executed outside the Kingdom over the past five years, in which countries were these transactions executed?
Client's appetite for risk Low Medium High
General investment objectives? protection of capital income balanced growth of capital create savings for retirement project financing purchase an asset (for example: real estate, or vehicle)
What are the client's preferred investment assets? (tick as many as required): denominated in Saudi Riyals? denominated in other foreign currencies? State the foreign currencies:
The period during which the client expects to cash out his invested money:
Short term (less than 1 year) Medium term (1 year-5 years) Long term (more than 10 years)
Client's investment portfolio profile:
Client's current investment portfolio profile:
Client's ideal investment portfolio profile:
Deposits and Murabaha
Debt instruments
Shares
Real-estates
Derivative contracts
Alternative investments

(Ensure that the sum of all Percentages of each portfolio above equal 100%)

Indicate where the following should be forwarded:

The client
The custodian
Other

Specify all details as instructed by client

1) Certificates
2) Dividends/other income
3) Sale proceeds

(In accordance with the Board of the Authority Resolution No. (2-75-2020) dated 22/12/1441H corresponding to 12/8/2020G, Annex 5.3 (B) of these Regulations shall become effective as of 28/5/1443H corresponding to 1/1/2022G, provided that Annex 5.3 of the Authorized Persons Regulations issued by the Board of the Authority Resolution No. (1-83-2005) dated 21/5/1426 H corresponding to 28/6/2005G and amended by the Board of the Authority Resolution No. (3-85-2017) dated 27/12/1438H corresponding to 9/18/2017G shall continue to be effective until the effectiveness date of Annex 5.3 (B) of these Regulations.)

5.12 ANNEX 5.4 FIDUCIARY DUTIES

1. Loyalty

A Capital Market Institution must act in all cases in good faith and in the interests of the client.

2. Conflict of Interest

A Capital Market Institution must comply with principle 10 provided for at paragraph (b) of Article 5 and with the provisions of Article 41 of these Regulations.

3. No Secret Profits

A Capital Market Institution must not use the client's property, information or opportunities for its own or anyone else's benefit unless the Capital Market Institution makes full disclosure of such usage to the client and obtains his consent.

4. Care, Skill and Diligence

A Capital Market Institution owes the client a duty to exercise the care, skill and diligence which would be exercised in the same circumstance by a person having both:

a. The knowledge and experience that may reasonably be expected of a person in the same position as the Capital Market Institution; and
b. The knowledge and experience which the Capital Market Institution has.

5.13 ANNEX 5.5 REQUIRED CONTENTS OF CONTRACT NOTES

Particulars

1. The Capital Market Institution's name and a statement that it is authorized by the Authority.

2. The trade date and time.

3. The client's name, account number, address or other identifier.

4. The security concerned, the size involved and the type of the transaction (sale or purchase), and:

1. the maturity and delivery or expiry date if the security is a contractually based security;
2. if the security is an option that has been exercised: the strike price of the option; and whether the exercise of the option creates a sale or purchase in the underlying asset.

5. The per security price at which the transaction was executed, or averaged and the total consideration due from or to the client, and a statement if applicable, that the price is an averaged price.

6. The settlement date where agreed.

7. The Capital Market Institution's charges to the client in connection with the transaction.

8. The amount of any front-end loading if the transaction is a purchase of a unit in an investment fund.

9. Whether the Capital Market Institution executed the transaction as principal, or with or through an affiliate.

10. Where any commission or other return which has accrued or will accrue on the relevant securities is accounted for separately from the transaction price, the amount of the commission or other return which the purchaser will receive or the number of days for which he will receive commission must be clarified.

11. A statement, if this is the case, that any dividend, bonus or other right which has been declared, but which has not been paid, allotted or otherwise become effective in respect of the relevant security, will not pass to the purchaser under the transaction.

12. The amount of any costs including transaction taxes which are incidental to the transaction and which will not be paid by the capital market institution out of the charges mentioned in 7 above.

13. If the transaction involved or will involve the purchase of one currency with another, the currency conversion rate involved or a statement that the rate will be supplied on request.

14. If the security to which the contract note relates closes out an open position in a derivatives contract, the contract note must set out:

1. each derivatives contract that forms part of the open position;
2. each derivatives contract that forms part of the closing of the position; and
3. the net profit or loss made by the client on closing out the position.

5.14 ANNEX 5.6 REQUIRED CONTENTS OF PERIODIC VALUATION STATEMENTS FOR CLIENT PORTFOLIOS

1. Contents and Value of Portfolio

1. Description of each security held in the portfolio, the number of shares, units or contracts held, and the current value of each security position;
2. Amount of cash balances;
3. Total value of the portfolio on the valuation date; and
4. Change in the value of the portfolio since the last valuation statement.

2. Basis of Valuation

1. A statement of the basis on which the value of each security has been determined and an explanation of any change in the basis for valuing any securities since the previous valuation report.
2. Where any securities are valued in a currency other than the currency used to value the portfolio, the relevant currency conversion rates as of the valuation date must be shown.

3. Transactions and Changes in Portfolio

1. Particulars of each transaction entered into for the portfolio during the period;
2. Total amount of money transferred into and paid out of the portfolio during the period;
3. Details of any securities transferred into or out of the portfolio during the period; and

4. Total amount of commissions, dividends and other returns received by the Capital Market Institution for the portfolio during the period.

4. Charges and Remuneration

1. Total amount of fees, charges and taxes paid out of the portfolio for purchases and sales of securities during the period;
2. Total amount of fees and charges for managing the portfolio and any other services provided by the Capital Market Institution during the period; and
3. Details of any remuneration received by the capital market institution from a third party in respect of transactions entered into for the portfolio, or a statement that the basis or amount of any such remuneration has been separately disclosed in writing to the client.

5. Securities Pledged or Charged

1. Particulars of any securities that have been pledged as collateral for or charged to secure borrowings on behalf of the portfolio, and the identity of the person the securities are pledged to; and
2. Total amount of any commission or other payments made in respect of such borrowings during the period.

6. Derivatives Positions

1. Profit or loss on each transaction to close out a derivatives position during the period (including any commissions or other fees payable for the transaction); and
2. Details of each open derivatives position on the valuation date, including:

- the underlying securities, commodity, index or any other asset;
- the trade price and date of the opening transaction;
- the current market price of the derivatives contract;
- the current unrealized profit or loss on the position; and
- the exercise price and expiry date of the contract.

5.15 ANNEX 5.7 PERSONAL ACCOUNT DEALING

A Capital Market Institution must provide every employee with a written notice (the personal dealing notice) which must contain statements as prescribed by this Annex. Employees must undertake that they will observe the requirements of the personal dealing notice by signing a copy of it and returning it to the Capital Market Institution.

This Annex sets out a model personal dealing notice. A capital market institution is free to impose more stringent requirements than those required by this Annex.

MODEL PERSONAL DEALING NOTICE

So as to comply with the requirements for personal dealing transactions, it is required to comply with the provisions of this notice.

1. Permission to Deal

It is permitted to buy and sell securities in these categories:

A Capital Market Institution should insert here types of securities or transactions in which the employee can deal. A capital market institution will also need to clarify its procedure for restricting or withdrawing its consent in relation to particular securities in special conflict of interest circumstances.

An employee may not buy or sell any other securities without having obtained consent from the compliance officer or his deputy.

Note that where a general or specific consent is given for a transaction, the other requirements set out in this notice (e.g. reporting) still need to be complied with.

2. Rights Issues, Takeovers The restrictions in this notice extend to making any formal or informal offer to buy or sell, taking up rights on a rights issue and exercising conversion or subscription rights and exercising an option.

The restrictions also extend to buying or selling securities under any offer, including a takeover or tender offer, which is made to the public or all (or substantially all) the holders of the security concerned.

3. Executors and Agents

The restrictions extend to dealings by the employee:

a. as an executor of a will in which the employee or a relative of the employee has a significant interest;
b. as an executor of any other will, unless the employee is relying entirely on the advice of another person (such as another broker or lawyer); or
c. for another person, unless the employee is dealing as an employee of the Capital Market Institution.

4. General Exemptions

The restrictions do not extend to any transaction in a managed or discretionary account if the transaction is entered into without consultation with the employee.

5. Selling to or Buying from a Client

The employee may not sell to or buy from any client of the capital market institution for his own account.

6. Reporting of transactions

The employee must immediately report to the Capital Market Institution in writing any purchase or sale of a security which the employee enters into otherwise than through (name of the Capital Market Institution) or (name of another group company that is a capital market institution, including those transactions falling within 1 above. If, however, the employee has made arrangements for the capital market institution promptly to receive a copy of the contract note (or similar report) in respect of the transaction, the employee does not have to report it to the Capital Market Institution.

7. Dealing Ahead of a Research Recommendation

This restriction applies when the employee knows that the capital market institution intends to publish a research recommendation and the employee knows, or should know, that the recommendation is likely to cause a price change in the security to which it relates. In that situation, the employee must not deal until the recommendation has been published and the clients for whom it was principally intended have had a reasonable opportunity to react to it. Dealing before the research recommendation has become public may also breach insider trading rules.

8. Dealing Contrary to a Client's Interest

The employee must not deal in a security where he knows that such dealing is likely to have a direct adverse effect on the particular interests of one of the Capital Market Institution 's clients.

9. Personal Benefits

If the employee's functions involve giving securities advice, including the preparation of research material, or entering into transactions in securities for the Capital Market Institution 's own account or the account of those for whom it deals, the employee must not accept any benefit or inducement which is likely to conflict with the employee's duties to the Capital Market Institution or any of the capital market institution's clients.

"Benefit or inducement" means credit or any other financial advantages, money, property or gift; any services, facilities, or any opportunity to make, receive or increase a gain or revenue or to avoid or reduce a loss or expense.

If in any doubt the employee should consult with the compliance officer or his deputy.

10. Counseling and Procuring

If the employee is precluded by the above provisions from entering into any transaction, the employee cannot advise or cause another person to enter into such a transaction or communicate any information or opinion to any other person if the employee knows, or has reason to believe, that that other person will as a result enter into such a transaction or cause or advise someone else to do so.

This does not apply to actions which the employee takes in the course of his employment with the Capital Market Institution.

11. Summary of Insider Trading Rules

The employee may not act contrary to the provisions of the Capital Market Law, its Implementing Regulations, especially insider trading rules. A broad guide to the insider trading rules now follows: Inside information is information that is not generally available, but would be price sensitive if it were generally available. An insider is a person who obtains inside information from a family, business or contractual relationship. The employee is likely to be an insider as a result of the employment, as is anyone to whom the employee passes the inside information. An insider may not trade in any security related to the inside information or communicate it to another person for him to trade in the security. Another person may not trade in a security after receiving inside information relating to it.

If the employee breaches these rules, the employee may face compensation claims, fines or prison.

MODEL UNDERTAKING

To: (name of the Capital Market Institution)

a. I undertake to observe the provisions of the Capital Market Law and of the Market Conduct Regulations in relation to insider trading as they may be amended or replaced in future, and the requirements regarding personal dealing transactions that are set out in the foregoing notice.

b. I agree that this undertaking extends to any amended or replacement requirements that (name of the Capital Market Institution) set out in any written notice which you subsequently give to me.

c. I further agree that this undertaking shall form part of the contract of employment (or contract for services) with you and that any breach of this undertaking will entitle you, among other things, to terminate that contract without notice.

(Print Name)

Signature: Date:

5.16 PART 6: SYSTEMS AND CONTROLS

5.16.1 Chapter One – Scope of Application

Article 52: Scope of Application This Part applies to all the activities carried on by the Capital Market Institution.

5.16.2 Chapter Two – Management Arrangements

Article 53: Division of Responsibilities

a. A Capital Market Institution must take appropriate measures to maintain a clear and appropriate division of the principal responsibilities among its governing body and senior executives so that:

1) it is clear who is responsible for each function; and
2) the business and affairs of the Capital Market Institution. are adequately monitored and overseen by the governing body and senior executives of the Capital Market Institution.

b. The governing body is responsible for arranging the division of responsibilities under paragraph (a) of this Article, and overseeing the establishment and implementation of the Capital Market Institution's systems and controls.

c. The formation of the Capital Market Institution's board of directors must include independent members not less than two or a third of the board members, whichever is more. By way of example and without limitation, the following negate the independence requirement for an independent board of directors member:

1) being an owner of 5% or more of the shares of the capital market institution or the shares of another company in its group;
2) being a representative of a legal person who owns 5% or more of the shares of a Capital Market Institution or shares of another company in its group;
3) being a member of the board of directors of another company from the group of the Capital Market Institution, which he is nominated for membership in its board of directors; and
4) is working or have worked as an employee during the past year at a Capital Market Institution or any party dealing with it or another company in its group, such as auditors and major suppliers, or controlled any of those parties during the past year.

d. The board of directors of a Capital Market Institution must establish the governance infrastructure, which is to set the necessary systems and policies to achieve its corporate governance objectives, develop its own governance policies and procedures for overseeing those systems and policies, monitor their implementation and their effectiveness and amend them when needed; to include, but not be limited to, the following:

1) determine the procedures and controls for nomination for membership of the board of directors of a Capital Market Institution and the responsibilities and main functions of the board of directors of a Capital Market Institution;
2) determine the powers of the board of directors and senior executives;
3) develop codes of conduct for employees of a capital market institution; and

4) forming supervisory committees such as the audit committee, nominations committee, and the remuneration committee.

e. A board of directors of a Capital Market Institution must issue an annual report that includes the operations of the capital market institution during the last financial year, and all factors affecting its business, and the report of the board of directors must include the information stipulated in Annex 6.1.

f. A Capital Market Institution must send a copy of the report of the board of directors referred to in paragraph (e) of this Article to the Authority within three months of the end of the financial year of the Capital Market Institution, and the sent report must be in Arabic language.

g. A Capital Market Institution, which is a subsidiary of a local bank, must establish the necessary procedures that guarantee independence and complete separation from the business of its local bank, and not rely on its financial, human and technical resources, including - but not limited to - opening investment accounts for clients and executing sales and purchase orders in securities, and effecting subscription and redemption transactions in investment funds through the branches of that local bank and by its employees.

h. A Capital Market Institution, whose legal form is not a joint stock company and a Capital Market Institution, which its authorization type is limited to managing investments or arranging or advising or combine any of these activities only, is exempted from implementing paragraphs (c), (d), (e) and (f) of this Article.

Article 54: Establishment and Maintenance of Systems and Controls

a. A Capital Market Institution must establish and maintain systems and controls that are appropriate to its business. The systems and controls must conform to the requirements of Chapter 3 of this Part and be sufficient to enable the Capital Market Institution to comply with the Capital Market Law and its Implementing Regulations.

b. The Capital Market Institution's governing body is primarily responsible for compliance with the Capital Market Law and its Implementing Regulations and all other regulatory requirements applicable to the Capital Market Institution. The governing body must make appropriate arrangements to ensure that the activities detailed in Chapter 3 of this Part are carried out.

5.16.3 Chapter Three – Systems and Controls

Article 55: General Provisions

a. The Capital Market Institution must establish systems and controls under this Part taking into account the following:

1) the nature, scale and complexity of its business;
2) the diversity of its operations;
3) the number and value of its transactions; and
4) the degree of risk associated with each area of its operation.

b. A Capital Market Institution must establish systems and controls to cover at a minimum:

1) the division of responsibilities and reporting lines in accordance with Article 53 of these Regulations;
2) risk management policies and systems;
3) anti-money laundering and combating the financing of terrorism procedures;
4) a compliance manual;
5) a compliance monitoring programme;
6) a code of conduct;
7) an operational procedures manual; and
8) continuity of business manuals and plans.

c. A Capital Market Institution that carries out dealing business as an agent must establish clients' conduct trading surveillance policies and systems, provided that such policies and systems are sufficient for the Capital Market Institution to ensure compliance of its clients with the Capital Market Law and its Implementing Regulations.

d. A Capital Market Institution must document its systems and controls appropriately and keep such documentation up to date.

e. The documentation described in this Article must be retained for ten years after it ceases to be used or is amended.

Article 56: Review by the Governing Body

a. A Capital Market Institution's governing body must carry out a regular review of the division of responsibilities and its systems and controls, including the documents referred to in paragraph (d) of Article 55 of these Regulations, at least once every three years.

b. A Capital Market Institution's governing body must expeditiously monitor the actions arising as a result of the review.

c. Each review conducted in accordance with paragraph (a) of this Article should be minuted and reports of such reviews must be retained for ten years.

Article 57: Compliance

a. A Capital Market Institution must appoint a senior officer as compliance officer.

b. The governing body of the Capital Market Institution is responsible for supervising the following:

1) ensuring that appropriate policies and procedures are in place to enable the Capital Market Institution to comply with the Capital Market Law, the Implementing Regulations and all other relevant regulatory requirements;
2) ensuring that the compliance officer and his department are appropriately resourced and have access to all of the capital market institution's records;
3) the establishment, implementation, enforcement and maintenance of the compliance manual and the compliance monitoring programme;
4) the establishment of and ensuring compliance with the code of conduct;
5) the preparation of reports and notifications to be filed with the Authority; and
6) the procedures for the periodic reporting to the governing body by the compliance officer regarding the Capital Market Institution compliance with the Capital Market Law and its Implementing Regulations and all other relevant regulatory requirements.

c. The Authority may review the appropriateness of a capital market institution's compliance arrangements at any time.

d. The compliance officer shall comply to periodically submitting reports to the governing body regarding the Capital Market Institution compliance with the Capital Market Law and its Implementing Regulations and all other relevant regulatory requirements.

Article 58: Risk Committee and Compliance Committee

a. Depending on the nature, scale and complexity of its business, a Capital Market Institution may establish a compliance committee, risk committee or both to monitor its securities business and its compliance programme.

b. The Authority may require a Capital Market Institution to appoint a compliance committee, risk committee or both if it considers one to be necessary based on the nature, scale and complexity of the business.

c. When a compliance committee is established, its members should include, but are not limited to, the CEO, the compliance officer and the MLRO, and it must be connected to the governing body of the capital market institution.

d. Meetings of compliance committee and risk committee must be minuted and retained for ten years.

Article 59: Outsourcing

a. A Capital Market Institution may delegate specific compliance or other functions to an external party, provided that appropriate safeguards are put in place, including:

1) an assessment of whether the delegate is suitable to carry out the delegated function or task, taking into account the degree of responsibility involved;
2) clear documentation of the extent and limits of any delegation and information confidentiality standards;
3) suitable arrangements to supervise the delegation, and to monitor the discharge of the delegate's functions or tasks and ensuring its continuity, including granting the Capital Market Institution the right to ensure the delegate's ability to continue carrying out the delegated functions or tasks, and to oblige the delegate to provide any information it requests regarding the delegated functions or tasks within a period not exceeding ten days from the date of the request; and
4) appropriate remedial action if any concern arises about the performance of the delegate's functions or tasks.

b. A Capital Market Institution must exercise due diligence in the selection of an external party to perform specific functions.

c. The outsourcing of any function by the Capital Market Institution will not derogate from the Capital Market Institution's, compliance officer's or the compliance committee's regulatory obligations.

d. The delegated to carry out any securities business must be a capital market institution authorized to carry out the delegated securities business.

(In accordance with the Board of the Authority Resolution No. (2-75-2020) dated 22/12/1441H corresponding to 12/8/2020G, Article 59 of these Regulations shall become effective as of 28/5/1443H corresponding to 1/1/2022G, provided that Article 59 of the Authorized Persons Regulations issued by the Board of the Authority Resolution No. (1-83-2005) dated 21/5/1426 H corresponding to 28/6/2005G and amended by the Board of the Authority Resolution No. (3-85-2017) dated 27/12/1438H corresponding to 9/18/2017G shall continue to be effective until the effectiveness date of Article 59 of these Regulations.)

Article 60: Audit Committee

a. Depending on the nature, scale and complexity of its business, a Capital Market Institution may appoint an audit committee.

b. The Authority may require a Capital Market Institution to appoint an audit committee if it considers one to be necessary based on the nature, scale and complexity of its business.

c. The audit committee must meet at least twice a year, and when necessary..

d. Meetings of the audit committee must be minuted and retained for ten years.

Article 61: Internal Audit

a. Depending on the nature, scale and complexity of its business, a Capital Market Institution may delegate part of the task of monitoring the appropriateness and effectiveness of its systems and safeguards to an internal audit function.

b. An internal audit function should have clear responsibilities and reporting lines to the audit committee or appropriate senior manager, be adequately resourced and staffed by competent individuals, be independent of the day-to-day activities of the capital market institution and have appropriate access to a capital market institution's records.

c. Reports of meetings of the internal audit function must be prepared and retained for a period of ten years.

Article 62: Audit and Inspections

a. A Capital Market Institution's internal auditor must review books, accounts and other records related to securities business at least once every three years, and when necessary.

b. All accounts, records, terms of business and other agreements to which a Capital Market Institution is party must be retained for the period specified in Part 3 of these Regulations and must be made available to the internal and external auditors.

c. A Capital Market Institution authorized to carry out dealing, arranging or managing business when appointing its auditor must ensure that the auditor is registered with the Authority in accordance with the Rules for Registering Auditors of Entities Subject to the Authority's Supervision.

Article 63: Resolution of Complaints

a. A Capital Market Institution must have written procedures to ensure:

1) timely and proper handling of complaints from clients;
2) that appropriate remedial action in respect of complaints is promptly taken; and
3) where a complaint arises from the conduct of a third party employed or recommended by a Capital Market Institution, a capital market institution shall intercede on behalf of the client, making best efforts to resolve the complaint.

b. The Capital Market Institution must design the procedures to resolve complaints to ensure that:

1) each employee working with clients is aware of them;
2) a complaint is investigated promptly and fully by an officer of the Capital Market Institution who was not originally involved in the matter giving rise to the complaint; and
3) records of the written complaints are made and any action taken documented.

Article 64: Anti-Money Laundering and Combating the Financing of Terrorism A Capital Market Institution must appoint a senior employee as MLRO. The MLRO is responsible for ensuring compliance with the requirements of the Anti-Money Laundering Law and its implementing regulations and the Combating-Terrorism Crimes and its Financing Law and its implementing regulations, and must report to the governing body on matters relating to money laundering and terrorism financing.

Article 65: Employees
a. A Capital Market Institution must establish adequate procedures for the recruitment, training, supervision and discipline of employees.

b. A Capital Market Institution must establish recruitment procedures to ensure that it recruits employees who are appropriately qualified for the role and honest.

c. A Capital Market Institution must establish a programme to ensure that employees are trained appropriately (including passing any examinations required under Part 4 of these Regulations).

d. A Capital Market Institution must maintain records of the names of any employee disciplined by a Capital Market Institution in connection with any breach of the Capital Market Law or its Implementing Regulations or any other conduct which may affect the conduct of the Capital Market Institution 's securities business. The records must also include particulars of:

1) the breach or conduct for which the employee was disciplined; and
2) the steps taken to discipline the employee.

e. A capital market institution must train its employees periodically and such training must cover updates to the Capital Market Law, its Implementing Regulations and any other laws relevant to the business of the capital market institution. Such training should occur at least annually.

f. A Capital Market Institution must retain appropriate records relating to its employees in connection with their recruitment procedure, experience and qualifications for a period of ten years from the date on which the Capital Market Institution recruited the employee.

Article 66: Business Continuity
a. A Capital Market Institution should have in place appropriate arrangements, having regard to the nature, scale and complexity of its business, to ensure that it can continue to operate and meet its regulatory obligations in the event of an unforeseen interruption to its activities. These arrangements should be documented and regularly updated and tested to ensure their effectiveness.

b. Appropriate records relating to the arrangements in connection with business continuity must be retained for a period of ten years after it ceases to be used or is amended.

Article 67: Record Retrieval
All records required to be maintained by a Capital Market Institution under the Capital Market Law or its Implementing Regulations must be available for inspection by the Authority. Article 68: Mandate Over an Account in the Client's Name

A Capital Market Institution must establish and maintain adequate records and internal controls in respect of a mandate it has over an account in the client's own name. A Capital Market Institution must in particular ensure that all transactions entered into pursuant to a mandate are within the scope of the authority conferred by the mandate and establish procedures for the giving and receiving of instructions under the mandate.

5.17 ANNEX 6.1 – REQUIRED CONTENTS OF THE BOARD OF DIRECTORS' REPORT

1) A description of all the main activities of the capital market institution.

2) Formation of the board of directors and classification of its members as follows: executive board member - non-executive board member - independent board member.

3) Names of companies inside and outside the Kingdom of which a member of the board of directors of the Capital Market Institution is a member of its boards of directors or one of its directors.

4) Name of each company affiliated with the Capital Market Institution, its capital, the percentage of ownership of the capital market institution in it, its main activity, the main country of its operations, and the country of its establishment.

5) A description of the plans and important decisions of a capital market institution (including structural changes, expansion of business, or suspension of operations), and future expectations of the business of the Capital Market Institution.

6) The number of board of directors' meetings held during the last financial year, their dates, and the attendance record of each meeting indicating the names of those present.

7) A brief description of the powers and functions of the committees, such as: the Audit Committee, the Nominations Committee, and the Remuneration Committee, stating the names of these committees, their chairmen and members, the number of their meetings, the dates of their meeting, and the attendance record of each meeting, indicating the names of those present.

8) Disclosure of remunerations and compensations paid to members of the board of directors of the Capital Market Institution and five of the senior executives who received the highest remunerations and compensations, in addition to the chief executive officer and chief financial officer if they are not among them, according to the table below:

Statement

Executive Board Members*
Non-Executive Board Members
Independent Board Members
Allowance for attendance of the board of directors' sessions
Allowance for attendance of the committees' sessions
Periodic and annual remunerations
Incentive plans
Any compensations or other in-kind benefits paid monthly or annually

Total:

*As members of the board of directors.

Statement:

Five of the senior executives who received the highest remunerations and compensations in addition to the CEO and CFO, if they are not among them
Salaries and wages
Allowances
Periodic and annual remunerations

Incentive plans
Commissions
Any compensations or other in-kind benefits paid monthly or annually

Total

9) A statement of any arrangement or agreement whereby a member of the board of directors of the Capital Market Institution or a senior executive waives any remunerations and compensations.

10) Any penalty, sanction, precautionary measure, or precautionary restriction imposed on a Capital Market Institution by the Authority or from any supervisory, regulatory, or judicial body, along with a statement of its signatory, the reasons for the violation, and the ways to address it and avoid its occurrence in the future.

11) The results of the audit report of a Capital Market Institution's system and controls, in addition to the audit committee's opinion on the adequacy of the internal audit system (where applicable).

12) Information related to any risks faced by a capital market institution (whether operational risks, financing risks or market risks) and the policy for managing and monitoring these risks.

13) If the auditor's report includes reservation to the annual financial statements, the report of the board of directors must clarify those reservations, their reasons and any information related to them.

14) Summary in the form of a table or diagram of the assets and liabilities of a Capital Market Institution and the results of its business in the last five financial years or since inception, whichever is shorter.

15) Clarification of any material differences in the operating results from the results of the previous financial year, or any expectations announced by the Capital Market Institution.

16) A description of any interest, contractual securities and rights issue belonging to the members of the board of directors of the capital market institution, the senior executives and their relatives in the shares or debt instruments of the Capital Market Institution or any of its affiliates, and any change in that interest, those securities or rights during the last financial year.

17) Information related to any loans on the Capital Market Institution (whether payable on demand or otherwise), a statement of the total indebtedness of the Capital Market Institution and its affiliates, and any amount paid for loans during the financial year, the amount of the loan principal, and the remaining amount, the amount of the loan's principal, the name of the lender, its duration, and the remaining amount, and in the event of the absence of loans on a capital market institution, it must provide an acknowledgment thereof.

18) A description of each transaction concluded between a capital market institution and a related person.

19) Information related to any business or contracts to which a capital market institution is a party, or in which it has an interest for one of the members of the board of directors of the Capital Market Institution or for senior executives or for any person related to any of them, so that it includes the names of those involved in the business or contracts and the nature of these business or contracts, their terms, duration and amount and in the absence of any such business or contracts, the Capital Market Institution must provide an acknowledgment thereof.

5.18 Part 7: Client Money and Assets

5.18.1 Chapter One – General Provisions

Article 69: Purpose and Scope

a. The provisions in this Part implement Principle 6, which is provided for at paragraph (b) of Article 5 of these Regulations.

b. A Capital Market Institution must segregate its own money and assets from client money and client assets, and client money and client assets must only be used for the benefit of a Capital Market Institution's clients.

c. Clients' money or assets kept in accordance with the provisions of this Part must be through a Capital Market Institution authorized to carry out custody business.

Article 70: Effect of Segregation

a. Clients' money and assets, which are segregated from capital market institution's money and assets, are deemed to be held for the capital market institution's clients and shall be not deemed money nor assets of the Capital Market Institution.

b. Creditors of a Capital Market Institution do not have any claim or entitlement to segregated money or assets.

5.18.2 Chapter Two – Client Money Rules

Article 71: Money Received by a Capital Market Institution

a. With regards to Article 72 of these Regulations, all money that a Capital Market Institution receives from or on behalf of a client in the course of carrying out securities business is client money.

b. Client money must be segregated and held in a client account, separately from the money of a Capital Market Institution, except where otherwise provided in this Part.

c. All money paid into a client account by a Capital Market Institution will be treated as client money.

d. Only client money should be held in a client account unless it is required to open or keep open the account or it is temporarily in the account.

e. A Capital Market Institution may transfer client money to another person for the purpose of settling a securities transaction with or through that other person or to provide collateral for a client.

Article 72: Money Which is Not Client Money

Money is not client money if it is immediately due and payable to the Capital Market Institution for its own account (including, fees and commissions which are lawfully due to the Capital Market Institution).

Article 73: Money to be Held With a Bank
a. A Capital Market Institution must hold client money in a client account with a local bank.

b. A Capital Market Institution must assess the risk of a local bank prior to opening a client account and consider whether it is necessary to open client accounts with more than one bank.

c. A Capital Market Institution may open a client account with a local bank in its own group, provided it notifies its client of its intention and the client has not objected.

d. Client money may be held with an overseas bank but only if this is necessary for the settlement of a transaction in securities outside the Kingdom. Dividends or other income received outside the Kingdom for a Capital Market Institution's client may be paid into an account with an overseas bank in the Capital Market Institution's name, provided that the funds in question are either transferred to a client account or paid to the client no later than three days after notification of receipt. A Capital Market Institution must notify its client of its intention to hold client money with a bank outside the Kingdom.

e. The requirements specified in paragraphs (b) and (c) of this Article and the requirements in Article 74 of these Regulations apply equally to an account with an overseas bank.

Article 74: Acknowledgement by the Bank
a. A Capital Market Institution must within 20 days of opening a client account obtain a written acknowledgement from the local bank with which a client account has been opened that:

1) the client account will hold client money and not money belonging to the Capital Market Institution; and
2) the local bank will not enforce any right or claim that it has against the Capital Market Institution against funds held in the client account and will not combine the client account with any other account.

b. If a Capital Market Institution does not receive the acknowledgement referred to in paragraph (a) of this Article within the 20 day period, it must withdraw all money in the account and pay it into another client account with another local bank.

Article 75: Client Accounts
a. Except as otherwise provided in this Part 7 a capital market institution must, where it receives client money, either:

1) pay the money into a client account no later than the next day after receipt; or
2) pay the money out in accordance with Article 76 of these Regulations.

b. If a remittance comprises part client money and part other money it must be paid in full into a client account. The part of the remittance that is not client money should be transferred out of the client account as soon as possible.

c. Client money may be held in a client account in a different currency from that of receipt.

In such a case a Capital Market Institution must daily ensure that the amount held in the different currency is at least equal to the amount of the original currency and must adjust the amount held in the different currency accordingly (if necessary by making up any deficit). In carrying out the currency conversion the Capital Market Institution should use the closing spot currency conversion rate on the business day preceding the day on which the conversion calculation is carried out.

Article 76: Money Ceasing to be Client Money Money ceases to be client money for which the Capital Market Institution is responsible if it is paid:

1) To the client;
2) To a third party on the instructions of the client;
3) Into a bank account in the name of the client (not being an account which is also in the name of the Capital Market Institution); or
4) To a Capital Market Institution itself, where it is lawfully due and payable to the Capital Market Institution.

Article 77: Returns
a. No returns are payable to a client in respect of client money held in a client account.

b. Without prejudice to the provisions of this Part, a capital market institution may deposit the client's money in an account that provides returns with a local or overseas bank, and obtain such returns or part of them, provided that the client's prior written approval has been obtained, in addition to satisfying the conditions stipulated in the Client Money Rules.

Article 78: Records and Auditor's Report
a. A Capital Market Institution must keep records which are sufficient to demonstrate compliance with the Client Money Rules.

b. A Capital Market Institution's auditors shall annually review the Capital Market Institution's compliance with the Client Money Rules and shall report on this review as part of its audit of the capital market institution.

c. A Capital Market Institution must provide the Authority with the auditor's report mentioned in paragraph (b) of this Article within 4 months of the end of its financial year.

Article 79: Amounts to be Held in Client Money Bank Accounts
a. A Capital Market Institution must:

1) daily confirm that the aggregate balance on all of its client accounts as at the close of the preceding business day was at least equal to the "client money requirement" calculated in the manner prescribed by the Authority; and
2) ensure that any shortfall is paid into a client account by the close of business on the day the calculation is performed, and any excess is withdrawn within the same time period.

b. For the purposes of paragraph (a) of this Article, a capital market institution should use the values contained in its accounting records, such as its cash book, rather than values contained on statements received from banks. Fees and commissions may be excluded from the calculation.

c. So as to satisfy paragraph (a) of this Article, a capital market institution may be required to pay money into a client account. Such money will be client money.

d. A Capital Market Institution must notify the Authority immediately if it is unable to perform the calculation required by this Article.

Article 80: Reconciliations
a. A Capital Market Institution must, at least once in every 7 days, reconcile:

1) the balance on each client account as recorded by the capital market institution with the balance on that account as set out on the statement or other form of confirmation issued by the local bank;
2) the balance on each client transaction account with exchanges, clearing centres, intermediate brokers, settlement agents and counterparties as recorded by the Capital Market Institution with the balance on that account as set out in the statement or other form of confirmation issued by the person with whom the account is held; and
3) its records of collateral received from clients with the statement of collateral or other form of confirmation issued by the person with whom that collateral is located.

b. A Capital Market Institution must perform the reconciliations in paragraph (a) of this Article within 10 days of the date to which the reconciliation relates.

c. Where any difference arises on any of the reconciliations in paragraph (a) of this Article, the Capital Market Institution must correct it as soon as possible and in any event within 3 days.

d. A Capital Market Institution must notify the Authority as soon as possible where it is unable to perform any of the reconciliations required by the provisions in this Chapter.

e. Where a Capital Market Institution is unable to resolve a difference arising from a reconciliation, but the records examined by the capital market institution during its reconciliation indicate that there might need to be a greater amount of money in the relevant client accounts or collateral than is in fact the case, the Capital Market Institution must assume, until the matter is finally resolved, that those records are accurate and pay the difference from its own money into a client account and the amount paid will be client money.

Article 81: Client Money Reporting Requirement A Capital Market Institution who holds client money must submit to the Authority such accounts as it requests.

5.18.3 Chapter Three – Client Asset Rules

Article 82: Assets Received by a Capital Market Institution
a. A Capital Market Institution must not hold client assets unless it is authorized to provide custody services.

b. All assets which include, or may include, securities that are received by a Capital Market Institution in the course of carrying out securities business shall be treated as client assets unless they consist of cash or collateral, to which Article 83(b) of these Regulations applies.

c. A Capital Market Institution must segregate the client assets that it holds from its own assets.

d. A Capital Market Institution must not use client assets for its own account or the account of another client unless it has obtained the prior consent of the client to whom the assets belong.

Article 83: Assets Which are Not Client Assets
a. Client assets shall include collateral taken by way of pledge to satisfy an obligation arising from that pledge until applied to satisfy that obligation.

b. Collateral retained by a Capital Market Institution as Other Collateral (as defined at paragraph (a) of Article 94 of these Regulations) for its own account is not a client asset, provided that the Capital Market Institution has complied with the requirements of paragraph (b) of that Article.

Article 84: Segregation
a. If a client asset is recorded in an account with a capital market institution, the Capital Market Institution must ensure that the title to the account makes it clear that such assets belong to the client and are segregated from the Capital Market Institution's assets.

b. A Capital Market Institution must require that where a client asset is recorded in an account with a custodian or with an overseas custodian, the custodian or overseas custodian makes it clear in the title of the account that the client asset belongs to one or more clients of the Capital Market Institution and that the assets are segregated.

Article 85: Holding and Registration of Client Assets
a. Securities that are eligible for the Depositary Centre must be held in an account in the relevant client's name with the Depositary Centre.

b. A Capital Market Institution must hold a document of title to a client asset in its physical possession, or with a custodian in an account designated for client assets.

c. Where a Capital Market Institution registers or records title to a client asset it must ensure that it is registered or recorded in the name of the client, unless the client is a Capital Market Institution acting on behalf of its own client, in which case the asset must be registered in the name of that client.

d. Where the asset concerned is a security acquired overseas, title to the asset may be registered or recorded in the name of an overseas custodian or in the name of the Capital Market Institution, provided that the Capital Market Institution has satisfied itself that is not feasible for the asset to be registered or recorded in the client's name. A Capital Market Institution must obtain the prior written agreement of a client to the client's assets being recorded or registered in the name of an overseas custodian or in the name of the Capital Market Institution and must notify the client in writing of any adverse consequences of the assets being registered or recorded other than in its name. A Capital Market Institution must in particular:

1) before holding or arranging for an overseas custodian to hold client assets outside the Kingdom, notify the client in writing that there may be different settlement, legal and regulatory requirements in the relevant jurisdiction to those which apply in the Kingdom, in particular in relation to the segregation of client assets; and
2) obtain the clients prior agreement to registering or recording legal title to their assets in the name of the Capital Market Institution and to the fact that the client assets may not be segregated from the Capital Market Institution's own assets and may be subject to claims from the Capital Market Institution creditors in the event of its failure.

Article 86: Lending of Client Securities

a. A Capital Market Institution must not lend securities belonging to a client or engage in such lending activities with a client except after obtaining the client's express consent to this in writing.

b. Any securities lending activity must be subject to appropriate terms and conditions, including, as relevant, those specified by Annex 5.2 to these Regulations.

c. A Capital Market Institution must at all times during the period of a securities transaction:

1) ensure that the borrower provides collateral to cover the realizable value of the securities being lent;
2) daily monitor whether the amount of the collateral is sufficient to cover the realizable value of the securities; and
3) if the amount of the collateral is not sufficient to cover the realizable value of the securities, make up the level of collateral, unless otherwise agreed in writing with the client.

d. Securities, which are registered or otherwise held together for more than one client must not be used for the purpose of a securities lending transaction unless all of the clients to whom the securities belong consent in writing and, if only some of the clients consent, the capital market institution must ensure and demonstrate that only securities belonging to clients who have given their consent are used for this purpose.

e. A Capital Market Institution must ensure that all securities lending transactions are appropriately documented.

Article 87: Assessment of Custodian

a. A Capital Market Institution person owes a duty of care to a client in deciding or recommending where to hold the client assets.

b. A Capital Market Institution must undertake a risk assessment prior to recommending or deciding to hold client assets with a custodian to ensure that the custodian has in place adequate arrangements to safeguard the assets, and is subject to appropriate standards of regulatory oversight. A Capital Market Institution must conduct a risk assessment of custodians holding client assets as frequently as required to be satisfied of the above matters on a continuing basis.

c. A Capital Market Institution must notify its client before holding that client's assets with a custodian in the capital market institution's group and must not hold the relevant client's assets with a custodian in its group if the client objects.

d. A Capital Market Institution must not hold client assets with or recommend an overseas custodian to a client unless the proposed arrangements with the overseas custodian are necessary for the purpose of the acquisition or holding of securities outside the Kingdom.

e. The requirements set out in paragraphs (a) to (c) of this Article apply in relation to overseas custodians. In carrying out a risk assessment in relation to an overseas custodian, a capital market institution must take into account the extent to which the overseas custodian is subject to regulatory obligations at least equivalent to those imposed on custodians under the Capital Market Law and the Implementing Regulations.

Article 88: Clients Agreements

a. Before a Capital Market Institution provides custody services to a client, it must agree in writing with that client appropriate terms of business which must cover the matters set out in paragraph (b) of this Article. Before a Capital Market Institution provides custody services to a counterparty, it must send a written notice to the counterparty which must cover the matters set out in paragraph (b) of this Article.

b. The agreement or the notice referred to in paragraph (a) of this Article must cover the following matters:

1) The manner in which the client assets will be registered;
2) Arrangements for the receiving and giving of instructions by the client in respect of custody services;
3) The Capital Market Institution's liability to the client;
4) Any lien or security interest taken over the client assets by the Capital Market Institution or other party;
5) The circumstances in which the Capital Market Institution may realize client assets which are held as collateral, to meet the client's liabilities;
6) How the Capital Market Institution will deal with the claiming and receipt of dividends, commissions and other income and entitlements accruing to the client;
7) How the Capital Market Institution will deal with corporate actions, such as the voting of shares, capital reorganizations and take-overs;
8) The information to be provided to the client in respect of client assets that the Capital Market Institution holds;
9) The provision of statements to the client;
10) The fees and charges to the client in respect of the custody services; and
11) An explanation of whether the client's assets will be pooled with the assets of other clients and an explanation of the effect of that pooling.

Article 89: Custodian Agreement

a. Before a Capital Market Institution holds client assets with a custodian, it must agree in writing with the custodian appropriate terms of business, which must cover the following:

1) that the title of the account in which any client assets will be held indicates that the assets credited to the account do not belong to the Capital Market Institution;
2) that the custodian is not to permit withdrawal of any client assets from the account other than to the Capital Market Institution or to another person as the custodian may be instructed by the capital market institution;
3) that the custodian will hold or record a client asset belonging to the Capital Market Institution's client separate from any securities or other assets of the custodian, and that it will treat the assets in the account as client assets;
4) that the custodian will deliver to the Capital Market Institution a statement as at a date or dates specified by the capital market institution which details the description and amounts of all the securities credited to the account and the statement must be delivered to the Capital Market Institution within 7 days of the date of the statement; and
5) that the custodian will not claim any lien, right of retention or sale, over the securities standing to the credit of any account designated in accordance with sub-paragraph (a)(1) of this Article, except:

- where the clients whose assets are held in the account have consented; or
- in respect of any charges relating to the administration or custody of the client asset.

b. The requirements of paragraph (a) apply if client assets are lodged in an account with an overseas custodian.

Article 90: Reconciliations

a. A Capital Market Institution must as often as necessary, but at least every 7 days, reconcile its record of client assets which it does not physically hold, with statements obtained from the Depository Centre, custodians or overseas custodians and, in the case of dematerialized securities not held with the Depository Centre or through a custodian or overseas custodian, statements obtained from the person who maintains the record of entitlement.

b. A Capital Market Institution must as often as necessary, but at least every six months, carry out:

1) a count of all client assets physically held by it, and reconcile the results of that count to its record in this regard; and
2) a reconciliation between the Capital Market Institution's record of client holdings, and its record of the location of client assets.

c. The count and reconciliation in paragraph (b) of this Article must cover all of the Capital Market Institution's books and records, and must be performed by counting and reconciling all securities and other client assets as at the same date.

d. A Capital Market Institution must perform the reconciliations within 10 days of the date to which the reconciliation relates.

e. A Capital Market Institution must within 3 days correct any discrepancy, which is revealed by any reconciliation that it has carried out. If the Capital Market Institution discovers any discrepancy, which amounts to a shortfall, it must within 3 days make good any shortfall and if the discrepancy is not resolved within 7 days, report the matter to the Authority.

Article 91: Client Statements

a. A Capital Market Institution must, as often as necessary, but not less frequently than annually, provide each client in writing with a statement prepared in accordance with paragraph (d) of this Article.

b. A Capital Market Institution is required to provide a statement in paragraph (a) of this Article to a client for whom a client asset, collateral or other asset has been held at any time during the capital market institution's financial year even when there are no holdings at the statement date. However, there is no requirement to provide a statement where the client's account with the Capital Market Institution has been closed, and the Capital Market Institution has sent the client a closing statement which demonstrates that the capital market institution no longer holds a client asset, collateral or other asset for the client.

c. Statements may be sent electronically with the client's prior written consent where the Capital Market Institution is capable of reproducing the statement and keeping a record of its dispatch.

d. All statements produced by or on behalf of a capital market institution in accordance with paragraph (a) of this Article must list all client assets, collateral and other assets owned by the client for which the Capital Market Institution is accountable and:

1) identify any securities registered in the client's name, separately from those registered in another name;
2) identify those securities and assets which are being used as collateral, or have been pledged to third parties, separately from any other securities and asset;
3) show the market value of any collateral held, as at the date of the statement; and
4) be based on information as of trade date or settlement date, and the basis must be notified to the client.

5.18.4 Chapter Four – Collateral and Money and Assets Passed to Third Parties

Article 92: Scope of Application

a. This Chapter applies to Capital Market Institutions which hold collateral or provide collateral to third parties, or which pass client money or client assets to settlement agents.

b. Article 93 of these Regulations applies to:

1) collateral that is subject to the Client Money Rules or the Client Asset Rules; and
2) client money and client assets passed to settlement agents.

c. Article 94 of these Regulations applies to collateral that is not subject to the Client Money Rules or the Client Asset Rules.

Article 93: Collateral Subject to the Client Money Rules or the Client Asset Rules

a. A Capital Market Institution must take reasonable steps to ensure that collateral is properly safeguarded. Where the capital market institution has reasonable grounds to believe that the collateral will not be properly utilized or safeguarded by a third party, then it must withdraw the collateral from the third party unless the client has indicated otherwise in writing.

b. Collateral held by the Capital Market Institution must be separately identifiable from assets of the Capital Market Institution. The capital market institution must be able to identify at all times the client providing the collateral.

c. Where a Capital Market Institution passes collateral of a client which is client money or client assets to a counterparty in the Kingdom, it must:

1) take reasonable steps to ensure that the counterparty treats the collateral as client money or client assets; or
2) have obtained the consent of the client in the terms of business not to treat the money or assets as client money or client assets.

d. A Capital Market Institution must not undertake a transaction for a client that involves client money or client assets being passed either as collateral to a counterparty or to a settlement agent outside the Kingdom before formally notifying the client that:

1) his money or assets may be passed to such person;
2) the regulatory regime applying to such persons is different from that of the Kingdom; and
3) it has taken reasonable steps to ensure that the counterparty or settlement agent will effectively segregate the collateral from its own assets under the law of the country in which the counterparty or settlement agent is located.

e. A Capital Market Institution who transfers clients' collateral to an exchange or clearing house must:

1) notify the exchange or clearing house that the collateral is client money or client assets, and that the Capital Market Institution is under an obligation to keep clients' collateral separate from the capital market institution's collateral; and
2) instruct the exchange or clearing centre to:

- credit the value of that collateral passed by the capital market institution to the Capital Market Institution's client transaction account with the exchange or clearing house; and
- treat the sale proceeds of that collateral in accordance with the requirements of that exchange or clearing house.

f. Before a Capital Market Institution deposits a client asset as collateral with, mortgages, pledges, charges or grants another encumbrance over any client asset to, a third party, it must:

1) properly consider the credit risk to its clients;
2) notify the client that the collateral will not be registered in the client's name; and
3) obtain the client's prior written consent whether in the terms of business or otherwise.

g. The Capital Market Institution must have prior written consent from its client if it proposes to return to the client collateral other than the original collateral, or original type of collateral, or money.

h. A Capital Market Institution must:

1) notify the Authority as soon as it is aware of the insolvency of a person to whom it has passed collateral; and
2) notify the Authority as soon as reasonably practicable, of its intentions regarding making good any shortfall in client money or client assets that has arisen or may arise, stating the amounts involved.

Article 94: Other Collateral

a. Other collateral is collateral that a Capital Market Institution is entitled to treat as its own provided the Capital Market Institution is obliged to return equivalent assets to the client upon conclusion of a transaction or satisfaction of an obligation.

b. A Capital Market Institution must not receive or hold other collateral under this Article in the case of collateral of a client before it has:

1) determined in accordance with Article 43 of these Regulations that the taking of collateral is suitable for the client;
2) taken reasonable steps to ensure that the client understands the nature of the risks involved in his providing other collateral to the Capital Market Institution;
3) disclosed to the client in the terms of business that his collateral will not be subject to the protections under the Client Asset Rules and as a consequence, his collateral will not be separated from the assets of the Capital Market Institution and will be used by the capital market institution in the course of the Capital Market Institution's business, and he will therefore rank as a general creditor of the capital market institution; and
4) ensured that it maintains adequate records to enable it to meet any prospective obligations including the return of equivalent assets to the client.

5.19 PART 8: INSOLVENCY PROVISIONS

Article 95: Supervision of Insolvency Proceedings The Authority shall supervise the compulsory and voluntary liquidation of Capital Market Institutions and shall have the power to take any of the steps set out in this Part, which it considers appropriate to ensure the proper protection of the rights of clients of the capital market institution.

Article 96: Rights of Clients on Insolvency of a Capital Market Institution Holding Client Money and Assets

a. If, on an insolvency event of a Capital Market Institution holding client money or client assets, the Capital Market Institution has or may have insufficient client assets or client money to satisfy its obligations to return such money and assets to its clients, then the claims of clients in respect of any shortfall in client assets and client money rank ahead of all other creditors.

b. The Authority may represent the interests of all clients who may be entitled to the return of client money or client assets, or who may have any other claim relating to their account, in insolvency, liquidation or settlement proceedings of Capital Market Institutions.

Article 97: Settlement Proceedings

a. If a Capital Market Institution proposes to submit a petition to request a settlement under the Bankruptcy Regulations, the capital market institution must:

1) notify the Authority of the proposed petition at least 14 days prior to its submission;
2) provide the Authority with any documentation it requests; and
3) cooperate with the Authority prior to initiating settlement proceedings in order to ensure that client money, client assets and all other claims of clients relating to their accounts are resolved.

b. The Authority may attend and be heard at any proceedings relating to the insolvency or bankruptcy of the Capital Market Institution, including:

1) any meeting of members or creditors of the Capital Market Institution; or
2) any application for conciliation with creditors or settlement to prevent bankruptcy under the Bankruptcy Regulations.

c. No settlement proceedings in respect of a Capital Market Institution may be granted unless the Authority consents to it.

d. From the initiation of settlement proceedings to the end of such proceedings, the Capital Market Institution may not, without the prior consent of the Authority, undertake any of the following actions:

1) accept further client money or client assets;
2) dispose of client money or client assets; or
3) compromise, effect a mortgage, charge or pledge, give a guarantee, donate any part of its assets or effect a transfer of ownership in relation to any of its assets.

e. The Authority is an interested party for the purposes of any proceedings relating to a Capital Market Institution under the Bankruptcy Regulations.

Article 98: Liquidation Proceedings

a. If a Capital Market Institution enters into the stage of liquidation under the Bankruptcy Regulations, the Capital Market Institution must:

1) notify the Authority of the liquidation and of the proposed date of any meeting of members or creditors relating to the liquidation;
2) provide the Authority with any documentation it requests in relation to the liquidation proceedings; and

3) cooperate with the Authority prior to initiating settlement proceedings in order to ensure that client money, client assets and all other claims of clients relating to their accounts are resolved.

b. No appointment of a liquidator in respect of a capital market institution will be effective unless the Authority consents to it.

c. The Authority may attend and be heard at any proceedings relating to the insolvency or bankruptcy of the Capital Market Institution, including:

1) any meeting of members or creditors of the capital market institution; and
2) any liquidation proceedings under the Bankruptcy Regulations.

d. From the initiation of liquidation under the Bankruptcy Regulations, the Capital Market Institution may not, without the prior consent of the Authority, undertake any of the following actions:

1) accept further client money or client assets; or
2) dispose of client money or client assets; or
3) compromise, effect a mortgage, charge or pledge, give a guarantee, donate any part of its assets or effect a transfer of ownership in relation to its assets.

e. The Authority may direct the liquidator to take such steps as the Authority considers fit to establish the entitlements of clients of the Capital Market Institution at any time, or to appoint a third party to take such steps.

5.20 PART 9: PUBLICATION AND ENTRY INTO FORCE

Article 99: Publication and Entry into Force These Regulations shall become effective upon their publication.

6 Capital Markets Law

(Article Headings have been added for convenience and do not constitute part of the law.)

6.0.1 Chapter 1: Definitions

Article 1: Definitions Unless the context otherwise indicates, the following words and phrases, wherever they appear in this Law, shall have the meaning herein specified:

Kingdom: the Kingdom of Saudi Arabia.

The Authority: the Capital Market Authority.

The Board: the Board of the Capital Market Authority.

The Chairman: the Chairman of the Board of the Capital Market Authority.

Person: any natural or legal person that is recognized as such under the laws of the Kingdom.

The Exchange: the Saudi Stock Exchange.

Trading: buying and selling of securities.

Issuer: a person who is issuing or intending to issue securities.

Affiliate: a person who controls another person or is controlled by that other person, or who is jointly being controlled with that person by a third person.

Control: the direct or indirect ability or power to exercise effective influence over the actions and decisions of another person.

Underwriter: a person who buys securities from the issuer or an affiliate of the issuer for the purpose of offering, placing and marketing such securities to the public, or a person who sells securities on behalf of the issuer or an affiliate of the issuer for the purpose of making a public offering and placement of such securities. Relatives: husband, wife and minor children.

Placement or offering of securities: issuing securities, inviting the public to subscribe therefor or the direct or indirect marketing thereof; or any statement, announcement or communication that has the effect of selling, issuing or offering securities, but does not include preliminary negotiations or contracts entered into with or among underwriters.

Investment Adviser: an adviser who provides, offers or agrees to provide, advice to others in their capacity as investors or potential investors, in relation to purchasing, selling, subscribing or underwriting a security, or exercising any right conferred by a security to acquire, dispose of, underwrite or convert a security.

The Center: the Securities Depositary Center.

The Committee: the Committee for the Resolution of Securities Disputes.

The Implementing Regulations: the rules, instructions and procedures issued by the Authority for the implementation of the provisions of this Law.

Internal Regulations: the regulations issued by the Authority in relation to the Authority's administrative and financial affairs and its personnel and staff affairs.

Article 2: Securities Defined Subject to the provisions of Article three hereof, for the purposes of this Law, the term "Securities" shall mean:

a. convertible and tradeable shares of companies;

b. Tradable debt instruments issued by companies, the government, public institutions or public organizations;

c. investment units issued by investment funds;

d. any instruments representing profit participation rights, any rights in the distribution of assets; or either or the foregoing;

e. any other rights or instruments which the Board determines should be included or treated as Securities if the Board believes that this would further the safety of the market or the protection of investors. The Board can exercise its power to exempt from the definition of Securities rights or instruments that otherwise would be treated as Securities under paragraphs (a, b, c, d) of this Article if it believes that it is not necessary to treat them as Securities, based on the requirements of the safety of the market and the protection of investors.

Article 3: Bills of Exchange Commercial bills such as cheques, bills of exchange, order notes, documentary credits, money transfers, instruments exclusively traded among banks, and insurance policies shall not be considered Securities.

6.0.2 Chapter 2: The Capital Market Authority

Article 4: The Capital Markets Authority
a. An Authority to be named "The Capital Market Authority" is hereby established in the Kingdom and shall directly report to the President of the Council of Ministers. It shall have a legal personality and financial and administrative autonomy. It shall be vested with all authorities as may be necessary to discharge its responsibilities and functions under this Law. The Authority shall enjoy exemptions and facilities enjoyed by public organizations. Its personnel shall be subject to the Labour Law.

b. The Authority shall not have the right to engage in any commercial activities, to have a special interest in any project intended for profit, to borrow or lend any funds, or to acquire, own or issue any Securities.

Article 5: Authority as Regulator
a. The Authority shall be the agency responsible for issuing regulations, rules and instructions, and for applying the provisions of this Law. To achieve these objectives, the Authority shall:

1. Regulate and develop the Exchange, seek to develop and improve methods of systems and entities trading in Securities, and develop the procedures that would reduce the risks related to Securities transactions.
2. Regulate the issuance of Securities and monitor Securities and dealing in Securities.
3. Regulate and monitor the works and activities of parties subject to the control and supervision of the Authority.

4. Protect citizens and investors in Securities from unfair and unsound practices or practices involving fraud, deceit, cheating or manipulation.
5. Seek to achieve fairness, efficiency and transparency in Securities transactions.
6. Regulate and monitor the full disclosure of information regarding Securities and their issuers, the dealings of informed persons and major shareholders and investors, and define and make available information which the participants in the market should provide and disclose to shareholders and the public.
7. Regulate proxy and purchase requests and public offers of shares.
8. license the establishment of special purposes entity, and regulate and control its business, uses, issuance of securities, the registration in its registry established by the Authority and the provisions of its articles of incorporation, and regulate the provisions of the registration of funds transferred to it, including documentation of the rights thereof and its legal standing against others, and the issuance of rules governing thereof.
9. Regulate the pledge of securities and its enforcement.

b. The Authority may publish a draft of regulations and rules before issuing or amending them. The regulations, rules and instructions issued by the Authority shall be effective in the manner prescribed under their provisions.

c. For the purpose of conducting all investigations which, in the opinion of the Board, are necessary for the enforcement of the provisions of this Law and other regulations and rules issued pursuant to this Law, the members of the Authority and its employees designated by the Board are empowered to subpoena witnesses, take evidence, and require the production of any books, papers, or other documents which the Authority deems relevant or material to its investigation.

The Authority shall have the power to carry out inspections of the records or any other materials, whoever the holder may be, to determine whether the person concerned has violated, or is about to violate any provision of this Law, the Implementing Regulations or the rules issued by the Authority.

d. The special purposes entity shall have legal personality and financial autonomy, and it shall cease to exist with the end of the purpose for which it was established for in accordance with the rules and regulations issued by the Authority.

Article 6: Powers of the Authority

a. The Authority shall have the power to carry out its functions under this Law as well as the regulations, rules and instructions issued pursuant thereto including, but not limited the power to:

1. Set forth policies and plans, conduct studies and issue necessary rules to achieve the Authority's objectives.
2. Issue and amend the Implementing Regulations as may be necessary to enforce the provisions of this Law.
3. Approve the offering of Securities.
4. Give advice and make recommendations to government authorities in respect of matters that would contribute to the development of the Exchange and the protection of investors in Securities.
5. Suspend the Exchange's activities for a period of not more than one day; and in cases where the Authority or the Minister of Finance deems it necessary to suspend the Exchange's activity for more than one day, the approval of this decision must be issued by the Minister of Finance.
6. Approve the listing, cancel or suspend the listing, of any Saudi Security traded on the Exchange of any Saudi issuer, on any stock exchange outside the Kingdom.
7. Prohibit any Security or suspend the issuance or trading of any Securities on the Exchange, as the Authority may deem necessary.
8. Determine the maximum or the minimum commissions to be charged by brokers to their clients if the Board deems it appropriate, and approve the fees and other commissions to be charged by the Exchange and the Depositary Center.
9. In addition to other provisions of relevant regulations, the Authority shall have the right to establish standards and conditions required for the auditors who audit the books and records of the Exchange, the Depositary Center, brokerage companies, investment funds and joint stock companies listed on the Exchange. The Authority, subject to its supervisory responsibilities, shall have the right to delegate this responsibility to the Saudi Organization for Certified Public Accountants.
10. Determine the contents of annual and periodical financial statements, reports and documents that should be submitted by issuers offering Securities for public subscription or the issuers whose Securities are listed on the Exchange.
11. Define and explain the terms and provisions set out in this Law.
12. Issue decisions, instructions and set the procedure as deemed necessary for the implementation of the provisions of this Law and the Implementing Regulations, and conduct inquiries and investigations regarding violations of the provisions of this Law and the Implementing Regulations.
13. Set Internal Regulations and issue instructions and set the procedures as necessary for the management of the Authority.
14. Approve the regulations, rules and policies of the Exchange and the Depositary Center.
15. Prepare the regulations and rules for the surveillance and supervision of entities subject to the provisions of this Law.
16. Approve the establishment, merger and liquidation of investment funds and their related operating rules in accordance with the provisions of Article Thirty-nine of this Law.
17. Appoint a licensed auditor to audit the Authority's financial statements and final accounts.
18. Grant the necessary licenses to be issued in accordance with the provisions of this Law and its Implementing Regulations, including the licensing of rating companies and agencies and the conditions thereof.
19. Prepare the Authority's annual budget. b. Upon starting to exercise its powers in accordance with this Law and its Implementing Regulations, the Authority shall coordinate with the Saudi Arabian Monetary Agency in connection with the procedures that it intends to undertake and which may have an impact on the monetary situation.

Article 7: The Board of the Authority

a. The Authority shall have a board known as the "Board of the Capital Market Authority" comprising five members, who shall be natural Saudi Arabian persons working on a full time basis, and shall be professionally qualified. The Board members shall be appointed, and their salaries and financial benefits determined, by Royal Order. The Royal Order shall specify from the Board members the chairman and deputy chairman who will replace the chairman in his absence.

b. The term of membership of the Board shall be five years, renewable once. The member shall remain in his office on the termination of his membership term until a successor is appointed.

c. The Board shall set forth the Internal Regulations of the Authority and the manner in which the personnel, advisors, auditors and any other experts shall be appointed as may be necessary for carrying out the responsibilities and functions entrusted to the Authority. The Board shall determine their salaries and remunerations.

d. The Board shall exercise all authorities entrusted to the Authority in accordance with the provisions of this Law. The Board will specify how the Authority's functions, responsibilities and operations will be organized among its divisions and departments. The Internal Regulations of the Authority will set forth the requirements for the operation of these departments and divisions. Except for the powers conferred by this Law exclusively upon the Board, the Board may delegate, by a published resolution, any of its functions. The Board shall, however, at its discretion, retain the power to review the actions and decisions made by those who had been delegated with such powers. Such a review will be made at the Board's initiative, upon the request of one of its members, or upon the request of a party to a lawsuit arising under the provisions of this Law and in compliance with the rules issued by the Authority.

Article 8: Board Employees Any person who becomes an employee or a member of the Board of the Authority must, immediately upon accepting its functions, disclose to the Authority, in the manner set forth in the regulations of the Authority, the Securities he owns or has at his disposal or the disposal of one of his relatives, and thereafter declare any change thereon, within three days of becoming aware of such change. Any of those who become agents for the Authority must also make this disclosure in connection to what is related to the work entrusted to them, in the manner specified in the regulations of the Authority.

Article 9: Limits on Outside Employment The members of the Board and the employees of the Authority shall not engage in any other profession or job, including occupying a position or a post in any company, in the government, or public or private institutions. Furthermore, they shall not provide advice to companies and private institutions.

Article 10: Board Meetings
a. The Board shall hold its meetings at the request of its chairman. Meetings should be attended by at least three of its members including the chairman or vice chairman. Its decisions shall be made upon a vote of a majority of the members attending the meeting. In case of equal votes, the chairman of the meeting will have a casting vote.

b. The Internal Regulations will set forth the conditions and requirements with respect to convening meetings of the Board, including the notice for a meeting. The rules issued by the Authority may provide that it is permitted to vote for resolutions to be passed by the Board in emergency situations by telephone or by any other means of communication.

Article 11: Board Chairman The chairman of the Board shall be the Authority's chief executive officer who shall implement the Authority's policy and shall be responsible for the management of its affairs, including the following:

a. Implementing the decisions taken by the Board.

b. Signing, alone or jointly with others, reports, accounting statements, financial statements, correspondence and the Authority's documents.

c. The Authority's administrative and financial affairs.

Article 12: Vice-Chairman
a. The vice chairman shall carry out the tasks and duties of the chairman if the chairman is absent, is unable to carry out his duties, or if his position becomes vacant.

b. The chairman may delegate to another member of the Board or to any employee of the Authority some of the powers entrusted to him provided that such delegation shall be specific and in writing.

Article 13: Funding the Authority
a. The financial resources of the Authority shall consist of the following:

1. Fees for services and commissions charged by the Authority in accordance with the provisions of this Law and the regulations and instructions issued in pursuance thereof.
2. Charges against using its facilities, return on its funds, and proceeds of the sale of its assets.
3. Fines and financial penalties imposed on violators of the provisions of this Law.
4. Funds provided by the government to the Authority.
5. Any other resources determined by the Board.

b. The Board shall determine the fees to be paid to the Authority for the following matters:

1. Registration of Securities with the Authority.
2. Listing of Securities on the Exchange.
3. Trading of Securities.
4. Licensing and renewal of licenses of brokerage companies or investment advisers.
5. Registration of investment funds.

Article 14: Annual Budget The Authority shall have a separate annual budget that will be submitted to the Minister of Finance and will be approved in accordance with applicable regulations. Surplus funds collected by the Authority under Article 13 of this Law and under the provisions, rules and instructions issued thereunder, shall be remitted to the Ministry of Finance after deducting all current and capital expenses or other expenses needed by the Authority. However, the Authority shall maintain a general reserve equal to the double of its expenditures as reported in its previous annual budget.

Article 15: Nature of Debts Owed to the Authority Any sums owed to the Authority by third parties shall be considered as public funds and enjoy the same treatment as debts owed to the Public Treasury and shall be collected in accordance with the procedures for the collection of debts due to the Public Treasury.

Article 16: Annual Report The chairman of the Board shall present to the President of the Council of Ministers an annual report on the Authority's activities and its financial position during the preceding year within ninety days from the end of the year.

Article 17: Confidential Information Any undisclosed information obtained by the Authority is considered confidential. The Authority may disclose any part of this information as the Board deems necessary for the protection of investors.

Article 18: Authority's Right to Information Government agencies and other persons must provide the Authority with the documents and information it requires for the purposes of carrying out its duties in accordance with the provisions of this Law.

Article 19: Internal Regulations The internal regulations issued pursuant to this Law will define the rules, instructions and procedures relating to the Authority's administrative and financial affairs and the Authority's personnel affairs, including rules of professional conduct and the means of development of the Authority's operations, realization of its objectives and the enhancement of the performance and professional and academic standards of its staff.

6.0.3 Chapter Three – The Stock Exchange

Article 20: Stock Exchange
a. A market shall be established in the Kingdom for the trading in Securities which shall be known as the "Saudi Stock Exchange", and will have the legal status of a joint stock company in accordance with the provisions of this Law. This Exchange shall be the sole entity authorized to carry out trading in Securities in the Kingdom.

b. Securities listed or traded in a regulated market outside the Kingdom are not subject to the provisions of this Law even though trading in such a market originates by orders transmitted telephonically or electronically from within the Kingdom, with the exception of what may be agreed upon by the Authority with other foreign authorities.

c. The objectives of the Exchange include the following:

1. Ensuring fair, efficient and transparent listing requirements, trading rules and technical mechanisms and information for Securities listed on the Exchange;
2. Providing sound and rapid settlement and clearance rules and procedures through its Securities Depositary Center;
3. Establishing and enforcing professional standards for brokers and their agents;
4. Ensuring the financial strength and soundness of brokers through the periodic review of their compliance with capital adequacy requirements, and setting such arrangements to protect the funds and Securities in the custody of brokerage companies.

d. The Exchange shall not distribute to its members any cash or in kind distributions by way of a dividend without the approval of the Board.

Article 21: Trading on the Exchange Securities listed on the Exchange shall be traded through transactions among brokers, each on behalf of its client, and shall be evidenced by entries in the Exchange records, in accordance with the provisions of Chapter Four of this Law, unless such transactions are excluded from trading pursuant to the rules and instructions issued by the Authority.

Article 22: Exchange Rules and Governance
a. The regulations and rules of the Exchange shall specify the terms and requirements of the membership of the Exchange.

b. The Exchange shall be managed by a Board of Directors comprising nine members who shall be appointed by a Council of Ministers Resolution upon nomination by the chairman of the Board of the Authority and who will choose from among them a chairman and a vice chairman. The membership will be as follows:

1. A representative of the Ministry of Finance.
2. A representative of the Ministry of Commerce and Industry.
3. A representative of the Saudi Arabian Monetary Agency.
4. Four members representing licensed brokerage companies.
5. Two members representing the joint stock companies listed on the Exchange.

c. The term of the membership at the board of directors of the Exchange shall be three years renewable one or more times.

d. The regulations and instructions issued by the Board of the Authority shall specify the procedures related to convening the meetings of the Board of Directors of the Exchange, the decisions making process at the board of directors, the plans for conducting the affairs of the board of directors, the powers and responsibilities entrusted to each of the board of directors and the executive manager and all other related administrative and financial affairs.

e. The board of directors of the Exchange shall appoint an executive manager with the approval of the Board of the Authority. The manager appointed shall not have the right to perform any other governmental or commercial work or to have any interest or ownership in any brokerage company on the Exchange. The executive manager may be removed from his position by decision of the board of directors of the Exchange.

Article 23: Board of the Exchange
a. The Board of Directors of the Exchange shall propose the necessary regulations, rules and instructions for the operation of the Exchange including the following matters:

1. Conditions for the listing of and the trading in Securities.
2. The minimum capital required for brokerage companies and the financial assurances required from such companies or their employees.
3. The immediate and timely publication of information regarding transactions executed in Securities traded on the Exchange, and the obligations of issuers of Securities, shareholders and members to disclose such information to the Exchange as the Exchange deems necessary.
4. Standards of professional conduct applicable to the Exchange's members and their employees, the members of the board of directors, the Exchange's executive manager and employees, including the procedures and disciplinary sanctions applicable against those who violate such standards or any other conditions or requirements set forth in the regulations and instructions.
5. Settling disputes among members of the Exchange and between the members and their clients.
6. Conditions and requirements for membership of the Exchange and the appropriate limitations and procedures that permit licensed brokerage companies but not members of the Exchange to execute their transactions on the Exchange.

7. The determination of the fees and commissions that brokers charge for their services.

8. Any other rules and instructions that the Exchange deems necessary for the protection of investors through ensuring fairness, efficiency and transparency in all of the Exchange's related affairs.

b. The Exchange shall submit to the Authority the regulations, rules and instructions for the operation of the Exchange and the amendments thereof for approval by the Board.

Article 24: Fees The Exchange may charge fees on its members, on issuers of Securities listed on the Exchange and others for services it provides to them.

Article 25: Disputes Committee

a. The Authority shall establish a committee known as the "Committee for the Resolution of Securities Disputes" which shall have jurisdiction over the disputes falling under the provisions of this Law, its Implementing Regulations, and the regulations, rules and instructions issued by the Authority and the Exchange, with respect to the public and private actions. The Committee shall have all necessary powers to investigate and settle complaints and suits, including the power to issue subpoenas, issue decisions, impose sanctions and order the production of evidence and documents.

b. The Committee will consist of legal advisors specialized in the doctrine of transactions and capital markets, and experts in commercial and financial affairs and Securities. The members of the Committee shall be appointed by a Board decision for a three-year term renewable. The members of the Committee must not have any direct or indirect financial or commercial interest or have a family relationship up to the fourth degree with the parties to the complaint or the suit brought before the Committee. The Committee must start considering the complaint or the suit within a period not to exceed fourteen days from the date of filing of the complaint or the suit with the Committee.

c. The Committee's jurisdiction shall include claims against decisions and actions taken by the Authority or the Exchange and the Committee shall have the right to issue a decision awarding damages and request to revert to the original status or issue another decision as appropriate and that would guarantee the rights of the aggrieved.

d. The regulations and rules of the Authority shall specify the procedures that the Committee must follow regarding the complaints and the suits presented to it.

e. No complaint or statement of claim may be filed with the Committee without being filed first with the Authority and a 90 day period has passed from the filing date, unless the Authority notifies the grievant otherwise of the permissibility of submitting before the expiration of this period.

f. The Committee's decision may be appealed before the Appeal Panel within thirty days from their notification date.

g. An Appeal Panel is to be formed by a Council of Ministers' decision, and it shall have three members representing the Ministry of Finance, the Ministry of Commerce and Industry and the Bureau of Experts at the Council of Ministers. The members of the Appeal Panel shall be appointed for a three-year term renewable. The Appeal Panel shall have the discretion to refuse to review the decisions of the Committee for the Resolution of Securities Disputes, to affirm such decisions, to undertake a de novo review of the complaint or suit based on the record developed at the hearing before the Committee and to issue such decision as it deems appropriate in relation to the complaint or the suit. The decisions of the Appeal Panel shall be final.

h. At the Authority or the Exchange's request, final decisions shall be enforced through the government agency responsible for the enforcement of judicial judgments. Decisions issued in favor of the parties pursuant to Articles 55, 56 and 57 of Chapter 10 of this Law shall be enforced by such parties in accordance with the procedure for enforcement of judicial judgment in civil proceedings.

i. Evidence in Securities cases shall be admissible in all forms including electronic or computer data, telephone recordings, facsimile messages and electronic mail.

6.0.4 Chapter Four – The Securities Depositary Center

Article 26: Depositary Center

a. The Board of Directors of the Exchange shall establish a department to be known as the "Securities Depositary Center" which shall be the sole entity in the Kingdom authorized to practice the operations of deposit, transfer, settlement, clearing and registering ownership of Saudi Securities traded on the Exchange. The Exchange's Board of Directors may convert the Securities Depositary Center into a company after obtaining the approval of the Authority's Board for the conversion. The Board may give its approval indicating the requirements of the company's structure and its operations, as it deems appropriate and necessary for the safety of the market and the protection of investors.

b. The Depositary Center's operating rules shall specify the sound and efficient procedures which shall ensure the efficient operations for registration, settlement and clearance of Securities traded on the Exchange in a regulatory manner, including the procedures to be followed for the disbursement of funds to investors following settlement. The Depositary Center may maintain cash accounts for settlement and clearance purposes of transactions in the context of its operations. The Authority has the power to adopt, amend, repeal or suspend any of the Depositary Center's operating regulations or rules if it deems appropriate.

Article 27: Registration and Procedures

a. The registration of ownership of Securities traded on the Exchange and the settlement and clearance of Securities shall be made by entries in the Depositary Center's records. Ownership of Securities traded on the Exchange must be registered with the Depositary Center in order to be protected against third party claims. The Depositary Center's records will also report pledges or other claims related to the Securities traded on the Exchange.

b. The Depositary Center shall be the sole entity to register all property rights in Securities traded on the Exchange. The final mentions reported in the records of the Depositary Center shall serve as conclusive evidence and proof of ownership of the Securities indicated therein together with the encumbrances and rights associated therewith, subject to the provisions of paragraph (d) of this Article.

c. Registration of ownership of Securities shall be effective from the time of final verification by the Depositary Center of the authenticity of the ownership documents. The Depositary Center shall promptly register all transactions effected upon being reported to and received by the Depositary Center with no delay. If the Depositary Center has reason to doubt actual or legal facts or consequences related to the registration of ownership or if the Depositary Center receives any notice that registration will cause damages to third parties, the Depositary Center may make a preliminary registration and, if it does so, it shall immediately commence an appropriate process to decide how the final registration for such Security shall be effected.

d. A person who believes that there is an error in the information entered into the registry so that the registry needs to be corrected or otherwise amended should make a written request to the manager of the Depositary Center or the person appointed by the manager to receive such requests. The Depositary Center shall correct or amend the registry after confirming the validity of the comments and information that are requested to be corrected or amended in the registry. Such correction or amendment can only be effected after notice and opportunity to comment by the person or persons the registry identifies as owning the Security, and giving them a reasonable opportunity to comment on the required correction or amendment.

e. The Depositary Center shall issue a certificate of registration upon request by the investor. The operating rules of the Depositary Center will specify the manner in which periodic reports to all the owners of Securities registered on the Depositary Center's records on the Securities owned by each owner and which are recorded with the Depositary Center's records.

f. Complaints about decisions with respect to the registration of Securities listed on the Exchange shall be brought before the Committee.

g. The Depositary Center shall be liable for any monetary damage suffered by an investor and resulting from the proven negligence or misconduct of the Depositary Center's employees that causes an error in the registration process.

h. The compensation due for the damage under paragraph (g) of this Article may be reduced or even eliminated if the claimant has contributed to causing the error in registration or if the error could have been avoided.

Article 28: Confidentiality of Depositary Center Records The employees of the Depositary Center and the Exchange and their independent auditors, advisors and consultants may not disclose any information about owners of Securities registered in the records except as set forth in the operating rules issued by the Depositary Center in this regard.

Article 29: Depositary Center Management The Board of Directors of the Exchange, with the approval of Board of the Authority, shall establish the necessary instructions for managing the Depositary Center's affairs, including the standards of professional conduct applicable to the Depositary Center's manager and personnel, to assure efficient and trustworthy operations of the Depositary Center.

Article 30: Depositary Center Fees The Depositary Center may charge fees and commissions for the provision of its services as may be provided for in the Implementing Regulations and the Depositary Center's operating rules.

6.0.5 Chapter Five – Brokers Regulation

Article 31: Brokerage Business, Eligibility Brokerage business is restricted to a person holding a valid license and who is an agent of a joint stock company that is licensed to perform brokerage activities, unless such person is exempt from these requirements in accordance with paragraph (c) of Article 32.

Article 32: Broker, Definition and Roles
a. Broker means a joint stock company that carries on brokerage activities and the broker agent who is working at the brokerage company and carries out all or part the following activities:

1. acts in a commercial capacity as an intermediary in the trading of Securities, other than persons working on the basis of a contractual arrangement as defined in paragraph (b) of this Article, including any person who commercially acts as a custodian for Securities;
2. presents in a commercial capacity an offer to others for obtaining financial assets in the form of Securities by opening an account through which transactions in Securities may be effected;
3. effects in a commercial capacity Securities transactions for its own account other than by way of issuing Securities, in order to create a market in Securities and make a profit out of the difference between offer prices for Securities and demand;
4. acquires or places Securities in a commercial capacity for an issuer or a person who controls an issuer;
5. acts as an intermediary in a commercial capacity - other than persons who act on the basis of a contractual arrangement as defined in paragraph (b) of this Article - including in arranging currency or securities swaps.

b. A portfolio manager means:

1. Any person acting in a commercial capacity who, on the basis of a contractual arrangement or otherwise, manages either Securities owned by a person or investment funds owned by a natural or judicial person which are intended for investment in Securities, and whose activities may include transactions in Securities or ordering Securities transactions to be effected for the account of the person with whom the contractual arrangements have been made;
2. Any person acting in a commercial capacity who, on the basis of a contractual arrangement, carries on the works mentioned in paragraph (a.5) of this Article. c. The Authority may specify, in the rules that it issues, such exemptions from the provisions of paragraphs (a) and (b) of this Article as it considers will achieve the safety of the market and the protection of the investor.

Article 33: Licensing, Capital Requirements
a. The Authority shall grant the license referred to under Article 31 within thirty days of receiving from the Exchange the information and documents that are required by the rules issued by the Authority and which demonstrate that the applicant satisfies the conditions and requirements necessary for obtaining a license to work as a broker or a broker's agent. The term of validity of the licenses must be defined and their holder must be subject to periodic qualification examination as set forth by the Implementing Regulations.

b. The regulations and rules of the Exchange shall set forth the requirements and conditions that must be met by applicants for obtaining a brokerage license. In addition to the requirements under the Exchange's regulations, the conditions for licensing or renewal of a license must include the following:

1. Criteria pertaining to an applicant's competence to act as a broker or a broker's agent;
2. Criteria of integrity or suitability for persons to conduct brokerage activities;
3. Minimum capital requirements that brokerage companies must continually meet, which must not be less than SR 50 million.

Article 34: Compliance with Regulations A broker and a broker's agent must observe the Exchange's regulations and rules pertaining to the regulation of brokers' business.

Article 35: Power to Investigate The Exchange may carry out investigations and inspections in connection with any licensed broker or broker's agent to verify whether that person or another person has violated, is violating or there is evidence substantiating that it is about to violate the regulations and instructions of the Exchange. The Exchange's investigation and inspection powers shall include the power to require the production of any person's testimony, papers, books and documents which the Exchange deems necessary or relevant to its inquiry. The Exchange may require the attendance of witnesses or the submission of documents and evidence. Inspection may take place wherever the records are situated. The Exchange can exercise its power to carry out such investigations and inspections by obtaining a subpoena or an order for interrogation or inspection or such other order from the Committee for Resolution of Securities Disputes. The Committee shall accept the Exchange's request for a subpoena or other order unless it is established to the Committee that the Exchange's request is arbitrary or involves abuse of power.

Article 36: Surrender of License Any broker or broker's agent may relinquish its license by filing a written notice of withdrawal with the Authority in accordance with such terms and conditions as the Authority may deem necessary or appropriate for the safety of the market or the protection of the investor.

Article 37: Filing of Reports Licensed brokers or broker's agents must file with the Authority and the Exchange such reports as required by the regulations and rules of the Authority and the Exchange.

Article 38: Liquidation The Authority shall supervise the compulsory and voluntary liquidation of the broker's business.

6.0.6 Chapter Six: Investment Funds and Collective Investment Schemes

Article 39: Investment Funds

a. An investment fund is a collective investment scheme aimed at providing investors therein with an opportunity to participate collectively in the profits of the scheme which is managed by a portfolio manager for specified fees.

b. The Authority shall assume the power to regulate the activities of investment funds managed by banks within two years from the enactment of this Law.

c. The Authority shall regulate portfolio managers and investment advisers and supervise them. This shall include setting the regulations, rules and instructions that pertain to the following:

1. The organizational structure;
2. Accounting systems and operational rules;
3. Investment fund governance and decision making;
4. Securities custody procedures and efficient provision of services to clients;
5. Services fees and commissions and management remuneration;
6. Entering into transactions with related parties;
7. Performance reports and the calculation of asset values and unit prices and advertisement;
8. Conditions and requirements for the approval of establishing new funds;
9. Financial and periodic reporting requirements of funds;
10. Liquidity requirements and risk limits;
11. Professional qualifications, personal suitability, financial responsibility and licensing requirements.

6.0.7 Chapter Seven – Disclosure [Prospectus]

Article 40: Publication of Prospectus

a. The contents of the prospectus set forth under Article 42 of this Law, or portions thereof, shall be published in such a manner and for such duration as required by the regulations and rules of the Authority.

b. An issuer or an affiliate of an issuer or an underwriter may not offer Securities of the issuer or the issuer's affiliate unless he has submitted a prospectus to the Authority, published the prospectus in the manner set forth in paragraph (a) of this Article, and has paid the requisite fees. The Authority may exempt the issuer from some requirements based on the manner of the offering, the amount of the offering, the number of investors and their characteristics, or the characteristic of the issuer of the Security or the Security itself.

c. Upon satisfying the requirements of paragraphs (a) and (b) of this Article, offers may be made in any of the forms listed below:

1. Verbally;
2. Through a prospectus satisfying the conditions of Article 42 of this Law;
3. Through an announcement containing a summary of the prospectus and any other information required by the Authority or authorized by it in accordance with the rules specified by the Authority;
4. Through other means, including electronic media, provided that such mean has been approved by the Authority.

Article 41: Approval of Prospectus Required An issuer, an affiliate of the issuer or an underwriter may not sell any Security owned by that issuer before the prospectus is approved by the Authority and becomes effective, provided that the approved prospectus shall be sent to the buyer prior to the sale date in accordance with such rules as the Authority may issue.

Article 42: Prospectus Contents The prospectus must contain the following information and statements:

a. Information required by the Authority's rules which give an adequate description of the issuer, the nature of its business, the individuals in charge of its management such as members of the board of directors, executive officers, senior staff and its major shareholders.

b. Information required by the Authority's rules which give an adequate description of the Securities to be issued, their number, price, and related rights, preferences or privileges of the issuer's other Securities, if any. The description will set forth how the issue proceeds will be disbursed, and the commissions levied by persons connected with the issue.

c. A clear statement of the financial position of the issuer and any significant financial data including the audited financial balance sheet, profit and loss account and cash flow statement as the rules of the Authority may require.

Any other information required or authorized by the Authority in accordance with rules issued by the Authority which it deems necessary to assist investors and their advisers in making decisions about investing in the Securities to be issued.

Article 43: Approval of Prospectus
a. After its review of the prospectus, the Authority shall announce its approval or rejection of the prospectus. If it approves the prospectus, the Authority may define a period of time during which the prospectus remains valid.

b. Every issuer offering Securities to the public through a prospectus must notify the Authority in writing of any material change to the statements set forth in the prospectus immediately upon becoming aware of such change provided such change may affect the price or value of the Security. The issuer should also prepare and publish a press release to disclose such change. The Authority's regulations and rules shall set forth the information to be disclosed and the conditions applicable regarding the press release.

Article 44: Rejection of Prospectus The Board of the Authority may reject a prospectus in any of the following cases:

a. If the prospectus does not contain the information required by Article 42 of this Law.

b. If the prospectus contains incorrect information pertaining to material matters, false or misleading statements or omits to state material information or statements that would under the circumstances render the prospectus misleading or incorrect.

c. The prospectus issuance fees have not been paid in full to the Authority. d. The issuer has failed to provide any of the reports stipulated in Article 45 of this Law.

Article 45: Issuers' Required Reports
a. Every issuer offering Securities to the public or whose Securities are traded on the Exchange must submit to the Authority quarterly and annual reports. Annual reports must be audited as required by the rules of the Authority. These reports shall contain the following:

1. The balance sheet;
2. The profit and loss account;
3. The cash flow statement; and
4. Any other information as required by the rules of the Authority.

b. In addition to the information required in paragraph (a) of this Article, the annual report must contain the following:

1. An adequate description of the issuing company, the nature of its business and its activities as required under the rules of the Authority;
2. Information regarding the members of its board of directors, executive officers, senior staff and major investors or shareholders as required under the rules of the Authority;
3. An evaluation of the issuing company management of current and future developments and any future possibilities that may have significant effect on the business results or financial position of the company as required under the rules of the Authority.
4. Any other information as may be required by the rules of the Authority as it deems necessary to assist investors and their advisers in making a decision to invest in the issuer's Securities.

c. All information and data described in paragraphs (a - 1, 2, 3) and (b.3) of this Article shall be deemed confidential. Before providing and disclosing such information and data to the Authority, the issuing company shall be prohibited from disclosing such information to parties not bound by a confidentiality obligation and an obligation to protect such information.

Article 46: Duty to Report Material Developments
a. A party who issues securities must inform the Authority in writing upon becoming aware of any material developments which may affect the prices of the Securities issued by such party. If such party has a Security traded on the Exchange, the Exchange must be informed of such developments in writing.

b. The Authority or the Exchange may request the party issuing Securities to provide any information or data pertaining to such party and the issuing party shall provide the same within the period of time specified in the request.

c. The Board of the Authority or the Exchange may, after reviewing the facts, require the issuing party to disclose any information or data related to that party. The Board or the Exchange shall also have the right to publish such information and data at the expense of the issuing party.

Article 47: Public Access to Prospectus and Reports
The public shall be allowed, in return for fees to be determined by the Authority, to review and make copies of the prospectuses, periodical reports, and information and data which have been filed with the Authority, made public and obtained.

Article 48: Disclosure Forms and Instructions
a. The Authority shall specify the disclosure forms and instructions, including the information which must be included in the prospectuses and periodical reports which must be provided to the Authority by the parties that are subject to its control and supervision or which must be announced to the public, as the case may be.

b. The Authority shall have no responsibility for the omission in prospectuses, periodical reports, advertisements, or any other document filed with it by any party of any important information or data or for including misleading information or data.

c. The publisher of the advertisement shall be responsible for any errors committed by it in publishing the contents of the advertisement pursuant to the regulations applicable in the Kingdom.

6.0.8 Chapter Eight Manipulation and Insider Trading

Article 49: Prohibited Conduct

a. Any person shall be considered in violation of this Law if he intentionally does any act or engages in any action which creates a false or misleading impression as to the market, the prices or the value of any security for the purpose of creating that impression or thereby inducing third parties to buy, sell or subscribe for such security or to refrain from doing so or to induce them to exercise, or refrain from exercising, any rights conferred by such Security.

b. The Authority shall set out rules determining the acts and practices which shall constitute violations of paragraph (a) of this Article. These rules shall specify the acts and practices excluded from the application of the provisions of paragraph (a) of this Article. The powers of the Authority provided for in this paragraph shall include the power to set forth the rules, define the circumstances and procedures aiming at stabilizing the prices of Securities offered to the public, and the manner in which and the period during which these actions must be taken.

c. The following acts and practices shall be among those which shall be considered types of manipulation that are prohibited by paragraph (a) of this Article:

1. To perform any act or practice aiming at creating a false or misleading impression of an existing active trading in a Security as may be contrary to the reality. These acts and practices shall include, but not be limited to the following:

    a. Undertaking transactions in Securities which do not involve a true transfer of ownership thereof.

    b. Entering an order or orders for the purchase of a particular Security with prior knowledge that an order or orders of substantially the same size, price and timing for the sale of the same Security has been or will be entered by a different party or parties.

    c. Entering an order or orders for the sale of a particular Security with prior knowledge that an order or orders of substantially the same size, price and timing for the purchase of the same Security has been or will be entered by the same party or different parties.

2. To affect, alone or with others, the price of a particular Security or Securities traded on the Exchange through executing a series of transactions in such Security or Securities creating actual or apparent active trading or causing an increase or decrease in the prices of such Securities, for the purpose of inducing third parties to buy or sell such Securities as the case may be.
3. To affect, alone or with others through any series of transactions such as buying or selling or buying and selling a Security traded on the Exchange for the purpose of pegging or stabilizing the price of such Security in violation of the rules set forth by the Authority for the safety of the market and the protection of investors.

Article 50: Insider Trading Prohibited

a. Any person who obtains, through family, business or contractual relationship, inside information (hereinafter an "insider") is prohibited from directly or indirectly trading in the Security related to such information, or to disclose such information to another person with the expectation that such person will trade in such Security.

Insider information means information obtained by the insider and which is not available to the general public, has not been disclosed, and such information is of the type that a normal person would realize that in view of the nature and content of this information, its release and availability would have a material effect on the price or value of a Security related to such information, and the insider knows that such information is not generally available and that, if it were available, it would have a material effect on the price or value of such Security.

b. No person may purchase or sell a Security based on information obtained from an insider while knowing that such person, by disclosing such insider information related to the Security, has violated paragraph (a) of this Article.

c. The Authority has the power to establish the rules for specifying and defining the terms provided for under paragraphs (a) and (b) of this Article, and such acts or practices which the Authority deems appropriate to exempt them from their application, as may be required for the safety of the market and the protection of investors.

6.0.9 Chapter Nine – Regulation of Proxy Solicitations, Restricted Purchase and Restricted Offer for Shares

Article 51: Solicitation of Proxies The Authority shall issue rules for the regulation of disclosure of information and other practices in connection with the solicitation of proxies if such solicitation pertains to any Security listed on the Exchange.

Article 52: Rules for Restricted Transactions The Authority shall issue rules for the regulation of restricted purchase of shares transactions and restricted offer for shares transactions. For the purpose of application of the provisions of this Law, these two terms mean the following:

a. A restricted purchase of shares is the purchase of voting shares listed on the Exchange when as a consequence of such purchase ten percent (10%) or more of such class of the relevant company shares is owned by, or under control of, the purchaser or those acting in concert with the purchaser.

b. A restricted offer for shares is making a public announcement by which the announcer offers to purchase voting shares of a particular class of shares listed on the Exchange if the amount of shares sought to be acquired by the offering party would increase its ownership or the ownership of those acting in concert with the offering party, or the shares under their control, to ten percent (10%) or more of the shares of the relevant company.

Article 53: Authority's Power to Regulate Restricted Transactions The Authority's powers to issue rules for the regulation of restricted purchases of shares and restricted offers for shares shall include, without limitation, the power to issue rules in connection with the following:

a. Amending the percentages prescribed under Article 52 of this Law and approving exceptions to the definitions of restricted purchases of shares and restricted offers for shares;

b. Specifying the timing, form and manner for announcements in connection with restricted purchases of shares and restricted offers for shares;

c. Setting forth the information which party purchasing the shares or offering party must disclose, and the manner for its disclosure, including any requirements for the continuous disclosure with respect to changes in share ownership;

d. Imposing any conditions or requirements on the company the shares of which are subject or target of a restricted purchase of shares or a restricted offer for shares that it announces its position or viewpoint regarding such restricted purchase or restricted offer;

e. Any other rules pertaining to restricted purchases of shares or restricted offers for shares as may be necessary for the safety of the market and the protection of investors. Article Fifty Four If any person increases its ownership of shares in a given company through a restricted purchase of shares or restricted offer for shares so that such person or those with whom such person is acting in concert become the owner of (50%) fifty percent or more of a given class of voting shares listed on the Exchange, the Board shall have the right, within sixty (60) days, if it believes it would achieve the safety of the market and the protection of shareholders, to order such person to offer to purchase the shares of the same class it does not own on such terms and conditions as the Board shall determine. In no case will the prospective purchaser be compelled to offer to purchase the remaining shares at a price exceeding the highest price he paid to purchase any of the shares of that company during the 12 months preceding the date of the Board order.

6.0.10 Chapter Ten – Sanctions and Penalties for Violations

Article 55: Liability for Material Mis-statements or Omissions

a. In case a prospectus, when approved by the Authority, contained incorrect statements of material matters or omitted material facts required to be stated in the prospectus, the person purchasing the Security that was the subject of such prospectus shall be entitled to compensation for the damages incurred by him as a result thereof. A statement or omission shall be considered material for the purposes of this paragraph if it is proven to the Committee that had the investor been aware of the truth when making such purchase it would have affected the purchase price.

b. The following persons shall be liable under paragraph (a) of this Article:

1. The party issuing the Security. The issuer shall be liable irrespective of whether it had acted reasonably, or it was not aware of the incorrect statements in connection with material matters, or of the omission of material facts that should have been disclosed in the prospectus.
2. The senior officers of the issuing party of the Security in accordance with the definition provided in the rules issued by the Authority. Such liability could be relieved according to paragraph (c.l and 2) of this Article.
3. The members of the board of directors of the issuing party, or persons performing similar functions, as of the date on which the prospectus was approved by the Authority. Such liability could be relieved in accordance with paragraph (c.l and 2) of this Article.
4. The underwriters who have undertaken to offer on behalf of the issuer the Security for sale to the public, provided that an underwriter shall not be liable for more than the total price of the Securities underwritten or amount of Securities distributed by him (whichever amount is greater).
5. The accountant, engineer or appraiser and others identified in the prospectus, who have consented in writing to be so identified, as having certified the accuracy and truthfulness of the information stated in the prospectus; however, such person's liability shall not extend to information in parts of the prospectus which are not so certified by him. That person shall be responsible for any part of the prospectus understood to have been prepared according to his statement and approval in his capacity defined under this paragraph, unless he proves that he was convinced after conducting reasonable investigations and on the basis of reasonable grounds, that that part of the prospectus is not in violation of paragraph (a) of this Article.

c. Any of the persons mentioned in paragraph (b.2, 3 and 4) of this Article shall be liable as provided for in the provisions of paragraph (a) of this Article unless it is proven that:

1. As to any part of the prospectus not certified by the person described in paragraph (b.5) of this Article that, after reasonable investigation, and on the basis of reasonable grounds, he was convinced that such part of the prospectus was not in violation of paragraph (a) of this Article;
2. As to any part of the prospectus purporting to have been made based on the statement of a person set forth in paragraph (b.5) of this Article, and the person invoking the defense is identified in paragraphs (b.2, 3, 4) of this Article, he had no reasonable ground at that time to believe that such part of the prospectus contained what could be deemed a violation of paragraph (a) of this Article.

d. In determining that investigation shall be deemed reasonable or what shall constitute reasonable ground for belief for the purposes of paragraph (c) of this Article, the standard of reasonableness for the purpose of this Article shall be that of the prudent man in the management of his property.

e. Damages may be obtained through a claim brought on the basis of paragraph (a) of this Article, which damages shall represent the difference between the price actually paid for purchasing the Security (not to exceed the price at which it was offered to the public) and the value thereof as of the date of bringing the legal action or the price which such Security could have been disposed of on the Exchange prior to filing the complaint with the Committee, provided that if the defendant proves that any portion in the decline in value of the Security is due to causes which are not related to the omission or the incorrect statement which is the substance of the suit, such portion shall be excluded from the damages for which the defendant is responsible. The defendants are individually and jointly and severally liable for damages for which they are responsible under this Article. The amount of indemnification shall be subject to the provisions of the contract or agreement entered into between the parties identified in paragraph (b) of this Article or as the Committee believes is equitable and does not harm the interest of investors or otherwise contravene the spirit of this Law.

Article 56: Untrue Statements

a. Any person who makes, or is responsible for another making, orally or in writing an untrue statement of material fact or omits to state that material fact, if it causes another person to be misled in relation to the sale or the purchase of a Security, shall be liable for compensation of the damages. For establishing responsibility for damages in pursuance of the provisions of this Article, it is not required that a relationship exists between the claimant and the defendant and the claimant should prove:

1. That he was not aware that the statement was omitted or untrue.
2. That either he would not have purchased or sold the Security in question had he known that information was omitted or untrue, or that he would not have purchased or sold such Security at the price at which such Security was purchased or sold.
3. That the person responsible for the disclosure of the statements or the giving of such incorrect information knew of the said untruthfulness or was aware that there was a substantial likelihood that the information disclosed omitted or misstated a material fact.

b. The damages recoverable under this Article from any defendant, and the rights of indemnity and contribution among the persons responsible shall be as provided in paragraph (e) of Article 55 of this Law.

c. For the purpose of this Article, a statement or omission shall be considered related to an important material fact in accordance with the standard provided for in paragraph (a) of Article 55 of this Law.

Article 57: Prohibition on Manipulation; Penalties Generally

a. Any person who violates Article 49 of this Law or any of the regulations or the rules issued by the Authority pursuant to the said Article by engaging in an act or transaction for the purpose of intentionally manipulating the price of a Security, or participating in such act or transaction, or is responsible for a person who undertakes such act or transaction shall be liable for damages to any person who purchases or sells the Security whose price has been significantly adversely affected by such manipulation for the amount such person's purchase or sale price was so affected.

b. The damages recoverable under this Article from any defendant, and the rights of indemnity and contribution among the persons responsible shall be measured in a manner that is consistent with the provisions of paragraph (e) of Article 55 of this Law.

c. In addition to the penalties and financial compensation provided for under this Law, the Committee may, based on a claim filed by the Authority, punish the persons who violate Articles 49 and 50 with imprisonment terms not exceeding five years.

Article 58: Limitations on Actions A suit under Articles 55, 56 and 57 of this Law shall not be heard if the complaint is filed with the Authority after the elapse of one year from the date when the claimant should reasonably have been aware of facts causing him to believe he had been the victim of a violation, and in no case may such complaint be heard by the Committee after five years from the occurrence of the violation subject of the claim.

Article 59: Penalties

a. If it appears to the Authority that any person has engaged, is engaging, or is about to engage in acts or practices constituting a violation of any provisions of this Law, or the regulations or rules issued by the Authority, or the regulations of the Exchange, the Authority shall have the right to bring a legal action before the Committee to seek an order for the appropriate sanction. The sanctions include the following:

1. Warning the person concerned.
2. Obliging the person concerned to cease or refrain from carrying out the act which is the subject of the suit.
3. Obliging the person concerned to take the necessary steps to avert the violation, or to take such necessary corrective steps to address the results of the violation.
4. Indemnifying the persons who have suffered damages as a consequence of a violation that has occurred, or obliging the violator to pay to the Authority's account the gains realized as a consequence of such violation.
5. Suspending the trading in the Security.
6. Barring the violating person from acting as a broker, portfolio manager or investment adviser for such period of time as is necessary for the safety of the market and the protection of investors.
7. Seizing and executing on property.
8. Travel ban.
9. Barring from working with companies whose Securities are traded on the Exchange.

b. The Authority may, in addition to taking the actions provided for under paragraph (a) of this Article, request the Committee to impose a financial fine upon the persons responsible for an intentional violation of the provisions of this Law, its Implementing Regulations, the rules of the Authority and the regulations of the Exchange. As an alternative to the foregoing, the Board may impose a financial fine upon any person responsible for the violation of this Law, its Implementing Regulations, the rules of the Authority and the regulations of the Exchange. The fine that the Committee or the Board can impose shall not be less than SR 10,000 and shall not exceed SR 100,000 for each violation committed by the defendant.

Article 60: Penalties for Unlicensed Business

a. Any person who carries on, or purports to carry on, the activities provided in Article 32 of this law without a license shall be considered violating the provisions of Article 31 of this Law and and the Committee may sentence the violator, in addition to the sanctions set out in Article 59 of this law, to imprisonment for a term not to exceed nine (9) months.

b. Any agreement or contract which is entered into in relation to a Security related transaction that is in violation of Article 31 of this Law shall be void and the violating broker may not complain on basis of such agreement or contract against the other party and that party shall be entitled to request the rescission of the agreement or contract and the recovery of any money or other property paid or transferred by him under the agreement or contract, provided the rescinding party restitutes any money or other property received through such agreement or contract. The Committee shall have jurisdiction over the suits brought pursuant to this provision.

Article 61: Broker Disciplinary Proceedings

a. The failure of a licensed broker or his agent to comply with any regulations and rules of the Exchange pertaining to the regulation of the work of brokers can give rise to disciplinary proceedings pursuant to the procedures established in the regulations of the Exchange. Upon discovering a violation of its regulations, the Exchange may file a claim with the Committee to impose a suitable sanction against the violator which may include the revocation of the license granted to it, suspension of said license, the imposition of a financial fine or obliging the broker to restitute the sums due to clients. A broker or his agent sanctioned may request the review of the decision by the Appeal Panel of the Committee.

b. The Authority may, pursuant to its powers under Article 59 of Chapter 10 of this Law, take necessary actions against brokers or their agents who fail to comply with the rules of operation of the Exchange.

Article 62: Board-imposed Penalties
a. The Board may issue a decision providing for a reprimand to the violator broker or broker's agent, or may, pursuant to the decision, place restrictions on the licensed activities, functions or operations of the broker or the broker's agent, suspend those activities for a period not exceeding twelve months, or revoke the license of any broker or his agent if the Board finds, after giving notice to the concerned broker or the broker's agent and giving it an opportunity for a hearing, that such broker or the broker's agent, whether prior or subsequent to obtaining a license has committed any of the following:

1. he deliberately gave or caused to be given materially false or misleading statements in the broker's or the broker agent's application to obtain a license, in any document or report submitted to the Exchange or to the Authority.
2. he deliberately violated, or assisted another person to violate any provision of this Law and its regulations.
3. the broker or the broker's agent violated a judgment or decision issued by any court of the Kingdom or by the Committee for Resolution of Securities Disputes prohibiting him permanently or temporarily from carrying on brokerage or portfolio manager business.
4. the Authority has formally been notified by a Securities regulator in another country that the broker or his agent willfully violated the Securities laws of that country or provided false and misleading information in the reports required to be submitted in such foreign jurisdiction.

b. The Board may issue a decision suspending the brokerage license pending the issuance of a final determination in relation to the revocation of the license, if such suspension appears to the Board, after giving the broker or the broker's agent concerned notice and an opportunity to be heard on an urgent basis, to be necessary for the safety of the market and the protection of investors.

c. The Board may, in urgent cases, and without prior notice or hearing being granted to the concerned party to the decision, issue a decision suspending the license of a broker or barring the broker from performing such functions as a broker for a period not to exceed 60 days. Issuing such a decision does not prevent the Authority or the Exchange from taking such other actions against the broker or his agent as provided by this Law.

Article 63: Suspension of License The license of the broker or the broker's agent may be suspended by order of the Board upon discovering that the broker ceases to exist or has for a period of twelve months ceased to carry out brokerage activities.

Article 64: Board's Authority to Settle Violations A person charged with violation of Article 50 of this Law may avoid proceedings before the Committee by reaching an agreement with the Authority pursuant to which he agrees to pay the Authority a sum not exceeding three times the profits he has realized, or three times the losses he has averted by committing the violation. Such arrangement shall be without prejudice to any compensation awardable as a result of the violation.

Article 65: Repeal of Prior Laws This Law shall repeal all provisions that are contrary hereto.

Article 66: Effective Date; Implementing Regulations The Implementing Regulations to this Law shall be issued 150 days after the publication of the date of publication of the Law and shall come into effect with the Law. Article Sixty Seven This Law shall be published in the Official Gazette and shall be effective 180 days after the date of the publication thereof.

7 Corporate Governance Regulations

Issued by the Board of the Capital Market Authority pursuant to Resolution Number 8-16-2017 dated 16/5/1438H (13/2/2017G) based on the Companies Law issued by Royal Decree No M/3 dated 28/1/1437H amended by Resolution of the Board of the Capital Market Authority Number 1-7-2021 dated 1/6/1442H (14/1/2021G)

Important Notice: the current version of these Regulations, as may be amended, can be found at the Authority website: www.cma.org.sa

Table of Contents

Part 1: Preliminary Provisions
Article 1: Definitions
Article 2: Preamble
Article 3: Objectives of the Regulations
Part 2: Rights of Shareholders
Chapter 1: General Rights
Article 4: Fair Treatment of Shareholders
Article 5: Rights related to shares
Article 6: Shareholder access to information
Article 7: Communicating with Shareholders
Article 8: Electing the Board Members
Article 9: Distribution of Dividends
Chapter 2: Rights Related to the Meeting of the General Assembly
Article 10: Preamble
Article 11: Competencies of the Extraordinary General Assembly
Article 12: Competencies of the Ordinary General Assembly
Article 13: Shareholders' Assembly
Article 14: The Agenda of the General Assembly
Article 15: Management of the Shareholders' Assembly
Part 3: The Board of Directors
Chapter 1: Formation of the Board
Article 16: Composition of the Board
Article 17: Appointment of the Board members
Article 18: Conditions for the Membership of the Board
Article 19: Termination of a Board Membership
Article 20: Issues Affecting Independence
Chapter 2: Responsibilities and Competencies of the Board
Article 21: Responsibility of the Board
Article 22: Main Functions of the Board
Article 23: Distribution of Competencies and Duties
Article 24: Separation of Positions
Article 25: Oversight over the Executive Management
Article 26: Competencies and Duties of the Executive Management
Chapter 3: Competencies of the Chairman and the Board Members
Article 27: Competencies and Duties of the Chairman of the Board
Article 28: Appointing the Chief Executive Officer after the end of his/her services as Chairman of the Board
Article 29: Principles of truthfulness, honesty and loyalty
Article 30: Tasks and Duties of the Board Members
Article 31: Duties of the Independent Director
Chapter 4: Procedures of the Board Activities
Article 32: The Board Meetings
rticle 33: Remarks of the Board Members
Article 34: Organising the Attendance of the Board Meetings
Article 35: The Agenda of Board Meetings
Article 36: Exercising the Competencies of the Board
Article 37: The Secretary of the Board
Article 38: Qualifications of the Secretary
Chapter 5: Training, Support and Assessment
Article 39: Training
Article 40: Providing Members with Information
Article 41: The Assessment
Chapter 6: Conflicts of Interest
Article 42: Dealing with Conflicts of Interest and Related Parties Transactions
Article 43: Conflicts of Interest Policy
Article 44: Avoiding Conflicts of Interest
Article 45: Disclosure of Conflicts of Interest by the Nominee
Article 46: Rules of Competing with the Company
Article 47: Concept of the Competing Businesses
Article 48: Rejecting to Grant Authorzation
Article 49: Accepting Gifts
Part 4: Company Committees
Chapter 1: General Provisions
Article 50: Forming the Committees
Article 51: Committees Membership
Article 52: Studying Subjects
Article 53: Committees Meetings
Chapter 2: The Audit Committee
Article 54 Audit Committee Formation
Article 55: Competencies, powers and responsibilities of the Audit Committee
Article 56: Conflict between the Audit Committee and the Board
Article 57: Audit Committee Meetings
Article 58: Arrangements for Providing Remarks
Article 59: Powers of the Audit Committee
Chapter 3: Remuneration Committee
Article 60: Composition of the Remuneration Committee
Article 61: Competencies of the Remuneration Committee
Article 62: Remuneration Policy
Article 63: Meetings of the Remuneration Committee
Chapter 4: Nomination Committee
Article 64: Composition of the Nomination Committee
Article 65: competences of the Nomination Committee
Article 66: The Nomination Procedures
Article 67: Meetings of the Nomination Committee
Article 68: Publishing the Nomination Announcement
Article 69: Nomination Rights of Shareholders
Chapter 5: Risk Management Committee
Article 70: Composition of the Risk Management Committee
Article 71: Competencies of the Risk Management Committee
Article 72: Meetings of the Risk Management Committee
Part 5: Internal Control
Article 73: Internal Control System
Article 74: Establishing Independent Units or Departments within the Company
Article 75: Duties of the Internal Audit Unit or Department
Article 76: Composing an Internal Audit Unit or Department

Article 77: Internal Audit Plan
Article 78: Internal Audit Report
Article 79: Maintaining Internal Audit Reports
Part 6: The Company's External Auditor
Article 80: Assigning the Audit Function
Article 81: Appointment of the External Auditor
Article 82: Duties of the External Auditor
Part 7: Shareholders
Article 83: Regulating the Relationship with Stakeholders
Article 84: Reporting Non-Compliant Practices
Article 85: Employee Incentives
Part 8: Professional and Ethical Standards
Article 86: Professional Conduct Policy
Article 87: Social Responsibility
Article 88: Social Initiatives
Part 9: Disclosure and Transparency
Article 89: Policies and Procedure of Disclosure
Article 90: The Board's Report
Article 91: The Audit Committee's Report
Article 92: Disclosure by the Board
Article 93: Disclosure of Remunerations
Part 10: Implementation of Corporate Governance
Article 94: Implementation of Effective Governance
Article 95: Formation of a Corporate Governance Committee
Part 11: Retaining of Documents
Article 96: Retaining of Documents
Part 12: Closing Provisions
Article 97: Providing the Additional data and Information
Article 98: Publication and Entry into Force
Appendix (1) Remuneration Schedule

7.1 PART 1: PRELIMINARY PROVISIONS

Article 1: Definitions The following terms and expressions shall have the meaning they bear as follows unless the contrary intention appears:

Companies Law: the Companies Law issued by Royal Decree No. (M/3) dated 28/1/1437 AH.

Capital Market Law: the Capital Market Law issued by Royal Decree No. (M/30) dated 2/6/1424 AH.

Rules on the Offer of Securities and Continuing Obligations: The Rules on the Offer of Securities and Continuing Obligations issued by the Board. Listing Rules: The Listing Rules approved by the Board Authority: the Capital Market Authority.

The Exchange: The Saudi Stock Exchange. Company: the listed joint stock company. Board: the company's Board of Directors.

Corporate Governance: rules to lead and guide the Company that includes mechanisms to regulate the various relationships between the Board, Executive Directors, shareholders and Stakeholders, by establishing rules and procedures to facilitate the decision making process and add transparency and credibility to it with the objective of protecting the rights of shareholders and Stakeholders and achieving fairness, competitiveness and transparency on the Exchange and the business environment.

Shareholders Assembly: an assembly consisting of the shareholders in the Company formed in accordance with the provisions of the Companies Law and the Company's bylaws.

Executive Director: a member of the Board who is a full time member of the executive management team of the Company and participates in its daily activities.

Non-Executive Director: a member of the Board who is not a full-time member of the management team of the Company and does not participate in its daily activities.

Independent Director: a non-executive member of the Board who enjoys complete independence in his/her position and decisions and none of the independence affecting issues stipulated in Article 20 of these Regulations apply to him/her.

Executive Management or Senior Executive: persons responsible for managing the daily operations of the Company, and proposing and executing strategic decisions, such as the Chief Executive Officer (CEO) and his/her delegates and the Chief Financial Officer (CFO).

Relatives:

-Fathers, mothers, grandfathers and grandmothers (and their ancestors).

-children and grandchildren and their descendants.

-siblings, maternal and paternal half-siblings.

-Husbands and wives.

Holding Company: a Joint Stock Company or Limited Liability Company aims to control other Joint Stock Companies or Limited Liability Companies called affiliates by owning more than half of those companies' share capitals or by controlling the composition of their management.

Person: any natural or legal person that is recognized as such under the laws of the Kingdom.

Related Parties:

A. Substantial Shareholders of the company.

B. Board members of the Company or any of its affiliates and their relatives.

C. Senior Executives of the Company or any of its affiliates and their relatives.

D. Board members and Senior Executives of Substantial Shareholders of the company.

E. Entities, other than companies, owned by a Board member or any Senior Executive or their relatives.

F. Companies in which a Board member or a Senior Executive or any of their relatives is a partner.

G. Companies in which a Board member or a Senior Executive or any of their relatives is a member of its Board of directors or is one of its Senior Executives.

H. Joint stock companies in which a member of the Board or a Senior Executive or any of their relatives owns (5%) or more, subject to the provisions of paragraph (D) of this definition.

I. Companies in which a Board member or a Senior Executive or any of their relatives has influence on their decisions even if only by giving advice or guidance.

J. Any person whose advice or guidance influence the decisions of the Company, the Board and the Senior Executives.

K. Holding companies or affiliates.

Advice or guidance that is provided on a professional basis by a person licensed to provide such advice shall be excluded from the provisions of paragraphs (I) and (J) of this definition.

The Group: When referring to a person, means the person and his affiliates.

Affiliate: a person who controls another person or is controlled by that other person, or who is under common control with that person by a third person. In any of the preceding, control could be direct or indirect.

Stakeholder: any person who has an interest in the Company, including employees, creditors, customers, suppliers and the community.

Substantial Shareholders: any person who owns (5%) or more of the shares of the Company or voting rights therein.

Cumulative voting: a method of voting for electing Board members that gives each shareholder a voting capacity equivalent to the number of shares he/she owns , and by which the shareholder is entitled to either exercise all of his/her votes towards one nominee or to divide his/her votes towards several nominees without any duplication of such votes.

Controlling Interest: The ability to influence actions or decisions of another person directly, indirectly, individually or collectively with a relative or an affiliate through: (A) owning %30 or more of the voting rights in a company, (B) having the right to appoint %30 or more of the administrative team members.

Administrative Team: A group of individuals who make strategic decisions of the person. The Board is the Company's Administrative Team.

Remunerations: amounts, allowances, dividends and the like, periodic or annual bonuses linked to performance, long or short term incentive plans and any other in-kind benefits except the actual reasonable expenses and fees incurred by the company to enable the Board member to perform his duties.

Day: Calendar day whether a business day or not.

Article 2: Preamble
a) These Regulations state the rules and standards that regulate the management of the companies to ensure its compliance with the best governance practices that ensure the protection of shareholder's rights as well as the rights of Stakeholders.

b) These Regulations are mandatory to companies except the provisions that contain a reference of being guiding.

c) Without prejudice to the provisions of these Regulations, laws and instructions of other supervisory authorities apply to companies that subject to them.

Article 3: Objectives of the Regulations These Regulations aim at establishing an effective legal framework to govern the Company, and particularly aim at the following:

1) enhancing the role of the Company's shareholders and facilitating the exercise of their rights;
2) Stating the competencies and responsibilities of the Board and the Executive Management;
3) enhancing the role of the Board and the committees and developing their capabilities to enhance the Company's decision making mechanisms;
4) achieving transparency, impartiality and equity in the Exchange, its transactions, and the business environment and enhance disclosure therein;
5) providing effective and balanced tools to deal with conflicts of interest;
6) enhancing accountability and control mechanisms for the Company's employees;
7) establishing the general framework for dealing with Stakeholders and protecting their rights;
8) supporting the effectiveness of the system for overseeing Companies and the tools thereof; and
9) raising the awareness of Companies in respect of the concept of professional conduct and encouraging them to adopt and develop such concept in accordance with their nature.

7.2 Part 2: RIGHTS OF SHAREHOLDERS

7.2.1 Chapter 1: General Rights

Article 4: Fair Treatment of Shareholders
a) The Board is obliged to seek shareholders' rights protection to ensure fairness and equality among them.

b) The Board and the Executive Management of the Company is obliged not to discriminate among shareholders who own the same class of shares nor prevent them from accessing any of their rights.

c) The Company shall specify in its internal policies the procedures that are necessary to guarantee that all shareholders exercise their rights.

Article 5: Rights related to shares All rights related to shares shall be guaranteed to the shareholder, and particularly the following:

1) to obtain his/her portion of the net profits which are to be distributed in cash or through the issuance of shares;

2) to obtain his/her share of the Company's assets upon liquidation;

3) to attend the General or Special Shareholders Assemblies, take part in their deliberations and vote on their decisions;

4) to dispose of his/her shares in accordance with the provisions of the Companies Law, The Capital Market Law and their implementing regulations;

5) to enquire and request viewing the books and documents of the Company, including the data and information related to the activities of the Company and its operational and investment strategy without prejudice to the interests of the Company or breach of the Companies Law and the Capital Market Law and their implementing regulations;

6) to monitor the performance of the Company and the activities of the Board;

7) to hold Board members accountable, to file liability lawsuits against them and appeal for nullification of the resolutions of the General and Special Shareholders Assemblies in accordance with the conditions and restrictions provided in the Companies Law and the bylaws of the Company;

8) preemptive rights to subscribe for new shares issued in exchange for cash unless otherwise specified in the Company's bylaws or when the Extraordinary General Assembly suspends the pre-emptive rights are per Article (140) of the Company's Law.

9) to record his/her name in the Company's shareholders register;

10) to request to view a copy of the Company's articles of association and bylaws unless the Company publishes them on its website; and

11) to nominate and elect the Board members.

Article 6: Shareholder access to information
a) The Board shall make available to the shareholder complete, clear, accurate and non- misleading information to enable him/her to properly exercise his/her rights. Such information shall be provided at the proper times and shall be updated regularly.

b) The method used to provide information to the shareholders shall be clear and detailed and shall include a list of the Company's information that the shareholders may obtain. This information shall be made available to all shareholders of the same class.

c) The Company shall use the most effective methods in communicating with shareholders and shall not discriminate among shareholders in respect of providing information.

Article 7: Communicating with Shareholders
a) The Board shall ensure communication between the Company and the shareholders based on the common understanding of the strategic objectives and interests of the Company.

b) The chairman of the Board and the Chief Executive Officer shall inform the remaining Board members of the opinions of the shareholders and discuss these opinions with them.

c) No shareholder may intervene in the operations of the Board or the work of the Executive Management of the Company unless he/she is a member of its Board or its management team; or unless his/her intervention is through the Ordinary General Assembly according to its powers or within the limits and situations permitted by the Board.

Article 8: Electing the Board Members
a) Upon calling for the General Assembly, the Company shall announce on the Exchange's website information about the nominees for the membership of the Board which shall include the nominees' experience, qualifications, skills and their previous and current jobs and memberships. The Company shall make a copy of the mentioned information available in the Company's head office and its website.

b) Cumulative voting shall be used in electing the Board, in which it is not allowed to use the voting right of a single share more than once.

c) Voting in the General Assembly shall be confined to the Board nominees whose information has been announced as per paragraph (a) of this Article.

Article 9: Distribution of Dividends
a) The Company's bylaws shall prescribe the percentage of the net profits to be distributed to the shareholders after setting aside the statutory reserve and the other reserves.

b) The Board shall establish a clear policy for the distribution of dividends to achieve the interests of the shareholders and the Company as per the Company's bylaw.

c) The shareholder is entitled to receive his/her share of dividends as per the decision of the General Assembly in respect of the distribution of dividends to shareholders or the Board resolution on distributing interim dividends. The resolution shall specify the record date and the distribution date provided that the resolution shall be executed as per the Regulatory Rules and Procedures issued pursuant to the Companies Law related to Listed Joint Stock Companies.

7.2.2 Chapter 2: Rights Related to the Meeting of the General Assembly

Article 10: Preamble General Shareholders Assemblies of the Company are competent in all of its affairs. A duly- constituted General Assembly represents all shareholders in exercising their powers in respect of the Company. The General Assembly shall exercise its role in accordance with the provisions of the Companies Law and Its Implementing Regulations and the Company's bylaws.

Article 11: Competencies of the Extraordinary General Assembly The Extraordinary General Assembly shall have the following Competencies:

1) amending the Company's bylaws, except for amendments which are deemed null and void pursuant to the provisions of the Companies Law;

2) increasing the Company's share capital in accordance with the situations provided by the Companies Law and Its Implementing Regulations;

3) decreasing the Company's share capital if it exceeds the Company's needs or in the event the Company incurs financial losses, in accordance with the situations provided by the Companies Law and Its Implementing Regulations;

4) resolving to form a consensual reserve for the Company as provided for in its bylaws to be set aside for a specific purpose, and the disposal thereof;

5) resolving to maintain or liquidate the Company before the end of the term specified in its bylaws;

6) approving the Company's shares buy-back;

7) issuing preferred shares or approving their buying, or converting ordinary shares into preferred shares or converting preferred shares into ordinary shares as per the Company's bylaws and the Regulatory Rules and Procedures issued pursuant to the Companies Law related to Listed Joint Stock Companies;

8) issuing debt instruments or financing deeds convertible into shares, and stating the maximum number of shares that may be issued against these instruments or deeds;

9) allocate Shares that are issued upon the capital increase or part of them for the employees of the Company, and its affiliates or some of them, or any of them; and

10) suspending preemptive rights of shareholders in subscribing for the capital increase in exchange for cash or giving priority to non-shareholders in cases as deemed in the interest of the Company if so is provided for in the Company's bylaws.

The Extraordinary General Assembly may issue resolutions that fall within the powers of the Ordinary General Assembly, provided that such resolutions are issued in accordance with the issuance requirements of Ordinary General Assembly resolutions which require that the absolute majority of shares be represented at the meeting.

Article 12: Competencies of the Ordinary General Assembly Except for the competencies reserved to the Extraordinary General Assembly, the Ordinary General Assembly shall have competencies in all affairs of the Company, and particularly the following:

1) appointing and dismissing Board members;

2) permitting a Board member to have direct or indirect interest in the business and contracts that are executed for the Company's account, in compliance with the provisions of the Companies Law and Its Implementing Regulations;

3) permitting a Board member to take part in any activities that may lead to competition with the Company, or competition in any of its activities, in compliance with the provisions of the Companies Law and its Implementing Regulations;

4) monitoring the compliance of the Board members with the provisions of the Companies Law and Its Implementing Regulations and other relevant laws and the Company's bylaws; inspecting any damage that may occur as a result of their violation of such provisions or mismanagement of the affairs of the Company; determine the liability resulting therefrom and undertaking the procedures it deems proper in this regard pursuant to the Companies Law and Its Implementing Regulations;

5) forming the audit committee pursuant to the provisions of the Companies Law and Its Implementing Regulations;

6) approving the Company's financial statement;

7) approving the Board report;

8) deciding on the proposals of the Board with respect to the method of distributing the net profits;

9) appointing the external auditors of the Company, specifying their remunerations, reappointing them, replacing them and approving their reports;

10) looking into the violations and errors committed by the external auditors of the Company when performing their duties and any difficulties, reported by the Company's external auditors, regarding their empowerment by the Company's Board or Management to review the books, records and other documents, statements and clarifications required to perform their duties, and respond to that as it deems appropriate in this regard;

11) resolving to withhold from setting aside statutory reserve when it reaches an amount equal to (30%) of the Company's paid share capital, and resolving to distribute the surplus of such percentage to the Company's shareholders in financial years where the Company does not generate net profits;

12) using the Company's consensual reserve, if such has not been set aside for a specific purpose, provided that using such reserve shall be based on a proposal submitted by the Board and used in ways that benefit the Company or the shareholders;

13) forming other reserves besides the statutory reserve and consensual reserve and disposal of the same;

14) setting aside amounts from the Company's net profits to set up social organizations for the benefit of the Company's employees or to assist any such existing establishments in accordance with Article (129) of the Companies Law; and

15) approving the sale of more than (50%) of the assets of the Company, whether in one or several transactions within a period of 12 months from the date of the first selling transaction. In case selling these assets includes what falls within the powers of the Extraordinary General Assembly, the approval of the said Assembly is required.

Article 13: Shareholders' Assembly
a) The Ordinary General assembly shall convene in accordance with the situations and circumstances stated in the Companies Law and Its Implementing Regulations and the Company's bylaws.

b) The Ordinary General Assembly shall convene at least once per year within the six months following the end of the Company's financial year.

c) The General and Special Shareholders' Assemblies shall convene upon an invitation from the Board in accordance with the situations stated in the Companies Law and Its Implementing Regulations and the Company's bylaws. The Board shall invite the Ordinary General Assembly to convene upon the request of the external auditor, the audit committee or a number of shareholders holding shares equal to at least (5%) of the share capital of the Company. The external auditor may invite the assembly to convene if the Board does not invite the assembly within thirty days from the date of the external auditor's request.

d) The date, place and agenda of the General Assembly shall be announced at least twenty one days prior to the date thereof; the invitation shall be published on the website of the Exchange, the Company's website and in a daily newspaper distributed in the province where the Company's head office is located. The Company may invite the General and Special Shareholders' Assemblies to convene using methods of contemporary technologies.

e) The Company may amend the agenda of the General Assembly within a period between publishing the announcement referred to in paragraph (d) of this Article and the date of convening the General Assembly meeting, provided that the Company shall announce this as prescribed in paragraph (d) of this Article.

f)Shareholders shall be granted the opportunity to effectively participate and vote in the General Assembly meetings. The meetings of the General Assemblies of shareholders may be convened and shareholders may participate in their deliberations and vote on their resolutions using methods of contemporary technologies pursuant to the Regulatory Rules and Procedures issued pursuant to the Companies Law related to Listed Joint Stock Companies.

g) The Board shall work on facilitating the participation of the largest number of shareholders in the meetings of the General Assembly, including choosing the appropriate place and time of such meeting.

h) The Company shall ensure recording the details of the shareholders who desire to attend at the Company's head office prior to the specified time for convening the assembly, unless the Company's bylaw state other means.

Article 14: The Agenda of the General Assembly
a) When preparing the General Assembly's agenda, the Board shall take into consideration the matters that the shareholders wish to list; shareholders holding no less than (5%) of the Company's shares are entitled to add one or more items to the agenda upon its preparation.

b) The Board shall separate each of the matters listed in the agenda of the General Assembly meeting as an independent item, and not combine significantly different matters under one item, and not combine the businesses and contracts in which

Board members have a direct or indirect interest under one item, for the purpose of obtaining the shareholders' vote for the item as a whole.

c) The shareholders shall be allowed through the Company's website and the Exchange's website, when the invitation for the convention of the General Assembly is published, to obtain the information related to the items of the General Assembly's agenda, particularly the reports of the Board and the external auditor, the financial statements and the audit committee's Report in order to enable them to make an informed decision in this regard. The Company shall update this information in case the General Assembly's agenda was amended.

d) The Authority may add any items it deems appropriate to the agenda of the General Assembly.

Article 15: Management of the Shareholders' Assembly
a) The Shareholders' General Assembly meetings shall be chaired by the chairman, his deputy (if the chairman is absent) or whom is delegated by the Board of directors of its members (when the chairman and his deputy are absent).

b) The chairman of the Shareholders' Assembly shall commit to grant the shareholders the opportunity to effectively participate and vote in the meetings of the General Assembly,, and avoid any procedure that may preventing their attendance to the assemblies or the exercise of the voting right. Shareholders shall be informed of the rules governing such meetings and the voting procedures.

c) Shareholders are entitled to discuss matters listed in the agenda of the General Assembly and raise relevant questions to the Board members and to the external auditor. The Board or the external auditor shall answer the questions raised by shareholders to the extent that does not jeopardise the Company's interest.

d) Shareholders shall be granted access to the minutes of the General Assembly meeting; and the Company shall provide the Authority with a copy of such minutes within (10) days of the date of any such meeting.

e) A Company shall announce to the public and inform the Authority and the Exchange, as per the rules prescribed by the Authority, of the results of a General Assembly meeting immediately following its conclusion.

7.3 PART 3: BOARD OF DIRECTORS

7.3.1 Chapter 1: Formation of the Board

Article 16: Composition of the Board The following shall be taken into consideration when composing the Board:

1) the number of its members shall be suitable for the size and nature of the Company's activities without prejudice to paragraph (a) of Article 17 of these Regulations.

2) the majority of the Board members shall be of Non-Executive Directors.

3) the number of Independent Directors shall not be less than two members or one-third of the Board members, whichever is greater.

Article 17: Appointment of the Board members Board
a) The Company's bylaws shall specify the number of the Board members, provided that such number shall not be less than three and not more than eleven.

b) The General Assembly shall elect the Board members for the term stated in the Company's bylaws, provided that such term shall not exceed three years. Board members may be re- elected, unless otherwise provided for in the Company's bylaws.

c) A Board member shall not be a member of the Boards of Directors of more than five listed joint stock companies at the same time.

d) The Company shall notify the Authority of the names of the Board members and description of their memberships within five business days from the commencement date of the Board term or from the date of their appointment ,whichever is shorter,, as well as any changes that may affect their membership within five business days from the occurrence of such changes.

Article 18: Conditions for the membership of the Board1 A member of the Board is required to be professionally capable and has the required experience, knowledge, skill and independence, which enable him/her to perform his/her duties efficiently. He/she shall have the following qualifications in particular:

1) Ability to lead: He/she shall enjoy leadership skills which enable him/her to delegate powers in order to enhance performance and apply best practices in effective management and compliance with professional ethics and values.

2) Competency: He/she shall have the academic qualifications and proper professional and personal skills as well as an appropriate level of training and practical experience related to the current and future businesses of the Company and the knowledge of management, economics ,accounting, law or governance, as well as the desire to learn and receive training.

3) Ability to guide: He/she shall have the technical, leadership, and administrative competencies as well as the ability to take prompt decisions, and understand technical requirements and developments related to the job. He/she shall also be able to provide strategic guidance and long-term planning and have a clear future vision.

4) Financial knowledge: He/she shall have the ability to read and understand financial statements and reports.

5) Physical fitness: He/she shall not suffer from any health issue that may hinder him/her from performing his/her duties and responsibilities.

The General Assembly shall take into account, when electing members to the Board, the recommendations of the nomination committee and the availability of the personal and professional capabilities required to perform their duties effectively pursuant to this Article.

Article 19: Termination of a Board Membership
a) The Company's bylaws shall specify the manner by which membership of the Board may be terminated. At all times, the Ordinary General Assembly may dismiss all or any of the Board members, even if the Company's bylaws provides for otherwise,

without prejudice to the dismissed member's right for compensation if the dismissal was on an unacceptable reason or at inappropriate time. The General Assembly may also, s per a recommendation of the Board, terminate the membership of the member who missed three consecutive meetings without a legitimate excuse.

b) Upon the termination of the membership of a Board member by any termination method, the Company shall promptly notify the Authority and the Exchange and shall specify the reasons for such termination.

c) If a member of the Board resigns and has comments on the performance of the Company, he/she shall submit a written statement explaining such comments to the chairman of the Board and such statement shall be presented to the Board members.

Article 20: Issues Affecting Independence
a) An Independent Director shall be able to perform his/her duties, express his/her opinions and vote on decisions objectively with no bias in order to help the Board make correct decisions that contribute to achieving the interests of the Company.

b) The Board shall annually evaluate the extent of the member's independence and ensure that there are no relationships or circumstances that affect or may affect his/her independence.

c) By way of example, the following negate the independence requirement for an Independent Director:

1) if he/she holds five percent or more of the shares of the Company or any other company within its group; or is a relative of who owns such percentage.
2) if he/she is a representative of a legal person that holds five percent or more of the shares of the Company or any company within its group;
3) if he/she is a relative of any member of the Board of the Company, or any other company within the Company's group;
4) if he/she is a relative of any Senior Executive of the Company, or of any other company within the Company's group;
5) if he/she is a Board member of any company within the group of the Company for which he/she is nominated to be a Board member.
6) if he/she is an employee or used to be an employee, during the preceding two years, of the Company, of any party dealing with the Company or any company within its group, such as external auditors or main suppliers; or if he/she, during the preceding two years, held a controlling interest in any such parties;
7) if he/she has a direct or indirect interest in the businesses and contracts executed for the Company's account;
8) if the member of the Board receives financial consideration from the Company in addition to the remuneration for his/her membership of the Board or any of its committees exceeding an amount of (SAR 200,000) or 50% of his/her remuneration of the last year for the membership of the board or any of its committees, whichever is less.
9) if he/she engages in a business where he competes with the Company, or conducting businesses in any of the company's activities.
10) if he/she served for more than nine years, consecutive or non-consecutive, as a Board member of the Company.

d) Unless the Nominations Committee considers otherwise, the businesses and contracts with the board member to meet his/her personal needs shall not be deemed as an interest that affect the independence of the board member which require an authorization from the ordinary general assembly, provided that such businesses and contracts are carried out in the same conditions and settings followed by the company with all contractors and dealers, and that such businesses and contracts must be within the normal course of the Company's activities.

(The Capital Market Authority Board issued its Resolution Number 1-35-2018 Dated 9/7/1439H Corresponding to 26/3/2018G stating that the sub-paragraph (10) of paragraph (c) of Article 20 of the Corporate Governance Regulations is to be a mandatory paragraph starting from the term of the listed company's board that will be after 1/1/2019G.)

7.3.2 Chapter 2: Responsibilities and Competencies of the Board

Article 21: Responsibility of the Board
a) The Board represents all shareholders; it shall perform its duties of care and loyalty in managing the Company's affairs and undertake all actions in the general interest of the Company and develop it and maximise its value.

b) The Board is responsible for the Company's business even if it delegates some of its powers to committees, individuals or other third parties. In any case, the Board may not issue a general or an open-ended delegation.

Article 22: Main Functions of the Board Without prejudice to the competencies of the General Assembly as per the Companies Law and Its Implementing Regulations and the Company's bylaws, the Board shall have the broadest powers in managing the Company and guiding its activities to achieve its objectives. Among the main functions and competencies of the Board are the following:

1) laying down the plans, policies, strategies and main objectives of the Company; supervising their implementation and reviewing them periodically; . And, ensuring that the human and financial resources required to fulfill them are available, including:

a.setting a comprehensive strategy for the Company, key business plans and policies and mechanisms of the risk management and review and guide them
b. determining the most appropriate capital structure for the Company, its strategies and financial objectives, and approving all kinds of estimated budgets;
c.overseeing the main capital expenditures of the Company and the acquisition or disposal of assets;
d. setting performance indicators, and monitoring the implementation thereof and the overall performance of the Company;
e.reviewing and approving the organizational and human resources structures of the Company on a periodic basis; and
f.ensuring that the financial and human resources required for achieving the objectives and main plans of the Company are available.

2) setting rules and procedures for internal control and generally overseeing them, including:

a.developing a written policy to remedy actual and potential conflicts of interest scenarios for each of the Board members, the Executive Management, and the shareholders. This includes misuse of the Company's assets and facilities

and the mismanagement resulting from transactions with Related Parties;
b. ensuring the integrity of the financial and accounting rules, including rules relating to the preparation of financial reports;
c.ensuring the implementation of appropriate control procedures for risk assessment and management by generally forecasting the risks that the Company may encounter and creating an environment which is aware of the culture of risk management at the Company level and disclosing such risks transparently to the Stakeholders and parties related to the Company ; and
d. reviewing the effectiveness of the Company's internal control procedures on an annual basis.

3) setting forth specific and explicit policies, standards and procedures for membership in the Board, without prejudice to the mandatory provisions of these Regulations, and implementing them following approval by the General Assembly;

4) developing a written policy that regulates the relationship with Stakeholders pursuant to the provisions of these Regulations;

5) setting policies and procedures to ensure the Company's compliance with the laws and regulations and the Company's obligation to disclose material information to shareholders and Stakeholders, and ensuring the compliance of the Executive Management with these policies and procedures;

6) supervising the management of the Company's finances, its cash flows as well as its financial and credit relationships with third parties;

7) providing recommendations to the Extraordinary General Assembly as to what it deems appropriate regarding the following:

a.increasing or decreasing the share capital of the Company; and
b. dissolving the Company before the end of its term as specified in its bylaws or deciding the continuity of the Company.

8) providing recommendation to the Ordinary General Assembly as to what it deems appropriate regarding:

a.using the consensual reserve of the Company, if such has been formed by the Extraordinary General Assembly and has not been allocated to a specific purpose;
b. forming additional financial allocations or reserves for the Company; and c.the method of distributing the net profits of the Company.

9) preparing the Company's interim and annual financial statements and approving them before publishing them;

10) preparing the Board report and approving it before publishing it.

11) ensuring the accuracy and integrity of the data and information which must be disclosed pursuant to the applicable policies and systems in respect of disclosure and transparency;

12) developing effective communication channels allowing shareholders to continuously and periodically review the various aspects of the Company's businesses as well as any material developments;

13) forming specialized committees of the Board pursuant to resolutions that shall specify the term, powers and responsibilities of such committees as well as the manner used by the Board to monitor such committees. Such resolutions shall also specify the names of the members and their duties, rights and obligations and shall evaluate the performance and activities of these committees and their members;

14) specifying the types of remunerations granted to the Company's employees, such as fixed remunerations, remunerations linked to performance and remunerations in the form of shares without prejudice to the Regulatory Rules and Procedures issued pursuant to the Companies Law related to Listed Joint Stock Companies;

15) setting the values and standards that govern the work at the Company.

Article 23: Distribution of Competencies and Duties
The organizational structure of the Company shall specify the competencies and distribute the duties between the Board and the Executive Management in accordance with the best practices in Corporate Governance, and to improve the efficiency of the Company's decision making and to achieve a balance of powers and authorities across the Board and the Executive Management, and to achieve this, the Board shall:

1) approve and develop internal policies in respect of the Company's business, including specifying the duties, competencies and responsibilities assigned to the various organizational levels;

2) approving a written and detailed policy that identifies the powers delegated to the Executive Management, a matrix stating these powers, means of implementation and the period of delegation. The Board may request the Executive Management to submit periodic reports in respect of its exercise of such delegated powers; and

3) identifying the matters on which the Board reserves the power to decide.

Article 24: Separation of Positions
a) without prejudice to the provisions of the Company's bylaws, The Board appoints a chairman, a vice chairman and may appoint a managing director of its members.

b) it is prohibited to hold, at the same time, the position of chairman of the Board and any other executive position in the Company, including the positions of the managing director, the Chief Executive Officer, or the general manager, even if the Company's bylaws provided for otherwise.

c) the Board shall define the competencies and specify the responsibilities of the chairman, the vice chairman, and the managing director (if any) explicitly and in writing if the Company's bylaws has no reference thereto.

d) in all cases, no person shall have the sole and absolute power to take decisions in the Company.

Article 25: Oversight over the Executive Management
The Board shall form the Executive Management of the Company, regulate its operating procedures, monitor and oversee it and ensure that it performs the duties assigned to it, and to achieve this, the Board shall:

1) develop the necessary administrative and financial policies;

2) ensure that the Executive Management operates in accordance with the policies approved by the Board;

3) select and appoint the Chief Executive Officer of the Company, and oversee his/her work;

4) appoint the manager of the internal audit unit or department, or the internal auditor and dismiss him and determine his remuneration, if any;

5) convene periodic meetings with the Executive Management to explore the work progress and any obstacles and problems in connection therewith, and review and discuss the important information in respect of the Company's business;

6) develop standards for the performance of the Executive Management consistent with the objectives and strategy of the Company;

7) review and evaluate the performance of the Executive Management; and

8) develop succession plans for the management of the Company.

Article 26: Competencies and Duties of the Executive Management Without prejudice to the competencies entrusted to the Board pursuant to the provisions of the Companies Law and Its Implementing Regulations, the Executive Management shall be responsible for implementing the plans, policies, strategies and main objectives of the Company in order to achieve its purposes. The competencies and duties of the Executive Management shall include the following:

1) implementing the Company's internal policies and rules approved by the Board;

2) suggesting the Company's comprehensive strategy as well as the principal and interim business plans and the policies and mechanisms for investment, financing, risk management and emergency administrative circumstances management plans and implementing them;

3) proposing the most appropriate capital structure for the Company and its strategies and financial objectives;

4) proposing the main capital expenditures of the Company and acquiring and disposing of assets;

5) proposing the organizational and human resources structures of the company and presenting them to the Board for approval;

6) implementing internal control systems and procedures, and generally overseeing them, which include:

a.implementing the conflicts of interest policy;
b. correctly applying the financial and accounting procedures, including the procedures relating to the preparation of financial reports;
c.applying appropriate control systems for measuring and managing risks by generally forecasting the risks that the Company may encounter and creating an environment which is aware of the culture of risk mitigation at the Company level, and transparently disclosing them to the Company's Board and other Stakeholders.

7) implementing the Company's Corporate Governance rules effectively, to the extent they do not conflict with the provisions of these Regulations, and proposing amendments thereto if needed;

8) implementing policies and procedures to ensure the Company's compliance with the laws and regulations and its obligation to disclose material information to shareholders and Stakeholders;

9) providing the Board with the information required to exercise its competencies and provide recommendations regarding the following:

a.increasing or decreasing the share capital of the Company;
b. dissolving the Company before the end of its term as specified in its bylaws or deciding the continuity of the Company;
c.using the consensual reserve of the Company;
d. forming additional reserves for the Company; and
e.the method for distributing the net profits of the Company.

10) proposing the policy and types of remunerations granted to employees, such as fixed remunerations, remunerations linked to performance and remunerations in the form of shares;

11) preparing periodic financial and non-financial reports in respect of the progress achieved in the business of the Company in light of the strategic plans and objectives of the Company, and presenting such reports to the Board;

12) managing the daily business and activity of the Company, in addition to managing its resources in the most appropriate form in accordance with the objectives and strategies of the Company;

13) participating effectively in building and developing a culture of ethical values within the Company;

14) implementing internal control and risk management systems and ensuring that they are effective and efficient, and ensuring compliance with the level of risks approved by the Board;

15) proposing and developing internal policies related to the business of the Company, including specifying the duties, competencies and responsibilities assigned to the various organizational levels;

16) proposing a clear policy to delegate tasks to the Executive Management and the method for implementing such policy; and

17) proposing the powers to be delegated to the Executive Management, the procedures for decision making and the period of delegation, provided that it shall present periodic reports to the Board in respect of its exercise of such powers.

7.3.3 Chapter 3: Competencies of the Chairman and the Board Members

Article 27: Competencies and Duties of the Chairman of the Board Without prejudice to the competencies of the Board, the chairman of the Board shall be responsible for leading the Board and supervising its operations and the effective performance of its duties. The competencies and duties of the chairman of the Board shall in particular include the following:

1) ensuring that the Board members obtain complete, clear, accurate and non-misleading information in due course;

2) ensuring that the Board effectively discusses all fundamental issues in due course;

3) representing the Company before third parties in accordance with the Companies Law and Its Implementing Regulations and the Company's bylaws;

4) encouraging the Board members to effectively perform their duties in order to achieve the interests of the Company;

5) ensuring that there are actual communication channels with shareholders and conveying their opinions to the Board;

6) encouraging constructive relationships and effective participation between the Board and the Executive Management on the one hand, and the Executive, Non-Executive and Independent Directors on the other hand, and creating a culture that encourages constructive criticism;

7) preparing agendas of the Board meetings, taking into consideration any matters raised by Board members or the external auditor and consult with the Board members and the Chief Executive Officer upon preparing the Board's agenda; and

8) convening periodic meetings with the Non-Executive Directors without the presence of any executive officers of the Company.

9) notifying the Ordinary General Assembly while convening of the businesses and contracts in which any Board member has direct or indirect interest, the notification shall include the information provided by the member to the Board as per paragraph (14) of Article (30) of these Regulations; this notification shall be accompanied by a special report of the Company's external auditor.

Article 28: Appointing the Chief Executive Officer after the end of his/her services as Chairman of the Board: It is prohibited to appoint the Chief Executive Officer, during the first year following the end of his/her service, as the chairman of the Board.

(The Capital Market Authority Board issued its Resolution Number 4-52-2018 Dated 28/8/1439H Corresponding to 14/5/2018G stating that Article 28 of the Corporate Governance Regulations is to be Guiding Article.)

Article 29: Principles of truthfulness, honesty and loyalty Each member of the Board shall comply with the principles of truthfulness, honesty, loyalty, and care of the interests of the Company and its shareholders, and prioritize their interests over his/her personal interests. This shall include, in particular, the following:

1) Truthfulness: is achieved when the relationship between the Board member and the Company is an honest professional relationship, and he/she discloses to the Company any significant information before entering into any transaction or contract with the Company or any of its affiliates.

2) Loyalty: is achieved when the Board member avoids transactions that may entail conflicts of interest and ensures fairness of dealing, in compliance with the provisions relating to conflicts of interest in these Regulations.

3) Care: is achieved by performing the duties and responsibilities set forth in the Companies Law, the Capital Market Law and their implementing regulations and the Company's bylaws and other relevant laws.

Article 30: Tasks and Duties of the Board Members Each member of the Board shall, being a Board member, perform the following tasks and duties:

1) providing proposals to develop the strategy of the Company;

2) monitoring the performance of the Executive Management and the extent to which it has achieved the objectives and purposes of the Company;

3) reviewing reports related to the performance of the Company;

4) ensuring the integrity and impartiality of the financial statements and information of the Company;

5) ensuring that the financial control and risk management systems are sound;

6) determining the appropriate level of remunerations of the members of the Executive Management;

7) expressing opinions as to the appointment and dismissal of members of the Executive Management;

8) participating in developing the succession and replacement plans of executive positions within the Company;

9) complying fully with the provisions of the Companies Law, Capital Market Law, their implementing regulations, the relevant regulations and the bylaws when performing his/her duties as a member of the Board and abstaining from taking or participating in any action that constitute mismanagement of the Company's affairs;

10) attending the Board and the General Assembly meetings, and not being absent except for legitimate excuse of which the chairman of the Board shall be notified by prior notice, or for emergency reasons;

11) allocating sufficient time to fulfill his/her responsibilities and preparing for the Board and its committees meetings and effectively participating therein, including raising relevant questions and carrying discussions with the Senior Executives;

12) studying and analyzing all information related to the matters looked into by the Board before expressing an opinion on the same;

13) enabling other Board members to express their opinions freely, and encouraging the Board to deliberate on the subjects and obtain the views of the competent members of the Company's Executive Management and others, when necessary;

14) notifying the Board fully and immediately of any interest, either direct or indirect, in the businesses and contracts that are executed for the Company's account, the notification shall include the nature and extent of such interest, the names of concerned persons, and the expected benefit to be obtained directly or indirectly from interest whether financial or non-financial. the concerned member shall abstain from voting on any decisions issued in connection therewith in compliance with the provisions of the Companies Law, the Capital Market Law and their implementing regulations;

15) notifying the Board fully and immediately of his/her participation, directly or indirectly, in any businesses that may compete with the Company or lead to competing with the Company, directly or indirectly, in respect of any of its activities, in compliance with the provisions of the Companies Law, the Capital Market Law and their implementing regulations;

16) refraining from disclosing or announcing any secrets he/she came across through his/her membership in the Board to any shareholder of the Company, unless such disclosure is made during the meetings of the General Assembly, or to a third party, in pursuance with the provisions of the Companies Law, the Capital Market Law and their implementing regulations;

17) working on the basis of complete information, in good faith and with the necessary care and diligence for the interest of the Company and all shareholders;

18) recognizing his/her duties, roles and responsibilities arising from the membership;

19) developing his/her knowledge in the field of the Company's business and activities and in the related financial, commercial and industrial fields; and

20) resigning from the membership of the Board if he/she is unable to fully fulfill his/her duties in the Board.

Article 31: Duties of the Independent Director Without prejudice to Article (30) of these Regulations, an Independent Director of the Board shall effectively participate in the following duties:

1) expressing his/her independent opinion in respect of strategic issues and the Company's policies and performance and appointing members of the Executive Management;

2) ensuring that the interest of the Company and its shareholders are taken into account and given priority in case of any conflicts of interest;

3) overseeing the development of the Company's Corporate Governance rules, and monitoring the implementation of the rules by the Executive Management.

7.3.4 Chapter 4: Board Meeting Procedures

Article 32: The Board Meetings
a) Without prejudice to the Companies Law and Its Implementing Regulations, the Board shall convene regular meetings to perform its duties effectively, and also convene meetings whenever needed.

b) The Board shall convene no less than four meetings per year, and no less than one meeting every three months.

c) The Board shall meet upon the invitation of its chairman or upon a request from two of its members. The invitation to the meeting shall be sent to each of the Board members no less than five days prior to the date of the meeting accompanied by its agenda and the necessary documents and information, unless circumstance require convening an emergency meeting, the invitation accompanied with the agenda and necessary documents and information may be sent within a period less than the five days.

d) The meeting shall not be valid unless attended by half of the Board members, provided that the number of attendees shall not be less than three, unless the Company's bylaws stated greater percentage or number.

Article 33: Remarks of the Board Members
a) If any member of the Board has any remarks in respect of the performance of the Company or any of the matters presented and which was not resolved in the Board meeting, such remarks shall be recorded and the procedures taken or to be taken by the Board in connection therewith must be set forth in the minutes of the Board meeting.

b) If a member of the Board expresses an opinion differs from the Board resolution, such opinion must be recorded in detail in the minutes of the Board meeting.

Article 34: Organising the Attendance of the Board Meetings.
a) The Attendance of Board meetings, and dealing with cases of irregular attendance by members of such meetings shall be organized.

b) An Independent Director of the Board shall make every effort to attend all meetings in which important and material decisions affecting the position of the Company are made.

Article 35: The Agenda of Board Meetings
a) The Board shall approve the agenda once the Board meeting is convened. Should any member of the Board raise any objection in respect of such agenda, such objection shall be recorded in the minutes of the meeting.

b) Each member of the Board is entitled to propose additional items to the agenda.

Article 36: Exercising the Competencies of the Board
a) The Board shall exercise its competencies and duties to lead the Company within a framework of effective and prudent controls that allow assessing and managing risks and limiting and mitigating their effects.

b) Without prejudice to Paragraph (b) of Article (21) of these Regulations, the Board may, within the scope of its competencies, delegate to one or more of its members or committees or a third party the performance of a specific function or functions.

c) The Board shall develop an internal policy that explains the procedures of the Board activities and aims at encouraging its members to work effectively to fulfill their obligations towards the Company.

d) The Board shall organise its activities and allocate sufficient time to perform the duties and responsibilities assigned to it, including preparing for Board and committees meetings and ensuring the coordination, recording and retaining of the minutes of its meetings.

Article 37: The Secretary of the Board
a) The Board shall appoint a secretary among its members or a third party, whose competencies and remunerations shall be specified by a Board resolution, unless the Company's bylaws include provisions in connection therewith, provided that such powers shall include:

1) documenting the Board meetings and preparing minutes therefor, which shall include the discussions and deliberations carried during such meetings, as well as the place, date, times on which such meetings commenced and concluded; and recording the decisions of the Board and voting results and retaining them in a special and organized register, and including the names of the attendees and any reservations they expressed (if any). Such minutes shall be signed by all of the attending members;
2) retaining the reports submitted to the Board and the reports prepared by it;
3) providing the Board members with the agenda of the Board meeting and related worksheets, documents and information and any additional information, related to the topics included in the agenda items, requested by any Board member;
4) ensuring that the Board members comply with the procedures approved by the Board;

5) notifying the Board members of the dates of the Board's meetings within sufficient time prior to the date specified for the meeting;
6) presenting the draft minutes to the Board members to provide their opinions on them before signing the same;
7) ensuring that the Board members receive, fully and promptly, a copy the minutes of the Board's meetings as well as the information and documents related to the Company;
8) coordinating among the Board members;
9) regulating the disclosure register of the Board and Executive Management as per Article (92) of these Regulations; and
10) providing assistance and advice to the Board members.

b) The Secretary of the Board may not be dismissed except pursuant to a decision of the Board.

Article 38: Qualifications of the Secretary The Board must specify the conditions that the secretary must meet, provided that they include at least one of the following:

1) he/she holds a bachelor degree in law, finance, accounting or administration or their equivalent, and has relevant practical experience of not less than three years; or

2) he/she has relevant practical experience of not less than five years.

7.3.5 Chapter 5: Training, Support and Assessment

Article 39: Training The Company shall pay adequate attention to the training and preparation of the Board members and the Executive Management, and shall develop the necessary programs required for the same, taking the following into account:

1) preparing programmes for the recently-appointed Board members and Executive Management to familiarise them with the progress of the Company's business and activities, particularly the following:

a.the strategy and objectives of the Company;
b. the financial and operational aspects of the Company's activities;
c.the obligations of the Board members and their duties, responsibilities and rights;
d. the duties and competencies of the committees of the Board.

2) developing the necessary mechanisms for Board members and the Executive Management to continuously enroll in training programmes and courses in order to develop their skills and knowledge in the fields related to the activities of the Company.

Article 40: Providing Members with Information The Executive Management of the Company shall provide the Board members, the Non- Executive Directors in particular, and the committees of the Company with all of the necessary information, details, documents and records, provided that they shall be complete, clear, correct and non-misleading, in due course to enable them to perform their duties and obligations.

Article 41: The Assessment
a) The Board shall develop, based on the proposal of the nomination committee, the necessary mechanisms to annually assess the performance of the Board, its members and committees and the Executive Management using key performance indicators linked to the extent to which the strategic objectives of the Company have been achieved, the quality of the risk management and the efficiency of the internal control systems, among others, provided that weaknesses and strengths shall be identified and a solution shall be proposed for the same in the best interests of the Company.

b) The procedures of performance assessment shall be in writing and clearly stated and disclosed to the Board members and parties concerned with the assessment.

c) The performance assessment shall entail an assessment of the skills and experiences of the Board, identification of the weaknesses and strengths of the Board and shall attempt to resolve such weaknesses using the available methods, such as nominating competent professional staff able to improve the performance of the Board. The performance assessment shall also entail the assessment of the mechanisms of the Board's activities in general.

d) The individual assessment of the Board members shall take into account the extent of effective participation of the member and his/her commitment to performing his/her duties and responsibilities, including attending the Board and its committees meetings and dedicating adequate time thereof.

e) The Board shall carry out the necessary arrangements to obtain an assessment of its performance from a competent third party every three years.

f) Non-Executive Directors shall carry out a periodic assessment of the performance of the chairman of the Board after getting the opinions of the Executive Directors, without the presence of the chairman of the Board in the discussion on this matter, provided that weaknesses and strengths shall be identified and a solution shall be proposed for the same in the best interests of the Company.

7.3.6 Chapter 6: Conflicts of Interest

Article 42: Dealing with Conflicts of Interest and Related Parties Transactions Without prejudice to the provisions of the Companies Law and Its Implementing Regulations, conflicts of interest situations and Related Parties transactions shall be dealt with in accordance with the provisions of this Chapter.

Article 43: Conflicts of Interest Policy The Board shall develop an explicit and written policy to deal with actual and potential conflicts of interest situations which may affect the performance of Board members, the Executive Management or any other employees of the Company when dealing with the Company or other Stakeholders. This policy shall include the following in particular:

1) informing Board members, Substantial Shareholders, Senior Executives and other employees of the Company of the importance of avoiding situations that may lead to a conflict between their interests and the interests of the Company, and dealing with them in accordance with the provisions of the Companies Law and Its Implementing Regulations.

2) providing examples of conflicts of interest situations that are relevant to the nature of the Company's activity.

3) clear procedures for disclosing conflicts of interest in the activities that may lead to such conflicts and obtaining authorization or the requisite approval.

4) the obligation to constantly disclose situations that may lead to conflicts of interest or upon the occurrence of such conflicts.

5) the obligation to abstain from voting or taking part in decision making when there is conflicts of interest.

6) clear procedures when the Company contracts or enters into a transaction with a Related Party, this shall include notifying the Authority and the public without any delay of that contract or transaction if it equals to or exceeds 1% of the Company's total revenues according to the last annual audited financial statements.

7) procedures to be taken by the Board when discovering that such policy is violated.

Article 44: Avoiding Conflicts of Interest
a) A member of the Board shall:

1) perform his/her duties with honesty and integrity, and prioritize the interests of the Company over his/her own interest, and not use his/her position to achieve personal interests;
2) avoid situations of conflicts of interest and notify the Board of situations of conflict which may affect his/her neutrality when looking into matters presented before the Board. The Board shall not allow such member to be involved in deliberations and shall not count his/her vote when voting on such matters in the Board and the Shareholders Assemblies meetings; and
3) protect the confidentiality of the information related to the Company and its activities, and not disclose any of such information to any person.

b) Each Board member is prohibited from:

1) voting on a decision taken by the Board or the General Assembly with respect to transactions and contracts that are executed for the Company's account, if he/she has a direct or indirect interest therein.
2) misusing or benefitting, directly or indirectly, from any of the Company's assets, information or investment opportunities presented to the Company or to him in his/her capacity as a member of the Board. This includes investment opportunities which are within the activities of the Company, or which the Company wishes to make use of. Such prohibition shall extend to Board member who resigns to, directly or indirectly, use investment opportunities that the Company wishes to use, which came to his/her knowledge during his/her membership in the Board.

Article 45: Disclosure of Conflicts of Interest by the Nominee A person who desires to nominate himself/herself for the membership of the Board shall disclose to the Board or the General Assembly any cases of conflicts of interest, including:

1) having direct or indirect interest in the contracts and businesses entered into for the benefit of the Company in which he/she desires to be nominated to the Board.

2) engaging in business that may compete with the Company or any of its activities.

Article 46: :Rules of Competing with the Company Without prejudice to Article (72) of the Companies Law and other relevant provisions in these regulations, if a member of the Board desires to engage in a business that may compete with the Company or any of its activities, the following shall be taken into account:

1) notifying the Board of the competing businesses he/she desires to engage in and recording such notification in the minutes of the Board meeting.

2) the conflicted member shall abstain from voting on the related decision in the Board meeting and General Assemblies.

3) the chairman of the Board informing the Ordinary General Assembly, once convened, of the competing businesses that the member of the Board is engaged in, after the Board assesses the board member's competition with the company's business or if he/she is in competition with one of the branch activities that it conducts in accordance with the standards issued by the Ordinary General Assembly upon a proposal from the Board and published on the company's website, provided that such businesses are assessed on annual basis.

4) obtaining an authorization of the Ordinary General Assembly of the Company for the member to engage in the competing business.

Article 47: Concept of the Competing Businesses The following shall be deemed a participation in any business that may compete with the Company or any of its activities:

1) the Board members' establishing a company or a sole proprietorship or the ownership of a controlling percentage of shares or stakes in a Company or any other entity engages in business activities that are similar to the activities of the Company or its group.

2) accepting membership in the Board of a company, an entity that competing with the Company or its group, or managing the affairs of a competing sole proprietorship or any competing company of any form, except the company's affiliates.

3) the Board member's acting as an overt or covert commercial agent for another company or entity competing with the Company or its group.

Article 48: Rejection to Grant Authorization If the General Assembly rejects granting the authorization pursuant to Article(72) of the Companies Law and Article (46) of these Regulations, the member of the Board shall resign within a period specified by the General Assembly; otherwise, his/her membership in the Board shall be deemed terminated, unless he/she decides to withdraw from competing the company or regularize his/her situation in accordance with the Companies Law and its Implementing Regulations prior to the end of the period set by the General Assembly.

Article 49: Accepting Gifts No member of the Board or Senior Executives may accept gifts from any person who has entered into commercial transactions with the Company if such acceptance of gifts may lead to a conflicts of interest.

7.4 PART 4: COMPANY COMMITTEES

7.4.1 Chapter 1: General Provisions

Article 50: Forming the Committees Without prejudice to Article (101) of the Companies Law and Article (54) of these Regulations, the Board shall form specialized committees as follows:

1. as may be needed depending on the Company's circumstances in order to enable it to effectively perform its duties.

2. the formation of the committees shall be made in accordance with general procedures developed by the Board, which shall determine the duties, duration and powers of each committee, and the manner in which the Board monitors the activities of each committee. The committee shall inform the Board of its findings or decisions with complete transparency. The Board shall regularly follow up the activities of such committees to ensure the performance of the duties delegated to them.

3. each committee shall be responsible before the Board for its activities, this shall not relief the Board of its responsibility for such activities, duties and powers that it has delegated to such committee.

4. the number of members of a committee shall not be less than three or more than five.

5. the chairmen or whom they delegate of each committee members, shall attend the General Assembly Meetings and answer any questions raised by the shareholders.

6. the Company shall provide the Authority with the names of the members and the types of their memberships in such Board's committees within five (5) days of their appointment, and shall notify the Authority of any changes thereto within five (5) days of the date of such changes.

7. a Company may combine remuneration and nomination committees into one committee named remuneration and nomination committee. In such case, the remuneration and nomination committee must satisfy the requirements related to any of them as set forth in Chapter 3 and 4 of this Part, and exercise all the powers set forth in Article (61) and (65) of these Regulations, provided that the committee convenes periodically at least every six months.

Article 51: Committees Membership
a) A sufficient number of Non-Executive Directors shall be appointed to the committees which perform duties that may involve a conflicts of interest, such as ensuring the integrity of financial and non-financial reports, reviewing Related Party transactions, nomination to membership of the Board, appointment of Senior Executives and determining the remuneration. Chairmen and members of these committees shall comply with principles of truthfulness, honesty, loyalty, and care and shall attend to the interests of the Company and its shareholders, and prioritize them over their personal interests.

b) The Company shall take into consideration while forming the remuneration and nomination committees that their members are of Independent Directors. The Board may appoint Non- Executive Directors or persons other than Board members either from shareholders or others, provided that the chairmen of committees mentioned in this paragraph are of the Independent Directors.

c) Chairman of the Board shall not be a member of the audit committee. He may be a member of other committees, provided that he is not the chairman of committees mentioned in these Regulations.

Article 52: Studying Subjects
a) Each committee shall assess the matters that fall within its authority or those referred to it by the Board and shall communicate its recommendations to the Board to issue decisions in connection therewith. The committees shall take decisions in regards to these matters if delegated by the Board, in pursuance to paragraph (b) of Article (21) of these Regulations.

b) The committees may seek assistance from any experts or specialists, whether internal or external, within the scope of its powers. This shall be included in the minutes of the committee meeting; the minutes states the name of the expert and his relation to the Company or its Executive Management.

Article 53: Committees Meetings
a) No member of the Board or the Executive Management except the secretary or a member of the committee may attend the meetings of a committee unless such committee requests his/her opinion or advice.

b) Committee meetings are valid if attended by a majority of its members. Resolutions of the committees shall be issued by a majority of the votes present and, in case of a tie, the chairman of the relevant committee shall have the casting vote.

c) Board meetings shall be documented and minutes including the discussions and deliberations carried during such meetings shall be prepared. Recommendations of the committees and voting results shall be documented and retained in a special and organized register, including the names of the attendees and any reservations they expressed (if any). Such minutes shall be signed by all of the attending members.

7.4.2 Chapter 2: The Audit Committee

Article 54: Audit Committee Formation
a) An audit committee shall be formed by a resolution of the Company's Ordinary General Assembly, and the members of the audit committee shall be from the shareholders or others, provided that at least one of its members is an Independent Director and that no Executive Director is among its members. The number of the members of the audit committee shall not be less than three or more than five, provided that one of its member is specialized in finance and accounting.

b) The chairman of the audit committee shall be an Independent Director.

c) The Company's General Assembly shall, upon a recommendation of the Board, issue a regulation for the audit committee which shall include the rules and procedures for the activities and duties of the committee, the rules for selecting its members, the means of their nomination, the term of their membership, their remunerations, and the mechanism of appointing temporary members in case a seat in the committee becomes vacant.

d) Any person who works or has worked in the Company's finance Department, the Executive Management or for the Company's external auditor during the preceding two years may not be a member of the audit committee.

Article 55: Competencies, powers and responsibilities of the Audit Committee The audit committee shall be competent in monitoring the Company's activities and ensuring the integrity and effectiveness of the reports, financial statements and internal control systems. The duties of the audit committee shall particularly include the following:

a) Financial Reports:

1) analyzing the Company's interim and annual financial statements before presenting them to the Board and providing its opinion and recommendations thereon to ensure their integrity, fairness and transparency;
2) providing its technical opinion, at the request of the Board, regarding whether the Board's report and the Company's financial statements are fair, balanced, understandable, and contain information that allows shareholders and investors to assess the Company's financial position, performance, business model, and strategy;
3) analyzing any important or non-familiar issues contained in the financial reports;
4) accurately investigating any issues raised by the Company's chief financial officer or any person assuming his/her duties or the Company's compliance officer or external auditor;
5) examining the accounting estimates in respect of significant matters that are contained in the financial reports; and
6) examining the accounting policies followed by the Company and providing its opinion and recommendations to the Board thereon.

b) Internal Audit:

1) examining and reviewing the Company's internal and financial control systems and risk management system;
2) analyzing the internal audit reports and following up the implementation of the corrective measures in respect of the remarks made in such reports; and
3) monitoring and overseeing the performance and activities of the internal auditor and internal audit department of the company, if any, to ensure the availability of the necessary resources and their effectiveness in performing the assigned activities and duties. If the Company has no internal auditor, the committee shall provide a recommendation to the Board on whether there is a need to appoint an internal auditor.
4) providing a recommendation to the Board on appointing the manager of the internal audit unit or department, or the internal auditor and suggest his/her remunerations.

c) External Auditor:

1) providing recommendations to the Board to nominate external auditors, dismiss them, determine their remunerations, and assess their performance after verifying their independence and reviewing the scope of their work and the terms of their contracts;
2) verifying the independence of the external auditor, its objectivity, fairness, and effectiveness of the audit activities, taking into account the relevant rules and standards;
3) reviewing the plan of the Company's external auditor and its activities, and ensuring that it does not provide any technical or administrative works that are beyond its scope of work, and provides its opinion thereon;
4) responding to queries of the Company's external auditor; and
5) reviewing the external auditor's reports and its comments on the financial statements, and following up the procedures taken in connection therewith.

d) Ensuring Compliance:

1) reviewing the findings of the reports of supervisory authorities and ensuring that the Company has taken the necessary actions in connection therewith;
2) ensuring the Company's compliance with the relevant laws, regulations, policies and instructions;
3) reviewing the contracts and proposed Related Party transactions, and providing its recommendations to the Board in connection therewith; and
4) reporting to the Board any issues in connection with what it deems necessary to take action on, and providing recommendations as to the steps that should be taken.

Article 56: Conflict between the Audit Committee and the Board If a conflict arises between the recommendations of the audit committee and the Board resolutions, or if the Board refuses to put the committee's recommendations into action as to appointing or dismissal the company's external auditor or determining its remuneration, assessing its performance or appointing the internal auditor, the Board's report shall include the committee's recommendations and justifications, and the reasons for not following such recommendations.

Article 57: Audit Committee Meetings
a) The audit committee shall convene periodically, provided that at least four meetings are held during the Company's financial year.

b) The audit committee shall convene periodically with the Company's external auditor and internal auditor, if any.

c) The internal auditor and the external auditor may call for a meeting with the audit committee at any time as may be necessary.

Article 58: Arrangements for Providing Remarks The audit committee shall develop arrangements that enable the Company's employees to confidentially provide their remarks in respect of any inaccuracies in the financial or other reports. The audit committee shall ensure that such arrangements have been put into action through an adequate independent investigation in respect of the error or inaccuracy, and shall adopt appropriate follow-up procedures.

Article 59: Powers of the Audit Committee In order to perform its duties, the audit committee may:

1) review the Company's records and documents.

2) request any clarification or statement from the Board members or the Executive Management.

3) request that the Board calls for a General Assembly Meeting if its activities have been impeded by the Board or if the Company has suffered significant losses and damages.

7.4.3 Chapter 3: Remuneration Committee

Article 60: Composition of the Remuneration Committee
a) The Company's Board shall, by resolution thereof, set up a committee to be named the "remuneration committee." Members of the committee shall not be Executive Directors, provided that there shall be at least one Independent Director among them.

b) The Company's General Assembly, as per the Board recommendation, issues a regulation for the remuneration committee including its procedure, duties and rules for selecting its members, the term of their membership and their remunerations.

Article 61: Competencies of the Remuneration Committee The competences of the Remuneration Committee are:

1) preparing a clear policy for the remunerations of the Board members and its committees and the Executive Management, and presenting such policy to the Board in preparation for approval by the General Assembly, provided that such policy follows standards that linked to performance, and disclosing and ensuring the implementation of such policy;

2) clarifying the relation between the paid remunerations and the adopted remuneration policy, and highlighting any material deviation from that policy.

3) periodically reviewing the remuneration policy and assessing its effectiveness in achieving its objectives; and

4) providing recommendations to the Board in respect of the remunerations of its members, the committees members and Senior Executives, in accordance with the approved policy.

Article 62: Remuneration Policy Without prejudice to the provisions of the Companies Law and the Capital Market Law and their implementing regulations, the remuneration policy shall:

1) be consistent with the Company's strategy and objectives;

2) provide remunerations with the aim of encouraging the Board members and Executive Management to achieve the success of the Company and its long-term development, by for example making the variable part of the remuneration linked to the long-term performance;

3) determine remuneration based on job level, duties and responsibilities, educational qualifications, practical experience, skills and level of performance;

4) be consistent with the magnitude, nature and level of risks faced by the Company;

5) take into consideration the practices of other companies in respect of the determination of remunerations, and avoid the disadvantages of such comparisons in leading to unjustifiable increases in remunerations and compensations;

6) attract talented professionals and retain and motivate them without exaggeration;

7) be prepared in coordination with the nomination committee in respect of new appointments;

8) take into consideration situations where remunerations should be suspended or reclaimed if it is determined that such remunerations were set based on inaccurate information provided by a member of the Board or the executive management, in order to prevent abuse of power to obtain unmerited remunerations; and

9) regulating the grant of Company's shares to theBoard members and the Executive Management, whether newly issued or purchased by the Company.

Article 63: Meetings of the Remuneration Committee The remuneration committee shall convene periodically at least once a year, and as may be necessary.

7.4.4 Chapter 4: Nomination Committee

Article 64: Composition of the Nomination Committee
a) The Company's Board shall, by resolution thereof, form a committee to be named the "nomination committee,". Members of the committee shall not be Executive Directors, provided that there shall be at least one Independent Director among them.

b) The Company's General Assembly, as per the Board recommendation, issues a regulation for the nomination committee including its procedures, duties and rules for selecting its members, the term of their membership and their remunerations.

Article 65: competences of the Nomination Committee The competences of the nomination committee shall include the following:

1) suggesting clear policies and standards for membership of the Board and the Executive Management;

2) providing recommendations to the Board for the nomination or re-nomination of its members in accordance with approved policies and standards, taking into account that nomination shall not include any person convicted of a crime involving moral turpitude or dishonesty;

3) preparing a description of the capabilities and qualifications required for membership of the Board and Executive Management positions;

4) determining the amount of time that the member shall allocate to the activities of the Board;

5) annually reviewing the skills and expertise required of the Board members and the Executive Management;

6) reviewing the structure of the Board and the Executive Management and providing recommendations regarding changes that may be made to such structure;

7) annually ensuring the independence of Independent Directors and the absence of any conflicts of interest if a Board member also acts as a member of the Board of directors of another company;

8) providing job descriptions for the Executive, Non-Executive and Independent Directors and the Senior Executive Management;

9) setting procedures to be followed if the position of a member of the Board or a Senior Executive becomes vacant; and

10) determining the strengths and weaknesses of the Board and recommending remedy solutions that serve the Company's interests.

Article 66: the Nomination Procedures
a) When nominating a Board member, the nomination committee shall take into consideration the provisions of these Regulations and the requirements set by the Authorities; and

b) The number of nominees to the Board whose names are presented to the General Assembly shall be more than the number of available seats to give a chance to the General Assembly to select the Board members among those nominees.9

Article 67: Meetings of the Nomination Committee The nomination committee shall convene periodically at least once a year, and as may be necessary.

Article 68: Publishing the Nomination Announcement The Company shall publish the nomination announcement on the websites of the Company and the Exchange and through any other medium specified by the Authority; to invite persons wishing to be nominated to the membership of the Board, provided that the nomination period shall remain open for at least a month from the date of the announcement.

Article 69: Nomination Rights of Shareholders None of the provisions of this Chapter shall prejudice the right of any shareholder to nominate him/herself or others to the membership of the Board in accordance with the provisions of the Companies Law and Its Implementing Regulations.

7.4.5 Chapter 5: Risk Management Committee

Article 70: Composition of the Risk Management Committee10 The Company's Board shall, by resolution therefrom, form a committee to be named the "risk management committee." Chairman and majority of its members shall be Non-Executive Directors. The members of that committee shall possess an adequate level of knowledge in risk management and finance.

Article 71: Competencies of the Risk Management Committee The competences of the risk management committee shall include the following:

1) developing a strategy and comprehensive policies for risk management that are consistent with the nature and volume of the Company's activities, monitoring their implementation, and reviewing and updating them based on the Company's internal and external changing factors;

2) determining and maintaining an acceptable level of risk that may be faced by the Company and ensuring that the Company does not go beyond such level;

3) Ensuring the feasibility of the Company continuation, the successful continuity of its activities and determining the risks that threaten its existence during the following twelve (12) months;

4) overseeing the Company's risk management system and assessing the effectiveness of the systems and mechanisms for determining and monitoring the risks that threaten the Company in order to determine areas of inadequacy therein;

5) Regularly reassessing the Company's ability to take risks and be exposed to such risks (through stress tests as an example);

6) preparing detailed reports on the exposure to risks and the recommended measures to manage such risks, and presenting them to the Board;

7) providing recommendations to the Board on matters related to risk management;

8) ensuring the availability of adequate resources and systems for risk management;

9) reviewing the organizational structure for risk management and providing recommendations regarding the same before approval by the Board;

10) verifying the independence of the risk management employees from activities that may expose the Company to risk;

11) ensuring that the risk management employees understand the risks threatening the Company and seeking to raise awareness of the culture of risk; and

12) reviewing any issues raised by the audit committee that may affect the Company's risk management.

Article 72: Meetings of the Risk Management Committee12 The risk management committee shall convene periodically at least once every six months, and as may be necessary.

7.5 PART 5: INTERNAL CONTROL

Article 73: Internal Control System The Board shall approve an internal control system for the Company in order to assess the policies and procedures relating to risk management, implementation of the provisions of the Company's governance rules approved by the Company and compliance with the relevant laws and regulations. Such system shall ensure compliance with clear accountability standards at all executive levels in the Company, and that Related Party transactions are implemented in accordance with the relevant provisions and controls.

Article 74: Establishing Independent Units or Departments within the Company

a) For purposes of implementing the approved internal control system, the Company shall establish units or departments for the assessment and management of risks and for internal auditing.

b) The Company may utilise external entities to perform the duties and competencies of the units or departments of risks assessments and management and internal control without prejudice to the Company's responsibility for those duties and competencies.

Article 75: Duties of the Internal Audit Unit or Department An internal audit unit or department assesses and monitors the implementation of the internal control system, and verifies that the Company and its employees comply with the applicable laws, regulations and instructions, and the Company's policies and procedures.

Article 76: Composing An Internal Audit Unit or Department The internal audit unit or department shall be composed of at least one internal auditor whose appointment is recommended by the audit committee. Such internal auditor shall be responsible before the audit committee. The formation and operation of the internal audit unit or department shall take into consideration the following:

1) employees of such department shall be competent, independent and adequately trained, and shall not be entrusted with any other functions other than internal audit duties and internal control system;

2) the department shall report to the audit committee, and shall be subordinate and accountable to it;

3) the remunerations of the manager of the audit unit or department shall be determined by the a recommendation of the audit committee as per Company's policies; and

4) the department or unit shall be given access to information and documents, and shall be able to obtain the same without any restrictions.

Article 77: Internal Audit Plan The internal audit unit or department shall operate pursuant to a comprehensive audit plan approved by the audit committee. Such plan shall be updated annually. Key activities and operations, including the activities of risk management and compliance departments, shall be reviewed at least annually.

Article 78: Internal Audit Report
a) The internal audit unit or department shall prepare and submit a written report on its activities at least quarterly to the Board and the audit committee. Such report shall include an assessment of the Company's internal control system and the final opinion and recommendations of the unit or department. Such report shall also specify the procedures taken by each department for addressing the findings and recommendations from the previous audit, and any remarks thereon, particularly failures to promptly address such findings and recommendations and the reasons for such failure;

b) The internal audit unit or department shall prepare a general written report to be submitted to the Board and the audit committee on the audit activities it carried during the fiscal year compared to the approved plan. Such report shall explain the reasons for any deviation from the plan, if any, during the quarter following the end of the relevant financial year;

c) The Board shall specify the scope of the report of the internal audit unit or department, based on recommendations from the audit committee and the internal audit unit or department. The report shall include the following in particular:

1) procedures for monitoring and overseeing the financial affairs, investments and risk management;
2) assessing the development of risk factors threatening the Company and the existing systems, in order to confront radical or unexpected changes in the Exchange;
3) an assessment of the performance of the Board and the Senior Management with respect to the implementation of internal control systems, including specifying the number of times the Board has been informed of control issues (including risk management) and a description of the method followed to address such issues;
4) failures or weaknesses in the implementation of internal control, or emergency situations that have affected or may affect the Company's financial performance, and the measures taken by the Company to address such failures (particularly the issues disclosed in the Company's annual reports and its financial statements);
5) the extent to which the Company has complied with the internal controls when determining and managing risks; and
6) information describing the Company's risk management operations.

Article 79: Maintaining Internal Audit Reports The Company shall keep records of the audit reports and business documents, which shall clarify its accomplishments, findings and recommendations, and all actions taken in their regard.

7.6 PART 6: COMPANY AUDITOR

Article 80: Assigning the Audit Function The Company shall assign the function of auditing its annual accounts to an independent and competent external auditor who possesses the necessary expertise and qualifications to prepare an objective and independent report to the Board and the shareholders, setting out whether the Company's financial statements clearly and impartially express the financial position of the Company and its performance in the significant areas.

Article 81: Appointment of the External Auditor The Ordinary General Assembly shall appoint the Company's external auditor based on a recommendation from the Board, provided that the following requirements are met:

1) the nomination shall be based on a recommendation from the audit committee;

2) the external auditor shall be authorized by the Competent Authority;

3) the external auditor's interests shall not conflict with the interests of the Company; and

4) the number of nominees shall not be less than two.

Article 82: Duties of the External Auditor The external auditor shall:

1) owe the duties of loyalty and care to the Company;

2) notify the Authority if the Board fails to take appropriate actions in respect of suspicious issues it raises; and

3) Request the Board to call for a General Assembly meeting if the Board has not facilitated his mission; and shall be liable to compensate the Company, the shareholders or third parties for the damages resulted from errors it commits in the course of its engagement. If an error is attributable to more than one external auditor, they shall be jointly responsible therefor.

7.7 PART 7: STAKEHOLDERS

Article 83: Regulating the Relationship with Stakeholders The Board shall establish clear and written policies and procedures regulating the relationship with Stakeholders with the aim of protecting them and safeguard their rights, which shall include the following, in particular:

1) methods to compensate Stakeholders when their rights established by laws or protected by contracts are infringed;

2) methods for resolving complaints or disputes that may arise between the Company and the Stakeholders;

3) methods for building good relationships with customers and suppliers and maintaining the confidentiality of their information;

4) rules of professional conduct for Company managers and employees that are prepared in compliance with the proper professional and ethical standards and regulate their relationship with Stakeholders, provided that the Board shall establish mechanisms for supervising the implementation of, and compliance with such rules;

5) the Company's social contributions;

6) ensuring that the Company's transactions with Board members and Related Parties are entered into on terms identical to the terms of transactions with Stakeholders without any discrimination or bias;

7) Stakeholders obtaining of information relevant to their activities to enable them to perform their duties. Such information shall be correct and sufficient and shall be provided in timely manner and on a regular basis; and

8) treating Company employees pursuant to the principles of justice and equality and without discrimination.

Article 84: Reporting Non-Compliant Practices The Board shall, based upon a proposal from the audit committee, develop the necessary policies and procedures to be followed by Stakeholders when submitting complaints or reporting any violations, taking the following into consideration:

1) facilitating the method by which Stakeholders (including Company employees) report to the Board conducts and practices of the Executive Management's that violate applicable laws, regulations and rules or raising doubts as to the financial statements or the internal audit controls or others, whether such conducts or practices are against them or not, and conducting the necessary investigation in that regard;

2) maintaining the confidentiality of reporting procedures through facilitating direct contact with an independent member of the audit committee or other specialized committees;

3) appointing an employee to receive and address complaints or reports sent by Stakeholders;

4) dedicating a telephone number or an email address for receiving complaints; and

5) providing the necessary protection to the Stakeholders.

Article 85: Employee Incentives The Company shall establish programmes for developing and encouraging the participation and performance of the Company's employees. The programmes shall particularly include the following:

1) forming committees or holding specialized workshops to hear the opinions of the Company's employees and discuss the issues and topics that are subject to important decisions;

2) establishing a scheme for granting Company shares or a percentage of the Company profits and pension programmes for employees, and setting up an independent fund for such programme; and

3) establishing social organizations for the benefit of the Company's employees.

7.8 PART 8: PROFESSIONAL AND ETHICAL STANDARDSrofessional and Ethical

Article 86: Professional Conduct Policy The Board shall establish a policy for professional conduct and ethical values at the Company, which shall particularly take the following into consideration:

1) ensuring that each member of the Board or the Executive Management and employees perform his/her duties of loyalty and care to the Company, and undertake the measures that may protect the Company's interests and contribute to its development and increase its value, and shall, at all times, prioritize the Company's interests over his/her own interests;

2) a Board member shall represent all shareholders of the Company and take all actions to achieve the best interests of the Company and its shareholders, while protecting the rights of the other Stakeholders rather than only the interests of the group that elected him;

3) entrench among the Board members and Senior Executives the principle of compliance with all relevant laws, regulations and instructions;

4) preventing the Board members or the Executive Management from abusing their positions with the aim of achieving benefits for himself/herself or a third party;

5) ensuring that the Company's assets and resources are only used to achieve the Company's purposes and objectives, and not to achieve personal interests; and

6) establishing accurate, well-formed, and clear rules regulating the authority to access the Company's internal information and timing to access it, in a way that prevents the Board members, the Executive Management and others from making personal use or disclosing the same to any person, except within the prescribed limits or as permitted by law.

Article 87: Social Responsibility The Ordinary General Assembly, based on the Board recommendation, shall establish a policy that guarantees a balance between its objectives and those of the community for purposes of developing the social and economic conditions of the community.

Article 88: Social Initiatives The Board shall establish programs and determine the necessary methods for proposing social initiatives by the Company, which include:

1) establishing indicators that link the Company's performance with its social initiatives and comparing it with other companies that engage in similar activities;

2) disclosing the objectives of the Company's social responsibility to its employees and raising their awareness and knowledge of social responsibility;

3) disclosing plans for achieving social responsibility in the periodical reports on the activities of the Company's; and

4) establishing awareness programmes to the community to familiarise them with the Company's social responsibility.

7.9 PART 9: DISCLOSURE AND TRANSPARENCY

Article 89: Policies and Procedure of Disclosure Without prejudice to the Rules on the Offer of Securities and Continuing Obligations, the Board shall set forth in writing the policies, procedures and supervisory rules related to disclosure pursuant to the disclosure requirements provided for in the Companies Law and the Capital Market Law, as the case may be, and their implementing regulations, taking into consideration the following:

1) such policies shall include proper disclosure methods that enable the shareholders and other Stakeholders to access the

financial and non-financial information pertaining to the Company's performance and information in respect of ownership of shares, and to obtain a comprehensive view of the Company's position;

2) disclosure to shareholders and investors shall be made without discrimination in a clear, correct and non-misleading fashion, and in a timely, regular and accurate manner in order to enable shareholders and other Stakeholders to exercise their rights to the fullest extent;

3) the Company's website shall include all information required to be disclosed and any details or other information that may be published through other disclosure methods;

4) reporting rules shall be established and shall describe the information required to be disclosed and the method of its classification in terms of its nature, and the frequency of its disclosure; and

5) the disclosure policies shall be reviewed periodically and their compliance with the best practices and the provisions of the Capital Market Law and its implementing rules shall be verified.

Article 90: The Board's Report The Board's report shall include the Board's operations during the last fiscal year and all factors that affect the company's businesses , such report shall include the following:

1) implemented and non-implemented provisions of these Regulations, and justifications therefor;

2) names, qualifications, and experience of the Board and committees members and Executive Management;

3) names of the companies inside and outside the Kingdom in which a Board member is a member of their current or previous Board member or manager;

4) composition of the Board and classification of its members, as follows: Executive Directors, Non-Executive Director, or Independent Director;

5) Procedure taken to the Board to inform its members , Non-Executive Directors in particular, of the shareholders' suggestions and remarks on the Company and its performance.

6) a brief description of the competencies and duties of the committees, such as the audit committee, the nomination committee and the remuneration committee indicating their names, names of their chairmen, names of their members, the number of their respective meetings, dates of those meetings and the members' attendance details of each meeting;

7) Where applicable, the means used by the Board to assess its performance, the performance of its committees and members and the external body which conducted the assessment and its relation with the Company, if any;

8) disclose the remuneration of the Board members and Executive Management as stated in Article (93) of these Regulations;

9) any punishment, penalty, precautionary procedure or preventive measure imposed on the Company by the Authority or any other supervisory, regulatory or judiciary authority, describing the reasons for non-compliance, the imposing authority and the measures undertaken to remedy and avoid such non-compliance in the future;

10) results of the annual review of the effectiveness of the internal control procedures of the Company and the opinion of the audit committee with respect to the adequacy of the Company's internal control system;

11) the audit committees recommendation on the need for appointing an internal auditor for the Company, if there is no internal auditor.

12) the audit committees recommendation with conflict with Board resolution or those which the Board disregards relating to the appointment, dismissal, assessment or determining the remuneration of an external auditor, as well as justifications for those recommendations and reasons for disregarding them.

13) details of the Company's social contributions, if any;

14) a list of the dates of the General Assembly meetings held during the last fiscal year and the names of the Board members who attended them.

15) a description of the main scope of business of the company and its affiliates. If there are two or more, a statement showing each activity and how it affects the company businesses and results shall be attached.

16) a description of the company's significant plans and decisions (including changes to the structure, expanding the company's operations or halting them) and the future expectations.

17) information on any risks facing the company (operational, financial or market related) and the policy of managing and monitoring these risks.

18) a summary in a form of table or graph showing the company's assets, liabilities and results of the last five fiscal year or since the incorporation date, whichever is shorter.

19) geographical analysis of the company's and its affiliates' revenues.

20) any material differences in the operational results compared to the preceding year's results, along with any expectations announced by the company.

21) any inconsistency with the standards approved by the Saudi Organizations for Certified Public Accountant.

22) name of each affiliate company, its capital, the company's ownership percentage, the main scope of business, country of operation and country of incorporation.

23) details of shares and debt instruments issued for each affiliate company.

24) a descriptions of the dividends distribution policy.

25) a description of any interest in a class of voting shares held by persons (other than the company's directors, Senior Executives and their relatives) who have notified the company of their holdings pursuant to Article 67 of the Rules on the Offer of Securities and Continuing Obligations, together with any change to such interests during the last fiscal year;

26) a description of any interest, contractual securities or rights issue of the Board members, Senior Executives and their relatives on shares or debt instruments of the company or its affiliates, and any change on these interest or rights during the last fiscal year.

27) information on any loans (payable upon request or not), a statement of the total indebtedness of the company and its affiliates, any amounts paid by the company in repayments of loans during the year, the amount of the principal debts, the creditor name, the loan term and remaining amount. In case there is no debts, a declaration thereof shall be presented.

28) a description of the class and number of any convertible debt instruments, contractual securities, preemptive right or similar rights issued or granted by the company during the fiscal year, as well as stating any compensation obtained by the company in this regard.

29) a description of any conversion or subscription rights under any convertible debt instruments, contractually based securities, warrants or similar rights issued or granted by the company;

30) description of any redemption, purchase or cancellation by the company of any redeemable debt instruments and the value of such securities outstanding, distinguishing between those listed securities purchased by the company and those purchased by its affiliates.

31) the number of Board meetings held during the last financial year, their dates and the attendance record of each meeting listing the names of the attendees.

32) numbers of company's requests of shareholders records, dates and reasons thereof.

33) a description of any transaction between the company and any Related Party.

34) information relating to any business or contract to which the company is a party and in which a director of the company, a Senior Executive or any person related to any of them is or was interested, including the names of persons in relation, the nature, conditions, durations and the amount of the business or contract. If there are no such businesses or contracts, the company must submit a statement thereof.

35) a description of any arrangement or agreement under which a director or a Senior Executive of the company has waived any remuneration.

36) a description of any arrangement or agreement under which a shareholder of the company has waived any rights to dividends.

37) a statement of the value of any paid and outstanding statutory payment on account of any zakat, taxes, fees or any other charges that have not been paid until the end of the annual financial period with a brief description and the reasons therefor.

38) a statement as to the value of any investments made or any reserves set up for the benefit of the employees of the company.

39) declarations that:

a. proper books of account have been maintained;
b. the system of internal control is sound in design and has been effectively implemented; and
c. there are no significant doubts concerning the company's ability to continue its activity.

40) if the external auditor's report contains reservations on the annual financial statements, the Board report shall highlight this mentioning the reasons and any relevant information.

41) if the Board recommended replacing the external auditor before the end of its term, the report shall indicate this mentioning the reasons for the replacement recommendation.

Article 91: The Audit Committee's Report

a) The report of the audit shall include details of its performance of its competencies and duties stated in the Companies Law and Its Implementing Regulations, provided that the report contains its recommendations and opinion on the adequacy of the internal and financial control systems and risk management systems in the Company.

b) The Board shall make available sufficient copies of the audit committees' report at the Company's head office, and publish them on the Company's and the Exchange's websites when publishing the invitation to convene the General Assembly, to enable shareholders to get a copy thereof. Summary of the report shall be read at the General Assembly.

Article 92: Disclosure by the Board The Board shall regulate the disclosures of each of its members and the members of the Executive Management, observing the following:

1) maintaining a register for the disclosures of the Board members and the Executive Management and updating it regularly based on disclosures required as per the Companies Law, the Capital Market Law and their implementing regulations; and

2) making such register available for review by the Company's shareholders free of charge.

Article 93: Disclosure of Remunerations

a) The Board shall:

1) disclose the remuneration policy and the method by which remunerations of the Board and executive management are determined;
2) provide an accurate, transparent and detailed disclosure in the Board report on the remunerations granted to the Board members and Executive Management, directly or indirectly, without any omission or misleading information, and whether these were in cash or other benefits of any nature. In case they were shares of the Company, the value of the shares is the market value on the due date;
3) explain the relationship between remunerations granted and applicable remuneration policy, highlighting any significant deviation from such policy;
4) a description of the necessary details with respect to the remunerations and compensations granted to each of the following, separately:

a.Board members;

b. five Senior Executives who have received the highest remuneration from the Company, provided that the chief executive officer and chief financial officer are among them.21

c.members of committees.

b) The disclosures in this article and in the Board report shall be pursuant to the appended schedule.

(The Capital Market Authority Board issued its Resolution Number 1-35-2018 Dated 9/7/1439H Corresponding to 26/3/2018G stating that the remunerations of senior executives mentioned in sub- paragraph (b) of paragraph (4) of Article 93 of the Corporate Governance Regulations is to be disclosed collectively.)

7.10 Part 10: IMPLEMENTATION

Article 94: Implementation of Effective Governance The Board shall establish governance rules for the Company in accordance with the provisions of these Regulations, and shall monitor their implementation, verify their effectiveness, and amend them as necessary. To that end, the Board shall:

1) verify that the Company is in compliance with these rules;

2) review and update the rules pursuant to statutory requirements and best practices;

3) review and develop codes of professional conduct representing the Company's values and other internal policies and procedures in order to fulfill the Company's requirements and in accordance with best practices; and

4) regularly inform the Board members of the developments in corporate governance and best practices, or authorize the audit committee or any other committee or department to undertake this task.

Article 95: Formation of a Corporate Governance Committee2 If the Board forms a corporate governance committee, it shall assign to it the competences stipulated in Article (94) of these Regulations. Such committee shall oversee any matters relating to the implementation of governance, and shall provide the Board with its reports and recommendations at least annually.

7.11 Part 11: DOCUMENT RETENTION

Article 96: Document Retention A company shall retain all minutes, documents, reports and other papers required to be maintained in the company's head office for at least ten years as per these Regulations. This shall include the Board report and audit committee report. Without prejudice to this period, a company, in case of any lawsuit (filed or threatened to be filed) or ongoing claim or any investigation relating to those minutes, documents, reports and other papers, shall maintain them until the end of the ongoing lawsuit, claim or investigation.

7.12 Part 12: CLOSING PROVISIONS

Article 97: Providing Additional data and Information The Authority may request from the Company any additional information or details it deems necessary to verify the extent of its compliance with the provisions of these Regulations.

Article 98: Publication and Entry into Force These Regulations shall be effective as per their approval resolution.

7.13 APPENDIX 1: Remuneration Schedule

Appendix (1) Remuneration Schedule

Board Remuneration

	Fixed remunerations							Variable remunerations								
	Specific amount	Allowance for attending Board meetings	Total Allowance for attending committee meetings committee	In-kind benefits	Remunerations for technical, managerial and consultative work	Remunerations of the chairman, Managing Director or Secretary, if a	Total	Percentage of the profits	Periodic remunerations	Short-term incentive plans	Long-term incentive plans	Granted shares (insert the value)	Total	End-of-service award	Aggregate Amount	Expenses Allowance
First: Independent Directors																
1-																
2-																
3-																
Total																
Second: Non-Executive Directors																
1-																
2-																
3-																
Total																
Third: Executive Directors																
1-																
2-																
3-																
Total																

Appendix (1) Remuneration Schedule

(For Independent Directors, Non-Executive Directors, Executive Directors)

Fixed Remuneration

Fixed remunerations

Allowance for attending Board meetings

Total Allowance for attending committee meetings committee

In-kind benefits

Remunerations for technical, managerial and consultative work

Remunerations of the chairman, Managing Director or Secretary, if a (sic)

Total:

Variable remunerations

Percentage of the profits

Periodic remunerations

Short-term incentive plans

Long-term incentive plans

Granted shares (insert the value)

Total:

(Other)

End-of-service award

Aggregate Amount

Expenses Allowance

Total:

Remunerations of Senior Executives

Remunerations of Senior Executives [23]

Senior Executives	Fixed remunerations				Variable remunerations						End-of-service award	Total remunerations for Board executives, if any	Aggregate Amount
	Salaries	Allowances	In-kind benefits	Total	Periodic remunerations	Profits	Short-term incentive plans	Long-term incentive plans	Granted shares (insert the	Total			
1- CEO													
2- CFO													
3-													
4-													
5-													
Total													

(CEO, CFO, Others)

Fixed remuneration

Salaries

Allowances

In-kind benefits

Total:

Variable remuneration

Periodic Remuneration

Profits

Short-term incentive plans

Long-term incentive plans

Granted shares (insert the

Total:

End-of- service award

Total:

Remunerations for Board executives, if any

Total:

Aggregate Amount:

Total:

(The Capital Market Authority Board issued its Resolution Number 1-35-2018 Dated 9/7/1439H Corresponding to 26/3/2018G stating that the table for disclosure of senior executive remunerations specified in Appendix (1) of the Corporate Governance Regulations is of guiding nature, and the disclosure of senior executives' remunerations in the Board of Directors' reports, which will be issued for the financial periods beginning on 1/1/2020, shall be detailed in accordance with the table for the disclosure of senior executives remunerations specified in Appendix (1) of the Corporate Governance Regulations.)

7.14 APPENDIX 2: Committee Members Remuneration

Committees Members Remuneration

	Fixed Remuneration (Except for the allowance for attending Board meetings)	Allowance for attending Board meetings	Total
Audit Committee Members			
1-			
2-			
3-			
Total			
Remuneration Committee Members			
1-			
2-			
3-			
Total			
Nomination Committee Members			
1-			
2-			
3-			
Total			
Risks Committee Members			
1-			
2-			
3-			
Total			
(.........) Committee Members			
1-			
2-			
3-			
Total			

(Audit Committee Members, Remuneration Committee Members, Nomination Committee Members, Risks Committee Members (Other committees)

Fixed Remuneration (Except for the allowance for attending Board meetings)

Allowance for attending Board meetings

Total:

8 CREDIT RATING AGENCIES REGULATIONS

Issued by the Board of the Capital Market Authority pursuant to its Resolution Number 3-58-2014 dated 17/1/1436H (10/11/2014G) gased on the Capital Market Law Issued by Royal Decree No. M/30 dated 2/6/1424H

Important Note: The current version of these Regulations, as may be amended, can be found at the Authority website: www.cma.org.sa

TABLE OF CONTENTS

Part 1: PURPOSE AND SCOPE
Article 1: Preliminary
Article 2: Definitions
Article 3: Scope
Article 4: Requirement for Authorization
Article 5: Waivers
Article 6: Right of appeal
Part 2: Authorization and Maintenance of Authorization
Article 7: Application for authorization
Article 8: Authorization requirements
Article 9: Additional Authorization requirements for applicants incorporated within the Kingdom
Article 10: Additional authorization requirements for foreign applicants
Article 11: Procedure and powers of the Authority in relation to an application for authorization
Article 12: Withdrawal from business and cancellation of authorization
Article 13: Cancellation or suspension of Authorization
Article 14: Fees
Part 3: Conduct of Business Requirements
Article 15: General conduct of business requirements
Article 16: Conflicts of interest
Article 17: Rating categories, methodologies, models and key rating assumptions
Article 18: Assignment of credit ratings
Article 19: Monitoring and updating of credit ratings
Article 20: Discontinued credit ratings
Article 21: Disclosure requirements
Article 22: Transparency report
Article 23: Record keeping
Part 4: System Controls
Article 24: Organizational requirements
Article 25: Fit and Proper
Article 26: Administrative or supervisory committee
Article 27: Remuneration of rating analysts, employees involved in rating activities
Article 28: Professional ethics
Article 29: Professional misconduct
Article 30: Training
Article 31: Recruitment and employment practices
Article 32: Controllers
Article 33: Outsourcing
Article 34: Notification requirements
Part 5: Registered Persons
Article 35: Scope of Application
Article 36: Registrable functions
Article 37: Performance of registrable functions
Article 38: Requirements for application for registration
Article 39: Procedure and powers of the Authority in relation to an applicant for registration
Article 40: Responsibilities of registered persons
Article 41: Cancellation of registration
Part 6: Closing provisions
Article 42: Publication and entry into force
Annex 1. Information and Documents Required for authorization Application
Annex 2. Standard Form Credit Rating Disclosure

8.1 PART 1: PURPOSE AND SCOPE

Article 1: Preliminary The purpose of these Regulations is to regulate and monitor the conduct of rating activities in the Kingdom and to specify the procedures and conditions for obtaining an authorization to conduct rating activities.

Article 2: Definitions

(a) Any reference to the "Capital Market Law" in these Regulations shall mean the Capital Market Law issued by Royal Decree No. M/30 dated 2/6/1424H.

(b) Expressions and terms in these Regulations have the meaning which they bear in the Capital Market Law and in the Glossary of defined terms used in the Regulations and Rules of the Capital Market Authority, unless the contrary intention appears.

Article 3: Scope
(a) These Regulations apply to rating activities which are carried out in the Kingdom.

(b) Rating activities are carried out in the Kingdom if such activities are conducted in whole or in part in the Kingdom and includes:

1) dissemination of credit ratings to the public by any means or medium, whether in the Kingdom or elsewhere; or
2) distribution of credit ratings by way of subscription or membership, whether in the Kingdom or elsewhere.

(c) A credit rating is excluded from the scope of these Regulations if it is issued by the government of the Kingdom or a governmental agency in the Kingdom.

(d) These Regulations do not apply to:

1) credit ratings issued by any person for its internal commercial or industrial purposes, including assessing creditworthiness of its counterparties, provided that such credit rating is not circulated to any third party;
2) credit ratings issued by financial sector entities for an internal purpose of assessing its economic capital position, internal modelling, or risk management, provided that such credit rating is not circulated to any third party, except to its regulator only; or
3) credit ratings issued by any person pursuant to an individual order, provided exclusively to the person who placed the order and not intended for public disclosure or distribution by subscription.

Article 4: Requirement for authorization No person may carry out rating activities in the Kingdom or hold itself out as an authorized credit rating agency unless it has been authorized by the Authority in accordance with these Regulations.

Article 5: Waivers The Authority may waive a provision of these Regulations in whole or in part as it applies to an applicant for authorization or an authorized credit rating agency either on an application from the applicant for authorization or the authorized credit rating agency or on its own initiative.

Article 6: Right of appeal Any person subject to these Regulations may appeal to the Committee in respect of any decision or action that the Authority takes under these Regulations.

8.2 PART 2: AUTHORIZATION AND MAINTENANCE OF AUTHORIZATION

Article 7: Application for authorization
(a) For the purposes of these Regulations, an applicant for authorization means a legal person that is applying for authorization to carry out rating activities in the Kingdom. An applicant for authorization becomes subject to these Regulations from the date of submission of its application.

(b) An application for authorization may be submitted by the founders or controlling shareholders of an applicant for authorization if the applicant for authorization is not yet established. The founders or controlling shareholders become subject to the provisions that apply to an applicant for authorization from the date of submission of the application for authorization.

(c) An application for authorization must be made on the application form prescribed by the Authority and be accompanied by the information and documents required in Annex 1 of these Regulations.

(d) An applicant for authorization must notify the Authority immediately of any material changes to the information provided to the Authority for the purposes of application for authorization.

Article 8: Authorization requirements
(a) An applicant for authorization must either be:

1) incorporated in the Kingdom; or
2) a foreign credit rating agency authorized, or registered (as applicable) in a jurisdiction whose regulatory standards and requirements are at least equivalent to those of the authority.

(b) For the purposes of sub-paragraph (2) of paragraph (a) of this Article, the Authority shall have the absolute discretion to assess whether the foreign regulator has regulatory standards and requirements at least equivalent to those of the Authority.

(c) An applicant for authorization must demonstrate to the Authority that:

1) it is fit and proper and has adequate expertise and resources to carry out rating activities in the Kingdom;
2) it has managerial expertise, financial systems, risk management policies and systems, technological resources, policies and procedures, and systems that are sufficient to fulfill its business and regulatory obligations; and
3) its governing body, rating analysts, employees and any other natural person who will be involved in the applicant's rating activities have the necessary qualifications, skills, experience and integrity.

(d) In addition to the authorization requirements stated in Article 9 and Article 10 of these Regulations, the Authority may stipulate additional authorization requirements to be met by, or specific conditions or limitations to be applied to either all applicants for authorization, or particular applicants or categories of applicants as it considers appropriate.

Article 9: Additional authorization requirements for applicants incorporated within the Kingdom An applicant for authorization incorporated in the Kingdom must demonstrate to the Authority that:

1) any person with whom the applicant for authorization has close links is of a satisfactory standard of integrity, regulatory status, business record and financial soundness, and such close links will not impair the effective supervision of the applicant, or its operations and compliance with these Regulations; and

2) it has paid up capital of not less than SR 2,000,000 or three months working capital (whichever is higher).

Article 10: Additional authorization requirements for foreign applicants
(a) An applicant for authorization that is a foreign credit rating agency must establish a branch in the Kingdom.

(b) An applicant for authorization that is a foreign credit rating agency must confirm to the Authority that:

1) it has given notice to its foreign regulator of its intention to establish a branch in the Kingdom; and
2) by conducting rating activities in the Kingdom it will not violate any laws or regulations to which it is subject or any relevant requirements imposed by its foreign regulator.

Article 11: Procedure and powers of the Authority in relation to an application for authorization
(a) In considering an application for authorization, the Authority may:

1) carry out any enquiries that it considers appropriate;
2) require the applicant for authorization, or its representative, to attend before the Authority to answer questions and explain any matter the Authority considers relevant to the application;
3) require the applicant for authorization to provide such additional information as the Authority considers appropriate within 30 days of the request; and
4) verify any information furnished by the applicant for authorization.

(b) The Authority may refuse to consider the application for authorization where an applicant has failed to provide information requested from it, or has failed to provide information requested from it within the time requested.

(c) The Authority will, upon receipt of all information and documents required, notify the applicant for authorization in writing of the same, and will take one of the following decisions within a maximum period of 30 days from the date of the notice:

1) approve the application;

2) approve the application subject to such conditions and limitations as it considers appropriate; or
3) reject the application, giving reasons.

(d) If the Authority resolves to authorize the applicant for authorization, it will notify the applicant for authorization of this in writing including any conditions and limitations that the Authority may consider appropriate.

(e) If the Authority resolves to refuse the application for authorization, it will notify the applicant for authorization of this in writing.

(f) The Authority may extend the period for assessment of an application for authorization referred to in paragraph (c) of this Article if the applicant for authorization intends to outsource any of its functions or requests a waiver in accordance with Article 5 of these Regulations.

(g) The applicant for authorization must pay such fees as may be prescribed by the Authority.

(h) The Authority may stipulate additional minimum authorization requirements to be met by, or specific conditions or limitations to be applied to either all applicants for authorization or particular categories of applicants.

Article 12: Withdrawal from business and cancellation of authorization

(a) An authorized credit rating agency that proposes to cease to carry out rating activities must notify the Authority in writing of the date on which it intends to cease to carry out rating activities and the reasons for the decision at least 45 days in advance of that date; or if such advance notice is not possible because cessation of business is caused by an external event of which the authorized credit rating agency was not aware, immediately on making a decision to cease carrying out rating activities.

(b) An authorized credit rating agency may request the cancellation of its authorization, and must in this case submit a written request to the Authority not less than three months prior to the proposed date of the cancellation.

(c) A request to cancel an authorization must include sufficient information concerning the circumstances of the cancellation.

(d) The Authority may refuse a request to cancel an authorization, or postpone the date of the cancellation, if it considers that the maintenance of the authorization is necessary to investigate any matter affecting the authorized credit rating agency.

(e) An authorized credit rating agency continues to be subject to the jurisdiction of the Authority in respect of any act or omission that occurred before the cancellation of its authorization and for two years thereafter. If at any time during this period the Authority commences any enforcement investigation or proceedings, the authorized credit rating agency shall continue to be subject to the jurisdiction of the Authority until the end of the enforcement investigation or proceedings.

Article 13: Cancellation or suspension of authorization

(a) The Authority may cancel or suspend the authorized credit rating agency's authorization, as it considers appropriate, after giving it an opportunity for a hearing, where:

1) the authorized credit rating agency does not carry out rating activities for a continuous period of 12 months, or 6 months following the date on which the authorized credit rating agency has ceased to carry out any rating activities after notification to the Authority in accordance with paragraph (a) of Article 12 of these Regulations;
2) the authorized credit rating agency fails to pay any fees imposed by the Authority under these Regulations;
3) the authorized credit rating agency becomes insolvent, or, in the opinion of the Authority, there is a material risk of the authorized credit rating agency becoming insolvent;
4) the authorized credit rating agency provides the Authority with false or misleading information or documents to obtain authorization.
5) the authorized credit rating agency, in the opinion of the Authority, no longer meets its minimum authorization requirements;
6) the authorized credit rating agency has violated the Capital Market Law or any of its Implementing Regulations;
7) the authorized credit rating agency is subject to litigation which may materially affect its ability to carry out its rating activities; or
8) in the opinion of the Authority, the revocation or suspension is necessary.

(b) Cancellation or suspension of an authorized credit rating agency's authorization under paragraph (a) of this Article shall take effect immediately following the giving of written notice by the Authority to the authorized credit rating agency.

(c) Where the Authority suspends an authorized credit rating agency's authorization under this Article, it will notify the authorized credit rating agency in writing within six months from the date of giving notice under paragraph (b) of this Article that the authorized credit rating agency's authorization is either:

1) cancelled;
2) suspended for a further period;
3) reinstated on the same terms as before the suspension became effective; or
4) reinstated subject to such further conditions or limitations as the Authority considers appropriate.

Article 14: Fees The authorized credit rating agency must pay such fees as the Authority may prescribe.

8.3 PART 3: CONDUCT OF BUSINESS REQUIREMENTS

Article 15: General conduct of business requirements

(a) An authorized credit rating agency must continue to meet the minimum authorization requirements at all times.

(b) An authorized credit rating agency may not carry out any activity other than rating activities its authorized to conduct, with the exception that it may carry out activities ancillary to rating activities, provided that the authorized credit rating agency demonstrates to the Authority that conducting ancillary activities do not create conflict of interest when provided in conjunction with rating activities.

(c) An authorized credit rating agency shall adopt, implement and enforce adequate measures to satisfy at all times that:

1) it has sufficient resources to carrying out high-quality credit assessments and the monitoring and updating thereof;

2) it has sufficient information to make a credit assessment and the information it uses in assigning a credit rating is of sufficient quality to support a credible credit rating;
3) its credit ratings reflect all information known, and believed to be relevant, to the authorized credit rating agency, consistent with its published methodology; and
4) if the credit rating involves a type of financial product presenting limited historical data, the authorized credit rating agency should make clear, in a prominent place, the limitations of the credit rating; and
5) it complies, and its rating analysts, employees and any other natural person who is involved in its rating activities comply, with all applicable laws and regulations governing its activities in each jurisdiction in which it operates.

(d) An authorized credit rating agency, its rating analysts, employees and any other natural person who is involved in its rating activities must deal fairly and honestly with the Authority, rated entities, investors and other users of credit ratings, other market participants, and the public.

(e) An authorized credit rating agency, its rating analysts, employees and any other natural person who is involved in its rating activities must use care and professional judgment to maintain both the substance and the appearance of independence and objectivity.

(f) An authorized credit rating agency, its rating analysts, employees and any other natural person who is involved in its rating activities must not use confidential information except for purposes related to its rating activities or otherwise in accordance with any confidentiality agreements with the rated entity.

(g) An authorized credit rating agency must take all reasonable steps to avoid issuing a credit rating or other communication that contains misrepresentations or is otherwise misleading as to the general creditworthiness of a rated entity or the relevant security.

(h) The determination of the credit rating must be influenced only by factors relevant to the credit assessment.

Article 16: Conflicts of interest

(a) An authorized credit rating agency must implement complete operational and legal separation of its rating activities and ancillary activities (which may not cause or may not be generally perceived as causing conflicts of interest) from any other businesses.

(b) An authorized credit rating agency must adopt, implement and enforce procedures and mechanisms designed to minimize the likelihood of conflicts of interest arising from any of its ancillary activities operations.

(c) An authorized credit rating agency must identify and disclose; and eliminates or manages any actual or potential conflicts of interest that may influence the opinions and analysis of its rating analysts, employees and any other natural person who is involved in rating activities of the authorized credit rating agency.

(d) An authorized credit rating agency is not required to disclose a conflict of interest if this information would constitute provision of inside information. In that instance, the authorized credit rating agency must disclose to the Authority immediately and take all necessary steps to ensure that no conflict of interest between its interest and the interest of potential users of its credit ratings affects its rating activities.

(e) An authorized credit rating agency must adopt and disclose its written conflict of interest avoidance and management measures to identify, disclose and eliminate or manage any actual or potential conflicts of interest.

(f) An authorized credit rating agency's disclosure required under paragraphs (c), (d) and (e) of this Article must be in writing, timely, complete, clear, concise, specific and prominent.

(g) An authorized credit rating agency must not conduct any rating activity where:

1) the rated entity, any of its affiliates, governing body, senior executives or any of their associates is an affiliate of the authorized credit rating agency, or a director or a manager within the authorized credit rating agency or a rating analyst which would be involved in any rating activity for the relevant credit rating;
2) the determination of the relevant credit rating would be affected by the existence of or potential for a business relationship between the authorized credit rating agency (or its affiliates) and the entity (or its affiliates) or any other party, or the non-existence of such a relationship;
3) in determining the relevant credit rating the authorized credit rating agency would not be independent;
4) it owns securities issued, guaranteed, or otherwise supported by the rated entity, other than holding in diversified investment funds;
5) its owns securities of any entity that is an affiliate of a rated entity, the ownership of which may cause or may be generally perceived as causing conflicts of interest, other than holdings in diversified investment funds; or
6) any of its rating analysts, employees or any other natural person who is involved in its rating activities has any business relationship with the rated entity or the rated entity's affiliates or a family relationship with any manager within the rated entity which may cause or may be generally perceived as causing conflicts of interest.

Article 17: Rating Categories, methodologies, models and key rating assumptions

(a) When conducting rating activities, an authorized credit agency must:

1) use an established and defined ranking system of rating categories.
2) use rating categories and methodologies that are rigorous, systematic, and, where possible, result in ratings that can be subjected to objective validation based on its past experience.
3) adopt, implement and enforce adequate measures to ensure that it uses appropriate rating categories, methodologies, models and key rating assumptions for determining credit ratings of structured products. Where due to the complexity or structure of a structured product or the lack of robust data about the assets underlying the structured product the authorized credit rating agency cannot determine a credible credit rating for the structured product, it must refrain from issuing a credit rating.
4) ensure that its rating analysts involved in the rating activities use rating methodologies, models and key rating assumptions established by the credit rating agency and apply such methodology, model and key rating assumption in a consistent manner.

(b) When rating categories, methodologies, models or key rating assumptions used in rating activities are changed, an authorized credit rating agency must:

1) immediately, using the same means of communication as used for the distribution of the affected credit ratings, disclose the likely scope of credit ratings to be affected;
2) review the credit rating affected by the change (both initial ratings and subsequent ratings) as soon as possible and no later than six months after the change, and place it during that period under observation; and
3) re-rate all credit ratings that have been based on those methodologies, models or key rating assumptions if, following the review, the overall combined effect of the changes affects those credit ratings.

(c) The authorized credit rating agency must base its credit ratings upon relevant information that is of quality and obtained from reliable sources.

(d) The ratings must be based on thorough analysis of all information obtained by the authorized credit rating agency pursuant to paragraph (c) of this Article.

Article 18: Assignment of credit ratings

(a) Credit ratings must be assigned by the authorized credit rating agency only.

(b) An authorized credit rating agency, its rating analysts, employees and any other natural person who is involved in its rating activities must not, either implicitly or explicitly, give any assurance or guarantee of a particular credit rating.

(c) An authorized credit rating agency must distribute an assigned credit rating simultaneously to all potential users as soon as reasonably possible.

Article 19: Monitoring and updating of credit ratings

Unless a credit rating clearly indicates that it is not subject to ongoing surveilla nce by the authorized credit rating agency responsible for the credit rating, an authorized credit rating agency must monitor and update all credit ratings on an ongoing basis by:

1) regularly reviewing the rated entity or the related security's creditworthiness;

2) initiating a review of the status of the rating upon becoming aware of any information that might reasonably be expected to result in a rating action (including termination of a credit rating), consistent with the applicable rating methodology; and

3) updating on a timely basis the credit rating, as needed, based on the results of such review.

Article 20: Discontinued credit ratings

(a) Where an authorized credit rating agency makes credit ratings available to the public, the authorized credit rating agency must publicly announce in a timely manner if such rating is discontinued.

(b) Where an authorized credit rating agency makes credit ratings available to its subscribers only, the authorized credit rating agency must announce in a timely manner to its subscribers if any such ratings are discontinued.

(c) Where an authorized credit rating agency makes a discontinued credit rating available to its subscribers or the public generally, the authorized credit rating agency must indicate the date the credit rating was last updated and the fact that the credit rating is no longer being updated.

Article 21: Disclosure requirements

(a) An authorized credit rating agency must attach with every credit rating a disclosure in the form set out in Annex 2.

(b) An authorized credit rating agency must disclose in timely manner to the public, on a non- selective basis and free of charge, any credit rating regarding publicly issued securities, or issuers of publicly issued securities, as well as any subsequent decisions to discontinue such a rating, if the rating action is based in whole or in part on non-public information.

(c) An authorized credit rating agency must make public and keep up-to-date the following information:

1) a description of its actual and potential conflicts of interest;
2) its policies and procedures adopted by the credit rating agency, including the policy concerning the publication of credit ratings, and other related communications, and its policy regarding credit ratings that are not requested by the rated entity or subscribers;
3) the nature of its compensation arrangements with rated entities, including compensation arrangements with rated entities or related third parties that provide more than 10% of the annual revenue of an authorized credit rating agency and any compensation unrelated to rating activities;
4) the rating categories, methodologies, and descriptions of models and key rating assumptions used in its rating activities as well as any material changes to the rating categories, methodologies, models and key rating assumptions;
5) its policies for distributing credit ratings, reports and updates;
6) any material modification to its systems, resources or procedures.
7) a list of its ancillary activities.
8) its code of conduct.

(d) An authorized credit rating agency must submit a copy of the information listed in this Article to the Authority annually and notify the Authority in writing of any material changes.

(e) An authorized credit rating agency must at least annually make public historical default rates of its rating categories, distinguishing between the ma in geographical areas and industry sectors of the entities and whether the default rates of these categories have changed over time.

(f) An authorized credit rating agency must submit the following information to the Authority annually:

1) a list of the largest 20 clients of the authorized credit rating agency by revenue generated from them; and
2) a list of those clients of the authorized credit rating agency whose contribution to the growth rate in the generation of revenue of the authorized credit rating agency in the previous financial year exceeded the growth rate in the total revenues of the authorized credit rating agency in that year by a factor of more than 1.5 times. Any such client shall be included on the list only where, in that year, it accounted for more than 0.25 % of the total revenues of the authorized credit rating agency (including the total revenue of the authorized credit rating agency's group).

(g) In the case of an authorized foreign credit rating agency, the provisions of paragraph (f) of this Article shall only apply insofar as related to its revenue generated from rating activities conducted in the Kingdom.

(h) An authorized credit rating agency must publish information required to be made public under these Regulations on the authorized credit rating agency's website, available to the public, in both Arabic and English and for a reasonable time.

Article 22: Transparency report

(a) An authorized credit rating agency must publish annually a transparency report which includes the following information:

1) a description of the authorized credit rating agency's compliance with these Regulations and other relevant laws and regulations;
2) detailed information on the legal structure and ownership structure of the authorized credit rating agency;
3) a description of the internal control mechanisms ensuring quality of the authorized credit rating agency's rating activities;
4) statistics on the allocation of the authorized credit rating agency's staff and rating analysts to new credit ratings, ongoing credit rating reviews, methodology or model appraisal and senior management;
5) a description of the record-keeping policy adopted by the authorized credit rating agency.
6) the outcome of the annual internal review of the authorized credit rating agency's independent compliance function;
7) financial information on the revenue of the authorized credit rating agency based on the fees from rating activities and other activities with a comprehensive description of each. In the case of an authorized foreign credit rating agency, this information should be based on revenues attributable to its rating activities and other activities in the Kingdom;
8) a governance statement, including details of the authorized credit rating agency's administrative or supervisory committee and executive committee structures and terms of reference. In the case of an authorized foreign credit rating agency, this information should be limited to details of its branch management structures and key personnel and the reporting lines of those structures and personnel within the authorized foreign credit rating agency as a whole;
9) the authorized credit rating agency's policies for distributing credit ratings, reports and updates;
10) a description of any material changes to the authorized credit rating agency's systems, resources and procedures including but not limited to its code of conduct, conflict of interest policies;
11) audited financial statements (if applicable) and any material information concerning the authorized credit rating agency's financial condition.

(b) An authorized credit rating agency must publish the transparency report, required according to paragraph (a) of this Article, no later than three months after the end of each financial year, and it must ensure that it is made available to the public on its website for at least five years.

Article 23: Record keeping

(a) An authorized credit rating agency must record and retain sufficient information about its rating activities to demonstrate compliance with these Regulations.

(b) An authorized credit rating agency must maintain internal records to support its credit ratings, reports and updates for five years.

(c) An authorized credit rating agency must maintain internal records of all significant risks to the independence of the rating activities, including those referred to in paragraph (f) of Article 26 of these Regulations for five years.

(d) An authorized credit rating agency must maintain internal records in connection with the recruitment procedure, experience and qualifications of any of its rating analysts, employees and any other natural person who are involved in its rating activities for a period of five years from the issuance date of the last credit rating where such person has been involved in.

(e) Records made by an authorized credit rating agency may be recorded in any form, but must be capable of reproduction in hard printed form.

(f) Except where the information is available to the public on the authorized credit rating agency's website, the authorized credit rating agency must keep copies of all information required to be made public under these Regulations on its premises in the Kingdom and must ensure that members of the public can access this information free of charge and make copies of this information at a reasonable cost.

(g) All records required to be maintained by an authorized credit rating agency under the Capital Market Law and its Implementing Regulations must be available for inspection by the Authority. The Authority may inspect the records directly or through a person it appoints for that purpose.

8.4 PART 4: SYSTEM AND CONTROLS

Article 24: Organzsational requirements

(a) An authorized credit rating agency must have written robust internal procedures, policies and controls necessary to ensure compliance with these Regulations.

(b) An authorized credit rating agency must establish an independent and effective compliance function department and must appoint a compliance officer for this purpose. The compliance function must monitor and report to the administrative or supervisory committee of the authorized credit rating agency referred to in Article 26 of these Regulations on compliance of the authorized credit rating agency and its rating analysts, employees and any other natural person who is involved in its rating activities with the authorized credit rating agency's obligations under these Regulations, and on other regulatory requirements, and compliance policies and procedures adopted by the authorized credit rating agency.

(c) An authorized credit rating agency must establish and implement a rigorous and formal review function made up of one or more senior executives for periodically reviewing and monitoring the credit rating agency's rating methodologies, categories, models and key rating assumptions and any material changes or modifications thereto as well as the appropriateness of those methodologies, categories, models and key rating assumptions when they are used or intended to be used for new types of rated entity or security. This function shall be independent of the business lines that are principally responsible for credit ratings and shall directly report to the administrative or supervisory committee referred to in Article 26 of these Regulations .

(d) An authorized credit rating agency must establish a function charged with communicating with market participants and the public about any questions, concerns or complaints that the authorized credit rating agency may receive and keeping the authorized credit rating agency's senior management informed of any such complaints.

Article 25: Fit and Proper An authorized credit rating agency must ensure that its rating analysts, employees and any other natural persons who is involved in its rating activities:

1) possess adequate qualifications and professional experience to carry out their responsibilities, including appropriate technical knowledge and skills;
2) have probity and soundness of judgement commensurate with their positions;
3) exercise of appropriate due diligence while carrying out their responsibilities.
4) have not committed an offense involving fraud or dishonesty; and
5) have not violated any provisions of the Capital Market Law, its Implementing Regulations or any other relevant laws or regulations.

Article 26: Administrative or supervisory committee
(a) An authorized credit rating agency must have an administrative or supervisory committee, which shall be responsible for ensuring compliance with the Capital Market Law, its Implementing Regulations, other relevant laws and regulations, and compliance policies and procedures adopted by the authorized credit rating agency.

(b) An authorized credit rating agency must ensure that at least one third, but no less than two, of the members of its administrative or supervisory committee are independent and are not involved in rating activities. A member of an administrative or supervisory committee is considered to be independent only if he/she is (and during the preceding two years was) free of any business, family or other relationship, with the credit rating agency, its controlling shareholder or the management of either, which may cause or may be generally perceived as causing conflicts of interest.

(c) The compensation of independent members of the administrative or supervisory committee must not be linked to the business performance of the authorized credit rating agency and must be arranged so as to ensure their independence.

(d) The term of office of the independent members of the administrative or supervisory committee must be for a pre-agreed fixed period not exceeding five years and must not be renewable. The dismissal of independent members of the administrative or supervisory committee must take place only in case of misconduct or professional underperformance.

(e) The majority of members of the administrative or supervisory committee of an authorized credit rating agency, including all of its independent members, must have sufficient expertise in appropriate areas of related financial services. If the authorized credit rating agency issues credit ratings of structured products, at least one independent member and one other member of the board must have in-depth knowledge and experience at a senior level of the markets in structured products.

(f) In addition to the overall responsibility of the administrative or supervisory committee, the independent members of the administrative or supervisory committee shall monitor:

1) the development of the credit rating policy and of the methodologies used by the authorized credit rating agency in its rating activities;
2) the effectiveness of the internal quality control system of the authorized credit rating agency in relation to its rating activities;
3) the effectiveness of measures and procedures instituted to ensure that any conflicts of interest are identified and disclosed; and eliminated or managed; and
4) the compliance and governance processes, including the efficiency of the review function referred to under paragraph (c) of Article 24 of these Regulations.

(g) Opinions of the independent members of administrative or supervisory committee issued on the matters referred to under paragraph (f) of this Article must be presented to the administrative or supervisory committee periodically and must be made available to the Authority on request.

Article 27: Remuneration of rating analysts, employees involved in rating activities
(a) An authorized credit rating agency must not evaluate or determine the remuneration of its rating analysts or employees directly involved in rating activities on the basis of the amount of revenue that the authorized credit rating agency derives from rated entities that the relevant rating analyst or employee is involved in the relevant rating activities or with which the rating analyst or employee regularly interacts.

(b) An authorized credit rating agency must conduct formal and periodic reviews of compensation policies and practices for its rating analysts and other employees who participate in or who might otherwise have an effect on its rating activities to ensure that these policies and practices do not compromise the objectivity of the authorized credit rating agency's rating activities.

Article 28: Professional ethics
(a) An authorized credit rating agency must take all reasonable steps to structure its credit rating teams to ensure continuity of personnel involved and avoid bias in rating activities.

(b) An authorized credit rating agency must take all reasonable steps to ensure the compliance of its rating analysts, employees and any other natural person who is involved in its rating activities with these Regulations.

(c) Rating analysts and employees of the authorized credit rating agency and any other natural person who is involved in its rating activities must:

1) take all reasonable measures to protect all property and records belonging to or in possession of the authorized credit rating agency from fraud, theft or misuse;
2) not engage in transactions in securities (other than investing in diversified investment funds) when:

   a. the relevant security is issued, guaranteed, or otherwise supported by any rated entity or entities to be rated within their area of primary analytical responsibility;

   b. they possess confidential information concerning the issuer of such security; or

   c. such transactions otherwise present conflicts of interest with the authorized credit rating agency's rating activities.

3) not disclose any non-public information about rating opinions or possible future rating actions of the authorized credit rating agency, except to the rated entity in question or its designated agents;
4) not share confidential information entrusted to the authorized credit rating agency with any person, including within the authorized credit rating agency, except where the disclosure is necessary for the purposes of the authorized credit rating agency's rating activities which may not cause or may not be generally perceived as causing conflicts of interest;
5) not use confidential information for the purpose of trading securities, or for any other purpose except the purposes of conducting the authorized credit rating agency's business which may not cause or may not be generally perceived as causing conflicts of interest;
6) not solicit money, gifts or favors from any person with whom the authorized credit rating agency does business or contemplates doing business and must not accept gifts offered in the form of cash or any gifts from that person, or from any other person which may cause or may be generally perceived as causing conflicts of interest.
7) comply with the internal securities trading policies maintained by the authorized credit rating agency, and at least annually certify their compliance as required by such policies.

(d) No rating analyst, employee of the authorized credit rating agency or any other natural person who is involved in its rating activities may be involved in rating activities or may participate in or otherwise influence the determination of the authorized credit rating agency's credit rating of any particular rated entity or security if he/she:

1) owns, or is aware that any relative of his\her owns, securities issued, guaranteed, or otherwise supported by the rated entity, other than holdings in diversified investment funds;
2) owns, or is aware that any relative of his\her owns, securities of any entity that is an affiliate of a rated entity, the ownership of which may cause or may be generally perceived as causing conflicts of interest, other than holdings in diversified investment funds;
3) has (or had) an employment, business or any other relationship with the rated entity or with any of its affiliates which may cause or may be generally perceived as causing conflicts of interest; or
4) has a family relationship with any manager within the rated entity which may cause or may be generally perceived as causing conflicts of interest.

(e) No rating analyst, employee of the authorized credit rating agency and any other natural person, who are involved in its rating activities may be allowed to initiate, or participate in, discussions regarding fees or payments with any rated entity or entities to be rated.

(f) No rating analyst. employee of the authorized credit rating agency and any other natural person, who are involved in its rating activities may be allowed to participate in making proposals or recommendations regarding the design of structured products that the authorized credit rating agency rates.

(g) Any rating analyst, employee of the authorized credit rating agency and any other natural person, who are involved in its rating activities who becomes involved in any personal relationship that creates the potential for any real or apparent conflict of interest must be required to disclose such relationship to the compliance officer of the authorized credit rating agency, as determined by the authorized credit rating agency's adopted compliance policies and procedures.

Article 29: Professional misconduct

(a) Any rating analyst, employee of an authorized credit rating agency or any other natural person who is involved in its rating activities must, upon becoming aware of any information that results in the rating analyst or employee believing that another rating analyst, employee of the authorized credit rating agency or any other natural person who is involved in its rating activities is, or has, engaged in conduct that is illegal, unethical or non-compliant with these Regulations, be required to report such information immediately to the compliance officer of the authorized credit rating agency, as appropriate and in accordance with the authorized credit rating agency's adopted compliance policies and procedures.

(b) Any compliance officer of an authorized credit rating agency who receives the report mentioned in paragraph (a) of this Article is required to take appropriate action to ensure compliance with these Regulations on a continuous basis and the adopted policies and procedures set forth by the authorized credit rating agency. Any conduct that is illegal, unethical or non-compliant which may materially impair the continuing compliance of the authorized credit rating agency with the conditions and obligations of its authorization or its other obligations under the Capital Market Law and its Implementing Regulations, or the soundness or the continuity of its relevant services and activities must be reported in writing to the Authority as soon as reasonably possible.

(c) An authorized credit rating agency is prohibited from retaliation against any rating analyst, employee or any other natural person who is involved in its rating activities who, in good faith, makes a report as stated in paragraph (a) of this Article.

(d) An authorized credit rating agency must ensure the conduct of an appropriate investigation on any report received in accordance with paragraph (a) of this Article, and as a result an appropriate disciplinary or other action be taken.

(e) An authorized credit rating agency must maintain records of the names of any rating analyst, employee or any other natural person who is involved in its rating activities disciplined by the authorized credit rating agency and/or the Authority in connection with any breach of the Capital Market Law and its Implementing Regulations or any illegal or unethical conduct. The records must also include particulars of:

1) the breach or conduct for which the rating analyst, employee or any other natural person who is involved in its rating activities was disciplined; and
2) the steps taken to discipline the rating analyst, employee or any other natural person who is involved in its rating activities.

Article 30: Training

(a) An authorized credit rating agency must establish an appropriate training programme to its rating analysts and other employees (including passing any examinations which may be required by the Authority).

(b) An authorized credit rating agency must at least annually organise training for its rating analysts and other relevant employees which includes compliance with the Capital Market Law and its Implementing Regulations and any other laws and regulations relevant to the authorized credit rating agency's rating activities.

Article 31: Recruitment and employment practices

(a) An authorized credit rating agency must establish recruitment procedures to ensure that it recruits and employs rating analysts and employees who meet requirements under Article 25 of these Regulations.

(b) The authorized credit rating agency must implement and maintain a written decision-making procedures and organizational structures which clearly specify reporting lines for its rating analysts, employees and any other natural persons who is involved in its rating activities, and the authorized credit rating agency must make arraignments related to their compensation in a way that eliminates or effectively manage actual and potential conflicts of interest.

(c) An authorized credit rating agency must establish policies and procedures for reviewing the past work of rating analysts or other employees that leave the employ of the authorized credit rating agency and join an entity the rating analyst or employee has been involved in rating, or a financial firm with which the rating analyst or employee has had significant dealings as part of his\her duties at the authorized credit rating agency.

Article 32: Controllers

(a) This Article shall only apply to an authorized credit rating agency that is incorporated in the Kingdom.

(b) An authorized credit rating agency must notify the Authority, in such form as the Authority may prescribe, that a person is intending to become, or cease to be, a controller of the authorized credit rating agency:

1) at least 30 days in advance of the proposed effective date; or
2) if such advance notice is not possible, immediately on the authorized credit rating agency becoming aware of such intention.

(c) An authorized credit rating agency must not permit any person to become or act as a controller unless the Authority has approved the controller in writing.

(d) A person who intends to become a controller of an authorized credit rating agency must notify the Authority in writing of such intention at least 30 days in advance of the proposed effective date, and must provide the Authority with such information as the Authority requires to satisfy itself of its identity, integrity, regulatory status, business record and financial soundness.

(e) Before approving a controller the Authority must be satisfied that the person's control of the authorized credit rating agency will not impair the effective supervision of the authorized credit rating agency or its operations and compliance with the Capital Market Law and its Implementing Regulations.

(f) In considering any application submitted under this Article, the Authority has all of the powers set out in Article 11 of these Regulations.

Article 33: Outsourcing

(a) In relation to an authorized foreign credit rating agency, this Article shall only apply insofar as it relates to its rating activities carried out in the Kingdom.

(b) An authorized credit rating agency may outsource any of its functions (other than those functions specified in paragraph (f) of this Article), provided that appropriate safeguards are put in place, including:

1) an assessment of whether the delegate is suitable to carry out the delegated function or task, taking into account the degree of responsibility involved;
2) clear documentation of the extent and limits of any delegation;
3) suitable arrangements to supervise the delegation, and to monitor the discharge of the delegate's functions or tasks;
4) procedures for the taking of appropriate remedial action if any concern arises about the performance of the delegate's functions or tasks;
5) exercise of appropriate due diligence in the selection of an external party to perform outsourced functions; and
6) satisfaction on the part of the authorized credit rating agency that the outsourcing of any function by the authorized credit rating agency does not affect the authorized credit rating agency's compliance with the Capital Market Law and its Implementing Regulations and any other relevant laws and regulations.

(c) The outsourcing of any important operational function must not be undertaken in such a way as to impair materially the quality of the authorized credit rating agency's internal control and the ability of the Authority to supervise the authorized credit rating agency's compliance with obligations under the Capital Market Law and its Implementing Regulations.

(d) An authorized credit rating agency must give the Authority prior written notice of any arrangements for outsourcing, or of any material change to its existing outsourcing arrangements.

(e) The outsourcing of any function by the authorized credit rating agency will not derogate from the authorized credit rating agency's compliance officer's or the compliance function department's regulatory obligations.

(f) The following functions may not be outsourced to any person that is not a member of the authorized credit rating agency's group:

1) Carrying out rating activities;
2) monitoring of a credit rating issued by the authorized credit rating agency.

Article 34: Notification requirements

(a) An authorized credit rating agency must notify the Authority in writing not less than 30 days before any material change in:

1) the name or registered name of the authorized credit rating agency or any trading name under which the authorized credit rating agency carries on rating activities in the Kingdom;
2) the address of the head office of the authorized credit rating agency, or, if different, the address of the place for service of notices or documents; or
3) the original or most recent business plan submitted by the authorized credit rating agency.

(b) An authorized credit rating agency must notify the Authority in writing within 7 days of the occurrence of any material change in the information originally submitted under the following headings:

1) the branches in the Kingdom from which the authorized credit rating agency carries out rating activities;
2) in the case of an authorized credit rating agency incorporated in the Kingdom only, the countries outside the Kingdom in which the authorized credit rating agency carries on rating activities whether this is done through a branch office, a subsidiary or otherwise; and
3) the standard contracts or arrangements for issuing credit ratings to clients, or the outsourcing arrangements of any of the authorized credit rating agency's functions (in each case as applicable to the authorized credit rating agency).

(c) An authorized credit rating agency must notify the Authority in writing as soon as possible on the occurrence of any of the following:

1) the presentation of a petition for the winding up or an insolvency (or similar to such) of the authorized credit rating agency or a company which is a subsidiary or controller of the authorized credit rating agency;
2) the imposition of disciplinary measures or disciplinary sanctions on the authorized credit rating agency or a member of its group in relation to its rating activities by any regulatory authority;
3) the conviction of the authorized credit rating agency, or any rating analyst or employee thereof, for any offense under legislation relating to rating activities or financial services, Companies Law, Bankruptcy Regulations, or for any offense involving fraud or any act involving dishonesty or a lack of integrity, or the imposition of any penalties for deliberate zakat or tax evasion;
4) in the case of an authorized credit rating agency incorporated in the Kingdom only, the granting or refusal of any application for, or revocation of, authorization to carry out rating activities in any country or territory outside the Kingdom;
5) the appointment of inspectors by an official or regulatory authority to investigate the affairs of the authorized credit rating agency;
6) a significant act of professional misconduct by the authorized credit rating agency, or any rating analyst or employee thereof;
7) the resignation or dismissal of any of the registered persons and the independent members of the administrative or supervisory committee, including full details of reasons in cases of dismissal;
8) any matter which would be material to the requirements of the authorized credit rating agency or (in the case of an authorized credit rating agency incorporated in the Kingdom) any of its controllers, or any of the authorized credit rating agency's registered persons to remain fit and proper in accordance with the requirements under these Regulations; or
9) any other matter which would be material to the Authority's supervision of the authorized credit rating agency.

(d) An authorized credit rating agency must inform the Authority as soon as possible in writing of any material event or change in its business or operations.

(e) An authorized credit rating agency must give the Authority prior written notice, or where the event has occurred, written notice as soon as it becomes aware, of:

1) a proposed reorganization or business expansion or other change that could have a material impact on the authorized credit rating agency's business, risk profile or resources, including, but not limited to, the following:

a. setting up a new business within an authorized credit rating agency's group, or establishing a new branch;

b. commencing the provision of cross border services into a new territory;

c. commencing the provision of a new class of credit rating;

d. sale or transfer of any material assets or parts of its business; or

e. significantly reducing the scope of rating activities.

2) any significant failure in the authorized credit rating agency's systems or monitoring procedures, including those reported to the authorized credit rating agency by the authorized credit rating agency's auditor; or
3) in the case of an authorized credit rating agency incorporated in the Kingdom only, any event related to the authorized credit rating agency that results in a material change in its capital adequacy, including:

a. any action that would result in a material change in the authorized credit rating agency's financial resources or financial resources requirements under these Regulations;

b. the payment of a special or unusual dividend or the repayment of share capital or a subordinated loan; or

c. any significant losses, whether recognized or unrecognized.

(f) In the case of an authorized foreign credit rating agency, subparagraphs (1) and (2) of paragraph (e) of this Article shall only apply insofar as material to the business, risk profile or resources of its local branch established in accordance with these Regulations.

(g) Upon receiving a notice under this Article, the Authority may:

1) require the authorized credit agency to provide any additional information that it considers necessary to properly assess that matter; and/or
2) impose any conditions, restrictions or additional requirements on that authorized credit rating agency that it reasonably considers to be necessary to address a regulatory concern raised by any matter of which it is notified under this Article.

8.5 PART 5: REGISTERED PERSONS

Article 35: Scope of Application This Part applies to authorized credit rating agencies, registered persons, applicants for registration and persons performing registrable functions.

Article 36: Registrable functions
(a) The Authority shall prescribe the registrable functions.

(b) In the case of an authorized credit rating agency incorporated in the Kingdom, the following functions are considered functions that must be performed by registered persons:

1) CEO or managing director;

2) a director or partner;
3) compliance officer;
4) lead rating analysts; and
5) any other function designated by the Authority as a registrable function.

(c) In the case of an authorized foreign credit rating agency, the following functions are considered functions that must be performed by registered persons:

1) branch managing director or branch manager;
2) branch compliance officer;
3) lead rating analysts engaged in carrying out rating activities in the Kingdom; and
4) any other function designated by the Authority as a registrable function.

Article 37: Performance of registrable functions

(a) No person other than a registered person may perform a registrable function without the Authority's prior written consent.

(b) Every authorized credit rating agency must at all times have a person who is registered for each of the following functions:

1) CEO, managing director or (in the case of an authorized foreign credit rating agency) branch managing director or branch manager;
2) compliance officer or (in the case of an authorized foreign credit rating agency) branch compliance officer.

(c) The Authority will not take action against an authorized credit rating agency for failure to comply with paragraph (b) of this Article where there is a temporary gap in the performance of the registrable functions, provided that the authorized credit rating agency actively seeks an appropriate substitute and notifies the Authority of another registered person who will temporarily take responsibility for that registrable function.

(d) A person may perform more than one registrable function for an authorized credit rating agency, except that:

1) the CEO or the managing director and the branch managing director or the branch manager, and compliance officer or branch compliance officer must be separate persons unless the Authority's prior written consent is obtained on another arrangement.
2) the compliance officer or branch compliance officer must not perform any other function.

Article 38: Requirements for application for registration

(a) An authorized credit rating agency must not apply for registration of a person to perform a registrable function without the consent of the relevant person.

(b) The application for registration must be made on the form prescribed by the Authority.

(c) An applicant for registration becomes subject to these Regulations from the date of submission of the application.

(d) An applicant for registration must have passed the qualification examinations required by the Authority, or secured an exemption from the Authority from such requirement.

(e) The Authority will specify the examination requirements associated with the registrable functions, together with guidance on eligible qualifications and criteria for any applicable exemption from the required examinations.

(f) The authorized credit rating agency must pay such fees as may be determined by the Authority.

Article 39: Procedure and powers of the Authority in relation to an applicant for registration

(a) In considering an application for registration, the Authority may take any of the following actions:

1) carry out any enquiries which it considers appropriate;
2) require the authorized credit rating agency or the applicant for registration to appear before the Authority to answer any questions and explain any matter it considers relevant to the application;
3) require that additional information be provided;
4) verify the accuracy of any information furnished by the applicant for registration;

(b) The Authority will aim to consider an application for registration within 30 days of receiving all information and documents that it considers pertinent.

(c) The Authority may, after considering the application, take any of the following actions:

1) approve the application for registration;
2) approve the application for registration subject to such conditions as it considers appropriate;
3) defer making a decision for such period as may be necessary to carry out further investigation or to allow for the provision of additional information; or
4) refuse the application for registration, giving reasons.

(d) If the Authority resolves to register the applicant for registration, the Authority will add the applicant's name to the register of registered persons that the Authority shall maintain for this purpose and so notify the authorized credit rating agency in writing.

(e) If the Authority resolves to reject the application, the Authority shall notify the authorized credit rating agency and the applicant for registration named in the application in writing.

(f) An applicant for registration must not perform the registrable function until he/she has been registered by the Authority.

Article 40: Responsibilities of registered persons

(a) Except for persons registered to perform the function prescribed in sub-paragraphs (2) and (3) of paragraph (c) of Article 36 of these Regulations, a registered person must be resident in the Kingdom unless the Authority exempts him\her from this requirement.

(b) Without prejudice to paragraph (a) of Article 37 of these Regulations, this Article applies to any person performing a registrable function who is not registered.

Article 41: Cancellation of registration

(a) If a registered person's registration is cancelled, the authorized credit rating agency must ensure that the person immediately ceases to perform a registrable function.

(b) Within seven days of a registered person ceasing to carry on a registrable function or ceasing to be employed or associated with an authorized credit rating agency, the authorized credit rating agency must notify the Authority of that fact on the form prescribed by the Authority. Upon receipt of the notice, the registration will be suspended, and the suspension shall remain in force until the Authority resolves any of the following:

1) to agree to the termination of the registration;
2) to consent to the person becoming employed by other authorized credit rating agency in a similar capacity; or
3) to remove the person's name from the register of registered persons.

(c) A registered person continues to be subject to the jurisdiction of the Authority in respect of any act or omission that occurred before the cancellation of his\her registration and for two years thereafter. If at any time during this period the Authority commences any enforcement investigation or proceedings, the registered person shall continue to be subject to the jurisdiction of the Authority until the end of the enforcement investigation or proceedings.

(d) The Authority shall have the power to cancel the registration of a registered person if the registered person violates any provision of the Capital Market Law or its Implementing Regulations.

8.6 PART 6: CLOSING PROVISIONS

Article 42: Publication and entry into force These Regulations shall be effective in accordance with their approval resolution.

8.7 ANNEX 1: INFORMATION AND DOCUMENTS REQUIRED FOR AUTHORIZATION APPLICATION

The requirements set out in this Annex apply to all applicants for authorization. An applicant for authorization which is a foreign credit rating agency should only submit information required in this Annex insofar as relevant to its local branch and its rating activities conducted in the Kingdom.

1. Administrative or supervisory committee – An applicant for authorization must submit information about the composition of its administrative or supervisory committee, including the number of the independent members.

2. Controllers – An applicant for authorization incorporated in the Kingdom must submit a list of all controllers of the applicant, and provide details of the identity, ownership (if applicable), integrity, regulatory status, business record and financial position of each proposed controller.

3. Close Links – An applicant for authorization incorporated in the Kingdom must submit a list of all persons that have, or are proposed to have, close links with the applicant, and provide details of the identity, ownership (if applicable), integrity, regulatory status, business record and financial position of each such person.

4. Governing Body Resolution – An applicant for authorization must submit to the Authority a resolution of its governing body in the form prescribed by the Authority approving the application and its contents, and certifying the accuracy and completeness of the accompanying information and documents.

5. Financial Statements - An applicant for authorization must submit financial statements prepared and accredited by the applicant's auditors and presented in the format prescribed by the Authority, and must:

1) show the applicant's current and projected financial position, including its capital, financial resources, revenues and expenses as at the date of the financial statements, the proposed commencement of business, and the financial position 12 months after the date of commencement of business;
2) provide supporting evidence of the capitalization and resources of the applicant for authorization and the presumptions on which the statements have been provided.

6. Registered Persons – An applicant for authorization must submit a list of each person who is to be a registered person and an application form for registration for each such person in the format prescribed by the Authority, including details of their qualifications and experience.

7. Business Plan – An applicant for authorization must submit a business plan, setting out:

1) a detailed description of the rating activities that the applicant proposes to undertake during, at least, the first 12 months after authorization;
2) a program of business operations, including where the applicant's main business activities are proposed to be carried out and (where applicable) branches to be established;
3) classes of credit ratings in relation to which the application for authorization is being made;
4) a description of the nature of the proposed clients of the applicant for authorization in relation to each relevant class of credit ratings;
5) whether the applicant for authorization intends to outsource any part of its rating activities to one or more third parties, and the identity of the third parties concerned;
6) details of relevant capabilities on which the applicant for authorization will draw on to conduct rating activities, including experience of its management and affiliates;
7) a feasibility study conducted by the applicant (including potential market share and financial projections to support the financial projections provided under paragraph 5 (1) of this Annex;
8) details of proposed fee structures and distribution channels for credit ratings;
9) details of the number of personnel expected to be employed and the intended functions of such persons, with reference to the Organization Chart provided under paragraph (16) on this Annex;
10) details of all jurisdictions other than the Kingdom in which it carries out or intends to carry out rating activities or distributes its credit ratings; and
11) details of any activity that the applicant may carry out ancillary to rating activities.

8. Systems and Controls – An applicant for authorization must submit the following systems and controls documentation:

1) risk management policies and systems;
2) compliance policies;
3) compliance monitoring program; and
4) code of conduct.

9. Policies and Procedures – An applicant for authorization must submit a policies and procedures manual detailing the procedures and systems to be employed in relation to all material business and administrative operations, including the following:

1) rating activities;
2) Reporting, publishing and dissemination of credit ratings; and
3) complying with all record-keeping requirements.

10. Contracts – An applicant for authorization must submit agreements, arrangements and understandings with third parties to provide any material services or operations, including:

1) standard contracts or arrangements for issuing credit ratings to clients
2) arrangements to offer products or services provided by, sponsored by, or associated with a third party;
3) information technology, databases and computer systems;
4) record-keeping;
5) compliance services;
6) audit services;
7) outsourcing arrangements; and
8) contracts for ancillary activities.

11. Methodologies and Rating Categories - An applicant for authorization must submit details of methodologies used to issue and review credit ratings, including any specific rating categories or methodologies used for structured products or other particular classes of credit ratings;

12. Policies and procedures - An applicant for authorization must submit details of the following policies and procedures:

1) policies and procedures to identify, manage and disclose any conflicts of interests;
2) policies and procedures for compensation and performance evaluation of rating analysts, persons responsible for compliance and other staff; and
3) if the applicant intends to outsource any part of its functions, details of policies and procedures for ensuring compliance with Article 33 of these Regulations.

13. Incorporation Documents – An applicant for authorization must submit a copy of its articles of association or by-laws, including (in the case of any applicant for authorization that is a foreign credit rating agency) details on the establishment of the branch.

14. Ownership Structure – An applicant for authorization must submit an ownership structure chart showing the group of which the applicant for authorization forms part, including (in the case of an applicant for authorization incorporated in the Kingdom only) each controller and each person with whom the applicant has close links.

15. Organization Chart – An applicant for authorization must submit an organization chart identifying the applicant's governing body, the CEO and senior management, the rating oversight function (demonstrating compliance with paragraph (c) Article (24) of these Regulations) the lead rating analyst, rating analysts and compliance officers. The chart must outline the reporting lines of each department within the business.

16. Business Continuity – An applicant for authorization must submit a copy of the applicant's business continuity plan.

8.8 ANNEX 2: STANDARD FORM CREDIT RATING DISCLOSURE

1. An authorized credit rating agency must ensure that every credit rating is accompanied with the following statements which must appear prominently:

1) The credit rating does not guarantee the performance of the rated entity or the relevant security.
2) A person should not rely on the credit rating for the purposes of making an investment decision.

2. An authorized credit rating agency must ensure that every credit rating is accompanied with the following information:

1) the name and job title of the related lead rating analyst in a clear and prominent manner.
2) the date when the credit rating was first released for distribution and when it was last updated;

3) the principal methodology or methodology version that was used in determining the credit rating including details of any significant adjustments and deviations, and where a description of that methodology and a discussion of how the other methodologies and other important aspects factored into the credit rating decision can be found;

4) the assumptions and limitations of each credit assessment, and the extent to which the authorized credit rating agency verifies information provided to it by the rated entity;

5) a description of all material sources used to prepare the credit rating, including (if relevant) the rated entity and any related third party;

6) clarify whether the credit rating was prepared on the basis of limited historical data;

7) clarify whether the credit rating has been disclosed to that rated entity or its related third party and amended following that disclosure before being issued;

8) the meaning of each rating category, the definition of default or recovery and any appropriate risk warning, including a sensitivity analysis of the relevant key rating assumptions;

9) clarify whether the credit rating concerns a newly issued security and whether the authorized credit rating agency is rating the security for the first time;

10) clarify whether the rated entity participated in the rating activities carried out with respect to the credit rating;

11) clarify whether the credit rating was initiated at the request of the rated entity; and

12) clarify whether the authorized credit rating agency has outsourced any rating activities in relation to the relevant credit rating.

9 The Depository Centre Procedures

Approved by the Board of the Capital Market Authority pursuant to its Resolution Number (1-2-2022) Dated 30/5/1443 H (3/1/2022 G)

Table of Contents

Section 1: Preliminary Provisions
1. Provisions and Definition
2. Conditions for Depository Centre Membership
3. Membership approval and Activation
4. Fees, Payment and Invoice
5. Notices
Section 2: Accounts Structure and Types
6. Depository Centre Accounts
7. Special Accounts
8. Accounts attributes
Section 3: Investors
9. Investors Identification
10. Investor Types and Identification Mechanism
Section 4: Cash Payments and Cash Accounts
11. Cash Payment
12. Cash accounts
13. Settlement agreements and Cash Settlement Headroom
14. Cash settlement
Section 5: Settlement Instructions
15. Settlement instructions
16. Holding Settlement
17. Releasing Settlement
18. Request to Cancel
19. Settlement Instructions cancellation by The Depository Centre
20. Settlement Instructions Amendments
21. Priority of Settlement Instructions
22. Partial settlement
Section 6: Settlement
23. Settlement
24. Free of Payment (FoP) Settlement
25. Delivery versus Payment Settlement
Section 7: CCP Settlement
26. Settlement related to CCP
Section 8: Securities Transfers
27. Transfer of Securities
28. Murabaha
29. Collateral transfers
30. Unlisted Securities transfers
31. Transfer of Foreign Securities
Section 9: Pledge
32. Pledge
Section 10: Restrictions
33. Restrictions
Section 11: Corporate actions
34. Corporate action Activities and Dates
35. Corporate Action Event and entitlement
36. Aggregation of Fractions
37. Capital Reductions
38. Bonus Shares Issuance and Capital Reductions
39. Tradeable Rights
40. Claims
41. Transformation of settlement instructions
42. SBL Agreement
43. Corporate Actions Activities on Foreign Securities Listed on The Exchange
Section 12: Securities Borrowing and Lending (SBL)
44. SBL Registration
45. Collateral
46. Loan Return
Section 13: Reconciliation
47. Reporting and Reconciliation

9.1 Section 1: Preliminary Provisions

9.1.1 1. Provisions and Definition

1.1. This document specifies the Depository Centre Procedures that Depository Centre Members must follow to comply with provisions of the Securities Depository Centre Rules.

1.2. The expressions and terms in these Procedures carry the same meaning as they do in the Capital Market Law and Glossary of Defined Terms Used in the Exchange Rules unless the text explicitly notes an alternate meaning.

1.3. These Procedures will enter into effect as per its approval resolution.

9.1.2 2. Conditions for Depository Centre Membership

2.1. Applicant that wishes to apply for a Depository Centre Membership must meet the conditions set out in the Securities Depository Centre Rules.

9.1.3 3. Membership approval and Activation

3.1. Upon approval by the Depository Centre, the applicant must pay the membership fee. Details of required documentation and relevant deadlines for membership application process shall be published on the Depository Centre's website.

3.2. After the conditions stipulated in (3.1) are fulfilled, the membership will be activated in the Depository and Settlement System.

9.1.4 4. Fees, Payment and Invoice

4.1. The Depository Centre will submit invoice to the Depository Centre Members on a periodic basis and define deadline for payment accordingly.

4.2. The Depository Centre shall publish all fee types and their calculation method on its website.

4.3. The Depository Centre shall notify the Depository Centre Members, at least, 30 days before imposing new fees or changing the fees.

9.1.5 5. Notices

5.1. The Depository Centre shall publish notices on its website for clarification and details related to The Depository Centre Procedure.

9.2 Section 2: Accounts Structure and Types

9.2.1 6. Depository Centre Accounts

6.1. Without prejudice to Section (4) of the Securities Depository Centre Rules the Depository Centre Accounts are opened and closed by the relevant Custody Member.

6.2. Investors may open one or more Depository Centre Account with more than one Custody Member. Investors can use the Depository Centre Account with more than one Exchange Member.

6.3. The Depository Centre Accounts are used for the following purposes:

6.3.1. Deposit Securities owned by the Depository Centre Account owner.
6.3.2. Transactions settlement.
6.3.3. Registration of restrictions.

6.4. The following table specify the mechanism of opening including, but not limited to, the Depository Centre Accounts:

Account Type Account Function The Account opened by		
Individual	Investor account	Custody Member
Organization	Investor account	Custody Member
House Account	Custody Member House Account	Custody Member

6.5. The Depository Centre may request any additional documents or information related to the Depository Centre Accounts.

9.2.2 7. Special Accounts

7.1. The Custody Member provides Settlement Pool Account for each Exchange Member for the purpose of Securities settlement in accordance with Section (7) of these Procedures.

7.2. The following table specify the mechanism of opening the Special Accounts:

Account Type	Account Function	The Account Opened By
Intermediary Account (mutual fund)	Transitory account between issuance account and investor account	Custody Member with Depository Centre approval
Lead Manager Rights Account	Unsubscribed rights account	Custody Member with Depository Centre approval
Custody Member Client Collateral Account	Transitory account against CCP Client Collateral Account. Safekeeping of Collateral.	Custody Member with Depository Centre approval
Custody Member Collateral Omnibus Account	Transitory account against CCP Collateral Omnibus Account Safekeeping of Collateral.	Custody Member with Depository Centre approval
CCP Collateral Omnibus Account	An account to hold CCP Clearing Members clients commingled Collaterals	CCP
CCP Client Collateral Account	An account to hold CCP Clearing Member client's Collaterals	CCP
CCP Collateral Account	An account to holds CCP Clearing Members Collaterals	CCP
CCP Settlement Pool Account	Settlement of Transactions against Exchange Member Settlement Pool Account and Exchange Member Clients Settlement Pool Account	CCP
Exchange Member Settlement Pool Account	Settlement of Transactions against CCP Settlement Pool Account	Custody Member with Depository Centre approval
Exchange Member Clients Settlement Pool Account	Settlement of Transactions against CCP Settlement Pool Account	Custody Member with Depository Centre approval
Distribution Account	Transitory account between issuance account and investor account	The Depository Centre
Issuance Account	Issuance of Securities	The Depository Centre
Corporate Action Distribution Account	Corporate Actions distribution	The Depository Centre

7.3. The Depository Centre may request any additional documents or information related to the Depository Centre Accounts.

9.2.3 8. Account Attributes

8.1. The Custody Member may activate the Holding settlement mechanism for any settlement instructions for each account opened by the Custody Member. Such instructions cannot be settled until the Custody Member activates the Releasing settlement mechanism.

8.2. The Custody Members may enable or prevent their employees to access their accounts opened by the relevant Custody Member.

8.3. The Custody Member must ensure that its accounts configured to flag the following activities:

8.3.1. Depository Receipts;
8.3.2. Exchange Traded Funds;
8.3.3. Investment Funds;
8.3.4. Corporate Actions fractions;
8.3.5. Discretionary Portfolio Management;
8.3.6. Employee Incentive Scheme;

8.3.7. Custody Member's Depository Receipts;
8.3.8. Certificates; and
8.3.9. Murabaha.

8.4. The interested parties accounts (guardian account for minor investors or CCP Collateral Accounts) are registered at the Depository and Settlement System for the purpose of reporting and special processing.

9.3 Section 3: Investors

9.3.1 9. Investors Identification

9.1. The Investors are identified by the Custody Member.

9.2. The Investor are identified by national identification or resident identification or commercial identification, and Country of residence and Investor type. The identification of an Investor in the Depository and Settlement System shall be by entering the Investor's information, as determined by the Depository Centre. Upon the completion of the identification process, the Investor will be provided with a unique "Identification Number". The creation of the Identification Number shall be as follows:

9.2.1. The National Identification Number for Saudi individuals and resident Identification Number for resident individuals in the Kingdom (10-digits number beginning with 1 or 2) is used as Identification Number.
9.2.2. The commercial number for Saudi companies is used as Identification Number.
9.2.3. 14-digit serial numbers are used as Identification Number for other Saudi Investors.
9.2.4. 14-digit serial numbers are used as Identification Number for other foreign investors (which includes GCC) and the first two digits are as country code.
9.2.5. If there is a conflict between the national Identification Number for Saudi individual and the commercial number for the Saudi companies, an additional code will be added to the Identification Number.

9.3. The Identification Number cannot be changed after creation.

9.4. The Custody Member may have separate records of Investors that allows having different addresses and contact details from other Custody Members using the same Identification Number. The Depository Centre shall notify Custody Members to confirm and update the provided addresses and contact details.

9.5. The Depository Centre may request any additional documents or information related to the Investors.

9.3.2 10.Investor Types and Identification Mechanism

10.1. The following table specifies the Investor Identification Mechanism:

Investor Category	Investor Types	Identified by
ETF foreign investor	Organization	Custody Member
Foreign fund	Organization	Custody Member
Individual foreign investor	Individual	Custody Member
Foreign institution	Organization	Custody Member
Individual	Individual	Custody Member
Investment Funds	Organization	Custody Member
QFI (Company)	Organization	Custody Member
QFI (Fund)	Organization	Custody Member
QFI (government and related entities)	Organization	Custody Member
Swap agreements	Organization Individual	Custody Member
Asset manager	Organization	Custody Member with The Depository Centre approval
Charity	Organization	Custody Member with The Depository Centre approval
Company	Organization	Custody Member with The Depository Centre approval
Endowments	Organization	Custody Member with The Depository Centre approval
Government	Organization	Custody Member with The Depository Centre approval
Government funds	Organization	Custody member with The Depository Centre approval
Public organizations	Organization	Custody member with The Depository Centre approval
Others	Organization, Individual	The Depository Centre
Special Case	Organization, Individual	The Depository Centre

9.4 Section 4: Cash Payments and Cash Accounts

9.4.1 11.Cash Payment

11.1. The Depository Centre use The Payment Systems - SAMA for cash settlement.

11.2. The Depository Centre provides cash settlement services for the following activities:

11.2.1. CCP instructions related to Securities settlement;
11.2.2. CCP instructions related to cash compensation;
11.2.3. CCP instructions related to cash substitution;
11.2.4. CCP instructions related to Default Management;
11.2.5. CCP instructions related to other Clearing activities;
11.2.6. The Depository Centre instructions related to corporate action claims;
11.2.7. The Depository Centre instructions related to tradable rights; and
11.2.8. The Depository Centre instructions related to SBL.

9.4.2 12.Cash Accounts

12.1. The Depository Centre shall define The Payment System - SAMA accounts for each Settlement Members.

9.4.3 13.Settlement agreements and Cash Settlement Headroom

13.1. The provided settlement agreement by the Depository Centre is defined based on the request from the relevant Settlement Member and Custody Member.

13.2. The Cash Settlement Limit is defined and updated by the Settlement Members. The Settlement Member may update the Cash Settlement Limit of the relevant Custody Member permanently or temporarily (effective during adjustment day).

13.3. The utilization of the Cash Settlement Limit is reset daily by the Depository and Settlement System.

13.4. The available funds that the Settlement Member is ready to settle are determined by calculating the Cash Settlement Headroom as follows: Cash Settlement Headroom = Cash Settlement Limit - Debited Cash + Credited Cash.

13.5. The Cash Settlement Headroom is used for the instructions stipulated in Paragraph (11.2) of these Procedures.

9.4.4 14.Cash Settlement

14.1. The Depository Centre shall request the Payment System - SAMA to credit the Depository Centre Account, and the Depository Centre shall credit the Depository Centre Accounts of the relevant Settlement Members.

14.2. The Payment System -SAMA may reject the request, if the relevant Settlement Members has insufficient balance.

14.3. In the event of rejection by the Payment System - SAMA, the Depository and Settlement System will notify the Settlement Member and Custody Members in relation with the relevant Settlement Member. The Depository and Settlement System will reset the relevant Cash Settlement Limit to zero, which shall be updated by the Settlement Members.

14.4. The Depository Centre calculates the total debited/credited amount related to Settlement Members on a daily basis. If the Custody Member cash exceeds its Cash Settlement Headroom, the Settlement Instructions that exceeds the Cash Settlement Headroom will not be settled in The Depository and Settlement System.

9.5 Section 5: Settlement Instructions

9.5.1 15.Settlement Instructions

15.1. The Settlement Instructions are generated by the Custody Members, the Depository Centre and CCP.

15.2. The Settlement Instructions require matched Settlement Instructions from the counterparty, except for the following cases:

15.2.1. CCP Settlement Instruction related to listed and unlisted Securities settlement and Collateral withdrawal if such Collaterals are Securities; and

15.2.2. The relevant Custody Member Settlement Instruction related to the distribution of public offer shares to the Investors accounts.

15.3. The following table specifies Settlement Instructions mechanism:

Transaction Type	Instructed by			Beneficial ownership change	Counter Party Account Mandate	Additional Rule Criteria
	The Depository and Settlement System	CCP	Custody Member			
TRAD (Trade)		X		Accept	No	Rejected if the instrument has Mecca/Medina flag set and delivering/receiving securities account holder's citizenship is not Saudi.
BIYI (Buy-in)		X		Accept	No	
SUBS (Subscription)			X	Accept	No	
ISSU (Issuance)			X	Accept	No	
REDM (Redemption)			X	Accept		
CORP (Corporate action)	X			Accept	No	
CLAI (Market claim)	X			Accept	No	
OWNI (Internal account transfer)			X	Reject	Yes	
OWNE (External account transfer)			X	Reject	Yes	
COLI (Collateral in)			X	Reject	Yes	Accepted if Interested Party matches
COLO (Collateral out)		X	X	Reject	Yes	Accepted if Interested Party matches
SECB (Securities borrowing)			X	Accept	No	Rejected if the instrument has Mecca/Medina flag set and delivering/receiving securities account holder's citizenship is not Saudi.
SECL (Securities lending)			X	Accept	No	
CONV (Depository receipt conversion)			X	Accept	No	
RELE (Depository receipt cancellation)			X	Accept	No	
PLCA (Pledge call)			X	Accept	No	

MURA (Murabaha)	X	Accept	Yes	Within same participant (intra transfer) only
GIFT (Gift within family)	X	On hold for The Depository Centre validation	Yes	
DONA (Donation to charity)	X	On hold for The Depository and Settlement System validation	Yes	
WILL (Will execution)	X	Accept	Yes	
VERD (Verdict)	X	On hold for The Depository and Settlement System validation	Yes	
INHE (Inheritance)	X	Accept	Yes	
EDOW (Endowment)	X	On hold for The Depository and Settlement System validation	Yes	
AUTA (Approved by authority)	X	On hold for The Depository and Settlement System validation	Yes	
EEIP (Employee incentive plan)	X	Accept	Yes	
UNLE (Unlisted Shares settlement)	X	On hold for The Depository and Settlement System validation	Yes	
CTSW (Conversion transfers from Swap to QFI end client)	X	On hold for The Depository and Settlement System validation	Yes	
CRSW (Correction transfer from Swap to QFI end client)	X	On hold for The Depository and Settlement System validation	Yes	

15.4. The following table specifies Settlement Instructions Matching criteria mechanism:

Matching field	Matching method	Comment
Mandatory for all instructions		
Securities movement type	Values are matched opposite	Receive vs Deliver
Payment type		FoP, DvP
ISIN code		Same instrument
Trade date		
Settlement quantity		
Intended settlement date		
The Depository Centre of Delivering party		The Depository Centre of counterparty have to match if provided
The Depository Centre of Receiving party		The Depository Centre of counterparty have to match if provided
Delivering (settlement) party		Participant code
Receiving (settlement) party		Participant code
Transaction type		Only additional matching for the transaction types specified below.
Mandatory for instructions involving payments		
Currency		
Settlement amount		May be subject to tolerance matching
Credit/debit indicator	Values are matched opposite	
Additional (have to match if provided by one instruction)		
Opt out indicator		
Cum/Ex indicator		
Optional (have to match if provided by both instructions)		
Common reference		
Client of delivering party		Identification Number
Client of receiving party		Identification Number
Securities account of delivering party (counterparty's account specified in the instruction)	Matched to securities account of the other instruction	For some transactions this field is mandatory.
Securities account of receiving party (counterparty's account specified in the instruction)	Matched to securities account of the other instruction	

15.5. The Depository and Settlement System verifies all settlement instructions generated from CCP or Custody Members. If the Settlement Instructions generated by CCP are rejected, the Depository Centre will notify CCP with rejection reasons.

15.6. The Depository and Settlement System will not verify the availability of cash, securities or Cash Settlement Limit of any Settlement Instructions.

15.7. Settlement Instructions are generated as follows:

15.7.1. FOP - Free of Payment- Transfer of Securities without a corresponding transfer of funds.
15.7.2. DVP - Delivery versus Payment - a Securities settlement mechanism that links a Securities transfer and a funds transfer in such a way as to ensure that delivery occurs if and only if the corresponding payment occurs.
15.7.3. FOD - Payment Free of Delivery - Transfer of funds without a corresponding transfer of securities.

15.8. Settlement Instructions statuses are reported by The Depository and Settlement System as the following:

15.8.1. Unmatched: upon receiving Settlement Instruction, without matching counterparty Settlement Instruction.

15.8.2. Matched: upon receiving Settlement Instruction, with matching counterparty Settlement Instruction. These Settlement Instructions will be settled in the indented settlement date. such Settlement Instructions appears as "accepted" status at CCP.
15.8.3. Rejected: upon rejecting Settlement Instructions after such Settlement Instruction are verified by The Depository and Settlement System. such Settlement Instructions appears as "failed" status at CCP. The Depository Centre will notify the CCP with the rejection reasons.
15.8.4. Cancelled: when a CCP, The Depository Centre or a Custody Member cancel matched Settlement Instructions. such instruction appears as "recalled "or "cancelled" status at CCP.
15.8.5. Settled: when a Settlement Instruction are settled. such Settlement Instruction appears as "completed" status at CCP.

9.5.2 16.Holding Settlement

16.1. The Custody Member and CCP may hold the settlement instructions in the following cases:

16.1.1. if the received information from the related client is incorrect; or
16.1.2. If there is insufficient cash to settle a transaction.

16.2. The Settlement Instructions which are in Holding Settlement status, will not be settled unless the Custody Member or CCP change the status to Releasing Settlement.

9.5.3 17.Releasing Settlement

17.1. All Settlement instruction received from CCP are in Releasing Settlement status. The Custody Member may set a Holding Settlement status for all Settlement Instructions received from CCP.

17.2. The Custody Member and CCP may Release the Settlement Instructions in the following cases:

17.2.1. If a confirmation is received from the clients to settle transaction; and
17.2.2. If there is sufficient cash to settle a Transaction.

17.3. If the Custody Member or CCP Release Settlement, the Depository and Settlement System will attempt to settle such Released Settlement Instruction on the intended settlement date.

9.5.4 18.Request to Cancel

18.1. The Custody Member and CCP may request to cancel any settlement instructions if there is a discrepancy between the client instructions and the settlement instructions generated. The CCP Settlement Instructions related to listed Securities may not be canceled unless such Settlement Instructions are between two different Custody Members.

18.2. The Custody Member and CCP may request to cancel the Settlement Instructions until the Depository and Settlement System automatically cancel such Settlement Instructions (3 days after intended settlement date).

18.3. If the relevant Custody Members or CCP request to cancel Settlement Instructions on the day before intended settlement date, CCP system allows the relevant Exchange Member to rectify such canceled Settlement Instructions in accordance with the Securities Clearing Centre Rules and Procedures. If the relevant Exchange Member does not rectify such Settlement Instruction in the period specified in this paragraph, CCP will rectify it automatically to relevant Exchange Member own account.

18.4. If the relevant Custody Members or CCP request to cancel Settlement Instructions on or after the intended settlement date, the relevant Exchange Member is responsible to settle such Settlement Instructions from its own account.

18.5. The relevant Custody Members may request late confirmation transfers from The Depository and Settlement System to settle the canceled Settlement Instructions in which they have requested to cancel after intended settlement date.

9.5.5 19.Settlement Instructions Cancellation by The Depository Centre

19.1. The Depository and Settlement System will cancel Settlement Instructions based upon the Authority's instruction.

19.2. The Depository and Settlement System will cancel the unsettled Settlement Instructions automatically on intended settlement date + 3.

9.5.6 20.Settlement Instructions Amendments

20.1. The generated Settlement Instructions by the relevant Custody Members at Depository and Settlement System can be amended as follows:

20.1.1. if the Settlement Instructions are not matched, such Settlement Instructions can be amended unilaterally; or
20.1.2. if the Settlement Instructions are matched, such Settlement Instructions can be amended bilaterally.

9.5.7 21.Priority of Settlement Instructions

21.1. Settlement Instructions with higher priority are executed before Settlement Instructions with lower priority.

21.2. There are four priority levels for the Settlement Instructions as follows:

21.2.1. Reserved priority: Settlement Instructions generated by the Depository Centre.
21.2.2. Top priority: Settlement Instructions generated by CCP.
21.2.3. High priority: The Custody Member may set or update priority level of their Settlement Instructions to high priority.
21.2.4. Normal priority: Settlement Instructions generated by the Custody Member.

9.5.8 22.Partial Settlement

22.1. The Custody Member and CCP may define the Settlement Instructions bilaterally to be settled partially.

22.2. The relevant Custody Members and CCP must set the partial settlement indicator on the Settlement Instructions to be settled partially.

9.6 Section 6: Settlement

9.6.1 23.Settlement

23.1. Each Settlement Instructions includes intended settlement date.

23.2. The released Settlement Instructions are settled at Depository and Settlement System between 07:00 AM to 16:10 PM. The Delivery Versus Payment (DvP)Settlement Instructions are settled at predetermined time (settlement batches).

9.6.2 24.Free of Payment (FoP) Settlement

24.1. The Free of payment Settlement Instructions are settled continuously between 07:00 AM to 16:10 PM.

9.6.3 25.Delivery versus Payment Settlement

25.1. Instructions related cash settlement are settled with batches during the day as follows:

25.1.1. First settlement batch: all Settlement Instructions generated by CCP.
25.1.2. Second settlement batch: all Settlement Instructions generated by the Depository Centre.

25.2. Cash settlement timings and updates are disclosed to the Depository Centre Members by the Depository Centre.

9.7 Section 7: CCP Settlement

9.7.1 26.Settlement related to CCP

26.1. Transactions are cleared and settled from Exchange Member Settlement Pool Account against CCP Settlement Pool Account. Each Exchange Member must have Exchange Member Settlement Pool Account and Exchange Member Clients Settlement Pool Account, which are linked to Position Account.

26.2. The CCP generate cash compensation and cash substitution instructions to replace the failed Transactions where a CCP is a party with cash.

26.3. In regards to any failure on indented settlement date; any remaining securities at the Exchange Member Settlement Pool Account shall be transferred to the account of the Exchange Member.

26.4. The CCP may generate Settlement Instructions on behalf of the relevant Custody Members. These instructions can be settling against CCP Pool account or across other Depository Centre accounts at Custody Members.

26.5. Settlement Instructions to or from Exchange Member Settlement Pool Account to CCP Settlement Pool account are settled on a net basis.

26.6. Settlement Instructions to or from Exchange Member Client Settlement Pool Account to the Investor Depository Centre account are settled on either gross or net basis and upon information inserted in the Trading Account on CCP.

26.7. The Settlement Instructions on CCP level and different Custody Members are Delivery versus Payment. 26.8. The Settlement Instructions of the same Custody Member are Free of Payment.

26.9. The Settlement Instructions related to the same investor account are settled on a net basis during settlement batches.

9.8 Section 8: Securities Transfers

9.8.1 27.Transfer of Securities

27.1. The Settlement Instructions related to changing the beneficial owner are settled with the Depository Centre approval.

27.2. The Settlement Instructions generated by CCP or Depository and Settlement System may change beneficial owner including, but not limited to, trades or Corporate Actions.

9.8.2 28.Murabaha

28.1. The Custody Member transfer Securities related to Murabaha through the Depository and Settlement System without executing a transaction.

28.2. The Settlement Instructions related to Murabaha transfers are generated by the relevant Custody Member through the Exchange Member account defined as Murabaha account within the same Custody Member.

9.8.3 29.Collateral transfers

29.1. The beneficial owners are changed in case the Collaterals are transferred from or to CCP Collateral Account by the Custody Members. Transfer of Collateral to CCP accounts is accepted by The Depository and Settlement System only if the interested party Identification Number is matching with the CCP Collateral Accounts.

29.2. Collaterals are transferred from Custody Member Collateral Omnibus account to CCP Collateral Account through the transitory account at the Depository and Settlement System. 29.3. Withdrawal of Collaterals can be done directly from CCP once the Collaterals are transferred to CCP Collateral Account.

9.8.4 30.Unlisted Securities Transfers

30.1. Unlisted deposited Securities and Designated Securities and Transactions shall be transferred without executing a transaction if the transfer instructions have been issued by a CCP, including DvP transfers between the Exchange Member settlement pool account and the Exchange Member's client settlement pool account.

30.2. Unlisted deposited Securities shall be transferred without executing a transaction if the transfer instructions have been approved by the Issuer to validate the Settlement Instructions issued by the Depository Centre or the Custody Member in the form prescribed for that purpose to settle at the Depository and Settlement System.

9.8.5 31.Transfer of Foreign Securities

31.1. Transfer of Foreign Securities from a Depository Centre account to the Foreign Depository Centre can be initiated by submitting a Securities transfer request form to the Depository Centre.

9.9 Section 9: Pledge

9.9.1 32. Pledge

32.1. Corporate Actions entitlements, excluding tradeable rights, are reflected in the Securities subject to the pledge.

9.10 Section 10: Restrictions

9.10.1 33. Restrictions

33.1. All restrictions on conducting any action or ownership on a deposited Securities shall be registered in the Depository and Settlement System through Custody Members or directly by the Depository Centre upon the instructions of the Authority, or the Issuer.

9.11 Section 11: Corporate actions

9.11.1 34.Corporate action Activities and Dates

34.1.1. Eligibility Date: The day of which Investors who are registered in the issuer's Securities Ownership Register are eligible to attend GA and vote on its decisions.
34.1.2. Ex-Date: The day where the securities are traded without the benefits/rights of the corporate actions. Security price is adjusted by the Exchange if the Corporate Actions resulted in (splits, bonus shares or rights issuance).
34.1.3. The Exchange does not adjust price in case of cash dividends.

34.2. Record Date: The day of which investors who are registered in the issuer's Securities Ownership Register are eligible to receive the benefits/rights of the corporate actions.

34.3. Payment Date of securities: (one business day after the Record Date) The day of which the Securities resulting from Corporate Actions are credited to the investors' Depository Centre accounts. Securities are credited into Depository Centre account before the start of trading session.

9.11.2 35.Corporate Action Event and Entitlement

35.1. All Corporate Action events recognized by The Exchange are applicable at the Depository Centre.

35.2. Corporate Action events, entitlements, status reporting, distributions and Custody Members subscriptions are available through messaging, The Depository and Settlement System features, and reports.

9.11.3 36.Aggregation of Fractions

36.1. Corporate Actions entitlements and distribution are paid on the investor account level.

36.2. Issuers are entitled to receive investor information subject to compensation from the Depository Centre. Compensation payments for fractions are completed by issuers outside the Depository Centre systems.

36.3. Corporate Actions fractions can be compensated by the issuers as the following:

36.3.1. Compensation by rump offer share sale price;
36.3.2. Compensation by reference price; or
36.3.3. No compensation for fractions.

9.11.4 37.Capital Reductions

37.1. If the GA decided on a capital reduction, trading of the issuer's security will be suspended until the end of the second trading day after the GA's relevant decision.

9.11.5 38.Bonus Shares Issuance and Capital Reductions

38.1. The Depository Centre adjusts the Trade volume (number of securities) according to the Corporate Action.

38.2. The value of the Trade (cash amount) will not change; however, the price is adjusted in accordance to the adjusted volume.

9.11.6 39.Tradable Rights

39.1. The Tradable Rights activities are covered as the following:

39.1.1. Rights distribution;
39.1.2. Exercise of rights during 9 days and the settlement is Delivery versus Payment; and
39.1.3. Conversion of subscribed rights to shares.

39.2. Subscription to Tradable Rights are settled in (T+0).

39.3. The subscription to Tradable Rights are completed with the Depository and Settlement System settlement batches. Subscription to Tradable Rights cannot be cancelled after settlement of rights.

39.4. The Investor may exercise the Tradable Rights during 9 days, or sell the Tradable Rights during 6 days, and if the relevant Investor take no action, the issuer compensates the Investor.

39.5. The lapsed Tradable Rights are transferred to the lead manager account for rump offering, and the Investors are compensated after the sale of the Tradable Rights.

9.11.7 40.Claims

40.1. The Depository Centre generates Corporate Actions claims instruction for the unsettled exchange Traded Transactions on the intended settlement date. Reverse claims are not applicable.

40.2. Corporate Actions claim instructions are generated independently from the underlying unsettled Settlement Instructions.

9.11.8 41.Transformation of settlement instructions

41.1. If the Settlement Instructions that are not settled by the end of record date, the Depository Centre cancels the original Settlement Instructions with new Settlement Instructions.

9.11.9 42. SBL Agreement

42.1. The Depository Centre generates new Settlement instructions if the relevant SBL agreement is affected by Corporate Actions.

9.11.10 43.Corporate Actions Activities on Foreign Securities Listed on The Exchange

43.1. In relation to corporate action's timing and activities of foreign securities, it will be dealt with in accordance to the market where the security is primarily issued.

43.2. When the foreign issuer increases its capital by rights issuance, the Depository Centre will allot shares based on the instruction from the foreign issuer.

9.12 Section 12: Securities Borrowing and Lending (SBL)

9.12.1 44. SBL Registration

44.1. Securities borrowing and lending transactions are created by custodians based on SBL Regulations. Settlement Instructions (Section 5) and Transfers (Section 8) procedures shall apply.

44.2. Lending Agents if any, or the Custody Members -where applicable- will be the main contact point of lenders/borrowers for the Centre.

44.3. Throughout the loan duration, the borrowed securities will be included in the lender's ownership limit (individual and group), and the borrowed securities are included in the borrower's ownership limit. 44.4. Registered SBL's can be cancelled by custodians bilaterally between the parties, and the loan and Collaterals returns will be cancelled.

44.5. The Securities borrowed by a Broker or Custody Member or Qualified Foreign Investor can be transferred to its Client with Onward Lending.

9.12.2 45.Collateral

45.1. SBL transactions may include Collateral transaction. Collateral can be cash or a specific instrument and asset class.

45.2. Members can top up or withdrawal the Collateral during the agreement.

9.12.3 46.Loan Return

46.1. The Depository and Settlement System generates SBL return instructions on the date set on the SBL agreement automatically, or at any time agreed between the parties.

9.13 Section 13: Reconciliation

9.13.1 47.Reporting and Reconciliation

47.1. Holdings, Transactions reports, and messages are available on scheduled and ad-hoc basis.

47.2. Custody Members shall reconcile on a daily basis, and inform the Depository Centre on reconciliation issues at least the following Day of the issue.

10 Depositary Receipts

(Instructions on Issuing Depositary Receipts out of the Kingdom)

Issued by the Board of the Capital Market Authority pursuant to its Resolution Number 2-86-2020 dated 19/1/1442H (7/9/2020G) based on the Capital Market Law issued by Royal Decree No. M/30 dated 2/6/1424H.

TABLE OF CONTENTS

Part 1: Preliminary
Part 2: Definitions
Part 3: Waiver
Part 4: General Provisions
Part 5: Authority's Approval for Issuing Depositary Receipts out of the Kingdom
Part 6: Issuer's Obligations
Part 7: Depositary Bank's Obligations
Part 8: Capital Market Institution's Obligations
Part 9: Investment Limits
Part 10: Authority's Powers in Relation to the Depositary Bank
Part 11: Publication and Entry into Force
Annex: Required Information and Documents to Apply for the Authority's Approval for Issuing Depositary Receipts out of the Kingdom

10.1 Part 1: Preliminary

a) The purpose of these Instructions is to set out the requirements and conditions for issuing Depositary Receipts out of the Kingdom for shares issued in the Kingdom and listed in the Exchange or shares issued in the Kingdom and its Issuer has made the necessary arrangements for listing them in the Exchange.

b) These Instructions shall not prejudice the provisions of the Capital Market Law, its Implementing Regulations, and the other related laws.

10.2 Part 2: Definitions

a) Any reference to the "Capital Market Law" in these Instructions shall mean the Capital Market Law issued by Royal Decree No. M/30 dated 2/6/1424H.

b) Expressions and terms in these Instructions shall have the meanings which they bear in the Capital Market Law and the Glossary of Defined Terms Used in the Regulations and Rules of the Capital Market Authority unless the context indicates otherwise.

c) For the purpose of implementing these Instructions, the following expressions and terms shall have the meaning they bear as follows, unless the context indicates otherwise:

Depositary Bank: A financial institution of legal personality authorized to issue and cancel Depositary Receipts out of the Kingdom, appointed by the Issuer in accordance with the provisions of these Instructions.

Foreign Market: A regulated market for the trade of securities out of the Kingdom.

Depositary Receipts: Financial instruments listed and traded in a Foreign Market, issued by the Depositary Bank for shares issued in the Kingdom and listed in the Exchange, or for shares issued in the Kingdom and its Issuer has made the necessary arrangements for listing them in the Exchange.

Ratio of Shares to Depositary Receipts: The number of Depositary Receipts for each of the Issuer's issued shares in the Kingdom.

10.3 Part 3: Waivers

The Authority may waive any person from applying any provision of these Instructions in whole or in part, upon the request of such person or on its own initiative.

10.4 Part 4: General Provisions

a) The issuance of Depositary Receipts out of the Kingdom must not prejudice any of the continuing obligations on the Issuers of the Securities in the Kingdom under the provisions of the Capital Market Law, its Implementing Regulations stipulated in the Rules on the Offer of Securities and Continuing Obligations and the Listing Rules.

b) The Depositary Bank must be licensed (or otherwise subject to regulatory oversight) by a regulatory authority, and must be incorporated in a jurisdiction that applies regulatory and monitoring standards equivalent to those of the Authority or acceptable to it. The Authority may determine, at its sole discretion, whether such regulatory and monitoring standards are equivalent to those of the Authority or acceptable to it.

c) Prior to listing the Depository Receipts in the Foreign Market, the Depository Receipts must be offered out of the Kingdom.

d) As an exception to the provisions of the Instructions for Book Building Process and Allocation Method in Initial Public Offerings, if the offering of shares in the Kingdom occurred simultaneously with the offering of the corresponding Depository Receipts out of the Kingdom, the financial advisor, in agreement with the Issuer, may take into consideration the subscription applications of the legal persons for the Depository Receipts out of the Kingdom during the book building process and the subscription price determination for the shares offered in the Kingdom, provided that the allocation for the shares that correspond to the Depository Receipts that are going to be issued out of the Kingdom are allocated to the Depository Bank. (IPO Book Building Exception)

e) For purposes of the Issuer's continuing obligations relating to sufficient liquidity requirements under the provisions of the Listing Rules, the shares held by the Depositary Bank shall be considered owned by the Public.

f) The Rules for Qualified Foreign Financial Institutions Investment in Listed Securities shall not apply to the Depositary Bank.

10.5 Part 5: Authority's Approval for Issuing Depositary Receipts out of the Kingdom

a) The Issuer must obtain the Authority's approval prior to issuing Depositary Receipts out of the Kingdom for its issued shares in the Kingdom.

b) The Issuer seeking to issue Depositary Receipts out of the Kingdom must submit an application to the Authority that includes the information and documents required in the Annex of these Instructions.

c) In considering an application, the Authority may:

1. carry on any enquiries that it considers appropriate;
2. require the Issuer, or his representative, to attend before the Authority to answer questions and explain any matter the Authority considers relevant to the application;
3. require the Issuer to provide additional information as the Authority considers appropriate within 30 days of the request; and
4. verify any information furnished by the Issuer.

d) The Authority may refuse to consider the application where the Issuer has failed to provide information requested from it, or has failed to provide information requested from it within the time requested.

e) The Authority, upon receipt of all information and documents required, shall notify the Issuer in writing, and shall take any of the following decisions within a maximum period of 45 days from the date of notice:

1. approve the application;
2. approve the application subject to conditions and limitations as it considers appropriate; or
3. reject the application and give the reasons thereof.

f) If the Authority decides to approve the application, it shall inform the Issuer in writing of such approval and of the limitations that the Authority may consider appropriate.

g) If the Authority decides to reject the application, it shall notify the Issuer in writing.

h) If a material change to the application documents arises after its submission to the Authority in accordance with requirements of these Instructions, the Issuer must immediately notify the Authority of such change upon knowledge. In such event, the Authority, in its own discretion, may then require the Issuer to re-submit the documents.

i) The Authority, when it decides to approve the application, may publish the identity of the Depositary Bank appointed by the Issuer.

10.6 Part 6: Issuer's Obligations

a) The Issuer, after obtaining the Authority's approval to issue Depositary Receipts out of the Kingdom, must notify the Authority and the Exchange with no delay of the listing, suspension, or delisting of its Depositary Receipts in the Foreign Market.

b) The Issuer must comply with the requirement that the maximum limit of the total number of shares agreed upon with the Depositary Bank that Depositary Receipts can be issued corresponding to it, does not exceed 10% of the total of its issued shares or the equivalent of one third of its shares owned by the Public, whichever is less.

c) The Issuer, in agreement with the Depositary Bank, must establish a mechanism for the distribution of voting rights related to shares to the holders of the Depositary Receipts, in accordance with voting mechanism set by the Depositary Center.

d) The Issuer must disclose to the Public in the Kingdom all information that must be disclosed to the Public under the Capital Market Law, its Implementing Regulations and the Exchange Rules, and all information disclosed in the Foreign Market simultaneously in a way that ensures that no information or material developments are leaked to the Foreign Market before disclosing them to the Public in the Kingdom in accordance with the Listing Rules.Public in the Kingdom in accordance with the Listing Rules.

e) If the Issuer submits a prospectus or any other equivalent document in the Foreign Market, the issuer must make such information available, with no delay, as a document available for the Public in the Kingdom.

f) Upon the receipt of a notice from the Authority based on the occurrence of any of the events specified in paragraph (d) of Part 10 of these Instructions in respect of the Depository Bank, the Issuer must appoint an alternative Depository Bank within a period not exceeding (45) days from the date of receipt of such notice.

10.7 Part 7: Depositary Bank's Obligations

a) The Depositary Bank, when the Issuer obtains the Authority's approval for issuing Depository Receipts out of the Kingdom, must open an account with the Depositary Center and appoint a custodian authorized to carry out custody business in the Kingdom to hold the shares that correspond to the Depositary Receipts that are going to be issued out of the Kingdom, in accordance with any regulations, rules or procedures the Authority, the Exchange or the Depositary Center issues.

b) The Depositary Bank, when the Issuer obtains the Authority's approval for issuing Depository Receipts out of the Kingdom, must open an investment account with a Capital Market Institution in the Kingdom, in which the transactions shall be limited to the transactions related to the Issuer's corporate actions for the shares that correspond to the Depositary Receipts.

c) The Depositary Bank may not dispose of the shares deposited in its account with the Depository Center, except for transferring the shares to a Capital Market Institution licensed to carry out dealing business, for the purpose of canceling the corresponding Depository Receipts; in accordance with any regulations, rules or procedures issued by the Authority, the Exchange or the Depository Center.

d) The Depository Bank must comply with the requirement that the total number of shares that correspond to the Depository Receipts it issues, shall not exceed the maximum limit under the Depository Receipts program agreed upon with the Issuer.

e) The Depositary Bank must without delay, notify the Exchange, in the event of any change in the Ratio of Shares to Depositary Receipts.

f) Without prejudice to the provisions of paragraph (c) of this Part, the Depositary Bank must enable the holder of Depositary Receipts, if such holder is among the categories of investors allowed to invest in the listed shares in the Kingdom, to cancel such

Depositary Receipts to become the holder of the corresponding shares, provided that such holder of Depositary Receipts holds an investment account with a Capital Market Institution in the Kingdom and an account with the Depository Center.

g) Without prejudice to the provisions of paragraph (d) of this Part, the Depositary Bank must enable the shareholder, if such shareholder is among the categories of investors allowed to invest in the Depositary Receipts listed in the Foreign Market, to convert shares to Depositary Receipts to become a holder of Depositary Receipts in the Foreign Market.

h) The Depositary Bank must prepare and maintain correct records of all transactions related to Depositary Receipts and corresponding shares. All records must, at all times, be current and sufficient to demonstrate compliance with the provisions of these Instructions.

i) The Depository Bank must maintain the records as stipulated in these Instructions for a period not less than ten years unless the Authority specifies otherwise. Without prejudice to this period and in case of any litigation or claim (including any litigation pending or threatened) or any on-going investigations relating to these documents, the Depository Bank must retain such documents until the closure of that litigation, claim or ongoing investigation.

j) All records required to be maintained by the Depositary Bank under the provisions of these Instructions must be available for review of the Authority at request.

10.8 Part 8: Capital Market Institution's Obligations

The Capital Market Institution, who deals or intends to deal with a shareholder or Depository Receipts holder for the purpose of issuing or canceling Depository Receipts by the Depository Bank, must designate an investment account and an account with the Depository Center, in which the transactions shall be limited to the transactions related to issuing or canceling Depository Receipts by the Depository Bank.

10.9 Part 9: Investment Limits

The shares held by the Depositary Bank for the purpose of issuing or cancelling Depositary Receipts shall be subject to the following limitations:

a) The maximum proportion of the shares of any issuer whose shares are listed or convertible debt instrument of the issuer that may be owned by all foreign investors (in all categories, whether residents or non-residents, except the foreign strategic investors pursuant to the Instructions for the Foreign Strategic Investors' Ownership in Listed Companies) in aggregate is 49
b) Other legislative limitations on foreign ownership in joint stock companies.
c) The limitations set forth in the articles of association or by-laws of the listed companies or any instructions issued by the supervisory or regulatory authorities to which these companies are subject.

10.10 Part 10: Authority's Powers in Relation to the Depositary Bank

a) If the Authority considers that any of the events specified in paragraph (d) of this Part has occurred or may occur in relation to a Depositary Bank, the Authority may:

1) Require the Depositary Bank to provide such information, documents and/or written explanation as the Authority deems necessary to verify the relevant situation;
2) Require the Depositary Bank or its representative, to attend before the Authority to answer questions and explain any matter the Authority considers relevant;
3) Carry on any enquiries that it considers appropriate;
4) Take any action to verify any information provided by the Depositary Bank, including communicating with foreign regulatory authorities;
5) Prohibit the Depositary Bank from disposing of shares held in its account with the Depositary Center;
6) Oblige the Issuer to appoint an alternative Depositary Bank; and
7) Exercise any of its other powers under the Capital Market Law and its Implementing Regulations.

b) Prohibition under sub-paragraphs (5) of paragraph (a) of this Part shall be effective immediately upon sending a written notice of such from the Authority to the Issuer and the Depositary Bank.

c) The Authority may publish the identity of the Depositary Bank, who has been prohibited from disposing of the shares held in its account with the Depositary Center under this Part.

d) The events referred to in paragraph (a) of this Part include the following:

1) The Depositary Bank no longer meets the conditions, obligations and requirements stated in these Instructions;
2) The Depositary Bank becomes insolvent;
3) The Depositary Bank has violated any of its obligations stipulated in the Capital Market Law and its Implementing Regulations or any other laws of the Kingdom;
4) The Depositary Bank has been subject to any material legal or regulatory sanction in any jurisdiction;
5) Any other event that the Authority believes necessitates its intervention to protect investors or safeguard the functioning of the Exchange in the Kingdom.

e) Following the prohibition imposed under this Part, the Depositary Bank may not dispose of any shares held in its account with the Depositary Center without the prior consent of the Authority.

10.11 Part 11: Publication and Entry into Force

These Instructions shall become effective upon its publication date.

10.12 Annex: Required Information and Documents to Apply for the Authority's Approval for Issuing Depositary Receipts out of the Kingdom

The Issuer must attach to its application to the Authority electronic copies of the following documents (and must retain the original copies of such documents and submit them to the Authority upon request):

1. A summary of a technical study that includes the objective of listing in the Foreign Market, the potential advantages and risks of such listing and a statement of the measures to be taken by the Issuer to mitigate those risks.
2. The required approvals under Issuer's bylaws, the Companies Law and its Implementing Regulations.
3. Name of the Depository Bank, its place of incorporation, details of its legal form, and demonstration of the regulatory and supervisory situation in which it is subject to.
4. A list prepared in coordination with a legal advisor that identifies any conflicts between the regulatory requirements in the Kingdom and the regulatory requirements in the Foreign Market that may have a material impact on the related listed shares, including the identification of any potential regulatory conflicts between the requirements of governance, disclosure and listing in the Kingdom, and the suggested methods of addressing them.
5. The total number of the Issuer's shares to be offered under the Depository Receipts program.
6. The maximum value of Depositary Receipts that may be issued under the Depository Receipts program.
7. The Ratio of Shares to Depositary Receipts.
8. The percentage of Depositary Receipts to be issued to the total number of Issuer's shares issued in the Kingdom.
9. The process and cost for canceling Depositary Receipts when a holder requests to be the owner of the shares corresponding to the Depositary Receipts, including the time needed for canceling Depositary Receipts and enabling the holder to trade the underlying shares in the Exchange.
10. The process and cost for issuing Depositary Receipts when a shareholder requests to be a holder of Depositary Receipts, including the time needed for issuing Depositary Receipts and enabling the holder to trade them in the Foreign Market.
11. Any other conditions or requirements determined by the Authority.

11 Instructions on the Direct Financing Investment Funds

Issued by the Board of Capital Market Authority pursuant to its Resolution No. 1-35-2022 dated 12/8/1443H.(15/3/2022G0.

The current version of these Regulations, as may be amended, can be found at the CMA website: www.cma.org.sa

TABLE OF CONTENTS

FIRST: PREAMBLE
SECOND: DEFINITIONS
THIRD: GENERAL PROVISIONS
FOURTH: CONDITIONS FOR ESTABLISHING AND OFFERING UNITS OF THE DIRECT FINANCING FUND
FIFTH: INVESTMENTS LIMITATIONS
SIXTH: ADDITIONAL DUTIES TO A DIRECT FINANCING FUND MANAGER
SEVENTH: CREDIT INFORMATION OF THE BENEFICIARY
E
IGHTH: BOARD OF DIRECTORS OF THE DIRECT FINANCING FUND
NINTH: REPORTING TO UNITHOLDERS
TENTH: PUBLICATION AND ENTRY INTO FORCE

Article 1: Preamble

a) These Instructions aim to regulate the offering of units of investment funds that are established for the purpose of carrying out direct financing activity, and the management and operations of those funds.

b) These Instructions are without prejudice to the Capital Market Law and its Implementing Regulations, including the provisions of the Investment Funds Regulations and other relevant regulations.

Article 2: Definitions

a) Any reference to the "Law" in these Instructions shall mean the Capital Market Law issued by Royal Decree No. M/30 dated 2/6/1424H.

b) Subject to paragraph (d) of this Article, expressions and terms in these Instructions have the meaning which they bear in the Capital Market Law and in the Glossary of Defined Terms Used in the Regulations and Rules of the Capital Market Authority, unless the context indicates otherwise.

c) Definitions of terms used in the Investment Funds Regulations stipulated in the Glossary of Defined Terms Used in the Regulations and Rules of the Capital Market Authority shall apply to the words and phrases mentioned in these Instructions, unless the context indicates otherwise.

d) For the purpose of implementing the requirements of these Instructions, expressions and terms shall have the meaning they bear as follows, unless the context indicates otherwise:

- Direct Financing Fund: An investment fund established for the purpose of carrying out the activity of direct financing for legal persons and investment funds.
- Beneficiary :The beneficiary of the financing.
- Fund size: It means the Fund's Total Assets Value plus any capital pledged to be paid by the unitholders.

Article 3: General Provisions

a) The offering of the units, operations and management of the Direct Financing Fund in the Kingdom must be in accordance with these Instructions and the Investment Funds Regulations.

b) The Authority may waive a provision of these Instructions in whole or in part as it applies to a person either on an application from such person to whom the relevant provisions of this Article would otherwise apply or on the Authority's own initiative.

Article 4: Conditions for Establishing and Offering Units of the Direct Financing Fund

The following conditions must be satisfied when offering units and establishing the Direct Financing Fund:

1) The fund's units shall be offered by a way of a private placement in accordance with the provisions of Part (5) of the Investment Funds Regulations.

2) The fund shall be closed ended.

3) The fund shall take the form of a special purpose entity in accordance with the Capital Market Law and its Implementing Regulations.

4) The total fund size at establishment shall not be less than (50) Million Saudi Riyals.

5) The Fund Manager shall submit to the Authority a detailed feasibility study that includes the targeted sectors and its details.

6) The fund's terms and conditions shall include the investment decision-making mechanism, and any relationships that may lead to a conflict of interests when the fund's practice its activity, and a statement that the fund investment would be in grant finance processes and the investment risk may extend to lose the value of the fund's assets.

Article 5: Investments Limitations

a) The Direct Financing Fund is prohibited from practicing in the activity of direct financing to individuals.

b) The duration of the financing granted through the Direct Financing Fund may not exceed the remaining period of the fund's lifetime, including any rescheduling or extension of the financing.

c) The Direct Financing Fund's total borrowing may not exceed (50%) of the total fund's size.

d) The total direct financing provided through the Direct Financing Fund may not exceed its total size.

e) The Direct Financing Fund may not bear any exposure to one beneficiary or more than one belonging to the same group at a rate of (25%) or more of the total fund's size.

f) When selling a financing contract for a beneficiary in the Kingdom to a person in the Kingdom, the Fund Manager must include the right of full recourse, provided that the purchaser of the financing contract has the right to refer to the fund to demand payment according to the arrangements indicated by the contract.

g) The Fund Manager may not sell financing contracts concluded outside the Kingdom to financial institutions licensed by the Saudi Central Bank (SAMA).

Article 6: Additional Duties to a Direct Financing Fund Manager

a) The policies and procedures set by the Fund Manager must include the aspects related to granting credit and the collection provisions and procedures. The Board of Directors of the fund must ensure the completeness and accuracy of those policies and procedures.

b) The Fund Manager must maintain all documents, records and files of the beneficiary in an orderly and secure manner, verify the completeness of the files and update them periodically, for a period of, at least, (10) years from the date of termination of the relationship.

c) The Fund Manager must set clear procedures for receiving and documenting the beneficiaries' complaints, studying them, and responding to them, and must commit to taking appropriate and immediate corrective actions related to those complaints. Provided that the complaints shall be registered in special records for this purpose, which include all the necessary information related to the subject matter of the complaint and the actions taken in this regard.

d) The Fund Manager must maintain the confidentiality of the beneficiaries' data and operations, and not disclose or detect it to other parties, or report it even after the termination of the relationship with the Fund, except as required by the relevant regulations and instructions.

e) The Fund Manager must disclose to the Fund's Board of Directors any conflict of interest that may arise between the Fund Manager and the Direct Financing Fund under his management caused by dealing with one of the beneficiaries - if any - or a related party, such conflict of interest must be approved or validated by the Fund's Board of Directors and disclosed to unitholders.

f) The Fund Manager must include in the financing contract concludes with the beneficiaries a mechanism for considering disputes that may arise from it; such as adding an arbitration clause in those contracts, provided that such a mechanism shall be disclosed in the Fund's terms and conditions.

g) The Fund Manager must calculate the provisions for potential losses and risks for the fund in accordance with the International Financial Reporting Standard.

Article 7: Credit Information of the Beneficiary

a) The Fund Manager must examine the beneficiary's credit record, after its approval, to verify its financial solvency, ability to fulfill and credit behavior, and document this in the financing file.

b) The Fund Manager must register the credit information of the beneficiary, after its approval, with one or more licensed companies for the credit information collection, in accordance with the Credit Information Law and its implementing regulation, and such information shall be updated throughout the period of dealing with the beneficiary.

c) In the event that the Fund Manager is not able to implement the provisions of paragraphs (a) and (b) of this Article, financing must not be provided.

d) The Fund Manager must follow clear and transparent written standards and procedures to assess the beneficiary's creditworthiness and ability to fulfill, and update them when needed. Such standards and procedures shall be approved and any update thereon by the Fund's Board of Directors. The Fund Manager must implement these procedures before granting the finance and document such in the financing file.

e) Subject to Article (59) of the Regulations of Capital Market Institutions, the Fund Manager may contract with finance companies licensed by the Saudi Central Bank (SAMA) to delegate any of the duties described in these Instructions.

Article 8: Board of Directors of the Direct Financing Fund The provisions governing the Board of Directors of the fund and the responsibilities of its members stipulated in Articles (84) and (85) of the Investment Funds Regulations shall apply to the Direct Financing Fund.

Article 9: Reporting to Unitholders The Fund Manager must include, as additional information, in its annual report stipulated in paragraph (a) of Article (93) of the Investment Funds Regulations the following:

1. The ratio of the fund's lending to the Direct Financing Fund's Total Assets Value.

2. The dual unit price of the fund.

3. Beneficiaries default ratio (90) days or more and (180) days or more of the total financing provided through the Direct Financing Fund (if any).

4. The actual ratio of asset-backed loans out of the total financing provided through the Direct Financing Fund.

Article 10: Publication and Entry Into Force

These Instructions shall become effective upon its publication.

12 Financial Technology Experimental Permit Instructions

Issued by the Board of the Capital Market Authority pursuant to its Resolution Number 1-4-2018 Dated 23/4/1439H (10/1/2018G) Based on the Capital Market Law Issued by Royal Decree No M/30 dated 2/6/1424H

TABLE OF CONTENTS

PART A
1: OVERVIEW
Introduction
Objectives & Principles
Target Applicants
PART B
REQUIREMENTS OF THE FINTECH
Authorization Requirements
Application Process for Authorization
Additional Regulatory Requirements
FinTech ExPermit Validity Period
Cancellation of Approval
APPENDICES
Appendix A: Application Process
Appendix B: Application Template 16

12.1 PART A OVERVIEW

Article 1: Introduction

1.1 The purpose of this Instructions is to provide a regulatory framework that is conducive for the innovation of financial technology ("FinTech") in capital market within the Kingdom of Saudi Arabia (The Kingdom).

1.2 For the purpose of implementing this Instructions, the following expressions and terms shall have the meaning they bear as follows unless the contrary intention appears: FinTech products: innovative FinTech products, services and business models related to the securities activities. FinTech ExPermit: a permit to enable applicants to participate in the FinTech Lab to deploy and test their innovative FinTech products related to capital market within specified parameters and timeframes.

1.3 The Capital Market Authority ("Authority") has the right to waive or modify the requirements set out in this Instructions at its discretion where appropriate.

1.4 The Authority will consider the number of applicants that can be effectively supported within the FinTech ExPermit at any one time to ensure that sufficient guidance can be provided to the applicants.

Article 2: Objectives & Principles

2.1 This section outlines the objectives and principles of this Instructions, and provides the eligibility and suitability of the FinTech product prior to application into the FinTech ExPermit.

2.2 The applicant should clearly understand the objectives and principles of the Instructions. It must be emphasized that the FinTech ExPermit cannot be used to avoid local laws and regulations.

2.3 These instructions shall be read in conjunction with and in addition to the Capital Market Law and its Implementing Regulations.

2.4 The FinTech ExPermit may NOT be suitable under the following circumstances:

(a) The proposed FinTech product is not related to securities activities.
(b) The proposed FinTech product is similar to those that are already being offered in the Kingdom, unless the applicant can show that either:

(i) a different technology is being applied; or

(ii) the same technology is being applied differently.

(c) The applicant has not done its due diligence, including knowing the relevant rules and regulatory requirements for deploying the proposed FinTech product.

2.5 In considering an application to participate in the FinTech ExPermit, the Authority will take into account, among others, the following:

(a) the potential benefits of the proposed FinTech product;
(b) the potential risks and mitigating measures associated with the proposed FinTech product; and
(c) the integrity, capability and track record of the FinTech applicant.

2.6 The FinTech ExPermit is not intended to create a risk-free FinTech environment. The FinTech ExPermit aims to promote FinTech innovation in a controlled environment which the consequences of failure can be contained.

Article 3: Target Applicants

3.1 Any applicant intends to test FinTech product related to securities activities can apply to FinTech ExPermit, even if it is not Authorized Person by the Authority.

3.2 An Authorized Person does not need to apply for FinTech ExPermit to test its FinTech product which complies with all relevant regulatory requirements to a wider market, if it has authorization for the activity it wishes to carry on. Alternatively, if it does not have the relevant authorization for the activity, it will need to apply to the Authority to amend its License to obtain that authorization in accordance to the Authorized Person Regulations.

3.3 FinTech ExPermit is not intended to be a platform for a person to launch an established FinTech product which complies with all relevant regulatory requirements to a wider market. A person, who intend to deploy its complying Fintech products will need to apply to the Authority to obtain a License for the activity it wishes to carry on in accordance to the Authorized Person Regulations.

3.4 If an Authorized Person / person considers that the FinTech ExPermit is the only appropriate regulatory framework to the testing of its Fintech product, it can apply for FinTech ExPermit and the Authority may accept or reject its application.

12.2 PART B: FINTECH REQUIREMENTS

Article 4: Authorization Requirements

4.1 An applicant seeking the Authority's approval to obtain a FinTech ExPermit to participate in the FinTech Lab must demonstrate to the satisfaction of the Authority that:

(a) the applicant permitted under the FinTech ExPermit will be required to establish a commercial presence in the Kingdom;
(b) the applicant has adequate and appropriate resources, including financial resources, to develop the FinTech product;
(c) the applicant must intend to roll-out its FinTech product in the Kingdom once it has successfully completed testing;
(d) the applicant is fit and proper;
(e) the applicant is acting with integrity and with due skill, care and diligence, including but not limited to the following:

(i) communicating information to its clients in a way which is clear, fair and not misleading;

(ii) paying due regard to clients' interests, by treating them fairly and paying due regard to their interests;

(iii) managing conflicts of interest fairly, both between its clients and between itself and its clients; and

(iv) the applicant has the ability to ensure confidentiality of client information;

(f) it complies with all obligations under the Anti-Money Laundering Law and the rules and regulations on anti-money laundering and terrorism financing as in force in the Kingdom; (g) it will disclose to the Authority any material event or change in its business model; (h) the applicant has conducted its due diligence, including knowing the relevant rules and regulatory requirements for deploying the proposed FinTech product; and (i) is able to satisfy all additional regulatory requirements that the Authority may prescribe.

4.2 The application should also contain the necessary supporting information to explain and depict on the following requirements:

(a) the applicant has relevant technical and business knowledge and experience to develop and test the FinTech product;
(b) is able to clearly define the FinTech product's targeted clients, the additional regulatory requirements, key milestones and intended outcomes;
(c) is able to propose an acceptable reporting schedule to report to the Authority on the status and progress of development and testing of its FinTech product;
(d) is able to satisfactorily detail the safeguards that have been put in place, and demonstrate how they are appropriate to the FinTech product being tested;
(e) significant risks arising from the FinTech product and how it should be assessed and mitigated; and
(f) is able to set out a fair and proper exit strategy for clients should the FinTech product be discontinued for any reasons, including but not limited to the following:

(i) to cease the offering of the FinTech product to its new and existing clients;

(ii) provides notification to its clients informing them of the decision and related reasons;

(iii) dispose all confidential information including client personal information collected during the FinTech ExPermit testing; and

(

iv) submit a report to the Authority on the actions taken under this paragraph.

4.3 A proposed FinTech product should meet the following criteria prior to submission of application for FinTech ExPermit:

(a) it must involve a security activity (i.e. it is within the scope of the activities that the Authority regulates);
(b) it promotes FinTech innovation, in terms of the business application and deployment model of the technology;
(c) it has the potential to:

(i) promote significant growth, efficiency or competition in the capital market;

(ii) promote better compliance and monitoring and risk management solutions for the capital market; or

(iii) improve the choices and welfare of clients.

(d) it is at a sufficiently advanced stage of development to mount a FinTech live test.

4.4 The Authority may at any time modify or impose additional criteria, that it reasonably considers to be necessary to address a regulatory concern.

Article 5: Application Process for Authorization

5.1 If the applicant is suitable to participate for the FinTech ExPermit framework (set out in Section 3 above) and meets the authorization requirements (set out in Section 4 above), it can proceed to complete and submit the FinTech ExPermit Application Form. A copy of the application form is attached at Appendix B to this Instructions and can be submitted to the Authority by email at FinTech.ExPermit@cma.org.sa.

5.2 Once the applicant has submitted its application form, the Authority will review the application and inform the applicant of its eligibility to qualify for the FinTech ExPermit.

5.3 The Authority will work with the applicant to determine the additional regulatory requirements (set out in Section 6 below) to be applied to the applicant and its FinTech product during the testing period. The applicant will then assess if it is able to meet these requirements.

5.4 If the applicant is able and willing to meet the additional regulatory requirements (set out in Section 6 below) as prescribed by the Authority during the testing period, the applicant will be granted a FinTech ExPermit.

5.5 Once the Authority grants the FinTech ExPermit, the applicant will be able to test its product within the additional regulatory requirements (set out in Section 6 below).

5.6 Details of the application process are set out in Appendix A.

Article 6: Additional Regulatory Requirements

6.1 To grant the FinTech ExPermit, the Authority may impose additional regulatory requirements including limitations and/or conditions on the applicant and its FinTech product. These regulatory requirements may be adapted from existing CMA's regulations as applicable. These may include, but are not limited to, any of the following:

(a) the number and type of clients with or for whom the applicant carries on, or intends to carry on within the FinTech ExPermit;
(b) the type and size of client transactions that the applicant is permitted to enter into;

(c) the suitability assessment and clients' written consent required prior to carrying on the regulated activity;
(d) the applicant's ability to protect client's assets;
(e) the requirements surrounding the applicant's handling and protection of client information;
(f) the manner and type of financial promotion that the applicant may undertake and the associated disclosures that the applicant is required to make to clients;
(g) the key information required to be contained in a client's agreement;
(h) the FinTech applicant's capital requirements (if any); and
(i) the FinTech applicant's financial and other reporting requirements.

6.2 The Authority may, at any time through the life cycle of the FinTech ExPermit, by notice in writing to the applicant, cancel or vary any additional regulatory requirements imposed on the applicant or impose such further additional regulatory requirements.

Article 7: FinTech ExPermit Validity Period
7.1 The FinTech ExPermit validity period (or testing period) shall not exceed two years from the date of approval by the Authority.

7.2 To extend the testing period, a written application must be submitted by the applicant to the Authority no later than three months before its expiry, or at such time as is otherwise agreed by the Authority. The application should state the additional time required and clearly explain reasons for requiring the extension.

7.3 The testing period may only be extended in exceptional circumstances and the Authority shall reserves the right to reject any application for an extension.

7.4 Upon the completion of the testing, the applicant can choose to either:

(a) execute the exit strategy; or
(b) proceed to deploy the FinTech product on a wider scale, provided that:

(i) both the Authority and the applicant are satisfied that the FinTech ExPermit has achieved its intended test outcomes;

(ii) a strategy is in-place for the deployment of the product on a wider scale; and

(iii) the applicant can and willing to fully comply with the Capital Market Law and its Implementing Regulations.

7.5 The Authority may also prohibit deployment of the FinTech product in the market upon the completion of the testing due to the following reasons:

(a) in the event of an unsuccessful testing based on agreed test measures; or
(b) the FinTech product has unintended negative consequences to the market. In such case, the applicant must immediately execute its exit strategy.

Article 8: Cancellation of Approval
8.1 The Authority may cancel an approval to participate in the FinTech ExPermit at any time before the end of the testing period if the applicant:

(a) has failed to achieve its intended purpose, based on the latest test scenarios, expected outcomes and schedule;
(b) is unable to fully comply with the relevant legal and regulatory requirements at the end of the testing period;
(c) a flaw has been discovered in the FinTech product where the risks posed outweigh the benefits of the product, and the applicant acknowledges that the flaw cannot be resolved within the duration of the testing;
(d) breaching any condition imposed for the duration of the FinTech ExPermit ; or
(e) contravenes any applicable of the CMA's Implementing Regulations or any applicable law in the Kingdom or abroad which may affect the applicant's integrity and reputation.

8.2 Upon cancellation of approval, the applicant must immediately execute its exit strategy.

12.3 APPENDIX A: APPLICATION PROCESS

Submit FinTech ExPermit application form to CMA

CMA reviews the application to determine applicant's preliminary eligibility based on the requirements in the Instructions Does applicant potentially qualify for the FinTech ExPermit?

Application is rejected and applicant is informed.

CMA informs applicant that its application will potentially qualify for the FinTech ExPermit

CMA works with the Applicant to determine the additional regulatory requirements

Is the Applicant able and willing to meet the proposed additional regulatory requirements?

FinTech ExPermit application is approved

FinTech ExPermit expires within 2 years

CMA grants the Applicant with FinTech ExPermit

12.4 APPENDIX B: APPLICATION TEMPLATE

1. Details on the Applicant

General Information

1.1. Full name of Applicant:

1.2. Main address:

1.3. Contact e-mail address:

1.4. Contact telephone number and facsimile number:

1.5. National Identity No. / Passport No. :

1.6. Has the application been prepared on behalf of the Applicant by an external service provider? If yes, please fill the following:

a) Full name of contact person :
b) Firm name and main address:
c) Contact e-mail address:
d) Contact telephone number and facsimile number:
e) National Identity / Passport No. Commercial Registration No.

Resources, Experience and Track Record of the Applicant

1.7. Details of the Applicant's resources, including financial resources, to develop and test its FinTech product:

1.8. Details of the Applicant's relevant technical and business knowledge and experience to develop and test the FinTech product:

1.9. Details of the Applicant's previous experience in FinTech (if any):

1.10.Details of the proposed project members' relevant technical and business domain knowledge and experience to develop and test the FinTech Proposal:

1.11. Is or has the Applicant been licensed by, or subject to, the oversight of other government / regulatory bodies? If so, provide details:

2. Establishment of the Applicant's Entity (if applicable)

2.1. If the Applicant has established an entity:

a. please indicate the legal form of Applicant (e.g. Joint Stock Company, Limited Liability Company, etc.):
b. Commercial Registration Number:
c. Full list of project members including the Applicant, designated founders, shareholders, management / Directors, team members / employees of the FinTech entity. Please provide organization chart as a separate attachment:

2.2. If the Applicant is individual:

a. Please indicate the propose name of FinTech entity and its legal form (to be established in the Kingdom):
b. Propose legal form of FinTech entity (e.g. Joint Stock Company, Limited Liability Company, etc.):
c
. Propose corporate and ownership structure of FinTech entity:
d. Full list of proposed project members including the Applicant, designated founders, shareholders, management / Directors, team members / employees of the FinTech entity. Please provide organization chart as a separate attachment.

2.3. Does the Applicant at the time of filling this application have a firm that is currently operating in FinTech business, securities business, or banking? If yes, please provide details:

2.4. Is the Applicant intending to carry or is carrying on FinTech business in other countries? If yes, please provide details:

3. Fit and Proper Requirements

3.1. In the past ten years, has the Capital Market Authority or any other governmental authority, professional body, self-regulatory organization in the Kingdom of Saudi Arabia or elsewhere ever:

a) found the Applicant or a person who directly or indirectly controls the Applicant to have made a false statement or omission? If yes, please provide details:
b) found the Applicant or a person who directly or indirectly controls the Applicant to have been involved in a violation of its rules or regulations? If yes, please provide details:
c) found the Applicant or a person who directly or indirectly controls the Applicant to have been a cause of an investment-related business having its Authorization to do securities business, Fintech business or other business refused, suspended, revoked, or restricted? If yes, please provide details:
d) Entered a judgment or order against the Applicant or a person who directly or indirectly controls the Applicant to in connection with securities business, Fintech business or any investment- related activity? If yes, please provide details:
e) Entered a judgment or order the Applicant or a person who directly or indirectly controls the Applicant to cease and desist from any activity? If yes, please provide details:
f) Imposed a civil money penalty on the Applicant or a person who directly or indirectly controls the Applicant to? If yes, please provide details:

3.2. In the past ten years, has any court in the Kingdom of Saudi Arabia or elsewhere done any of the following :

a) Restricted or restrained the Applicant or a person who directly or indirectly controls the Applicant in connection with securities business, FinTech business, or any investment-related activity? If yes, please provide details:
b) Ever found the Applicant or a person who directly or indirectly controls the Applicant was involved in a violation of any Saudi Arabian laws or regulations? If yes, please provide details:
c) Ever dismissed any investment-related civil action brought against the Applicant or a person who directly or indirectly controls the Applicant by any foreign financial regulatory authority? If yes, please provide details:

3.3. Currently, is the Applicant or any person who directly or indirectly controls the Applicant subject of any civil or criminal proceeding that could result in a "yes" answer to any part of Items 3.1 or 3.2? If yes, please provide details:

3.4. In the past ten years, has the Applicant or any of the Applicant's registered or proposed executive directors, or officers declared insolvency or been declared insolvent by authority in the Kingdom of Saudi Arabia or elsewhere? If yes, please provide details:

4. Details on the Fintech Product

4.1 Describe how the FinTech product is addressing the needs (or issues) in relation to securities business:

4.2 Describe how the FinTech product will promotes FinTech innovation in terms of the business application and deployment model of the technology:

4.3 In relation to Item 4.2 above, explain how the FinTech product address gaps in or open up new opportunities for financial market:

4.4 Describe the benefits of the FinTech product, including how it may: (i) promote significant growth, efficiency, or competition in the capital market; (ii) promote better compliance and monitoring and risk management solutions for the capital market; or (iii) improve the choices and welfare of consumers.

4.5 Demonstrate how the FinTech product is at a sufficiently advanced stage of development to mount a live test in the FinTech Lab. Provide details of actual funding raised or potential funding sought for the FinTech product (if any).

4.6 Provide a brief description of the FinTech product to be experimented in the ExPermit including but not limited to the following:

a) Explain why the FinTech product needs to be tested within the FinTech Lab, and cannot be implemented otherwise:

b) Describe the market research carried out to assess the state, demand and readiness of the relevant financial segments and target customers in the Kingdom to adopt the FinTech product (please provide relevant statistics and supporting data where applicable):

4.7 Describe in detail the proposed test program for the FinTech product, including the:

a) Test objectives and outcomes:
b) Test parameters to measure the success of the test objectives / outcomes:
c) Control boundaries / limits for the test, including but not limited to:

- Clientele type and number
- Transaction size and total exposure limits

d) Client communications plan and risk disclosures for the live-tests
e) Any other safeguards (if applicable) that the Applicant proposed to put in place prior to commencing the testing of the FinTech product
f) Key milestones and timelines to achieve the milestones

4.8 Describe the proposed control program for the tests, including:

a) Significant risks arising from the FinTech product
b) Measures to mitigate the risks and impact to customers and the arising from any test failures
c) Measures for prevention of money laundering and countering the financing of terrorism (if applicable)

4.9. Describe the proposed reporting schedule to the CMA on the status and progress of development and testing of the FinTech product:

4.10.Describe the exit strategy for clients upon completion or discontinuation of the testing or revocation by the CMA:

4.11.Describe the business strategy / plan to deploy the FinTech product in the broader market after successfully exiting from the testing:

4.12.Attach any other relevant information such as process flow diagrams, promotional presentations, etc. on the FinTech product:

5. Applicant's Declaration and Undertaking

5.1. The Applicant hereby represents and undertakes that he and all of his employees will follow all laws, rules, and regulations relating to carrying on Fintech business in the Kingdom of Saudi Arabia.

5.2. The Applicant represents that the information and statements contained herein, including exhibits attached hereto, and other information filed herewith, all of which constitute part of this Application, are complete, clear, accurate and not misleading.

5.3. The Applicant further represents that to the extent any information previously submitted is not amended, such information is currently accurate and complete up to the date that this application is executed.

5.4. The Applicant also undertakes if any information or statement in this application changes before this application is approved, he will notify the CMA in writing immediately of the changes.

5.5. The Applicant declares that to the best of his knowledge and belief, having made due enquiry, the individuals are fit and proper to perform the functions to which this application relates.

5.6. The Applicant confirms that he have the authority to make this notification, to declare as specified above and sign this form for, or on behalf of, the Applicant.

Signature
Date of the Application
Name of the Applicant
Name of the authorized representative of the Applicant

13 INSTRUCTIONS FOR THE FOREIGN STRATEGIC INVESTORS OWNERSHIP IN LISTED COMPANIES

Issued by the Board of the Capital Market Authority pursuant to its Resolution Number 3-65-2019 dated 14/10/1440H (17/6/2019G) Based on the Capital Markets Law, issued by Royal Decree No. M/30 dated 2/6/1424H

TABLE OF CONTENTS

Part 1: Preliminary
Part 2: Definitions
Part 3: Waivers
Part 4: Right to Appeal
Part 5: Requirements of Strategic Shareholdings Ownership by Foreign Strategic Investors
Part 6: Investment Limits
Part 7: Publication and Entry into Force

13.1 Part 1: Preliminary

a) The purpose of these Instructions is to set out the provisions, requirements and conditions necessary for the Foreign Strategic Investors ownership of Strategic Shareholdings in listed companies, and determine their obligations and the obligations of the Authorized Persons in this regard.

b) These Instructions shall have no prejudice to the provisions of the Capital Market Law and its Implementing Regulations, especially the Rules on the Offer of Securities and Continuing Obligations and the Merger and Acquisition Regulations, and the other related laws.

c) The Foreign Strategic Investors are entitled to exercise all rights related to the shares of the listed companies they own, including trading in rights issue.

d) The Rules for Qualified Foreign Financial Institutions Investment in Listed Securities shall not apply to the Foreign Strategic Investors.

e) These Instructions shall not apply to the Citizens of the Cooperation Council for the Arab States of the Gulf.

13.2 Part 2: Definitions

a) Any reference to the "Capital Market Law" in these Instructions shall refer to the Capital Market Law issued by the Royal Decree No. M/30 dated 2/6/1424H.

b) Without prejudice to paragraph (c) of this Part, expressions and terms in these Instructions have the meaning which they bear in the Capital Market Law and in the Glossary of Defined Terms Used in the Regulations and Rules of the Capital Market Authority, unless the context indicates otherwise.

c) For the purpose of implementing these Instructions, the following expressions and terms shall have the meaning they bear as follows, unless the context indicates otherwise:

Foreign Strategic Investor: a foreign legal entity that aims to own a Strategic Shareholding in listed companies.

Strategic Shareholding: the direct ownership percentage in the listed company's shares, and through which the aim is to contribute in promoting the financial or operational performance of the listed company.

Citizens of the Cooperation Council for the Arab States of the Gulf: natural persons who hold citizenship of one of the Cooperation Council for the Arab States of the Gulf countries , or legal persons that (i) the capital of which is majority owned by citizens or governments of the Cooperation Council for the Arab states of the Gulf; and (ii) are holding the citizenship of one of the Cooperation Council for the Arab states of the Gulf countries ,in accordance with the definition set out in the resolution of the Supreme Council of the Cooperation Council for the Arab States of the Gulf in its 15th session approved by the Council of Ministers Resolution Number (16) dated 20/1/1418H.

13.3 Part 3: Waivers

The Authority may waive the Foreign Strategic Investor from applying the provision of these Instructions in whole or in part, upon the Foreign Strategic Investor's request or on its own initiative.

13.4 Part 4: Right to Appeal

Any person subject to these Instruction may appeal to the Committee in respect of any decision or action that the Authority takes under these Instructions.

13.5 Part 5: Requirements for the Foreign Strategic Investor Ownership of Strategic Shareholdings

a) Without prejudice to the provisions of the Capital Market Law and its Implementing Regulations and the other related laws, for Foreign Strategic Investor to own Strategic Shareholdings in listed companies, the following requirements shall be fulfilled:

1. The Foreign Strategic Investor shall be established or licensed in a country that applies regulatory and supervisory measures similar to those applied by the Authority or are accepted by it. The Authority may, at its sole discretion, determine whether such regulatory and supervisory measures are similar to those applied by the Authority or accepted by it or not.
2. Have a client account and a Depositary Center account.
3. Any other requirements or conditions as the Authority require.

b) The Authorized Person shall ensure that the Foreign Strategic Investor has fulfilled the requirements stipulated in paragraph (a) of this Part.

13.6 Part 6: Investment Limits

a) The investments of the Foreign Strategic Investor shall be subject to the following limitations:

1. The limitations set forth in the Articles of Association of the listed companies or any instructions issued by the regulatory and supervisory authorities which such companies are subject to.
2. Other legislative limitations on foreigner's ownership in joint stock companies.
3. The Foreign Strategic Investor, may not dispose of any of the shares it owned in accordance with these Instructions within a period of two years after the date of ownership of such shares.

b) The Authorized Person shall not enable any procedure that may violate the provisions of subparagraph (a\3) of this Part.

c) The Exchange shall publish on its website, as determined by the Authority in this regard, the following information:

1. A statistic reflecting the ownership percentage of the Foreign Strategic Investors in listed companies.
2. The limitations specified in subparagraphs (a/1) and (a/2) of this Part, according to the information received by the Exchange from listed companies in this regard.

13.7 Part 7: Publication and Entry into Force

These Instructions shall become effective upon their publication.

14 INSTRUCTIONS ON ISSUING DEPOSITARY RECEIPTS OUT OF THE KINGDOM

Issued by the Board of the Capital Market Authority pursuant to its Resolution Number 2-86-2020 dated 19/1/1442H (7/9/2020G), based on the Capital Markets Law, issued by Royal Decree No. M/30 dated 2/6/1424H.

TABLE OF CONTENTS

Part 1: Preliminary
Part 2: Definitions
Part 3: Waiver
Part 4: General Provisions
Part 5: Authority's Approval for Issuing Depositary Receipts out of the Kingdom
Part 6: Issuer's Obligations
Part 7: Depositary Bank's Obligations
Part 8: Capital Market Institution's Obligations
Part 9: Investment Limits
Part 10: Authority's Powers in Relation to the Depositary Bank
Part 11: Publication and Entry into Force
Annex: Required Information and Documents to Apply for the Authority's Approval for Issuing Depositary Receipts out of the Kingdom

Article 1: Preliminary

a) The purpose of these Instructions is to set out the requirements and conditions for issuing Depositary Receipts out of the Kingdom for shares issued in the Kingdom and listed in the Exchange or shares issued in the Kingdom and its Issuer has made the necessary arrangements for listing them in the Exchange.

b) These Instructions shall not prejudice the provisions of the Capital Market Law, its Implementing Regulations, and the other related laws.

Article 2: Definitions

a) Any reference to the "Capital Market Law" in these Instructions shall mean the Capital Market Law issued by Royal Decree No. M/30 dated 2/6/1424H.

b) Expressions and terms in these Instructions shall have the meanings which they bear in the Capital Market Law and the Glossary of Defined Terms Used in the Regulations and Rules of the Capital Market Authority unless the context indicates otherwise.

c) For the purpose of implementing these Instructions, the following expressions and terms shall have the meaning they bear as follows, unless the context indicates otherwise:

Depositary Bank: A financial institution of legal personality authorized to issue and cancel Depositary Receipts out of the Kingdom, appointed by the Issuer in accordance with the provisions of these Instructions.

Foreign Market: A regulated market for the trade of securities out of the Kingdom.

Depositary Receipts: Financial instruments listed and traded in a Foreign Market, issued by the Depositary Bank for shares issued in the Kingdom and listed in the Exchange, or for shares issued in the Kingdom and its Issuer has made the necessary arrangements for listing them in the Exchange.

Ratio of Shares to Depositary Receipts: The number of Depositary Receipts for each of the Issuer's issued shares in the Kingdom.

Article 3: Waivers The Authority may waive any person from applying any provision of these Instructions in whole or in part, upon the request of such person or on its own initiative.

Article 4: General Provisions

a) The issuance of Depositary Receipts out of the Kingdom must not prejudice any of the continuing obligations on the Issuers of the Securities in the Kingdom under the provisions of the Capital Market Law, its Implementing Regulations stipulated in the Rules on the Offer of Securities and Continuing Obligations and the Listing Rules.

b) The Depositary Bank must be licensed (or otherwise subject to regulatory oversight) by a regulatory authority, and must be incorporated in a jurisdiction that applies regulatory and monitoring standards equivalent to those of the Authority or acceptable to it. The Authority may determine, at its sole discretion, whether such regulatory and monitoring standards are equivalent to those of the Authority or acceptable to it.

c) Prior to listing the Depository Receipts in the Foreign Market, the Depository Receipts must be offered out of the Kingdom.

d) As an exception to the provisions of the Instructions for Book Building Process and Allocation Method in Initial Public Offerings, if the offering of shares in the Kingdom occurred simultaneously with the offering of the corresponding Depository Receipts out of the Kingdom, the financial advisor, in agreement with the Issuer, may take into consideration the subscription applications of the legal persons for the Depository Receipts out of the Kingdom during the book building process and the subscription price determination for the shares offered in the Kingdom, provided that the allocation for the shares that correspond to the Depository Receipts that are going to be issued out of the Kingdom are allocated to the Depository Bank. [IPO Book Building Exception]

e) For purposes of the Issuer's continuing obligations relating to sufficient liquidity requirements under the provisions of the Listing Rules, the shares held by the Depository Bank shall be considered owned by the Public.

f) The Rules for Qualified Foreign Financial Institutions Investment in Listed Securities shall not apply to the Depositary Bank.

Article 5: Authority's Approval for Issuing Depositary Receipts out of the Kingdom

a) The Issuer must obtain the Authority's approval prior to issuing Depositary Receipts out of the Kingdom for its issued shares in the Kingdom.

b) The Issuer seeking to issue Depositary Receipts out of the Kingdom must submit an application to the Authority that includes the information and documents required in the Annex of these Instructions.

c) In considering an application, the Authority may:

1. carry on any enquiries that it considers appropriate;
2. require the Issuer, or his representative, to attend before the Authority to answer questions and explain any matter the Authority considers relevant to the application;
3. require the Issuer to provide additional information as the Authority considers appropriate within 30 days of the request; and
4. verify any information furnished by the Issuer.

d) The Authority may refuse to consider the application where the Issuer has failed to provide information requested from it, or has failed to provide information requested from it within the time requested.

e) The Authority, upon receipt of all information and documents required, shall notify the Issuer in writing, and shall take any of the following decisions within a maximum period of 45 days from the date of notice:

1. approve the application;
2. approve the application subject to conditions and limitations as it considers appropriate; or
3. reject the application and give the reasons thereof.

f) If the Authority decides to approve the application, it shall inform the Issuer in writing of such approval and of the limitations that the Authority may consider appropriate.

g) If the Authority decides to reject the application, it shall notify the Issuer in writing.

h) If a material change to the application documents arises after its submission to the Authority in accordance with requirements of these Instructions, the Issuer must immediately notify the Authority of such change upon knowledge. In such event, the Authority, in its own discretion, may then require the Issuer to re-submit the documents.

i) The Authority, when it decides to approve the application, may publish the identity of the Depositary Bank appointed by the Issuer.

Article 6: Issuer's Obligations

a) The Issuer, after obtaining the Authority's approval to issue Depositary Receipts out of the Kingdom, must notify the Authority and the Exchange with no delay of the listing, suspension, or delisting of its Depositary Receipts in the Foreign Market.

b) The Issuer must comply with the requirement that the maximum limit of the total number of shares agreed upon with the Depositary Bank that Depositary Receipts can be issued corresponding to it, does not exceed 10% of the total of its issued shares or the equivalent of one third of its shares owned by the Public, whichever is less.

c) The Issuer, in agreement with the Depositary Bank, must establish a mechanism for the distribution of voting rights related to shares to the holders of the Depositary Receipts, in accordance with voting mechanism set by the Depositary Center.

d) The Issuer must disclose to the Public in the Kingdom all information that must be disclosed to the Public under the Capital Market Law, its Implementing Regulations and the Exchange Rules, and all information disclosed in the Foreign Market simultaneously in a way that ensures that no information or material developments are leaked to the Foreign Market before disclosing them to the Public in the Kingdom in accordance with the Listing Rules.Public in the Kingdom in accordance with the Listing Rules.

e) If the Issuer submits a prospectus or any other equivalent document in the Foreign Market, the issuer must make such information available, with no delay, as a document available for the Public in the Kingdom.

f) Upon the receipt of a notice from the Authority based on the occurrence of any of the events specified in paragraph (d) of Part 10 of these Instructions in respect of the Depository Bank, the Issuer must appoint an alternative Depository Bank within a period not exceeding (45) days from the date of receipt of such notice.

Article 7: Depositary Bank's Obligations

a) The Depositary Bank, when the Issuer obtains the Authority's approval for issuing Depository Receipts out of the Kingdom, must open an account with the Depositary Center and appoint a custodian authorized to carry out custody business in the Kingdom to hold the shares that correspond to the Depositary Receipts that are going to be issued out of the Kingdom, in accordance with any regulations, rules or procedures the Authority, the Exchange or the Depositary Center issues.

b) The Depositary Bank, when the Issuer obtains the Authority's approval for issuing Depository Receipts out of the Kingdom, must open an investment account with a Capital Market Institution in the Kingdom, in which the transactions shall be limited to the transactions related to the Issuer's corporate actions for the shares that correspond to the Depositary Receipts.

c) The Depositary Bank may not dispose of the shares deposited in its account with the Depository Center, except for transferring the shares to a Capital Market Institution licensed to carry out dealing business, for the purpose of canceling the corresponding Depository Receipts; in accordance with any regulations, rules or procedures issued by the Authority, the Exchange or the Depository Center.

d) The Depository Bank must comply with the requirement that the total number of shares that correspond to the Depository Receipts it issues, shall not exceed the maximum limit under the Depository Receipts program agreed upon with the Issuer.

e) The Depositary Bank must without delay, notify the Exchange, in the event of any change in the Ratio of Shares to Depositary Receipts.

f) Without prejudice to the provisions of paragraph (c) of this Part, the Depositary Bank must enable the holder of Depositary Receipts, if such holder is among the categories of investors allowed to invest in the listed shares in the Kingdom, to cancel such Depositary Receipts to become the holder of the corresponding shares, provided that such holder of Depositary Receipts holds an investment account with a Capital Market Institution in the Kingdom and an account with the Depository Center.

g) Without prejudice to the provisions of paragraph (d) of this Part, the Depositary Bank must enable the shareholder, if such shareholder is among the categories of investors allowed to invest in the Depositary Receipts listed in the Foreign Market, to convert shares to Depositary Receipts to become a holder of Depositary Receipts in the Foreign Market.

h) The Depositary Bank must prepare and maintain correct records of all transactions related to Depositary Receipts and corresponding shares. All records must, at all times, be current and sufficient to demonstrate compliance with the provisions of these Instructions.

i) The Depository Bank must maintain the records as stipulated in these Instructions for a period not less than ten years unless the Authority specifies otherwise. Without prejudice to this period and in case of any litigation or claim (including any litigation pending or threatened) or any on-going investigations relating to these documents, the Depository Bank must retain such documents until the closure of that litigation, claim or on-going investigation.

j) All records required to be maintained by the Depositary Bank under the provisions of these Instructions must be available for review of the Authority at request.

Article 8: Capital Market Institution's Obligations The Capital Market Institution, who deals or intends to deal with a shareholder or Depository Receipts holder for the purpose of issuing or canceling Depository Receipts by the Depository Bank, must designate an investment account and an account with the Depository Center, in which the transactions shall be limited to the transactions related to issuing or canceling Depository Receipts by the Depository Bank.

Article 9: Investment Limits The shares held by the Depositary Bank for the purpose of issuing or cancelling Depositary Receipts shall be subject to the following limitations:

a) The maximum proportion of the shares of any issuer whose shares are listed or convertible debt instrument of the issuer that may be owned by all foreign investors (in all categories, whether residents or non-residents, except the foreign strategic investors pursuant to the Instructions for the Foreign Strategic Investors' Ownership in Listed Companies) in aggregate is 49%.

b) Other legislative limitations on foreign ownership in joint stock companies.

c) The limitations set forth in the articles of association or by-laws of the listed companies or any instructions issued by the supervisory or regulatory authorities to which these companies are subject.

Article 10: Authority's Powers in Relation to the Depositary Bank
a) If the Authority considers that any of the events specified in paragraph (d) of this Part has occurred or may occur in relation to a Depositary Bank, the Authority may:

1) Require the Depositary Bank to provide such information, documents and/or written explanation as the Authority deems necessary to verify the relevant situation;
2) Require the Depositary Bank or its representative, to attend before the Authority to answer questions and explain any matter the Authority considers relevant;
3) Carry on any enquiries that it considers appropriate;
4) Take any action to verify any information provided by the Depositary Bank, including communicating with foreign regulatory authorities;
5) Prohibit the Depositary Bank from disposing of shares held in its account with the Depositary Center;
6) Oblige the Issuer to appoint an alternative Depositary Bank; and
7) Exercise any of its other powers under the Capital Market Law and its Implementing Regulations.

b) Prohibition under sub-paragraphs (5) of paragraph (a) of this Part shall be effective immediately upon sending a written notice of such from the Authority to the Issuer and the Depositary Bank.

c) The Authority may publish the identity of the Depositary Bank, who has been prohibited from disposing of the shares held in its account with the Depositary Center under this Part.

d) The events referred to in paragraph (a) of this Part include the following:

1) The Depositary Bank no longer meets the conditions, obligations and requirements stated in these Instructions;
2) The Depositary Bank becomes insolvent;
3) The Depositary Bank has violated any of its obligations stipulated in the Capital Market Law and its Implementing Regulations or any other laws of the Kingdom;
4) The Depositary Bank has been subject to any material legal or regulatory sanction in any jurisdiction;
5) Any other event that the Authority believes necessitates its intervention to protect investors or safeguard the functioning of the Exchange in the Kingdom.

e) Following the prohibition imposed under this Part, the Depositary Bank may not dispose of any shares held in its account with the Depositary Center without the prior consent of the Authority.

Article 11: Publication and Entry into Force These Instructions shall become effective upon its publication date.

14.1 ANNEX: REQUIRED INFORMATION AND DOCUMENTS TO APPLY FOR THE AUTHORITY'S APPROVAL FOR ISSUING DEPOSITARY RECEIPTS OUT OF THE KINGDOM

The Issuer must attach to its application to the Authority electronic copies of the following documents (and must retain the original copies of such documents and submit them to the Authority upon request):

1. A summary of a technical study that includes the objective of listing in the Foreign Market, the potential advantages and risks of such listing and a statement of the measures to be taken by the Issuer to mitigate those risks.

2. The required approvals under Issuer's bylaws, the Companies Law and its Implementing Regulations.

3. Name of the Depository Bank, its place of incorporation, details of its legal form, and demonstration of the regulatory and supervisory situation in which it is subject to.

4. A list prepared in coordination with a legal advisor that identifies any conflicts between the regulatory requirements in the Kingdom and the regulatory requirements in the Foreign Market that may have a material impact on the related listed shares, including the identification of any potential regulatory conflicts between the requirements of governance, disclosure and listing in the Kingdom, and the suggested methods of addressing them.

5. The total number of the Issuer's shares to be offered under the Depository Receipts program.

6. The maximum value of Depositary Receipts that may be issued under the Depository Receipts program.

7. The Ratio of Shares to Depositary Receipts.

8. The percentage of Depositary Receipts to be issued to the total number of Issuer's shares issued in the Kingdom.

9. The process and cost for canceling Depositary Receipts when a holder requests to be the owner of the shares corresponding to the Depositary Receipts, including the time needed for canceling Depositary Receipts and enabling the holder to trade the underlying shares in the Exchange.

10. The process and cost for issuing Depositary Receipts when a shareholder requests to be a holder of Depositary Receipts, including the time needed for issuing Depositary Receipts and enabling the holder to trade them in the Foreign Market.

11. Any other conditions or requirements determined by the Authority.

15 Instructions for Companies Announcements

Issued by the Board of Capital Market Authority pursuant to its Resolution Number 1-199-2006 dated 18/7/1427H (12/8/2006G); amended by Resolution No. 1-104-2019 dated 01/02/1441H (30/09/2019G) (Eighth version.)

Table of Contents

Part: Introduction

Chapter: General Instructions

1. Instructions for Companies' Announcements of Financial Results
2. Announcement Form for Annual Financial Results for Companies except Banks and Insurance Companies
3. Announcement Form for Interim Financial Results for Companies except Banks and Insurance Companies
4. Announcement Form for Annual Financial Results for Banks
5. Announcement Form for Interim Financial Results for Banks
6. Announcement Form for Annual Financial Results for Insurance Companies
7. Announcement Form for Interim Financial Results for Insurance Companies
8. Instructions for Companies' Announcements of Administrative Changes
9. Announcement Form for the Nomination for Board of Directors Membership
10. Announcement Form for the Resignation of a Board Member
11. Announcement Form for the Appointment of a New Board Member
12. Announcement Form for the Resignation of a Board Member and the Appointment of a New Board Member
13. Announcement Form for the Resignation of the Chief Executive Officer of the Company
14. Announcement Form for the Appointment of a New Chief Executive Officer for the Company
15. Announcement Form for the Resignation of the Chief Executive Officer and the Appointment/Delegation of a New Chief Executive Officer of the Company
16. Announcement Form for the Resignation of an Audit Committee Member
17. Announcement Form for the Appointment of an Audit Committee Member
18. Instructions for Companies Announcements Regarding Capital Alternation
19. Announcement Form for Board's Recommendation for Capital Increase by Offering Rights Issue
20. Announcement Form for the Appointment of a Financial Advisor to Manage the Subscription in the Rights Issue
21. Announcement Form for Submitting an Application File for Capital Increase by Offering
22. Rights Issue to the Capital Market Authority for Approval
23. Announcement Form for Material Developments Regarding the Application File for Capital Increase by Offering Rights Issue Submitted to the Capital Market Authority
24. Announcement Form for Determining the Period for Rights Issue Trading and Subscriptions in the New Shares
25. Reminder Announcement Form Reminder Announcement Form for the Start of the Period for Rights Issue Trading and Subscriptions in the New Shares
26. Reminder Announcement Form for the Last Day for Trading Rights Issue and the Last Day for Subscriptions in the New Shares
27. Announcement Form for the Process Details for the Sale of Un-Subscribed Shares and the Start of the Offering Stage, in Addition to the Results of Trading Rights Issue and Subscription in the New Shares
28. Announcement Form for Rump Offering Results and the Allocation of the Rights Issue shares
29. Announcement Form for the Distribution of Compensation (if any) among Rights Issue Holders Who Did Not Exercise Their Right of Subscribing in the New Shares
30. Announcement Form for the Deviation of 5% or more between the Actual Usage of the Proceeds of Issuing Rights Issue than What Has Been Disclosed in the Prospectus
31. Announcement Form for Board's Recommendation for Capital Increase by way of Issuing Bonus Shares
32. Announcement Form for the Completion of Shares Fractions Sale (if any) and Distribution of Sales Proceeds among Eligible Shareholders
33. Announcement Form for the Non-Completion of Shares Fractions Sale (if any) and Distribution of the Sales Proceeds Amount among Eligible Shareholders within the Specified Period
34. Announcement Form for the Board's Recommendations of Any Suggested Company's Capital Reduction
35. Announcement Form for the Appointment of a Financial Advisor for Capital Reduction.
36. Announcement Form for Submitting an Application File for Capital Reduction to the Authority to Obtain Its Approval
37. Announcement Form for Material Developments on the Application File for Capital Reduction Submitted to the Authority
38. Announcement Form for the Completion of Shares Fractions Sale (if any) and Distribution of Sales Proceeds among Eligible Shareholders
39. Announcement Form for the Non-Completion of the Shares Fractions Sale (if any) and the Distribution of Sales Proceeds among Eligible Shareholders within the Time Frame Mentioned in the Shareholders' Circular
40. Announcement Form for the Board of Directors' Recommendation for the Company's Capital Increase by Way of Debt Conversion
41. Announcement Form for the Appointment of a Financial Advisor to Manage the Application File for the Company's Capital Increase by Debt Conversion
42. Announcement Form for Submitting the Application File for the Company's Capital Increase by Way of Debt Conversion to the Authority for Approval
43. Announcement Form for the Material Developments on the Application File Submitted to the Authority for the Company's Capital Increase by Debt Conversion
44. Announcement Form for the Company's Signature of a Memorandum of Understanding for the Acquisition of a Company/Purchase of an Asset
45. Announcement Form for the Company's Signature of an Agreement for the Acquisition of a Company/Purchase of an Asset through Capital Increase by Issuing Shares to the Owners of the Company/Asset
46. Announcement Form for the Completion of the Procedures

of the Acquisition of a Company/Purchase of an Asset through Capital Increase by Issuing Shares to the Owners of the Company/Asset
47. Instructions for Companies' Announcements Regarding Reverse Take-Over
48. Announcement Form for the Reverse Take-Over Agreement
49. Instructions for Companies' Announcements Regarding General Assemblies
50. Announcement Form for the call for a General Assembly (Ordinary or Extraordinary)
51. Announcement Form for Announcing the General Assembly's Results (Ordinary or Extraordinary)
52. Announcement Form for Non-Convening the General Assembly (Ordinary or Extraordinary)
53. A Statement of the Supporting Documents of the General Assembly Meeting Items
54. Form No.(1) Resume
55. Instructions for Companies' Announcements Regarding Cash Dividends
56. Announcement Form for the Distribution of Cash Dividends to Shareholders of the Company.
57. Announcement Form for the Non-Distribution of Cash Dividends to Shareholders of the Company
58. Instructions for Companies' Announcement Regarding Contracts
59. Announcement Form for Awarding a Contract or Project
60. Announcement Form for Signing a Contract
61. Instruction for Companies Announcements Regarding SAMA's (Saudi Arabian
62. Monetary Authority) Approval on Insurance Products
63. Announcement Form for SAMA's Approval Regarding Insurance Products
64. Instruction for Companies Announcements Regarding Addendum and Corrective
65. Announcement Addendum Announcement Form
66. Corrective Announcement Form
67. Instruction for Companies' Announcement Regarding Signing a Memorandum of Understanding
68. Announcement Form for Signing a Memorandum of Understanding
69. Instructions for Companies' Announcement Regarding their Projects
70. Announcement Form for Projects
71. Instructions for Companies' Announcements for Transactions of Sale, Purchase,
72. Mortgage or Leasing of an Asset
73. Announcement Form for the Transactions of Sale, Purchase, Mortgage or Leasing of an Asset
74. Instructions for Companies' Announcements for Obtaining Financing
75. Announcement Form for Obtaining Financing
76. Announcement Form for Defaulting on the Repayment of Financing
77. Announcement Form for Rescheduling the Financing
78. Instructions for Companies' Announcements Related to Debt Instruments
79. Announcement Form for the Determination to Issue Debt Instruments
80. Announcement Form for Beginning the Offer of Debt Instruments
81. Announcement Form for Completing the Offer of Debt Instruments
82. Announcement Form for the Redemption of Issued Debts Instruments
83. Instructions for Companies' Announcements Regarding the Company's Shares Buy- Back and Sale
84. Announcement Form for the Company's Determination to Buy-Back Its Shares
85. Announcement Form for the Results of the Company's Shares Buy-Back
86. Announcement Form for the Company's Determination to Sell Its Shares
87. Announcement Form for the Results of the Company's Sale of Its Shares
88. Instruction for Companies' Announcements Regarding the Company Pledge of Its Shares
89. Announcements Form Relating to the Company's Determination to Pledge Its Shares
90. Announcement Form for the Company's Release of Its Pledged Shares
91. Instructions for Companies' Announcement Regarding Lawsuits
92. Announcement Form for Lawsuits
93. Instructions for Companies' Announcement of Previously Announced Development
94. Announcement Form for Previously Announced Developments
95. Instructions for Companies' Announcements for Companies with Accumulated Losses Reaching 20% or More of Their Share Capital
96. Announcement Form for Accumulated Losses Reaching 20% or More and Less Than 35% of Share Capital
97. Announcement Form for the Reduction of the Accumulated Losses Below 20% of Share Capital
98. Announcement Form for Accumulated Losses Reaching 35% or More and Less Than 50% of Share Capital
99. Announcement Form for the Reduction of the Accumulated Losses Below 35% of Share Capital
100. Announcement Form for Accumulated Losses Reaching 50% or More of Share Capital
101. Announcement Form for the Reduction of the Accumulated Losses Below 50% of Share Capital
102. Announcement Form for the Recommendation of the Board of Directors to the Extraordinary General Assembly Regarding the Accumulated Losses of 50% or More of the Share Capital
103. Instructions for Companies' Announcement Pursuant to the Requirements of Article (150) of the Companies Law
104. Announcement Form for Procedures that Must be Taken and their Periods According with Article (150) of the Companies Law Before the Trading Period Begins on the Day Following the Company's Announcement of Accumulated Losses Reaching 50% or More of Its Capital
105. Announcement Form for the Deadline for Convening the Extraordinary General Assembly Meeting to Address the Accumulated Losses after the Company's Announcement for the call for the Extraordinary General Assembly Meeting
106. Reminder Announcement Form for the Deadline for Convening the Extraordinary General Assembly Meeting to Address the Accumulated Losses Two Days Prior to Convening the Extraordinary General Assembly Meeting to Address the Accumulated Losses
107. Announcement Form for the Last Period for the Completion of the Subscription in Capital Increase to Address the Accumulated Losses

15.1 Introduction

The Capital Market Authority (the Authority) has updated and amended these Instructions to assist companies whose securities are listed in the Exchange to comply with the provisions of the Companies Law and the Capital Market Law and their Implementing Regulations, especially those relating to continuing obligations stipulated in the Rules on the Offer of Securities and Continuing Obligations issued by the Authority, and the Listing Rules issued by the Saudi Stock Exchange Company (Tadawul) and approved by the Authority's Board. These Instructions are aimed at enhancing the level of transparency and disclosure in the Capital Market and helping investors in making their investment decisions based on correct and adequate information.

These Instructions determine the main elements that must be met in all the companies' announcements published on the Saudi Stock Exchange's (Tadawul) website.

15.2 General Instructions

a) The following are the information that must be included in any company's announcements of any event or material development that has occurred or is expected to occur:

1. The announcement title must be complete, clear, true, not misleading and reflects the material development to be announced.
2. Provide detailed description of the material development with clarification of all relating information and its dates.
3. Clarification of the factors and justifications that led to such material development.
4: If the material development has financial affect in the financial statements, such affect must be mentioned. If such is not possible, reasons must be stated.
5. The company must perform due diligence to ensure that any events or information, related to such material development, are accurate and not misleading.
6. The company shall not delete, exclude or hide any information that may affect the content or the results of the material development.
7. If the material development resulted in any financial obligation on the company, or providing guarantees or mortgage of assets, the announcement must include the conditions, period and amount of such obligation, guarantee or mortgage, as well as the entities to which it is a party, and its impact to the financial statements.
8. In case the announced event has related parties, their identities must be disclosed.
9. In case of any transaction between the company and related party, or any arrangement under which the company and the related party are investing in a project or asset, or providing it with financing, if this transaction or arrangement equals or exceeds 1% of the company's total revenues according to the last audited financial statements, the nature of interest associated with such arrangement or transaction, the range of such interest and the names of any concerned persons must be disclosed, as well as the direct or indirect benefit expected to be obtained from such interest, whether the benefit was financial or not. Further, the ownership percentage of the related persons in both parties associated with the announced event (if any).

b) The announcement must be published through the specified method set forth on the Listing Rules and fulfill all the formality requirements.

c) The financial statement must be published on the Saudi Stock Exchange's (Tadawul) website within a period not exceeding (6) business days from the date of publishing the related financial results announcement.

d) If the company announces a material development which might have future material developments, the company must announce any new material development occurring on that event.

e) In case where the company has two material developments, the company must announce each one of them separately.

f) If any material developments stipulated under Chapters 7 and 8 of the Rules on the Offer of Securities and Continuing Obligations or under Chapter 5 of the Listing Rules occurs during the trading period, the company shall wait until the end of the trading period, then announce it on the Saudi Stock Exchange's (Tadawul) website. All necessary precautions must be taken to ensure that such news of material developments are not leaked before publishing the announcement. However, in case the news of the material development is of a type that cannot be guaranteed not to leak (such as; being related to other parties which the company may not guarantee their commitment to maintain confidentiality, or that the development is a media material (e.g. natural disasters, fire, ... or such) then the company may request the temporary suspension.

g) Meetings of the company's board of directors, audit committees or any other committees, in which a subject that must be disclosed is discussed in accordance with the Rules on the Offer of Securities and Continuing Obligations, must be held within a period that would enable the company to publish an announcement on the Saudi Stock Exchange's (Tadawul) website before starting the trading period following convening the meeting.

h) The specialized department in the company shall set policies and procedures regarding the disclosure of the material developments in which ensure the fulfillment of the company's obligations in this regard. Also, it shall set announcement procedures of financial information which ensure that such announcement is consistent with these Instructions, and the continuance following up by the company's employees with the specialized employees of the Saudi Stock Exchange (Tadawul) until the announcement form is accepted and published. The aforementioned policies and procedures must include the names of the persons responsible for publishing in case of emergency and determine the degree of their powers in scope of publishing. In addition to the names of other persons in cases where the assigned person is out of reach during the event.

i) The listed company must be aware that the material developments might occur during preparing the periodic financial statements, and in this case the company must announce such development immediately and should not delay the announcement until issuing its financial statements, even if it happens shortly before publishing the financial statements.

j) Response to Rumors: the company must determine the need to publish an announcement on the Saudi Stock Exchange's (Tadawul) website in order to respond to the rumors related to any material developments. The Authority may oblige companies to publish announcements when it deems necessary.

k) Companies must not prejudice any other related obligations stipulated in the Capital Market Law and its Implementing Regulations.

l) The company must comply with the Arabic language sound rules while preparing their announcement.

m) Where the company publishes an announcement in English Language, the text must be identical to the Arabic Language version. In case of any conflict between the texts, the Arabic text shall prevail.

n) Companies must comply with the announcements forms set forth in these Instructions.

o) Foreign companies listed on the main market in accordance with the Listing Rules may disclose the financial information in Saudi Riyals or an equivalent in other currencies.

15.3 Instructions for Companies' Announcements of Financial Results

(1) The Basic Elements that Must be met in the Companies' Announcements of Their Financial Results:

1. Statement of the Sales/Revenue during the current quarter and a comparison with the same quarter of last year, with a clarification of the percentage of change.

2. Statement of the gross profit (loss) during the current quarter and a comparison with the same quarter of last year, with a clarification of the percentage of change.

3. Statement of the total operational profit (loss) during the current quarter and a comparison with the same quarter of last year, with a clarification of the percentage of change.

4. Statement of the net profit (loss) during the current quarter and a comparison with the same quarter of last year, with a clarification of the percentage of change. In addition to a comparison with previous quarter with a clarification of the percentage of change.

5. Statement of the total comprehensive income during current quarter and a comparison with the same quarter of last year, with a clarification of the percentage of change. In addition to a comparison with previous quarter with a clarification of the percentage of change.

6. Statement of the Sales/revenues during the current period and a comparison with the same period last year with a clarification of the percentage of change.

7. Statement of the gross profits (loss) during the current period and a comparison with the same period of last year with a clarification of the percentage of change.

8. Statement of the operational profit or (loss) during the current period and a comparison with the same period of last year with a clarification of the percentage of change.

9. Statement of the net profit (loss) during the current period and a comparison with the same period of last year with a clarification of the percentage of change.

10. Statement of the total comprehensive income during the current period and a comparison with the same period of last year with a clarification of the percentage of change.

11. The amount of profit (loss) per share during the current period and a comparison with the same period of last year.

12. Statement of the total shareholders' equity during the current period (after deducting minority' equity) and a comparison with the same period of last year with a clarification of the percentage of change.

13. Statement of the amount of the accumulated losses and its percentage of the capital at the end of the current period.

14. The material reasons and effects that impact the net profit (loss) between the current and the previous period set forth in paragraphs (4) and (9), including the exceptional, non-recurrent reasons or the reasons that do not fall within the company's main activity.

15. Statement of the type of external auditor's report: (Audited: Unmodified opinion, Unmodified opinions with additional communication: Emphasis of matter, other matter. Modified audit opinions: qualified opinion, Adverse opinion and Disclaimer of opinion) or (Reviewed: Unmodified conclusion, Modified conclusions: Qualified conclusion, Adverse conclusion and Disclaimer of conclusion).

16. Statement of any comment mentioned in the external auditor's report, mentioned in any of the following paragraphs (Emphasis of Matter and Other Matter, Qualified Opinion, Adverse Opinion and Disclaimer of Opinion, Modified Conclusions: Qualified Conclusion, Adverse Conclusion and Disclaimer of Conclusion) in the announcement exactly as mentioned in the external auditor's report.

17. When changing the amount of the profit (loss) per share for the same period of the previous year as a result of changing the capital, such change shall be clarified in the announcement by adding a statement that the change of the profit (loss) per share for the same period was the result of capital alternation.

18. Upon re-classification of the comparison items of the same or previous period, it must be clarified in the announcement that the comparison items have been re-classified.

19. When the announcement includes the re-classification of the comparison items in the same or previous period, which was mentioned in former company's announcement, it must be clarified in the announcement that numbers were amended or reissued with statement of reasons.

20. The company must mention any change in the accounting policies or adopting new accounting standards.

Notes:

- The gross profit (loss) means: net sales (revenues) minus cost of sales (revenues cost).

- The operational profit (loss) means: the gross profit (loss) minus operational expenses.

- The net profit (loss) means: the net profit (loss) in the income statements (after Zakat and Tax).

- The comprehensive income (loss) means: the net profit (loss) in addition to other comprehensive income (loss) items.

- The other comprehensive income (loss) means: income and expenses items that are not included in the net profit (loss).

- The numbers of the compared periods must appear in the announcement as mentioned in the financial statements (reviewed / audited) by the external auditor for the current period.

- In case that the company has gained profit during the current period compared to the losses on the same period (or vice versa), the paragraph may not include the percentage of change.

- Paragraphs (6, 7, 8, 9 and 10) are excluded from announcement of the interim financial results, if such announcement is related to the first quarter results of the financial year.

- The company must clarify all the material reasons and effects of the change in its results, whether positive or negative, clearly, accurately and directly, in a manner that would enable the investors to determine the real reason of the change in the result. Also the company must mention the reasons for the change compared to the same period last year, and the reasons of such change compared to the previous period.

- When announcing the estimated financial result, the company must clarify that these results are the management of the company's estimations and have not been reviewed or examined by its external auditor. In case the numbers of the reviewed and examined financial results were different from the announced on the estimated financial results, it must clarify the reasons of the differences.

15.4 Announcement Form for the Interim and Annual Financial Result

15.4.1 (1) Announcement Form for Annual Financial Results for Companies except Banks and Insurance Companies

a) The Announcement Title Must be as Follow: "[*] Company announces its annual financial results ended on **/**/****".

b) The Announcement Must at Least Contain the Following Elements:

1. The sales/revenue amounted to *** Saudi Riyals, compared to *** Saudi Riyals in the last year, with increase (decrease) of **%.
2. The gross profit (loss) amounted to *** Saudi Riyals compared to *** Saudi Riyals in the last year, with increase (decrease) of **%.
3. The operational profit (loss) amounted to *** Saudi Riyals compared to *** Saudi Riyals in the last year, with increase (decrease) of **%.
4. The net profit (loss) after Zakat and Tax amounted to *** Saudi Riyals compared to *** Saudi Riyals in the last year, with increase (decrease) of **%.
5. The total comprehensive income amounted to *** Saudi Riyals compared to *** Saudi Riyals in the last year, with increase (decrease) of **%.
6. The profit (loss) per share amounted to *** Saudi Riyal compared to *** Saudi Riyals in the last year, with increase (decrease) of **%.
7. The total shareholders' equity (after deducting the minority equity) amounted to *** Saudi Riyals compared to *** Saudi Riyals in the last year, with increase (decrease) of **%.
8. The reason of the increase (decrease) in the net profit during the current year compared to the last year is [*%].
9. Statement of the type of external auditor's report: (Audited: Unmodified opinion, Unmodified opinions with additional communication: Emphasis of matter, other matter. Modified audit opinions: Qualified opinion, Adverse opinion and Disclaimer of opinion).
10. Statement any comment mentioned in the external auditor's report, mentioned in any of the following paragraphs (Emphasis of matter and other matter, qualified opinion, Adverse Opinion and Disclaimer of Opinion,) in the announcement exactly as mentioned in the external auditor's report.
11. In case of re-classification of the comparison items, it should be mentioned in the announcement.
12. Mention any information the company wishes to add.

15.4.2 (2) Announcement Form for Interim Financial Results for Companies except Banks and Insurance Companies

a) The Announcement Title Must be as Follow: "[*]Company announces its interim financial results ended on **/**/**** (three\ six\ nine\ twelve months)". b) The Announcement Must at Least Contain the Following Elements:

1. The sales\revenue during the current quarter amounted to *** Saudi Riyals, compared to *** Saudi Riyals in the same quarter of the last year, with increase (decrease) of **%.

2. The gross profit (loss) during the current quarter amounted to *** Saudi Riyals compared to *** Saudi Riyals in the same quarter of the last year, with increase (decrease) of **%

3. The operational profit (loss) during the current quarter amounted to *** Saudi Riyals compared to *** Saudi Riyals in the same quarter of the last year, with increase (decrease) of **%.

4. The net profit (loss) during the current quarter, after Zakat and Tax, amounted to *** Saudi Riyals, with increase (decrease) of **%, compared to *** Saudi Riyals in the same quarter of the last year, with increase (decrease) of **%.

5. The total comprehensive income during the current quarter amounted to *** Saudi Riyals, with increase (decrease) of **%, compared to *** Saudi Riyals in the same quarter of the last year, with increase (decrease) of **%,

6. The sales\revenues during the current period amounted to *** Saudi Riyals compared to *** Saudi Riyals in the same period of the last year, with increase (decrease) of **%.

7. The gross profit (loss) during the current period amounted to *** Saudi Riyals compared to *** Saudi Riyals in the same period of the last year, with increase (decrease) of **%.

8. The operational profit (loss) during the current period amounted to *** Saudi Riyals compared to *** Saudi Riyals in the same period of the last year, with increase (decrease) of **%.

9. The net profit (loss) during the current period after Zakat and Tax amounted to *** Saudi Riyals compared to *** Saudi Riyals in the same quarter of the last year, with increase (decrease) of **%.

10. The total comprehensive income during the current period amounted to *** Saudi Riyals compared to *** Saudi Riyals in the same period of the last year, with increase (decrease) of **%.

11. The profit (loss) per share during the current period amounted to *** Saudi Riyals compared to *** Saudi Riyals in the same period of the last year, with increase (decrease) of **%.

12. The total shareholders' equity (after deducting the minority's equity) during the current period amounted to *** Saudi Riyals compared to *** Saudi Riyals in the same quarter of the last year, with increase (decrease) of **%.

13. The accumulated losses amount by the end of the current period amounted to

*** Saudi Riyals with a percentage of **% of the capital.

14. The reason of the increase (decrease) in the net profit during the current quarter compared to the same quarter of the last year is (•).

15. The reason of the increase (decrease) in the net profit during the current quarter compared to the previous period of the current year is (•).

16. The reason of the increase (decrease) in the net profit during the current period compared to the same period of the last year is (•).

17. Statement of the type of external auditor's report: (Reviewed: Unmodified conclusion, Modified conclusions: Qualified conclusion, Adverse conclusion and Disclaimer of conclusion).

18. Statement of any comment mentioned in the external auditor's report, mentioned in any of the following paragraphs Modified conclusions: Qualified conclusion, Adverse conclusion and Disclaimer of conclusion in the announcement exactly as mentioned in the external auditor's report.

19. In case of reclassification of the comparison items, it should be mentioned in the announcement.

20. Mention any information the company wishes to add.

15.4.3 (3) Announcement Form for Annual Financial Results for Banks

a) The Announcement Title Must be as Follows: "[*]Bank announces its annual financial results ended on **/**/****".

b) The Announcement Must at Least Contain the Following Elements:

1. The total income from special commission \ financing and investment amounted to *** Saudi Riyals, compared to *** Saudi Riyals in the last year, with increase (decrease) of **%.

2. The net income from special commission \ financing and investment amounted to *** Saudi Riyals, compared to *** Saudi Riyals in the last year, with increase (decrease) of **%.

3. The total operations profit (loss) amounted to *** Saudi Riyals, compared to *** Saudi Riyals in the last year, with increase (decrease) of **%.

4. The net profit (loss) amounted to *** Saudi Riyals, compared to *** Saudi Riyals in the last year, with increase (decrease) of **%.

5. The total comprehensive income amounted to *** Saudi Riyals, compared to *** Saudi Riyals in the last year, with increase (decrease) of **%.

6. The profit (loss) per share amounted to *** Saudi Riyals, compared to *** Saudi Riyals in the last year.

7. The total shareholders' equity (after deducting the minority's rights) amounted to *** Saudi Riyals, compared to *** Saudi Riyals in the last year, with increase (decrease) of **%.

8. The assets amounted to *** Saudi Riyals, compared to *** Saudi Riyals in the last year, with increase (decrease) of **%. The investment amounted to

*** Saudi Riyals compared to *** Saudi Riyals in the last year, with increase (decrease) of **%. The loans and advances portfolio (financing and investment) amounted to *** Saudi Riyals compared to *** Saudi Riyals in the last year, with increase (decrease) of **%. The clients' deposits amounted to *** Saudi Riyals compared to *** Saudi Riyals in the last year, with increase (decrease) of **%.

9. The reason of the increase (decrease) in the net profit during the current year compared to the last year is [*]

10. Statement of the type of external auditor's report: (Audited: Unmodified opinion, Unmodified opinions with additional communication: Emphasis of matter, other matter. Modified audit opinions: Qualified opinion, Adverse opinion and Disclaimer of opinion).

11. Statement of any comment mentioned in the external auditor's report, mentioned in any of the following paragraphs (Emphasis of Matter and Other Matter, Qualified Opinion, Adverse Opinion and Disclaimer of Opinion) in the announcement exactly as mentioned in the external auditor's report .

12. In case of re-classification of the comparison items, it should be mentioned in the announcement.

13. Mention any information the bank wishes to add.

15.4.4 (4) Announcement Form for Interim Financial Results for Banks

a) The Announcement Title Must be as Follows: "[*]Bank announces its interim financial results ended on **/**/**** (three\ six\ nine\ twelve months)".

b) The Announcement Must at Least Contain the Following Elements:

1. The total income from special commission\financing and investment amounted to *** Saudi Riyals during current quarter, compared to *** Saudi Riyals in the same quarter the last year, with increase (decrease) of **%.

2. The net income from special commission \ financing and investment amounted to *** Saudi Riyals during current quarter, compared to *** Saudi Riyals in the same quarter the last year, with increase (decrease) of **%.

3. The total of the operations profits (loss) amounted to *** Saudi Riyals during current quarter, compared to *** Saudi Riyals in the same quarter the last year, with increase (decrease) of **%.

4. The net profit (loss) amounted to *** Saudi Riyals during the current quarter, compared to the same quarter last year with increase (decrease) of **%, and compared to the previous quarter *** Saudi Riyals, with increase (decrease) of **%.

5. The total of comprehensive income amounted to *** Saudi Riyals during current quarter, compared to *** Saudi Riyals in the same quarter last year with increase (decrease) of **%, and compared to *** Saudi Riyals in the previous quarter, with increase (decrease) of **%.

6. The total income from special commission\financing and investment amounted to *** Saudi Riyals during current period compared to the same period last year with increase (decrease) of **%.

7. The net income from special commission \ financing and investment amounted to *** Saudi Riyals during current period compared to *** Saudi Riyals in the same period last year with increase (decrease) of **%.

8. The total operations profit (loss) amounted to *** Saudi Riyals during current period compared to *** Saudi Riyals in the same period last year with increase (decrease) of **%.

9. The net profit (loss) amounted to *** Saudi Riyals during current period compared to *** Saudi Riyals in the same period last year with increase (decrease) of **%.

10. The total comprehensive income amounted to *** Saudi Riyals during current period compared to *** Saudi Riyals in the same period last year, with increase (decrease) of **%.

11. The profit (loss) per share amounted to *** Saudi Riyals during current period compared to *** Saudi Riyals in the same period last year, with increase (decrease) of **%.

12. The total shareholders' equity (after deducting the minority's equity) amounted to *** Saudi Riyals, compared to *** Saudi Riyals in the same period last year, with increase (decrease) of **%.

13. The accumulated losses at the end of the current period amounted to *** Saudi Riyals from the capital.

14. The assets amount at the end of the current period is *** Saudi Riyals, compared to *** Saudi Riyals in the same period last year, with increase (decrease) of **%. The investment amounted to *** Saudi Riyals compared to *** Saudi Riyals in the last year, with increase (decrease) of **%. The loan and advances portfolio (financing and investment) at the end of current period amounted to *** Saudi Riyals compared to *** Saudi Riyals in the same period last year, with increase (decrease) of **%. the clients' deposits at the end of current period amounted to *** Saudi Riyals, compared to *** Saudi Riyals in the end of same period last year, with increase (decrease) of **%.

15. The reason of the increase (decrease) in the net profit during the current quarter compared to the same quarter of last year is (•)

16. The reason of the increase (decrease) in the net profit during the current quarter compared to the previous quarter of current year is (•)

17. The reason of the increase (decrease) in the net profit during the current period compared to the previous period of current year is (•)

18. Statement of the type of external auditor's report: (Reviewed: Unmodified conclusion, Modified conclusions: Qualified conclusion, Adverse conclusion and Disclaimer of conclusion).

19. Statement of any comment mentioned in the external auditor's report, mentioned in any of the following paragraphs Modified conclusions: qualified conclusion, Adverse conclusion and Disclaimer of conclusion in the announcement exactly as mentioned in the external auditor's report

20. In case of re-classification of the comparison items, it should be mentioned in the announcement.

21. Mention any information the Bank wishes to add.

15.4.5 (5) Announcement Form for Annual Financial Results for Insurance Companies

a) The Announcement Title Must be as Follows: "[*]Company announces its annual financial result ended on **/**/****".

b) The Announcement Must at Least Contain the Following Elements:

1. The Gross Written Premiums (GWP) amounted to *** Saudi Riyals, compared to *** Saudi Riyals in the last year with increase (decrease) of **%.

2. The Net Written Premiums (NWP) amounted to *** Saudi Riyals compared to *** Saudi Riyals in the last year with increase (decrease) of **%.

3. The net incurred claims amounted to *** Saudi Riyals compared to *** Saudi Riyals in the last year with increase (decrease) of **%.

4. The net profit (loss) of policy holders' investment amounted to *** Saudi Riyals compared to *** Saudi Riyals in the last year with increase (decrease) of **%.

5. The Surplus (deficit) of insurance operations minus the revenues of policy holders' investments (operational procedures results) amounted to *** Saudi Riyals compared to *** Saudi Riyals in the last year with increase (decrease) of **%.

6. The net profit (loss) of shareholders' capital investment amounted to *** Saudi Riyals compared to *** Saudi Riyals in the last year with increase (decrease) of **%.

7. The net profit (loss) before Zakat amounted to *** Saudi Riyals compared to *** Saudi Riyals in the last year with increase (decrease) of **%.

8. The total comprehensive income amounted to *** Saudi Riyals compared to *** Saudi Riyals in the last year with increase (decrease) of **%.

9. The profit (loss) per share amounted to *** Saudi Riyals compared to *** Saudi Riyals in the last year.

10. The total shareholders' equity (after deducting the minority's equity) amounted to *** Saudi Riyals, compared to *** Saudi Riyals in the last year, with increase (decrease) of **%.

11. The perpetrating expenses amounted to** Saudi Riyals (if the company is in the first operation year).

12. The reason of the increase (decrease) in the net profit during the current year compared to the previous year is (•)

13. Statement of the type of external auditor's report: (Audited: Unmodified opinion, Unmodified opinions with additional communication: Emphasis of matter, other matter. Modified audit opinions: Qualified opinion, Adverse opinion and Disclaimer of opinion).

14. Statement any comment mentioned in the external auditor's report, mentioned in any of the following paragraphs (Emphasis of matter and other matter, qualified opinion, Adverse Opinion and Disclaimer of Opinion,) in the announcement exactly as mentioned in the external auditor's report .

15 In case of re-classification of the comparison items, it should be mentioned in the announcement.

16. Mention any information the Company wishes to add

15.4.6 (6) Announcement Form for Interim Financial Results for Insurance Companies

a) The Announcement Title Must be as Follows: "[*]Company announces interim financial results ended on **/**/**** (three/six/nine/ twelve months)".

b) The Announcement Must at Least Contain the Following Elements:

1. The Gross Written Premiums (GWP) during the current quarter amounted to

*** Saudi Riyals, compared to *** Saudi Riyals in the same quarter last year with increase (decrease) of **%.

2. The Net Written Premiums (NWP) during the current quarter amounted to *** Saudi Riyals, compared to *** Saudi Riyals in the same quarter last year with increase (decrease) of **%.

3. The net incurred claims during the current quarter amounted to *** Saudi Riyals, compared to *** Saudi Riyals in the same quarter last year with increase (decrease) of **%.

4. The net profit (loss) of policy holders' investment during the current quarter amounted to *** Saudi Riyals compared to *** Saudi Riyals in the same quarter last year with increase (decrease) of **%.

5. The Surplus (deficit) of insurance operations minus the revenues of policy holders' investments (operational procedures results) during the current quarter amounted to *** Saudi Riyals compared to *** Saudi Riyals in the same quarter last year with increase (decrease) of **%.

6. The net profit (loss) of shareholders' funds investment during the current quarter amounted to *** Saudi Riyals compared to *** Saudi Riyals in the same quarter last year with increase (decrease) of **%.

7. The net profit (loss) before Zakat during the current quarter amounted to *** Saudi Riyals compared to *** Saudi Riyals in the same quarter last year with increase (decrease) of **%, and compared to *** Saudi Riyals of the previous quarter with increase (decrease) of **%.

8. The total comprehensive income during the current quarter amounted to *** Saudi Riyals compared to *** Saudi Riyals in the same quarter last year with increase (decrease) of **%, and compared to *** Saudi Riyals of the previous quarter with increase (decrease) of **%.

9. The Gross Written Premiums (GWP) during the current period amounted to *** Saudi Riyals, compared to *** Saudi Riyals in the same period last year with increase (decrease) of **%.

10. The Net Written Premiums (NWP) during the current period amounted to *** Saudi Riyals, compared to *** Saudi Riyals in the same period last year with increase (decrease) of **% compared to *** Saudi Riyals in the same period last year with increase (decrease) of **%.

11. The net incurred claims during the current period amounted to *** Saudi Riyals, compared to *** Saudi Riyals in the same period last year with increase (decrease) of **%.

12. The net profit (loss) of policy holders' investment during the current period amounted to *** Saudi Riyals compared to *** Saudi Riyals in the same period last year with increase (decrease) of **%.

13. The Surplus (deficit) of insurance operations minus the revenues of policy holders' investments (operational procedures results) during the current period amounted to *** Saudi Riyals compared to *** Saudi Riyals in the same period last year with increase (decrease) of **%.

14. The net profit (loss) of shareholders' funds investment during the current period amounted to *** Saudi Riyals compared to *** Saudi Riyals in the same period last year with increase (decrease) of **%.

15. The net profit (loss) before Zakat during the current period amounted to *** Saudi Riyals compared to *** Saudi Riyals in the same period last year with increase (decrease) of **%.

16. The total comprehensive income during the current period amounted to *** Saudi Riyals compared to *** Saudi Riyals in the same period last year with increase (decrease) of **%.

17. The profit (loss) per share during current period amounted to *** Saudi Riyals compared to *** Saudi Riyals in the same period last year.

18. The total shareholders' equity (after deducting the minority's equity) during the same period amounted to *** Saudi Riyals, compared to *** Saudi Riyals in the same period last year, with increase (decrease) of **%.

19. The accumulated losses at the end of the current period amounted to *** Saudi Riyals from the capital.

20. The reason of the increase (decrease) in the net profit during the current quarter compared to the same quarter of last year is (•)

21. The reason of the increase (decrease) in the net profit during the current quarter compared to the previous quarter of current year is (•)

22. The reason of the increase (decrease) in the net profit during the current period compared to the previous period of current year is (•)

23. Statement of the type of external auditor's report: (Reviewed: Unmodified Conclusion, Modified conclusions: qualified conclusion, Adverse conclusion and Disclaimer of conclusion).

24. Statement of any comment mentioned in the external auditor's report, mentioned in any of the following paragraphs Modified conclusions: qualified conclusion, Adverse conclusion and Disclaimer of conclusion in the announcement exactly as mentioned in the external auditor's report.

25. In case of re-classification of the comparison items, it should be mentioned in the announcement.

26. Mention any information the Company wishes to add.

15.5 Instructions for Companies' Announcements of Administrative Changes

15.5.1 (1) Announcement Form for the Nomination for Board of Directors Membership

a) The Announcement Title Must be as Follows: "[*]Company announces the opening of the nomination period for the board of directors' membership for the next term".

b) The Announcement Must at Least Contain the Following Elements:

1. The starting and ending dates of the term.

2. The opening and the ending dates of the nomination.

3. The method of receiving the nomination requests.

4. The standards for nomination set out in the nomination committee regulations. issued by the General Assembly (attach a copy of these standards).

15.5.2 (2) Announcement Form for the Resignation of a Board Member

a) The Announcement Title Must be as Follows: "[*] Company announces the resignation of the board of director's member (members)".

b) The Announcement Must at Least Contain the Following Elements:

1. Name of the resigned member (members).

2. The description of his (their) membership.

3. The resignation submission date by the member (members) to the board of directors, the acceptance and the effective date.

4. Reasons for resignation.

5. Membership starting date of the resigned member.

15.5.3 (3) Announcement Form for the Appointment of a New Board Member

a) The Announcement Title Must be as Follows: "[*]Company announces the appointment of the board member (members)".

b) The Announcement Must at Least Contain the Following Elements:

1. The name of the appointed member (members) of board of directors.
2. The description of his (their) membership.
3. The date of the board of directors' meeting in which a new board member (members) was (were) appointed.
4. The membership effective date.
5. The board's approval shall not be deemed final. Such appointment will be discussed at the first General Assembly for ratification.
6. Mention a brief description of the appointed member's (members) resume.

15.5.4 (4) Announcement Form for the Resignation of a Board Member and the Appointment of a New Board Member

a) The Announcement Title Must be as Follows:"[*]Company announces the resignation of the board member (members) and the appointment of a new board member (members)".

b) The Announcement Must at Least Contain the Following Elements:

1. The name of the resigned member (members) and his (their) membership description.
2. The resignation submission date by the member (members) to the board of directors, the acceptance and the effective date.
3. Reasons for resignation.
4. The starting date of the membership of the resigned member.
5. The name of the appointed member (members), and his (their) membership description.
6. The date of the board of directors' meeting in which a new board member (members) was (were) appointed.
7. The membership effective date.
8. The board's approval shall not be deemed final. Such appointment will be discussed at the first General Assembly for ratification.
9. Mention a brief description of the appointed member's (members') resume.

15.5.5 (5) Announcement Form for the Resignation of the Chief Executive Officer of the Company

a) The Announcement Title Must be as Follows: "[*]Company announces the resignation of its Chief Executive Officer".

b) The Announcement Must at Least Contain the Following Elements:

1. The name of the resigned person.
2. The acceptance date of the resignation and its effective date.
3. Reasons for resignation.

15.5.6 (6) Announcement Form for the Appointment of a New Chief Executive Officer for the Company

a) The Announcement Title Must be as Follows: "[*]Company announces the appointment of a new Chief Executive Officer".

b) The Announcement must at least contain the following elements:

1. The name of the appointed person.
2. The date of the board's resolution on which the new Chief Executive Officer was appointed.
3. The work commencement date.
4. Mention a brief description of the appointed member's resume.

15.5.7 (7) Announcement Form for the Resignation of the Chief Executive Officer and the Appointment\Delegation of a New Chief Executive Officer for the Company

a) The Announcement Title Must be as Follows:"[*]Company announces the resignation of the Chief Executive Officer and appointment\ delegation of a new Chief Executive Officer for the Company".

b) The Announcement Must at Least Contain the Following Elements:

1. The name of the resigned person.
2. The acceptance date of resignation acceptance and its effective date.
3. Reasons for resignation.
4. The name of the delegated person for the position until appointing a new Chief Executive Officer (in case of delegation).
5. The name of the appointed person (in case of appointment)

6. The starting date of the (appointment\ delegation).
7. The date of board's resolution of the (appointment\ delegation).
8. Mention a brief description of the appointed\delegated member's resume.

15.5.8 (8) Announcement Form for the Resignation of an Audit Committee Member

a) The Announcement Title Must be as Follows: "[*]Company announces the resignation of the Audit Committee Member (Members)".

b) The Announcement Must at Least Contain the Following Elements:

1. The name of the resigned member (members).
2. The date of submitting the resignation and its effective date.
3. The resignation reasons.
4. The starting date of the membership of the resigned member.

15.5.9 (9) Announcement Form for the Appointment of an Audit Committee Member

a) The announcement title must be as follows: "[*]Company announces the appointment of an Audit Committee Member (Members)".

b) The announcement must at least contain the following elements:

1. The name of the appointed member (members).
2. The date of the board's resolution on which the new Audit Committee Member (Members) was\were appointed.
3. The membership effective date.
4. The board's approval shall not be deemed final. Such appointment will be discussed at the first General Assembly Meeting for ratification.
5. Mention a brief description of the appointed member's (members') resume.

15.6 Instructions for Companies Announcements Regarding Capital Alternation

15.6.1 (1) Offering Rights Issue Shares

15.6.2 (1) Announcement Form for Board's Recommendation for Capital Increase by Offering Rights Issue

a) The announcement title must be as the following: "[*]Company announces the board's recommendation for capital increase by offering rights issue".

b) The announcement must contain at least the following elements:

1. The date of the board's meeting.
2. The total amount that the company wishes to receive, without reporting the amount or numbers of shares that intended to offer or its percentage of current capital.
3. Reasons of capital increase.
4. Eligibility date, provided that the eligibility shall be for the shareholders on the Extraordinary General Assembly day, in which the capital increase by offering rights issue is decided, and whose names appear in the issuer's shareholders register at the Depository Center on the end of the second trading day following the assembly meeting date.
5. Indicate that an announcement will be made upon appointing a financial advisor for offering, as well as upon submitting the request for capital increase to the Capital Market Authority for approval.

15.6.3 (2) Announcement Form for the Appointment of a Financial Advisor to Manage the Subscription in the Rights Issue

After the board's recommendation to increase the company's capital by way of rights issue, the company announces the appointment of a financial advisor in line with the following:

a) The announcement title must be as follows: "[*] Company announces the appointment of a financial advisor to manage the subscription of rights issue".

b) The announcement must at least contain the following elements:

1. The name of the financial advisor.
2. The appointment date of the financial advisor.
3. In case of changing the current financial advisor, the company shall announce the name of the new financial advisor and the reason behind changing the old financial advisor.
4. Any other information the company wishes to add.

15.6.4 (3) Announcement Form for Submitting an Application File for Capital Increase by Offering Rights Issue to the Capital Market Authority for Approval

a) The announcement title must be as the following: "[*] Company announces the submission of an application to increase the company's capital by offering the rights issue to the Capital Market Authority".

b) The Announcement Must at Least Contain the Following Elements:

1. The date of submitting the application to the Capital Market Authority.
2. Reference to the subject of the application.

3. Reference to the announcement of the board's recommendation regarding the company's capital increase by offering rights issue.

15.6.5 (4) Announcement Form for Material Developments Regarding the Application File for Capital Increase by Offering Rights IssueSubmitted to the Capital Market Authority.

After the announcement of submitting an application of the capital increase by offering rights issue to the Capital Market Authority for approval, the company must announce any material changes regarding the application submitted to the Authority. Upon the Authority's approval, the company shall publish the prospectus within a period not exceeding (14) days prior to the convening date of the General Assembly.

a) The announcement title must be as the following: "[*]Company announces the developments regarding the submitted application of the company's capital increase by offering the rights issue to the Capital Market Authority".

b) The Announcement Must at Least Contain the Following Elements:

1. Reference to the subject of the application submitted to the Authority and the application's date of submission.
2. Clarification and elaboration of the application status at the Authority (including, but not limited to: Completion or fulfillment of the requirements and remarks on the application, or whether the application is under review by the Authority).
3. Any other material developments (including, but not limited to: permanent withdrawal of the application with a clarification of the reasons, the Authority's rejection of the application with reasons, suspension of the application for not fulfilling the requirements...etc).

15.6.6 (5) Announcement Form for Determining the Period for Rights Issue Trading and Subscriptions in the New Shares.

After the issuance of approvals by the official entities and Extraordinary General Assembly on the capital increase, the company shall announce the following:

a) The announcement title must be as the following: "[*]Company announces the determination of the rights issue trading period and subscription in the new shares".

b) The Announcement Must at Least Contain the Following Elements:

1. Determine the start and end dates of the rights issue trading period and subscription in the new shares. (Note that the shareholders of the rights issue are able to exercise their rights to subscribe (partially or completely) in the new shares within the limits of the number of the rights issue existing in their portfolios, and that the trade of the rights issue and subscription in the new shares is according to the prospectus for the registered shareholders and new investors).
2. Clarification of the Rump Offering details: (Note that in case of remaining unsubscribed shares, these shares and fractions shares (if any) will be offered to the institutional investors in accordance with the prospectus).
3. Notify the investors who do not wish to subscribe of the importance of selling what they own of rights issue during the specified trading period; in order not to be subject to a reduction of the value of their investment portfolios as a result of not taking advantage of their rights to sell or subscribe.
4. To obtain a daily Price Volatility percentage of rights issue after closing the rights issue trading period visit the Saudi Stock Exchange Company's (Tadawul) website via the link (....)
5. To obtain the Indicative Value of a Right visit the Saudi Stock Exchange Company's (Tadawul) website via the link (....)
6. To obtain more details regarding the mechanism of trading the rights issue and subscription in the new shares, kindly visit the ....'s website via the link (....)
7. To obtain the prospectus related to the company's capital increase by rights issue kindly visit the ......'s website via the link (....)

15.6.7 (6) Reminder Announcement Form for the Start of the Period for Rights Issue Trading and Subscriptions in the New Shares.

a) The announcement title must be as the following: "[*] Company announces a reminder of starting period of the rights issue trading and subscription in the new shares".

b) The Announcement Must at Least Contain the Following Elements:

1. The start date of the rights issue trading period and subscription in the new shares.
2. The end date of the rights issue trading period.
3. The end date of the subscription in the new shares period.

15.6.8 (7) Reminder Announcement Form for the Last Day for Trading Rights Issue and the Last Day for Subscriptions in the New Shares

a) The announcement title must be as the following: "[*] Company announces a reminder of the last day for trading rights issue and the last day for subscription in the new shares".

b) The Announcement Must at Least Contain the Following Elements:

1. The end date of the rights issue trading period.
2. The end date of the subscription in the new shares period.

15.6.9 (8) Announcement Form for the Process Details of the Sale of the Un-Subscribed Shares and the Start of the Offering Stage, in Addition to the Results of Trading Rights Issue and Subscription in the New Shares.

a) The announcement title must be as the following: " [*] Company announces the results of trading rights issue and subscribing in the new shares, and the process details of the Sale of the un-subscribed shares".

b) The Announcement Must at Least Contain the Following Elements:

1. The number of subscribed shares, its value and the coverage percentage of the total new offered shares.
2. The total number and value of the subscribed shares and the coverage percentage of the total new offered shares.
3. The details of the rump offering mechanism, and its start and end dates.
4. Determine the rump offering period hours.

15.6.10 (9) Announcement Form for Rump Offering Results and the Allocation of the Rights Issue shares.

a) The announcement title must be as the following: "[*] Company announces the rump offering results and the allocation of the rights issue shares".

b) The Announcement Must at Least Contain the Following Elements:

1. The number of sold shares.
2. The total refunded amount from sale process of the un-subscribed shares and shares fractions (if any).
3. Average selling price for the sold shares.
4. The net amount of the compensations refunded to the shareholders of rights issue and shares fractions.
5. Date of the Shares deposit in shareholders' accounts.

15.6.11 (10) Announcement Form for the Distribution of Compensations (if any) among Rights Issue Holders Who Did Not Exercise Their Right of Subscribing in the New Shares

a) The announcement title must be as the following:"[*]Company announces the distribution of compensations (if any) to the shareholders of rights issue who did not exercise their right to subscribe in the new shares".

b) The Announcement Must at Least Contain the Following Elements:

1. The date of the distribution of the compensations among the eligible persons who did not exercise their rights in subscription, and shares fractions of eligible persons.
2. The total amount that will be distributed among the eligible persons who did not exercise their rights in subscriptions, and shares fractions of eligible persons.
3. The delivery method of the compensations to the eligible persons who did not exercise their right in subscriptions, and shares fractions of eligible persons.
4. The name and contact method of the responsible entity for the depositing process.

15.6.12 (11) Announcement Form for the Deviation of 5% or more between the Actual Usage of the Proceeds of Issuing Rights Issue than What Has Been Disclosed in the Prospectus

a) The Announcement Title Must be as Follows: "[*] Company announces the developments of the use of proceeds of issuing rights issue".

b) The Announcement Must at Least Contain the Following Elements:

1. Disclosure of any deviations of 5% or more in the actual usage of the proceeds than what have been disclosed in the prospectus, and the reasons and justification of such deviations.
2. Any other important information that the company deems necessary to disclose.

15.6.13 Second: Bonus Shares (1) Announcement Form for Board's Recommendation for Capital Increase by way of Issuing Bonus Shares

a) The Announcement Title Must be as Follows: "[*] Company announces the board's recommendation for the capital increase by way of issuing bonus shares"

b) The Announcement Must at Least Contain the Following Elements:

1. The date of the board's meeting.
2. The company's capital before and after the increase
3. The increase percentage in the capital.
4. The number of shares before and after the capital increase.
5. The reasons for the capital increase.
6. The number of bonus shares granted per existing share.
7. The nature and value of the reserves that will be used in the capitalization issue.
8. The eligibility date, provided that the eligibility is for the shareholders who own the shares on the due date registered in the issuer's shareholders record at the Depository center at the end of second day following the eligibility date.
9. In case of shares fractions, the company must mention that "all the shares fractions will be collected in one portfolio for all shareholders and will be sold at the market price, then the amount will be distributed among the eligible shareholders for the bonus shares proportionately as per ownership percentage within a period not exceeding (...Specify Period...) days from the date of determining the due shares for each shareholder.
10. Indicate the necessity of obtaining approvals form the official entities and Extraordinary General Assembly regarding the capital increase, in addition to the number of the bonus shares.

15.6.14 (2) Announcement Form for the Completion of Shares Fractions Sale (if any) and Distribution of the Sale Proceeds among Eligible Shareholders

a) The Announcement Title Must be as Follows: "[*]Company announces the deposit of the amounts from selling the shares fractions resulted from the company's capital increase in the eligible shareholders' accounts".

b) The Announcement Must at Least Contain the Following Elements:

1. The date of completing the sale of the shares fractions process.
2. The number of sold shares.
3. The return amount from selling the shares' fractions process.
4. Average selling price per share.
5. The deposit date of the return amounts from selling the shares fractions process in the eligible shareholders' accounts.
6. The name and contact method of the responsible entity of distributing the return amounts from the selling the shares fractions process among the eligible shareholders.

15.6.15 (3) Announcement Form for the Non-Completion of Shares Fractions Sale (if any) and Distribution of the Sales Proceeds Amount among Eligible Shareholders within the Specified Period

(a) The Announcement Title Must be as Follows: "[*] Company announces the non-completion of selling shares fractions resulting from the company's capital increase during the specified period".

(b) The Announcement Must at Least Contain the Following Elements:

1. The reason of non-completion of selling the shares fractions process and deposit the amounts at the eligible shareholders' accounts within the specified period.
2. The excepted end date of completing the sale process of shares fractions and distributing the amounts among the eligible shareholders.

15.6.16 Third: Capital Reduction. (1) Announcement Form for the Board's Recommendations of Any Suggested Company's Capital Reduction

(a) The Announcement Title Must be as Follows: "[*] Company announces its board's recommendation for the company's capital reduction".

(b) The Announcement Must at Least Contain the Following Elements:

1. The date of the board's meeting
2. The company's capital before and after the reduction.
3. The reduction percentage in the capital.
4. The number of shares before and after the capital reduction.
5. The reason and method of capital reduction.
6. Any material impact of the reduction in the company's commitments, process or the company's financial, operational or organizational performance.
7. State that the reduction date is at the end of the second trading day following the Extraordinary General Assembly meeting in which the capital reduction was decided.
8. Indicate the necessity of obtaining the approvals of the official entities and Extraordinary General Assembly regarding the capital reduction and the number of shares.
9. Indicate that an announcement will be made upon appointing a financial advisor, and upon submitting the application for capital reduction to the Capital Market Authority for approval.

15.6.17 (2) Announcement Form for the Appointment of a Financial Advisor for Capital Reduction

After the announcement of the recommendation of board of directors for capital reduction, the company must announce the appointment of a financial adviser in line with the following:

a) The Announcement Title Must be as Follows: "[*]Company announces the appointment of a financial advisor for capital reduction".

b) The Announcement Must at Least Contain the Following Elements:

1. The name of the financial advisor.
2. The date of appointing the financial advisor.
3. In case of changing the current financial advisor, the company shall announce the name of the new financial advisor and the reason behind changing the old financial advisor
4. Any other information the company wishes to add.

15.6.18 (3) Announcement Form for Submitting an Application File for Capital Reduction to the Authority to Obtain Its Approval

a) The Announcement Title Must be as Follows: "[*] Company announces submitting an application for capital reduction to the Capital Market Authority".

b) The Announcement Must at Least Contain the Following Elements:

1. The date of submitting the application for capital reduction to the Authority.

2. Indicate the subject of the application.

3. Indicate the announcement of the board's recommendation for the company's capital reduction.

15.6.19 (4) Announcement Form for Material Developments on the Application File for Capital Reduction Submitted to the Authority.

After the announcement of submitting an application of capital reduction to the Authority for approval. The company must announce any material changes regarding the application submitted to the Authority. Upon the Authority's approval, the shareholders' circular must be published within a period no less than 14 days prior to the date of convening the general assembly.

a) The Announcement Title Must be as Follows: "[*] Company announces the developments on the application submitted to the Capital Market Authority regarding the capital reduction".

b) The Announcement Must at Least Contain the Following Elements:

1. Indicate the subject of the application submitted to the Authority and the date of submission.

2. Detailed description of the application status submitted to the Authority (including, but not limited to: fulfilling the requirements and remarks on the application, or whether the application is under review by the Authority).

3. Any other material developments (permanent withdrawal of the application with a clarification of the reasons, the Authority's rejection of the application with justifications, suspension of the application for not fulfilling the requirements...etc.).

(5) Announcement Form for the Completion of Shares Fractions Sale (if any) and Distribution of the Sales Proceeds among Eligible Shareholders

a) The Announcement Title Must be as Follows: "[*] Company announces the deposit of the amounts resulted from selling the shares fractions in order to reduce the company's capital to the eligible shareholders' accounts".

b) The Announcement Must at Least Contain the Following Elements:

1. The date on which the selling of shares fractions process ended.
2. The number of sold shares.
3. The amounts resulted from selling the shares fractions process.
4. Average selling price for each sold share.
5. The deposit date of the amounts resulted from selling the shares fractions process in the eligible shareholders' accounts.
6. The name and contact method of the responsible entity of distributing the resulted amounts from selling the shares fractions process among the eligible shareholders.

(6) Announcement Form for the Non-Completion of the Shares Fractions Sale (if any) and the Distribution of Sales Proceeds among eligible Shareholders within the Time Frame Mentioned in the Shareholders' Circular

a) The Announcement Title Must be as Follows: "[*]Company announces the non-completion of the shares fractions sale resulted from capital reduction within the term mentioned in the shareholders' circular".

b) The Announcement Must at Least Contain the Following Elements:

1. The justification for the company's failure to complete the sale of the shares fractions and the deposit of the sale proceeds in the eligible shareholders' accounts.
2. The estimated date of completion of the shares fractions sale and the distribution of sales proceeds among eligible shareholders.

Fourth: Capital Increase by Debt Conversion (1) Announcement Form for the Board of Directors' Recommendation for the Company's Capital Increase by Way of Debt Conversion

a) The Announcement Title Must be as Follows: "[*] Company announces the board of directors' recommendation to increase the company's capital by way of debt conversion".

b) The Announcement Must at Least Contain the Following Elements:

1. Date of the board meeting.

2. The total amount of debts that the company intends to convert, without mentioning the number or value of the shares intended to be offered or their percentage of the current capital.

3. Reasons for the capital increase.

4. Indicate the necessity of obtaining approvals from the official entities and the Extraordinary General Assembly to increase capital by way of debt conversion.

5. Indicate that an announcement shall be made upon the appointment of a financial advisor for the offering and upon submitting the application for the increase of the capital by way of debt conversion to obtain the approval of the Capital Market Authority.

(2) Announcement Form for the Appointment of a Financial Advisor to Manage the Application File for the Company's Capital Increase by Debt Conversion

After announcing the board of directors' recommendation to increase the company's capital by way of debt conversion, the company announces the appointment of a financial advisor in line with the following:
a) The Announcement Title Must be as Follows: "[*]Company announces the appointment of a financial advisor to manage the application for the increase of the capital by way of debt conversion".

b) The Announcement Must at Least Contain the Following Elements:

1. The name of the financial advisor.

2. The date of appointing the financial advisor.

3. In the case of changing the current financial advisor, the name of the new financial advisor and the reason for changing the old financial advisor must be announced.

4. Any other information that the company may want to add.

(3) Announcement Form for Submitting the Application File for the Company's Capital Increase by Way of Debt Conversion to the Authority for Approval

a) The Announcement Title Must be as Follows: "[*]Company announces the submission of an application for the increase of the company's capital by way of debt conversion to the Capital Market Authority".

b) The Announcement Must at Least Contain the Following Elements:

1. The date of submitting the application to the Authority.
2. Statement of the subject of the application.
3. Reference to the announcement of the boards' recommendation to increase the company's capital by way of debt conversion.

(4) Announcement Form for Announcing the Material Developments on the Application File Submitted to the Authority for the Company's Capital Increase by Debt Conversion

After announcing the submission of the application for the increase of the company's capital by way of debt conversion to the Authority to obtain its approval, the company must announce any material developments to the application with the Authority upon their occurrence. Upon the Authority's approval, the shareholders' circular must be published within a period no less than 14 days prior to the date of convening the general assembly.

a) The Announcement Title Must be as Follows: "[*] Company announces the material developments to the application for the increase of the company's capital by way of debt conversion with the Capital Market Authority".

b) The Announcement Must at Least Contain the Following Elements:

1. Reference to the subject of the application and the date of submitting it.
2. Clarifying and detailing the status of the application with the Authority (including but limited to: fulfilling the requirements and remarks on the application, or whether the application is under review by the Authority).
3. Any other material changes (including but limited to: permanent withdrawal of the application with a clarification of the reasons, the Authority's rejection of the application with justifications, suspension of the application for not fulfilling the requirements...etc).

Fifth: Announcements Related to the Acquisition of a Company/Purchase of an Asset through Increasing the Company's Capital by Issuing Shares for the Owners of the Acquired Company/ Purchased Asset

Phase 1: Announcement Form for the Company's Signature of a Memorandum of Understanding for the Acquisition of a Company/Purchase of an Asset

a) The Announcement Title Must be as Follows: "(•) Company announces the signing of a memorandum of understanding with (•) name of the second party (•) for the acquisition/purchase of a (•)".

b) The Announcement Must at Least Contain the Following Elements:

1. The date of signing the memorandum of understanding.
2. The period of the memorandum of understanding.
3. The name of the party who the memorandum of understanding is signed with.
4. The financial advisor of each party in the agreement.
5. The most prominent terms of the memorandum of understanding.
6. In case of related parties, their identities must be disclosed.
7. The actions to be taken by the company during the agreement period.
8. Indicate the necessity of obtaining the official entities and Extraordinary General Assembly's approval regarding capital increase for the purpose of acquisition/purchase.

2: Announcement Form for the Company's Signature of an Agreement for the Acquisition of a Company/Purchase of an Asset through Capital Increase by Issuing Shares to the Owners of the Company/Asset Phase

a) The Announcement Title Must be as Follows: "(•) Company announces the signing of an agreement for the acquisition of (•) name of the company to be acquired (•) company/purchase of an asset by means of capital increase by issuing shares to the owners of (•) name of the company to be acquired (•) company/asset".

b) The Announcement must at least contain the following elements:

1. The size and percentage of the capital increase.
2. Number of shares before and after the capital increase.
3. Name of (the company to be acquired)/(asset to be purchased).
4. Value of (the company to be acquired)/(asset to be purchased).
5. Value of the listed company.
6. Percentage of the shares swap with indication of the possible impacts and risks to the company's shareholders, the company and the decision making process in it.
7. The ownership percentage of the listed company in (the company to be acquired)/ (asset to be purchased) after issuing the shares.
8. The ownership percentage of the partners for whom new shares are issued after the end of the acquisition process.
9. The date of signing the acquisition agreement.
10. Any related material information or conditions which may affect the share price.
11. In case of related parties, their identities must be disclosed.
12. The end date of the agreement and its termination conditions.
13. Indicate the necessity of obtaining the official entities and Extraordinary General Assembly's approval regarding capital increase for the purpose of acquisition/purchase.

Note: In regards of the required announcements, if the company to be acquired is a listed company, the provisions of the Merger and Acquisition Regulation must be complied with.

Phase 3: Announcement Form for the Completion of the Procedures of the Acquisition of a Company/Purchase of an Asset through Capital Increase by Issuing Shares to the Owners of the Company/Asset

a) The Announcement Title Must be as Follows: "(•) Company announces the completion of the procedures of the acquisition/purchase of (•)".

b) The Announcement must at least contain the following elements:

1. The date of completion of the acquisition procedures.
2. Summary regarding the acquisition/purchase.
3. Related parties.
4. Financial Impact.
5. The date of completing the ownership transfer and the legal documents that have been amended to reflect the transfer of ownership. Or clarify that an announcement will be made later.

Reverse Take-Over (1) Announcement Form for the Reverse Take-Over Agreement

a) The Announcement Title Must be as Follows: "[*] Company announces the agreement to the reverse take-over terms with (...... name of the other party ......) to acquire [*]".

b) The Announcement Must at Least Contain the Following Elements:

1. The Details of the transaction, including the name of the other party.
2. Summary of the company's activity or the asset subject to the transaction.
3. Compensation and the extent to which it is satisfied (including the terms related to any arrangements necessary for delaying compensation).
4. The value of the total assets of the transaction.
5. The profits related to the assets of the transaction.
6. The effect of the transaction on the listed company, including any benefits expected to be received by the issuer as a result of the transaction.
7. Details of any service contracts for the proposed members of the issuer's board of directors.
8. Indicate the necessity of obtaining the official entities and Extraordinary General Assembly's approval regarding the reverse take-over.

General Assemblies (1) Announcement Form for the call for a General Assembly (Ordinary or Extraordinary)

a) After obtaining the official authorities' approval, the Announcement Title Must be as Follows: "[*] Company calls its shareholders to attend the (Ordinary or Extraordinary) General Assembly meeting (First/Second/Third meeting)".

b) The Announcement Must at Least Contain the Following Elements:

1. The general assembly meeting agenda.
2. Date and time of convening the general assembly.
3. Location for convening the general assembly including the name of the city, and a hyperlink of the meeting location (Google Maps link).
4. The company must attach the supporting documents for each item of the (ordinary or extraordinary) general assembly meeting's agenda in accordance with the attached table in page (42).
5. Indicate who has the right to attend the Assembly from the shareholders who are registered in the issuers' shareholders record at the Depositary Center by the end of the trade session prior to the general assembly meeting and in accordance with the laws and regulations.
6. Clarification on the quorum required for convening the general assembly meeting.
7. In the event where the first general assembly meeting was not convened, and if the company wishes to convene the second meeting one hour after not convening the first meeting, the announcement of the call for the first meeting must include an indication of that, as well as stating the quorum required for convening the second meeting.
8. If the call for convening the general assembly was made under the request of the Auditor, the Audit Committee or by a number of shareholders representing at least (5%) of the capital, the announcement must state such fact.
9. Attach the Proxy Letter\form in the call announcements for the Shareholders' Assembly meeting in accordance with the form set out in Annex (1) of the Regulatory Rules and Procedures Issued Pursuant to the Companies Law Relating to Listed Joint Stock Companies.
10. Reference in the announcement to the availability of e-voting, to vote on the items of the assembly's agenda, in addition to the date and time of its commencement if determined, or state that another announcement will be made regarding the date and time of the e-voting commencement.
11. Reference that the right to register a name to attend the general assembly meeting ends at the time of convening the general assembly meeting.
12. Reference that the attendees right to vote on the items of the assembly's agenda ends upon the end of screening the votes by the Screening Committee.
13. If the agenda includes voting on the company's buy-back of its shares, the following must be determined; the maximum limit of the number of shares to be purchased and the purposes of the purchase, the method of financing the purchase, the number of stages of the purchase, the maximum time period during which the company may keep the treasury stocks without selling them or allocating them to the employee shares program.
14. Reference that in case of any enquiries, contact the Investors Relations department (Phone Number/Email).

(2) In the Event Where the Agenda Includes an Item for Changing the Company's Capital

a) After Obtaining the Official Authorities' Approval, the Announcement Title Must be as Follows: "[*] Company calls its shareholders to attend the Extraordinary General Assembly meeting which include the increase/reduction of the company's capital (First/Second/Third meeting)".

b) The Announcement Must at Least Contain the Following Elements in Addition to the Elements Mentioned in (1(b)):

1. The company's capital before and after the change (in case of increase of capital by bonus shares or reduction of capital).
2. The percentage of change in the capital before and after the change (in case of increase of capital by bonus share or reduction of capital).
3. Number of shares before and after the capital alternation (in case of increase of capital by bonus share or reduction of capital).
4. Reasons and methods of changing the capital.
5. Increase/reduction rate for each share (in case of increase of capital by bonus share or reduction of capital).
6. In case of capital increase, the eligibility date must be determined.
7. In case of capital reduction, the effective date of the reduction must be determined.
8. In case of capital increase by means of offering rights issue, the total offer price must be clarified.
9. In case of capital alternation for the purpose of merger or acquisition of the shares of other company, all related details and the effective date of the capital increase must be disclosed.
10. In case the capital alternation is for the purpose of acquisition, and the acquisition process, which included related parties, a clarification must be made that the votes of the related parties will not be included when voting on the decisions of the acquisition deal in the extraordinary general assembly pertaining to capital increase.

(3) Announcement Form for Announcing the General Assembly's Results (Ordinary or Extraordinary)

a) The Announcement Title Must be as Follows: "[*] Company announces the results of the (Ordinary or Extraordinary) General Assembly meeting (First/Second/Third meeting)".

b) The Announcement Must at Least Contain the Following Elements:

1. Location, date and time of convening the assembly meeting.
2. Attendance percentage.
3. Names of the board members attending the assembly meeting and the names of the absent board members.
4. Names of the committees' chairmen attending the assembly meeting or their representatives from the members of each committee.
5. Voting Results on the assembly's agenda.
6. In case the assembly approves distribution of dividends (cash or shares), all details related to such dividends and their eligibility and distribution dates must be announced.
7. In case of (electing members to the board /appointing a representative for a legal person), state the names of the (elected/appointed) members and the start and end date of their term.
8. In case of appointing an external auditor for the company, state the auditor's name and the financial periods during which the auditor will review the company's relevant financial statements.

(4) In the Event Where the General Assembly Approves the Company's Capital Alteration

a) The Announcement Title Must be as Follows: "[*] Company announces the results of the extraordinary general assembly meeting including the approval on the company's capital increase (reduction) (First/Second/Third meeting)".

b) The Announcement Must at Least Contain the Following Elements in Addition to the Elements Mentioned in (3(b)):

1. The company's capital before and after the change.
2. Percentage of change in the capital.
3. Number of shares before and after the change.
4. Reasons and methods of changing the capital.
5. Increase/reduction percentage for each share.
6. In case of capital increase, the eligibility date must be determined.
7. In case of capital reduction, the effective date of the reduction must be determined.
8. In case of capital increase by means of offering rights issue, the offer value for each share and its par value in addition to the number of offered shares must be clarified.
9. In case of capital alternation for the purpose of acquisition of a company/asset, all related details and the effective date of the capital increase must be clarified.

(5) Announcement Form for Non-Convening the General Assembly (Ordinary or Extraordinary)

a) The Announcement Title Must be as Follows: "[*]Company announces the non-convening of the (Ordinary or Extraordinary) General Assembly of the Company's (first/second/ third) meeting"

b) The Announcement Must at Least Contain the Following Elements:

1. Indicate the date of the non-convened assembly.
2. The reason behind non-convening the assembly.
3. The Attendance percentage.
4. The impact of non-convening the assembly upon matters relating to the recommendations of the board of directors on profits and capital alterations or on the work of the External Auditor (where applicable).

General note on the announcements of the Ordinary and Extraordinary General Assemblies: The Ordinary General Assembly call or its results must be in a separate announcement than that of the Extraordinary General Assembly.

A Statement of the Supporting Documents of the Shareholders' General Assembly Agenda Items

List of Supporting Documents

1. Vote on the composition of the Audit Committee Resume of the candidates according to resume Form No. (1) attached on page (43)
2. Vote on the board of directors' decision regarding the dividends distributed to the shareholders A statement of all details relating to these profits

3. Voting on business and contracts in which the member of the board of directors has any direct or indirect interest therein Limited examination report, notification of the Chairman of the board of directors including a description of such transactions, name of the relevant board member, the nature of the transaction, the amount of the transaction, the period of the transaction, the conditions of the transaction
4. Voting on the participation of a board member in a competitive activity A statement and description of the company in which the member practices a competing activity, including the member's role in that company
5. Voting on the decision of the board of directors for appointing a member of the board of directors Resume of the appointed member according to resume Form No. (1) attached on page [*].
6. Voting on the amendment of the company's policies and regulations (e.g. The Company's Corporate Governance Regulations) Statement of the articles before and after the amendment
7. Vote on the adoption of regulations such as corporate governance and rules for the selection of members of the Audit Committee A copy of such regulations
8. Voting on the election of the board of directors from among the candidates Resume of the candidates according to resume Form No. (1) attached on page (43)
9. Voting on the amendment of an article(s) of the company's bylaws A copy of the article(s) before and after the amendment(s)
10. Voting on the alteration of the company's capital Prospectus / Shareholders Circular (as applicable)

Note: The mentioned items in the above statement are not exclusive. In case where the assembly agendas include an additional item with supporting documents that are not mentioned above, such relevant supporting documents must be included in the announcement.

Form No. (1) Resume

a) Personal information of the Nominated Member:

Full name

Nationality / Date of birth

b) Academic Qualifications of the Nominated Member

No. Qualifications / Specialization

Date of obtaining the qualifications

The issuer of the qualification:

c) Experience of the Nominated Member Period / Experience

d) Current membership in the board of directors of other joint stock companies (listed or non-listed) or any other company, regardless of its legal form or the committees deriving from it:

- Company name
- Main activity
- Membership type (executive, non- executive, independent)
- Nature of the membership (in personal capacity, representative of legal person)
- Membership of committees
- Legal form of the company

Instructions for Companies' Announcements Regarding Cash Dividends

(1) Announcement Form for the Distribution of Cash Dividends to Shareholders of the Company.

a)The Announcement Title Must be as Follows: "[*]Company announces the board of directors' recommendation to distribute cash dividends for (the distribution period)"

b) The Announcement Must at Least Contain the Following Elements:

1. Date of the board's decision.
2. The dividends period.
3. The Total amount distributed.
4. Number of shares eligible for dividends.
5. Dividend per share.
6. Percentage of Dividend to the share par value.
7. Date of eligibility, provided that the eligibility of Cash dividend shall be to Shareholders who own the shares on the eligibility date, who are enrolled in the issuer's shareholders register at the Depository Center by the end of the second trading day following the eligibility.
8. Date of distribution (If no specific distribution date is specified, it shall be stated that "the distribution date will be announced later").

(2) Announcement Form for the Non-Distribution of Cash Dividends to Shareholders of the Company.

a) The Announcement Title Must be as Follows: "[*] Company announces the board of directors' recommendation to not distribute dividends for (the related distribution period)".

b) The Announcement Must at Least Contain the Following Elements:

1. Date of the board's decision.
2. The related distribution period.
3. Reason for the recommendation to not distribute dividends.
4. Indicate that the recommendation will be submitted to the General Assembly for vote.

Instructions for Companies' Announcement Regarding Contracts

(1) Announcement Form for Awarding a Contract or Project

a) The Announcement Title Must be as Follows "[*]Company announces awarding (contract/ project) with (the other party's name)".

b) The Announcement Must at Least Contain the Following Elements:

1. Date of the awarding.
2. Other party's name.
3. The contract/ project value.
4. The estimated date of signing the contract (if any).
5. Contract/ project details.
6. In case of having related parties, their identities must be disclosed.

(2) Announcement Form for Signing a Contract
a) The Announcement Title Must be as Follows: "[*] Company announces signing a contract with (the other party's name) for (the purpose)".

b) The Announcement Must at Least Contain the Following Elements:

1. Reference of the awarding announcement.
2. The entity with which the contract was signed.
3. Date of signing the contract.
4. Value of the contract.
5. Contract details and period.
6. In case of having related parties, their identities must be disclosed.
7. Financial impact and the period in which it will be reflected.

15.6.20 SAMA's (Saudi Arabian Monetary Authority) Approval on Insurance Products

(1) The Announcement Form for SAMA's Approval Regarding Insurance Products

a) The Announcement Title Must be as Follows: "[*]Company announces obtaining SAMA's (Final\Temporary) approval on the company's product/products".

b) The Announcement Must at Least Contain the Following Elements:

1. Approval letter's issuing date from SAMA and the date of receiving it.
2. Approved products based on the letter from SAMA.
3. Approved period (for temporary approvals).

15.6.21 Addendum and Corrective Announcement (1) Addendum Announcement Form

a) The Announcement Title Must be as Follows: "Addendum announcement from [*] regarding (announcement subject)".

b) The Announcement Must at Least Contain the Following Elements:

1. Date of the pervious announcement on (Tadawul)'s website preceding the development.
2. The change on the development.
3. Financial impact of the change (if any), in case of otherwise, the reason must be clarified. Note: the addendum announcement is only used if the company wishes to provide additional information not disclosed or the company did not comply with on its pervious announcement. However, in cases where the company's announcement of the latest developments regarding the material developments already announced, then the company's announcement form for previously announced developments must be used.

15.6.22 (2) Corrective Announcement Form

a) The Announcement Title Must be as Follows: "A corrective announcement from [*] regarding (announcement subject)".

b) The Announcement Must at Least Contain the Following Elements:

1. Date of the pervious announcement on (Tadawul)'s website preceding the development.
2. The misstatement on the previous announcement.
3. Correction for the misstatement.

15.6.23 Instruction for Companies' Announcement Regarding Signing a Memorandum of Understanding (1)

Announcement Form for Signing a Memorandum of Understanding
a) The Announcement Title Must be as Follows: "[*]Company announces signing a memorandum of understanding with (the other entity's name)".

b) The Announcement Must at Least Contain the Following Elements:

1. Date of signing the Memorandum of Understanding.
2. The name of the entity with which the memorandum was signed
3. The Memorandum subject.
4. The Memorandum period.
5. In case of having related parties, their identities must be disclosed.
6. Financial impact (if any).

15.6.24 Instructions for Companies' Announcement Regarding their Projects

(1) Announcement Form for Projects
a) The Announcement Title Must be as Follows: "[*] Company announces (project name)".

b) The Announcement Must at Least Contain the Following Elements:

1. Date of board of directors' resolution regarding the project (if any).
2. Project starting date.
3. Project cost.
4. Financing method for the project.
5. Expected completion date of the project.
6. Expected financial impact of the project on the company's results.
7. The start of the expected impact of the project on the company's results.
8. Expected date of commencement of the pilot production of the project.
9. Period for the pilot production of the project.
10. The expected date of commercial production of the project.
11. The executing entity or the other party of the project.
12. In case of having related parties, their identities must be disclosed.

13. In case of inability to obtain any previous information, the announcement shall indicate that "an announcement of any development to such will be made when such information is available" with reasons.

15.6.25 Instructions for Companies' Announcements for Transactions of Sale, Purchase, Mortgage or Leasing of an Asset

(1) Announcement Form for the Transactions of Sale, Purchase, Mortgage or Leasing of an Asset.
a) The Announcement Title Must be as Follows: "[*] Company announces of (the purchase or sale) of [*] in the amount of [*]".

b) The Announcement Must at Least Contain the Following Elements (as applicable):

1. Details and cost of the transaction, with mention of its conditions, parties and financing method.
2. Date of entering into the transaction.
3. Description of activity of the asset subject of the transaction.
4. Statement of the book value of the asset in case of sale.
5. Financial statements for the last three years for the asset subject of the transaction where financial information for it are available.
6. Transaction's reasons and expected impact on the company and its operations.
7. Statement of the use of proceeds in case of sale the asset.
8. In case of having related parties, their identities must be disclosed.

15.6.26 Instructions for Companies' Announcements for Obtaining Financing

(1) Announcement Form for Obtaining Financing.
a) The Announcement Title Must be as Follows: "[*] Company announces obtaining of (finance type)".

b) The Announcement Must at Least Contain the Following Elements:

1. Date of obtaining the financing.
2. Financing entity.
3. Financing amount.
4. Financing duration.
5. Any guarantees offered for the financing.
6. Financing objective.
7. In case of any related parties, their identities must be disclosed.

(2) Announcement Form for Defaulting on the Repayment of Financing.
a) The Announcement Title Must be as Follows: "[*] Company announces the default on the payment of the finance provided by (financing entity)".

b) The Announcement Must at Least Contain the Following Elements:

1. Date of obtaining the funding and its due date.
2. Financing entity.
3. Financed amount.
4. Reasons for defaulting the payment.
5. Company's plan to address the default.
6. Impacts, costs and risks on the company in the event of non-payment on time or in case of disagreement with the financing entity to postpone repayment.

(3) Announcement Form for Rescheduling the Financing.
a) The announcement title must be as follows: "[*] Company announces rescheduling the (Finance type) provided by (Financing entity).

b) The Announcement Must at Least Contain the Following Elements:

1. Date of singing the rescheduling of finance.
2. Financing entity.
3. Reasons for rescheduling the Finance.
4. The Financing amount and rescheduled part.
5. The Financing duration before and after the rescheduling.
6. Guarantees offered for the rescheduled Financing.
7. In case of any related parties, must disclose their identities.

15.6.27 Instructions for Companies' Announcements Related to Debt Instruments

(1) Announcement Form for the Determination to Issue Debt Instruments
a) The Announcement Title Must be as Follows: "[*] Company announces its determination to issue (sukuk/ bonds)".

b) The Announcement Must at Least Contain the Following Elements:

1. Date of the board of directors' decision.
2. Value of the offer.
3. The purpose of the offer.
4. Indicate the necessity for obtaining the approval of the regulatory authorities.

(2) Announcement Form for Beginning the Offer of Debt Instruments
a) The Announcement Title Must be as Follows: "[*]Company announces beginning of offering (sukuk/bonds)".

b) The Announcement must at least contain the following elements:

1. Value of the offer.
2. Starting and ending dates of the offer.
3. Determine the targeted class of the issuance.
4. Name of the issuance manager.
5. Minimum Subscription (if any).
6. Offer price (sukuk/bond) and the par value.
7. Return of (sukuk/bond).
8. Maturity of (sukuk/bond).
9. Terms of redemption (if any).

(3) Announcement Form for Completing the Offer of Debt Instruments
a) The Announcement Title Must be as Follows: "[*] Company announces the end of the debts instruments offer (sukuk/bonds)".

b) The Announcement Must at Least Contain the Following Elements:

1. Value of the offer.
2. Total number of (sukuk\ bonds).
3. Par value (sukuk/bond).
4. Return of (sukuk/bond).
5. Maturity of (sukuk/bond).
6. Terms of redemption (if any).

8. Indicate the company's fulfillment of financial solvency requirements contained in paragraph (3) of Article (12) of Regulatory Rules and Procedures issued pursuant to the Companies Law, and attach a report by the external auditor of the company.
9.Indicate that the shares that the company buys-back shall not have voting rights in the shareholders' assemblies.

15.6.28 (4) Announcement Form for the Redemption of Issued Debts Instruments

a)The Announcement Title Must be as Follows: "[*]Company announces its determination to redeem the issued (sukuk/bonds)"

b) The Announcement Must at Least Contain the Following Elements:

1. Value of the redeemed (sukuk/bonds) and its percentage of the total issuance.
2. The total number of the redeemed (sukuk/bonds).
3. Date of Issuance.
4. End of trading date.
5. The par value of the redeemed sukuk.
6. The total issuance value after the redemption.
7. Date of depositing the amounts of (sukuk/bonds) holders' account.
8. Name of the responsible entity for the deposit and its contact method.

15.6.29 Instructions for Companies' Announcements Regarding the Company's Shares Buy-Back and Sale

Note: The controls over the Company's Shares Buy-Back and sale stipulated in Chapter 4 of the Regulatory Rules and Procedures issued pursuant to the Companies Law Relating to Listed Joint Stock Company must be complied with.

15.6.30 First: Instructions for Companies' Announcements Regarding the Buy-Back of its shares

(1) Announcement Form for the Company's Determination to Buy-Back Its Shares

a) The Announcement Title Must be as Follows: "[*]Company announces its determination to buy-back its shares".

b) The Announcement Must at Least Contain the Following Elements

1. Board of directors' approval date.
2. Purpose of the purchase.
3. If the purpose of the buy-back is to maintain them as treasury shares, it must clarify such purpose.
4. Number of shares to be bought-back and their class.
5. Financing method of the purchase.
6. The percentage of the treasury shares currently with the company in relation to the total share of the same class that the company buys-back (if any).
7.Indicate the necessity of obtaining the Extraordinary General Assembly's approval on the shares buy-back transaction.

(2) Announcement Form for the Results of the Company's Shares Buy-Back

a) The announcement title must be as follows: "[*] Company announces the results of its shares buy-back (stage [*])".

b) The Announcement Must at Least Contain the Following Elements:

1. Reference to the company's announcement regarding the shares buy-back approval by the assembly.
2. Buy-back transaction period.
3. Number of the shares that the company buys-back.
4. Value of the shares that the company buys-back.
5. Average price for a share that the company buys-back.

15.6.31 Second: Instructions for Companies' Announcements Regarding a Company's Sale of its Shares.

(1) Announcement Form for the Company's Determination to Sell Its Shares.

a) The Announcement Title Must be as Follows: "[*]Company announces the company determination to sell its shares".

b) The Announcement Must at Least Contain the Following Elements:

1.Board of directors' approval date.
2. Number of the shares to be sold and their percentage from the company's treasury shares.
3.The purpose of the sale.

(2) Announcement Form for the Results of the Company's Sale of Its Shares

a) The Announcement Title Must be as Follows: "[*] Company announces the results of selling its shares (stage...)".

b) The Announcement Must at Least Contain the Following Elements:

1.Date of sale of shares.
2.Number of sold shares.
3.Value of sold shares.
4.Sold shares price average.
5.Realized profit (loss) from the sale of shares.
6.Statement of the use of the sale proceeds.

15.6.32 Instruction for Companies' Announcements Regarding the Company Pledge of Its Shares

Note: Must comply with the rules for company's pledge of its shares stipulated in Chapter 5 of the Regulatory Rules and Procedures Issued Pursuant to the Companies Law Relating to Listed Joint Stock Company.

(3) Announcements Form Relating to the Company's Determination to Pledge Its Shares.
a) The Announcement Title Must be as Follows: "[*]Company announces its determination to pledge its shares".

b) The Announcement Must at Least Contain the Following Elements:

1. Board of directors' approval date.
2. The reasons for the pledge and its financial or commercial fees.
3. The number of pledged shares.
4. The date and period for the pledge.
5. The shares pledgee.
6. Indicate that the pledgee creditor may not attend or vote on the general shareholders' assemblies.
7. Indicate whether if the pledgee creditor may receive profits and use the rights related to the share.
8. Indicate if there are any related parties.
9. Indicate that the Ordinary General Assembly's approval on the company's pledge of its shares must be obtained.

(10) Announcement Form for the Company's Release of Its Pledged Shares.
a) The Announcement Title Must be as Follows: "[*] Company announces the release of its pledged shares".

b) The Announcement Must at Least Contain the Following Elements:

1. Date of releasing the pledged shares.
2. Numbers of pledged shares.
3. The source of the financing used to release the pledged shares.
4. Reasons for pledge expiration.

15.6.33 Instructions for Companies' Announcement Regarding Lawsuits Announcement Form for Lawsuits:

a) The Announcement Title Must be as Follows: "[*] Company announces (the lawsuit type and the other party name in such lawsuits").

b) The Announcement Must at Least Contain the Following Elements:

1. The other party of such lawsuit, with a statement of who filed the suit.
2. The lawsuit type, place and the competent judicial entity's name.
3. Date of lawsuit.
4. A brief of the lawsuit including an explanation of it, and the reasons for filing it.
5. The expected financial impact, including the claimed amount and any other fees or burdens.
6. Clarification of any consequences or significant legal, regulatory or operational risks that may result from the lawsuit with stating the impact of such consequences on the company's financial, legal and operational position.
7. The taken procedures, including the estimate of liability that the Company may incur as a result of the lawsuit.

15.6.34 Instructions for Companies' Announcement of Previously Announced Developments Announcement Form for Previously Announced Developments.

a) The Announcement Title Must be as Follows: "[*] Company announces the latest developments on (previously announced event)".

b) The Announcement Must at Least Contain the Following Elements:

1. The previously announced event.
2. Date of the previous announcement.
3. Percentage of fulfilled achievement.
4. Expected date of ending the event.
5. Reasons for the delay on the date of the event previously announced (if any).
6. The costs associated with the event, and if they have changed or not with indication of the reasons.
7. Delay consequences (if any) on the Company's financial results.

15.6.35 Instructions for Companies' Announcements for Companies with Accumulated Losses Reaching 20% or More of Their Share Capital

First: Companies with Accumulated Losses of 20% or More and Less Than 35% of their Share Capital.

15.6.36 (1) Announcement Form for Accumulated Losses Reaching 20% or More and Less Than 35% of Share Capital.

a) The Announcement Title Must be as Follows: "[*] Company announces its accumulated losses reaching [*]% of its capital."

b) The Announcement Must at Least Contain the Following Elements:

1. Date of reaching the losses.
2. Accumulated losses amount.
3. Accumulated losses percentage of the capital.
4. The main reasons that led to such losses.
5. Indicate that it will apply the Procedures and Instructions Related to Listed Companies with Accumulated Losses Reaching 20% or more of their Share Capital.
6. Reference to any other laws or instructions (if any) that regulate such case that shall be applied.

Note: In accordance with the Procedures and Instructions Related to Listed Companies with Accumulated Losses Reaching 20% or more of their Share Capital, in case that the announcement of the company's accumulated losses happens together with the announcement of the interim or annual financial results, the Company shall be exempted from disclosure in a separate announcement of the Company's accumulated losses if it is included in the announcement of the interim or annual financial results.

15.6.37 (2) Announcement Form for the Reduction of the Accumulated Losses Below 20% of Share Capital

a) The Announcement Title Must be as Follows: "[*] Company announces the reduction in its accumulated losses to reach [*]% of its capital".

b) The Announcement Must at Least Contain the Following Elements:

1. Date of the losses reduction.
2. Accumulated losses amount.
3. Accumulated losses percentage of the capital.
4. The procedure taken by the company to reduce its accumulated losses.
5. The external auditor's report clarifying the financial position of the company after the reduction in its accumulated losses (attached).

15.6.38 Second: Companies with Accumulated Losses Reaching 35% or More and Less Than 50% of Share Capital (1) Announcement Form for Accumulated Losses Reaching 35% or More and Less Than 50% of Share Capital

a) The Announcement Title Must be as Follows: "[*] Company announces that its accumulated losses reaching [*]% of its capital"

b) The Announcement Must at Least Contain the Following Elements:

1. Date of reaching the losses.
2. Accumulated losses amount.
3. Accumulated losses percentage of the capital.
4. The main reasons that led to such losses.
5. The procedure taken by the company regarding such accumulated losses.
6. Indicate that it will apply the Procedures and Instructions Related to Listed Companies with Accumulated Losses Reaching 20% or more of their Share Capital.
7. Reference to any other laws or instructions (if any) that regulate such case and that will be applied.

Note: In accordance with the Procedures and Instructions Related to Listed Companies with Accumulated Losses Reaching 20% or more of their Share Capital, in case the announcement of the company's accumulated losses happens together with the announcement of the interim or annual financial results, the Company shall be exempted from disclosure in a separate announcement of the Company's accumulated losses if it is included in the announcement of the interim or annual financial results.

15.6.39 (2) Announcement Form for the Reduction of the Accumulated Losses Below 35% of Share Capital.

a) The Announcement Title Must be as Follows: "[*] Company announces the reduction in its accumulated losses to reach [*] % of its capital".

b) The Announcement Must at Least Contain the Following Elements:

1. Date of losses reduction.
2. Accumulated losses amount.
3. Accumulated losses percentage of the capital.
4. The procedure taken by the company to reduce its accumulated losses.
5. The external auditor's report clarifying the financial position of the company (attached).

Note: When accumulated losses of the company are reduced below 35% and not less than 20% of its capital, Article 3 of the Procedures and Instructions Related to Listed Companies with Accumulated Losses Reaching 20% or more of their Share Capital shall be applied on the company. Accordingly, the Company shall commit to announce its accumulated losses of over 20% or more and less than 35% of its capital, in addition to announcing the reduction of the accumulated losses below 35% of share capital.

15.6.40 Third: Companies with Accumulated Losses Reaching 50% or More of Share Capital

(1) Announcement Form for Accumulated Losses Reaching 50% or More of Share Capital
a) The Announcement Title Must be as Follows: "[*] Company announces its accumulated losses reaching [*]% of its capital".

b) The Announcement Must at Least Contain the Following Elements:

1. Date of reaching losses.
2. Date on which the board of directors of the company was informed of the losses of the company reaching...% of the capital.
3. Accumulated losses amount.
4. Accumulated losses percentage of the capital.
5. The main reasons that led to such losses.
6. Indicate that it will apply the Procedures and Instructions Related to Listed Companies with Accumulated Losses Reaching 20% or more of their Share Capital.
7. Reference to any other laws or instructions (if any) that regulate such case and that will be applied.

Note: In accordance with the Procedures and Instructions Related to Listed Companies with Accumulated Losses Reaching 20% or more of their Share Capital, in case that the announcement of the company's accumulated losses happens together with the announcement of the interim or annual financial results, the Company shall be exempted from disclosure in a separate announcement of the Company's accumulated losses if it is included in the announcement of the interim or annual financial results.

(2) Announcement Form for the Reduction of the Accumulated Losses Below 50% of Share Capital
a) The Announcement Title Must be as Follows: "[*] Company announces the reduction of its accumulated losses to reach [*]% of its capital".

b) The Announcement Must at Least Contain the Following Elements:

1. Date of losses reduction.
2. Accumulated losses amount.

3. Accumulated losses percentage of the capital.
4. The procedure taken by the company to reduce its accumulated losses.
5. The external auditor's report clarifying the financial position of the company (attached).

Note: When accumulated losses of the company are reduced below 50% and not less than 35% of its capital, Article 4 of the Procedures and Instructions Related to Listed Companies with Accumulated Losses Reaching 20% or more of their Share Capital shall be applied on the company. Accordingly, the Company shall commit to announce its accumulated losses reaching 35% or more and less than 50% of the share capital, in addition to announcing the accumulated losses reduction below 50% of its share capital. When accumulated losses of the company are reduced below 35% and not less than 20% of its capital, Article 3 of the Procedures and Instructions Related to Listed Companies with Accumulated Losses Reaching 20% or more of their Share Capital shall be applied on the company. Accordingly, the Company shall commit to announce its accumulated losses reaching 20% or more and less than 35% of its share capital, in addition to announcing the accumulated losses reduction below50% of its share capital.

15.6.41 (3) Announcement Form for the Recommendation of the Board of Directors to the Extraordinary General Assembly Regarding the Accumulated Losses of 50% or More of the Share Capital In case the recommendation is to dissolve the company before the prescribed date in its articles of association

a) The Announcement Title Must be as Follows: "[*] Company announces the recommendation of the board of directors to the Extraordinary General Assembly to dissolve the company before its term prescribed in its articles of association, due to the accumulated losses exceeding [*]% of the capital".

b) The Announcement Must at Least Contain the Following Elements:

1. Reference to the company's announcement of reaching accumulated losses of 50% or more of its capital.
2. Date of board of directors' meeting.
3. Board of directors' recommendation. In case the recommendation is for capital increase or reduction, must refer to the relevant announcement forms in these Instructions.

15.6.42 Instructions for Companies' Announcement Pursuant to the Requirements of Article (150) of the Companies Law

(1) Announcement Form for Procedures that Must Be Taken and Their Periods According with Article (150) of the Companies Law Before the Trading Period Begins on the Day Following the Company's Announcement of Accumulated Losses Reaching 50% or More of Its Capital.

a) The Announcement Title Must be as Follows: "[*] Company announces the procedures that must be taken and their periods after reaching accumulated losses of [*]% of its capital".

b) With regards to Article (150) of the Companies Law, the Announcement Must at Least Contain the Following Elements:

1. Reference to the company's announcement dated **/**/**** of reaching accumulated losses of 50% or more of its capital.
2. Date on which the board of directors of the company was informed of the losses of the company reaching ...% of the capital.
3. The date of the last day on which the board of directors can call for an extraordinary general assembly meeting pursuant to Article (150) of the Companies Law.
4. Date of the last day for convening the extraordinary general assembly to address accumulated losses pursuant to Article (150) of the Companies Law.
5. A clarification that in case the extraordinary general assembly meeting was not convened within 45 days from the date of the board of directors being aware of the company's losses (which ends on **/**/****) or in case the meeting was convened but unable to issue a decision in this regard. The company will be deemed terminated by the operation of law as set out in Article (150) of the Companies Law.

15.6.43 (2) Announcement Form for the Deadline for Convening the Extraordinary General Assembly Meeting to Address the Accumulated Losses after the Company's Announcement for the call for the Extraordinary General Assembly Meeting

a) The Announcement Title Must be as Follows: "[*] Company announces the deadline for convening the Extraordinary General Assembly meeting to address the accumulated losses".

b) With Regards to Article (150) of the Companies Law, the Announcement Must at Least Contain the Following Elements:

1. Reference to the company's announcement dated */*/* of reaching accumulated losses of 50% or more of its capital, the company's announcement dated **/**/**** of board of directors' recommendation to address the accumulated losses and the company's announcement dated **/**/**** of call for extraordinary general assembly meeting to address the accumulated losses.
2. Clarification of that in case the extraordinary general assembly meeting was not convened within 45 days from the date of the board of directors being aware of the company's losses (which ends on **/**/****) or in case it was convened but was unable to issue a decision in this regard, the company will be deemed terminated by the operation of law as set out in Article 150 of the Companies Law.
3. The announcement of the extraordinary general assembly's approval of capital increase must state that if the full amount of capital increase was not subscribed in within 90 days of the assembly's decision to increase, the company will be deemed terminated by the operation of law as set out in Article (150) of the Companies Law.
4. The company's assurance of the necessity of shareholders attending the extraordinary general assembly or the e-voting on the assembly's items, in order to avoid the expiration of period for convening the assembly.

15.6.44 (3) Reminder Announcement Form for the Deadline for Convening the Extraordinary General Assembly Meeting to Address the Accumulated Losses Two Days Prior to Convening the Extraordinary General Assembly Meeting to Address the Accumulated Losses.

a) The announcement title must be as follows: "[*] Company announces the deadline for convening the Extraordinary General Assembly meeting to address the accumulated losses (reminder announcement)"

b) With Regards to Article (150) of the Companies Law, The Announcement Must at Least Contain the Following Elements:

1. Reference to the company's announcement dated **/**/**** of reaching accumulated losses of 50% or more of its capital, the company's announcement dated **/**/**** of board of directors' recommendation to address the accumulated losses and the company's announcement dated **/**/**** of the call for extraordinary general assembly meeting to address the accumulated losses.
2. A clarification that in case the extraordinary general assembly meeting was not convened within 45 days from the date of the board of directors being aware of the company's losses (which ends on **/**/****), or in case it was convened but was unable to issue a decision in this regard, the company will be deemed terminated by the operation of law as set out in Article (150) of the Companies Law.
3. The announcement of the Extraordinary General Assembly's approval of capital increase must state that if the full amount of capital increase is not subscribed in within 90 days of the assembly's decision to increase, the company will be deemed terminated by the operation of law as set out in Article (150 of the Companies Law.
4. The company's assurance of the necessity of the shareholders attending the extraordinary general assembly or the e-voting on the assembly's items, in order to avoid the assembly time expiration.

(4)Announcement Form for the Last Period for the Completion of the Subscription in Capital Increase to Address the Accumulated Losses.

a) The Announcement Title Must be as Follows: "[*]Company announces the last period for completing the subscription of capital increase".

b) The Announcement Must at Least Contain the Following Elements:

1. Reference to the company's announcement date (**/**/**) of accumulated losses of 50% or more of its capital and the company's announcement date (**/**/**) on the results of the Extraordinary General Assembly meeting in which it was announced the approval of capital increase to address the accumulated losses.
2. Clarification that in the event of non-completion of the subscription to increase the capital within 90 days from the issuance of the Extraordinary General Assembly's decision to increase (ending on **/**/**), the Company will be deemed terminated by the operation of law as set out in Article (150) of the Companies Law.

16 INVESTMENT ACCOUNTS INSTRUCTIONS

Issued by the Board of the Capital Market Authority Pursuant to its Resolution Number 4 -39-2016 dated 25/6/1437H (3/4/2016G) based on the Capital Market Law Issued by Royal Decree No. M / 30 dated 2/6/1424H, as amended by Board Resolution No.2-124-2018 dated 13/3/1440H (21/11/2018G)

TABLE OF CONTENTS

PART 1: GENERAL PROVISIONS
Article 1: Preliminary Provisions
Article 2: Definitions
P
ART 2: INSTRUCTIONS FOR OPENING INVESTMENT ACCOUNTS
A
rticle 3: Clients Acceptance
Article 4: Information Required in the Investment Account Opening Agreement
Article 5: Investment Accounts Identification Card
Article 6: Instructions for Opening Investment Accounts for Natural Persons
Article 7: Instructions for Opening Investment Accounts for Legal Persons
Article 8: Opening Investment Accounts for Other Persons
PART 3: INSTRUCTIONS FOR OPERATING INVESTMENT ACCOUNTS
Article 9: Transactions on the Investment Account
Article 10: Opening and Operating the Investment Account by Power of Attorney
Article 11: Appointment of Court-Appointed Receiver over the Investment Account
Article 12: Closing the Investment Account
PART 4: REGULATORY AND SUPERVISORY INSTRUCTIONS
Article 13: Electronic Record
Article 14: Updating the Investment Accounts Information
Article 15: Freezing the Investment Accounts
Article 16: Instruction on the Attachment of Investment Accounts and Disclosure of their Information
PART 5: PUBLICATION AND ENTRY INTO FORCE
Article 17: Publication and Entry into Force
Annex 1: Guidance List of Documents for Opening an Investment Account for Saudi Companies or Companies from GCC Member States
Annex 2: Guidance List of Documents for Opening an Investment Account for Qualified Foreign Investors
Annex 3: Guidance List of Documents for Opening an Investment Account for Investment Funds Established in the Kingdom or GCC Member States
Annex 4: Required Information in the Investment Account Statement

16.1 PART 1: GENERAL PROVISIONS

Article 1: Preliminary Provisions

a. These Instructions aim to regulate the opening and operation of investment accounts by Authorized Persons licensed to conduct dealing, management, or custody activities and define the regulatory and supervisory rules related to investment accounts.

b. These Instructions are without prejudice to the Capital Market Law and its Implementing Regulations, the Anti-Money Laundering Law and its Implementing Regulations, and the Combating-Terrorism Crimes and its Financing Law and its Implementing Regulations.

Article 2: Definitions

a. Any reference to the "Capital Market Law" in these Instructions shall mean the Capital Market Law issued by the Royal Decree No. M/30 dated 2/6/1424H.

b. Subject to paragraph (c) of this Article, expressions and terms in these Instructions have the meaning which they bear in the Capital Market Law and the Glossary of Defined Terms Used in the Regulations and Rules of the Capital Market Authority, unless the context indicates otherwise.

c. For the purpose of implementing these Instructions, the following expressions and terms shall have the meaning they bear as follows, unless the context indicates otherwise:

Freezing the Investment Account: The temporary block on all money transfers from the investment account, the utilization of its balance, and the transfer or pledge of securities in the investment portfolios linked to it. The freezing of the investment account shall not prevent the client from selling securities and receiving its proceeds or profits on the investment account or transferring funds from his bank account to his investment account.

Investment Account: An accounting record created by the Authorized Person for the client's money deposited in a client account opened by the Authorized Person to fund the client's transactions in securities and reflects all the details of the transactions in respect of that account.

Investment Portfolio: An account linked to the investment account that reflects the client's assets received by the Authorized Person in the course of carrying out securities business as per the Client Asset Rules stipulated in the Authorized Persons Regulations and reflects all the details of the transactions in respect of that account.

GCC Legal Persons: A legal person whose capital is majority owned by citizens or governments of the GCC member states and holds the nationality of one of the GCC member states.

GCC: The Cooperation Council for the Arab States of the Gulf.

Identification Document: The valid identification document issued by the competent authorities and accepted for opening an investment account for the client in accordance with these Instructions.

Non-profit Organization: Any legal entity licensed to engage in collecting, receiving, or paying money for charitable, religious, cultural, educational, social, or solidarity purposes or other charitable activities.

Combating -Terrorism Crimes and its Financing Law: The Combating-Terrorism Crimes and its Financing Law issued by the Royal Decree No. M/21 dated 12/2/1439H.

Anti-Money Laundering Law: The Anti-Money Laundering Law issued by the Royal Decree No. M/20 dated 5/2/1439H.

16.2 PART 2: INSTRUCTIONS FOR OPENING INVESTMENT ACCOUNTS

Article 3: Client Enrollment

a. The Authorized Person, before accepting any client and opening an investment account for him, must ensure his compliance with all of his obligations stated in the Capital Market Law and its Implementing Regulations, the Anti-Money Laundering Law and its Implementing Regulations, and the Combating-Terrorism Crimes and its Financing Law and its Implementing Regulations.

b. The Authorized Person, when accepting any client, must not provide any services related to dealing, managing, or custody activities until signing an investment account opening agreement with such client that contains all the information mentioned in Article (4) of these Instructions.

c. The Authorized Person may rely on a third party to carry out the customer due diligence measures in accordance with the related provisions of the Anti-Money Laundering Law and its Implementing Regulations, and the Combating-Terrorism Crimes and its Financing Law and its Implementing Regulations for any person for whom these Instructions permit the opening of an investment account.

d. The Authorized Person must verify the actual relationship between the clients and the natural persons who open or operate investment accounts on their behalf such as guardians, agents, trustees, or authorized signatories in accordance with the relevant provisions in the Anti-Money Laundering Law and its Implementing Regulations, and the Combating-Terrorism Crimes and its Financing Law and its Implementing Regulations.

e. In all situations in which these Instructions require the verification of copies of documents, data, or information, such verification must be done through documents, data or information from a reliable and independent source.

f. Depending on the risk profile of a particular client, the Authorized Person, when carrying out the customer due diligence measures, must determine if original copies of any of the documents should be checked in order to verify their validity.

Article 4: Information Required in the Investment Account Opening Agreement

In addition to the terms of business with clients requirements mentioned in the Authorized Persons Regulations, the investment account opening agreement must include, as a minimum, the following:

a. Information of the client's identification document, address, contact information, occupation and, if the client is a legal person, its main business activity.

b. An acknowledgment by the client that he understands the terms and conditions of the investment account opening agreement, and that all data and information provided to the Authorized Person are correct, complete, valid and not misleading.

c. An undertaking by the client of his commitment to update his data and information or confirm, upon the Authorized Person's request, that there are no changes to such data and information at the end of the relevant time period specified by the Authorized Person (provided that such period does not exceed 3 years); and provide information of his renewed identification documents upon the expiration of the original identification documents. The client shall provide an acknowledgment of his awareness that the Authorized Person will freeze his investment account upon his failure to meet such commitment, and also provide an undertaking to adhere to the Capital Market Law and its Implementing Regulations, and other laws and regulations of the Kingdom, especially the Anti- Money Laundering Law and its Implementing Regulations, and the Combating-Terrorism Crimes and its Financing Law and its Implementing Regulations.

d. Unless the company is listed on an exchange, the investment account opening agreement signed with any company must include an undertaking to immediately notify the Authorized Person upon any change to any of the documents, information or data that were previously provided when opening the investment account.

Article 5: Investment Account Identification Card

Upon the client's request, the Authorized Person must issue and deliver an investment account identification card to the client, which shall contain the client's name and number of the investment account as well as the Authorized Person's name.

Article 6: Instructions for Opening Investment Accounts for Natural Persons

a. Opening Investment Accounts for Saudi Natural Persons

To open an investment account for a Saudi natural person, the Authorized Person must obtain and verify the client's valid national identification card information.

b. Opening Investment Accounts for the Citizens of the GCC Member States

To open an investment account for a citizen of a GCC member state, the Authorized Person must obtain and verify the client's valid passport or national identification card information.

c. Opening Investment Accounts for Foreign Residents in the Kingdom

1. Foreign Residents Carrying a Residence Permit (Iqama) or Resident Identity

To open an investment account for a foreign resident who holds a residence permit (Iqama) or resident identity, the Authorized Person must obtain and verify his valid residence permit (Iqama) or resident identity information.

2. Holders of the Five Year Residency Card

To open an investment account for a holder of a five year residency card, the Authorized Person must obtain and verify the valid five year residency card information.

3. Members of the Diplomatic Missions in the Kingdom

To open an investment account for a member of a diplomatic mission in the Kingdom, the Authorized Person must obtain and verify an identification letter from the member's embassy and the member's valid diplomatic identity card information.

d. Opening Investment Accounts for Foreign Natural Persons not Residing in the Kingdom

To open an investment account for a foreign natural person not residing in the Kingdom for the purpose of investing in the permitted securities in accordance with the Capital Market Law and its Implementing Regulations and the related instructions issued by the Authority, the Authorized Person must obtain and verify the client's valid passport information.

e. Special Provisions for Opening Investment Accounts for Natural Persons

1. Opening an Investment Account for a Blind Person or a Person Unable to Read

a) When opening an investment account for a blind client or a client unable to read, the client shall be entitled to have a personal referee in attendance to explain to him the investment account opening procedures and terms and conditions stated in the investment account opening agreement. In cases where the client does not have a personal referee in attendance, an employee of the Authorized Person must explain the procedures to him, and an officer in the branch or the main offices of the Authorized Person must certify that the client was provided with all information of Know Your Customer Form and investment account opening agreement, and that terms and conditions of the investment account were read to him, and he acknowledged that he bears all responsibilities of opening that investment account.
b) The referee of the blind person or the person unable to read must be a natural person with full legal capacity who personally knows the blind person or the person unable to read intending to open an investment account; hold a valid identification document; be able to explain the investment account opening procedures to the blind person or the person unable to read; be able to read the terms and conditions of the investment account opening agreement; and provide an acknowledgement in writing of such.
c) The valid identification document information of the personal referee must be obtained and verified.
d) When an investment account is opened for a blind client or a client unable to read, such client shall not be allowed to use any services provided by telephone or electronic channels for operating the investment account until one of the Authorized Person's employees or his personal referee reads to him the terms and conditions related to such services and the Authorized Person informs him that such services are provided to him based on his will, choice, and awareness of the risks associated with using such services and the client's legal liability for all transactions executed through such services. The Authorized Person shall also obtain a written acknowledgement signed by the client indicating that he understands the above terms.
e) The Authorized Person may use the client's fingerprint or personal stamp as his personal signature in all of his transactions.
f) With the exception of any transactions carried out by telephone or electronic channels, in order for the Authorized Person to accept any instructions from a blind client or a client unable to read, the Authorized Person must obtain the client's signature on such instructions with the client's awareness and responsibility of the instructions he signs. Also, if the blind client or the client unable to read was accepted as a client with a personal referee when opening the account, the Authorized Person must obtain an acknowledgement in writing signed by a personal referee that meets the conditions stated in subparagraph (b-1) of paragraph (e) of this Article that the client is aware of the procedure's nature and that he bears liability as a personal referee.

2. Opening an Investment Account for Persons Under the Age of (18) Hijri Calendar Years:

a) An investment account for a person under the age of (18) Hijri calendar years is opened by a guardian, provided that the investment account is under the name of the client and operated by the guardian.
b) The valid identification document information of the client who is under the age of (18) Hijri calendar years and the identification document information of his guardian must be obtained and verified.
c) If the client is a Saudi citizen under the age of (15) Hijri calendar years, the family card information that shows the client's information and the valid national identification card information of his guardian must be obtained and verified, without requiring the client to provide a national identification card.
d) If the client is under the age of (18) Hijri calendar years and under legal guardianship, the Authorized Person must obtain and verify a copy of the guardian's deed issued by the competent court and comply with all its provisions.
e) If the client is a foreigner under the age of (18) Hijri calendar years and his name is added to another person's residence permit (Iqama) or resident identity, the information of the valid residence permit (Iqama) or resident identity (to which the client's name is added) must be obtained and verified, provided that the investment account is under the name of the client and opened and operated by the holder of the residence permit (Iqama) or the resident identity to which the client is added.
f) The Authorized Person must carry out customer due diligence measures in relation to the guardian, and the guardian when acting on behalf of the client under the age of (18) Hijri calendar years shall comply with all legal responsibilities applicable to such client.

3. Opening an Investment Account for an Incapacitated Person

a) An investment account for an incapacitated person is opened by his guardian, provided that the account is in the name of the client and operated by his guardian.
b) The Authorized Person must obtain and verify information of the guardian identification document and information of the identification card of the incapacitated client above the age of (18) Hijri calendar years or information of the family card if the client is below the age of (15) Hijri calendar years.
c) A copy of a final decision or a decision subject to expeditious execution issued by the competent court which illustrates that the client for whom the investment account is to be opened is considered incapacitated must be obtained and verified, and the Authorized Person must comply with all its provisions.
d) The Authorized Person must carry out customer due diligence measures in relation to the guardian, and the guardian when acting on behalf of the incapacitated client shall comply with all legal responsibilities applicable to such client.

4. Opening an Investment Account for a Person Unable to Write and Sign

The Authorized Person must open the investment account for a client unable to write and sign in the same procedures of opening an investment account for natural persons. However, the Authorized Person must take the fingerprints or personal stamp of such client as a substitute for his personal signature.

5. Opening Investment Accounts for the Interdicted Person

a) The investment account of an interdicted person is opened by his guardian, provided that the investment account is under the name of the interdicted person and operated by his guardian.
b) Information of the valid identification documents of the interdicted person and his guardian must be obtained and verified.

c) A copy of a final decision or a decision subject to expeditious execution issued by the competent court must be obtained and verified, and the Authorized Person must comply with all its relevant provisions.
d) The Authorized Person must carry out customer due diligence measures in relation to the guardian, and the guardian when acting on behalf of the interdicted person shall comply with all legal responsibilities applicable to such client.

Article 7: Instructions for Opening Investment Accounts for Legal Persons

a. Opening Investment Accounts for Saudi Companies and Companies from GCC Member States

1) To open an investment account for a Saudi company, the company must be incorporated in accordance with the Companies Law, and to open an investment account for a company from a GCC member state, the company must fall within the scope of the definition of a GCC legal person.
2) Unless the company is listed on the Exchange, the company's bylaws, shareholders assembly resolution, articles of association, or partners' resolution must provide that the company is permitted to invest in securities.
3) To open an investment account for a Saudi or GCC company, the Authorized Person may use the guidance list of documents provided in Annex (1) of these Instructions by obtaining copies of the documents and verifying them.
4) When opening an investment account for a listed company on the Exchange (excluding banks and insurance companies) or an affiliate of the listed company included in its consolidated financial statements, the Authorized Person must comply with the following additional conditions:

- The listed company's investment in securities listed on the Exchange shall be based on a Board of Directors' resolution of the listed company and the company that the investment account is to be opened for (if it is an affiliate of that company). Such resolution shall also determine the investment controls, and prior to opening the investment account, the Authorized Person must obtain and verify a copy of the resolution.
- Unless the investment of the listed company, or that of its affiliate, is for one year (in which period the company commits not to sell the security before the elapsing of one year from the time of last purchase of the security issued by the same issuer), the investment in securities must be through an investment fund or investment portfolio managed by an Authorized Person based on a management contract, which clearly states that there is a complete segregation between the listed company, its affiliates, and the investment decisions, and that the terms of contract do not conflict with such requirement. The Authorized Person must ensure that the terms of contract are in accordance with these controls prior to signing the management contract with the listed company or its affiliate.
- The Authorized Person must notify the Authority without delay of any management contract signed with any listed company or its affiliate and refer to the number of the investment account opened for such purpose and the number of the investment portfolio linked to it.

b. Opening Investment Accounts for Foreign Legal Persons
The Authorized Person may open an investment account for a foreign legal person who has no premises in the Kingdom for the purpose of investing in the permitted securities in accordance with the Capital Market Law and its Implementing Regulations and the relevant instructions issued by the Authority, including opening an investment account for a foreign legal person for the purpose of entering into a swap agreement in accordance with the Authority's instructions related to swap agreements.

c. Opening Investment Accounts for Qualified Foreign Investors
To open an investment account for a qualified foreign investor in accordance with the provisions of the Rules for Qualified Foreign Financial Institutions Investment in Listed Securities, the Authorized Person may use the guidance list of documents provided in Annex (2) of these Instructions by obtaining copies of the documents and verifying them.

d. Opening Investment Accounts for Funds Owned by a Governmental Entity

1) An Authorized Person may open an investment account for a fund of a governmental entity, provided that the fund is fully owned by a Saudi governmental entity or a governmental entity of a GCC member state.
2) The Authorized Person, when opening an investment account for the fund referred to in paragraph (1) above, must obtain copies of the following documents and verify them:

- The fund's bylaws.
- The issued resolution assigning the authorized signatories to open and operate the investment account of the fund and their valid identity documents.
- The fund's articles of association (if any) and its annexes, which clearly show the structure of the fund's capital and its management.
- Documents that show the names of members of the Board of Directors.

e. Opening Investment Accounts for Non-profit Organizations in the Kingdom:
When opening an investment account for a Non-profit Organization in the Kingdom, the Authorized Person must obtain copies of the following documents and verify them:

- The license issued by the competent authority.
- The bylaws that have an express provision permitting the Non-profit Organization to invest in securities, and if the Non-profit Organization's bylaws do not explicitly state that, the Authorized Person must obtain a letter from the Non-profit Organization licensing authority stating its approval to invest in securities.
- The Board of Directors' resolution approving the opening of the investment account and assigning the authorized signatories to operate the investment account.

f. Opening Investment Accounts for Endowments

1) When opening an investment account for an endowment in the Kingdom, the Authorized Person must obtain copies of the following documents and verify them:

- The deed of endowment and the deed of trusteeship.
- National identification card of the endowment's trustee / board of trustees.
- The resolution of the trustee or the board of trustees (if there is a board of trustees) approving the opening of the investment account and

assigning the authorized signatories to operate the investment account.

2) The deed of endowment must include a provision that permits investment in securities, or the trustee must provide a letter from the governmental authority that supervises the endowment granting its approval to invest in securities and also granting permission to the authorized signatories to operate the investment account (if the endowment's trustee or the board of trustees delegates the power to operate such account.)

g. Opening Investment Accounts for Governmental Entities
To open an investment account for a governmental entity (Saudi or from another GCC member state), the Authorized Person must obtain copies of the following documents and verify them:

- - The main documents of the governmental entity according to its administrative regulations and relevant laws.
- - The resolution of the competent person in the governmental entity to assign the authorized signatories that will open and operate the investment account, and the identification documents of such signatories.
- - The approval of the Ministry of Finance (or its equivalent in the GCC member state) to open the investment account, unless there are legal provisions issued by the competent authority that explicitly give the right to such governmental entity to invest in securities.

h. Opening Investment Accounts for International Organizations and Institutions:
To open an investment account for international organizations and institutions that have premises in the Kingdom, the Authorized Person must obtain copies of the following documents and verify them:

- The Association Agreement and/or bylaws.
- The premises agreement signed with the government of the Kingdom that permits the international organization or institution to invest in securities.
- The resolution of the competent person in accordance with the Association Agreement and/or bylaws assigning the authorized signatories to open and operate the investment account.

i. Opening Investment Accounts for Investment Funds Established in the Kingdom or in a GCC member state:
To open an investment account for an investment fund established in the Kingdom or in a GCC member state, the Authorized Person may use the guidance list of documents provided in Annex (3) of these Instructions by obtaining copies of the documents and verifying them.

Article 8: Opening Investment Accounts for Other Persons If the Authorized Person is approached by a natural or legal person for whom these Instructions do not state the procedures for opening an investment account, the Authorized Person must obtain the Authority's approval to open an investment account for that person.

16.3 PART 3: INSTRUCTIONS FOR OPERATING INVESTMENT ACCOUNTS

Article 9: Transactions on the Investment Account
a. The Authorized Person must not enable his client to buy securities unless the purchase is made from the client's investment account balance.

b. The Authorized Person, in respect of the investment account, must ensure his compliance with the provisions related to clients' money and assets stated in the Authorized Persons Regulations.

c. The Authorized Person must not accept any cash amounts from the client or from a third party for the benefit of the client for investment purposes or in exchange for a services provided by the Authorized Person, and the Authorized Person must not deliver to the client or any third party any cash amounts from the investment account.

Article 10: Opening and Operating the Investment Account by Power of Attorney
a. The Authorized Person shall accept a power of attorney to open or operate an investment account for his client whenever the following conditions are met:

1) The power of attorney is issued by the Notary Public, a person licensed as a notary, or out of the Kingdom and certified by the Saudi Embassy or Consulate at the issuing country and the Ministry of Foreign Affairs in the Kingdom.

2) The attorney-in-fact is a relative of the client as a parent, son, daughter, spouse, brother, or sister or appointed by heirs to liquidate the investment account of the deceased and close it.

3) The power of attorney must be issued by the client or the guardian if the client is under the age of (18) Hijri calendar years, and any power of attorney issued by the attorney-in-fact on behalf of the client shall not be accepted.

b. The Authorized Person must verify the validity of the power of attorney and that it explicitly states the powers given to the attorney-in-fact, whether it is opening an investment account, operating it, performing transfers, purchasing or selling securities, or closing the investment account, and the Authorized Person must comply with the provisions of the power of attorney.

c. The Authorized Person shall not accept any power of attorney except for that set out in paragraph (a) of this Article.

Article 11: Appointment of Court-Appointed Receiver over the Investment Account When a court-appointed receiver is appointed over an investment account, the Authorized Person must comply with the following:
a. The Authorized Person, before permitting a judicial receiver to have access to an investment account, must obtain and verify a copy of a final decision or a decision subject to expeditious execution issued by the competent judicial authority that includes the appointment of judicial receiver and its authorities, and also obtain and verify information of the judicial receiver's valid national identification card if he is a natural person, or a copy of the commercial register of the judicial receiver and the information of the national identification card of its representative if it is a legal person.
b. The investment account information must show that the investment account is under judicial receivership.
c. Only the court-appointed receiver shall have the authority to operate the investment account and sign for its transactions, unless the judicial authority's decision provides otherwise.

Article 12: Closing the Investment Account
a. If a client requests to close his investment account, he must submit a written request to the Authorized Person.

b. Without prejudice to paragraphs (c) and (d) of this Article, the Authorized Person must accept the client's request to close his investment account and notify him of such, unless the investment account is attached, or the client has financial obligations owing to the Authorized Person.
c. The Authorized Persons must permit their Saudi and GCC clients to close their frozen investment accounts without updating their information, provided that the investment account is not subject to attachment, there are no restrictions or balance on the account, any securities in the investment portfolios linked to it, or any claims in relation to it.
d. Unless the Authority instructs otherwise, the Authorized Person must not permit the foreign resident in the Kingdom to close his investment accounts if his residence permits (Iqama) or resident identity is expired, until such client provides a renewed residence permit (Iqama) or resident identity or a final exit visa.
e. After the Authorized Person ensures that the investment account of the foreign resident in the Kingdom is not subject to attachment or under any restrictions or claims, the Authorized Person, after (12) months of the account being frozen, must liquidate the securities in any investment portfolio linked to that account and transfer its sale proceeds to the client and then close the investment account.
f. If five years elapse from the date of freezing the investment account without the client providing the required updated information, and the investment account is not subject to attachment, has no securities linked to it and is not under any restrictions or claims, the Authorized Person may transfer the available balance on the investment account to a bank account under the client's name, close the investment portfolios linked to the investment account and the client account opened by the Authorized Person (unless it is linked to more than one investment account), and then close the investment account.
g. If a year elapses without any balance on the investment account of the client and without any securities in any investment portfolio linked to it, and if such account is not subject to attachment or under any restrictions or claims, the Authorized Person may close the investment account after (30) days from notifying the client of such.

16.4 PART 4: REGULATORY AND SUPERVISORY INSTRUCTIONS

Article 13: Electronic Record For the purpose of establishing a unified electronic database for investment accounts, the Authorized Person that holds investment accounts for clients must create an electronic record to link the investment account with all the information set out in the documents provided by the client for opening the investment account.

Article 14: Updating the Investment Accounts Information

a. The Authorized Person shall require his clients to update the information that were provided when opening the investment account as and when there are any changes to the original information provided or at least once every three years from the date of opening the investment account or date of last update, and the Authorized Persons must maintain policies and procedures to fulfill this requirement.
b. The Authorized Person must inform his clients at least ninety calendar days in advance of the expiry date that the original documents are going to expire shortly.
c. Ninety calendar days prior to the Saudi minor client reaching the age of (15) Hijri Calendar years, the Authorized Person must request the guardian to update the information of the client's investment account, and obtain and verify the client's national identification card information.
d. Ninety calendar days prior to the Saudi minor client reaching the age of (18) Hijri Calendar years, the Authorized Person must notify the guardian of the necessity of updating the information of the client's investment account, obtain and verify the client's national identification card information, and sign a new investment account opening agreement with the client as soon as he becomes (18) Hijri Calendar years' old, provided that it contains all the information mentioned in Article (4) of these Instructions.

Article 15: Freezing the Investment Accounts

a. The Authorized Person must freeze all the investment accounts of the client at the expiration date of the documents provided when opening the investment account if the client has not updated them or if the client has not updated his investment accounts information upon the Authorized Person's request in accordance with paragraph (a) of Article 14 of these Instructions.
b. The Authorized Person must notify his clients of the date of freezing the investment account at least one month prior to the freezing date. The Authorized Person must also maintain policies and procedures to fulfill this requirement and keep records of its applications.
c. If the documents provided when opening the investment account for the legal person do not include a specific expiration of the validity date, the Authorized Person must freeze such investment account after the elapsing of three years from the date of opening the investment account or the date of the last update of the investment account, until the client updates the account's information.
d. The Authorized Person must monitor the validity of identification documents for the authorized signatories of the legal persons as well as the persons who provided information of their identification documents upon opening the investment account, and the Authorized Person must freeze their authority to operate the investment account until they provide renewed identification documents information.

Article 16: Instruction on the Attachment of Investment Accounts and Disclosure of their Information

a. Provisional Attachment of the Investment Account and Disclosure of its Information Upon the Authority's Request

1) Subject to the provisions of Article (25) of the Capital Market Law and Article (29) of the Authorized Persons Regulations, the Authorized Person is not permitted to provisionally attach or disclose the information of any investment account, unless requested by the Authority or a competent judicial authority through the Authority.
2) When the Authorized Person receives a request from the Authority to disclose any information related to an investment account of any of its clients, the Authorized Person must provide the Authority with the requested information in a maximum period of (3) business days, unless the Authority specifies otherwise.
3) Unless the Authority's request is specific, the Authorized Person must disclose information of all of the

client's investment accounts.

4) When the Authorized Person receives a request from the Authority to disclose an investment account statement related to any of its clients, the Authorized Person must provide the Authority with the requested investment account statement, containing, as a minimum, the required information stipulated in Annex (4) of these Instructions.

5) When the Authorized Person provisionally attaches the investment accounts of a certain client at the Authority's request, the Authorized Person must not allow that client to take any action in relation to the balances of any attached investment accounts, unless the Authority's request was to provisionally attach a specific amount, then the client shall be allowed to take action in respect of any amount exceeding the specified amount.

6) When the Authorized Person receives a request from the Authority to provisionally attach the investment accounts of a client, the Authorized Person must attach the investment account and immediately provide the Authority with information of the attached investment accounts.

7) When an investment account is provisionally attached based on subparagraph (a-5) of this Article, the Authorized Person must stop all money transfer and withdrawal transactions and must not allow the utilization of the investment account balance in any form.

8) The Authorized Person must not remove the provisional attachment of any investment account that was attached based on subparagraph (a-5) of this Article until the Authorized Person receives a request from the Authority.

b. Blocking the Investment Account Upon the Client's Bankruptcy, Insolvency, or Loss of Legal Competence

1) If the Authorized Person receives a notification, enclosing official documents as evidence, regarding the client's insolvency, bankruptcy, or loss of legal competence, the Authorized Person must block all the investment accounts of that client without delay.

2) When an investment account is blocked based on subparagraph (b-1) of this Article, the Authorized Person must stop all money transfer and withdrawal transactions and must not allow the utilization of the investment account balance in any form.

3) The Authorized Person must not unblock the investment account that was blocked based on subparagraph (b-1) of paragraph (b) of this Article until the Authorized Person receives a request from the Authority.

c. Disclosing the Investment Account information, Blocking it, and Liquidating it Upon the Client's Being Deceased

1) If the Authorized Person is officially notified or becomes aware that the client is deceased, the Authorized Person must block all of the client's investment accounts without delay.

2) When any person requests to be provided with information of the investment accounts of the deceased client, the Authorized Person must provide him in writing with detailed and clear information of the investment accounts of the deceased client after verifying the identity of that person and ensuring that he is one of the heirs or attorney-in-fact of one of them. The Authorized Person must also obtain and verify the valid identification document information of that person, a copy of the power of attorney if that person was an attorney-in-fact of the heirs or one of them, a copy of the death certificate of the deceased client, and a copy of the determination of heirs.

3) The Authorized Person, after freezing the investment account of the deceased client, must not carry out any transactions from such account except for liquidating the investment account for the benefit of the heirs.

4) The Authorized Person must not liquidate the investment account for the benefit of the heirs unless all heirs, guardians of the minor heirs, or their attorneys-in-fact are present and provide copies of the heirs determination deed, the guardianship deed for the minor heirs (if there is minor heirs) and power of attorney (if any) and verify them. The Authorized Person must also obtain and verify the identification document of the guardian, attorney-in-fact, and heirs who have no guardian or attorney-in-fact, and if there is a judicial deed for the distribution of the inheritance issued by the competent court, the Authorized Person must obtain a copy of the deed and verify it.

5) If the heirs of the deceased client are non-resident foreigners, the Authorized Person must not liquidate the investment accounts of the deceased client until the requirements aforementioned in sub-paragraph (4) are fulfilled, and ensure, if the documents were issued outside the Kingdom, that they are authenticated by the Saudi Embassy or Consulate at the issuing country and the Ministry of Foreign Affairs in the Kingdom.

6) After the investment account of the deceased client and all investment portfolios linked to it are liquidated, the Authorized Person must close the investments portfolios linked to the investment account and the client account opened by the Authorized Person, then close the client's investment account.

7) After the Authorized Person completes, upon the Authority's instructions, the liquidation of the investment account of the deceased client and all of the investment portfolio linked to it, the Authorized Person must notify the Authority, immediately, if he receives any dividends or bonus shares belonging to that client.

16.5 PART 5: PUBLICATION AND ENTRY INTO FORCE

Article 17: Publication and Entry into Force
These Instructions shall be effective in accordance with its approval resolution.

16.6 Annex 1: Guidance List of Documents for Opening an Investment Account for Saudi Companies or Companies from GCC Member States

- The commercial register issued by the competent authority.
- The company's articles of association, bylaws, and their annexes and amendments.
- A list of the Board of Directors and senior managers' names.
- The Board of Directors' or partners' resolution approving the opening of the investment account and assigning authorized signatories to operate the investment account.
- A list of authorized signatories to operate the investment account in accordance with the company's commercial regis-

ter, articles of association, bylaws and the Board of Directors' resolution.
- Any licenses issued for the company by any government entity to conduct certain activities.

16.7 Annex 2: Guidance List of Documents for Opening an Investment Account for Qualified Foreign Investors

- The license or the commercial register for the foreign investor obtained from the relevant authority in the county of establishment.
- The by-laws and its annexes, or a copy of the article of association and its annexes.
- A list of the names of the legal entity's managers and authorized signatories on behalf of the foreign investor in regard to the account.
- A delegation from the Board of Directors specifying names of authorized signatories in relation to the account.

16.8 Annex 3: Guidance List of Documents for Opening an Investment Account for Investment Funds Established in the Kingdom or GCC Member States

- The commercial register of the fund manager.
- The Bylaws or Articles of Association of the fund manager and any amendments to them.
- The authorization issued by the Authority or the competent authority in the GCC member state for the fund manager to conduct managing activities and the commencement letter.
- The notification issued by the Authority or the competent authority in GCC member states approving the establishment of the investment fund and offering its units.
- The investment fund's Terms and Conditions and any amendments to them.
- The issued resolution approving the opening of the investment account and assigning the authorized signatories to operate the investment account.

16.9 Annex 4: Required Information in the Investment Account Statement

The investment account statement must be printed, at the request of the Authority to be disclosed, in Arabic and on the official letter head of the Authorized Person, and shall contain at minimum the following information:

1. Formal information:
    - The Authorized Person's stamp on the investment account statement.
    - The date and time of printing the investment account statement.
    - The beginning and the end dates of the period of the investment account statement in the Hijri and Gregorian dates.
    - Number of the printed pages and its total number.
2. Basic information:
    - For a natural person: the client's full name and identity number as per the identification document, address and contact information.
    - For a legal person: the client's full name as per the proof of incorporation, commercial register number (if any), address and contact information.
    - The full name of the person authorized to operate the investment account and his identity number as per the identification document (if any).
    - The client's investment account number.
    - The client's Center Account number at the depository center.
    - The investment account status – including but not limited to: active, frozen, pledged, closed.
3. Investment Account Statement Information:

• The balance available on the investment account and its currency.

• The transactions log, provided that it includes as minimum: all cash transfers to and from the investment account, its time, date and source, a brief and clear description of the transaction and all transactions executed on securities, indicating the date, time, type, the name of the issuer and its symbol, the amount of securities, the price, the value of the transaction, the commission, the total value, and the executed channel. In addition, the accumulated balance, the transaction executor, all actions performed on shares as split and reverse split of shares, bonus shares, and priority rights shares.

17 Instructions for Investment Funds Announcements

Issued by the Board of the Capital Market Authority Pursuant to its Resolution Number 4-01-2018 dated 14/04/1439H (01/01/2018G)

These Instructions were issued pursuant to the Capital Market Authority Board Resolution No. 4-01-2018 dated 14/04/1439H (01/01/2018) regarding the approval of the Instructions for Investment Funds Announcements.

Table of Contents

General Instructions:

Chapter 1: Public Investment Funds Announcements

1. Announcement for Conflict of Interest
2. Announcement for Appointing a Replacement Custodian by the Fund Manager
3. Announcement for the Public Fund's Distributions.
4. Announcement for the Termination and Liquidation of Public Fund
5. Announcement for a Membership Change in the Public Fund's Board of Directors.
6. Announcement for the Details of Fundamental Changes to a Public Fund
7. Announcement for the Details of Significant Changes to a Public Fund
8. Announcement for the Details of Notifiable Changes to a Public Fund
9. Announcement for Extending the Initial Public Offer Period For a Public Fund
10. Announcement for the Results of the Initial Public Offer for a Public Fund
11. Announcement for the Suspension of Subscription or Redemption of a Public Fund's Units
12. Announcement for the End of Suspension of Subscription or Redemption of a Public Fund's Units
13. Announcement for an Incorrect Valuation or Pricing of a Public Fund's Units
14. Announcement for the Call for a Meeting of the Public Fund's Unitholders

14.1 Announcement for the Call for a Meeting of the Public Fund's Unitholders.

14.2 Announcement for the Call for the Second Meeting of the Public Fund's Unitholders for Not Meeting the Quorum at the First Meeting

15. Announcement for the Results of Unitholders Meeting
16. Announcement for Not Convening the Unitholders Meeting
17. Announcement for the Details of Investment Funds Merger
18. Announcement for Providing the Public with the Fund's Interim Reports, Including The Interim Audited Financial Statements
19. Announcement for Providing the Public with the Annual Reports, Including the Annual Audited Financial Statements
20. Announcement for Updating the Terms and Conditions of the Public Fund.
21. Announcement for Updating the Information Memorandum / Key Fact Sheet of the Public Fund
22. Corrective Announcement
23. Addendum Announcement
24. Corrective Announcement for Fund's Information on the Fund Manager's Website and Exchange's Website

Chapter 2: Announcement of Real Estate Investment Traded Funds

1. Announcement for Appointing a Replacement Custodian by the Fund Manager
2. Announcement of the Fund Distributions
3. Announcement for the Termination of the Fund's Term and Liquidation Period
4. Announcement for a Membership Change in the Fund's Board of Directors
5. Announcement for the Call for a Meeting of the Fund's Unitholders

5.1 Announcement for the Call for a Meeting of the Fund's Unitholders.

5.2 Announcement for the Call for the Second Meeting of the Fund's Unitholders for Not Meeting the Quorum at the First Meeting

6. Announcement for the Results of Unitholders Meeting
7. Announcement for Non-Convention the Unitholders Meeting
8. Announcement for Providing the Public with the Interim Financial Reports
9. Announcement for Providing the Public with the Annual Financial Reports
10. Announcement for the Occurrence of a Specific Event
11. Announcement for the Occurrence of a Material Development
12. Announcement for Updating the Fund's Terms and Conditions
13. Announcement for the Details of the Material Changes to the Fund's Terms and Conditions
14. Corrective Announcement
15. Addendum Announcement

17.1 General Instructions:

Without prejudice to the relevant Articles of the Capital Market Law, the Investment Funds Regulations, the Real Estate Investment Funds Regulations and the Instructions for Real Estate Investment Traded Funds, the Fund Manager must comply with these Instructions and announce when any of the cases mentioned in Chapters 1 and 2 of these Instructions occur. The announcement must be made available on the Exchange's website/the Fund Manager's website (as described in each case) according to the following rules:

1- The Announcement must be in Arabic language and shall be in compliance with the Arabic language sound rules.

2- If the Fund Manager wishes to publish an announcement in English language, the text must be identical to the Arabic language version. The Fund Manager shall be responsible for ensuring that the Arabic and English version are identical, and in case of any conflict between the texts, the Arabic text shall prevail.

3- The Fund Manager must comply with announcements forms set forth in these Instructions.

4- The announcement shall not be published during the trading times of the Saudi Stock Exchange.

5- The title and content of the announcement must be clear and reflect what is intended to be announced.
6- The name of the fund approved by the Authority must be used.
7- After the Fund Manager makes the announcement, the Fund Manager must update all information of the fund related to the announcement on The Exchange's website.
8- In addition to the provisions of the general instructions abovementioned, the public investment funds are subject to Chapter 1 of these Instructions, and the Real Estate Investment Traded Funds are subject to Chapter 2 of these Instructions.

Chapter 1: Public Investment Funds Announcements

1. Announcement for Conflict of Interest

a) Announcement Website:
- The Fund Manager's website.
- The Exchange's website.
b) The announcement title must be as follows:
"(The Fund Manager's Name) announces a conflict of interest in (The Fund's Name)".
c) The Detailed Announcement:
"(The Fund Manager's Name) announces a conflict of interest in (The Fund's Name) which is as follows: (state the details of conflict of interest approved or endorsed by the board of directors of the relevant fund)".

2. Announcement for Appointing a Replacement Custodian by the Fund Manager

a) Announcement Website:
- The Fund Manager's website.
- The Exchange's website.
b) The announcement title must be as follows:
"(The Fund Manager's Name) announces the appointment of (Name of the replacement custodian) as a Custodian for (The Fund's Name)".
c) The Detailed Announcement:
"(The Fund Manager's Name) announces the appointment of (Name of the replacement custodian) as a Custodian for (The Fund's Name) effective as of the date of (day) dated (00/00/0000H.) corresponding to (00/00/0000G.)".

3. Announcement for the Public Fund's Distributions

a) Announcement Website:
- The Fund Manager's website.
- The Exchange's website
b) The announcement title must be as follows:
"(The Fund Manager's Name) announces the distribution of dividends to the unitholders of (The Fund's Name)".
c) The Detailed Announcement:
"(The Fund Manager's Name) announces the distribution of (cash dividends / investment units) to the unitholders of (The Fund's Name) for (the dividends maturity period) as follows:
1. Total distributed dividends ...... (Currency).
2. Cash distributions will be made on the basis of ...... (Number of units) outstanding units.
3. The amount of dividends distributed is ...... (Currency) for each unit, and its percentage to the initial price of the unit is ......%.
4. The distribution ratio is ... % of the net asset value as of the date of (day) dated (00/00/0000H.) corresponding to (00/00/0000G.).
5. The cash distributions entitlement will be for unitholders as per the unitholders register on the end of (day) dated (00/00/0000H.) corresponding to (00/00/0000G.).
6. The distributions will be paid within (number of days). The Fund Manager would like to remind the unitholders to update their bank information to ensure the direct deposit of their due distributions".

4. Announcement for the Termination and Liquidation of Public Fund

a) Announcement Website:
- The Fund Manager's website.
- The Exchange's website.
b) The announcement title must be as follows:
"(The Fund Manager's Name) announces the term termination and the liquidation period for (The Fund's Name)".
c) The Detailed Announcement:
"(The Fund Manager's Name) announces the term termination of (The Fund's Name) on (date of term termination of the Fund). The fund will be liquidated and the investment amounts will be distributed to unitholders within (period - week\month) from the date of fund's termination. ".

5. Announcement for a Membership Change in the Public Fund's Board of Directors.

a) Announcement Websites:
- The Fund Manager's website.
- The Exchange's website.
b) The announcement title must be as follows:
"(The Fund Manager's Name) announces a change in the membership of the (The Fund's Name) Board of Directors".
c) The Detailed Announcement:
"(The Fund Manager's Name) announces a change in the membership of the (the Fund's Name) Board of Directors, due to the (resignation\ removal\ appointment\death) of a member of the Board of Directors, (member name) (membership status: independent\ dependent) commencing from (00/00/0000H.) corresponding to (00/00/0000G.) the members of the Board of Directors shall become after the change as follows:
1- (Name of the member) (membership status: independent\ dependent)
2- (Name of the member) (membership status: independent\ dependent)
3- (Name of the member) (membership status: independent\ dependent)"

6. Announcement for the Details of Fundamental Changes to a Public Fund

a) Announcement Website:
- The Fund Manager's website.
- The Exchange's website.
b) The announcement title must be as follows:
"(The Fund Manager's Name) announces a fundamental change in (The Fund's Name)".
c) The Detailed Announcement:
"(The Fund Manager's Name) announces the approval of the unitholders and the Capital Market Authority on a fundamental change in (The Fund's Name), and such changes will become effective on (00/00/0000H.) corresponding to (00/00/0000G.)".
Details of the fundamental change are: (............................)
In the event where the fundamental change is for an open-ended public fund that imposes redemption fees, the following text must be added:

Unitholders have the right to redeem their units before any fundamental change is effective; without incurring any redemption fees".

7. Announcement for the Details of Significant Changes to a Public Fund

a) Announcement Website:
- The Fund Manager's website.
- The Exchange's website.
b) The announcement title must be as follows:
"(The Fund Manager's Name) announces significant changes to (The Fund's Name)".
c) The Detailed Announcement:
"(For an open-ended public fund: (The Fund Manager's Name) announces significant changes to (The Fund's Name), and such changes will become effective on (00/00/0000H.) corresponding to (00/00/0000G.)".
Details of the significant change are: (•). The unitholders have the right to redeem their units before any significant change is effective without incurring any redemption fees (if any).
"(For a closed-ended public fund: "(The Fund Manager's Name) announces the approval of the unitholders on a significant change to (The Fund's Name), and such changes will become effective on (00/00/0000H.) corresponding to (00/00/0000G.).
Details of the significant change are: [•]".

8. Announcement for the Details of Notifiable Changes to a Public Fund

a) Announcement Website:
- The Fund Manager's website.
- The Exchange's website.
b) The announcement title must be as follows:
"(The Fund Manager's Name) announces the details of notifiable change to (The Fund's Name)".
c) The Detailed Announcement:
"For an open-ended public fund: "(The Fund Manager's Name) announces a notifiable change to (The Fund's Name), such change will become effective on (00/00/0000H.) corresponding to (00/00/0000G.)".
Details of the notifiable change are: (..................)".
"For a closed-ended public fund: "(The Fund Manager's Name) announces the approval of the Fund's Board of Directors on a notifiable change to (The Fund's Name), such change will become effective on (00/00/0000H) corresponding to (00/00/0000G)".
Details of the notifiable change are: [•]".

9. Announcement for Extending the Initial Public Offer Period for a Public Fund

a) Announcement Website:
- The Fund Manager's website.
b) The announcement title must be as follows:
"(The Fund Manager's Name) announces the extension of the initial public offer period for (The Fund's Name)".
c) The Detailed Announcement:
"(The Fund Manager's Name) announces obtaining the approval of the Capital Market Authority to extend the period of the initial public offer of (The Fund's Name), as the initial public offer has commenced on (day) dated (00/00/0000H.) corresponding to (00/00/0000G.), and will be extended until (00/00/0000H.) corresponding to (00/00/0000G.)".

10. Announcement for the Results of the Initial Public Offer for a Public Fund

a) Announcement Website:
- The Fund Manager's website.
b) The announcement title must be as follows:
"(The Fund Manager's Name) announces the results of the initial public offer for (The Fund's Name)".
c) The Detailed Announcement:
"(The Fund Manager's Name) announces that the initial public offer period for (The Fund's Name) has ended as of (the date of the end of the initial public offer period: (day) dated (00/00/0000H.) corresponding to (00/00/0000G.). Thus, the Fund's operation date shall be: (00/00/0000H.) corresponding to (00/00/0000G.), as the amounts raised for the Fund during the period of the initial public offer has reached (the amount) Saudi Riyal".

11. Announcement for the Suspension of Subscription or Redemption of a Public Fund's Units

a) Announcement Website:
- The Fund Manager's website.
- The Exchange's website.
b) The announcement title must be as follows:
"(The Fund Manager's Name) announces the suspension of subscription or redemption of units for (The Fund's Name)".
c) The Detailed Announcement:
"(The Fund Manager's Name) announces the suspension of subscription or redemption of units for (The Fund's Name), as of (date of suspension of subscription or redemption the Fund units: (day) dated (00/00/0000H.) corresponding to (00/00/0000G.). (The reason for suspension must be stated)".

12. Announcement for the End of Suspension of Subscription or Redemption of a Public Fund's Units

a) Announcement Website:
- The Fund Manager's website.
- The Exchange's website.
b) The announcement title must be as follows:
"(The Fund Manager's Name) announces the end of suspension of subscription or redemption of units for (The Fund's Name)".
c) The Detailed Announcement:
"Following the announcement regarding the suspension of subscription or redemption of units for (The Fund's Name) published on (00/00/0000H.) corresponding to (00/00/0000G.), (The Fund Manager's Name) announces the end of suspension of subscription or redemption of units for (The Fund's Name), as of (date of the end of suspension for the subscription or redemption of the fund's units): (day) dated (00/00/0000H.) corresponding to (00/00/0000G.). (The reason for ending the suspension must be stated)".

13. Announcement for an Incorrect Valuation or Pricing of a Public Fund's Units

a) Announcement Website:
- The Fund Manager's website.
- The Exchange's website.
b) The announcement title must be as follows:
"(The Fund Manager's Name) announces an incorrect valuation or pricing of units for (The Fund's Name)".
c) The Detailed Announcement:
"(The Fund Manager's Name) announces the incorrect valuation or pricing of units for (The Fund's Name) during

the period (period (duration) of incorrect valuation/pricing). The following is the total assets of the fund and the unit price after correction:
- Total assets (•) Saudi Riyal.
- Unit price (•) Saudi Riyal.
- Error percentage in the unit price (•) %
- Date of publishing the incorrect valuation or pricing (00/00/0000H.) corresponding to (00/00/0000G.).
All affected unitholders will be compensated (including former unitholders) for all valuation and pricing errors without delay.

14. Announcement for the Call for a Meeting of the Public Fund's Unitholders.
a) Announcement websites:
- The Fund Manager's website.
- The Exchange's website.
b) The Announcement Title Must be as follows:
"(The Fund Manager's Name) announces the call for a meeting of (The Fund's Name) unitholders".
c) The Detailed announcement:
"(The Fund Manager's Name) invites (The Fund's Name) unitholders to attend unitholders meeting, which will take place in (meeting venue) at (meeting time), on (00/00/0000H.) corresponding to (00/00/0000G.) to discuss the following agenda: (suggested decisions)".

14.2 Announcement for the Call for a Meeting of the Public Fund's Unitholders.

a) Announcement Websites:
- The Fund Manager's website.
- The Exchange's website.
b) The announcement title must be as follows:
"(The Fund Manager's Name) announces the call for the second meeting of (The Fund's Name) unitholders".
c) The Detailed announcement:
"(The Fund Manager's Name) invites the (The fund's Name) unitholders to attend the second unitholders meeting, which will take place at (meeting venue) at (meeting time), on (00/00/0000H.) corresponding to (00/00/0000G.) to discuss the following agenda: (suggested decisions)".

15. Announcement for the Results of Unitholders Meeting
a) Announcement Websites:
- The Fund Manager's website.
- The Exchange's website.
b) The announcement title must be as follows:
"(The Fund Manager's Name) announces the results of (The Fund's Name) unitholders meeting".
c) The Detailed Announcement:
"(The Fund Manager's Name) announces the results of (The Fund's Name) unitholders meeting held on (00/00/0000H.) corresponding to (00/00/0000G.) as follows: (state the meeting results)".

16. Announcement for Not Convening the Unitholders Meeting
a) Announcement Websites:
- The Fund Manager's website.
- The Exchange's website.
b) The announcement title must be as follows:
"(The Fund Manager's Name) announces the non-convention of (The Fund's Name) unitholders meeting".
c) The Detailed Announcement:
"(The Fund Manager's Name) announces the non-convention of (The Fund's Name) unitholders meeting, which was scheduled on (00/00/0000H.) corresponding to (00/00/0000G.) due to (state the reasons for not convening the meeting)".

17. Announcement for the Details of Investment Funds Merger
a) Announcement Website:
- The Fund Manager's website.
- The Exchange's website in regards of public funds
b) The announcement title must be as follows:
"(The Fund Manager's Name) announces the approval of the unitholders and the Capital Market Authority on merging the following funds: (The Fund's Name) and (The Fund's Name)".
c) The Detailed Announcement:
"(The Fund Manager's Name) announces the approval of the unitholders and the Capital Market Authority on merging the following funds: (The Fund's Name) and (The Fund's Name)". The details of the merger are: (........................)".

18. Announcement for Providing the Public with the Fund's Interim Reports, Including the Interim Audited Financial Statements
a) Announcement Website:
- The Fund Manager's website.
- The Exchange's website.
b) The announcement title must be as follows:
"(The Fund Manager's Name) announces that the (The Fund's Name)'s interim reports, including the interim audited financial statements, for the period ended on 00/00/0000 are available to the public".
c) The Detailed Announcement:
"(The Fund Manager's Name) announces the availability of the interim financial reports. The following is a summary of the interim financial results for the period ended on 00/00/0000.
- Net assets on the end of period of (•) (currency).
- Total expenses and fees for the period (•) (currency).
- Net profit \ (loss) for the period of (•) (currency).
- Number of outstanding units at the end of period (•) units.
- Net unit value (by currency).
- Revenue of the period (•)%
Must insert a link on the Exchange and the Fund Manager's website that refers to the Fund's interim reports".

19. Announcement for Providing the Public with the Annual Reports, Including the Annual Audited Financial Statements
a) Announcement Website:
- The Fund Manager's website
- The Exchange's website.
b) The announcement title must be as follows:
"(The Fund Manager's Name) announces that (The Fund's Name)'s annual reports, including the annual audited financial results, for the period ended on 00/00/0000 are available to the public".
c) The Detailed Announcement:
"(The Fund Manager's Name) announces that (The Fund's Name)'s annual audited results are available to the public. The following is a summary of the annual financial results for the period ended on 00/00/0000.
- Net assets on the end of period of (....) (currency).
- Total expenses and fees for the period (....) (currency).

- Net profit (loss) for the period of (...) (currency).
- Number of outstanding units in the end of period (....) units.
- Net unit value.
- Revenue of the period (•)%.
Must insert a link on the Exchange and The Fund Manager's website that refers to the Fund's annual reports".

20. Announcement for Updating the Terms and Conditions of the Public Fund

a) Announcement Website:
- The Fund Manager's website.
- The Exchange's website.
b) The announcement title must be as follows:
"(The Fund Manager's Name) announces an update to the terms and conditions of (The Fund's Name)".
c) The Detailed Announcement:
"(The Fund Manager's Name) announces an update to the terms and conditions of (The Fund's Name) staring from 00/00/0000 corresponding to 00/00/0000 as the updated terms and conditions can be viewed via the following link: (insert a link to the terms and conditions)".

21. Announcement for Updating the Information Memorandum\ Key Fact Sheet of the Public Fund

a) Announcement Website:
- The Fund Manager's website.
- The Exchange's website.
b) The Announcement Title must be as follows:
"(The Fund Manager's Name) announces the update of the Information Memorandum\ Key Fact Sheet of (The Fund's Name)".
c) The Detailed Announcement:
"(The Fund Manager's Name) announces the update of the Information Memorandum / Key Fact Sheet of (The Fund's Name), starting from (00/00/0000H.) corresponding to (00/00/0000G.) The updated Information Memorandum / Key Fact Sheet can be viewed via the following link: (insert a link to the Information Memorandum\ Key Fact Sheet"

22. Corrective Announcement

a) Announcement Websites:
- The Fund Manager's website
- The Exchange's website (as applicable).
b) The announcement title must be as follows:
" Corrective announcement from the fund manager of (The Fund's Name) regarding (announcement subject) "
c) The detailed Announcement must contain the following elements:
1- Date of the pervious announcement on the Saudi Stock Exchange (Tadawul)'s website and the Fund Manager's website (as applicable).
2- The misstatement on the pervious announcement.
3- Correction of the error.
4- The resulted impact from the misstatement (if any).
d) The Detailed Announcement:
"A corrective announcement for the (The Fund Manager's Name)'s announcement published on 00/00/0000G. The Fund Manager wishes to clarify (state the correction details)".

23. Addendum Announcement

a) Announcement Websites:
- The Fund Manager's website
- The Exchange's website (as applicable).
b) The announcement title must be as follows:
"(The Fund Manager's Name) announces an addendum announcement regarding (announcement subject)".
c) The detailed announcement must contain the following elements:
1- Date of the pervious announcement on the Saudi Stock Exchange (Tadawul)'s website and the Fund Manager's website (as applicable).
2- Subject of change.
3- The resulted impact from the change (if any).
d) The Announcement Form:
"An addendum announcement for the (The Fund Manager's Name)'s announcement published on 00/00/0000G. (The Fund Manager's Name) wishes to clarify (state the details)".

24. Corrective Announcement for Fund's Information on the Fund Manager's Website and Exchange's Website "Note: This announcement is intended to correct the Fund's information required to be disclosed by the Fund Manager on its website and The Exchange's website. For example, without limitation, the net asset value of each unit, the requirements stated in paragraph (h) of Article (71), and the financial statements".
a) Announcement Websites:
- The Fund Manager's website.
- The Exchange's website (as applicable).
b) The announcement title must be as follows:
"(The Fund Manager's Name) announces a corrective announcement for correcting the information relating to (state the information to be corrected)".
c) The detailed announcement must contain the following elements:
1- Date of the pervious announcement on the Saudi Stock Exchange (Tadawul)'s website and the Fund Manager's website (as applicable).
2- The misstatement on the pervious announcement.
3- Correction of the error.
4- The resulted impact from the misstatement (if any).
d) The Detailed Announcement:
"(The Fund Manager's Name) announces a correction in the information of (The Fund's Name) (state the elements stipulated in paragraph (c) mentioned above)".

Chapter 2: Announcement of Real Estate Investment Traded Funds

1. Announcement for Appointing a Replacement Custodian by the Fund Manager

a) Announcement Websites:
- The Fund Manager's website.
- The Exchange's website.
b) The announcement title must be as follows:
"(The Fund Manager's Name) announces the appointment of (the Name of the replacement custodian) as a Custodian of (The Fund's Name)".
c) The Detailed Announcement:
"(The Fund Manager's Name) announces the appointment of (the Name of the replacement custodian) as a Custodian of (The Fund's Name), commencing from: (day) (00/00/0000H.) corresponding to (00/00/0000G.)".

2. Announcement of the Fund Distributions

a) Announcement Websites:
- The Fund Manager's website
- The Exchange's website.

b) The announcement title must be as follows:
"(The Fund Manager's Name) announces the distribution of dividends to (the Fund's Name)'s unitholders".
c) The Detailed Announcement:
"(The Fund Manager's Name) announces the distribution of (cash dividends / investment units) to the unitholders of (The Fund's Name) for (the dividends maturity period) as follows:
1. Total distributed dividends ...... (Saudi Riyal).
2. Cash distributions will be made on the basis of ...... (Number of units) outstanding units.
3. The amount of dividends distributed is [*](Saudi Riyal) for each unit, and its percentage to the initial price of the unit is [*]%.
4. The distribution ratio is [*]% of the net asset value as of the date of (day) dated (00/00/0000H.) corresponding to (00/00/0000G.).
5. The cash distributions entitlement will be for unitholders as per the unitholders register on the end of (day) dated (00/00/0000H.) corresponding to (00/00/0000G.).
6. The distributions will be paid within (number of days). The Fund Manager would like to remind the unitholders to update their bank information to ensure the direct deposit of their due distributions".

3. Announcement for the Termination of the Fund's Term and Liquidation Period
a) Announcement Websites:
- The Fund Manager's website.
- The Exchange's website.
b) The announcement title must be as follows:
"(The Fund Manager's Name) announces the term termination and liquidation period for (of The Fund's Name)".
c) The Detailed Announcement:
"(The Fund Manager's Name) announces the term termination of (The Fund's Name) on (date of term expiration of the Fund). The Fund will be liquidated and the investment amounts will be distributed to unitholders within (period: week\month - to distribute the investment amounts to the unitholders) from the date of termination of the Fund".

4. Announcement for a Membership Change in the Fund's Board of Directors
a) Announcement Websites:
- The Fund Manager's website.
- The Exchange's website.
b) The announcement title must be as follows:
"(The Fund Manager's Name) announces the change of the membership of (the Fund's Name)'s Board of Director".
c) The Detailed Announcement:
"(The Fund Manager's Name) announces a change to the membership of (The Fund's Name)'s Board of Director, due to the (resignation\ removal\ appointment\death) of the Board of Directors' member, (the member name) (membership status: independent\ dependent) starting from (00/00/0000H.) corresponding to (00/00/0000G.) the members of the Board of Directors shall become after the change as follows:
1. (Name of the member) (membership status: independent\ dependent)
2. (Name of the member) (membership status: independent\ dependent)
3. (Name of the member) (membership status: independent\ dependent)".

5. Announcement for the Call for a Meeting of the Fund's Unitholders 5.1. Announcement for the Call for a Meeting of the Fund's Unitholders.
a) Announcement Websites:
- The Fund Manager's website.
- The Exchange's website.
b) The announcement title must be as follows:
"(The Fund Manager's Name) announces the call for a meeting of (the Fund's Name)'s unitholders".
c) The Detailed Announcement:
"(The Fund Manager's Name) invites the unitholders to attend the Fund's unitholders meeting, which will take place in (meeting venue) at (meeting time), on (00/00/0000H.) corresponding to (00/00/0000G.) to discuss the following agenda: (suggested decisions)".
5.2. Announcement for the Call for the Second Meeting of the Fund's Unitholders for not Meeting the Quorum at the First Meeting
a) Announcement Websites:
- The Fund Manager's website.
- The Exchange's website.
b) The announcement title must be as follows:
"(The Fund Manager's Name) announces the call for the second meeting of (the Fund's Name)'s unitholders".
c) The Detailed Announcement:
"(The Fund Manager's Name) invites (The Fund's Name) unitholders to attend the second unitholders meeting, which will take place in (meeting venue), at (meeting time), on (00/00/0000H.) corresponding to (00/00/0000G.) to discuss the following agenda: (suggested decisions)".

6. Announcement for the Results of Unitholders Meeting
a) Announcement Websites:
- The Fund Manager's website.
- The Exchange's website.
b) The announcement title must be as follows:
"(The Fund Manager's Name) announces the results of (The Fund's Name) unitholders meeting".
c) The Detailed Announcement:
"(The Fund Manager's Name) announces the results of (The Fund's Name) unitholders meeting, which was held on (00/00/0000H.) corresponding to (00/00/0000G.) as follows: (state the meeting results)".

7. Announcement for Non-Convention the Unitholders Meeting
a) Announcement Websites:
- The Fund Manager's website.
- The Exchange's website.
b) The announcement title must be as follows:
"(The Fund Manager's Name) announces the non-convention of (The Fund's Name) unitholders meeting".
c) The Detailed Announcement:
"(The Fund Manager's Name) announces the non-convention of (The Fund's Name) unitholders meeting, which was scheduled to be held on (00/00/0000H.) corresponding to (00/00/0000G.) due to (state the reasons for not convening the meeting)".

8. Announcement for Providing the Public with the Interim Financial Reports
a) Announcement Websites:
- The Fund Manager's website.
- The Exchange's website.

b) The announcement title must be as follows:
"(The Fund Manager's Name) announces the availability of the interim financial report of (Fund's Name) for the period ending on (00/00/0000) to the Public".
c) Detailed Announcement:
"(The Fund Manager's Name) announces the availability of the interim financial report of (Fund's Name). The following is a summary of the interim financial results for the period ended on 00/00/0000.
- Net assets on the end of the period of (•) (currency).
- Total expenses and fees for the period (•) (currency).
- Net profit (loss) for the period of (•) (currency).
- Number of outstanding units at the end of the period (•) units.
- Net unit value (•) (currency).
- Revenue of the period (•)%.
Must insert a link on the Exchange and the Fund Manager's website that refers to the interim financial statements".

9. Announcement for Providing the Public with the Annual Financial Reports
a) Announcement Websites:
- The Fund Manager's website.
- The Exchange's website.
b) The announcement title must be as follows:
"(The Fund Manager's Name) announces the availability of the Annual Financial Report of (Fund's Name) for the financial year ending on (financial year end date) to the public".
c) The Detailed Announcement:
"(The Fund Manager's Name) announces the availability of the Annual Financial Report of (Fund's Name) for the financial year ending on (financial year end date) to the public. The following is a summary of the annual financial results for the financial year ended on 00/00/0000.
- Net assets on the end of the period of (....) (currency).
- Total expenses and fees for the year\period (....) (currency).
- Net profit (loss) for the year\period of (...) (currency).
- Number of outstanding units in the end of year\ period (....) units.
- Net unit value (...) (currency).
- Revenue of the period ...%
Must insert the link of the Exchange and The Fund Manager's website that refers to the financial statements".

10. Announcement for the Occurrence of a Specific Event
a) Announcement Websites:
- The Fund Manager's website.
- The Exchange's website.
b) The announcement title must be as follows:
"(The Fund Manager's Name) announces the occurrence of a specific event to (The Fund's Name)".
c) The detailed announcement must contain the following:
1- Description of the event.
2- The resulted impact from the occurrence of the event.

11. Announcement for the Occurrence of a Material Development
a) Announcement Websites:
- The Fund Manager's website.
- The Exchange's website.
b) The announcement title must be as follows:
"(The Fund Manager's Name) announces a material development to (The Fund's Name)".
c) The detailed announcement must contain the following:
1- Description of the event.
2- The resulted impact from the occurrence of the event.

12. Announcement for Updating the Fund's Terms and Conditions
a) Announcement Websites:
- The Fund Manager's website.
- The Exchange's website.
b) The announcement title must be as follows:
"(The Fund Manager's Name) announces an update to the Terms and Conditions of (The Fund's Name)".
c) The Detailed Announcement:
"(The Fund Manager's Name) announces updating (The Fund's Name)'s Terms and Conditions, which will be effective from (00/00/0000H.) corresponding to (00/00//0000G.). The updated Terms and Conditions can be viewed via the link: - (insert the Terms and Conditions link)".

13. Announcement for the Details of the Material Changes to the Fund's Terms and Conditions
a) Announcement Websites:
- The Fund Manager's website.
- The Exchange's website.
b) The announcement title must be as follows:
"(The Fund Manager's Name) announces the details of the material changes to the Terms and Conditions of (The Fund's Name)".
c) The Detailed Announcement:
"(The Fund Manager's Name) announces the material changes to the Terms and Conditions of (The Fund's Name). Such change will become effective on (00/00/0000H.) corresponding to (00/00/0000G.)
The details of the material change are (...................................)".

14. Corrective Announcement
a) Announcement Websites:
- The Fund Manager's website.
- The Exchange's website (as applicable).
b) The announcement title must be as follows:
"(The Fund Manager's Name) announces a corrective announcement regarding (announcement subject)".
c) The detailed announcement must contain the following elements:
1- Date of the pervious announcement on Saudi Stock Exchange (Tadawul)'s website and the Fund Manager's website (as applicable).
2- The misstatement made on the previous announcement.
3- Correction of the error.
4- The resulted impact from the misstatement (if any).
d) The Detailed Announcement:
"A corrective announcement for the (Fund Manager's Name)'s announcement published on (00/00/0000G.) The Fund Manager wishes to clarify that (state the correction details)".

15. Addendum Announcement
a) Announcement Websites:
- The Fund Manager's website
- The Exchange's website (as applicable).
b) The announcement title must be as follows:
"(The Fund Manager's Name) announces an addendum announcement regarding (announcement subject)".

c) The detailed announcement must contain the following elements:
1- Date of the pervious announcement on Saudi Stock Exchange (Tadawul)'s website and the Fund Manager's website (as applicable).
2- Subject of change.
3- The resulted impact from the change (if any).
d) The Announcement Form:
"An addendum announcement for the (The Fund Manager's Name)'s announcement published on 00/00/0000G. (The Fund Manager's Name) wishes to clarify that (state the details)".

18 INVESTMENT FUNDS REGULATIONS

Issued by the Board of the Capital Market Authority Pursuant to its Resolution Number 1 - 219 - 2006 dated 3/12/1427H (24/12/2006G), based on the Capital Market Law issued by Royal Decree No. M/30 dated 2/6/1424H, as amended by Resolution of the Board of the Capital Market Authority Number 2-22-2021 Dated 12/7/1442H (24/2/2021G).

(According to the Authority's Board Resolution no. (2-22-2021) Dated 12/07/1442H. Corresponding to 24/02/2021G these Regulations shall become effective as of 19/09/1442H. corresponding to 01/05/2021G. Moreover, the Investment Funds Regulations issued pursuant to the Authority's Board Resolution no. (1-219-2006) dated 03/12/1427H. corresponding to 24/12/2006G. amended pursuant to the Authority's Board Resolution No. (1-61-2016) dated 16/08/1437H. corresponding to 23/05/2016G., which can be viewed via the following link: (https://cma.org.sa/RulesRegulations/Regulations/DocLib/IFRs Regulations- Final English_EN.pdf) shall remain effective until the effective date of these Regulations.)

TABLE OF CONTENTS

PART 1: GENERAL PROVISIONS
Article 1: Preliminary Provisions
Article 2: Definitions
3: Compliance With The Regulations
Article 4: Waivers
Article 5: Fees
Article 6: Right Of Appeal
PART 2: FUNDS MANAGEMENT
Article 7: Scope And Application
Article 8: Eligibility Requirements
Article 9: Fund Management And Duties Of The Fund Manager
Article 10: Books And Records Keeping
Article 11: Financial Statements
Article 12: Register Of Unitholders
Article 13: Conflicts Of Interest
Article 14: Investment Policies And Practices
Article 15: Fund's Subscriptions
Article 16: Special Commission Arrangements
Article 17: Delegation By The Fund Manager
Article 18: Appointment Of Advisors Article
Article 19: Services, Commissions And Management Fees
Article 20: Power Of The Authority To Remove And Replace Fund Manager
Article 21: Investment Decisions
Article 22: Termination And Liquidation Of The Fund
PART 3: CUSTODY
Article 23: Scope And Application
Article 24: Appointment Of The Custodian
Article 25: Ownership And Custody Of The Assets Of The Investment Fund
Article 26: Segregation Of Assets
Article 27: Delegation by Custodian
Article 28: Responsibilities Of The Custodian
Article 29: Power Of The Authority To Remove And Replace Custodian
Article 30: Removal Of Custodian By The Fund Manager
PART 4: PUBLIC FUNDS
Article 31: Application To The Authority For The Offer Of Units In A Public Fund
Article 32: Procedures And Power Of The Authority Toward The Application
Article 33: Contractual Format Of A Public Fund
Article 34: Units
Article 35: Permitted Fees, Commissions And Expenses
Article 36: Public Fund Distributions
Article 37: Fund's Subscription In Securities
Article 38: Public Fund Board
Article 39: Responsibilities of the Members of the Fund Board
Article 40: Investments Areas
Article 41: Investment Limitations
Article 42: Notification Relating to Substantial Holdings in Shares or Convertible Debt Instruments
Article 43: Principal Transactions
Article 44: Real Estate Investment Fund
Article 45: Index Fund
Article 46: Exchange Traded Fund
Article 47: Closed-Ended Investment Traded Fund
Article 48: Conditions For Offering Closed-Ended Investment Traded Fund
Article 49: Net Assets Of Closed-Ended Investment Traded Fund Units
Article 50: Offer Requirements For Closed-Ended Investment Traded Fund
Article 51: Closed-Ended Investment Traded Fund Buy-Back And Sale Of Its Units
Article 52: Disclosure Requirements Of Closed-Ended Investment Traded Fund
Article 53: Specialized Public Funds
Article 54: Money Market Fund
Article 55: Feeder Fund
Article 56: Fund Of Funds
Article 57: Capital Protected Fund
Article 58: Endowment Fund
Article 59: Breach Of Investment Limitations
Article 60: Exercise Of Rights In Respect Of Public Fund Assets
Article 61: Requirement To Produce Terms And Conditions
Article 62: Approval Of The Authority And Consent Of Unitholders To Fundmental Changes
Article 63: Notification to the Authority and Unitholders of Non-Fundamental Changes
Article 64: Initial Offer Period
Article 65: Subscription And Redemption
Article 66: Deferring Redemptions
Article 67: Suspension Of Subscription Or Redemption Of Units
Article 68: Transaction Fees
Article 69: Borrowing to Meet Redemption Requests
Article 70: Securities Advertisements and Promotional Materials
Article 71: Valuation
Article 72: Pricing of Units
Article 73: Incorrect Valuation or Pricing

Article 74: Audit Requirements
Article 75: Meetings Of Unitholders
Article 76: Reporting To Unitholders
Article 77: Reporting to the Authority
PART 5: PRIVATE FUNDS
Article 78: Submitting a Notice to the Authority for the Offer of Units in a Private Fund
Article 79: Capital Call In Installments
Article 80: Private Placement Of A Private Fund And Eligibility Of Investors
Article 81: Private Placement Requirements
Article 82: Contractual Format Of A Private Fund
Article 83: Units
Article 84: Private Real Estate Fund Board
Article 85: Responsibilities Of The Members Of The Private Real Estate Fund's Board
Article 86: General Rules And Restrictions
Article 87: Private Fund Documentation
Article 88: Securities Advertisements And Promotional Materials
Article 89: Financial Statement Auditing Requirements
Article 90: Valuation
Article 91: Meetings Of Unitholders
Article 92: Consent Of Unitholders To Changes
Article 93: Reporting To Unitholders
Article 94: Reporting To The Authority
Article 95: Notification Relating to the Substantial Holdings in Shares or Convertible Debt Instruments
Article 96: Restriction On Secondary Market Activity
PART 6: FOREIGN FUNDS
Article 97: Offer Of Securities Issued By a Foreign Fund in the Kingdom
Article 98: Private Placement of a Foreign Fund And Eligibility of Investors
Article 99: Private Placement Requirements Of A Foreign Fund
Article 100: Information To Securities Holders and Offer Documentation
Article 101: Securities Advertisements And Promotional Materials
Article 102: Power of the Authority To Suspend A Distributor
Article 103: Distributor Responsibilities
Article 104: Reporting To The Authority
Article 105: Restriction On Secondary Market Activity
PART 7: MERGE OF THE INVESTMENT FUNDS
Article 106: Application To The Authority For The Merging Of Investment Funds
Article 107: Additional Information To Be Provided To The Unitholders
PART 8: INVESTMENT FUNDS THAT TAKE THE FORM OF A SPECIAL PURPOSES ENTITY
Article 108: General Provisions
Article 109: Custodian
Article 110: Board of an Investment Fund that Takes the Form of a Special Purposes Entity
PART 9: PUBLICATION AND ENTRY INTO FORCE
Article 111: Publication And Entry Into Force
Annexes
Annex 1: Requirements of the Fund's Terms and Conditions
Annex 2: Contents of the Application for Offering of a Public Fund's Units
Annex 3: Contents of Fund's Reports
Annex 4: Contents of the Quarter Statements
Annex 5: Valuation Methodologies for Public Funds
Annex 6: Private Placement Notification to the Authority – Private Funds And Foreign Funds
Annex 7: Fund's Declaration to the Authority – Private Fund
Annex 8: Fund's Declaration to the Authority – Foreign Fund
Annex 9: Statement to Be Included in the Private Placement Offering Documents
Annex 10: Approval and Notification Requests Provided to the Authority
Annex 11: Requirements of the Private Fund's Terms and Conditions
Annex 12: Legal Advisor Letter Form
Annex 13: Fund Manager Letter Form
Annex 14: Fund Termination Report

18.1 PART 1: GENERAL PROVISIONS

Article 1: Preliminary Provisions
a. These Regulations aim to regulate the registration, offering and management of investment funds and associated activities in the Kingdom.
b. These Regulations shall have no prejudice to the provisions of the Capital Market Law and its Implementing Regulations, including, the Market Conduct Regulations, the Capital Market Intuitions Regulations, the Securities Business Regulations and the Rules for Special Purposes Entities.

Article 2: Definitions
a. Any reference to the "Capital Market Law" in these Regulations shall mean the Capital Market Law issued by Royal Decree No. M/30 dated 2/6/1424H.
b. Expressions and terms in these Regulations have the meaning which they bear in the Capital Market Law and in the Glossary of defined terms used in the Regulations and Rules of the Capital Market Authority, unless the context indicates otherwise.

Article 3: Compliance with the Regulations
a. A person who intends to offer units in an investment fund in the Kingdom, must comply with these Regulations, and the provisions of the Rules for Special Purposes Entities (where applicable).
b. A fund manager, fund operator, custodian, distributor, market maker, adviser and any member of the fund board of an investment fund in the Kingdom must comply with these Regulations, and the provisions of the Rules for Special Purposes Entities (where applicable).

Article 4: Waivers
The Authority may waive a provision of these Regulations in whole or in part as it applies to a person either on an application from such person to whom the relevant provisions of this Article would otherwise apply or on the Authority's own initiative.

Article 5: Fees The Authority may impose a fee on the fund manager and the distributor as the Authority may prescribe.

Article 6: Right of Appeal Any person subject to these Regulations may appeal to the Committee in respect of any decision or action that the Authority takes under these Regulations.

18.2 PART 2: FUNDS MANAGEMENT

Article 7: Scope and Application This Part shall apply to both public funds and private funds.

Article 8: Eligibility Requirements

a. The fund manager must be a Capital Market Institution licensed to carry out the activity of managing investments and operating funds or the activity of managing investments.
b. Where the fund manager was licensed to carry out managing investments activity, without the license to carry out operating funds activity, it must appoint a Capital Market Institution licensed to carry out managing investments and operating funds activity to operate the investment funds under its management.
c. A Capital Market Institution appointed under Paragraph (b) of this Article may be a custodian of the relevant investment fund.
d. A Capital Market Institution appointed under Paragraph (b) of this Article shall be responsible for the fund's compliance with the provisions of the Capital Market Law and its Implementing Regulations.
e. As an exception to the provisions of Paragraph (a) of this Article, the fund manager of the private real estate investment fund must be a Capital Market Institution licensed to carry out the activity of managing investments and operating funds.
(According to Authority Board Resolution no. (2-22-2021) Dated 12/07/1442H. Corresponding to 24/02/2021G. Article (8) of these Regulations shall become effective as of 28/05/1443 H. corresponding to 01/01/2022 G. Moreover, Article (8) of the Investment Funds Regulations issued pursuant to the Authority's Board Resolution No. (1-219-2006) dated 03/24/1427 H. Corresponding to 24/12/2006 G., and amended by the Authority's Board Resolution No. (1-61-2016) dated 16/08/1437 H. corresponding to 23/05/2016 G., which can be viewed via the following link: (https://cma.org.sa/RulesRegulations/Regulations/DocLib/IFRs Regulations- Final English_EN.pdf), shall remain effective until the effective date of Article (8) of these Regulations.)

Article 9: Fund Management and Duties of the Fund Manager

a. The fund manager must act for the benefit of unitholders in accordance with these Regulations, the Capital Market Institutions Regulations and the Fund's Terms and Conditions.
b. The fund manager shall comply with all principles and duties required under the Capital Market Institutions Regulations including the fiduciary duty towards unitholders, which includes the duty to act in the best interests of the unitholders and duty to exercise all reasonable care and skill.
c. With respect to the investment funds, fund manager's responsibilities shall include:

1) Fund management.
2) Offering of fund units.
3) Ensuring the accuracy of the Fund's Terms and Conditions, and verify that the terms and conditions are complete, clear, accurate, and not misleading.

d. In relation to investment funds, the fund operator shall be responsible for operating investment funds.
e. The fund manager shall have the primary responsibility for compliance with these Regulations, whether it directly performs its responsibilities and duties or delegated them to an external party under these Regulations and the Capital Market Institutions Regulations. The fund manager shall be responsible toward unitholders for losses incurred by the investment fund, which are caused by, fraud, negligence, misconduct or willful default of the fund manager.
f. The fund manager must develop policies and procedures that detect risks effecting the fund's investments and ensure treatment of these risks as soon as possible. These policies and procedures must include conducting risks assessment, at least, once a year.
g. Unless the Authority determines otherwise, the fund manager may not limit the eligibility of the investment in the fund to nationals of any state or group of states or in a particular fund. This clause does not prevent the fund manager from rejecting investment from any person or entity that is deemed unqualified for such investment by any other relevant law.
h. All disclosures by the fund manager must be complete, clear, accurate and not misleading.
i. The fund manager must comply with the provisions of Annex (10) of these Regulations when applying for an approval from or notifying the Authority requests.
j. The fund manager must implement a compliance monitoring program for every fund under its management. The fund manager must provide the Authority with the results of the implementation of the program upon its request.
k. The fund manager must cooperate with all persons concerned with the performance of tasks for the fund, including the custodian and the auditor, and the fund manager must provide them with whatever necessary to perform their duties and tasks in accordance with these Regulations.
l. The fund manager must prepare an annual report that includes an assessment of the performance and quality of services provided by the parties involved in providing material services to the fund - including the custodian, developer and property manager (as applicable) - and the fund manager must submit the report referred to in this Paragraph to the fund's board of directors.
m. The fund manager must prepare an annual report that includes all complaints and actions taken towards them. The fund manager must submit the report referred to in this Paragraph to the fund's board of directors.
n. The fund manager must comply with the Instructions for Investment Funds Announcements.

Article 10: Books and Records Keeping

a. The fund manager must maintain the books and records of all investment funds, which the fund manager manages. In addition, the fund operator must maintain the books and records related to the operation of all the funds it operates.
b. The fund operator must maintain -at all times- records of all units issued and cancelled, and must maintain an up to date record of the balance of outstanding units for each fund under its operation.
c. Without prejudice to Paragraph (b) of this Article, the fund manager and fund operator must maintain all books and records in accordance with these Regulations for a period of (10) years unless the Authority determines otherwise. The fund manager and fund operator must maintain copies of all books and records required pursuant to this Article for a

longer period in the event such books and records relate to any litigation or claim (including any pending or threatened litigation) or any on-going investigations procedures, the fund manager and fund operator must maintain such books and records until the closure of that litigation, claim or on-going investigation procedures.

Article 11: Financial Statements

a. The financial statements for an investment fund must be prepared in Arabic, and in a semi- annual basis at least for public fund and private real estate fund, and must be reviewed in accordance with the accounting standards approved by the Saudi Organization of Certified Public Accountants. Additional copies may be prepared in other languages, and in the event of any conflict between those copies, the Arabic text shall prevail.
b. The annual financial statements for an investment fund must be audited in accordance with the accounting standards approved by the Saudi Organization of Certified Public Accountants, and the auditor, through reviewing the annual financial statements and based on the information provided to it, must include in its report what may come to its attention of breaches to the provisions of the Investment Funds Regulations and the Fund's Terms and Conditions.
c. Copies of all financial statements required by Paragraphs (a) and (b) of this Article must be included in the fund reports prepared by the fund manager pursuant to Article (76) of these Regulations in the case of public funds and pursuant to Article (93) of these Regulations in the case of private funds.

Article 12: Register of Unitholders

a. The fund operator must establish a register of unitholders and must maintain it in the Kingdom.
b. The register shall be conclusive evidence as to the persons entitled to units entered on the register.
c. The fund operator must maintain at least the following information in the register:

1) The name, address and contact numbers of each unitholder;
2) The national identification number, residence number (Iqama), passport number or commercial registration number of the unitholder when applicable, or any other identification as determined by the Authority;
3) The nationality of the unitholder;
4) The date on which the unitholder was registered in the register;
5) Details of all transactions in relation to units conducted by each unitholder; and
6) The current balance of the number of units (including fractions of a unit) held by each unitholder.
7) Any restriction or right attached to units owned by the unitholder.

d. The register of unitholders must be made available for inspection by the Authority at its request. A summary must be provided by the fund manager to any unitholder free of charge upon request, such summary must show all the information that is relevant to the requesting unitholder only.
e. The fund operator must update the register of unitholders immediately to reflect changes to information referred to in Paragraph (c) of this Article.
f. The traded funds shall be exempted from the provisions of this Article.

Article 13: Conflicts of Interest

a. Without prejudice to Paragraphs (b), (c), and (d) of this Article, the fund manager must treat any conflicts of interest in accordance with the provisions of the Capital Market Institutions Regulations.
b. If the fund manager (or the fund sub-manager) does not carry out a prior (where possible) or immediate disclosure of the conflict of interest to the relevant fund board, and obtain the fund board's approval on that action, the fund manager or the fund sub-manager may not engage in any action that involves:

1) A material conflict between the interests of the fund manager or fund sub-manager and the interests of any investment fund it manages; or
2) A conflict between the interests of any investment fund it manages and another investment fund or another client account.

c. The fund manager (and fund sub-manager), must ensure their affiliates do not engage in any action that involves any conflict of interest as described in Paragraph (b) of this Article.

d. The fund manager of a public investment must disclose immediately, on its website and the Exchange's website or any other website available to the public according to the controls set out by the Authority (where applicable), and on the public fund's annual reports that has been prepared by the fund manager in accordance to Article (76) of these Regulations.

Article 14: Investment Policies and Practices

The investment decisions of the fund manager must conform to well and prudent investment practice in relation to the investment objectives of the fund as set out in the Terms and Conditions, including using its best efforts to ensure:
1) in the case of an open-ended fund, that the investment fund is sufficiently liquid in order to meet anticipated redemption requests;
2) that the investment fund does not unduly concentrate investments in a certain security or securities, in a country, geographic area, industry or sector, except to the extent any such concentration is disclosed in the Fund's Terms and Conditions; and
3) that the investments of the fund provide a prudent spread of risk whilst having due regard to the investment objectives, investment policies and Terms and Conditions of the relevant investment fund.

Article 15: Fund's Subscriptions

a. A fund manager and any of its affiliates may only subscribe, for their own accounts, in units in an investment fund which is managed by the fund manager if the intention of such subscription is disclosed in the Fund's Terms and Conditions, if the following requirements are satisfied:

1) the terms of the fund manager's (or its affiliates') subscriptions, and the rights attached to the units which they hold must be no more favorable than those of other unitholders of the same class;
2) the fund manager and its affiliates shall not be entitled to vote on the units which they hold; and
3) the public fund manager shall disclose at the end of each quarter details of its investments in the fund's units on the fund manager's website and the Exchange's website, or any other website available to the public according to the controls set out by the Authority (where applicable), as well as in the reports

that the fund manager prepares in accordance with Article (76) of these Regulations.

b. A unitholder whose subscription in a closed-ended fund was made in kind may reduce its ownership to a minimum of (50%) of the number of units issued for its in kind contribution after one year from the date of subscription in the fund or the date of operation of the fund, whichever is further, unless the relevant Fund's Terms and Conditions state a longer period.

c. Without prejudice to the restrictions stipulated in Article (47) of these Regulations, a closed-ended investment traded fund shall be excluded from the provisions of Paragraph (b) of this Article.

Article 16: Special Commission Arrangements

a. Any special commission arrangement entered into by a fund manager is subject to the Capital Market Institutions Regulations and must be disclosed in the Fund's Terms and Conditions.

b. Goods and services received by a fund manager under a special commission arrangement must be restricted to those that are related to the execution of transactions on behalf of an investment fund or comprise the provision of research for the benefit of relevant investment fund.

c. The fund manager may not obtain direct sums of money under special commission or any other arrangements.

Article 17: Delegation by the Fund Manager

a. A fund manager may, in respect to any investment fund, which the fund manager manages, delegate one or more third parties or affiliates as a fund sub-manager. The remuneration of any fund sub-manager must be paid by the fund manager out of its own resources.

b. With exception for cases described in Paragraph (c) of this Article, Any fund sub-manager delegated pursuant to Paragraph (a) of this Article must be delegated pursuant to a contract in writing and must be a Capital Market Institution licensed to carry out the activity of managing investments and operating funds or the activity of managing investments.

c. A fund manager may delegate a fund sub-manager operating in a jurisdiction other than the Kingdom to manage foreign investments of the investment fund, however the sub- manager shall be established, authorized and supervised in a jurisdiction that employs regulatory standards and requirements at least equivalent to those of the Authority, and must be delegated pursuant to a contract in writing.

d. The Authority shall have the discretion to assess whether the jurisdiction in which any fund sub-manager operates has regulatory standards and requirements at least equivalent to those of the Authority.

e. The fund manager may delegate a third party or more, or any of its affiliate to work as distributor to units of an investment fund managed by the fund manager. The distributor's remuneration must be paid from the fund manager's own resources.

f. The distributor that has been delegated in the Kingdom pursuant to Paragraph (e) of this Article, must be one of the following:

1) a Capital Market Institution licensed to carry out dealing activity.
2) a Capital Market Institution licensed to carry out advising activity.
3) a local bank.

g. The delegation referenced in Paragraph (e) of this Article must be made pursuant to a contract in writing, and where the distributor is a local bank it must include the following controls at minimum:

1) That the units of the publicly offered investment funds shall be distributed through the distributer's website only.
2) The website of the delegated distributor provides the ability to fill and sign the required documents, including:
   a) The fund manager's investment account opening agreement.
   b) The "Know Your Client" form provided in the Capital Market Institutions Regulations.
   c) The fund's subscription form, and the Fund's Terms and Conditions in which a client wishes to participate.

h. Where the fund manager has delegated the distributor under Paragraph (e) of this Article, the fund manager is responsible for complying with the Capital Market Law and its Implementing Regulations, and the Anti-Money Laundering Law, and its Implementing Regulations. The fund manager may rely on the delegated distributor to take due diligence measures towards the client according to the relevant provisions contained in the Anti- Money Laundering Law and its Implementing Regulations.

i. The fund manager may delegate a third party or more, to carry out the fund operations, including administrative services for the fund.

j. With exception for cases described in Paragraph (k) of this Article, any third party delegated pursuant to Paragraph (i) of this Article must be a Capital Market Institution licensed to carry out the activity of managing investments and operating funds4, and must be delegated pursuant to a written contract.

k. A fund manager may delegate a third party operating in a jurisdiction other than the Kingdom to carry out the fund operations in relation to investment fund's foreign investments. The third party must be established, authorized and supervised in a jurisdiction that employs regulatory standards and requirements at least equivalent to those of the Authority, and must be delegated pursuant to a contract in writing.

l. The Authority shall have the discretion to assess whether the jurisdiction in which any third party, which delegated to carries out the operations of the fund outside the Kingdom, it has regulatory standards and requirements at least equivalent to those of the Authority.

(According to Authority Board Resolution no. 2-22-2021 Dated 12/07/1442H. Corresponding to 24/02/2021G. Paragraph (b) of Article (17) of these Regulations shall become effective as of 28/05/1443 H. corresponding to 01/01/2022 G. Moreover, Paragraph (b) of Article (17) of the Investment Funds Regulations issued pursuant to the Authority's Board Resolution No. (1-219-2006) dated 03/12/1427 H. Corresponding to 24/12/2006 G., and amended by the Authority's Board Resolution No. (1-61-2016) dated 16/08/1437 H. corresponding to 23/05/2016 G., which can be viewed via the following link:(https://cma.org.sa/RulesRegulations/Regulations/DocLib/IFRs Regulations- Final English_EN.pdf), shall remain effective until the effective date of Paragraph (b) of Article (17) of these Regulations.)

(According to Authority Board Resolution no. 2-22-2021 Dated 12/07/1442H. Corresponding to 24/02/2021G. Paragraph (j) of Article (17) of these Regulations shall become effective as of 28/05/1443 H. corresponding to 01/01/2022 G. Moreover, Paragraph (h) of Article (17) of the Investment

Funds Regulations issued pursuant to the Authority's Board Resolution No. (1-219-2006) dated 03/12/1427 H. Corresponding to 24/12/2006 G., and amended by the Authority's Board Resolution No. (1-61-2016) dated 16/08/1437 H. corresponding to 05/23/2016 G., which can be viewed via the following link: (https://cma.org.sa/RulesRegulations/Regulations/DocLib/IFRs Regulations- Final English_EN.pdf), shall remain effective until the effective date of Paragraph (j) of Article (17) of these Regulations.)

Article 18: Appointment of Advisors

a. The fund manager may, in respect to any investment fund which the fund manager manages, appoint a person to provide advice. The remuneration of any such person must be paid from the fund manager's own resources.

b. With exception for cases described in Paragraph (c) of this Article, any person appointed by the fund manager as an adviser, must be a Capital Market Institution licensed to carry out the advising activity, and must be appointed pursuant to a written contract.

c. A fund manager may appoint a person in a jurisdiction other than the Kingdom to provide advice in relation to investment fund's foreign investments. The person that has been appointed pursuant to this Paragraph must be established, authorized and supervised in a jurisdiction that employs regulatory standards and requirements at least equivalent to those of the Authority, and must be delegated pursuant to a contract in writing.

d. The Authority shall have the discretion to assess whether the jurisdiction in which any adviser operates has regulatory standards and requirements at least equivalent to those of the Authority.

Article 19: Services, Commissions and Management Fees Any fees, commissions or charges levied on the fund for its management must be on arm's length terms (and at least equivalent to the terms entered into by persons dealing independently) and in no event shall such charges exceed the limit specified in the Fund's Terms and Conditions.

Article 20: Power of the Authority to Remove and Replace Fund Manager

a. The Authority shall have the power to remove a fund manager in relation to a particular investment fund and to take any action it deems appropriate to appoint a replacement fund manager for that investment fund or to take any other measures it deems necessary in the event of:

1) the fund manager ceasing to carry out managing investments and operating funds activity or managing investments activity without notification to the Authority under the Capital Market Institutions Regulations;

2) the cancellation, withdrawal or suspension by the Authority of the fund manager's authorization(s) to carry out managing investments and operating funds activity or managing investments activity under the Capital Market Institutions Regulations;

3) a request by the fund manager to the Authority to cancel its relevant authorization to carry out managing investments and operating funds activity or managing investments activity;

4) the Authority believing that the fund manager has failed, in a manner which the Authority considers material, to comply with the Capital Market Law or its Implementing Regulations;

5) the death, incapacity or resignation of a portfolio manager who manages the assets of the investment fund, if no other registered person employed by the fund manager can manage the assets of the relevant investment fund or the assets of the funds managed by the portfolio manager;

6) the issuance of a special fund resolution by unitholders of a close ended fund requesting the Authority of removal of the fund manager; or

7) any other event determined by the Authority on reasonable grounds to be of sufficient material.

b. Notice of any event described in Subparagraph (5) of Paragraph (a) of this Article must be provided by the fund manager to the Authority within (2) days from the date of its occurrence.

c. Upon removal of the fund manager in accordance with the cases stipulated in Subparagraphs (1), (2), (3), (4), (5) and (7) of Paragraph (a) of this Article, the Authority shall directs the removed fund manager to call for a unitholders meeting within (15) days from the date of the Authority's removal decision, in order to appoint the custodian or other party, through an ordinary fund resolution, to find and negotiate with a replacement fund manager and specify the time limit for finding and negotiation.

d. Upon removal of the fund manager in accordance with the case stipulated in Subparagraph (6) of Paragraph (a) of this Article, the fund manager must issue an ordinary fund resolution at the same meeting in which unitholders voted on the request to remove the fund manager, in order to appoint the custodian or other party, to find and negotiate with a replacement fund manager and specify the time limit for finding and negotiation.

e. When any of the two cases stipulated in Paragraphs (c) and (d) of this Article occurs, the fund manager must notify the Authority of the results of the unitholders meeting within two days of its convening date.

f. The fund manager must cooperate and provide the custodian or the party assigned to find and negotiate any documents required by it for the purpose of appointing a replacement fund manager within (10) days from the date of the request, and both parties must maintain the confidentiality of the information.

g. The fund manager must, upon approval of the replacement fund manager to manage the fund and transfer of the fund management to it, send a written consent of the replacement fund manager to the Authority as soon as it is received.

h. If the Authority exercises any of its powers pursuant to Paragraph (a) of this Article, the relevant fund manager shall co-operate fully in order to help facilitate a smooth transfer of responsibilities to the replacement fund manager during the initial (60) days period after the appointment of the replacement fund manager. The fund manager shall where necessary and applicable and at the discretion of the Authority, novate all of the contracts relating to the relevant investment fund to which it is a party to the replacement fund manager.

i. In case a replacement fund manager has not been appointed within the time limit for finding and negotiation with a replacement fund manager referred to in Paragraphs (c) and (d) of this Article, unitholders are entitled to request the liquidation of the fund through a special fund resolution.

Article 21: Investment Decisions If a fund manager is removed pursuant to Article (20) of these Regulations, it must cease to make any investment decisions in relation to the relevant fund as soon as the replacement fund manager is appointed or at any earlier time determined by the Authority.

Article 22: Termination and Liquidation of the Fund

a. The fund manager shall specify the termination provisions of a fund in the Terms and Conditions of the relevant fund.
b. The fund manager must complete the process of selling the fund's assets and distribute the unitholders' dues among them prior to the end of the fund's term.
c. The fund manager may extend the fund's term to complete the sale process of the fund's assets or any other event in accordance with the provisions of Articles (62) and (92) of these Regulations.
d. For the purpose of terminating a fund, the fund manager must prepare a plan and procedures for the termination of the fund consistent with the unitholders interests and must obtain the fund board of directors' approval – where applicable – on such plan and procedures prior to carrying out any procedure in this regard.
e. The fund manager must notify the Authority and the unitholders, in writing, of the details of the plan and procedures for the fund termination at least (21) days prior to the intended date for terminating the fund, without prejudice to the Fund's Terms and Conditions.
f. The fund manager must comply with the plan and procedures for fund's termination approved as per Paragraph (d) of this Article.
g. The fund manager must notify the Authority and unitholders, in writing, regarding the fund's termination within (10) days from the end of the fund term in accordance with the requirements in Paragraph (d) of Annex (10) of these Regulations.
h. In case the Fund's Terms and Conditions provide that the fund will be terminated upon the occurrence of specified events, the fund manager must terminate the fund immediately upon the occurrence of such event and notify the Authority and unitholders in writing within (5) days from the occurrence of a specified event triggering the termination of the fund.
i. In the event of expiry of the fund's term and the fund manager has not completed the sale of the fund's assets before the expiry of its term, the fund manager must liquidate the assets and distribute the unitholders' dues among them within a period not exceeding (6) months from the date of the expiry of the fund's term.
j. For the purpose of liquidating a fund, the fund manager must obtain the fund's board of directors' approval on the plan and procedures for the liquidation of the fund (where applicable) prior to carrying out any action in this regard.
k. The fund manager must comply with the plan and procedures for fund liquidation approved as per Paragraph (j) of this Article.
l. The fund manager must notify the Authority and the unitholders, in writing, of the end of the fund liquidation within (10) days from the end of the fund liquidation in accordance with the requirements in Paragraph (d) of Annex (10) of these Regulations.
m. The fund manager must treat all unitholders equally during the fund termination or liquidation process.
n. The fund manager must immediately upon the end of fund term or liquidation distribute the dues of the unitholders among them, without delay and in a manner that does not conflict with the interest of unitholders and the Fund's Terms and Conditions.
o. The public fund manager must disclose, on its website and the Exchange's website or any other website available to the public according to the controls set out by the Authority (where applicable), regarding end of term of the fund or its liquidation period. Moreover, the private fund manager must notify the unitholders of such in the places and means specified in the Fund's Terms and Conditions.
p. The fund manager must provide the unitholders with the fund termination report, in accordance with the requirements of Annex (14) of these Regulations within a period not exceeding (70) days from the date of completion of its termination or liquidation, including the final audited financial statements of the fund for the period subsequent to the last annual audited financial statements.
q. The Authority may remove the fund manager from the liquidation process in the event of a special fund resolution issued by the unitholders, provided that a replacement liquidator is appointed on the same meeting in which unitholders voted on removing the fund manager.
r. If the fund manager was removed from the liquidation process, it should fully cooperate to transfer liquidation responsibilities to the appointed liquidator. It must also transfer to the appointed liquidator all the documents of the relevant investment fund, that will enable it to complete the liquidation within (20) days from the issuance of the Authority's resolution to remove the fund manager and appoint a replacement liquidator.
s. The fund manager must notify the unitholders, in writing, in the event where the Authority issues a resolution of the removal of the fund manager and the appointment of a replacement liquidator under Paragraph (q) of this Article.
t. In all cases, the fund manager must notify the Authority and the unitholders, in writing, immediately and without any delay of any material events or developments during the liquidation period of the fund.
u. The traded funds shall be exempted from the requirement to send the written notice to all unitholders mentioned in Paragraphs (e), (g), (h) (l), (s), and (t) of this Article, provided that the announcement for such is made on the fund manager's website and the Exchange's website.
(According to Authority Board Resolution no. 2-22-2021 Dated 12/07/1442H. Corresponding to 24/02/2021G. Article (22) of these Regulations shall become effective as of 28/07/1443 H. corresponding to 01/03/2022 G. Moreover, Articles (37) and (78) of the Investment Funds Regulations issued pursuant to the Authority's Board Resolution No. (1-219-2006) dated 03/12/1427 H. Corresponding to 24/12/2006 G., and amended by the Authority's Board Resolution No. (1-61-2016) dated 16/08/1437 H. corresponding to 23/05/2016 G., which can be viewed via the following link: (https://cma.org.sa/RulesRegulations/Regulations/DocLib/IFRs Regulations- Final English_EN.pdf) shall remain effective until the effective date of Article (22) of these Regulations.)

18.3 PART 3: CUSTODY

Article 23: Scope and Application This Part shall apply to public funds and private funds.

Article 24: Appointment of the Custodian

a. The fund manager must appoint one or more custodians in the Kingdom to take custody of the assets of the investment funds which the fund manager manages. The custodian must be appointed pursuant to a written contract.

b. The custodian appointed pursuant to Paragraph (a) of this Article must not be a fund manager or a fund sub-manager to the relevant fund, or an affiliate of the fund manager or to the fund sub-manager.

c. The custodian appointed pursuant to Paragraph (a) of this Article must be a Capital Market Institution licensed to carry out custody activity.

d. As an exception to the provisions of Paragraph (b) of this Article, the custodian of a feeder fund for public and private investment funds may become a fund manager for the relevant fund, a sub-manager of the relevant fund or an affiliate to the fund manager or the fund sub-manager, when fulfilling the following criteria:

1) Investing the feeder fund's assets in another investment fund, whether that investment is in or outside the Kingdom.

2) The custodian of the feeder fund shall not impose any additional fees on the fund.

3) The investment fund in which the feeder fund invests in shall be a closed ended fund.

Article 25: Ownership and Custody of the Assets of the Investment Fund

a. The assets of an investment fund shall be owned collectively by the unitholders in that fund. A fund manager, fund sub-manager, fund operator, custodian, sub-custodian, advisor or distributor may not have any interest in or claims against such assets, other than, when the fund manager, fund sub-manager, fund operator, custodian, sub- custodian, advisor or distributor is a unitholder (within the limits of its ownership), or for claims permitted under these Regulations and disclosed in the Fund's Terms and Conditions.

b. With the exception of units owned by the fund manager, fund sub-manager, fund operator, custodian, sub-custodian, advisor, or distributor, and within the limits of what is owned by the debtor, creditors of such fund manager, fund sub-manager, fund operator, custodian, sub-custodian, advisor, or distributor may not have any claim or entitlement to money or assets of the investment fund.

Article 26: Segregation of Assets

a. The custodian must, in relation to each investment fund to which it acts as custodian, open a separate account in a local bank under its name with the account designated as being for the benefit of the relevant investment fund.

b. The custodian must segregate each investment fund's assets from its own assets and from the assets of its other clients, and must separately identify, by registration in the name of the custodian for the benefit of the relevant investment fund the securities and other assets of such investment fund. The custodian must register the real estate assets of the fund and the ownerships in unlisted companies that are not deposited at the Depositary Center in the name of a company fully owned by the custodian. The custodian must maintain all necessary records to support the performance of its contractual responsibilities6.

c. As an exception to the provisions of Paragraph (a) of this Article, in the case of an investment fund that takes the form of a special purposes entity, the custodian must open a separate account with a local bank in the name of such special purposes entity.

d. As an exception to the provisions of Paragraph (b) of this Article, in the case of an investment fund that takes the form of a special purposes entity, the custodian must segregate the assets of each investment fund from its own assets and the assets of its other clients. Such assets must be specified independently by registering the securities and other assets in the name of the special purposes entity. It shall also maintain all necessary records and other documents that support the performance of its contractual obligations.

e. The custodian must deposit all cash belonging to the investment fund into the relevant bank account referred to in Paragraph (a) or Paragraph (c) of this Article, whichever applies, and must deduct from the relevant bank account payments for investments and expenses incurred in the management and operation of the investment fund in accordance with these Regulations, the updated Fund's Terms and Conditions that it received from the fund manager, and the contract by which the custodian was appointment by the fund manager.

f. Real estate assets of a fund may be pledged to an entity licensed to provide loans that extended a loan to the fund. (According to the Authority's Board Resolution no. (2-22-2021) Dated 12/07/1442H. Corresponding to 24/02/2021G. Paragraph (b) of Article (26) of these Regulations shall become effective as of 28/07/1443H. corresponding to 01/03/2022G. Moreover, Paragraph (b) of Article (25) of the Investment Funds Regulations issued pursuant to the Authority's Board Resolution No. (1-219-2006) dated 03/12/1427 H. corresponding to 24/12/2006 G. and amended by the Authority's Board Resolution No.)2016-61-1(dated 16/08/1437 H. corresponding to 23/05/2016 G., which can be viewed via the following link: (https://cma.org.sa/RulesRegulations/Regulations/DocLib/IFRs Regulations- Final English_EN.pdf) shall remain effective until the effective date of Paragraph (b) of Article (26) of these Regulations.)

Article 27: Delegation by the Custodian

a. A custodian, in respect of any investment fund in relation to which the custodian acts, may delegate one or more third parties or affiliates as a fund sub-custodian. The remuneration of the fund sub-custodian shall be paid by the custodian out of its own resources.

b. With exception for cases described in Paragraph (c) of this Article, any fund sub-custodian delegated pursuant to Paragraph (a) of this Article must be delegated pursuant to a contract in writing and must be a Capital Market Institution licensed to carry out the custody activity.

c. A fund sub-custodian operating in a jurisdiction other than the Kingdom may be delegated to take custody of the fund's assets in relation to the fund's foreign investments, and must be delegated pursuant to a contract in writing and shall be established, authorized and supervised in a jurisdiction that employs regulatory standards and requirements at least equivalent to those of the Authority.

d. The Authority shall have the discretion to assess whether the jurisdiction in which any fund sub-custodian, who operates outside the Kingdom, has regulatory standards and requirements at least equivalent to those of the Authority.

e. The fund sub-custodian delegated pursuant to the provisions of this Article, must not be the fund manager, the fund sub-manager, or any of their affiliates.

Article 28: Responsibilities of the Custodian

a. Notwithstanding the delegation by a custodian to one or more third parties under the provisions of these Regulations or the Capital Market Institutions Regulations, the custodian shall remain fully responsible for compliance with its responsibilities in accordance to the provisions of these Regulations. The custodian shall be held responsible to the fund manager and unitholders for any losses caused to the investment fund due to the custodian fraud, negligence, misconduct or wilful default.

b. The custodian shall be responsible for taking custody and protecting the fund's assets on behalf of unitholders, and taking all necessary administrative measures in relation to the custody of the fund's assets.

Article 29: Power of the Authority to Remove and Replace Custodian

a. The Authority shall have the power to remove the custodian which was appointed by the fund manager of an investment fund and take any other measures it deems necessary, as appropriate, in the event of:

1) The custodian ceasing to carry out custody activity without notification to the Authority under the Capital Market Institutions Regulations;

2) The cancellation or suspension by the Authority of the custodian's relevant authorization to carry out custody activity;

3) A request by the custodian to the Authority to cancel its authorization to carry out custody activity;

4) The Authority believing that the custodian has failed, in a manner which the Authority considers material, to comply with the Capital Market Law or its Implementing Regulations; or

5) Any other event determined by the Authority - based on reasonable grounds- to be of sufficient significance.

b. If the Authority exercises its power pursuant to Paragraph (a) of this Article, the relevant fund manager must appoint a replacement custodian to that investment fund in accordance with the Authority's instructions, the fund manager as well as the isolated custodian shall co-operate fully in order to facilitate a smooth transfer of responsibilities to the replacement custodian during the first (60) days of the appointing the replacement custodian. The custodian must transfer, where the Authority decides its necessary and applicable, all the contracts related to the relevant investment fund to the replacement custodian.

Article 30: Removal of Custodian by the Fund Manager

a. The custodian appointed by the fund manager of an investment fund may be subject to removal by written notice by the fund manager of that investment fund upon the fund manager forming the reasonable opinion that the removal is for the interest of the unitholders, the fund manager shall notify the Authority and the unitholders in writing immediately.

b. upon removing the custodian, the fund manager must appoint a replacement custodian within (30) days of the custodian's receipt of the written notification issued in accordance with Paragraph (a) of this Article. The removed custodian must co-operate fully with the fund manager in order to facilitate a smooth transfer of responsibilities to the replacement custodian, and must transfer, where necessary and applicable, all contracts related to the relevant investment fund to the replacement custodian.

c. The fund manager must immediately disclose on its website the appointment of a replacement custodian. The fund manager of a public fund shall also disclose on any other website available to the public according to the controls set out by the Authority regarding the appointment of a replacement custodian for the public fund.

d. The traded funds shall be exempted from the requirement to notify unitholders in writing stipulated in Paragraph (a) of this Article. Provided the announcement of such shall be on the fund manager's website and the Exchange's website.

18.4 PART 4: PUBLIC FUNDS

Article 31: Application to the Authority for the Offer of Units in a Public Fund

a. Any person seeking to offer units in a public fund must submit an application to the Authority which contains the information specified in Annex (2) of these Regulations. The Applicant must be a capital market institution licensed to carry out the activity of managing investments and operating funds or the activity of managing investments7.

b. The applicant must notify the Authority immediately of any change in the documentation and information provided to the Authority.

c. The applicant must pay the fees set by the Authority.

(According to the Authority's Board Resolution no. (2-22-2021) Dated 12/07/1442H. Corresponding to 24/02/2021G. Paragraph (a) of Article (31) of these Regulations shall become effective as of 28/05/1443 H. corresponding to 01/01/2022 G. Moreover, Paragraph (a) of Article (30) of the Investment Funds Regulations issued pursuant to the Authority's Board Resolution No. (1-219-2006) dated 03/12/1427 H. corresponding to 24/12/2006 G. and amended by the Authority's Board Resolution No.)2016-61-1(dated 16/08/1437 H. corresponding to 23/05/2016 G., (which can be viewed via the following link: () shall remain effective until the effective date of Paragraph (a) of Article (31) of these Regulations.)

Article 32: Procedures and Power of the Authority toward the Application

a. The Authority, after receiving all the required information and documents referred to in Paragraph (a) of Article (31) of these Regulations, shall notify the applicant of the completion of its application and shall review the application within (30) days from the date of the notification, and it shall take any of the following decisions:

1) a decision to approve the application, and the Authority will provide the applicant with a notice;

2) a decision to approve the application subject to such conditions and limitations as it considers appropriate by the Authority, and the Authority will provide the applicant with a notice; or

3) a decision to reject the application, and the Authority will provide the applicant with a notice with a statement of reasons.

b. If the Authority deems that offering the proposed fund units may not be in the interest of the investors, or may result in a breach of the Capital Market Law, its Implementing Regulations or the Exchange Rules, then it may take any of the following actions:

1) carry out any enquiries which it considers appropriate;

2) require the applicant or its representative, to appear

before the Authority to answer questions and explain any matters that the Authority considers relevant to the application;

3) require the applicant to provide additional information or confirm in such manner as the Authority may specify, that the information provided is accurate; and

4) defer making a decision for such period as may be reasonably necessary to carry out further study or examination.

c. If having taken actions pursuant to Paragraph (b) of this Article, the Authority determines that the offer to be made pursuant to the application may not be in the interest of the investors or may result in a breach of the Capital Market Law, its Implementing Regulations or the Exchange Rules, the Authority may issue a notification to the applicant stating that the application has been rejected.

d. An applicant may not offer or hold itself out as offering units in a public fund unless it has received the Authority's decision in a written notice referred to in Subparagraphs (1) or (2) of Paragraph (a) of this Article.

e. An applicant must commence the offer and issuance of units in a public fund within (12) months from the date of the Authority's decision referred to in Subparagraph (1) or (2) of Paragraph (a) of this Article. If the applicant did not commence the offer and issuance of units during such period, the Authority's approval shall be deemed to be cancelled. (According to the Authority's Board Resolution no. (2-22-2021) Dated 12/07/1442H. Corresponding to 24/02/2021G. Paragraph (c) of Article (32) of the Investment Funds Regulations issued pursuant to the Authority's Board Resolution No. (1-219-2006) dated 03/12/1427 H. corresponding to 24/12/2006 G. and amended by the Authority's Board Resolution No. (1-(1-219-2006) dated 16/08/1437 H. corresponding to 23/05/2016 G. which can be viewed via the following link: (https://cma.org.sa/RulesRegulations/Regulations/DocLib/IFRs Regulations- Final English_EN.pdf) and which states that: "c) A unitholder who has signed terms and conditions of the relevant fund shall be deemed to be a customer of the fund manager for the purposes of the Authorized Persons Regulations", shall remain effective until the date of 28/05/1443 H. corresponding to 01/01/2022 G.)

Article 33: Contractual format of a Public Fund

a. A public fund shall be established by the signing of the Terms and Conditions of the relevant Fund between the first potential unitholders and the fund manager. The Terms and Conditions shall contain the information required by Annex)1) of these Regulations and the relevant provisions of these Regulations.

b. The contractual relationship between the potential unitholders and the fund manager is established by signing the Terms and Conditions of the relevant fund.

Article 34: Units

a. The potential unitholder shall be the owner of the units to which it has subscribed for as soon as executing the subscription request in the next dealing day deadline for submission of subscription and redemption request.

b. The unitholder shall be entitled to exercise all rights in relation to the units (including, but not limited to, the right to vote at meetings of unitholders);

c. Other than losing his\her investment in the fund or part of it, the unitholder shall not be liable for the debts and obligations of the relevant public fund.

d. A public fund may issue more than one class of units, all unitholders from the same class shall have the same rights as each other and shall be treated equally by the fund manager. No class of unitholders shall have a deferent investment strategies and objectives from the investment strategies and objectives of another class in the same investment fund.

e. A class of a unitholders may not benefit from the rights that prejudice the rights of unitholders of another class.

Article 35: Permitted Fees, Commissions And Expenses

a. The only payments which may be made by the fund manager from the assets of the public fund managed by the fund manager are those in respect of:

1) the costs of dealing in the assets of that public fund, including brokerage fees;

2) costs associated with borrowings related to that public fund;

3) management fees, including any performance or incentive element if applicable;

4) the fees of the custodian;

5) the fees and expenses of the auditor;

6) the fees of the Shariah committee (including Shariah oversight), if any;

7) The expenses for publishing the quarter statement, interim financial statements, and annual reports (including annual financial statements).

8) fees and expenses of the fund board directors; and

9) any other charges or expenses associated with the operation and administration of that public fund (including, but not limited to, the cost of holding unitholder meetings).

b. The fund manager must pay all costs of the offer of units of any public fund and the promotion for it out of its own resources, such costs shall include the preparation of the Fund's Terms and Conditions and other documents required to be submitted to the Authority under these Regulations, beside copying and publication of such.

c. The fund manager shall, in its annual report to unitholders, disclose the ratio of the aggregate fees for the year in question to the average net asset value of the public fund.

Article 36: Public Fund Distributions

a. The fund manager is obliged to distribute dividends to unitholders, unless stated otherwise in the Fund's Terms and Conditions.

b. The fund operator shall be responsible for the process of dividends distribution to unitholders.

c. If dividends are distributed to unitholders, the distribution must be in accordance to the public Fund's Terms and Conditions, and must be announced immediately on the fund manager's website and the Exchange's website or any other website available to the public according to the controls set out by the Authority (where applicable), and it must be reported in the public funds reports prepared by the fund manager and pursuant to Article (76) of these Regulations.

d. The fund manager may not claw back any dividends made to the unitholders.

Article 37: Fund's Subscription in Securities

a. With regards to the provisions of Article (41) of these Regulations and the investment limitations on specialized public funds stipulated in these Regulations, a public fund may subscribe in securities according to the following conditions:

1) The securities are being offered in a public offer within the Kingdom or outside the Kingdom. If the public offer was made in a jurisdiction outside the Kingdom, the offer must be subject to regulatory standards and requirements at least equivalent to those applied on public offering in the Kingdom. The Authority shall have the discretion to assess whether the regulatory standards and requirements applied on the offer is at least equivalent to those applied by the Authority.

2) With the exception of Initial Public Offering that are made in accordance with the Instructions of Book Building Process and Allocation Method in Initial Public Offering, the securities may be subscribed by the public fund at a price which is no more than the offering price;

b. With regards to the provisions of Article (41) of these Regulations, a public fund may subscribe in debt instruments offered by way of private placement with the following conditions:

1) The debt instruments shall be issued by a listed company on the Exchange.

2) The debt instruments shall be rated in as an Investment Grade by an authorized credit rating agency or by an authorized foreign credit rating agency or by a foreign credit rating agency authorized, or registered in a jurisdiction whose regulatory standards and requirements are at least equivalent to those of the Authority; or

3) Such debt instruments shall be guaranteed by the government of the Kingdom;

Article 38: Public Fund Board

a. A public fund shall be supervised by a fund board appointed by the public fund manager since its establishment. The approval of the Authority shall be obtained (10) days prior to any appointment of the fund's board, or any subsequent change in such composition.

b. The number of directors in a fund board must not be less than three (3) directors. The number of independent fund directors of a fund board must not be less than two, or one third of the total number of directors, whichever is greater.

c. If the quorum set forth in Paragraph (b) of this Article is not fulfilled with regard to independent members, the fund manager shall appoint independent members, which fulfill the qualification requirements mentioned in Paragraph (i) of this Article.

d. The fund manager has no right to remove any independent board member, and the removal shall only be made by the unitholders in accordance with the provisions of Article (75) of these Regulations.

e. The fund manager must remove any member of the board of directors of the fund if a special fund resolution is issued by the fund's unitholders requesting the fund manager to remove that member.

f. When more than one public fund is managed by the same fund manager, those public funds may be supervised by a single fund board unless the number of public funds is estimated by the fund manager to be too high to be supervised effectively by a single fund board. The fund board and the fund manager must review annually the number of public funds supervised by that board and assess whether the number is such that effective supervision is compromised and a different board should be appointed for one or more of those public funds. The Authority reserves the right to require a fund manager to appoint another fund board if the Authority considers that the number of public funds the fund board supervises is too high.

g. The fund board shall conduct an annual assessment for each independent member to ensure that there are no relationships or circumstances that affect or may affect his/her independency.

h. A fund board director may not vote on any resolution taken by the fund's board of directors to be taken on any matter in which such fund board director has any direct or indirect particular interest and shall disclose any such interest to the fund board.

i. Any person appointed by the fund manager as a member of the fund board shall fulfill the following eligibility requirements:

1) the person must not be bankrupt or subject to any bankruptcy or insolvency proceedings;

2) the person must not have committed an offense involving fraud or acted in breach of integrity and honesty; and

3) the person must possess the necessary experience and expertise.

j. If a member of the fund board ceases to meet the eligibility requirements set out in Paragraph (i) of this Article, the fund manager must:

1) notify the Authority immediately; and

2) replace a member of the fund board with another person who fulfils the eligibility requirements within (45) days from the date of his knowledge of such, in case the requirements set out in Paragraph (b) of this Article are not met.

k. If any board director resigned or ceased to provide services, the fund manager must:

1) notify the Authority within (10) days.

2) replace the member of the fund's board of director with another person within (45) days from the day the fund manager becomes aware of such resignation or cessation of services, in case the requirements set out in Paragraph (b) of this Article are not met.

l. The fund manager must disclose immediately, on its website and the Exchange's website or any other website available to the public according to the controls set out by the Authority (where applicable), any changes in the membership of the fund's board of directors.

m. The fund manager must provide all necessary information about the public fund to all members of the fund's board in order to enable them to carry out their duties efficiently, the fund manager shall also provide any other information or documentation requested by the fund's board to enable it to perform its duties.

Article 39: Responsibilities of the Members of the Fund Board The responsibilities of the members of the fund board shall include the following:

1) approving material contracts, decisions and reports involving the public fund, including, but not limited to, contracts for the provision of fund management services, contracts for the provision of custody services but excluding contracts entered into pursuant to investment decisions regarding underlying investments made or to be made by the fund;

2) approve a written policy in regards to the voting rights related to the public fund assets.

3) overseeing and, where appropriate, approving or ratifying any conflicts of interest the fund manager has identified;
4) meeting at least twice annually with the fund manager's compliance committee or its compliance officer to review the fund manager's compliance with all applicable rules, laws and regulations, including (without limitation) the requirements of these Regulations;
5) Approving all changes stipulated in Articles (62) and (63) of these Regulations before the fund manager obtains the approval or notification of the unitholders and the Authority (as applicable);
6) confirming the completeness and accuracy (complete, clear, accurate, and not misleading), and compliance with these Regulations, of the Terms and Conditions and of any other document, contractual or otherwise, that includes disclosures relating to the public fund and/or the fund manager and its conduct of the public fund;
7) ensuring that the fund manager carries out its obligations in the best interests of the unitholders, in accordance with these Regulations, the Fund's Terms and Conditions;
8) Reviewing the report that includes assessment of the performance and quality of services provided by the parties involved in providing significant services to the fund referred to in Paragraph (l) of Article (9) of these Regulations, in order to ensure that the fund manager fulfils his responsibilities in the interest of unitholders in accordance with the Fund's Terms and Conditions and the provisions stipulated in these Regulations.
9) Assessing the mechanism of the fund manager's handling of the risks related to the fund's assets in accordance with the fund manager's policies and procedures that detect the fund's risks and how to treat such risks.
10) have a fiduciary duty to unitholders, including a duty to act in good faith, a duty to act in the best interests of the unitholders and a duty to exercise all reasonable care and skill; and
11) taking minutes of meetings that provide all deliberations and facts of the meetings and the decisions taken by the fund's board of director.
12) Review the report containing all complaints and the measures taken regarding them referred to in Paragraph (m) of Article (9) of these Regulations, in order to ensure that the fund manager carries out his responsibilities in a way that serves the interest of unitholders in accordance with the Fund's Terms and Conditions and what contained in this Regulation.

Article 40: Investments Areas

a. The assets and money of a public fund must be invested in investments in accordance with these Regulations, other applicable laws and regulations, and the Fund's Terms and Conditions.
b. The fund manager must invest the assets and money of a public fund, in the following types of investments only:

1) securities;
2) money market transactions concluded with a party subject to Saudi Central Bank supervision or equivalent regulator to the Saudi Central Bank in a jurisdiction outside the Kingdom;
3) Bank deposits with a local bank or institution regulated by an equivalent regulator to the Saudi Central Bank in a jurisdiction outside the Kingdom;
4) real estate assets, without prejudice to the provisions of Paragraph (h) of this Article; and
5) commodities.

c. The fund manager may not invest the money and assets of a public fund in securities issued by the fund manager or its affiliates unless this is permitted by the Terms and Conditions of the relevant public fund.
d. The subscription monies received from a unitholder may not be placed on deposit which is not invested with an affiliate of the fund manager other than on Terms and Conditions equivalent to at least the terms entered into by persons dealing at arm's length.
e. With regards to the provision of Paragraph (b) of this Article, the public fund manager may not lend the fund's assets or money to any person, except in these two cases:

1. The lending of securities by a closed-ended public fund.
2. The lending of securities by an open-ended public fund in a maximum of)30%(of the fund's net assets value.

f. The fund manager may not invest the public fund's money and assets in any type of assets that would result in the fund assuming, guaranteeing, endorsing or otherwise become directly or contingently liable for any obligation or indebtedness of any person.
g. The public fund's money and assets may not be used to acquire any asset that involves the assumption of any liability which is unlimited.
h. Money and assets of a non-real estate closed-ended investment traded fund may not be invested in real estates.

Article 41: Investment Limitations

a. Unless a public fund is established and approved by the Authority as a specialized public fund or a specific waiver has been obtained from the Authority, the following investment limitations shall apply.
b. Investments of the public fund's money and assets must be in another investment fund in accordance with the following conditions:

1.) The investment of the public fund's money and assets shall be limited to investment in the funds registered with the Authority or investment funds outside the Kingdom subject to an equivalent regulatory oversight in a jurisdiction recognized by the Authority as having equivalent regulation. The Authority shall have the discretion to assess whether the jurisdiction has regulatory standards and requirements at least equivalent to those of the Authority.
2.) The investment of the public fund's money and assets in private funds or illiquid assets, in accordance with Paragraph (j) of this Article, shall not exceed (10%) of the public fund's net assets value.
3.) The investment of the money and assets of the public fund shall not exceed (25%) of its net asset value in the units of another investment fund, or in the units of different investment funds issued by the same Capital Market Institution.

c. Not more than)10%(of the issued securities of any single issuer may be held for the benefit of the public fund.
d. With regards to the provisions of Subparagraph (3) of Paragraph (b) of this Article, not more than)10%(of the public fund's net asset value may be invested in a class of securities issued by any single issuer, and in all cases not more than (20%) of fund's net assets value may be invested in all classes of securities issued by any single issuer.
e. The following investment shall be exempted from the provisions of Paragraph (d) of this Article:

1) Investment in debt instruments issued by the Gov-

ernment of the Kingdom in the currency of the fund, and if its currency is other than the currency of the fund, investment in such may not comprise more than (35%) of the net asset value of the public fund.

2) Investment in debt instruments issued by sovereign issuer other the government of the Kingdom, which may comprise not more than 35% of the net asset value of the public fund;

3) Investment of more than 10% of the public fund net asset value in one class of listed debt instruments issued by a single issuer, which may comprise not more than)20%(of the net asset value of the fund

4) Investment of more than (10%) of the public fund's net asset value in shares issued by any single issuer listed on the Exchange or any other regulated exchange. Provided that the issue's percentage of market value does not exceed the total market value of all listed shares on the relevant exchange. This is for a public fund that aims to invest in shares listed on the Exchange or any other regulated exchange, provided that investment in such does not exceed (20%) of the fund's net assets value.

5) Investment of more than 10% of the public fund's net asset value in shares listed in the Exchange or any other regulated exchange by any single issuer affiliated with a field or sector in which the fund's general objective is to invest in it. Provided that the market value of the issue percentage shall not exceed the total market value of that particular field or sector, for the public fund whose Terms and Conditions state that its investment objective is specified in a field or sector of listed shares, provided that the investment in it shall not exceed (20%) of the fund's net asset value.

f. With regards to the provisions of Paragraph (c) of Article (40) of these Regulations, and except for the investment in investment funds, not more than (25%) of the public fund's net asset value may be invested in deferent parties belonging to the same group, including all investments in securities issued by them, money market transactions with them and bank deposits to them.

g. Not more than 20% of the net asset value of the units of another investment fund may be held for the benefit of a public fund.

h. The borrowing of the public fund may not exceed (15%) of its net asset value.

i. Not more than (15%) of the public fund's net asset value may be invested in derivatives.

j. Not more than (10%) of the public fund's net asset value may be invested in illiquid assets.

k. The portfolio of a public fund may not include any security where a call is to be made for any sum unpaid on that security unless it is feasible to pay the entire amount of cash or securities that can be converted into cash from the portfolio of the fund within (5) days.

Article 42: Notification Relating to Substantial Holdings in Shares or Convertible Debt Instruments

a. The fund manager must notify the Exchange when the fund becomes owner or has an interest of)5%(or more of any class of voting shares or convertible debt instrument of the issuer, during a maximum period not exceeding the end of the third trading day following the executing of the transaction or the occurrence of the event which results such ownership or interest. The person notification to the Authority shall also include a list of persons, in which those persons, have an interest in the shares or convertible debt instruments which they own or control.

b. The fund manager referred to in Paragraph (a) of this Article must notify the Exchange in the event of any change to the list of persons referred to in Paragraph (a) of this Article including any event which requires the inclusion of a person to that list or the exclusion of any person who has been previously included in that list, during a period not exceeding the third trading day following the occurrence of the event that led to the relevant event.

c. For the purpose of this Article, when calculating the total number of shares or convertible debt instruments in which the fund is interested, the fund shall be deemed to be interested in any shares or convertible debt instrument owned or controlled by any of the following:

1) a company controlled by that fund.

2) any person or fund acting in concert with the public fund referred to in Paragraph (a) of this Article to acquire interest in or exercise voting rights in the shares or convertible debt instrument of an issuer listed on the Exchange.

d. The notice referred to in Paragraph (a) of this Article must include, at a minimum, the following information:

1) the names of the persons who own or have the right to dispose of the subject shares or convertible debt instruments;

2) details of the ownership process;

3) details of any loans or financial support for the ownership process that the person has received from any other persons.

Article 43: Principal Transactions

a. A fund manager, or any of its affiliates, or any fund sub-manager, or any of its affiliates may not act as principal for their own account or accounts when dealing for public funds managed by them, other than money market funds provided that the exposure of the money market fund to the fund manager, or any of its affiliates, and any fund sub-manager, or any of its affiliates, does not exceed (25%) of the value of all its assets.

b. A fund manager or fund sub-manager may not cause a public fund (other than a money market fund in accordance with Paragraph (a) of this Article) to deal as principal with any other investment fund managed with the same fund manager or fund sub-manager, or with any unitholder the value of whose investment in the public fund exceeds (5%) of the net asset value of that public fund.

Article 44: Real Estate Investment Fund

a. Public real estate investment funds shall be subject to the Real Estate Investment Funds Regulations not these Regulations.

b. Real estate investment funds, whose units are offered for private placement, shall be subject to the relevant provisions of these Regulations, and shall not be subject to the Real Estate Investment Funds Regulations.

Article 45: Index Fund

a. An index fund may only invest in constituent securities of a specified index. b. A specified index for the purposes of this Article is an index which:

1) is published in a manner and place which enables it to be accessed by the public;

2) represents an adequate and appropriate benchmark

for the market to which it refers, clearly defined, has a sufficiently diversified composition, and has sufficiently liquid composition;

3) is solely comprised of securities traded on the Exchange or any other exchange which is subject to regulatory standards and requirements at least equivalent to those of the Exchange.

c. If the index fund does not, at any time during its lifetime, fulfill the requirements in Paragraph (b) of this Article, the fund manager must notify the Authority in writing within (5) days of such requirements not being met and take the necessary measures to ensure compliance with the provisions of this Article

Article 46: Exchange Traded Fund

a. The unitholder of an exchange traded fund shall be deemed to have read and accepted the Fund's Terms and Conditions upon purchasing any unit of an exchange traded fund from the Exchange.

b. Units of an exchange traded fund must be deposited with the Depository Center.

c. The exchange traded fund may invest in its own measurement indicator, provided that the securities weights in the fund's portfolio are matching the weights of those securities in its own measurement to the extent that does not conflict with the Fund's Terms and Conditions.

d. Units in an exchange traded fund may be issued and cancelled for in kind or cash transactions, provided that they are in a pre-determined block size in accordance with the Fund's Terms and Conditions.

e. The custodian of an exchange traded fund must ensure that any units issued or cancelled in the exchange traded fund (and the value of such units) match with fund assets received or paid for those units (and their value), and to rectify any mis-match between exchange traded fund units and its underlying assets.

f. The fund manager of an exchange traded fund must appoint one or more Capital Market Institution which are licensed to carry out dealing activity and as a market maker for the exchange traded fund.

g. The market maker must, at all times, comply with the market making requirements agreed upon with the fund manager and disclosed in the Fund's Terms and Conditions.

h. The total indicative net asset value and indicative net asset value per unit for an exchange traded fund must be regularly calculated by the fund manager during a trading day and must be disclosed on the Exchange on a real-time basis or at any other frequency acceptable to the Authority.

i. The fund manager must calculate the total net asset value and net asset value per unit and disclose this information on the Exchange at the end of each trading day.

j. The exchange traded fund's component securities and their respective weightings must be disclosed by the fund manager on the Exchange.

k. All documents and information of an exchange traded fund and changes thereof shall be deemed to have been made available to unitholders once they have been published on the Exchange.

l. Unitholders shall be deemed to have accepted and signed the Terms and Conditions of the exchange traded fund, upon purchase of units in an exchange trade fund.

m. An exchange traded fund must comply with any conditions or additional continuing obligations as the Authority may specify.

n. The exchange traded fund manager may submit a request for a temporary suspension of trading in accordance with the provisions of the Listing Rules.

o. An index fund may request to be listed on the Parallel Market after the issuance of a special fund resolution by the unitholders, approving of such.

p. In the event of offering the exchange traded fund units in the Parallel Market, the offering of those units shall be limited under the provisions of this Part to the categories of Qualified Investors.

q. As an exception from the provisions of Paragraph (h) of Article)41) of these Regulations, the borrowing of the exchange traded fund in the Parallel Market may not exceed)75%(of the fund's net assets value.

r. As an exception from the provisions of Paragraph (i) of Article (41) of these Regulations, the investments in derivatives of the exchange traded fund in the Parallel Market may not exceed (25%) of the fund's net assets value.

s. The fund manager seeking to register and offer the exchange traded fund units must submit a request to the Authority that includes the information required under these Regulations, and simultaneously submit an application to the Exchange for listing those units in accordance with the provisions of the Listing Rules.

t. The provisions of these Regulations shall apply to the exchange traded fund to the extent that they apply to nature of the exchange traded fund.

Article 47: Closed-Ended Investment Traded Fund

a. The offer, operations and management of a closed-ended investment traded fund in the kingdom must be in accordance with the provisions of this Part and these Regulations, to the extent that does not conflict with the nature of the fund.

b. The unitholder of a Closed-Ended Investment Traded Fund shall be deemed to have read and accepted the Fund's Terms and Conditions upon purchasing any unit of a Closed-Ended Investment Traded Fund from the Exchange.

c. The units of the closed-ended investment traded funds must be deposited with the Securities Depository Center.

d. The fund's total assets value may increase by accepting cash contributions or in-kind contributions, or both, through the following mechanism:

1.) the fund manager must obtain the Authority's approval to offer additional units of the fund by accepting cash or in-kind contributions, or both.

2.) after obtaining the Authority's approval referred to in Subparagraph (1) of Paragraph (d) of this Article, the fund manager must obtain the approval of the unitholders - by an ordinary fund resolution - to offer additional units of the fund by accepting cash contributions or in-kind contributions, or both.

3.) if the fund total assets value is to increase by accepting cash contributions, or cash and in-kind contributions, the new units offering period shall be a minimum of (5) days within a period not later than (6) months from the date of the Authority's approval.

4.) In the event that the value of the units to be offered has been collected, the offered units must be first allocated to the unitholders registered on the day of the unitholders' meeting, then allocate the remaining units (if any) to the remaining subscribers, within a period not exceeding (15) days after the end of the offering period, which is set out in the Fund's Terms and Conditions. The ownership of the in-kind contributions that is to be acquired must be transferred for the interest of the fund, and the new units shall be listed on the Exchange within a period not exceeding (60) days from the end of the offering period. It is not permissible to dispose of the units allocated to subscribers by in-kind contributions of (5%) or more through the process of increasing the fund's total assets value in accordance with Paragraph (d) of this Article within the first year of their trading commencement.

5.) where the fund's total assets value increase is made through accepting in-kind contributions, the additional units shall be allocated to the subscribers by in-kind contributions immediately after obtaining the unitholders' approval referred to in Subparagraph (2) of Paragraph (d) of this Article, provided that the ownership of the in-kind contribution to be acquired is transferred for the interest of the fund, and the new units are listed on the Exchange within a period not exceeding (60) days after the end of the offering period. It is not permissible to dispose the units allocated to subscribers by in-kind contributions of (5%) or more through the process of increasing the fund's total assets value in accordance with Paragraph (d) of this Article within the first year of their trading commencement.

6.) With regards to Subparagraph (3) of Paragraph (d) of this Article, and where the minimum amount required to be raised and which is set out in the Fund's Terms and Conditions was not fulfilled, the fund manager must cancel the offer and return the subscribers' money with no deduction within a period not exceeding (5) days of the end of the offering period.

e. In-kind contributions, referred to in Paragraph (d) of this Article, must be valuated by two accredited valuers independent from the fund manager after ensuring that such accredited valuers have obtained all the required licenses and authorizations from the related government entities to practice their profession.

f. The unitholder shall be entitled to exercise all rights in relation to the units including, but not limited to, the right to vote at the meetings of unitholders.

g. In the event of breaching any of the restrictions forth in these Regulations or in the Fund's Terms and Conditions due to a change of circumstances that is beyond the control of the fund manager or the sub-manager and the breach has not been rectified within (5) days from the date of the occurrence of such breach, the fund manager shall immediately notify the Authority of such event in writing, indicating the action taken and the period of time required to rectify such violation. The Authority may at its absolute discretion vary the time limit for rectifying such breach.

h. The Fund's Terms and Conditions shall allocate a percentage of the total offer amount for institutional investors.

i. No person or group of persons having their names listed in the Fund's Terms and Conditions that they, upon establishment, indicating their ownership of (5%) or more of the fund units (through in-kind contributions), may dispose any of the units in which they subscribed, during the first year of trading commencement of the relevant fund's units.

j. To achieve the independence of a member of the fund's board of directors, the following must be complied:

1.) an independent director of a closed-ended investment traded fund shall be able to perform his/her duties, express his/her opinions and vote on decisions objectively with no bias in order to help the board make correct decisions that contribute to achieving the interests of the fund.

2.) the board of a closed-ended investment traded fund shall conduct an annual assessment of the member's independence and ensure that there are no relationships or circumstances that affect or may affect his/her independence.

3.) with regards to the definition of "Independent Fund Director" in the Glossary of Defined Terms Used in the Regulations and Rules of the Capital Market Authority, cases that negate the independence requirement for an independent director in the board of a closed-ended investment traded fund, include but are not limited to, the following:

a.) if he/she holds 5% or more of the fund's units or the units of another fund under the management of the same fund manager; or is a first degree relative of someone who owns such percentage.

b.) if he/she is a representative of a legal person that holds 5% or more of the fund's units or the units of another fund under the management of the same fund manager;

c.) if he/she is a representative of a legal person that holds 5% or more of the shares of the fund manager, an affiliate of the fund manager, the custodian or an affiliate of the custodian;

d.) if he/she is a first degree relative of any member of the board of the fund or any other fund under the management of the same fund manager;

e.) if he/she is a first degree relative of any employees of any related party of the fund.

f.) if he/she is an employee or used to be an employee during the preceding two years, of the fund manager or any party related to the fund, or if he/she, during the preceding two years, held a controlling interest in any of these parties.

g.) if he/she receives financial consideration from the fund in addition to the remuneration for his/her membership of the board.

k. In the event of offering the closed-ended investment traded fund units in the Parallel Market, the offering of those units shall be limited under the provisions of this Part to the categories of Qualified Investors.

l. A closed-ended investment fund may request to be listed on the Parallel Market after the issuance of a fund special resolution consented by the unitholders.

m. A closed-ended investment traded fund may invest its money and assets in private funds provided that it does not exceed 25% of the fund net asset value. Further, a closed-ended investment traded feeder fund or fund of funds may not invest in private funds.

n. As an exception from the provisions of Paragraph (h) of Article (41) of these Regulations, the borrowing of a closed-ended investment traded fund in the Main Market may not exceed 30% of the fund's net assets value.

o. As an exception from the provisions of Paragraph (h) of Article (41) of these Regulations, the loans of a closed-ended investment traded fund in the Parallel Market may not exceed 100% of the fund's net assets value.

p. As an exception from the provisions of Paragraph (j) of Article (41) of these Regulations, a closed-ended investment traded fund may invest more than 10% of its net asset value in illiquid assets, provided that investment in a single illiquid asset may not exceed (25%) of the fund's net assets value.

Article 48: Conditions for Offering Closed-Ended Investment Traded Fund The following must be must be satisfied when submitting an application for the offer of closed- ended investment traded fund units:
a. The fund type: the investment traded fund shall be a closed-ended fund.
b. The minimum requirement for establishment: the fund's total assets value, at the establishment, must be (300) million Saudi Riyals at least to offer its units in the Main Market, and not less than (100) million to offer its units in the Parallel Market.
c. The nominal value per unit: the nominal value per unit must be (10) Saudi Riyals.
d. Subscription consideration: public unitholders may only subscribe by way of cash contributions. e. Subscription limit: the minimum subscription must not exceed (1000) units per unitholder.

Article 49: Net Assets of Closed-ended Investment Traded Fund Units With regards to the provisions of Articles (71) and (72) of these Regulations, the fund manager must publish the net assets value of each unit during a period consistent with the nature of the fund's assets, provided that such period does not exceed (6) months at most.

Article 50: Offer Requirements for Closed-Ended Investment Traded Fund
a. A fund manager seeking to offer a closed-ended investment traded fund units on the Exchange must submit an application to the Authority that includes the information required under these Regulations, and simultaneously submit an application to the Exchange for listing those units in accordance with the provisions of the Listing Rules. b. In addition to the requirements set forth in Article (61) of these Regulations, the Fund's Terms and Conditions must include all necessary information to enable the potential unitholders to make an informed judgement based on sufficient information regarding the investment offered to them, in addition to the following information:

1. Key dates and initial subscription procedures: this section must include the following information: a. timetable showing the expected dates of the initial offering. b. description of the initial subscription procedures. c. the mechanism of the fund manager to allocate units among subscribers.
2. The mechanism of increasing the fund's total assets value, through accepting cash or in- kind contributions, or both.
3. A letter by the fund manager's legal advisor, who is licensed to practice the profession in the Kingdom, regarding the legal due diligence report in the form set out in Annex (12) of these Regulations.
4. A letter by the fund manager regarding the due diligence report in the form set out in Annex (13) of these Regulations.

c. When submitting an application for offering, the fund manager must provide the Authority with any contracts related to the fund or the fund's assets management.
d. When submitting an application for offering, the fund manager must provide the Authority with the names of two receiving agents, at least. e. The fund manager may not offer units publicly without making prior arrangements for listing those units on the Exchange in accordance with the Listing Rules. f. The approval of the application for offering will only be given by the Authority if:

1. the Authority has received a notification from the Exchange regarding the Exchange's conditional approval of the corresponding application for listing pursuant to the Listing Rules;
2. the conditional approval mentioned under Subparagraph (1) of Paragraph (f) of this Article has not been withdrawn by the Exchange; and
3. the Authority is satisfied that the information contained in the Terms and Conditions is complete and fulfills the requirements of the Capital Market Law and its Implementing Regulations.

Article 51: Closed-Ended Investment Traded Fund Buy-Back and Sale of its Units
a. For the purposes of implementing these Regulations, the process of a closed-ended investment traded fund buying-back and selling its units is excluded in accordance with the provisions of these Regulations from the actions and practices mentioned in Paragraph (a) of Article (49) of the Capital Market Law.
b. The closed-ended investment traded fund may buy-back its units unless the fund's terms and conditions stipulate otherwise, in accordance with the following controls:

1. The buy-back of the fund's units is for the purpose of keeping them as treasury units or in order to cancel them.
2. The percentage of treasury units for the fund shall not exceed (10%), at any time, of the units issued by the fund.
3. Issuance of a special fund resolution by the unitholders approving the buy-back process, specifying the maximum number of units subject to the buy-back and its purposes, the sources of financing the buy-back process, and authorising the fund manager to complete the buy-back within a period not exceeding twelve months from the date of the issuance of the referenced special fund resolution. Moreover, unitholders may, at any time, issue a special fund resolution to change the purposes of the buy-back.
4. Unless the purpose of buying-back the units of the fund is to cancel them, the units buy- backs must be made not exceeding (10%) of the quantity approved at the meeting of the unitholders for buy-back within one trading day, unless the approved quantity, or the remainder of the approved quantity that is not bought-back yet, is less than (10%) of the trading volume of the fund's units the day before the buy-back.
5. The buy-back price shall not exceed (5%) of the market closing price on the day preceding the day on which the buy-back is executed.
6. The buy-back does not result in a decrease in the ownership of public unitholders to less than the liquidity requirements stipulated in the Listing Rules (where applicable) for the units issued by the Fund.
7. The buy-back shall be made through the Exchange and not through a special transaction.
8. The treasury units bought-back by the fund shall have any no voting rights at the unitholders meeting and shall not have any right in fund distributions.

c. The closed ended investment traded fund may not buy-back its units for use as treasury units except for the following purposes:

1. If the fund's board of directors or whoever they may delegate believes that the price of the units in the

Exchange is less than their fair value.

2. Swaps operations in return for purchase of an asset.

3. Any other purpose approved by the Authority.

d. A closed-ended investment traded fund manager regarding buy-back of the fund's units must comply with the following:

1. Disclose on its website and the Exchange's website, the decision of the Fund's Board of Directors to approve the Fund's buy-back of its units, at least half an hour before the start of the trading period for the next day.

2. Call for a meeting of unitholders in accordance with the provisions of Paragraph (d) of Article (75) of these Regulations.

e. In the event of a special fund resolution issued by the unitholders approving the buy-back process, the closed ended investment traded fund manager must disclose this on its website and the Exchange's website, at least half an hour before the start of the trading period for the next day.

f. The closed ended investment traded fund manager must immediately notify the Exchange, according to the method determined by the Exchange, of the fund's buy-back of its units and the purpose of the buy-back, in order for the Exchange to publish that information in its periodic report on the funds buy-back of their units.

g. The closed ended investment traded fund manager must include the annual report of the fund details of the treasury units held by the fund, and the details of disposal of these units.

h. The closed ended investment traded fund may sell its treasury units if the Fund's Terms and Conditions stipulate that this is permissible, according to the following controls:

1. Executing the sale of treasury units shall not exceed (10%) of the total amount of treasury units to be sold within one trading day, unless the approved quantity, or the remainder of the quantity to be sold is less than (10%) of the trading volume of the fund's units the day before the buy-back.

2. The sale of the treasury units shall be through the Exchange and not through a special transaction. As an exception to this, the sale of these units is not required to be through the Exchange if the purpose of the treasury units is to be used as a compensation in the swaps in exchange for buying an asset in accordance with the Fund's Terms and Conditions.

Article 52: Disclosure Requirements of Closed-Ended Investment Traded Fund

a. Disclosure of material developments

1.) The fund manager must disclose to the Authority and the unitholders without delay any material developments in its sphere of activity which are not public knowledge and which may affect the fund's assets and liabilities, its financial position or the general course of its business, and which may:

a. which leads to movements in the price of the fund's listed units; or

b. significantly affect the fund's ability to meet its commitments in respect to the debt instruments.

2.) In determining whether a development falls within the scope of Paragraph (a) of this Article, the fund manager must assess whether a prudent investor would be likely to consider information about the development in making his/her investment decision.

b. Disclosure of specific events

The fund manager must disclose without any delay to the Authority and the unitholders any of the following developments (whether a material development as per Paragraph (a) of this Article or not):

1.) any transaction to buy, sell, mortgage or lease an asset at a price equal to or greater than (10%) of the fund's net assets value according to the latest reviewed interim financial statements or audited annual financial statements, whichever is later;

2.) any losses equal to or greater than (10%) of the fund's net assets according to the latest reviewed interim financial statements or audited annual financial statements, whichever is later;

3.) any dispute, including any litigation, arbitration or mediation where the value involved is equal to or greater than (5%) of the fund's net assets according to the latest reviewed interim financial statements or audited annual financial statements, whichever is later;

4.) the increase or decrease in the fund's net assets equal to or greater than (10%) according to the latest reviewed interim financial statements or audited annual financial statements, whichever is later;

5.) the increase or decrease of the fund's gross profit equal to or greater than (10%) according to the latest audited annual financial statements;

6.) any transaction between the fund and a related party or any arrangement through which the fund and a related party invest in any project or asset or provide financing thereof if such transaction or arrangement is equal to or greater than (1%) of the fund's gross revenues according to the latest audited annual financial statements;

7.) any interruption in the principal activities of the fund equal to or greater than (5%) of the fund's gross revenues according to the latest audited annual financial statements;

8.) the issuance of any judgement, decision, order or declaration by a court or judicial body, whether at first instance or on appeal, which may adversely affect the Fund's utilization of any portion of its assets which is equal to or exceeds (5%) of the fund's net assets according to the latest reviewed interim financial statements or audited annual financial statements, whichever is later; or

9.) any proposed change to the fund's total assets value.

c. Disclosure relating to substantial unitholder dealings:

1.) Any person must notify the Exchange if such person becomes the owner of, or is interested in, (5%) or more of the fund's units, within a maximum period not exceeding the end of the third trading day following the execution of the transaction or the occurrence of the event which results such ownership or interest; the notification shall also include a list of persons who have an interest in the units that they own or control.

2.) The person referred to in Subparagraph (1) of Paragraph (c) of this Article must notify the Exchange in the event of any change to the list of persons referred to in Subparagraph (1) of Paragraph (c) of this Article, including any event which requires the inclusion of a person to that list or the exclusion of any person who has been previously included in that list. Such notification must be made during a period not exceeding the end of the third trading day following the occurrence of the event that led to the relevant change.

3.) For the purposes of this Paragraph, in calculating

the total number of the fund's units in which a person is interested, that person shall be deemed to be interested in any units owned or controlled by any of the following persons:

a. a relative of that person;

b. a company controlled by that person; or

c. any other persons with which that person has agreed to act in concert to acquire an interest in the fund units.

4.) the notification referred to in Subparagraph (1) of Paragraph (c) of this Article must contain at least the following information:

a. the names of the persons who own the units or who have the right to dispose of the subject units;

b. details of the ownership process; and

c. details of any loans or financial support for the ownership process that the person has received from any other persons.

d. Where, in the opinion of the fund manager, disclosure of any matter required under the provisions of this Part would be unduly detrimental to the fund and the omission is not likely to mislead unitholders with regard to facts and circumstances, knowledge of which is essential for the assessment of the fund units in question, the fund manager may apply to postpone the relevant requirement or waive it. The fund manager must in that case provide the Authority on a strictly confidential basis with a statement of the request together with the reasons why the fund manager believes that the information shall not be disclosed at that time. The Authority may approve the application for postponing or waiving the relevant requirement or reject it. If the Authority approves the application, the Authority may at any time require the fund manager to disclose any information on the waiver or postponement of the disclosure.

e. All information and material developments set forth in this Article shall be deemed confidential until they are disclosed. Before disclosing such information, the fund manager is prohibited from communicating such information to parties not bound by a confidentiality obligation and an obligation to protect such information. A fund manager must also take all necessary steps to prevent the leakage of any information or material developments before disclosing it as per these Regulations.

f. The fund manager must determine the need to publish a disclosure to the public in response to rumors related to any material developments, and the Authority may require such publication to be made by the fund manager as it sees appropriate

.

g. The fund manager must comply with the provisions of the Investment Funds Announcements Instructions.

h. The fund manager must publish all information required to be disclosed under this Article on its website and the Exchange's website, and such information must be complete, clear, accurate and not misleading.

Article 53: Specialized Public Funds

Specialized public funds which are regulated by the provisions of these regulations shall include:

1. money market funds;
2. feeder funds;
3. fund of funds; and
4. capital protected funds.
5. endowment funds.

Applications to offer other types of specialized public funds may be made to the Authority, to consider each application individually.

Article 54: Money Market Fund

a. A money market fund manager must invest the fund's assets and money only in the following types of investments:

1 Money market transactions concluded with a party regulated by the Saudi Central Bank or an equivalent regulator to the Saudi Central Bank in a jurisdiction outside the Kingdom.

2 Debt instruments.

3 Derivatives.

4 Bank deposits with institutions regulated by the Saudi Central Bank or equivalent regulator to the Saudi Central Bank in a jurisdiction outside the Kingdom.

5 Units of money market funds with a similar strategy.

6 Units of debt instruments funds with fixed income.

b. A money market fund may not invest in derivatives contracts except for the purposes of hedging, and the value of such investment must not exceed (5%) of the fund's net assets value and the issuer entity of these contracts should be subject to prudential rules issued by an equivalent regulator to the Authority.

c. The value of a money market fund investments in securitization must not exceed (10%) of the fund's net assets value.

d. With regards to Paragraph (a) of this Article, the investments of a money market fund with or in a single counterparty, or with or in parties belonging to the same group, may not not exceed (25%) of the fund's net assets. This includes all investments in money market transactions concluded with one counterparty or different parties belonging to the same group, securities issued by one person or different parties belonging to the same group, and bank deposits with one or different parties belonging to the same group.

e. Units of investment funds are excluded from the provisions of Paragraph (d) of this Article, provided that the total money market fund investments in units of another investment fund, or in different investment fund units issued by the same Capital Market Institution, shall not exceed (25%) of the net asset value of the fund.

f. Debt instruments issued by the Kingdom's government are excluded from the provisions of Paragraphs (c) and (d) of this Article.

g. Money market fund must have a foreseen average of the date of maturity not exceeding (180) calendar days.

h. A money market fund manager must ensure, at all times, that it has liquidity equalling to at least (10%) of the fund's net assets value or that it has investments that have a maturity, or a remaining maturity, period not more than (7) days.

i. A money market fund manager must carry out a Stress Testing at least twice a year to detect risks related to the fund and ensure treatment of these risks as soon as possible.

Article 55: Feeder Fund

a. A public fund which is a feeder fund may not invest in another feeder fund.
b. A public fund which is a feeder fund may not invest in more than one investment fund.

Article 56: Fund of Funds

a. A fund of funds may retain up to (5%) of its total assets as cash and cash equivalents.
b. A fund of funds shall invest in a minimum of (3) investment funds. The minimum investments in each such investment funds shall be (5%) of the fund of funds' net asset value, this percentage does not apply to the fund's investments in additional investment funds.
c. Not more than (50%) of a fund of funds' net asset value may be invested in a single investment fund.
d. A fund of funds may invest its money and assets in private funds, provided that does not exceed (10%) of the fund net assets value.

Article 57: Capital Protected Fund

a. The name of capital protected fund must be included the phrase "capital protected" in all the fund's relevant documents.
b. All investments of the capital protected fund must be consistent with the investment objectives of the fund for the protection of the capital invested by the unitholders and to returning their capital to them in a predetermined future date.
c. Without prejudice to Paragraph (b) of Article (40) of these Regulation, the investments of a capital protected fund with or in a single entity, or with or in parties belonging to the same group, may not not exceed (25%) of the fund's net assets. These investments shall include money market transactions concluded with one counterparty or different parties belonging to the same group, debt instruments issued by one or different parties belonging to the same group, and bank deposits with one or different parties belonging to the same group.

Article 58: Endowment Fund

a. The endowment fund manager must comply with the requirements set by the General Authority of Awqaf without prejudice to the requirements contained in the Capital Market Law and its Implementing Regulations.
b. The endowment fund shall be exempted from the provisions of redemption requests mentioned in Article (65) of these Regulations.
c. An endowment fund may invest its money and assets in private funds, provided that does not exceed (25%) of the fund net assets value.

Article 59: Breach of Investment Limitations

a. If any of the investment limitations referred to in these Regulations or in the Fund's Terms and Conditions are breached due to an act of the fund manager or the fund sub- manager, the fund manager shall notify the Authority in writing immediately and shall take, within five (5) days from the date of the occurrence of such breach, the necessary steps to rectify the breach, and the Authority may change this period at its discretion.
b. If any of the investment limitations referred to in these Regulations or in the Fund's Terms and Conditions are breached due to a change of circumstance that is beyond the control of the fund manager or the fund sub-manager, and the breach has not been rectified within (5) days from the date of the occurrence of such breach, the fund manager shall notify the compliance officer and/or compliance committee of such event immediately, indicating the rectification plan and ensure the rectification of the matter as soon as possible.
c. The fund manager must report all breaches of the investment limitations referred to in Paragraph (a) of this Article to the compliance officer and/or compliance committee and to the fund board upon occurrence.
d. The compliance officer and/or compliance committee must maintain a permanent record of all breaches of the investment limitations referred to in Paragraphs (a) and (b) of this Article, and document the action taken and period of time required to rectify any such breach.
e. The fund manager must include in the annual report all breaches of the investment limitations referred to in Paragraph (a) of this Article, and disclose cases of non- compliance with the rectification plan referred to in Paragraph (b) of this Article.

Article 60: Exercise of Rights in Respect of Public Fund Assets

a. The fund manager must exercise or not exercise any rights associated with any assets of any public fund a fund manager must act in accordance with the best interests of the unitholders of the relevant public fund.
b. With respect to voting rights (if any) associated with any assets of any public fund which the manager manages, the fund manager must:

1. develop a written policy regarding such voting rights which shall be approved by the fund board; and
2. exercise or not exercise voting rights in accordance with the written policy approved by the fund board and maintain full records documenting the exercise of voting rights (including the reasons for exercising or not exercising voting rights in a particular way).

c. The fund manager must disclose on its website and the Exchange's website or any other website available to the public according to the controls set out by the Authority (where applicable) its policies regarding voting rights, in relation to each fund the fund manager manages.

Article 61: Requirement to Produce Terms and Conditions

a. A public fund manager must provide to unitholders and potential unitholders and the custodian the Terms and Conditions in Arabic and free of charge.
b. A public Fund's Terms and Conditions must contain the basis upon which potential unitholders are to enter into contractual relations with the fund manager regarding the investment being offered to them and must include the information specified in Annex (1) of these Regulations.
c. The Terms and Conditions shall be deemed as satisfying the terms of business requirements of the Capital Market Institutions Regulations.
d. Before accepting an initial subscription to a public fund, the fund manager must ensure that the unitholder has received and signed a copy of the Terms and Conditions.
e. Identical Terms and Conditions must apply to all unitholders of the same class in a public fund.
f. The fund manager must file an updated version of the Fund's Terms and Conditions with the Authority within (10) days of any change being made to the Terms and Conditions, and to the custodian as soon as them being updated.

g. The fund manager must publish, on its website and the Exchange's website or any other website available to the public according to the controls set out by the Authority (where applicable) of the Fund's Terms and Conditions, as well as announce of any updates or of any updated version of the Fund's Terms and Conditions in its website and the Exchange's website or any other website available to the public according to the controls set out by the Authority (where applicable) within (10) days of any update.

Article 62: Approval of the Authority and Consent of Unitholders to Fundamental Changes

a. A fund manager must obtain the consent of the unitholders in the relevant fund to the proposed fundamental change by way of an ordinary fund resolution.

b. As an exception to Paragraph (a) of this Article, the fund manager must obtain the approval of the unitholders in the concerned fund for the proposed fundamental change mentioned in Subparagraph (9) of Paragraph (d) of this Article through a special fund resolution.

c. A fund manager, having obtained the approval of the unitholders specified in Paragraphs (a) and (b) of this Article, must obtain the consent of the Authority in the relevant fund to the proposed fundamental change.

d. For the purposes of these Regulations, "fundamental change" means:

1) a change which significantly changes the purposes, nature or class of the public fund;
2) a change which may have a material adverse effect on the unitholders or their rights in relation to the closed-ended public fund;
3) a change which alters the risk profile of the public fund; or
4) the voluntary withdrawal of a fund manager from its position as the fund manager.
5) would reasonably be expected to cause the unitholders to reconsider their participation in the closed-ended public fund;
6) results in any increased payments out of the assets of the closed-ended public fund to a fund manager or any member of the fund board or an affiliate of either;
7) introduces any new type of payment out of the assets of the closed-ended public fund;
8) materially increases other types of payment out of the assets of the closed-ended public fund.
9) change in the eligibility date or the termination of the closed-ended public fund.
10) increase the total value of the closed-ended public fund's assets by accepting cash or in-kind contributions, or both.
11) any other instances determined by the Authority from time to time and reported to the fund manager.

e. The fund manager must obtain the fund board approval before carrying out any fundamental change.

f. The fund manager must notify the unitholders and disclose details of fundamental changes on its website and any other website available to the public according to the controls set out by the Authority (10) days before of the date in which the change becomes effective.

g. Details of all fundamental changes must be included in the next fund report prepared by the fund manager pursuant to Article (76) of these Regulations.

h. The unitholders of an open-ended public fund have the right to redeem their units before any fundamental changes are effective; without incurring any redemption fees)if any(.

i. The traded funds shall be exempted from the requirement to notify unitholders in writing, stipulated in Paragraph (f) of this Article. Provided that the announcement of such shall be made on the fund manager's website and the Exchange's website.

Article 63: Notification to the Authority and Unitholders of non-Fundamental Changes

a. The fund manager must notify the Authority and unitholders, and disclose on its website and any other website available to the public according to the controls set out by the Authority regarding any non-fundamental changes in the public fund that it manages (10) days before the change becomes effective, and unitholders of an open-ended public fund have the right to redeem their units before any non-fundamental change takes effect without imposing any redemption fees (if any).

b. The fund manager must obtain the fund board approval before carrying out any non- fundamental change.

c. For the purposes of these Regulations, "non-fundamental change" means a change, excluding Article (62) provisions of these Regulations.

d. Details of all non-fundamental changes must be included in the next fund report prepared by the fund manager pursuant to Article (76) of these Regulations.

e. The traded funds shall be exempted from the requirement to send the notice to all unitholders mentioned in Paragraph (a) of this Article, provided that the announcement of such shall be made on the fund manager's website and the Exchange's website.

Article 64: Initial Offer Period

a. Details of any initial offer (including the duration of the initial offer period and the initial price of the units) must be provided in the Fund's Term and Conditions.

b. During the initial offer period, units may only be offered by the fund manager at the initial price.

c. The duration of any initial offer period must not exceed (60) days. During such period and until the elapse of the initial offer no investment of subscription monies raised to be made except investing them in money market funds, deposits, or money market transactions concluded with a party subject to the Saudi Central Bank supervision or equivalent regulator to the Saudi Central Bank in a jurisdiction outside the Kingdom, without prejudice to Paragraph (d) of Article (40) of these Regulations.

d. The fund manager must specify a minimum amount that must be raised through investors subscriptions during the initial offer period, without prejudice to Paragraph (d) of Article (40) of these Regulations, no investment of subscription monies raised may be made until this minimum sum has been achieved, except for its investment in money market funds, or in bank deposits and money market transactions concluded with a party subject to the Saudi Central Bank supervision or equivalent regulator to the Saudi Central Bank in a jurisdiction outside the Kingdom. The fund manager must disclose the required minimum amount that must be raised in the Fund's Terms and Conditions.

e. In case the minimum amount referred to in Paragraph (d) of this Article is not raised during the initial offer period, the fund manager must return to the unitholders their full subscriptions monies together with any returns generated from investing the subscriptions monies as per the Paragraphs (c) and (d) of this Article without any deduction.

f. At the end of the offer period, the fund manager must

provide the Authority within (10) days the offer results, and disclose them on its website, in accordance with the requirements of Annex (10) of these Regulations.

Article 65: Subscription and Redemption

a. Units in a public fund may only be subscribed for or redeemed on a dealing day. A public fund, which is not a closed-ended fund, shall have not less than two dealing days during each week. A public fund which is a closed-ended investment fund shall have such dealing days as the fund manager specifies in the Fund's Terms and Conditions.
b. The deadlines for submission of requests for subscriptions and redemptions for a public fund must be specified in the public Fund's Terms and Conditions.
c. The fund operator must process requests for subscriptions or redemption at the price calculated at the next valuation point following the deadline for submission of requests for subscription or redemption.
d. A fund operator must be obliged to meet subscription or redemption requests, subject to any provisions to the contrary in the public Fund's Terms and Conditions or in these Regulations.
e. The fund operator must pay the unitholder proceeds of redemption no later than the close of business on the fifth day at the latest of the following the valuation point at which the price for the redemption was determined.

Article 66: Deferring Redemptions

a. A fund manager may defer fulfilling a request for redemptions from an open-ended public fund until the next dealing day if the total of all unitholders' redemption requests to be fulfilled on any dealing day amounts to a total of (10%) or more of the net asset value of the fund.
b. Each fund manager must adopt fair and equitable procedures by which those redemption requests which are to be deferred are selected and disclose those procedures in the Fund's Terms and Conditions.

Article 67: Suspension of Subscription or Redemption of Units

a. The fund manager must suspend the subscription and redemption of units if the Authority orders any such suspension.
b. The fund manager may not suspend the subscription and redemption of units, unless in the following circumstances:

1) if the fund manager reasonably believes that any such suspension is in the best interests of the unitholders in the public fund; or
2) if there has been a suspension of dealing on the principal market in which the securities or other assets held by the public fund are dealt, either in general or in relation to assets of the public fund which the fund manager reasonably believes to be material to the net asset value of the public fund.

c. For any suspension imposed by the fund manager pursuant to Paragraph (b) of this Article, the fund manager must:

1) ensure that any suspension continues only for as long as it is necessary and justified having regard to the best interests of the unitholders;
2) review the suspension on a regular basis and shall consult with the fund's board of directors, the custodian and the fund operator on a regular basis regarding that;
3) notify both the Authority and the unitholders immediately of any suspension, and give the reasons for the suspension, and shall similarly notify both the Authority and the unitholders as soon as the suspension ends and disclose it on its website and any other website available to the public according to the controls set out by the Authority;

d. the Authority shall have the power to lift such suspension if the Authority believes that to do so is in the best interests of unitholders.

Article 68: Transaction Fees The only transaction charges which may be charged in relation to a public fund are subscription charges, redemption charges and transfer of ownership charges. Any of these charges must be disclosed in full in the Terms and Conditions of the relevant Fund.

Article 69: Borrowing to Meet Redemption Requests

a. A fund manager shall use its best efforts to retain sufficient liquidity to meet redemption requests.
b. A fund manager may borrow to meet redemption requests where the money available in the account designated as being for the benefit of the relevant public fund is insufficient to meet redemption requests in a manner that serves the interest of unitholders and does not conflict with the Fund's Terms and Conditions.
c. Borrowing to meet redemption requests pursuant to this Article shall not be subject to the percentage set out in Paragraph (h) of Article (41) of these Regulations.

Article 70: Securities Advertisements and Promotional Materials

a. A securities advertisement which is communicated to unitholders or potential unitholders in relation to a public fund must satisfy the requirements of this Article and the applicable provisions of the Capital Market Institutions Regulations and the Securities Business Regulations.
b. Any securities advertisement relating to a public fund must include information about how to obtain a copy of the Fund's Terms and Conditions and fund reports to unitholders, and a reference to the disclosure in the Fund's Terms and Conditions of the risks of investing in the fund.
c. If a securities advertisement includes performance information for a fund or any representations about the performance of a fund or its manager, the securities advertisement must comply with the following requirements:

1) total return information must be shown net of all actual historical expenses of the fund and the securities advertisement may include the total return of a fund that is gross of fees and expenses if the return is presented in addition to, and with no greater prominence than, returns of the fund that are net of actual expenses;
2) total return information for a fund must be presented in comparison to the total return for the same period of an appropriate index or other benchmark disclosed in the Fund's Terms and Conditions. If the index or other benchmark does not include all elements of total return, the presentation must disclose what elements of return are not included in the index or other benchmark and how that omission affects the comparison of the fund's total return to the index other benchmark; and
3) the securities advertisement must disclose that the

value of an investment in a public fund is variable and may increase or decrease.

d. If any total return is shown for a fund, the securities advertisement must show total returns for periods of one, (3), (5) and (10) years (or since inception if the life of the fund is shorter than these periods, but no performance shall be provided for a period of less than one year).

e. Total returns shown for a fund in accordance with Paragraph (d) of this Article must be current through the end of the most recent calendar quarter (using the same calendar as for the preparation of the fund's financial statements).

f. If there is any respect in which the fund performance information may be misleading to potential unitholders, the securities advertisement must include relevant explanatory disclosure of the circumstances relating to the performance information.

g. A securities advertisement must include the risk warnings required under the Capital Market Institutions Regulations, as applicable.

h. A securities advertisement may include a list of all of a fund's portfolio holdings or a list of selected holdings. If a securities advertisement includes only a list of selected holdings, the holdings listed must be selected in an objective, balanced manner, and the securities advertisement must disclose the basis for selecting the holdings listed.

i. A securities advertisement may not include:

1) a projection or prediction of the total return or investment performance of the public fund or of unitholders of a public fund (except that a securities advertisement for a public fund with a guarantee or other principal protection feature may disclose any guaranteed minimum return); or

2) any form of testimonial, that is, statements about the experience of actual or fictitious unitholders of that fund or other funds with the same manager.

j. The fund manager must provide to the Authority copies of any securities advertisement communicated to unitholders or potential unitholders no later than (5) days following the first communication of such securities advertisement.

Article 71: Valuation

a. The fund operator shall be responsible for valuing the assets of the public fund. In so doing, the fund operator shall conduct a full and fair valuation.

b. The assets of a public fund must be valued by the fund operator each dealing day at such time as specified in the Terms and Conditions of such public fund, and for the duration not exceeding one day from the deadline for submission of requests for subscription or redemption.

c. The fund manager must, in the Fund's Terms and Conditions, document the basis of the valuation of units and, where appropriate, any valuation methodology, and must ensure that the valuation methodology and procedures are applied in a fair and consistent manner.

d. The fund manager must develop, maintain and state in the Fund's Terms and Conditions a clear policy covering valuation, valuation points, pricing and dealing in units. The fund manager must adopt a consistent approach to the valuation of units for the purposes of meeting the subscription and redemption requests and transfer of ownership.

e. The fund operator must comply with the provisions of Annex (5) of these Regulations in relation to valuation of the public funds.

Article 72: Pricing of Units

a. The fund operator shall be responsible for calculating the price of the units in a public fund that it operates. The price of units for subscriptions and redemptions on any dealing day shall be calculated by reference to the net asset value per unit of the public fund at the valuation point on the relevant dealing day.

b. The fund operator must state the Unit prices to at least four decimal places.

c. The fund manager must publish the net asset value per unit on the business day following the dealings day on its website and any other website available to the public according to the controls set out by the Authority;

Article 73: Incorrect Valuation or Pricing

a. The fund operator must record each instance where an asset of the public fund is valued incorrectly or the price of a unit is calculated incorrectly.

b. The fund operator must compensate all harmed unitholders (including former unitholders) as soon as reasonably practicable for all valuation or pricing errors

c. The fund manager must immediately report to the Authority any valuation or pricing error of 0.5% or more of the price of a unit and disclose it immediately on its website and any other website available to the public according to the controls set out by the Authority and in the public fund's reports prepared in accordance to articles (76) of these Regulations

d. The fund manager, in its reports to the Authority pursuant to Article (77) of these Regulations, must provide a summary of all valuation and pricing errors.

Article 74: Audit Requirements

a. The fund manager must appoint an auditor prior to the establishment of a public fund. The auditor of the public fund must be registered with the Authority in accordance with the Rules for Registering Auditors of Entities Subject to the Authority's Supervision and must be independent from the fund manager according to the independence standard stated in Certified Public Accountants Regulations and its Implementing Regulations.

b. Where (9) months have lapsed since the establishment of a public fund before the end of such public fund's fiscal year, an audit must be conducted by the end of the first fiscal year.

c. Where (9) months or less have lapsed since the establishment of a public fund before the end of such public fund's fiscal year, an audit may be conducted at the end of the second fiscal year of the public fund.

d. The appointment or the substitution of any auditor must be approved by the fund board.

e. The fund board must reject the appointment of an auditor, or instruct the fund manager to replace an auditor which has already been appointed in relation to the public fund, if:

1) there are any outstanding and material allegations of professional misconduct in relation to audit functions by the auditor;

2) the auditor of the public fund ceases to be an independent auditor;

3) the auditor of the public fund is no longer registered with the Authority;

4) the fund board determines that the auditor does not have sufficient qualifications and experience to perform a satisfactory auditing functions; or

5) the Authority, in its absolute discretion, instructs the public fund manager to replace the auditor appointed in relation to the public fund.

f. The audit fees of the auditor shall be determined by the fund manager with the approval of the fund board.

Article 75: Meetings of Unitholders

a. The fund manager may call for a meeting of unitholders on its own initiative, provided that the subject of the invitation does not conflict with the duties and responsibilities of the fund manager in accordance with the provisions of these Regulations.

b. The fund manager must call for a meeting of unitholders within (10) days of receiving a written request from the custodian.

c. The fund manager must call for a meeting of unitholders within (10) days of receiving a written request from the unitholder or unitholders own collectively or individually at least (25%) in value of the units in the fund, and the fund manager must state it in the Fund's Terms and Conditions.

d. The fund manager shall call for a meeting of unitholders by announcing it on its website and any other website available to the public according to the controls set out by the Authority, and by sending a notice in writing to all unitholders and the custodian giving not less than (10) days' prior notice of the meeting and not more than (21) days' notice before the meeting. The announcement and notice must specify the date, place, time and agenda of the meeting and the resolutions proposed. The fund manager must at the same time as sending a notice to unitholders convening any meeting of unitholders also send a copy of any such notice to the Authority.

e. When preparing the unitholders meeting's agenda, the fund manager must take into consideration the matters that unitholders wish to list; unitholders holding no less than)10%(of the value of the public fund units are entitled to add one or more items to the unitholders meeting's agenda, provided that the proposed items does not overlap with the duties and responsibilities of the fund manager in accordance with the provisions of these Regulations.

f. The fund manager may amend the unitholders meeting's agenda during the announcement period referred to in Paragraph (d) of this Article, provided that it is announced on the fund manager's website and on any other website available to the public according to the controls set out by the Authority and by sending a written notice to all the unitholders and the custodian at least (10) days' prior to the meeting and not more than (21) days' notice before the meeting.

g. If the unitholders approve to any of the proposed decisions at the unitholders meeting, which necessitated amending the Fund's Terms and Conditions, the fund manager must amend such Terms and Conditions in accordance with the approved decision.

h. The quorum required to conduct a meeting of the unitholders shall be a such number of unitholders own collectively at least (25%) in value of the units in the public fund, unless the Terms and Conditions of the fund specified a greater percentage.

i. If the quorum requirements set out in Paragraph (h) of this Article are not met, the fund manager must call for a second meeting by announcing it on its website and any other website available to the public according to the controls set out by the Authority and shall send a notice in writing to all unitholders and the custodian giving not less than (5) days' notice of the second meeting (excluding the day on which the notice is sent and the day of the meeting). The second meeting is considered valid regardless of the percentage of units represented in the meeting.

j. Every unitholder may be entitled to appoint a proxy to represent such unitholder at a meeting of the unitholders.

k. Every unitholder may be entitled to exercise one vote at the meeting of the unitholders for each unit which the unitholder holds as at the time of the meeting.

l. The unitholders meetings and its deliberations and voting on decisions may be conducted through modern technology in accordance with requirements set by the Authority.

m. The traded funds shall be exempted from the requirement to notify unitholders in writing, stipulated in Paragraphs (d), (f) and (i) of this Article. Provided that the announcement of such shall be made on the fund manager's website and the Exchange's website.

Article 76: Reporting to Unitholders

a. The fund manager must prepare the annual reports that include (audited annual financial statement) and quarter statement in accordance with the requirements of Annex (3) and Annex (4) of these Regulations and must be provided by the fund manager to unitholders on request and without charge.

b. Annual reports must be made available to the public no later than (3) months from the end of the period to which the report relates in such locations and by such means as specified in the Terms and Conditions as well as on the fund manager's website and the Exchange's website or any other website available to the public according to the controls set out by the Authority (where applicable).

c. The interim financial statements must be prepared and made available to the public within a period not exceeding (30) days from the end of the period to which the statements relates in such locations and by such means as specified in the Terms and Conditions, as well as in the fund manager website and the Exchange's website or any other website available to the public according to the controls set out by the Authority (where applicable).

d. The fund manager must publish the quarter statement in accordance with the requirements of Annex (4) within a period not exceeding (10) days from the end of such quarter, in such locations and by such means as specified in the Fund's Terms and Conditions as well as on the fund manager's website and the Exchange's website or any other website available to the public according to the controls set out by the Authority (where applicable).

e. A feeder fund or fund of funds must make its fund reports available within (21) days after the release of the fund reports of the fund(s) in which it invests.

f. The fund manager must make available for inspection by unitholders the current net asset value of the public funds to which it is fund manager free of charge, and all historical net asset value figures at the registered offices of the fund manager.

g. The traded funds shall be exempted from the provisions of Paragraph (f) of this Article.

(According to the Authority's Board Resolution no. (2-22-2021) Dated 12/07/1442H. Corresponding to 24/02/2021G. Paragraph (c) of Article (76) of the Investment Funds Regulations issued pursuant to the Authority's Board Resolution No. (1-219-2006) dated 03/12/1427 H. corresponding to 24/12/2006 G. and amended by the Authority's Board Resolution No. (1-(1-219-2006) dated 16/08/1437 H. corresponding to

23/05/2016 G. which can be viewed via the following link: (https://cma.org.sa/RulesRegulations/Regulations/DocLib/IFRs Regulations- Final English_EN.pdf) and which states that "c) A unitholder who has signed terms and conditions of the relevant fund shall be deemed to be a customer of the fund manager for the purposes of the Authorized Persons Regulations"., shall remain effective until the date of 28/05/1443 H. corresponding to 01/01/2022 G.)

Article 77: Reporting to the Authority

a. After making the annual fund reports available to the public pursuant to Article (76) of these Regulations (including the annual audited financial statements) of the public fund, the fund manager must submit such reports to the Authority no later than (5) days following the day of which the reports request was made.
b. After making the quarter statement and interim financial statements available to the public pursuant to Article (76) of these Regulations. The fund manager must submit such reports to the Authority no later than (5) days from the Authority request.

18.5 PART 5: PRIVATE FUNDS

Article 78: Submitting a Notice to the Authority for the Offer of Units in a Private Fund

a. A notification to the Authority to offer units in a private fund must be submitted by a capital market Institution licensed to carry out the activity of managing investments and operating funds or the activity of investments management9 (where applicable). Any such notice must be in the form specified in Annex (6) of these Regulations. Requirements of a private placement referred to in Paragraph (a) of Article (81) of these Regulations must be met.
b. Units in a private fund may only be offered in the Kingdom by way of private placement in accordance with Article (80) of these Regulations.
(According to the Authority's Board Resolution no. (2-22-2021) Dated 12/07/1442H. Corresponding to 24/02/2021G. Paragraph (a) of Article (78) of these Regulations shall become effective as of 28/05/1443 H. corresponding to 01/01/2022 G. Moreover, Paragraph (a) of Article (73) of the Investment Funds Regulations issued pursuant to the Authority's Board Resolution No. (1-219-2006) dated 03/12/1427 H. corresponding to 24/12/2006 G. and amended by the Authority's Board Resolution No.)2016-61-1(dated 16/08/1437 H. corresponding to 23/05/2016 G., which can be viewed via the following link: (https://cma.org.sa/RulesRegulations/Regulations/DocLib/IFRs Regulations- Final English_EN.pdf) shall remain effective until the effective date of Paragraph (a) of Article (78) of these Regulations.)

Article 79: Capital Call in Installments

a. The fund manager may call the capital in installments, provided that this is included in the Fund's Terms and Conditions at the time of offering, with a statement of the minimum for fund operation, and that the fund manager notify the Authority of the results within (10) days of the completion of all capital calls. Moreover, capital call in installments shall be available to all unitholders in closed-ended private funds.
b. The fund manager who wishes to call the capital in installments must specify in the Fund's Terms and Conditions the minimum period for notifying unitholders and a policy to deal with such capital call, and in case of non-compliance with that policy, the fund manager must clarify in the Fund's Terms and Conditions the followed procedures in these cases.

Article 80: Private Placement of a Private Fund and Eligibility of Investors

a. An offer of units in a private fund is a private placement where the offerees are investors under the categories of institutional and qualified clients and if the maximum amount payable per offeree (from investors of the retail clients' category) is not more than (200) thousand Saudi Riyals or an equivalent amount.
b. The Authority may, in circumstances other than those described in Paragraph (a) of this Article and upon application of a capital market institution seeking to make an offer of units in a private fund, determine that such an offer shall be treated as a private placement subject to compliance with such limitation as the Authority may impose.
c. If the units are offered in a private real estate fund, the fund must be a closed-ended investment fund.
(According to the Authority's Board Resolution no. (2-22-2021) Dated 12/07/1442H. Corresponding to 24/02/2021G. Paragraph (a) of Article (80) of these Regulations shall become effective as of 28/05/1443 H. corresponding to 01/01/ 2022 G. Moreover, Paragraphs (a) and (b) of Article (74) of the Investment Funds Regulations issued pursuant to the Authority's Board Resolution No. (1-219-2006) dated 03/12/1427 H. corresponding to 24/12/2006 G. and amended by the Authority's Board Resolution No. (1-61-2016) dated 16/08/1437 H. corresponding to 23/05/2016 G., which can be viewed via the following link: (https://cma.org.sa/RulesRegulations/Regulations/DocLib/IFRs Regulations- Final English_EN.pdf) shall remain effective until the effective date of Paragraph (a) of Article (80) of these Regulations.)

Article 81: Private Placement Requirements

a. A Capital Market Institution may not offer units in a private fund unless the following fulfilled:

1) notifies the Authority in writing in accordance with the format set out in Annex (6) of these Regulations at least (15) days prior to the proposed date of an offer;
2) submits to the Authority a declaration in accordance with the terms set out in Annex (7) of these Regulations;
3) submits to the Authority copies of the Fund's Terms and Conditions in accordance with the requirements of Annex (11) of these Regulations and any offering documents to be used in advertising the offer; and
4) provide details of the organizational structure of the Fund Manager, including a description of the investment decision-making process of fund manager or sub- fund manager, and the name and function of any registered person in that decision-making process to the Authority.
5) provide a compliance monitoring program for the relevant investment fund.
6) pays such registration fees as the Authority may prescribe.
7) any other information that the Authority requires.

b. If having received a private placement notification and the relevant information and documents provided under Paragraph (a) of this Article the Authority considers that the proposed offer of units may not be commensurate with the fund manager's ability or may result in a breach of the Capital Market Law or its Implementing Regulations, then it may take the following actions:

1) carry out any enquiries which it considered appropriate including requiring the concerned person or its representative to appear before the Authority to answer the questions of the Authority and to explain any matters that the Authority considers relevant to the private placement offering; or

2) require the concerned person or others to provide additional information or to confirm, in such manner as the Authority may specify, that the information provided is accurate.

c. Where the Authority determines that the private placement may not be commensurate with the fund manager's ability or may result in a breach of the Capital Market Law or its Implementing Regulations, the Authority may issue a "notification" to the Capital Market Institution stating that the private offer is not to be made or publish a "Notice" prohibiting the offer.

d. Where the Authority has not taken any actions stated in Paragraph (c) of this Article, the Authority shall, at the request of the capital market institution, issue a notice stating it has no objection to offering units in the private fund.

e. The Capital Market Institution must provide the Authority within (10) days of the end of the offer period of the private fund with the results of the offer, in the form set out in Annex (10) of these Regulations.

f. Where the offer is not completed by the proposed offer end date (if any) specified in the private placement notification provided to the Authority in accordance with Subparagraph (1) of Paragraph (a) of this Article and of the Fund's Terms and Conditions, the capital market institution must provide the Authority within (10) days with a notification in writing signed by the Capital Market Institution confirming that the offer has failed to complete. The capital market institution must return to the unitholders their full subscriptions monies together with any returns generated from investing the subscriptions monies without any deduction.

Article 82: Contractual Format of a Private Fund

a. A private fund shall be established by the signing of the Terms and Conditions of the relevant fund between the first potential unitholders and the fund manager.

b. The contractual relationship between a potential unitholder and the fund manager shall be established by signing the fund's Terms and Conditions.

c. The fund manager must include in the Fund's Terms and Conditions the related requirements in these Regulations, and the private investment fund manager must, in addition to that, include the Terms and Conditions to the requirements and the information contained in Annex (11) of these Regulations.

d. The Terms and Conditions referred to in Paragraph (b) of this Article shall be considered as satisfying the terms of business requirements in the Capital Market Institutions Regulations.

Article 83: Units

a. The subscribed units shall be owned by the potential unitholder when the subscription request is executed on the dealing day following the deadline for submission of requests for subscription and redemption.

b. The unitholder shall be entitled to exercise all rights in relation to the units (including, but not limited to, the right to vote at meetings of unitholders).

c. Other than losing his\her investment in the fund or part of it, the unitholder shall not be liable for the debts and obligations of the relevant private fund.

d. The private fund may issue more than one class of units, and all unitholders from the same class must have equal rights and be treated equally by the fund manager. No class of unitholders shall have a different investment strategies and goals that differ from the investment strategies and goals of another class of the same investment fund.

e. The owners of a class of units shall not have the rights that will prejudice the rights of the owners of another class of units.

Article 84: Private Real Estate Fund Board

a. A private real estate fund shall be supervised by a fund board appointed by the fund manager.

b. The fund manager must remove a board member of the real estate private fund if a special fund resolution is issued to request the removal of that member.

c. The number of directors in a private real estate fund board must not be less than three (3) directors. The number of independent fund directors of a fund board shall not be less than two, or one third of the total number of directors, whichever is greater.

d. A fund board director may not be entitled to vote on any resolution to be taken by the fund board of on any matter in which such fund board director has any direct or indirect particular interest and shall disclose any such interest to the fund board.

e. Any person appointed by the fund manager as a member of the fund board must fulfill the following eligibility requirements:

1) the person must not be bankrupt or subject to any bankruptcy or insolvency proceedings;

2) the person must not have committed an offense involving fraud or acted in breach of integrity and honesty;

3) the person must possess the necessary experience and expertise.

f. If a member of the fund board ceases to meet the eligibility requirements set out in Paragraph (e) of this Article, the fund manager must replace a member of the fund board with another person who fulfils the eligibility requirements set out in Paragraph (e) of this Article.

g. The fund manager must provide all necessary information about the private real estate fund to all members of the fund's board in order to enable them to carry out their duties efficiently, the fund manager must also provide any other information or documentation required by the fund's board to enable it to perform its functions.

Article 85: Responsibilities of the Members of the Private Real Estate Fund's Board The responsibilities of the members of the private real estate fund board shall include the following:

1) approving material contracts, decisions and reports involving the private real estate fund, including, but not limited to, contracts for the provision of real estate development, custody contract, and marketing contract, valuation contract, and the contract with an engineering office;

2) approving of the appointment of the auditor of the fund nominated by the fund manager.

3) making a decision regarding any transaction involving a conflict of interest disclosed by the fund manager.
4) meeting at least twice annually with the fund manager's compliance officer or the fund's Money Laundering and Terrorism Financing Reporting Officer (MLRO) to review the fund manager's compliance with all applicable rules, laws and regulations;
5) approving the Terms and Conditions of a private real estate fund and any changes thereto;
6) ensuring that the fund manager carries out its obligations in the best interests of the unitholders, in accordance with the provision of these Regulations, the Terms and Conditions of a private real estate fund;
7) ensuring that the fund manager is disclosing material information to the Unitholders and other stakeholders;
8) have a fiduciary duty to unitholders, including a duty to act in good faith, a duty to act in the best interests of the unitholders and a duty to exercise all reasonable care and skill; and
9) taking minutes of meetings that provide all deliberations and facts of the meetings and the decisions taken by the fund board of director.
10) reviewing the report that includes assessment of the performance and quality of services provided by the parties involved in providing significant services to the fund referred to in Paragraph (l) of Article (9) of these Regulations, in order to ensure that the fund manager fulfils his responsibilities in the interest of unitholders in accordance with the Fund's Terms and Conditions and the provisions stipulated in these Regulations.
11) assessing the mechanism of the fund manager's handling of the risks related to the fund's assets in accordance with the fund manager's policies and procedures that detect the fund's risks and how to treat such risks.
12) Review the report containing all complaints and the measures taken regarding them referred to in Paragraph (m) of Article (9) of these Regulations, in order to ensure that the fund manager carries out his responsibilities in a way that serves the interest of unitholders in accordance with the Fund's Terms and Conditions and in accordance in this Regulation.

Article 86: General Rules and Restrictions

a. The investments of a private fund may consist of assets of any types and descriptions; however, the fund manager must clearly state the permitted investments together with the investment objective, investment policies and any investment restrictions or limitations in the Fund's Terms and Conditions and in the offering documents of the relevant private fund.
b. The fund manager must comply at all times with the Fund's Terms and Conditions, the offering documents, investment objective, investment policies and any investment restrictions or limitations of the relevant private fund.
c. The fund manager must disclose all payments out of assets of the fund in the Terms and Conditions.
d. The fund manager must disclose all expenses of offering the units of a private investment fund if it's incurred by the fund in the Fund's Terms and Conditions.

Article 87: Private Fund Documentation

a. The Capital Market Institution shall submit to the Authority any documentation which it distributes in relation to the offer of a private fund. Such documentation must include the disclaimer that stated in such format set out in Annex (9) of these Regulations.
b. The manager of a private fund shall comply with notifying the Authority and the unitholders upon any change to the fund documentations, provided that the mechanism of such is determined in the Fund's Terms and Conditions.

Article 88: Securities Advertisements and Promotional Materials A Capital Market Institution may not advertise or communicate securities advertisements and promotional materials in respect of a private fund unless the following conditions are fulfilled:
1) the securities advertisement is sent solely to persons to whom a private placement of a private fund may be made in accordance with Article (80) of these Regulations; and
2) the securities advertisement complies with the applicable provisions of the Capital Market Institutions Regulations and the Securities Business Regulations.

Article 89: Financial Statement Auditing Requirements

a. The fund manager must appoint an auditor upon the establishment of a private fund. An audit must be conducted at the end of the first full calendar year after the establishment of a private fund, but may be conducted earlier.
b. The auditor must be registered with the Authority in accordance with the Rules for Registering Auditors of Entities Subject to the Authority's Supervision and shall be an independent auditor according to criterion of the independence defined in Certified Public Accountants Regulations and its implementing regulations.

Article 90: Valuation

a. The fund operator shall be responsible for valuing the fund's assets, as well as pricing and dealing in the units of the private fund in accordance with a clear policy.
b. The fund manager must disclose the policy referred to in Paragraph (a) of this Article in the Fund's Terms and Conditions and annual reports of the fund, and must establish a similar method for pricing the units for the purpose of issuing, transferring and redeeming.
c. The fund manager must notify the unitholders of any amendments to the valuation, pricing and dealing policy in the private fund units within a period not exceeding (5) days.
d. A fund manager of a private real estate fund must, before purchasing or selling any real estate assets, obtain valuation from at least two accredited valuers.
e. The real estate fund manager must ensure that any accredited valuer appointed pursuant to Paragraph (d) of this Article meets the following conditions:
 1) the accredited valuer must be independent from all related parties
 2) the accredited valuer must join the Saudi Authority for Accredited Valuers.
f. At the time of the purchasing or selling of the real estate asset, the accredited valuers' valuation report issued pursuant to Paragraph (d) of this Article must not be more than three (3) months old.
g. In the case of a one investment goals of the fund includes Initial development or structural development, the fund manager of a private real estate fund must appoint a developer, and an engineering office that is independent of any of the relevant parties, after ensuring that they have obtained the necessary approvals and licenses to carry out their business and activities from the relevant governmental

bodies, and the engineering office shall – at least- oversee the implementation of the Fund's business plan, and the approval of disbursements to the developer and contractor.
h. For the purposes of this Article, the term related party shall mean any of the followings:

1) the fund manager.
2) the custodian.
3) the developer.
4) accredited valuer, where applicable.
5) the auditor.
6) board members, or any of the executives or employees of any of the parties above.
7) any unitholder whose ownership exceeds (5%) of the net assets of the private real estate investment fund.
8) any person under or in control of any of the previously mentioned persons.

i. For the purposes of this article, it is intended that meanings of the initial development and construction development set forth in the Real Estate Investment Funds Regulations.
(According to the Authority's Board Resolution no. (2-22-2021) Dated 12/07/1442H. Corresponding to 24/02/2021G. Subparagraph (2) of Paragraph (e) of Article (90) shall become effective as of 08/06/1444 H. corresponding to 01/01/2023G.)

Article 91: Meetings of Unitholders

a. The fund manager shall develop a policy regarding meetings of unitholders. The fund manager shall include the details of such policy in the Terms and Conditions of the private fund.
b. The fund manager must call for a unitholders meeting upon receiving a written request from the unitholder or of unitholders own collectively or individually at least (25%) in value of the units in the fund, or from the custodian.
c. When calling for a unitholders meeting, the fund manager must state the items of the agenda and the quorum of the meeting and the required percentage to approve to these items, provided that the policy of such is determined in the Fund's Terms and Conditions.
d. The fund manager may call for a unitholders meeting on its own initiative, provided that the subject of the invitation does not conflict with the responsibilities and duties of the fund manager in accordance with the provisions of these Regulations.
e. The fund manager shall call for a meeting of unitholders by sending a written notice to all unitholders and the custodian by giving not less than (10) days' prior notice of the meeting and not more than (21) days' notice before the meeting. The notice must specify the date, place, time and agenda of the meeting and the resolution proposed. The fund manager must at the same time as sending a notice to unitholders convening any meeting of unitholders also send a copy of any such notice to the Authority.
f. The fund manager must immediately notify the Authority of all resolutions issued in the unitholders' meetings.
g. When preparing the unitholders meeting's agenda, the fund manager of a private fund must take into consideration the matters that unitholders wish to list; unitholders holding no less than (10%) of the value of the private fund units are entitled to add one or more items to the unitholders meeting's agenda, provided that the proposed items does not overlap with the duties and responsibilities of the fund manager in accordance with the provisions of these Regulations.
h. The fund manager may amend the agenda of the unitholders meeting during the notification period referred to in Paragraph (e) of this Article, provided that a written notice is sent to all the unitholders and the custodian by giving not less than (10) days' prior notice of the meeting and not more than (21) days' notice before the meeting.
i. If the unitholders approve to any of the proposed decisions at the unitholders meeting, which necessitated amending the Fund's Terms and Conditions, the fund manager must amend such Terms and Conditions in accordance with the approved decision.
j. The fund manager must call for a unitholders meeting upon the Authority's request within a period not exceeding (10) days.

Article 92: Consent of Unitholders to Changes

a. A fund manager must obtain the consent of unitholders in the relevant fund by way of an ordinary fund resolution on the following changes:

1) a change which significantly changes the purposes, nature or class of the private fund;
2) the change that has an impact on the risk level of the private fund;
3) the change that results in a material increase of the aggregate payments made out of the assets of the closed-ended private fund;
4) the change that will make a negative or material effect on the rights of unitholders in relation to the closed-ended private fund;
5) the change of the due date or maturity date of private fund.
6) Any other cases determined by the Authority from time to time and reported to the fund manager.

b. As an exception to Paragraph (a) of this Article, the fund manager must obtain the approval of the unitholders in the concerned fund for the proposed change mentioned in Subparagraph (5) of Paragraph (a) of this Article through a special fund resolution.
c. Details of changes referred to in this Article must be listed in the private fund's reports made by the fund manager pursuant to Article (93) of these Regulations.
d. The fund manager must notify the Authority and the unitholders of the details of the changes referred to in Paragraph (a) of this Article, (10) days prior to the effective date of the change.
e. In case of an open-ended fund, unitholders may redeem their units before the date the changes referred to in Paragraph (a) of this Article are effective, without imposing redemption fees (if any).

Article 93: Reporting to Unitholders

a. Annual reports (including the annual audited financial statements) of the private fund must be prepared in accordance with the requirements set out Annex (3) of these Regulations and must be provided by the fund manager to unitholders on request and without charge. Annual reports should be made available to unitholders no later than (90) days from the end of the period to which it relates by such means as specified in the Fund's Terms and Conditions.
b. Interim reports for a private real estate funds must be prepared every (6) months in accordance with the requirements of Annex (3) of these Regulations, and make available to unitholders within (35) days from the end of the reporting period, in the places and the means specified in the Fund's

Terms and Conditions, and the fund manager must provide Unitholders interim reports of the Fund upon request at no charge.

Article 94: Reporting to the Authority

a. After making the annual reports available to unitholder pursuant to Article (93) of these Regulations (including the annual audited financial statements), the fund manager must submit such reports to the Authority no later than (5) days following the day of which the reports request was made.
b. The fund manager must submit to the Authority any information regarding the subscription or redemption of units in a private fund and no later than (10) days following the day of which the information request was made.

Article 95: Notification Relating to the Substantial Holdings in Shares or Convertible Debt Instruments

a. The fund manager must notify the Exchange when the fund becomes owner or has an interest of (5%) or more of any class of voting shares or convertible debt instrument of the issuer, during a period not exceeding the end of the third trading day following the executing of the transaction or the occurrence of the event which result in such ownership or interest. The person notification to the Authority shall also include a list of persons, in which those persons, have an interest in the shares or convertible debt instruments which they own or control.
b. The fund manager referred to in Paragraph (a) of this Article must notify the Exchange in the event of any change to the list of persons referred to in Paragraph (a) of this Article including any event which requires the inclusion of a person to that list or the exclusion of any person who has been previously included in that list. Such notification must be made during a period not exceeding the end of the third trading day following the occurrence of the relevant event.
c. For the purpose of this Article, when calculating the total number of shares or convertible debt instruments in which the fund is interested, the fund will be deemed to be interested in any shares or convertible debt instrument owned or controlled by any of the following:

1) A company controlled by that fund.
2) Any person or fund acting in concert with the private fund referred to in Paragraph (a) of this Article to acquire interest in or exercise voting rights in the shares or convertible debt instrument of an issuer listed on the Exchange.

d. The notice referred to in Paragraph (a) of this Article must at least include the following information:

1) the names of the persons who own or have the right to dispose of the subject shares or convertible debt instruments;
2) details of the ownership process;
3) details of any loans or financial support for the ownership process that the person has received from any other persons.

Article 96: Restriction on Secondary Market Activity Subsequent transfers of units in a private fund offered in accordance to the provisions of Article (81) of these Regulations may only be made to any of the following:
1) to existing unitholders,
2) to investors under the categories of institutional and qualified clients,
3) where the maximum amount payable for such units is not more than (200) thousand Saudi Riyals, or an equivalent amount.
(According to the Authority's Board Resolution no. (2-22-2021) Dated 12/07/1442H. Corresponding to 24/02/2021G. Paragraphs (2) and (3) of Article (96) of these Regulations shall become effective as of 28/05/1443 H. corresponding to 01/01/2022 G. Moreover, Paragraphs (2) and (3) of Article (92) of the Investment Funds Regulations issued pursuant to the Authority's Board Resolution No. (1-219-2006) dated 03/12/1427 H. corresponding to 24/12/2006 G. and amended by the Authority's Board Resolution No.2016-61-1 dated 16/08/1437 H. corresponding to 23/05/2016 G., which can be viewed via the following link: (https://cma.org.sa/RulesRegulations/Regulations/DocLib/IFRs Regulations- Final English_EN.pdf) shall remain effective until the effective date of Paragraphs (2) and (3) of Article (96) of these Regulations.)

18.6 PART 6: FOREIGN FUNDS

Article 97: Offer of Securities Issued By a Foreign Fund in the Kingdom

a. Securities issued by a foreign fund may not be offered in the Kingdom except in accordance with this Part.
b. No person may offer securities issued by a foreign fund in the Kingdom unless the offer is being made through a distributor and the offering of securities shall be a private placement in accordance with the requirements set out in Article (99) of these Regulations.
c. The distributer referred to in Paragraph (b) of this Article, must be a Capital Market Institution licensed to carry out dealing activity or the activity of managing investments and operating funds.
d. A foreign offered fund manager must be authorized in a jurisdiction that employs regulatory standards and requirements at least equivalent to those of the Authority. The Authority shall have the discretion to assess whether the jurisdiction has regulatory standards and requirements at least equivalent to those of the Authority.
(According to the Authority's Board Resolution no. (2-22-2021) Dated 12/07/1442H. Corresponding to 24/02/2021G. Paragraph (c) of Article (97) of these Regulations shall become effective as of 28/05/1443 H. corresponding to 01/01/2022 G. Moreover, Paragraph (c) of Article (93) of the Investment Funds Regulations issued pursuant to the Authority's Board Resolution No. (1-219-2006) dated 03/12/1427 H. corresponding to 24/12/2006 G. and amended by the Authority's Board Resolution No. (1-61-2016) dated 16/08/1437 H. corresponding to 23/05/2016 G., which can be viewed via the following link: (https://cma.org.sa/RulesRegulations/Regulations/DocLib/IFRs Regulations- Final English_EN.pdf) shall remain effective until the effective date of Paragraph (c) of Article (97) of these Regulations.)

Article 98: Private Placement of a Foreign Fund and Eligibility of Investors

a. An offer of securities issued by a foreign fund is a private placement where the offerees are investors under the categories of institutional and qualified clients, and if the maximum amount payable per offeree (from investors of the retail clients' category) is not more than (200) thousand Saudi Riyals, or an equivalent amount.
b. The Authority may, in circumstances other than those described in Paragraph (a) of this Article and upon a request

from a distributor seeking to make an offer of securities issued by a foreign fund, determine that such an offer shall be treated as a private placement subject to compliance with such limitation as the Authority may impose.
(According to the Authority's Board Resolution no. (2-22-2021) Dated 12/07/1442H. Corresponding to 24/02/2021G. Paragraph (a) of Article (98) of these Regulations shall become effective as of 28/05/1443 H. corresponding to 01/01/2022 G. Moreover, Paragraph (a) of Article (94) of the Investment Funds Regulations issued pursuant to the Authority's Board Resolution No. (1-219-2006) dated 03/12/1427 H. corresponding to 24/12/2006 G. and amended by the Authority's Board Resolution No. (1-61-2016) dated 16/08/1437 H. corresponding to 23/05/2016 G., which can be viewed via the following link: (https://cma.org.sa/RulesRegulations/Regulations/DocLib/IFRs Regulations- Final English_EN.pdf) shall remain effective until the effective date of Paragraph (a) of Article (98) of these Regulations.)

Article 99: Private Placement Requirements of a Foreign Fund
a. No securities issued by a foreign fund may be offered unless the distributor meets the following requirements:

1) notify the Authority in writing in accordance with the format set out in Annex (6) of these Regulations at least (15) days prior to the proposed date of the offer;
2) submit to the Authority a declaration in accordance with the terms set out in Annex)8) of these Regulations;
3) submit to the Authority copies of any offering documents to be used in advertising the offer; and
4) conduct a due diligence check of the foreign fund and its manager before the distribution of securities issued by such fund, and provide the Authority with it upon request within (5) days from the date of request.
5) pay such registration fees as the Authority may prescribe.
6) submit any another information that the Authority requires.

b. If having received a private placement notification and the information and documents provided under paragraph (a) of this Article and the Authority considers that the proposed offer of securities may not be commensurate with the distributor's ability or may result in a breach of the Capital Market Law or its Implementing Regulations, then it may take any of following actions:

1) carry out any enquiries which it considered appropriate including requiring the concerned person or its representative to appear before the Authority to answer the questions of the Authority and to explain any matters that the Authority considers relevant to the private placement offering; or
2) require the concerned person or others to provide additional information or to confirm that the information provided is accurate, in such manner as the Authority may specify.

c. Where the Authority determines that the private placement may not be commensurate with the distributor's ability or may result in a breach of the Capital Market Law or its Implementing Regulations, the Authority may issue a "notification" to the distributor stating that the private offer is not permissible or publish a "notice" prohibiting the offer.
d. Where the Authority has not taken any actions stated in Paragraph (c) of this Article, the Authority shall, on the request of the distributor, issue a notice stating it has no objection to the offering of securities in the foreign fund.
e. The distributor must provide the Authority within (10) days of the end of the initial offer period of the foreign fund (if any) a statement of the results of the offer.
f. Where the offer is not completed by the proposed offer end date (if any) specified in the private placement notification provided to the Authority in accordance with Subparagraph (1) of Paragraph (a) of this Article, the Fund's Terms and Conditions, and relevant offering documents, the distributor must provide the Authority within (10) days with a notification in writing signed by the distributor confirming that the offer has failed to complete, the distributor must return to the securities holders their full subscriptions monies together with any returns generated from investing the subscriptions monies without any deduction to securities holders.

Article 100: Information to Securities Holders and Offer Documentations
a. The distributor of securities issued by a foreign fund must make available to securities holders in the Kingdom the same documentation which is made available by the foreign fund manager to securities holders of the same class in other jurisdictions.
b. The distributor of securities issued by a foreign fund must ensure that securities holders are provided with sufficient information on the private placement to enable them to make an informed investment decision and that such information is are complete, clear, accurate, and not misleading.
c. The private placement offering documents to be used in advertising the offer of securities issued by the foreign fund must contain a prominent statement in the form set out in Annex (9) of these Regulations.

Article 101: Securities Advertisements and Promotional Materials Distributors may not advertise or communicate securities advertisements and promotional materials in respect of a foreign fund unless the following conditions are fulfilled:
1) the securities advertisement is sent solely to persons to whom a private placement of a foreign fund may lawfully be made in accordance with this Part;
2) the securities advertisement is to satisfy the relevant requirements of the Securities Business Regulations and the Capital Market Institutions Regulations.
(Moreover, Paragraphs (2) and (3) of Article (101) of the Investment Funds Regulations issued pursuant to the Authority's Board Resolution No. (1-219-2006) dated 03/12/1427 H. corresponding to 24/12/2006 G. and amended by the Authority's Board Resolution No. (1-61-2016) dated 16/08/1437 H. corresponding to 23/05/2016 G., which can be viewed via the following link: (https://cma.org.sa/RulesRegulations/Regulations/DocLib/IFRs Regulations- Final English_EN.pdf) shall remain effective until the effective date of Paragraphs (2) and (3) of Article (105) of these Regulations.)

Article 102: Power of the Authority to Suspend a Distributor The Authority shall have the power to suspend a distributor in relation to a particular foreign fund or to take any other measures it deems necessary in the event of:
1) the distributor ceasing to carry out activities of dealing or the activity of managing investments and operating funds

without notification to the Authority under the Capital Market Institutions Regulations;
2) the cancellation or suspension by the Authority of the distributor's relevant authorization(s);
3) a request by the distributor to the Authority to cancel its relevant authorization;
4) the Authority considering it necessary for the protection of securities holders or maintenance of an orderly market;
5) the Authority believing that the distributor has failed, in a manner which the Authority considers material, to comply with the Capital Market Law and its Implementing Regulations; or
6) any other event determined by the Authority on reasonable grounds to be of sufficient significance.

Article 103: Distributor Responsibilities The distributor of securities issued by a foreign fund must comply with the followings:
1) Sending all reports and documentation issued by the foreign fund manager to the securities holders in the Kingdom. And ensuring that all securities holders within the Kingdom in a foreign fund shall be directly entitled to the rights prescribed in the fund documentation.
2) Notifying all securities holders in writing of all fundamental changes related to the foreign fund.
3) Conveying all requests and letters of securities holders within the Kingdom to the foreign fund manager.
4) Notifying the securities holder in the kingdom (90) days prior to the termination of the relationship with the foreign open-ended fund manager.
5) Taking all appropriate actions to ensure continuity of relationship with the manager of the closed-ended foreign fund until the end of the fund's term.

Article 104: Reporting to the Authority
a. The distributor of securities issued by a foreign fund must report to the Authority all fundamental changes in relation to a foreign fund, and any other information the Authority requires.
b. The distributor of securities issued by a foreign fund must submit to the Authority any information regarding the subscription or redemption of securities issued by a foreign fund and no later than (10) days following the day of which the information request was made.

Article 105: Restriction on Secondary Market Activity Subsequent transfers of securities issued by a foreign fund offered in accordance to the provisions of Article (99) of these Regulations to any person in the Kingdom may only be made:
1) to existing securities holders,
2) to investors under the categories of institutional and qualified clients,
3) where the maximum amount payable for such securities is not more than (200) thousand Saudi Riyals, or an equivalent amount.
(According to the Authority's Board Resolution no. (2-22-2021) Dated 12/07/1442H. Corresponding to 24/02/2021G. Paragraphs (2) and (3) of Article (105) of these Regulations shall become effective as of 28/05/1443 H. corresponding to 01/01 / 2022 G. Moreover, Paragraphs (2) and (3) of Article (101) of the Investment Funds Regulations issued pursuant to the Authority's Board Resolution No. (1-219-2006) dated 03/12/1427 H. corresponding to 24/12/2006 G. and amended by the Authority's Board Resolution No. (1-61-2016) dated 16/08/1437 H. corresponding to 23/05/2016 G., which can be viewed via the following link: (https://cma.org.sa/RulesRegulations/Regulations/DocLib/IFRs Regulations- Final English_EN.pdf) shall remain effective until the effective date of Paragraphs (2) and (3) of Article (105) of these Regulations.)

18.7 PART 7: MERGER OF INVESTMENT FUNDS

Article 106: Application to the Authority for the Merging of Investment Funds
a. After obtaining the approval of the unitholders of all the related funds offered in accordance with Articles (32) or Article (80) of these Regulations by way of fund special resolutions, the fund manager may apply to the Authority for approval to merge a number of investments fund it manages.
b. The merger shall be through combining one fund or more into an existing fund.
c. The funds that are planned to be merged must have the same type and have the same class, and share similar investment objectives and policies.
d. The unitholders must be notified about the merger details, which must be disclosed on the fund manager's website (21) days before executing the merger. as well as announcing of such on any other website available to the public according to the controls set out by the Authority for public funds.
e. The merger details must be incorporated in the fund's report prepared by the fund manager pursuant to Article (76) or Article (93) of these Regulations, according to the offering type.
f. The unitholders of an open-ended fund have the right to redeem their units before the merger closure, without imposing any redemption fees if any.
g. The fund manager shall pay the merger costs from its own recourses.

Article 107: Additional Information to be Provided to the Unitholders The fund manager must provide all the unitholders with complete information about the proposed merger that will enable them to reach a proper decision as per followings:
1) It is written in a way that is clear, accurate, and not misleading.
2) It contains, in a detailed way, all the expected consequences of the proposed merger.
3) It contains a detailed comparison of the charges of all services, commissions and management fees that are imposed on the relevant funds.

18.8 PART 8: INVESTMENT FUNDS THAT TAKE THE FORM OF A SPECIAL PURPOSES ENTITY

Article 108: General Provisions
a. Investment funds that take the form of a special purposes entity shall be subject to all the provisions of these Regulations and the Rules for Special Purposes Entities, unless these Regulations states otherwise. b. To establish an investment fund that takes the form of a special purposes entity, the fund manager must satisfy the requirements to establish a special purposes entity in accordance with the provisions contained in the Rules for Special Purposes En-

tities, and the provisions contained in these regulations, as applicable. c. For the purposes of this Part, any reference to the "investment fund" in these Regulation or the Capital Market Law and its Implementing Regulations, applies to the investment fund that takes the form of a special purposes entity.

Article 109: Custodian The custodian of the investment fund that takes the form of a special purposes entity shall be subject to the provisions contained in Part (3) of these Regulations, in manners consistent with the nature of this entity.

Article 110: Board of an Investment Fund that Takes the Form of a Special Purposes Entity The board of directors of the investment fund that takes the form of special purposes entity is the board of directors of a special purposes entity, and shall be subject to all the provisions related to the fund's board of directors stipulated in these Regulations (where applicable).

18.9 PART 9: PUBLICATION AND ENTRY INTO FORCE

Article 111: Publication and Entry into Force These Regulations shall become effective in accordance to its approval resolution.

Annexes

(According to the Authority's Board Resolution no. (2-22-2021) Dated 12/07/1442H. Corresponding to 24/02/2021G. Annex (1) of these Regulations shall become effective as of 28/07/1443 H. corresponding to 01/03/2022 G. Moreover, Annex (1), Annex (2) and Annex (3) of the Investment Funds Regulations issued pursuant to the Authority's Board Resolution No. (1- 219-2006) dated 03/12/1427 H. corresponding to 24/12/2006 G. and amended by the Authority's Board Resolution No. 2016-61-1 dated 16/08/1437 H. corresponding to 23/05/2016 G., which can be viewed via the following link: (https://cma.org.sa/RulesRegulations/Regulations/DocLib/IFRs%20Regulations-%20Final%20English_EN.pdf) shall remain effective until the effective date of Annex (1) of these Regulations.)

18.10 ANNEX 1: REQUIREMENTS OF THE FUND'S TERMS AND CONDITIONS

The Fund Manager shall present the Terms and Conditions in Arabic language and in a way that is comprehensible and easy for unitholders or potential unitholders to understand. The Terms and Conditions must comprise at least the following, in the sequence of the items set out in this Annex:

Contents of the Cover Page

a) Name of the investment fund, its class and type.

b) Name of the fund manager c) Acknowledgements and explanatory statement:

1) The cover page must contain an explanatory statement and an acknowledgment of responsibility according to the following form:

"The Fund's Terms and Conditions has been reviewed and approved by the Fund's Board of Directors. The Fund Manager and the members of the Fund's Board of Directors collectively and individually bear full responsibility for the accuracy of the information presented herein. Having made all reasonable inquiries, the fund board directors and the fund manager confirm the validity and completeness of the information in the Terms and Conditions, and further confirm that the information and data maintained in the Terms and Conditions are not misleading".

2) The cover page must contain a statement of disclaimer according to the following form:

"The Capital Market Authority has approved the offering of units in the investment fund. The Capital Market Authority does not, however, take any responsibility for the contents of the Fund's Terms and Conditions, nor does it make any representation as to its accuracy or completeness. The Capital Market Authority does not make any recommendation as to the soundness or otherwise of investing in the investment fund, and the approval of offering the fund does not mean that the Authority recommends to invest in the fund, and the Authority emphasizes that the decision to invest in the fund is up to the investor or his representative."

3) For a Shariah-compliant investment fund, the following statement must be additionally stated:

"[Name of fund] has been certified as being Shariah compliant by the Shariah Committee appointed for the investment fund."

4) Must add the following statement: (If the investment fund is taking the form of a special purposes entity):

"[Name of fund] has been approved as an investment fund that takes the form of a special purposes entity in accordance with the Investment Funds Regulations and the Rules for Special Purposes Entities".

5) A statement that the Fund's Terms and Conditions and all other documentation comply with the Investment Funds Regulations and contain are complete, clear, accurate, and not misleading information on the investment fund and shall be updated and amended.

6) A statement that the Fund's Terms and Conditions shall be read in conjunction with the other documentation.

7) A statement that, unitholders shall be deemed to have accepted and signed the Fund's Terms and Conditions, upon subscribing in any listed unit of the fund (where applicable).

8) A statement that the performance of the fund can be viewed within the fund's reports.

9) A warning statement as follows:

"Investors are advised to read and understand the Fund's Terms and Conditions. if in doubt, please consult a professional adviser."

d) Fund summary, containing at least the following:

1. Name of the investment fund
2. Class/type of the fund
3. Name of the fund manager
4. Purpose of the fund
5. Risks level
6. Minimum amount for subscription and redemption
7. Days of dealing/valuation
8. Days of announcement
9. Date for paying redemption amount
10. Unit price at initial offer (nominal value)
11. Currency of the fund
12. Period of the investment fund and its maturity date (where applicable)
13. Date of commencing the fund
14. Date of issuing the Terms and Conditions, and latest update of it (if any)
15. Early redemption fees (if any)
16. Benchmark

17. Name of the fund operator
18. Name of the custodian
19. Name of the auditor
20. Fund management fees
21. Subscription and redemption fees
22. Custodian fees
23. Dealing expenses
24. Other fees and expenses
25. Performance fees (if any)

1) Investment Fund:

a. Name of the investment fund, its type and class.

b. Date of issuing the Terms and Conditions of the investment fund, and the last update, (if any).

c. Date of the Authority's approval on the offering of the fund's units.

d. The duration of the investment fund and maturity date (where applicable).

2) a. Governing Laws:

A statement that the investment fund and the fund manager are subject to the Capital Market Law and its Implementing Regulations as well as other relevant laws and regulations applicable in the Kingdom of Saudi Arabia.

3) Investment Policies and Practices

a. The Investment objectives of the investment fund.

b. Type or types of securities in which the investment fund will invest in primarily.

c. Any concentrated policy of investment in specific securities, or in an industry or group of sectors, or in a specific country or geographic region, provided that it includes the minimum and maximum for such securities.

d. A table showing the percentage of investment in each investment field, with its minimum and highest limits.

e. The markets in which the investment fund intends to invest in.

f.Disclose if the fund manager intends to invest in the investment fund.

g. Specific techniques and instruments that the fund manager can use to make investment decisions for the investment fund.

h. Types of securities that cannot be included in the fund's investments.

i. Any other restriction on the type(s) of securities or other assets the fund can invest in.

j. The limit that investments of the Fund's assets can be in a unit of an investment fund or units of investment funds managed by that manager or by managers of other funds.

k. The investment fund lending and borrowing powers, and fund manager policy on the exercise of the lending and borrowing powers, and a statement of fund manager policy with respect to pledging assets of the fund.

l. Disclosure of the maximum limit to deal with any counterparty.

m. Statement on the fund manager policy for the management of investment fund risks.

n. The benchmark, as well as information about the provider of the benchmark and the bases and the methodology used to calculate the benchmark.

o. Where derivatives are used, there must be a prominent statement that states the purpose of using such instruments (e.g. efficient portfolio management, meeting investment objectives or merely for hedging purposes from the price volatility).

p. Any waivers approved by the Capital Market Authority for any investment limits and restrictions;

4) The Main Risks of Investing in the Fund:

a. Where an investment fund is likely to have a high volatility due to the composition of its investment portfolio, there must be a prominent statement to that effect.

b. A statement that the performance history of the investment fund or the benchmark is considered irrelevant in terms of future performance of the fund.

c. A prominent statement that there is no guarantee for unitholders that the investment fund's absolute performance or its performance relative to the index will repeat or match past performance.

d. A prominent statement that investment in the investment fund is not a deposit with any bank.

e. A prominent statement that warns investors from the risk of loss of money when investing in the investment fund; and

f. Must contain a list of potential risks associated with investing in an investment fund, risk exposure to the investment fund and any conditions likely to affect the net asset value of the Fund's assets and revenues.

5) Mechanism for Assessing Risks

Must contain an acknowledgment statement by the fund manager to the fact that an internal mechanism for assessment of the risks related to the fund is in place.

6) Targeted Class for Investing in the Fund

A statement for the targeted class for investing in the fund (specify the most suitable type of investors to invest in the relevant fund).

7) Investments Restrictions/Limitations

A statement that the fund manager, in managing investments fund, shall comply with any restrictions imposed by the Investment Funds Regulations, the Fund's Terms and Conditions.

8) Currency

State the base currency of the fund and describe any procedures for converting subscriptions received in other currencies.

9) Fees, Charges and Expenses

a. Statement of details on all payments from the assets of the investment fund, and the method for calculating them.

b. A table showing all fees and expenses, how the fees, charges and expenses are calculated and when it is paid by the investment fund.

c. Hypothetical table that shows the percentage of the fund expenses against the total fund asset value for the fund and the unitholder throughout the lifespan of the fund. Such fund shall include percentage of recurring non-recurring expenses.

d. Statement of details on charges imposed for subscription, redemption and ownership transfer, paid by unit holders, and the method for calculating it.

e. Information on rebates and special commissions and explanation of the fund manager's policy on rebates and special commissions.

f. Information regarding tax and/or zakat (if any).

g. Statement of any special commission concluded by the fund manager (if any).

h. Hypothetical example that illustrates all fees, charges and expenses, paid from the fund's assets or unitholders based on the currency of the fund.

10) Valuation and Pricing

a. A statement of the valuation method of each asset

held by the fund.

b. A statement Frequency of valuation and number of valuation points.

c. A statement of actions to be taken in case of mis-valuation or mis-pricing.

d. A statement of the method for calculating the unit price for the purpose of executing subscription or redemption requests.

e. The publication time and place of the unit price, and its frequency.

11) Dealings

a. A statement on details of the initial offer (e.g. start date, period, initial price).

b. A statement clarifies the date set and the deadlines for submission of requests for subscriptions and redemptions, in any dealing day, and the responsibilities of the fund manager in relation to subscription and redemption requests.

c. A statement of the procedures for subscriptions and redemptions, including where to submit applications and the period between request for redemption and payment of redemption proceeds, or transfer the ownership (if applicable)

d. A statement showing any restrictions on dealing in units of the fund.

e. A statement showing the circumstances in which dealing in units may be deferred or suspended, and the procedures followed in those cases.

f. A statement of the procedures by which those redemption requests which are to be deferred are selected.

g. A statement of the provisions governing the transfer the ownership of units to other investors.

h. A description of any minimum number or value of units that a unitholder must subscribe or transfer or redeem; and

i. A statement on details of any minimum of the amount which the fund manager intends to raise, and the actions to be taken in case of not reaching that minimum.

12) Distribution Policy

a. A statement relating to the policy of distribution of income and gains, including details of the unclaimed distributions.

b. Approximate maturity and distribution date, if applicable.

c. A statement on how distribution will be paid.

13) Reporting to Unitholders

a. Relevant information regarding annual reports, including the quarterly statement and the interim, annual and financial statements.

b. Information on the locations and means of making available fund reports prepared by the fund manager.

c. Information on the means of providing the annual financial statement to unitholders.

d. Must contain a declaration stating the availability of the first audited financial statement at the end of the fiscal year of the fund and stating the end date of that year.

e. Must contain a declaration stating that the fund's audited annual financial statement are available free of charge upon request.

14) Unitholders Register a. Statement regarding the maintenance of an up-to-date register of unitholders in the Kingdom. b. Statement of details on the unitholders register (e.g. the location of the register where it can be obtained by unitholders.).

15) Meeting of Unitholders

a. A statement of the circumstances in which a meeting of unitholders is called.

b. A statement of the procedures for calling a meeting of unitholders.

c. A statement showing the manner in which unitholders' cast their votes and their voting rights at meetings.

16) Unitholders' Rights a. List of unitholders' rights.

b. The fund manager's policy regarding the voting rights associated with any assets of the public fund which it manages.

17) Unitholders' Liability

A statement providing that other than losing his investment in the fund or part of it, the unitholder shall not be liable for the debts and obligations of the fund.

18) Units Characteristics

Provide a description of the various classes of units, if the fund has more than one class, including the class name and details.

19) Changes to the Fund's Terms and Conditions

a. A statement of the provisions governing changes to the Fund's Terms and Conditions including any approvals and/or notifications required by the Investment Funds Regulations.

b. A description of the procedures to be employed on notifying changes to the Fund's Terms and Conditions.

20) Termination and liquidation of the Investment Fund

a. A statement of any events of which will result in the termination of the investment fund and procedures for termination of the investment fund under the Investment Funds Regulations.

b. Must include a statement of the followed procedures for the liquidation of the Fund.

c. In case of end of term of the investment fund, the fund manager may not take any fees deducted from the fund's assets.

21) Fund Manager

a. Name, duties and responsibilities of the fund manager.

b. Authority authorization number and date.

c. Registered address and business head office address of the fund manager.

d. The fund manager's website and any website, related to the fund manager, contain information on the investment fund, if any.

e. A statement of the paid up capital to the fund manager.

f. A summary of financial information of the fund manager, highlighting, substantial shareholders, revenues and profits in the preceding financial year.

g. A statement of the primary roles, responsibilities and duties of the fund manager in relation to the investment fund.

h. Any other business activities or interests of the fund manager that are of significance or could potentially conflict with those of the investment fund

i. Right of the fund manager to appoint a fund sub-manager.

j. Provisions governing the removal/replacement of fund manager.

22) Fund Operator

a. Name of the fund operator.

b. Authority authorization number and date.

c. Registered address and business address of fund operator.

d. A statement of the primary roles for the fund operator, functions in relation to the investment fund.

e. Statement that the operator may appoint a sub-operator.

f. Statement of the functions to which the operator has delegated a third party in relation to the investment fund.

23) Custodian

a. Name of the custodian.

b. Authority authorization number and date.

c. Registered address and business address of custodian.

d. A statement of the primary roles, functions in relation to the investment fund.

e. Right of custodian to appoint a sub-custodian.

f. Functions that have been delegated to a third party by the custodian in relation to the investment fund.

g. Provisions governing the removal/replacement of custodian.

24) Fund Board

a. Names of Fund Board members, indicating the membership type.

b. A brief about the fund board members' qualifications.

c. A description of the roles and responsibilities of the Fund Board.

d. Details on the remuneration of fund board members.

e. A statement of any conflict or potential conflict of interest between the interests of a fund board member and the interests of the fund.

f. A statement showing all the funds boards that the relevant board member is participating in.

25) Shariah Supervisory Committee (if any)

a. Names and qualifications of the Shariah Supervisory Committee members.

b. A description of the roles and responsibilities of Shariah Supervisory Committee.

c. Details on the remuneration of Shariah Supervisory Committee members.

d. Details of the standards used to determine the Shariah-compliant assets to be used for investment, and the periodic review of such assets, and the procedures in the event of non-compliance with the Shariah standards.

26) Investment Advisor (if any)

a. Name of investment advisor.

b. Registered address and business address of investment advisor.

c. A description of primary role and responsibility of investment advisor in relation to the investment fund.

27) Distributor (if applicable)

a. The name of the distributor.

b. The registered address and business address of the distributor.

c. The distributor's website (as applicable).

d. The license issued by the Authority for the distributor (if any).

e. A description of primary roles and responsibilities of the distributor in relation to the investment fund.

28) Auditor

a. Name of the auditor of the investment fund.

b. The registered address and business address of the auditor.

c. A description of the primary role and responsibility of the auditor.

d. Provisions governing the replacement of the investment fund's auditor.

29) Fund's assets

a. A declaration that the assets of the investment fund is held by the custodian on behalf of the investment fund.

b. A statement clarifying that the custodian must segregate the assets of each investment fund from its assets and from the assets of its other clients.

c. A statement that the assets of an investment fund are owned collectively by the unitholders. A fund manager, fund sub manager, fund operator, custodian, sub custodian, distributor or investment advisor may not have any interest in or claims against such assets, other than when the fund manager, fund sub manager, fund operator, custodian, sub custodian, distributor or investment advisor is a unitholder, and for claims permitted under the Investment Funds Regulations and disclosed by way of statement in these Terms and Conditions.

30) Complaints Procedures

It must contain a statement that includes the procedures for remediating complaints that will be presented upon request without charge, including the means that can be used to submit the complaint and where to submit complaints.

31) Other Information

a. Must contain a statement that the policies and procedures to be followed in addressing conflicts of interests, and any potential and/or actual conflicts of interests will be made available upon request.

b. A statement that the "Committee For The Resolution of Securities Disputes" has the jurisdiction to adjudicate disputes arising from investing in the investment funds.

c. A list of documents available for unitholders, which includes, the Fund's Terms and Conditions, each contract mentioned in the Terms and Conditions, and the financial statements of the fund manager.

d. Any other information known to, or that ought reasonably to be known to, the fund manager or the fund board and that unitholders, potential unitholders and their professional advisors might reasonably require or expect to be included in the Fund's Terms and Conditions upon which an investment decision is to be made.

e. Any waivers from limitations in the Investment Funds Regulations approved by the Capital Market Authority, except those stipulated in investment policies and practices.

32) Additional Information Requirements for Certain Types of Funds

a. In the case of a money market fund:

1) a statement that the subscription in a unit in such a fund is not the same as placing cash on deposit with a local bank.

2) that the fund manager has no obligation to redeem units at the subscription price, and that the value of units and the income from them can go down as well as up.

3) a statement of the methodology that will be adopted by the fund manager for the classification of the fund's investments or counterparties, which will deal with the Fund.

4) If the fund will deal with any issuer of money market transactions outside the Kingdom, the fund manager acknowledges that the issuer is subject and regulated by a regulator equivalent to the Saudi Central Bank.

5) If the fund will invest in derivative contracts for the purpose of hedging, the fund manager acknowledges that the issuer is subject to the Prudential Rules issued by the Authority or issued by an equivalent regulator.

b. In the case of a feeder fund:

1) The criteria used by the fund manager in selecting

those target investment funds.

2) The feeder fund manager must disclose full details of the applicable fees and charges at all levels of the fund structure, including the aggregate of the underlying fees of the investment fund in which the feeder fund invests and the fees charged by the fund manager of the feeder fund.

c. In the case of a capital protected fund, a statement that the capital will be protected only if the units are held until the maturity of the fund and the redemption of the units prior to the maturity of the fund may be at a price lower than the invested value, and where there is a better treatment for redemption requests before the maturity of the fund, they must contain a statement of such treatment.

d. In the case of an exchange traded fund:

1) A statement that, upon subscription in units in an exchange traded fund, unitholders are deemed to have acknowledged and accepted the Fund's Terms and Conditions of such exchange traded fund;

2) A disclosure of the valuation points of the indicative net asset value and net asset value per unit; and

3) A disclosure of market maker information and the details of the agreed market- making requirements (which include, for example, a price range that the market maker is committed to enter the purchase order and the sell order within it and the minimum values of purchase and sell orders).

4) A statement that there is no guarantee that the fund and the performance of the index are accurate or identical.

5) An indication of the circumstances that may lead to errors in tracking the indicator performance, and the strategies used to reduce such errors.

6) A brief description of the indicator methodology / rules with mentioning the means by which unitholders can obtain the most recent information, news and components of the index.

7) A statement of any circumstance or circumstances that may affect the accuracy and completeness of the indicator's calculation.

8) A description of the fund manager's plan in case the index account is suspended by the service provider

9) A statement of the margin of deviation factor for the index.

e. In case of index fund:

1) A statement that there is no guarantee that the fund and the performance of the index are accurate or identical.

2) An indication of the circumstances that may lead to errors in tracking the indicator performance, and the strategies used to reduce such errors.

3) A brief description of the indicator methodology / rules with mentioning the means by which unitholders can obtain the most recent information, news and components of the index.

4) A statement of any circumstance or circumstances that may affect the accuracy and completeness of the indicator's calculation.

5) A description of the fund manager's plan in case the index account is suspended by the service provider

6) A statement of the Margin of deviation factor for the index.

f. In case of a fund of funds, a disclosure that the underlying funds are subject to other fees.

g. The criteria for determining the investment field must be stated in case the investment field in the fund is specified.

h. In the case of an investment fund that takes the form of a special purposes entity, must include the special purposes entity by-laws form.

33) Unitholder Declaration

A declaration from the unitholder that he has read the Fund's Terms and Conditions, as well as agreeing to consent to units characteristics in which he has subscribed.

(According to the Authority's Board Resolution no. (2-22-2021) Dated 12/07/1442H. Corresponding to 24/02/2021G. Annex (1) of these Regulations shall become effective as of 28/07/1443 H. corresponding to 01/03/2022 G. Moreover, Annex (1), Annex (2) and Annex (3) of the Investment Funds Regulations issued pursuant to the Authority's Board Resolution No. (1- 219-2006) dated 03/12/1427 H. corresponding to 24/12/2006 G. and amended by the Authority's Board Resolution No.)2016-61-1(dated 16/08/1437 H. corresponding to 23/05/2016 G., which can be viewed via the following link: (https://cma.org.sa/RulesRegulations/Regulations/DocLib/IFRs Regulations- Final English_EN.pdf) shall remain effective until the effective date of Annex (1) of these Regulations.)

18.11 ANNEX 2: CONTENTS OF THE APPLICATION FOR OFFERING OF A PUBLIC FUND'S UNITS

This Annex highlights the documents that are required to be included in an application file, in the manner specified by the Authority, for submission to the Capital Market Authority. The application file must include the following:

a. Form (1) of this Annex.

b. Submission Checklist of the provided documents.

c. Draft of the Fund's Terms and Conditions (with the Fund's Terms and Conditions revised checklist according to Annex (1)).

d. A copy of the identification card of the board member.

e. Subscription and Redemption Forms (where applicable).

f. A detailed investment decision-making process, highlighting the names of any registered persons involved.

g. A detailed description of risk management policies and procedures for the relevant fund.

h. A declaration by the fund manager of the setting an administrative body that will be adopted regarding the operational aspects related to the investment funds, including Compliance Monitoring Program for the relevant investment fund.

i. A declaration by the fund manager that all candidates of the fund's board meet the qualification and requirements contained in these Regulation, and that the definition of independent fund director in the Glossary of Defined Terms Used in the Regulations and Rules of the Capital Market Authority applies on that fund's independent directors.

j. Any other supporting documents.

k. Fees.

l. Electronic copies of all documents required under the above paragraphs.

m. Approvals required from relevant government bodies (where applicable).

n. Any contracts entered into by the fund manager for the benefit of the fund, including, but not limited to, contracts related to independent members of the fund's board, auditor, custodian, and the administrative manager.

Application form is available for public at the official Capital Market Authority website: www.cma.org.sa

FORM – 1 THE APPLICATION FOR OFFERING A PUBLIC FUND

Instructions to complete the form:

This form can be filled out electronically. Where there are supporting documents required under this form, please include them. Please tick in the relevant boxes, where appropriate. If a question is not applicable, please state "N/A" in the space provided. If the space provided is insufficient for your requirements, please continue on a separate sheet of paper. Please indicate which question your additional information relates to. Please fill up one application form for each fund. A copy of this form and any supporting documents submitted to the Capital Market Authority shall be kept.

THE INVESTMENT FUND

Information about the Investment Fund to be offered

1. Name of Fund
2. Fund Class and Type
3. Investment Objectives
4. Investment Policies and practices
5. The start date of the proposed initial public offering period
6. The end date of the proposed initial public offering period
7. Duration of Investment Fund (if any)
8. Reasons of offering the investment fund's units.
9. The fund's marketing strategy (3-5 years plan)
10. Names of the proposed fund board members.
11. For a Feeder Fund, please fill up the following:
    - a Name of Target Fund
    - b Name of Fund Manager
    - c Name of Custodian
    - d Date of Inception
    - e Place of Fund Inception
    - f Name of Regulatory Authority
    - g Target Fund's Investment Objectives
    - h Target Fund's Investment Policies and practices
    - i Special / Distinctive Features of Target Fund (if any)

Note: Please submit Due Diligence Report on the targeted fund and its' Fund Manager.

THE FUND MANAGER

Information on the Capital Market Institution managing the investment fund

1. Name of the Capital Market Institution (the fund manager)
2. The Authorization Number granted by the Capital Market Authority
3. Organizational Structure (Whole Company and Asset Management Division) Please use a separate sheet of paper if space is insufficient.
4. Name(s) of the Registered Portfolio Manager Responsible for the Fund
5. Name(s) of Compliance Officer and/or Compliance Committee
6. Will a fund sub-manager be appointed? Yes/No. If yes, please submit a copy of the service contract.
7. If yes, name of fund sub-manager(s)
8. Name of Portfolio Manager Responsible for the Fund at the Fund Sub-Manager
9. The authorization number granted by the Capital Market Authority of the fund sub- manager (if applicable)
10. If the fund sub-manager is a foreign entity, please provide the following information
    - a) Place of Incorporation
    - b) Regulatory Authority
    - c) Address and contact details of fund sub-manager
        - Address
        - Phone No
        - Email
    - d) Is the fund sub-manager supervised in a jurisdiction that employs regulatory standards and requirements at least equivalent to those of the Authority?

If there are more than one fund sub-manager, please give the information required under paragraphs 6 – 10 above for each fund sub-manager.

11. Will there be any other functions of the fund manager that are delegated to service providers? Yes/No If yes, please submit copies of the service contracts.
12. If yes, please list the functions that are delegated and give details of the service provider(s). Please use a separate sheet of paper if space is insufficient.

THE CUSTODIAN

Information on the Capital Market Institution that carries out the custody activity

1. Name of the Capital Market Institution (the custodian)
2. The Authorization Number granted by the Capital Market Authority
3. Relationship with Fund Manager: Related Party / Independent Please submit a copy of the service contract / service level agreement.
4. Organizational Structure (Custody Division) Please use a separate sheet of paper if space is insufficient.
5. Will a sub-custodian be appointed? Yes/No If yes, please submit a copy of the service contract.
6. If yes, name of the sub-custodian
7. the authorization number granted by the Capital Market Authority of the sub-custodian (if applicable)
8. If the sub-custodian is foreign, please provide the following information –
    - a) Place of Incorporation
    - b) Regulatory Authority
    - c) Address and contact details of sub-custodian
        - Address
        - Phone No
        - Email
    - d) Is the sub-custodian supervised in a jurisdiction that employs regulatory standards and requirements at least equivalent to those of the Authority? If there are more than one sub-custodian, please give the information required under para 5 – 8 above for each sub-custodian.
9. Will there be any other functions of the custodian that are delegated to service providers? Yes/No If yes, please submit copies of the service contracts.
10. If yes, please list the functions that are delegated and give details of the service provider and the arrangements.

Please use a separate sheet of paper if space is insufficient.

DECLARATION

Declaration by, the Fund Manager and Custodian

On behalf of the Capital Market Institution (Fund Manager)

I declare, to the best of my knowledge and belief and (after taken reasonable care to ensure that such) information given in this application form is complete, correct, accurate and not misleading at the time of this application. In addition, the proposed investment fund and the contents of the Fund's Terms and Conditions do not conflict with the Capital Market Law and Investment Funds Regulations.

- Name Position Signature Date
- Name of person responsible for the application with the fund manager
- Position
- Phone number
- Email

On behalf of the Capital Market Institution (the Custodian)

I declare that the (name of the Capital Market Institution) acts as a Custodian for the proposed investment fund. I acknowledge and confirm that I will fulfill the responsibilities entrusted to me according to the Investment Funds Regulations, the Fund's Terms and Conditions and the Capital Market Law and its implementing Regulations.

- Name Position Signature Date
- Name of person responsible for the application with the Custodian
- Position
- Phone number
- Email
- Offeror/Distributor
- Information regarding the Capital Market Institution that offer/distribute investment fund units/securities
- Name and address of the Capital Market Institution or person delegated to offer/distribute investment fund units/securities
- Authority's authorization number (where applicable)

18.12 ANNEX 3: CONTENTS OF FUND'S REPORTS

A fund report is used to provide regular and relevant information that would enable unitholders to valuate the performance of the investment fund. Annual Reports must contain all the information required in this Annex. Interim Reports of the private real estate fund must contain at least the information required under Paragraphs (C) and (F) of this Annex.

Content of Fund Annual Reports

a. Investment Fund Information

1) Name of investment fund.
2) Investment objectives, policies and polices.
3) Distribution of income and gain policy.
4) A statement that the fund's Reports are available upon request free of charge.
5) Description of the fund's benchmark and the service provider's website (if any).

b. Fund Performance

1) A comparative table covering the last (3) financial years (or since inception), highlighting:
    a) the fund net assets value at the end of each financial year.
    b) the fund net assets value per unit at the end of each financial year.
    c) highest and lowest net asset value per unit for each financial year.
    d) the number of units in issue at the end of each financial year.
    e) income distribution per unit (where applicable).
    f) expense ratio.
    g) percentage of borrowed assets from the total asset value, the period of their exposure period and due date (if any).
    h) results of comparing the performance of the benchmark of the fund with performance of the fund.
2) A performance record that covers the following:
    a) the total return for 1 year, 3 years and 5 years (and since inception (where applicable).
    b) the Annual total return for each of the last 10 financial years (or since inception).
    c) a table showing actual fees and fund expenses paid by the investment fund during the year. The Total Expense Ratio should also be clearly disclosed. If there are any circumstances in which a fund manager may elect to waive or rebate any fees, this must also be disclosed.
    d) The bases for calculating the performance data and any assumption made must be consistently applied.
3) If there were material changes that occurred during the period and that affected the performance of the fund, these changes must be clearly disclosed.
4) Disclosure of the exercise of annual voting rights and it must include the issuer's name and the date of the General Assembly and the subject of the vote and the decision to vote (agree / disagree / abstain from voting).
5) The fund's board annual report including, but not limited to, the following:
    a) Names of Fund Board members, and indicating membership type.
    b) A brief about of the fund board members' qualifications.
    c) Description of the roles and responsibilities of the Fund Board.
    d) Details on the remuneration of fund board members.
    e) A statement of any conflict or potential conflict of interest between the interests of a fund board member and the interests of the fund.
    f) A statement showing all the funds boards that the relevant board member is participating in.
    g) topics discussed and issued resolutions, as well as the fund performance and fund acievement of its objectives.

c. Fund Manager

1) Name and address of the fund manager.
2) Names and addresses of sub-manager and/or investment adviser (if any).
3) A review of the investment activities during the period.
4) A report of investment fund's performance during the period.
5) Details of any material changes to the Fund's Terms and Conditions (for a public fund) or fund documents (for private fund) made during the period.
6) Any other information that would enable unitholders to make an informed judgment about the fund's activities during the period.
7) Where an investment fund invests substantially in other investment funds, a statement must disclose on the proportion of the management fees charged to the fund itself and

to funds in which the funds invests.
8) A statement on any special commission received by the fund manager during the period, clearly identifying what they are and the manner in which they were utilized (if any).
9) Any other data and other information required by these Regulations to be included in this report.
10) Period for the management of the person registered as fund manager.
11) A disclosure of the expense ratio of each underlying fund at end of year and the weighted average expense ratio of all underlying funds that invested in (where applicable).

d. Custodian

1) Name and address of custodian.
2) A brief description of its duties and responsibilities.

e. Fund Operator

1) Name and address of fund operator.
2) A brief description of its duties and responsibilities.

o. [sic] Auditor

Name and address of auditor.

f. Financial Statements

Financial statements for the annual accounting period (or the interim period covered in the report) of the investment fund must be prepared in accordance with the accounting standards approved by the Saudi Organization of Certified Public Accountants.

18.13 ANNEX 4: CONTENTS OF QUARTERLY STATEMENTS

The quarter statement must include the following information as a minimum:

a. The objective of the fund.

b. Fund information as follows:

1) Fund start date.
2) Unit price upon offering.
3) Size of the fund.
4) Type of fund.
5) Currency of the Fund.
6) Level of risk.
7) Benchmark.
8) Number of distributions (if any)
9) Percentage of fees for the management of the invested funds (if any).
10) The investment advisor and fund sub-manager (if any).
11) The number of days of the weighted average (if any).

c. Definitions (optional)

If the definitions are available on another webpage, the link to the definitions page shall suffice.

1) Standard deviation.
2) Sharp indicator.
3) Tracking Error.
4) Beta.
5) Alpha.
6) Information Index.

d. The Fund Manager's comment (optional).

e. Contact information as follows:

1) Phone number.
2) Website.
3) Email.

f. Price information as at the end of the relevant quarter (month / year):

1) Unit Price (as at the end of the relevant quarter) Saudi Riyals
2) Change in unit price (compared to the previous quarter) %
3) Dual unit price for money market funds, and debt instruments funds with fixed income (if any) Saudi Riyals
4) Total units of the fund Number of units
5) Total net assets Saudi Riyals
6) P/E ratio (if any)

g. Fund information as at the end of the relevant quarter (month / year):

Item Value* %*

1) Total Expense Ratio (TER) (if any) From the average of the net asset of the fund
2) Borrowing percentage (if any) (if any) From the total asset value of the fund
3) Dealing expenses From the average of the net asset of the fund From the average of the net asset of the fund
4) Investment of the fund manager (if any) From the net asset of the fund From the net asset of the fund
5) Distributed profits SAR 00.00 (if any)

h. Details of the fund's ownership investments:

Details are for the purpose of clarifying the calculation method, it is not required to be included if made available in the fund manager's website

1) Full Ownership %
2) Usufruct right %

i. Disclaimer

j. A graph indicating the top 10 investments of the fund.

k. A graph indicating the fund's asset distribution (sector/geographic)

l. Revenue:

- 3 months (end of current quarter)
- Year to date
- One year
- 3 years
- 5 years
  - 1) Fund performance
  - 2) Benchmark performance
  - 3) Performance difference

m. Performance and risks:

Performance and risks standards

- 3 months (end of current quarter)
- Year to date
- One year
- 3 years
- 5 years
  - 1) Standard deviation
  - 2) Sharp indicator
  - 3) Tracking Error
  - 4) Beta
  - 5) Alpha
  - 6) Information Index

n. A graph indicating the performance of the fund since its beginning.

18.14 ANNEX 5: VALUATION METHODOLOGIES FOR PUBLIC FUNDS

Assets to be included in the Valuation:

a) All the investment fund assets must be part of the valuation.

b) The assets of the investment fund are deemed to include all assets of every kind and nature, including but not limited to:

1) cash or deposits including interest owing thereon;
2) dividends and distributions payable in stocks, cash or other property received by the investment fund;
3) all investments and other assets owned; and
4)any interest accrued on any assets or investments.

c) The liabilities of the investment fund are deemed to include all liabilities of every kind d nature, including but not limited to:

1) all loans, and accounts payable; and
2) all accrued or payable expenses and fees chargeable to the investment fund.

Method of Valuation:

a) The investment fund is to be valued on each valuation day. The valuation is to be the currency based and will be determined in respect of all the assets of which the portfolio comprises minus the liabilities attributable to the investment fund at that time.

b) The method of valuing the individual asset will depend on the type of the asset and the fund manager may rely upon any trustable system for the determination of values, prices or exchange rates.

c) The following principles shall be followed to value the fund's assets:

1) if the assets are securities which are listed or traded on any regulated securities exchange or automated quotation system, the closing price may be used of such market or system;
2) where the securities are suspended, it should be valued at the suspended price, unless there is conclusive evidence to indicate that the value of such securities have gone below the suspended price;
3) non-listed Bond and Sukuk, book value plus accrued interest or profit must be used;
4) listed Bond and Sukuk, or traded on any organized securities market or through automatic pricing system, and market conditions does not allow the valuation of the bond, or sukuk, as stated in Subparagraph (1) referred to above, it may valuate those sukuk and bonds as stated in Subparagraph (3) provided that this is disclosed in the terms and conditions of the fund.
5) Investment Funds, last published Net Asset Value per unit;
6) Deposit, nominal value and accrued interest/profit; and
7) Any other investment, fair value, as determined in good faith by the fund manager based on methods, which disclosed in the Fund's Terms and Conditions and have been verified by the auditor of the fund.

d) Net Assets Value per Unit = (Total Assets – Liabilities – Accrued Expenses) / Outstanding unit at the valuation time

18.15 ANNEX 6: PRIVATE PLACEMENT NOTIFICATION TO THE AUTHORITY – PRIVATE FUNDS AND FOREIGN FUNDS

Instructions to fill up the form: Please tick in the relevant boxes, where appropriate. If a question is not applicable, please state "N/A" in the space provided. If the space provided is insufficient for your requirements, please continue on a separate sheet of paper. Please indicate which question your additional information relates to. Please fill up one notification form for each fund. You must keep a copy of your completed form and any supporting documents submitted to the Capital Market Authority for future reference.

THE INVESTMENT FUND

Information about the Investment Fund to be Offered:

Private Fund Foreign Fund

1. Name of Fund
2. Fund Type and Class
3. (For foreign fund) Please provide the following information -
    a) Place of Establishment
    b) Name of Regulatory Authority
    c) Date of Registration
4. Brief Description of the fund (Objectives and practices)
5. The start date of the proposed initial public offering period
6. The end date of the proposed initial public offering period
7. Please specify which category of private placement specified in Articles (80) or (98) of Investment Funds Regulations
8. Number and type of securities /units to be offered (where applicable).
9. The price to be paid for the offered securities/units (in SAR) (where applicable).
10. The minimum amount (if any) to be paid by each offeree.
11. The duration of the investment fund and maturity, if applicable.
12. Required approvals from relevant government entities (where applicable)

THE OFFEROR

Information on the Capital Market Institution offering/distribute units/securities in the investment fund

1. Name and address of the Capital Market Institution offering/distribute units/securities of the private or foreign fund in the Kingdom
2. The Authorization Number granted by the Capital Market Authority.
3. (For foreign fund) Please provide the following additional information about the foreign fund manager.
    a) Foreign Fund Manager and Place of Incorporation
    b) Name of Regulatory Authority
    c) Date of License / Authorization / Registration
    d) Address and contact details of the foreign fund manager:
        - Address
        - Contact Person
        - Phone Number
        - Email

e) Is the manager of the foreign fund authorized in a jurisdiction that employs regulatory standards and requirements at least equivalent to those of the Authority?

4. Where the fund, fund manager or any of the directors, senior executives, controlling shareholders, or founding shareholders of the fund manager have been convicted by a judicial authority of any violation involving fraud or dishonesty or a violation under the Capital Market Law, its Implementing Regulations, or any legislation relating to companies or money laundering of which, details of such violation including details of the convicted party, the name of the judicial authority by which such party was convicted, the date of conviction and full particulars of the violation and the penalty imposed.

THE CUSTODIAN

Information on the Capital Market Institution that carries out the custody activity

1. (For private fund) Name of the Capital Market Institution (the custodian)

2. (For private fund) the Authorization Number granted by the Capital Market Authority.

3. (For foreign fund) Please provide the following additional information about the foreign custodian.

a) Name of the Foreign Custodian and Place of Incorporation

b) Name of Regulatory Authority

c) Date of License / Authorization / Registration

d) Address and contact details of the foreign custodian:

- Address
- Contact Person
- Phone Number
- Email

e) Is the custodian of the foreign fund authorized in a jurisdiction that employs regulatory standards and requirements at least equivalent to those of the Authority?

18.16 ANNEX 7: FUND'S DECLARATION TO THE AUTHORITY – PRIVATE FUND

[To be provided on the letterhead of the manager of the private fund]

To: The Capital Market Authority

We, being (insert name of the manager of the private fund), hereby jointly and severely declare that to the best of our knowledge and belief (having taken reasonable care to ensure that such is the case) the information contained in the private placement notification and offering documents for (the private fund name) to be used in advertising the offer is in accordance with the facts and contains no omission likely to affect the import of such information and is fair, clear and not misleading.

We further declare that all the relevant conditions for making a private placement have been satisfied and have submitted or will submit all the information and documentation required to be provided to the Authority under the Investment Funds Regulations.

We hereby authorize the Authority to request or exchange any relevant information with any authorities, agencies or bodies having responsibility for the supervision of financial services or any other relevant authorities.

Name: _ Signature:

Date:

18.17 ANNEX 8: FUND'S DECLARATION TO THE AUTHORITY – FOREIGN FUND

[To be provided on the letterhead of the distributor]

To: The Capital Market Authority

We,

(insert name of the distributor) (Hereinafter referred to as "the

distributor") hereby confirm that we have been appointed by name of offeror) (the offeror) to offer securities of the offeror.

(insert

We further declare that all the relevant conditions for making a private placement of (Name of the foreign fund) have been satisfied and have submitted or will submit all the information and documentation required to be provided to the Authority under the Investment Funds Regulations.

We hereby authorize the Authority to request or exchange any relevant information with any authorities, agencies or bodies having responsibility for the supervision of financial services or any other relevant authorities.

Name: _ Signature:

Date:

18.18 ANNEX 9: STATEMENT TO BE INCLUDED IN THE PRIVATE PLACEMENT OFFERING DOCUMENTS

The private placement offering documents must include the following statement:

"This document may not be distributed in the Kingdom except to such persons as are permitted under the Investment Funds Regulations issued by the Capital Market Authority.

The Capital Market Authority does not make any representation as to the accuracy or completeness of this document, and expressly disclaims any liability whatsoever for any loss arising from, or incurred in reliance upon, any part of this document. Prospective subscribers of the securities offered hereby should conduct their own due diligence on the accuracy of the information relating to the securities to be offered. If you do not understand the contents of this document, you should consult an authorized financial adviser."

18.19 ANNEX 10: APPROVAL AND NOTIFICATION REQUESTS PROVIDED TO THE AUTHORITY

Approvals Requests and notifications must be submitted in the manner specified by the Authority, according to the following:

a. Approvals and notifications that require changes in the Fund's documents:

1) Fund's name.

2) The subject of the notice.

3) Detail the current version and the proposed amendment and detailed justifications for such change.

4) If the change requires the consent of parties other than the fund manager, their consent must be taken before sending the request or the notice, with the necessity to refer to that in the request sent to the Authority.

5) Declaration of the fund manager that the proposed change does not conflict with the Investment Funds Regulations and other implementing regulations and any applicable Law in the Kingdom.

6) Any other documents in support of the request.

b. Approval and notifications that do not require changes in the Fund's documents:

1) Fund's name.

2) The subject of the notice.

3) If the change requires the consent of parties other than the fund manager, their consent must be taken before sending the request, with referring to that in the request sent to the Authority.

c. Notifications relating to the end of the offering period:

1) Fund's name.

2) the subject of the notice.

3) the date of the end of the offering period.

4) the amount collected (in SAR).

5) In the case of private funds, a list of the names of all investors and the amount paid from each investor and their categories, according to the Article (80) of these Regulations.

6) In the case of private funds, the investment opportunities that were acquired for the benefit of the fund, and any information related to them.

7) Date of fund operation

d. Notification on the termination or liquidation of the Fund:

1) Fund's name.

2) the date of the distribution of investment amounts to unitholders.

3) the return on investment as a percentage (where applicable).

18.20 ANNEX 11: REQUIREMENTS OF THE PRIVATE FUND'S TERMS AND CONDITIONS

Fund manager must present the Fund's Terms and Conditions in Arabic and in a manner easy to comprehend and understand by the unitholders and potential unitholders, the Terms and Conditions must include the following information according to the sequence shown in this annex:

Content of Cover Page:

a. Name of the fund, its type and class.

b. Name of the fund manager. c. Name of the fund operator. d. Name of the custodian. e. Name of the developer (if any).

f. Must include the following statement:

"This document may not be distributed in the Kingdom except to such persons as are permitted under the Investment Funds Regulations issued by the Capital Market Authority. The Capital Market Authority does not make any representation as to the accuracy or completeness, and expressly disclaims any liability whatsoever for any loss arising from, or incurred in reliance upon, any part of this document. Prospective subscribers of the securities offered hereby should conduct their own due diligence on the accuracy of the information relating to the securities subject of the offer. If you do not understand the contents of this document, you should consult an authorized financial adviser."

g. If the investment fund is in compliance with the Shariah standards approved by the Shariah Supervisory Committee appointed for the investment fund, the following statement must be additionally stated:

"[Name of fund] has been certified as being Shariah compliant by the Shariah Supervisory Committee appointed for the investment fund."

h. Must add the following statement: (If the investment fund is taking the form of a special purposes entity):

"[Name of fund] has been approved as an investment fund that takes the form of a special purposes entity in accordance with the Investment Funds Regulations and the Rules for Special Purposes Entities".

i. A statement that the Fund's Terms and Conditions shall be read in conjunction with the other documentation of the investment fund.

j. Issue date of the Fund's Terms and Conditions and last updated (if any).

k. The date of the notification to the Authority for the offering of units of an investment fund.

Inside the cover page:

1) Name and Type of the fund.

2) Address of the head office of the Fund Manager and the website for obtaining any information about the fund or its Manager.

3) Fund duration, with extension duration (if any).

4) Fund objectives.

5) A description of the Fund's objectives and its investment objectives, and clarification of the funds policy on the distribution of dividends to Unitholders.

6) A summary of the Fund's strategies to achieve its objective, which includes at least the following:

a. A description of type (or types) of the assets of real estate or investments such Fund will invest in (where applicable).
b. Any policy that may result in concentrating investment in a certain type of assets or specific geographical region.
c. Information on the deed of ownership of the property (properties) subject in the projects (where applicable).
d. A clear course of business plan approved by the developer (where applicable).
e. Lending and borrowing powers for the Fund and the Fund Manager policy in the exercise of these powers.
f. Methods and ways to invest the liquidity available in the fund.

7) Risks of Investing in the Fund:

a. Setting out a description of the main risks related to investing in the Fund, which could affect the Fund investments or any other circumstances that could affect the Fund net assets and the return on investment.
b. A statement that, investment in the Fund does not guarantee profits and does not protect from losses.

8) Subscription:

a. Providing sufficient information on the subscription which includes subscription and termination dates.
b. Clarifying whether the fund take or accept an in-kind subscriptions.
c. Shall include a commitment from the fund manager to comply with Law of Real Estate Ownership and Investment by Non-Saudis (as applicable).
d. A detailed statement of any minimum amount that the fund manager intends to collect, and the action taken in the absence of reaching that minimum limit in the fund.
e. A statement to clarifies the targeted group that are fitted to invest in the fund (qualified investors to invest in the fund).

9) Fund Unit Trading:

a. Specifying the days of accepting requests for subscription and redemption of the units of a fund.
b. Description of the provisions governing the transference of units to other investors.
c. Must contain a statement that the register of unitholders shall be conclusive evidence as to the persons entitled to units entered.
d. A statement that the fund manager will make a reasonable effort to facilitate the trading of units, and the transfer of its ownership.

10) Termination and Liquidation of the Investment Fund

a. Statement of any events of which will result in the termination of the investment fund.
b. In case of end of term of the investment fund, the fund manager may not take any fees out of the fund's assets (where applicable).
c. A statement about recovering in-kind investments or not, with a pledged by the fund manager to comply with the Law of Real Estate Ownership and Investment by Non-Saudis (as applicable).

11) Fees, Charges and Expenses:

It must include a disclosure of all fees and charges will be incurred by the Fund's assets in detail to clarify the amounts of the fees and expenses and their percentage of the total assets of the Fund with the stating of ceiling limit for all the expenses and charges. It should contain a table showing all fees and commissions and management fees, whether paid by the Unitholders or from the Fund's assets, and shall include:

a. charges imposed for subscription and redemption.
b. all charges made from the assets of the investment fund to the fund manager. Any fees owed to the fund manager from the fund's assets for management fees from the fund's net assets.
c. custody services fees, or any other service provided by the custodian.
d. Fees paid to the auditor.
e. Any commission resulting from loans made to the Fund.
f. Any fees related to the registration of units, and any other administrative service.
g. Fees paid to the developer and the engineering office (if any)
h. Clarification of all types of deduction or payments paid out of the investment fund assets and any other amount paid by the unitholders. All cases or circumstances in which the fund manager has the right to resolve or deduct any of the dues mentioned above must be mentioned.

12) The Fund's Assets:

a. A statement of registration mechanism of the fund's assets.
b. A detailed statement of each:
1) How to valuate each asset owned by Fund.
2) Method of calculating the unit price.
3) The number of valuation and its timing.
4) Procedures to be taken in case valuations or pricing where wrong or incorrect.
c. A statement that the assets of an investment fund are owned collectively by the unitholders. A fund manager, fund sub manager, fund operator, custodian, sub custodian, investment advisor or distributor shall not have any interest in or claims against such assets, other than when the fund manager, fund sub manager, fund operator, custodian, sub custodian, investment advisor or distributor is a unitholder (within the limits of its ownership), and for claims permitted under the Investment Funds Regulations and disclosed by way of statement in these Terms and Conditions.

13) Fund Board (where applicable)

1. Names of fund board members and a statement of their qualifications, and to clearly indicate independent fund directors of a fund board.

2. Details on the expected total compensation to be paid to the fund board members during the term of the fund.

3. A description of the nature of the services provided by the members of the fund's board.

4. A statement of any other investment fund managed by any member of the Fund's Board.

a. Any person appointed by the fund manager as a member of the fund board must fulfill the following eligibility requirements:
1) the person must not be bankrupt or subject to any bankruptcy or insolvency proceedings;
2) the person must not have committed an offense involving fraud or acted in breach of integrity and honesty;
3) the person must possess the necessary experience and expertise.
b. Declaration by the fund manager that the definition of "an independent fund director" in the glossary of Defined Terms Used in the Regulations And Rules of The Capital Market Authority applies to the independent fund board members.

14) Fund Manager

a. Name of the fund manager and its address.

b. A statement that the fund manager is a Capital Market Institution licensed under the Capital Market Institutions Regulations, in addition to its authorization number granted by the Authority.

c. Functions, duties and responsibilities of the fund manager.

d. Provisions governing the removal/replacement of fund manager.

e. Any other business activities or interests of the fund manager that are of significance that could potentially conflict with those of the investment fund.

f. A description of any material conflict of interests could potentially effect the performance and implementation of the duties of the fund manager towards the investment fund.

g. Functions that have been delegated to a third party by the fund manager in relation to the investment fund. h. Disclose if the fund manager intends to invest in the investment fund and the amount of such investment.

15) Fund operator

a. Name of the fund operator and the Authorization number granted by the Authority to the fund operator.

b. Functions, duties and responsibilities of the fund operator.

c. The functions delegated to the fund operator by a third party in relation to the investment fund.

16) Custodian

a. Name and address of the custodian and the Authorization Number granted by the Authority.

b. Functions, duties and responsibilities of the custodian.

c. The functions delegated to the custodian by a third party in relation to the investment fund.

d. Provisions governing the removal/replacement of custodian.

17) Developer (if any):

a. the developer name, and address.

b. A statement of the developer's functions, duties, and responsibilities.

c. Disclosure of whether the developer intends to invest in the units of the Fund and the value of these investments.

18) Engineering office (if any):

a. Engineering office name, and address.

b. A statement of the engineering office functions, duties and responsibilities.

19) Auditor:

a. The name of the auditor of the Fund, and its address.

b. A statement of the auditor tasks and duties and responsibilities.

20) Fund Financial Reports

A statement that indicates that the fund financial reports are available to unitholders upon request and free of charge, with an explanation of how to obtain them. Also, the end date of the fund's financial year must be specified.

21) Conflict of Interest

A statement stating that the policies and procedures to be followed to address conflicts of interest and any potential and / or actual conflicts of interest will be provided upon request free of charge.

22) Reporting to Unitholders

a. Description of the periodic reports that will be provided to unitholders and the fund's financial statements, and how to submit these reports and statements to them.

b. A statement that the fund manager will include the periodic reports that will be provided to unit holders the following items:

1) Full disclosure of all fund expenses that explains each item of expenditure separately and the beneficiary of those. Detailed report from the engineering office (if any) about the percentage of completion and any changes to the course of the project progress, and it must be provided to the unitholders upon request at no charge.
2) Fees of acquisition, sale or lease related to the real estate(s) under investment by the fund (where applicable).
3) The functioning of the business plan along with an engineering office summary report of the percentage completed, and any changes to the business plan (where applicable)
4) Any wrong valuation of any of the assets of the Fund or the pricing of units.

23) Meeting of Unitholders

a. Statement of the circumstances in which a meeting of unitholders is called.

b. Statement of the processes and procedures for calling a meeting of unitholders with mentioning the minimum attendance limit.

c. A statement explaining how unitholders vote and their voting rights in unitholders' meetings.

24) A list of unitholders rights.

A list that contains the rights of unitholders.

25) Unitholders' Liability

A statement providing that other than losing his investment in the fund or part of it, the unitholder shall not be liable for the debts and obligations of the fund.

26) Other Information

Include any other important information that is known (or supposed to be known) to the fund manager or the fund board at the time of issuing the Fund's Terms and Conditions.

27) Additional Information Requirements for Certain Types of Funds In the case of an investment fund that takes the form of a special purposes entity, must include the special purposes entity by-laws form.

28) Shariah Supervisory Committee

a. Names and qualifications of the Shariah Supervisory Committee members;

b. Description of the roles and responsibilities of Shariah Supervisory Committee.

c. Details on the remuneration of Shariah Supervisory Committee's members.

29) Unit Characteristics

Provide a description of the various classes of units, if the fund has more than one category, including name of all class, and its details.

30) Changes to the Fund's Terms and Conditions

a. A statement of the provisions regulating changing the Fund's Terms and Conditions and the approvals and notifications specified under the Investment Funds Regulations.

b. A statement of the procedures that will be followed to notify of any changes in the Fund's Terms and Conditions.

31) Governing Laws:

A statement that the investment fund and the fund manager are subject to the Capital Market Law and its Implementing Regulations as well as other relevant laws and regulations applicable in the Kingdom of Saudi Arabia.

18.21 ANNEX 12: LEGAL ADVISOR LETTER FORM

[To be provided on the legal advisor's letterhead] To: The Capital Market Authority We, acting as legal advisor to (-------) [name of the fund manager] "Fund Manager" in respect of the fund manager's request to offer Closed-Ended Investment Traded Funds units and list them on the Exchange (details of the Closed-Ended Investment Traded Fund),

We refer to the Terms and Conditions prepared in relation to the fund (details of the offer), and more specifically, in connection with the application submitted to the Capital Market Authority (the Authority) for the offer of Closed-Ended Investment Traded Fund units and listing them on the Exchange, and in accordance with the requirements of the Capital Market Law, and the Investment Funds Regulations, we particularly advised the fund manager of the requirements that must be included in the legal sections of the Terms and Conditions, and regarding the fulfillment of the assets to all regulatory requirements and the soundness of the acquired assets. In this respect, we have carried out such further review and enquiries as we consider appropriate in the circumstances, and we conducted an official study of the legal due diligence in this respect.

In this advisory capacity, we confirm that we are not aware of any material matter which constitutes a violation by the fund manager of its compliance with the requirements of the Capital Market Law or any conditions required under the Investment Funds Regulations in relation to the offering and listing of the Closed-Ended Investment Traded Fund units, including the requirements of the content of the Terms and Conditions as is at the date of this letter.

18.22 ANNEX 13: FUND MANAGER LETTER FORM

[To be provided on the Fund Manager's letterhead]

To: The Capital Market Authority

In our capacity acting as the fund manager of (name of the fund) in respect of offering a Closed- Ended Investment Traded Fund under the name (name of the fund), and registering and listing its units on the Saudi Stock Exchange (Tadawul), we (name of the fund manager) confirm, to the best of our knowledge, and through conducting due diligence and making enquiries of the fund, that the fund has satisfied all conditions required for registration, offer and listing of its units and has satisfied all other matters required by the Capital Market Authority (the Authority) as of the date of this letter. (name of the fund manager) further confirms that it has, to the best of its knowledge and within its capacity as fund manager, provided to the Authority all information or clarifications in such form and within such time limit as the Authority requires for the purpose of verifying whether (name of the fund manager) and the fund have complied with the Capital Market Law, and the Investment Funds Regulations.

In particular, (name of the fund manager) further confirms that:

It has provided all the relevant services required in the Investment Funds Regulations, with due care and skill. It has taken reasonable steps to ensure that the members of the directors of the fund understand the nature and extent of their responsibilities under the Capital Market Law and its Implementing Regulations. It has come to a reasonable opinion, based on due enquiries and professional experience, that: o The fund has satisfied all relevant requirements in the Investment Funds Regulations (including provisions regarding the Terms and Conditions).

All nominated members of the fund's board of directors satisfy the eligibility requirements set out in the Authority's Rules and Regulations, and that the independent members of the board satisfy the definition of the "independent fund directors" as provided in Glossary of Defined Terms Used in The Regulations and Rules of the Capital Market Authority and the Investment Funds Regulations.

Assets are free of any regulatory violations that prevent or may result in the non- utilization or operation of buildings, and that the assets are technically intact and free of any major engineering faults or defects that may prevent or may result in the non-utilization or operation of buildings, or that may in turn cause costly repairs and major changes. In addition to that the main activities of the assets are sound and able to fulfill their obligations to the fund. o All matters known to (name of the fund manager) which must be taken into account by the Authority when considering the application for registration and listing have been disclosed to the Authority.

18.23 ANNEX 14: FUND TERMINATION REPORT

The fund termination report is used to provide relevant information regarding the process of the investment fund's termination or liquidation. The fund termination and liquidation report must contain all the information required under this Annex.

Content of the fund reports:

a) Investment fund information:

1. Name of the investment fund.
2. Investments objectives and policies and practices
3. A statement that the fund's Reports are available upon request free of charge.
4. Number of the fund's units at establishment.

b) Fund performance (including liquidation period):

1. Net assets value of the fund at the end of each financial year.
2. Net assets value of the fund upon liquidation.
3. Net assets value of the fund per unit at the end of each financial year.
4. Net assets value of the fund per unit upon liquidation.
5. Highest and lowest net assets value per unit for each financial year.
6. The number of units in issue at the end of each financial year.
7. Income distribution per unit (gross and net).
8. The total return for 1 year, 3 years and 5 years (or since inception).

9. The annual total return for each year of the last 10 financial years (or since inception).
10. Expenses percentage for each year.
11. a table showing the fees, commissions and expenses incurred by the investment fund during the year including the liquidation period. The Total Expense Ratio must be clearly disclosed. If there are any circumstances in which a fund manager may elect to waive or rebate any fees, this must also be disclosed.

c) Fund's Termination or liquidation process information:

1. Name and address of the fund manager.
2. Name and address of the fund sub-manager and/or investment advisor (if any).
3. Reasons for termination or liquidation of the fund.
4. Name of liquidator (if any).
5. Date of commencing the termination or liquidation.
6. Number of fund units.
7. Description of the termination or liquidation process and its latest updates.
8. Any material events occurring during the termination or liquidation period.

d) Fund operator:

1. Name and address of the fund operator.
2. Brief description of its duties and responsibilities.

e) The custodian:

1. Name and address of the custodian.
2. Brief description of its duties and responsibilities.

f) Fund Board members

1. Names of Fund Board members, and indicating membership type.
2. A brief description of the fund board members' qualifications.
3. Description of the roles and responsibilities of the Fund Board.
4. Details on the remuneration of fund board members.
5. A statement of any conflict or potential conflict of interest between the interests of a fund board member and the interests of the fund.
6. A statement showing all the fund boards that the relevant board member is participating in. g) Name and address of the auditor. h) Financial statements:

The final audited financial statements of the investment fund for the period following the last annual audited financial statements must be prepared in accordance with the accounting standards approved by the Saudi Organization for Certified Public Accountants.

19 Instructions for Book Building Process and Allocation Method in Initial Public Offerings (IPOs)

Issued by the Board of the Capital Market Authority Pursuant to its Resolution Number 2-94-2016 Dated 15/10/1437H Corresponding to 20/07/2016G Based on the Capital Market Law Issued by Royal Decree No M/30 dated 2/6/1424H Amended by the Board of the Capital Market Authority Resolution Number 3-102-2019 Dated 18/01/1441H Corresponding to 17/09/2019G

Contents

Part 1: Preamble
Part 2: Definitions
Part 3: General Provisions
Part 4: Requirements for Book building and Changing the Price Range
Part 5: Participating Parties
Part 6: Subscription Price
Part 7: Shares Allocation for Participating Entities after Completing the Book Building.
Part 8: Offering for Retail Subscribers]
Part 9: Publication and Entry into Force

19.1 Part 1: Preamble

1) These Instructions aim to regulate the book building process and the allocation method in initial public offerings (IPOs).

2) These Instructions shall have no prejudice to the provisions of the Capital Market Law and its Implementing Regulations.

19.2 Part 2: Definitions

a) Any reference to the "Capital Market Law" in these Instructions shall mean the Capital Market Law issued by the Royal Decree No. M/30 dated 2/6/1424H.

b) Expressions and terms in these Instructions shall have the meaning which they bear in the Capital Market Law and the Glossary of defined terms used in the Regulations and Rules of the Capital Market Authority.

c) For the purpose of implementing these Instructions, the following expressions and terms shall have the meaning they bear as follows unless the context indicates otherwise:

Government Entities: Refers to any of the following: a) Entities which the Custodian of The Two Holy Mosques or the Council of Ministers are their point of reference for their financial and administrative affairs, including Ministries, Departments, Authorities, General Agencies, Government Funds or Funds managed by government entities. b) Legal persons affiliated to one of the GCC countries.

Government-owned Companies: Companies fully owned by the government or any government entity.

GCC companies: Companies that have the nationality of one of the GCC countries, and are incorporated according to the Companies Law of such country, and which the majority of their capital is owned by citizens of the GCC countries or their governments.

GCC Funds: The investment funds which have legal personality that are established in one of the GCC countries, the units of which are publicly or privately offered to investors in these countries according to the applicable laws in these countries, and which the majority of their capital is owned by citizens of the GCC countries or their governments.

GCC citizens: Natural persons who have the nationality of one of the GCC countries, and legal persons that the majority of their capital is owned by citizens of GCC countries or governments and has the nationality of one of the GCC countries.

Conflict of Interest: Refers to the conflict of interest between the issuer and any of the participating entities involved in the book building process, including but not limited to the following circumstances:

a) A director or an executive of any of the participating entities is a substantial shareholder in the issuer or any company that controls the issuer or any of the issuer's subsidiaries or vice versa.
b) A participating entity is a substantial shareholder in the issuer or any of the issuer's subsidiaries or vice versa.
c) Any of the persons, referred to in paragraph (a) and (b) above, is a director of the issuer or any of the issuer's subsidiaries.

Book building: The process by which a financial advisor registers bids from participating entities in order to determine the offering price.

Book Building Period: A period determined by the financial advisor, after obtaining the consent of the issuer, without prejudice to paragraph (d) of Part (3) of these Instructions. It starts from the first day of the financial advisor offering the issuer's shares to the participating entities in accordance with paragraph (a) of Part (3) of these Instructions.

Bidding Participation Application: The application submitted by the participating entities to the financial advisor of the issuer in order to participate in the book building process, and submitted to the financial advisor in time no later than the last day of the book building period.

Appended Bidding Application: The application submitted to the financial advisor of the issuer when the price range is changed, in accordance with paragraph (b) of Part (4) of these Instructions, in time no later than the last day of the Book building period, and submitted by participating parties in order to participate in the book building or by the participating entities for the purpose of changing their requests concerning the price range.

Participating parties: Those whom are entitled to participate in the Book building process as specified in Part (5) of these Instructions.

Participating entities: Entities involved in the Book building process from the specified parties in Part (5) of these Instructions.

Tick Size: The minimum price increment and decrement allowed for share price as applied by the Saudi Stock Exchange Company (Tadawul).

19.3 Part 3: General Provisions

a) The financial advisor of the issuer is permitted – after obtaining the Authority's approval of the IPO – to offer the shares to the participating entities only during the Book building period.

b) The financial advisor, in coordination with the issuer, shall determine a percentage of the full offering to be allocated to institutional investors, subject to the Authority's approval of such percentage.

c) The issuer must sign an underwriting agreement before the beginning of the subscription process.

d) The Book building period shall not exceed (14) fourteen calendar days.

e) The participating entities provide their bidding participation applications in the Book building; in the manner that the financial advisor of the issuer determines, provided that the financial advisor of the issuer makes the necessary arrangements and procedures to ensure documenting the bidding participation applications and verify their validity.

f) The participating entities shall not submit a bid with an amount of (5%) or more of the issued securities of the issuer.

g) The participating entities shall comply with the provisions of the Capital Market Law and its Implementing Regulations and any other investment conditions that regulate their business.

h) Where a conflict of interest with the issuer exists, the conflicted participating entities are prohibited from participating in the Book building.

i) The participating entities may change or cancel their bids at any time during the book building period, provided that the change must be made by submitting an amended bidding participation application or an appended bidding application (as applicable).

j) The Authority may waive any person subject to these Instructions from applying any of its provisions in whole or in part, upon his/her request or on its own initiative.

19.4 Part 4: Requirements for Book building and Changing the Price Range

a) During Book building, the following requirements must be satisfied:

1) The issuer's financial advisor must announce the Book building period without prejudice to paragraph (d) of Part (3) of these Instructions.
2) The issuer's financial advisor must announce the price range, and ensure its availability to all participating parties.
3) The announcement made by the issuer's financial advisor regarding the book building period and price range must be available to all participating parties on its website and the website of the issuer

b) The financial advisor may, after obtaining the underwriter and the issuer's consent, change the price range, with consideration of the following the following:

1) The financial advisor must announce the new price range to all participating parties.
2) The underwriter must provide the Authority with an updated underwriting commitment letter reflecting the new price range.
3) The change in participating entities' bids shall be by submitting an appended bidding participation application. c) At the end of the book building period, the financial advisor shall announce the offer coverage percentage by all participating parties on its website and the website of the issuer.

19.5 Part 5: Participating Parties

Those whom are entitled to participate in the Book building are:

a) Public and private funds that invest in securities listed on the Saudi Stock Exchange as permitted by the fund's terms and conditions and in accordance with the provisions and limitations stipulated in the Investment Funds Regulations. In addition, public funds must comply with the following when submitting the bidding participation application:

1) The value of the shares in the bid of a public fund and all other funds with the same fund manager shall not exceed (25%) of the total offer value.
2) The public fund shall not submit a bid with an amount in excess of (10%) of the total offer value.
3) The public fund shall not submit a bid on securities of the issuer with an amount exceeding (20%) of the fund's net asset value.
4) The public fund shall not submit a bid with an amount that exceeds (10%) of its net asset value in the issuer's offered shares.
5) Public funds are exempted from paragraph (4) above, in the following cases:

a. If the public fund whose investment objective is to invest in the shares listed on the Exchange, provided that it does not exceed the market capitalization of the issue expressed as a percentage of the total market value of all shares listed on the Exchange.

b. If the public fund's terms and conditions and information memorandum state an investment objective of investing in a specific investable universe which is a sub-category of the issuers listed on the Exchange provided that such investment does not exceed the market capitalization of the issuer expressed as a percentage of the investable universe.

6) The public fund must disclose in the bidding participation application, the market capitalization of the investable universe of the public fund as of the end of the previous day of submitting the bidding participation application.

b) Authorized Persons who are licensed to deal as a principle, in accordance with the Prudential Rules when submitting the bidding participation application.

c) Clients of a person authorized by the Authority to conduct managing activities provided that:

1. The Authorized Person has been appointed on terms which enable it to make decisions concerning the acceptance of the participation in the offering and investing in the exchange on the client's behalf without reference to the client.
2. The participation in Book building shall be directed through the Authorized Person, and all related communication are made through the Authorized Person.

d) Any legal persons allowed to open an investment account in the Kingdom, and an account with the depositary center, including foreign legal persons who are allowed to invest in the market where the shares of an issuer are to be listed, with regards to the conditions of listing companies investments in listed securities stipulated in the Authority's circular number (6/05158) dated 11/08/1435H corresponding to 09/06/2014G based on the Capital Market Authority's board resolution number (9-28-2014) dated 20/07/1435H corresponding to 19/05/2014G.

e) Government entities, any supranational authority recognized by the Authority, the Exchange, or any other stock exchange recognized by the Authority, or the Depositary Center.

f) Government-owned Companies whether investing directly or through a portfolio manager.

g) GCC companies, and GCC funds if the terms and conditions of the fund permit that.

19.6 Part 6: Subscription Price

The financial advisor in coordination with the issuer determines the subscription price according to the supply and demand, with consideration to the following:

1) The subscription price must not exceed the price specified in underwriting agreement.

2) The subscription price must be in accordance with to the tick size applied by the Saudi Stock Exchange (Tadawul).

19.7 Part 7: Shares Allocation for Participating Entities after Completing the Book building

1) The allocation percentage for participating entities is specified in the prospectus.

2) Without prejudice to paragraph (b) of Part (3) of these instructions, the allocation of the offered shares is made as the financial advisor deems appropriate in coordination with the issuer.

19.8 Part 8: Offering for Retail Subscribers

The allocation percentage for retail subscribers shall be set forth in the prospectus.

19.9 Part 9: Publication and Entry into Force

These instructions shall be effective in accordance with the approval resolution.

20 INSTRUCTIONS ON THE PRICE STABILIZATION MECHANISM IN INITIAL PUBLIC OFFERINGS

Issued by the Board of the Capital Market Authority Pursuant to its Resolution Number 4-87-2018 dated 24/11/1439H (6/8/2018G) based on the Capital Market Law issued by Royal Decree No. M/30 dated 2/6/1424H Amended by Resolution of the Board of the Capital Market Authority Number 1-7-2021 dated 1/6/1442H (14/1/2021G)

TABLE OF CONTENTS

Part 1: Preliminary
Part 2: Definitions
Part 3: General Provisions
Part 4: Obligations of the Price Stabilization Manager
Part 5: Exemptions
Part 6: Records for the Price Stabilization Transactions
Part 7: Publication and Entry Into Force

20.1 Part 1: Preliminary

a) The purpose of these Instructions is to regulate the price stabilization activities on shares of companies newly listed on the Exchange after the initial public offering. b) These Instructions shall not prejudice the provisions of the Capital Market Law and its Implementing Regulations.

20.2 Part 2: Definitions

a) Any reference to the "Capital Market Law" in these Instructions shall refer to the Capital Market Law issued by the Royal Decree No. M/30 dated 2/6/1424H. b) Expressions and terms in these Instructions have the meaning which they bear in the Capital Market Law and in the Glossary of Defined Terms Used in the Regulations and Rules of the Capital Market Authority, unless the context indicates otherwise. c) For the purpose of implementing these Instructions, the following expressions and terms shall have the meaning they bear as follows, unless the context indicates otherwise:

Price Stabilization Mechanism: A mechanism that contribute to the price stabilization of the newly listed shares on the Exchange, by means of Over- Allotment, and where all or any of the following transactions are conducted:

a) Borrowing a number of shares from lending-shareholders prior to the initial public offering, in an amount not exceeding the number resulted from the maximum limit allowed for Over-Allotment.
b) The short selling of shares during the offer period.
c) The Over-Allotment of shares not exceeding the limit set out in paragraph (a) of Part 3 of these Instructions.
d) Purchasing of shares from the Exchange during the Price Stabilization Period or by a Purchase Option in order to close any position under paragraph (a) above.

Over-Allotment: A process upon which a number of additional shares is allocated to the shares offered for subscription. Such shares are borrowed from the lending-shareholders and sold to the public during the initial public offering at the subscription price, in accordance with the over-allotment agreement.

Purchase Option: A contractual option whereby the price stabilization manager is granted the right to buy an amount of shares not exceeding the amount of the shares included in the Over-Allotment at the subscription price in the initial offer period, during the price stabilization period or after its end.

Price Stabilization Period: A period of time for the Price Stabilization Mechanism that is agreed upon between the price stabilization manager and the issuer, provided that such period shall not exceed (30) calendar days from the first day of listing the shares on the Exchange.

20.3 Part 3: General Provisions

a) The maximum amount allowed for an Over-Allotment shall not exceed 15% of the number of shares offered for subscription in the initial public offering.

b) The issuer shall, in case of conducting a Price Stabilization Mechanism, disclose the following in the prospectus:

1. Maximum number of additional shares to be over-allotted in accordance with the Over-Allotment agreement.
2. The Price Stabilization Period.
3. Any other restrictions imposed by the issuer or the underwriter on the price stabilization manager.
4. The price stabilization manager.

c) The Price Stabilization Period is deemed concluded in the event that the entire over-allotted shares were purchased by the price stabilization manager.

d) The price stabilization manager must be an Authorized Person by the Authority to carry out dealing activities as principal.

20.4 Part 4: Obligations of the Price Stabilization Manager

a) Upon completion of the book building process, the price stabilization manager, before the trading session of the next day, must disclose to the public the following:

1. The percentage of over-allotted shares among the total amount of shares offered, during the offer period.
2. The number of over-allotted shares.
3. The Price Stabilization Period, with indication that the Price Stabilization Mechanism may not be conducted and may end at any time.

b) At the end of the Price Stabilization Period, the price stabilization manager, before the trading session of the next day, must disclose to the public the following:

1. Whether the Purchase Option has been exercised.
2. The number of shares that the Purchase Option has been exercised upon.
3. The start and the end of the Price Stabilization Period.
4. The price range in which the purchase orders were executed in order to achieve the price stabilization.

c) The price stabilization manager must hold an account with the Depositary Center, in which its operations are limited to transferring the shares purchased during the exercise of the Price Stabilization Mechanism to the lending- shareholders without executing a transaction.

d) The price stabilization manager must have an investment account to hold the amounts obtained from the Over-Allotment, and which the transactions in it are limited to carrying out price stabilization transactions.

e) Starting from the first day of listing the shares on the Exchange, the price stabilization manager must disclose to the public at the end of every fifth trading day and until the end of the Price Stabilization Period the details of all price stabilization transactions it conducted, including the disclosure of the amount of shares purchased and the price range of such shares.

f) The price stabilization manager, during the Price Stabilization Period, shall not cancel the order entered in the last two minutes of the opening and closing auctions on the Exchange.

g) The price stabilization manager shall not execute any sale transactions on the shares purchased to conduct the Price Stabilization Mechanism during the Price Stabilization Period.

h) The Price Stabilization Mechanism shall be exercised at a price not exceeding the offer price or at a price not exceeding 2% of the last trade price, whichever is lower.

i) The price stabilization manager must treat any conflict of interest in accordance with the provisions of the Authorized Persons Regulations.

j) The price stabilization manager shall act in the interest of the issuer when carrying out the Price Stabilization Mechanism, and in line with these Instructions.

20.5 Part 5: Exemptions

a) For the purposes of implementing these Instructions, the shares purchase transactions from the Exchange executed by the price stabilization manager during the Price Stabilization Period in accordance with the provisions of these Instructions shall be exempted from the acts and actions stated in paragraph (a) of Article 49 of the Capital Market Law and Article 2 and subparagraph (5) of paragraph (b) of Article 3of the Market Conduct Regulations.

b) For the purpose of implementing these Instructions, the price stabilization manager shall be waived from the obligations and restrictions stated in paragraph (a) of Article 12 of the Market Conduct Regulation and Article 86 of the Authorized Persons Regulations.

c) For the purposes of implementing these Instructions, the lending-shareholders shall be waived from the obligations and restrictions stated in Article 23 and Article 24 of the Merger and Acquisition Regulations and paragraph (a) of Article 69 of the Rules on the Offer of Securities and Continuing Obligations.

20.6 Part 6: Records for the Price Stabilization Transactions

a) The price stabilization manager shall establish and maintain an updated record of each transaction conducted in accordance with these Instructions.

b) The price stabilization manager shall ensure that the record referred to in paragraph (a) of this Part contains the following information:

1. Quantity and price of shares per transaction during the conduct of the Price Stabilization Mechanism.
2. Date and time of the transaction.
3. Details of the counter party in the purchase transaction executed during the Price Stabilization Mechanism, or a statement explaining that the purchase has been executed through the Exchange.

c) The record referred to in paragraph (a) above shall be maintained for a period not less than ten years after the end of the Price Stabilization Period.

20.7 Part 7: Publication and Entry Into Force

These instructions shall be effective in accordance with the approval resolution.

21 Regulatory Rules and Procedures issued pursuant to the Companies Law relating to Listed Joint Stock Companies

Issued by the Board of the Capital Market Authority pursuant to Resolution No. 8-127-2016 dated 16/1/1438H (17/10/2016G) as amended by Board Resolution No. 4-122-2020 dated 3/4/1442H (18/11/2020G)

[Editor's Note: this document has been merged with the Guidance Note to the Regulatory Rules and Procedures issued pursuant to the Companies Law relating to Listed Joint Stock Companies, issued by the Board of the Capital Market Authority pursuant to Resolution No. (8-127-2016) dated 16/1/1438H (17/10/2016G) based on the Companies Law issued by Royal Decree No. M/3 dated 28/1/1437AH Amended by Resolution of the Board of the Capital Market Authority Number (3-57-2019) Dated 15/9/1440H (20/5/2019G)

The Guidance Note clarifies the meaning of certain Articles of the Regulatory Rules. This is accomplished by printing the various paragraphs of the Regulatory Rules in full, accompanied by a Clarification. For convenience in this edition, each Clarification is set-off in parentheses with each paragraph beginning with the word "Clarification." Not all articles are accompanied by a clarification.

The full text of the Regulatory Rules has been compared with the reprint in the Guidance Note.

The CMA did not name the articles in this law or in the Guidance Note. The titles of the articles are not a part of the law and are provided for convenience only.]

Guidance Note: Third Version

The Capital Market Authority hereby highlights that this note is for guidance only and not a substitute to the Regulatory Rules and Procedures Issued Pursuant to the Companies Law in addition to other related laws, rules and regulations. This note should not be relied upon regarding any legal procedures and responsibilities imputed to any related party or person.

21.1 INTRODUCTION

This guidance note (the "Guidance Note") is intended to assist listed joint stock companies and its boards of directors; shareholders; and any related party in implementing the Regulatory Rules and Procedures issued pursuant to the Companies Law issued by decision of the Board of the Capital Market Authority (hereinafter referred to as the "Regulatory Rules and Procedures") which aims to provide companies and its boards of directors; shareholders; and any related party to achieve a higher degree of compliance with the requirements of these Regulatory Rules and Procedures as well as the related provisions of the Companies Law. Therefore, the main objective of this Guidance Note is to further clarify a number of these requirements and provide practical examples related to such requirements.

Regulatory Rules and Procedures relating to Listed Joint Stock Companies with Integrated Guidance Note

21.2 PART 1: PRELIMINARY PROVISIONS

Article 1: [Scope and Waiver; Definitions]

a) These rules and procedures shall not prejudice the provisions of the Companies Law, the Capital Market Law, any of their implementing regulations, and other relevant Laws.

b) The Authority may waive a provision of these rules and procedures, in whole or in part as they apply to any person, upon his/her request or on its own initiative.

c) Unless the context indicates otherwise, the following words and phrases, whenever they appear in these rules and procedures, shall have the meanings herein specified.

Shares: shares of listed joint stock companies.

Treasury Shares: Purchased Shares which are retained by the Company, including Employees' Shares which are retained by the Company.

(Clarification: According to the details specified in the Regulatory Rules and Procedures, the company may dispose or sell its Treasury Shares for any of the purposes mentioned herein.)

Employees' Shares: Treasury Shares which are allocated by the Company to its employees.

(Clarification: These shares are included in the employee's incentive plans through which Treasury Shares owned by the Company are granted to the Company's employees.)

Purchased Shares: shares bought back by the Company pursuant to Article 112 of the Companies Law.

(Clarification: These are shares bought back by the Company for the purposes specified in these Regulatory Rules and Procedures, including, capital reduction, shares allocation to the Company's employees or having the Company retain such shares for a specific time as determined by the General Assembly upon approving the buy-back of shares pursuant to the provisions of these Regulatory Rules and Procedures.)

Preferred Shares: shares issued by the Company which entitle their holders to receive a percentage of the Company's net profits larger than the percentage received by holders of ordinary shares, after setting aside the statutory reserve, without entitling them to vote in the General Assembly.

General Assembly: the general assembly held with the attendance of the shareholders of the Company pursuant to the provisions of the Company's bylaws and the Companies Law.

Special Assembly: the special assembly held with the attendance of holders of preferred shares of the same class in accordance with the Companies law, Company's bylaws and these rules and procedures.

The Public: any person other than the persons mentioned in the definition of "public" set out in the Glossary of Defined Terms Used in the Regulations and Rules of the Authority. For purposes of these Rules and Procedures, the shares retained by the Company do not count as a part of the ownership of the public.

Shareholders Register: a register of shareholders prepared and maintained by the Depository Centre which includes names of shareholders, their nationality, place of residence, Shares numbers in which all relevant dealings related to the Shares issued by the Company are recorded.

Exchange: the Saudi Stock Exchange {Tadawul}.

Authorized Person: a person authorized by the Authority to conduct securities business activities.

Company: a joint stock company listed in the Exchange.

Rules on the Offer of Securities and Continuing Obligations: The Rules on the Offer of Securities and Continuing Obligations issued by the Board.

Depository Centre Regulations: The Securities Depository Centre Regulations approved by the board of the Authority.

Rules for Qualified Foreign Financial Institutions Investment in Listed Securities: {Those} Rules for Qualified Foreign Financial Institutions Investment in Listed Securities issued by the Board of the Capital Market Authority.

Corporate Governance Regulations: the Corporate Governance Regulations for listed joint stock companies issued by the Board of the Authority.

Remuneration Committee: a committee formed pursuant to the provisions of the Corporate Governance Regulations.

Board: The Company's board of directors.

Registered Shareholders: the shareholders registered in the Shareholders Register at the end of the day on which the Extraordinary General Assembly's meeting is held to approve the increase of the Company's share capital and issuance of related new shares or at the end of the day specified by the ordinary General Assembly or by the Board on which shareholders become entitled to dividends as to dividends distribution.

Remunerations: amounts, allowances, profits and their equivalent, periodic and annual performance-related bonuses, short and long term incentive plans, in addition to any other in- kind benefits, except for reasonable costs and expenses actually incurred by the Company on behalf of a Board member in performing his work.

Prospectus: the document required to offer securities in accordance with the Capital Market Law, and the Rules on the Offer of Securities and Continuing Obligations.

Capital Market Law: the Capital Market Law issued by Royal Decree No. (M/30) dated 2/6/1424H.

Companies Law: the Companies Law issued by Royal Decree No. (M/3) dated 28/1/1437H.

Depository Centre: the Securities Depository Centre.

Authority: the Capital Market Authority.

Day: a working day in the Kingdom according to official working days of the Authority.

Calendar Day: any day, whether a working or non-working day.

Affiliate: a person who controls another person or is controlled by that other person, or who is under common control with that person by a third person. In any of the preceding, control could be direct or indirect.

Controlling Interest: The ability to influence actions or decisions of another person directly, indirectly, individually or collectively with a relative or an affiliate through: (A) owning 0 or more of the voting rights in a company, (B) having the right to appoint 0 or more of the administrative team members.

21.3 PART 2: REMUNERATION OF BOARD MEMBERS:

Article 2: Determining Board Remuneration

a) Without prejudice to other relevant Laws and regulations issued by other supervisory authorities and in addition to the relevant provisions of the Companies Law and the Corporate Governance Regulations, when determining and paying Remunerations of each Board member, the Board must comply with the following standards:

1) the Remuneration must be fair and proportionate to the Board member's activities carried out and responsibilities borne by the Board members, in addition to the objectives set out by the Board to be achieved during the financial year.

(Clarification: The Company's Remuneration Committee may set an internal regulation which includes detailed standards and policies on the scale of Board members' remuneration and the extent of their entitlements, all in accordance with standards listed in this sub-article and the Corporate Governance Regulation.)

2) the Remuneration must be based on the recommendation of the Remuneration Committee;

(Clarification: This recommendation specifies remunerations that each of the Board members is entitled to in accordance with any other relevant standards or policies on which such recommendation was based, if any.)

3) the Remuneration must be proportionate to the Company's activities and the required skills for its management;

4) taking into consideration the sector in which the Company operates, its size and experience of its Board members; and

(Clarification: For example, sectors that require special skills and professional expertise such as banks, insurance companies, or complex industries; In addition to the Company's size and scale of its activities, other foreign countries in which it operates and the Board members' experience in the Company's business, should be taken into account.)

5) the remuneration must be reasonably sufficient to attract and retain highly qualified and experienced Board members.

(Clarification: Subject to the maximum amount (SR 500,000) set out in Article 76 (3) of the Companies Law.)

b) Board members shall not vote on the agenda item relating to the Remuneration of Board members at the General Assembly's meeting.

(Clarification: The purpose of this paragraph is to guarantee the independence of the resolution of the General Assembly in respect of the agenda item related to the Board members' remuneration. Such restriction applies to the Board member either his/her votes in the General Assembly meeting is on his/her behalf or on others behalf.)

Article 3: Additional Board Member Compensation A Board member may receive a Remuneration for his/her membership in the audit committee formed by the General Assembly, additional executive, technical, managerial or consultative duties – pursuant to a professional license - or positions carried out by the Board member, and such Remuneration should be in addition to the Remuneration he/she may receive in his/her capacity as a member in the Board and in the committees formed by the Board, pursuant to the Companies Law and the Company's bylaws.

(Clarification: This means the total remuneration received by a board member for his/her membership in the audit committee formed by the General Assembly and for any additional executive, technical, managerial or consultative duties – pursuant to a professional license - or positions carried out by the Board member, shall not be subject to the maximum limit set forth in Article 76 (3) of the Companies Law.)

Article 4: Non-Uniform Board Member Compensation; Prohibition on Tying Compensation to Profitability
a) The Remunerations of different Board members may vary depending on the Board member's experience, expertise, duties he/she undertakes, independence and number of Board meetings he/she attends in addition to other considerations.

(Clarification: Remunerations paid to board members may vary according to the standards stipulated in this article or any other standards based on which the remuneration can be determined.)

b) The Remuneration of independent Board members shall not be a percentage of the profits that are realized by the company, nor shall it be based directly or indirectly on the Company's profitability.

(Clarification: Independent board members remunerations shall not be linked to the Company's profit, as such link may affect the independence of their decisions.)

Article 5: Remuneration and Meeting Attendance If the General Assembly decides to terminate the membership of any Board member who fails to attend three consecutive Board meetings without a legitimate excuse, then such Board member shall not be entitled to any Remuneration for the period starting from the last Board meeting he/she failed to attend, and he/she shall pay back any Remuneration he/she received for that period.

Article 6: False Representations If it is evidenced to the audit committee or the Authority that the Remuneration paid to any Board member was based on false or misleading information presented to the General Assembly or included in the annual Board report, the Board member shall return such Remuneration to the Company, and the Company may request such Board member to return such Remuneration.

(Clarification: As a result of such false or misleading information, all Remuneration paid to any Board member shall be returned to the Company. Repaying all Remuneration received, will not relieve the said Board members from being liable for any damages incurred by the Company, the shareholders, or any related party.)

Article 7: Disclosure of Board Remuneration Policies The Board must disclose in its annual report details of the Remuneration policies, and mechanisms for determining such Remuneration, including amounts in cash and in-kind benefits paid to each Board member in exchange for any executive, technical, managerial, or advisory work or positions.

21.4 PART 3: CONVENING GENERAL AND SPECIAL ASSEMBLY SHAREHOLDER MEETINGS AND CONTEMPORARY TECHNOLOGY

Article 8: Virtual Attendance Permitted
a) Contemporary technology may be used to allow the shareholders to participate in General Assembly and Special Assembly meetings and their deliberation, review agendas of such meetings and related documents, in accordance with the following rules:

1) the shareholders' participation at the General and Special Assembly must be through instant video and audio transmission;

2) the participation must be through a live connection between the Company and the shareholders, which shall enable the shareholder to actively and instantaneously participate in the General Assembly and Special Assembly, and to listen to and follow presentations, present opinions and discuss and vote on resolutions;

b) the company must allow shareholders to vote on the agenda of the General and Special assembly meetings electronically, even if they did not attend those meetings, in accordance with the following rules:

1) electronic voting must allow shareholders to cast their votes, whether before or during the General Assembly and Special Assembly meeting, without the need to appoint a proxy to attend such meetings on their behalf; and

2) The electronic voting on the agenda items of any General Assembly and Special Assembly meeting commences after the date of publishing the meeting's invitation, provided that such period shall not be less than three (3) days prior to the date of the meeting. The electronic voting on any item of the meeting agenda shall stop when the discussion and the voting on the item are concluded in that General or Special Assembly.

c) The provisions of this Part shall not apply to non-shareholding Board members' participation in meetings of the General Assemblies and Special Assemblies.

(Clarification: This should allow the shareholder to actively engage in the discussions and events of the General Assembly through instant video and audio transmission, in a manner that would allow him/her to watch and listen to the speakers and any video or audio presentations, in addition to the ability to speak with the speakers, and to vote electronically on the resolutions and agenda items of the General Assembly. The General Assembly's attendees of shareholders or the Company's management are not required to view other shareholders who participate remotely in the General Assembly meetings. Shareholders may also vote on the General and Special Assembly's resolutions via contemporary technology without being present in person. Attendees and voters of the General and Special Assembly are counted through the automated system adopted by the company towards the quorum for validly held General and Special Assembly meetings, provided that all Rules in this Part are satisfied. The company may contract a service provider to provide such services.)

Article 9: Virtual Meetings Guidelines If contemporary technology is used in General Assembly or Special Assembly meetings, the Board must establish the rules and guidelines for checking the identity of the shareholder who votes electronically and participates in General Assembly and Special Assembly meetings through contemporary technology; the Board shall also verify the eligibility of each shareholder to vote on any of the meeting's agenda items.

(Clarification: If contemporary technology is used in General Assembly or Special Assembly meetings, the Board shall comply with any regulatory requirements - for example: the Electronic Transactions Law - and technical requirements to ensure that the identity of shareholders who remotely participate is verified.)

Article 10: Quorum The attendance and votes of shareholders who participate in General Assemblies and Special Assemblies meetings by means of contemporary technology and shareholders who vote electronically are counted towards the quorum required for a validly held meeting of the General Assemblies and Special Assemblies.

(Clarification: The votes of participating shareholders through contemporary technology (even if they do not attend the meeting) are counted towards the quorum required for a validly held meeting of the General Assemblies and Special Assemblies. In the event of losing the connection with any shareholder, such shareholder is considered as a shareholder who personally attends the meeting and leaves it prior to the end of the meeting. Such event does not prejudice counting such shareholder towards the attendance and votes quorum if such shareholder had voted electronically prior to the end of the meeting.)

Article 11: Meeting Notices Without prejudice to Article 91 of the Companies Law, the Company may send General Assemblies and Special Assemblies meeting invitations through means of contemporary technology.

21.5 PART 4: BUY-BACK, SALE, PLEDGE OF SHARES

21.5.1 CHAPTER 1: Share Buy-back Rules RULES:

Article 12: Share Buy-Back A Company may, if so provided and permitted in its bylaws, buy-back its ordinary or preferred shares, in accordance with the following rules:

(Clarification: The Company, in this case, should comply with any other laws, regulations, rules or instructions issued by another supervisory authority - to which it is subject - that restrict the Company issuance of Preferred Shares or prohibit it from such issuance.)

1) the purpose of the share buy-back shall be to either reduce the Company's capital or to retain them as Treasury shares;

(Clarification: The Company may buy-back its shares to reduce its capital directly after the buy-back or later. The company may also buy these shares and retain them as Treasury Shares. If the purpose of the Company's buy-back of its Shares is reducing its capital, the Company must take all relevant regulatory procedures and obtain any necessary approval.

2) the Treasury Shares of the Company, must not at any time exceed 10% of the total Shares in the class of Shares subject of the buy-back;

3) the Company, based on a report issued by the Company's auditor, must satisfy the following solvency requirements:

- prior to buying its Shares the Company must have, on its own or with its subsidiaries, sufficient working capital for the twelve (12) months immediately following the date of completion of the share buy-back transaction.

(Clarification: After deducting the value of the buy-back transaction, the Company must have sufficient working capital for a period of twelve (12) months.)

- The amount of Treasury Shares held must not exceed the amount of the retained profits of the Company.

4) the extraordinary General Assembly approval of the Share buy-back transaction and determining its purposes, the maximum number of Shares subject to the buy-back and the buy-back funding method. The extraordinary General Assembly must also authorize the Board to finalize the buy-back transaction, within a maximum period of twelve (12) months from the date of the above mentioned extraordinary General Assembly's resolution. The Company must announce the approval of the buy-back transaction and its conditions, immediately after the relevant resolution of the extraordinary General Assembly is issued. The extraordinary General Assembly may at any time issue a resolution to change the purposes of the Shares buy-backs.

(Clarification: For example, if the General Assembly approved buy-back of 60.000 shares of the company's shares, the extraordinary General Assembly may delegate the Board to conduct the buy-back on as many phases as it deems appropriate. In such case, the Board may, for example, complete the buy-back transaction in three phases, so 20.000 shares are bought in each phase.)

5) Unless the purpose of Share buy-back transaction is reducing the share capital of the company, the buy-back must not exceed 10% of the total quantity approved for buy-back by the General Assembly in one trading day, unless the total approved quantity, or the remaining of the approved quantity that has not been bought-back, is lower than 10% of the trading volume on the day preceding the buy-back transaction;

(Clarification: The buy-back transaction must not exceed 10% of the total quantity approved by the General Assembly in one trading day. Such percentage is calculated based on the total quantity approved for all phases (if the transaction is meant to be conducted through multiple phases). This, however does not apply if the total quantity approved by the General Assembly (or the remaining of the approved quantity) is lower than 10% of the trading volume on the day preceding the buy-back transaction.)

6) The purchase price shall not exceed 5% of the closing price on the day preceding the day the Share buy-back transaction is executed;

(Clarification: For example, if the closing price of the share on the proceeding day was SR 10, the purchase order price shall not exceed SR 10.5 on the trading day when buy-back transaction is executed.)

7) The buy-back transaction must not cause the ownership of the public in Shares of the same class to decrease to less than 30%

or any other percentage specified in the prospectus approved by the Authority.

(Clarification: The Company's buy-back transaction must not cause the ownership percentage of the public in the Company's shares to decrease below the statutory limit i.e. 30% or any other percentage specified by the Authority.)

8) Unless the purpose of Share buy-back transaction is reducing the share capital of the company, the Share buy-back transactions must be executed through the Exchange – must not be through a private transaction –;

9) the Company must not buy-back its Shares during the following periods:

• during the fifteen (15) calendar days preceding the end of the financial quarter and until the date of the Company's announcement of its reviewed interim financial statements; and

• during the thirty (30) calendar days preceding the end of the financial year and until the date of the Company's announcement of its reviewed interim financial statements or its audited annual financial statements;

10) the Company must not have a sale order in place while buying Shares.

(Clarification: The Company shall not enter or execute purchase orders when it is simultaneously selling its shares through entering or executing sale orders.)

Article 13: Permitted Buy-Back Purposes A Company may not buy-back its shares to use them as Treasury Shares except for the following purposes:

1) If the Board or its authorized representative, considers that the Share price on the Exchange is lower than its fair value.

(Clarification: The Company may purchase its shares for purposes of stabilizing the fluctuating share price when it is lower than its fair value.)

2) To fulfill convertible debt instruments holders right to convert them into Shares in accordance with the terms and conditions of those instruments.

3) Share swap transactions for the acquisition of shares or limited liability company's interests or an asset purchase.

(Clarification: These bought Shares would consist of the full or partial consideration paid by the Company to the sellers of shares, stakes or the acquired asset.)

4) To allocate them to Company's employee as part of an Employees' Shares plan.

(Clarification: The shares allocated to the Company's employee as part of an employee's share incentive plan.)

5) Any other purpose approved by the Authority.

Article 14: Notification Required The Company shall immediately notify the Exchange – according to the mechanism set out by the Exchange - of its transactions related to shares buy-back and the purpose of such buy-back. In order for the Exchange to publish the shares buy-back transactions in the listed companies shares buy-back periodic report.

Article 15: Inclusion in Annual Report The Board's annual report must contain details relating to Treasury Shares retained by the company and details on the use of these shares.

Article 16: Limitation on Buy-Backs The amount the Company will pay to buy-back its shares must not exceed the amount of distributable profits, whether the buy-back will be made through its own cash accounts or external sources of financing.

(Clarification: The Company may use its own cash accounts or external sources of financing (such as loans), provided that the financing sources shall not exceed the total amount of the distributable profits at the time of buying these shares, after deducting the used amounts of these profits for dividends , zakat and previous capitalization.

Distributable Profits are defined as per the accounting definition approved by the competent authority.)

Article 17: Buy-Backs and Capital Decrease If the purpose of a Company's buy-back of its Shares is to decrease its share capital, the provisions of Article 148 of the Companies Law must be taken into consideration.

21.5.2 CHAPTER 2: Effect of Buy-Back Transaction

Article 18: Preferred Shares Buy-Back Requirements
a) If a Company buys-back its Preferred Shares, they are deemed cancelled upon completion of the buy-back transaction and the Company must then take necessary regulatory procedures prior to purchasing these Preferred Shares.

(Clarification: When a Company intends to buys-back its Preferred Shares, It has to take the required regulatory procedures, for example but not limited to, amend its articles of association and finalise the capital reduction process.)

b) The Company planning to purchase a class of its Preferred Shares must make an offer to all the holders of that class of Preferred Shares. The holders of that class of the Preferred Shares shall have an equal opportunity to offer their Preferred Shares to the Company to purchase them in accordance with the provisions of Article 148 of the Companies Law.

(Clarification: The company in this case shall not make an offer to buy a class of its preferred shares to specific persons of the holders of these shares, rather it must make an offer to all holders of the shares.)

Article 19: General Assembly Approval Required The extraordinary General Assembly shall determine, within its resolution approving the Share buy-back transaction, the maximum time period during which the Company may retain its Treasury Shares without selling them or allocating them to its employees as Employees' Shares Plan, and the Company must not dispose of these Shares after the elapse of the mentioned period, and must take necessary regulatory procedures to cancel these Shares within a period not exceeding six months after the end of that period, unless the extraordinary General Assembly resolved to extend the period for which the company may retain the Treasury Shares before the said six month elapses.

(Clarification: if the time period specified by the extraordinary General Assembly elapsed without either reselling the treasury shares or allocating them for Employees Shares Plan, the company then must take the required regulatory procedures within six month after the end of this period, for example but not limited to, amending its articles of association and finalizing the capital reduction procedures. The company shall not dispose these shares during the period in between the end of the period specified by the Assembly up to finalizing the aforementioned regulatory procedures.)

Article 20: No Rights Issue if Holding Treasury Shares Unless the Treasury Shares are allocated to the Company's employees as part of the Employees' Shares Plan, a Company may not increase its share capital through a rights issue if it retains Treasury Shares or if the extraordinary General Assembly approved a Share buy-back transaction, and did not cancel such approval.

Article 21: Status of Treasury Shares Post-Capitalization If a Company which retains Treasury Shares increases its share capital through a capitalization issue, it shall have rights similar to those of other shareholders with respect to such Shares.

21.5.3 CHAPTER 3: Rules for Sale and Pledge of Treasury Shares

Article 22: (Sale of Treasury Shares) A Company may sell its Treasury Shares, if so provided and permitted in its bylaws, in accordance with the following rules:

1) the approval of the Board on the sale of Treasury Shares without prejudice to the extraordinary General Assembly's resolution on the approval of buying these shares.

(Clarification: This includes specifying whether the sale transaction will take place in one or multiple phases.)

2) the sale of Treasury Shares transaction must not exceed 10% of the total Treasury Shares to be sold, during one trading day, unless the total quantity of Treasury Shares to be sold is lower than 10% of the trading volume of the Company's Shares on the day preceding the buy-back transaction;

(Clarification: (This means that no transaction shall be conducted to sell more than 10% of the quantity approved by the board in one trading day. This percentage is calculated of the total quantity approved for all phases (if the sale is to be conducted in multiple phases. This, however does not apply if the quantity approved by the General Assembly or the remaining quantity is lower than 10% of the trading volume on the day preceding the buy-back transaction.)

3) the sale transactions must be executed through the Exchange – must not be through a private transaction –. As an exception, the sale of these Shares is not required to be executed through the Exchange if the purpose of the Treasury Shares is to fund share swap transactions for acquiring a company or an asset or to fulfill convertible debt instruments holders right to convert them into Shares in accordance with the terms and conditions of those instruments;

(Clarification: When a company intends to sell its shares, this must be done through the Exchange except those cases when the purpose of using these shares is as non-cash consideration in an exchange transactions for the acquisition of a company or selling an asset. Also, if the company intends to sell these shares to fulfill convertible debt instruments holders' right to convert them into shares, the company may sell these shares through a private transaction.)

4) the company must not sell its Treasury Shares during the following periods:

- during the fifteen (15) calendar days preceding the end of the financial quarter and until the date of the Company's announcement of its reviewed interim financial statements; and

- during the thirty (30) calendar days preceding the end of the financial year and until the date of the Company's announcement of its reviewed interim financial statements or its audited annual financial statements; and

5) the Company must not have a buy order in place while selling Shares.

(Clarification: This means the company shall not place or execute any sale order for its shares and simultaneously purchase its shares by placing or executing any purchase order.)

Article 23: Pledge of Shares A Company may pledge its Shares as security for a debt, if so provided and permitted in its bylaws, in accordance with the following rules:

1) the pledge must benefit the Company and its shareholders, this shall be based on a statement issued by the Board;

2) the ordinary General Assembly must approve the Share pledge transaction, and a pre-approval may be granted for several transactions; and

3) the pledge must not result in a breach of the Companies Law and any other relevant rules and regulations.

21.5.4 CHAPTER 4: Employee Shares

Article 24: Buy-Back for Employee Share Plan Requirements If a Company is buying-back its Shares for the purpose of allocating them to its employees within an Employees' Shares plan, the Company must, in addition to the other requirements of a share buy-back, comply with the following rules:

1) the Company's bylaws must provide and permit that;

2) obtain the extraordinary General Assembly's approval on the Employees' Shares plan. The General Assembly may authorize the Board to determine the terms of the plan including the allocation price for each Share offered to employees if offered for consideration; and

3) non-executive Board members shall not participate in the Employees' Shares plan, and executive Board members shall not vote on Board resolutions relating to the plan.

21.6 PART 5: PLEDGE OF SHARES

21.6.1 CHAPTER 1: SHARE PLEDGE RULES

Article 25: Right to Pledge Without prejudice to other relevant Laws and regulations, anyone who has the right to own Shares of a Company or hold Shares for and on behalf of a third party may take a pledge over Shares in accordance with the rules set forth in this Part.

(Clarification: "who has the right to own Shares on behalf of a third party" refers to banks and Authorized Persons and their counterparts of lenders or contractors with the shareholder in the kingdom or abroad in the scope of providing loans or commercial deals guarantees and other commercial transactions.)

Article 26: Pledge Requirements A shareholder of a Company may pledge some or all of his/her Shares, in accordance with the following rules:

1) obtaining any regulatory approvals necessary to create the pledge, if any; and

(Clarification: This refers to the required regulatory approvals within the company (in case the company is the pledgor) and the necessary regulatory approvals from other relevant authorities such as supervisory authorities that supervise the company's activities.)

2) the pledge agreement between the pledging shareholder and pledgee creditor must comply with the rules set forth in Chapter Two of this Part.

21.6.2 CHAPTER 2: Pledge Agreements and Registration

Article 27: Creation of a Pledge a) A pledge of Shares of a Company is created pursuant to a written or an electronic agreement between the pledging shareholder and the pledgee creditor, which shall include the following information.

(Clarification: This is pursuant to other relevant laws such as Electronic Transactions Law issued under royal decree (M/18) dated 08/03/1428H.)

1) names of the pledging shareholder, pledgee, and the beneficiary creditor (if other than the pledgee), their identifications numbers, and their addresses;
2) number of the pledged Shares and their nominal value, name of the issuing Company and its commercial registration number;
3) the amount of the debt secured by the pledge or the maximum debt amount permitted by it;

(Clarification: The debt may be defined as if it is created on these shares to secure a One Million SR debt. The debt may have a maximum permitted limit as if it is created to secure a debt or debts not exceeding One Million SR in total.)

4) the name of the debtor (if the debtor is other than the pledging shareholder), his/her identification number, and his/her address.
5) date of the pledge agreement;
6) conditions and terms of releasing the pledge; and
7) any other conditions agreed upon by both parties.

b) The Depositary Centre and the custodian of the pledged shares, should be provided with a certified copy of the pledge agreement upon recording the pledge on the relevant Shares.

c) A pledge over Shares is recorded, registered and released in the Shareholders Register in accordance with the provisions of the Depository Centre Regulations.

Article 28: Notice of Pledge and Third Parties A share pledge shall have no legal effect towards third parties unless it is recorded in the Shareholders Register. This is to be done at the Securities Depository Centre.

Article 29: Pledgee Creditor Receipt of Dividends The pledgee creditor may receive the dividends resulting from the pledged Shares and may enjoy all rights attached to them, unless the pledge agreement provides otherwise.

Article 30: Prohibition on Pledgee Creditor Attendance and Voting As an exception to Article 29 of these Rules and Procedures, the pledgee creditor shall not be permitted to attend or vote at the General Assembly meetings and the Special Assembly meetings.

21.6.3 CHAPTER 3: Foreclosure of Pledged Shares

Article 31: Foreclosure Permitted
a) The foreclosure on pledged Shares shall be in accordance relevant laws, regulations, and rules.

b) An Authorized Person may foreclose on Shares deposited for its benefit or Shares available in its customer's portfolio as a guarantee for the margin lending through directly selling them on the Exchange, in accordance with the relevant applicable rules and the margin lending agreements entered into between both parties, even if such Shares are not pledged for the benefit of the Authorized Person.

21.6.4 CHAPTER 4: General Provisions

Article 32: Multiple Pledges Permitted It is permitted to record more than one pledge over any Share of the Shares subject to a pledge in accordance with the provisions of the Commercial Mortgage Law.

21.7 PART 6: ISSUANCE, BUY-BACK AND CONVERSION OF PREFERRED SHARES BY THE COMPANY:

Article 33: Issuance and Conversion The Company may issue or buy-back Preferred Shares, convert ordinary Shares into Preferred Shares or convert the Preferred Shares into ordinary Shares, in accordance with the following rules:

1) the Company's bylaws must provide and permit it;

2) obtain the extraordinary General Assembly's approval;

(Clarification: It is a specific separate approval for each specific issuance of preferred shares. However, more than one issuance can be included under one approval of the Assembly if the maximum limit of all issuances is determined and a timeframe is specified to finalize all issuances. Amending the company's articles of association to include clauses allowing the company to issue preferred shares shall not be considered a permission to a specific issuance of Preferred Shares.)

3) obtain the approval of holders of Preferred Shares convened in a Special Assembly if the resolution relates to converting Preferred Shares into ordinary Shares or amending the rights of any holders of such Shares;

(Clarification: The extraordinary General Assembly approval is required on converting Preferred Shares into ordinary shares, or on amending the rights of any holders of such Shares.)

4) the Preferred Shares must not exceed 10 % of the Company's share capital;

5) the Company's share capital must be fully paid; and

6) Compliance with other relevant laws and regulations.

Article 34: Preferred Shares Special Assemblies Requirements Special assemblies of holders of Preferred Shares must be held in accordance with the provisions of Article 89 of the Companies Law.

Article 35: Preferred Shares Right to Vote Preferred Shares shall not grant its holders the right to vote in General Assemblies unless the Company fails to pay to holders of such Shares the specified percentage of the Company's net profits after setting aside the statutory reserve for three consecutive years.

Article 36: Preferred Shareholders Ratification Required If the General Assembly resolution results in amending the rights of holders of Preferred Shares, including the liquidation of the Company or conversion of Preferred Shares into ordinary Shares or vice-versa, such resolution shall not be effective unless ratified by holders of Preferred Shares allowed to vote in a Special Assembly.

Article 37: Failure to Pay Preferred Shareholders If the Company fails to pay holders of Preferred Shares the specified percentage of the Company's net profits after setting aside the statutory reserve for three consecutive years, the Special Assembly of holders of Preferred Shares, held in accordance with the provisions of Article 89 of the Companies Law, may resolve either to allow them to attend the Company's General Assembly and participate in voting, or to appoint representatives in the Board in proportion to the value of their Shares in the share capital, until the Company is able to pay all profits allocated to holders of such Shares from all previous years. Each Preferred Share shall have one vote in the General Assembly, and the holder of a Preferred Share may, in this case, vote on all agenda items of the General Assembly without any exceptions.

21.8 PART 7: DIVIDEND DISTRIBUTION TO SHAREHOLDERS OF THE COMPANY

21.8.1 CHAPTER 1: Dividend Payment Timing

Article 38: Dividend Distribution Timing The Board must implement the General Assembly resolution with respect to dividend distribution to the Registered Shareholders within fifteen (15) days from the date they become entitled to such dividends as determined in such resolution, or the Board's resolution for the distribution of interim dividends.

(Clarification: The company that declares distributing dividends either by a resolution of the General Assembly or the Board (for interim dividends) shall commit to pay the amounts (representing the shares of each shareholder in dividends) to the respective shareholders within 15 business days from the issuance of the resolution.)

CHAPTER 2: Interim Dividend Distribution

Article 39: Interim Dividend Distribution Permitted A Company may, if so provided and permitted in its bylaws, distribute interim dividends to its shareholders on a biannual or quarterly basis after fulfilling the following requirements:

1) The issuance of a resolution by the General Assembly renewed annually authorizing the Board to distribute interim dividends.

2) The company shall enjoy regular positive profitability.

3) The company shall enjoy reasonable liquidity, and is able to reasonably foresee the scale of its profits.

4) The Company shall have distributable profits from one or more previous years – according to the latest audited annual financial statements - sufficient to cover the proposed dividend distribution, after deducting the amounts distributed and capitalized of the profits after the date of the these financial statements.

Article 40: Annual Report Dividend Disclosure The Board must include in its annual report submitted to the General Assembly of the Company the portion of dividends distributed to shareholders during different periods of the financial years in addition to the portion of dividends proposed for distribution at the end of the financial year, and the aggregate dividend amounts.

(Clarification: The Board report which is prepared at the end of every fiscal year and presented to the General Assembly shall include the details of all interim profits that were distributed during the fiscal year and its percentage of the total realized profits for the same year (if any) in addition to any other profits and the aggregate dividend amounts. distributions recommended by the Board.)

Article 41: Accounting for Interim Dividend Distributions

a) Dividend distributions must be recorded to the cumulative retained earnings account of preceding years, or the contractual reserves, or both. The Company must take a sequential and consistent approach in determining the manner and percentage of dividend distributions in light of the Company's capabilities and available liquidity. The Board must disclose and announce the portion of regular interim dividends approved for distribution to the shareholders on the specified dates.

b) A Company must, upon resolving to distribute interim dividends, disclose and announce such resolution immediately, and provide the Authority with a copy thereof immediately.

(Clarification: Upon resolving to distribute interim dividends to shareholders by the Board, the company must disclose this in the Exchange and send a copy of this resolution to the Authority.)

21.9 PART 8: ISSUANCE AND SALE OF PRE-EMPTIVE RIGHTS RESULTING FROM CAPITAL INCREASE

21.9.1 CHAPTER 1: Definition of Pre-Emptive Rights

Article 42: Pre-Emptive Rights Definition Pre-emptive Rights are tradable securities issued by a Company which grant their holder the right to subscribe for new cash Shares offered upon the extraordinary General Assembly's approval of the capital increase through the issuance of new cash Shares. Each pre-emptive right grants its holder the right to subscribe for one new Share at the offer price. The extraordinary General Assembly may issue a resolution to allocate the new Shares resulting from a capital increase to any shareholder (excluding others) or a new investor who is not a shareholder, and in this event the capital increase does not result in rights issue.

Article 43: Capital Increase Calculations After the extraordinary General Assembly's approval of the capital increase through a rights issue, the price of the Share is adjusted by the Exchange, and the pre-emptive rights are deposited as securities in the portfolios of the Registered Shareholders based on their eligibility and in proportion to the percentage they each own in the share capital, within a maximum of two (2) days from the date of the extraordinary General Assembly meeting. The pre-emptive rights will appear in the portfolios of Registered Shareholders under a new symbol that designates these rights, and cannot be traded and subscribed for except in accordance with what is disclosed in the Prospectus. The value of such pre-emptive rights will not appear in the Registered Shareholders' portfolios before the trading period, however, only the number of pre- emptive rights will appear. The Exchange will regularly calculate and publish an indicative value on its website during the period for trading of pre-emptive rights.

(Clarification: see table below.)

	Calculation	Results
Market Value	The number of existing and issued shares x the closing price on the day of holding the Assembly	1,000,000 x SR 40 =SR 40,000,000
The Total Value of the Offering	As per the company's request	SR 2,000,000 (example)
Offering Price	Determined based on studies	SR 10
Number of the Offered Shares	Total value of the offering/offering price	200,000
The offering ratio	Number of the offered shares/number of the existing and issued shares	1,000,000/200,000 =1 for every 5 shares (20%)
The total of existing and issued shares after the offering	The number of existing and issued shares + the number of the offered shares	1,000,000 + 200,000 = 1,200,000
Market value after the offering	Market value + offering value	SR 40,000,000 =SR 2,000,000 = SR 42,000,000
The amended priceM (after holding the Assembly)	Market value after the offering/total number of shares	SR 42,000,000/1,200,000 shares = SR35.

21.9.2 CHAPTER 2: Trading of Pre-Emptive Rights

Article 44: Trading Pre-Emptive Rights The process of trading of pre-emptive rights include the following steps:

1) Period for trading of pre-emptive rights and the subscription in the new Shares:

The period of the trading in the pre-emptive rights and the subscription in the new Shares by the registered shareholders and the new investors shall be determined in the relevant prospectus.

(Clarification: The trading period is the period during which the Registered Shareholders and investors in the Exchange sell and buy rights from the Exchange.)

2) Rump Offering Period (if any):

a) If there Shares that are unsubscribed for (rump Shares) or fractional Shares (if any), such Shares shall be offered at a minimum at the offer price to a number of institutional investors according to the procedures set out in the prospectus.
b) The subscription price of the rump Shares shall not be less than the offer price during that period.

(Clarification: Institutional Investors wishing to subscribe in new shares shall present their offers to buy the rump share at a price not less than the offer price.

c) If the price of rump Shares is higher than the offer price, the difference (if any) shall be distributed, after deducting the subscription monies and expenses incurred by the Company in relation to selling these rights, as a compensation to holders of pre-emptive rights, whether they are Registered Shareholders or the new investor who purchased the pre-emptive rights and did not subscribe for their pre-emptive rights or did not sell their pre-emptive rights in proportion to the pre-emptive rights they own.

(Clarification: Any surplus resulting from the investment institutions buying of shares at a price higher than the offer price (if any) shall be distributed by the subscription manager to the Registered Shareholders or the new investors who did not subscribe for their rights nor sell these rights in proportion to the rights they own. This is after deducting the subscription amounts and fees incurred by the company.)

3) Allocation of shares to subscribers: The prospectus determines the period of allocation of Shares to subscribers, and the date of transferring the compensation (if any).

(Clarification: This includes allocating the new shares resulting from the capital increase to the Registered Shareholders and investors who bought pre- emptive rights in the Exchange and then subscribe for relevant shares.)

21.9.3 CHAPTER 3: Options Available to Registered Shareholders and New Investors

Article 45: Shareholders Pre-Emption Rights A Registered Shareholder shall have the following options:

1) Exercise its right to subscribe for the entire pre-emptive rights deposited in its portfolio to maintain its shareholding percentage in the Company.

2) Sell the pre-emptive rights deposited in its portfolio or part thereof through the Exchange and receive the consideration for such entire or partial sale.

3) Purchase additional pre-emptive rights through the Exchange, and all purchasers shall have the right to subscribe for the Shares during the subscription period in accordance to what is disclosed in the Prospectus.

4) Maintain its pre-emptive rights without any change, whether by selling them or exercising the right to subscribe for them, and in this case, the rump Shares resulting from not exercising such pre-emptive rights or selling them shall be offered during the rump offering period. The Registered Shareholder may not receive any consideration for such pre-emptive rights if the sale occurs in the rump offering period at the offer price.

Article 46: New Investors Pre-Emption Rights A new investor may purchase pre-emptive rights during the trading period and subscribe for such pre-emptive rights in accordance with the procedures set out in the prospectus. If it does not subscribe for such Shares before the end of the second subscription period, the rump Shares resulting from not exercising such pre-emptive rights or selling them shall be offered during the remaining rump offering period.

21.9.4 CHAPTER 4: Pre-emptive Rights Indicative Value

Article 47: Pre-Emptive Rights Value The indicative value of the pre-emptive rights shall reflect the difference between the market value of the Company's Shares during the trading period and the offer price regularly calculated and published by the Exchange on its website during the trading period. The indicative value may also be published on websites of market information providers to enable investors to view the reference value upon entering orders.

(Clarification: The indicative value of the pre-emptive rights shall reflect the difference between the market value of the Company's Shares during the trading period and the offer price. For example, if the share price was SR 45 (the amended price after the capital increase), and the offer price was ten riyals, then the indicative value equals to the share market price minus the offer price = SR 35. The market will calculate and publish the indicative value on its website continuously during the trading period in addition to market information providers to enable investors to view the reference value upon entering orders.)

21.10 PART 9: PROXY PROCEDURES FOR ATTENDING GENERAL AND SPECIAL ASSEMBLIES

Article 48: Shareholder Proxy Authorization Rights
a) A shareholder in a Company may authorize, pursuant to a written proxy letter, another natural person, either from shareholders of the Company or others, provided that he is not a Board member or employee of the Company, to attend the General Assembly or Special Assembly meetings and vote on its agenda items on his/her behalf. Such proxy letter must be in accordance with the proxy form attached to the meeting notice issued by the Company, which shall be in the form set out in Annex (1) and shall include the following information:

- full name of the authorising shareholder if he is a natural person, or its name according its commercial registration, or equivalent, if it is a legal person;
- name of the Company according to its commercial registration;
- Identification number if the shareholder is a natural person, or commercial registration number if it is a legal person, or equivalent;
- full name and identification number of the proxy;
- name and capacity of the proxy letter signatory, provided that a copy of the legal power of attorney is attached if the signatory is a legal agent;

(Clarification: In case the signatory is a legal agent of the assigning shareholder under a power of attorney before a notary, a copy of the said power of attorney shall be attached along with the proxy letter.)

- date of proxy letter and period of validity; and
- type of assembly meeting for which the proxy letter is granted.

(Clarification: State that the proxy letter is for attending the General or extraordinary Assembly or the Special Assembly.)

b) Notwithstanding the information required in paragraph (a) of this Article, a shareholder may authorize another person, from shareholders of the Company or others, provided that he is not a Board member or employee of the Company, to attend the General Assembly or Special Assembly meetings on its behalf pursuant to a legal power of attorney, provided that such power of attorney shall explicitly state the representative's right to attend General Assembly and Special Assembly meetings of the Company (as applicable) and vote on its agenda items.

(Clarification: The power of attorney is the authorization prepared before a notary in the Kingdom of Saudi Arabia. The legal authorization is prepared before the competent authorities overseas or before the licensed notaries in the Kingdom.)

Article 49: Proxy Attestation
a) A shareholder who is a Saudi natural person or resident in the Kingdom, or a legal person duly established in the Kingdom, must attest his/her signature in the proxy letter by any of the following authorities:

1) chambers of Commerce and Industry if the shareholder is a member of the same, a company, or a legal entity;
2) a licensed bank or an Authorized Person in the Kingdom, provided that the authorising shareholder holds an account with the attesting bank or Authorized Person; or
3) Notary public or persons licensed to take oaths.

b) A shareholder who is a legal person established outside the Kingdom may send a proxy letter to the Company, attested by the Kingdom's diplomatic authorities and embassy in its country and the Saudi Ministry of Foreign Affairs, specifying its representatives who have the right to attend the Company's General Assembly or Special Assembly meetings on its behalf. Such proxy letter must be sent to the Company within the first three (3) months of the financial year or within one (1) month from the date of acquiring Shares in the Company. Such letter shall be deemed an official proxy letter which allows such representatives to attend General Assembly or Special Assembly meetings held within one (1) year from the date of the proxy letter. As an exception to the above, the qualified foreign investor may have the letter referred to in this paragraph attested by the Assessing Authorized Person with whom he transacts, in accordance to the Rules for Qualified Foreign Financial Institutions Investment in Listed Securities.

(Clarification: This proxy letter is different from the authorization referred to in Article 48(a) for the attendance of the assignee is considered an attendance of the legal person itself and not by proxy.)

c) A shareholder who is a non-resident natural person may send a proxy letter to the Company, attested by the Kingdom's diplomatic authorities and embassy in his/her country of residence, specifying his/her proxy who have the right to attend the Company's General Assembly or Special Assembly meetings on his/her behalf, in accordance with Articles 51, 52, and 53 of these Rules and Procedures.

Article 50: Proxy Limitations The Company's bylaws may determine a maximum number of shares that a single proxy may represent in attending meetings and vote on behalf of its holders. If the Company's bylaws do not include such limitation, a single proxy may accept more than one proxy letter from the Company's shareholders, attend meetings and vote on their behalf regardless of the number of shares he represents in a meeting, except where the proxy is issued by a shareholder if he/she solely owns a number of Shares exceeding the maximum number determined in the bylaws.

Article 51: Proxy Specificity Requirement Without prejudice to paragraph (b) of Article 48 of these rules and procedures, and unless otherwise stated in the proxy, a proxy letter must be to a specific General Assembly or Special Assembly meeting. Such proxy shall be valid if a meeting is adjourned to a second or third meeting for failure to reach the quorum of the first meeting to which the proxy letter was issued.

Article 52: Prohibition on Use of Proxy It is prohibited for a shareholder (who is a natural person) to authorize another person in any of the following cases:

a) To attend the Company's General Assembly or Special Assembly meeting on his/her behalf using contemporary technology.

b) To attend the Company's General Assembly or Private Assembly meeting on his/her behalf if the shareholder intends to personally attend the meeting at the same time through Contemporary Technology.

(Clarification: A shareholder shall choose whether to assign an agent to attend the meeting on his/her behalf or to attend the meeting via contemporary technology without assigning an agent. The agent shall not represent the assigning shareholder by attending the meeting via contemporary technology.)

Article 53: Delivery of Proxy The shareholder or its proxy must deliver the original copy of the proxy letter to the Company at least two days prior to the assembly meeting, and the proxy shall present the original proxy letter prior to the assembly meeting.

Article 54: Validity of Non-Compliant Proxy Any proxy letter issued in violation of the Part must be excluded and considered void. The Company may accept proxies that are not received within the period specified in Article 53 of these rules and procedures, provided that it is handed over to the Company prior to the close of the registration process of shareholders to attend the General Assembly or Special Assembly.

21.11 PART 10: RULES OF AUTHORIZATION FOR BUSINESSES AND CONTRACTS THAT ARE EXECUTED FOR THE COMPANY'S ACCOUNT, IN WHICH A BOARD MEMBER HAS DIRECT OR INDIRECT INTEREST

Article 55: Personal Needs Business Excluded The businesses and contracts that are executed for personal needs shall not be deemed as a direct or indirect interest that require an authorization from the ordinary general assembly, provided that such businesses and contracts are carried out in the same conditions and settings followed by the company with all contractors and dealers, and that such businesses and contracts must be within the normal course of the Company's activities.

Article 56: General Assembly Delegation of Authorization
a) The Ordinary General Assembly shall have the right to delegate the authorization powers stipulated in paragraph (1) of Article 71 of the Companies Law to the company's Board of Directors, provided that the delegation is in accordance with the following conditions:

1. The total amount of business or contract or the total of the businesses and contracts during the fiscal year - is less than (1%) of the company's revenues according to the latest audited financial statements and less than 10 million Saudi Riyals.
2. The business or contract falls within the normal course of the Company's business.
3. The business or contract shall not include preferential terms to the Board members and shall be in accordance with the same terms and conditions followed by the company with all contractors and dealers.
4. The business or contract shall not be part of the business and consultation contracts which a board member carries out by a professional license for the company in accordance with Article 3 of these Regulations.

b) The board member shall be responsible for calculating the business, stipulated in paragraph (1) above, (in which he has a direct or indirect interest during the same fiscal year).

c) The period for the delegation shall be a maximum of one year from the date of approval by the General Assembly to delegate its powers, stipulated in paragraph (1) of Article 71 of the Companies Law, to the company's Board of Directors, or until the end of the session of the delegated Board of Directors, whichever is earlier.

d) Any member of the Board of Directors shall not be allowed to vote on the items of delegation and the revocation (in the Ordinary General Assembly).

e) The Ordinary General Assembly shall have the right to add additional terms to the terms stated in this Article, provided that such terms are included in the conflict of interest policy referred to in Article 43 of the Corporate Governance Regulations.

Article 57: Effect of Failure to Delegate; Authorization Required If the Ordinary General Assembly does not delegate the authorization powers stipulated in Article 56 of these Rules and Procedures, or if the terms of authorizations powers are not fulfilled stipulated in paragraph (a) of Article 56 of these Rules and Procedures are not fulfilled, an authorization must obtained from the Ordinary General Assembly on the business and contracts that are executed for the Company's account, and in which a board member has a direct or indirect interest.

Article 58: Definition of Indirect Interest An interest shall be considered indirect if the business and contract executed for the company's account may result in financial or non- financial benefits to, but not limited to, the following categories:

1. The relatives of the board member.
2. A partnership, limited partnership or limited liability company where any board member or any of his/her relatives is a partner in it or among its managers.
3. A joint stock company in which a board member or any of his/her relatives, individually or collectively, own (5%) or more of its total ordinary shares.
4. An entity - other than companies - in which a board member or any of his/her relatives has ownership, or is managing it.
5. An entity or a company where a board member or any of his/her relatives is a member of its Board of Directors or a senior executive, except for the Company's affiliates .
6. A legal person represented by a board member.

For the purposes of Implementing this Article, the meaning of the term "Relatives" is as stipulated in the Corporate Governance Regulations.

Article 59: Board Member Resignation Required
a) If the Board of Directors rejects granting the authorization pursuant to Article (56) of these Rules and Procedures, the member of the Board shall resign within a period specified by the Board of Directors; otherwise, his/her membership in the Board shall be deemed terminated, unless he/she decides to withdraw from such contract, transaction or competing venture or regularize his/her situation in accordance with the Companies Law and its Implementing Regulations prior to the end of the period set by the Board of Directors.

b) If the Ordinary General Assembly rejects granting the authorization pursuant to Article (72) of the Companies Law and Article (56) of these Regulatory Rules and Procedures, the member of the Board shall resign within a period specified by the General Assembly; otherwise, his/her membership in the Board shall be deemed terminated, unless he/she decides to withdraw from such contract, transaction or competing venture or regularize his/her situation in accordance with the Companies Law and its Implementing Regulations prior to the end of the period set by the General Assembly.

21.12 PART 11: PUBLICATION AND ENTRY INTO FORCE

Article 60: Entry into Force These Rules and Procedures shall become effective upon their publication.

21.13 Annex 1: Proxy Form

Proxy Form Date: Corresponding to: I [authorising shareholder's full name][[*]] with national with ID number [[*]]/ residence permit (for non-Saudis) or its equivalent, issued by [[*]] in my [personal]capacity or]an authorized signatory/ chairman/manger[] name of authorising company[and the owner of [[*]] shares of]name of the joint stock company[with commercial registration number [[*]] and pursuant to article [[*]] of the company's by-laws herby authorize [name of the representative] to attend the [type of assembly] assembly meeting held in [place of meeting] in [name of city] in the Kingdom of Saudi Arabia at [[*]] of the [[*]]th day of [[*]] dated[[*]H.] according to Hijri calendar and corresponding to [[*]]G to vote on my behalf on the agenda and to sign on my behalf on all resolutions and documents related to these meetings. This authorization is valid for this meeting and any subsequent adjourned meeting.

Full name of the person signing the proxy:

Capacity the person signing the proxy:

National ID number of the person signing the proxy or residence permit (for non-Saudis) or its equivalent:

Signature/ official seal (if a legal entity):

22 MARKET CONDUCT REGULATIONS

Issued by the Board of the Capital Market Authority Pursuant to its Resolution Number 1-11-2004 Dated 20/8/1425 (4/10/2004G) based on the Capital Market Law issued by Royal Decree No. M/30 dated 2/6/1424H amended by Resolution of the Board of the Capital Market Authority Number 2-11-2021 dated 12/6/1442H (25/1/2021G)

TABLE OF CONTENTS

PART 1: PRELIMINARY PROVISIONS
Article 1: Definitions
PART 2: PROHIBITION OF MARKET MANIPULATION
Article 2: Prohibition of manipulative and deceptive acts or practices
Article 3: Manipulative and deceptive acts or practices
PART 3: INSIDER TRADING
Article 4: Disclosure of inside information and insider trading defined
Article 5: Prohibition of disclosure of inside information
Article 6: Prohibition of insider trading
PART 4: UNTRUE STATEMENTS
Article 7: Prohibition of untrue statements
Article 8: Rumors
Article 9: Untrue statements defined
Article 10: Responsibility for untrue statements
PART 5: CAPITAL MARKET INSTITUTIONS' CONDUCT
Article 11: Conduct in case of market manipulation and insider trading by clients
Article 12: Clients priority
Article 13: Timely execution
Article 14: Best execution
Article 15: Timely allocation
Article 16: Churning
Article 17: Aggregation of client orders
Article 18: Dealing ahead of research
Article 19: Prohibition of dealing contrary to a recommendation
PART 6: LIABILITY FOR ACTS OF OTHERS
Article 20: Liability for acts of others
PART 7: PUBLICATION AND ENTRY INTO FORCE
Article 21: Publication and entry into force

22.1 PART 1: PRELIMINARY PROVISIONS

Article 1: Definitions

a. Any reference to the "Capital Market Law" in these Regulations shall mean the Capital Market Law issued by Royal Decree No. M/30 dated 2/6/1424H.

b. Expressions and terms in these Regulations have the meaning which they bear in the Capital Market Law and in the Glossary of defined terms used in the Regulations and Rules of the Capital Market Authority, unless the contrary intention appears.

22.2 PART 2: PROHIBITION OF MARKET MANIPULATION

Article 2: Prohibition of manipulative and deceptive acts or practices

a. It is prohibited for any person to engage in or participate in any manipulative or deceptive acts or practices in connection with an order or transaction in a security, if the person knows or has reasonable grounds to know the nature of the act or practice.

b. It is prohibited for any person to, directly or indirectly, enter an order or execute a trade in a security for the purpose of creating any of the following:

1) a false or misleading impression of trading activity or interest in the purchase or sale of the security; or
2) an artificial bid price, ask price or trade price for the security or any related security.

c. The prohibition referred to in this Article shall apply when any person enters an order or executes a trade in a security by using any means, including using technical tools to generate and enter orders automatically based on pre-defined instructions or calculations.

Article 3: Manipulative and Deceptive Acts or Practices

a. The following actions shall be among those considered as manipulative or deceptive acts or practices:

1) making a fictitious trade;
2) promoting the purchase of a security for the purpose of selling that security, or arranging for another person to sell it; or
3) promoting the sale of a security for the purpose of purchasing that security, or arranging for another person to purchase it.

b. The following acts shall be among those considered as manipulative or deceptive acts or practices when committed for the purpose of creating a false or misleading impression of trading activity in a security or interest in the purchase or sale of the security, or for the purpose of creating an artificial bid price, ask price or trade price for a security:

1) effecting a trade in a security that involves no change in its beneficial ownership.
2) entering an order or orders for the purchase of a security with the prior knowledge that an order or orders of substantially the same size, time and price for the sale of that security, has been or will be entered;
3) entering an order or orders for the sale of a security with the prior knowledge that an order or orders of substantially the same size, time and price for the purchase of that security, has been or will be entered;
4) purchasing or making offers to purchase, a security at successively higher prices or in a pattern of successively higher prices;
5) selling or making offers to sell a security at successively lower prices or in a pattern of successively lower prices; or
6) entering an order or orders for the purchase or sale of a security in order to:

- establish a predetermined sale price, ask price or bid price;
- effect a high or low opening or closing sale price, ask price or bid price;
- affect the theoretical price of volatility auction;
- maintain the sale price, ask price or bid price within a predetermined range;
- entering an order or a series of orders for a security that are not intended to be executed; or
- affect the price of another security.

c. The following acts shall not be among those considered as manipulative or deceptive acts or practices:

1) a company buying-back its own shares, if such is in accordance with the provisions of the Regulatory Rules and Procedures issued pursuant to the Companies Law relating to Listed Joint Stock Companies;
2) a price stabilization manager buying the shares, if such is in accordance with the provisions of the Instructions on the Price Stabilization Mechanism in Initial Public Offerings; or
3) a market maker buying or selling securities, if such is in accordance with any regulations, rules or procedures that the Authority or the Exchange issues.

22.3 PART 3: INSIDER TRADING

Article 4: Disclosure of Inside Information and Insider Trading Defined

a. For purposes of the application of Article 50 of the Capital Market Law and the provisions of this Part:

1) A security related to inside information must be a traded security.
2) A security related to inside information shall mean any security whose price or value would be materially affected if the information was disclosed or made available to the general public.
3) A person shall be considered directly trading in a security in any of the following two situations:

- if he executes a trade in the security for any account in which he has an interest; or
- if he makes a bid or offer on the Exchange for the security.

- 4) A person shall be considered indirectly trading in a security in any of the following situations:
  - if he executes a trade as an attorney-in-fact for another person;
  - - if he arranges a trade to which a relative or person with whom he has a business or a contractual relationship is party; or
  - - if he arranges for his attorney-in-fact or any other person acting on his behalf or at his direction to trade in the related securities.

5) Trading shall constitute insider trading, if it is directly or indirectly effected in a security related to inside information.

b. For greater certainty, insider means any of the following:

1) a director, a senior executive or an employee of the issuer of a security related to inside information;
2) a director, a senior executive or an employee of a capital market institution related to inside information;
3) an authorized signatory or an attorney-in-fact over an account for which the orders, entered or to be entered, constitute inside information;
4) a person who obtains inside information through a family relationship, including from any person related to the person who obtains the information;
5) a person who obtains inside information through a business relationship, including obtaining the information:

- from the issuer of a security related to inside information;
- from a Capital Market Institution related to inside information;
- from a person who owns an account for which the orders, entered or to be entered, constitute inside information;
- from any person who has a business relationship with the person who obtains the information; or
- from any person who is a business associate of the person who obtains the information.

6) a person who obtains inside information through a contractual relationship, including obtaining the information:

- from the issuer of a security related to inside information;
- from a Capital Market Institution related to inside information;
- from a person who owns an account for which the orders, entered or to be entered, constitute inside information; or
- from any person who has a contractual relationship with the person who obtains the information.

c. For greater certainty, inside information means information that fulfills the following:

1) information that relates to a security or orders entered or to be entered for it;
2) that has not been disclosed to the general public, and that is not otherwise available to the general public; and
3) that a normal person would realize that, in view of the nature and content of the information, disclosing it or making it available to the public would have a material effect on the price or value of the security.

Article 5: Prohibition on Disclosure of Inside Information

a. An insider is prohibited from disclosing any inside information to any other person where he knows or should have known that it is possible that such other person may trade in the security related to the inside information.

b. A person who is not insider is prohibited from disclosing to any other person any inside information obtained in whatever manner, where he knows or should have known that it is possible that such other person to whom the disclosure has been made may trade in the security related to the inside information.

c. Without prejudice to the provisions of Part 2 of these Regulations and paragraph (a) of this Article, a Capital Market Institution and a registered person may disclose the client's orders for the purpose of negotiating a private transaction for such client, provided the following:

1) the disclosure is in the client's interest to complete the transaction.

2) the client's prior approval has been obtained and documented.

Article 6: Prohibition on Insider Trading
a. An insider is prohibited from engaging in insider trading.

b. A person who is not insider is prohibited from engaging in insider trading where he knows or should have known, that the information is inside information.

22.4 PART 4: UNTRUE STATEMENTS

Article 7: Untrue Statements Prohibited A person is prohibited from making an untrue statement of material fact verbally or in writing or from failing to make a statement required to be made under the Capital Market Law, the Implementing Regulations, or the rules of the Exchange or the Depositary Center, including the financial data, if the statement is made, or the person fails to make the required statement, for the purpose of influencing the price or value of a security, inducing another person to purchase or sell a security, inducing him to exercise or refrain from exercising rights under a security, or any other manipulative or deceptive purpose.

Article 8: Rumors
a. A person is prohibited from circulating, directly or indirectly, an untrue statement of material fact or a statement of opinion for the purpose of influencing the price or value of a security or for any manipulative or deceptive purpose.

b. The prohibition in paragraph (a) applies to a statement made by the person who circulates the statement or to a statement made by another person.

Article 9: Untrue Statements defined
a. A person makes an untrue statement of material fact in any of the following circumstances:

1) if he makes a statement that is false or inaccurate in a material respect;
2) if he procures another person to make a statement that is false or inaccurate in a material respect;
3) if he makes a statement that contains a misrepresentation of a material fact;
4) if he procures another person to make a statement that contains a misrepresentation of a material fact; or
5) if he omits a material fact when making a statement.

b. A material fact is any information relating to a security which, if the investor knew about, would have materially affected the price or value at which the investor purchased or sold the security.

Article 10: Responsibility for Untrue Statements For the purposes of application of Article 56 of the Capital Market Law and the provisions of this part:

a. A person shall be liable for damages to a claimant if he makes an untrue statement of material fact and the statement is made:

1) for the purpose of profit or commercial benefit; and
2) in relation to the purchase or sale of a security.

b. A claimant for damages under paragraph (a) of this Article must establish that:

1) he was not aware that the statement was untrue;
2) he would not have purchased or sold the security in question if he was aware of the untrue statement, or that he would not have purchased or sold the security at the price at which such security was purchased or sold; and
3) the person who made the untrue statement knew, or knew that there was a substantial likelihood, that the statement was untrue in relation to a material fact.

c. A person shall be liable for damages to a claimant, if he is obliged under the Capital Market Law, the Implementing Regulations, or the rules of the Exchange or the Depositary Center to make a statement and fails to do so provided that:

1) the claim for damages is in relation to the purchase or sale of a security; and
2) what has been omitted relates to a material fact.

d. A claimant for damages under paragraph (c) of this Article must establish that:

1) he was not aware of the failure to make the statement; and
2) he would not have purchased or sold the security in question had he known in advance that the statement was omitted, or that he would not have purchased or sold the security at the price at which such security was purchased or sold.

22.5 PART 5: CAPITAL MARKET INSTITUTIONS CONDUCT

Article 11: Conduct in Case of Market Manipulation and Insider Trading by Clients
a. A Capital Market Institution and a registered person must not accept or execute a client order if any of them has reasonable grounds to believe that the client:

1) is engaging in market manipulation or insider trading;
2) would be engaging in market manipulation or insider trading in another market if these Regulations applied to that market; or
3) would be considered in breach of the Capital Market Law, regulations or rules applicable in the relevant market.

b. Where a Capital Market Institution or registered person has decided not to accept or execute an order under paragraph (a) of this Article, the circumstances of, and reasons for, such decision must be documented in writing, and the Capital Market Institution must notify the Authority of the decision within three days.

c. Without prejudice to the provisions of this Article, if a capital market institution or a registered person accepts or executes a client's order, then became aware of reasonable grounds to believe the client is in violation of the Capital Market Law, the Implementing Regulations or the Exchange's Rules, the Capital Market Institution must notify the Authority of such within three days from the date of becoming aware of these grounds.

d. A Capital Market Institution must retain the records in relation to any decision under this Article for ten years from the date of the decision.

Article 12: Clients Priority A Capital Market Institution or a registered person must execute client orders for a security before executing any order on the same security for any of their own accounts.

Article 13: Timely Execution If a Capital Market Institution accepts a client order or decides in its discretion to execute a client order, it must execute the order as soon as is practical in the circumstances.

Article 14: Best Execution
a. Where a Capital Market Institution deals with or for a client, it must provide best execution.

b. A Capital Market Institution is considered to provide best execution if:

1) acting as an agent, it ensures that the order is executed at the best prevailing price in the relevant market or markets for the size of the order; or
2) acting as a principal, it executes the transaction at a better price for the client than it would have obtained if it executed the order in accordance with the preceding paragraph.

Article 15: Timely Allocation A Capital Market Institution who executes a transaction based on a client order must ensure that the transaction is promptly allocated to the account of that client. A Capital Market Institution who executes a discretionary transaction must ensure that the transaction is promptly allocated to the account of the client for whom the capital market institution decided to transact.

Article 16: Churning A Capital Market Institution must not advise or solicit a client to deal or deal or arrange a deal in the course of managing for a client if the dealing would reasonably be regarded as contrary to the interest of the client, having regard to the number and frequency of trades relative to the client's investment objectives, financial situation and the size and character of his account.

Article 17: Aggregation of Client Orders
a. A Capital Market Institution must not aggregate a client's orders with those of other clients or with the Capital Market Institution's own orders if the order is for a security traded on the Saudi Stock Exchange, unless such aggregation is performed in accordance with any regulations, rules or procedures the Authority or the Exchange issues.

b. If the order is for a security that is not traded on the Saudi Stock Exchange, a Capital Market Institution may aggregate a client's orders with those of other clients or with the Capital Market Institution's own orders if the following is fulfilled:

1) the Capital Market Institution has provided a written explanation to the client of the advantages and disadvantages of aggregation and obtained written consent from the client to aggregate orders;
2) the Capital Market Institution ensures that no client will be disadvantaged by aggregation of his orders; and
3) all clients' orders that are aggregated receive the average price of execution for all of the orders that are executed.

c. A Capital Market Institution must establish a written policy setting out its method of allocating trades to client and principal orders.

Article 18: Dealing Ahead of Research
a. Where a Capital Market Institution intends, or knows that an affiliate intends, to issue to a client or clients an investment recommendation, or a research, study or analysis relating to a security, subject to paragraph (b) below, the Capital Market Institution must not knowingly make a trade for its own account in the security concerned or in any related security until the clients for whom the recommendation or research was intended have had a reasonable opportunity to react to it.

b. A Capital Market Institution may make a trade for its own account if the recommendation, research, study or analysis could not reasonably be expected to affect the price of the security concerned or any related security.

Article 19: Prohibition of Dealing Contrary to a Recommendation Where a Capital Market Institution or any of its affiliates issues an investment recommendation, research, study or analysis relating to a security it is prohibited from:

1) providing advice to a client or making a trade for a client that is contrary to the recommendation unless the Capital Market Institution, prior to providing the advice or making the trade, discloses to the client the recommendation and the potential conflict of interest between the Capital Market Institution and the client; or

2) making a trade for its own account in the security that is contrary to the recommendation unless reasonable grounds exist to make the trade.

22.6 PART 6: LIABILITY FOR ACTS OF OTHERS

Article 20: Liability for Acts of Others Where a person is found to have violated the provisions of the Capital Market Law or the Implementing Regulations on market manipulation, insider trading or untrue statements while acting on behalf of another person and at the direction of the person on whose behalf the relevant act is carried out, that other person is liable and is subject to any sanctions to which the person carrying out the relevant acts is subject unless the person on whose behalf the act is carried out:

1) took reasonable steps to prevent the violation of the provisions of the Capital Market Law and its Implementing Regulations; and

2) did not authorize the acts in question.

22.7 PART 7: PUBLICATION AND ENTRY INTO FORCE

Article 21: Publication and Entry into Force These Regulations shall become effective upon their publication.

23 MERGER AND ACQUISITION REGULATIONS

Issued by the Board of the Capital Market Authority pursuant to its Resolution Number 1-50-2007 dated 21/9/1428H (3/10/2007G) based on the Capital Market Law issued by Royal Decree No. M/30 dated 2/6/1424H amended by Resolution No. 3-45-2018 dated 7/8/1439H (23/4/2018 G) and the Companies Law issued by Royal Decree No. M/3 dated 28/1/1437H

Important Notice:

The current version of these Regulations, as may be amended, can be found at the CMA website: www.cma.org.sa

Table of Contents

Part 1 GENERAL PROVISIONS
Article 1 : Preliminary Provisions
Article 2 : Extent and Scope of the Regulations
Article 3 : General Provisions
Article 4 : General Principles of Announcements
Article 5 : Compliance with Competition Law
Article 6 : Waiver
Part 2 ACQUISITIONS
Chapter 1: RULES OF PRIVATE TRANSACTIONS
Article 7 :Negotiation between Selling Shareholder and Offeror
Article 8 :Approaching the Offeree Company
Article 9 :Access to Confidential Information of the Target Company
Article 10:Announcements
Article 11 :Prohibitions and Restrictions on Dealings
Article 12 :Appointment of Financial Advisors and Legal Advisors
Article 13 :Mandatory Offer Triggers
Article 14 :Purchase Price
Article 15 :Exemptions from the Offer of Securities Regulation
Chapter 2: RULES OF OFFERS
Article 16: Approaching the Offeree Company
Article 17: Announcement and Offer Timetable
Article 18:Independent Advice
Article 19 :Prohibitions and Restrictions on Dealings
Article 20 :Purchases Resulting in an Obligation to Offer a Minimum Level of Payment
Article 21 :Consequences of Certain Dealings
Article 22 :Disclosure of Dealings during the Offer Period, Indemnity and other Arrangements
Article 23 :The Mandatory Offer
Article 24: Restrictions on the control of shares representing 40% of the voting rights
Article 25: The Partial Offer
Article 26: Securities Exchange Offer for all the offeree company's shares
Article 27: The Acceptance Condition
Article 28: Nature of Payment to be Offered
Article 29: Subjective and Financing Conditions
Article 30: Offer to a Company with more than One Class of Shares
Article 31: Special Deals with Favourable Conditions
Article 32: Announcement of Acceptance Results
Article 33: The Use of Proxies and Other Authorities in Relation to Acceptances
Article 34: Information Relating to an Offer
Article 35: Equality of Information
Article 36: Restrictions on Frustrating Actions
Article 37: Responsibilities of the Offeree Company to Update its Shareholders' Register
Article 38: Offer Document
Article 39: Offeree Board Circular
Article 40: Documents Available for Inspection
Article 41: Profit Forecasts
Article 42: Asset Valuations
Article 43: Publication of the Offer Document and the Offeree Company Board Circular
Article 44: Timing of the Offer
Article 45: Revision of the Offer
Article 46: Right to Withdraw Acceptance
Article 47: Reduction or Increase of Company's Shares
Article 48: Related Parties' Offers
Part 3 MERGER
Article 49: Types of Merger Transactions
Article 50: Rules of Merger Transactions
Article 51: Required Acceptance and Approvals for a Merger Transactions
Part 4 PUBLICATION AND ENTRY INTO FORCE
Article 52: Publication and Entry into Force

23.1 PART 1: GENERAL PROVISIONS

Article 1: Preliminary Provisions

a) Any reference to the "Capital Market Law" in these Regulations shall mean the Capital Market Law issued by Royal Decree No. M/30 dated 2/6/1424H and any reference to the "Companies Law" in these regulations shall mean the Companies Law issued by Royal Decree No. M/3 dated 28/1/1437H.

b) Expressions and terms in these Regulations have the meaning which they bear in the Capital Market Law and in the Glossary of defined terms used in the Regulations and Rules of the Capital Market Authority, unless the contrary intention appears.

Article 2: Extent and Scope of the Regulations

a) The purpose of these Regulations is to regulate the following:

1) Acquisitions activities, based on the Authority's powers as stated in the Capital Market Law; and
2) Merger activities, based on the Authority's powers as stated in the Companies Law.

b) The provisions of the Regulations apply to the following:

1) any purchase or sale of shares with voting rights of listed companies, resulting in an ownership or control of a person, individually or collectively by acting in concert, over ten percent (10%) or more of the relevant Offeree Company; or
2) any Offer to purchase shares with voting rights of listed companies, if the percentage of shares sought to be acquired by the Offeror would increase its ownership, individually or collectively by acting in concert, or the shares under their Control, to ten percent (10%) or more of the shares of the relevant Offeree Company, and of that same shares class.

c) The parties to whom the Regulations apply include:

1) Any person who deals in the Exchange, including (without limitation) issuers, shareholders, Authorized Persons, and any person involved directly or indirectly in participating or giving an advice on any transaction regulated by these Regulations;
2) directors of companies which are subject to these Regulations; and
3) any person who seek the Acquisition of, or increase its shares in, any company subject to this regulation.

d) This Regulation shall not contradict the provisions of the Capital Market Law and its implementing regulations.

e) Any reference to a person or persons in these Regulations applies to private investment fund(s).

Article 3: General Provisions

a) Except in private transactions, an Offeror or Offeree Company must appoint their Independent Financial Advisor who shall be approved by the Authority, and an Independent Legal Advisor, who shall be authorized to practice law in Saudi Arabia. The Independent Financial Advisors of the Offeror or Offeree Company shall be the point of contact to coordinate with the Authority on behalf of the party each of them represents, in respect of the potential Acquisition or the potential Merger.

b) Parties involved in Acquisitions or Mergers must take care that information made available for the purpose of the Acquisition or Merger are not made in a way that may mislead shareholders or the Exchange.

c) In the case of an Offer, all shareholders of the same class of an Offeree Company must be treated equally by an Offeror.

d) Any document or announcement related to an Offer or potential Offer, addressed by the Offeror, the board of the Offeree Company or their respective advisors, to shareholders, must be true, fair and not misleading.

e) During the course of an Offer, or when an Offer is in contemplation by the Offeree Company, neither an Offeror, nor the Offeree Company, nor any of their respective advisors may furnish information to some shareholders which is not readily made available to all shareholders. This principle does not apply to the following:

1) the furnishing of information in confidence by the Offeree Company to a bona fide potential Offeror or vice versa in the context of an Offer; or
2) the furnishing of information in confidence by the selling shareholder and/or Offeree Company to an Offeror in the context of a Private Transaction.

f) An Offeror should only announce an Offer after the most careful consideration in accordance with the provisions of these Regulations, and if it firmly believes that it can and will continue to be able to implement the Offer; responsibility for advising the Offeror and ensuring all reasonably steps are taken in this respect rests on the financial advisor of the Offeror.

g) In case of a merger or acquisition by an offer to exchange securities against securities that'll be listed in the exchange, the offeror shall comply with relevant provisions stated in the Capital Market Law and its implementing regulation.

h) In case of an Offer, the Offeror and the board of directors of the Offeree Company must give sufficient information and advice to the shareholders of the Offeree Company to enable them to reach a properly informed decision to accept or reject the offer, and must have sufficient time to do so. No relevant information should be withheld from them.

i) All persons who have access to confidential information, especially information that are price sensitive, regarding the acquisition or any similar transaction, shall deal with such information in confidential manner, and it shall not be provided to any person unless it's necessary to do so, provided that such person is aware of the importance of confidentiality. Moreover, such persons shall act in manner that eliminates the chances of a leak of the information that are price sensitive.

j) In case the board of the Offeree Company has reason to believe that a bona fide Offer might be imminent, the board of the Offeree Company may not take any action in relation to the affairs of the company, that may cause the rejection of the offer or preventing shareholders from making a decision on it, without the approval of the shareholders convened in a general assembly

k) Where there are Related Parties to an Acquisition to which these Regulations apply, there must be full disclosure of the Related Party's interest in the transaction to the affected shareholders prior to completion of that transaction. Any such transaction must be on arm's length terms.

l) The board of an Offeree Company must always act in the best interests of its shareholders.

m) Directors of the Offeree Company must always, in advising their shareholders, act only in their capacity as directors and not have regard to their personal shareholdings, the shareholdings through Related Parties, the shareholdings of the shareholders they represent in the board, or to their personal relationships with the Offeror or Offeree Company, as applicable, and must at all times have regard to advice given in accordance with Article 18 of these Regulations. It is the shareholders' interests taken as a whole, together with those of employees and creditors, that should be considered when the directors are giving advice to shareholders. Directors of the Offeree Company should give careful consideration before they enter into any commitment with an Offeror (or anyone else) which would restrict their freedom to advise their shareholders in the future.

n) A shareholder who owns shares with offeror (or Merging Company) and the offeree company (or the merged company) may not vote in shareholders general assembly on decisions related to offers subject to this regulation, except in one of these companies.

o) A director shall not vote at a meeting of board or of its committees or a general assembly meeting on any resolution concerning an offer subject to these Regulations or any other relevant matter where the director, any relative or representative of his/her has a conflict of interest. In this context such a conflict of interest would arise if:

1) the director has, directly or indirectly, an interest related to the offer or the potential offer.
2) the director is a shareholder in the Offeror and at the same time he/she is a director of the Offeree Company board, or vice versa.
3) the director is a director of the Offeror board and at the same time he/she is a board member of, or a manager in the Offeree Company, or vice versa.

p) For the purposes of these Regulations, an interest of a person who is a relative or an affiliate of a director shall be treated as an interest of the director.

q) If a person is intending to enter into an acquisition, which will result in an obligation to extend an Offer to all shareholders, he/she must, before making the Acquisition, ensure that he/she can and will continue to be able, financially and practically, to implement such an Offer.

r) A false market must not be created where the securities value fluctuate, weather of the Offeree Company/merged company, or the Offeror company/Merging Company or of any other company concerned by the Acquisition/Mergers or any other company concerned by the offer in such way that the rise or fall of the prices of the relevant securities becomes artificial and the normal functioning of the market is distorted.

s) An Offeree Company activities must not be affected longer than reasonable as a consequence of an Acquisition or a Merger.

Article 4: General Principles of Announcements

a) Any announcement or statement related to a transaction, required under these Regulations, must be complete, clear, accurate and not misleading, and it must comply with the Instructions of announcement issued by the Authority and the provisions of these Regulations.

b) Parties of an offer or Private Transactions, other than listed companies, that are required to make a public announcement pursuant to these Regulations, and which are not a members in the exchange, may use the Exchange website to make such announcements, or use other Regulatory Information Service Providers.

Article 5: Compliance with Competition Law

a) Notification

Where the Competition Law, its Implementing Regulations and other related instructions are applicable on an offer, or where it's required to obtain other local or foreign regulatory approvals or non-objection, the Offeror must state that in its announcement. The Offeree Company and the Offeror must notify and obtain the approval of the General Authority for Competition pursuant to the provisions of the Competition Law.

b) Transaction lapse

Where the Competition Law, its Implementing Regulations and other related instructions are applicable on an offer, the transaction will lapse if the General Authority for Competition notifies the Offeror or the Offeree Company in writing, or through any other formal means of notification, that it objects to the transaction.

c) The end of Offer period

1) When the Offeror or the Offeree Company is notified of the General Authority for Competition objection on the Offer or potential Offer, the Offer period will end, and any new Offer must be announced within 21 days after the General Authority for Competition's approval of the transaction under the provisions of the Competition Law. In all cases, a new Offer period will be deemed to begin on the date of the General Authority for Competition's approval of the transaction.

2) If there is no announcement of a new Offer within 21 days after the General Authority for Competition's approval of the transaction under the provisions of the Competition Law, the Offer period will last until either the expiry of the referred to period, or the announcement by all relevant Offerors (affected by the General Authority for Competition's approval of the transaction under the provisions of the Competition Law) that they do not intend to make an Offer, whichever is earlier.

Article 6: Waiver The Authority reserves the right to waive any person subject to this regulation from applying the provision of these Regulations in whole or in part, upon his/her request or on its own initiative.

23.2 PART 2: ACQUISITIONS

23.2.1 Chapter 1: Private Transactions Rules

Article 7: Negotiation between Selling Shareholder and Offeror

a) Negotiations or discussions between a selling shareholder and an Offeror regarding a Private Transaction must remain strictly confidential and be restricted to a limited number of concerned people within the selling shareholder and Offeror and their immediate advisors (if any).

b) A selling shareholder and an Offeror who are in negotiation or discussions regarding a Private Transaction must take adequate measures to limit any potential leakage or unlawful usage of confidential/price sensitive information.

Article 8: Approaching the Offeree Company

a) The parties involved in a Private Transaction (the selling shareholder and the Offeror) may inform the board of the Offeree Company or its advisors of the potential transaction, at their discretion, in order to provide the offeror with price sensitive confidential information, conditioning the absence of any of the events requiring disclosure as per paragraph (d) of this Article.

b) The Offeree Company is deemed informed of a potential Private Transaction upon formally notifying and informing its board of directors. Following its formal notification of a potential Private Transaction, the board of director of an Offeree Company shall act independently to serve the best long term interests of the Offeree Company and its shareholders. The knowledge of individual board members of a potential private transaction shall not be imputed to the Offeree Company, unless the board of directors is formally notified of the potential Private Transaction.

c) Upon formally approaching an Offeree Company in respect of a potential Private Transaction, an Offeror or potential Offeror must make clear the identity of its substantial shareholders.

d) In the event of a leakage of confidential and/or price sensitive information about the Offeree Company or the potential Private Transaction or in the event of the Offeree Company becoming subject of rumors relating to the potential Private Transaction, the Offeror should promptly notify the Offeree Company's board of directors and the Authority of the Private Transaction and announce the Transaction to the public in accordance with Article 10 of these Regulations.

Article 9: Access to Confidential Information of the Target Company

a) If and when an Offeree Company is formally approached in respect of a potential Private Transaction in accordance with paragraph (b) of Article 8 of these Regulations, such Offeree Company may share confidential/price sensitive information with a bona fide Offeror, to assist such Offeror in conducting its due diligence over the Offeree Company to evaluate the merits of the potential Private Transaction, provided this is made in strict confidence.

b) The Offeree Company (through its board of directors) shall have the discretion to determine the nature and extent of confidential/price sensitive information to be shared with a bona fide Offeror. Any such determination shall be considered on a case by case basis and be made by the board of directors of the Offeree Company, taking into consideration the interests of the Offeree Company and its shareholders. The board of directors of the Offeree Company must also take adequate measures to limit any potential leakage or unlawful usage of confidential/price sensitive information.

Article 10: Announcements

a) An announcement to the public is required to be promptly made by each of the Offeror and the selling shareholder when:

1) definitive agreements (including the share sale and purchase agreement and excluding entering into preliminary agreements such as memorandum of understanding) relating to a Private Transaction, entered into by and between the Offeror and the selling shareholder; or

2) prior to formally notifying the Offeree Company of a potential Private Transaction in accordance with paragraph (b) of Article 8 of these Regulations, the Offeree Company is the subject of rumours and speculations or where there is an untoward price movement since the start of the negotiations between the selling shareholder and the Offeror, of 10% or more within a single day or 20% or more of the lowest share price since the start of the negotiations between the selling shareholder and the Offeror, and there are reasonable grounds for concluding that it is the potential Private Transaction which have led to the situation.

b) An announcement to the public is required to be promptly made by each of the Offeree Company's board of directors, the Offeror and/or the selling shareholder when, after the Offeree Company is formally notified of a potential Private Transaction in accordance with paragraph (b) of Article 8 of these Regulations and the Offeree Company is the subject of transaction related rumors and speculations or where there is an untoward price movement in the Offeree Company since the start of the negotiations between the selling shareholder and the Offeror, of 10% or more within a single day or 20% or more of the lowest share price since the start of the negotiations between the selling shareholder and the Offeror, and there are reasonable grounds for concluding that it is the potential Private Transaction which have led to the situation.

Article 11: Prohibitions and Restrictions on Dealings

a) Restrictions on dealings by the selling shareholder, the Offeror or persons acting in concert with any of them:

No dealings of any kind in securities of the Offeree Company by the selling shareholder, the Offeror or any party acting in concert with them may take place between the time during the preliminary consideration regarding a potential Private Transaction (including entering into a memorandum of understanding or other relevant agreements) is reached, between the selling shareholder and the Offeror, and the announcement of the closing of the transaction or termination of discussions and negotiations.

b) Prohibition on dealings by persons with access to confidential price sensitive information

1) No dealings of any kind in securities of the Offeree Company by any person, who is privy to confidential price-sensitive information concerning a potential Private Transaction, may take place between the time when a preliminary understanding regarding a potential Private Transaction (including entering into a memorandum of understanding or other relevant agreements) is reached, between the selling shareholder and the Offeror, and the announcement of the closing of the transaction or termination of discussions and negotiations.

2) No person who is privy to confidential price-sensitive information concerning a potential Private Transaction or contemplated transaction may make any recommendation to any other person as to dealing in the relevant securities.

3) If the transaction wasn't completed, the offeror who have obtained confidential price-sensitive information concerning the Private Transaction may not, in any kind, trade in the offeree company's securities for 6 months from the date of announcing the non-completion of the transaction.

Article 12: Appointment of Financial Advisors and Legal Advisors Each Offeror and selling shareholder that is party to a Private Transaction may appoint an Independent Financial Advisor and an Independent Legal Advisor, provided that they'll be responsible for advising in regards of the requirements of this regulation.

Article 13: Mandatory Offer Triggers

a) An Offeror who, in a Private Transaction which results in the purchase or an increase in the aggregate ownership or interest in the shares so that such Offeror or persons acting in concert with it become the owner (or Controller) of 40% or more of the offeree company's shares carrying voting rights, becomes subject to Article 23 of these Regulations.

b) The provision set out in paragraph (a) of this Article shall also apply to any beneficiary on behalf of whom the selling shareholder or Offeror is acting in the context of the Private Transaction. A person shall be treated as a beneficial owner of shares of the Offeree Company if he/she has the ultimate beneficial ownership or Control of such shares, whether through multiple entities or a contractual arrangement.

Article 14: Purchase Price

a) The selling shareholder and Offeror may agree, in a Private Transaction, on any purchase price they deem appropriate for the acquired shares by applying a premium or discount on the market price of the shares of the Offeree Company on the Exchange.

b) The selling shareholder, Offeror and/or Offeree Company (as applicable), each must disclose the agreed purchase price for the Private Transaction, in the announcement they are required to make in accordance with Article 10 of these Regulations.

Article 15: Exemptions from the Offer of Securities Regulation

The solicitation by a selling shareholder of multiple potential Offerors to enter into a Private Transaction for the sale of part or all of its shares in the Offeree Company shall not constitute an Offer of securities subject to the private placement requirements of the Rules Of Offering Securities And Continuing Obligations , as long as the shares of the Offeree Company are listed in the Exchange.

Chapter 2: Offer Rules

Article 16: Approaching the Offeree Company

a) An Offer must be put forward to the board of the Offeree Company or to its Independent Financial Advisor on or before it is made to the shareholders of the offeree company.

b) Any Offer, or an approach with a view to an Offer being made, must make clear the identity of the substantial shareholders of the Offeror or potential Offeror or any persons Acting in Concert with the Offeror or potential Offeror.

c) If the Offer, or an approach with regard to a possible Offer, is not made by the Offeror or potential Offeror, the identity of that Offeror or potential Offeror must be disclosed to the board of the Offeree Company at the outset of the Offer or the approach with regard to a possible Offer.

Article 17: Announcement and Offer Timetable

a) Mandatory public announcement

A public announcement is required to be promptly made in the following circumstances:

1) When firm intention to make an Offer (the making of which is not, or has ceased to be, subject to any pre-condition, other than the General Authority for Competition's approval in accordance with Article 5 of these Regulations) is notified to the board of the Offeree Company in accordance with paragraph (e) of this Article, irrespective of the attitude of the board of directors of the Offeree Company to the Offer;

2) upon an Acquisition of shares by a person which gives rise to an obligation to make an Offer under paragraph (a) of Article 23 of these Regulations. The announcement shall not be delayed even if all relevant information was not obtained, as additional information can be the subject of a later supplementary announcement;

3) when a person, individually or acting in concert with the others, owns 40% of the shares carrying voting rights in the offeree company as per Article 24 of this regulation;

4) When, before a bid approach has been made, the Offeree Company is the subject of rumors and speculations or where there is an untoward price movement of 10% or more within a single day and there are reasonable grounds for concluding that it is the potential Offeror's actions which have led to the situation;

5) When, following a bid approach, an Offeree Company is the subject of Offer- related rumors and speculations, or where there is an untoward price movement in the Offeree Company shares of 20% or more of the lowest share price since the time of the approach or a price movement of 10% or more in a single day;

6) When negotiations or discussions regarding an Acquisition relating to shares listed on the Exchange carrying 30% or more of the voting rights of a company, or when the board of a listed company is seeking one or more potential Offerors, to include more than a very restricted number of people (outside those who need to know in the companies concerned and their immediate advisors).

b) Responsibilities of Offeror and the Offeree Company

1) Before the board of the Offeree Company is approached, the responsibility for making the announcement required under paragraph (a) of this Article lies only with the Offeror. The Offeror should, therefore, keep a close watch on the Offeree Company's share price for any signs of untoward movements in the Offeree Company's share price or where the Offeree Company is the subject to Offer- related rumors or speculations. The Offeror is also responsible for making an announcement once an obligation is incurred as per Article 23 of these Regulations .

2) Following an approach to the board of the Offeree Company which may or may not lead to an Offer, the primary responsibility for making the announcement required under paragraph (a) of this Article will rest with the board of the Offeree Company which must, therefore, keep a close watch on its share price for any untoward movement or if it is the subject of Offer-related rumors or speculations.

3) Where there is a recommendation from the Offeree Company's board of directors to accept the Offer and to submit an application to the Authority to grant a temporary suspension of trading, and the Authority has granted such suspension, the Offeree Company may instead of announcing, obtain the temporary suspension and make the announcement afterwards.

4) A potential Offeror must not attempt to prevent the board of an Offeree Company from making an announcement or requesting the Authority to grant a temporary suspension of trading.

c) Offer timetable

1) The Offeror must approach the Authority for the purpose of submitting its proposed Offer timetable by no later than three days from the date of the announcement required under sub-paragraphs (1) or (2) of paragraph (a) of this Article. Provided that the timetable includes the following stages:

a. the delivery of the final Offer Document to the Authority for approval;

b. the publication of the Offer Document approved by the Authority and prepared by the Offeror and providing the same to the board and to the shareholders of the Offeree Company which shall take place no later than 3 days from obtaining the Authority's approval;

c. the publication of the Offeree Company's board circular in accordance with Article 39 of these Regulations (if such information has not been published with the Offer Document), which shall take place no later than 14 days from step (b) of this sub-paragraph;

d. Offeror shareholders' approval (if any), which shall take place no later than 28 days from step (b) of this sub-paragraph, provided that the period between announcing the general assembly meeting and convening it must not be less than 21 days;

e. Offeree Company shareholders' approval which shall take place no later than 28 days from step (b) of this sub-paragraph, provided that the period between announcing the general assembly meeting and convening it must not be less than 21 days;

f. the earliest permitted closing date of the Offer, which shall be no earlier than 28 days from step (b) of this sub-paragraph;

g. the right of withdrawal of acceptances if the Offer has not become unconditional as to acceptances, which shall be no later than 14 days from the first closing date mentioned in step (f) of this sub-paragraph;

h. the last date on which the Offeree Company may announce profit or dividend forecasts, asset valuations or proposals for dividend payments, which shall be no later than 60 days from step (b) of this sub-paragraph;

i. the last date on which the Offeror may revise its Offer or publish new information which shall be no later than 60 days from step (b) of this sub-paragraph;

j. the last date on which the Offer can be declared unconditional as to acceptances, which shall be no later than 60 days from step (b) of this sub- paragraph;

k. the last date on which the Offer must remain open for acceptance after it is declared unconditional as to acceptance, which shall be no earlier than 21 days from step (j) of this sub-paragraph;

l. the last date for satisfaction of all other conditions, which shall be no later than 21 days from step (j) of this sub-paragraph; and

m. the last date for cash or other consideration to be provided to the shareholders of the Offeree Company, which shall be no later than 10 days from step (i) of this sub-paragraph.

2) All parties related to the Offer must comply with the timetable as specified in sub- paragraph (1) of paragraph (c) of this Article.

3) The Authority must be notified immediately if the Offeror or the Offeree Company considers that it cannot comply with the adopted timetable as specified in sub-paragraph (1) of paragraph (c) of this Article. The Authority may, in any circumstances, amend the periods in the adopted timetable.

4) The offeror, while approaching the Authority as per sub-paragraph (1) of paragraph (c) of this Article, shall provide the offer document prepared in line with the provisions of Article 38 of these regulations.

5) The Offeror must notify the Authority, at any time after publishing the offer document and before the offer becomes unconditional in respect of acceptance, or before the meeting of the general assembly (if applicable) of any significant changes in the offering document or any other document required by the offeror under these Regulations, or the rise of any important issues that should've been added to this document.

6) The offer timetable as per sub-paragraph (1) of paragraph (c) of this Article shall be published in the manner specified by the Authority.

d) The setting of deadline to make a firm Offer announcement

When an announcement has been made in accordance with paragraph (a) of this Article other than the announcement of a firm intention to make an Offer, the Offeree Company's board of directors may request that the Authority to set a time limit for the Offeror to clarify its intentions in respect of the Offeree Company. If such a time limit is approved by the Authority, at some time on or before the expiry of that limit the Offeror must publicly announce either a firm intention to make an Offer, or that it does not intend to make an Offer.

e) The announcement of a firm intention to make an Offer

1) The announcement of a firm intention to make an Offer should be made only when an Offeror has every reason to believe that it can and will continue to be able to implement the Offer. Responsibility for advising the Offeror in this connection rests on the Independent Financial Advisor of the Offeror.

2) When a firm intention to make an Offer is announced, the announcement must contain at least the following information:

a. the terms of the Offer;

b. the identity of the Offeror and any persons Acting in Concert with the Offeror;
c. details of any existing holding in the Offeree Company:

1. which the Offeror owns or Controls;

2. which is owned or controlled by any person Acting in Concert with the Offeror;

3. in which the Offeror has received an irrevocable commitment to accept the Offer;

4. in which the Offeror or any person Acting in Concert with it holds an option to purchase;

d. all conditions (including any conditions relating to acceptances, listing and increase of capital and any consent or regulatory approval) to which the Offer or the publication of the Offer Document is subject; and
e. details of any indemnity arrangement involving the Offeror, the Offeree Company or any person Acting in Concert with any of them in relation to relevant securities.

3) The announcement of a firm intention to make an Offer should include confirmation by the Independent Financial Advisor that financial and practical capabilities available to the Offeror are sufficient to satisfy full acceptance of the Offer. The Independent Financial Advisor must act responsibly in accordance with paragraph (f) and paragraph (d) of Article 38 of these Regulations and take all reasonable steps to assure itself that capabilities are available.

f) Obligation on the Offeree Company to circulate announcements

The offeree company promptly after the Authority's approval on publishing the offer document, shall announce its board's circular, summarizing the terms and conditions of the Offer.

g) Consequences of a "firm announcement"

When there has been an announcement of a firm intention to make an Offer, the Offeror must, except with the consent of the Authority, proceed with the Offer unless the Offer is subject to the prior fulfillment of a specific condition which has been made public and which has not been met. The Offeror must proceed with the Offer in accordance with the timetable referred to in sub-paragraph (1) of paragraph (c) of this Article.

h) Issuing a statement of intention not to make an Offer

An Offeror making a statement that he/she does not intend to make an Offer for the Offeree Company should ensure that the statement is clear and unambiguous. Such Offeror (and persons acting in concert) will be bound by that statement for a period of six months unless there is a material change of circumstances related to the statement or there has occurred an event which the Offeror specified in its statement as an event which would enable it to be set aside.

Article 18: Independent Advice The board of the Offeror (if the Offeror is a listed company) and the board of the Offeree Company must obtain competent independent advice from Independent Financial Advisors, appointed in accordance with paragraph (a) of Article 3 of these Regulations, and inform their respective shareholders of the substances of such advice.

Article 19: Prohibited and Restricted Dealings
a) Prohibited dealings

1) No dealings of any securities of the Offeree Company by any person (including persons Acting in Concert), who is privy to confidential price-sensitive information concerning an Offer or potential Offer, from the time when there is reason to suppose that an approach or an Offer is contemplated and the announcement of the approach or Offer or of the termination of the discussions.

2) No person who is privy to confidential price-sensitive information concerning an Offer or contemplated Offer may make any recommendation to any other person as to dealing in the relevant securities.

b) Restriction on dealings by the Offeror

1) During an Offer period, the Offeror must not sell any securities of the Offeree Company without obtaining the Authority's prior approval, and in any cases it may not sell with price less than the offer price.

2) During an Offer period, the Offeror (including persons Acting in Concert) must not deal in Offeror securities (if the Offeror is a listed company) where any information concerning an Offer or potential Offer is considered by the Offeror to be price sensitive in respect of those Offeror securities.

c) Gathering of irrevocable commitments

1) The Offeror's Independent Financial Advisor shall inform the Authority before any offeree shareholder or Offeror shareholder, where Offeror shareholder consent is required, is contacted with a view to seeking an irrevocable commitment to accept/approve or refrain from accepting/approving an Offer.

2) Any person proposing to contact any shareholder with a view to seek an irrevocable commitment to accept or refrain from accepting an Offer or potential Offer may consult the Authority in advance, and the Independent Financial Advisor of the Offeree Company must ensure that such shareholder (other than a sophisticated investor) fully knows the nature of the commitment being requested.

d) Dealings in Offeree Company's securities by certain persons

During the Offer period, Independent Financial Advisor or Independent Legal Advisor (as applicable) to an Offeree Company, any other person in its group, any person Acting in Concert with it or any of their subsidiaries, shall not:

1) either for its own account or on behalf of discretionary account, purchase Offeree Company shares or deal in their derivatives of such shares; 2) make any loan to a person to assist him in making any such purchases or carrying out any such dealings referred to in sub-paragraph (1) of this paragraph except for lending in the ordinary course of business and on normal commercial terms to persons with which they have an established client relationship and in accordance with the Authorized Persons Regulations; or

3) enter into any indemnity or option arrangement, or any arrangement, agreement or understanding, formal or informal, of whatever nature, which may be an inducement for a person to retain, deal or refrain from dealing in relevant securities of the Offeree Company.

Article 20: Purchases Resulting in an Obligation to Offer a Minimum Level of Payment
a) Purchases before announcement referred to in paragraph (e) of Article 17

When an Offeror has purchased shares in the Offeree Company within the three month period prior to the announcement of firm intention to provide an offer, or prior to these three months (if required by the Authority), the Offer to the shareholders of the same class shall not be on less price than the price of the purchase made prior to the announcement of firm intention.

b) Purchases after announcement referred to in paragraph (e) of Article 17

1) If, during the period from the announcement made in accordance with sub- paragraphs (1) or (2) of paragraph (a) of Article 17 of these Regulations until the end of the Offer period, an Offeror purchases shares at more than the Offer price (being the then current value of the Offer), or otherwise acquires any other interest in shares giving it Control of the voting rights of such shares, it shall increase its Offer to not less than the highest price paid for the shares so acquired during that period.

2) An Offeror must announce, immediately after the purchase, that a revised Offer will be made in accordance with this Article. The announcement should also state the number of shares purchased, or the interest otherwise acquired, and the price paid.

Article 21: Consequences of Certain Dealings An Offeror (or any persons acting in concert) who purchase shares in an Offeree Company must fulfill any obligations arising under Article 23, 24 or 25 of these Regulations. An announcement shall be made by the offeror immediately after such a purchase, or immediately upon becoming a substantial shareholder of the Offeree Company, and shall include the number of shares purchased and the price paid.

Article 22: Disclosure of Dealings during the Offer Period, Indemnity and other Arrangements
a) Dealings by Offer parties and by persons Acting in Concert

1) Dealings in relevant securities by an Offeree Company, and by any person Acting in Concert with it, for their own account in the offeror's securities (if the offeror is a listed company) or the offeree company's, must be publicly disclosed during the Offer period by the end of the third trading day following the day of the relevant dealing.

2) Dealings in relevant securities by an Offeror, and by any person Acting in Concert with it, for their own account in the offeree company's securities or the offeror's (if the offeror is a listed company), must be publicly disclosed during the Offer period by the end of the third trading day following the day of the relevant dealing.

b) Dealings by offer parties or any persons Acting in Concert with them for non- discretionary account

Dealings in relevant securities during an Offer period by the Offeror or the Offeree Company, and by any person Acting in Concert with them, for the favor of clients in securities of the offeror (if it was a listed company) or the offeree company must be privately disclosed to the Authority by the end of the third trading day following the day of the relevant dealing.

Article 23: The Mandatory Offer

a) The mandatory Offer

Where a person (or persons Acting in Concert with it) increase an aggregate interest in shares through a restricted purchase of shares or restricted Offer for shares so that such person's ownership (individually or collectively with persons Acting in Concert with it) becomes 50% or more of a given class of shares listed on the Exchange carrying voting rights, the Board shall have the right to exercise its discretionary power in accordance with Article 54 of the Capital Market Law to order such person (and any person or persons Acting in Concert with it) to Offer to purchase the shares of the same class it does not own of the Offeree Company on the terms set out in this Article and in accordance with the other relevant provisions of these Regulations. When an obligation to make a general Offer is incurred under this Article, it is not necessary for the Offer to extend to treasury shares in the Offeree Company .

b) Conditions, third party consents and regulatory approvals

No Acquisition of shares which would give rise to an obligation of providing an Offer under this Article, if the making or implementation of such Offer would or might be dependent on the passing of a resolution at any general assembly of shareholders of the Offeror or upon any other conditions, consents or arrangements, including the relevant regulatory approvals.

c) Payment Method and Takeover Consideration

1) An Offer made under this Article must, in respect of each class of share of the Offeree Company, be in cash or be accompanied by a cash alternative at not less than the highest price paid by the Offeror, or persons acting in concert, for shares of that class during the Offer period and within 12 months prior to its commencement. The Authority should be consulted where there is more than one class of share capital involved.

2) If the Offeror considers that the highest price as specified in sub-paragraph (1) of paragraph (c) of this Article should not apply in a particular case, the Offeror should approach the Authority, which has discretion to agree on an adjusted price.

3) In no case will the Offeror be compelled under this Article to Offer to purchase the remaining shares at a price exceeding the highest price it paid, or paid by persons acting in concert with it, to purchase (or otherwise gain Control over) any of the shares of that company during the 12 months preceding the date of the Board order in accordance with paragraph (a) of this Article.

d) Restrictions on exercise of rights by an Offeror

From the time when the Offeror announces the firm intention to make an Offer, no person who formally represents the interests of an Offeror, or persons acting in concert, may be appointed to the board of directors of the Offeree Company, nor may an Offeror, or persons acting in concert with it, exercise the votes attached to any shares held by them in the Offeree Company, on items of the general assembly meetings related to the offer, until the Offer Document has been published.

e) Filing with the Authority

When an Offer to which this Article applies is to be made, the Offeror must file a report with the Authority detailing all relevant purchases of the Offeree Company's shares in the prior 12 month period no later than the end of the trading day on which the announcement of the mandatory Offer is made.

Article 24: Restrictions on the control of shares representing 40% of the voting rights

a) Any person obtaining shares (or have control over them) by a deal or number of deals (in owned or controlled shares, or which is controlled by persons acting in concert with it) that represent 40% or more of a specific class of shares that carry voting rights, may not have control over its shares during the following 6 months of obtaining such percentage without the Authority's approval and in accordance with the conditions it specifies.

b) Any person obtaining shares (or have control over them) by a deal or number of deals (in owned or controlled shares, or which is controlled by persons acting in concert with it) that represent 40% or more of shares that carry voting rights of a listed company, shall disclose such information to the public in period not exceeding the end of the third trade day following the day on which its ownership reached the aforementioned percentage, provided that its disclosure includes the following as minimum:

1) the ownership details of such person and persons acting in concert with it, before and after the transaction.
2) The purchase method and the price for share.
3) Parties of the purchase (if the shares were bought through private transactions).
4) The purpose of such purchase and the future plans (with persons acting in concert) toward the offeree company's activity, shareholders and employees resulting from the purchase.

c) When a person obtains shares (or have control over them) by a deal or number of deals (in owned or controlled shares, or which is controlled by persons acting in concert with it) that represent 40% or more of shares, the offeree company shall disclose such information to the public, in period not exceeding the end of the third trade day following the day on which the announcement was made, as per paragraph (b) of this Article, provided that its disclosure includes the following as minimum:

1) Details of structure changes of the company.
2) The most significant rights and obligations on the buyer in light of the relevant laws and regulation beside the company's Article of Association.
3) The opinion of offeree company's board regarding the person's (and persons acting in concert with it) plans toward the company's activity, shareholders and employees.
4) Any financial impact on the offeree company as a result of the takeover.

d) Any person may consult the Authority in advance in any matter relating to the application of the provisions of this Article.

e) The Authority may add any additional obligations to any person to whom this Article applies as it deems appropriate to market safety and investor protection.

Article 25: The Partial Offer

a) An Offeror may, subject to obtaining the Authority's prior approval, make a Partial Offer to the board of an Offeree Company.

b) The partial offer for the purpose of owning 30% or more shall not be conditional unless the Offeror obtains the approvals relating to the shares which, together with the shares acquired or agreed to be acquired by the Offeror before or during the offer, result in the offeror obtaining 30% or more of the voting rights (in the absence of any other regulatory approvals necessary to implement the offer).

c) If the Offeror receives a level of acceptance that is higher than the one initially planned for, it may, subject to obtaining the Authority's prior approval, allocate the shares to the accepting shareholders in proportion to each accepting shareholder's current ownership stake in the Offeree Company.

d) A Partial Offer is subject to the provisions of these Regulations including Article 23 of these Regulations.

Article 26: Securities Exchange Offer for all the shares of the Offeree Company

a) An Offeror (who is a joint stock company) may provide, after obtaining the Authority's prior approval, the Offeree Company with a Securities Exchange with the Offeror in consideration of all the shares in the Offeree Company.

b) The provisions of these Regulations shall apply to a Securities Exchange Offer for all the shares in the Offeree Company, except the provisions of sub-paragraphs (1/f), (1/g), (1/h), (1/i), (1/j), (1/k), (1/l) and (1/m) of paragraph (c) of Article 17 of these Regulations.

c) With no prejudice to the Companies Law, to the decision to complete the acquisition offer by offering an exchange of securities for all the shares of the offeree Company, shall not be deemed valid unless it is issued by the votes of 75% of the shares represented in Extraordinary General Assembly.

Article 27: The Acceptance Condition

a) with consideration to paragraph (a) of article 25 of these regulations, in the event of any takeover offer, to which article 23 of these regulations apply, for shares carrying voting rights which, if accepted in full, would result in the offeror holding shares carrying over 90% of the voting rights of the offeree company (including a merger of the offeree company), the offer shall not become or be announced as unconditional in regards of acceptances unless the offeror has acquired or agreed to acquire (either pursuant to the offer or otherwise) shares carrying over 50% of the voting rights attributable to any class of shares of the offeree company.

b) Any announcement made pursuant to Article 32 of these Regulations must state whether the Offer has reached the required acceptance level to announce unconditional acceptances (if permitted by the Offer timetable), or whether the Offer is to remain open for acceptance and whether the Offeror shall maintain or reduce the acceptance level.

c) The offer presented to acquire all shares of the offeree company must be only conditioned with the offeror obtaining the approvals related to shares, which result in (along with acquired shares or agreed to be acquired by the offeror during or after the offer) the offeror (or any persons acting in concert with it) owning shares that carry more than 50% percent of the voting rights.

d) An Offeree Company may accept a Takeover Offer in respect of treasury shares until after the Offer is unconditional as to acceptances.

Article 28: Nature of Payment to be Offered

a) Cash Offer

In the event where shares of any class in the Offeree Company are purchased in exchange for cash by an Offeror (or any persons acting in concert) during the Offer period or in the 12 months prior to it, in which case the Offer for that class shall be in cash or accompanied by a cash alternative at not less than the highest price paid by the Offeror (or any persons acting in concert) for shares of that class during the Offer period or in the 12 months prior to it.

b) Exemption from highest price

If the Offeror considers that the highest price (for the purpose of paragraph (a) of this Article) should not apply in a particular case, the Offeror should approach the Authority, which has discretion to agree on an adjusted price.

c) Non-cash payment

If the Offeror is a company, it may make an Offer that includes in whole or in part non- cash consideration (including issuing share by Offeror to the shareholders of the Offeree Company) as per the following conditions:

a. all shareholders of the same class of the Offeree Company are treated equally by the Offeror; and
b. where the Offeree Company's shareholders are offered shares in the Offeror or other non-cash consideration, the Offeror must provide a valuation report of the non-cash consideration prepared by the Offeror's Independent Financial Advisor and which shall be required to be published in accordance with paragraph (f) of Article 38 of these Regulations.

Article 29: Subjective and Financing Conditions

a) An Offer must not be subject to conditions which depend solely on subjective judgements by the Offeror or the Offeree Company, or in either case, their respective directors, or that the fulfillment of such conditions is subject to their opinions.

b) An Offer must not be made subject to conditions relating to financing.

Article 30: Offer to a Company with more than One Class of Shares

a) Where an Offeree Company has more than one class of share capital, an Offer (that is comparable) must be made for each class (whether such classes of shares carry voting rights or not); and the Authority should be consulted in advance. An Offer for non-voting shares shall not be made conditional on any particular level of acceptances in respect of that class unless the Offer for the voting shares is also conditional on the success of the Offer for the non-voting shares.

b) Provisions of this Article shall apply to an Offeree Company which has options or subscription rights that are outstanding.

Article 31: Special Deals with Favorable Conditions

An Offeror (or any person acting in concert with it) may not make any arrangements with shareholders and may not deal, enter into arrangements to deal in shares of the Offeree Company, or enter into arrangements which involve acceptance of an Offer, if there are favorable conditions attached which are not being extended to all shareholders.

Article 32: Announcement of Acceptance Results

a) Timing and contents

An Offeror must make an announcement regarding the Offer acceptance result no later than half an hour before the time on which the Exchange is due to open and not exceeding the day following the time on which an Offer is due to expire, the next day when the offer becomes, or is declared unconditional as to acceptances, or the next day following the offer revising or extension. The announcement must state the total number of shares and rights over shares as follows:

1) Shares which acceptances of the Offer have been received;
2) Shares held by the Offeror before the Offer period; and
3) Shares acquired or agreed to be acquired during the Offer period,

Such announcement must specify the percentages of the relevant classes of shares represented by these figures.

b) Consequences of failure to announce

1) If an Offeror (having announced the Offer to be unconditional as to acceptances) fails to comply with any of the requirements of paragraph (a) of this Article, any shareholder having accepted the Offer will be entitled to withdraw his acceptance, unless the Authority decides otherwise.
2) If an Offeror fails to make an announcement as required by paragraph (a) of this Article, the Authority may suspend the trading of the Offeree Company's shares until an appropriate announcement is made.

Article 33: The Use of Proxies and Other Authorities in Relation to Acceptances An Offeror may not require a shareholder as a term of his acceptance of an Offer to appoint a proxy to vote in respect of his shares in the Offeree Company, or to exercise any other rights or take any other action in relation to those shares, other than as may be required following the Offer being declared unconditional as to acceptances and a power of attorney being granted in favor of the Offeror in respect of the transfer of the Offeree Company's shares.

Article 34: Information Relating to an Offer

a) Standards of care

1) Each announcement, or document, or statement related to an Offer issued during the course of an Offer must, as is the case with a prospectus issued in accordance with the Capital Market Law and its Implementing Regulations, satisfy the highest standards of accuracy and the information given must be adequately and fairly presented. This applies whether it is issued by the Offeree Company or the Offeror directly or by their Independent Financial Advisor(s) on their behalf.

2) If any announcement, document, or statement published in connection with an Offer includes an advice, opinion, report or an independent valuation prepared by third party advisors then such a document or announcement must include a statement that each of the parties giving these particulars (such as Independent Financial Advisor(s), the auditor and/or the independent evaluator) has given and not withdrawn its consent to the inclusion of its advice, report or opinion (as applicable) in the relevant document in the form and context in which it is included.

b) Inaccurate announcements

Parties to an Offer and their advisors must not issue inaccurate or imprecise announcements, which may mislead shareholders or the Exchange.

c) Distribution and availability of documents and announcements

Copies of all documents and announcements bearing on an Offer and of advertisements and any material released to the media must, at the time of request, be provided to the Authority, the Independent Financial Advisors and all parties of the Offer. When the release is outside normal business hours, such Independent Financial Advisors must be informed of the release immediately; special arrangements may need to be made to ensure that the material is delivered directly to them and to the Authority. No party to an Offer should be put at a disadvantage through delay in the release of new information to it.

Article 35: Equality of Information

a) Equality of information to shareholders

Information about the Offer, including announcements, statements, presentations, circulars and information concerning companies involved in an Offer must be made equally available to all shareholders as nearly as possible at the same time and in the same manner, including publication on the website of the Offeror and Offeree Company, through the exchange or other Regulatory Information Service Providers (as applicable), no later than the end of the trading day.

b) Equality of information to competing Offerors

Any information, including particulars of shareholders, given to one Offeror or potential Offeror must, upon request, be given equally and promptly to another Offeror or bona fide potential Offeror.

Article 36: Restrictions on Frustrating Actions

a) Shareholders' consent in the general assembly

During the course of an Offer, or even before the date of the Offer if the board of the Offeree Company has reason to believe that a bona fide Offer might be imminent, the board must not, except in pursuance of a binding contract entered into earlier, and without the approval of the shareholders convened in a general assembly, effect any of the following:

1) Issue any undisclosed unissued shares;
2) issue or grant rights in respect of any unissued shares;
3) create or issue, or permit the creation or issuance of, any convertible securities into shares or subscription for shares;
4
) sell, dispose of or acquire, or agree to sell, dispose of or acquire, assets of a value equal to 10% of the net asset of the Offeree Company according to the latest reviewed interim financial statements or audited annual financial statements, whichever is later, whether through a transaction or various transactions;
5) buy-back of offeree company's shares; or
6) enter into contracts otherwise than in the ordinary course of business.

The notice convening such a general assembly of shareholders must include information about the Offer or potential Offer.

b) Break-up Fees

1) For the purposes of these Regulations a break-up fee is an arrangement which may, with the consent of the Authority, be entered into between an Offeror or a potential Offeror and the Offeree Company pursuant to which a cash sum will be payable by the Offeree Company if certain specified events occur which have the effect of preventing the Offer from proceeding or causing it to fail, including, without limitation, a recommendation by the Offeree Company board of a higher competing Offer.

2) Any break-up fee that is proposed must be of a minimal size (no more than 1% of the Offer value) and the Offeree Company

board of directors and its Independent Financial Advisor must confirm to the Authority in writing that the fee is in the best interests of the Offeree Company's shareholders. Any break-up fee arrangement must be fully disclosed in the Offer Document and in the announcement made under paragraph (e) of Article 17.

Article 37: Responsibilities of the Offeree Company to Update its Shareholders' Register

The board of the Offeree Company shall keep the Depository Center and/or the Exchange informed of an Offer to ensure that its shareholder register is kept up to date during the Offer period in accordance with the relevant laws and regulations.

Article 38: Offer Document

a) Financial and other information about the offeror, the offeree company and the offer.

1) The Offer Document (including, where relevant, any amendments to the Offer Document) must include the following requirements:

a. A statement at the beginning of the document asserting on the need of consulting an independent financial advisor approved by the Authority in case of any doubts regarding the offer.

b. The date of publishing the document, the offeror's name and address and the persons who presented the offer on its behalf (if any).

c. Details regarding the securities subject to the offer, and clarifying if they are going to be transferred with profits or without it.

d. Total amount of the presented offer.

e. Details of all needed documents and procedures that need to be followed to accept the offer.

f. Closing price of the securities to be acquired, and offered securities (in the event of a merger or securities exchange), for the first day of each month for past 6 months prior to the date of publishing the offer document, the last day prior to beginning of the offer period and the last available date before the publishing of the offer document (provided that the price of listed securities in exchange is obtained from the exchange, and if securities aren't listed, then information about all transactions made in the last 6 months and its values must be disclosed, in addition to the source of such information, or provide a clarification of the non-availability of any of that).

g. Details of the first patch of profits and revenues that the new securities will participate in (in the event of a merger or securities exchange offer) and the priority classification of such securities in respect of profits, revenues, capital and redemption. In addition to a statement clarifying the impact of accepting the offer on capital and income earned by shareholders of the offeree company. In the event that the new securities are not identical with the listed securities, the offer document shall contain all the details of the rights associated with the securities and a statement indicating whether or not a request has been or will be submitted to the Authority for listing.

h. In the event of a merger or offer of a securities exchange, reference should be made to the effect of accepting the offer (in full) for the purpose of controlling the assets of the offeror, its profits and its business that may be important for the proper valuation of the offer.

2) The Offer Document must include a statement as follows: "The Capital Market Authority and the Saudi Stock Exchange do not assume any responsibility for the contents of this Offer Document and make no assurances as to its accuracy or completeness, and expressly disclaim any liability whatsoever for any loss arising from this document or reliance on any part thereof "

3) In the event of the offer of a securities exchange in which the offeror is a non- listed company, or where the offer for the purpose of control results in merger with an non-listed company, the offer document shall include:

a. Sales and net profit or loss before and after the deduction of Zakat or tax, the value of Zakat or tax paid, any exceptional items, minority interests, and the total amount of dividends, revenues and profits per share for the last three financial years in which this information was published.

b. Statement of assets and liabilities in accordance with the most recent audited financial statements.

c. Cash flows when available in accordance with the most recent audited financial statements.

d. All material changes in the financial or commercial position of the offeror in accordance with the most recent audited financial statements, or a statement that none have occurred.

e. Details of the items referred to in sub-paragraph (3) of paragraph (a) of this Article on any quarterly announcement or any interim financial statements issued since the last audited financial statements were published.

f. Any information on any of the above that has been adjusted to take inflation impact into account.

g. Significant accounting policies and any key notes to the financial statements relating to the adjustment of the data, including any data adjusted to take inflation impact into account. If the data cannot be compared due to a change in accounting policy, it should be disclosed and the approximate amount of variation arising from the change is specified.

h. The names of the members of the board of directors of the offeror and their contributions to the offeree company and the offeror.

i. The nature of the offeror's activity and the financial and commercial expectations.

j. A summary of the basic contents of each essential contract entered into by the offeror or any of its subsidiaries outside the ordinary course of business of the company during the two years preceding the beginning of the offer period. The summary shall include a clarification of the date of the contract, its parties, terms and conditions and any amounts paid by the offeror (or any of its subsidiaries) Or paid to it on the basis of each contract.

4) The offer document shall contain a description of how the offer is financed and the financing source, and identify the names of the major lenders or the person arranging the

financing. If the offeror decides that the payment of the fee or payment or the provision of security for any obligation (conditional or otherwise) will depend to a large extent on the business of the offeree company, the planned arrangements shall be described, or provide a statement that there is no such arrangement.
5) If any document issued to the shareholders of the offeree company contains a recommendation or opinion of a financial advisor regarding the acceptance of the offer or not; the document, unless issued by the financial advisor itself, shall contain a statement stating the approval of the financial advisor (and without withdrawing its consent) to issue the document containing its recommendation or opinion in the form and text contained in the document.

b) Shareholdings and dealings

The offer document should indicate the following:

1. the shareholdings, and the size of any control shareholding, of the Offeree Company in the Offeror;
2. the shareholdings, and the size of any control shareholding of directors of the Offeree Company, in the Offeree Company and in the Offeror (or in which the directors of the Offeree Company have interests).
3. shareholdings and the size of any control shareholding in the offeror (in the event of merger or offer of securities exchange), the shareholdings and the size of any control shareholding in the offeree company which is owned or controlled by persons acting in concert with the offeror, with their names stated.
4. shareholdings and the size of any control shareholding in the offeror (in the event of merger or offer of securities exchange), the shareholdings and the size of any control shareholding in the offeree company which is owned or controlled by persons who have committed to accept the offer irrevocably prior to publishing the offer document, with their names stated.
5. shareholdings and the size of any control shareholding in the offeror (in the event of merger or offer of securities exchange), the shareholdings and the size of any control shareholding in the offeree company which is owned or controlled by a person with whom the offeror (or any person acting in concert with it) have any arrangements mentioned in subparagraph (3) of paragraph (d) of Article 19 of these Regulations.
6. In the absence of ownership shares or control shares as set out in the above cases, this shall be stated in the offer document, except for the cases mentioned in subparagraphs (4) and (5) of paragraph (b) of this Article if there are no irrevocable arrangements or obligations.
7. If a person whose shareholding is required to be disclosed under this Article (whether existing or not) has dealt in the shares in question during the period beginning 12 months prior to the Offer period and ending with the last day prior to the publication of the circular, the details, must be stated (Including dates and prices). In the absence of such transactions, this should be stated in the offer document.

c) Special arrangements or conditions

The offer document shall contain a statement indicating the existence (or absence) of any agreement, arrangement or understanding (including any arrangement for compensation) between the offeror (or any person acting in concert with it) and any of the board members of the offeree company, its current shareholders or any person who was a member of the Board of Directors of the Offeree Company or a shareholder within the twelve months prior to the date of publication of the Offer Document, as well as the substantial details of any such agreements, arrangements or understandings.

d) Confirmation of cash sufficiency

If the offer or any part thereof is to be paid in cash, the offer document must contain a bank guarantee issued by a local bank that ensures that the bidder can fulfill the full value of the offer.

e) The final owner of the shares acquired and the controlling shareholders in the offeror

The offer document shall contain a description of any person or persons who own or have control over 30% or more of the offeree company's capital, or is able to direct and manage its decisions, as well as to clarify whether there is a transfer of any securities acquired under the offer to other persons or not, with the names of the parties in any relevant agreement, arrangement of understanding (If any), besides the details of the securities held by such persons in the offeree company, or a statement that there is no such securities.

f) Estimated value of unlisted securities

If the offer includes the issuance of securities not listed in the market as compensation, and will remain unlisted, or the consideration is non-cash, the offer document and any subsequent document made by the offeror shall include, an estimate of the value of these securities or any other non-monetary consideration and issued by a financial advisor.

g) Information not applicable to other offers

The information contained in sub-paragraphs (1/g), (1/h), and (3) of paragraph (a) of this Article shall not apply to the partial offer that is not intended for the takeover of the shares of the offeree company.

Article 39: Offeree Board Circular

a) Views of the board

The board of the Offeree Company must circulate its views on the Offer to the shareholders, including any alternative Offers, and must, at the same time, make known to its shareholders the substance of the advice given to it by the Independent Financial Advisor appointed pursuant to Article 18 of these Regulations. An Offeree Company board circulars shall be published in accordance with the Offer timetable announced by the Authority pursuant to paragraph (c) of Article 17 of these Regulations.

b) Views of the Offeree Company's board on the Offeror's plans for the company and its employees

The circular of the board of the Offeree Company (referred to in paragraph (a) of this Article) should, insofar as relevant, include its views on the Offeror's plans in respect of the Offeree Company and its employees.

c) Shareholdings and dealings

1) The first circular from the board of the Offeree Company advising shareholders on an Offer (whether recommending acceptance or rejection of the Offer) must state:

a. the shareholdings, and the size of any control shareholding, of the Offeree Company in the Offeror;

b. the shareholdings, and the size of any control shareholding of directors of the Offeree Company, in the Offeree Company and in the Offeror (or in which the directors of the Offeree Company have interests).

c. the shareholdings, and the size of any control shareholding, in the Offeree Company and (in the case of a Merger or Securities Exchange Offer) in the Offeror owned or subject to shareholder Control by a subsidiary of the Offeree Company, by a pension fund of the Offeree Company or of a subsidiary of the Offeree Company, or by an advisor to the Offeree Company, or by any person Acting in Concert with the Offeree Company;

d. the shareholdings and the size of any control shareholding, in the Offeree Company and (in the case of a Merger or a Securities Exchange Offer) in an arrangement of the kind referred to in sub-paragraph (3) of paragraph (d) of Article 19 of these Regulations;

e. the shareholdings in the Offeree Company and (in the case of a Merger or a Securities Exchange Offer) in the Offeror which are managed on a discretionary basis by a Connected Fund Manager, unless the Authority consents of otherwise; and

f. whether the directors of the Offeree Company intend, in respect of their own shareholdings, to accept or reject the Offer.

2) If there are no shareholdings or controlled shareholdings as prescribed above, then this fact shall be stated.

3) If any person whose shareholdings or substantial shareholdings are required by sub-paragraphs (1/a) or (1/b) of paragraph (c) of this Article to be disclosed (whether there is an existing holding or not) has dealt in the shares in question during the period beginning 12 months prior to the Offer period and ending with the last day prior to the publication of the circular, the details, including dates and prices, must be stated. In all cases, if no such dealings have taken place this fact should be stated.

4) If any person whose shareholdings or substantial shareholdings are required by sub-paragraphs (1/c), (1/d) or (1/e) of paragraph (c) of this Article to be disclosed (whether there is an existing holding or not) has dealt in the shares in question during the Offer period and ending with the last day prior to the publication of the circular, details of such dealing, including dates and prices, must be stated. In all cases, if no such dealings have taken place this fact shall be stated.

d) Material contracts

The first circular from the board of the Offeree Company advising shareholders on an Offer must contain a summary of the principal contents of each material contract entered into by the Offeree Company (or any of its subsidiary companies) out of the ordinary course of business during the period beginning two years before the commencement of the Offer period where the total amount of consideration for such contract is 10% or more of the Offeree Company's annual revenues according to the latest reviewed interim financial statements or latest audited annual financial statements, whichever is later. Such summary must include particulars of dates, parties, terms and conditions and any consideration passing to or from the Offeree Company (or any of its subsidiaries) on each contract basis.

Article 40: Making Documents Available for Review

a) Copies of the following documents must be made available for review from the date the Offer Document or Offeree Company board circular is published until the end of the Offer period:

1) memorandum and articles of association of the Offeror (if it is a legal entity) and the Offeree Company or any equivalent documents;

2) consolidated and audited financial statements of the Offeror (if it is a legal entity), if any, and the Offeree Company for the last two financial years for which these have been published;

3) any report, letter, valuation or other document which is exhibited or referred to in any document issued by or on behalf of the Offeror and the Offeree Company;

4) written consents of the Independent Financial Advisors given in accordance with subparagraph (5) of paragraph (a) of Article 38 of these Regulations;

5) any document evidencing an irrevocable commitment to accept an Offer;

6) documents relating to the financing arrangements for the Offer where such arrangements are described in the Offer Document in compliance with subparagraph (4) of paragraph (a) of Article 38 of these Regulations; and

7) documents relating to break-up fees or similar arrangements.

b) The Offer Document or Offeree Company board circular must state the place, being the registered address of the Offeror company or the Offeree Company respectively or such other place as the Authority may agree, where document required to be on display in accordance with paragraph (a) of this Article, can be inspected.

c) A copy of each document required to be on display in accordance with paragraph (a) of this Article must, upon request, promptly be made available by the Offeror or the Offeree Company to the other party and to any competing Offeror or potential Offeror.

Article 41: Profit Forecasts

a) Standards of care

A profit forecast must be compiled with due care and consideration by the relevant board of directors with the assistance of such professional advice, whose sole responsibility it is; the Independent Financial Advisors must ensure that the forecast has been prepared in care and consideration by the board of directors.

b) Assumptions

When a profit forecast appears in a document addressed to shareholders in connection with an Offer, or in a press announcement, any assumptions on which the forecast is based should be included.

c) Publication of a profit forecast

Unless the Authority consents of otherwise, if, during an Offer period (or in an announcement which commences an Offer period), the Offeree Company or the Offeror in a securities exchange offer, must include in the document or announcement in which the forecast or statement is first published, the following:

1) a report from the auditor of the Offeree Company or the Offeror (as applicable), who is authorized to practice in Saudi Arabia, ensuring that the forecast or statement has been properly compiled on the assumptions stated and the accounting policies applied in the offeree company or the offeror (as applicable).

In addition to ensuring that (in the case of a profit forecast only) the basis of accounting used are consistent with the company's accounting policies; and

2) an acknowledgement from the Independent Financial Advisor(s) of the Offeree Company or the Offeror (as applicable) stating that, in its (or their) opinion, the forecast or statement has been prepared with due care and consideration.

d) Statements which will be treated as profit forecasts

1) An estimate of profit for a period which has already expired shall be treated as a profit forecast.
2) Unless the Authority consents of otherwise, any unaudited profit figures published during an Offer period must be prepared based on the same standards as a profit forecast, except the following:

a. unaudited statements of annual or interim results which have been published prior to the commencement of the Offer period; and

b. any other unaudited statements of results which comply with the Capital Market Law and its Implementing Regulations.

3) A profit forecast for a limited period (such as for the following quarter) is subject to this Article.
4) The Authority must be consulted in advance of publishing any announcement of guaranteed profits in connection with an Offer.

e) Earnings enhancement and Offer benefits statements:

Parties related to an Offer wishing to make earnings enhancement statements which are not intended to be profit forecasts must include within the statement an explicit and clear disclaimer to the effect that such statements should not be interpreted to mean that earnings per share will necessarily be greater than those for the relevant preceding financial period.

Article 42: Asset Valuations

a) Valuation Report

When a value of real or intangible property assets is stated in connection with an Offer, it shall be supported at the time of publication by a valuation report containing the opinion of a named independent licensed valuator, and the basis of valuation must be clearly stated. The document containing the valuation must also state that the evaluator has given and not withdrawn his consent to the publication of his valuation report.

b) Validity of Valuation

A valuation report related to the Offer made in accordance with this Article must state the effective date as at which the assets were valued and the address of the valuator and his professional qualifications. If a valuation is not current, the valuator must state that a current valuation would not be materially different. If this statement cannot be made, the valuation must be updated.

Article 43: Publication of the Offer Document and the Offeree Company Board Circular

a) Approval of the Offer Document

1) The Offeror must submit the Offer Document to the Authority for its approval to publish it.

2) An Offer Document may not be published without the prior approval of the Authority.

3) The Authority will grant its approval to the Offer Document within 30 days of receiving all information and documentation required under these regulations.

4) If the Authority considers that the proposed Offer may not be in the interest of investors or may result in a breach of the Capital Market Law or its Implementing Regulations, then it may take any of the following actions:

a. carry out any investigation which it considers appropriate including requiring the concerned person or its representative to appear before the Authority to answer the questions of the Authority and to explain any matters that the Authority considers relevant to the Offer;

b. require the concerned person or third parties to provide additional information or documents, or to confirm, in such manner as the Authority may specify, that the information provided is accurate; or

c. defer making any decision for such period as may be reasonably necessary to carry out a further study and examination or to allow for additional information to be provided.

5) If, having taken actions pursuant to sub-paragraph (4) of paragraph (a) of this Article, the Authority determines that the Offer to be made pursuant to the Offer Document is still not in the interest of investors or may result in a breach of the Capital Market Law or its Implementing Regulations, the Authority shall, after giving the Offeror a suitable opportunity to be heard, issue a notification to the Offeror stating that the approval of the Authority to publish the Offer Document is not granted. A notification under this sub-paragraph may include a prohibition on a further Offer for the Offeree Company on such terms as the Authority sees appropriate.

6) On receipt of a notification under sub-paragraph (5) of paragraph (a) of this Article, an Offeror must notify the Offeree Company of, and publicly announce, the rejection of publishing the Offer Document.

b) Publication of the Offer Document

The Offer Document must be published by, or on behalf of, the Offeror in accordance with the timetable referenced in sub-paragraph (1) of paragraph (c) of Article 17 of these Regulations.

c) The Offeree Company board circular

The board of the Offeree Company shall publish the circular containing its advise to shareholders regarding the Offer in accordance with the Offer timetable referenced in sub-paragraph (1) of paragraph (c) of Article 17 of these Regulations.

d) Material changes

1) Unless the Authority approves otherwise, following the publication of the initial Offer Document or Offeree Company's board circular (as applicable) and until the end of the Offer period, the Offeror or the Offeree Company (as applicable) must promptly announce the following:

a. any material changes in information disclosed in any document or announcement published in connection with the Offer; and

b. any material new information which would have been required to have been disclosed in any previous document or announcement published during the Offer period, had it been known at the time.

2) Where an announcement is required to be made under sub-paragraph (1) of this paragraph, the Authority may, in addition, require:

a. a document setting out the relevant information to be sent to shareholders in the Offeree Company and persons with the right to view information;

b. making the documents including relevant information available to the Offeree Company's employee representatives (or, where there are no employee representatives, to the employees themselves); and

c. the Offeror to publish an updated Offer timetable, after the Authority approves such updates.

e) Subsequent documents

If, following the publication of the Offer Document or Offeree Company's board circular (as applicable) and before the end of the Offer period, an Offeror or the Offeree Company publishes any subsequent document in connection with the Offer, that document must include any material changes in information (relating to the Offeror, Offeree Company or the Offer), intentions or opinions disclosed in any previous document published by it in connection with the Offer which are material in the context of that document, or a statement that there have been no such material changes.

Article 44: Timing of the Offer

a) Periods related to the offer

1) All periods relating to an Offer (whether revised or not) must be in accordance with the timetable proposed by the Offeror referenced in sub-paragraph (1) of paragraph (c) of Article 17 of these Regulations, including the period during which the Offer will be open, and the period when the Offer may become or be declared unconditional as to acceptances.

2) Where an Offer is subject to the Competition Law, the Offer may not become or be declared unconditional as to acceptances after the end of the period prescribed in the Offer timetable referenced in sub-paragraph (1/j) of paragraph (c) of Article 17 of these Regulations.

3) Where an Offeror has stated that its Offer will not be extended beyond a particular day, that Offer may not become or be declared unconditional as to acceptances after that day.

4) After an Offer has become or is declared unconditional as to acceptances, the Offer must remain open for acceptance for not less than the period prescribed in sub-paragraph (1/k) of paragraph (c) of Article 17 of these Regulations. When, however, an Offer is unconditional as to acceptances from the outset, an extension is not required provided that the position should be set out clearly in the Offer Document.

b) Announcement that Offer is unconditional as to acceptances

On the last business day on which an Offer may be declared unconditional as to acceptances an announcement shall be made immediately after closing of trading in the Exchange as to whether the Offer is unconditional as to acceptances or has lapsed. Such announcement shall include, if possible, the details required in paragraph (a) of Article 32 of these Regulations, and must include a statement of the offer acceptance result.

c) Extension of Offer

1) There is no obligation to extend an Offer, the conditions of which are not met by the first or any subsequent closing date.

2) In any announcement of an extension of an Offer, either announce the next closing date must be stated, or, if the Offer is unconditional as to acceptances, a statement may be made that the Offer will remain open until further notice in accordance with sub-paragraph (1/k) of paragraph (c) of Article 17 of these Regulations.

d) Time for fulfillment of all other conditions

All conditions must be fulfilled or the Offer must lapse within the period prescribed in the timetable referred sub-paragraph (1/l) of paragraph (c) of Article 17 of these Regulations.

e) Settlement of payment

The Offer payment must be made within the period prescribed in the timetable adopted in accordance with sub-paragraph (1/m) of paragraph (c) of Article 17 of these Regulations.

f) Offeree Company announcements

The board of the Offeree Company may not announce any material new information including trading results, profit or dividend forecasts, asset valuations or proposals for dividend payments after the date prescribed in the timetable referred to in sub-paragraph (1/g) of paragraph (c) of Article 17 of these Regulations. Where the publication of such results would be required by the Capital Market Law and its Implementing Regulations, the board of directors of the Offeree Company shall, as soon as possible, raise the issue to the Authority that will decide as it deems appropriate.

g) Effect of lapsing

The lapsing of an Offer, before it becomes unconditional as to acceptance, will result in the Offer ceasing to be capable of further acceptance and the shareholders and the Offeror thereafter shall not be bound by prior acceptances. Such effect shall be clearly stated in the Offer Document.

Article 45: Revision of the Offer

a) Entitlement to revised payment

If an Offer is revised, it must be revised on terms making it not less favorable to Offeree Company's shareholders, and all shareholders who accepted the original Offer must be entitled to the revised payment.

b) New conditions for the Offer

Subject to the prior approval of the Authority, and only to the extent necessary to implement an improved or increased Offer, the Offeror may introduce new conditions.

Article 46: Right to Withdraw Acceptance A person who has accepted an Offer must be entitled to withdraw his acceptance from the time prescribed in the timetable referenced in sub-paragraph (1/i) of paragraph (c) of Article 17 of these Regulations.

Article 47: Reduction or Increase of Company's Shares

a) Possible requirements to make an Offer as per Article 23 of these regulations or impose restriction period and disclosure requirement as per Article 24 of these regulations

When for any reason the total number of a particular class of shares of a company listed on the Exchange is reduced or increased, whether by redemption, repurchase or cancellation, resulting in each case in an increase in the percentage of voting rights held by a shareholder or group of shareholders Acting in Concert with it, the provisions of Article 23 and 24 of these Regulations shall apply (as the case may be).

b) Subsequent Acquisitions of shares

Subsequent to the reduction or increase referred to in paragraph (a) of this Article, all shareholders will be subject, in making further Acquisitions of shares in the company, to the relevant provisions of these Regulations.

c) Redemption or purchase of shares by the Offeree Company

1) Providing information to shareholders

If a notice for the general assembly of shareholders of the Offeree Company is sent for approval of redemption or purchase by the Offeree Company of its own shares during the course of an Offer, or before the date of the Offer, and the board of the Offeree Company has reason to believe that a bona fide Offer might be imminent, the board of the Offeree Company must include information about the Offer, Merger or anticipated Offer in the notice convening the general assembly.

2) Public disclosure

For the purpose of applying the provisions of paragraph (a) of Article 22 of these Regulations, dealings in relevant securities by the Offeree Company include the redemption or purchase of, or taking or exercising an option over, any of its own relevant securities. The total amount of securities of the relevant class remaining in issue following the redemption or purchase must also be disclosed.

3) Disclosure in the Offeree Company board circular

The Offeree Company board circular advising shareholders on an Offer must state the amount of relevant shares of the Offeree Company which the Offeree Company has redeemed or purchased during the period commencing 12 months prior to the Offer period and ending with the latest date prior to the publication of the circular, and the details of any such redemptions and purchases, including dates and prices.

d) Redemption or purchase of securities by the Offeror

1) Public disclosure

For the purpose of applying the provisions of paragraph (a) of Article 22 of these Regulations, dealings in relevant securities include the redemption or purchase of, or taking or exercising an option over, any of its own relevant securities by an Offeror (if it is a listed joint stock company).

2) Disclosure in the Offer Document

The Offer Document must state the amount of relevant securities of the Offeror which the Offeror has redeemed or purchased during the period commencing 12 months prior to the Offer period and ending with the latest date prior to the publication of the Offer Document and the details of any such redemptions and purchases, including dates and prices.

Article 48: Related Parties' Offers

a) Requirements to Related Parties' Offers

Where an Offeror makes an Offer to which these Regulations apply, and there exists any Related Party, the Offer shall be made subject to the additional conditions set out in this Article.

b) Shareholders consent as a precondition to Offer

1) Any Offer made in relation to which there is a Related Party shall be conditional to obtaining the independent and disinterested shareholders' approval, in accordance with this Article.

2) The announcement of any Offer made under Article 17 of these Regulations shall include the following:

a. the name of the Related Party, and of any person Acting in Concert with it, and with reference that such person is a Related Party; and

b. the fact that, by virtue of the existence of a Related Party in relation to the Offer, the Offer will be subject to the independent and disinterested shareholders' vote as required by these Regulations.

3) Where this Article applies to an Offer, it must be a term of the Offer that it will lapse if, by the earliest approved closing date for the Offer, the Offeror has not obtained approval of a majority of the Offeree Company's independent and disinterested shareholders in voting in general meeting on the completion of the Offer.

4) If requested by the Offeror who owns 5% or more of the Offeree Company, the board of the Offeree Company must convene a general assembly of shareholders and send a circular to shareholders prior to the date of such general assembly in accordance with the terms of its bylaws and the provisions of the Companies Law and the Corporate Governance Regulations. Such circular must include at least the following:

a. a copy of the Offer Document;

b. the details of any existing holdings of Related Party in each of the Offeror and the Offeree Company, including:

1. any holdings which such Related Party (or any person Acting in Concert with it) owns or over which it has shareholding Control;

2. any holdings in respect of which such Related Party (or any person Acting in Concert with it) holds an option to purchase;

c. the details of any position of such Related Party (and any person Acting in Concert with it) in the Offeror or the Offeree Company (as applicable);

d. details of any outstanding derivative referenced to the securities of the Offeror or the Offeree Company (or any of their affiliates) entered into by such Related Party and any person Acting in Concert with it;

e. a statement whether the directors (excluding the Related Party) are of the view that the proposed Offer is fair and reasonable so far as the shareholders are concerned, and that the directors have reached such a view without the Related Party taking any role in the matter, and that the directors have been so advised by a competent Independent Financial Advisor; and

5) The board of directors of the Offeree Company shall ensure the compliance with relevant provisions included in the Capital Market Law and Companies Law and their Implementing Regulations, related to counting the votes of the Related Party (or any person Acting in Concert with it) in determining the resolution approving the Offer at the shareholders' general assembly convened in accordance with sub- paragraph (4) of paragraph (b) of this Article.

6) In the event that the resolution approving the proposed Offer is not passed, the Offer shall lapse and the Offeror shall promptly notify the Authority of such.

23.3 PART 3: MERGER

Article 49: Types of Merger Transactions Without prejudice to the Capital Market Law, Companies Law, and their Implementing Regulations, a company may enter into a Merger transaction through any of the following:

a) Merger by way of absorption

A merged Company may merge into another entity by way of absorption by a Merging Company, whether the shares of Merging Company are listed on the Exchange or not.

1) Merged Company absorbed by another listed Company

a. If a Merger involves the absorption of a Merged Company by a Merging Company which shares are listed on the Exchange, a Security Exchange Offer to purchase all of the Merged Company's shares shall be made by the Merging Company in accordance with Part 2 of these Regulations, and new shares in the Merging Company shall be offered and issued to the shareholders of the Merged Company in accordance with the provisions of Capital Market Law, Companies Law and their Implementing Regulations.

b. Upon successful completion of the share exchange mentioned in sub- paragraph (1/a) of paragraph (a) of this Article and closing of the Merger transaction, all assets of the Merged Company are transferred to the Merging Company, which will continue to exist. The listing of the Merging Company will remain in place while the Merged Company will cease to exist and its shares will be delisted from the Exchange in accordance with the Capital Market Law and its Implementing Regulations.

2) Merged Company absorbed by a non-listed company

a. If a Merger involves the absorption of a Merged Company by a Merging Company which shares are not listed on the Exchange, a Security Exchange Offer to purchase all of the Merged Company's shares shall be made by the Merging Company in accordance with Part 2 of these Regulations, and new shares in the Merging Company shall be offered and issued to the shareholders of the Merged Company in accordance with the provisions of Capital Market Law, Companies Law and its Implementing regulations.

b. Upon successful completion of the share exchange mentioned in sub- paragraph (2/a) of paragraph (a) of this Article and closing of the Merger transaction, all assets of the Merged Company are transferred to the Merging Company which will continue to exist. The Merged Company will cease to exist and its shares will be delisted from the Exchange in accordance with the Capital Market Law and its Implementing Regulations.

b) Merger by way of forming a new legal entity

1) If a Merger involves the formation of a newly formed legal entity into which the Merged Company and another Merging Company will merge, a Security Exchange Offer for the purchase of all the shares of the Merged Company's shareholders shall be made by the newly formed legal entity in accordance with Part 2 of these Regulations, and shares in the newly formed legal entity shall be issued to the shareholders of the Merged Company and the other Merging Company in accordance with the provisions of the Capital Market Law, Companies Law and its Implementing Regulations.

2) Upon successful completion of the Offers mentioned in sub-paragraph (1) of paragraph (b) of this Article and closing of the Merger transaction, the assets of the Merged Company and of the other Merging Company are transferred to the newly formed legal entity, the Merged Company and other Merging Company will cease to exist, and the Merged Company's shares will be delisted from the Exchange in accordance with the Capital Market Law and its Implementing Regulations.

3) Should the newly formed legal entity wish to list its shares on the Exchange, it shall submit a new application to list the shares of the new legal entity to the Authority in accordance with the Capital Market Law and its Implementing Regulations.

Article 50: Rules of Merger Transactions The provisions of Chapter 2 of Part 2 of these Regulations, applicable to Takeover Offers, shall apply mutatis mutandis to Merger transactions.

Article 51: Required Approvals for a Merger Transactions 1) The Offer related to a Merger transaction shall not be declared unconditional as to acceptances unless the Offeror has acquired or agreed to acquire (either pursuant to the Offer or otherwise) shares carrying over 50% of the voting rights attributable to any class of shares of the Offeree Company.

2) Notwithstanding paragraph (1) of this Article, the implementation and closing of a Merger transaction is not permitted until the passing of resolutions of the extraordinary general assembly of shareholders of the Offeror and the Offeree Company, in accordance with the provisions of the Companies Law.

23.4 PART 4: PUBLICATION AND ENTRY INTO FORCE

Article 52: Publication and Entry into Force These Regulations shall become effective upon their publication.

24 The Guidance Note for the Investment in the Parallel Market by Non-Resident Foreigners

Issued by the Board of the Capital Market Authority pursuant to Resolution Number 4-59-7102 dated 27/01/1439H (16/10/2017)G based on the Capital Market Law issued by Royal Decree No M/30 dated 2/6/1424H amended by Resolution No.3-65-2019 dated 14/10/1440H (17/6/2019G)

24.1 Part 1: The Objective of the Guidance Note

A. This guidance note aims to clarify the investment of non-resident foreigners mechanism in the Parallel Market, and the restrictions related to that.

B. This guidance note should be read in conjunction with and in addition to the provisions of the Capital Market Law and its Implementing Regulations and in particular the Authorized Persons Regulations, Anti-Money Laundering and Counter-Terrorist Financing Rules, Investment Accounts Instructions, Rules on the Offer of Securities and Continuing Obligations, Listing Rules, Rules for Qualified Foreign Financial Institutions Investment in Listed Securities, conditions and requirements of Swap Agreements issued by the Authority, and other relevant laws.

24.2 Part 2: Categories of Non-resident Foreigners who are Allowed to Invest in the Parallel Market

The following categories of foreigners who do not reside in the Kingdom are allowed to invest in the Parallel Market:

1. Qualified foreign investor according to the Rules for Qualified Foreign Financial Institutions Investment in Listed Securities.

2. Ultimate beneficiary in Swap agreement with an Authorized Person.

3. Legal person allowed to open an investment account in the Kingdom and an account at the Depositary Center and are licensed or incorporated in a jurisdiction that applies regulatory and monitoring standards equivalent to those of the Authority or acceptable to it in accordance with the list of jurisdictions issued by the Authority as required in sub-paragraph (2), and sub-paragraph (3) of paragraph (a) of article 6 of the Rules for Qualified Foreign Financial Institutions Investment in Listed Securities.

4. Natural person holding the nationality of a country that applies regulatory and monitoring standards equivalent to those of the Authority or acceptable to it in accordance with the list of jurisdictions issued by the Authority as required in sub-paragraph (2), and sub- paragraph (3) of paragraph (a) of article 6 of the Rules for Qualified Foreign Financial Institutions Investment in Listed Securities, and resides in such countries, and fulfill any of the following criteria:

a. Has conducted transactions in security markets of not less than 40 million Saudi riyals in total, and not less than ten transactions in each quarter during the last twelve months.
b. His net assets is not less than 5 million Saudi Riyals.
c. Works or has worked for at least three years in the financial sector.
d. Holds the General Securities Qualification Certificate which is recognized by the Authority.
e. Holds a professional certificate that is related to securities business and accredited by an internationally recognized entity.

24.3 Part 3: Investment Restrictions

The investments of non-resident foreigners of all categories in the Parallel Market are subject to the following limitations:

1. Each non-resident foreign investor may not own 10% or more of the shares of any issuer whose shares are listed or convertible debt instrument of the issuer.

2. The maximum proportion of the shares of any issuer whose shares are listed or convertible debt instrument of the issuer that may be owned by all foreign investors (in all categories, whether residents or non-residents, except the foreign strategic investors pursuant to the Instructions for the Foreign Strategic Investors' Ownership in Listed Companies) in aggregate is 49%.

3. Other legislative limitations on foreign ownership in joint stock companies.

4. The limitations set forth in the articles of association or by-laws of the listed companies or any instructions issued by the supervisory or regulatory authorities to which these companies are subject.

24.4 Part 4: Requirements for Opening an Investment Account

A. Opening Investment Accounts for Foreign Natural Persons not Residing in the Kingdom:

To open an investment account for a foreign natural person not residing in the Kingdom for the purpose of investing in the permitted securities in accordance with the Capital Market Law and its Implementing Regulations and instructions issued by the Authority, the Authorized Person must check his valid passport and obtain copy of it, and obtain the client's residential address and place of work and work address. The Authorized Person also, must perform the customer due diligence in accordance with the provisions of the Anti- Money Laundering and Counter-Terrorist Financing Rules.

B. Opening Investment Accounts for Foreign Legal Persons out of the Kingdom:

1. Without prejudice to Clause (c) of this section and the provisions of the Rules for Qualified Foreign Financial Institutions

Investment in Listed Securities, to open an investment account for a foreign legal person for the purpose of investing in the permitted securities in accordance with the Capital Market Law and its Implementing Regulations and instructions issued by the Authority, the Authorized Person must perform the customer due diligence in accordance with the provisions of the Anti- Money Laundering and Counter-Terrorist Financing Rules.

2. To open an investment account for a foreign legal person out of the Kingdom for the purpose of entering in swap agreements in accordance with the conditions and requirements of the swap agreements, the Authorized Person must perform the customer due diligence requirements in accordance with the relevant conditions and requirements of the swap agreements.

C. Opening Investment Accounts for Qualified Foreign Financial Institutions:

1. When opening an investment account for any foreign financial institution as a qualified foreign investor, the Authorized Person must obtain the following documents:

-Where applicable, a copy of the license or the commercial registrar for the foreign investor obtained from the relevant authority in the county of establishment.
-Where applicable, a copy of the by-laws and its appendices, or a copy of the article of association and its appendices.
-A list of names of the foreign investor's managers that are authorized signatory in regard to the account.
-Where applicable, a list of all foreign investor's owners whose names are included in the article of association. An exception of this requirement is when the foreign investor is a joint-stock company listed in any exchange.
-Where applicable, a delegation from the board of director's specifying names of authorized signatory in regard to the account.

24.5 Part 5: Reliance on Third Parties for CDD

Authorized Person may rely on third party to perform elements in subparagraph (a) to (c) of the CDD measures in paragraph (2) article (8) of the Anti-Money Laundering and Anti-Terrorist Financing Rules, if the client is located in a country other than Saudi Arabia and must either be a commercial bank or financial institution that engages in securities activities, without prejudice to what is specified in the Anti-Money Laundering and Anti-Terrorist Financing Rules.

24.6 Part 6: Continuing Obligations

1. Legal foreign persons out of the Kingdom are not allowed to be direct investors and qualified foreign investors in the Parallel Market at the same time, and in case the foreign investor out of the Kingdom is willing to transfer from qualified foreign investor to direct investor in the Parallel Market or vice versa, the investor shall transfer all securities from the qualified foreign investor account to the direct account or vice versa.

2. Authorized person must take costumer due diligence measurements towards his client in accordance with the provisions of the Anti-Money Laundering and Counter-Terrorist Financing Rules.

3. Foreign investor must comply with the applicable provisions stated in the Capital Market Law and its Implementing Regulations, as well as the rules and the regulations of the Exchange and other relevant laws.

4. Authorized person must comply with the applicable provisions stated in the Capital Market Law and its Implementing Regulations, as well as the rules and the regulations of the Exchange and other relevant laws.

25 RULES ON THE OFFER OF SECURITIES AND CONTINUING OBLIGATIONS

Issued by the Board of the Capital Market Authority pursuant to its Resolution No. 3-123-2017 dated 9/4/1439H (27/12/2017G) based on the Capital Market Law issued by Royal Decree No. M/30 dated 2/6/1424H amended by Board Resolution No. 1-7-2021 dated 1/6/1442H (14/1/2021G)

Important Notice: The current version of these Rules, as may be amended, can be found at the CMA website: www.cma.org.sa

TABLE OF CONTENTS

Part 1: General Provisions
Article 1 : Scope and application
Article 2 : Preliminary Provisions
Article 3 : Types of offers of securities
Article 4 : Liability for incorrect or incomplete documents
Part 2: Exempt Offers
Article 5: Scope and application
Article 6: Exempt offers
Part 3: Private Placement Offer
Article 7 : Scope and application
Article 8 : Types of private placement offer
Article 9 : Limited Offers
Article 10 : Private placement requirements
Article 11 : Responsibilities and obligations of Capital Market Institutions
Article 12 : Information to investors and private placement advertisements
Article 13 : No continuing obligations
Article 14 : Secondary market activity
Part 4: Public Offer
Chapter 1 : General Provisions
Article 15 : Application of the provisions on public offers
Article 16 : Requirement to comply with the Listing Rules
Article 17 : Required approvals
Article 18 : Appointment of representatives of the issuer
Article 19 : Fees
Chapter 2 : Advisors to the Issuer
Article 20 : Appointment of advisors
Article 21 : Requirements and obligations of the financial advisor
Article 22 : Requirements and obligations of the legal advisor
Chapter 3 : Conditions for a Public Offer
Article 23 : Conditions for a public offer of shares
Article 24 : Conditions for a public offer of debt instruments
Article 25 : Additional conditions for a public offer of convertible debt instruments
Chapter 4 : Application for Registration and Offer
Article 26 : Underwriting
Article 27 : Requirement to submit an application for registration and offer to the Authority
Article 28 : Supporting documents
Article 29 : The Prospectus
Article 30 : Issuances not requiring a prospectus
Article 31 : Supplementary prospectus and supplementary circular
Article 32 : Authority powers in relation to the application for registration and offer
Article 33 : Publication of prospectus, shareholders circular and formal notices
Article 34 : Dissemination of information
Article 35 : Application to employee share schemes
Article 36 : Dormant applications
Part 5: Financing Transactions for Special Purposes Entity
Chapter 1 : New Financing Transactions For Special Purposes Entity
Article 37 : Scope and Application
Article 38 : Approval of new financing transactions by the Authority
Article 39 : Procedures and powers of the Authority in relation to a financing transaction application
Chapter 2 : Financing Transactions Conditions for Special Purposes Entity
Article 40 : Scope and Application
Article 41 : Financing structures
Article 42 : Appointment of a custodian
Article 43 : Investor protection
Article 44 : Use of proceeds
Article 45 : Payments and bank accounts
Article 46 : Investments
Article 47 : Enforceability
Article 48 : Financing transactions involving the issue of asset-linked recourse debt instruments or asset backed debt instruments
Article 49 : Multiple financing transactions
Chapter 3 : Investors Protection
Article 50 : Investors protection
Article 51 : Stop orders
Part 6: Capital Alteration
Chapter 1 : Capital Increase for Issuers of Listed Shares
Article 52 : Scope and application
Article 53 : Application submission for capital increase of issuer of listed securities and supporting documents
Article 54 : Conditions and requirements applicable to a rights issue
Article 55 : Conditions and requirements applicable to a capitalization issue
Article 56 : Conditions and requirements applicable to capital increase by debt conversion
Article 57 : Conditions and requirements applicable to a capital increase to acquire a company or purchase an asset
Chapter 2 : Capital Reduction for Issuers of Listed Shares
Article 58 : Conditions and requirements applicable to a capital reduction
Part 7: Continuing Obligations
Chapter 1 : Disclosures
Article 59 : Scope and application
Article 60 : Complete, clear, accurate and not misleading disclosures
Article 61 : Obligation to disclose material developments
Article 62 : Disclosure of specific events
Article 63 : Disclosure of financial information
Article 64 : Board of directors' report
Article 65 : Duties of directors and senior executives
Article 66 : Provision of Documents to the Authority
Chapter 2 : Restrictions on Dealings

Article 67 : Dealings by substantial holders of shares and convertible debt instruments
Article 68 : Dealings of directors and senior executives
Article 69 : Restrictions on shares
Part 8: Offer or Registration in the Parallel Market
Article 70 : Scope and application
Article 71 : Appointment of representative of the issuer
Article 72 : Appointment of advisers
Article 73 : Required approvals
Article 74 : Conditions for an issuer
Article 75 : Requirement to submit the application to the Authority
Article 76 : Dormant applications
Article 77 : The Prospectus and the Registration Document
Article 78 : Issuances not requiring Prospectus or Shareholders' Circular
Article 79 : Supplementary Prospectus, supplementary Shareholders' Circular or Supplementary Registration Document
Article 80 : Authority powers in relation to the application
Article 81 : Publication of Prospectus, Shareholders' Circular, Registration Document and formal notices
Article 82 : Dissemination of information
Article 83 : Application submission for capital increase of issuers of shares listed in the Parallel Market
Article 84 : Conditions related to issuance of rights issue
Article 85 : Conditions related to a capitalization issue
Article 86 : Conditions related to increasing the capital by debt conversion
Article 87 : Conditions related to capital increase for acquiring a company or purchasing an asset
Article 88 : Capital reduction for issuers of shares listed on the Parallel Market
Article 89 : Continuing obligations
Article 90 : Fees for the Parallel Market
PART 9: Provisions Related to Reverse Takeover and Demerger
Article 91 : Scope of Application
Article 92 : General Provisions
Article 93 : Announcement and Conditions of a Reverse Takeover
Article 94 : Potential Suspension of Listing when Announcing a Reverse Takeover
Article 95 : Applying Class Tests and Calculating Percentage Ratios
Article 96 : Aggregation of Transactions
Article 97 : Condition Relating to the Listed Company
Article 98 : Shareholders' Approval
Article 99 : Specialized Committee and Independent Financial Advisor
Article 100 : Circular to Shareholders
Article 101 : Requirements for Registration, Offering and Listing of Shares of the De-merged Entity
Article 102 : Announcement of a Demerger
Part 10: Publication and Entry into Force
Article 103 : Publication and entry into force
Part 11: Annexes
Annex 1 : Contents of A Private Placement Notification in Respect of Shares and Other Securities
Annex 2 : Contents of A Private Placement Notification in Respect of Debt Instruments
Annex 3 : Offeror's Declaration
Annex 3(a) : Sponsor's Declaration
Annex 4 : Capital Market Institutions's Declaration
Annex 5 : Statement to Be Included in The Private Placement Offering Documents
Annex 5 (a) : Contents of the Private Placement Offer Document for Securities issued by a Special Purposes Entity
Annex 6 : Content Of Application
Annex 7 : Issuer's Declaration
Annex 7 (a) : Sponsor's Declaration
Annex 7 (b) : Issuer's Declaration to Request the Registration of its Shares in the Parallel Market
Annex 8 : Director's Declaration
Annex 8 (a) : Director's Declaration in a Structure with right to recourse
Annex 9 : Content of a Prospectus for Shares
Annex 10 : Content Of A Prospectus For A Rights Issue
Annex 11 : Content Of A Prospectus For Debt Instruments For An Issuer Without Securities Listed On The Exchange
Annex 11 (a) : Contents Of A Prospectus For Debt-Bases Recourse Debt Instruments
Annex 11 (b) : Contents Of A Prospectus For Asset-Linked Recourse Debt Instruments
Annex 12 : Content Of A Prospectus For Debt Instruments For An Issuer With Securities Listed on The Exchange
Annex 13 : Content of a Circular for a Capital Increase by Debt Conversion
Annex 14 : Contents of a Circular for a Capital Increase to Acquire a Company or Purchase an Asset
Annex 15 : External Auditor's Report
Annex 16 : Form of a Financial Advisor's Letter
Annex 16 (a) : Form of a Financial Advisor's Letter for a Special Purposes Entity
Annex 17 : Form of a Legal Advisor's Letter
Annex 17 (a) : Form of a Legal Advisor's Letter for a Special Purposes Entity
Annex 18 : Content of Letter Required for a Capitalization Issue
Annex 19 : Content of Letter Required for Capital Reduction
Annex 20 : Content of A prospectus for parallel Market offers
Annex 20 (a) : Content of A Registration Document
Annex 21 : Form Of Financial Advisor's Letter With Regards To An Application For Registration And Offer On The Parallel Market
Annex 22 : Contents Of Shareholders' Circular For A Capital Increase Of A Company Which Shares Are Listed On The Parallel Market By Debt Conversion
Annex 23 : Contents Of Shareholders' Circular For A Capital Increase Of A Company Which Shares Are Listed On The Parallel Market To Acquire A Company Or Purchase An Asset
Annex 24 : Class Tests

25.1 PART 1: GENERAL PROVISIONS

Article 1: Scope and application

a) Securities may not be offered in the Kingdom except in accordance with these Rules.

b) For the purpose of the application of these Rules, offering securities shall mean:

1) issuing securities;
2) inviting the public to subscribe in securities or the direct or indirect marketing of securities; or
3) any statement, announcement or communication that has the effect of selling, issuing or offering securities.

c) Offering securities mentioned in paragraph (b) of this Article shall not include preliminary negotiations or contracts entered into with or among underwriters.

d) The provisions of these Rules shall not apply to units in investment funds including Real Estate Investment Funds.

Article 2: Preliminary Provisions
a) Any reference to the "Capital Market Law" in these Rules shall mean the Capital Market Law issued by Royal Decree No. M/30 dated 2/6/1424H.

b) Expressions and terms in these Rules have the meaning which they bear in the Capital Market Law and in the Glossary of Defined Terms Used in the Regulations and Rules of the Capital Market Authority, unless the contrary intention appears.

c) Any person subject to these Rules may appeal to the Committee in respect of any decision or action that the Authority takes under these Rules.

Article 3: Types of offers of securities Securities may be offered in the Kingdom by way of:

1) an exempt offer;

2) a private placement offer;

3) a public offer; or

4) a Parallel Market offer.

Article 4: Liability for incorrect or incomplete documents Liability for an incorrect or incomplete prospectus, supplementary prospectus or registration document, supplementary registration document, shareholders' circular, supplementary shareholders' circular, offering document or other documents relating to an offer or registration shall be determined in accordance with the Capital Market Law or the Companies Law, as applicable.

25.2 PART 2: EXEMPT OFFER

Article 5: Scope and application The provisions of this part apply to an exempt offer of securities in the Kingdom.

Article 6: Exempt Offer
a) Without prejudice to the Securities Business Regulations and the Capital Market Institutions Regulations, an offer shall be exempt from the requirements of these Rules in any of the following cases:

1) where the securities are issued by the government of the Kingdom
2) offers of contractually based securities, provided that the offer of unlisted contractually based securities shall be limited to any of the following cases:

a. Where all offerees are investors under the categories of Institutional and Qualified Clients.

b. Where all offerees are employees of the issuer or of any of its affiliates.

3) where an issuer whose shares are not listed on the Exchange increases its capital by offering new shares to existing shareholders;
4) where the offeree is an affiliate of the issuer unless it is an offer of a class of shares that is listed on the Exchange;
5) where all of the offerees are employees of the issuer or of any of its affiliates unless it is an offer of a class of shares that is listed on the Exchange; or
6) offers in an insolvency situation where shares are offered to creditors.
7) where an issuer whose shares are not listed on the Exchange increases its capital by way of debt conversion.
8) where the subscription in total value for the securities being offered is less than 10 million SR or an equivalent amount, in accordance to the following conditions:

a. The offer shall be not made more than one time during the twelve months after the completion of the offer.
b. Subscription in the offered securities shall be limited to (50) offerees or less (excluding investors under the categories of Institutional and Qualified Clients) provided that the amount payable per offeree (excluding investors under the categories of Institutional and Qualified Clients) shall not exceed (200,000) two hundred thousand SR or an equivalent amount.
c. Declaration by the offeree who participate in the subscription for such offered securities (excluding investors under the categories of Institutional and Qualified Clients) to the offeror or the Capital Market Institution (if the offer is carried out through a Capital Market Institution) of its acknowledgment to the risks associated with the investment, including what may result in loss of the full amount of the investment, and the that the Authority shall not give any assurance as to the accuracy and completeness of the documents related to the Offering or its completeness, and expressly disclaim any liability whatsoever for any loss arising from or incurred in reliance upon any part of these documents, and its acknowledgment that the offeror or the Capital Market Institution (if the offer is carried out through a Capital Market Institution) does not have to notify the Authority of the suitability of such an investment.

b) The offeror or the Capital Market Institution (if the offer is carried out through a Capital Market Institution) shall, when making an exempt offer, notify the Authority on a quarterly basis of the total number and value of the exempt offers the Capital Market Institutionhas made. In addition, the following information must be submitted to the Authority in respect of each exempt offer:

1) type of exempt offer;
2) categories of the offerees;
3) amount paid by each offeree category in Saudi riyals;
4) date of the commencement of the offering;
5) date of the completion of the offering;
6) name and nationality of the issuer;
7) name and nationality of the offeror;
8) price paid for each security;
9) type of security; and
10) total size of the offering.
11) Declaration by the offeree indicated in subparagraph (c) of paragraph (8) of this Article, including the following information:

a. The total amount payable per offeree who participate in the subscription for such securities and the number and description of the securities.
b. Name of the offeree who participate in the subscription for such securities and its passport number or National ID and signature.
c. Declaration date.

c) The notification referred to in paragraph (b) of this Article must contain the information related to offers that are not complete as follows:

1) on-going offerings;
2) name of relevant issuer;
3) name of relevant offeror;
4) the expected date of completion of the offering; and
5) type and class of the offered securities.

(In accordance with the Board of the Authority Resolution no. (1-7-2021) Dated 1/6/1442H Corresponding to 14/1/2021G, sub-paragraph (2), and sub- paragraphs (8/b) and (8/c) of paragraph (a) of Article (6) of these Rules shall become effective as of 28/05/1443H. corresponding to 01/01/2022G, provided that sub-paragraph (2), and sub-paragraphs (8/b) and (8/c) of paragraph (a) of Article (6) of the Rules on the Offer of Securities and Continuing Obligations issued by the Board of the Authority Resolution no. (3-123-2017) dated 09/04/1439H. corresponding to 27/12/2017G and amended by the Board of the Authority Resolution no. (1-104-2019) dated 01/02/1441H. corresponding to 30/09/2019G, which can be viewed via the following link:

(https://cma.org.sa/RulesRegulations/Regulations/DocLib/OSRCI_en.pdf), shall continue to be effective until the effectiveness date of sub-paragraph (2), and sub-paragraphs (8/b) and (8/c) of paragraph (a) of Article (6) of these Rules.)

25.3 PART 3: PRIVATE PLACEMENT OFFER

Article 7: Scope and application The provisions of this Part apply to a private placement of securities in the Kingdom.

Article 8: Types of Private Placement Offer

a) An offer of securities is a private placement where it is not an exempt offer, public offer or a Parallel Market Offer and falls under any of the following cases:

1) the subscription is restricted to investors under the categories of Institutional and Qualified clients; or

2) the offer is a limited offer.

b) The Authority may, in circumstances other than those described in paragraph (a) of this Article and upon application of a person seeking to make an offer of securities, determine that such an offer shall be treated as a private placement subject to compliance with such limitations as the Authority may impose.

(In accordance with the Board of the Authority Resolution no. (1-7-2021) Dated 1/6/1442H Corresponding to 14/1/2021G, Article (8) of these Rules shall become effective as of 28/05/1443H. corresponding to 01/01/2022G, provided that Article (8) and Article (9) of the Rules on the Offer of Securities and Continuing Obligations issued by the Board of the Authority Resolution no. (3-123-2017) dated 09/04/1439H. corresponding to 27/12/2017G and amended by the Board of the Authority Resolution no. (1-104-2019) dated 01/02/1441H. corresponding to 30/09/2019G, which can be viewed via the following link: (https://cma.org.sa/RulesRegulations/Regulations/DocLib/OSRCI_en.pdf), shall continue to be effective until the effectiveness date of Article (8) of these Rules.)

Article 9: Limited Offers

a) An offer of securities is a limited offer if at the subscription is limited to no more than 100 offerees (excluding investors under the categories of Institutional and Qualified Clients) and the amount payable per offeree does not exceed 200,000 (two hundred thousand SR) or an equivalent amount.

b) Securities of the same class may not be offered as a limited offer under paragraph (a) of this Article more than once in a twelve-month period ending with the date of the offer in question.

(In accordance with the Board of the Authority Resolution no. (1-7-2021) Dated 1/6/1442H Corresponding to 14/1/2021G, Article (9) of these Rules shall become effective as of 28/05/1443H. corresponding to 01/01/2022G, provided that Article (10) of the Rules on the Offer of Securities and Continuing Obligations issued by the Board of the Authority Resolution no. (3-123-2017) dated 09/04/1439H. corresponding to 27/12/2017G and amended by the Board of the Authority Resolution no. (1-104-2019) dated 01/02/1441H. corresponding to 30/09/2019G, which can be viewed via the following link:

(https://cma.org.sa/RulesRegulations/Regulations/DocLib/OSRCI_en.pdf), shall continue to be effective until the effectiveness date of Article (9) of these Rules.)

Article 10: Private Placement Requirements

a) No person may offer securities by way of private placement unless the following requirements are met:

1) the offer is made through a Capital Market Institution licensed to carry out arranging activities; and

2) the offeror notifies the Authority in accordance with Annexes 1 or 2 of these Rules (as applicable) at least ten days prior to the proposed date of the offer and submits the following to the Authority:

a. a declaration by the offeror in the form set out in Annex 3 of these Rules. Or a declaration by the sponsor in the form set out in Annex 3(a) of these Rules if the offer was made by a special purposes entity;

b. a declaration from the Capital Market Institution through which the offer is made, in the form set out in Annex 4 of these Rules; and

c. copies of any offering documents to be used in advertising the offer.

b) If a material change to the offering documents mentioned in paragraph (a) of this Article arises after their date of submission to the Authority and prior to the start of the offer or after the start of the offer and before its end, the offeror must immediately notify the Authority of such change upon knowledge. The Authority, in its own discretion, may then require the offeror to re-file the offering documents. At the discretion of the Authority, such re-filing may re-start the ten-day notice period referred to in subparagraph (2) of paragraph (a) of this Article.

c) If having received the private placement notification and the information provided under in subparagraph (2) of paragraph (a) of this Article the Authority considers that the proposed offer of securities may not be in the interest of the investors or may result in a breach of the Capital Market Law or its Implementing Regulations, then it may take the following actions:

1) carry out any enquiries which it considers appropriate including requiring the concerned person or its representative to

appear before the Authority to answer the questions of the Authority and to explain any matters that the Authority considers relevant to the private placement offering; or

2) require the concerned person or others to provide additional information or to confirm, in such manner as the Authority may specify, that the information provided is accurate.

d) If, having taken action pursuant to paragraph (c) of this Article, the Authority determines that the private placement is not in the interest of the investors or may result in a breach of the Capital Market Law or its Implementing Regulations, the Authority may after giving the offeror a suitable opportunity to be heard, issue a notification to the offeror stating that the offer is not to be made, or publish a notice prohibiting the offer, sale or transfer of the securities to which the private placement relates.

e) After the offer has completed, the offeror or the Capital Market Institution must provide the Authority within ten days a list of the categories of all persons who have acquired the securities and details of the total proceeds of the offer.

f) Where the offer is not completed by the proposed offer end date specified in the private placement notification provided to the Authority in accordance with subparagraph (2) of paragraph (a) of this Article, the offeror or the Capital Market Institution must provide the Authority within ten days with a notification in writing signed by the offeror confirming that the offer has failed to complete. The offeror or the Capital Market Institution may extend the offering period, provided that such extension shall be notified to the Authority before the end date of the offer period.

g) Without prejudice to paragraph (e) of this Article, the offeror or the Capital Market Institution, in case where the offer is a debt instruments issuance program, must provide the Authority within ten days from the completion of the offering of each issuance of a programme the details of the total proceeds and the issuance terms and conditions.

Article 11: Responsibilities and Obligations of the Capital Market Institution The Capital Market Institution through which the offer is made must ensure that all of the conditions and requirements in paragraphs (a), (e), (f), and (g) of Article 10 and Article 12 of these Rules have been fulfilled.

Article 12: Information to Investors and Private Placement Advertisements
a) The offeror must ensure that investors are provided with sufficient information on the private placement to enable them to make an informed investment decision and that such information is complete, clear, correct and not misleading.

b) The private placement offering documents to be used in advertising the offer must contain a prominent statement in the form set out in Annex 5 of these Rules. The private placement offer documents, used in the announcement by a special purposes entity, shall contain a clear statement in the form set out in Annex 5(a) of these Rules.

c) No person may make or communicate a securities advertisement (as defined in the Securities Business Regulations) in respect of a private placement unless the securities advertisement complies with the applicable provisions of the Securities Business Regulations and the Capital Market Institutions Regulations.

Article 13: No Continuing Obligations Except as set out in the provisions of this Part, an offeror of securities by way of a private placement is not required to inform the Authority of any material developments relating to such securities.

Article 14: Secondary Market Activity
a) A person (referred to as a "transferor") who has acquired securities pursuant to a private placement may not offer or sell such securities to any person (referred to as a "transferee") unless the offer or sale is made through a Capital Market Institution and where one of the following requirements is met:

1) the price to be paid for the securities in any one transaction does not exceed 200 thousand SR or an equivalent amount;

2) the securities are offered or sold to an investor under the categories of Institutional and Qualified Clients; or

3) the securities are being offered or sold in such other circumstances as the Authority may prescribe for these purposes.

b) If the requirement in subparagraph (1) of paragraph (a) of this Article cannot be fulfilled because the price of the securities being offered or sold to the transferee has increased since the date of the original private placement, the transferor may offer or sell securities to the transferee if their purchase price during the period of the original private placement did not exceed 200 thousand SR or an equivalent amount.

c) If the requirement in paragraph (b) of this Article cannot be fulfilled, a transferor may offer or sell the securities if he sells his entire holding of such securities to one transferee.

d) The provisions of paragraphs (a), (b) and (c) of this Article shall apply to all subsequent transferees of such securities.

e) The restrictions in this Article shall cease to apply upon approval of listing on the Exchange of securities of the same class as the securities that are subject to such restrictions.

(In accordance with the Board of the Authority Resolution no. (1-7-2021) Dated 1/6/1442H Corresponding to 14/1/2021G, Article (14) these Rules shall become effective as of 28/05/1443H. corresponding to 01/01/2022G, provided that Article (15) of the Rules on the Offer of Securities and Continuing Obligations issued by the Board of the Authority Resolution no. (3-123-2017) dated 09/04/1439H. corresponding to 27/12/2017G and amended by the Board of the Authority Resolution no. (1-104-2019) dated 01/02/1441H. corresponding to 30/09/2019G, which can be viewed via the following link:

(https://cma.org.sa/RulesRegulations/Regulations/DocLib/OS-RCI_en.pdf), shall continue to be effective until the effectiveness date of Article (14) of these Rules.)

25.4 PART 4: PUBLIC OFFER

25.4.1 Chapter 1: General Provisions

Article 15: Application of the Provisions on Public Offers a) The purpose of this Part is to regulate the registration and public offering of securities in the Kingdom.

b) Securities may not be offered by way of a public offer except in accordance with this Part.

c) A foreign issuer who submits an application for listing its shares in the Main Market pursuant to the Listing Rules shall be subject to Article 18 of these Rules.

Article 16: Compliance with Listing Rules An offeror may not offer securities to the public without making prior arrangements for listing those securities on the Exchange in accordance with the Listing Rules.

Article 17: Required Approvals An offeror may not offer securities to the public without obtaining all approvals required pursuant to the issuer's bylaws, the Companies Law and its implementing regulations. In case where securities are publicly offered by a special purposes entity, such securities may not be offered unless the approval of the special purposes entity's and the sponsor's boards' approvals are obtained.

Article 18: Appointment of Representatives of the Issuer

a) The issuer must appoint two representatives, one of whom must be a director and the other must be a senior executive, to act as its representatives before the Authority for all relevant purposes relating to the Capital Market Law, the Companies Law, their Implementing Regulations, other relevant laws and these Rules. In case where the offer is made by a special purposes entity, such entity and the sponsor shall appoint representatives for each of them, to attend before the authority in matters related to these Rules, provided that the entity's representatives shall be from the board members, while the sponsor's representatives are a board member and a senior executive.

b) The issuer must provide details in writing of how its representatives may be contacted including office, mobile number, and electronic mail address, in addition to written details regarding the methods of contacting the sponsor's representatives if the offer was made by a special purposes entity.

c) The issuer and its representatives, referred to in paragraph (a) of this Article, must provide the Authority, without delay, with all the information, clarifications, books, records and forms that the Authority requests from them, for the purpose of implementing the Capital Market Law, the Companies Law, their Implementing Regulations, other relevant laws and these Rules. Which must be complete, clear, correct, and not misleading.

Article 19: Fees

a) An issuer who submits an application for registration and offer of its securities is required to pay such fees to the Authority as the Authority specifies.

b) An issuer whose securities are registered and have been listed is required to pay such fees to the Authority as the Authority specifies.

25.4.2 Chapter 2: Advisors to the Issuer

Article 20: Appointment of Advisors

a) Where an issuer makes an application for registration and offer of its securities that requires the production of a prospectus or a shareholders' circular (as applicable), the issuer must appoint financial advisor and legal advisor.

b) Where an issuer whose securities are listed submits an application for the voluntary cancellation of listing pursuant to the Listing Rules, the issuer must appoint financial advisor and legal advisor.

c) Where an issuer whose securities are listed submits an application to reduce its capital, the issuer must appoint financial advisor.

d) The Authority may, at any times, require the issuer to appoint a financial advisor and legal advisor or both, or any other advisors, to advise the issuer on the application of the Capital Market Law, its Implementing Regulations, the Exchange Rules, the Companies Law or its Implementing Regulations.

e) Where a financial advisor or a legal advisor gives advice to an issuer in relation to the application for registration and offer of its securities or any matter related to the application of these Rules, the Capital Market Law, its Implementing Regulations or the Exchange Rules, it must ensure that it gives appropriate advice in accordance with the rules of its profession.

Article 21: Requirements and Obligations of the Financial Advisor

a) The financial advisor must be authorized by the Authority to carry out arranging activities and any other securities business related to the services which the financial advisor agreed with the issuer to provide.

b) Upon an application to the Authority of an issuer for registration and offer of securities, the financial advisor must:

1) be the main point of contact for the Authority in relation to the application for registration and offer of the securities;

2) satisfy itself, having conducted due diligence and made enquiry from the issuer and its advisors, that the issuer has satisfied all conditions required for the registration and offer of the securities and has satisfied all other relevant requirements;

3) provide to the Authority any information or clarifications in such form and within such time limit as the Authority may require for the purpose of verifying whether the financial advisor and the issuer have complied with the Capital Market Law, its Implementing Regulations or the Exchange Rules; and

4) provide the Authority with a letter in the form set out in Annex 16 of these Rules.

c) If matters which should be taken into account by the Authority come to the attention of the financial advisor during the period between the provision of the letter described in subparagraph (4) of paragraph (b) or subparagraph (4) of paragraph (d) of this Article (as applicable) and the completion of the offer, the financial advisor must notify the Authority thereof without delay.

d) In the event that the offer is made by a special purpose entity, the financial advisor shall, upon submitting an application to the Authority for offering and listing securities, comply with the following:

1) To be the main point of contact with the Authority in relation to the application.

2) Ensure, after performing due diligence, and ask the special purpose entity, the sponsor and their advisors, that the sponsor and the special purpose entity have met all the conditions required to list and offer the entity's securities and any other related requirements.

3) provide any information or clarifications to the Authority as required within the time limit set by it for the purpose of verifying the compliance of the financial advisor, sponsor and special purpose entity of the Capital Market Law and its Implementing Regulations and Exchange Rules.

4) Submit a letter to the Authority as contained in Annex 16(a) of these Rules.

Article 22: Requirements and Obligations of the Legal Advisor
a) The legal advisor must be licensed to practise law in the Kingdom.

b) On an application of an issuer for the registration and offer of its securities, the legal advisor to the issuer must provide the Authority with a letter in the form set out at Annexes 17 or 17(a) of these Rules.

25.4.3 Chapter 3: Conditions for a Public Offer

Article 23: Conditions for a Public Offer of Shares
The conditions for making a public offer of shares are:

1) The issuer must be a joint stock company.

2) Any application for registration and offer of securities must be accompanied by a prospectus, except where a prospectus is not required under these Rules.

3) When submitting an application for registration and offer of securities, the issuer must have been carrying on, either by itself or through one or more of its subsidiaries, the same main activity for at least the previous three years before submitting the application for registration and offer of securities.

4) When submitting an application for registration and offer of securities, the issuer must have audited financial statements that cover at least the previous three financial years and that were prepared in accordance with the accounting standards adopted by SOCPA.

5) If the period covered by the most recent audited financial statements has ended more than six months prior to the expected date of approval of the application for registration and offer of securities, it shall submit to the Authority a reviewed interim financial statements covering any period from the date of the end of the period covered by the latest audited financial statements until the expected date of approval of the application for registration and offer of securities, or submit audited annual financial statements (as applicable).In all cases, the period covered by the latest audited interim financial statements submitted to the Authority shall not have ended more than (6) months before the date of approval of the application for registration and offer of securities.

6) Where the issuer has undergone material restructuring, an application for registration and offer of securities may not be submitted until one financial year has elapsed from the date of completion of that material restructuring. For the purposes of this paragraph, "material restructuring" shall mean:

a. disposing any of the issuer's asset that has contributed in generating 30% or more of the issuer's revenue or net income as per the most recent annual financial statements;

b. acquiring assets with a value exceeding 30% or more of the net asset value of the issuer as per the most recent annual financial statements;

c. acquiring a company with a shareholder equity constituting 30% or more of the issuer's shareholder equity as per the most recent annual financial statements.

7) The senior executives of the issuer must have an appropriate expertise and experience for the management of the issuer's business.

8) An issuer must, on its own or with its subsidiaries (if any) hold sufficient working capital to continue operating for at least the twelve months immediately following the date of publication of the prospectus.

9) If reviewed interim financial statements are issued during the application period, the issuer must provide a copy of such statements to the Authority as soon as reasonably practicable.

10) An application for registration and offer of securities may be accepted if it does not meet the requirements of this Article if the Authority is satisfied that it will be in the interest of the investors and that the investors have received the necessary information to arrive at an informed judgment concerning the issuer and the securities that are the subject of the application.

11) Where an issuer already has securities that are listed on the Exchange, paragraphs (3), (4), (5), (6), (8) and (9) of this Article shall not apply.

Article 24: Conditions for a Public Offer of Debt Instruments
a) The issuance of debt instruments shall be in accordance with the conditions set out in Article 23 of these Rules as applicable. And where the offer is made by a special purposes entity, the issuer must be a special purposes entity authorized in accordance with Special Purposes Entity's Rules.

b) Where an issuer wishes to launch a debt instrument issuance programme, it must produce a single prospectus which covers the maximum value of debt instruments which may be issued under the programme. If the Authority approves the prospectus, all debt instruments which may be issued under that programme must be offered within 24 months after the approval of the prospectus.

c) An application for registration and offer of debt instruments may be accepted even if it does not meet the requirements of this Article if the Authority is satisfied that it will be in the interest of the investors, provided that the issuer must provide the investors with the necessary information to arrive at an informed judgment concerning the issuer and the securities that are the subject of the application.

d) In relation to an offer of debt instruments by a special purposes entity, the provisions of the paragraphs (3), (4), (5), (6) and (7) of Article 23 of these Rules shall apply only on the sponsor

e) In relation to an offer of debt instruments by a special purposes entity, the provisions of the paragraph (9) of Article 23 of these Rules shall apply on the special purposes entity and the sponsor.

f) The provisions of paragraph (8) of Article 23 of these Rules shall not apply in case of issuing debt instruments.

Article 25: Additional Conditions for a Public Offer of Convertible Debt Instruments
a) The issuance of convertible debt instruments shall be subject to the following conditions:

1) The conditions set out in Article 24 of these Rules, as applicable.

2) Convertible debt instruments may be registered and offered only if the shares into which they are convertible are already listed.

3) A prospectus for convertible debt instruments, which would be converted into shares which are already listed on the Exchange, must in addition to all of the information stipulated in Annex 12 of these Rules, contain the applicable information as required by Annex 10 of these Rules.

4) The Authority's approval of the application for registration and offer of a convertible debt instrument is regarded as approval of the issuance of the relevant share upon conversion.

b) The issuer may not issue convertible debt instruments of the same class already issued unless such instruments have been registered and offered in accordance with the provisions of this Part.

25.4.4 Chapter 4: Application for Registration and Offer

Article 26: Underwriting
a) The offer of securities must be fully underwritten by one or more Capital Market Institutions licensed to carry out underwriting activities, and that Capital Market Institution must comply with the Prudential Rules.

b) The provisions of paragraph (a) of this Article shall not apply to:

1) capital increases to acquire a company or an asset;
2) capital increases by way of capitalization issues;
3) capital increases by way of debt conversion;
4) issuance of debt instruments; or
5) issuance of convertible debt instruments.

Article 27: Requirement to Submit an Application for Registration and Offer to the Authority An issuer seeking to register and offer its securities must submit an application to the Authority which contains the information required under these Rules, and submit to the Exchange, at the same time, an application for listing of such securities in accordance with the provisions of the Listing Rules.

Article 28: Supporting Documents
a) The issuer, or the sponsor if the issuer is a special purposes entity, must submit to the Authority with its application for registration and offer electronic copies of the following documents (it shall maintain original copies of such documents and submit it to the Authority at its request):

1) the letter of appointment of the financial advisor;
2) the letter of appointment of the legal advisor;
3) the authorization letters or powers of attorney of the representatives of the issuer empowering them to sign the prospectus or the shareholders' circular (as applicable);
4) the issuer's employees list providing the contact details involved with the application at the issuer, in addition to the details of the financial advisor and the legal advisor;
5) a list containing the names and civil registry numbers (or the equivalent to it for non-Saudi nationals) of the directors and their relatives, senior executives and their relatives and shareholders;
6) a formal letter of application for registration and offer, signed by a representative of the issuer that contains the applicable information as required by Annex 6 of these Rules;
7) a declaration by the issuer in the form set out in Annex 7 of these Rules, and in case the issuer is a special purposes entity, a declaration by the sponsor in the form set out in Annex 7(a) of these Rules;
8) a declaration and undertaking signed by the directors of the issuer and by each proposed director of the issuer in the form set out in Annex 8 of these Rules, and in case the issuer is a special purposes entity, a declaration and undertaking signed by the directors of the sponsor and by each proposed director of the sponsor in the form set out in Annex 8(a) of these Rules;
9) approvals required by the relevant governmental agencies, where applicable;
10) evidence of the issuer obtaining the required approvals to offer its securities to the public as required under Article 17 of these Rules;
11) the draft prospectus or shareholders' circular (as applicable) in Arabic;
12) the issuer's certificate of commercial registration, or equivalent;
13) the issuer's articles of association and bylaws and all amendments to date, and in case the issuer is a special purposes entity, the sponsor's articles of association and bylaws and all amendments to date;
14) the audited annual financial statements of the issuer for each of the three financial years immediately preceding submission of the application;
15) the latest interim financial statements produced since the date of the most recent audited annual financial statements;
16) the legal due diligence report issued by the legal advisor regarding the application;
17) the financial due diligence report regarding the application;
18) a presentation detailing the structure of the issuer and its subsidiaries, along with a detailed description of the most recent restructuring of the issuer (if applicable);
19) the letters of consent from all the advisors on the use of their names, logos and statements in the prospectus or the shareholders' circular (as applicable);
20) a copy of the subscription application forms;
21) a letter from the financial advisor and the issuer setting out the inapplicable requirements, if no disclosure requirements under these Rules are applicable;
22) a letter from the issuer's financial advisor in the form set out in Annex 16 of these Rules, and in case the issuer is a special purposes entity, a letter from the entity's financial advisor in the form set out in Annex 16(a) of these Rules;
23) a letter from the issuer's legal advisor in the form set out in Annex 17 of these Rules, and in case the issuer is a special purposes entity, a letter from the issuer's legal advisor in the form set out in Annex 17(a) of these Rules;
24) in the case of debt instruments or convertible debt instruments, a copy of the debenture agreement or any other document constituting or securing such instruments must be included;
25) the issuer's internal governance regulations including the policies for conflict of interests, standards and procedures for board membership and the charters for the audit committee and the nomination and remuneration committee;
26) all underwriting commitment letters;
27) in case the issuer is a special purposes entity, the agreement governing the finance with the sponsor;
28) in case the issuer is a special purposes entity, the agreement with the custodian (where applicable);
29) in case the issuer is a special purposes entity, any agreement governing the special purposes entity's investment or

management; and
30) any other documentation that may be required by the Authority.

b) Following the approval of the application for registration and offer by the Authority and prior to the listing, the issuer, or the sponsor if the issuer is a special purposes entity, must submit an electronic copy (and shall maintain the original copies for submission at the Authority's request) of the following documents:

1) a prospectus or the shareholders' circular (as applicable) in Arabic signed on every page by the representatives of the issuer who are appointed as authorized signatories;
2) its updated commercial registration (as applicable), and in case the issuer is a special purposes entity, the entity's updated commercial registration, and the sponsor's commercial registration;
3) the securities allocation model;
4) the latest reviewed interim financial statements (where applicable);
5) all signed underwriting, sub-underwriting and distribution agreements entered into in connection with the offer and the lead manager agreement (as applicable);
6) an updated and signed letter that contains the applicable information as required by Annex 6 of these Rules; and

c) Following the approval of the application for registration and offer by the Authority, and after the completion of the offering of each tranche of a debt issuance programme but prior to the listing thereof, the following requirements must be complied with:

1) the issuer must submit the following documents to the Authority:

a. a pricing supplement for each tranche under the programme, signed by a duly authorized representative of the issuer, must be submitted in writing to the Authority as soon as the issuer submits it to the Exchange for consideration under the Listing Rules; and

b. the issuer's written confirmation to the Authority that the debt instruments in question have been offered.

2) the issuer must notify the Authority as soon as possible of the final allocation of the debt instruments offered as well as the total amount paid compared to the total value offered under the prospectus;

3) the pricing supplement of each tranche under the programme must include details in respect of the issue, maturity and redemption dates (if any) of the debt instruments offered as well as the pricing details; and

4) the pricing supplement must provide the terms and conditions of an issue, in addition to those set out in the prospectus related to the debt instrument issuance programme.

d) The issuer, or the sponsor if the issuer is a special purposes entity, must retain original copies (or certified copy where appropriate) of all documents required pursuant to this Article for a period not less than ten years from the completion of the offer. Without prejudice to this period, in the event such documents relate to any litigation or claim (including any litigation pending or threatened) or any on-going investigations, the issuer must retain such documents until the closure of that litigation, claim or on-going investigation.

e) For an issuer who does not have securities already listed on the Exchange and is seeking to register and offer debt instruments or convertible debt instruments subparagraphs (16), (17), (25) and (26) of paragraph (a) of this Article shall not apply.

f) If the issuer has its securities already listed on the Exchange:

1) subparagraphs (5), (12), (13), (14), (15), (16), (17), (18), (20), (24), (25), (26), (27), (28), (29) and (30) of paragraph (a), and subparagraphs (3), (4) and (5) of paragraph (b) of this Article shall not apply to the application for capital increase for acquisition of a company or purchasing an asset;

2) subparagraphs (5), (12), (13), (14), (15), (16), (17), (18), (20), (24), (25), (26), (27), (28), (29) and (30) of paragraph (a) and subparagraph, (3), (4) and (5) of paragraph (b) of this Article shall not apply to the application for capital increase for debt conversion;

3) subparagraphs (5), (12), (13), (14), (15), (16), (17), (18), (24) (25), (27), (28), (29) and (30) of paragraph (a) and subparagraph (4) of paragraph (b) of this Article shall not apply to the application for capital increase by way of rights issues;

4) subparagraphs (5), (12), (13), (14), (15), (16), (17), (25) and (26), of paragraph (a) and subparagraph (4) of paragraph (b) of this Article shall not apply to the application for the issuance of debt instruments or convertible debt instruments; and

5) the provisions of this Article shall not apply to capitalization issues. g) In case the offer is made by a special purposes entity:

1) Subparagraphs (3), (4), (5), (10), (14), (15), (21) and (23) of paragraph (a), subparagraphs (1) and (4) of paragraph (b) and paragraph (d) of this Article shall apply to the sponsor in addition to the special purposes entity.

2) Subparagraphs (16) and (19) of paragraph (a) of this Article shall apply only to the sponsor.

3) Subparagraphs (25) and (26) of paragraph (a) of this Article shall not apply.

Article 29: The Prospectus

a) The prospectus must contain all information which is necessary to enable an investor to make an assessment of the activities, assets and liabilities, financial position, management and prospects of the issuer and of its profits and losses and must include information in relation to the number and price of the securities and any obligations, rights, powers and privileges attaching to them. If the Issuer is a Special Purpose Entity, the Prospectus shall include all information necessary to enable the Investor to evaluate the activity, assets and liabilities of the special purposes entity, in addition to the sponsor's assets, liabilities, financial position, management, expected opportunities, profits and losses. and it shall include information on the number and price of securities and any obligations Rights, powers and privileges associated with them.

b) Annex 9 of these Rules sets out the minimum information which must be included in a prospectus for shares.

c) Annex 10 of these Rules sets out the minimum information which must be included in a prospectus for a rights issue.

d) Annex 11 of these Rules sets out the minimum information which must be included in a prospectus for debt instruments where the issuer does not have securities listed on the Exchange. If the Issuer is a Special Purpose Entity, Annex 11(a) of these Rules shall determine the minimum required information to be included in prospectus of issuing debt-based debt instruments for a special purposes entity. Moreover, annex 11(b) of these Rules shall determine the minimum required information to be included in prospectus of issuing asset-linked debt instruments for a special purposes entity

e) Annex 12 of these Rules sets out the minimum information which must be included in a prospectus for debt instruments where that issuer has securities currently listed on the Exchange and continues to have them listed throughout the offer and listing process.

f) A prospectus for the offering of convertible debt instruments must contain the combined minimum information set out in Annex12 of these Rules and the relevant information set out in Annex 10 of these Rules.

g) The draft of the prospectus that is submitted to the Authority must be in the Arabic language.

h) The draft prospectus submitted to the Authority must be annotated in the margin to indicate where the information required by the applicable paragraphs of these Rules has been included and any changes from any previous drafts must be clearly marked. Each draft prospectus must indicate the draft number and date of submission on its cover page.

Article 30: Issuances not Requiring a Prospectus

a) A prospectus is not required for the issue of further securities by an issuer whose securities are already listed where:

1) the securities to be issued would increase the securities of a class already listed by no more than 10% in any 12-month period. For the purpose of determining this percentage a series of issues in connection with a single transaction will be deemed a single issue, and a series of transactions that is regarded by the Authority as a single transaction will be deemed a single issue;

2) shares issued as a result of capitalization issue;

3) an employee share scheme;

4) shares issued as a result of the conversion of debt instruments that convert into shares already listed;

5) shares issued as a result of capital increase by conversion of debt, provided that a shareholders' circular must be produced in accordance with Article 56 of these Rules;

6) shares issued as a result of a capital increase that is made to acquire a company or purchase an asset provided that a shareholders' circular must be produced in accordance with Article 57 of these Rules; or

7) split of shares already issued.

b) Where an issuer wishes to issue securities in the circumstances specified in paragraph (a) of this Article it must make an application for registration and offer to the Authority in accordance with any applicable requirements under these Rules or as prescribed by the Authority. The relevant securities may not be issued prior to the approval of such application by the Authority.

c) The issuer must disclose any issuance made under this Article in the manner prescribed by the Authority.

d) If the issuer is a special purposes entity, the provisions of subparagraphs (2), (3), (4), (5), (6) and (7) of paragraph (a) of this Article shall not apply.

Article 31: Supplementary Prospectus and Circular

a) A supplementary prospectus or supplementary shareholders' circular must be submitted (as applicable) to the Authority if, at any time after that prospectus or circular has been published and before completion of the offer (in the case of a prospectus) or before the extraordinary general assembly is convened (in the case of a shareholders circular), the issuer, and the sponsor in relation to issuance of debt instruments by a special purposes entity, becomes aware that:

1) there has been a significant change in material matters contained in the prospectus or the shareholders' circular (as applicable); or

2) additional significant matters have become known which would have been required to be included in the prospectus or the shareholders' circular (as applicable).

b) A supplementary prospectus or supplementary circular must contain the following (as applicable):

1) details of the change or new matters in accordance with paragraph (a) of this Article;

2) a declaration in the form specified at paragraph (10) of section (1) of Annex 9 of these Rules, paragraph (7) of section (1) of Annex 10 of these Rules, paragraph (9) of section (1) of Annex 11 of these Rules, paragraph (10) of section (1) of Annex 11 of these Rules, paragraph (10) of section (1) of Annex 11 of these Rules, paragraph (9) of section (1) of Annex 12 of these Rules, paragraph (11) of section (1) of Annex 13 of these Rules or paragraph (11) of section (1) of Annex 14 of these Rules as the case may be;

3) a declaration by the directors, and the sponsor's directors if the issuer is a special purposes entity, that there have been no significant changes in material matters nor additional significant matters have arisen other than what has been disclosed in the supplementary prospectus or supplementary circular; and

4) a declaration by the directors, and the sponsor's directors if the issuer is a special purposes entity, that a copy of the supplementary prospectus or supplementary circular has been submitted to the Authority.

c) Where a supplementary prospectus or supplementary circular is submitted to the Authority under this Article, it must be signed on every page by the relevant representatives of the issuer who are appointed as authorized signatories.

d) Where a supplementary prospectus is submitted to the Authority under this Article, an investor who subscribed for securities prior to the disclosure of the supplementary prospectus is permitted to rescind or amend his subscription for such securities prior to the end of the offering period.

e) Where a supplementary prospectus or supplementary circular is submitted to the Authority under this Article, the Authority must be satisfied that the information contained in such supplementary prospectus or supplementary circular is complete and fulfills the requirements of the Capital Market Law, its Implementing Regulations and the Exchange Rules. If the information supplied suggests to the Authority that the proposed offer of securities may not be in the interest of the investors or may result in a breach of the Capital Market Law, its Implementing Regulations or the Exchange Rules, then it may require the issuer to terminate the offer.

f) The supplementary prospectus or supplementary shareholders' circular must not be published or otherwise made available to the public without obtaining the approval of the Authority.

Article 32: Authority Powers in Relation to the Application for Registration and Offer
a) The approval of the application for registration and offer of securities will only be given by the Authority if:

1) the Authority has received notification from the Exchange of the Exchange's conditional approval of the corresponding application for listing pursuant to the Listing Rules;
2) the conditional approval mentioned under sub-paragraph (1) of this paragraph has not been withdrawn by the Exchange; and
3) the Authority is satisfied that the information contained in the prospectus or the shareholders' circular (as applicable) is complete and fulfils the requirements of the Capital Market Law and its Implementing Regulations.

b) The Authority will review the application within 45 days of receiving all information and documentation required pursuant to these Rules. If the application is for registration and offer of debt instruments, or registration and offer of convertible debt instruments, the Authority will review the application within 20 days of receiving all information and documentation required pursuant to these rules. The commencement of the period is not subject to the Authority's receipt of the notification referred to in subparagraph (1) of paragraph (a) of this Article provided that the notification must be submitted to the Authority prior to the end of the review period, otherwise the Authority may extend the review period for a term not exceeding 10 days from the date of receipt of the notification.

c) If, having reviewed the application, the Authority considers that the proposed offer of securities may not be in the interest of the investors or may result in a breach of the Capital Market Law, its Implementing Regulations or the Exchange Rules, then it may take any of the following actions:

1) carry out any enquiries which it considers appropriate;
2) require the issuer or its representative to appear before the Authority to answer questions and explain any matters that the Authority considers relevant to the application. In case the issuer is a special purposes entity, the Authority may require the entity or its representative and the issuer or its representative to appear before the Authority to answer questions and explain any matters that the Authority considers relevant to the application;
3) require the issuer or third parties to provide additional information or to confirm, in such manner as the Authority may specify, that the information provided is accurate; or
4) defer making a decision for such period as may be reasonably necessary to carry out further study or examination.

d) If, having taken action pursuant to paragraph (c) of this Article, the Authority determines that the offer to be made pursuant to the application may not be in the interest of the investors or may result in a breach of the Capital Market Law its Implementing Regulations or the Exchange Rules, the Authority may issue a "notification" to the issuer stating that the application has not been approved, or publish a "notice" prohibiting the offer, sale or transfer of title of the securities to which the application relates.

e) The approval of the application for registration and offer of securities by the Authority shall be considered as an approval of the prospectus or the shareholders' circular, as applicable.

f) The prospectus or shareholders' circular (as applicable) must not be published and made available to the public without the approval of the application for registration and offer of securities by the Authority.

g) The Issuer and its financial advisor - prior to the Authority's approval of the application for registration and offer of securities – are allowed to provide information on the Issuer and its financial statements to the group of potential investors; In order to ascertain the extent to which potential investors are willing to participate in the subscription of the Issuer's shares if they are offered, provided that this does not result in taking a binding undertaking to subscribe.

h) The Issuer and its financial advisor may, prior to obtaining the approval of the Authority, request the registration and presentation of securities by providing information on the issuer and its financial statements to a specific group of Capital Market Institutions to conduct the advice activity for the purpose of preparing research and financial reports on the issuer, provided that such research and reports shall not be published before obtaining the approval of the Authority for the application of registration and offer of securities.

Article 33: Publication of Prospectus, Shareholders Circular and Formal Notices
a) The issuer must publish the prospectus and must ensure that it is made available to the public at least 14 days prior to the start of the offering.

b) As an exception from paragraph (a) of this Article, an issuer must publish the prospectus and must ensure that it is made available to the public at least 14 days prior to the date of the general assembly meeting where an offering of a rights issue is to be made.

c) Where an issuer must publish a shareholders' circular in accordance with these Rules, it must ensure that it is made available to the public at least 14 days prior to the date of the relevant general assembly meeting.

d) The prospectus, the shareholders' circular, any supplementary prospectus or any supplementary circular (as applicable) shall be made available to the public on the websites of the issuer, the Exchange, the Authority and the financial advisor

e) Where an issuer has published a disclosure after the publication of the prospectus or the shareholders' circular in a local newspaper, the disclosure must contain at least the following (if applicable):

1) the name and commercial registration number of the issuer, and in case the issuer is a special purposes entity; the name and commercial registration number of the entity and the name and commercial registration number of the sponsor;
2) the securities that are the subject of the relevant application for registration and offer and their value, type and class;
3) the addresses and locations where the public may obtain the prospectus or the shareholders' circular;
4) the date of publication of the prospectus or the shareholders' circular;
5) a statement that the disclosure is for information only and does not constitute an invitation or offer to acquire, purchase or subscribe for securities;
6) the names of the subscription lead manager (if any), underwriter, financial advisor, legal advisor and receiving agents;
7) a statement of the total value of securities that could be issued under an issuance programme (if applicable); and

8) a disclaimer as follows:
"The Capital Market Authority and the Saudi Stock Exchange take no responsibility for the contents of this disclosure, make no representations as to its accuracy or completeness, and expressly disclaim any liability whatsoever for any loss arising from, or incurred in reliance upon, any part of this disclosure."

Article 34: Dissemination of Information
a) The Authority may require the publication of further information by, or impose additional continuing obligations on, the issuer where it deems this appropriate. The Authority will notify the issuer of its intentions in this regard and will allow representations by the issuer before imposing any such requirements or obligations.

b) Except as permitted in paragraph (c) of this Article, information that is required to be disseminated pursuant to these Rules must not be given to a third party before the information has been filed with the Authority and has been published.

c) The issuer may disclose information that is required to be disseminated pursuant to these Rules before the information has been filed with the Authority and has been published to any of the following persons:

1) the issuer's advisors to the extent necessary for those advisors to provide advice in relation to these Rules;
2) the issuer's agent employed to release the information; and
3) persons with whom the issuer is negotiating with a view to effecting a transaction or raising finance, including prospective underwriters of an issue of securities or lenders.
d) The issuer must advise the above mentioned persons in writing that the information is confidential and that they must not deal in the issuer's securities (or any other related securities) before the information has been made available to the public.
e) Where, in the opinion of the issuer, disclosure of any matter required by these Rules would be unduly detrimental to the issuer, and omission is not likely to mislead investors with regard to facts and circumstances, knowledge of which is essential for the assessment of the securities in question, the issuer may apply for a waiver from the relevant requirement. The issuer must in that case provide to the Authority on a strictly confidential basis a statement of the requested waiver together with the reasons why the issuer believes that the information should not be disclosed at that time. The Authority may approve or reject the application for a waiver. If the Authority approves the application for a waiver, the Authority may at any time require the issuer to disclose any information in relation to the waiver.
f) The provisions of this Article shall apply to the sponsor if the issuer is a special purposes entity.

Article 35: Application to Employee Share Schemes
a) Where an application for registration and offer of securities includes a distribution of shares which are not already listed to employees through an employee share scheme, the following requirements must be fulfilled:

1) subscription to such shares is to be restricted to directors and employees of the issuer or its subsidiaries; and

2) the issuer must ensure that the total number of shares to be issued under the scheme does not exceed 15% of the paid-up capital of the issuer at any time.

b) The provisions of this Article shall not apply on special purposes entity.

Article 36: Dormant Applications The Authority may, at its absolute discretion, cancel an application for registration and offer of securities where such application has in the opinion of the Authority remained dormant. The effect of such cancellation is that if the issuer then wishes to seek approval for registration and offer of the same securities, it must make a new application in accordance with the process set out in these Rules.

25.5 PART 5: FINANCING TRANSACTIONS FOR SPECIAL PURPOSE ENTITY

25.5.1 Chapter 1: New Financing Transactions For Special Purposes Entity

Article 37: Scope and Application This Part sets out requirements applicable to each financing transaction entered into in relation to the issuance of a new class or series of debt instruments by a special purposes entity.

Article 38: Approval of New Financing Transactions by the Authority
a) No financing transaction may be entered into in relation to the issuance of a new class or series of debt instruments by a special purposes entity without obtaining an approval from the Authority for the financing transaction application required under paragraph (a) of Article 39 of these Rules.

b) A financing transaction shall meet each of the applicable transaction conditions specified in this Part.

c) For the purposes of this Chapter, the Authority's approval may include multiple issues of debt instruments under a single issuance program. If the Authority approves the financing transaction, all debt instruments to be issued under the program will be offered within 24 months following the approval of the Authority provided that the sponsor complies with the following requirements:

1) submit to the Authority, as soon as possible, the following documents:

a. pricing annex for each segment of the debt instrument issuance program signed by a representative of the entity and the sponsor authorized to sign; and

b. A confirmation letter by the sponsor to the Authority that the debt instruments in question have been offered.

2) The pricing annex for each issue of debt instrument shall include details of the issuance, maturity and redemption dates (if any) of the debt instruments to be included, and their price details.

3) The Pricing Annex shall explain all terms and conditions of the issue.

4) The Sponsor shall notify the Authority in writing of the final allocation results of the debt instruments offered, and the total amounts paid against the total amount specified in the application.

d) Neither a sponsor nor a special purposes entity shall offer or hold itself out, or allow a third party to offer or hold itself out, as offering debt instruments in the special purposes entity which are subject of the application unless it has received the Authority's approval referred to in paragraph (a) of this Article.

e) An applicant shall commence the offer of debt instruments within one year of receipt of the Authority's approval under paragraph (a) of this Article, failing which the approval shall lapse.

Article 39: Procedures and Powers of the Authority in Relation to a Financing Transaction Application
a) The sponsor shall submit an application to the Authority which contains the information required in Annex 24 of these Rules.

b) The Authority shall, upon receipt of all information and documents required, notify the sponsor in writing of the same, and it may make any of the following decisions within the period specified in paragraph (c) of this Article:

1) approve the financing transaction application, and in respect of a financing transaction in relation to offering debt instruments privately, the approval of the Authority is considered obtained upon the lapse of 10 days from the date of the Authority notification referred to in paragraph (b) of this Article unless the Authority perform any of the actions mentioned in this Article before the lapse of the period specified in this sub-paragraph;

2) approve the financing transaction application subject to such conditions and restrictions as it considers appropriate; or

3) reject the financing transaction application.

c) For the purposes of paragraph (b) of this Article, the Authority shall make its decision in respect of a financing transaction within (20) days, if the financing transaction is in relation to the public offering debt instruments, but if the transaction is related to privately offered debt instruments, the Authority shall make its decision within 10 days.

d) If the authority, in considering an application made under paragraph (a) of this Article, found that approving the financing transaction application may not be in the interest of the investors or may result in a breach of the Capital Market Law, its Implementing Regulations or the Exchange Rules the Authority may:

1) carry out any enquiries that it deems appropriate;

2) request the sponsor, its representative or the representative of the special purposes entity, to attend before the Authority to answer questions and explain any matter the Authority considers relevant to the application;

3) request the special purposes entity or the sponsor to provide such additional information as the Authority considers appropriate within fourteen (14) days of the request, unless the Authority states otherwise;

4) verify any information provided by the sponsor or the special purposes entity.

e) The Authority may refuse to consider the application where the sponsor or the special purposes entity has failed to provide information requested from it within the time specified in subparagraph (3) of paragraph (d) of this Article.

f) The Authority may refuse the financing transaction application if the Authority believes that the proposed financing transaction may not be in the interest of the investors or may result in a breach of the Capital Market Law or its Implementing Regulations.

25.5.2 Chapter 2: Financing Transactions Conditions for Special Purposes Entity

Article 40: Scope and Application
a) This Part sets out the conditions that a special purposes shall ensure that they are met with respect to a financing transaction entered into by it in relation to the issuance of a new class or series of debt instruments.

b) A special purposes entity shall ensure that the conditions in Articles 42 to 47 of these rules are met with respect to every financing transaction.

c) Where a special purposes entity enters into a financing transaction involving the issue of asset-linked recourse debt instruments or asset-backed debt instruments, it shall also ensure that the conditions in Article 48 of these Rules are met.

d) Where a special purposes entity enters into multiple financing transactions, it shall also ensure that the condition in Article49 of these Rules are met.

Article 41: Financing Structures There is no limit on the type of financing structure that may be utilized by the special purposes entity in a financing transaction

Article 42: Appointment of a custodian The special purposes entity must have a custodian in accordance with Article 32 of the Rules for Special Purpose Entities.

Article 43: Investor Protection The documentation associated with the financing transaction shall include appropriate arrangements to protect the interests of investors in accordance with Article 50 of these Rules.

Article 44: Use of Proceeds The proceeds of issuance of the debt instruments shall be realized, held, managed (where relevant) and invested in consistence with the disclosure made under these Rules, as applicable, and with the terms and conditions of the debt instruments.

Article 45: Payments and Bank Accounts Without prejudice to Article 44 of these Rules:

1) where the terms and conditions of the debt instruments provide for such payments to be made to the special purposes entity, all payments made by or on behalf of investors on subscription for debt instruments of a special purposes entity shall be received into the account of the designated bank;

2) all payments made by the special purposes entity shall be realized and made in accordance with these Rules, all applicable laws and regulations, the by-laws of the special purposes entity and the terms and conditions of the debt instruments issued by the special purposes entity; and

3) where the terms and conditions of the debt instruments provide for such payments to be made by the special purposes entity to the investors, all payments made shall be paid from an account of special purposes entity.

Article 46: Investments Without prejudice to Article 44 of these Rules, all investments made by the special purposes entity shall be subject, monitored, managed (where applicable) and realized in accordance with the Rules for Special Purpose Entities, all applicable laws and regulations, the by-laws of the special purposes entity and the terms and conditions of the debt instruments issued by the special purposes entity.

Article 47: Enforceability Each financing contract entered into by the special purposes entity in relation to a financing transaction shall be:

1) legal, valid and binding on each party to it insofar as relevant to the interests of investors, except as clearly disclosed in the prospectus or private placement offering document; and

2) consistent with the disclosure provided under these Rules, as applicable.

Article 48: Financing Transactions Involving the Issue of Asset-linked Recourse Debt Instruments or Asset Backed Debt Instruments Financing transactions involving the issue of asset-linked recourse debt instruments or asset-backed debt instruments are subject to the following requirements:

1) In relation to issuing asset-linked recourse debt istruments, the sponsor shall be a Saudi joint stock company, a Capital Market Institution licensed to carry on securities business related to the business of special purposes entities, a local bank or a finance company with the required licenses to carry on their businesses and activities from the relavant government entities, in accordance with sub-paragraph (1) of paragraph (a) of Article 11 of the Rules for Special Purpose Entities.

2) In relation to issuing asset-backed debt istruments, the sponsor shall be a Saudi joint stock or limited liability company, a Capital Market Institution licensed to carry on securities business related to the business of special purposes entities, a local bank or a finance company with the required licenses to carry on their business and activities from the relavant government entities, in accordance with sub-paragraph (2) of paragraph (a) of Article 11 of the Rules for Special Purpose Entities.

3) As an exception to the provisions of paragraph (1) of this Article, if a special purposes entity issues, or intends to issue, asset-linked recourse debt instruments through a private placement, the sponsor may be a Saudi limited liability Company, in accordance with sub-paragraph (3) of paragraph (a) of Article 11 of the Rules for Special Purpose Entities.

4) the custodian shall hold custody of the real estate assets and securities owned by the special purposes entity (if any), in accordance with Article 31 of the Rules for Special Purpose Entities.

Article 49: Multiple Financing Transactions The sponsor shall be able to demonstrate to the Authority that adequate legal safeguards are in place to ensure that investors in a financing transaction are not at risk of losses arising from the liability of the special purposes entity under any other financing transaction to which the special purposes entity is party, unless the transaction is a part of a financing transaction and it was clearly disclosed in the prospectus or private placement offering document, as applicable.

Chapter 3: Investors Protection

Article 50: Investors Protection
a) The documentation associated with the financing transaction shall include adequate protections for holders of debt instruments issued by the special purposes entity. This shall include at a minimum the arrangements set out in this Article.

b) The documentation associated with the financing transaction shall include a valid, legally binding and irrevocable arrangement enabling holders of debt instruments, acting by a majority of the holders (by par value) eligible to vote of each class of holders of debt instrument issued by the special purposes entity, to compel the special purposes entity:

1) to act in accordance with the instructions of the holders in relation to the financing transaction to which their debt instruments relate; and

2) to repay all rights and claims of the special purposes entity with respect to the financing transaction.

c) Neither the sponsor nor any affiliate of it, nor any person acting on behalf of the sponsor, may exercise any voting rights with respect to debt instruments issued to it in a meeting of holders of a class of debt instruments.

Article 51: Stop Orders
a) The Authority may at any time issue an order to a special purposes entity or its sponsor prohibiting or restricting the marketing or sale of debt instruments in the special purposes entity if the Authority believes that the marketing or sale of those debt instruments may result in a breach of the Capital Market Law or its Implementing Regulations.

b) A special purposes entity or sponsor served with a notice under paragraph (a) of this Article shall:

1) immediately cease, and procure that any person acting on its behalf ceases, the marketing or sale of the debt instruments;
2) immediately notify any other person of whom it is aware marketing or selling the debt instruments of the issue of the order; and
3) on request from the Authority, notify the Authority of the identity of any person involved in the marketing or selling of the debt instruments.

25.6 PART 6: CAPITAL ALTERATION

25.6.1 Chapter 1: Capital Increase for Issuers of Listed Shares

Article 52: Scope and Application
a) The purpose of this Part is to regulate the issuance, registration and offering or cancelation of shares as a result of a capital alteration of an issuer whose shares are listed on the Main Market.

b) The Special purposes entities shall not be subject to the provisions of this Part.

c) A foreign issuer whose shares are listed on the Main Market pursuant to the Listing Rules shall not be subject to the provisions of this Part.

Article 53: Application Submission for Capital Increase of Issuers of Listed Securities and Supporting Documents Where an issuer wishes to register and offer new shares of a class already listed by raising its capital, either by way of rights issue, capitalization issue, debt conversion, acquisition of a company or asset purchase, it must obtain the Authority's approval prior to calling for the issuer's extraordinary general assembly meeting. The approval of the extraordinary general assembly of the issuer must be obtained within six months of the approval of the Authority. If the assembly's approval is not obtained during such time, the Authority's approval shall be deemed to be cancelled and the issuer will be required to resubmit its letter of application if it still wishes to increase its capital.

Article 54: Conditions and Requirements Applicable to a Rights Issue
a) In addition to any other applicable requirements under Article 28 of these Rules, where an issuer wishes to submit an application for registration and offer of securities to the Authority in respect of a rights issue the following conditions must be satisfied:

1) details of the proceeds of any previous rights issues must be provided and such details must be compared with the disclosure made under the previous prospectus;

2) details of any qualifications made in the audited financial statements for the preceding financial year must be provided; and

b) The issuer must, in the event of any deviation of 5% or more from the planned use of proceeds as set out in the relevant rights issue prospectus, disclose each such case to the public before the opening of the trading session following the relevant deviation.

Article 55: Conditions and Requirements Applicable to a Capitalization Issue Where an issuer wishes to increase its capital by way of a capitalization issue it must submit to the Authority a letter of application that includes the minimum information set out in Annex 18 of these Rules.

Article 56: Conditions and Requirements Applicable to Capital Increase through Debt Conversion
a) In addition to any other applicable requirements under Article 28 of these Rules, where an issuer wishes to increase its capital by way of a debt conversion, the issuer must submit the following documents to the Authority:

1) a statement of the origin and amount of the debt; signed and certified by the board of directors and the auditors of the issuer; and

2) a legal review report and a legal opinion issued by the issuer's legal advisor on the extent to which the debt conversion transaction complies with the relevant laws.

b) Where an issuer wishes to increase its capital by way of a debt conversion it must produce a circular for its shareholders stating the information required to enable the shareholders to make an informed vote at the relevant extraordinary general assembly. This circular shall include, but is not limited to the items set out in Annex 13 of these Rules.

c) The shareholders' circular - submitted to the Authority in respect of a request of a capital increase by way of a debt conversion- must be produced in Arabic and be annotated in the margin to indicate where the information required by the applicable paragraphs of these Rules have been included and any changes from any previous drafts must be clearly marked. Each draft shareholders' circular must indicate the draft number and date of submission on its cover page.

Article 57: Conditions and Requirements Applicable to a Capital Increase to Acquire a Company or Purchase an Asset In addition to any other applicable requirements under Article 28 of these Rules, where the purpose of a capital increase is to acquire a company or purchase an asset, the following requirements must be complied with as applicable:

1) the issuer must submit to the Authority a report prepared by the issuer's financial advisor comprising the issuer's valuation and a valuation of the target company to be acquired or the asset to be purchased;

2) the issuer must submit to the Authority a financial due diligence report and a legal due diligence report issued by the legal advisor for the target company to be acquired or assets to be purchased;

3) the issuer must produce a circular for its shareholders stating the information required to enable the shareholders to make an informed vote at the extraordinary general assembly. This circular shall include, but is not limited to the items set out in Annex 14 of these Rules.

4) The shareholders' circular – submitted to the Authority in respect of a request of a capital increase to acquire a company or purchase an asset- must be produced in Arabic and be annotated in the margin to indicate where the information required by the applicable paragraphs of these Rules have been included and any changes from any previous drafts must be clearly marked. Each draft shareholders' circular must indicate the draft number and date of submission on its cover page.

25.6.2 Chapter 2: Capital Reduction for Issuers of Listed Shares

Article 58: Conditions and Requirements Applicable to a Capital Reduction
a) Where an issuer wishes to reduce its share capital, it must submit to the Authority a letter of application that includes the minimum information set out in Annex 19 of these Rules, for the Authority's approval prior to obtaining the approval of the relevant extraordinary general assembly of the issuer on the capital reduction. The application must be accompanied by the following:

1) the letter of appointment for the financial advisor;
2) the letter of appointment for the legal advisor (if any);
3) an external auditor's report on the reasons for the capital reduction and the impact of the capital reduction on the issuer's liabilities;
4) the proposed method of capital reduction and the expected effect of such reduction;
5) a copy of the shareholders' circular as per paragraph b) below; and
6) any other documentation as may be required by the Authority.

b) Where an issuer wishes to reduce its share capital, it must also produce a circular for its shareholders stating the information required to enable the shareholders to make an informed vote at the relevant extraordinary general assembly. This circular shall include, but is not limited to, the following:

1) the general structure of the proposed reduction in share capital;
2) the rationale behind the proposed reduction in share capital, including a reasoned discussion from management in this regard;
3) the risk factors related to the proposed reduction in share capital;
4) the proposed timing of the process; and
5) a statement from the directors of the issuer confirming that in the board's view, the proposed reduction in share capital is in the best interests of the issuer and the shareholders.

c) The shareholders' circular - submitted to the Authority in respect of a capital reduction request - must be produced in Arabic language and be annotated in the margin to indicate where the information required by the applicable paragraphs of these Rules have been included and any changes from any previous drafts must be clearly marked. Each draft shareholders' circular must indicate the draft number and date of submission on its cover page.

25.7 PART 7: CONTINUING OBLIGATIONS

25.7.1 Chapter 1: Disclosures

Article 59: Scope and Application
a) The purpose of this Part is to regulate the continuing obligations of issuers whose securities are listed on the Main Market.

b) Provisions of Article 60, paragraphs (1), (2), (3), (6), (10), (11), (12), (13), (14), (15), (16), (26), (27), (28) and (29) of Article 62, paragraphs (a) and (e) of Article 63, and Articles 64, 66 and 68 of these Rules shall apply to the sponsor.

c) Provisions of paragraphs (4), (30) and (31) of Article 62 of these Rules shall only apply to the sponsor, in case the issuer is a special purposes entity.

d) Provisions of Article 67, Article 69, and paragraph (b) of Article 68 of these Rules shall not apply to the issues made by a special purposes entity.

e) A foreign issuer whose shares are listed on the Main Market pursuant to the Listing Rules shall be subject to the provisions of Article 60, Article 61, and paragraphs (1),(2),(3),(4),(5),(6),(7),(8),(9),(10),(11),(12),(13),(14),(15),(16),(26),(27),(28),(29), (30),(31),(32),(33) and (34) of Article 62, subparagraph (1) of paragraph (a) and paragraphs (b) and (e) of Article 63, Article 64, Article 65, Article 66, Article 67 and Article 68 of these Rules.

Article 60: Complete, Clear, Accurate and not Misleading Disclosures
a) All disclosures made by an issuer must be complete, clear, accurate and not misleading and shall comply with the means of disclosure specified by the Exchange in the Listing Rules.

b) Where, in the opinion of the issuer, disclosure of any matter required by these Rules would be unduly detrimental to the issuer, and omission is not likely to mislead investors with regard to facts and circumstances, knowledge of which is essential for the assessment of the securities in question, the issuer may apply for a waiver from the relevant requirement or otherwise request to delay the disclosure. The issuer must in that case provide to the Authority on a strictly confidential basis a statement of the requested waiver or delay together with the reasons why the issuer believes that the information should not be disclosed at that time. The Authority may approve or reject the application for a waiver or delay. If the Authority approves the application for a waiver or delay, the Authority may at any time require the issuer to disclose any information in relation to the waiver or delay.

c) All information and material developments stated in this Chapter shall be deemed confidential until they are disclosed. Before disclosing such information and material developments, the issuer shall be prohibited from communicating such information to parties not bound by a confidentiality obligation and an obligation to protect such information. An issuer must also take all necessary steps to prevent the leakage of any information and material developments before disclosing them as described in the Listing Rules.

d) An issuer must determine the need to publish a disclosure to the public in response to rumors related to any material developments, and the Authority may require such publication to be made by the issuer as it sees appropriate.

Article 61: Obligation to Disclose Material Developments
a) An issuer must disclose to the Authority and the public without delay any material developments in its sphere of activity which are not public knowledge, and which may affect the assets and liabilities or financial position or the general course of business of the issuer or its subsidiaries and which may reasonably lead to movements in the price of the issuer's listed securities or significantly affect an issuer's ability to meet its commitments in respect of listed debt instruments.

b) Exception from paragraph (a) of this Article, if the issuer is a special purposes entity, the special purposes entity shall disclose to the Authority and the public without delay any material developments that fall within the scope of its activity and the knowledge of which is not available to the general public, and which may affect the assets or liabilities of the special purposes entity and can reasonably lead to a change in the price of the listed securities or have a significant impact on the ability of the special purpose entity to meet its debt instrument related obligations

c) In determining whether a development falls within the scope of this Article, an issuer must assess whether a prudent investor would be likely to consider information about the development in making his investment decisions.

Article 62: Disclosure of Specific Events The issuer must immediately and without delay disclose to the Authority and the public any of the following developments (regardless of whether or not they qualify as "material" under Article 61 of these Rules):

1) any transaction to purchase, sell, lease or mortgage an asset at a price equal to or greater than 10% of the net assets of the issuer according to the latest reviewed interim financial statements or audited annual financial statements, whichever is later;

2) any debt outside the issuer's ordinary course of business, of a value equal to or greater than 10% of the issuer's net assets; according to the latest reviewed interim financial statements or audited annual financial statements, whichever is later;

3) any losses equal to or greater than 10% of the issuer's net assets; according to the latest reviewed interim financial statements or audited annual financial statements, whichever is later;

4) any significant change in the issuer's production environment or activity including (but not limited to) the availability of resources and the possibility of obtaining them;

5) any changes in the composition of the directors, the audit committee or to CEO's position of the issuer, and in case the issuer is a special purposes entity, any changes in the composition of the directors, the audit committee or to CEO's position of the sponsor and the special purposes entity;

6) any dispute including any litigation, arbitration, or mediation where the value involved is equal to or greater than 5% of the net assets of the issuer according to the latest reviewed interim financial statements or audited annual financial statements, whichever is later;

7) any judicial decision issued against the board or any of the directors where the subject of the decision involved relates to the business of the board or any of the directors in the issuer;

8) the increase or decrease in the net assets of the issuer equal to or greater than 10% according to the latest reviewed interim financial statements or audited annual financial statements, whichever is later;

9) the increase or decrease in the gross profit of the issuer equal to or greater than 10% according to the latest audited financial statements;

10) the entering into, or the unexpected termination of, any contract with revenues equal to or greater than 5% of the gross revenues of the issuer according to the latest audited annual financial statements;

11) any transaction between the issuer and a related party or any arrangement through which the issuer and a related party invest in any project or asset or provide financing therefore if this transaction or arrangement is equal to or greater than 1% of the gross revenues of the issuer according to the latest audited annual financial statements;

12) any interruption in the principal activities of the issuer or its subsidiaries equal to or greater than 5% of the gross revenues according to the latest audited annual financial statements;

13) any changes in the issuer's articles of association or the location of the issuer's principal office;

14) any change in its external auditors;

15) the presentation of any winding-up petition, the making of any winding-up order or the appointment of a liquidator in respect of the issuer or its affiliates under the Companies Law, or under any regulations applicable to a foreign issuer whose shares are listed on the Main Market in accordance with the Listing Rules including the commencement of any proceedings under the Bankruptcy Regulations;

16) the passing of a resolution by the issuer or its affiliates that it be dissolved or liquidated, or the occurrence of an event or termination of a period of time which would require the issuer to be put into liquidation or dissolution;

17) Upon the issuance of any recommendation or a resolution by the person of authority in the issuer to submit an application to the court for commencing any of the bankruptcy procedures under the Bankruptcy Law, with a statement of its impact on the issuer's financial position or the general course of its business:

18) Upon receiving a notification from the court regarding others registering an application with the court for commencing a financial restructuring procedure or commencing the liquidation procedure or the administrative liquidation procedure for the issuer in accordance with the Bankruptcy Law, with a statement of its impact on the issuer's financial position or the general course of its business:

19) Upon registering an application with the court for commencing any of the bankruptcy procedures for the issuer in accordance with the Bankruptcy Law, with clarification of the subsequent steps and durations therefor and a statement of its impact on the issuer's financial position or the general course of its business.

20) Upon the issuance of the court's decision (first instance or final) ordering the commencement of any of the bankruptcy procedures for the issuer in accordance with the Bankruptcy Law, with clarification of the subsequent steps and durations therefor and a statement of its impact on the issuer's financial position or the general course of its business.

21) Upon the issuance of the court's decision (first instance or final) rejecting the application of commencing any bankruptcy procedures for the issuer in accordance with the Bankruptcy Law, or rejecting any of them and commencing the appropriate bankruptcy procedure, with a statement of the reasons for such rejection and a statement of its impact on the issuer's financial position or the general course of its business.

22) Upon the issuance of the court's decision (first instance or final) terminating the financial restructuring procedure or the protective settlement procedure for the issuer in accordance with the Bankruptcy Law, or terminating any of them and commencing the appropriate bankruptcy procedure in accordance with Bankruptcy Law with a statement of its impact on the issuer's financial position or the general course of its business.

23) Objecting before the competent court regarding the commencing or rejecting of the commencement of any bankruptcy procedures under the Bankruptcy Law, or the termination or non-termination of the protective settlement procedure or the financial restructuring procedure under the Bankruptcy Law with a statement of its impact on the issuer's financial position or the general course of its business.

24) Upon the issuance of the court's decision in the objection referred to in paragraph (23) of this Article to affirm or reverse the Court decision and to adjudicate the case under the Bankruptcy Law with a statement of its impact on the issuer's financial position or the general course of its business.

25) Any material developments included in the reports the issuer provides during the commenced bankruptcy procedures in accordance with the Bankruptcy Law with a statement of its impact on the issuer's financial position or the general course of its business, unless the officeholder, the bankruptcy committee or the competent authority decides that such developments are confidential according the Implementing Regulation of the Bankruptcy Law.

26) the making of any judgement, decision, order or declaration by a court or judicial body, whether at first instance or on appeal, which may adversely affect the issuer's utilization of any portion of its assets which in aggregate value represents a value in excess of 5% or more of the net assets of the issuer according to the latest reviewed interim financial statements or audited annual financial statements, whichever is later;

27) the call for convening a general or special assembly and its agenda;

28) the outcome of the general or special assembly;

29) any proposed change in the capital of the issuer;

30) any decision to declare, recommend to declare or pay dividends or to make any other distributions to the holders of its listed securities;

31) any decision or a recommendation not to pay dividends which would otherwise have been expected to have been paid;

32) any decision to call, repurchase, draw, redeem or propose to buy any of its securities and the total amount and value thereof;

33) any decision not to make payment in respect of debt instruments or convertible debt instruments; or

34) any change in the rights attaching to any class of listed shares or to the debt instruments convertible to such shares.

35) If the issuer is a special purposes entity, any court proceedings taken or threatened against the special purposes entity, any criminal or disciplinary procedures or sanctions to be inflicted on or likely to be inflicted on the special purposes entity.

36) If the issuer is a special purposes entity, any court proceedings taken or threatened against members of the board of directors of a special purposes entity, any criminal or disciplinary proceedings or sanctions to be inflicted on or likely to be inflicted on members of the board of directors of the special purpose entity, If the subject matter of the procedure or sanction relates to the work of the Board of Directors or one of its members in the Special Purpose Entity.

37) Paragraphs (27), (28) and (29) shall not apply where the issuer is a special purposes entity.

Article 63: Disclosure of Financial Information
a) The annual financial statements and the first, second, and third interim financial statements of an issuer must be disclosed to the Authority and the public upon their approval and prior to their publication to shareholders or third parties. Where the issuer is a special purposes entity, such entity must disclose its annual financial statements to the Authority and the public upon their approval and prior to publishing it to third parties. For the purposes of this Article:

1) interim financial statements are approved after being (a) approved by the board of directors and (b) signed by (i) a director authorized by the board of directors, (ii) by the CEO and (iii) the CFO; and

2) annual financial statements are approved in accordance with the provisions of the Companies Law and the Corporate Governance Regulations. Where the issuer is a special purposes entity, the financial statements of such entity are approved after being approved by the entity's board of directors.

b) The issuer shall disclose its interim and annual financial statements through the electronic system specifically designated for such purpose by the Exchange.

c) The issuer must prepare its interim financial statements in accordance with the accounting and auditing standards adopted by SOCPA, and disclose them to the public within a period not exceeding 30 days after the end of the financial period included in such financial statements.

d) The issuer must prepare its annual financial statements in accordance with the accounting and auditing standards adopted by SOCPA, and disclose them to the public within a period not exceeding three months after the end of the annual financial period included in such financial statements. The issuer must disclose these annual financial statements not less than 21 calendar days before the date of convening the issuer's annual general assembly. Where the issuer is a special purposes entity, the disclosure to the public shall be within a maximum period of 3 months after the end of the annual financial period included in such statements.

e) The certified public accountant or the accounting firm that audits the issuer's financial statements must be registered with the Authority in accordance with the Rules for Registering Auditors of Entities Subject to the Authority's Supervision, and the issuer must ensure that the certified public accountant or the accounting firm that audits its financial statements and any of their partners comply with the SOCPA rules and regulations in relation to the ownership of shares or securities of the issuer or any of its subsidiaries in order to ensure the independency of the certified public accountant or the accounting firm and any partner or employee of that firm.

f) If the issuer is a special purposes entity, the sponsor shall provide the special purposes entity of its interim and annual financial statements and the report of the board of directors in a timely manner to enable the special purposes entity to fulfill its obligations under this article.

g) In the event where the issuer is a foreigner whose shares are listed on the Main Market in accordance with the Listing Rules, it shall prepare its interim and annual financial statements in accordance with international standards issued by the International Accounting Standard Board. For the purposes of this paragraph, the interim and annual financial statements shall be disclosed as follows:

1) In respect of the interim financial statements; disclosure shall be made to the public within a period not exceeding (30) days after the end of the financial period included in such financial statements.

2) In respect of the annual financial statements; disclosure shall be made to the public within a period not exceeding (3) months of the end of the annual financial period mentioned in those statements, and must disclose such financial statements within a period not less than (21) calendar days prior to the date of its annual general assembly.

Article 64: Board of Directors Report The issuer must provide the Authority with, and disclose to the shareholders, within three months from the end of the financial year, a report issued by the board of directors containing the required information pursuant to the Corporate Governance Regulations and including a review of the operations of the issuer during the last financial year and of all relevant factors affecting the issuer's business which an investor requires to assess the assets, liabilities and financial position of the issuer.

Article 65: Duties of Directors and Senior Executives
The directors and senior executives of an issuer must exercise their powers and carry out their duties in such a way as to serve the interests of the issuer.

Article 66: Provision of Documents to the Authority
The issuer must send copies to the Authority of any notices, documents or information that are sent or otherwise made available to its shareholders, unless they were disclosed on the Exchange.

25.7.2 Chapter 2: Restrictions on Dealings

Article 67: Dealings by Substantial Holders of Shares and Convertible Debt Instruments

a) Any person must notify the Exchange if such person becomes the owner of, or is interested in, 5% or more of any class of voting shares or convertible debt instruments of the issuer at the end of the third trading day following the execution of the transaction or the occurrence of the event which results such ownership or interest; The person notification to the Authority shall also include a list of persons, in which those persons, have an interest in the shares or convertible debt instruments which they own or control.

b) The person referred to in paragraph (a) of this Article must notify the Exchange in the event of any change to the list of persons referred to in paragraph (a) of this Article including any event which requires the inclusion of a person to that list or the exclusion of any person who has been previously included in that list. Such notification must be made at the end of the third trading day following the occurrence of the relevant event.

c) For the purposes of this Article, a person's notification to the Exchange pursuant to paragraph (a) of this Article, regarding its ownership or interest in 5% or more of any class of voting shares of the foreign issuer whose shares are listed on the Main Market in accordance with the Listing Rules, limited to those listed in the Main Market pursuant to the Listing Rules

d) For the purposes of this Article, in calculating the total number of shares or convertible debt instruments in which a person is interested, that person will be deemed to be interested in any shares or convertible debt instruments owned by or controlled by any of the following persons:

1) a relative of that person;
2) a company controlled by that person; or
3) any other persons with which that person has agreed to act in concert to acquire an interest in or exercise voting rights in the shares or in the convertible debt instruments of the issuer.

e) The notices referred to in this Article shall be in accordance with the form prepared for this regard. The notice referred to in paragraph (a) of this Article must contain at least the following information:

1) the names of the persons who own or have the right to dispose of the subject shares or convertible debt instruments;
2) details of the ownership process;
3) details of any loans or financial support for the ownership process that the person has received from any other persons; and

Article 68: Dealings of Directors and Senior Executives

a) The directors, senior executives or audit committee members of the issuer and any of their associates may not deal in any securities of the issuer during the following periods:

1) during the 15 calendar days preceding the end of the financial quarter and until the date of the disclosure of the reviewed interim financial statement of the issuer that is required to be disclosed pursuant to paragraph (a) of Article 63 of these Rules; and

2) during the 30 calendar days preceding the end of the financial year and until the date of disclosing the issuer's audited annual financial statements, or the interim financial statements for the fourth quarter if the issuer has disclosed them after reviewing them and fulfilling the requirements of Article 63 of these Rules.

b) The prohibition referred to in paragraph (a) of this Article shall not apply to exercising the subscription's right in rights issues and the sale of such rights.

c) Upon termination of a director's membership in the board of directors or director's dismissal from the board of directors, termination of any of the audit committee's membership, or resignation of any of senior executives of the issuer during any of the periods referred to in paragraph (a) of this Article, this period (where applicable) shall apply to the director, audit committee's member, or senior executive, and any of their associates.

Article 69: Restrictions on Shares

a) The substantial shareholders in the issuer shown in the prospectus or registration document as owners of the issuer's shares must not dispose any of their shares during a period of six months from the date on which the issuers shares' trading first commences on the Exchange, except where the issuer states a longer lock up period in the prospectus or registration document.

b) If the registered owner specified in the prospectus or registration document is different to the beneficial owner, then the beneficial owner must undertake that the registered holder shall not dispose any of such shares for a period of six months from the date on which trading in the shares first commences on the Exchange. A person shall be treated as a beneficial owner of shares if he has the ultimate beneficial ownership or control of the shares, whether through a chain of companies or otherwise.

c) Shares granted to the persons described in paragraph (a) of this Article-during the lock- up period-as a result of a capital increase by way of a capitalization issue must not be disposed until lock-up period described in paragraphs (a), and (b)of this Article is lifted.

25.8 PART 8: OFFER OR REGISTRATION IN PARALLEL MARKET

Article 70: Scope and Application

a) The purpose of this Part is to regulate the registration and offering of shares on the Parallel Market beside regulating the registration of shares in the Parallel Market.

b) Shares may not be offered in the Parallel Market or registred unless pursuant to this Part.

c) The Instructions of Book Building Process and Allocation Methods in Initial Public Offerings shall not apply to shares offerings conducted under these Rules.

d) The Corporate Governance Regulation shall be deemed indicative to all issuers whose shares are listed on the Parallel Market unless another law, regulations or a resolution of the Board of the Authority states that some provisions thereof are mandatory on issuers whose shares are listed on the Parallel Market.

e) The offer, under this Part, shall be limited to the categories of qualified investors, and the financial advisor of the issuer is responsible for ensuring compliance with this paragraph.

f) In all cases, Capital Market Institutions shall ensure that their clients of qualified investors are aware of the risks involved in subscribing of shares offered in the Parallel Market.

Article 71: Appointment of Representative of Issuer
a) The issuer must appoint two representatives, one of whom must be a director and the other must be a senior executive, to act as its representatives before the Authority for all purposes relating to the Capital Market Law, the Companies Law, their implementing regulations, other relevant laws and these Rules.

b) The issuer must provide details in writing of how its representatives may be contacted including office, mobile number, and electronic mail address.

c) The issuer and its representatives, referred to in paragraph (a) of this Article, must provide the Authority, without delay, with all the information, clarifications, books, records and forms that the Authority requests from them, for the purpose of implementing the Capital Market Law, the Companies Law, their Implementing Regulations, other relevant laws and these Rules, which must be complete, clear, correct, and not misleading.

Article 72: Appointment of Advisors
a) Where an issuer makes an application for registration and offering of shares in the Parallel Market or the registration of its shares that requires the production of a prospectus, shareholders' circular or the registration document (where applicable), the issuer must appoint a financial advisor authorized by the Authority to carry out arranging activities and any other securities activities related to the agreed services to be provided.

b) The financial advisor, who is appointed pursuant to paragraph (a) of this Article, is subject to the obligations set out under paragraphs (b) and (c) of Article 21 of these Rules, and the reference to Annex 16 shall be replaced with Annex 21.

c) Where an issuer whose shares are listed on the Parallel Market undertakes a voluntary cancellation of listing, the issuer must appoint a financial advisor.

d) Where an issuer whose shares are listed on the Parallel Market submits an application to reduce its capital, the issuer must appoint a financial advisor.

e) The financial advisor and the legal advisor (if any) shall take into account the principles of the profession when providing advice to the issuer on the application for registration and offer of its securities, the registration of its shares in the Parallel Market or complying with Capital Market Law and its implementing regulations and Exchange Rules.

f) The Authority may, at all times, require the issuer to appoint a financial advisor, a legal advisor, or any other advisor to advise the issuer on the application of the provisions of the Capital Market Law, its Implementing Regulations, the Exchange Rules or the Companies Law or its Implementing Regulations.

Article 73: Approval of the Issuer An issuer may not make a Parallel Market offer of shares or registration unless the issuer has obtained all necessary corporate approvals required pursuant to its bylaws, the Companies Law and its Implementing Regulations.

Article 74: Conditions for an Issuer
a) An issuer applying to the Authority to register its shares and offer them by way of a Parallel Market Offer or for the registration of its shares in the Parallel Market must meet the following conditions:

1) The issuer must be a joint stock company.
2) The issuer must have been carrying on, either by itself or through one or more of its subsidiaries, a main activity for at least one year.
3) The issuer must have prepared its audited financial statements for the financial year preceding the application in accordance with the accounting standards adopted by SOCPA.
4) If the period covered in the latest audited financial statements was ended six months prior to the expected date of approval of the application, audited reviewed interim financial statements for any period from the end date of the period covered by the latest Audited financial statements to the expected date of approval of the application must be submitted to the Authority. Or submit the audited financial statements (as applicable), and in all cases, the period covered by the latest audited interim financial statements submitted to the Authority shall not have ended more than (6) months before the date of approval of the application for registration of securities.

b) Where an issuer already has securities that are listed on the Exchange, subparagraphs (2), (3) and (4) of paragraph (a) of this Article shall not apply.

c) An application may be accepted if it does not meet the requirements of this Article if the Authority is satisfied that the offer or registration will be in the interest of the investors, and that the issuer has provided the investors with the necessary information to arrive at an informed judgment concerning the issuer and the shares that are the subject of the application.

Article 75: Requirement to Submit the Application to the Authority
a) An issuer seeking registration and offering of its shares in the Parallel Market or the registration of its shares in the Parallel Market must submit an application to the Authority for approval which contains the information required under this part, and pay any fees set by the Authority.

b) The issuer must submit an electronic of the following documents to the Authority (and it shall maintain the original copies of such documents and submit them to the Authority at request):

1) the letter of the appointment of the financial advisor;
2) the authorization letters or powers of attorney of the representatives of the issuer empowering them to sign the prospectus, the shareholders' circular or the registration document (as applicable);
3) a list containing the names and contact numbers of the persons working for the issuer, the financial advisor and the legal advisor (if any) concerned with the application;
4) a formal letter of application for registration and offer in the Parallel Market or the registration of shares in the Parallel Market (as applicable), signed by a representative authorized to sign on behalf of the issuer in the form set out in Annex 6 of these Rules;
5) a declaration by the issuer in the form set out in Annex 7 or Annex 7 (b) of these Rules (as applicable).
6) approvals required by the relevant governmental agencies;
7) evidence of the issuer obtaining the required approvals under Article 73 of these Rules;
8) the draft prospectus, shareholders' circular or the registration document (as applicable) in Arabic;
9) the issuer's certificate of commercial registration;
10) the issuer's articles of association and bylaws;
11) the issuer's annual audited financial statements for the financial year preceding the submission of the application;

12) the latest audited interim financial statements since the financial position date of most recent annual audited financial statements;
13) the letters of consent from all the advisors on the use of their names, logos and statements in the prospectus, the shareholders' circular or the registration document (as applicable);
14) a letter from the issuer's financial advisor in the form set out in Annex 21 of these Rules;
15) a list containing the names and civil registry numbers (or the equivalent to it for non- Saudi nationals) of the directors;
16) A declaration and undertaking signed by the directors of the issuer and by each proposed director of the issuer in the form set out in Annex 8 of these Rules.
17) any other documentation that may be required by the Authority.

c) Following the approval of the registration and offer of shares on the Parallel Market by the Authority or the registration of shares in the Parallel Market and prior to the listing, the issuer must submit an electronic copy of the following documents to the Authority (and it shall maintain the original copies of such documents and submit them to the Authority at request):

1) the prospectus, the shareholders' circular or the registration document (where applicable) in Arabic signed on every page by the representatives of the issuer who are appointed as authorized signatories;

2) a list of shareholders and shares allocated to, except where the application is for a capital increase for acquisition of a company or purchasing an asset or for debt conversion or the registration of shares in the Parallel Market.

3) an updated and signed letter in the form set out in Annex 6 of these Rules; unless the application is related to the registration of shares in the Parallel Market.

d) The issuer must retain original copies (or certified copies where appropriate) of all documents required pursuant to this Article for a period not less than ten years from the completion of the offer or the direct listing in the Parallel Market, and without prejudice to this period, in case of any litigation or claim (including any litigation pending or threatened) or any on-going investigations relating to these documents, the issuer must retain such documents until the closure of that litigation, claim or on-going investigation.

e) If the issuer has its shares already listed on the Parallel Market, the subparagraphs (9), (10, (11), (12) and (15) of paragraph (b) of this Article shall not apply to the application for capital increase for acquisition of a company or purchasing an asset, issuing new shares for debt conversion or rights issue.

f) Where the offer is not completed by the prescribed offer end date specified in the prospectus provided to the Authority, the financial advisor must provide the Authority within ten days with a notification in writing signed by the financial advisor confirming that the offer has not completed. The financial advisor may, in consultation with the issuer, extend the period of the offer before end date of the offer, the qualified investor who has subscribed to the shares prior to the extension of the offer period may cancel or amend its subscription.

g) The provision of this Article shall not apply to the capitalization issue.

Article 76: Dormant Applications The Authority may, at its absolute discretion, cancel an application for registration and offer of shares in the Parallel Market or an application for the registration of shares in the Parallel Market where such application has, in the opinion of the Authority, remained outstanding. Should the issuer wish to continue such application, a new application must be made by the issuer in accordance with the application process set out in this Part if it wishes to register and offer the shares of the cancelled application in the Parallel Market or its registration in the Parallel Market.

Article 77: The Prospectus and the Registration Document
a) The Prospectus must contain the information set forth in Annex 20 of these Rules, and may contain additional information, provided that such information must be within the requirements set forth in Annex 9 of these Rules.

b) The registration document must contain the information set forth in Annex (20) (a) of these Rules, and may contain additional information, provided that such information must be within the requirements set forth in Annex 9 of these Rules

c) The draft prospectus and the draft registration document provided to the Authority shall be in Arabic.

d) The draft prospectus and the draft registration document provided to the Authority must be annotated to indicate where the information required by the applicable paragraphs of these Rules has been included and any changes from any previous drafts must be clearly marked. Each draft prospectus and draft registration document must indicate the draft number and the submission date on its cover page.

e) The provisions of paragraphs (c) and (d) of this Article shall apply to the shareholders' circular produced pursuant to this Part.

Article 78: Issuances not Requiring Prospectus
a) The prospectus is not required for the issue of further shares by an issuer whose shares are already listed on the Parallel Market, if the shares are categorized as:

1) shares result in an increase of not more than 10% of a share class already listed on the Parallel Market. For the purpose of determining this percentage, series of issues conducted during the twelve months are deemed a single issue, and series of transactions deemed as single transaction by the Authority are deemed a single issue.

2) shares issued as a result of capitalization issue.

3) employees share scheme;

4) shares issued as a result of capital increase by conversion of debt, provided that a shareholders' circular must be produced in accordance with Article 86 of these Rules;

5) shares issued as a result of capital increase to acquire a company or purchase an asset, provided that a shareholders' circular must be produced in accordance with Article 87 of these Rules; or

6) split of shares already issued.

b) Where an issuer wishes to issue securities in the circumstances specified in paragraph (a) of this Article it must make an application for registration and offer to the Authority in accordance with any applicable requirements under these Rules or as prescribed by the Authority. The relevant securities may not be issued prior to the approval of such application by the Authority.

c) The issuer must disclose any issuance made under this Article in the manner prescribed by the Authority.

Article 79: Supplementary Prospectus and Supplementary Shareholders Circular or Supplementary Registration Document

a) The issuer must submit a supplementary prospectus, supplementary shareholders' circular or supplementary registration document (as applicable) to the Authority if at any time after the prospectus, the shareholders' circular or the registration document has been published and before completion of the offer (in the case of a prospectus) or before the extraordinary general assembly is convened (in the case of a shareholders' circular) or prior to the direct listing in the Parallel Market (in the case of a registration document), the issuer becomes aware that:

1) there has been a significant change in material matters contained in the prospectus, the shareholders' circular or the registration document (as applicable); or

2) additional significant matters have become known which would have been required to be included in the prospectus, the shareholders' circular or the registration document (as applicable).

b) A supplementary prospectus, supplementary shareholders' circular or supplementary registration document must contain the following (as applicable):

1) details of the change or new matters in accordance with paragraph (a) of this Article; and

2) a declaration in the form specified at paragraph (10) of section (1) of Annex 20 of these Rules or paragraph (8) of section (1) of Annex (20) (a) of these Rules, or paragraph (2) of section (1) of Annex 22 of these Rules, or paragraph (2) of section (1) of Annex 23 of these Rules (as applicable).

c) Where a supplementary prospectus, supplementary shareholders' circular or supplementary registration document is submitted to the Authority under this Article, it must be signed on every page by the representatives of the issuer who are appointed as authorized signatories.

d) Where a supplementary prospectus is submitted to the Authority under this Article, a qualified investor who subscribed for shares prior to the publishing of the supplementary prospectus is permitted to rescind or amend his subscription for such shares prior to the end of the offering period.

Article 80: Powers of Authority in Relation to the Application

a) The approval of the application for registration and offer of securities in the parallel market or the application for registration in the Parallel Market is subject to the following conditions:

1) the Authority has received notification from the Exchange its conditional approval of the corresponding application for listing pursuant to the Listing Rules;
2) the conditional approval mentioned under sub-paragraph (1) of this paragraph has not been withdrawn by the Exchange; and
3) the Authority is satisfied that the information contained in the prospectus, the shareholders' circular or the registration document (as applicable) is complete and fulfils the requirements set out in the Capital Market Law and its Implementing Regulations.

b) The Authority will review the application within 30 days of receiving all information and documentation required pursuant to these Rules. The commencement of this period is not subject to the Authority's receipt of the notification referred to in subparagraph (1) of paragraph (a) of this Article provided that the notification must be submitted to the Authority at least (10) days prior to the end of the review period, otherwise the Authority may extend the review period for a term not exceeding 10 days from the date of receipt of the notification.

c) If, having reviewed the application, the Authority considers that the proposed offer of shares or registration in the Parallel Market may not be in the interest of the investors or may result in a breach of the Capital Market Law, its Implementing Regulations or the Exchange Rules, then it may take any of the following actions:

1) carry out any enquiries which it considers appropriate;
2) require the issuer or its representative to appear before the Authority to answer questions and explain any matters that the Authority considers relevant to the application;
3) require the issuer or third parties to provide additional information or to confirm, in such manner as the Authority may specify, that the information provided is accurate; or
4) defer making a decision for such period as may be reasonably necessary to carry out further study or examination.

d) If, having taken action pursuant to paragraph (c) of this Article, the Authority determines that the offer or registration to be made pursuant to the application may not be in the interest of the investors or may result in a breach of the Capital Market Law its Implementing Regulations or the Exchange Rules, the Authority may issue a "notification" to the issuer stating that the application has not been approved, or publish a "notice" prohibiting the offer, sale or transfer of title of the shares to which the application relates. The Authority's approval on the application of offer and registration of securities in the parallel market is considered an approval of the prospectus or shareholders' circular as applicable.

e) The Authority's approval of the application for registration and offer of shares on the parallel market or the application for shares registration on the parallel market shall be deemed as an approval of the prospectus, the shareholders' circular or the registration document, as applicable.

f) The prospectus, the shareholders' circular or the registration document (as applicable) must not be published and made available to the public without the approval of the application for registration and offer of shares or application for the registration on the parallel market by the Authority.

g) The Issuer and its financial advisor may, prior to the Authority's approval of the application for registration and offer of shares, be allowed to provide information on the Issuer and its financial statements to the group of potential investors; In order to ascertain the extent to which potential investors are willing to participate in the subscription of the Issuer's shares if they are offered, provided that this does not result in taking a binding undertaking to subscribe.

h) The Issuer and its financial advisor may, prior to the Authority's approval of the application for registration and offer of shares, be allowed to provide information on the Issuer and its financial statements to a specific group of Capital Market Institutions to conduct the advice activity for the purpose of preparing research and financial reports on the issuer, provided that such research and reports shall not be published before obtaining the approval of the Authority for the application of registration and offer of shares.

i) The issuer and its financial advisor may, prior to the Authority's approval of the application for shares registration, be allowed to provide information on the Issuer and its financial statements to the group of potential investors; In order to ascertain the extent to which potential investors are willing to invest in the Issuer's shares if they are directly listed in the Parallel Market.

j) The issuer and its financial advisor may, prior to the Authority's approval of the application for shares registration for direct listing in the Parallel Market, be allowed to provide information on the Issuer and its financial statements to a specific group of Capital Market Institutions to conduct the advice activity for the purpose of preparing research and financial reports on the issuer, provided that such research and reports shall not be published before obtaining the approval of the Authority for the application for registration of shares on the parallel market.

Article 81: Publication of Prospectus, Shareholders' Circular, Registration Document and Formal Notices
a) The issuer must publish the prospectus or the registration document (where applicable) and must ensure that it is made available to the qualified investors at least 14 days prior to the start of the offering (In case of prospectus) and before direct listing (in case of registration document).

b) Where an issuer must publish a shareholders' circular in accordance with the provisions of these Rules, it must ensure that it is made available to the qualified investors at least 14 days prior to the relevant general assembly meeting.

c) The prospectus, the shareholders' circular, the registration document (where applicable) any supplementary prospectus, any supplementary shareholders' circular or any supplementary registration document (as applicable) shall be made available to the public in electronic form on the official websites of the issuer, the Authority, the Exchange and the financial advisor.

Article 82: Dissemination of Information An issuer who is seeking to register and offer its securities in the Parallel Market, an issuer who is seeking to register its shares in the Parallel Market or an issuer whose securities are listed on the Parallel Market is subject to the provisions of Article 35 of these Rules.

Article 83: Application Submission for Capital Increase of Issuers Shares Listed in the Parallel Market Where an issuer whose shares are listed on the Parallel Market wishes to register and offer new shares of a class already listed, either by way of rights issue, capitalization issue, issuing new shares for debt conversion, acquisition of a company or asset purchase, it must obtain the Authority's approval prior to calling for the issuer's extraordinary general assembly meeting. The approval of the extraordinary general assembly of the issuer must be obtained during six months of the approval of the Authority. If the assembly's approval is not obtained during such time, the Authority's approval shall be deemed to be cancelled and the issuer will be required to resubmit its letter of application if it still wishes to increase its capital.

Article 84: Conditions related to Rights Issue In addition to any other applicable requirements under Article 75 of these Rules, where an issuer wishes to submit an application for registration and offer of securities to the Authority in respect of a rights issue the following conditions must be satisfied:

1) details of the proceeds of any previous rights issues must be provided and such details must be compared with the disclosure made under the previous prospectus; and

2) details of any qualifications made in the audited financial statements for the preceding financial year must be provided.

3) The issuer shall disclose to the public where there is discrepancy of 5% between the actual use of proceeds from issuing priority shares and what has been disclosed in the prospectus as it becomes aware.

Article 85: Conditions related to a Capitalization Issue Where an issuer wishes to increase its capital by way of a capitalization issue it must submit to the Authority a letter of application in the form set out in Annex 18 of these Rules.

Article 86: Conditions related to Increasing the Capital by Debt Conversion
a) Where an issuer whose shares are listed on the Parallel Market wishes to increase its capital by way of a debt conversion, it must produce a circular for its shareholders stating the information required to enable the shareholders to vote at the extraordinary general assembly.

b) The shareholders' circular must contain at least the information set out in Annex 22 of these Rules.

Article 87: Conditions related to Capital Increase for Acquiring a Company or Purchasing an Asset
a) In addition to any other applicable requirements under Article 75 of these Rules, where an issuer whose shares are listed on the Parallel Market wishes to increase its capital to acquire a company or purchase an asset, it must produce a circular for its shareholders stating the information required to enable the shareholders to vote at the extraordinary general assembly.

b) Shareholders' Circular shall contain at least the information set out in Annex 23 of these Rules.

Article 88: Capital Reduction for Issuers of Shares Listed on the Parallel Market
a) Where an issuer wishes to reduce its share capital, it must submit to the Authority a letter of application that includes the minimum information set out in Annex 19 of these Rules for the Authority's approval prior to obtaining the approval of the relevant extraordinary general assembly of the issuer on the capital reduction. The application must be accompanied by the following:

1) Financial advisor appointing letter.
2) Legal advisor appointing letter.
3) an external auditor's report on the reasons for the capital reduction and the impact of the capital reduction on the issuer's liabilities;
4) the proposed method of capital reduction and the expected effect of such reduction;
5) Copy of shareholders' circular referred to in paragraph (b) of this Article; and

6) any other documentation as may be required by the Authority.

b) The Issuer shall issue a circular to its shareholders containing the necessary information to enable shareholders to vote at the Extraordinary General Assembly Meeting on the basis of awareness and knowledge. The circular shall include, at a minimum, the following information:

1) The general structure of the proposed capital reduction.
2) Reasons for capital reduction, including discussion and management analysis in this regard.
3) risk factors related to capital reduction.
4) The time period of the operation.
5) A statement from the Board of Directors of the Issuer stating that they believe that the capital reduction is in the interest of the Issuer and the shareholders.

c) The shareholders' circular - submitted to the Commission on the request for reduction of the issued capital - shall be prepared in Arabic and the reference to the relevant paragraphs of these Rules shall be indicated in the margin of the Circular, indicating any change from previous drafts. Every circular draft on the first page of the draft number and date of submission.

Article 89: Continuing Obligations An issuer of securities listed on the Parallel Market must comply with Part 7 of these Rules subject to the following:

1) The phrase "the first, second, and third interim financial statements of an issuer" mentioned in paragraph (a) of Article 63 of these Rules shall be replaced with "the semi-annual interim financial statements of an issuer".

2) The issuer must disclose its interim financial statements which must be prepared and reviewed in accordance with the accounting standards approved by SOCPA as soon as they have been approved and within a maximum of 45 days of the end of the financial period covered by these statements.

3) The phrase "the financial quarter" mentioned in subparagraph (1) paragraph (a) of Article 68 of these Rules shall be replaced with "the half of the financial year".

4) Information, set forth in the Corporate Governance Regulations, that is required to be included in the board of directors' report are indicative to issuers whose shares are listed on the Parallel Market.

5) The "six months" period set forth in Article 69 of these Rules shall be replaced with "twelve months".

6) Exception from the provisions of paragraph (a) of Article 69 of these Rules, a Capital Market Institution assigned in accordance with the Listing Rules by an issuer whose shares are directly listed on the Parallel Market may sell the issuer's shares in its own discretion, provided that it is within the scope of implementing the liquidity requirement fulfillment plan provided to the Exchange pursuant to the Listing Rules.

(In accordance with the Board of the Authority's Resolution no (1-104-2019) dated 1/02/1441H corresponding to 30/9/2019G, the provisions of paragraphs (1) and (3) of this Article shall enter into force starting from 1/1/2020G.)

Article 90: Fees for the Parallel Market
a) An issuer who submits an application for approval under this Part is required to pay such fees to the Authority as the Authority specifies.

b) An issuer of securities listed on the Parallel Market is required to pay such fees to the Authority as the Authority specifies.

25.9 Part 9: PROVISIONS FOR REVERSE TAKEOVER AND DEMERGER

Article 91: Scope of Application
a) The purpose of this section is to regulate reverse takeover and demerger the merger under the Authority's powers stipulated in the Capital Market Law.

b) The provisions of this section shall apply to the following:

1) Market participants, including issuers of securities, shareholders, Capital Market Institutions, and any person who has participated or provided advice directly or indirectly in any transaction subject to the provisions of this Part.

2) Members of the Board of Directors of issuers subject to the provisions of this Part.

Article 92: General Provisions
a) The issuer, when calculating the percentage, to determine whether the transaction (or multiple transactions) constitute a demerger that requires the consent of the shareholders, shall apply all criteria for determining the applicable category, so the value of the percentage rate is the most recent published numbers of the assets value, revenues Or profits as shown in the most recent audited interim financial statements or audited annual financial statements, whichever is more recent, in addition to the market value of the issuer at the time the transaction (or multiple transactions) is declared, as applicable.

b) When making an assessment to determine whether there has been a material change in the issuer as a result of the transaction, the issuer shall consider the following:

1) The extent of the change resulting from the transaction in the direction or strategic nature of the company's business.

2) Whether the issuer's business will be considered a part of a different sector after the transaction is completed.

Article 93: Announcement and Conditions of a Reverse Takeover With regards to the provisions of Part 6 of these Rules, the issuer, when a party to the reverse takeover, shall do the following:

1) Announcing to the public, as soon as possible, after the terms of the reverse takeover have been agreed upon, and following it with supplementary announcements relating to any material changes in any matter contained in the original announcement or if an important new issue arose which should have been mentioned in the original announcement. The original announcement must include the following:

a) details of the transaction, including the name of the other party.

b) a summary of the company's activity or the asset subject to the transaction.

c) compensation and the extent to which it is satisfied (including terms related to any necessary arrangements for delaying compensation).

d) the value of the total assets of the transaction.

e) profits relating to the assets of the transaction.

f) the effect of the transaction on the listed company including any benefits expected to be received by the issuer as a result of the transaction.

g) details of any service contracts for proposed members of the Board of Directors of the Issuer.

2) Assign a financial advisor to evaluate the target entity.

3) Ensure that any agreement related to the transaction is conditional upon the approval of the shareholders.

Article 94: Potential Suspension of Listing when Announcing a Reverse Takeover
a) The issuer shall communicate with the Authority as soon as possible in the following cases:

1) prior to the announcement of any reverse takeover approved or under consideration, to discuss the appropriateness of trading suspension.

2) If the reverse takeover details leak, for the purpose of requesting suspension of trading.

b) Reverse takeover is being under consideration in any of the following cases:

1) The issuer contacting the board of directors of the target entity.

2) Entry of the issuer in an exclusive period with the target entity.

3) The issuer giving the permission to start preparing for the necessary studies (whether limited or unlimited).

Article 95: Applying Class Tests and Calculating Percentage Ratios
a) To determine whether the transaction represents a demerger that requires shareholders' approval, by reference to the percentage, the issuer shall evaluate the size of the transaction against the size of the company or the asset of the demerger transaction. The size is determined by using the percentages resulting from Applying Class Tests calculations to this transaction according to the details in Annex 24 of these Rules.

b) If any percentage calculations result in an unusual or inappropriate result of the scope of the issuer's activities, the Authority may ignore such calculations and replace it with other size related indicators, including the sector-specific measures. The listed company shall submit the alternative measures it deems appropriate to the Authority for its consideration.

c) In case of any percentage changes between the time a transaction with the Authority is discussed (as applicable) and the time of its announcement, the Issuer shall inform the Authority of such change. Moreover, the Issuer shall comply with the relevant requirements applicable to the Transaction at the time of its declaration.

Article 96: Aggregation of Transactions The Authority may request the Issuer to combine a series of transactions and act on them as if they were a single transaction, provided that all of them were completed within twelve months or were linked to each other. In such cases, the issuer must comply with the Class Tests of the transaction when aggregated and the figures to be used to determine percentages are those shown in the most recent audited financial statements or audited annual financial statements, whichever is earlier.

Article 97: Conditions relating to the Listed Company
The issuer seeking demerger shall have completed at least 3 financial years as a listed company.

Article 98: Shareholder Approval If any of the percentages set in Annex (24) of these Rules reaches 50% or more of the planned demerger, the Issuer shall obtain the prior approval of its shareholders at the General Assembly meeting. Any shareholder having a direct or indirect interest in the proposed demerger must abstain from voting on such transaction at the General Assembly meeting.

Article 99: Specialized Committee and Independent Financial Advisor
a) In respect of any demerger transaction subject to the approval of the shareholders in accordance with Article 98 of these Rules, the Issuer shall establish a Specialized Committee (consisting solely of independent Board members or of other independent persons or both of whom have no substantial interest in the proposed demerger). That's to advise shareholders on whether the terms of the relevant demerger are fair and reasonable and whether the demerger transaction is in the interest of the issuer and all of its shareholders.

b) The Issuer shall appoint a Financial Advisor authorized by the Authority to provide advisory services and make recommendations to the Specialized Committee and the Shareholders as to whether the terms of the relevant demerger are fair and reasonable and whether the demerger transaction is in the interest of the issuer and all of its shareholders.

Article 100: Circular to Shareholders
a) In respect of any demerger transaction subject to the approval of the shareholders in accordance with Article 98 of these Rules, the Issuer shall prepare a circular on the proposed demerger to be submitted to shareholders, published and made available to the public at least 14 days prior to the date of the General Assembly In which the shareholders will vote on the demerger. The circular shall include, at a minimum, the following:

1) sufficient information on the proposed demerger, provided that such information includes a minimum:

a. Proposed structure and purpose of the demerger.
b. The most prominent financial information illustrating the financial impact of demerger.
c. The most prominent legal information related to the terms of the demerger, which the shareholders need to make a decision based on knowledge and awareness.
d. Risk factors related to demerger.

2) a separate letter from the specialized committee advising shareholders as to whether the relevant terms of demerger are fair and reasonable in accordance with Article 99 of these Rules and whether such a demerger is in the interest of the issuer and all

of its shareholders, taking into account the recommendations of the financial advisor.

3) A separate letter from the financial advisor, including its recommendations to the specialized committee and shareholders, on whether the relevant terms of demerger are fair and reasonable, and whether this demerger is in the interest of the issuer and all of its shareholders.

4) The circular shall include the following disclaimer: "The Capital Market Authority and the Saudi Stock Exchange (Tadawul) shall not assume any responsibility for the contents of this Circular, and shall not give any assurance regarding its accuracy or completeness, and expressly disclaim any liability whatsoever for any loss Resulting from what is stated in this circular or from reliance on any part thereof ".

b) The circular and the two letters referred to in paragraph (a) of this article shall indicate the reasons behind the opinion and its main assumptions and the factors taken into account in forming the opinion.

Article 101: Requirements for Registration, Offering and Listing of Shares of the De-merged Entity In case a demerged company wishes to register, offer and list its shares in the market, all the requirements for registration and offering of securities provided for in these rules and the listing requirements stipulated in the Listing Rules must be fulfilled.

Article 102: Announcement of a Demerger The Issuer must announce that it has submitted an application for registration, offer of its securities and listing of the demerged entity as soon as the completed applications have been submitted to the Authority and the Exchange (or its equivalent in any foreign country). If the foreign state regulations require that the application for registration, offering and listing be filed confidentially, then the listed company must announce to the public its intention to file a registration, offering and listing application of the demerged entity in another country without mentioning the name of that country or market on which the demerged entity intends to list its security in.

25.10 PART 10: Publication and Entry into Force

Article 103: Publication and entry into force These Rules shall be effective as per its approval resolution.

25.11 PART 11: ANNEXES

25.12 ANNEX 1: CONTENTS OF A PRIVATE PLACEMENT NOTIFICATION IN RESPECT OF SHARES AND OTHER SECURITIES

[To be provided on the offeror's letterhead]

The following information, as applicable, must be signed and dated by the offeror or an authorized officer of the offeror and notified to the Authority at least ten days prior to the proposed date of the offer.

1) The name of the issuer, its principal place of registration and the address of its principal place of the business, in addition to the number and types of securities to be offered;

2) The name of the offeror(s), its principal place of registration and the address of its principal place of the business;

3) An acknowledgement that the offeror(s) intend(s) to make a private placement, specifying which category of private placement in Article 8 of these Rules that private placement falls into;

4) The name and address of the Capital Market Institution through which the offer is made;

5) The proposed start and end dates of the offer;

6) The class/classes of securities to be offered;

7) The offer price for each security offered (in SR);

8) The total offer size (in SR)

9) In case of limited offers, the number of offerees;

10) The number and types of securities previously issued by the offeror (and the issuer if different from the offeror) within the past 12 months;

11) The minimum amount (if any) to be paid by each offeree;

12) The total number of securities to be offered plus the total number of securities already issued by the offeror (and the issuer if different from the offeror);

13) Whether the securities to be offered are identical or, where there are differences, details of these differences;

14) Where the offeror or any of the directors, senior executives, controlling shareholders, or founding shareholders of the offeror have been convicted by a judicial authority of any violation involving fraud or dishonesty or a violation under the Capital Market Law, its Implementing Regulations or the Exchange Rules, or any legislation relating to companies or money laundering of which, details of such violation including details of the convicted party, the name of the judicial authority by which such party was convicted, the date of conviction and full particulars of the violation and the penalty imposed.

[This Annex shall be submitted electronically through the automated system determined by the Authority for this purpose and the offeror shall retain the original copies (or, where appropriate, certified copies) for a period not less than ten years. In case of a lawsuit or claim (including any existing or threatened action) or any existing investigation procedures relating to such documents, the offeror shall retain such documents until the completion of such litigation, claim or investigation procedures. Moreover, such documents must be submitted to the Authority upon request].

25.13 ANNEX 2: CONTENTS OF A PRIVATE PLACEMENT NOTIFICATION IN RESPECT OF DEBT INSTRUMENTS

[To be provided on the offeror's letterhead]

The following information, must be signed and dated by the offeror or an authorized officer of the offeror and notified to the Authority at least ten days prior to the proposed date of the offer.

1) The name of the issuer, its principal place of registration and the address of its principal place of the business, in addition to the number and types of debt instruments to be offered;

2) The name of the offeror(s), its principal place of registration and the address of its principal place of the business;

3) The category of the issuer (for example: government, semi-government, central bank, bank, corporate, insurance, special purpose vehicle);

4) The sector in which the offeror operates (for example: financial, non-financial or government);

5) The fact that the offeror(s) intend(s) to make a private placement specifying which category of private placement in Article 8 of these Rules that private placement falls into;

6) The name and address of the Capital Market Institution through which the offer is made;

7) The proposed start and end dates of the offer;

8) The currency of debt securities to be offered;

9) The types of debt securities to be offered;

10) The price of the principal and coupon (or method of calculation of return) of the offered debt securities (in SR);

11) The total offer size (in SR);

12) In case of limited offers, the number of offerees;

13) The number and types of securities, including any debt securities, previously issued by the offeror (and the issuer if different from the offeror) within the past 12 months;

14) The total number of securities to be offered plus the total number of securities already issued by the offeror (and the issuer if different from the offeror)

15) Whether the securities to be offered are identical or, where there are differences, details of these differences;

16) Where the offeror or any of the directors, senior executives, controlling shareholders, or founding shareholders of the offeror have been convicted by a judicial authority of any violation involving fraud or dishonesty or a violation under the Capital Market Law, its Implementing Regulations or the Exchange Rules, or any legislation relating to companies or money laundering of which, details of such violation including details of the convicted party, the name of the judicial authority by which such party was convicted, the date of conviction and full particulars of the violation and the penalty imposed.

[This Annex shall be submitted electronically through the automated system determined by the Authority for this purpose and the offeror shall retain the original copies (or, where appropriate, certified copies) for a period not less than ten years. In case of a lawsuit or claim (including any existing or threatened action) or any existing investigation procedures relating to such documents, the offeror shall retain such documents until the completion of such litigation, claim or investigation procedures. Moreover, such documents must be submitted to the Authority upon request].

25.14 ANNEX 3: OFFEROR DECLARATION

[To be provided on the offeror's letterhead]

To: The Authority

We, being

(insert name of the offeror(s)), hereby jointly and severally declare that to the best of our knowledge and belief (having taken reasonable care to ensure that such is the case) the information contained in the private placement notification and offering documents to be used in advertising the offer is in accordance with the facts and contains no omission likely to affect the veracity of such information and is fair, clear and not misleading.

We further declare that all the relevant conditions for making a private placement have been satisfied and have submitted or will submit all the information and documentation required to be provided to the Authority under the Rules on the Offer of Securities and Continuing Obligations.

We hereby authorize the Authority to exchange any relevant information with any authorities, agencies or bodies having responsibility for the supervision of financial services or any other relevant authorities.

Name: Signature:

Date:

Name: Signature:

Date:

[This Annex shall be submitted electronically through the automated system determined by the Authority for this purpose and the offeror shall retain the original copies (or, where appropriate, certified copies) for a period not less than ten years. In case of a lawsuit or claim (including any existing or threatened action) or any existing investigation procedures relating to such documents, the offeror shall retain such documents until the completion of such litigation, claim or investigation procedures. Moreover, such documents must be submitted to the Authority upon request].

25.15 ANNEX 3A: SPONSOR'S DECLARATION

To: The Authority

We, being (insert name of sponsor) ("the sponsor"), hereby jointly and severally declare that to the best of our knowledge and belief (having taken reasonable care to ensure that such is the case) that all information included in the private placement notification and offering documents to be used in advertising the offer are similar to the facts, clear, not misleading and have no insufficiency that may affect such information.

We confirm that all the relevant conditions for registration and admission to listing has been satisfied, and that all the information required to be delivered under the Rules on the Offer of Securities and Continuing Obligations, has been or will supplied.

We hereby authorize the Authority to exchange any relevant information with the authorities, agencies or bodies having responsibility for the supervision of financial services or other relevant authorities.

Name: Signature: Date:

Name: Signature: Date:

[This Annex shall be submitted electronically through the automated system determined by the Authority for this purpose and the offeror shall retain the original copies (or, where appropriate, certified copies) for a period not less than ten years. In case of a lawsuit or claim (including any existing or threatened action) or any existing investigation procedures relating to such documents, the offeror shall retain such documents until the completion of such litigation, claim or investigation procedures. Moreover, such documents must be submitted to the Authority upon request].

25.16 ANNEX 4: CAPITAL MARKET INSTITUTION'S DECLARATION

[To be provided on the Capital Market Institution's letterhead] To: The Authority

We,

(insert name of the "Capital Market Institution") (the Capital

Market Institution), hereby confirm that we have been appointed by

(insert name of offeror) (the offeror) to offer securities of the

offeror.

We further declare that to the best of our knowledge and belief (having taken reasonable care to ensure that such is the case) that the offeror has satisfied all the relevant conditions for making a private placement and has submitted or will submit all the information and documentation required to be provided to the Authority under the Rules on the Offer of Securities and Continuing Obligations.

We hereby authorize the Authority to exchange any relevant information with the authorities, agencies or bodies having responsibility for the supervision of financial services or other relevant authorities.

Signed on behalf of the Capital Market Institution: [the authorized officer]: Name:

Signature: Date:

[This Annex shall be submitted electronically through the automated system determined by the Authority for this purpose and the offeror shall retain the original copies (or, where appropriate, certified copies) for a period not less than ten years. In case of a lawsuit or claim (including any existing or threatened action) or any existing investigation procedures relating to such documents, the offeror shall retain such documents until the completion of such litigation, claim or investigation procedures. Moreover, such documents must be submitted to the Authority upon request].

25.17 ANNEX 5: STATEMENT TO BE INCLUDED IN THE PRIVATE PLACEMENT OFFERING DOCUMENTS

The private placement offering documents must include the following statement:

"This document may not be distributed in the Kingdom except to such persons as are permitted under the Rules on the Offer of Securities and Continuing Obligations issued by the Capital Market Authority.

The Capital Market Authority does not make any representation as to the accuracy or completeness of this document, and expressly disclaims any liability whatsoever for any loss arising from, or incurred in reliance upon, any part of this document. Prospective purchasers of the securities offered hereby should conduct their own due diligence on the accuracy of the information relating to the securities. If you do not understand the contents of this document, you should consult an authorized financial advisor."

ANNEX 5A: CONTENTS OF THE PRIVATE PLACEMENT OFFER DOCUMENT FOR SECURITIES ISSUED BY A SPECIAL PURPOSES ENTITY The Private Placement Offer Documents shall contain the following statement:

"The securities offered hereby are issued by a special purposes entity licensed by the Capital Market Authority. The Capital Market Authority maintains a register of special purposes entities and regulates the special purposes entity. The Capital Market Authority does not approve, and is not responsible for, the terms of the securities the special purposes entity issues, the financing structure the special purposes entity employs, or the investment risks and rewards associated with the securities. The Capital Market Authority does not regulate or monitor the value of the assets of the special purposes entity or the ability of the special purposes entity to meet its obligations and makes no endorsement of or recommendation about the securities."

25.18 ANNEX 6: CONTENTS OF APPLICATION

The application must be submitted on the letterhead of the issuer and contain the following information:

First: Shares

[*] Number of issued shares
[*] Class
[*] Nominal value per share (in SR)
[*] Amount paid up per share (in SR)
[*] Total amount paid up for issued shares

Second: Debt instruments and convertible debt instruments

[*] Number of debt instruments or convertible debt instruments issued
[*] Class
[*] Nominal Value
[*] Redemption value
[*] Total nominal value of the debt instruments

Third: Ownership of shares

[*] Number of holders of shares
[*] Number of issued shares
[*] Directors of the issuer
[*] Substantial shareholders
[*] Shares in public hands
[*] Shares in hands of employees
[*] Shares in hands of directors

Fourth: Type of issue for which application is being made

[*] Number or value of securities for which application is being made
[*] Description of securities for which application is being made
[*] Are the securities for which application is made identical in all respects? If not, how do they differ and when will they become identical?
[*] Details of documents of title

The application must be by way of a letter dated and signed by the issuer or an authorized officer of the issuer and contain an authorization in the form below:

"The issuer hereby authorizes the Authority to exchange any relevant information with the authorities, agencies or bodies having responsibility for the supervision of financial services or any other relevant authorities."

[This Annex shall be submitted electronically through the automated system determined by the Authority for this purpose and the offeror shall retain the original copies (or, where appropriate, certified copies) for a period not less than ten years. In case of a lawsuit or claim (including any existing or threatened action) or any existing investigation procedures relating to such documents, the offeror shall retain such documents until the completion of such litigation, claim or investigation procedures. Moreover, such documents must be submitted to the Authority upon request].

25.19 ANNEX 7: ISSUER'S DECLARATION

[To be provided on the Issuer's letterhead]

To: The Authority

We, being directors of

(insert name of "issuer") (referred to hereinafter as "the issuer"), hereby jointly and severally declare that to the best of our knowledge and belief (having taken reasonable care to ensure that such is the case) the issuer:

1) has satisfied all the relevant conditions for approval of its application for registration and offer of securities and all other relevant requirements of the Capital Market Law its Implementing Regulations and the Exchange Rules;

2) has included all the information required to be included in the prospectus or shareholders' circular [use as applicable]pursuant to the Capital Market Law and the Rules on the Offer of Securities and Continuing Obligations; and

3) has or will supply all the documents required by the Rules on the Offer of Securities and Continuing Obligations.

We confirm that there are no other facts bearing on the issuer's application for registration and offer of securities which in our opinion should have been disclosed to the Authority. We further confirm that we:

1) have read and understood the Capital Market Law, the Listing Rules of the Saudi Stock Exchange (the "Listing Rules") and the Rules on the Offer of Securities and Continuing Obligations;

2) have understood the nature of our responsibilities and obligations as directors of a company whose securities are listed; and

3) have understood in particular what is required of us to enable holders of the listed securities and the public to appraise the issuer.

We acknowledge that the issuer's securities will be entitled to remain listed only if the issuer and securities comply with the applicable requirements of the Rules on the Offer of Securities and Continuing Obligations and in the Listing Rules. We hereby jointly and severally undertake and agree to comply with the Capital Market Law and applicable regulations and rules from time to time issued by the Authority and in particular undertake and agree to comply with the continuing obligations vis-à-vis the Authority set out in the relevant Part of the Capital Market Law and the Rules on the Offer of Securities and Continuing Obligations and the Companies Law. We further jointly and severally undertake to use our best endeavors to procure that the issuer shall also comply with the Capital Market Law, the Companies Law, the Listing Rules and the Rules on the Offer of Securities and Continuing Obligations, as well as other rules from time to time issued by the Authority. We acknowledge the power of the Authority to suspend or cancel the listing of the issuer's securities and to take other actions in accordance with its rules.

We jointly and severally confirm that the funds and assets raized through the offer of any securities shall be utilized in accordance with the reasons disclosed in the relevant prospectus or shareholders' circular [use as applicable], unless we obtain the general assembly's approval for any alternative use. We further confirm that the financial information in the relevant prospectus or shareholders' circular [use as applicable] has been extracted without material adjustment from the audited financial statements, and that such financial statements have been prepared and audited in accordance with the auditing standards issued by ("please insert the accounting standard").

We hereby authorize the Authority to exchange any relevant information with the authorities, agencies or bodies having responsibility for the supervision of financial services or other relevant authorities.

Signed on behalf of the issuer: the directors

Name: Signature:

Date:

Name: Signature: Date: Name: Signature: Date:

[This Annex shall be submitted electronically through the automated system determined by the Authority for this purpose and the offeror shall retain the original copies (or, where appropriate, certified copies) for a period not less than ten years. In case of a lawsuit or claim (including any existing or threatened action) or any existing investigation procedures relating to such documents, the offeror shall retain such documents until the completion of such litigation, claim or investigation procedures. Moreover, such documents must be submitted to the Authority upon request].

25.20 ANNEX 7A: SPONSOR'S DECLARATION

To: The Authority

We, being directors of

(insert name of sponsor) ("the sponsor"),

hereby jointly and severally declare that to the best of our knowledge and belief (having taken reasonable care to ensure that such is the case) the sponsor:

1. has satisfied all the relevant conditions for registration and admission to listing and all other relevant requirements of the Capital Market Law and the Exchange Rules;

2. has included all the information required to be included in the prospectus pursuant to the

Capital Market Law and Rules on the Offer of Securities and Continuing Obligations; and

3. has or will supply all the documents required by the Capital Market Law and Rules on the

Offer of Securities and Continuing Obligations.

We confirm that there are no other facts bearing on the issuer's application for registration and admission to listing which in our opinion, should have been disclosed by the sponsor to the Authority. We further confirm that we:

1. have read and understood the Capital Market Law and the Listing Rules of the Saudi Capital Market ("Listing Rules") and the Rules on the Offer of Securities and Continuing Obligations;

2. have understood the nature of our responsibilities and obligations as directors of a sponsor; and

3. have understood in particular what is required of us to enable holders of the listed securities and the public to appraise the issuer and the sponsor.

We acknowledge that the issuer's securities will be entitled to remain listed only if the securities comply with the applicable requirements of the Listing Rules and the Rules on the Offer of Securities and Continuing Obligations, and the special purposes entity and the sponsor compliance with these requirements. We hereby jointly and severally undertake and agree to comply with the Capital Market Law, the Listing Rules, the Rules on the Offer of Securities and Continuing Obligations and other rules issued from time to time by the Authority. We, in particular, undertake and agree to comply with the continuing obligations to the Authority, as set out in the relevant part of the Capital Market Law, the Listing Rules and the Rules on the Offer of Securities and Continuing Obligations. We further jointly and severally undertake to use our best efforts to ensure that the special purposes entity and the sponsor also comply with the Capital Market Law, the Listing Rules, the Rules on the Offer of Securities and Continuing Obligations and other rules issued from time to time by the Authority. We acknowledge the power of the Authority to suspend or cancel the listing of the special purposes entity's securities and to take any other actions in accordance with its rules.

We jointly and severally confirm that the funds raized through the offer of any securities shall be utilized in accordance with the purposes disclosed in the relevant prospectus, unless we inform the Authority and the shareholders otherwise and obtain their approval for any alternative use. We further confirm that the financial information in the relevant prospectus has been obtained, without any material adjustment, from the audited financial statements and that such financial statements have been prepared and audited in accordance with the (auditing standards).

We hereby authorize the Authority to exchange any relevant information with the authorities, agencies or bodies having responsibility for the supervision of financial services or other relevant authorities.

Signed on behalf of the sponsor: the directors

Name: Signature:

Date:

Name: Signature: Date:

Name: Signature: Date:

[This Annex shall be submitted electronically through the automated system determined by the

Authority for this purpose and the offeror shall retain the original copies (or, where appropriate, certified copies) for a period not less than ten years. In case of a lawsuit or claim (including any existing or threatened action) or any existing investigation procedures relating to such documents, the offeror shall retain such documents until the completion of such litigation, claim or investigation procedures. Moreover, such documents must be submitted to the Authority upon request].

25.21 ANNEX 7B: ISSUER'S DECLARATION TO REQUEST THE REGISTRATION OF IT'S SHARES IN THE PARALLEL MARKET

[To be provided on the Issuer's letterhead]

To: The Authority

We, being directors of

(insert name of "issuer") (referred to hereinafter as "the issuer"), hereby jointly and severally declare that to the best of our knowledge and belief (having taken reasonable care to ensure that such is the case) that the issuer:

1) Has satisfied all the relevant conditions for registration of its shares and all other relevant requirements of the Capital Market Law its Implementing Regulations and the Exchange Rules;

2) Has included all the information required to be included in the registration document pursuant to the Capital Market Law and the Rules on the Offer of Securities and Continuing Obligations; and

3) Has or will supply all the documents required by the Rules on the Offer of Securities and Continuing Obligations.

We confirm that there are no other facts bearing on the issuer's application for registration and offer of securities that in our opinion should have been disclosed to the Authority. We further confirm that we:

1) have read and understood the Capital Market Law, the Listing Rules of the Saudi Stock Exchange (the "Listing Rules") and the Rules on the Offer of Securities and Continuing Obligations;

2) have understood the nature of our responsibilities and obligations as directors of a company whose securities are listed; and

3) Have understood in particular what is required of us to enable holders of the listed securities and the public to appraise the issuer.

We acknowledge that the issuer's securities will be entitled to remain listed only if the issuer and securities comply with the applicable requirements of the Rules on the Offer of Securities and Continuing Obligations and in the Listing Rules. We hereby, jointly and severally, undertake and agree to comply with the Capital Market Law and the regulations and rules issued by the Authority. We particularly undertake and agree to comply with the continuing obligations vis-à-vis the Authority set out in the relevant Part of the Capital Market Law and the Rules on the Offer of Securities and Continuing Obligations and the Companies

Law. We further jointly and severally undertake to use our best endeavors to procure that the issuer shall also comply with the Capital Market Law, the Companies Law, the Listing Rules and the Rules on the Offer of Securities and Continuing Obligations, as well as other rules from issued by the Authority time to time. We acknowledge the power of the Authority to suspend or cancel the listing of the issuer's securities and to take other actions in accordance with its rules.

We further confirm that the financial information in the relevant registration document has been extracted without material adjustment from the audited financial statements, and that such financial statements have been prepared and audited in accordance with the auditing standards issued by ("please insert the accounting standard").

We hereby authorize the Authority to exchange any relevant information with the authorities, agencies or bodies having responsibility for the supervision of financial services or other relevant authorities.

Signed on behalf of the issuer: the directors

Name: Signature: Date: Name: Signature: Date: Name: Signature: Date:

[This Annex shall be submitted electronically through the automated system determined by the Authority for this purpose and the offeror shall retain the original copies (or, where appropriate, certified copies) for a period not less than ten years. In case of a lawsuit or claim (including any existing or threatened action) or any existing investigation procedures relating to such documents, the offeror shall retain such documents until the completion of such litigation, claim or investigation procedures. Moreover, such documents must be submitted to the Authority upon request].

25.22 ANNEX 8: DIRECTOR'S DECLARATION

Each director (or comparable official) of an issuer must sign and submit a declaration containing the following information:

I: Information regarding board members:

1) Full name.
2) Passport / Civil Registry number.
3) Date of birth.
4) Residential address.
5) Nationality.
6) Professional and academic qualifications, if any.
7) Business experience during the last five years (to include name of the organization, the nature of its business, dates of employment and the positions held).

II: Answer the following questions:

1) Are you a director of any other organization or a partner in any partnership? If yes, state the name of any such organization or partnership, its legal status, the nature of its business, and date you became a director or partner.

2) Have you at any time been declared bankrupt in any jurisdiction? If so, state the court by which you were adjudged bankrupt and, if discharged, the date and conditions on which you were granted your discharge.

3) Have you at any time been a party to a deed of arrangement or made any other form of composition with your creditors?

4) Are there any unsatisfied judgements outstanding against you? If so, give full particulars.

5) Are you aware of any lawsuits, litigation, investigations or any similar regulatory or governmental action against you? If so, give full particulars.

6) Has any company or special purposes entity been put into compulsory liquidation or has an administrator or an administrative or other receiver been appointed during the period when you were one of its directors? If so, give full particulars.

7) Has any partnership been put into compulsory liquidation or been sequestrated during the period when you were one of its partners? If so, in each case state the name, nature of business, date of commencement of winding up, administration or receivership and the amount together with an indication of the outcome or current position.

8) Have you at any time or has a company or special purposes entity of which you were a director at the time of the offense been convicted in any jurisdiction of any offense involving fraud or dishonesty or an offense under legislation relating to companies or money laundering. If so, all such convictions must be disclosed together with the name of the court by which you were or the company was convicted, the date of conviction and full particulars of the offense and the penalty imposed.

9) Have you, in connection with the formation or management of any company, partnership or unincorporated institution been adjudged by a court in any jurisdiction civilly liable for any fraud, misfeasance or other misconduct by you towards it or towards any of its members? If so, give full particulars.

10) Have you ever been disqualified by a court from acting as a director of a company or special purposes entity, or from acting in the management or conduct of the affairs of any company or special purposes entity? If so, give full particulars.

11) Have you been refused membership or renewal of membership in any professional body, institution or association, or stock exchange or been censured or disciplined or had membership withdrawn by any such body to which you belong or belonged or have you held a practicing certificate subject to conditions? If so, give full particulars.

III: A declaration in the following form:

"I [Insert Name] being a director of the company or special purposes entity [state name of company or special purposes entity] declare that to the best of my knowledge and belief (having taken all reasonable care to ensure that such is the case) the answers to all the above questions are true and complete. I hereby authorize the Authority to exchange any relevant information with the authorities, agencies or bodies having responsibility for the supervision of financial services or any other relevant authorities."

Name: Signature:

Date:

[This Annex shall be submitted electronically through the automated system determined by the Authority for this purpose and the offeror shall retain the original copies (or, where appropriate, certified copies) for a period not less than ten years. In case of a lawsuit or claim (including any existing or threatened action) or any existing investigation procedures relating to such documents, the offeror shall retain such documents until the completion of such litigation, claim or investigation procedures. Moreover, such documents must be submitted to the Authority upon request].

25.23 ANNEX 8(A): DIRECTOR'S DECLARATION IN A STRUCTURE WITH RIGHT TO RECOURSE

Each director (or comparable official) of an issuer must sign and submit a declaration containing the following information:

I: Information regarding the board member:

1) Full name.
2) Passport / Civil Registry number.
3) Date of birth.
4) Residential address.
5) Nationality.
6) Professional and academic qualifications, if any.
7) Business experience during the last five years (to include name of the organization, the nature of its business, dates of employment and the positions held).

II: Answer the following questions:

1) Are you a director of any other organization or a partner in any partnership? If yes, state the name of any such organization or partnership, its legal status, the nature of its business, and date you became a director or partner.

2) Have you at any time been declared bankrupt in any jurisdiction? If so, state the court by which you were adjudged bankrupt and, if discharged, the date and conditions on which you were granted your discharge.

3) Have you at any time been a party to a deed of arrangement or made any other form of composition with your creditors?

4) Are there any unsatisfied judgements outstanding against you? If so, give full particulars.

5) Are you aware of any lawsuits, litigation, investigations or any similar regulatory or governmental action against you? If so, give full particulars.

6) Has any company been put into compulsory liquidation or appointed to an administrator or a receiver during the period when you were one of its directors? If so, give full particulars.

7) Has any partnership been put into compulsory liquidation or been sequestrated during the period when you were one of its partners? If so, in each case state the name, nature of business, date of commencement of liquidation, the administration or receivership appointed by the court and the amount, together with an indication of the outcome or current position.

8) Have you at any time or has a company of which you were a director at the time of the offense been convicted in any jurisdiction of any offense involving fraud, dishonesty or an offense under legislation relating to companies or money laundering. If so, all such convictions must be disclosed together with the name of the court by which you were or the company was convicted, the date of conviction and full particulars of the offense and the penalty imposed.

9) Have you, in connection with the formation or management of any company, partnership or unincorporated institution been adjudged, by a court in any jurisdiction, as civilly liable for any fraud, misfeasance or other misconduct by you towards it or towards any of its members? If so, give full particulars.

10) Have you ever been disqualified by a court in any jurisdiction from acting as a director of a company, or from acting in the management or conduct of the affairs of any company? If so, give full particulars.

11) Have you been denied membership or renewal of membership in any professional body, institution, association, or stock exchange in any jurisdiction? Or have you been censured or disciplined or had membership withdrawn by any such body to which you belong or belonged? or have you held a practicing certificate subject to conditions? If so, give full particulars.

III: A declaration in the following form:

"I [Insert Name] being a director of [state name of sponsor] declare that to the best of my knowledge and belief (having taken all reasonable care to ensure that such is the case) the answers to all the above questions are true and complete. Thus, I hereby authorize the Authority to exchange any relevant information with the authorities, agencies or bodies having responsibility for the supervision of financial services or any other relevant authorities."

[This Annex shall be submitted electronically through the automated system determined by the Authority for this purpose and the offeror shall retain the original copies (or, where appropriate, certified copies) for a period not less than ten years. In case of a lawsuit or claim (including any existing or threatened action) or any existing investigation procedures relating to such documents, the offeror shall retain such documents until the completion of such litigation, claim or investigation procedures. Moreover, such documents must be submitted to the Authority upon request].

25.24 ANNEX 9: CONTENTS OF A PROSPECTUS FOR SHARES

A prospectus submitted as part of an application for registration and offer of shares must contain the information under the following sections at a minimum:

1. Cover page

This section must include the following information (where applicable):

1) the issuer's name, incorporation date and commercial registration number;
2) capital and number of shares;
3) a summary of the offer including share class and rights;
4) substantial shareholders;
5) targeted types of investors;
6) offer period and conditions;
7) shares that have been listed prior to the particular offer by the issuer (if applicable);
8) a statement that the issuer has submitted the application for registration and offer of securities subject to this prospectus to the Authority, and an application for listing of shares on the Exchange, and that all required documents have been submitted to the relevant authorities;
9) a statement referring to the "Important Notice" and the "Risk Factors" under section (2) and section (10) of this Annex, respectively before making an investment decision; and

10) the following declaration:

"This prospectus includes information provided as part of the application for registration and offer of securities in compliance with the Rules on the Offer of Securities and Continuing Obligations of the Capital Market Authority of the Kingdom of Saudi Arabia (the "Authority") and the application for listing of securities in compliance with the Listing Rules of the Saudi Stock Exchange. The directors, whose names appear on page [ ], collectively and individually accept full responsibility for the accuracy of the information contained in this prospectus and confirm, having made all reasonable enquiries, that to the best of their knowledge and belief, there are no other facts the omission of which would make any statement herein misleading. The Authority and the Exchange do not take any responsibility for the contents of this prospectus, do not make any representation as to its accuracy or completeness, and expressly disclaim any liability whatsoever for any loss arising from, or incurred in reliance upon, any part of this prospectus."

2. Important notice

This section must include a notice which shows the purpose and the nature of information mentioned in the prospectus.

3. Corporate directory

This section must include the following:

1) the issuer's and its representatives' contact information, including addresses, telephone and fax numbers, e-mail addresses, and the issuer's website.

2) the contact information, including addresses, telephone and fax numbers, and website and e-mail addresses, for each of the parties listed below, and any other expert to whom a statement or report included in the prospectus has been attributed:

a) the financial advisor;
b) the legal advisor;
c) the external auditor;
d) the underwriter; and
e) receiving entities

4. Offer summary

This section must include a disclaimer to the targeted investors on the importance of reading the prospectus prior to making an investment decision and include the following information (where applicable):

1) the issuer's name, description and incorporation information;
2) the issuer's activities;
3) substantial shareholders showing their ownership percentages and number of shares pre- and post-offering;
4) the capital of the issuer;
5) issuer's total number of shares;
6) the nominal value per share;
7) the total number of offered shares;
8) the percentage of offered shares to the capital of the issuer;
9) the offer price;
10) the total value of offer;
11) the use of the proceeds;
12) the number of offer shares underwritten;
13) the value of offer shares underwritten;
14) types of targeted investors;
15) the total number of offered shares available to each type of targeted investors;
16) subscription procedure for each type of targeted investors;
17) the minimum number of shares to be subscribed for by each type of targeted investors;
18) the minimum value of shares to be subscribed for by each type of targeted investors;
19) the maximum number of shares to be subscribed for by each type of targeted investors;
20) the maximum value of shares to be subscribed for by each type of targeted investors;
21) allocation method and description of the process where an excess of subscription monies has been received for each type of targeted investors;
22) the offer period;
23) the rights to dividends;
24) voting rights;
25) restrictions on shares;
26) a statement regarding whether or not there has been a prior listing of the issuer's shares; and
27) a statement emphasizing the importance of considering the "Important Notice" and "Risk Factors" under section (2) and section (10) of this Annex, respectively prior to making an investment decision in the offered shares.

5. Key dates and subscription procedure

This section must include:

1) a timetable showing the expected dates of the offering; and

2) a description of the subscription procedure.

6. Summary of basic information

This section must include a summary of the basic information contained in the prospectus, including:

1) a disclaimer to investors about consideration of the prospectus as a whole, and not merely the summary;
2) a description of the issuer;
3) the issuer's mission and overall strategy;
4) the issuer's key strengths and competitive advantages; and
5) an overview of the market.

7. Summary of financial information

This section must include a summary of key financial information contained in the prospectus, including issuer's operational performance, financial condition, cash flows, and key performance indicators.

8. Table of contents

This section must include the prospectus table of contents.

9. Terms and definitions

This section must include the terms and definitions used through the prospectus.

10. Risk factors

This section must include information in relation to risk factors specific to:

1) the issuer;
2) the market or industry in which the issuer operates; and
3) the securities being offered.

11. Market and industry information

This section must include information on market trends and industry information specific to the issuer's operations and the source of the information contained therein.

12. Issuer's background and business nature

This section must include the following information:

1) the official name, commercial registration number and the address shown in the commercial registration and, if different, the principal address of the issuer;

2) the date of incorporation of the issuer;

3) the authorized shares of the issuer, the number of shares issued or agreed to be issued, the value paid up, the nominal value and a description of the shares;

4) a description and organization chart of the group showing the issuer's position within that group (if applicable);

5) the general nature of the business of the issuer and the issuer's substantial subsidiaries (if applicable) and details of the main products sold or services performed and an indication of any significant new products or activities;

6) if the issuer or the issuer's substantial subsidiaries (if applicable) trades outside the Kingdom, a statement showing the location of such trading operations must be provided. Where a material portion of the issuer or the issuer's subsidiaries assets' are outside the Kingdom, the value and location of such assets and the value of the assets located in the Kingdom;

7) information concerning the policy of the issuer and the issuer's substantial subsidiaries (if applicable) on the research and development of new products and production processes over the past three financial years, where significant;

8) particulars of any interruption in the business of the issuer and the issuer's substantial subsidiaries (if applicable) which may have or has had a significant effect on the financial position in the last 12 months;

9) the number of people employed by the issuer and the issuer's substantial subsidiaries (if applicable) and any material changes to that number over the last two financial years, with a breakdown of persons employed by main categories of activity and by Saudization ratio; and

10) a statement that no material change in the nature of the business is contemplated or, if one is contemplated, a detailed description of that change and its impact on the issuer's business and profitability.

For the purpose of measuring the substantiality of a subsidiary, the issuer and its financial advisors must consider its impact on the investment decision in the securities and its price, including but not limited to, a subsidiary is considered substantial if it constitutes 5% or more of the total assets, liabilities, revenues or profits of the issuer, or any potential obligations or on it.

13. Ownership and Organizational structure

This section must include the following information:

1) Ownership structure pre- and post-offering

2) Management:

a) the issuer's organizational chart showing the directors structure, supervisory committees, and the functions of senior executives;

b) the full names and description of the most significant professional and academic qualifications and area of expertise and the date of appointment of all the directors or proposed directors (showing whether the director is independent or executive or non-executive), in addition to the senior executives and the secretary of the board;

c) details of other previous or current board positions held by all the directors or proposed directors, senior executives, and the secretary of the board. The details should include the name of the company, legal entity, membership dates, and the sector in which the company operates;

d) details of any bankruptcies of each director or proposed director, senior executives, or the secretary of the board;

e) details of any company insolvency in the preceding five years where any of the directors or proposed directors, senior executives, or the secretary of the board were employed by the insolvent company in a managerial or supervisory capacity;

f) a statement showing the direct or indirect interests of each director or proposed director, senior executives, secretary of the board, and any of their relatives in (i) the shares or debt instruments of the issuer or (ii) the issuer's subsidiaries (if applicable) or (iii) that may in any way affect the business of the issuer, or provide an appropriate negative statement;

g) the aggregate remuneration and benefits in kind granted by the issuer or any affiliate during the three financial years prior to offering to the directors and the five senior executives who received the highest payments, including the CEO and CFO if they were not within the top five;

h) a summary of existing or proposed service contracts, if any, of the directors, the CEO, and CFO;

i) full particulars of any contract or arrangement in effect or contemplated at the time of submission of the prospectus in which a director or senior executive or any of their relatives is interested in relation to the business of the issuer or the issuer's subsidiaries (if applicable), or provide an appropriate negative statement;

j) information about the issuer's directors' committees, including the names of each committee member and a summary of the terms of reference under which the committee operates; and

k) information on the issuer's compliance with Corporate Governance Regulations.

3) Employees

a. any employee share-schemes in place prior to the application for registration and offer of securities that are subject to this prospectus along with details on the aggregate amount of shares owned by the employees in the issuer; and

b. any other arrangements involving the employees in the capital of the issuer.

14. Financial information and management discussion and analysis

The information required below must be provided in relation to the issuer and the issuer's substantial subsidiaries (if applicable) for the three financial years immediately preceding the application for registration and offer of the securities that are subject to this prospectus as well as the period covered in the interim financial statements as per paragraph (4) of Article 23 of the Rules on the Offer of Securities and Continuing Obligations:

1. comparative tables of financial information with commentary and analysis by management. The comparative tables must:

a) be prepared on a consolidated basis;

b) be extracted without material adjustment from audited financial statements; and

c) include financial information presented in a form consistent with that which is adopted in the issuer's annual financial statements.

2. a report by certified external auditor to be prepared in accordance with the requirements of Annex 15 of the Rules on the Offer of Securities and Continuing Obligations in any of the following circumstances:

a) where the external auditors' report on the financial statements of the issuer for any of the last three financial years immediately preceding the application for registration and offer of securities that are subject to this prospectus has been qualified;

b) where the issuer has undergone restructuring in the three financial years immediately preceding the date of the application for registration and offer of securities that are subject to this prospectus;

c) where any material change has been made to the accounting policies of the issuer; or

d) where any material adjustment has been made or is required to be made to the published audited financial statements during the periods referred to in sub- paragraph (a) above.

3. details of holdings, including holdings in contractually based securities or other assets whose value may be subject to fluctuations or be difficult to ascertain with certainty, significantly affecting the assessment of the issuer's financial position.

4. the information required below must be provided in relation to the financial, operating performance, and results of operations:

a) performance indicators;
b) the financial, operating performance, and results of operations of the main lines of business;
c) any seasonal or business cycles which affect the business or the financial condition;
d) an explanation of any material changes from year to year in the financial information;
e) information regarding any governmental, economic, fiscal, monetary or political policies or other factors that have materially affected, or could materially affect, directly or indirectly, the operations;
f) the funding structure;
g) particulars of any alterations in the capital of the issuer, or where material, any of the issuer's substantial subsidiaries (if applicable) within the three years immediately preceding the date of the application for registration and offer of securities that are subject to this prospectus. Such particulars must state the price and terms of any issues by the issuers or its subsidisers; and
h) a table showing any capital of the issuer or any subsidiaries subsidiary which is under option, including the consideration for which the option was granted, and the price and duration of the option, and the name and address of the grantee, or provide an appropriate negative statement.

5. property, plant and equipment

a) a breakdown of any existing material fixed assets, including leased properties;
b) an explanation of the issuer's depreciation policy and any changes contemplated in that policy; and
c) any planned material fixed assets, including leased properties.

6. in relation to debt, a statement on a consolidated basis as at the most recent date must be prepared covering the following:

a) a breakdown and classification of any debt instruments issued and outstanding, and authorized or otherwise created but unissued, and term loans, distinguishing between guaranteed, unguaranteed, secured (whether the pledge is provided by the issuer or by third parties) and unsecured loans, or provide an appropriate negative statement;

b) a breakdown and classification of all other borrowing or indebtedness, including bank overdrafts, liabilities under acceptances, acceptance credits or hire purchase commitments, distinguishing between guaranteed, unguaranteed, secured and unsecured borrowing and debt, or provide an appropriate negative statement;

c) a breakdown and classification of all mortgages, rights and charges on the issuer, and its subsidiaries' properties, or provide an appropriate negative statement; and

d) a breakdown of any contingent liabilities or guarantees, or provide an appropriate negative statement.

7. a working capital statement in accordance with paragraph (8) of Article 23 of the Rules on the Offer of Securities and Continuing Obligations.

8. a statement by the directors of any material adverse change in the financial or trading position in the three financial years preceding the application for registration and offer of securities that are subject to this prospectus and during the period from the end of the period covered in the external auditors' report up to and including the date of approval of the prospectus, or provide an appropriate negative statement.

9. particulars of any commissions, discounts, brokerages or other non-cash compensation granted within the three years immediately preceding the application for registration and offer of securities that are the subject of this prospectus in connection with the issue or offer of any securities by the issuer or any of the issuer's subsidiaries (if applicable), together with the names of any directors, proposed directors, senior executives, persons offering or placing the securities or experts who received any such payment or benefit, or provide an appropriate negative statement.

For the purpose of measuring the substantiality of a subsidiary, the issuer and its financial advisors must consider its impact on the investment decision in the securities and its price, including but not limited to, a subsidiary is considered substantial if it constitutes 5% or more of the total assets, liabilities, revenues or profits of the issuer, or any potential obligations or on it.

15. Dividend policy

This section must include an explanation of the issuer's dividend policy, as well as details on any dividend payments made during the last three years.

16. Use of proceeds and future projects

a) This section must include an estimate of the proceeds of the offer and the offer expenses and a statement as to how such proceeds are intended to be used.

b) Where the proceeds are to be used to fund future projects, the nature of these projects should be described and the following information included:

1) future projects' key milestones and timetable; and

2) an estimate and breakdown of future projects costs, showing the stage in which such costs will be incurred, in addition to details regarding the sources of financing.

17. Statements by experts

Where the prospectus includes a statement made by an expert, a statement should be included specifying the qualifications of the expert and whether such expert or any relative has any shareholding or interest of any kind in the issuer or any of its subsidiaries. In addition, the statement should confirm that the expert has given and not withdrawn his written consent to the publication in the prospectus of the expert's statement included in the form and context in which it is included.

18. Declarations

The directors of the issuer must make the following declarations:

1) other than what has been mentioned on page ( ) of this prospectus, there has not been any interruption in the business of the issuer or any of the issuer's subsidiaries (if applicable) which may have or has had a significant effect on the financial position in the last 12 months.

2) other than what has been mentioned on page ( ) of this prospectus, no commissions, discounts, brokerages or other non-cash compensation have been granted within the three years immediately preceding the application for registration and offer of securities that are the subject of this prospectus in connection with the issue or offer of any securities by the issuer or any of the issuer's subsidiaries (if applicable).

3) other than what has been mentioned on page ( ) of this prospectus, there has not been any material adverse change in the financial or trading position of the issuer or its subsidiaries (if applicable) in the three financial years preceding the application for registration and offer of securities that are subject to this prospectus and during the period from the end of the period covered in the external auditors' report up to and including the date of approval of the prospectus.

4) other than what is mentioned on page ( ) of this prospectus, they do not have any shareholding or interest of any kind in the issuer or any of the issuer's subsidiaries (if applicable), and nor does any relative of theirs.

5) The Issuer - individually or jointly with its subsidiaries (if any) – has a working capital sufficient for a period of at least 12 months immediately following the date of publication of the Prospectus.

19. Legal information

This section must include the following legal information:

1) the following declarations from the board of directors that:

a) the issuance does not constitute a breach of the relevant laws and regulations in Saudi Arabia;

b) the issuance does not constitute a breach of any contract/agreement entered into by the issuer;

c) all material legal issues concerning the issuer have been disclosed in the prospectus;

d) other than what has been mentioned on page (•) of this prospectus, the issuer and its subsidiaries are not subject to any claims, litigious cases or any other type of legal proceedings that could individually or collectively have a material effect on the business of the issuer or its subsidiaries or their financial position; and

e) other than what has been mentioned on page (•) of this prospectus, the directors are not subject to any claims, litigious cases or any other type of legal proceedings that could individually or collectively have a material effect on the business of the issuer or its subsidiaries or their financial position.

2) a summary of the provisions of the issuer's bylaws and other constitutional documents, including but not limited to:

a) the object clause;
b) provisions relating to the issuer's administrative, management and supervisory bodies;
c) provisions relating to the rights and restrictions attached to the issuer's securities;
d) provisions governing the alteration of share rights or classes;
e) provisions governing the conduct of general assembly meetings;
f) provisions governing liquidation and winding up;
g) any power enabling a director or the CEO to vote on a contract or proposal in which he has an interest;
h) any power enabling a director or the CEO to vote on remuneration to themselves; and
i) any powers allowing the directors or the senior executives to borrow from the issuer.

3) a summary of all material contracts.

4) a summary of all related party material contracts.

5) in relation to the issuer and its subsidiaries (if applicable), the following must be included:

a) particulars of any intangible assets such as trademarks, patents, copyright or other intellectual property rights which are material in relation to the issuer's or any of its subsidiaries (if applicable) business or profitability, and a statement regarding the extent to which the issuer or any of its subsidiaries (if applicable) is dependent on such assets; and

b) particulars of any litigation or claim (including any litigation pending or threatened) or any ongoing investigations which may have a material effect on the issuer's or any of its subsidiaries business or financial position, or an appropriate negative statement.

6) as to the shares that are the subject of the application, a description of the rights of the holders of the shares must be provided, as follows:

a) the voting rights, rights to dividends, rights to redemption or repurchase or to surplus assets on liquidation, winding up or otherwise, and all other significant information regarding the rights of the holders of such shares; and

b) a summary of the approvals necessary for the variation of such rights.

20. Underwriter

This section must include information about the underwriter of the offer, as follows:

1) the name and address of the underwriter; and

2) the principal terms of the underwriting agreement, including the compensation arrangement between the issuer and the underwriter.

21. Expenses

This section must include details of the aggregate offer expenses.

22. Waivers

This section must include details on all requirements that have been waived for the issuer by the Authority.

23. Information concerning the shares and terms and conditions of the offer

This section must include the following information:

1) a statement that application has been made to the Authority for the application for registration and offer of securities and to the Exchange for listing;
2) the type and total value of the offer including the number of shares being offered;
3) the offer price and the nominal value of each share;
4) the subscription method;
5) the offer period and conditions;
6) the method of allocation of the shares and refund of excess monies;
7) when and under what circumstances the offer may be suspended;
8) a description of the resolutions, and approvals by virtue of which the shares will be offered;
9) details of any lock-up arrangement in place restricting the disposal of particular shares; and
10) if a public or private offer has been or is being made simultaneously on the markets of two or more countries at the same time, and if a tranche has been or is being reserved for certain of these markets, details of any such offer or tranche must be provided.

24. Subscription Declarations

This section must include information on the subscription declarations, allocation process, and the Exchange's details.

25. Documents available for inspection

This section must include information in relation to the place in the Kingdom at which the following documents may be inspected and the period of time during which the inspection may take place (being not less than 20 days before the end of the offer period):

1) the bylaws and other constitutional documents of the issuer;
2) any document or order granting permission to offer securities to the public;
3) each contract disclosed pursuant to sub-paragraph (i) of paragraph (2) of section (13) of this Annex or, if the contract is not produced in writing, a memorandum giving full particulars of the agreement;
4) all other reports, letters, documents, value estimates or statements by any expert any part of which is extracted or referred to in the prospectus; and
5) the audited financial statements of the issuer for each of the three financial years immediately preceding the date of the publication of the prospectus, in addition to the most recent interim financial statements.

26. External auditor's report

The issuer's audited financial statements for the three years immediately preceding the date of the publishing the prospectus, in addition to the most recent interim financial statements.

25.25 ANNEX 10: CONTENTS OF A PROSPECTUS FOR A RIGHTS ISSUE

A prospectus submitted as part of an application for registration and offer of preference shares must contain the information under the following sections at a minimum:

1. Cover page

This section must include the following information (where applicable):

1) a summary of the offer including share class and rights;

2) targeted types of investors;

3) offer period and conditions;

4) shares that have been listed prior to the particular offer by the issuer;

5) a statement that the issuer has submitted the application for registration and offer of securities that are subject to this prospectus to the Authority and the application for listing to the Exchange and has submitted all the required documents to the relevant authorities;

6) a statement referring to the "Important Notice" and the "Risk Factors" under section (2) and section (10) of this Annex, respectively before making an investment decision; and (7) the following declaration:

"This prospectus includes information provided as part of the application for registration and offer of securities in compliance with the Rules on the Offer of Securities and Continuing Obligations of the Capital Market Authority of the Kingdom of Saudi Arabia (the "Authority") and the application for listing of securities in compliance with the Listing Rules of the Saudi Stock Exchange. The directors, whose names appear on page [ ], collectively and individually accept full responsibility for the accuracy of the information contained in this prospectus and confirm, having made all reasonable enquiries, that to the best of their knowledge and belief, there are no other facts the omission of which would make any statement herein misleading. The Authority and the Saudi Stock Exchange do not take any responsibility for the contents of this prospectus, do not make any representation as to its accuracy or completeness, and expressly disclaim any liability whatsoever for any loss arising from, or incurred in reliance upon, any part of this prospectus."

2. Important notice

This section must include a notice which shows the purpose and the nature of information mentioned in the prospectus.

3. Corporate directory

This section must include the following:

1) the issuer's and its representatives' contact information, including addresses, telephone and fax numbers, e-mail addresses, and the issuer's website.

2) the contact information, including addresses, telephone and fax numbers, and website and e-mail addresses, for each of the parties listed below, and any other expert to whom a statement or report included in the prospectus has been attributed:

a) the financial advisor;
b) the legal advisor;
c) the external auditor;
d) the underwriter; and
e) receiving entities

4. Offer summary

This section must include a disclaimer to the targeted investors on the importance of reading the prospectus prior to making an investment decision and contain the following information (where applicable):

1) the issuer's name, description and incorporation information;

2) the issuer's activities;

3) substantial shareholders showing their ownership percentages and number of shares pre- offering;

4) the purpose(s) of the issuance of the proposed rights issue;

5) the total proceeds expected to be raized and a detailed breakdown and description of the proposed use of the proceeds;

6) the total proceeds raized on the most recent rights issue, its breakdown and description as well as the use, or (where applicable) the expected use of such proceeds not yet utilized;

7) any information required under Annex 9 of the Rules on the Offer of Securities and Continuing Obligations that has materially changed since approval of the most recent prospectus;

8) any additional information required by the Authority to be provided in the rights issue prospectus as it deems appropriate;

9) the capital of the issuer;

10) issuer's total number of shares;

11) the nominal value per share;

12) the total number of offered shares;

13) the percentage of offered shares to the capital of the issuer;

14) the offer price;

15) the total value of offer;

16) the number of offer shares underwritten;

17) the value of offer shares underwritten;

18) types of targeted investors;

19) the total number of offered shares available to each type of targeted investors;

20) the minimum number of shares to be subscribed for by each type of targeted investors;

21) the minimum value of shares to be subscribed for by each type of targeted investors;

22) the maximum number of shares to be subscribed for by each type of targeted investors;

23) the maximum value of shares to be subscribed for by each type of targeted investors;

24) allocation method and description of the process where an excess of subscription monies has been received for each type of targeted investors;

25) the offer period;

26) the rights to dividends;

27) voting rights;

28) restrictions on shares or rights;

29) a statement regarding whether or not there has been a prior listing of the issuer's shares; and

30) a statement emphasizing the importance of considering the "Important Notice" and "Risk Factors" under section (2) and section (10) of this Annex, respectively prior to making an investment decision in the offered shares.

5. Key dates and subscription procedure

This section must include:

1) a timetable showing the expected dates of the offering; and

2) a description of the subscription procedure.

6. Summary of basic information

This section must contain a summary of the basic information contained in the prospectus, including:

1) a disclaimer to investors about consideration of the prospectus as a whole, and not merely the summary;

2) a description of the issuer;

3) the issuer's mission and overall strategy;

4) the issuer's key strengths and competitive advantages; and

5) an overview of the market.

7. Summary of financial information

This section must contain a summary of key financial information contained in the prospectus, including issuer's operational performance, financial condition, cash flows, and key performance indicators.

8. Table of contents

This section must include the prospectus table of contents.

9. Terms and definitions

This section must include the terms and definitions used through the prospectus.

10. Risk factors

This section must contain information in relation to risk factors specific to:

1) the issuer;

2) the market or industry in which the issuer operates; and

3) the securities being offered.

11. Employees

1) Any employee share schemes in place prior to the application for registration and offer of securities that are subject to this prospectus along with details on the aggregate amount of shares owned by the employees in the issuer; and

2) Any other arrangements involving the employees in the capital of the issuer.

12. Financial information and management discussion and analysis

The information required below must be provided in relation to the issuer and the issuer's substantial subsidiaries (if applicable) for the three financial years immediately preceding the application for registration and offer of securities that are subject to this prospectus as well as the period covered in the interim financial statements as per paragraph (4) of Article 23 of the Rules on the Offer of Securities and Continuing Obligations:

1) comparative tables of financial information with commentary and analysis by management. The comparative tables must:

a) be prepared on a consolidated basis;
b) be extracted without material adjustment from audited financial statements; and
c) include financial information presented in a form consistent with that which is adopted in the issuer's annual financial statements.

2) a report by certified external auditor to be prepared in accordance with the requirements of Annex 15 of the Rules on the Offer of Securities and Continuing Obligations in any of the following circumstances:

a) where the external auditors' report on the financial statements of the issuer for any of the last three financial years immediately preceding the application for registration and offer of securities that are subject to this prospectus has been qualified;

b) where the issuer has undergone restructuring during the three financial years immediately preceding the date of the application for registration and offer of securities that are subject to this prospectus;

c) where any material change has been made to the accounting policies of the issuer; or

d) where any material adjustment has been made or is required to be made to the published audited financial statements during the periods referred above.

3) details of holdings, including holdings in contractually based securities or other assets whose value may be subject to fluctuations or be difficult to ascertain with certainty, significantly affecting the assessment of the issuer's financial position.

4) the information required below must be provided in relation to the financial, operating performance, and results of operations:

a) performance indicators;
b) the financial, operating performance, and results of operations of the main lines of business;
c) any seasonal or business cycles which affect the business or the financial condition;
d) an explanation of any material changes from year to year in the financial information;
e) information regarding any governmental, economic, fiscal, monetary or political policies or other factors that have materially affected, or could materially affect, directly or indirectly, the operations;
f) the funding structure;
g) particulars of any alterations in the capital of the issuer, or where material, any of the issuer's substantial subsidiaries (if applicable) within the three years immediately preceding the date of the application for registration and offer of securities that are subject to this prospectus. Such particulars must state the price and terms of any issues by the issuers or its subsidizers; and
h) a table showing any capital of the issuer or any substantial subsidiary which is under option, including the consideration for which the option was granted, and the price and duration of the option, and the name and address of the grantee, or provide an appropriate negative statement.

For the purpose of measuring the substantiality of a subsidiary, the issuer and its financial advisors must consider its impact on the investment decision in the securities and its price, including but not limited to, a subsidiary is considered substantial if it constitutes 5% or more of the total assets, liabilities, revenues or profits of the issuer, or any potential obligations or on it.

5) property, plant and equipment

a) a breakdown of any existing material fixed assets, including leased properties;

b) an explanation of the issuer's depreciation policy and any changes contemplated in that policy; and

c) any planned material fixed assets, including leased properties.

6) in relation to debt, a statement on a consolidated basis as at the most recent date must be prepared covering the following:

a) a breakdown and classification of any debt instruments issued and outstanding, and authorized or otherwise created but unissued, and term loans, distinguishing between guaranteed, unguaranteed, secured (whether the pledge is provided by the issuer or by third parties) and unsecured loans, or provide an appropriate negative statement;

b) a breakdown and classification of all other borrowing or indebtedness, including bank overdrafts, liabilities under acceptances, acceptance credits or hire purchase commitments, distinguishing between guaranteed, unguaranteed, secured and unsecured borrowing and debt, or provide an appropriate negative statement;

c) a breakdown and classification of all mortgages, rights and charges on the issuer, and its subsidiaries' properties, or provide an appropriate negative statement; and

) a breakdown of any contingent liabilities or guarantees, or provide an appropriate negative statement.

7) a statement by the directors of any material adverse change in the financial or trading position in the three financial years preceding the application for registration and offer of securities that are subject to this prospectus and during the period from the end of the period covered in the external auditors' report up to and including the date of approval of the prospectus, or provide an appropriate negative statement.

8) particulars of any commissions, discounts, brokerages or other non-cash compensation granted within the three years immediately preceding the application for registration and offer of securities that are subject to this prospectus in connection with the issue or offer of any securities by the issuer or any of the issuer's subsidiaries (if applicable), together with the names of any directors, proposed directors, senior executives, persons offering or placing the securities or experts who received any such payment or benefit, or provide an appropriate negative statement.

13. Use of proceeds and future projects

a) This section must include an estimate of the proceeds of the offer and the offer expenses and a statement as to how such proceeds are intended to be used.

b) Where the proceeds are to be used to fund future projects, the nature of these projects should be described and the following information included:

1) future projects' key milestones and timetable; and

2) an estimate and breakdown of future projects costs, showing the stage in which such costs will be incurred, in addition to details regarding the sources of financing.

14. Statements by experts

Where the prospectus includes a statement made by an expert, a statement should be included specifying the qualifications of the expert and whether such expert or any relative has any shareholding or interest of any kind in the issuer or any of its subsidiaries. In addition, the statement should confirm that the expert has given and not withdrawn his written consent to the publication in the prospectus of the expert's statement included in the form and context in which it is included.

15. Declarations

The directors of the issuer must make the following declarations:

1) other than what has been mentioned on page (•) of this prospectus, there has not been any interruption in the business of the issuer or any of the issuer's subsidiaries (if applicable) which may have or has had a significant effect on the financial position in the last 12 months.

2) other than what has been mentioned on page (•) of this prospectus, no commissions, discounts, brokerages or other non-cash compensation have been granted within the three years immediately preceding the application for registration and offer of securities that are the subject of this prospectus in connection with the issue or offer of any securities by the issuer or any of the issuer's subsidiaries (if applicable).

3) other than what has been mentioned on page (•) of this prospectus, there has not been any material adverse change in the financial or trading position of the issuer or its subsidiaries (if applicable) in the three financial years preceding the application for registration and offer of securities that are subject to this prospectus and during the period from the end of the period covered in the external auditors' report up to and including the date of approval of the prospectus.

4) other than what is mentioned on page (•) of this prospectus, they do not have any shareholding or interest of any kind in the issuer or any of the issuer's subsidiaries (if applicable), and nor does any relative of theirs.

16. Legal Information

This section must include the following declarations from the board of directors that:

a) the issuance does not constitute a breach of the relevant laws and regulations in Saudi Arabia.

b) the issuance does not constitute a breach of any contract/agreement entered into by the issuer.

c) all material legal issues concerning the issuer have been disclosed in the prospectus.

d) other than what has been mentioned on page (•) of this prospectus, the issuer and its subsidiaries are not subject to any claims, litigious cases or any other type of legal proceedings that could individually or collectively have a material effect on the business of the issuer or its subsidiaries or their financial position.

e) other than what has been mentioned on page (•) of this prospectus, the directors are not subject to any claims, litigious cases or any other type of legal proceedings that could individually or collectively have a material effect on the business of the issuer or its subsidiaries or their financial position.

17. Underwriter

This section must include information about the underwriter of the offer, as follows:

a) the name and address of the underwriter; and

b) the principal terms of the underwriting agreement, including the compensation arrangement between the issuer and the underwriter.

18. Waivers

This section must include details on all requirements that have been waived for the issuer by the Authority.

19. Information concerning the shares and terms and conditions of the offer

This section must include the following information:

1) a statement that application has been made to the Authority for the registration and offer of the securities that are subject to this prospectus and to the Exchange for listing;

2) the type and total value of the offer including the number of shares being offered;

3) the offer price and the nominal value of each share;

4) the subscription method;

5) the offer period and conditions;

6) the method of allocation of the shares and refund of excess monies;

7) when and under what circumstances the offer may be suspended;

8) a description of the resolutions, and approvals by virtue of which the shares will be offered;

9) details of any lock-up arrangement in place restricting the disposal of particular shares;

and

10) if a public or private offer has been or is being made simultaneously on the markets of two or more countries at the same time, and if a tranche has been or is being reserved for certain of these markets, details of any such offer or tranche must be provided.

20. Price dilution

This section must include information on the price dilution effects and its impact on the shareholders.

21. Subscription Declarations

This section must include information on the subscription declarations, allocation process, and the Exchange's details.

22. Documents available for inspection

This section must include information in relation to the place in the Kingdom at which the following documents may be inspected and the period of time during which the inspection may take place (being not less than 14 days before the extraordinary general assembly and such documents must remain available for inspection until the end of the offer period):

1) the bylaws and other constitutional documents of the issuer;

2) any document or order granting permission to offer securities to the public;

3) any feasibility studies prepared in relation to the projects that will be financed from the proceeds of the offer;

4) all other reports, letters, documents, value estimates or statements by any expert any part of which is extracted or referred to in the prospectus; and

25.26 ANNEX 11: CONTENT OF A PROSPECTUS FOR DEBT INSTRUMENTS FOR AN ISSUER WITHOUT SECURITIES LISTED ON THE EXCHANGE

Inclusion of information in the prospectus

A prospectus submitted for the registration and the offer of debt instruments from an issuer which does not have any listed securities on the Exchange at the time of submission must contain the information under the following sections at a minimum:

1. Cover page

This section must include the following information (where applicable):

1) the issuer's name, incorporation date and commercial registration number;
2) capital and number of shares;
3) a summary of the offer including debt instruments details and rights;
4) target participants;
5) offer period and conditions;
6) shares and debt instruments that have been listed prior to the particular offer by the issuer (if applicable);
7) a statement that the issuer has submitted the application for registration and offer of securities that are subject to this prospectus to the Authority, has submitted the application for listing to the Exchange and has submitted all the required documents to the relevant authorities;
8) a statement referring to the "Important Notice" and the "Risk Factors" under section (2) and section (9) of this Annex, respectively before making an investment decision; and
9) the following declaration:

"This prospectus includes information provided as part of the application for registration and offer of securities in compliance with the Rules on the Offer of Securities and Continuing Obligations of the Capital Market Authority of the Kingdom of Saudi Arabia (the "Authority") and the application for listing of securities in compliance with the Listing Rules of the Saudi Stock Exchange. The directors, whose names appear on page [ ], collectively and individually accept full responsibility for the accuracy of the information contained in this prospectus and confirm, having made all reasonable enquiries, that to the best of their knowledge and belief, there are no other facts the omission of which would make any statement herein misleading. The Authority and the Saudi Stock Exchange do not take any responsibility for the contents of this prospectus, do not make any representation as to its accuracy or completeness, and expressly disclaim any liability whatsoever for any loss arising from, or incurred in reliance upon, any part of this prospectus."

2. Important notice

This section must include a notice which shows the purpose and the nature of information mentioned in the prospectus.

3. Corporate directory

This section must include the following:

1) the issuer's and its representatives' contact information, including addresses, telephone and fax numbers, e-mail addresses, and the issuer's website.

2) the contact information, including addresses, telephone and fax numbers, and website and e-mail addresses, for each of the parties listed below, and any other expert to whom a statement or report included in the prospectus has been attributed:

a) the financial advisor;

b) the legal advisor;

c) the external auditor; and

d) the Capital Market Institutions authorized to place or sell the securities.

e) the underwriter (if any)

4. Offer summary

This section must include a disclaimer to the target investors on the importance of reading the prospectus prior to making an investment decision and include the following information (where applicable):

1) the issuer's name, description and incorporation information;

2) the issuer's activities;

3) substantial shareholders showing their ownership percentages and number of shares;

4) the capital of the issuer;

5) the issuer's total number of shares;

6) the nominal value for offered debt instrument;

7) the use of proceeds;

8) types of targeted investors;

9) subscription method for each type of targeted investors;

10) the minimum number of offer debt instruments to be subscribed for by each type of targeted investors;

11) the minimum value of offer of debt instruments to be subscribed for by each type of targeted investors;

12) the maximum number of offer debt instruments to be subscribed for by each type of targeted investors;

13) the maximum value of offer debt instruments to be subscribed for by each type of targeted investors;

14) allocation method and description of the process where an excess of subscription monies has been received for all types of targeted investors;

15) the offer period;

16) full information of rights granted to holders of the debt instruments;

17) debt instruments particulars;

18) details of repayment related dates including final maturity date and early repayment dates, specifying whether exercisable at the issuer's or the holder of debt instruments' request and the date from which payments are due to start;

19) restrictions on debt instruments;

20) details of the arrangements for transfer of the debt instruments;

21) the names and addresses of the paying agents, and any registrar and transfer agents for the debt instruments;

22) details of the early redemption of the debt instruments; and

23) a statement referring the reader to the "Important Notice" and the "Risk Factors" under section (2) and section (9) of this Annex, respectively before making an investment decision.

5. Summary of basic information

This section must include a summary of the basic information contained in the prospectus, including:

1. a disclaimer to investors about consideration of the prospectus as a whole, and not merely the summary;

2. a description of the issuer;

3. the issuer's mission and overall strategy;

4. the issuer's key strengths and competitive advantages; and

5. an overview of the market.

6. Summary of financial information

This section must include a summary of key financial information contained in the prospectus, including issuer's operational performance, financial condition, cash flows and key performance indicators.

7. Table of contents

This section must include a table of contents.

8. Terms and definitions

This section must include the terms and definitions used through the prospectus.

9. Risk factors

This section must include information in relation to risk factors specific to:

1) the issuer;

2) the market or industry in which the issuer operates; and

3) the securities being offered.

10. Issuer's background and business nature

This section must include the following information:

1) the official name, commercial registration number and the address shown in the commercial registration and, if different, the principal address of the issuer;

2) the date of incorporation of the issuer;

3) the authorized shares of the issuer, the number of shares issued or agreed to be issued, the value paid up, the nominal value and a description of the shares;

4) a description and organization chart of the group showing the issuer's position within that group (if applicable);

5) the general nature of the business of the issuer and the issuer's subsidiaries (if applicable) and details of the main products sold or services performed and an indication of any significant new products or activities;

6) if the issuer or the issuer's subsidiaries (if applicable) trades outside the Kingdom, a statement showing the location of such trading operations must be provided. Where a material portion of the issuer or the issuer's subsidiaries assets' are outside the Kingdom, the value and location of such assets and the value of the assets located in the Kingdom;

7) information concerning the policy of the issuer and the issuer's subsidiaries (if applicable) on the research and development of new products and production processes over the past three financial years, where significant;

8) particulars of any interruption in the business of the issuer and the issuer's subsidiaries (if applicable) which may have or has had a significant effect on the financial position in the last 12 months;

9) the number of people employed by the issuer and the issuer's subsidiaries (if applicable) and any material changes to that number over the last two financial years, with a breakdown of persons employed by Saudization ratio; and

10) a statement that no material change in the nature of the business is contemplated or, if one is contemplated, a detailed description of that change and its impact on the issuer's business and profitability.

11. Organizational structure

This section must include the following information:

1) Management

a) the issuer's organizational chart showing the directors structure, supervisory committees, and the functions of senior executives;
b) the full names and description of the most significant professional and academic qualifications and area of expertise and the date of appointment of all the directors or proposed directors (showing whether the director is independent or executive or non-executive), in addition to the senior executives and the company secretary of the issuer;
c) details of other previous or current board positions held by all directors or proposed directors or senior executives and the company secretary of the issuer. The details should include, the name of the company, legal entity, membership dates, and the sector in which the company operates;
d) details of any bankruptcies of each director or proposed director, senior executives, or the company secretary of the issuer;
e) details of any company insolvency in the preceding five years where any of the directors or proposed directors, senior executives, or the company secretary of the issuer were employed by the insolvent company in a managerial or supervisory capacity;
f) a statement showing the direct or indirect interests of each director or proposed director, senior executives, secretary of the board, and any of their relatives in (i) the shares or debt instruments of the issuer or (ii) the issuer's subsidiaries (if applicable), or provide an appropriate negative statement;
g) the aggregate remuneration and benefits in kind granted by the issuer or any subsidiary during the three financial years prior to offering to the directors and the five senior executives who received the highest payments, including the CEO and CFO if they were not within the top five;
h) full particulars of any contract or arrangement in effect or contemplated at the time of submission of the prospectus in which a director or senior executive or any of their relatives is interested in relation to the business of the issuer or the issuer's subsidiaries (if applicable), or provide an appropriate negative statement;
i) information about the issuer's directors' committees, including the names of each committee member and a summary of the terms of reference under which the committee operates; and

j) information on the issuer's compliance with corporate governance.

2) Employees

a) any employee share schemes in place prior to the application for registration and offer of securities subject to this prospectus along with details on the aggregate amount of shares owned by the employees in the issuer; and

b) any other arrangements involving the employees in the capital of the issuer.

12. Financial information

The information required below must be provided in relation to the issuer for the three financial years immediately preceding the application for registration and offer of securities that are subject to this prospectus as well as the period covered in the interim financial statements as per paragraph (4) of Article 23 of the Rules on the Offer of Securities and Continuing Obligations:

1) comparative tables of financial information with commentary and analysis by management of financial material information. The comparative tables must:

a) be prepared on a consolidated basis;

b) be extracted without material adjustment from audited financial statements; and

c) include financial information presented in a form consistent with that which is adopted in the issuer's annual financial statements.

2) a report by certified external auditor must be prepared in accordance with the requirements of Annex 15 of the Rules on the Offer of Securities and Continuing Obligations in any of the following circumstances:

a) where the external auditors' report on the financial statements of the issuer for any of the last three financial years immediately preceding the application for registration and offer of securities that are subject to this prospectus has been qualified;

b) where the issuer has undergone restructuring in the three financial years immediately preceding the date of the application for registration and offer of securities that are subject to this prospectus;

c) where any material change has been made to the accounting policies of the issuer; or

d) where any material adjustment has been made or is required to be made to the published audited financial statements during the periods referred to in sub-paragraph (a) above.

3) details of holdings, including holdings in contractually based securities or other assets whose value may be subject to fluctuations or be difficult to ascertain with certainty, significantly affecting the assessment of the issuer's financial position.

4) the information required below must be provided in relation to the financial, operating performance, and results of operations:

a) performance indicators;

b) the financial, operating performance, and results of operations of the main lines of business;

quad c) any seasonal or business cycles which affect the business or the financial condition;

d) an explanation of any material changes from year to year in the financial information;

e) information regarding any governmental, economic, fiscal, monetary or political policies or other factors that have materially affected, or could materially affect, directly or indirectly, the operations;

f) the funding structure;

g) particulars of any alterations in the capital of the issuer, or where material, any of the issuer's subsidiaries (if applicable) within the three years immediately preceding the date of the application for registration and offer of securities that are subject to this prospectus. Such particulars must state the price and terms of any issues by the issuers or its subsidisers; and

h) a table showing any capital of the issuer or any subsidiary which is under option, including the consideration for which the option was granted, and the price and duration of the option, and the name and address of the grantee, or provide an appropriate negative statement.

5) property, plant and equipment

a) a breakdown of any existing material fixed assets, including leased properties;

b) an explanation of the issuer's depreciation policy and any changes contemplated in that policy; and

c) any planned material fixed assets, including leased properties.

6) in relation to debt, a statement on an individual and consolidated basis as at the most recent date must be prepared covering the following:

a) a breakdown and classification of any debt instruments issued and outstanding, and authorized or otherwise created but unissued, and term loans, distinguishing between guaranteed, unguaranteed, secured (whether the pledge is provided by the issuer or by third parties) and unsecured loans, or provide an appropriate negative statement;

b) a breakdown and classification of all other borrowing or indebtedness, bank overdrafts, liabilities under acceptances, acceptance credits or hire purchase commitments, distinguishing between guaranteed, unguaranteed, secured and unsecured borrowing and debt, or provide an appropriate negative statement;

c) a breakdown and classification of all mortgages, rights and charges on the issuer and its subsidiaries' properties, or provide an appropriate negative statement; and

d) a breakdown of any contingent liabilities or guarantees, or provide an appropriate negative statement.

7) A statement by the directors of any material adverse change in the financial or trading position in the three financial years preceding the application for registration and offer of securities that are subject to this prospectus and during the period from the end of the period covered in the external auditors' report up to and including the date of approval of the prospectus or provide an appropriate negative statement.

8) Particulars of any commissions, discounts, brokerages or other non- cash compensation granted within the three years immediately preceding the application for registration and offer of securities that are subject to this prospectus in connection with the issue or offer of any securities by the issuer or any of the issuer's subsidiaries (if applicable), together with the names of any directors, proposed directors, senior executives, persons offering or placing the securities or experts who received any such payment or benefit or provide an appropriate negative statement.

13. Use of proceeds

This section must include a statement as to how such proceeds are intended to be used.

14. Statements by experts

Where the prospectus includes a statement made by an expert, a statement should be included specifying the qualifications of the expert and whether such expert or any relative has any shareholding or interest of any kind in the issuer or any of its subsidiaries. In addition, the statement should confirm that the expert has given and not withdrawn his written consent to the publication in the prospectus of the expert's statement included in the form and context in which it is included.

15. Declarations

The directors of the issuer must make the following declarations:

1) other than what has been mentioned on page ( ) of this prospectus, there has not been any interruption in the business of the issuer or any of the issuer's subsidiaries (if applicable) which may have or has had a significant effect on the financial position in the last 12 months.

2) other than what has been mentioned on page ( ) of this prospectus, no commissions, discounts, brokerages or other non-cash compensation have been granted within the three years immediately preceding the application for registration and offer of securities that are the subject of this prospectus in connection with the issue or offer of any securities by the issuer or any of the issuer's subsidiaries (if applicable).

3) other than what has been mentioned on page ( ) of this prospectus, there has not been any material adverse change in the financial or trading position of the issuer or its subsidiaries (if applicable) in the three financial years preceding the application for registration and offer of securities that are subject to this prospectus and during the period from the end of the period covered in the external auditors' report up to and including the date of approval of the prospectus.

4) other than what is mentioned on page ( ) of this prospectus, they do not have any shareholding or interest of any kind in the issuer or any of the issuer's subsidiaries (if applicable), and nor does any relative of theirs.

16. Legal information

This section must include the following legal information:

1) the following declarations from the board of directors that:

a) the issuance does not constitute a breach of the relevant laws and regulations in Saudi Arabia;

b) the issuance does not constitute a breach of any contract/agreement entered into by the issuer;

2) a summary of all material contracts.

3) a summary of all related party material contracts.

4) in relation to the issuer and its subsidiaries (if applicable), the following must be included:

a) particulars of any intangible assets such as trademarks, patents, copyright or other intellectual property rights which are material in relation to the issuer's or any of its subsidiaries (if applicable) business or profitability, and a statement regarding the extent to which the issuer or any of its subsidiaries (if applicable) is dependent on such assets; and

b) particulars of any litigation, claim (including any litigation pending or threatened) or ongoing investigation which may have a material effect on the issuer's or any of its subsidiaries business or financial position, or an appropriate negative statement.

17. Underwriter

This section must include information about the underwriter of the offer, as follows:

1) the name and address of the underwriter; and

2) the principal terms of the underwriting agreement, including the compensation arrangement between the issuer and the underwriter.

18. Expenses

This section must include details of the aggregate offer expenses.

19. Waivers

This section must include details on all requirements that have been waived for the issuer by the authority.

20. Information concerning the debt instruments and terms and conditions of the offer

This section must include the following information:

1) a statement that application has been made to the Authority for the registration and offer of the securities that are subject to this prospectus and to the Exchange for the listing;

2) the nominal value of the offer;

3) full information on the rights conferred upon holders of debt instruments;

4) particulars of the debt instruments;

5) subscription method;

6) details of the early redemption of the offer;

7) the names and addresses of the paying agents, and any registrar and transfer agents for the debt instruments;

8) details of the arrangements for transfer of the debt instruments;

9) details of repayment related dates including the final maturity date and early repayment dates, specifying whether exercisable at the issuer's or the holder of debt instruments' request and the date from which payments are due;

10) procedures and time limits for allocation and delivery of the debt instruments and, where there will be temporary documents of title, the procedures for the delivery and exchange thereof;

11) a description of the resolutions, and approvals by virtue of which the debt instruments will be offered;

12) whether there are any guarantees, pledges or commitments intended to be provided to guarantee the offer;

13) details of any agreements with the representative of the holders of the debt instruments, if any, the name and function and head office of such representative, the conditions under which the representative may be replaced together with an indication of where the public may inspect copies of the documents detailing the obligations of the representative;

14) a description of any subordination of the offer to any other debts or debt instruments of the issuer;

15) a description of the applicable law related to the offer;

16) details of any restrictions on the transferability of the debt instruments;

17) the date upon which it is expected that trading in the debt instruments will commence, if the issuer can anticipate such date; and

18) if a public or private offer has been or is being made simultaneously on the markets of two or more countries at the same time, and if a tranche has been or is being reserved for certain of these markets, details of any such offer or tranche must be provided.

21. Subscription declarations

This section must include information on the subscription declarations, allocation process, and the Exchange's details.

22. Documents available for inspection

This section must include information in relation to the place in the Kingdom at which the following documents may be inspected and the period of time during which the inspection may take place (being not less than 3 days before the start of the offer):

1) the bylaws and other constitutional documents of the issuer;

2) any document or order granting permission to offer securities to the public;

3) each contract disclosed pursuant to sub-paragraph (h) of paragraph (1) of section (12) of this Annex or, if the contract is not produced in writing, a memorandum giving full particulars of the agreement;

4) all other reports, letters, documents, value estimates or statements by any expert any part of which is extracted or referred to in the prospectus; and

5) the reviewed financial statements of the issuer for each of the three financial years immediately preceding the date of the publication of the prospectus, in addition to the most recent interim financial statements.

23. External auditor's report

The issuer's audited financial statements for the three years immediately preceding the date of the publication of the prospectus, in addition to the most recent interim financial statements.

24. Guarantees

Where a guarantee, pledge or other similar commitment is to be provided the following information must be included:

1) details regarding the terms, conditions and scope of the guarantee, pledge or other similar commitment including any conditionality on the application of the guarantee, pledge or similar commitment; and

2) copies of the external auditors' and the directors' report on the accounts of the guarantor company.

25. Bylaws

The issuer's bylaws.

25.27 ANNEX 11(A): CONTENTS OF A PROSPECTUS FOR DEBT-BASED RECOURSE DEBT INSTRUMENTS

Inclusion of information in the prospectus

A prospectus submitted for registration and admission to listing of debt-based recourse securities must contain the information under the following sections at a minimum. Additionally, such prospectus for registration and admission to listing of debt-based recourse debt instruments submitted by a Special Purposes Entity with listed securities are exempted from satisfying the requirement of sections (5), (11), (12), (13), (14/4/g) and (17/1).

1. Cover page

This section must include the following information (where applicable):

1) A license to establish a special purposes entity;
2) The sponsor's commercial registration.
3) The capital of the sponsor;
4) a summary of the offer including debt instruments details and rights;
5) substantial shareholders of the sponsor;
6) target participants;
7) offer period and conditions;
8) Shares and debt instruments that have been listed prior to the particular offer by the special purposes entity and the sponsor (if applicable);
9) a statement that the special purposes entity has submitted the application for admission to listing to the Authority and that all requirements have been met;
10) a statement referring to the "Important Notice" and the "Risk Factors" under section (2) and section (9), respectively before making an investment decision; and
11) the following declarations:

"This prospectus includes information given in compliance with the Listing Rules of the Capital Market Authority of the Kingdom of Saudi Arabia (the "Authority"). The directors of the special purposes entity and the sponsor, whose names appear on page [ ], collectively and individually accept full responsibility for the accuracy of the information contained in this prospectus and confirm, having made all reasonable enquiries, that to the best of their knowledge and belief, there are no other facts the omission of which would make any statement herein misleading. The Authority and the Saudi Stock Exchange do not take any responsibility for the contents of this prospectus, do not make any representation as to its accuracy or completeness, and expressly disclaim any liability whatsoever for any loss arising from, or incurred in reliance upon, any part of this prospectus"

and

"The securities offered hereby are issued by a special purposes entity licensed by the Capital Market Authority. The Capital Market Authority maintains a register of special purposes entities and regulates the special purposes entity. The Capital Market Authority does not approve, and is not responsible for, the terms of the securities the special purposes entity issues, the financing structure the special purposes entity employs, or the investment risks and rewards associated with the securities. The Capital Market Authority does not regulate or monitor the value of the assets of the special purposes entity or the ability of the special purposes entity to meet its obligations and makes no endorsement of or recommendation about the securities."

2. Important notice

This section must include a notice which shows the purpose and the nature of information mentioned in the prospectus.

3. Corporate directory

This section must include the following:

1) the special purposes entity's, the sponsor's and its representatives' contact information, including addresses, telephone and fax numbers, e-mail addresses, and the issuer's and the sponsor's website addresses.

2) the contact information, including addresses, telephone and fax numbers, and website and e-mail addresses, for each of the parties listed below, and any other expert to whom a statement or report included in the prospectus has been attributed:

a) the financial advisor;

b) the legal advisor;

c) the external auditor;

d) the underwriter (if any);

e) the Capital Market Institutions authorized to place or sell the securities;

f) the custodian (where applicable); and

g) the board members of the special purposes entity.

4. Offer summary

This section must include a disclaimer to the target investors on the importance of reading the prospectus prior to making an investment decision. This section must include the following information (where applicable):

1) the special purposes entity's name, description and incorporation information;
2) the special purposes entity's activities;
3) substantial shareholders of the sponsor showing their ownership percentages and number of shares.
4) the capital of sponsor;
5) the nominal value for offered debt instrument;
6) the use of proceeds of the offer;
7) the sponsor ensuring the due payments are paid as per the debt instruments;
8) types of targeted investors of the issuer;
9) subscription method for each type of targeted investors of the issuer;
10) the minimum number of debt instruments to be subscribed for by each type of targeted investors;
11) the value of minimum number of debt instruments to be subscribed for by each type of targeted investors;
12) the maximum number of debt instruments to be subscribed for by each type of targeted investors;
13) the value of the maximum number of debt instruments to be subscribed for by each type of targeted investors;
14) allocation method and description of the process where an excess of subscription monies is returned to all types of targeted investors;
15) the offer period;
16) full information of rights granted to holders of the debt instruments;
17) debt instruments particulars;
18) details of repayment related dates including final maturity date and early repayment dates, specifying whether exercisable at the special purposes entity's or the holder of debt instruments' request and the date from which payments are due to start;
19) restrictions on debt instruments;
20) details of the arrangements for transfer of the debt instruments;
21) the names and addresses of the paying agents, and any registrar and transfer agents of the issuer for the debt instruments;
22) the names and addresses of the special purposes entity's board members;
23) details of the early redemption of the debt instruments; and
24) a statement referring to the "Important Notice" and the "Risk Factors" under section (2) and section (9), respectively before making an investment decision.
25) a statement confirming that arrangements have been implemented to protect holders of debt instruments in accordance with Article 50 of the Rules on the Offer of Securities and Continuing Obligations.

5. Summary of basic information

This section must include a summary of the basic information contained in the prospectus, including:

1) a disclaimer to investors about consideration of the prospectus as a whole, and not merely the summary;
2) a description of the issuer;
3) the issuer's mission and overall strategy;
4) the issuer's key strengths and competitive advantages;
5) an overview of the market.
6) a summary of the financial transaction provided to the special purposes entity and the sponsor shall ensure that the due payments are paid as per the debt instruments

6. Summary of financial information

This section must include a summary of key financial information contained in the prospectus, including issuer's operational performance, financial condition, cash flows and key performance indicators.

7. Table of contents

This section must include the table of contents of the prospectus.

8. Terms and definitions

This section must include the terms and definitions used through the prospectus.

9. Risk factors

This section must include information in relation to risk factors specific to:

1) the sponsor;
2) the market or industry in which the sponsor operates;
3) the special purposes entity
4) the securities being offered.

10. Information about the market and sector

This section must include information on the market and sector in which the sponsor operates.

11. The special purposes entity background, business nature

This section must include the following information:

1) the official name, commercial registration number and the address shown in the commercial registration and, if different, the principal address of the special purposes entity;
2) the date of incorporation of the special purposes entity;
3) the purpose of the special purposes entity;
4) the board of the special purposes entity;

5) the dates of appointment of all the directors or proposed directors of the special purposes entity;
6) details of other previous and current board positions held by all directors or proposed directors the special purposes entity. The details should include, the name of the entity, legal status, membership dates, and the sector in which the entity operates;
7) details of any bankruptcies of each director or proposed director, of the special purposes entity;
8) details of any company insolvency in the preceding five years where any of the directors or proposed directors of the special purposes entity were employed by the insolvent company in a managerial or supervisory capacity;
9) a summary of existing or proposed service contracts, if any, of the directors;
10) a statement showing the direct or indirect interests of each director or proposed director of the special purposes entity, and every senior executives and any of their relatives in the shares, and the secretary of the special purposes entity (if any), in shares or debt instruments of the special purposes entity, the sponsor or the sponsor's subsidiaries (if any), or provide an appropriate negative statement;

12. Sponsor background, business nature

This section must include the following information:

1) the official name, commercial registration number and the address shown in the commercial registration and, if different, the principal address of the sponsor;

2) the date of incorporation of the sponsor;

3) the authorized shares of the sponsor, the number of shares issued or agreed to be issued, the value paid up, the nominal value and a description of the shares;

4) a description and organization chart of the group showing the sponsor's position within that group (if applicable);

5) the general nature of the business of the sponsor and the sponsor's subsidiaries (if applicable) and details of the main products sold or services performed and an indication of any significant new products or activities;

6) if the sponsor or the sponsor's subsidiaries (if applicable) trades outside the Kingdom, a statement showing the location of such trading operations must be provided. Where a material portion of the sponsor or the sponsor's subsidiaries assets are outside the Kingdom, the value and location of such assets and the value of the assets located in the Kingdom;

7) information concerning the policy of the sponsor and the sponsor's subsidiaries (if applicable) on the research and development of new products and production processes over the past three financial years, where significant;

8) particulars of any interruption in the business of the sponsor and the sponsor's subsidiaries (if applicable) which may have or has had a significant effect on the financial position in the last 12 months;

9) the number of people employed by the sponsor and the sponsor's subsidiaries (if applicable) and any material changes to that number over the last two financial years, with a breakdown of persons employed by main categories of activity and by Saudization ratio; and

10) a statement that no material change in the nature of the business is contemplated or, if one is contemplated, a detailed description of that change and its impact on the sponsor's business and profitability.

13. Sponsor's organizational structure

This section must include the following information:

1) management

(a) the sponsor's organizational chart showing the directors structure, supervisory committees, and the functions of senior executives;

(b) the full names and description of the professional and academic qualifications and area of expertise and the date of appointment of all the directors or proposed directors (showing whether the director is independent or non- independent and executive or non-executive), in addition to the senior executives and the company secretary of the sponsor;

(c) details of other previous or current board positions held by all directors or proposed directors or senior executives and the company secretary of the sponsor. The details should include, the name of the company, legal entity, membership dates, and the sector in which the company operates;

(d) details of any bankruptcies of each director or proposed director, senior executives, or the company secretary of the sponsor;

(e) details of any company insolvency in the preceding five years where any of the directors or proposed directors, senior executives, or the company secretary of the sponsor were employed by the insolvent company in a managerial or supervisory capacity;

(f) a statement showing the direct or indirect interests of each director or proposed director, senior executives, company secretary of the sponsor, and any of their relatives in the shares or debt instruments of the sponsor, the sponsor or the sponsor's subsidiaries (if applicable), or provide an appropriate negative statement;

(g) the aggregate remuneration and benefits in kind granted by the sponsor or any subsidiary during the three financial years prior to listing to the directors and the five senior executives who received the highest payments, including the CEO and CFO if they were not within the top five;

(h) a summary of existing or proposed service contracts, if any, of the directors or the CEO and CFO of the sponsor;

(i) full particulars of any contract or arrangement in effect or contemplated at the time of submission of the prospectus in which a director or senior executive or any of their relatives is interested in relation to the business of the sponsor or the sponsor's subsidiaries (if applicable), or provide an appropriate negative statement;

(j) information about the sponsor's directors committees, including the names of each committee member and a summary of the terms of reference under which the committee operates; and

(k) information on the sponsor's compliance with corporate governance.

2) employees

(a) any employee share schemes in place prior to the application for registration and admission to listing of the securities along with details on the aggregate amount of shares owned by the employees in the sponsor; and

(b) any other arrangements involving the employees in the capital of the sponsor.

14. Sponsor Financial Information

The information required below must be provided in relation to the sponsor for the three financial years immediately preceding the application for registration and admission to listing subject to this prospectus and the period referred to in preliminary financial statements according to paragraph (4) of Article 23 of the Rules for the Offer of Securities and Continuing Obligations:

1) comparative tables of financial information with commentary and analysis by management. The comparative tables must:

(a) be prepared on a consolidated basis;

(b) be extracted without material adjustment from audited financial statements; and

(c) include financial information presented in a form consistent with that which is adopted in the sponsor's annual financial statements.

2) a report by certified external auditor must be prepared in accordance with the requirements of Annex 6 of the Listing Rules in any of the following circumstances:

(a) where the external auditors' report on the consolidated financial statements of the sponsor for any of the last three financial years immediately preceding the application for registration and admission to listing has been qualified;

(b) where the sponsor has undergone restructuring or an alteration in capital using external financing in the three financial years immediately preceding the date of application for registration and admission to listing;

(c) where any material change has been made to the accounting policies of the sponsor; or

(d) where any material adjustment has been made or is required to be made to the published audited financial statements during the periods referred to in sub-paragraph (a) above.

3) details of holdings, including holdings in contractually based securities or other assets whose value may be subject to fluctuations or be difficult to ascertain with certainty, significantly affecting the assessment of the sponsor's financial position.

4) the information required below must be provided in relation to the financial, operating performance, and results of operations of the sponsor:

(a) performance indicators;

(b) the financial, operating performance, and results of operations of the main lines of business;

(c) any seasonal or business cycles which affect the business or the financial condition;

(d) an explanation of any material changes from year to year in the financial information;

(e) information regarding any governmental, economic, fiscal, monetary or political policies or other factors that have materially affected, or could materially affect, directly or indirectly, the operations;

(f) the funding structure;

(g) particulars of any alterations in the capital of the sponsor, or where material, any of the sponsor's subsidiaries (if applicable) within the three years immediately preceding the date of application for registration and admission to listing. Such particulars must state the price and terms of any issues by the sponsor; and

(h) details of any capital of the sponsor which is under option, including the consideration for which the option was granted, and the price and duration of the option, and the name and address of the grantee, or provide an appropriate negative statement.

5) property, plant and equipment

(a) a breakdown of any existing material fixed assets, including leased properties;

(b) an explanation of the issuer's depreciation policy and any changes contemplated in that policy; and

(c) any planned material fixed assets, including leased properties.

6) in relation to debt, a statement on an individual and consolidated basis as at the most recent date must be prepared covering the following:

(a) a breakdown and classification of any debt instruments issued and outstanding, and authorized or otherwise created but unissued, and term loans, distinguishing between guaranteed, unguaranteed, secured

(whether the pledge is provided by the sponsor or by third parties) and unsecured loans, or provide an appropriate negative statement;

(b) a breakdown and classification of all other borrowing or indebtedness, bank overdrafts, liabilities under acceptances, acceptance credits or hire purchase commitments, distinguishing between guaranteed, unguaranteed, secured and unsecured borrowing and debt, or provide an appropriate negative statement;

(c) a breakdown and classification of all mortgages, rights and charges on the sponsor, its subsidiaries' properties (if any) and the special purposes entity's, or provide an appropriate negative statement; and

(d) a breakdown of any contingent liabilities or guarantees, or provide an appropriate negative statement.

7) A statement by the directors of any material adverse change in the financial or trading position in the three financial years preceding the application for registration and admission to listing and during the period from the end of the period covered in the external auditors' report up to and including the date of approval of the prospectus or provide an appropriate negative statement.

8) Particulars of any commissions, discounts, brokerages or other non-cash compensation granted within the three years immediately preceding the application for registration and admission to listing in connection with the issue or offer of any securities by the sponsor or any of the sponsor's subsidiaries (if applicable), together with the names of any directors, proposed directors, senior executives, persons offering or placing the securities or experts who received any such payment or benefit or provide an appropriate negative statement.

15. Financing Structure and Use of proceeds

This section must include the following:

1) Information regarding the financial structure including details of:

(a) the use of the proceeds of issuance by the special purposes entity; (b) the rights to be acquired by the special purposes entity under the financing structure (including their ranking on the event of insolvency of the sponsor or any other person, where applicable);

(c) the nature of the claim of the special purposes entity on the sponsor; (d) any direct rights of recourse of the holders against the sponsor;

(e) details of any security interest to be granted in favor of the special purposes entity, including a description of the assets secured and any rights to substitute such assets, or a description of any variation in such security;

2) a description of any obligation on the special purposes entity in relation to the transaction, including the order of priority of any payments.

3) Information of any investment powers associated with the special purposes entity's assets.

4) a description of how the cash flows will be used to meet the special purposes entity's obligations including details of:

5) particulars of how payments will be made by the sponsor.

6) a statement as to how the proceeds of issuance are intended to be used by the sponsor.

7) an estimate of the offer expenses.

16. Statements by experts

Where the prospectus includes a statement made by an expert, a statement should be included specifying the qualifications of the expert and whether such expert or any relative has any shareholding or interest of any kind in the sponsor or any of its subsidiaries. In addition, the statement should confirm that the expert has given and not withdrawn his written consent to the publication in the prospectus of the expert's statement included in the form and context in which it is included.

17. Declarations

The directors of the sponsor must make the following declarations:

1) other than what has been mentioned on page ( ) of this prospectus, there has not been any interruption in the business of the special purposes entity and of the special purposes entity's subsidiaries (if applicable), which may have or has had a significant effect on the financial position in the last 12 months.

2) other than what has been mentioned on page ( ) of this prospectus, there has not been any commissions, discounts, brokerages or other non-cash compensation granted within the three years immediately preceding the application for registration and admission to listing in connection with the issue or offer of any securities by the sponsor or any of the sponsor's subsidiaries (if applicable).

3) other than what has been mentioned on page ( ) of this prospectus, there has not been any material adverse change in the financial or trading position of the sponsor or its subsidiaries (if applicable) in the three financial years preceding the application for registration and admission to listing and during the period from the end of the period covered in the external auditors' report up to and including the date of approval of the prospectus.

4) other than what is mentioned on page ( ) of this prospectus, the Board directors do not have any shareholding or interest of any kind in the special purposes entity, the sponsor, or any of the sponsor's subsidiaries (if applicable), and nor does any relative of theirs.

18. Legal information

This section must include the following legal information, as relevant:

1) a summary of the provisions of the special purposes entity and the sponsor's by- laws and other constitutional documents, including:

(a) the object clause of the special purposes entity and the sponsor;

(b) provisions relating to the special purposes entity and the sponsor's administrative, management and supervisory bodies;

(c) provisions relating to the rights and restrictions attached to the special purposes entity's securities and the financing transaction. including;

1. any pledges not to apply for new loans which give privileges to new creditors;

2. any control rights granted to investors by the special purposes entity;

(d) provisions governing the alteration of securities rights or classes of the special purposes entity, where applicable, and the sponsor;

(e) provisions governing liquidation and winding up of the special purposes entity, where applicable, and the sponsor;

(f) any power enabling a director or the CEO, of the special purposes entity, where applicable, or the sponsor, to vote on a contract or proposal in which he has an interest;

(g) any power enabling a director or the CEO, of the special purposes entity, where applicable, or the sponsor, to vote on remuneration to themselves; and

(h) any powers allowing the directors or the senior executives, of the special purposes entity, where applicable, or the sponsor, to borrow from the sponsor.

2) a summary of all material contracts of the special purposes entity and the sponsor, including summaries of any contract which is material to the financing arrangement.

3) a summary of all related party contracts of the special purposes entity and the sponsor.

4) in relation to the special purposes entity and the sponsor and its subsidiaries (if applicable), the following information must be included:

a) particulars of any intangible assets such as trademarks, patents, copyright or other intellectual property rights which are material in relation to the special purposes entity's, the sponsor's or any of its subsidiaries (if applicable) business or profitability, and a statement regarding the extent to which the special purposes entity, the sponsor or any of its subsidiaries (if applicable) is dependent on such assets.

b) in relation to the special purposes entity, the sponsor and the sponsor's subsidiaries, particulars of any litigation or claim (including any litigation pending or threatened) which may have a material effect on the special purposes entity's, the sponsor's or any of its subsidiaries' business or financial position, or an appropriate negative statement.

19. Underwriter

This section must include information about the underwriter of the offer, as follows:

1) the name and address of the underwriter; and

2) the principal terms of the underwriting agreement, including the compensation arrangement between the special purposes entity and the underwriter.

20. Expenses

This section must include details of the aggregate offer expenses.

21. Waivers

This section must include details on all requirements that have been waived for the special purposes entity and the sponsor by the Authority.

22. Information concerning the debt instruments and terms and conditions of the offer

This section must include the following information:

1) a statement that application has been made to the Authority for the registration and admission to listing;
2) the nominal value of the offer;
3) full information on the rights conferred upon holders of debt instruments;
4) particulars of the debt instruments;
5) subscription method;
6) details of the early redemption of the offer;
7) the names and addresses of the paying agents, and any registrar and transfer agents for the debt instruments;
8) details of the arrangements for transfer of the debt instruments;
9) details of repayment related dates including the final maturity date and early repayment dates, specifying whether exercisable at the sponsor's or the holder of debt instruments' request and the date from which payments are due;
10) procedures and time limits for allocation and delivery of the debt instruments and, where there will be temporary documents of title, the procedures for the delivery and exchange thereof;
11) a description of the resolutions, and approvals by virtue of which the debt instruments will be offered;
12) whether there are any guarantees, pledges or commitments intended to be provided to guarantee the offer;
13) details of any agreements with the representative of the holders of the debt instruments, if any, the name and function and head office of such representative, the conditions under which the representative may be replaced together with an indication of where the public may inspect copies of the documents detailing the obligations of the representative;
14) a description of any subordination of the offer to any other debts or debt instruments of the special purposes entity;
15) a description of the applicable law related to the offer;
16) details of any restrictions on the transferability of the debt instruments;
17) the date upon which it is expected that trading in the debt instruments will commence, if the sponsor can anticipate such date; and
18) if a public or private offer has been or is being made simultaneously on the markets of two or more countries at the same time, and if a tranche has been or is being reserved for certain of these markets, details of any such offer or tranche must be provided.

23. Subscription declarations

This section must include information on the subscription declarations, allocation process, and the Exchange details.

24. Documents available for inspection

This section must include information in relation to the place in the Kingdom at which the following documents may be inspected and the period of time during which the inspection may take place (being not less than 3 days before the end of the offer period):

1) the by-laws and other constitutional documents of the special purposes entity and the sponsor;

2) any document or order granting permission to offer securities to the public;

3) each contract disclosed pursuant to sub-paragraph (i) of paragraph (1) of section (13) of this Annex or, if the contract is not produced in writing, a memorandum giving full particulars of the agreement;

4) all other reports, letters, documents, value estimates or statements by any expert any part of which is extracted or referred to in the prospectus; and

5) the reviewed financial statements of the sponsor for each of the three financial years immediately preceding the date of the publication of the prospectus, in addition to the most recent interim financial statements.

25. External auditor's report

The special purposes entity's audited financial statements for the three years immediately preceding the date of the publication of the prospectus, in addition to the most recent interim financial statements.

26. Guarantees

Where a guarantee, pledge or other similar commitment is to be provided the following information must be included:

1) details regarding the terms, conditions and scope of the guarantee, pledge or other similar commitment including any conditionality on the application of the guarantee, pledge or similar commitment; and

2) copies of the external auditors' and the directors' report on the accounts of the guarantor company.

25.28 ANNEX 11(B): CONTENTS OF A PROSPECTUS FOR ASSET-LINKED RECOURSE DEBT INSTRUMENTS

Inclusion of information in the prospectus

A prospectus submitted for registration and admission to listing of asset-linked recourse debt instruments must contain the information under the following sections at a minimum. Additionally, such prospectus for registration and admission to listing of asset-linked recourse debt instruments submitted by a Special Purposes Entity with listed securities are exempted from satisfying the requirement of sections (5), (11), (12), (13), (14/4/g) and (17/1):

1. Cover page

This section must include the following information (where applicable):

1) A license to establish a special purposes entity;
2) The sponsor's commercial registration.
3) The capital of the sponsor;
4) a summary of the offer including debt instruments details and rights;

5) substantial shareholders of the sponsor;
6) target participants;
7) offer period and conditions;
8) Shares, debt instruments and any other asset-linked recourse securities that have been listed prior to the particular offer by the special purposes entity and the sponsor (if applicable);
9) a statement that the special purposes entity has submitted the application for admission to listing to the Authority and that all requirements have been met;
10) a statement referring to the "Important Notice" and the "Risk Factors" under section (2) and section (9) of this Annex, respectively before making an investment decision; and
11) the following declarations:

"This prospectus includes information given in compliance with the Rules on the Offer of Securities and Continuing Obligations issued by the Capital Market Authority of the Kingdom of Saudi Arabia (the"Authority"). The directors of the special purposes entity and the sponsor, whose names appear on page [ ], collectively and individually accept full responsibility for the accuracy of the information contained in this prospectus and confirm, having made all reasonable enquiries, that to the best of their knowledge and belief, there are no other facts the omission of which would make any statement herein misleading. The Authority and the Saudi Stock Exchange do not take any responsibility for the contents of this prospectus, do not make any representation as to its accuracy or completeness, and expressly disclaim any liability whatsoever for any loss arising from, or incurred in reliance upon, any part of this prospectus"

and

"The securities offered hereby are issued by a special purposes entity licensed by the Capital Market Authority. The Capital Market Authority maintains a register of special purposes entities and regulates the special purposes entity. The Capital Market Authority does not approve, and is not responsible for, the terms of the securities the special purposes entity issues, the financing structure the special purposes entity employs, or the investment risks and rewards associated with the securities. The Capital Market Authority does not regulate or monitor the value of the assets of the special purposes entity or the ability of the special purposes entity to meet its obligations and makes no endorsement of or recommendation about the securities."

2. Important notice

This section must include a notice which shows the purpose and the nature of information mentioned in the prospectus.

3. Corporate directory

This section must include the following:

1) the special purposes entity's, the sponsor's and its representatives' contact information, including addresses, telephone and fax numbers, e-mail addresses, and the special purposes entity's and the sponsor's website addresses.

2) the contact information, including addresses, telephone and fax numbers, and website and e-mail addresses, for each of the parties listed below, and any other expert to whom a statement or report included in the prospectus has been attributed:

(a) the financial advisor;
(b) the legal advisor;
(c) the external auditor;
(d) the underwriter;
(e) the Capital Market Institutions authorized to place or sell the securities;
(f) the custodian (where applicable); and
(g) Board members of the special purposes entity.

4. Offer summary

This section must include a disclaimer to the target investors on the importance of reading the prospectus prior to making an investment decision. This section must include the following information (where applicable):

1) the special purposes entity and the sponsor's name, description and incorporation information;
2) the special purposes entity and the sponsor's activities;
3) substantial shareholders of the sponsor showing their ownership percentages and number of shares.
4) the capital of the special purposes entity and the sponsor;
5) the nominal value for offered debt instrument;
6) the use of proceeds by the issuer and the financing transaction to be entered into by the issuer;
7) the commitment of the sponsor to ensure payment of amounts due under the debt instruments;
8) types of targeted investors of the issuer;
9) subscription method for each type of targeted investors of the issuer;
10) the minimum number of offer debt instruments to be subscribed for by each type of targeted investors;
11) the minimum value of offer of debt instruments to be subscribed for by each type of targeted investors;
12) the maximum number of offer debt instruments to be subscribed for by each type of targeted investors;
13) the maximum value of offer debt instruments to be subscribed for by each type of targeted investors;
14) allocation method and description of the process where an excess of subscription monies has been received for all types of targeted investors;
15) the offer period;
16) full information of rights granted to holders of the debt instruments;
17) debt instruments particulars;
18) details of repayment related dates including final maturity date and early repayment dates, specifying whether exercisable at the issuer's or the holder of debt instruments' request and the date from which payments are due to start;
19) restrictions on debt instruments;
20) details of the arrangements for transfer of the debt instruments;
21) the names and addresses of the paying agents, and any registrar and transfer agents of the issuer for the debt instruments;
22) the name and address of the board members of the special purposes entity ;
23) details of the early redemption of the debt instruments;
24) a statement referring to the "Important Notice" and the "Risk Factors" under section (2) and section (9), respectively before making an investment decision; and
25) a statement confirming that arrangements have been implemented to protect holders of debt instruments in accordance with Article 51 of the Rules on the Offer of Securities and Continuing Obligations.

5. Summary of basic information

This section must include a summary of the basic information contained in the prospectus, including:

1) a disclaimer to investors about consideration of the prospectus as a whole, and not merely the summary;

2) a description of the sponsor;
3) the sponsor's mission and overall strategy;
4) the sponsor's key strengths and competitive advantages;
5) an overview of the market in which the sponsor operates; and
6) a summary of the special purposes entity's financing transaction and commitment of the sponsor to ensure payment of amounts due under the debt instruments.

6. Summary of financial information

This section must include a summary of key financial information contained in the prospectus, including sponsor's operational performance, financial condition, cash flows and key performance indicators.

7. Table of contents

This section must include a table of contents.

8. Terms and definitions

This section must include the terms and definitions used through the prospectus.

9. Risk factors

This section must include information in relation to risk factors specific to:

1) the sponsor;
2) the market or industry in which the sponsor operates;
3) the special purposes entity; and
4) the securities being offered.

10. Market and industry information

This section must include information on market trends and industry information specific to the sponsor's operations.

11. Issuer background, business nature

This section must include the following information:

1) the official name, commercial registration number and the address shown in the commercial registration and, if different, the principal address of the special purposes entity;
2) the date of incorporation of the special purposes entity;
3) the purpose of the special purposes entity;
4) the directors of the special purposes entity;
5) the date of appointment of all the special purposes entity's directors or proposed directors;
6) details of other previous or current board positions held by all directors or proposed directors. The details should include, the name of the company, legal status, membership dates, and the sector in which the company operates;
7) details of any bankruptcies of each of the special purposes entity's director or proposed director;
8) details of any company insolvency in the preceding five years where any of the special purposes entity's directors or proposed directors were employed by the insolvent company in a managerial or supervisory capacity; and
9) a summary of existing or proposed service contracts, if any, of the directors.
10) a statement showing the direct or indirect interests of each director or proposed director, or senior executives of the special purposes entity, and any of their relatives in the shares or debt instruments of the special purposes entity, the sponsor or the sponsor's subsidiaries (if applicable), or provide an appropriate negative statement.

12. Sponsor background, business nature

This section must include the following information:

1) the official name, commercial registration number and the address shown in the commercial registration and, if different, the principal address of the sponsor;

2) the date of incorporation of the sponsor;

3) the authorized shares of the sponsor, the number of shares issued or agreed to be issued, the value paid up, the nominal value and a description of the shares;

4) a description and organization chart of the group showing the sponsor's position within that group (if applicable);

5) the general nature of the business of the sponsor and the sponsor's subsidiaries (if applicable) and details of the main products sold or services performed and an indication of any significant new products or activities;

6) if the sponsor or the sponsor's subsidiaries (if applicable) trades outside the Kingdom, a statement showing the location of such trading operations must be provided. Where a material portion of the sponsor or the sponsor's subsidiaries assets are outside the Kingdom, the value and location of such assets and the value of the assets located in the Kingdom;

7) information concerning the policy of the sponsor and the sponsor's subsidiaries (if applicable) on the research and development of new products and production processes over the past three financial years, where significant;

8) particulars of any interruption in the business of the sponsor and the sponsor's subsidiaries (if applicable) which may have or has had a significant effect on the financial position in the last 12 months;

9) the number of people employed by the sponsor and the sponsor's subsidiaries (if applicable) and any material changes to that number over the last two financial years, with a breakdown of persons employed by main categories of activity and by Saudization ratio; and

10) a statement that no material change in the nature of the business is contemplated or, if one is contemplated, a detailed description of that change and its impact on the sponsor's business and profitability.

13. Sponsor's organizational structure

This section must include the following information:

1) Sponsor's management

(a) the sponsor's organizational chart showing the directors structure, supervisory committees, and the functions of senior executives;

(b) the full names and description of the professional and academic qualifications and area of expertise and the date of appointment of all the directors or proposed directors (showing whether the director is independent or non-independent and executive or non-executive), in addition to the senior executives and the company secretary of the sponsor;

(c) details of other previous or current board positions held by all directors or proposed directors or senior executives and the company secretary of the sponsor. The details should include, the name of the company, legal status, membership dates, and the sector in which the company operates;

(d) details of any bankruptcies of each director or proposed director of the special purposes entity, or senior executives or the company secretary of the sponsor;

(e) details of any company insolvency in the preceding five years where any of the directors or proposed directors, senior executives, or the company secretary of the sponsor were employed by the insolvent company in a managerial or supervisory capacity;

(f) a statement showing the direct or indirect interests of each director or proposed director, senior executives, company secretary of the sponsor, and any of their relatives in the shares or debt instruments of the issuer, the sponsor or the sponsor's subsidiaries (if applicable), or provide an appropriate negative statement;

(g) the aggregate remuneration and benefits in kind granted by the sponsor or any subsidiary during the three financial years prior to listing to the directors and the five senior executives who received the highest payments, including the CEO and CFO if they were not within the top five;

(h) a summary of existing or proposed service contracts, if any, of the directors or the CEO and CFO of the sponsor;

(i) full particulars of any contract or arrangement in effect or contemplated at the time of submission of the prospectus in which a director or senior executive or any of their relatives is interested in relation to the business of the sponsor or the sponsor's subsidiaries (if applicable), or provide an appropriate negative statement;

(j) information about the sponsor's directors committees, including the names of each committee member and a summary of the terms of reference under which the committee operates; and

(k) information on the sponsor's compliance with corporate governance.

2) Sponsor's employees

(a) any employee share-schemes in place prior to the application for registration and admission to listing of the securities along with details on the aggregate amount of shares owned by the employees in the sponsor; and

(b) any other arrangements involving the employees in the capital of the sponsor.

14. Sponsor financial information

The information required below must be provided in relation to the sponsor and the sponsor's subsidiaries (if applicable) for the three financial years immediately preceding the application for registration and admission to listing:

1) comparative tables of financial information with commentary and analysis by management of the sponsor. The comparative tables must:

(a) be prepared on a consolidated basis;

(b) be extracted without material adjustment from audited financial statements; and

(c) include financial information presented in a form consistent with that which is adopted in the sponsor's annual financial statements.

2) a report by certified external auditor must be prepared in accordance with the requirements of Annex 15 of the Listing Rules in any of the following circumstances:

(a) where the external auditors have reservations regarding its report on the consolidated financial statements of the sponsor for any of the last three financial years immediately preceding the application for registration and admission to listing;

(b) where the sponsor has undergone restructuring in the three financial years immediately preceding the date of application for registration and admission to listing;

(c) where any material change has been made to the accounting policies of the sponsor; or

(d) where any material adjustment has been made or is required to be made to the published audited financial statements during the periods referred to in sub-paragraph (a) above.

3) details of holdings, including holdings in contractually based securities or other assets whose value may be subject to fluctuations or be difficult to ascertain with certainty, significantly affecting the assessment of the sponsor's financial position.

4) the information required below must be provided in relation to the financial, operating performance, and results of operations:

(a) performance indicators;

(b) the financial, operating performance, and results of operations of the main lines of business;

(c) any seasonal or business cycles which affect the business or the financial condition;

(d) an explanation of any material changes from year to year in the financial information;

(e) information regarding any governmental, economic, fiscal, monetary or political policies or other factors that have materially affected, or could materially affect, directly or indirectly, the operations;

(f) the funding structure;

(g) particulars of any alterations in the capital of the sponsor, or where material, any of the sponsor's subsidiaries (if applicable) within the three years immediately preceding the date of application for registration and admission to listing. Such particulars must state the price and terms of any issues by the sponsor; and

(h) details of any capital of the sponsor, or any subsidiary, which is under option, including the consideration for which the option was granted, and the price and duration of the option, and the name and address of the grantee, or provide an appropriate negative statement.

5) property, plant and equipment:

(a) a breakdown of any existing material fixed assets, including leased properties;

(b) an explanation of the sponsor's depreciation policy and any changes contemplated in that policy; and

(c) any planned material fixed assets, including leased properties.

6) in relation to debt, a statement on an individual and consolidated basis as at the most recent date must be prepared covering the following:

(a) a breakdown and classification of any debt instruments issued and outstanding, and authorized or otherwise created but unissued, and term loans, distinguishing between guaranteed, unguaranteed, secured (whether the pledge is provided by the sponsor or by third parties) and unsecured loans, or provide an appropriate negative statement;

(b) a breakdown and classification of all other borrowing or indebtedness, bank overdrafts, liabilities under acceptances, acceptance credits or hire purchase commitments, distinguishing between guaranteed, unguaranteed, secured and unsecured borrowing and debt, or provide an appropriate negative statement;

(c) a breakdown and classification of all mortgages, rights and charges on the sponsor and its subsidiaries' properties, and special purposes entity's or provide an appropriate negative statement; and

(d) a breakdown of any contingent liabilities or guarantees, or provide an appropriate negative statement.

7) A statement by the directors of any material adverse change in the financial or trading position in the three financial years preceding the application for registration and admission to listing and during the period from the end of the period covered in the external auditors' report up to and including the date of approval of the prospectus or provide an appropriate negative statement.

8) Particulars of any commissions, discounts, brokerages or other non-cash compensation granted within the three years immediately preceding the application for registration and admission to listing in connection with the issue or offer of any securities by the sponsor or any of the sponsor's subsidiaries (if applicable), together with the names of any directors, proposed directors, senior executives, persons offering or placing the securities or experts who received any such payment or benefit or provide an appropriate negative statement.

15. Financing structure and use of proceeds

This section must include the following:

1) Information regarding the financial structure including details of:

(a) the use of the proceeds of issuance by the special purposes entity;
(b) the rights to be acquired by the special purposes entity under the financing structure (including their ranking on the event of insolvency of the sponsor or any other person, where applicable);
(c) the nature of the claim of the special purposes entity on the sponsor;
(d) any direct rights of recourse of the holders against the sponsor;
(e) details of any security interest to be granted in favor of the special purposes entity, including a description of the assets secured and any rights to substitute such assets, or a description of any variation in such security;

2) a description of any obligation on the special purposes entity in relation to the transaction, including the order of priority of any payments.

3) Information regarding the underlying assets of the asset-linked structure including, where relevant, details of:

a. in respect of the assets to which the debt instruments are linked:

1. the jurisdictions in which the assets will be held and by which they will be governed;
2. in the case of a small number of easily identifiable obligors, a general description of each obligor. In all other cases, a description of: the general characteristics of the obligors; and the economic environment, as well as global statistical data referred to the securitized assets;
3. the legal nature of the assets;
4. the expiry or maturity date(s) of the assets;
5. the amount of the assets;
6. any loan to value ratio or level of collateralization, where relevant;
7. the method of origination or creation of the assets, and for loans and credit agreements, the principal lending criteria and an indication of any loans which do not meet these criteria and any rights or obligations to make further advances;
8. an indication of significant representations and collateral given to the special purposes entity relating to the assets;
9. any rights to substitute the assets and a description of the manner in which and the type of assets which may be so substituted; if there is any capacity to substitute assets with a different class or quality of assets a statement to that effect together with a description of the impact of such substitution;
10. a description of any relevant insurance policies relating to the assets. Any concentration with one insurer must be disclosed if it is material to the transaction;
11. If a relationship exists that is material to the issue, between the special purposes entity or the sponsor and an obligor, details of the principal terms of that relationship.
12. Where the assets comprise obligations that are not actively traded on an exchange, a description of the principal terms and conditions of the obligations.
13. Where the assets comprise equity securities that are traded on an exchange indicate the following:

a. a description of the securities;
b. a description of the market on which they are traded including its date of establishment, how price information is published, an indication of daily trading volumes, information as to the standing of the market in the country and the name of the market's regulatory authority;
c. the frequency with which prices of the relevant securities, are published.

14. a description of the method and date of the sale, transfer, novation or assignment of the assets or of any rights and/or obligations in the assets to the special purposes entity or, where applicable, the manner and time period in which the proceeds from the issue will be fully invested by the special purposes entity;

15. where relevant, the name, address and significant business activities of the originators of the securitized assets;

16. the name, address and significant business activities of the administrator, calculation agent or equivalent, together with a summary of the administrator's/calculation agents responsibilities, their relationship with the originator or the creator of the assets and a summary of the provisions relating to the termination of the appointment of the administrator/calculation agent and the appointment of an alternative administrator/calculation agent;

17. the name and addresses and brief description of:

(a) any swap counterparties and any providers of other material forms of credit/liquidity enhancements;

(b) the banks with which the main accounts relating to the transaction are held; and

18. an indication in the prospectus whether or not it intends to provide post-issuance transaction information regarding securities to be admitted to trading and the performance of the underlying collateral. Where the special purposes entity has indicated that it intends to report such information, specify in the prospectus what information will be reported, where such information can be obtained, and the frequency with which such information will be reported.

b. In respect of an actively managed pool of assets linked to the issue:

1. equivalent information to that contained in items 15(3/i) to allow an assessment of the type, quality, sufficiency and liquidity of the asset types in the portfolio which will secure the issue;

2. the parameters within which investments can be made, the name and description of the entity responsible for such management including a description of that entity's expertise and experience, a summary of the provisions relating to the termination of the appointment of such entity and the appointment of an alternative management entity, and a description of that entity's relationship with any other parties to the issue.

c. Valuation of the assets to which the debt instruments are to be linked, where known:

1. In respect of marketable securities traded on an exchange or other market approved by the Authority, a valuation at a mid-market basis based on a market price verified by the financial advisor.

2. In respect of assets not falling within paragraph (1) above, a valuation by a third party valuer of the assets and any cash flow/income streams. In this respect, the third party valuer must:

a) not be the special purposes entity, the sponsor, the financial advisor or an affiliate of any of them; and

b) be appropriately qualified and have relevant expertise in valuing the relevant asset class;

4) particulars of any investment powers associated with the special purposes entity's assets.

5) a description of how the cash flows will be used to meet the special purposes entity's obligations including details of:

(a) how the cash flow from the assets will meet the issuer's obligations to holders of the securities;

(b) information on any credit enhancements, an indication of where material potential liquidity shortfalls may occur and the availability of any liquidity supports and indication of provisions designed to cover interest/principal shortfall risks;

(c) without prejudice to item (b) above, details of any subordinated debt finance;

(d) an indication of any investment parameters for the investment of temporary liquidity surpluses and description of the parties responsible for such investment;

(e) how payments are collected in respect of the assets;

(f) the order of priority of payments made by the issuer to the holders of the class of securities in question; and

(g) details of any other arrangements upon which payments of interest and principal to investors are dependent.

6) particulars of how payments will be made by the sponsor.

7) a statement as to how the proceeds of issuance are intended to be used by the sponsor.

8) an estimate of the offer expenses.

16. Statements by experts

Where the prospectus includes a statement made by an expert, a statement should be included specifying the qualifications of the expert and whether such expert or any relative has any shareholding or interest of any kind in the sponsor or any of its subsidiaries. In addition, the statement should confirm that the expert has given and not withdrawn his written consent to the publication in the prospectus of the expert's statement included in the form and context in which it is included.

17. Declarations

The directors of the special purposes entity and the sponsor must make the following declarations:

1) other than what has been mentioned on page ( ) of this prospectus, there has not been any interruption in the business of the special purposes entity, the sponsor or any of the sponsor's subsidiaries (if applicable), which may have or has had a significant effect on the financial position in the last 12 months.

2) other than what has been mentioned on page ( ) of this prospectus, there has not been any commissions, discounts, brokerages or other non-cash compensation granted within the three years immediately preceding the application for registration and admission to listing in connection with the issue or offer of any securities by the sponsor or any of the sponsor's subsidiaries (if applicable).

3) other than what has been mentioned on page ( ) of this prospectus, there has not been any material adverse change in the financial or trading position of the sponsor or its subsidiaries (if applicable) in the three financial years preceding the application for registration and admission to listing and during the period from the end of the period covered in the external auditors' report up to and including the date of approval of the prospectus.

4) other than what is mentioned on page ( ) of this prospectus, the directors of the or their relatives have no shareholdings or interest of any kind in the special purposes entity, the sponsor or any of the sponsor's subsidiaries (if applicable), and nor does any relative of theirs.

18. Legal information

This section must include the following legal information, as relevant:

1) a summary of the provisions of the special purposes entity and the sponsor's by-laws and other constitutional documents, including but not limited to:

(a) the object clause of the special purposes entity and the sponsor;

(b) provisions relating to the special purposes entity and the sponsor's administrative, management and supervisory bodies;

(c) provisions relating to the rights and restrictions attached to the financing transaction including;

1) any pledges not to apply for new loans which give privileges to new creditors;

2) any control rights granted to of investors by the special purposes entity;

(d) provisions governing the alteration of securities rights or classes of the special purposes entity, where applicable, and the sponsor;

(e) provisions governing liquidation and winding up of the special purposes entity, where applicable, and the sponsor;

(f) any power enabling a director or the CEO, of the issuer, where applicable, or the sponsor, to vote on a contract or proposal in which he has an interest;

(g) any power enabling a director or the CEO, of the special purposes entity, where applicable, or the sponsor, to vote on remuneration to themselves; and

(h) any powers allowing the directors or the senior executives, of the special purposes entity, where applicable, or the sponsor, to borrow from the sponsor.

2) a summary of all material contracts of the special purposes entity and the sponsor, including summaries of any contract which is material to the financing arrangement.

3) a summary of all related party contracts of the special purposes entity and the sponsor.

4) in relation to the special purposes entity and the sponsor and its subsidiaries (if applicable):

1. particulars of any intangible assets such as trademarks, patents, copyright or other intellectual property rights which are material in relation to the special purposes entity's, the sponsor's or any of its subsidiaries (if applicable) business or profitability, and a statement regarding the extent to which the special purposes entity, the sponsor or any of its subsidiaries (if applicable) is dependent on such assets.

2. in relation to the special purposes entity, the sponsor and the sponsor's subsidiaries, particulars of any litigation or claim (including any litigation pending or threatened) which may have a material effect on the special purposes entity's, the sponsor's or any of its subsidiaries' business or financial position, or an appropriate negative statement.

19. Underwriter

This section must include information about the underwriter of the offer, as follows:

1) the name and address of the underwriter; and

2) the principal terms of the underwriting agreement, including the compensation arrangement between the issuer and the underwriter.

20. Expenses

This section must include details of the aggregate offer expenses.

21. Waivers

This section must include details on all requirements that have been waived for the special purposes entity and the sponsor by the Authority.

22. Information concerning the debt instruments and terms and conditions of the offer

This section must include the following information:

1) a statement that application has been made to the Authority for the registration and admission to listing;

2) the nominal value of the offer;

3) full information on the rights conferred upon holders of debt instruments;

4) particulars of the debt instruments;

5) subscription method;

6) details of the early redemption of the offer;

7) the names and addresses of the paying agents, and any registrar and transfer agents for the debt instruments;

8) details of the arrangements for transfer of the debt instruments;

9) details of repayment related dates including the final maturity date and early repayment dates, specifying whether exercisable at the sponsor's or the holder of debt instruments' request and the date from which payments are due;

10) procedures and time limits for allocation and delivery of the debt instruments and, where there will be temporary documents of title, the procedures for the delivery and exchange thereof;

11) a description of the resolutions, and approvals by virtue of which the debt instruments will be offered;

12) whether there are any guarantees, pledges or commitments intended to be provided to guarantee the offer;

13) details of any agreements with the representative of the holders of the debt instruments, if any, the name and function and head office of such representative, the conditions under which the representative may be replaced together with an indication of where the public may inspect copies of the documents detailing the obligations of the representative;

14) a description of any subordination of the offer to any other debts or debt instruments of the special purposes entity and/or the sponsor;

15) a description of the applicable law related to the offer;

16) details of any restrictions on the transferability of the debt instruments;

17) the date upon which it is expected that trading in the debt instruments will commence, if the sponsor can anticipate such date; and

18) if a public or private offer has been or is being made simultaneously on the markets of two or more countries at the same time, and if a tranche has been or is being reserved for certain of these markets, details of any such offer or tranche must be provided.

23. Subscription declarations

This section must include information on the subscription declarations, allocation process, and the Exchange details.

24. Documents available for inspection

This section must include information in relation to the place in the Kingdom at which the following documents may be inspected and the period of time during which the inspection may take place (being not less than 3 days before the end of the offer period):

1) the by-laws and other constitutional documents of the special purposes entity and the sponsor;

2) any document or order granting permission to offer securities to the public;

3) each contract disclosed pursuant to sub-paragraph (i) of paragraph (1) of section (13) of this Annex or, if the contract is not

produced in writing, a memorandum giving full particulars of the agreement;

4) all other reports, letters, documents, value estimates or statements by any expert any part of which is extracted or referred to in the prospectus; and

5) the audited financial statements of the sponsor for each of the three financial years immediately preceding the date of the publication of the prospectus, in addition to the most recent interim financial statements.

25. External auditor's report

The special purposes entity's audited financial statements for the three years immediately preceding the date of the publication of the prospectus, in addition to the most recent interim financial statements.

26. Guarantees

Where a guarantee, pledge or other similar commitment is to be provided the following information must be included:

1) details regarding the terms, conditions and scope of the guarantee, pledge or other similar commitment including any conditionality on the application of the guarantee, pledge or similar commitment; and

2) copies of the external auditors' and the directors' report on the accounts of the guarantor company.

25.29 ANNEX 12: CONTENT OF A PROSPECTUS FOR DEBT INSTRUMENTS FOR AN ISSUER THAT HAS SHARES CURRENTLY LISTED ON THE EXCHANGE

Inclusion of information in the prospectus

A prospectus submitted for the registration and offering of debt instruments from an issuer which has shares currently listed on the Exchange at the time of submission must contain the information under the following sections at a minimum:

1) Cover page

This section must include the following information (where applicable):

1. the issuer's formation, incorporation and commercial registration information;

2. capital and number of shares;

3. a summary of the offer including debt instruments details and rights;

4. target participants;

5. offer period and conditions;

6. shares and debt instruments that have been listed prior to the particular offer by the issuer (if applicable);

7. a statement that the issuer has submitted the application for registration and offer of securities subject to the prospectus to the Authority, has submitted the application for listing to the Exchange and has submitted all the required documents to the relevant authorities;

8. a statement referring to the "Important Notice" and the "Risk Factors" under section (2) and section (8) of this Annex, respectively before making an investment decision; and

9. the following declaration:

"This prospectus includes information provided as part of the application for registration and offer of securities in compliance with the Rules on the Offer of Securities and Continuing Obligations of the Capital Market Authority of the Kingdom of Saudi Arabia (the "Authority") and the application for listing of securities in compliance with the Listing Rules of the Saudi Stock Exchange. The directors, whose names appear on page [ ], collectively and individually accept full responsibility for the accuracy of the information contained in this prospectus and confirm, having made all reasonable enquiries, that to the best of their knowledge and belief, there are no other facts the omission of which would make any statement herein misleading. The Authority and the Saudi Stock Exchange do not take any responsibility for the contents of this prospectus, do not make any representation as to its accuracy or completeness, and expressly disclaim any liability whatsoever for any loss arising from, or incurred in reliance upon, any part of this prospectus."

2) Important notice

This section must include a notice which shows the purpose and the nature of information mentioned in the prospectus

.

3) Corporate directory

This section must contain the following:

1. the issuer's and its representatives' contact information, including addresses, telephone and fax numbers, e-mail addresses, and the issuer's website.

2. the contact information, including addresses, telephone and fax numbers, and website and e-mail addresses, for each of the parties listed below, and any other expert to whom a statement or report included in the prospectus has been attributed:

a) the financial advisor;

b) the legal advisor;

c) the external auditor;

d) the underwriter (if any); and

e) the Capital Market Institutions authorized to place or sell the securities.

4) Offer summary

This section must contain a disclaimer to the target investors on the importance of reading the prospectus prior to making an investment decision and include the following information (where applicable):

1. the issuer's name, description and incorporation information;

2. the issuer's activities;

3. substantial shareholders showing their ownership percentages and number of shares;

4. the capital of the issuer;

5. the issuer's total number of shares;

6. the nominal value for offered debt instrument;

7. the use of proceeds;

8. types of targeted investors;

9. subscription method for each type of targeted investors;

10. the minimum number of offer debt instruments to be subscribed for by each type of targeted investors;

11. the minimum value of offer of debt instruments to be subscribed for by each type of targeted investors;

12. the maximum number of offer debt instruments to be subscribed for by each type of targeted investors;

13. the maximum value of offer debt instruments to be subscribed for by each type of targeted investors;

14. allocation method and description of the process where an excess of subscription monies has been received for all types of targeted investors;

15. the offer period;

16. full information of rights granted to holders of the debt instruments;

17. debt instruments particulars;

18. details of repayment related dates including final maturity date and early repayment dates, specifying whether exercisable at the issuer's or the holder of debt instruments' request and the date from which payments are due to start;

19. restrictions on debt instruments;

20. details of the arrangements for transfer of the debt instruments;

21. the names and addresses of the paying agents, and any registrar and transfer agents for the debt instruments;

22. details of the early redemption of the debt instruments; and

23. a statement referring the reader to the "Important Notice" and the "Risk Factors" under section (2) and section (8) of this Annex, respectively before making an investment decision.

5) Summary of financial information

This section must contain at least summary of key financial information contained in the prospectus, including the issuer's operational operation, financial condition cash flow and key performance indicators.

6) Table of contents

This section must include a table of contents.

7) Terms and definitions

This section must include the terms and definitions used through the prospectus.

8) Risk factors

This section must contain information in relation to risk factors specific to:

1. the issuer;

2. the market or industry in which the issuer operates; and

3. the securities being offered.

9) Financial information

The information required below must be provided in relation to the issuer and the issuer's subsidiaries (if applicable) for the three financial years immediately preceding the application for registration and offer of securities that are subject to this prospectus as well as the period covered in the interim financial statements as per paragraph (4) of Article 23 of the Rules on the Offer of Securities and Continuing Obligations.

1. comparative tables of financial information with commentary and analysis by management of financial material information. The comparative tables must:

a. be prepared on a consolidated basis;

b. be extracted without material adjustment from audited financial statements; and

c. include financial information presented in a form consistent with that which is adopted in the issuer's annual financial statements.

2. a report by certified external auditor must be prepared in accordance with the requirements of Annex 15 of the Rules on the Offer of Securities and Continuing Obligations in any of the following circumstances:

a. where the external auditor has reservations on the report of the audited financial statements of the issuer for any of the last three financial years immediately preceding the application for registration and offer of securities that are subject to this prospectus;

b. where the issuer has undergone restructuring in the three financial years immediately preceding the date of the application for registration and offer of securities that are subject to this prospectus;

c. where any material change has been made to the accounting policies of the issuer; or

d. where any material adjustment has been made or is required to be made to the published audited financial statements during the periods referred to in subparagraph (a) above.

3. details of holdings, including holdings in contractually based securities or other assets whose value may be subject to fluctuations or be difficult to ascertain with certainty, significantly affecting the assessment of the issuer's financial position.

4. the information required below must be provided in relation to the financial, operating performance, and results of operations:

a. performance indicators;

b. the financial, operating performance, and results of operations of the main lines of business;

c. any seasonal or business cycles which affect the business or the financial condition;

d. an explanation of any material changes from year to year in the financial information;

e. information regarding any governmental, economic, fiscal, monetary or political policies or other factors that have materially affected, or could materially affect, directly or indirectly, the operations;

f. the funding structure;

g. a table showing any capital of the issuer or any subsidiary which is under option, including the consideration for which the option was granted, and the price and duration of the option, and the name and address of the grantee, or provide an appropriate negative statement.

5. property, plant and equipment

a. a breakdown of any existing material fixed assets, including leased properties;

b. an explanation of the issuer's depreciation policy and any changes contemplated in that policy; and

c. any planned material fixed assets, including leased properties.

6. in relation to debt, a statement on an individual and consolidated basis as at the most recent date must be prepared covering the following:

a. a breakdown and classification of any debt instruments issued and outstanding, and authorized or otherwise created but unissued, and term loans, distinguishing between guaranteed, unguaranteed, secured (whether the pledge is provided by the issuer or by third parties) and unsecured loans, or provide an appropriate negative statement;

b. a breakdown and classification of all other borrowing or indebtedness, bank overdrafts, liabilities under acceptances, acceptance credits or hire purchase commitments, distinguishing between guaranteed, unguaranteed, secured and unsecured borrowing and debt, or provide an appropriate negative statement;

c. a breakdown and classification of all mortgages, rights and charges on the issuer and its subsidiaries' properties, or provide an appropriate negative statement; and

d. a breakdown of any contingent liabilities or guarantees, or provide an appropriate negative statement.

7. A statement by the directors of any material adverse change in the financial or trading position in the three financial years preceding the application for registration and offer of securities that are subject to this prospectus and during the period from the end of the period covered in the external auditors' report up to and including the date of approval of the prospectus or provide an appropriate negative statement.

8. Particulars of any commissions, discounts, brokerages or other non- cash compensation granted within the three years immediately preceding the application for registration and offer of securities that are subject to this prospectus in connection with the issue or offer of any securities by the issuer or any of the issuer's subsidiaries (if applicable), together with the names of any directors, proposed directors, senior executives, persons offering or placing the securities or experts who received any such payment or benefit or provide an appropriate negative statement.

10) Use of proceeds

This section must include a statement as to how such proceeds are intended to be used.

11) Statements by experts

Where the prospectus includes a statement made by an expert, a statement should be included specifying the qualifications of the expert and whether such expert or any relative has any shareholding or interest of any kind in the issuer or any of its subsidiaries. In addition, the statement should confirm that the expert has given and not withdrawn his written consent to the publication in the prospectus of the expert's statement included in the form and context in which it is included.

12) Declarations

The directors of the issuer must make the following declarations:

1. other than what has been mentioned on page (•) of this prospectus, no commissions, discounts, brokerages or other non-cash compensation have been granted within the three years immediately preceding the application for registration and offer that are the subject of this prospectus in connection with the issue or offer of any securities by the issuer or any of the issuer's subsidiaries (if applicable).

2. other than what has been mentioned on page (•) of this prospectus, there has not been any material adverse change in the financial or trading position of the issuer or its subsidiaries (if applicable) in the three financial years preceding the application for registration and offer of securities that are subject to this prospectus and during the period from the end of the period covered in the external auditors' report up to and including the date of approval of the prospectus.

3. other than what is mentioned on page (•) of this prospectus, they do not have any shareholding or interest of any kind in the issuer or any of the issuer's subsidiaries (if applicable), and nor does any relative of theirs.

13) Legal Information

This section must include the following declarations from the board of directors that:

1. the issuance does not constitute a breach of the relevant laws and regulations in Saudi Arabia.

2. the issuance does not constitute a breach of any contract/agreement entered into by the issuer.

3. all material legal issues concerning the issuer have been disclosed in the prospectus.

4. details of any bankruptcies of each director or proposed director, senior executives, or the company secretary of the issuer;

5. details of any company insolvency in the preceding five years where any of the directors or proposed directors, senior executives, or the company secretary of the issuer were employed by the insolvent company in a managerial or supervisory capacity;

14) Underwriter

This section must include information about the underwriter of the offer, as follows:

1. the name and address of the underwriter; and

2. the principal terms of the underwriting agreement, including the compensation arrangement between the issuer and the underwriter.

15) Expenses

This section must include details of the aggregate offer expenses.

16) Waivers

This section must include details on all requirements that have been waived for the issuer by the authority.

17) Information concerning the debt instruments and terms and conditions of the offer

This section must include the following information:

1. a statement that application has been made to the Authority for the application for registration and offer of securities that are subject to this prospectus and to the Exchange for the listing;

2. the nominal value of the offer;

3. full information on the rights conferred upon holders of debt instruments;

4. particulars of the debt instruments;

5. subscription method;

6. details of the early redemption of the offer;

7. the names and addresses of the paying agents, and any registrar and transfer agents for the debt instruments;

8. details of the arrangements for transfer of the debt instruments;

9. details of repayment related dates including the final maturity date and early repayment dates, specifying whether exercisable at the issuer's or the holder of debt instruments' request and the date from which payments are due;

10. procedures and time limits for allocation and delivery of the debt instruments and, where there will be temporary documents of title, the procedures for the delivery and exchange thereof;

11. a description of the resolutions, and approvals by virtue of which the debt instruments will be offered;

12. whether there are any guarantees, pledges or commitments intended to be provided to guarantee the offer;

13. details of any agreements with the representative of the holders of the debt instruments, if any, the name and function and head office of such representative, the conditions under which the representative may be replaced together with an indication of where the public may inspect copies of the documents detailing the obligations of the representative;

14. a description of any subordination of the offer to any other debts or debt instruments of the issuer;

15. a description of the applicable law related to the offer;

16. details of any restrictions on the transferability of the debt instruments;

17. the date upon which it is expected that trading in the debt instruments will commence, if the issuer can anticipate such date; and

18. if a public or private offer has been or is being made simultaneously on the markets of two or more countries at the same time, and if a tranche has been or is being reserved for certain of these markets, details of any such offer or tranche must be provided.

18) Subscription declarations

This section must include information on the subscription declarations, allocation process, and the Exchange's details.

19) Documents available for inspection

This section must include information in relation to the place in the Kingdom at which the following documents may be inspected and the period of time during which the inspection may take place (being not less than three days before the start of the offer):

1. the bylaws and other constitutional documents of the issuer;

2. any document or order granting permission to offer securities to the public;

3. any contract or arrangement, in effect or contemplated, in which a director or senior executive or any of their relatives has an interest and that is related to the business of the issuer or any of the issuer's subsidiaries (if applicable). If such a contract is not produced in writing, a memorandum giving full particulars of the agreement;

4. all other reports, letters, documents, value estimates or statements by any expert any part of which is extracted or referred to in the prospectus; and

5. the audited financial statements of the issuer for each of the three financial years immediately preceding the date of the publication of the prospectus, in addition to the most recent interim financial statements.

20) External auditor's report

The issuer's audited financial statements for the three years immediately preceding the date of the publication of the prospectus, in addition to the most recent interim financial statements.

21) Guarantees

Where a guarantee, pledge or other similar commitment is to be provided the following information must be included:

1. details regarding the terms, conditions and scope of the guarantee, pledge or other similar commitment including any conditionality on the application of the guarantee, pledge or similar commitment; and

2. copies of the external auditors' and the directors' report on the accounts of the guarantor company.

22) Bylaws

The issuer's bylaws.

25.30 ANNEX 13: CONTENTS OF A SHAREHOLDERS' CIRCULAR FOR A CAPITAL INCREASE BY DEBT CONVERSION

A shareholders' circular for the registration and offering of capital increase shares by debt conversion shall contain the following information:

1. Cover page

This section must include the following information (where applicable):

1) a summary of the offer including share class and rights;
2) purpose of the capital increase and the identity of the creditor;
3) a brief description of the debt conversion;
4) the issuer's current capital and number of shares previously listed;
5) whether the debt conversion is deemed to be a related party transaction;
6) the names and shareholdings of related parties (if any);
7) the creditor's pre and post capital ownership in the issuer;
8) the total value of the debt that is subject to the transaction, and the value and number of shares to be issued;
9) a statement that the issuer has submitted the application for registration and offer of the securities and the application for listing to the Exchange and that all requirements have been met;
10) a statement referring to the "Important Notice" and the "Risk Factors" under section (2) and section (8) of this Annex, respectively before voting on the capital increase; and

11) the following declarations:
"This circular includes information provided as part of the application for registration and offer of securities in compliance with the Rules on the Offer of Securities and Continuing Obligations of the Capital Market Authority of the Kingdom of Saudi Arabia (the "Authority") and the application for listing of securities in compliance with the Listing Rules of the Saudi Stock Exchange. The directors, whose names appear on page [ ], collectively and individually accept full responsibility for the accuracy of the information contained in this circular and confirm, having made all reasonable enquiries, that to the best of their knowledge and belief, there are no other facts the omission of which would make any statement herein misleading. The Authority and the Saudi Stock Exchange do not take any responsibility for the contents of this circular, do not make any representation as to its accuracy or completeness, and expressly disclaim any liability whatsoever for any loss arising from, or incurred in reliance upon, any part of this circular. If understanding the contents of such circular is difficult, an authorized financial advisor must be appointed"; and
12) a statement from the directors of the issuer confirming that having done the due diligence they deemed sufficient in the circumstances, the debt conversion is in the best interests of the issuer and the shareholders.

2) Important notice

This section must include a notice which shows the purpose and the nature of information mentioned in the circular.

3) Corporate directory

This section must include the following:

1) the issuer's and its representatives' contact information, including addresses, telephone and fax numbers, e-mail addresses, and the issuer's website.

2) the contact information, including addresses, telephone and fax numbers, and website and e-mail addresses, for each of the parties listed below, and any other expert to whom a statement or report included in the circular has been attributed:

a. the financial advisor of the issuer;
b. the legal advisor of the issuer; and
c. the external auditor of the issuer.

4) Summary

This section must contain the following information (where applicable):

1) the issuer's name, description and incorporation information;

2) the issuer's activities;

3) substantial shareholders and their current ownership percentages;

4) the public, substantial shareholders of the issuer and the creditor showing their ownership percentages and number of shares pre- and post-capital increase

5) the capital of the issuer;

6) issuer's total number of shares;

7) the nominal value per shares;

8) the total number of new shares;

9) the percentage of the new shares to the capital of the issuer;

10) the issue price;

11) the total value of the issue;

12) description of the debt conversion including the identity of the creditor and key details in relation thereto;

13) structure of the debt conversion;

14) rationale behind the debt conversion;

15) statement on whether the debt conversion constitutes a related party transaction and if so the identity, and ownerships of such parties;

16) a summary of the key steps required until the completion of the capital increase and the listing of new shares;

17) the rights to dividends of the new shares;

18) consents and approvals required to complete the capital increase;

19) voting rights of the new shares;

20) restrictions on new shares;

21) a statement that the proposed capital increase is subject to the shareholders' approval at the extraordinary general assembly.

22) a statement to the issuer's current shareholders about the consideration of the circular as a whole and not merely the summary in an identifiable font); and

5) Key dates and debt conversion milestones

This section must include a timetable showing the detailed timeline of the debt conversion.

6) Table of contents

This section must include the circular table of contents.

7) Terms and definitions

This section must include the terms and definitions used through the circular.

8) Risk factors

This section must include information in relation to all risk factors relating to the debt conversion including but not limited to:

1) commercial risks, legal risks, and risks relating to the issuance of the new shares;

2) the dilution of current shareholders' ownership, and the associated reduction in voting power; and

3) any risk related to the potential control by the creditor (if post capital increase will result in owning 30% or more by such parties).

9) The Debt Conversion

This section must include all information relating to the debt conversion including:

1) the rationale behind the debt conversion and its implications on the issuer;

2) any envisaged changes in the issuer's board of directors or the executive management as a result of the debt conversion;

3) the issuer's ownership structure pre and post the capital increase;

4) the valuation of debt that is subject to the transaction and the resulting share valuation and number of shares to be issued, the

agreed debt conversion valuation terms including agreed debt valuation, and the resulting share valuation and number of shares to be issued;

5) details of any related parties who have direct or indirect interest in the transaction if the debt conversion is considered as a related party transaction;

6) the proposed timing of the debt conversion and its key steps;

7) pre and post capital increase ownership structure;

8) the pro-forma financial statements reflecting the financial position of the issuer following the debt conversion;

9) a comparison of the issuer's performance indicators as per the pro-forma vs. the issuer's audited financials;

10) earnings per share accretion/dilution analysis; and

11) the issuer's share price performance, covering at least one year prior to the date of the application for registration and offer of securities.

10) Financial information

This section must include at least the pro-forma financial statements of the issuer post-capital increase and covering pro-forma balance sheet, income statement and statement of cash flows.

11) Legal Information

This section must include all legal information relating to the debt conversion including but not limited to the following information:

1) board and senior executive declarations as to the following:

a. the debt conversion does not constitute a breach of the relevant laws and regulations in Saudi Arabia.

b. the issuance does not constitute a breach of any contract/agreement entered into by the issuer.

c. all material legal issues concerning the issuer have been disclosed in the circular.

d. this section includes all the material legal information about the debt conversion's documents, which the issuer's shareholders should take into consideration to make a well informed voting decision; and

e. that there is no other material legal information within this section the omission of which would make any statement herein misleading.

2) details on the debt conversion documents and agreements;

3) governmental approvals and third party consents required to complete the transaction;

4) particulars of any litigation or claim (including any litigation pending or threatened) or any ongoing investigations which may have a material effect on the issuer or any of its subsidiaries business or financial position, or an appropriate negative statement;

5) details of any bankruptcies of each director or proposed director, senior executives, or the company secretary of the issuer (or a negative statement thereto);

6) details of any company insolvency in the preceding five years where any of the directors or proposed directors, senior executives, or the company secretary of the issuer were employed by the insolvent company in a managerial or supervisory capacity.

7) (where the debt conversion is a related party transaction) that the independent members of the board of the issuer, other than the related parties, acknowledge that they do not have any direct or indirect interest in any of the issuer's shares or in any of the shares or businesses (as applicable) of the creditor, or in any contracts, signed or to be signed, between the parties of the transaction, and that they confirm their full independency in respect of the shares issuance subject of this circular.

12) Statements by experts

Where the circular includes a statement made by an expert, a statement should be included specifying the qualifications of the expert and whether such expert or any relative has any shareholding or interest of any kind in the issuer or any of its subsidiaries. In addition, the statement should confirm that the expert has given and not withdrawn his written consent to the publication in the circular of the expert's statement included in the form and context in which it is included.

13) Expenses

This section must include details of the aggregate debt conversion expenses.

14) Waivers

This section must include details on all requirements that have been waived for the issuer by the Authority.

15) Documents available for inspection

This section must include information in relation to the place in the Kingdom at which the following documents may be inspected and the period of time during which the inspection may take place (being not less than 14 days before the date of convening the extraordinary general assembly):

1) the transaction documents and agreements;

2) the examined issuer's pro-forma financials;

3) the valuation report;

4) the advisors' consent letters to the use their names, logos and statements in the circular;

5) a statement of the origin and amount of the debt subject of the transaction which is signed and certified by the board of directors and the auditors of the issuer; and

6) any other documents/information requested by the Authority.

16. Annexes

This section should include the following annexes to the circular:

1) the issuer's annual audited financials for the past three years; and

2) the reviewed pro-forma financial statement reflecting the financial position of the issuer following the debt conversion.

25.31 ANNEX 14: CONTENTS OF A CIRCULAR FOR A CAPITAL INCREASE TO ACQUIRE A COMPANY OR PURCHASE AN ASSET

The shareholders' circular for the registration and offering of capital increase to acquire a company or purchase an asset shall contain the following information as minimum:

1. Cover page

This section must include the following information (where applicable):

1. a summary of the offer including share class and rights;

2. purpose of the capital increase and the identity of the target company/assets;

3. whether the transaction is deemed to be a related party transaction;

4. the names and shareholdings of related parties (if any);

5. a brief description of the acquisition transaction or purchase;

6. details of ownership of the public, the substantial shareholders and the owners of the target company/asset.

7. total value of the transaction with the details of consideration provided to the owners of the target company/asset.

8. the current capital of the issuer and the number of shares that have been listed prior to the particular offer by the issuer;

9. a statement that the issuer has submitted the application for registration and offer of securities to the Authority and the application for listing to the Exchange and that all requirements have been met;

10. a statement referring to the "Important Notice" and the "Risk Factors" under section (2) and section (8) of this Annex, respectively before voting to the resolution of capital increase;

11. the following declarations:

"This circular includes information provided as part of the application for registration and offer of securities in compliance with the Rules on the Offer of Securities and Continuing Obligations of the Capital Market Authority of the Kingdom of Saudi Arabia (the "Authority") and the application for listing of securities in compliance with the Listing Rules of the Saudi Stock Exchange. The directors, whose names appear on page [ ], collectively and individually accept full responsibility for the accuracy of the information contained in this circular and confirm, having made all reasonable enquiries, that to the best of their knowledge and belief, there are no other facts the omission of which would make any statement herein misleading. The Authority and the Saudi Stock Exchange do not take any responsibility for the contents of this circular, do not make any representation as to its accuracy or completeness, and expressly disclaim any liability whatsoever for any loss arising from, or incurred in reliance upon, any part of this circular"; and

12. a statement from the directors of the issuer confirming that having done the due diligence they deemed sufficient in the circumstances, the acquisition or purchase is in the best interests of the issuer and the shareholders.

2. Important notice

This section must include a notice which shows the purpose and the nature of information mentioned in the circular.

3. Corporate directory

This section must include the following:

1. the issuer's and its representatives' contact information, including addresses, telephone and fax numbers, e-mail addresses, and the issuer's website.

2. the contact information, including addresses, telephone and fax numbers, and website and e-mail addresses, for each of the parties listed below, and any other expert to whom a statement or report included in the circular has been attributed:

a. the issuer's financial advisor;

b. the issuer's legal advisor; and

c. the issuer's external auditor.

4. Summary

This section must contain the following information (where applicable):

1. the issuer's name, description and incorporation information;

2. the issuer's activities;

3. substantial shareholders showing their ownership percentages and number of shares pre- and post-capital increase;

4. the capital of the issuer;

5. issuer's total number of shares;

6. the nominal value per shares;

7. the total number of new shares;

8. the percentage of the new shares to the capital of the issuer;

9. the issue price;

10. the total value of the issue;

11. description of the acquisition or purchase including the identity of the target company/asset and key details in relation thereto;

12. description of the target company/asset and incorporation information of the target company;

13. activities of the target company/asset;

14. substantial shareholders of the target (or the owners of the asset as applicable) showing their ownership percentages and number of shares (or stakes as the case may be) pre- and post-offering;

15. collective and individual ownership of the selling shareholders/ owners of the target company/asset in the issuer should the acquisition or purchase take place

16. the capital of the target;

17. target's total number of share (or stakes as the case may be);

18. statement on whether the acquisition or purchase constitutes a related party acquisition or purchase and if so the identity, and ownerships of such parties;

19. names of the selling shareholders of the target company to be acquired and the stakes/shares sought (collectively and from each selling shareholder);

20. the total value of the consideration and a break down (where applicable);

21. structure of the acquisition or purchase;

22. pre and post capital increase ownership structure in the issuer;

23. pre and post capital increase ownership structure in the target company or asset (as applicable);

24. ownership dilution effects;

25. earnings per share accretion/dilution;

26. rationale behind the acquisition or purchase;

27. a summary of the key steps required until the completion of the capital increase and the listing of new shares;

28. the rights to dividends of the new shares;

29. consents and approvals required to complete the capital increase;

30. voting rights of the new shares;

31. restrictions on new shares; and

32. a statement that the proposed capital increase is subject to the shareholders' approval at the extraordinary general assembly; and

33. include a disclaimer in identifiable font to the shareholders on the importance of reading the entire circular (and not just the summary) prior to voting at the extra ordinary general assembly on the capital increase.

5. Key dates and acquisition or purchase milestones

This section must include a timetable showing the detailed timeline of the acquisition or purchase.

6. Table of contents

This section must include the circular table of contents.

7. Terms and definitions

This section must include the terms and definitions used through the circular.

8. Risk factors

This section must include information in relation to all risk factors relating to the acquisition or purchase including but not limited to:

1) commercial risks, legal risks, and risks relating to the transaction and the issuance of the new shares;

2) the dilution of current shareholders' ownership, and the associated reduction in voting power.

3) any risk related to the potential control by selling shareholders (if post capital increase will result in owning 30% or more by such parties).

9. Market details of the relevant industry and trends of the target company/asset to be acquired

10. The Acquisition or Purchase

This section must include all information relating to the acquisition or purchase including:

1) a detailed break-down of the acquisition's or purchase's consideration, indicating the amount designated to each selling shareholder of the target company to be acquired or the asset to be purchased;

2) the rationale behind the acquisition or purchase and its implications on the issuer;

3) any envisaged changes in the issuer's board of directors or the executive team as a result of the acquisition or purchase;

4) an outline of the business of the target company/asset to be acquired;

5) the valuation of the target company/asset including a description of the valuation methodologies and assumptions utilized, the final agreed proposed valuation of the target company to be acquired/asset to be purchased, the final agreed value of the stakes/shares sought in the target company to be acquired, the corresponding value of acquisition or purchase consideration and the value and number of shares to be issued by the issuer, the agreed acquisition or purchase terms in lights of the above (for instance, the agreed upon consideration, portion of the consideration which will be paid in cash and in the proposed issued shares) ; covering at least the agreed value of the stakes/shares sought, a break-down of the consideration (i.e. shares vs. cash), the resulting share swap ratio and cash component per share (if any);

6) details of any related parties who have direct or indirect interest in the acquisition or purchase;

7) pre and post capital increase ownership structure;

8) the Pro-forma financial statements reflecting the financial position of the issuer following the acquisition or purchase;

9) a comparison of the issuer's performance indicators as per the pro-forma vs. the issuer's audited financials;

10) earnings per share accretion/dilution analysis; and

11) the issuer's share price performance, covering at least one year prior to the date of the application for registration and offer of securities.

11. Financial information

This section must include a reasoned management discussion and analysis on the target company/asset.

12. Legal Information

This section must include all legal information relating to the acquisition or purchase, including but not limited to the following:

1) the directors of the issuer must make the following declarations:

a) the acquisition or purchase does not constitute a breach of the relevant laws and regulations in Saudi Arabia;

b) the issuance does not constitute a breach of any contract/agreement entered into by the issuer;

c) this section includes all the material legal information about the acquisition's or purchase's documents, which the issuer's shareholders should take into consideration to make a well informed voting decision;

d) that there are no other material legal information within this section the omission of which would make any statement herein misleading; and

e) (where the acquisition or purchase is a related party transaction) that the independent members of the board of the issuer, other than the related parties, acknowledge that they do not have any direct or indirect interest in any of the issuer's shares or in any of the shares or businesses of the target (or the asset to be purchased), or in any contracts, signed or to be signed, between the parties of the acquisition or purchase, and that they confirm their full independency in respect of the acquisitions or purchases subject of this circular.

2) description of the legal structure of the acquisition or purchase;

3) governmental approvals and third party consents required to complete the acquisition or purchase;

4) a summary of all material contracts and agreements relating to the capital increase for the purpose stated in this circular;

5) material terms, conditions and any conditions precedent\undertakings as per the acquisition agreement;

6) material terms and conditions and any conditions precedent/undertakings for the other acquisition or purchase documents\agreements;

7) particulars of any litigation or claim (including any litigation pending or threatened) or any ongoing investigations which may have a material effect on the issuer or any of its subsidiaries business or financial position, or an appropriate negative statement.

8) particulars of any litigation or claim (including any litigation pending or threatened) or any ongoing investigations which may have a material effect on the target or any of its subsidiaries business or financial position, or an appropriate negative statement.

9) details of any bankruptcies of each director or proposed director, senior executives, or the company secretary of the issuer (or a negative statement thereto).

10) details of any company insolvency in the preceding five years where any of the directors or proposed directors, senior executives, or the company secretary of the issuer were employed by the insolvent company in a managerial or supervisory capacity (or a negative statement thereto).

13. Statements by experts

Where the circular includes a statement made by an expert, a statement should be included specifying the qualifications of the expert and whether such expert or any relative has any shareholding or interest of any kind in the issuer or any of its subsidiaries. In addition, the statement should confirm that the expert has given and not withdrawn his written consent to the publication in the circular of the expert's statement included in the form and context in which it is included.

14. Expenses

This section must include details of the aggregate acquisition or purchase expenses.

15. Waivers

This section must include details on all requirements that have been waived for the issuer by the Authority.

16. Documents available for inspection

This section must include information in relation to the place in the Kingdom at which the following documents may be inspected and the period of time during which the inspection may take place (being not less than 14 days before the date of convening the extraordinary general assembly):

1) the bylaws and the articles of association of the target and any amendments thereto (if any);

2) the acquisition or purchase documents and agreements;

3) the target's audited financials for the past three years (if any);

4) the issuer's pro-forma financials;

5) the valuation report;

6) the advisors consent letters to the use their names, logos and statements in the circular; and

7) any other documents/information requested by the Authority.

17. Annexes

This section should include the following annexes to the circular:

1. the annual audited financial statements for the past three years (if any) preceding the date of the application for the target company/asset (where applicable);

2. the reviewed pro-forma financial statement reflecting the financial position of the issuer following the acquisition or purchase; and

3. where the target is a company, a copy of the target's bylaws, and articles of association including all amendments to date.

25.32 ANNEX 15 EXTERNAL AUDITOR'S REPORT

This Annex details the external auditor's report which is prepared pursuant to Annex 9 (Contents of a Prospectus for Shares), Annex 10 (Content of a Prospectus for a Rights Issue), Annex 11 (Contents of a Prospectus for Debt Instruments and Convertible Debt Instruments for an issuer without securities listed on the Exchange) and Annex 12 (Content of a Prospectus for Debt Instruments for an issuer that has securities currently listed on the Exchange) to the Rules on the Offer of Securities and Continuing Obligations. The Authority must be consulted in cases where the issuer is uncertain as to whether an external auditor's report is required.

The external auditor's report must be prepared by an independent external auditor who is a current member certified by SOCPA.

1) Contents of external auditor's report:

a) The report must cover the issuer and its subsidiaries (if applicable).

b) The report must be extracted from the audited financial statements and adjusted as considered necessary by the reporting external auditor.

c) The report must be prepared in accordance with the accounting standards issued by SOCPA.

d) The report must include the following financial information, presented in a form consistent with that which is adopted in the issuer's annual financial statements, and must cover the three financial years immediately preceding the application for registration and offer of securities subject to the relevant prospectus:

1. balance sheet;

2. income statement;

3. cash flow statement;

4. accounting policies; and

5. any notes to the financial statements covering, as a minimum, the last three financial years.

e) The report must contain an opinion by the external auditor as to whether or not, for the purposes for which it was prepared, the report gives a true and fair view of the financial matters set out therein.

f) If the opinion in paragraph (e) above is qualified, the report must refer to all material matters about which the external auditor has reservations, give all reasons for the qualifications and, if both relevant and practicable, quantify its effect.

g) In the event that the issuer is applying for registration and offer of the securities for the first time, the report must not contain any qualification unless the Authority is satisfied that the qualification is acceptable to the Authority and has been adequately explained so as to enable the investors to make a proper and appropriate assessment of the significance of the matter that is the subject of the qualification.

2) Statement of adjustments

If the external auditor, when preparing his report, considers it necessary to effect adjustments to previously published figures, such adjustments must be limited to those that the external auditor considers necessary. The external auditor must prepare and sign a written statement of the adjustments, and submit it to the Authority for each period to which the report relates, in such form and detail and with such explanation as will show how the reported figures reconcile to the corresponding information in the published accounts. The statement of adjustments must be made available for inspection.

3) Material acquisitions and disposals made during the period under review

a) Where the issuer has acquired at any time during the three financial years immediately preceding the application for registration and offer of securities that are subject to the report, an undertaking or assets which would be classified as material by the Authority, financial information on the undertaking or assets must be given covering the last three years. An acquisition or disposition will be material where the consideration due in respect of such acquisition or disposition is greater than 15% of the net book value of the existing net assets of the issuer and its subsidiaries (if applicable).

b) The external auditor's report must include the post-acquisition information on the issuer and its subsidiaries and relevant undertaking referred to in paragraph (a) above.

c) Where the issuer has, since the date to which the latest published annual financial statements have been made up, acquired or disposed of an undertaking or assets which would be classified as material by the Authority, a pro forma net assets statement showing the effect of the acquisition or disposal on the net assets must be submitted.

In the case of a new application for registration and offer of securities, where the external auditor's report on the audited financial statements for the last three financial years of any undertaking acquired by the issuer during the period under review has been qualified, the issuer will be regarded as unsuitable for registration and offer of the securities unless the Authority is satisfied that the qualification has been adequately explained so as to enable the investors to make a proper and appropriate assessment of the significance of the matter that is the subject of the qualification.

25.33 ANNEX 16: FORM OF A FINANCIAL ADVISOR'S LETTER

[To be provided on the financial advisor's letterhead]

To: The Authority

In our capacity acting as the financial advisor to (please insert the name of the "issuer") (referred to hereinafter as "issuer") in respect of the issuer's application for registration and offer of securities (please provide details of the securities) / capital increase by way of a debt conversion (please provide details of the debt conversion) [use as applicable], and in accordance with Article 21 of the Rules on the Offer of Securities and Continuing Obligations, we [please insert the name of the financial advisor] confirm, to the best of our knowledge, and through conducting due diligence and making enquiries of the issuer and its advisors, that the issuer has satisfied all conditions required for registration and offer of securities and has satisfied all other matters required by the Capital Market Authority (the "Authority") as of the date of this letter. [please insert the financial advisor name] further confirms that it has, to the best of its knowledge and within its capacity as financial advisor, provided to the Authority any information or clarifications in such form and within such time limit as the Authority required for the purpose of verifying whether [please insert the financial advisor name] and the issuer have complied with the Capital Market Law, Listing Rules and the Rules on the Offers of Securities and Continuing Obligations.

In particular, [please insert the financial advisor name] confirms that:

1. it has provided all the relevant services required by the Rules on the

Offer of Securities and Continuing Obligations with due care and skill;

2. it has taken reasonable steps to satisfy itself that the directors of the issuer understand the nature and extent of their responsibilities under the Capital Market Law, its Implementing Regulations and the Exchange Rules; and

3. it has come to a reasonable opinion, based on due enquiry and professional experience, that:

a) the issuer has satisfied all relevant requirements for the registration and offer of securities (including provisions regarding the prospectus) (including provisions regarding the shareholder circular) [use as applicable];

b) the directors of the issuer have established adequate procedures, controls and systems which enable the issuer to comply with the requirements of the Rules on the Offer of Securities and Continuing Obligations, the Listing Rules, the Capital Market Law, its Implementing Regulations and the Exchange Rules; and

c) that all matters known to [please insert the financial advisor name] which should be taken into account by the Authority when considering the application for registration and offer of securities have been disclosed to the Authority.

d) that the scope of the financial due diligence report is proper for the purposes of the issuer's application for registration and offer of securities [use as applicable].

[This Annex shall be submitted electronically through the automated system determined by the Authority for this purpose and the offeror shall retain the original copies (or, where appropriate, certified copies) for a period not less than ten years. In case of a lawsuit or claim (including any existing or threatened action) or any existing investigation procedures relating to such documents, the offeror shall retain such documents until the completion of such litigation, claim or investigation procedures. Moreover, such documents must be submitted to the Authority upon request].

25.34 ANNEX 16(A): FORM OF A FINANCIAL ADVISOR'S LETTER

[To be provided on the legal advisor's letterhead]

To: The Authority

In our capacity acting as the financial advisor to (please insert the name of the "special purposes entity") (referred to hereinafter as "special purposes entity") in respect of the special purposes entity's application for registration and offer of securities (please provide details of the securities) in accordance with Article 21 of the Rules on the Offer of Securities and Continuing Obligations, we [please insert the name of the financial advisor] confirm, to the best of our knowledge, and through conducting due diligence and making enquiries of the special purposes entity, the sponsor and their advisors, that the issuer and the sponsor have satisfied all conditions required for registration and offer of securities and has satisfied all other matters required by the Capital Market Authority (the "Authority") as of the date of this letter. [please insert the financial advisor name] further confirms that it has, to the best of its knowledge and within its capacity as financial advisor, provided to the Authority any information or clarifications in such form and within such time limit as the Authority required for the purpose of verifying whether [please insert the financial advisor name], the sponsor and the special purposes entity have complied with the Capital Market Law, Listing Rules and the Rules on the Offers of Securities and Continuing Obligations.

In Particular, [please insert the financial advisor name] confirms that:

1) It has provided all relevant services required by the Rules on the Offer of Securities and Continuing Obligations, with the required care and experience.

2) That it has taken reasonable steps to verify that the members of the board of directors of the Special Purpose Entity and the Sponsor understand the nature and extent of their responsibilities in accordance with the Capital Market Law and its Implementing Regulations and Exchange Rules

3) It has reached a reasonable opinion, based on adequate investigations and professional experience, to ensure that:

a. The Special Purpose Entity and the Sponsor have met all requirements relating to the registration and placement of securities (including provisions relating to the Prospectus).

b. The members of the board of directors of the special purpose entity and the sponsor have developed procedures, controls and systems sufficient to enable the special purpose entity and the sponsor to meet the requirements of the Rules On The Offer Of Securities And The Continuing Obligations, the Listing Rules, the Capital Market Law and its implementing regulations, and the Exchange Rules.

c. All known issues of [insert name of the financial advisor] that the Authority should consider when reviewing the application for registration and the offering of securities Has been disclosed to the Authority.

[This Annex shall be submitted electronically through the automated system determined by the Authority for this purpose and the offeror shall retain the original copies (or, where appropriate, certified copies) for a period not less than ten years. In case of a lawsuit or claim (including any existing or threatened action) or any existing investigation procedures relating to such documents, the offeror shall retain such documents until the completion of such litigation, claim or investigation procedures. Moreover, such documents must be submitted to the Authority upon request]

25.35 ANNEX 17: FORM OF A LEGAL ADVISOR'S LETTER

[To be provided on the legal advisor's letterhead]

To: The Authority

We act as legal advisor to [please insert the name of the issuer] (referred to hereinafter as "issuer") in respect of the issuer's application for registration and offer of securities (please provide details of the securities).

We further refer to the draft prospectus / shareholders circular [use as applicable] prepared in relation to the issuer [please provide details of the offer], and more specifically, in connection with the application to the Capital Market Authority (the "Authority") for the registration and offer of the securities of the issuer. We have, in relation to the application, and in consultation with the financial advisor to the application, advised the issuer in relation to the requirements of the Capital Market Law its Implementing Regulations and the Exchange Rules including the Rules on the Offer of Securities and Continuing Obligations.

In particular, we have advised the issuer on the content of the legal sections of the prospectus / shareholders circular [use as applicable]. In this respect, we have carried out such further review and enquiries as we consider appropriate in the circumstances and (have undertaken a formal legal due diligence review [use as applicable]).

In our capacity as such counsel, we confirm that we are not aware of any material matter of noncompliance by the issuer with the requirements of the Capital Market Law its Implementing Regulations and the Exchange Rules including any conditions imposed by the Rules on the Offer of Securities and Continuing Obligations and the Listing Rules, including the content requirements in relation to the prospectus/ shareholders circular [use as applicable] as at the date hereof.

[This Annex shall be submitted electronically through the automated system determined by the Authority for this purpose and the offeror shall retain the original copies (or, where appropriate, certified copies) for a period not less than ten years. In case of a lawsuit or claim (including any existing or threatened action) or any existing investigation procedures relating to such documents, the offeror shall retain such documents until the completion of such litigation, claim or investigation procedures. Moreover, such documents must be submitted to the Authority upon request]

25.36 ANNEX 17(A): FORM OF A LEGAL ADVISOR'S LETTER FOR A SPECIAL PURPOSES ENTITY

[To be provided on the legal advisor's letterhead] To: The Authority

We, acting as legal advisor to [please insert the name of the special purposes entity] ("referred to hereinafter as "special purposes entity") in respect of the special purposes entity's application for registration and offer of securities (please provide details of the securities).

We further refer to the draft prospectus prepared in relation to the special purposes entity [please provide details of the offer], and more specifically, in connection with the application submitted to the Capital Market Authority (the "Authority") for the registration and offer of its securities, and after consultation with the financial advisor regarding the application in relation to the requirements of the Capital Market Law its Implementing Regulations and the Exchange Rules including the Rules on the Offer of Securities and Continuing Obligations, we particularly advised the special purposes entity of the requirements that should be included in the legal chapters of the prospectus. In this respect, we have carried out such further review and enquiries as we consider appropriate in the circumstances.

In our advisory capacity, we confirm that we are not aware of any material matter consisting a violation by the special purposes entity to the requirements of the Capital Market Law its Implementing Regulations and the Exchange Rules including any conditions imposed by the Rules on the Offer of Securities and Continuing Obligations and the Listing Rules, including the requirements of the content of the prospectus as at the date hereof.

[This Annex shall be submitted electronically through the automated system determined by the Authority for this purpose and the offeror shall retain the original copies (or, where appropriate, certified copies) for a period not less than ten years. In case of a lawsuit or claim (including any existing or threatened action) or any existing investigation procedures relating to such documents, the offeror shall retain such documents until the completion of such litigation, claim or investigation procedures. Moreover, such documents must be submitted to the Authority upon request]

25.37 ANNEX 18: FORM OF LETTER REQUIRED FOR A CAPITALIZATION ISSUE

The issuer must provide the Authority with an application letter to obtain the Authority's approval on any capitalization issue and the registration of shares. The letter shall contain the following information on the relevant issue according to the most recent audited annual financial statements:

1. The nominal value of the issuer's listed share capital before and after the issue;

2. The number of shares issued before and after the issue;

3. The ratio of shares to be issued as a result of the issue to the number of shares issued prior to the issue;

4. The value of the reserves to be utilized in the issue;

5. The nature of the reserves to be utilized in the issue;

6. A statement that the reserves used for any capital alteration are sufficient for such capital alteration and that the capital alteration complies with applicable rules and regulations.

7. The details on share fraction treatment (if any);

8. The date of the audited annual financial statements from which the value of the reserves to be utilized was taken and a certified copy of such statements; and

9. Details of any dividends or other actions that may impact the retained earnings and the reserves that appear in the financial statements referred to in paragraph (8) above or an appropriate negative statement.

10. Include a statement on the approval from the relevant regulatory authorities as well as a copy of this approval (where applicable).

[This Annex shall be submitted electronically through the automated system determined by the Authority for this purpose and the offeror shall retain the original copies (or, where appropriate, certified copies) for a period not less than ten years. In case of a lawsuit or claim (including any existing or threatened action) or any existing investigation procedures relating to such documents, the offeror shall retain such documents until the completion of such litigation, claim or investigation procedures. Moreover, such documents must be submitted to the Authority upon request]

25.38 ANNEX 19: CONTENT OF LETTER REQUIRED FOR CAPITAL REDUCTION

The issuer must provide the Authority with a signed and dated application letter to obtain the Authority's approval on any capital reduction. The letter shall contain the following information:

1. The nominal value of the issuer's listed share capital before and after the capital reduction.

2. The total number of shares of the issuer before and after the capital reduction.

3. The ratio of remaining shares of the issuer after the capital reduction to the number of shares of the issuer prior to the capital reduction.

4. The value of the capital reduction.

5. The method of the capital reduction.

6. The details on share fraction treatment (if any).

7. The date of the financial statements from which the required numbers for valuations of the capital reduction were taken and a certified copy of such statements.

8. Include a statement on the approval from the relevant regulatory authorities (if any) as well as a copy of this approval.

[This Annex shall be submitted electronically through the automated system determined by the Authority for this purpose and the offeror shall retain the original copies (or, where appropriate, certified copies) for a period not less than ten years. In case of a lawsuit or claim (including any existing or threatened action) or any existing investigation procedures relating to such documents, the offeror shall retain such documents until the completion of such litigation, claim or investigation procedures. Moreover, such documents must be submitted to the Authority upon request]

25.39 ANNEX 20: CONTENT OF A PROSPECTUS FOR PARALLEL MARKET OFFERS

The prospectus for the registration and offering of securities in the Parallel Market shall contain the following as minimum:

1. Cover page

This section must include the following information (where applicable):

1) the issuer's name;

2) the issuer's incorporation date and commercial registration number;

3) capital and number of shares;

4) a summary of the offer including share class and rights;

5) substantial shareholders;

6) targeted types of investors;

7) offer period and conditions;

8) shares that have been listed prior to the particular offer by the issuer (if applicable);

9) a statement that the issuer has submitted the application for registration and offer of shares in the Parallel Market to the Authority, and all requirements have been met; and

10) the following declaration:

"This prospectus includes information provided in compliance with the Rules on the Offer and Continuing Obligations issued by Capital Market Authority of the Kingdom of Saudi Arabia (the "Authority"). The directors, whose names appear on page [ ], collectively and individually accept full responsibility for the accuracy of the information contained in this prospectus and confirm, having made all reasonable enquiries, that to the best of their knowledge and belief, there are no other facts the omissions of which would make any statement in the prospectus misleading. The Authority and the Exchange do not take any responsibility for the contents of this prospectus, do not make any representation as to its accuracy or completeness, and expressly disclaim any liability whatsoever for any loss arising from, or incurred in reliance upon, any part of this document. Those wishing to buy listed shares under this prospectus shall verify the information related to the shares being offered; and consult a licensed financial advisor when facing any difficulty understanding the contents of this prospectus."

2. Important notice

This section must include a notice which shows the purpose and the nature of information mentioned in the Prospectus.

3. Corporate directory

This section must include the following:

1) issuer's and its representatives' contact information, including addresses, telephone and fax numbers, e-mail addresses, and the issuer's website.

2) the contact information, including addresses, telephone and fax numbers, and website and e-mail addresses, for each of the parties listed below, and any other expert to whom a statement or report included in the Prospectus has been attributed:

a) the financial advisor;
b) the legal advisor (if any);
c) the external auditor; and
d) the Capital Market Institutions authorized to place or sell the shares.

4. Offer summary

This section must include the following information (where applicable):

1) the issuer's name, description and incorporation information;
2) the issuer's activities;
3) substantial shareholders showing their ownership percentages and number of shares pre- and post-offering;
4) the capital of the issuer;
5) issuer's total number of shares;
6) the nominal value per share;
7) the total number of offered shares;
8) the percentage of offered shares to the capital of the issuer;
9) the offer price;
10) the total value of offer;
11) the use of the proceeds;
12) types of targeted investors;
13) subscription method;
14) the minimum number of shares to be subscribed for;
15) the minimum value of shares to be subscribed for;
16) the maximum number of shares to be subscribed for;
17) the maximum value of shares to be subscribed for;
18) the method of allocation of the shares and refund of excess monies;
19) the offer period;
20) the rights to dividends;
21) voting rights;
22) restrictions on shares; and
23) shares that have been listed prior to the particular offer by the issuer (if applicable).

5. Key dates and subscription procedure

This section must include:

1) a timetable showing the expected dates of the offering; and

2) a description of the subscription procedure.

6. Summary of basic information

This section must include a summary of the following basic information:

1) a description of the issuer;

2) the issuer's mission and overall strategy; and

3) the issuer's key strengths and competitive advantages.

7. Summary of financial information

This section must include a summary of the following key financial information:

1) issuer's operational performance;

2) financial condition;

3) cash flows; and

4) the issuer's key performance indicators.

8. Table of contents

This section must include the prospectus table of contents.

9. Terms and definitions

This section must include the terms and definitions used through the prospectus.

10. Risk factors

This section must include the following statement:

a) "Investment in the shares offered under this Prospectus involves high risks, and may only suit investors capable of assessing the benefits and risks of this investment, and bear any losses may result thereof".

b) This section must include information in relation to risk factors specific to:

1) the issuer;

2) the market and industry in which the issuer operates; and

3) the shares being offered.

11. Issuer's background and business nature

This section must include the following information:

1) the official name, commercial registration number and the address shown in the commercial registration and, if different, the principal address of the issuer;

2) the date of incorporation of the issuer;

3) the authorized shares of the issuer, the number of shares issued or agreed to be issued, the value paid up, the nominal value and a description of the shares;

4) a description and organization chart of the group showing the issuer's position within that group (if applicable);

5) the general nature of the business of the issuer and details of the main products sold or services performed and an indication of any significant new products or activities;

6) if the issuer trades outside the Kingdom, a statement showing the location of such trading operations must be provided. Where a material portion of the issuer's assets is outside the Kingdom, the value and location of such assets and the value of the assets located in the Kingdom must be specified;

7) information concerning the policy of the issuer on the research and development of new products and production processes over the last financial year, where significant;

8) particulars of any interruption in the business of the issuer which may have or has had a significant effect on the financial position in the last 12 months;

9) the number of people employed by the issuer and any material changes to that number, with a breakdown of persons employed by main categories of activity and by Saudization ratio; and

10) a statement that no material change in the nature of the business is contemplated or, if one is contemplated, a detailed description of that change and its impact on the issuer's business and profitability.

12. Ownership and Organizational structure

This section must include the following information:

1. Ownership structure pre- and post-offering

2. Management:

a) the issuer's organizational chart showing the directors structure, supervisory committees, and the functions of senior executives;

b) the full names and description of the most significant professional and academic qualifications and area of expertise and the date of appointment of all the directors or proposed directors (showing whether the director is independent or executive or non-executive), in addition to the senior executives and the secretary of the board; and

c) information about the issuer's board committees, including the names of each committee member and a summary of the terms of reference under which the committee operates.

13. Dividend policy

This section must include an explanation of the issuer's dividend policy, as well as details on any dividend payments made during the last year.

14. Use of proceeds and future projects

a) This section must include an estimate of the proceeds of the offer and the offer expenses and a statement as to how such proceeds are intended to be used.

b) Where the proceeds are to be used to fund future projects, the nature of these projects should be described and the following information included:

1) future projects' key milestones and timetable to execute those future projects; and

2) an estimate and breakdown of future projects costs, showing the stages in which such costs will be incurred, in addition to details regarding the sources of financing.

15. Declarations

The directors of the issuer must make the following declarations:

1) other than what has been mentioned on page ( ) of this Prospectus, there has not been any interruption in the business of the issuer or any of its subsidiaries (if any) which may have or has had a significant effect on the financial position in the last 12 months.

2) other than what has been mentioned on page ( ) of this Prospectus, no commissions, discounts, brokerages or other non-cash compensation have been granted within the last year preceding the application for registration and offer of shares that are the subject of this prospectus in connection with the issue or offer of any securities by the issuer or any of the issuer's subsidiaries (if applicable).

3) other than what has been mentioned on page ( ) of this Prospectus, there has not been any material adverse change in the financial and trading position of the issuer or any of its subsidiaries (if any) in the last year preceding the application for registration and offer of shares.

4) other than what is mentioned on page ( ) of this Prospectus, no director nor any of their relatives have interest of any kind in the issuer or any of its subsidiaries (if any).

16. Information concerning the shares and terms and conditions of the offer

This section must include the following information:

1) a statement that application has been made to the Authority for registration and offer of shares in the Parallel Market;
2) the type and total value of the offer including the number of shares being offered;
3) the offer price and the nominal value of each share;
4) the subscription method;
5) the offer period and conditions;
6) the method of allocation of the shares and refund of excess monies;
7) when and under what circumstances the offer may be suspended;

8) a description of the resolutions, and approvals by virtue of which the shares will be offered; and

9) details of any lock-up arrangement in place restricting the disposal of particular shares.

17. Price dilution

If the offer is a result of an increase in the issuer's capital, this section must include information on the price dilution effects and its impact on the shareholders.

18. Subscription declarations

This section must include information on the subscription declarations, allocation process, and the Exchange details.

19. Procedures of Incomplete Offer

This section must include procedures to be taken by the issuer in case the offer is not completed.

20. Documents Available for Inspection

This section must include information in relation to the place at which the following documents may be inspected and the period of time during which the inspection may take place (being not less than 7 days before the end of the offer period):

1) the by-laws and other constitutional documents of the issuer;

2) any document or order granting permission to offer securities to the public;

3) all other reports, letters, documents, value estimates or statements prepared by any expert and any part of which is extracted or referred to in the Prospectus; and

4) the audited annual financial statements of the issuer for the most recent financial year prior to the date of publication of the prospectus, in addition to the most recent interim financial statements.

21. External auditor's report

The issuer's audited annual financial statements for the last year preceding the date of the publishing the Prospectus, in addition to the most recent interim financial statements, if any.

25.40 ANNEX 20A: CONTENT OF A REGISTRATION DOCUMENT

The registration document for direct listing in the Parallel Market shall contain the following as minimum:

1. Cover page

This section must include the following information (where applicable):

1) the issuer's name;

2) the issuer's incorporation date and commercial registration number;

3) capital and number of shares;

4) share class and rights;

5) substantial shareholders;

6) shares that have been listed (if any);

7) a statement that the issuer has submitted the application to the Authority, and all requirements have been met; and

8) the following declaration:

"This prospectus includes information provided in compliance with the Rules on the Offer and Continuing Obligations issued by Capital Market Authority of the Kingdom of Saudi Arabia (the "Authority"). The directors, whose names appear on page [ ], collectively and individually accept full responsibility for the accuracy of the information contained in this prospectus and confirm, having made all reasonable enquiries, that to the best of their knowledge and belief, there are no other facts the omissions of which would make any statement in the prospectus misleading. The Authority and the Exchange do not take any responsibility for the contents of this prospectus, do not make any representation as to its accuracy or completeness, and expressly disclaim any liability whatsoever for any loss arising from, or incurred in reliance upon, any part of this document. Those wishing to buy listed shares under this prospectus shall verify the information related to the shares being offered; and consult a licensed financial advisor when facing any difficulty understanding the contents of this document."

2. Important notice

This section must include a notice which shows the purpose and the nature of information mentioned in the registration document.

3. Corporate directory

This section must include the following:

1) issuer and its representatives' contact information, including addresses, telephone and fax numbers, e-mail addresses, and the issuer's website.

2) the contact information, including addresses, telephone and fax numbers, and website and e-mail addresses, for each of the parties listed below, and any other expert to whom a statement or report included in the Prospectus and the registration document has been attributed:

a. the financial advisor;

b. the legal advisor (if any);

c. the external auditor; and

d. the Capital Market Institution authorized to offer or sell the shares.

e. The Capital Market Institution for the purpose of fulfilling the liquidity requirements for the shares subject in the direct listing application (if any).

4. Summary

This section must include the following information (where applicable):

1) the issuer's name, description and incorporation information;

2) the issuer's activities;

3) substantial shareholders showing their ownership percentages and number of shares prelisting;

4) substantial shareholders who assigned the Capital Market Institution, under the Listing Rules, to sell their shares at their discretion, the number of their shares and the percentage of their ownership before listing and after applying the liquidity requirement fulfillment plan provided to the Exchange pursuant to the Listing Rules;

5) the capital of the issuer;

6) issuer's total number of shares;

7) the nominal value per share;

8) the guiding share price upon listing;

9) the rights to dividends;

10) voting rights;

11) restrictions on shares; and

12) shares that have been listed (if any).

5. Summary of basic information

This section must include the following:

1) a description of the issuer;

2) the issuer's mission and overall strategy; and

3) the issuer's key strengths and competitive advantages.

6. Summary of financial information

This section must include a summary of the following key financial information:

1) issuer's operational performance;

2) financial condition;

3) cash flows; and

4) the issuer's key performance indicators.

7. Table of contents

This section must include the table of contents for the registration document.

8. Terms and definitions

This section must include the terms and definitions used through the registration document.

9. Risk factors

a) This section must include the following statement:

"Investment in the shares directly listed in the Parallel Market involves high risks, and may only suit investors capable of assessing the benefits and risks of this investment, and bear any losses may result thereof".

b) This section must include information in relation to risk factors specific to:

1) the issuer;

2) the market and industry in which the issuer operates; and

3) the shares being directly listed in the Parallel Market.

10. Issuer' s background and business nature

This section must include the following information:

1) the official name, commercial registration number and the address shown in the commercial registration and, if different, the principal address of the issuer;

2) the date of incorporation of the issuer;

3) the authorized shares of the issuer, the number of shares issued or agreed to be issued, the value paid up, the nominal value and a description of the shares;

4) a description and organization chart of the group showing the issuer's position within that group (if applicable);

5) the general nature of the business of the issuer and details of the main products sold or services performed and an indication of any significant new products or activities;

6) if the issuer trades outside the Kingdom, a statement showing the location of such trading operations must be provided. Where a material portion of the issuer's assets is outside the Kingdom, the value and location of such assets and the value of the assets located in the Kingdom must be specified;

7) information concerning the policy of the issuer on the research and development of new products and production processes over the last financial year, where significant;

8) particulars of any interruption in the business of the issuer which may have or has had a significant effect on the financial position in the last 12 months;

9) the number of people employed by the issuer and any material changes to that number, with a breakdown of persons employed by main categories of activity and by Saudization ratio; and

10) a statement that no material change in the nature of the business is contemplated or, if one is contemplated, a detailed description of that change and its impact on the issuer's business and profitability.

11. Ownership and Organizational structure

This section must include the following information:

1. Ownership structure in the issuer.

2. Management:

a) the issuer's organizational chart showing the directors structure, supervisory committees, and the functions of senior executives;

b) the full names and description of the most significant professional and academic qualifications and area of expertise and the date of appointment of all the directors or proposed directors (showing whether the director is independent or executive or non-executive), in addition to the senior executives and the secretary of the board; and

c) information about the issuer's board committees, including the names of each committee member and a summary of the terms of reference under which the committee operates.

12. Dividend policy

This section must include an explanation of the issuer's dividend policy, as well as details on any dividend payments made during the last year.

13. Costs of direct listing

This section must include an estimation of the costs of direct listing in the Parallel Market.

14. Declarations

The directors of the issuer must make the following declarations:

1) other than what has been mentioned on page ( ) of this document, there has not been any interruption in the business of the issuer or any of its subsidiaries (if any) which may have or has had a significant effect on the financial position in the last 12 months.

2) other than what has been mentioned on page ( ) of this document, no commissions, discounts, brokerages or other non-cash compensation have been granted within the last year preceding the application for registration for the issuance and offer of shares

that are the subject of this prospectus in connection with the issue or offer of any securities by the issuer or any of the issuer's subsidiaries (if applicable).

3) other than what has been mentioned on page ( ) of this document, there has not been any material adverse change in the financial and trading position of the issuer or any of its subsidiaries (if any) in the last year preceding the application for registration for the issuance and offer of shares.

4) other than what is mentioned on page ( ) of this document, no director nor any of their relatives have interest of any kind in the issuer or any of its subsidiaries (if any).

15. Information concerning the shares and terms of direct listing

This section must include the following information:

1) a statement that application has been made to the Authority for the registration of shares in the Parallel Market;

2) the guiding share price upon listing and the nominal value of each share;

3) when and under what circumstances the shares may be suspended;

4) a description of the resolutions, and approvals by virtue of which the shares will be listed; and

5) details of any lock-up arrangement in place restricting the disposal of particular shares.

16. Documents Available for Inspection

This section must include information in relation to the place at which the following documents may be inspected and the period of time during which the inspection may take place (being not less than 7 days before the end of the offer period):

1) the by-laws and other constitutional documents of the issuer;

2) any document or order granting permission to directly list shares in the Parallel Market;

3) all other reports, letters, documents or statements prepared by any expert and any part of which is extracted or referred to in the registration document; and;

4) The mechanism by which the guiding price is determined.

5) the audited annual financial statements of the issuer for the most recent financial year prior to the date of publication of the registration document, in addition to the most recent interim financial statements.

17. External auditor's report

The issuer's audited annual financial statements for the last year preceding the date of the publishing the registration document for direct listing of shares in the Parallel Market, in addition to the most recent interim financial statements, if any.

25.41 ANNEX 21: FORM OF FINANCIAL ADVISOR'S LETTER WITH REGARDS TO AN APPLICATION FOR REGISTRATION AND OFFER ON THE PARALLEL MARKET OR AN APPLICATION FOR REGISTRATION IN THE PARALLEL MARKET

[To be provided on the Financial Advisor's letterhead]

To: The Capital Market Authority

In our capacity acting as the financial advisor to [please insert the name of the issuer] (referred to hereinafter as the "issuer") in respect of the issuer's application for registration and offer of shares [please provide details of the shares] in the Parallel Market or the issuer's application for registration in the Parallel Market, and in accordance with Article 72 of the Rules on the Offer of Securities and Continuing Obligations, we [please insert the name of the financial advisor] confirm, to the best of our knowledge, and through conducting due diligence and making enquiries from the issuer and its directors, that the issuer has satisfied all conditions required for registration and offer of shares in the Parallel Market or for the registration in the Parallel Market (use as applicable) and has satisfied all other matters required by Capital Market Authority ("the Authority") as of the date of this letter.

[please insert the financial advisor name] further confirms that to the best of its knowledge and within its capacity as financial advisor, provided to the Authority any information or clarifications in such form and within such time limit as the Authority requires for the purpose of verifying whether [please insert the financial advisor name] and the issuer have complied with the Capital Market Law and the Rules on the Offer of Securities and Continuing Obligations.

In particular, [please insert the financial advisor name] confirms that:

1) It has provided all relevant services as per the Rules on the Offer of Securities and Continuing Obligations with due care and skill.

2) It has taken reasonable steps to satisfy itself that the directors of the issuer understand the nature and extent of their responsibilities under the Capital Market Law and its Implementing Regulations;

3) It has come to a reasonable opinion, based on due enquiry and professional experience, that:

a) the issuer has satisfied all requirements relevant to the registration and offer in the Parallel Market or for the registration in the Parallel Market (use as applicable), (including provisions regarding the prospectus)/(including provisions regarding the shareholder circular)/ (including the registration document) [use as applicable];

b) the directors of the issuer have established adequate procedures, controls and systems which enable the issuer to comply with the requirements of the Rules on the Offer of Securities and Continuing Obligations, Capital Market Law and its Implementing Regulations; and

c) that all matters known to [please insert the financial advisor name] which should be taken into account by the Authority when considering the application for registration and offer of shares on the Parallel Market or the registration in the Parallel Market (use as applicable) have been disclosed to the Authority.

d) that the scope of the financial due diligence report is proper for the purposes of the issuer's application for registration and offer of shares or the registration in the Parallel Market-if any- [use as applicable].

[This Annex shall be submitted electronically through the automated system determined by the Authority for this purpose and the offeror shall retain the original copies (or, where appropriate, certified copies) for a period not less than ten years. In case of a lawsuit or claim (including any existing or threatened action) or any existing investigation procedures relating to such documents, the offeror shall retain such documents until the completion of such litigation, claim or investigation procedures. Moreover, such documents must be submitted to the Authority upon request]

25.42 ANNEX 22: CONTENTS OF SHAREHOLDERS' CIRCULAR FOR A CAPITAL INCREASE OF A COMPANY THE SHARES OF WHICH ARE LISTED ON THE PARALLEL MARKET BY DEBT CONVERSION

The shareholders' circular submitted for registration and offering of shares for capital increase by debt conversion of a company the shares of which are listed on the parallel market shall contain the following information:

1. Cover page

This section must include the following information (as applicable):

1) a summary of the transaction, its reasons and details about the creditor.

2) the following declaration:

"This shareholders' circular contains information provided in compliance with the Rules on the Offer of Securities and Continuing Obligations issued by Capital Market Authority of the Kingdom of Saudi Arabia (the "Authority"). The directors, whose names appear on page [ ], collectively and individually accept full responsibility for the accuracy of the information contained in this shareholders' circular and confirm, having made all reasonable enquiries, that to the best of their knowledge and belief, there are no other facts the omissions of which would make any statement herein misleading. The Authority and the Exchange do not take any responsibility for the contents of this circular, do not make any representation as to its accuracy or completeness, and expressly disclaim any liability whatsoever for any loss arising from, or incurred in reliance upon, any part of this circular. A licensed financial advisor shall be consulted when facing any difficulty understanding the contents of this circular."

2. Description and structure of the transaction.

3. Risk factors related to the transaction.

4. Timeframe of the transaction.

5. Key accounting items of the issuer's audited financial statements.

6. Key accounting items for the pro-forma financial statements which reflect the issuer's condition following the capital increase.

7. The origin of the current debt (to be converted into shares) and its assessments based on the opinion of an expert or a certified assessor.

8. The material legal information which the Issuer's shareholders should take into consideration to make a well informed voting decision on the capital increase for the reason disclosed in the circular.

9. Related parties to the transaction.

10. Any new proposed members of the board or the executive management in the issuer as a result of the transaction;

11. A statement from the directors of the issuer confirming that in the board's view the proposed capital increase to acquire a company/ asset is in the best interests of the issuer and the shareholders.

12. The issuer must refer to the place in the Kingdom where the following documents may be reviewed and the timeframe during which such review may take place (provided that this timeframe must not be less than 14 days prior to the extraordinary general assembly meeting):

1. The documents and agreements related to the debt conversion;

2. The issuer's pro-forma financial statements;

3. The valuation report;

4. The statement prepared and signed by the issuer's board of directors and its auditor (who are jointly liable on its correctness) on the origin of the debt and its value;

5. Any additional document required by the Authority.

25.43 ANNEX 23: CONTENTS OF SHAREHOLDERS'S CIRCULAR FOR A CAPITAL INCREASE OF A COMPANY WHICH SHARES ARE LISTED ON THE PARALLEL MARKET TO ACQUIRE A COMPANY OR PURCHASE AN ASSET

The shareholders' circular submitted for registration and offering of shares for capital increase of a company the shares of which are listed on the parallel market, to acquire a company or purchase an asset, shall contain the following information:

1. Cover page

This section must include the following information:

1) a summary of the acquisition and purchasing transaction, purpose of the capital increase and the identity of the target company/assets.

2) the following declaration:

"This shareholders' circular contains information provided in compliance with the requirements of the Rules on the Offer of Securities and Continuing Obligations issued by Capital Market Authority of the Kingdom of Saudi Arabia (the "Authority") The directors, whose names appear on page [ ], collectively and individually accept full responsibility for the accuracy of the information contained in this shareholders' circular and confirm, having made all reasonable enquiries, that to the best of their knowledge and belief, there are no other facts the omissions of which would make any statement in the circular misleading. The Authority and the Exchange do not take any responsibility for the contents of this circular, do not make any representation as to its accuracy or completeness, and expressly disclaim any liability whatsoever for any loss arising from, or incurred in reliance upon, any part of this circular. A licensed financial advisor shall be consulted when facing any difficulty understanding the contents of this circular."

2. Description and structure of the transaction.

3. Risk factors related to the transaction.

4. Timeframe of the transaction.

5. Description of the targeted asset /company and the company's operations and industry.

6. Key accounting items of the issuer's audited financial statements.

7. Key accounting items of the audited financial statements (if any) for the targeted asset or company (as applicable).

8. Key accounting items for the pro-forma financial statements which reflect the issuer's condition following the capital increase.

9. Valuation of the asset or the company to be acquired;

10. The material legal information which the Issuer's shareholders should take into consideration to make a well informed voting decision on the capital increase for the reason disclosed in the circular.

11. Related parties to the transaction;

12. Any new proposed members of the board or the executive management in the issuer as a result of the transaction;

13. A statement from the directors of the issuer confirming that in the board's view the proposed capital increase to acquire a company/ asset is in the best interests of the issuer and the shareholders.

14. The issuer shall indicate the place in the kingdom where the following documents can be viewed and the timeframe for that (provided that this timeframe is no less 14 days prior to the Extraordinary General Assembly meeting):

1. The documents and agreements related to the acquisition;

2. The issuer's pro-forma financial statements, and the audited financial statements for the target company/asset (if any).;

3. The valuation report;

4. Any additional document required by the Authority.

25.44 ANNEX 24: CLASS TEST

This Annex sets out the following Class Tests:

1. The Assets test:

The assets test is calculated by dividing the total gross assets which are the subject of the transaction by the total gross assets of the Listed Company, according to the latest reviewed interim financial statements or audited annual financial statements, whichever is later.

2. The Profits test:

The profits test is calculated by dividing the net profits attributable to the assets which are the subject of the transaction by the net profits of the Listed Company, according to the latest reviewed interim financial statements or audited annual financial statements, whichever is later.

3. Revenues test:

The revenues test is calculated by dividing the gross revenues attributable to the assets which are the subject of the transaction divided by the gross revenues of the Listed Company, according to the latest reviewed interim financial statements or audited annual financial statements, whichever is later.

4. Consideration test:

The consideration test is calculated by dividing the consideration (i.e. the amount paid to the contracting party in the transaction) by the total market capitalization of the Listed Company (excluding treasury shares). The total market capitalization is the average closing price of the Listed Company's securities as listed on the Exchange for the five business days preceding the date of signing the final agreement or announcing the transaction.

26 PROCEDURES AND INSTRUCTIONS RELATED TO LISTED COMPANIES WITH ACCUMULATED LOSSES REACHING 20% OR MORE OF THEIR SHARE CAPITAL

Issued by the Board of the Capital Market Authority Pursuant to its Resolution Number 4-48-2013 dated 15/1/1435H (18/11/2013G) based on the Capital Market Law issued by Royal Decree No. M/30 dated 2/6/1424H amended by Board Resolution Number 1-77-2018 dated 5/11/1439H (18/7/2018G0

To keep abreast with the accelerated changes to the Authority's rules and regulations, please refer always to the rules and regulations posted on the Authority's website www.cma.org.sa

PART ONE: PRELIMINARY PROVISIONS

Article One: Definitions

Article Two: Scope and Application

PART TWO: PROCEDURES

Article Three: When accumulated losses of a company reach 20% or more and less than 35% of its share capital

Article Four: When accumulated losses of a company reach 35% or more and less than 50% of its share capital

Article Five: When accumulated losses of a company reach 50% or more of its share capital

PART THREE: DELISTING

Article Six: Delisting

26.1 PART ONE: PRELIMINARY PROVISIONS

26.1.1 Article One: Definitions

a) Unless the context otherwise indicates, the words and phrases as they appear in these procedures shall have the same meaning as set forth in the Capital Market Law and the Glossary of Defined Terms used in the Regulations and Rules of the Capital Market Authority.

b) For the purpose of applying these Procedures and Instructions, the words and phrases listed below shall have the meanings set in front of each of them, unless the context otherwise indicates:

- Accumulated Losses: The company's results for the current period added to the company's accumulated results from prior periods, which in aggregate represent a loss, and appear as a separate item under shareholder's equity on the balance sheet.

- Share Capital: The balance which appears as a separate item under shareholders' equity on the balance sheet.

26.1.2 Article Two: Scope and Application

a) These Procedures and Instructions aim at regulating the mechanism for dealing with a company whose shares are listed in the Exchange when its Accumulated Losses reach 20% or more of its Share Capital.

b) These Procedures and Instructions do not contravene with the Capital Market Law and its Implementing Regulations and other relevant laws and regulations.

c) Companies, in addition to the provisions set out in these Procedures and Instructions, should comply with all other provisions set forth in the Capital Market Law and its Implementing Regulations, and other relevant laws and regulations.

26.1.3 Article Three: When Accumulated Losses of a company reach 20% or more and less than 35% of its Share Capital

a) The company should, immediately and without delay, disclose to the public in a separate announcement when its Accumulated Losses reach 20% or more and less than 35% of its Share Capital. The announcement should reflect the total Accumulated Losses, its percentage of the capital, and the main reasons that caused the losses, with reference that these procedures will be applicable. In case the announcement coincides with the interim or annual financial results announcement, the company is exempt from the disclosure as a separate announcement if it disclosed the required information as per this paragraph in the interim or annual financial results announcement.

b) Following the public announcement referred to in paragraph (a) of this Article, the Exchange shall add a flag next to the company's name on the Exchange website indicating that the company's Accumulated Losses reached 20% or more and less than 35% of its Share Capital.

c) Upon receiving an external auditor's report illustrating its financial position, the company should, immediately and without delay, disclose to the public by a separate announcement upon reduction of its Accumulated Losses from 20% of its Share Capital. The announcement should reflect the remedial steps taken by the company to restore its position including attaching the external auditor's report referred to in this paragraph.

d) The Exchange shall delete the flag referred to in paragraph (b) of this Article following the company's announcement of its financial position remedy as indicated in paragraph (c) of this Article.

26.1.4 Article Four: When Accumulated Losses reach 35% or more and less than 50% of the Share Capital

a) The company should, immediately and without delay, disclose to the public in a separate announcement when its Accumulated Losses reach 35% or more and less than 50% of its Share Capital. The announcement should reflect the total Accumulated Losses, its percentage of the capital, and the main reasons that caused the losses, with reference that these procedures will be applicable. In case the announcement coincides with the interim or annual financial results announcement, the company is exempt from the disclosure in a separate announcement if it disclosed the required information as per this paragraph in the interim or annual financial results announcement.

b) Following the public announcement referred to in paragraph (a) of this Article, the Exchange shall add a flag next to the company's name on the Exchange website indicating that the company's Accumulated Losses reached 35% or more and less than 50% of its Share Capital.

c) Upon receiving an external auditor's report illustrating its financial position, the company should, immediately and without delay, disclose to the public by a separate announcement upon reduction in its Accumulated Losses from 35% of its Share Capital. The announcement should reflect the remedial steps taken by the company to restore its positions including attaching the external auditor's report referred to in this paragraph.

d) The Exchange shall delete the flag referred to in paragraph (b) of this Article following the company's announcement of its financial position remedy as indicated in paragraph (c) of this Article.

e) Upon the reduction of Accumulated Losses of a company below 35% and not less than 20% from its Share Capital, Article (3) of these Procedures and Instructions shall be applicable.

26.1.5 Article Five: When Accumulated Losses reach 50% or more of the Share Capital

a) The company should, immediately and without delay, disclose to the public in a separate announcement when its Accumulated Losses reach 50% or more of its Share Capital. The announcement should reflect the total Accumulated Losses, its percentage of the capital, and the main reasons that caused the losses, with reference that these procedures will be applicable. In case the announcement coincides with the interim or annual financial results announcement, the company is exempt from the disclosure in a separate announcement if it disclosed the required information as per this paragraph in the preliminary or yearly financial results announcement.

b) Following the public announcement referred to in paragraph (a) of this Article, the Exchange shall add a flag next to the company's name on the Exchange website indicating that the company's Accumulated Losses reached 50% or more of its Share Capital.

c) Subject to the provisions of Article (150) of the Companies Law, the company shall, after announcing that its Accumulated Losses reached 50% or more of its Share Capital, announce the following:-

1. The date of the last day on which the Board of Directors may invite the extraordinary general assembly to convene, and the date of the last day for convening the extraordinary general assembly to address the Accumulated Losses.

2. The Board of Directors' recommendation to the extraordinary general assembly regarding its Accumulated Losses immediately following its issuance, either to increase or decrease the company's capital, or to dissolve the company before the prescribed date in its by-laws.

3. The date of the last day to complete the process of subscription of the capital increase to address the Accumulated Losses, where applicable.

d) Upon receiving an external auditor's report illustrating its financial position, the company should, immediately and without delay, disclose to the public by a separate announcement the reduction in its Accumulated Losses from 50% of its Share Capital. The announcement should reflect the remedial steps taken by the company to restore its positions including attaching the external auditor's report referred to in this paragraph.

e) The Exchange shall delete the flag referred to in paragraph (b) of this Article following the company's announcement of its financial position remedy as indicated in paragraph (d) of this Article.

f) Upon the reduction of Accumulated Losses of a company below 50% and not less than 20% from its Share Capital, Articles (3) or (4) of these Procedures and Instructions shall be applicable, depending on the situation.

26.2 PART THREE: DELISTING

26.2.1 Article Six: Delisting

A company's shares will be delisted where the company is dissolved by force of law according to paragraph (2) of Article (150) of the Companies' Law or when the extraordinary general assembly decides to dissolve the company before the prescribed date in its by-laws according to paragraph (1) of Article (150) of the Companies' Law.

27 Prudential Rules

Issued by the Board of the Capital Market Authority pursuant to its Resolution No. 1-40-2012 dated 17/2/1434H (30/12/2012G) based on the Capital Market Law issued by Royal Decree No. M/30 dated 2/6/1424H

Important Notice: The current version of these Rules, as may be amended, can be found at the Authority website: www.cma.org.sa

Table of Contents

(Article names are not included in the Official Translation, are not part of the law and are provided for convenience).

Part 1: Introduction
Chapter 1: Scope, Purpose and Definitions
Part 2: Capital Base
Chapter 2: Capital Base Requirement
Chapter 3: Composition of Capital
Part 3: Pillar I - Minimum Capital Requirements
Chapter 4: General Provisions for the Trading Book
Chapter 5: Management Requirements for the Trading Book
Chapter 6: General Provisions for non-Trading Activities
Chapter 7: Calculating a Risk-Weighted Exposure Amount for non-Trading Activities
Chapter 8: Use of Credit Ratings
Chapter 9: General Provisions Regarding Operational Risks
Chapter 10: Basic Indicator Approach for Operational Risk
Chapter 11: Standardized Approach for Operational Risk
Chapter 12: Expenditure-based Approach for Operational Risk
Chapter 13: General Provisions Regarding Foreign Exchange Rate Risk
Chapter 14:Valuation and Conversion to Local Currency
Chapter 15: Calculating the Capital Requirement for Foreign Exchange Rate Risk
Chapter 16: General Provisions Regarding Commodities Risk
Part 4: Large and Excess Exposures
Chapter 17: General Provisions Regarding Large and Excess Exposures
Part 5: Minimum Liquidity Requirements
Chapter 18: General Provisions Regarding Liquidity Requirements
Chapter 19: Organizational Requirements
Part 6: Pillar II - Assessment of All Risks
Chapter 20: Internal Capital Adequacy Assessment Process (ICAAP)
Part 7: Pillar III - Disclosure and Reporting
Chapter 21: Disclosure
Chapter 22: Reporting
Part 8: Financial Groups
Chapter 23: General Provisions Regarding Financial Groups
Chapter 24: Consolidated Accounts
Chapter 25: Foreign Undertakings
Chapter 26: Systems and Controls Part 9: Closing Provisions
Chapter 27: Publication and Entry into Force
Annexes
Annex 1: Capital Base
Chapter 1:Tier-1 Capital
Chapter 2:Tier-2 Capital
Chapter 3: Deductions From Capital
Annex 2:Trading Book
Chapter 1: Interest Rate Risks
Chapter 2: Equity Price Risks
Chapter 3: Risks Related to Investment Funds
Chapter 4: Underwriting
Chapter 5: Excess Exposure
Chapter 6: Settlement Risks
Chapter 7: Counterparty Risks
Annex 3: Non-Trading Activities
Chapter 1: Exposure Classes and Risk Weights
Chapter 2: Calculating Exposure Amounts for off-Balance Sheet Items
Chapter 3: Calculating the non-Trading Book Exposure Amount for Derivatives
Chapter 4: Credit Protection
Chapter 5: Guarantees and Credit Derivatives
Chapter 6: Financial Collateral
Chapter 7: Netting Agreements
Chapter 8: Other Credit Protection
Annex 4: Operational Risks
Chapter 1: Basic Indicator Approach
Chapter 2: Standardized Approach
Annex 5: Foreign Exchange Rate Risks
Chapter 1:Two-Step Method
Chapter 2: Calculating the Capital Requirement
Chapter 3: Options
Chapter 4: Investment Funds
Chapter 5: Composite Currencies
Chapter 6: Collateral in a Third Country's Currency
Chapter 7: Exceptions
Annex 6: Commodities Risks
Chapter 1: Calculating Positions and Netting Long and Short Positions
Chapter 2: Maturity-Based Method
Chapter 3: Simple Method
Annex 7: Large Exposures
Chapter 1: Management Requirements
Chapter 2: Determining Exposure Amounts in non-Trading Activities
Chapter 3: Determining Exposure Amounts in the Trading Book
Annex 8: Liquidity Risks
Chapter 1: Identification and measurement of liquidity risks
Chapter 2: Liquidity risk management
Annex 9: Internal Capital Assessment
Chapter 1: Internal Capital Adequacy Assessment Process (ICAAP)
Chapter 2: Strategies on how to reach and maintain capital targets
Chapter 3: Self assessment and stress testing
Annex 10: Disclosure
Chapter 1: Disclosure Regarding Authorized Person and Financial Group
Chapter 2: Disclosure Regarding Capital Base
Chapter 3: Disclosure Regarding Capital Requirements
Chapter 4: Disclosure Regarding non-Trading Activities
Chapter 5: Disclosure Regarding Liquidity Risks
Chapter 6: Disclosure Regarding Counterparty Risks
Chapter 7: Disclosure Regarding Operational Risks

Chapter 8: Periodic Disclosure .
Annex 11: Long-Term Mapping
Annex 12: Short-Term Mapping

27.1 Part 1: INTRODUCTION

27.1.1 Chapter 1: Scope, Purpose and Definitions

Article 1: Scope, Capital Requirements

(a) The purpose of these Rules is to specify the requirements for the Authorized Persons' financial prudence.

(b) A person authorized to carry out the businesses of (dealing, managing or custody) shall comply with the provisions set forth in these Rules.

(c) A person authorized to carry out the businesses of (arranging or advising) shall maintain at all times owners' equity of not less than SR 200,000 and three months working capital; and comply with all requirements set forth in Chapter 22 of these Rules except Article 71 thereof.

(d) These Rules shall be read in conjunction with all Implementing Regulations.

(e) The Authority, if it deems necessary, may impose additional requirements to Authorized Persons' financial prudence.

(f) Definitions:

1) Any reference to the "Capital Market Law" in these Rules shall mean the Capital Market Law issued by Royal Decree No. M/30 dated 2/6/1424H.

2) Expressions and terms in these Rules have the meaning which they bear in the Capital Market Law and in the Glossary of defined terms used in the Regulations and Rules of the Capital Market Authority, unless otherwise stated in these Rules.

3) for the purpose of implementing these Rules, the following expressions and terms shall have the meaning they bear as follows unless the contrary intention appears:

Revaluation Reserve: a reserve account considered as a part of an Authorized Person's Tier-2 capital, that records the surplus created when a revaluation finds that the current value of an asset is higher than its recorded historical cost. The revaluation surplus may be reduced where a subsequent revaluation finds that the current value of an asset has decreased.

Exposures: items reported as assets in the balance sheet, derivatives reported as liabilities or off-balance sheet commitments.

Large Exposures: an exposure to a counterparty or group of connected counterparties that exceeds 10% of the Authorized Person's capital base.

Excess Exposures: large exposures in the trading book that exceed 25% of the Authorized Person's capital base.

Trading Book: the accounting book for the positions held with trading intent.

Commodities: food, metal, natural resources or other fixed physical substances in which contracts for future delivery are presently or in the future dealt in.

Tier-1 Capital: the most loss-absorbing form of capital, which includes (i) paid- up capital, (ii) audited retained earnings, (iii) share premium, (iv) reserves (other than revaluation reserves), and (v) Tier-1 capital contributions. Tier-1 capital is the net figure after applicable deductions.

Tier-2 Capital: a less loss-absorbing form of capital compared to Tier-1 capital. Tier-2 capital is the net figure after applicable deductions.

Internal Capital Adequacy Assessment Process or "ICAAP": an internal process in which all the Authorized Person's risks are identified and assessed, including risks not captured in Pillar 1 of these Rules.The process also includes capital planning.

Capital Base: comprised of Tier-1 capital and Tier-2 capital.

Subordinated Loans: the loans with conditions stating that in the event of liquidation or bankruptcy, the principal of the loans and its interest, shall not be paid until all other creditors have been paid in full.

Perpetual Subordinated Loans: the subordinated loans with no fixed term.

Fixed-term Subordinated Loans: the subordinated loans with a fixed term. These also include fixed term promissory notes.

Group of Connected Counterparties: two or more natural or legal persons who, unless otherwise shown, constitute a single risk because:

1) One of them, directly or indirectly, has control over the other or others in the group; or

2) they are so interconnected in a way that if one of them were to experience financial problems, the other or all of the others would be likely to encounter repayment difficulties.

Financial Group: Comprises an Authorized Person and:

1) The Authorized Person's local and foreign subsidiaries that are regulated by these Rules or by similar rules;

2) Companies with which the Authorized Person has a joint, or essentially joint, management or exercises a significant influence over ; and

3) Private equity investments in which the Authorized Person owns a majority of the voting rights.

And for the purposes of these Rules, the Authorized Person's parent bank shall not be included in the financial groups.

Credit Risks: risk of loss resulting from fluctuations in the credit standing of issuers of securities, counterparties and any debtors to which Authorized Persons are exposed.

Market Risk: risk of loss resulting from fluctuations in the level and in the volatility of market prices of assets, liabilities and financial instruments.

Positions Held With Trading Intent: the positions that are held intentionally for short-term resale and/or with the intent of benefiting from actual or expected short-term price movements or to lock in arbitrage profits.

Position: the Authorized Person's own market position and market position that derive from its activities on behalf of clients or as a market maker.

Non-Trading Activities: the positions that are held for non-trading purposes.

Risk-Weight: a percentage that describes a risk level of an exposure under the non-trading activities.

27.2 Part 2: CAPITAL BASE

27.2.1 Chapter 2:The Capital Base Requirement

Article 2: Minimum Capital An Authorized Person shall continuously possess a capital base which corresponds to not less than the total of the minimum capital requirements in accordance with Chapter 4 to Chapter 16 of Part 3 of these Rules.

Article 3: Authority's Discretion to Require Capital
(a) The Authority may decide that an Authorized Person's capital base shall be of certain minimum amount, higher than stated in Article 2 of these Rules, where:

1) The Authorized Person does not fulfill the requirements in Pillar I, II or III; and

2) It is unlikely that any other measure is sufficient in order to cause the Authorized Person to rectify the deficiencies within a reasonable period of time.

(b) Paragraph (a) of this Article shall not apply where the violation of these Rules is of such degree that the Authorized Person's license instead should be suspended or revoked as decided by the Authority.

Chapter 3: Composition of Capital

Article 4: Types of Capital Required The capital base of an Authorized Person shall comprise the total of:

1) Tier-1 capital calculated according to Chapter 1 of Annex 1 after applying the deductions according to Chapter 3 of Annex 1, plus

2) Tier-2 capital calculated according to Chapter 2 of Annex 1 after applying the deductions according to Chapter 3 of Annex 1.

Article 5: Tier-2 Capital Restrictions Tier-2 capital shall only be allowed up to an amount corresponding to 50% of Tier-1 capital in the calculation of the capital base for an Authorized Person.

27.3 Part 3: PILLAR I – MINIMUM CAPITAL REQUIREMENTS

27.3.1 Chapter 4: General Provisions for the Trading Book

Article 6: Risk Calculation The Authorized Person shall apply the rules regarding trading book exposures when calculating the risk associated with an Authorized Person's positions or as a market maker in securities which:

1) The Authorized Person holds with trading intent or in order to hedge other positions in the trading book; or

2) Are not subject to terms and conditions that limit the possibility to trade in them or, if they are subject to such terms and conditions, can be completely hedged.

Article 7: Trading Book Exposure Capital is required for trading book exposures which amounts to the total of the capital requirements for:

1) Counterparty risks for trading book exposures;

2) Settlement risks for trading book exposures;

3) Market risk (that is the risk of market price movements) for trading book operations; and

4) Foreign exchange risks and commodity risks in the entire operations.

Article 8: Capital Required for Trading Book Exposure
The capital requirement for trading book exposures shall be calculated in accordance with Chapter 4 to Chapter 5 of this Part and Annex 2, unless otherwise provided in a decision by the Authority pursuant to Article 9 of these Rules.

Article 9: Authority Approval Required
(a) For such trading book exposures as referred to in Article 6 of these Rules, an Authorized Person may, after obtaining an approval from the Authority, calculate the capital requirement in accordance with the rules for non-trading activities as defined in Chapter 6 to Chapter 8 of this Part. Approval shall be granted by the Authority where the total market value of the positions in the trading book and receivables attributable thereto:

1) Normally does not exceed 5% of the sum of the Authorized Person›s balance sheet total and total off-balance sheet commitments;
2) Normally does not exceed an amount equivalent to SAR 75 million; and
3) On no occasion exceeds 6% of the sum of the Authorized Person›s balance sheet total and total off-balance sheet commitments, nor exceeds an amount equivalent to SAR 100 million.

(b) Where an Authorized Person that has been granted an approval pursuant to paragraph (a) of this Article no longer fulfills the requirements for that approval, such Authorized Person shall calculate the capital requirement in accordance with Article 8 of these Rules and immediately notify the Authority thereof.

Article 10: Market Value for Balance Sheet Items
When calculating the values that form the basis for the granting of exceptions in accordance with Article 9 of these Rules, all items on the balance sheet that are assigned to the trading book are to be valued at their market value. Items on the balance sheet assigned to non-trading activities are to be valued at their book value. Off-balance sheet items and off-balance sheet commitments are to be valued at their market value. The Authorized Person's trading book positions shall be aggregated irrespective of whether they are long or short.

Article 11: Non-Trading Activities Exposure (a) Any positions and exposures not assigned to the trading book according to the provisions set out in Article 6 of these Rules shall be classified as a non-trading activities exposure.

(b) A position in an individual financial instrument or a commodity cannot be assigned to both the trading book and non-trading activities at the same time. However, the same types of financial instruments or commodities may appear in both the trading book and non-trading activities.

Article 12: Trades on Behalf of a Client Receivables and liabilities in the current trading account arising in conjunction with trades in the name of the Authorized Person but on behalf of a client, that is commission transactions, shall be treated in the context of capital adequacy when calculating the capital requirement in the same way as exposures pursuant to the rules on settlement risks and counterparty risks.

Article 13: Written Policy Required The Authorized Person shall establish a written policy that shows which financial instruments/ commodities or portfolios of such financial instruments/commodities are to be assigned to the trading book and non-trading activities respectively.

The intent of the holding of a financial instrument or commodity shall be established by the date of acquisition at the latest. Deviation from the written policy stated in paragraph (a) of this Article is only permitted under the circumstances contained in Article 14 of these Rules.

If the Authorized Person has an internal audit function, this internal audit function shall regularly review the compliance with the written policy.

Article 14: No Transfer of Financial Instruments Transfers of financial instrument or commodity from the trading book to non-trading activities and vice versa shall only occur in exceptional cases and where there is specific cause, in accordance with a written policy established by the Authorized Person.This written policy shall show how completed transfers are to be documented and which criteria shall be met to allow transfers between the trading book and non-trading activities.

27.3.2 Chapter 5: Management Requirements for the Trading Book

Article 15: AP Compliance Required An Authorized Person with a trading book shall comply with the provisions in this Chapter.

Article 16: Written Trading Strategy An Authorized Person shall have a written trading strategy for positions held with trading intent and have robust and well-documented control processes in place to ensure compliance with the set trading strategy. The Authorized Person's governing body shall approve the strategy.

Article 17: Management of Trading Book Positions An Authorized Person shall have clear procedures for the management of trading book positions. These procedures shall be set out in a written policy, which as a minimum shall include the following:

1) Trading limits and procedures for monitoring;

2) To what extent dealers have the autonomy to enter into/manage the position within agreed limits and according to the agreed strategy;

3) Clearly defined procedures for monitoring risk-taking activities against set trading strategy mentioned in Article 16 of these Rules, including monitoring of turnover and stale positions in the trading book; and

4) Procedures for actively monitoring the positions and assessing the marketability or hedgeability of the position.

Article 18: Values of Trading Book Positions
(a) An Authorized Person shall have procedures and control systems that ensure that the values of trading book positions correspond to their current market values.

(b) If the relevant market provides easily accessible closing prices independent of the Authorized Person, these shall be used to value positions. This type of valuation is referred to as marking-to-market.

(c) Where the valuation mentioned in paragraph (b) of this Article is not possible, the Authorized Person may use a mark to model valuation, which is a valuation that is derived from market prices or other market parameters.

Article 19: Valuation Principles and Controls
(a) An Authorized Person shall specify in its written policy:

1) Valuation principles that the Authorized Person shall apply for the trading book positions;

2) From where the market prices and other market parameters that may be needed for the valuation shall be acquired, and when this shall be carried out;

3) Controls to verify that the market prices and other market parameters used in the valuation are correct;

4) How any adjustments to the market prices and market parameters are carried out; and

5) How responsibility for the various steps in the valuation process is distributed within the Authorized Person.

Article 20: Independence of Market Prices Unit The unit within the Authorized Person responsible for verifying market prices and other market parameters shall be independent of the position-taking units.Verification of market prices and market parameters shall occur regularly, at least once every month.

27.3.3 Chapter 6: General provisions for Non-trading Activities

Article 21: Non-Trading Activities Capital Requirements For positions relating to non-trading activities, capital is required which corresponds to not less than 14% of the Authorized Person's risk-weighted exposure amounts calculated in accordance with Annex 3.

27.3.4 Chapter 7: Calculating a Risk-Weighted Exposure Amount for non-Trading Activities

Article 22: Risk-Weighted Exposure For each exposure, the risk weighted exposure amount shall be calculated by multiplying the exposure amount in accordance with Article 23 of these Rules by the risk weight that applies for that exposure, as set out in Annex 3.

Article 23: Balance Sheet Exposure Amounts
(a) The exposure amount for items on the balance sheet shall be the value net of write offs and specific provisions.

(b) When calculating the capital requirement for risks in non-trading activities, exposures may only be netted in those cases set out in Section 114 to Section 133 of Annex 3. This applies irrespective of what applies to external accounting.

(c) The exposure amount for off-balance sheet commitments shall consist of the nominal amount multiplied by a conversion factor as set out in Chapter 2 of Annex 3.

(d) The exposure amount for counterparty risk in derivatives shall be calculated in accordance with Chapter 3 of Annex 3.

(e) For counterparty risk in derivatives, repurchase transactions, margin lending transactions and securities lending and borrowing transactions, the exposure amount may be set to 0 (zero) if the following requirements are met:

1) The exposures shall be to a central clearing organization;
2) Participants in the clearing organization shall post collateral on a daily basis for the exposure they represent to the clearing organization; and
3) The collateral shall cover all those exposures.

Article 24: Non-Trading Activities Exposure Each non-trading activities exposure shall be assigned to one of the following exposure classes:

1) Exposures to governments and/or central banks;
2) Exposures to administrative bodies and non-profit organizations;
3) Exposures to Authorized Persons, banks and foreign equivalents that are subject to capital adequacy rules similar to those applied in the Kingdom;
4) Exposures to corporates;
5) Retail exposures;
6) Past due items;
7) High-risk items;
8) Exposures to securitization positions and re-securitization positions;
9) Exposures to investment funds;
10) Exposures to real estate funds, venture capital funds, private equity funds and other closed-ended funds;
11) Real estate investments; or
12) Other items.

Article 25: Sales and Repurchase Agreements Sales and repurchase agreements and outright forward purchases shall be assigned to the exposure class that applies to the assets in question and not to the counterparty.

Article 26: Capital Base Deductions Exposure Exposures that are deducted from capital base shall, regardless of which exposure class they are assigned to, be assigned a 0% risk weight in calculations of risk-weighted exposure amounts.

Article 27: Subsidiary Exposure
(a) An Authorized Person's risk-weighted exposure amounts for exposures to its subsidiaries, regardless of which exposure class they are assigned to, be assigned a risk-weight of 0%, if the following requirements are fulfilled:

1) The counterparty is another Authorized Person which is fully consolidated in the same financial group as the Authorized Person;

2) The counterparty is subject to the same risk evaluation, measurement and control procedures as the Authorized Person; and

3) There are no current or foreseen material practical or legal impediments to the prompt transfer of capital or repayment of liabilities from the counterparty to the Authorized Person.

(b) The exceptions to the approach provided in paragraph (a) of this Article are equity exposures or exposures in the form of other items that can be included in the issuing Authorized Person's capital base.

Article 28: Credit Calculation When calculating a risk-weighted exposure amount for an exposure, the Authorized Person may take into account any credit protection in accordance with Chapter 4 of Annex 3.

27.3.5 Chapter 8: Use of Credit Ratings

Article 29: Rating Exposures
(a) An Authorized Person may use credit ratings to determine which credit quality step an exposure corresponds to. To determine this, the Authorized Person shall use the correspondence tables in Annex 11 and Annex 12 between the credit rating agency's credit ratings and the steps in the credit quality scales determined by the Authority.

(b) An Authorized Person may only use credit ratings from authorized credit rating agencies or credit rating agencies regulated by a foreign authority equivalent to the Authority. This applies to credit ratings carried out on the initiative of the credit rating agency itself, and to credit ratings carried out at the behest of borrowers or other interested parties.

Article 30: Consistent Use
(a) When determining the risk weight of an exposure, credit ratings shall be used consistently and continuously.

(b) Credit ratings may not be used selectively.

Article 31: Uniform Use An Authorized Person which uses credit ratings for a particular exposure category shall use these credit ratings consistently for all exposures belonging to that category.

Article 32: Principal and Interest Amounts An Authorized Person may only use credit ratings that take into account all amounts, that are principal and interest amounts, included in the Authorized Person's exposure.

Article 33: Highest Risk Rate Application If two or more credit ratings are available for one exposure and they correspond to different credit quality steps, the step that corresponds to the highest risk weight shall be applied.

Article 34: Specific Credit Ratings If a credit rating exists for a specific issuing program or a facility to which the exposure belongs, this credit rating shall be used to determine the exposure's credit quality step.

Article 35: Use of Similar Credit Ratings
(a) If a credit rating which can be applied directly to a particular exposure is not available but a credit rating exists for a specific issuing program or a facility to which the exposure does not belong, this credit rating shall be used if:

1) It produces a lower credit quality step than would otherwise apply; or
2) It produces a better credit quality step and the relevant exposure is ranked equal to the issuing program, facility or unsecured exposures of the issuer.

(b) Paragraph (a) of this Article applies even if a general credit rating is available for the issuer.

Article 36: Use of Group Credit Ratings Prohibited Credit ratings for an issuer within a group may not be used as a credit rating for another issuer within the same group.

Article 37: Credit Ratings and Foreign Currency Exposure A credit rating for an exposure denominated in the counterparty's domestic currency may not be used to determine the credit quality step for another exposure, to the same counterparty, denominated in another currency.

Article 38: Short-Term Credit Ratings Short-term credit ratings may be used only for short-term exposures with an original maturity of three months or less to Authorized Persons and corporates. An Authorized Person may only use a short-term credit rating for the specific exposure to which it refers. The credit rating may not be used to derive the credit quality step of other exposures.

27.3.6 Chapter 9: General Provisions Regarding Operational Risks

Article 39: Operational Risks Capital Calculation For operational risks, capital is required which is calculated in accordance with any of the approaches stated in Chapter 10 or Chapter 11 of this Part. However, the capital requirement for operational risks shall correspond to not less than 25% of the Authorized Person's overhead expenses calculated in accordance with Chapter 12 of this Part.

27.3.7 Chapter 10:The Basic Indicator Approach for Operational Risk

Article 40: Operational Risk Capital The capital requirement for operational risk under the basic indicator approach is equal to 15% of the income indicator calculated in accordance with Annex 4.

27.3.8 Chapter 11:The Standardized Approach for Operational Risk

Article 41: Authority Approval Required

After obtaining the approval of the Authority, an Authorized Person may calculate the capital requirement for operational risk in accordance with the standardized approach according to Article 42 of these Rules rather than the basic indicator approach.

Article 42: Standardized Approach Capital Requirement Calculation In order to calculate the capital requirement in accordance with the standardized approach, the following requirements must be met:

1) The Authorized Person shall have written policies approved by the governing body for management and assessment of its exposure to operational risks, including extreme events with significant impact on the activities of an Authorized Person. In addition to stating the Authorized Person's applied definition of operational risk, the written policies shall state which forms of operational risk are relevant in the operations;

2) The Authorized Person shall have processes for handling its exposure to operational risks;

3) The Authorized Person shall have contingency and business continuity plans in place to ensure its ability to operate on an on-going basis and limit losses in the event of a severe business disruption;

4) The Authorized Person shall have documented risk management for operational risks with a clear allocation of responsibilities. The Authorized Person shall identify and assess its exposure to operational risks and track relevant data in an organized and structured manner. The risk management shall be regularly subject to an independent review;

5) The operational risk management shall be part of the Authorized Person's risk management process. The risk management outcome shall be an integral part of the monitoring and control of the Authorized Person's operational risk profile;

6) The Authorized Person shall have an internal reporting structure for operational risks reaching the governing body, of which the reporting structure provides operational risk reports to relevant Authorized Person functions. Procedures shall be in place to take appropriate action according to the information in these reports; and

7) The Authorized Person shall have written policies and documented criteria for assigning operations and the income indicatorto the appropriate business lines. These written policies and criteria shall be regularly reviewed by an independent review function. The criteria shall be updated regularly and adjusted for new and changing business lines, products and risks.The CEO of the Authorized Person shall approve that written policy.

Article 43: Business Lines Operational Capital Calculation The Authorized Person's operations shall be divided into business lines in accordance with Annex 4. The capital requirement for each such line is calculated using the income indicator multiplied by the percentage that applies for each business line in accordance with Annex 4.

27.3.9 Chapter 12: Expenditure-Based Approach for Operational Risk

Article 44: Capital Calculation
(a) When calculating capital requirements for expenditure-based risks, all overhead expenses except extraordinary expenses (such as write-offs) for the most recent audited annual financial statement shall be included.

(b) If the Authorized Person has operated for less than one year, expenditure-based risks shall be calculated as 25% of the overhead expenses set out in the business plan for the first year. Where the operations have changed significantly since the previous year, the Authority may decide to amend the capital requirement.

27.3.10 Chapter 13: General Provisions Regarding Foreign Exchange Rate Risk

Article 45: Foreign Currency and Gold Positions Capital requirement for foreign exchange rate risk shall be calculated for positions in foreign currency and for positions in gold, in accordance with the provisions set out in Chapter 13 to Chapter 15 of this Part and Annex 5.

Article 46: Capital Requirement Calculation for Foreign Exchange Rate Risk The Authorized Person shall calculate the capital requirement for foreign exchange rate risk that it is exposed to throughout the business, that is both for positions in the trading book and non-trading activity exposures.The calculation shall cover all assets, liabilities, provisions and off-balance sheet commitments.This calculation shall include gold and every individual currency in which the Authorized Person has positions except in the reporting currency.

27.3.11 Chapter 14: Valuation and Conversion to Local Currency

Article 47: Asset Valuation
(a) When calculating capital requirements with regard to foreign exchange rate risk, all assets, liabilities, provisions, positions and off-balance sheet commitments shall be valued at their market value. With regard to non-trading activities or instruments included in capital, if market values do not provide a fair picture, or market values are not available, book values may be used or, if relevant, hedge accounting can be applied when calculating the capital requirement.

(b) Conversion of assets, liabilities, provisions and positions as well as off-balance sheet commitments in currencies other than Saudi Riyal (SAR), shall be carried out using the current spot rates at the time of calculation. The conversion of all positions in foreign currency shall be carried out on the same date.

27.3.12 Chapter 15: Calculating the Capital Requirement for Foreign Exchange Rate Risk

Article 48: Use of Two-Step Method The Authorized Person shall use the two-step method provided in Chapter 1 of Annex 5 when calculating capital requirements for foreign exchange rate risks.

Article 49: Aggregation of Positions
(a) The Authorized Person shall aggregate the absolute values of the following positions:

1) Total net position in foreign currency in accordance with Chapter 1 of Annex 5;
2) The net position in gold in accordance with Chapter 1 of Annex 5; and
3) Currency positions in investment fund units in accordance with Chapter 4 of Annex

(b) Exposures to foreign currency assets which have been deducted in full from the Authorized Person's capital base or subjected to risk weight of 714% under the non- trading activities shall be excluded from the calculation of capital requirements for foreign exchange rate risks.

(c) The capital requirement for foreign exchange rate risk shall be calculated in accordance with Chapter 2 of Annex 5 of the sum resulted from the calculation provided in paragraph (a) and (b) of this Article.

27.3.13 Chapter 16: General Provisions Regarding Commodities Risk

Article 50: Calculation of Commodities Risk
(a) The Authorized Person shall calculate the capital requirements for commodities risk according to either the simple method or the maturity-based method for positions in commodities and commodity derivatives throughout the business for positions in the trading book and non-trading activities in accordance with this Chapter and Annex 6.

(b) Positions in gold and gold derivatives are exempted from the provisions provided in paragraph (a) of this Article when calculating a capital requirement for commodities risk. Capital requirements for positions in gold and gold derivatives are instead calculated in accordance with Chapter 13 to Chapter 15 of this Part and Annex 5. In addition, positions in commodities and commodities derivatives that entail pure stock financing are exempted when calculating capital requirements for commodities risk. Pure stock financing means that stock has been sold forward and the cost of funding has been locked in until the date of the forward sale.

(c) Each position in commodities or commodity derivatives shall be expressed in terms of standard units of measurement (for example barrel, MWh, kg).

(d) Capital requirements for commodities risk shall be calculated on the basis of the Authorized Person's long and short net positions in each individual commodity. When determining long and short net positions, positions in contracts maturing the same day and contracts maturing within ten days of each other may be netted if they are traded on markets that have daily delivery dates.

(e) In addition to positions in identical commodities, the following positions are also considered to be positions in the same commodity:

1) Positions in different categories of commodity if they can be delivered instead of each other ; or
2) Positions in similar commodities, if they are close substitutes and if a minimum correlation of 0.9 between price movements can be clearly established over a minimum period of one year.

(f) The application of this article shall in accordance with Annex 6.

27.4 Part 4: LARGE AND EXCESS EXPOSURES

27.4.1 Chapter 17: General Provisions for Large and Excess Exposures

Article 51: Large Exposure Determination An Authorized Person shall apply the provisions set out in this Chapter and Annex 7 when determining its large exposures.

Article 52: 25% Exposure Limitation The value of an Authorized Person's exposures to a single counterparty, or group of connected counterparties, may not exceed 25% of the Authorized Person's capital base.

Article 53: 800% Exposure Limitation The total value of an Authorized Person's large exposures may not exceed 800% of the Authorized Person's capital base.

Article 54: Exposures Excluded from Calculation The following exposures shall not be included upon calculation of an Authorized Person's exposures pursuant to Article 52 and Article 53 of these Rules:

1) Exposures which, in conjunction with foreign exchange transactions, arise in connection with the normal settlement of a transaction during the two days immediately after payment;

2) Exposures which, in conjunction with the purchase or sale of securities or commodities, arise in connection with the normal settlement of a transaction during five working days immediately after the date on which either payment has occurred or the securities or commodities have been delivered;

3) Exposures which an Authorized Person has towards another group undertaking, where the undertakings are the subject of super vision on a consolidated basis which is exercised by a competent authority or equivalent super vision in a third country;

4) Exposures which arise in connection with an underwriting where the Authority has given its approval pursuant to paragraph (c) of Section 63 of Annex 2;

5) Exposures in form of cash deposited by Authorized Person in local banks; and

6) Exposures that are deducted from the Authorized Person's capital base or subjected to the risk weight of 714% under the non-trading activities.

Article 55: Estimate of Exposures Permitted
(a) An Authorized Person may estimate the value of the exposures taking into consideration the risk-mitigating effect of credit protection.

(b) Where an Authorized Person utilises the possibility of risk-mitigation, that part of the exposure that is covered by collateral shall be treated as an exposure to the issuer of the collateral and not to the counterparty.

Article 56: Permission Required to Exceed Limits The value of an Authorized Person's exposures in the trading book to a counterparty or a group of connected counterparties may, after obtaining an approval from the Authority, exceed the limits stated in Article 52 and Article 53 of these Rules, provided that the Authorized Person fulfills the special capital requirements and the other conditions set forth in Chapter 5 of Annex 2.

27.5 Part 5 MINIMUM LIQUIDITY REQUIREMENTS

27.5.1 Chapter 18: General Provisions Regarding Liquidity Requirements

Article 57: Management of Liquidity Risks An Authorized Person shall manage its liquidity risks in accordance with the provisions set out in this Chapter and Annex 8.

27.5.2 Chapter 19 ORGANIZATIONAL REQUIREMENTS

Article 58: Risk Tolerance Written Policy Required
An Authorized Person shall have a written policy regarding risk tolerance that is partly based on an explicit quantitative and qualitative approach to the liquidity risk that is appropriate, and tailored to the Authorized Person's business objectives, strategic direction and general risk preference. The governing body of the Authorized Person shall take decisions on risk tolerance.

Article 59: Management of Liquidity Risk An Authorized Person shall have strategies, policies and instructions as set out in Annex 8, as to manage liquidity risk in accordance with the risk tolerance pursuant to Article 58 of these Rules and to ensure that the Authorized Person maintains sufficient liquidity.

Article 60: Liquidity Risk Regular Reports Required
The Authorized Person's CEO shall monitor and regularly report on its liquidity risk management and the liquidity development to the Authorized Person's governing body.

Article 61: Governing Body Approval
(a) The governing body of the Authorized Person shall at least annually review and approve the strategies, policies and instructions set out in Annex 8 relating to the Authorized Person's liquidity risk management.

(b) The governing body shall ensure that the Authorized Person's senior management handles liquidity risk in accordance with its risk tolerance.

Article 62: Liquidity Risk Strategies
(a) Strategies, policies and instructions on the management of liquidity risk provided in Article 59 of these Rules shall ensure that the Authorized Person monitors and meets future liquidity needs for normal day-to-day management as well as at temporary and protracted emergencies. They shall also provide guidance on responsibility of work, measurement methods, limits, monitoring and reporting. The guidelines and instructions referto the Authorized Person as a whole, including any branches and, where appropriate, coordination between them.

(b) An Authorized Person that is a part of a financial group shall consider the strategies, policies and instructions that apply to the group in setting their own strategies, policies and instructions.

Article 63: Communication of Policies to Employees
The strategies, policies and instructions mentioned in Article 59 of these Rules shall be communicated to all relevant staff in the Authorized Person.

Article 64: Liquidity Risk Control
(a) Each Authorized Person shall have a central function for independent oversight of liquidity risk (liquidity risk control) that report directly to the CEO or a member of the Authorized Person's governing body which is not responsible for position-taking business units.

(b) The central liquidity risk control function must have good working knowledge of financial instruments, liquidity risks and methods of governance and oversight of liquidity risk. If the Authorized Person has a central risk control, then the function for liquidity risk management can be part of it.

(c) If an Authorized Person is part of a financial group, the central function for liquidity risk control could be placed in the parent company.

(d) The central liquidity risk control function is responsible for the on-going reporting and analysis of the Authorized Person's and, where appropriate, the group's liquidity risk.

(e) If an Authorized Person has an internal function for liquidity risk control within a position-taking unit the internal function shall report to the central liquidity risk control function or the central risk control function, if any.

(f) An Authorized Person that is a part of a financial group shall adjust its liquidity risk control to the common group liquidity risk control function.

Article 65: Regular Review and Evaluation
(a) An Authorized Person shall regularly review and perform independent evaluation of the following:

1) its governance and oversight of liquidity risk;
2) the liquidity risk management to identify weaknesses or problems with the procedures, methods and systems for calculating and reporting of liquidity risk;
3) the established policies and procedures to ensure that they are followed and that the processes meet the set goals; and
4) Whether it has an appropriate organization for their liquidity management.

(b) The function for independent review shall report directly to the Authorized Person's governing body. If the Authorized Person has an internal audit function, the independent audit shall be conducted by it.

27.6 Part 6 PILLAR II – ASSESSMENT OF ALL RISKS

27.6.1 Chapter 20: Internal Capital Adequacy Assessment Process (ICAAP)

Article 66: ICAAP Features
(a) Authorized Persons shall have in place ICAAP pursuant to Annex 9. Authorized Persons shall ensure that their ICAAP consists of five main features:

1) Governing body oversight;
2) Sound capital assessment;
3) Comprehensive assessment of risks;
4) Monitoring and reporting; and
5) Internal control review.

(b) The ICAAP shall be reviewed and revised annually by the Authorized Person's governing body. The CEO shall have the responsibility over the ICAAP and ensure that the ICAAP is an integrated part of the business environment.

(c) The ICAAP shall be proportionate to the nature, scale and complexity of the activities of the Authorized Persons concerned.

(d) Authorized Persons shall at least annually conduct a comprehensive review and investigation according to the ICAAP.The annual investigation shall lead to a yearly report submitted to the Authority.

27.7 PART 7 PILLAR III – DISCLOSURE AND REPORTING

27.7.1 Chapter 21: Disclosure

Article 67: Additional Disclosure Requirements
(a) The disclosure obligations in this Chapter and Chapter 22 of this Part shall be in addition to any notification requirements that an Authorized Person has under the Authorized Persons Regulations.

(b) Where stated in these Rules that an Authorized Person shall submit information to the Authority or disclose information to the public, and the Authorized Person is part of a financial group, then the Authorized Person is obligated to disclose in addition to its own information the group's information.

Article 68: Annual Reports Required
(a) The information referred to in Annex 10 shall be disclosed at least once a year and shall, where applicable, include the financial status on the balance sheet date of the Authorized Person's annual report or, where applicable, the consolidated accounts for the financial group.

(b) The information referred to in Annex 10 shall be disclosed as quickly as possible, although, where applicable, no laterthan in conjunction with the public disclosure of the annual report.

Article 69: Publication Required Authorized Persons must have a website on which they shall publish the information stipulated in Annex 10. Listed Authorized Persons must also include that information in their annual report.

27.7.2 Chapter 22: Reporting

Article 70: Submission of Financial Statements to Authority An Authorized Person shall submit their financial statements to the Authority.

Article 71: Required Calculations An Authorized Person shall submit information regarding the calculation of capital base, minimum capital requirements and large exposures in accordance with the capital adequacy model.

Article 72: Time Period for Submissions The information in Article 70 and Article 71 of these Rules shall be submitted to the Authority within 5 days after the end of the month for the monthly statements, and within 60 calendar days after the financial year end for the audited annual financial statements.

Article 73: Record Retention An Authorized Person shall keep and preserve all financial and non-financial records and documents in accordance with the relevant provisions provided in the Authorized Persons Regulations.

Article 74: Audited Financial Statements
(a) Audited annual financial statements shall be prepared in accordance with the Saudi Organization for Certified Public Accountants (SOCPA) accounting standards or, after obtaining an approval from the Authority, internationally accepted accounting standards, and audited by an external audit firm who is a member of SOCPA.

(b) The external audit firm shall report whether, from its test examinations and after making due inquiry, the Authorized Person's minimum capital computations have been correctly computed and have been maintained in compliance with these Rules.

Article 75: Failure to Meet Requirements An Authorized Person shall report all deviations from these Rules to the Authority. Simultaneously the Authorized Person shall submit a plan to rectify these deviations.

27.8 PART 8 FINANCIAL GROUPS

27.8.1 Chapter 23: General Provisions Regarding Financial Groups

Article 76: Consolidated Reporting With respect to a financial group, responsibility for fulfillment of the requirements on a consolidated basis shall be borne by the Authorized Person that is not an affiliate of another Authorized Person.

27.8.2 Chapter 24: Consolidated Accounts

Article 77: Compliance Responsibility
1) The responsible Authorized Person pursuant to Article 78 of these Rules shall ensure that the financial group as a whole fulfills the requirements set forth in:

2) Chapter 2 and Chapter 3 of Part 2 and Chapter 19 of Part 5 and associated annex regarding capital base;

3) Chapter 4 to Chapter 15 of Part 3 and associated annexes regarding capital requirements;

4) Chapter 17 of Part 4 and associated annex regarding large exposures requirements; and

5) Chapter 18 and Chapter 19 of Part 5 and associated annexes regarding liquidity risk requirements.

Article 78: Preparation Consolidated accounts shall be prepared for a financial group by applying relevant rules applicable to the preparation of consolidated balance sheets and consolidated income statements. Upon preparation of the accounts, the Authorized Person shall consolidate all the companies that are a part of its financial group, in full.

Article 79: Exclusion of Financial Group Companies
(a) The Authority may decide that any company that is a part of the Authorized Person's financial group or an undertaking participation by the Authorized Person shall be excluded from the consolidated accounts mentioned in Article 78 of these Rules.

(b) The Authorized Person may submit an application to the Authority to exclude any company that is a part of its financial group or any undertaking in which a participation is held from the consolidated accounts mentioned in Article 78 of these Rules, where:

1) The undertaking is situated in a country that there are legal obstacles to the transfer of necessary information;
2) The undertaking is of negligible significance in light of the purpose of the supervision; or
3) A compilation of the financial position of the company that is a part of the Authorized Person's financial group would be inappropriate or misleading in light of the purpose of the supervision.

Article 80: Profit and Loss Statements An Authorized Person's profit and loss statement, balance sheet and off-balance sheet commitments may, if there are special grounds and with the approval of the Authority, be included in the consolidated accounts on the basis of financial statements referring to another point in time than the reporting date.

Article 81: Full Consolidation Required When producing the consolidated accounts, all parts of the Authorized Person's financial group shall be fully consolidated.The Authority can allow account consolidation by another method where special grounds exist.

Article 82: Contents of Submission An Authorized Person shall, on the dates and for the accounting periods determined by the Authority for each individual case, provide the Authority with the following consolidated information:

1) Information about the financial group's consolidated financial position;

2) Information about the purchase and sale of assets between the Authorized Person and any company that is a part of its financial group;

3) Information about the receivables and liabilities between the Authorized Person and any company that is a part of its financial group;

4) Information about agreements between the Authorized Person and any company that is a part of its financial group (for example cooperation or guarantee agreements); and

5) Information about commitments and any contingent liability between the Authorized Person and any company that is a part of its financial group (for example letters of guarantee or intent).

27.8.3 Chapter 25: Foreign Undertakings

Article 83: Foreign Companies
(a) When calculating the financial group's capital requirements, the Authorized Person may treat a foreign company that is a part of its financial group in accordance with this Chapter, after receiving the approval of the Authority.

(b) The capital requirement for the Authorized Person's exposures in the foreign company that is a part of its financial group may be calculated in accordance with the rules of the country in which the foreign company has its registered office if that country's rules are equivalent to these Rules.

(c) Netting shall not occur for long and short positions in the same financial instrument issued by an issuer outside the financial group and which are held by different companies within the same financial group. The netting is allowed, however, if a position belongs to the trading book in all of the relevant countries. If this method is utilized to include a foreign company that is a part of the Authorized Person's financial group, it shall be used consistently.

Article 84: Capital Calculation When calculating capital, the instruments which are included in the capital of the foreign company that is a part of the Authorized Person's financial group may only be included in the capital of the financial group if these instruments fulfill the conditions applying to Tier-1 capital or Tier-2 capital in accordance with Annex 1.

27.8.4 Chapter 26: Systems and Controls

Article 85: Obligation of Authorized Person In discharging its duties pertaining to systems and controls requirements as set out in the Authorized Persons Regulations, an Authorized Person shall have regard to the provisions of these Rules.

27.9 PART 9 CLOSING PROVISIONS

27.9.1 Chapter 27: Publication and Entry into Force

Article 86: Effective Date These Rules shall be effective in accordance with their approval resolution.

27.10 Annex 1: Capital Base

27.10.1 Chapter 1:Tier-1 Capital

Section 1

Tier-1 capital shall include the following:

1) Paid-up capital;
2) Audited retained earnings;
3) Share premium;
4) Reserves (other than revaluation reserves); and
5) Tier-1 capital contributions.

Section 2

(a) Unconditional Tier-1 capital contributions shall be included as Tier-1 capital.

(b) Conditional Tier-1 capital contributions shall only be included as Tier-1 capital if their conditions state that the governing body decides on the repayment of the contributions.

(c) In order for an Authorized Person to include a Tier-1 capital contribution as Tier-1 capital, the contribution must have been paid in to the Authorized Person.

Section 3

(a) Profit generated in the current financial year by an Authorized Person or financial group may be included in the capital of the Authorized Person or financial group as Tier-1 capital, if the Authorized Person's external auditors have verified the profit for both the individual Authorized Person and the financial group. Profit refers to profit after estimated taxes and zakat.

(b) External auditor's verification of profit means that the Authorized Person's external auditors have examined the accounts that form the basis of the capital adequacy report for the Authorized Person or financial group.

Section 4

An Authorized Person or financial group that later reports a smaller profit than what was most recently verified shall only include the smaller profit in the Tier-1 capital.

Section 5

If financial liabilities that are not held fortrading intent or are not the subject of an effective and documented fair value hedge are reported at fair value, accumulated value change which can be assigned to changes in own creditworthiness shall not affect the size of capital.

Section 6

When calculating capital base, Tier-1 capital contribution instruments may represent a maximum of 15% of the Authorized Person's Tier-1 capital after the reductions of Tier-1 capital in accordance with these Rules.

Section 7

Interest payment fortier-1 capital contribution instruments shall only be made if there are distributable funds available in the Authorized Person. Interest conditions for the Tier-1 capital contribution instrument shall not be cumulative.

Section 8

Tier-1 capital contribution instruments may not contain conditions stipulating that the interest can be raised after a period (step-up).

Section 9

The terms of the Tier-1 capital contribution instrument shall state that the contribution has subordinated terms of payment. A Tier-1 capital contribution can be considered equal with other Tier-1 capital instruments in terms of subordination, but it shall be subordinated to all other borrowings or deposits.

Section 10

(a) The terms of the Tier-1 capital contribution instrument shall state that the contribution is unsecured and in principle open term (perpetual).

(b) Fortier-1 capital contribution to be considered open term, the interest rate may not be unreasonably high at the beginning of the term of the loan only to then fall drastically (step-down).

(c) An instrument structure with a high interest rate at the beginning of the term of the instrument and a large decline in the interest rate later can be seen as a form of hidden amortization.

Section 11

Tier-1 capital contribution should be limited to the actual amount of funds the Authorized Person has received regardless of if the instrument was issued at a discount or a premium.

Section 12

(a) The terms of the Tier-1 capital contribution instrument shall state that the investor has the right to repayment only if the Authorized Person has been declared bankrupt and on obtaining an approval from the Authority. Such approval may be given at the earliest five years after the contribution has been taken up or issued.

(b) The Authority, where it deems necessary and in accordance with paragraph (d) of this Section, may permit the Tier-1 capital contribution to be repaid or repurchased less than five years after the contribution was taken up or issued.

(c) When applying for approval of the Authority for the repayment or repurchase of a Tier-1 capital contribution mentioned in paragraph (b) of this Section, the Authorized Person shall describe how the repayment or repurchase will affect the Authorized Person's capital adequacy. In addition, the Authorized Person shall specify which short-term changes it expects to the capital requirement and capital.

(d) The Authority may give its approval mentioned in paragraph (b) of this Section if the Authorized Person's capital adequacy ratio is deemed satisfactory in the long- term, even after the Tier-1 capital contribution has been repaid or repurchased. Otherwise, approval cannot be given unless theTier-1 capital contribution is replaced by at least an equal amount of capital of the same or higher quality. A new Tier-1 capital contribution may not have better preferential rights than the contribution that is to be repaid or repurchased.

Section 13

The Authority may give approval to an Authorized Person to repurchase a portion of an issued Tier-1 capital contribution intended for resale as part of securities-related operations. An Authorized Person that has received the approval shall deduct the portion of the contribution repurchased from the Tier-1 capital.When later selling the repurchased Tier-1 capital contribution notes, a corresponding amount may again be included in the Tier-1 capital.

Section 14

The terms of the Tier-1 capital contribution instrument shall state that the Tier-1 capital contribution, including accrued and unpaid interest can be appropriated to cover losses, so the Authorized Person can, by doing so, continue its activities without having to go into liquidation.

Section 15

(a) An Authorized Person that has drawn up a balance sheet for liquidation purposes and finds that it is thereby liable to go into liquidation may appropriate all or part of a Tier-1 capital contribution, including accrued interest amounts, in order to restore Tier-1 capital to a level equal to the paid-up capital. The Authorized Person shall in the first instance appropriate the Tier-1 capital contribution and its accrued interest. Accrued interest amount shall be entered as liabilities before they can be appropriated.

(b) The Annual (or Extraordinary) General Meeting, or where not relevant the meeting of the shareholders, shall decide whether the Tier-1 capital contribution and accrued interest entered as liabilities shall be appropriated. Such decision may, however, only be implemented after the auditors have examined the balance sheet and the Authority has given its approval.

(c) The appropriation mentioned in paragraph (b) of this Section shall be irrevocable and final. Provisions regarding the right of contribution providers to future payment shall only cover cases in which the restoration of the appropriated amount can be made from distributable profits in accordance with an adopted balance sheet.

(d) Interest shall at any time be charged only on the remaining portion of the Tier-1 capital contribution that has not been appropriated.

27.10.2 Chapter 2: Tier-2 Capital

Section 16

Tier-2 capital may include perpetual subordinated loans and fixed term subordinated loans with an original term to maturity of not less than five years.

Section 17

An Authorized Person may include cumulative preference shares in Tier-2 capital after obtaining the approval of the Authority. In the application for approval, the Authorized Person shall report on the rules in the Authorized Person's articles of association regarding how the accumulation shall occur.

Section 18

(a) Revaluation reserves shall be included in Tier-2 capital.

(b) Unrealized accumulated value changes to loans and receivables or other interest-bearing financial instruments classified as available-for-sale financial assets, may not affect the amount of Tier-2 capital other than for value changes reported as write downs or reversed write-downs in the profit and loss statement.

Section 19

A revaluation reserve that has been formed in conjunction with the write-up of a fixed asset may, after obtaining the approval of the Authority, be included in Tier-2 capital. In the application for approval, the Authorized Person shall report on the circumstances that served as the basis for the establishment of the reserve.

Section 20

Unrealized accumulated profit from investment property and tangible non-current assets at fair value shall be included in Tier-2 capital.

Section 21

A perpetual subordinated loan is allowed to contain conditions establishing how interest shall be determined during the entire term of the loan.

Section 22

The perpetual subordinated loan may not contain conditions stipulating that the interest can be raised after a period (step-up).

Section 23

(a) The terms of the perpetual subordinated loan shall state that the Authorized Person shall be able to defer payment of the interest on the loan, when:

1) The Authorized Person reports a negative operating income; or
2) The governing body has decided not to pay a dividend.

(b) The interest on the deferred amount of interest may at the most be 300 basis points above the interest that otherwise applies to the loan.

Section 24

The terms of the perpetual subordinated loan agreement shall state that the loan has subordinated terms of payment. A perpetual subordinated loan can be considered equal to other perpetual subordinated loans in terms of subordination, but must rank lower than fixed-term subordinated loans.

Section 25

(a) It shall be stated in the contract terms for a perpetual subordinated loan that the loan is unsecured and that it in principle has an open term.

(b) For a perpetual subordinated loan to be considered open term, the interest rate may not be unreasonably high at the beginning of the term of the loan only to then decline drastically (step-down). A credit agreement structure with a high interest rate at the beginning of the term of the loan and a large decline in the interest rate later can be seen as a form of hidden amortization of the loan.

Section 26

A perpetual subordinated loan shall be limited to the actual amount of funds the Authorized Person has received regardless if the perpetual subordinated loan was issued at a discount or a premium.

Section 27

(a) The terms of the perpetual subordinated loan agreement shall state that the investor has the right to repayment only if the Authorized Person has been declared bankrupt and on obtaining an approval from the Authority. Such approval may be given at the earliest five years after the loan has been issued.

(b) The Authority, where it deems necessar y and in accordance with paragraph (d) of this Section, may approve the perpetual subordinated loan to be repaid or repurchased less than five years after the loan was issued.

(c) When applying for the approval of the authority for the repayment or repurchase of a perpetual subordinated loan mentioned in paragraph (b) of this Section, the Authorized Person shall describe how the repayment or repurchase will affect the Authorized Person's capital adequacy. In addition, the Authorized Person shall specify which short-term changes it expects to the capital requirement and capital.

(d) The Authority may give its approval mentioned in paragraph (b) of this Section if the Authorized Person's capital adequacy ratio is deemed satisfactor y in the long- term, even after the perpetual subordinated loan has been repaid or repurchased. Otherwise, approval cannot be given unless the perpetual subordinated loan is replaced by at least an equal amount of capital of the same or higher quality. A new perpetual subordinated loan may not have better preferential rights than the loan that is to be repaid or repurchased.

Section 28

The Authority may give approval to an Authorized Person to repurchase a portion of an issued perpetual subordinated loan intended for resale as part of securities-related operations. An Authorized Person that has received approval shall deduct that portion of the loan repurchased from the Tier-2 capital. When later selling the repurchased perpetual subordinated loan notes, a corresponding amount may again be included in the Tier-2 capital.

Section 29

The terms of the perpetual subordinated loan agreement shall state that the perpetual subordinated loan, including accrued and unpaid interest, can be appropriated to cover losses so that the Authorized Person can, by doing so, continue its activities without having to enter into liquidation.

Section 30

(a) An Authorized Person that has drawn up a balance sheet for liquidation purposes and finds that it is thereby liable to go into liquidation may appropriate all or part of a perpetual subordinated loan, including accrued interest, in order to restore shareholders' equity to a level equal to the registered share capital.The Authorized Person shall in the first instance appropriate any Tier-1 capital contributions and their accrued interest. Accrued interest amounts shall be entered as liabilities before they can be appropriated.

(b) The Annual (or Extraordinary) General Meeting, or where not relevant the meeting of the shareholders, shall decide whether the perpetual subordinated loan and accrued interest entered as liabilities shall be appropriated. Such a decision may, however, only be implemented after the auditors have examined the balance sheet and the Authority has given its approval.

(c) The appropriation mentioned in paragraph (b) of this Section shall be irrevocable and final. Provisions regarding the right of contribution providers to future payment shall only cover cases in which the restoration of the appropriated amount can be made from distributable profits in accordance with an adopted balance sheet.

(d) Interest shall at any time be charged only on the portion of the perpetual subordinated loan that has not been appropriated.

(e) The payment of interest, may, like the repayment of the appropriated amount, only be made from distributable profits. With regard to perpetual subordinated loans, the interest on the amount of interest calculated on the fictitious debt may not exceed by more than three percentage points the interest that otherwise applies to the loan.

(f) When the Annual (or Extraordinary) General Meeting, or where not relevant the meeting of the shareholders, decides to appropriate all or part of the perpetual subordinated loan, including accrued interest, in order to restore shareholders' equity, the General Meeting, or where not relevant the meeting of the shareholders, may also decide to enter a provision into the articles of association with the following content:

"The Authorized Person may not pay dividends or make other repayment to shareholders unless the following conditions are met:

1) the appropriated amount of the perpetual subordinated loan, including appropriated interest, has been re-entered as a liability; and

2) the Authorized Person has entered as a liability and paid an amount corresponding to the interest which – if appropriation for covering losses has not taken place – should have accrued and been paid on the loan".

Section 31

That indicated in Section 32 to Section 41 of this Annex regarding fixed-term subordinated loans with subordinated terms of payment also applies to other similar fixed-term promissory notes with subordinated terms of payment.

Section 32

Fixed-term subordinated loans may be included in Tier-2 capital if the loans are paid in cash and no collateral is posted for the loans.

Section 33

The terms of the fixed-term subordinated loan agreement shall state that the loan has subordinated terms of payment. It shall also state that the loan has preferential rights over perpetual subordinated loans and Tier-1 capital contributions.

Section 34

For a fixed-term subordinated loan to be included in Tier-2 capital, the period from the issue date of the loan to the date at which the Authorized Person may terminate the loan for early repayment shall be at least five years. If an Authorized Person has issued a fixed-term subordinated loan with the right to terminate the loan for early repayment, the date of this right (the call date) must form the basis for the calculation of the loan's effective term. However, this does not apply if agreed early repayment is conditional on the Authority's approval.

Section 35

Fixed-term subordinated loans with a residual term less than five years may be included in Tier-2 capital up to a maximum of 20% of the notional value for each full year remaining until the maturity date.

Section 36

The terms of the fixed-term subordinated loan agreement shall state that the investor has the right to repayment before the agreed maturity date only if the Authorized Person has been declared bankrupt or has entered liquidation.

Section 37

(a) When notifying or applying for approval for the early repayment or repurchase of a fixed-term subordinated loan, the Authorized Person shall describe how the repayment or repurchase will affect the Authorized Person's capital adequacy. In addition, in both cases, the Authorized Person shall specify which short-term changes it expects to the capital requirement and capital.

(b) A condition for the repayment or repurchase is that the Authority judges the Authorized Person's capital adequacy ratio to be satisfactor y in the long-term, even after the loan has been repaid or repurchased. Otherwise, repayment or repurchase may not take place unless the loan is replaced by at least a corresponding amount of capital of the same or higher quality. A new fixed-term subordinated loan may not have better preferential rights than the loan that is to be redeemed.

Section 38

The Authority can give approval to an Authorized Person to repurchase a portion of an issued fixed-term subordinated loan intended for resale as part of securities-related operations. An Authorized Person that has received approval shall deduct the portion of the loan that was repurchased from the Tier-2 capital. When later selling the repurchased subordinated loan notes, a corresponding amount may again be included in the Tier-2 capital.

Section 39

If a fixed-term subordinated loan is extended, the entire loan shall be considered to be a new loan.The residual term shall, after the extension be at least five years in order for the loan, after the extension, to be included in the Tier-2 capital.

Section 40

20% of amounts that shall be amortized on a fixed-term subordinated loan may be included in Tier-2 capital for each full year remaining until the amortization date. A loan with several amortizations may therefore be included on the same conditions as if the corresponding amount had been taken up by several loans maturing on the respective amortization dates.

Section 41

Fixed-term subordinated loans, issued at a discount or premium, may, when issued, be included in Tier-2 capital to a maximum of the amount that the Authorized Person or borrower received at that time.

27.10.3 Chapter 3: Deductions from Capital

Section 42

An Authorized Person shall deduct losses in accordance with the annual accounts from the Tier-1 capital even if the Authorized Person's external auditors have not yet verified the losses.

Section 43

A deduction shall be made from the verified profit for the current financial year of an Authorized Person or financial group for as much of the annual cash dividend, or other similar allocations of these funds, bearing upon the current financial year for the period up to the relevant calculation date.

Section 44

Losses arising from price adjustments for all positions booked at fair value or provisions to the revaluation reserves shall be deducted from the Tier-1 capital.

Section 45

Goodwill and intangible non-current assets shall be deducted from Tier-1 capital. Shortfalls/ negative goodwill shall not be offset against surpluses/goodwill.

Section 46

Deferred zakat or taxes assets (where applicable) reported on the balance sheet shall be deducted from Tier-1 capital.

Section 47

Acquired own shares included in the Authorized Person's trading book shall be deducted from Tier-1 capital.

Section 48

Tier-1 capital contributions, subordinated loans, and other subordinated promissory notes may be included in the capital base only to the amounts placed in the market. This means that that portion of the issued instruments not placed in the market, or which the Authorized Person has redeemed or repurchased –

and where the Authorized Person has booked as an asset its own instruments related to the Tier-1 capital contribution, subordinated loan and other subordinated promissory notes—shall be deducted from the Tier-1 capital or Tier-2 capital accordingly when calculating the capital base.

Section 49

(a) The Authorized Person shall, in the manner stated in Section 50 of this Annex, deduct from the Tier-1 capital and Tier-2 capital the book value of the shares or other risk bearing capital (contribution) in an Authorized Person, a bank, an insurance company or equivalent foreign subsidiary. Such a deduction shall be made where the Authorized Person's holdings exceeds 10% of the undertaking's capital.

(b) Deductions shall not be made for contributions that relate to undertakings covered by the same consolidated accounts as the Authorized Person through complete consolidation or through a proportional consolidation.

Section 50

(a) Of the total amount deducted pursuant to Section 49 of this Annex, 50% shall be deducted from the Tier-1 capital and the remaining 50% from Tier-2 capital.

(b) Where the amount to be deducted from Tier-2 capital exceeds Tier-2 capital, the excess amount shall be deducted from Tier-1 capital.

Section 51

Deductions from Tier-1 capital related to unsettled exposures shall be made according to Section 71 of Annex 2.

27.11 ANNEX 2: Trading Book

27.11.1 Chapter 1: Interest Rate Risks

Section 1

(a) Interest rate risks shall be calculated for positions in interest rate linked financial instruments included in an Authorized Person's trading book. Calculating capital requirements for specific and general risk may be carried out on the Authorized Person's net positions in interest rate linked financial instruments. Net position refers to the difference between a long and a short position in financial instruments of the same type and issued by the same issuer. Same issuer refers to the same legal entity.

(b) Financial instruments issued by different issuers may be treated in the same way as instruments issued by the same issuer on the condition that a clearing organization can confirm that bonds issued by these issuers are fully deliverable against one another.

(c) In the case of cheapest-to-deliver futures or forwards an Authorized Person may net a short notional position in the cheapest to deliver security, arising from a short future or forward where the seller has a choice of which debt security it may use to settle its obligations, against a long position in any deliverable security.This exception is only applicable where the Authorized Person has sold the future or forward and netting is not allowed where the Authorized Person has bought a cheapest-to- deliver future or forward.

(d) Financial instruments are considered to be of the same type if they are denominated in the same currency and their coupons and maturities are the same. An Authorized Person may not net positions in financial instruments that are denominated in different currencies. The financial instruments shall also afford equal rights if the issuer enters liquidation.

Section 2

(a) A long (purchased) position in a future, synthetic future, forward or option shall be treated as:

1) A notional long position in the underlying security (or the cheapest to deliver (taking into account the conversion factor) where the contract can be satisfied by deliver y of one from a range of securities); and
2) A notional short position in a zero coupon zero-specific-risk security with a maturity equal to the expiry date of the future or forward.

(b) A short (sold) position in a future, synthetic future, forward or option is treated as:

1) A notional short position in the underlying security (or the cheapest to deliver (taking into account the conversion factor) where the contract can be satisfied by deliver y of one from a range of securities); and
2) A notional long position in a zero coupon zero-specific-risk security with a maturity equal to the expiry date of the future, synthetic future or forward.

(c) Long and short positions deriving from an option shall be delta-weighted in accordance with Section 9 of this Annex.

(d) A zero coupon bond deriving from the partition of derivatives into a long and a short position shall in this context be considered to be issued by a government which qualifies for credit quality step 1, alternatively to have a risk weight of 0% in non-trading activities.

(e) Netting long and short positions in zero coupon bonds shall be carried out in accordance with Section 1 of this Annex.

(f) The positions which arise from the partitioning into long and short positions shall be included in the calculation of specific and general risk unless otherwise set out in Section 3 to Section 31 of this Annex.

Section 3

(a) The calculation of capital requirements for the specific risk of the underlying security shall be based on the issuer of the underlying security.

(b) The capital requirement for specific risk in the zero coupon zero-specific-risk security, irrespective of whether it is long or short position, shall be calculated in accordance with Section 33 of this Annex.

(c) With regard to forwards with a constructed underlying instrument and several deliverable bonds, the underlying instrument shall be made up of the bond that is cheapest to deliver.

Section 4

(a) Forwards based on an index of interest rate linked financial instruments (including delta-weighted equivalents of options based on an index consisting of interest rate linked financial instruments) shall be treated as combined long and short positions in the same way as other derivatives. A long or short position in such an index may be split up among the instruments included in the index.These instruments may be netted against opposite positions in the same financial instrument to that extent that the instrument is included in the index. Forwards based on an index consisting of interest rate linked financial instruments not split up among the instruments included in the index shall be treated as individual financial instruments.

(b) The calculation of specific risk for both the underlying financial instrument and the zero coupon bond shall be carried out in accordance with Section 2 to Section 3 of this Annex.

Section 5

(a) A long (sold) position in a forward rate agreements shall be treated as a combination of a long position in a zero coupon bond with a maturity date corresponding to the settlement date for the forward rate agreements contract plus the number of days which correspond to the maturity of the contract and a short position in a zero coupon bond which expires on the settlement date.

(b) A short (purchased) position in forward rate agreements shall similarly be treated as a short position in a zero coupon bond with a maturity date corresponding to the settlement date coupon for the contract plus the number of days which correspond to the maturity of the contract and a long position in a zero coupon bond which matures on the settlement date.

(c) The amount due for the zero coupon bond with a maturity date corresponding to the settlement date for the contract plus the number of days corresponding to its maturity shall be comprised of the contract's notional amount plus the agreed amount of interest. The amount due for the zero coupon bond which matures on the settlement date of the contract shall be comprised of the contract's notional amount.

(d) These zero coupon bonds shall be considered to be issued by a government which qualifies for credit quality step 1, alternatively to have a risk weight of 0% in non- trading activities. Netting long and short positions in zero coupon bonds shall be carried out in accordance with Section 1 of this Annex.

(e) The capital requirement for specific risk in both long and short zero coupon bonds may be calculated in accordance with Section 33 of this Annex.

Section 6

(a) An interest rate swap shall be considered to be a combination of a short and a long position. For example, an interest rate swap designed to give its holder variable interest or while paying fixed interest is treated as a combination of a long position in a financial instrument with a variable interest rate maturing on the next interest rate adjustment date and a short position in a financial instrument with a fixed interest rate and the same maturity that applies to the swap.

(b) A currency swap shall be considered a combination of a short and a long position in each currency.

(c) A currency swap in which the holder pays and receives a variable interest rate in different currencies shall be treated as a combination of a long and a short position in financial instruments with a variable interest rate maturing on the next interest rate adjustment date.

(d) Capital requirements for specific risk in both long and short positions may be calculated in accordance with Section 33 of this Annex.

Section 7

(a) A currency forward shall be considered to be a combination of a long and a short position in a zero coupon bond in each currency.

(b) The zero coupon bonds shall be considered to be issued by a government which qualifies for credit quality step 1, alternatively to have a risk weight of 0% in non- trading activities.

(c) Netting long and short positions in zero coupon bonds shall be carried out in accordance with Section 1 of this Annex.

(d) Capital requirements for specific risk in both long and short positions in zero coupon bonds may be calculated in accordance with Section 33 of this Annex.

Section 8

(a) The transferring party in a repurchase transaction (repo) based on financial instruments assigned to the trading book shall be considered to have a short position in a zero coupon bond maturing when the contract expires. The capital requirement for specific risk for the short position may be calculated in accordance with Section 33 of this Annex. The receiving party in a repurchase transaction (reversed repo) shall be considered to have a long position in a zero coupon bond maturing when the contract expires.

(b) The capital requirement for the specific risk for the long position may be calculated in accordance with Section 33 of this Annex. Real repurchase transactions (repos and reversed repos) in which the settlement date for the repurchase/re-selling is three working days or less after the trade day are exempted from the treatment set out in this Section.

Section 9

(a) Options based on interest rates, interest rate swaps or other similar interest rate linked financial instruments shall be treated as a combination of long and short positions in the same way as other derivatives. Both positions shall be converted into delta-weighted positions by multiplying the underlying instrument's market value by the option's delta value. The delta-weighted positions may be netted against any offsetting positions in the same type of underlying financial instruments.

(b) If the exchange which lists the options does not publish the delta values of the options, or if they are over the counter options, the Authorized Person shall calculate the delta values of its options.

(c) When calculating capital requirements for specific risk for bought and sold options, the underlying debt instruments shall be treated on the basis of the issuer of the instrument.

(d) Calculation of capital requirements for specific risk of the zero coupon bonds arising from options in interest rate swaps or currency swaps (swaptions) and interest rate options (e.g. caps and floors) may be calculated in accordance with Section 33 of this Annex.

(e) A bought option does not need to be converted to a delta-weighted position and included in the calculation of specific risk as set out in Section 31 to Section 39 of this Annex or general risk as set out in Section 45 to Section 46 of this Annex.The capital requirement for such a position may instead be set at equal to the market value of the option. Netting against an offset position in the underlying instrument cannot be carried out in this case. An Authorized Person shall have systems in place and apply protective measures such that account is taken of other risks associated with options trading, such as:

1) The sensitivity of the delta value to price changes in the underlying financial instrument (gamma);
2) The sensitivity of the option price to changes in maturity (theta);

3) The sensitivity of the option price to changes in standard deviation (vega); and
4) The sensitivity of the option price to changes in the risk-free interest rate (rho).

Section 10

(a) Warrants entailing rights to the purchase or other acquisition of financial instruments which can be assigned to an on-going or future new bond issue shall be treated in the same way as the financial instruments in the issue.This type of position may be netted against corresponding positions in the opposite direction.

(b) Warrants entailing rights to the purchase or other acquisition of previously issued financial instruments, shall be treated in the same way as options.Warrants entailing rights other than those contained in the first and second paragraphs shall be treated in the same way as options.

Section 11

Unless otherwise specified, calculating capital requirements for specific and general risk shall be based on the notional amount of the credit derivative.

Section 12

Credit derivatives are of the same type if they are denominated in the same currency and have the same maturity at the same time as the reference assets are issued by the same legal entity, afford equal rights if the issuer enters into liquidation and have the same coupon and maturity. In addition, for credit derivatives that are designed so that the risk seller receives payment only in the case of a credit event, the selection of credit event and contractual calculation models for establishing payment shall be identical.

Section 13

If the risk seller has the right to terminate the credit derivative prematurely and this right is associated with an increase (step-up) in the cost of the derivative, the date of this right shall form the basis of determining the maturity of the credit derivative.

Section 14

Calculation of capital requirements for general and specific risk may be carried out on the Authorized Person's net positions in credit derivatives. Net position refers to the difference between a long and a short position in credit derivatives of the same kind.

Section 15

When calculating capital requirements for general risk the positions in credit derivatives may not be netted against positions in underlying assets.

Section 16

The position on which the capital requirement for specific risk shall be based shall be determined in accordance with Section 17 to Section 22 of this Annex. When calculating the capital requirement for specific risk, positions in credit derivatives may be netted against other positions in credit derivatives or positions in other assets in accordance with Section 17 of this Annex. A reduced capital requirement for specific risk may also be granted in accordance with Section 18 to Section 22 of this Annex when the Authorized Person has credit derivatives that protect other credit derivatives or underlying assets.

Section 17

An Authorized Person which holds a position in a total return swap may net a long/ short position in the reference asset against a short/long position in a protected asset on condition that the reference asset and the protected asset are identical in all respects. However, the maturity of the swap does not need to coincide with the maturity of the protected asset.

Section 18

(a) An Authorized Person may treat positions in credit derivatives and positions in underlying assets in accordance with that set out in paragraph (b) of this Section if the following conditions are met:

1) The market value of both positions shall always move in opposite directions;
2) The conditions associated with the credit derivative shall not be designed so that there can be reason to believe that the market value of the credit derivative has changed to a different extent than that of the market value of the underlying asset;
3) The reference asset and the underlying asset shall be identical;
4) The maturity of the credit derivative shall coincide with the maturity of the underlying asset; and
5) The credit derivative and the underlying asset shall be denominated in the same currency.

(b) If the conditions in paragraph (a) of this Section have been met, the Authorized Person only needs to calculate capital requirements for the position which gives rise to the highest capital requirement for specific risk. The size of the position is determined by multiplying the market value by 20%. Capital requirements for specific risk for the other position do not need to be calculated.

Section 19

(a) An Authorized Person may treat total return swaps and positions in underlying assets in accordance with that set out in the paragraph (b) of this Section if the following conditions are met:

1) The underlying asset and reference asset shall be issued by the same company;
2) The reference asset shall be ranked equal or junior to the protected asset in the event of bankruptcy; and
3) There are cross clauses in place between the reference asset and the protected asset which mean that if the borrower defaults (e.g. suspends payments) on other loans, this will also be treated as a default on the reference asset.

(b) If the conditions mentioned in paragraph (a) of this Section have been met, the Authorized Person need only calculate capital requirements for specific risk for either the credit derivative or the underlying asset. In this case the Authorized Person shall only calculate capital requirements for the position which gives rise to the highest capital requirement for specific risk.

Section 20

An Authorized Person may calculate the capital requirement for specific risk in accordance with Section 19 of this Annex, if the positions fulfill the requirements set out in points 1 until 3 of paragraph (a) in Section 18 of this Annex.

Section 21

The capital requirement for specific risk for short and long positions in credit derivatives which fulfill the requirements for being of the same type as set out in Section 12 of this Annex, apart from the requirement of having the same maturity and being denominated in the same currency, may be calculated in accordance with paragraph (b) of Section 19 of this Annex.

Section 22

An Authorized Person may calculate the capital requirement for the specific risk in accordance with Section 19 of this Annex, if the positions fulfill the requirements set out in Section 18 of this Annex, apart from the requirement that the reference asset and the underlying asset be identical. However, the underlying asset shall be deliverable in accordance with the conditions of the credit derivative.

Section 23

(a) A position in a credit default swap shall, when calculating specific risk, be treated as a synthetic position in the reference asset. However, the reference asset shall be considered to have a maturity corresponding to the maturity of the credit derivative. It shall be assumed that the risk seller holds a short position in the reference asset and the risk purchaser a long position. If the credit event payment is defined as a fixed amount, the size of the position corresponds to the amount received should a credit event occur. If the payment is defined as a notional amount reduced by the recover y value, or alternatively the payment of a notional amount in exchange for a physical deliver y of the reference asset, the size of the position corresponds to the notional amount of the reference asset.

(b) If the risk seller, through a credit default swap, has an obligation to pay interest or a periodic premium to the risk purchaser, both parties in the contract shall take this payment into account when calculating the capital requirements for general risk. It shall be assumed that the risk seller holds a short position in a bond issued by a government and the risk purchaser a long position.

Section 24

(a) A position in a credit-linked note shall be treated as a combination of a bond and a credit default swap.The risk seller shall treat a position in a credit-linked note as:

1) A short position corresponding to a notional amount in the bond issued by the risk seller that gives rise to the capital requirement for general risk based on the bond's coupon or interest; and
2) A short position in the reference asset for which capital requirement for specific risk shall be calculated (the reference asset shall however be considered to have a maturity equal to that of the credit derivative).

(b) The risk purchaser shall treat a position in a credit-linked note as:

1) A long position corresponding to a notional amount in the bond issued by the risk seller which gives rise to the capital requirement for specific risk based on the issuer of the bond and general risk based on the bond's coupon or interest; and
2) A long position in the reference asset for which capital requirement for specific risk shall be calculated (the reference asset shall however be considered to have a maturity equal to that of the credit derivative).

(c) The provisions of this Section do not need to be applied to a credit linked note which has a credit rating from a credit rating agency and which meets the requirements for risk weight assignment in accordance with Section 33 to Section 37 of this Annex.

Section 25

(a) The risk seller shall treat a position in a total return swap as a short position corresponding to a notional amount in the reference asset for which the capital requirement for specific and general risk shall be calculated.The risk purchaser shall treat a position in a total return swap as a long position corresponding to a notional amount in the reference asset for which capital requirement for specific and general risk is to be calculated.

(b) Where the derivative contract includes interest or premium payments, the derivative contract shall be considered a short or alternatively long position in a bond issued by a government which has a risk weight of 0% in non-trading activities.The bond's maturity shall be the period until the next interest or premium payment.The position shall be included in the calculation of the capital requirement for general risk.

Section 26

Credit derivatives tied to a basket of assets shall be treated in accordance with Section 23 to Section 25 of this Annex unless otherwise stated in Section 27 to Section 29 of this Annex.

Section 27

A credit derivative which refers to more than one asset and where the design of the derivative is such that it becomes due for payment when the first default occurs among the assets in the basket shall, when calculating the specific risk, be treated as if the Authorized Person held positions in all of the reference assets. Each position shall be considered to have a notional amount which corresponds to the notional amounts of the credit derivative. However, a cap for the capital requirement for specific risk in the reference assets is set that equals to the maximum amount which can be paid out during the contract.

Section 28

When calculating specific risk, a credit derivative which refers to more than one asset and is designed such that it becomes due for payment when the second default occurs among the assets in the basket shall be treated as if the Authorized Person held positions in all of the assets in the basket except for the asset which gives rise to the lowest capital requirement for specific risk. Each position shall be considered to have a notional amount which corresponds to the notional amounts of the credit derivative. However, a cap for the capital requirement for specific risk in the reference assets is set that equals the maximum amount which can be paid out during the contract.

Section 29

With regard to a credit linked note which refers to more than one asset and where the yield of these assets is transferred in accordance with their proportion in the basket (green bottle structure), the Authorized Person shall be considered to be exposed to all the assets in the basket.The proportion of each asset in the basket determines the size of the exposures. If several debt instruments for a particular reference asset are deliverable, the Authorized Person shall base the calculation of the specific risk on the debt instrument which gives rise to the highest capital requirement.

Section 30

An Authorized Person shall calculate capital requirements for specific and general interest rate risk separately for each individual currency in which the Authorized Person has positions. Positions in foreign currency shall be converted before the capital requirement is calculated.

Section 31

An Authorized Person's holdings in their own debt instruments shall be disregarded when calculating capital requirement for the specific risk.

Section 32

The capital requirement for the specific risk is calculated in two steps. First, the net position in each financial instrument is multiplied by the weights set out in Section 33 to Section 39 of this Annex. Second, the absolute values of the weighted positions calculated in this way are then totalled to determine the total capital requirement for specific risk. If the Authorized Person judges that a financial instrument has a higher risk than that indicated in Section 33 to Section 38 of this Annex, the Authorized Person shall assign the financial instrument a weight of 21%. For securitization positions and re-securitization positions, the net position in each financial instrument is first multiplied by the weights set out in Table 2 in Section 40 of this Annex.The absolute values of the weighted positions calculated in this way are then totalled to determine the total capital requirement for specific risk.

Section 33

Net positions in the following financial instruments shall have a weight of 0% if they qualify for credit quality step 1:

1) Financial instruments issued or guaranteed by governments; and
2) Financial instruments issued by central banks.

Section 34

(a) Net positions in the following financial instruments shall have a weight that varies depending on the remaining maturity of the instrument in accordance with Table 1 below:

Table 1

months 6 ≥	months 24 ≥ 6 <	months 24 <
0.5%	1.8%	2.8%

(b) The remaining maturity of the instrument refers to the time until the instrument matures. The following financial instruments shall have a weight in accordance to Table 1 above:

1) Financial instruments issued or guaranteed by governments that would qualify for credit quality steps 2 or 3;
2) Financial instruments issued by central banks that would qualify for credit quality steps 2 or 3;
3) Financial instruments issued or guaranteed by Authorized Persons, banks or foreign equivalents that would qualify for credit quality steps 1 or 2; and
4) Financial instruments issued or guaranteed by companies that would qualify for credit quality steps 1 or 2.

Section 35

Financial instruments which do not have a credit rating from a credit rating agency may be assigned a weight in accordance with Section 34 of this Annex if the following conditions are met:

1) The Authorized Person considers the financial instrument to have high liquidity;
2) The Authorized Person considers the financial instrument to have a creditworthiness corresponding to the creditworthiness of the financial instruments set out in Section 34 of this Annex; and
3) The financial instrument shall be traded on the Exchange, on obtaining the approval of the Authority, on a regulated market outside the Kingdom.

Section 36

Financial instruments issued by a foreign financial institution maybe assigned a weight in accordance with Section 34 of this Annex if the following conditions are met:

1) The foreign financial institution must be subject to capital adequacy rules similar to the rules applied in the Kingdom;
2) The Authorized Person has determined that the financial instrument has high liquidity; and
3) The Authorized Person considers the financial instrument to have a creditworthiness corresponding to the creditworthiness of the financial instruments set out in Section 34 of this Annex.

Section 37

Financial instruments issued by companies conducting activities similar to that of Authorized Persons may be assigned a weight in accordance with Section 34 of this Annex if the following conditions have been met:

1) The Authorized Person considers the financial instrument to have a creditworthiness corresponding to credit quality step 2; and
2) The company must be subject to regulations equivalent to the rules applied in the Kingdom.

Section 38

Net positions in the following financial instruments shall have a weight of 14%:

1) Financial instruments issued or guaranteed by governments that would qualify for credit quality steps 4 or 5;
2) Financial instruments issued by central banks that would qualify for credit quality steps 4 or 5;
3) Financial instruments issued or guaranteed by Authorized Persons, banks or foreign equivalents that would qualify for credit quality steps 35-; and
4) Financial instruments issued or guaranteed by companies that would qualify for credit quality steps 3 or 4.

Section 39

Net positions in the following financial instruments shall have a weight of 21%:

1) Financial instruments issued or guaranteed by governments that would qualify for credit quality step 6;
2) Financial instruments issued by central banks that would qualify for credit quality step 6;
3) Financial instruments issued by Authorized Persons, banks or foreign equivalents that would qualify for credit quality step 6;
4) Financial instruments issued or guaranteed by companies that would qualify for credit quality steps 5 or 6; and
5) Financial instruments which have no credit rating from a credit rating agency.

Section 40

Net positions in securitization and re-securitization shall have a weight in accordance to Table 2 below.

Table 2

Credit quality step	1	2	3	4	5	6
Securitisation	2.8%	7%	14%	49%	100%	100%
Re-securitisation	5.6%	14%	32%	91%	100%	100%

Section 41

(a) The method, either maturity-based or duration-based, selected by the Authorized Person to calculate the capital requirement for general interest rate risk shall be applied consistently for all interest rate linked financial instruments. The calculation methods may not be replaced without the approval of the Authority.

(b) If the maturity-based or duration-based method selected by an Authorized Person for calculating the capital requirement proves difficult to apply for certain types of interest rate linked financial instruments, the Authorized Person may, after obtaining the approval of the Authority, use the other method for this type of financial instrument, on condition that this model is applied consistently. Authorized Persons applying for such approval shall justify the application of the other method.

Section 42

(a) In addition to the conditions applying to netting under Section 1 of this Annex, when calculating general interest rate risk, Authorized Persons may net positions in derivatives in accordance with Section 3 to Section 7 of this Annex and against offsetting positions in derivatives in accordance with Section 9 and Section 10 of this Annex, if all conditions below are met:

1) The positions are denominated in the same currency;
2) The reference interest rates (for floating rate positions) or coupons (for fixed rate positions) do not deviate by more than 0.15 percentage points (fifteen basis points); and
3) The remaining maturity or time until the next interest rate adjustment date corresponds to the following:
   i. if there is less than one month until maturity/interest rate adjustment, the same day;
   ii. if there is between one month and one year until the maturity/interest rate adjustment, the difference may not exceed seven days; and
   iii. if there is more than one year until the maturity/interest rate adjustment, the difference may not exceed 30 days.

(b) The net positions obtained shall be included when calculating the capital requirement for the general interest rate risk in accordance with Section 45 or Section 46 of this Annex.

Section 43

Authorized Persons which mark-to-market and calculate the interest rate risk of derivatives in accordance with Section 3 to Section 7 of this Annex and Section 9 and Section 10 of this Annex on the basis of the present value of future cash flows may, on obtaining the Authority's approval, use a sensitivity model to calculate the positions. Positions obtained in this way shall be included when calculating the capital requirement for general interest rate risk according to the maturity-based method or duration-based method in accordance with Section 45 or Section 46 of this Annex.

Section 44

(a) A sensitivity model shall be used to calculate the present value of all future cash flows that the different instruments give rise to using selected zero-coupon rates. The present value of each cash flow shall then be distributed among the maturity bands set out in Section 45 of this Annex. Within each maturity band, short and long positions may be netted so that there is only one position, long or short, per maturity band. These positions shall then be multiplied by the weight for that maturity band.

(b) Alternatively to what has been mentioned in paragraph (a) of this Section, the interest rate risk, that is the sensitivity of the present values of the cash flows to changes in the zero-coupon interest rates, may be calculated directly.The interest rate risk shall be assessed taking into account independent movements in interest rates along the yield curve/zero coupon cur ve with at least one sensitivity point for each of the maturity bands set out in Section 45 of this Annex and the assumptions about the size of interest rate changes made according to the maturity based method or the duration-based method.The interest rate risks shall then be distributed among the maturity bands set out in Section 45 of this Annex or the zones set out in Section 46 of this Annex.

(c) The model shall be well documented, be used continuously and the Authorized Person shall be able to justify the use of the proposed model to the Authority. An Authorized Person's application for approval to apply a sensitivity model shall contain information about the model's algorithms, underlying assumptions, a justification and explanation of the selection of the zero coupon method and a description of the information technology system and control procedures.

Section 45

When the maturity based approach is used to calculate the capital requirement for the general interest rate risk, the subsequent eight steps shall be followed:

Step 1: The Authorized Person shall assign net positions, both long and short, in each individual interest rate linked financial instrument to one of the maturity bands in Table 3 below. The factors that determine which maturity band is applied to each financial instrument are the remaining maturity and whether the interest rate according to the coupon is 3% or more.With regard to instruments with variable interest rates, remaining maturity refers to the time remaining until the next interest rate adjustment date.

Table 3

	Maturity band	Remaining maturity		(%) Weight
		Coupon with 3% interest or more	Coupon with less than 3% interest	
One	1	0 ≤ 1 month	0 ≤ 1 month	0.00
	2	> 1 ≤ 3 months	> 1 ≤ 3 months	0.20
	3	> 3 ≤ 6 months	> 3 ≤ 6 months	0.40
	4	> 6 ≤ 12 months	> 6 ≤ 12 months	0.70
Two	5	> 1 ≤ 2 years	> 1.0 ≤ 1.9 years	1.25
	6	> 2 ≤ 3 years	> 1.9 ≤ 2.8 years	1.75
	7	> 3 ≤ 4 years	> 2.8 ≤ 3.6 years	2.25
Three	8		> 3.6 ≤ 4.3 years	2.75
	9	> 4 ≤ 5 years	> 4.3 ≤ 5.7 years	3.25
	10	> 5 ≤ 7 years	> 5.7 ≤ 7.3 years	3.75
	11	> 7 ≤ 10 years	> 7.3 ≤ 9.3 years	4.50
	12	> 10 ≤ 15 years	> 9.3 ≤ 10.6 years	5.25
	13	> 15 ≤ 20 years	> 10.6 ≤ 12 years	6.00
	14	> 20 years	> 12 ≤20 years	8.00
	15		> 20 years	12.50

Step 2: The Authorized Person's net position in each individual financial instrument shall be multiplied by the weight that applies to the net position's maturity band. Long and short net positions shall be weighted separately.

Step 3: The weighted long and short net positions are then aggregated individually within each maturity band. The portion of the sum of the weighted long net positions corresponding to the sum of the weighted short net positions, or vice versa, within each maturity band, is the matched position within the maturity band.The resulted matched position is sum 1 and is weighted by 17.5%. The difference between both sums is the unmatched position within the same maturity band.

Step 4: All weighted long and short unmatched net positions are aggregated separately within each zone. The sum of weighted long and the sum of the weighted short unmatched positions are then matched within each zone. The matched positions resulting from this matching are sum 2 for zone 1, sum 3 for zone 2 and sum 4 for zone

3. Sum 2 is weighted by 70%, sum 3 by 52.5% and sum 4 by 52.5%.

Step 5:The remaining unmatched positions, long or short, within each zone after matching in accordance with step 4 shall then be matched between the zones as follows.

First the long (short) unmatched position in zone 1 is matched with the short (long) unmatched position in zone 2. The resulting matched position is sum 5. The remaining long (short) unmatched position in zone 2 is then matched with the short (long) unmatched position in zone 3. The resulting matched position is sum 6. Both sums are weighted by 70%. In the matching process described in the previous paragraph, an Authorized Person may instead first match zones 2 and 3 and then zones 1 and 2.

Step 6: The remaining long (short) unmatched position in zone 1 is then matched with the remaining short (long) unmatched position in zone 3. The resulting matched position is sum 7.This sum is weighted by 250%.

Step 7: All unmatched positions remaining after the maturity bands and zones are matched are aggregated. The aggregated unmatched positions is sum 8. This sum is weighted by 175%.

Step 8: The weighted sums obtained in steps 3–7 above are aggregated and provide the capital requirement for general interest rate risk for interest rate linked financial instruments. Matching of positions and calculation of the capital requirement shall be carried out separately for each individual currency.

Section 46

When the duration-based method is used to calculate the capital requirement for general interest rate risk, the subsequent eight steps shall be followed:

Step 1: With regard to each individual interest rate linked financial instrument with a fixed interest rate, the yield to maturity of the instrument is calculated based on the market value. The yield is calculated in the same way for each individual interest rate linked financial instrument with a variable interest rate but with the assumption that the principal of the instrument falls due on the next interest rate adjustment date.

Step 2: With regard to each interest rate linked financial instrument, the modified duration is calculated on the basis of the yield calculated in step 1.The modified duration shall be calculated using the following formula.

$$\text{Modified duration} = \frac{\text{Duration}}{(1+r)}$$

$$\text{Duration} = \frac{\sum_{t-1}^{m} \frac{tc_t}{(1+r)^t}}{\sum_{t-1}^{m} \frac{c_t}{(1+r)^t}}$$

Where:

r = return to maturity as a percentage

Ct = payment at time t

t = time to payment (years)

m = time to maturity (years)

Step 3: Each individual net position is assigned to the zone which, according to Table 4 below, can be applied to each financial instrument. The division into zones is based on the modified duration of the individual financial instrument.

Table 4

Zone	Modified Duration (years)	Assumed change in interest (percentage points)
One	1.0 ≥ 0 <	1.00
Two	3.6 ≥ 1.0 <	0.85
Three	3.6 <	0.70

Step 4: The Authorized Person shall calculate the duration-weighted net position of each individual financial instrument by multiplying the instrument's market value by the modified duration and the assumed change in interest rate.The duration-weighted long net positions and duration-weighted short net positions are then aggregated separately within each zone.

The portion of the sum of the weighted long net positions corresponding to the sum of the weighted short net positions, or vice versa, within each zone, comprises the matched position within the zone. The difference between the weighted sums comprises the unmatched position within the zone.

The matched position comprises sum 1 for zone 1, sum 2 for zone 2 and sum 3 for zone 3. All sums are weighted by 3.5%.

Step 5: The remaining unmatched duration-weighted positions within each zone after matching in accordance with step 4 shall then be matched between the zones as follows.

First the long (short) unmatched duration-weighted position in zone 1 is matched with the short (long) unmatched duration-weighted position in zone 2. The resulting matched position is sum 4. The remaining long (short) unmatched position in zone 2 is then matched with the short (long) unmatched position in zone 3.The resulting matched position is sum 5. Both sums are weighted by 70%. In the matching process described in the previous paragraph, an Authorized Person may instead first match zones 2 and 3 and then zones 1 and 2.

Step 6: The remaining duration-weighted long (short) unmatched position in zone 1 is then matched with the remaining duration-weighted short (long) unmatched position in zone 3.The resulting matched position is sum 6.This sum is weighted by 250%.

Step 7: All remaining unmatched positions after the matching process within and between the zones are aggregated and become sum 7.This sum is weighted by 175%.

Step 8:The weighted sums obtained in steps 4–7 are aggregated and provide the capital requirement for general interest rate risk for interest rate linked financial instruments.

Matching of positions and calculation of capital requirements shall be carried out separately for each individual currency.

27.11.2 Chapter 2: Equity Price Risks

Section 47

(a) Equity price risks shall be calculated for positions in equity and equity linked financial instruments included in an Authorized Person's trading book. Capital requirements for equity price risks shall be calculated based on both the Authorized Person's gross and net position as they are defined in Section 55 and Section 56 of this Annex.

(b) Netting of the Authorized Person's long and short positions in equity and equity linked financial instruments may be carried out if they are issued by the same legal entity. Long and short positions in equity and equity linked financial instruments which belong to different classes may be netted against each other only if they have equal order of priority, dividend rights or rights in a future issue, and the difference between the equities' voting rights of a share of any class may not exceed ten times that of a share of another class.

(c) With regard to netting financial instruments and any underlying instruments, e.g. depository receipt, the underlying instruments shall be issued in the same currency.

(d) Positions in derivatives shall first be treated as positions in underlying financial instruments in accordance with Section 48 of this Annex.

Section 48

(a) Forwards and options shall be treated as combined long and short positions.

(b) A long (purchased) position in a forward or an option shall be treated as a combination of:

1) A long position comprised of underlying financial instruments in the contract; and
2) A short position corresponding to a zero coupon bond, for which the forward price for forwards or the exercise price of options consists of the amount due of the bond, and has a maturity date on the deliver y date or exercise date for the contract.

(c) A short (sold) position in a forward or an option shall be treated as a combination of:

1) A short position comprised of underlying financial instruments in the contract; and
2) A long position corresponding to a zero coupon bond, for which the forward price for forwards or the exercise price of options consists of the amount due of the bond, and has a maturity date on the delivery date or exercise date for the contract. Long and short positions deriving from an option shall be delta- weighted in accordance with Section 51 of this Annex.

(d) A zero coupon bond deriving from the partition of derivatives into a long and a short position shall be considered to be issued by a government which qualifies for credit quality step 1, alternatively to have a risk weight of 0%, in non-trading activities. When calculating specific and general risk, the zero coupon bond shall be considered to be an interest rate linked financial instrument and be treated in accordance with Section 1 to Section 46 of this Annex. The positions which arise from the partitioning into long and short positions shall be included in the calculation of specific and general risk unless otherwise set out in Section 49 to Section 56 of this Annex.

Section 49

(a) Calculating capital requirements for specific risk for zero coupon bonds deriving from equity forwards may be carried out in accordance with Section 33. An underlying financial instrument shall be included when calculating the Authorized Person's gross position for specific risk, irrespective of whether the position is long or short.

(b) When calculating capital requirements for general risk, the zero coupon bond shall, irrespective of whether the position is long or short, be included when calculating matched and unmatched positions in interest rate linked financial instruments in accordance with Section 45 to Section 46 of this Annex. An underlying financial instrument shall be included when calculating the Authorized Person's net position for general risk, irrespective of whether the position is long or short.

Section 50

(a) Equity index forwards (including delta-weighted equivalents to options on equity index forwards and equity indices) shall be treated as combined long and short positions in the same way that applies to other derivatives. A long or short position in such an index may be divided among the shares included in the index. These may be netted against opposite positions in the same share to the extent that the share is included in the index. Equity index forwards not divided among the shares included in the index shall be treated as individual shares.

(b) Calculating capital requirement for specific risk in zero coupon bonds may be carried out in accordance with Section 33 of this Annex.

(c) Forwards or options traded on regulated markets and based on a broadly diversified index or its equivalent may be assigned a capital requirement of 0% for specific risk.

(d) When calculating capital requirements for general risk, the zero coupon bond shall, irrespective of whether the position is long or short, be included when calculating matched and unmatched positions in interest rate linked financial instruments in accordance with Section 45 and Section 46 of this Annex.

Section 51

(a) Options based on equity or equity indices shall be treated as combined long and short positions in the same way as other derivatives. Both positions shall be converted into delta-weighted positions by multiplying the underlying instrument's market value by the option's delta value.The delta-weighted positions may be netted against any offsetting positions in the same type of underlying financial instrument. If the exchange that lists the options does not publish the delta values of the options, or if they are over the counter options, the Authorized Person shall calculate the delta values of its options.

(b) When calculating the capital requirement for specific risk for bought and sold options, the underlying debt instruments shall be included in the calculation of the Authorized Person's gross position. Calculating the capital requirement for specific risk in zero coupon bonds may be carried out in accordance with Section 33 of this Annex.

(c) When calculating the capital requirement for general risk for bought and sold options, the underlying debt instruments shall be included in the calculation of the Authorized Person's net position. The zero coupon bond shall be included when calculating matched and unmatched positions in interest rate linked financial instruments, in accordance with Section 45 or Section 46 of this Annex, irrespective of whether the position is long or short.

(d) A bought option does not need to be converted to a delta-weighted position and included in the calculation of specific risk as set out in Section 55 of this Annex or general risk as set out in Section 56 of this Annex. The capital requirement for such an option may instead be set equal to the market value of the option. Netting against an offset position in the underlying instrument cannot be carried out in this case.

(e) An Authorized Person shall have systems in place and apply protective measures such that sufficient account is taken of other risks associated with options trading, such as:

1) The sensitivity of the delta value to price changes in the underlying financial instrument (gamma);
2) The sensitivity of the option price to changes in maturity (theta);
3) The sensitivity of the option price to changes in standard deviation (vega); and
4) The sensitivity of the option price to changes in the risk-free interest rate (rho).

Section 52

(a) Warrants entailing rights to the purchase or other acquisition of financial instruments, which can be assigned to an on-going or future new share issue, shall be treated in the same way as the financial instruments in the issue. Such a position may be netted against corresponding positions in the opposite direction.

(b) Warrants entailing rights to the purchase or other acquisition of previously issued financial instruments shall be treated in the same way as options.Warrants entailing rights other than those contained in the first and second paragraphs shall be treated in the same way as options.

Section 53

(a) A convertible debt instrument shall be treated as if the conversion to the underlying instrument has taken place if the intent is that such a conversion shall take place, or if the current market conditions are such that the conversion may be expected to take place. Such a position shall be delta-weighted and may be netted against a short position in an equivalent underlying financial instrument. A convertible debt instrument that is not treated as if the conversion to the underlying instrument has taken place shall be treated as a debt instrument. Such a position may be netted against a short position in an equivalent underlying financial instrument.The capital requirement for such a position shall be calculated according to the rules for calculating capital requirements for interest rate linked financial instruments, pursuant to Chapter 1.

(b) Alternatively to what has been mentioned in paragraph (a) of this Section, a convertible debt instrument may be treated as a combination of the above alternatives. The portion corresponding to the underlying instrument is comprised of a subscription right or a subscription option and shall be treated in the same way as options. The portion corresponding to the debt instrument is comprised of the discounted present value of the portion of the debt instrument in the convertible debt. Such a position may be netted against a short position in an equivalent underlying financial instrument.The capital requirement for such a position shall be calculated according to the rules for calculating a capital requirement for equity linked financial instruments and interest rate linked financial instruments, as prescribed in this Chapter.

Section 54

An Authorized Person shall calculate capital requirements for specific and general equity risk separately for each individual currency in which the Authorized Person has positions. Positions in foreign currency shall be converted before the capital requirement is calculated. With regard to depositor y receipt, the underlying instruments shall be assigned to the currency in which the instrument was issued.

Section 55

(a) The capital requirement for specific risk shall be set at 4% of the Authorized Person's gross position.

(b) In exceptional cases the capital requirement for specific risk may be reduced to 2% of the Authorized Person's gross position for share portfolios that fulfill the following conditions:

1) Based on an objective evaluation the shares shall be considered to have a high liquidity;
2) Shares issued by the same issuer may not exceed 5% of the value of the share portfolio, or 10% if the total sum of such individual positions does not exceed 50% of the share portfolio; and
3) The shares may not be issued by an issuer whose interest rate linked financial instruments receive a capital requirement of 14% or 21% in accordance with Section 38 and Section 39 of this Annex.

(c) Gross position refers to the sum of all of the Authorized Person's net positions in financial instruments irrespective of whetherthey are long or short.

Section 56

(a) The capital requirement for general risk shall be set to 14% of the Authorized Person's net position.

(b) Net position refers to the difference between the sum of the Authorized Person's long net positions in financial instruments and the sum of the Authorized Person's short net positions in financial instruments.

27.11.3 Chapter 3: Risks Related to Investment Funds

Section 57

The capital requirement for general and specific risk for positions in investment funds shall, unless otherwise stated, be calculated by the market value of the position multiplied by 16%.

Section 58

Positions in investment funds may be treated in accordance with Section 59 to Section 61 of this Annex if they either satisfy the requirement of the Investment Funds Regulations, or meet the following criteria:

1) The investment fund is managed by a company subject to super vision by a competent supervisory authority;

2) The investment fund's terms and conditions and\or information brochure or equivalent documentation includes:

(a) the categories of assets in which the investment fund is authorized to invest;
(b) how any investment limits on the investment fund shall be calculated;
(c) the investment fund's rules for limiting counterparty risk in repurchase transactions and over the counter derivatives if the investment fund has the right to make such transactions; and
(d) how comprehensive the leverage may be if the investment fund has the right to use leverage in investments;

3) Information about the investment fund's activities and assets, liabilities and revenue shall be reported at least every six months;

4) It shall be possible for investment fund units to be redeemed in cash on a daily basis at the request of the unitholder ;

5) The positions in the investment fund shall be separate from the investment fund manager's positions; and

6) The Authorized Person shall have evaluated the risks of investing in the investment fund.

Section 59

Where an Authorized Person is aware of all positions included in the investment fund, they may be treated as if they were held directly by the Authorized Person.The netting of such positions against other positions held by the Authorized Person may be carried out. A condition for this is that the Authorized Person has a sufficient amount of investment fund units for these to be converted into holdings in the financial instruments which are part of the investment fund.

Section 60

If an investment fund replicates an index, an Authorized Person may treat the holding in the investment fund as if it had positions in the securities included in the index or basket. However, the following conditions shall be met:

1) The investment fund shall aim to replicate an index or basket of securities; and

2) The correlation coefficient between the daily price of the investment fund units and the daily price of the index or basket shall be at least 0.9.The correlation coefficient shall be calculated on the basis of a minimum of six months.

Section 61

(a) If an Authorized Person is not aware on a day-to-day basis of the positions included in the investment fund, the Authorized Person may treat holdings in the investment fund as follows:

1) The Authorized Person shall assume that the investment fund is investing to the maximum extent allowed under the relevant law, rules, or the investment fund's terms and conditions in the asset classes attracting the highest capital requirement for specific and general risk. The Authorized Person shall then assume that the investment fund is investing to the maximum extent allowed in the asset classes attracting successively lower capital requirement for specific and general risk. When calculating specific and general risk, the Authorized Person shall be considered to hold positions in all of these asset classes; and

2) The Authorized Person shall take account of the maximum indirect exposure that it could achieve by taking leveraged positions through the investment fund when calculating its position risk, by proportionally increasing the position in the investment fund up to the maximum exposure to the underlying investment items resulting from the investment mandate.

(b) Where an Authorized Person applies the method mentioned in paragraph (a) of this Section, the capital requirement for the position in the investment fund shall not be more than the capital requirement calculated pursuant to Section 57 of this Annex.

27.11.4 Chapter 4: Underwriting

Section 62

(a) An Authorized Person that underwrites a new or previously issued equity and/or interest bearing financial instruments or that gives a commitment to a person to sub-underwrite an issue or offer for sale of financial instruments shall calculate the capital requirement following the same principles which would apply if the financial instruments were part of the Authorized Person's trading book pursuant to Chapter 4 and Chapter 5 of Part 3 and Annex 2.

(b) If an Authorized Person only guarantees that a subscriber will pay cash for an issue or offer for subscribed financial instruments on the settlement date, that is payment guarantee, the guarantee is not covered by the provisions regarding the capital requirements for risks in the trading book.The capital requirement for such a guarantee shall instead be calculated in accordance with the capital requirements for non-trading activities pursuant to Chapter 6 and Chapter 7 of Part 3 and Annex 3.

Section 63

(a) An alternative method that an Authorized Person may use on obtaining the approval of the Authority allows the Authorized Person to deduct the portions of the issue or offer underwritten by a third party pursuant to a formal agreement from the portion of the issue or offer underwritten by the Authorized Person. In order for an issue or offerto be considered underwritten by a third party, the written contract shall contain the third party's unconditional liability for the issue or offer.

(b) When the Authorized Person's positions have been determined, the Authorized Person shall calculate the capital requirement for the underwritten and reduced positions in accordance with the rules which apply to calculating a capital requirement for the holding of such financial instruments.

(c) An Authorized Person that intends to underwrite any issue or offer of securities shall notify the Authority of its intention to underwrite prior to entering into an underwriting commitment. The Authorized Person shall describe how the underwriting will affect its capital adequacy. If the underwriting will result in an excess exposure for the Authorized Person or the Authorized Person's exposure to a single counterparty or group of connected counterparties to exceed the amount stipulated in Article 53 of these Rules, the Authorized Person shall apply for an approval from the Authority to underwrite such amount.The Authority may give its approval if the Authorized Person's capital adequacy ratio is deemed satisfactory in the long term.

27.11.5 Chapter 5: Excess Exposure

Section 64

(a) With regard to excess exposures pursuant to Article 56 of these Rules, special additional capital requirement applies to the capital requirements normally calculated for the Authorized Person's portfolio. When calculating the additional capital requirement, the excess exposure shall be comprised of the individual exposures in the trading book that have the highest capital requirement for specific risk and/or counterparty and settlement risk.

(b) The additional capital requirement is 200% of the sum of the capital requirements that apply to the individual exposures included in the excess exposure, if ten days or less have passed since an excess exposure has arisen.

(c) If an excess exposure has existed for longer than ten days, the exposures included in the excess exposure shall be entered into Table 5 below.The excess exposures shall be slotted into the respective bands starting with those trading book exposures which have the lowest capital requirements for specific risk under the market risk capital requirement or the lowest capital requirements under the counterparty risk capital component and taking those with the highest capital requirements last.

(d) The limits in the first column of Table 5 below refer to the proportion of capital of the aggregated exposure. Only the exposures included in the excess exposure are to be entered into the table.

Table 2

Excess Exposure	Factor
Up to 40%	200%
60% ≥ 40% <	300%
80% ≥ 60% <	400%
100% ≥ 80% <	500%
250% ≥ 100% <	600%
over 250%	900%

(e) The additional capital requirement for the excess exposure is the lowest of:

1) The sum of the capital requirements which, in accordance with this Chapter, apply to the individual exposures included in the excess exposure; and

2) The sum of the capital requirements which, if added to the existing capital requirements that apply to the individual exposure would amount to 100% of the exposure.

Chapter 6: Settlement Risks

Section 65

(a) The capital requirements for settlement risks shall be calculated for positions that are included in the trading book of an Authorized Person. Repos, reverse repos, securities borrowing and securities lending are exempted from this provision.

(b) When calculating the capital requirement for settlement risks, account must be taken of the risk of losses to the Authorized Person for a transaction that is not completed on the due settlement date. Either the purchaser or seller is assigned the capital requirement in an individual transaction.

Section 66

(a) With regard to transactions in interest, equity, currency and commodity-linked financial instruments as well as commodities which are not settled on the due settlement date, the Authorized Person shall calculate the loss, that is the negative difference in price which the Authorized Person risks suffering, without regard to potential positive differences in price. Netting of positive and negative differences in price in different transactions may not occur. The negative difference in price is made up of the difference between the agreed price of the financial instrument or commodity and the current market value on the calculation date.

(b) If a financial instrument or commodity is purchased, a negative price difference arises if the current market value of the instrument or commodity exceeds the agreed price. If a financial instrument or commodity is sold, a negative price difference arises if the agreed price exceeds the current market value of the instrument or commodity.

(c) The capital requirement is calculated by multiplying the absolute value of the negative price difference by the capital requirement factor in accordance with Table 6 below.

Table 3

Number of working days after due settlement date

(%) Capital requirement 3-0 0 5-4 100 or more 6 175

Chapter 7: Counterparty Risks

Section 67

(a) An Authorized Person shall calculate a risk-weighted exposure amount for counterparty risk in:

1) Transactions in which the counterparty has not fulfilled its deliver y/payment liability;

2) Over the counter derivatives and other derivatives giving rise to credit exposure;

3) Repos, reverse repos, securities lending or borrowing transactions; and

4) Margin lending transactions based on securities or commodities.

(b) Calculating a risk-weighted exposure amount shall be carried out in accordance with Chapter 6 and Chapter 7of Part 3 and Annex 3.

Section 68

An Authorized Person shall apply the provisions set out in Section 69 to Section 71 of this Annex if the Authorized Person has paid for securities, foreign currency or commodities before receiving them, or if the Authorized Person has delivered securities, foreign currency or commodities before receiving payment for them.

Section 69

An Authorized Person shall, as of the due settlement date and up to and including the fourth day after the settlement date, treat that component of the transaction which the counterparty has not fulfilled as an exposure, for which the Authorized Person shall calculate a risk-weighted amount. With regard to cross-border transactions an exposure shall not be considered to arise before the day after the due settlement date.

Section 70

If the exposures set out in Section 68 and Section 69 of this Annex are insignificant in relation to the total exposure of the Authorized Person, the Authorized Person may apply a risk weight of 100%. This may be done on condition that this method is applied for all such exposures.

Section 71

As of the fifth day after the due settlement date and until the transaction terminates, the Authorized Person shall deduct the value of what has been delivered to the counterparty from Tier-1 capital. If the transaction has a positive price difference, this value shall also be deducted from Tier-1 capital.

Section 72

(a) When calculating potential risk change, the credit derivative shall be assigned a risk factor of 10%. If the reference asset is an asset that may be assigned a risk weight for specific risk in accordance with Section 33 or Section 34 of this Annex, the risk factor may be 5%.

(b) If the credit derivative is a credit default swap, the Authorized Person may use a risk factor of 0% if the following requirements have been met:

1) Through the credit default swap the Authorized Person shall have a long position in the underlying asset, which is the Authorized Person has purchased risk; and

2) The credit default swap agreement may not contain provisions which entail that the derivative closes in the event of insolvency of the party with a short position in the underlying asset.

(c) When a credit derivative is designed so that it becomes due for payment when the nth default occurs in a basket of assets, the Authorized Person shall base the calculation on the asset in the basket that has the nth worst credit quality to determine the risk factor. If this asset is an asset that may be assigned a risk weight for specific risk in accordance with Section 33 or Section 34 of this Annex, the risk factor shall be 5%. Otherwise the risk factor shall be 10%.

Section 73

(a) Collateral that meets the conditions in Section 83 to Section 85 of Annex 3 are eligible collateral.

(b) Financial instruments and commodities assigned to the trading book are eligible as collateral if these are also included in repurchase transactions or in securities lending or borrowing transactions which are also assigned to the trading book.

(c) If the Authorized Person uses the prescribed volatility adjustments in accordance with Section 103 to Section 113 of Annex 3, eligible collateral shall be adjusted for volatility in accordance with the category "Other eligible collateral".

Section 74

Authorized Persons which, in accordance with Section 114 to Section 133 of Annex 3, take account of netting agreements when calculating a risk-weighted exposure amount, shall take the following into consideration with regard to repurchase transactions, securities lending or other capital market driven transactions.With regard to this type of transaction, netting between transactions that are on the trading book and non-trading activities, respectively, may only take place when the following conditions have been met:

1) All transactions shall be marked to market daily; and

2) All financial instruments or commodities borrowed, purchased or received as part of the transactions shall be recognizable collateral in accordance with the provisions in Section 83 to Section 85 of Annex 3.

27.12 ANNEX 3: Non-Trading Activities

27.12.1 Chapter 1: Exposure Classes and Risk Weights

Section 1

Where a credit rating is used to determine the risk weight of the exposure, the risk weight shall be assigned based on the exposure's credit quality step in accordance with the rules for using credit ratings as set out in Chapter 8 of Part 3.

Section 2

Exposures to governments or central banks for which a credit rating is available shall be assigned a risk-weight according to one of the credit quality steps set out in Table 7 below.

Table 4

Credit quality step	1	2	3	4	5	6
Risk weight	0%	20%	50%	100%	100%	150%

Section 3

Exposures to governments or central banks for which a credit rating is not available shall be assigned a risk-weight of 150%.

Section 4

An Authorized Person shall apply a risk-weight of 0% for exposures to SAMA regardless of what is stated in Section 2 and Section 3.

Section 5

Exposures to administrative bodies and non-profit organizations shall be assigned a risk- weight of 100%.

Section 6

(a) Where exposures to administrative bodies are treated by the Authority as exposures to governments and central banks, such exposures may be assigned the same risk weight as governments and central banks.

(b) Where the Authority treats exposures to administrative bodies as exposures to Authorized Persons, such exposures may, with the approval of the Authority, be assigned the same risk weight as exposures to Authorized Persons.

Section 7

(a) Exposures to Authorized Persons, banks and foreign equivalents in countries where credit ratings for the government are available shall be assigned a risk-weight according to one of the credit quality steps set out in Table 8 below.

(b) Cash deposited with local banks shall be assigned a risk weight according to the credit quality step 1 set out in Table 8 below. Otherwise, a risk-weight of 150% shall be used for exposures to Authorized Persons, banks and foreign equivalents.

Table 5

Credit quality step	1	2	3	4	5	6
Risk weight	20%	50%	100%	100%	100%	150%

Section 8

Exposures to Authorized Persons, banks and foreign equivalents in countries where credit ratings for the government are not available shall be assigned a risk-weight of 150%.

Section 9

Exposures to Authorized Persons, banks and foreign equivalents with an original maturity of three months or less and for which a credit rating for the specific exposure is available shall be assigned a risk-weight according to one of the credit quality steps set out in Table 9 below.

Table 6

Credit quality step	1	2	3	4	5	6
Risk weight	20%	20%	20%	50%	50%	150%

Exposures to corporates for which a credit rating is available shall be assigned a risk weight in accordance with Table 10 below. Otherwise, a risk-weight of 714% shall be used for exposures to corporates.

Table 7

Credit quality step	1	2	3	4	5	6
Risk weight	20%	50%	100%	200%	400%	714%

Section 12

(a) Past due item shall refer to an exposure where, interest or principal are more than 90 days past due, calculated from the original agreed payment date.

(b) The unsecured part of any item that is past due (net of provision) shall be assigned a risk weight of 714%.

Section 13

Exposures associated with particularly high risks such as venture capital investments shall be assigned a risk weight of 500%. Other private equity investments/unlisted shares and other participations shall be assigned a risk weight of 400%.

Section 14

Exposures to securitization positions and re-securitization positions for which a credit rating is available shall be assigned a risk-weight according to one of the credit quality steps set out in Table 11 below. Otherwise, a risk-weight of 714% shall be used.

Table 11

Credit quality step	1	2	3	4	5	6
Securitisation	20%	50%	100%	350%	714%	714%
Re-securitisation	40%	100%	225%	650%	714%	714%

Section 15

(a) Sections from 15 to 20 of this Annex contain provisions for investment funds other than the funds mentioned in Section 21 of this Annex.

(b) Exposures to investment funds for which a credit rating is available shall be assigned a risk-weight according to one of the credit quality steps set out in Table 12 below.

Table 12

Credit quality step	1	2	3	4	5	6
Risk weight	20%	50%	100%	100%	150%	150%

Exposures to investment funds for which a credit rating is not available shall be assigned a risk weight of 150%.

Section 17

Where the Authorized Person is aware of all of the underlying exposures of an investment fund, exposures to an investment fund may be assigned a risk weight as if the underlying exposures were owned directly by the Authorized Person.

Section 18

If the Authorized Person is not aware of the underlying exposures of an investment fund, the Authorized Person may calculate an average risk weight for the investment fund. This assumes that the investment fund first invests, to the maximum extent allowed under its mandate in the exposure classes attracting the highest risk weights, and then continues making investments in descending order in the remaining exposure classes.

Section 19

An Authorized Person may rely on a third party to calculate a risk weight for the investment fund in accordance with the methods set out in Section 17 and Section 18 of this Annex, provided the correctness of the calculation may be adequately ensured.

Section 20

To assign a risk weight for an investment fund in accordance with Section 17 to Section 19 of this Annex, the following criteria shall be met:

1) The investment fund is administered by an Authorized Person or a foreign equivalent subject to supervision of a competent authority;

2) The investment fund's information brochure or equivalent document includes:

(a) the categories of assets in which the investment fund is authorized to invest; and

(b) clarification of whether investment limits apply, that is the threshold values and the methods to calculate them; and

3) The business of the investment fund shall be reported on at least an annual basis to enable an assessment of the assets, liabilities, income and operations.

Section 21

Exposures to real estate funds, venture capital funds, private equity funds and other closed- ended funds shall be assigned a risk-weight of 300%.

Section 22

Real estate investments shall be assigned a risk-weight of 400%.

Section 23

Items referred to in Section 24 to Section 29 of this Annex shall be classified in the exposure class "Other items".

Section 24

Tangible assets shall be assigned a risk weight of 300%.

Section 25

Deferred expenditures and accrued income for which an Authorized Person is unable to determine the counterparty, or if it would be unreasonably burdensome for the Authorized Person to determine the counterparty, shall be assigned a risk weight of 300%.

Section 26

Holdings of listed equity shall be assigned a risk weight of 150%.

Section 27

Cash in hand and equivalent items shall be assigned a risk weight of 0%.

Section 28

Gold bullion held in own vaults or at an assigned location to the extent the Authorized Person has bullion liabilities shall be assigned a 0% risk weight.

Section 29

Exposures in any other form of items for which rules regarding risk-weighted amounts are not provided in Section 24 to Section 28 of this Annex shall be assigned a risk weight of 714%.

Chapter 2: Calculating Exposure Amounts for Off-Balance Sheet Items

Section 30

To determine the exposure values for off-balance sheet commitments, such items shall be multiplied by the appropriate conversion factors. The resulted exposure values shall be assigned relevant risk weights provided in Sections 2 to Section 29 of this Annex.

Section 31

A conversion factor of 100% applies to the following commitments:

1) Guarantees having the character of credit substitutes and other similar commitments, such as guarantees issued by Authorized Persons to a central clearing institution which entail that the Authorized Person shall upon request pay a maximum amount to the clearing institution pursuant to the guarantee as an issuer in the clearing system;

2) Repurchase transaction:

(a) In a repurchase agreement the transferring party shall calculate the capital requirement for counterparty risk with regard to the transferred asset; and

(b) An Authorized Person which is the seller at the spot phase of an optional repurchase agreement and which is obliged at a later date to repurchase a previously sold asset shall, for the agreed exercise price, be assigned the risk weight applying to the underlying asset in the transaction;

3) Securities lending and other similar commitments:

(a) The risk weight for lent assets is based on which party is the counterparty; and

(b) The risk weight for collateral for borrowed assets is based on which party is the counterparty;

4) Commitment to provide margin lending facilities; and

5) Commitments to make payments and other similar commitments:

(a) Commitments such as the unpaid portion of shares and other securities that sellers upon request may require to be settled and other full risk items; and

(b) Where an Authorized Person on the settlement date receives from the seller a deliver y commitment instead of the purchased security, the capital requirement is calculated from the deliver y commitment. The deliver y commitment shall be assigned a risk weight based on the issuer of the commitment.

Section 32

A conversion factor of 50% applies to the following commitments:

1) Other guarantees:

(a) Warranties and indemnities e.g. tender, performance, customs and tax;

(b) A guarantee issued by an "Authorized Person" on behalf of a third Authorized Person which entails that the "Authorized Person" shall be responsible for the fulfillment of the Authorized Person's obligations to the stock market clearing house; and

(c) Guarantees for commercial paper programs or other domestic borrowing programs with an original maturity of more than one year ; and

2) Guarantees for borrowing facilities:

(a) Commitments in the form of Note Issuance Facilities (NIFs) and Revolving Underwriting Facilities (RUFs).

Section 33

A conversion factor of 20% applies to guarantees for commercial paper programs or other domestic borrowing programs with an original maturity of at the most one year.

Section 34

A conversion factor of 0% applies to guarantees for commercial paper programs or other domestic borrowing programs that may be unconditionally cancelled at any time without notice.

27.12.2 Chapter 3: Calculating the non-Trading Book Exposure Amount for Derivatives

Section 35

(a) An Authorized Person shall apply eitherthe marking-to-market or risk approach for calculating exposure amounts for counterparty risk in derivatives.

(b) Within a financial group, the marking-to-market and risk approaches may be combined. An individual legal entity shall only use one approach.

Section 36

Derivatives based on different types of indices shall be classified as interest rate, equity, commodity or exchange rate derivatives depending on the relevant type of index in each individual case.

Section 37

An Authorized Person that purchases credit protection through credit derivatives for an exposure that is not assigned to the trading book or for an exposure to counterparty risk may set the exposure amount for the credit derivative to zero (0).

Section 38

An Authorized Person may take netting agreements into account when establishing exposure amounts in accordance with the provisions in Section 114 to Section 133 of this Annex.

Section 39

The exposure amount under the marking-to-market approach is the sum of the current replacement cost on the balance sheet date according to Section 40 of this Annex and the amount of possible risk change according to Section 41 of this Annex. For interest rate swaps where both legs are denominated in the same currency and are based on floating rates, the exposure amount shall only constitute replacement cost.

Section 40

Current replacement cost for an existing contract refers to the cost which the Authorized Person would incur for acquiring an equivalent new contract on the balance sheet date. Where the contract is of a type regularly traded on the market, replacement cost may be set at current market value. Where current market prices are not available, the contract's present value shall be calculated using current market interest rates and exchange rates. The calculation shall be based on current quotations that are professionally assessed to be correct for the currencies and maturities of the contract. For contracts with negative market value, the replacement cost shall be deemed to be zero.

Section 41

Amount for possible risk change refers to an amount which expresses the possibility that the replacement cost increases during the residual term of the contract calculated from the balance sheet date. Possible risk change is calculated for each contract (even for contracts that have a negative market value on the balance sheet date) by multiplying the contract's notional principal amount by a risk factor as set out in Table 13 below.

Table 13

Residual maturity	Interest rate contracts	Contracts concerning foreign exchange rates and gold	Contracts concerning equities	Contracts concerning precious metals except gold	Contracts concerning commodities except precious metals including gold
≤ 1 year	0%	1%	6%	7%	10%
> 1 ≤ 5 years	0.5%	5%	8%	7%	12%
> 5 years	1.5%	7.5%	10%	8%	15%

Contracts which do not fall within one of the five categories specified in Table 13 above shall be treated as contracts concerning commodities except precious metals including gold. For contracts where outstanding exposures are settled periodically so that the market value of the contract is reset to zero on each such occasion, the residual maturity shall be equal to the time until the next reset date.

Section 42

Notional principal refers to the amount in the reporting currency which the original contract covers. When determining a contract's notional amount where the reporting currency is not included at any stage, the value shall be calculated in accordance with the applicable spot rates at the time of calculation. The notional amount shall be the higher of the two values obtained as a result of the translation to the reporting currency. The Authorized Person shall ensure that the notional amounts that may be used are relevant for the risk the contract entails.

Section 43

Authorized Persons which have received approval from the Authority to calculate commodities risk in accordance with Section 7 of Annex 6 may use the risk factors presented in Table 14 below instead of those presented in Table 13.

Table 14

Residual maturity	Contracts concerning precious metals except gold	Contracts concerning base metals	Contracts concerning agricultural products	Contracts concerning other commodities (incl. (energy
≤ 1 year	2.0%	2.5%	3.0%	4.0%
> 1 ≤ 5 years	5.0%	4.0%	5.0%	6.0%
> 5 years	7.5%	8.0%	9.0%	10%

Section 44

A risk approach may only be used for derivatives.

Section 45

(a) An exposure amount under the risk approach shall be calculated separately for each netting set taking into account any collateral as follows: Exposure amount = (ß * max(CMV-CMC;Oj ORPTij-Oi RPCij * CCRMj) i i

where

CMV = the current market value of all transactions within the netting set with a counterparty gross of collateral, where

CMV=OCMVi i

CMVi = the current market value for the transaction i,

CMC = the current market value of the collateral assigned to the netting set, where

CMC=OCMCl l

CMCl = the current market value of collateral l, i = refers to the transaction, l = refers to the collateral, j = refers to hedging set category

These hedging sets correspond to risk factors for which risk positions of opposite sign may be offset to yield a net risk position on which the exposure measure is then based.

RPTij = Risk position from transaction i with respect to hedging set j, RPClj = Risk position from collateral l with respect to hedging set j, CCRMj = Multiplier set out in Section 59 for counterparty credit risk with respect to hedging set j, and

ß = 1.4.

(b) Collateral that is recognisable with the approach clarified in paragraph (a) of this Section is limited to the collateral that is eligible under Annex 3 and commodities assigned to the trading book.

Section 46

For a credit default swap, the risk position consists of the notional value of the reference debt instrument multiplied by the remaining maturity of the credit default swap.

Section 47

For options or other similar instruments (e.g. swaptions), the risk position consists of the delta equivalent market value of the underlying financial instrument for the transaction except in the case of an underlying debt instrument.Where the underlying instrument is a debt instrument or a payment leg, the risk position consists of the delta equivalent market value of the financial instrument or payment leg multiplied by the modified duration for the debt instrument or the payment leg.

Section 48

(a) For other derivatives the risk position is the market value of the underlying financial instrument (also commodities) converted to SAR. For debt instruments and payment legs, however, the risk position is the market value of the outstanding gross payments (including notional amounts), converted to SAR and multiplied by the modified duration of the debt instrument or payment leg, respectively.

(b) Where the underlying financial instruments are equity (also equity index) or commodities, these shall be allocated a risk position for the respective equity (or equity index) or commodity and an interest rate risk position for the payment leg. If the payment leg is expressed in foreign currency the currency shall also be allocated a risk position.

(c) Where the underlying instrument is a debt instrument, one interest rate risk position shall be allocated for the debt instrument and another for the payment leg. Where payment shall take place against payment (including foreign currency forwards), an interest rate risk position is allocated for each payment leg. Where the underlying debt instrument is expressed in foreign currency, a risk position is allocated for the foreign currency.

Where a payment leg is expressed in foreign currency, this is also allocated a risk position for the currency concerned.The exposure amount assigned to an interest basis swap is zero.

Section 49

For the determination of risk positions, collateral received from a counterparty shall be treated as a long position that is due today whereas collateral posted shall be treated as a short position that is due today.

Section 50

For payment legs with a remaining maturity of less than a year, the Authorized Person shall disregard the interest rate risk. For transactions that consist of two payment legs denominated in the same currency, for example interest rate swaps, the Authorized Person may treat the transaction as a single transaction.

Section 51

An Authorized Person shall use the following formulae to determine the amount and sign of its risk position:

1) For all other instruments than debt instruments: market value, or delta equivalent market value = Pref [illegible]v

where Pref = the price of the underlying instrument, expressed in the reference currency, V = the option price for an option or the value of the underlying instrument for other transactions, and

p = the price of the underlying instrument expressed in the same currency as V.

2) for the debt instrument and payment legs for all transactions: market value multiplied by the modified duration, or delta equivalent market value multiplied by the modified duration [illegible]v [illegible]r

where

V = the option price for an option or the value of the underlying instrument or payment leg for other derivatives, and

r = interest rate.

If V is expressed in another currency than the reference currency the derivative shall be converted to the reference currency.

Section 52

Sections from 52 to 57 of this Annex contain provisions for the hedging sets. for the calculation of the exposure amount, risk positions shall be grouped in hedging sets. The net risk position shall be calculated for each hedging set, that is the absolute value of the sum of the resulting risk positions. The net risk position is calculated in Section 45 of this Annex by the following: ORPTij - Oi RPClj i l

Section 53

For interest rate risk positions from payment legs, from money deposits received from the counterparty as collateral as well as from underlying debt instruments, which in accordance with Section 33 to Section 37 of Annex 2 shall be assigned a capital requirement of a maximum of 1.6%, there are three hedging sets set out in Table 15 below. The hedging amount shall be calculated for each separate currency.

Table 15

	Government referenced interest rates
Maturity	≤ 1 year
Maturity	> 1 ≤ 5 years
Maturity	> 5 years

Section 54

For interest rate risk positions from payment legs or underlying debt instruments with interest rates linked to a reference interest rate that represents a general market interest level, the remaining maturity is equivalent to the time interval up to the next adjustment of the interest rate. In all other cases the maturity is the remaining life of the underlying debt instrument or, in the case of a payment leg, the remaining life of the transaction.

Section 55

There is one hedging set for each issuer of a reference debt instrument underlying a credit default swap.

Section 56

(a) In the case of interest rate risk positions from money deposits that are posted with a counterparty as collateral, when that counterparty has no outstanding debt obligations with low specific risk and from underlying debt instruments, which according to Section 38 and Section 39 of Annex 2 shall be assigned a capital requirement of over 1.6%, there is a hedging set for each issuer. When a payment leg emulates such a debt instrument, there is also a hedging set for each issuer.

(b) Authorized Persons may assign risk positions arising from debt instruments of a certain issuer or from reference debt instruments of the same issuerthat are emulated by payment legs orthat underlie a credit default swap to the same hedging set.

Section 57

(a) Underlying financial instruments other than debt instruments shall be assigned to the same hedging sets only if they are identical or similar instruments. In all other cases, they shall be assigned to separate hedging sets.

(b) The similarity of instruments is established as follows:

1) For equities, similar instruments are those of the same issuer. An equity index is treated as a separate issuer ; and

2) For precious metals, similar instruments are those of the same metal. A precious metal index is treated as a separate precious metal; and

3) For electric power, similar instruments are electricity supply rights and obligations that referto the same peak and off-peak load interval over 24 hours; and

4) For commodities, similar instruments are those of the same commodity. A commodity index is treated as a separate index.

Section 58

(a) Multipliers for counterparty credit risk (CCRM) for the different hedging set categories shall be assigned in accordance with Table 16 below:

Table 16

	Hedging set categories	CCRM
1	Interest rates	0.2%
2	Interest rates for risk positions from a reference debt instrument that underlies a credit default swap and which, in accordance with Section 33 to Section 37 of Annex 2, shall be assigned a capital requirement of a maximum of 1.6%	0.3%
3	Interest rates for risk positions from a debt instrument or reference instrument and which in accordance with Section 38 and Section 39 of .Annex 2, shall be assigned a capital requirement of over 1.6%	0.6%
4	Exchange rates	2.5%
5	Electric power	4.0%
6	Gold	5.0%
7	Equity	7.0%
8	(Precious metals) except gold	8.5%
9	(Other commodities) except precious metal, gold and electric power	10.0%
10	Underlying financial instruments of derivative contracts that are not in any of the above categories	10.0%

(b) The underlying instruments of derivatives according to point 10 in Table 16 above shall be assigned to separate individual hedging sets for each categor y of underlying financial instrument.

Section 59

Fort ransactions with options where an Authorized Person cannot establish a delta value or modified duration, the Authorized Person may instead use the marking-to-market approach to determine the exposure amount. In this case netting may not be taken into account, that is the exposure amount shall be determined as if there was a netting set which only contains the individual transaction.

Chapter 4: Credit Protection

Section 60

An Authorized Person intending to utilize the effect of credit protection when calculating a risk-weighted exposure amount shall apply Chapter 4 to Chapter 8 of this Annex.

Section 61

An Authorized Person may only consider the effect of recognizable protection. Protection is recognizable if the form is eligible and if the Authorized Person meets the specific requirements related to the management of each respective form of protection.

Section 62

Where an individual exposure has more than one type of recognizable credit protection the Authorized Person shall distribute the exposure among the different types of credit protection. A risk-weighted exposure amount shall be calculated separately for each component.

27.12.3 Chapter 5: Guarantees and Credit Derivatives

Section 63

Guarantees and credit derivative are recognisable if they are eligible in accordance with Section 64 of this Annex and the Authorized Person meets the management requirements set out in Section 73 of this Annex.

Section 64

Guarantees and credit derivative are eligible as credit protection if they are issued by an eligible protection provider in accordance with Section 65 of this Annex and meet the conditions pursuant to Section 66 to Section 72 of this Annex.

Section 65

(a) Eligible issuers of guarantees and credit derivatives are issuers whose commitments are assigned to one of the following exposure classes:

1) Exposures to governments and central banks;

2) Exposures to administrative bodies treated as governments and central banks or Authorized Persons; or

3) Exposures to Authorized Persons and banks.

(b) In addition to what has been mentioned in paragraph (a) of this Section, companies with a credit rating corresponding to credit quality step 2 or better are deemed to be eligible issuers of guarantees and credit derivative

Section 66

In order for a guarantee or a credit derivative to provide eligible protection, the following requirements shall be met:

1) The protection is direct;

2) The protection applies to clearly defined and identifiable claims; and

3) The protection agreement is legally enforceable in all relevant jurisdictions.

Section 67

(a) The protection agreement may not contain conditions outside the control of the Authorized Person that entail that:

1) The issuer of the guarantee or credit derivative has a unilateral right to revoke the protection;

2) The cost of the protection increases due to the deteriorating quality of the protected asset;

3) The issuer of the guarantee or credit derivative is not obliged to pay out in a timely manner in the event the obligor fails to make payments due; or

4) It is possible for the issuer of the guarantee or credit derivative to reduce the maturity of the guarantee or credit derivative.

(b) The following shall also apply to the agreement referred to in paragraph (a) of this Section:

1) Protection in the form of guarantees shall meet the conditions set out in Section 65 of this Annex; and

2) Protection in the form of credit derivatives must meet the conditions in Section 66 to Section 69 of this Annex.

Section 68

(a) In the event of a failure to pay, the Authorized Person shall have the right to, without undue delay, make a claim for payment against the protection issuer, without first being required to make a claim against the obligor.

(b) This requirement mentioned in paragraph (a) of this Section does not need to be met for counter-guarantees or guarantees issued by credit guarantee associations or guarantors, on condition that one of the following conditions have been met:

1) The terms of the contract give the Authorized Person the right to, without undue delay, receive a provisional payment corresponding to a reliable estimate of the amount constituting the guaranteed portion of the Authorized Person's expected financial loss, including losses arising from the non-payment of interest

and other amounts for which the borrower is obligated to make; or

2) The Authorized Person can demonstrate that the loss-protecting effects, including losses resulting from non-payment of amounts for which the borrower is liable, justify the above. Guarantees which protect exposures using collateral in residential real estate are also eligible where the period before the Authorized Person can demand payment from the issuer is up to 24 months.

Section 69

(a) The following types of credit derivatives are eligible:

1) Credit default swaps;

2) Total return swaps; and

3) Credit linked note for the amount paid in.

(b) Financial instruments composed of or financially equivalent to these types of credit derivatives are also eligible.

(c) A total return swap is not eligible if the Authorized Person books the net payments from this credit derivative as income but does not take up a corresponding reduction in the value of the asset which the credit derivative protects as a cost.

Section 70

(a) Events that mean that the credit derivative becomes due for payment (credit events) shall at least include:

1) The obligor defaults on amounts due;

2) The obligor stops payments or applies for bankruptcy; and

3) A grace period for the obligor in which to pay installments and interest due or any other change to the terms of payment, in a manner that results in a financial loss for the Authorized Person.

(b) Where in accordance with the underlying debt instrument, the obligor can obtain a grace period regarding the payment of amounts due, the definition of the credit event pursuant to point 1 of paragraph (a) of this Section, must take account of this. Where the credit event does not include that set out in point 3 of paragraph (a) of this Section, the credit derivative may still be taken into account, although the protected amount shall be reduced in accordance with Section 77 of this Annex.

(c) It shall be clearly defined which parties are responsible for deciding if a credit event has occurred. This decision may not rest solely with the protection issuer. The protection purchaser shall have both the right and possibility to inform the protection issuer if a credit event occurs.

Section 71

For credit derivatives with cash settlement, the Authorized Person shall have procedures for reliably estimating losses. A period shall be set during which the Authorized Person may obtain post-credit event assessments of the reference exposure. If the cash settlement is conditional on the protection purchaser's transfer of the reference exposure to the issuer of the protection, the contract shall provide that any required approval between the parties to such a transfer may not unduly delay the transfer.

Section 72

Even if the reference exposure of a credit derivative does not exactly correspond to the exposure that the Authorized Person wishes to protect, the credit derivative is eligible if the following conditions are met:

1) The reference exposure refers to the same counterparty;

2) The reference exposure is ranked equal to or juniorto the protected asset in the event of bankruptcy; and

3) There are cross clauses in place between the reference asset and the protected asset that mean that if the borrower defaults (e.g. stops payments) on other loans the borrower has taken, this will be treated as a default on the reference asset as well.

Section 73

An Authorized Person shall have set guidelines regarding the use of guarantees and credit derivatives related to the Authorized Person's overall risk management strategy. The Authorized Person shall have procedures and systems for following up and managing potential concentrations of credit risk arising as a result of this protection.

Section 74

When a recognizable credit derivative or guarantee is available for an exposure, the obligor's risk weight may be replaced by the protection issuer's risk weight for the protected amount. When an Authorized Person has a guarantee or credit derivative for off-balance sheet commitments, the effect of these shall be included before the Authorized Person applies the relevant conversion factor.

Section 75

(a) Protected amount refers to the maximum amount that the protection provider has undertaken to pay, reduced by the adjustments specified in this paragraph.

(b) Where the protection does not cover all types of payment that can arise from the exposure, the protected amount shall be adjusted in order to take account of this. Where the protection is denominated in a currency other than that of the direct exposure, the protected amount shall be reduced by the exchange rate volatility adjustment factor (Hfx) that shall be determined in accordance with Section 100 to Section 113 of this Annex.

Section 76

Where a credit derivative pursuant to the terms of the contract cannot be redeemed because the obligor received a grace period to pay installments due and interest due or other changes to the terms of payment that result in a financial loss, in cases in which the protection does not exceed the exposure amount, the protected amount shall be reduced by 40%. If the protection exceeds the exposure amount, the protected amount shall not exceed 60% of the exposure amount.

Section 77

(a) Where a credit derivative covers several exposures and the credit derivative is designed so that it becomes due for payment when the first exposure occurs, the Authorized Person may only include protection for the exposure which in the absence of protection would give rise to the lowest risk weighted exposure amounts, provided that the protection at least covers the exposure.

(b) Where a credit derivative covers several exposures and the credit derivative is designed so that it becomes due for payment when the nth default occurs, the Authorized Person may apply the method specified in paragraph (a) of this Section, appropriately tailored, provided that either another protection has been obtained for default 1 to n-1 or that n-1 default has already occurred.

Section 78

Where there is a maturity mismatch, that is when the residual maturity of the credit protection is less than that of the protected exposure, the credit protection may not be taken into account when calculating risk-weighted exposure amounts if the residual maturity of the credit protection is less than three months or if the original term is less than one year.

Section 79

The residual maturity of the protected exposure refers to the time until the obligor must have fulfilled its obligations. However, the residual maturity shall be subject to a maximum of five years.

Section 80

(a) The residual maturity of the credit protection shall be the time to the earliest point of time at which the protection expires or may be terminated. Where the protection seller has the option to terminate the agreement the residual maturity of the protection shall be considered to be the time to the earliest date at which that option may be exercised.

(b) Where the credit protection buyer has the right to terminate the agreement, and the original agreement terms contain a positive incentive for the buyer to terminate the protection before contractual maturity, the residual maturity of the protection shall be considered to be the time to the earliest date at which this option may be exercised.

(c) The residual maturity shall be reduced by the amount of the grace period for credit derivatives that become repayable without consideration for the possibility that the protected asset may be subject to a grace period before default is considered to have occurred.

Section 81

Where there is a maturity mismatch the protected amount shall be reduced by multiplying it by the result of following expression:

$(t-0.25)/(T-0.25)$,

where

T is the residual maturity of the protected exposure, though a maximum of five years,

t is the residual maturity of the credit protection, though a maximum of T.

Section 82

Recognizable credit linked notes issued by the Authorized Person may be treated as cash collateral in accordance with the requirements set out in Section 83 to Section 85 of this Annex.

Chapter 6: Financial Collateral

Section 83

Collateral is recognizable if it is eligible as set out in Section 84 and Section 85 of this Annex and the Authorized Person fulfills the management requirements in accordance with Section 87 to Section 89 of this Annex.

Section 84

The following financial collaterals are eligible:

1) Cash deposited in the client account with a local bank and cash equivalent instruments held by the Authorized Person. Cash equivalent instruments in these Rules referto certificates of deposits or other money market instruments issued by a bank;

2) Debt instruments:

(a) Assigned to exposures to governments and central banks that have a credit rating or a credit rating by an export credit agency corresponding to credit quality steps 4 or better ;

(b) Issued by foreign authorities and comparable associations or administrative bodies which may be treated as exposures to their government;

(c) Issued by an Authorized Person or other legal entity with a credit rating corresponding to credit quality step 3 or better for the relevant type of counterparty;

(d) Issued by foreign authorities or comparable associations with a credit rating corresponding to credit quality step 3 or better ;

(e) Issued by administrative bodies with the same risk-weight as exposures to Authorized Persons and with a credit rating corresponding to credit quality step 3 or better ; or

(f) Issues by Authorized Persons and corresponding foreign companies which do not have a credit rating are still eligible provided that the following conditions are met:

i. They are traded on a regulated market;

ii. They are not subordinated;

iii. Where there are other debt instruments issued by the same counterparty with the same seniority for which there is a credit rating, all of these profit- bearing securities' credit ratings shall correspond to credit quality 3 or better ; and

iv. The Authorized Person has no information to suggest that that the liquidity of the debt instrument is insufficient.

3) Equity and convertibles included in one of the indices recognized by the Authority; and

4) Gold.

Section 85

(a) Investment fund units are eligible financial collateral if the following conditions are met:

1) The price of units in investment funds is updated and made public daily; and

2) The terms and conditions of the investment fund only allow the investment fund to invest in the securities specified in Section 84 of this Annex.

(b) What has been mentioned in paragraph (a) of this Section does not prevent the investment fund from using derivatives to hedge investments in such securities.

Section 86

(a) The creditworthiness of the counterparty and the value of the collateral may not have a material positive correlation.

(b) Securities issued by the counterparty or by other companies within the same group as the counterparty are not recognizable.

Section 87

The agreement regarding the grant of collateral shall be legally binding in all relevant jurisdictions. Where a third party holds the collateral, the Authorized Person shall take all necessary steps to ensure that the third party segregates the collateral from its own assets.

Section 88

The forms of the grant of collateral shall be documented, including the procedures for timely liquidation of collateral. The Authorized Person shall have written policies that regulate the type and volumes of assets that it accepts as collateral.

Section 89

An Authorized Person shall have well-functioning procedures and processes for verifying the risks arising due to the utilization of the collateral, including:

1) Risk of failed or reduced credit protection, for example the risk that the Authorized Person cannot immediately freely dispose of or liquidate the collateral;

2) The risk of incorrect valuations; and

3) Concentration risk arising from the utilization of financial collateral, and its effect on the Authorized Person's collective risk profile.

Section 90

Where there is a maturity mismatch, that is when the residual maturity of the financial collaterals is less than that of the protected exposure, the Authorized Person shall take into account Section 95 or of this Annex when calculating risk-weighted exposure amounts.

Section 91

An Authorized Person may disregard maturity mismatches if the following requirements are met:

1) The protected exposure and the collateral are valued daily;

2) The collateral agreement specifies that the collateral shall be delivered without undue delay if a collateral deficit has arisen; and

3) Where the financial collateral consists of debt instruments, the collateral agreement shall imply that if the collateral expires the funds shall be paid into an account at the Authorized Person which the counterparty cannot utilize without the approval of the Authorized Person.

Section 92

The residual maturity of the protected exposure refers to the time until the obligor must have fulfilled its obligations. However, maturity shall never be longer than five years.

Section 93

Subject to this Chapter, the residual maturity of the credit protection shall be the time to the earliest date at which the protection expires or can be terminated.

Section 94

When determining risk-weighted exposure amounts the Authorized Person may use recognizable financial collateral by using either the simple method pursuant to Section 95 to Section 99 of this Annex or the comprehensive method pursuant to Section 100 to Section 102 of this Annex.

Section 95

If the Authorized Person applies the simple method, the residual maturity of the protection must be at least as long as the residual maturity of the exposure, otherwise the credit protection may not be considered when calculating risk-weighted exposure amounts.

Section 96

(a) When an exposure has recognizable financial collateral, the risk weight of the counterparty may be replaced by the risk weight of the collateral instrument for the portion that the collateral covers. However, the new risk weight for the portion of the exposure covered by the collateral shall be at least 100%, except when applying Section 97 to Section 99 of this Annex.

(b) When the Authorized Person has financial collateral for off-balance sheet commitments, the effect of these shall be used before the Authorized Person applies the relevant conversion factor.The remainder of the exposure shall be assigned the risk weight that would be assigned to an unsecured exposure to the counterparty.

Section 97

(a) The value of the financial collateral shall be the market value.

(b) A 0% risk weight shall be assigned to the collateralized portion of an exposure arising from transactions with a counterparty in accordance with point 8 of Section 103 of this Annex or with companies assigned a risk weight that does not exceed 20%.

(c) A 20% risk weight shall be assigned to the collateralized portion of an exposure arising from transactions with companies assigned a risk weight that exceed 20% but does not exceed 100%.

Section 98

(a) Derivatives subject to daily marking-to-market and collateralized by cash deposited in local banks pledged and assigned to the Authorized Person or cash equivalent instruments and where there is no currency mismatch, shall be assigned, to the extent of the collateralization, a 0% risk weight.

(b) Derivatives collateralized by debt instruments issued by governments or central banks assigned a 0% risk weight shall be assigned a 10% risk weight.

(c) Debt instruments issued by foreign authorities and comparable associations must be treated in the same way as exposures to their government.

Section 99

Where the exposure and the collateral are denominated in the same currency a 0% risk weight may be assigned to the collateralized exposure if one of the following conditions is met:

1) The collateral is deposited cash in the client account with a local bank or a cash equivalent instrument held by the Authorized Person; or

2) The collateral is in the form of debt instruments issued by governments or central banks assigned a 0% risk weight and the collateral's market value has been discounted by 20%.

Section 100

(a) under the financial collateral comprehensive method, the Authorized Person shall calculate volatility-adjusted amounts to be applied to the exposure amount and the collateral to determine the extent to which the collateral is considered to cover the exposure.

(b) Eunsec is the portion of the exposure not considered protected by the collateral and is calculated as follows: $Eunsec = \max\{0, (EVA - CVA)\}$ $EVA = E^{*} \times (1 + HE)$ $CVA = C \times (1 - HC - Hfx)$ C is the market value of the collateral.

E^* is an adjusted exposure amount where off-balance sheet commitments are included, that is conversion factors are not taken into account.

EVA and CVA are the volatility-adjusted amounts of the exposure and collateral respectively. Where there is a maturity mismatch, CVA shall be adjusted in accordance with Section 101 of this Annex.

HE and HC are factors for the volatility adjustment of the amounts of the exposure and collateral, respectively, with regard to changes in market prices. Both HE and HC will henceforth be called H.

Hfx is a factor for volatility adjustment with regard to changes in exchange rates.

(c) When determining the volatility adjustment factors, the Authorized Person may use the prescribed volatility adjustments according to Section 103 to Section 113 of this Annex.

Section 101

(a) Where there is a maturity mismatch, the value of the collateral shall be reduced according to the following formula:

$$CVAM = CVA \times (t-0.25)/(T-0.25)$$

where

CVAM is CVA adjusted for the maturity mismatch,

CVA is the value of the credit protection in accordance with Section 100 of this Annex,

T is the residual maturity of the protected exposure, though a maximum of five years,

t is the residual maturity of the credit protection, though a maximum of T.

CVAM replaces CVA when calculating Eunsec pursuant to Section 100 of this Annex.

(b) The credit protection may not be taken into account if either the residual maturity of the credit protection is less than three months or if the original maturity of the credit protection is less than one year.

Section 102

Where several different financial collateral are recognizable for an exposure, the volatility adjustment factor shall be a weighted average of the factors applying to each individual collateral. The portion of the aggregated market value that each individual collateral represents is used as the weight.

Section 103

The volatility adjustment may be set to 0% if the following conditions are met:

1) The exposure and its collateral are debt instruments issued by governments and central banks and assigned a 0% risk weight;

2) The exposure and its collateral are denominated in the same currency;

3) The maturity of the transaction is a maximum of one day, alternatively that the marking-to-market for both the exposure and collateral is set daily and that the mark-to-market margin is set daily;

4) The Authorized Person judges that the time between the last market valuation and liquidation of the collateral has not exceeded four business days in situations where the counterparty fails to discharge its obligation to set a mark-to-market margin;

5) The transaction is cleared and settled in a clearing and settlement system suitable for this type of transaction;

6) The agreement governing the transaction is a standard market agreement for repurchase transactions and securities lending transactions;

7) Pursuant to the agreement mentioned in point 6 of this Section, the transaction may be terminated immediately if the counterparty fails to satisfy its obligation to deliver cash or securities orto provide collateral or if the counterparty in any other way fails to discharge its obligations; and

8) The counterparty is one of the following:

(a) governments and central banks assigned a 0% risk weight;

(b) Other Authorized Persons, banks or insurance companies assigned a risk weight that does not exceed 20%;

(c) Investment fund companies or equivalent foreign companies that are obligated under law to meet capital adequacy standards; or

(d) Clearing organizations.

Section 104

Volatility adjustments for changes in market prices do not need to be made for cash deposited in the client account with a local bank and cash equivalent instruments held by the Authorized Person.Volatility adjustments for changes in market prices do not need to be made for cash lent by the Authorized Person.

Section 105

The values of H in Section 106 to Section 109 of this Annex apply to collateral and exposures for which mark-to-market revaluations are conducted daily. If marking-to- market is less frequent, the values for H shall be adjusted upwards in accordance with Section 113 of this Annex.

Section 106

The debt instruments referred to in point 2 (a-b) of Section 84 of this Annex issued by counterparties shall be adjusted for volatility in accordance with Table 17 below.

Table 17

H in %		Liquidation period		
Credit quality step	Residual maturity in years	days 20	days 10	days 5
1	≤ 1 year	0.707	0.5	0.354
1	> 1 ≤ 5 years	2.828	2	1.414
1	> 5 years	5.657	4	2.828
3-2	≤ 1 year	1.414	1	0.707
3-2	> 1 ≤ 5 years	4.243	3	2.121
3-2	> 5 years	8.485	6	4.243
4		21.213	15	10.607
Debt instruments with a credit rating for short-term exposures				
1		0.707	0.5	0.354
3-2		1.414	1§	0.707

Section 107

The debt instruments referred to in point 2 (c-e) of Section 84 of this Annex issued by counterparties shall be adjusted for volatility, irrespective of the issuer, based on credit quality steps 2-3 in accordance with Table 18 below.

Table 18

H in %		Liquidation period		
Credit quality step	Residual maturity in years	days 20	days 10	days 5
1	≤ 1 year	1.414	1	0.707
1	> 1 ≤ 5 years	5.657	4	2.828
1	> 5 years	11.314	8	5.657
3-2	≤ 1 year	2.828	2	1.414
3-2	> 1 ≤ 5 years	8.485	6	4.243
3-2	> 5 years	16.971	12	8.485
Debt instruments with a credit rating for short-term exposures				
1		1.414	1	0.707
3-2		2.828	2	1.414

Section 108

Other types of exposures or recognizable financial collateral shall be adjusted for volatility in accordance with Table 19 below.

Table 19

H in %	Liquidation period		
Type of exposure or collateral	20 days	10 days	5 days
Shares included in one of the eligible indices recognised by the Authority	21.213	15	10.607
Other eligible collateral	35.355	25	17.678
Gold	21.213	15	10.607

Section 109

For volatility adjustment of units in investment funds which are recognizable collateral, a weighted average H is calculated for the assets in which the investment fund has invested. When adjustments are being made, the liquidation period for each transaction type must be applied. If the assets are not known to the Authorized Person, the Authorized Person shall use the maximum value of H that would apply to one of the assets permitted in accordance with terms and conditions of this investment fund.

Section 110

The factor for volatility adjustment for changes in exchange rates, Hfx, is expressed as a percentage in Table 20 below and applies to collateral and exposures which are subject to daily mark-to-market.

Table 20

Liquidation period		
days 20	days 10	days 5
11.314	8	5.657

Section 111

(a) With regard to over the counter derivatives, volatility adjustments for changes in exchange rates shall be carried out if the collateral currency is different from the settlement currency.

(b) With regard to over the counter derivatives for which the Authorized Person has recognizable netting agreements, volatility adjustments for currency fluctuations shall be applied if there is a mismatch between the collateral currency and the settlement currency. Only a single volatility adjustment shall be applied even if the netting agreement includes transactions in multiple currencies.

Section 112

The liquidation period used to determine H and Hfx, respectively, is the following:

1) Five business days for securities loans and for repurchase transactions that do not include the transfer of commodities or commodities or guaranteed rights relating to title to commodities;

2) Ten business days for capital market-driven transactions other than those indicated in point 1 of this Section; or

3) 20 business days for other exposures.

Section 113

If the Authorized Person does not mark-to-market its collateral and exposures daily, H and Hfx, which are defined in Section 106 to Section 110 of this Annex, shall be adjusted upwards according to the following formula.

$$HA= HM\sqrt{\{NR+(TM-1)\}/TM}$$

HA is the factor for the final volatility adjustment after adjustment for the frequency of the market valuation carried out by the Authorized Person. It is this value that is used in the calculation in Section 100 of this Annex.

HM refers to the volatility adjustment that is specified in Section 106 to Section 110 of this Annex.

NR refers to the number of business days between each valuation.

TM is the liquidation period for the relevant security in accordance with Section 112 of this Annex.

27.12.4 Chapter 7: Netting Agreements

Section 114

Bilateral netting agreements are recognizable if they are eligible under Section 115 to Section 119 of this Annex and the Authorized Person fulfills the requirements for managing them as contained in Section 120 to Section 124 of this Annex.

Section 115

(a) The eligible netting agreement shall be legally binding in all relevant jurisdictions. The agreement shall provide that the party which has not defaulted pursuant to the terms of the contract may terminate all contracts covered by the agreement without delay when a credit event occurs. Credit events shall include the insolvency or bankruptcy of the counterparty.

(b) The eligible netting agreement shall create a single obligation covering all receivables and liabilities contained in the agreement and covered by netting, so that, if the Authorized Person or counterparty do not fulfill their payment obligations, are declared bankrupt, go into liquidation, become the subject of public composition proceedings or start any other insolvency proceedings, the liability of the counterparty is only for the net sum of the receivables and liabilities.

(c) The eligible netting agreement may not contain conditions that would permit a non-defaulting party to make limited payments only, or no payments at all, to the defaulting party, even if the defaulter is a net creditor.

Section 116

An Authorized Person shall have written and reasoned legal opinions in its possession that demonstrate that the agreed netting would be recognized by the relevant courts and administrative authorities in the relevant jurisdictions. The legal opinions shall show that even if a netting agreement is terminated as a result of an event such as those set out in Section 115 of this Annex, a legal review by the relevant courts and administrative authorities would, in all reasonable probability, find the Authorized Person's receivables and liabilities limited to the net sum of the positive and negative market values of all the contracts included in the agreement and covered by netting, or limited to the net sum of all the receivables and liabilities covered by netting. The evaluation of the outcome of the legal review must be based on:

1) Governing law in the jurisdiction in which the parties have their respective registered offices and, if the commitments of the counterparty or Authorized Person were entered into through a foreign branch office, governing law in the jurisdiction in which the branch office is situated, pursuant to that set out in Section 117 of this Annex;

2) Governing law which pursuant to the agreement regulates the individual contracts and receivables and liabilities covered by the agreement; and

3) Governing law regulating every contract or agreement necessary to effect the netting agreement.

Section 117

(a) In cases where the parties have entered into a netting agreement in which several foreign branch offices are included, the legal opinions indicated in Section 116 of this Annex shall be requested from all the jurisdictions in which the branch offices are situated.

(b) If it is not possible to obtain a legal opinion pursuant to Section 116 of this Annex for one of the branch offices, this branch office can still be included in the agreement on condition that a legal opinion is available that finds that the netting agreement will not be declared null and void in its entirety merely for the reason that such agreements do not have any legal standing for the contracts and receivables and liabilities entered into with such a branch office. Agreements that include branch offices situated within the jurisdiction where the netting agreement is not legally binding may not be considered.

Section 118

A legal opinion pursuant to Section 116 of this Annex shall include the following:

1) A judgment that states that the netting agreement and the contracts and receivables and liabilities covered by the agreement do not breach laws, regulations or court judgments in the relevant jurisdictions;

2) Reference to existing netting agreements and a reference to the netting provisions contained in each such agreement; and

3) A judgment that states that the netting agreement will be deemed legally binding in the situations specified in Section 115 of this Annex in the relevant jurisdictions, if action is taken by an administrator, liquidator, receiver or the equivalent in other jurisdictions.

Section 119

The legal opinion pursuant to Section 116 of this Annex shall be issued by an external, independent licensed lawyer/law firm with considerable experience in the field. The opinion can be either given directly to the Authorized Person orto the organization behind the netting agreement that the Authorized Person has utilized. The opinion can also be a common legal opinion for a specific netting agreement for several Authorized Persons together or an organization representing the Authorized Person.The opinion can be drawn up for different types of netting agreement.

Section 120

(a) Before a netting agreement can influence the calculation of a risk-weighted amount for the first time, the Authorized Person shall notify the Authority that a legally binding netting agreement exists.

(b) The Authorized Person shall certify to the Authority in writing that:

1) All conditions pursuant to Section 115 of this Annex are met;

2) The Authorized Person has legal opinions pursuant to Section 116 to Section 119 of this Annex;

3) The Authorized Person has the necessary technical systems or manual procedures for calculating counterparty exposures as a net amount instead of a gross amount; and

4) The Authorized Person has the necessar y technical systems or manual procedures for calculating the risk arising when the counterparty's contracts or liabilities cease.

Section 121

An Authorized Person is responsible for documenting each individual netting agreement and legal opinion. Netting agreements and legal opinions must be kept well arranged.

Section 122

An Authorized Person shall continuously verify that:

1) Its netting agreements have legal standing with respect to the relevant counterparties, contracts, receivables and liabilities and jurisdictions, with regard to amendments to law; and

2) The conclusions of the legal opinions obtained are legally valid and no older than one year. If a legal opinion is older than one year, the Authorized Person shall request a new legal opinion stating that the conclusions of the previous opinion still apply.

Section 123

If an Authorized Person learns that the competent authorities in a counterparty's homeland do not consider a netting agreement to have legal standing in accordance with existing law in that country, the netting agreement may not be considered.This applies irrespective of the legal opinions obtained.

Section 124

If a legal opinion issued in accordance with Section 116 of this Annex is missing a piece of significant information regarding the sustainability of a netting agreement, the Authorized Person must assess whether an eligible netting agreement exists. If the Authorized Person judges the requirements have not been met, the exposure amount may not be adjusted.

Section 125

Authorized Persons that treat financial collateral according to the comprehensive method may take eligible netting agreements into account when calculating the exposure for capital market driven transactions, such as repurchase transactions and securities lending or borrowing transactions in accordance with either the prescribed method pursuant to Section 127 and Section 128 of this Annex.

Section 126

To qualify for recognition under the netting agreement, the collateral received should be eligible in accordance with Section 84 of this Annex.

Section 127

The management requirements shall be met for the assets covered by the netting agreement.

Section 128

for the repurchase transactions, securities lending or borrowing transactions and other capital market-driven transactions covered by a recognizable netting agreement, a net amount, E*, shall replace the individual exposure amounts for these transactions.

$E^* = \max\{0, E - C + Tnet \times HT + Efx \times Hfx\}$

E* therefore cannot be a negative amount.

E is the exposure amount for each separate exposure without regard to credit protection.

C is the market value of the assets that the Authorized Person has borrowed, purchased or received as collateral under the netting agreement.

Tnet is the amount of the net position (whether positive or negative) of each asset type. Asset type refers to securities which have been issued by the same legal entity, have the same issue date, the same terms of contract and liquidation period in accordance with Section 112.

HT is the volatility adjustment factor for changes in market value, H, for each asset and is calculated in accordance with Section 105 to Section 109 of this Annex.

Efx is the amount of the net position (whether positive or negative) in each currency that is not the settlement currency.

Hfx is the volatility adjustment factor for changes in foreign exchange rates and shall be calculated in accordance with Section 110 of this Annex.

Section 129

An Authorized Person may adjust the exposure amount in line with Section 130 and Section 131 of this Annex in order to take account of recognizable netting agreements for derivatives.

Section 130

When calculating the sum of the current replacement cost for contracts with a specific counterparty, the Authorized Person may reduce it by the sum of the negative market values for contracts that the Authorized Person has with the same counterparty.

Section 131

(a) For derivatives covered by a recognisable netting agreement, the amount for potential change in risk is calculated in accordance with the following formula.

$PCEred = 0.4 * PCEgross + 0.6 * NGR * PCEgross$

where

PCEred = the reduced amount for potential future credit exposure for all contracts with a specific counterparty included in a netting agreement.

PCEgross= the sum of the figures for potential change in risk for all contracts with a specific counterparty included in a netting agreement and calculated by multiplying their notional value with a risk factor in accordance with Table 13 in Section 41 of this Annex.

NGR = "net-gross ratio": the ratio between the net replacement cost for all contracts included in a netting agreement with a given counterparty (numerator) and the gross replacement cost for all contracts included in a netting agreement with that counterparty (denominator).

(b) If netting leads to a net debt when calculating the net replacement cost, the net replacement cost shall be set at zero in the above formula. PCEred may therefore never be less than 0.4*PCEgross.

Section 132

(a) An Authorized Person may adjust the exposure amount in accordance with Section

133 of this Annex to take account of recognizable netting agreements for other receivables and liabilities in the balance sheet.

(b) Recognizable netting agreements for other receivables and liabilities are limited to mutual cash receivables between the Authorized Person and the Authorized Person›s counterparty that constitute loans or deposits in the client accounts with local banks as well as other deposits in local banks pledged or assigned to the Authorized Person.

Section 133

With regard to receivables covered by the netting agreement, a net amount, Eunsec, may replace the individual exposure amounts when determining a risk-weighted exposure amount.

$Eunsec = \max\{0, (E - CVA)\}$ $CVA = C \times (1 - Hfx)$ E is the net book value of the receivables. C is the net book value of the liabilities. CVA is the volatility-adjusted amount of the liabilities.

Hfx is a factor for volatility adjustment with regard to changes in exchange rates.

27.12.5 Chapter 8: Other Credit Protection

Section 134

Cash deposited with a local bank, or cash equivalent instruments held by another Authorized Person, in a non-custodial arrangement can be considered to be recognizable collateral if the following conditions have been met:

1) The client's claim against the local bank or the other Authorized Person is pledged or assigned to the Authorized Person;

2) The local bank or the other Authorized Person shall have been notified of the pledge or assignment;

3) It may not be possible for the local bank or the other Authorized Person to make payments to any party other than the Authorized Person without the approval of the latter ;

4) The pledge or assignment shall be unconditional and irrevocable; and

5) The agreement regarding the grant of collateral shall be legally binding in all relevant jurisdictions. Collateral pursuant to the above shall be treated as a guarantee issued by a local bank.

27.13 ANNEX 4: Operational Risk

27.13.1 Chapter 1:The Basic Indicator Approach

Section 1

(a) The income indicator consists of the average of operating income for the last three audited annual financial statements in accordance with Section 2 of this Annex. Where an Authorized Person terminates a large portion of its operations and as a consequence the income indicator no longer provides a fair view of its operating income, the Authorized Person may, after receiving approval from the Authority, during a transition period, calculate the capital requirement for operational risk based on a different indicator.

(b) Where the operating income is negative or zero for any of the three financial years referred in paragraph (a) of this Section, these years shall not be included when calculating the income indicator. The income indicator shall be calculated as the operating income sum of the positive financial years divided by the number of positive financial years. If any of the three most recent financial years was shortened or extended, the operating income shall be recalculated to a twelve-month basis using simple proportions.

(c) Where an Authorized Person has been in business for less than one year, the income indicator shall correspond to the operating income given in the Authorized Person's business plan for the first year.

Section 2

(a) Operating income is calculated as the balance of the following items:

1) Interest receivable income;

2) Dividends received;

3) Fees and commissions receivable;

4) Net income on financial transactions; and

5) Other operating income.

(b) The operating income shall be calculated before deductions for provisions and operating expenses. Operating expenses shall include fees paid for outsourced services rendered by third parties that are not included in the Authorized Person's financial group. Expenditure for outsourced services rendered by third parties may be deducted from operating income if they were paid to a company subject to the super vision of the Authority.

(c) The following items shall not be taken into account when calculating operating income:

1) Dividends from companies in the Authorized Person's financial group; and

2) Realized profits/losses from the sale of assets in non-trading activities

27.13.2 Chapter 2:The standardized Approach

Section 3

(a) The income indicator for each business line shall be calculated as an average of the operating income for the last three audited annual financial statements. Operating income is calculated in accordance with Section 2 of this Annex.Where the operating income is negative for any of the three financial years in question, the operating income for each business line during the year in question shall be set as zero when calculating the income indicator.Where the operating income for a certain business line is negative, though the operating income for the entire year is not negative, the negative figure may be used.

(b) Where an Authorized Person terminates a large portion of its operations and as a consequence the income indicator no longer provides a fair view of its operating income, the Authorized Person may apply for approval to calculate, during a transition period, the capital requirement for operational risk based on a different indicator. If any of the three most recent financial years was shortened or extended, the operating income shall be recalculated to a twelve-month basis using simple proportions.

(c) Where an Authorized Person has been in business for less than one year, the income indicator shall correspond to the operating income given in the Authorized Person's business plan for the first year.

Section 4

Under the standardized approach, the capital requirement for operational risk is the sum of the capital requirements calculated across the business lines.

Section 5

The following conditions apply for the division of operations into business lines:

1) All of an Authorized Person's operations shall be consistently assigned to one of the five business lines;

2) An operation that cannot be assigned to a specific business line but which represents an ancillary function to an activity shall be allocated to the same business line to which that activity is assigned. Where the ancillary function supports more than one business line, the division shall be made on objective criteria;

3) If an activity or an ancillary function for an activity cannot be assigned to a specific business line in accordance with point 2 above, the activity shall be assigned to the business line with the highest percentage; and

4) The Authorized Person shall decide how to allocate income between business lines. Costs generated in one business line that can be attributed to another line may be reassigned to the business line to which they pertain, for example by using internal pricing between two business lines.

Section 6

Table 21 below presents the business lines, the corresponding licenses and the percentages for calculating the capital requirement.

Table 21

Business Line	Risk charge	License
Corporate Finance	18%	Arranging
Research and Advisory	18%	Advising
Trading and Sales	18%	Dealing
Custody	15%	Custody
Asset Management	12%	Managing

27.14 ANNEX 5: Foreign Exchange Rate Risk

27.14.1 Chapter 1:The Two-Step Method

Section 1

When using the two-step method, the calculation of the Authorized Person's total net position (long or short) in foreign currency is carried out in two steps. In addition, the net position in gold is calculated. Positions in the reporting currency shall not be included in the calculations.

Step 1: Net position in individual foreign currency and in gold

(a) First, the Authorized Person's open net position, long or short, in each currency and in gold, in which the Authorized Person has positions, is calculated.The net position in each currency and in gold is calculated as the net of the positive and negative items respectively, in accordance with the following:

1) The net spot position, that is all asset items less all liability items and provisions, including accrued income/expenses and deferred expenses/income, or, for gold, the net spot position in gold;
2) The net forward position, that is all outstanding amounts less all liabilities in currency and gold forwards transactions and the principal on currency swaps not included in the net spot position;
3) Irrevocable guarantees and similar instruments that is certain to be called and for which repayment most likely will not take place;
4) Net future income/expenditure not yet accrued but already fully hedged (application shall be carried out consistently overtime);
5) The net delta corresponding to the total holding in foreign currency and gold options;
6) The market value of other derivatives based on financial instruments in foreign currency or gold;
7) Other off-balance sheet commitments; and
8) The net position (long or short) in each currency and in gold shall be converted into SAR in accordance with Article 47 of these Rules.

(b) If an Authorized Person conducts activities abroad through a company that is a part of its financial group or through participating undertakings, profits shall continuously be taken into account when calculating the position (after deductions for taxes in accordance with applicable national tax rates for that company or the participating undertaking) in the relevant currency.

Step 2: Total Net Position in Other Foreign Currencies

After completing Step 1, the converted long net positions in other foreign currencies (excluding position in the United States dollar (USD) and the currencies of the members of the Cooperation Council for the Arab States of the Gulf (GCC currencies), closely correlated currencies and currencies covered by a legally binding exchange rate) shall be aggregated. The sum of the short net positions in other foreign currencies (excluding position in the USD and the GCC currencies, closely correlated currencies and currencies covered by a legally binding exchange rate) shall be calculated in the same way.The higher of these sums shall be the Authorized Person's total net other foreign currencies position.

27.14.2 Chapter 2: Calculating the Capital Requirement

Section 2

(a) With regard to positions in USD and the GCC currencies, a capital requirement corresponding to 2% shall be multiplied by the higher of the sum of the net short or the net long position of these currencies.

(b) With regard to matched positions in closely correlated currencies, a capital requirement corresponding to 7% of the value of the matched position may be applied. A pair of currencies are only to be treated as closely correlated if the likelihood of a loss – calculated on the basis of daily exchange rate data for the preceding three or five years – occurring on equal and opposite positions in such currencies over the following 10 working days, which is 4% or less of the value of the matched position in question (valued in terms of the reporting currency) has a probability of at least 99%, when an observation period of three years is used, or 95%, when an observation period of five years is used. Unmatched positions in closely correlated currencies shall be treated in the same way as other foreign currencies.

(c) In addition to what is mentioned in paragraph (b) of this Section, a lower capital requirement may be applied for currencies covered by a legally binding exchange rate.The capital requirement for matched positions in such currencies shall comprise of half of the maximum permitted exchange rate fluctuation variation set by the governments in question for the currencies. Unmatched positions in currencies covered by a legally binding exchange rate shall be treated in the same way as other foreign currencies.

(d) The capital requirement on unmatched positions in closely correlated currencies, unmatched currencies covered a by legally binding exchange rate and all positions in other foreign currencies, shall be 14%, multiplied by the higher of the sum of the net short or the net long positions in those currencies as calculated in Step 2 under Section 1 of this Annex after the removal of all positions in USD and the GCC currencies pursuant to paragraph (a) of this Section, matched positions in closely correlated currencies pursuant to paragraph (b) of this Section and matched positions in currencies covered by a legally binding exchange rate pursuant to paragraph (c) of this Section.

27.14.3 Chapter 3: Options

Section 3

(a) Options based on currencies shall be treated as combined long and short positions. Both positions shall be converted into delta-weighted positions by multiplying the notional amounts in each currency by the option's delta value. The net delta in a currency is calculated as the net of the delta-weighted short and long positions in that currency in accordance with Section 1 of this Annex.

(b) If the exchange which lists the options does not publish the delta values of the options, or if they are over the counter options, the Authorized Person shall calculate the delta values of its options.

(c) An Authorized Person shall have systems in place and apply protective measures that take sufficient account of other risks associated with options trading, such as:

1) The sensitivity of the delta value to price changes in the underlying financial instrument (gamma);
2) The sensitivity of the option price to changes in maturity (theta);
3) The sensitivity of the option price to changes in standard deviation (vega), and
4) The sensitivity of the option price to changes in the risk-free interest rates (rho) in both countries.

27.14.4 Chapter 4: Investment Funds

Section 4

If the Authorized Person is aware of all currency positions included in the investment fund, these shall be included in the calculation of the net position and total net position in accordance with Article 48 of these Rules. The netting of such currency positions against other currency positions may be carried out in accordance with Chapter 1 of Annex 5.

Section 5

If the Authorized Person is not aware of all of the currency positions included in the investment fund, the Authorized Person shall use the following method:

1) The Authorized Person shall assume that the investment fund's currency position is the maximum currency exposure that it can have by law and under investment fund's terms conditions;

2) The Authorized Person shall then take into consideration whether the investment fund uses derivatives to leverage investments by increasing the currency position in accordance with point 1 of this Section proportionally to the leverage; and

3) The currency position calculated in this way shall be treated as a separate currency and may not be netted against another currency.

Section 6

The fund manager may calculate the currency positions in the investment fund, provided that the Authorized Person ensures that the manager can carry out the calculations in accordance with that set out in this Chapter.The netting of such currency positions against other currency positions may be carried out in accordance with the rules in Article 48 of these Rules.

27.14.5 Chapter 5: Composite Currencies

Section 7

Net positions in composite currencies or baskets of currencies may be distributed across the component currencies following the quotas of these currencies in force. Alternatively, such currencies may be treated as one currency. Authorized Persons shall apply either of these methods consistently overtime.

27.14.6 Chapter 6: Collateral in a Third Country's Currency

Section 8

If a claim denominated in foreign currency is classified as doubtful according to the Authority's Regulations and Rules on financial reporting and the collateral for such a claim is denominated in a third country's currency, the calculation of the position shall be based on the currency in which the collateral is denominated. The calculation of positions with regard to current claims shall be based on the lending currency.

27.14.7 Chapter 7: Exceptions

Section 9

If an Authorized Person has hedged the exchange rate for a result or forecast result in another Authorized Person within the same financial group, the Authorized Person may take into consideration both the exchange rate hedge and the other Authorized Person's result or forecast result when calculating the net position. However this applies only to results or forecast results in the current financial year.

Section 10

(a) Any positions which an Authorized Person has deliberately taken to hedge against the adverse effect of the exchange rate on its capital adequacy ratio may, on obtaining the Authority's approval, be excluded from the calculation of net open currency positions. Such positions shall not be positions held with trading intent, but long term positions used to hedge structural foreign exchange rate risks. Ever y change in the conditions for excluding such positions requires the approval of the Authority.

(b) In addition to what has been mentioned in paragraph (a) of this Section, on obtaining the approval of the Authority, such structural positions comprised of units/equity in companies that are a part of the Authorized Person's financial group and/or in which the Authorized Person has a participating undertaking and which shall be deducted from the capital may be exempted. In order for the structural positions to be exempted from the calculation of the open net position, they must be treated consistently.

27.15 ANNEX 6: Commodities Risk

Chapter 1: Calculating Positions and Netting Long and Short Positions

Section 1

(a) Forwards and options shall be treated as combined long and short positions.

(b) A long (purchased) position in a forward or option shall be treated as a combination of:

1) A long position made up of underlying commodities or financial instruments in the contract; and

2) A short position corresponding to a zero coupon bond for which the forward price for forwards or the exercise price of options comprises the amount due of the bond and has a maturity date on the deliver y date or exercise date for the contract.

(c) A short (sold) position in a forward or option shall be treated as a combination of:

1) A short position comprised of underlying financial instruments in the contract; and

2) A long position corresponding to a zero coupon bond, for which the forward price for forwards or the exercise price of options comprises the amount due of the bond and has a maturity date on the deliver y date or exercise date for the contract.

(d) Long and short positions deriving from an option shall be delta-weighted in accordance with Section 4 of this Annex.

(e) A zero coupon bond deriving from the partition of derivatives into a long and a short position shall be considered to be issued by a government which qualifies for credit quality step 1, or is assigned a risk weight of 0% in non-trading activities.

(f) When calculating specific and general risk, the zero coupon bond shall be considered to be an interest rate linked financial instrument and treated in accordance with Annex 2.

Section 2

Commodity forwards and forward commitments to buy or sell individual commodities shall be incorporated into the maturity ladder approach as notional amounts in terms of the standard units of measurement and assigned a maturity corresponding to the period until the maturity date.

Section 3

(a) Commodity swaps where one leg of the transaction is a fixed price and the other leg the current market price shall be incorporated into the maturity ladder approach as a series of positions equal to the notional amount of the contract, with each position corresponding to each payment in the swap and slotted into the maturity ladder in accordance with this.The positions are long if an Authorized Person pays a fixed price and receives a floating price and short if the Authorized Person receives a fixed price and pays a floating price.

(b) Each leg of a commodity swap where the legs of the transaction are in different commodities shall be placed in the relevant categor y of commodities in the maturity ladder approach.

Section 4

(a) Options based on commodities or commodity derivatives shall be treated as combined long and short positions in the same way that applies to other derivatives. Both positions shall be converted into delta-weighted positions by multiplying the underlying asset's market value by the option's delta value. The delta-weighted positions may be netted against any offsetting positions in the same underlying commodities.

(b) If the exchange that lists the options does not publish the delta values of the options, or if they are over the counter options, the Authorized Person shall calculate the delta value of its options.

(c) An Authorized Person shall have systems in place and apply protective measures that take sufficient account of other risks associated with options trading, such as:

1) The sensitivity of the delta value to price changes in the underlying financial instrument (gamma);

2) The sensitivity of the option price to changes in maturity (theta);

3) The sensitivity of the option price to changes in standard deviation (vega); and

4) The sensitivity of the option price to changes in the risk-free interest rate (rho).

Section 5

To the extent permitted by the Authority, Authorized Persons that transfer or guarantee the title of commodities in a repurchase agreement and lend commodities in a commodities lending agreement shall include such positions when calculating the capital requirement for commodities risk.

27.15.1 Chapter 2: The Maturity-Based Method

Section 6

When the maturity-based method is used to calculate the capital requirement for commodities risk, the steps below shall be followed for each individual commodity.

Step 1: All positions in a commodity and positions which, in accordance with Article 50 of these Rules, are considered positions in the same commodity shall be expressed in terms of the standard units of measurement (barrel, kWh, kg, etc.).

Step 2: Long and short net positions in a commodity are calculated in accordance with that prescribed in paragraph (d) of Article 50 of these Rules.

Step 3: The long and short net positions in the commodity are multiplied by the spot price and placed in the relevant maturity band in the Table 22 below. Physical stocks of commodities shall be assigned to the first maturity band.

Table 22

Maturity band
$0 \leq 1$ month
$> 1 \leq 3$ months
$> 3 \leq 6$ months
$> 6 \leq 12$ months
$> 1 \leq 2$ years
$> 2 \leq 3$ years
> 3 years

Step 4: Long and short net positions within each maturity band shall be aggregated.

Step 5: Matched long and short positions within a maturity band comprise the matched position within a maturity band. The matched long and short positions in each maturity band are aggregated and multiplied by the spread rate of 2.6%.

Step 6: Unmatched long or short positions in each maturity band comprise the unmatched position within a maturity band. Unmatched long (or short) positions within a maturity band may be moved to a higher maturity band in order to match short (or long) positions in those maturity bands. The portion of an unmatched position within a maturity band moved in order to match positions in a higher maturity band comprises the matched position between two maturity bands. This position is multiplied by a carry rate of 1.1% for each maturity band the position is moved forward.The matched position arising in the higher maturity band due to an opposing position being moved from a lower maturity band is treated in the same way as matched long and short positions in step 5.

Step 7: Remaining long or short positions which cannot be matched within a maturity band or between two maturity bands comprise the unmatched position. This position is multiplied by an outright rate of 26%.The Authorized Person's total capital requirement for commodities risk is calculated by aggregating the capital requirements calculated in steps 5, 6 and 7 for each individual commodity.

Section 7

(a) Authorized Persons may, after receiving approval from the Authority, use the values of the spread rate, carry rate and outright rate set out in Table 23 below instead of those set out in Section 6 of this Annex.

Table 23

	Precious metals (except gold)	Base metals	Agricultural products	Other (incl. energy)
Spread rate (%)	1.0	1.2	1.5	1.5
Carry rate (%)	0.3	0.5	0.6	0.6
Outright rate (%)	8.0	10.0	12.0	15.0

(b) In order to obtain the approval from the Authority referred to in paragraph (a) of this Section, the Authorized Person must:

1) Conduct extensive trading in commodities;

2) Have a diversified commodities portfolio; and

3) Have sound procedures, methods and systems for measuring and monitoring commodities risk.

27.15.2 Chapter 3: The Simple Method

Section 8

When the simple method is used to calculate the capital requirement for an Authorized Person's commodities risk, the following steps shall be applied to each individual commodity.

Step 1: The Authorized Person's net position in the commodity shall be calculated in terms of the standard units of measurement (barrel, MWh, kg, etc.). The net position in each commodity equals the difference between an Authorized Person's long and short net positions in the commodity. Long and short net positions in a commodity are calculated in accordance with that prescribed in paragraph (d) of Article 50 of these Rules.

Step 2: 26% of the net position is multiplied by the spot price.

Step 3: The Authorized Person's gross position in the commodity shall be calculated in terms of the standard units of measurement (barrel, MWh, kg, etc.). The gross position is calculated as the sum of an Authorized Person's long and short net positions in the commodity.

Step 4: 5% of the gross position is multiplied by the spot price. The Authorized Person's total capital requirement for commodities risk is calculated by aggregating the capital requirements calculated in steps 2 and 4 for each individual commodity.

27.16 Annex 7: Large Exposures

27.16.1 Chapter 1: Management Requirements

Section 1

An Authorized Person shall have sound administrative and accounting procedures and adequate internal control procedures for the purpose of identifying and recording all large exposures in order to be able to monitor them using the Authorized Person's own exposure strategy.

Section 2

(a) When an exposure to a client is protected by a third party through a recognizable guarantee or credit derivative, except credit linked notes, the exposure may be treated as if it referred to the third party rather than the client.

(b) If the risk weight for an exposure, when calculating a risk-weighted exposure amount in accordance with the rules for non-trading activities, is determined on the basis of the protection provider, this provider shall be considered as the counterparty also when calculating large exposures.

Chapter 2: Determining Exposure Amounts in non-Trading Activities

Section 3

(a) When determining large exposures, the exposure amount shall be the following:

1) On-balance sheet items shall be taken at the net accounting value;

2) Off-balance sheet commitments shall consist of the nominal amount;

3) Derivatives shall be calculated in accordance with paragraph (d) of Article 23 of these Rules; and

4) Repurchase transactions, margin lending transactions and securities lending or borrowing transactions may be handled in accordance with paragraph (e) of Article 23 of these Rules.

(b) The Authorized Person may, when calculating its exposure amounts, take into account any netting agreements for these exposures.

Chapter 3: Determining Exposure Amounts in the Trading Book

Section 4

An Authorized Person shall calculate exposure to individual clients by aggregating the following items:

1) The sum, if it is positive, of the net positions in interest and equity linked financial instruments issued by the client.The net position in each instrument is calculated in accordance with the methods set out in Section 1 to Section 29 of Annex 2 and Section 47 to Section 53 of Annex 2;

2) Net positions arising due to underwriting commitments in conjunction with issues calculated in accordance with Section 63 of Annex 2; and

3) Exposures in activities exposed to settlement and counterparty risks are calculated in accordance with Section 65 to Section 74 of Annex 2. Exposures arising from transactions not settled on

the due settlement date shall not be multiplied by the factors set out in Section 66 of Annex 2. Transactions that are assigned a capital requirement of zero in accordance with Section 66 of Annex 2 may be exempted when determining large exposures.

Section 5

After a calculation in accordance with Section 4 of this Annex, exposures with regard to individual counterparties shall be aggregated to the group of connected counterparties to which the individual counterparty belongs.

Section 6

Exposures in the form of units in investment funds shall be reported as an exposure to the investment fund.The holdings in various investment funds do not need to be aggregated if they are administered by the same investment fund manager.

27.17 Annex 8: Liquidity Risk

27.17.1 Chapter 1: Identification and Measurement of Liquidity Risk

Section 1

(a) An Authorized Person shall identify and measure their exposure to liquidity risk and its funding needs within and between business lines and currencies.

(b) An Authorized Person that is a part of a financial group shall pay particular attention to, and document, the various legal and operational limitations to freely transfer cash and securities between companies that are part of its financial group.

Section 2

An Authorized Person shall calculate the cost of liquidity and take the costs into account in pricing and performance measurement.The cost of liquidity shall reflect the Authorized Person's current cost of refinancing, for the relevant maturities, and the cost that this entails for the Authorized Person to keep a liquidity reserve in accordance with Section 15 of this Annex.

Section 3

An Authorized Person shall use several customized risk measures and ratios to calculate the liquidity risk in a comprehensive manner.The Authorized Person must have a forward looking perspective on liquidity risk and assess the balance sheet structure, cash flows, liquidity positions and risks of off-balance. Risk measures and ratios shall identify vulnerabilities in normal operations and during periods of stress. Measurement procedures shall, where appropriate, distinguish between liquidity risks in different currencies.

Section 4

(a) An Authorized Person shall calculate the cash flows expected to arise when all assets, liabilities and off-balance sheet items are settled. Cash flows will be allocated to the different time intervals in which they are normally expected to occur. Cash inflows from assets in the liquidity reserve in accordance with Section 15 of this Annex shall be attributed to the time interval in which the asset at the earliest can be converted into cash.

(b) The Authorized Person shall in the cash flow calculation use daily intervals. If, having regard to the Authorized Person's size of business, it is not appropriate and reasonable to use the daily time intervals, the Authorized Person shall use at least seven time intervals: one day, more than one day up to one week, more than a week up to a month, more than one month up to three months; more than three months up to six months, more than six months up to a year, more than a year.

(c) The time intervals referred to in paragraph (b) of this Section shall be mutually exclusive and collectively exhaustive (MECE principle).

(d) For each time interval, the Authorized Person must calculate the net cash flow as the sum of expected cash outflows less the sum of expected cash inflows. The Authorized Person will then accumulate net cash flow over all time intervals to show how long it has a positive cash flow.

Section 5

(a) An Authorized Person shall, when calculating expected cash flows, distinguish contracted cash flows with fixed payment dates from such cash flows for which the payment dates and the size of payments is controlled by the Authorized Person's own decisions, customer behavior or market trends. In cases where customer behavior or market trend is the basis for the calculation of expected cash flows, the calculation shall be based on empirical observations.

(b) The Authorized Person shall ensure that the methods and assumptions used to calculate the expected cash flows are relevant.

Section 6

An Authorized Person shall also measure its structural liquidity risk.The Authorized Person shall calculate and overtime, follow the appropriate ratios from the balance sheet in order to highlight the financial structure and specific elements of the Authorized Person's liquidity risk.

Section 7

(a) An Authorized Person shall be well prepared to manage their liquidity under conditions that deviate from normal conditions. The Authorized Person shall carry out regular stress tests to identify and measure liquidity risk under different scenarios and make sure that the Authorized Person's current exposure to liquidity risk is consistent with the established risk tolerance.

(b) The Authorized Person shall develop appropriate scenarios based on their current risk profile. The scenarios shall be based on varying degrees of stress and duration and cover both the idiosyncratic as well as market related problems. Problems shall be illustrated both individually and in combination with each other.The stress tests shall take into account the evolution of liquidity and the need for intraday liquidity for time critical payments.

Section 8

(a) The Authorized Person shall design its stress tests based on its own and customers' risk exposure and the focus and complexity. The Authorized Person shall conduct market-wide stress tests based on assumptions about the erosion of market values of certain assets and a general deterioration in the conditions of market financing.

(b) The Authorized Person shall regularly review the assumptions underlying the stress test scenarios used, to ensure that they are relevant.

Section 9

An Authorized Person shall use the results of stress tests to adjust their strategies, policies and positions.The results of stress tests shall be coordinated with the Authorized Person's risk tolerance.

Section 10

An Authorized Person that is apart of a financial group shall consider its role and position in the group for the purposes of Section 7 to Section 9 of this Annex.

27.17.2 Chapter 2: Liquidity Risk Management

Section 11

An Authorized Person's long-term plan for the Authorized Person to meet its payment obligations (liquidity policy) shall include:

1) How liquidity management shall be organized;
2) How the assets and liabilities are put together ;
3) The distribution of various maturities and currencies;
4) Transfer of liquidity among different countries;
5) The use of borrowing instruments;
6) Possession of realizable assets; and
7) Preparedness for uneven intraday cash flows.

Section 12

(a) An Authorized Person shall in a long term plan for its future financing (financing strategy) seek to ensure that there is a sufficient degree of diversification of funding sources with regard to the appropriate number and type of counterparties, type of financial instruments, secured and unsecured borrowings, maturities, currencies and geographic markets.

(b) The Authorized Person will attend its chosen funding markets and ensure that they have a strong relationship with its funders to promote effective diversification of its sources of funding. The Authorized Person shall identify the key factors that affect the ability to raise financing and closely monitor these factors to ensure that the estimated financing ability is still valid under various possible circumstances.

Section 13

An Authorized Person shall manage their intraday liquidity positions and associated risks so that it can meet its payment and settlement obligations in various currencies and in different payment systems. The Authorized Person shall meet its commitments on time, both during normal times or emergency and shall specifically identify and prioritize the most critical obligations.The Authorized Person must also take account of such obligations that may arise in its role as a custodian.

Section 14

(a) An Authorized Person shall manage their collateral and oversee those of its subsidiaries with respect to jurisdiction and currency exposure. The Authorized Person must differentiate between assets that are utilized as collateral and other assets.

(b) The Authorized Person shall learn about the securities eligible as collateral for major counterparties and financiers of secured borrowing in the private market. A market value of securities shall be adjusted using an appropriate haircut.

(c) The Authorized Person must follow the location of the available securities to ensure that these securities may be used to provide liquidity.

Section 15

(a) An Authorized Person shall keep a separate pool of high quality liquid assets that can be used to secure the Authorized Person's short-term ability to pay for loss or reduced access to commonly available sources. The assets of the liquidity reserve may not be utilized as collateral. The size of the liquidity reserve shall be such that it is possible for an Authorized Person to withstand a severe liquidity strain, without having to change its business model.

(b) The liquidity reserve referred to in paragraph (a) of this Section shall consist of such assets that liquidity can be created in a short time at predictable values.The liquidity reserve shall consist of assets that are both liquid in private markets and that allows financing with central banks.

(c) An Authorized Person shall satisfy itself that there are no barriers to using reserve funds for short term financing.

(d) An Authorized Person shall, in determining the size and location of its financial group's liquidity reserve, take into account the degree to which companies that are part of its financial group shall be self-sufficient in liquidity and the extent of liquidity support to these companies.

(e) An Authorized Person with liquidity risk in different currencies shall where possible, allocate the liquidity in relevant currencies in order to avoid potential interference in the swap markets.

Section 16

An Authorized Person shall evaluate what other measures might create liquidity in a near future without that the Authorized Person needs to change its business model.

Section 17

(a) An Authorized Person shall set limits to control its exposure to liquidity risk. The limits shall be reviewed periodically and adjusted as circumstances or the governing body's risk tolerance change. The choice of the limits imposed by the Authorized Person shall be selected according to the methods it uses to measure liquidity risk and is therefore a consequence of the nature, scope and complexity.

(b) The Authorized Person shall under normal circumstances use the exposure limits in the current management of liquidity within and across business units and legal entities. Such a limit structure must also ensure that the Authorized Person can continue to act during times of market stress, business stress and a combination thereof.

(c) An Authorized Person shall have a procedure for the allocation of limits referred to in paragraph (a) of this Section. A decision scheme shall include details of how, by whom and to who limit excesses are reported and documented. It must also clarify whether and under what conditions limits can be redistributed and the steps to be taken for breaches of limits.

Section 18

An Authorized Person shall identify and use internal Authorized Person-specific indicators of liquidity risk and, where possible, market-related indicators that provides early warning of negative trends and increased risk.

Section 19

(a) An Authorized Person shall have a contingency plan for liquidity crises.

(b) The contingency plan for liquidity crises shall contain clear instructions for how it shall

respond to crisis situations involving different time horizons (options) to overcome liquidity shortage.The plan shall outline the measures to deal with various crises and contain definitions for events that trigger the application of any of the various policy options.The contingency plan shall be periodically tested and updated on the basis of such results of stress tests.

Section 20

An Authorized Person that is a part of a financial group shall consider its role and position in the group for the purposes of Section 19 of this Annex.

27.18 ANNEX 9: INTERNAL CAPITAL ASSESSMENT

27.18.1 Chapter 1: Internal Capital Adequacy Assessment Process (ICAAP)

Section 1

The purpose of Pillar II is to ensure that Authorized Persons have sufficient capital to support all material risks to which their business exposes them. It shall therefore reinforce the link between the risks and the capital, so that the Authorized Person's risk management strategy, approaches and systems are integrated with its capital planning.Authorized Persons are expected to develop and use sound risk management techniques in monitoring and measuring all their risks.

Section 2

(a) Each Authorized Person is responsible for its ICAAP, and for setting internal capital targets that are consistent with its risk profile and operating environment. The ICAAP should be tailored to the Authorized Person's circumstances and needs, and it should use the inputs and definitions that the Authorized Person normally uses for internal purposes.

(b) The Authorized Person should be able to demonstrate how the ICAAP meets super visor y requirements. Authorized Persons retain full responsibility for their ICAAP regardless of the degree of outsourcing, as outsourcing does not relieve Authorized Persons from the need to ensure that their ICAAP fully reflects their specific situation and individual risk profile.

Section 3

(a) The responsibility for initiating and designing the ICAAP rests with the executive management. The governing body should approve the conceptual design (at a minimum, the scope, general methodology and objectives) of the ICAAP.

(b) The executive management is responsible for integrating capital planning and capital management into the Authorized Person's overall risk management culture and approach. They should ensure that capital planning and management policies and procedures are communicated, implemented and supported by sufficient authority and resources.

(c) The Authorized Person's ICAAP (that is the methodologies, assumptions and procedures) and capital policy should be formally documented and written, and it should be reviewed and approved by the governing body.

Section 4

The ICAAP should form an integral part of Authorized Persons' management processes so as to enable the governing body to assess, on an on-going basis, the risks that are inherent in their activities and material to the Authorized Person. This could range from using the ICAAP to allocate capital to business units orto having it play a role in the individual business decision process.

Section 5

(a) The Authorized Person shall ensure that risks are covered adequately and that capital coverage reflects the actual risk profile of the Authorized Person.This review should take place at least annually.

(b) The ICAAP and its review process should be subject to independent internal review. Any changes in the Authorized Person's strategic focus, business plan, operating environment or other factors that materially affect assumptions or methodologies used in the ICAAP should initiate appropriate adjustments to the ICAAP. New risks that occur in the business of the Authorized Person should be identified and incorporated into the ICAAP.

Section 6

(a) The adequacy of an Authorized Person's capital is a function of its risk profile. The Authorized Person should set capital targets that are consistent with their risk profile and operating environment.

(b) Authorized Persons may take other considerations into account in deciding how much capital to hold, such as external rating goals, market reputation and strategic goals. However, the Authorized Person in this case shall be able to explain to the Authority how those considerations have influenced its decisions concerning the amount of capital to hold.

(c) The focus of the ICAAP for less readily quantifiable risks should be more on qualitative assessment, risk management and mitigation. The Authorized Person should clearly establish for which risks a quantitative measure is warranted, and for which risks a qualitative measure is the correct risk mitigation tool.

(d) Authorized Persons that take a Pillar I approach as the starting point for their ICAAP may also consider developing a fully risk based approach.

Section 7

(a) The ICAAP should capture all the material risks to which the Authorized Person is exposed, albeit that there is no standard categorization of risk types and definition of materiality. The Authorized Person may use its own terminology and definitions,

albeit that it should be able to explain these in detail to the Authority, including the methods used, the coverage of all material risks and how its approach relates to its obligations under Pillar I.

(b) The ICAAP should cover the following:

1) Pillar I risks, including major differences between the treatment of Pillar I risks in the calculation of capital base requirements and their treatment under the ICAAP;

2) Pillar II risks, such as concentration risk, liquidity risk, reputation and strategic risk. Some of these risks are less likely to lend themselves to quantitative approaches, in which cases Authorized Persons are expected to employ more qualitative methods of assessment and mitigation; and

3) Risk factors external to the Authorized Person. These include risks that may arise from the regulatory, economic or business environment and which are not included in the risks mentioned in 1 and 2 above.

Section 8

(a) The ICAAP should take into account the Authorized Person's strategic plans and how they relate to macroeconomic factors.The Authorized Person should develop an internal strategy for maintaining capital levels that can incorporate factors such as business growth expectations, future sources and uses of funds and dividend policy.

(b) The Authorized Person should have an explicit, approved capital plan, which states the Authorized Person's objectives and the time horizon for achieving those objectives, and in broad terms the capital planning process and the responsibilities for that process.The plan should state the following:

1) How the Authorized Person will comply with capital requirements in the future;

2) Any relevant limits related to capital; and

3) A general contingency plan for dealing with divergences and unexpected events (for example, raising additional capital, restricting business, or using risk mitigation techniques).

(c) Authorized Persons should conduct appropriate stress tests which take into account, for example, the risks specific to the jurisdiction(s) in which they operate and the particular stage of the business cycle. Authorized Persons should analyze the impact that new legislation, the actions of competitors or other factors may have on their performance, in order to determine what changes in the environment they could sustain.

Section 9

The ICAAP should produce a reasonable overall capital number and assessment. The Authorized Person should be able to explain to the Authority the similarities and differences between its ICAAP (which should cover all material risks) and its capital base requirements under Pillar I.

27.18.2 Chapter 2: Strategies on How to Reach and Maintain Capital Targets

Section 10

The ICAAP shall take into account the Authorized Person's strategic plans and how they relate to macroeconomic factors. The Authorized Person shall develop an internal strategy for maintaining capital levels that can incorporate factors such as business growth expectations, future sources and uses of funds and dividend policy.

Section 11

In designing an ICAAP, the Authorized Person must address core issues and define its general strategic conditions based on its fundamental attitude toward risk and risk management.The result of this process is the Authorized Person's risk strategy, which shall be documented in writing.The scope and level of detail of this strategy depend on the size, complexity and risk levels of the specific Authorized Person, but a concise strategic outline shall be preferred over an excessively long description.

Section 12

Every Authorized Person is characterized by a fundamental attitude toward risk and risk management. This basic attitude manifests itself in the Authorized Person's risk policy principles, its risk appetite, its (current and planned) risk structure as well as the structure and positioning of risk management within the Authorized Person.These elements already exist in every Authorized Person, for example, in the existing organization or in the instruments used for risk management.

27.18.3 Chapter 3: Self-Assessment and Stress Testing

Section 13

(a) Authorized Persons shall, if possible, conduct appropriate stress tests and self- assessment which take into account, for example, the risks specific to the jurisdiction(s) in which they operate and the particular stage of the business cycle. Authorized Persons shall analyze the impact that new legislation, the actions of competitors or other factors may have on their performance, in order to determine what changes in the environment they could sustain.

(b) The stressed scenarios shall be developed by the Authorized Persons, reflecting the risk factors that affect their specific business. However, the Authority also has the right to develop generic stressed scenarios that the Authorized Persons must assess its risks according to.

27.19 ANNEX 10: Disclosure

27.19.1 Chapter 1: Disclosure Regarding Authorized Person And Financial Group

Section 1

An Authorized Person shall, when it discloses information in accordance with these Rules, state its full name and Authorized Person license number.

Section 2

If an Authorized Person is part of a financial group, the Authorized Person shall describe the organizational structure of the financial group.

Section 3

An Authorized Person shall describe its objective and guidelines for risk management for each individual risk category.The information shall include:

1) Strategies and processes for risk management;

2) How the risk management and compliance function is organized and structured;

3) The scope and nature of risk reporting and measurement systems; and

4) The guidelines for hedging and mitigating risk and the strategies and procedures the Authorized Person has to monitor the continuing effectiveness of hedges and mitigations of risks.

27.19.2 Chapter 2: Disclosure regarding Capital Base

Section 4

An Authorized Person shall disclose a summary of the terms and conditions that apply to all capital items and components thereof.

Section 5

(a) An Authorized Person shall disclose the amount of the capital base pursuant to Article 4 of these Rules with separate disclosure of all capital base items and deductions.

(b) The Authorized Person shall also submit information about the deductions made from Tier-1 capital and Tier-2 capital so as not to exceed the threshold values set out in these Rules.The Authorized Person shall also submit information concerning total eligible capital base, net of deductions and threshold values, in accordance with these Rules.

Section 6

An Authorized Person shall disclose all current or foreseen material or legal impediments to the prompt transfer of capital or repayment of liabilities between the Authorized Person and its subsidiaries.

Chapter 3: Disclosure Regarding Capital Requirements

Section 7

An Authorized Person shall state whether the requirements for the minimum level for capital are fulfilled and report its strategies and methods for valuing and maintaining capital requirement in accordance with these Rules.

Section 8

An Authorized Person shall summarize its strategy and approach for assessing the adequacy of its internal capital to support current and future activities.

Section 9

An Authorized Person shall disclose information regarding the capital requirement for:

1) Risks in the trading book;
2) Risks in non-trading activities;
3) Operational risk;
4) Foreign exchange rate risk; and
5) Commodity risk.

27.19.3 Chapter 4: Disclosure Regarding non-Trading Activities

Section 10

An Authorized Person shall submit the following information concerning its credit risk exposures:

1) The definitions in accordance with the external accounts of past due claims and impaired liabilities; and

2) Information concerning the approaches adopted to determine impairments and specific provisions.

Section 11

An Authorized Person shall disclose the total amount of all exposures, in accordance with the applicable accounting regulations, after offsets but without taking into account the effects of credit risk mitigation, and the average amount of the exposures over the period broken down by different types of exposure classes.

Section 12

An Authorized Person shall disclose information broken down by significant industries and counterparty type, concerning:

1) Impaired exposures and past due exposures, provided separately;

2) Impairments and specific provisions; and

3) Charges for impairments and specific provisions during the last financial year.

Section 13

(a) A report for changes in impairments and specific provisions for impaired exposures shall be submitted separately.This information shall include:

1) Opening balances;
2) The amounts impaired or reversed during the report period;
3) The amounts set aside or reversed for estimated probable losses on exposures during the report period, any other adjustments including those determined by exchange rate differences, business combinations, acquisitions and disposals of subsidiaries and transfers between provisions; and
4) Closing balances.

(b) Specific provisions and recoveries recorded directly to the income statement shall be stated separately.

Section 14

Where credit risk protection is utilized to decrease the capital requirement, the Authorized Person shall disclose the following:

1) The policies and processes for, and indication of the extent to which it makes use of, on and off-balance sheet netting;

2) The policies and processes for collateral valuation and management;

3) A description of the most important types of collateral accepted by the Authorized Person;

4) Information on the most important types of guarantor and credit derivative counterparties and their creditworthiness; and

5) Information about market or credit risk concentrations within the credit risk mitigation taken.

Section 15

(a) An Authorized Person shall, separately for each exposure class, indicate the total exposure amount that is covered by eligible collateral.

(b) The exposure amount shall, where relevant, be calculated after netting on and off- balance sheet as well as after application of volatility adjustments.

Section 16

(a) An Authorized Person shall indicate the total exposure value that is covered by guarantees or credit derivatives separately for each exposure class.

(b) The exposure amount shall, where relevant, be calculated after netting on and off- balance sheet as well as after application of volatility adjustments.

Section 17

Each Authorized Person shall submit information concerning all exposure classes. The information shall include the following:

1) Names of the credit rating agencies used and the reasons for any changes;

2) The exposure classes for which each credit rating agency are used;

3) A description of the process used to transfer the issuer and to issue credit ratings onto non-trading activities items;

4) The mapping between the credit rating from each credit rating agency with the credit quality steps in regards to non-trading activities.This information need not be disclosed if the Authorized Person uses ratings from credit rating agencies mentioned in Annex 11 and Annex 12; and

5) Exposure amounts before and after credit risk protection associated with each credit quality step in regards to non-trading activities, as well as the exposure amounts that are deducted from capital.

27.19.4 Chapter 5: Disclosure Regarding Liquidity Risk

Section 18

An Authorized Person shall regularly publish such information as in Section 19 and Section 20 of this Annex which means that market participants can assess the Authorized Person's ability to manage liquidity risk and its liquidity position on an informed manner.

Section 19

An Authorized Person shall describe in the public information both the strategy and guidelines for its liquidity risk management, and how the function of liquidity risk management is organized, including the scope and nature of risk reporting and risk measurement systems involved.The Authorized Person shall also describe the stress tests conducted and how the Authorized Person's contingency plan is designed.

Section 20

An Authorized Person shall disclose quantitative information on their liquidity positions, making it possible for market participants to get an idea of its liquidity risk.The Authorized Person shall at least provide information on the size and composition of its liquidity reserves, the size and distribution of funding sources and the values of the various risk measures and ratios, which are periodically reported to the Authority. The Authorized Person shall provide sufficient qualitative information on the use of ratios and risk measures so that market participants can understand them.

27.19.5 Chapter 6: Disclosure Regarding Counterparty Risk

Section 21

An Authorized Person shall provide a description of:

1) The methodology used to assign internal capital and credit limits for counterparty risk exposures;

2) The policies for securing collateral and establishing credit reserves; and

3) The policies for the Authorized Person's wrong-way risk exposures.

Section 22

An Authorized Person shall also provide a description of the methodology used to calculate the risk exposure amount for counterparty risk.

Section 23

Information concerning counterparty risk shall include:

1) The impact of the amount of collateral the Authorized Person would have to provide following a downgrade in the Authorized Person's credit rating;
2) The notional value of credit derivative hedges;
3) The gross positive fair value of contract;
4) Netting benefits;
5) Netted current credit exposure;
6) Held collateral; and
7) Net derivative credit exposures.

Section 24

An Authorized Person shall provide information concerning its credit derivative transactions (notional values). The information shall be divided among transactions that are used in own credit portfolios and intermediation activities to assist client needs. The Authorized Person shall furthermore provide information about the distribution of the type of credit derivative products used, broken down further by protection bought and sold within each product group.

27.19.6 Chapter 7: Disclosure Regarding Operational Risk

Section 25

An Authorized Person shall disclose which method that is used to calculate the capital requirements for operational risk.

27.19.7 Chapter 8: Periodic Disclosure

Section 26

Periodic disclosure information shall as a minimum include the following information concerning capital:

1) The amount of Tier-1 capital;
2) The amount of Tier-2 capital;
3) The amount of an alternative determination of capital;
4) Deductions and threshold values in accordance with these Rules; and
5) Total capital, net after deductions and threshold values in accordance with these Rules.

Section 27

Periodic disclosure information shall as a minimum include the following information about the capital requirement:

1) The capital requirement for non-trading activities;
2) The capital requirement for risks in the trading book;
3) The capital requirement for operational risk;
4) The capital requirement for foreign exchange risk;
5) The capital requirement for commodities risk; and
6) The total minimum capital requirement.

Annex 11: Long-Term Mapping

Credit quality Step	Assessment			
	S & P	Fitch	Moody's	Capital Intelligence
1	AAA to AA-	AAA to AA-	Aaa to Aa3	AAA
2	A+ to A-	A+ to A-	A1 to A3	AA to A
3	BBB+ to BBB-	BBB+ to BBB-	Baa1 to Baa3	BBB
4	BB+ to BB-	BB+ to BB-	Ba1 to Ba3	BB
5	B+ to B-	B+ to B-	B1 to B3	B
6	CCC+ and below	CCC+ and below	Caa1 and below	C and below

Annex 12: Short-Term Mapping

Credit quality step	Assessment			
	S & P	Fitch	Moody's	Capital Intelligence
1	A-1+, A-1	F1+, F1	P-1	A1
2	A-2	F2	P-2	A2
3	A-3	F3	P-3	A3
4	Below A-3	Below F3	Not Prime	Below A3

28 Procedures Guide for Public Consultation on the Implementing Regulations Projects

Issued by the Board of the Capital Market Authority Pursuant to Resolution No. 2-20-2014 dated 09/06/1435H (09/04/2014G) based on the Capital Market Law issued by Royal Decree No. M/30 dated 02/06/1424H as amended by Board Resolution No. 1-109-2018 dated 29/01/1440H (09/10/2018G)

Important Notice: The current version of this Guide, as may be amended, can be found at the Authority website: www.cma.org.sa

Table of Contents

Part 1: General Provisions
Article 1: Preliminary Provisions
Article 2: Definitions
Part 2: Public Consultation
Article 3: Public Consultation
Article 4: Public Consultation Methods
Article 5: Public Consultation Period
Article 6: Receiving Public Comments
Part 3: Publishing Public Comments
Article 7: Publishing Public Comments
Article 8: Participants' Names and Information Confidentiality
Part 4: Entry Into Force
Article 9: Entry Into Force

28.1 PART 1: GENERAL PROVISIONS

28.1.1 Article 1: Preliminary Provisions

a) The purpose of this Guide is to regulate the public consultation process in respect of any implementing regulations project, prior to issuing or amending it.

b) Prior to consulting the public, the Authority shall consult experts in relation to any implementing regulations project prior to issuing or amending it, when needed.

28.1.2 Article 2: Definitions

a) Any reference to the "Capital Market Law" in this Guide shall mean the Capital Market Law issued by the Royal Decree No. M/30 dated 2/6/1424H.

b) Without prejudice to paragraph (c) of this Article, expressions and terms in this Guide have the meaning which they bear in the Capital Market Law and in the Glossary of Defined Terms Used in the Regulations and Rules of the Capital Market Authority, unless the contrary intention appears.

c) For the purpose of implementing this Guide, the following expressions and terms shall have the meaning they bear as follows, unless the contrary intention appears.:

- Public Consultation: A request for public comments on an implementing regulations project.

- Public Comments Report: A report summarizing the comments received by the Authority in relation to an implementing regulations project.

- The Guide: The Procedures Guide for Public Consultation on the Implementing Regulations Projects.

- Public: All who are invited to provide comments on an Implementing Regulations project, including, but not limited to, government entities, authorities, public institutions, the Exchange the Depositary Center, all participating parties in the Exchange including listed joint stock companies, Authorized Persons, investment corporations, private and public funds, professional companies, individual investors and any other person who has access to the Authority's announcement inviting for providing comments on an Implementing Regulations project.

- Implementing Regulations: Rules, instructions and procedures issued by the Authority for the implementation of the provisions of the Capital Market Law or any other law as per the powers vested in the Authority.

- Implementing Regulations Project: Each project that includes issuing or amending an Implementing Regulations.

- Public Comments: Opinions, comments and suggestions related to an Implementing Regulations project, requested or received by the Authority.

- Publishing Public Comments: Publishing the public comments received on an Implementing Regulations project, as specified in Article (7) of this Guide.

28.2 PART 2: PUBLIC CONSULTATION

28.2.1 Article 3: Public Consultation

a) The Authority shall carry out a public consultation in relation to any new Implementing Regulations project prior to issuing it.

b) The Authority shall determine the need to carry out a public consultation in relation to any project related to amending an existing Implementing Regulations, taking into consideration the scope of such amendment and its expected impact.

28.2.2 Article 4: Public Consultation Methods

The public consultation shall be made through the Authority's website, and the available methods for public consultations include the following:

1. Publishing the Implementing Regulations draft on the Authority's website.

2. Publishing a questionnaire to the public that covers the operational and technical aspects of the project.

3. Publishing a public consultation memorandum that summarizes the Implementing Regulations project and contains a list of questions.

4. Any other method as the Authority may specify.

28.2.3 Article 5: Public Consultation Period

The period of public consultation on an Implementing Regulations project shall be (30) calendar days, unless the Authority determines otherwise in line with the nature of the project.

28.2.4 Article 6: Receiving Public Comments

Receiving public comments on an Implementing Regulations project shall be through one of the following channels:

1. The link provided in the announcement inviting for public consultation.

2. The communication channels specified in the announcement inviting for public consultation.

3. Any other channel as the Authority may specify.

28.3 Part 3: PUBLISHING PUBLIC COMMENTS

28.3.1 Article 7: Publishing Public Comments

a) Upon the issuance of a Board resolution to approve the implementing Regulations and the method of publishing the comments received from the public, the Authority shall publish on its website a summary of the major public comments it received in relation to the final draft of the Implementing Regulations project.

b) Publishing the public comments shall be made in any manner the Authority deems appropriate, including, but not limited to, publishing the major comments received from the public in the press release or announcement in which issuance of the relevant Implementing Regulations is announced; publishing the original text of the comments as received by the Authority; or by preparing a public comments report.

28.3.2 Article 8: Participants' Names and Information Confidentiality

The Authority shall, along with publishing the public comments as per Article (7) of this Guide, publish the names and personal information of the participants in the public consultation, unless a participant (natural or legal person) requests not to publish such information, or if the Authority, as the case may be, decides not to publish such person's name or personal information.

28.4 PART 4: ENTRY INTO FORCE

28.4.1 Article 9: Entry Into Force

This Guide shall be effective in accordance to its approval resolution.

29 Rules for Qualified Foreign Financial Institutions Investment in Listed Securities

Issued by the Board of the Capital Market Authority pursuant to its Resolution Number 1-42-2015 dated 15/7/1436H (4/5/2015G) based on the Capital Market Law issued by Royal Decree No. M/30 dated 2/6/1424H as amended by Resolution of the Board of the Capital Market Authority Number 3-65-2019 dated 14/10/1440H (17/6/2019G)

Important Notice: The current version of these Rules, as may be amended, can be found at the Authority website: www.cma.org.sa

TABLE OF CONTENTS

Part 1 : GENERAL PROVISIONS
Article 1: Preliminary
Article 2: Definitions
Article 3: Waivers
Article 4: Right to appeal
Part 2 : APPLICATIONS FOR QUALIFICATION
Chapter One: Qualification conditions
Article 5: Qualification
Article 6: The qualification conditions
Chapter Two: Qualification procedures
Article 7: Application for Qualification
Article 8: Accuracy of information and documents submitted to the assessing Authorized Person Chapter Three: Determination of applications
Article 9: Determination by the Assessing Authorized Person
Article 10 : QFI assessment agreements
Article 11 : Record Keeping
Chapter Four: Further requirements following qualification
Article 12 : Commencement of trading
Annex 2.1 Information and documents for Qualification check
Part 3 : CONTINUING OBLIGATIONS
Article 13: Compliance with laws and regulations
Article 14: Investment limits
Article 15: Authorized persons and foreign portfolio managers engaged with the QFI, and authorization requirements
Article 16: Disclosure requirements
Annex 3.1 Information and documents to be disclosed by QFIs to assessing Authorized Persons
Part 4 : AUTHORIZED PERSONS OBLIGATIONS
Article 17: Obligations of Authorized Persons and their eligibility
Article 18: Monitoring of QFIs
Article 19: Powers of the Authority in relation to Authorized Persons engaged with QFIs
Part 5 : POWERS OF THE AUTHORITY IN RELATION TO QFIs
Article 20: Powers of the Authority in relation to QFIs
Part 6 : CLOSING PROVISIONS Article 21 : Publication and entry into force

29.1 PART 1: GENERAL PROVISIONS

Article 1: Preliminary

a. The purpose of these Rules is to set out the procedures, requirements and conditions for qualifying foreign investors to invest in listed securities, and to specify their obligations and the obligations of Authorized Persons in this regard.

b. These Rules shall be read in conjunction with and in addition to the Capital Market Law and its Implementing Regulations, including, the Rules of Offering Securities and Continuing Obligations , the Market Conduct Regulations, the Authorized Persons Regulations, the Merger and Acquisition Regulations and the Anti-Money Laundering and Counter-Terrorist Financing Rules.

c. Without prejudice to paragraph (e) of Article (15) of these Rules, these Rules shall not apply to Citizens of the Cooperation Council for the Arab States of the Gulf.

d. Qualified foreign investors ("QFIs") are entitled to exercise all rights related to listed securities owned by them, including trading in rights issues.

Article 2: Definitions

a. Any reference to the "Capital Market Law" in these Rules shall mean the Capital Market Law issued by Royal Decree No. M/30 dated 2/6/1424H.

b. Subject to paragraph (c) of this Article, expressions and terms in these Rules have the meaning which they bear in the Capital Market Law and the Glossary of defined terms used in the Regulations and Rules of the Capital Market Authority, unless the contrary intention appears.

c. For the purpose of implementing these Rules, the following expressions and terms shall have the meaning they bear as follows unless the contrary intention appears:

- QFI assessment agreement: an agreement between the Assessing Authorized Person and the QFI meeting the requirements set out in Article (10) of these Rules.

- Bank: a financial institution that has a legal personality which engages in banking business.

- Assessing Authorized Person: an Authorized Person who has agreed with an applicant to assess its application for registration as a QFI, or an Authorized Person who has executed a QFI assessment agreement with a QFI.

- Insurance company: a financial institution that has a legal personality which engages in insurance business.

- Brokerage and securities firm: a financial institution that has a legal personality which engages in securities business, including portfolio managers.

- Investment fund: means any of the following legal persons:

1) a pension fund in which its main objective is to collect fees or periodic contributions from participants or for their interest,

for the purpose of compensating them according to a specific mechanism.

2) Endowment fund with a principal purpose of making grants to organizations, institutions, or individuals for scientific, educational, cultural purposes, including university endowments fund.

3) a collective investment scheme aimed at providing investors therein with an opportunity to participate collectively in the profits of the scheme.

- Authorization Requirement: authorization requirement stated in Article (5) of the Securities Business Regulations.

- Foreign portfolio manager: a foreign financial institution that has a legal personality which manages the assets of clients, that meets the requirements stated in sub paragraph (a/2) of Article (6) of these Rules, which engages or intend to engage with the QFI or the applicant for the purpose of investing on its behalf in listed securities.

- Qualified foreign investor: a qualified foreign investor in accordance with these Rules to invest in listed securities.

- Applicant: a foreign investor that submits an application for qualification to an Assessing Authorized Person.

- Citizens of the Cooperation Council for the Arab States of the Gulf: natural persons who hold the citizenship of one of the Cooperation Council for the Arab States of the Gulf countries, or legal persons that (i) capital of which is majority owned by citizens or governments of the Cooperation Council for the Arab States of the Gulf; and (ii) holding the citizenship of one of the Cooperation Council for the Arab States of the Gulf countries, in accordance with the definition set out in the resolution of the Supreme Council of the Cooperation Council for the Arab States of the Gulf in its 15th session approved by the Council of Ministers Resolution number (16) dated 20/01/1418H.

- Government related entities: central banks, and investment funds -including sovereign funds and funds which take the form of pension and endowments funds- fully owned (directly or indirectly) by a government entity.

Article 3: Waivers The Authority may waive a provision of these Rules in whole or in part as it applies to an applicant, a QFI or an Authorized Person either on an application from any of the aforementioned persons or on the Authority's own initiative.

Article 4: Right to appeal Any person subject to these Rules may appeal to the Committee in respect of any decision or action that the Authority takes under these Rules.

29.2 PART 2: APPLICATIONS FOR QUALIFICATION

29.2.1 Chapter One: Qualification conditions

Article 5: Qualification An applicant may not be qualified as a QFI unless it meets each of the conditions prescribed by Article(6) of these Rules.

Article 6: The Qualification Conditions

a. Type of the financial institution

1) The applicant must be a financial institution that has a legal personality which falls within one of the following types:

a) Banks;

b) Brokerage and securities firms;

c) Insurance companies.

d) Government and government related entities.

e) Investment funds.

f) Any other financial institution considered eligible by the Authority.

2) The financial institutions referred to in sub-paragraphs a (1), b (1), c (1) of paragraph (a) of this Article must be licensed or otherwise subject to regulatory oversight by a regulatory authority and incorporated in a jurisdiction that applies regulatory and monitoring standards equivalent to those of the Authority or acceptable to it.

3) The financial institutions referred to in sub-paragraphs d (1) and e (1) of paragraph (a) of this Article must be incorporated in a jurisdiction that applies regulatory and monitoring standards equivalent to those of the Authority or acceptable to it.

4) For the purposes of this Article, the Authority may, at its absolute discretion, determine whether the regulatory and monitoring standards are equivalent to those of the Authority or acceptable to it, and the Authority shall provide Authorized Persons duly authorized to conduct custody or dealing activities with a list of jurisdictions that applies regulatory and monitoring standards equivalent to those of the Authority or acceptable to it, and any update occurs to that list.

5) The affiliates of a QFI or a foreign portfolio manager who meets the requirements stated in paragraph (b) of this Article, and the managed funds by them, shall be considered as a qualified foreign investor without applying for a separate application conditioned by meeting paragraph (a) of this article.

b. Size of the financial institution

1) With the exception of sub paragraph d (1) of paragraph (a) of this Article, the applicant must have assets under management or custody of SAR 1,875,000,000 one billion eight hundred and seventy five million Saudi Riyals (or an equivalent amount) or more. And the Authority may reduce these assets.

2) For the purposes of these Rules, assets under management include:

a) Assets owned by the applicant or its group for the purpose of investment; and in relation to the financial institution referred to in sub paragraph e (1) of paragraph (a) of this Article, including assets owned by the foreign portfolio manager or its group, for the purpose of investment.

b) Assets managed by the applicant or its group for the account of another person or persons, and in relation to the financial institution referred to in sub paragraph e (1) of paragraph (a) of this Article, including assets owned by the foreign portfolio manager or it's group, for the account of another person or persons.

29.2.2 Chapter Two: Qualification procedures

Article 7: Application for Qualification
a. An application for qualification must be made to an Assessing Authorized Person accompanied by the information and documents needed to prove the fulfillment of qualification conditions, as the Assessing Authorized Person can use the guidance list provided in Annex 2.1 paragraph (1) of these Rules or other documents proving the fulfillment of qualification conditions.

b. The Assessing Authorized Person must assess the application in accordance with the criteria and procedures set out in Chapter Three of this Part.

Article 8: Accuracy of information and documents submitted to the Assessing Authorized Person All information and documents submitted by the applicant to the Assessing Authorized Person must be complete, clear, accurate and not misleading.

29.2.3 Chapter Three: Determination of Applications

Article 9: Determination by the Assessing Authorized Person
a. The Assessing Authorized Person must not accept the application until after conducting the following:

1) Ensuring that the application complies with the requirements prescribed by these Rules; and
2) Ensuring that the applicant meets the applicable qualification conditions prescribed by these Rules.

b. The Assessing Authorized Person must provide the foreign investor with a written notice of its determination upon his request. Where the Assessing Authorized Person has rejected the application, the notice shall include a statement of the reasons for its determination. And if the Assessing Authorized Person has accepted the application, it shall submit to the foreign investor a written declaration with a minimum of the following:

1. Confirming that the applicant meets the qualification conditions stated in these Rules.
2. Confirming that the Assessing Authorized Person has conducted all of the customer due diligence checks required by the Capital Market Law and its Implementing Regulations, including preparing ("KYC") form, as required by the Anti-Money Laundering and Counter- Terrorist Financing Rules issued by the Board of the Capital Market Authority.
3. The Assessing Authorized Person declaring that the draft form of Qualified Foreign Investor Assessment Agreement meets the minimum requirements specified by Article (10) of these Rules.

c. The Assessing Authorized Person must accept the QFI as a client in accordance with the Authorized Persons Regulations

Article 10: QFI Assessment Agreement
a. An Assessing Authorized Person must agree with the applicant on a draft form of QFI assessment agreement meeting the minimum requirements specified in this Article.

b. A QFI assessment agreement must include the following minimum requirements:

1) A representation by the applicant that it meets the qualification conditions stated in these Rules.
2) Disclosure of any suspension or revocation by a regulatory authority of any license or permission in any jurisdiction or the imposition by a regulatory authority of any restriction or condition upon any such license or permission, If no suspension or revocation by a regulatory authority of any license or permission currently imposed on the applicant, a declaration by the applicant to this effect.
3) An undertaking by the applicant to provide the Assessing Authorized Person with all information and documents required under these Rules;
4) An undertaking by the applicant to notify the Assessing Authorized Person within a reasonable period of time not exceeding 30 days of any event or circumstance requiring such notification under these Rules;
5) A confirmation by the applicant of its consent that the Assessing Authorized Person may disclose to the Authority or the Exchange information or documents which the Assessing Authorized Person receives under these Rules or the Capital Market Law and its Implementing Regulations, and that such information may also be disclosed to other government agencies of the Kingdom in accordance with the relevant laws; and
6) An undertaking by the applicant to abide by the Capital Market Law and its Implementing Regulations and the rules of the Exchange and other relevant laws.

c. All requirements specified in paragraph (b) of this Article must be in such form as the Authority may require.

Article 11: Record-Keeping The Assessing Authorized Person must retain, and make available to the Authority on request, the information and documentation proving the fulfillment of qualification conditions under these Rules, in accordance with Article (16) of the Authorized Persons Regulations.

29.2.4 Chapter Four: Further Requirements Following Qualification

Article 12: Commencement of Trading A QFI may not invest in any listed securities unless it:

1) Holds a client account;
2) Holds an account with the Depositary Center; and
3) Has satisfied any other conditions as may be imposed by the Authority.

29.3 ANNEX 2.1 Information and Documents for Qualification

1. Guidance list for information and documents for applicant's qualification check:

The Assessing Authorized Person can use the guidance list provided below or other information and documents proofing the fulfillment of qualification conditions:

a. Details of the applicant's legal form and jurisdiction of establishment or foreign portfolio managers (if applicable).
b. A list of the QFI's affiliates or foreign portfolio managers that meets the requirements stated in paragraph (b) of Article (6) and their managed funds intends to qualify.
c. In relation to the financial institution referred to in sub paragraphs a (1), b (1), c (1) of paragraph (a) of Article (6), Evidence of the applicant's regulatory status.

d. A copy of the most recent annual report and consolidated accounts of the applicant or its group or the foreign portfolio managers (if applicable).
e. Disclosure of any suspension or revocation by a regulatory authority of any license or permission in any jurisdiction or the imposition by a regulatory authority of any restriction or condition upon any such license or permission, If no suspension or revocation by a regulatory authority of any license or permission currently imposed on the applicant, a declaration by the applicant to this effect.
f. Financial statements prepared and accredited by the applicant's or its group auditors in accordance with accounting standards prescribed by the relevant authorities in the applicant's jurisdiction of establishment.
g. Such other documents or other evidence as may be sufficient to satisfy each of the qualification conditions under these Rules.

2. Information and documents to be provided by applicants under this Rules:

a. A QFI assessment agreement must include the requirements of Article (10) of these Rules.
b. Where an applicant intends to engage with foreign portfolio managers to invest in listed securities, it must provide a list with all foreign portfolio managers intends to engage with.

29.4 PART 3: CONTINUING OBLIGATIONS

Article 13: Compliance with Laws and Regulations A QFI must at all times comply with the applicable provisions stated in the Capital Market Law and its Implementing Regulations, as well as the rules and the regulations of the Exchange and other relevant laws.

Article 14: Investment Limits
a. Investments of QFIs shall be subject to the following limitations:

1) Each QFI, may not own 10% or more of the shares of any issuer whose shares are listed or convertible debt instrument of the issuer.
2) The maximum proportion of the shares of any issuer whose shares are listed or convertible debt instrument of the issuer that may be owned by all foreign investors (in all categories, whether residents or non-residents, except the foreign strategic investors pursuant to the Instructions for the Foreign Strategic Investors' Ownership in Listed Companies) in aggregate is 49%.
3) Other legislative limitations on foreign ownership in joint stock companies.
4) The limitations set forth in the articles of association or by-laws of the listed companies or any instructions issued by the supervisory or regulatory authorities to which these companies are subject.

b. The Exchange shall publish on its website, as determined by the Authority in this regard, the following information:

1) A statistic reflecting the ownership percentages specified in sub-paragraph a (2) of this Article.
2) The limitations specified in sub-paragraphs a (3) and a (4) of this Article, according to the information received by the Exchange from listed companies in this regard.

Article 15: Authorized Persons and Foreign Portfolio Managers Engaged with the QFI, and Authorization Requirements:
a. A QFI must have, for as long as it remains as a QFI, an Assessing Authorized Person engaged by it.

b. For the purposes of these Rules, a QFI has engaged an Assessing Authorized Person if it has executed a QFI assessment agreement with the Assessing Authorized Person and that agreement remains valid and in force.

c. A QFI's qualification shall not be revoked by reason of the lapse or termination by either party of a QFI assessment agreement, provided that the QFI engages a replacement Assessing Authorized Person within 30 days. The replacement Assessing Authorized Person shall without delay notify the Authority in writing of its appointment.

d. If a QFI fails to engage a replacement Assessing Authorized Person within the period prescribed by paragraph (c) of this Article, it must notify the Authority of this fact without delay., whereupon the Authority may either grant an extension or revoke the QFI's qualification.

e. A QFI may engage with Authorized Persons, or foreign portfolio managers, or foreign custodians, or foreign advisors, for the purpose of investing in listed securities.

f. A QFI is excluded from the authorization requirement for carrying on dealing activity, when dealing as principal in listed securities.

g. A QFI and a foreign portfolio manager are excluded from the authorization requirement for carrying on managing activity, when managing listed securities belonging to a QFI.

h. A foreign custodian is excluded from the authorization requirement for carrying on custody activity, when safeguarding listed securities belonging to a QFI.

i. A foreign advisor is excluded from the authorization requirement for carrying on advising activity, when providing advice to a QFI.

Article 16: Disclosure Requirements a. Subject to paragraph (b) of this Article, a QFI must within a reasonable period of time not exceeding 30 days notify the Assessing Authorized Person engaged by it if any of the notifiable events set out in Annex 3.1 of these Rules occurs.

b. Where a notifiable event set out in Annex 3.1 of these Rules has occurred and the QFI reasonably believes that disclosure of the event to an Assessing Authorized Person in accordance with paragraph (a) of this Article would materially prejudice the operations and businesses of the QFI or a third party, the QFI may make a notification to the Authority in substitution for the notification required under paragraph (a) of this Article.

c. The QFI must provide without delay to the Authority any information, documents or written explanation as it may request.

d. All information and documents disclosed and notifications made to the Assessing Authorized Person or to the Authority under this Article must be complete, clear, accurate and not misleading.

29.5 ANNEX 3.1: Information and documents to be disclosed by QFIs to Assessing Authorized Persons

Notifiable Events

a. The QFI must notify the Assessing Authorized Person in the event in which the QFI engages with a new foreign portfolio manager for the purpose of investing in listed securities.

b. The QFI becoming aware that it no longer meets or will no longer meet the qualification conditions stated in these Rules, excluded from that any decline in the assets under management for market conditions or funds redemption reasons, and any decline for the these reasons will not be considered a violation of the qualification conditions under these Rules.

29.6 PART 4: AUTHORIZED PERSONS OBLIGATIONS

Article 17: Obligations of Authorized Persons and their Eligibility

a. An Authorized Person must not consider any applications for qualification in accordance with these Rules or engage with a QFI as an Assessing Authorized Person unless such person is duly authorized to conduct custody or dealing activities.

b. An Authorized Person must not accept a QFI as a client for the purpose of investing in listed securities unless it is satisfied that the QFI is qualified in accordance with these Rules.

c. An Authorized Person that was a party of a QFI assessment agreement must notify the Authority immediately upon the lapse or termination of such agreement.

d. An Authorized Person must at all times comply with the applicable provisions stated in the Capital Market Law and its Implementing Regulations, as well as the rules and the regulations of the Exchange and other relevant laws.

e. The Authority may impose any conditions and/or limitations that it sees fit on Authorized Persons in relation to their dealings with QFIs.

Article 18: Monitoring of QFIs

a. If an Assessing Authorized Person finds at any time that a QFI by which it is engaged no longer meets the applicable qualification conditions stated in these Rules or has breached any of its obligations under these Rules, the Assessing Authorized Person must report such findings to the Authority in writing without delay.

b. An Assessing Authorized Person must report to the Authority in writing immediately after being aware of any of the following events in relation to each QFI by which it is engaged:

1) The QFI must notify the Assessing Authorized Person in the event in which the QFI engages with a new foreign portfolio manager for the purpose of investing in listed securities.

2) The QFI becoming aware that it no longer meets or will no longer meet the qualification conditions stated in these Rules, excluded from that any decline in the assets under management for market conditions or funds redemption reasons, and any decline for the these reasons will not be considered a violation of the qualification conditions under these Rules.

Article 19: Powers of the Authority in Relation to Authorized Persons Engaged with QFIs

a. The Authority may at any time by issuing a written notice prohibit an Authorized Person from engaging with QFIs.

b. The Authority may require an Authorized Person to provide the Authority without delay any information, documents or written explanation relating to the Authorized Person dealings with QFIs.

c. The Authority may require an Authorized Person, or its representative, to attend before the Authority to answer questions and explain any aspect of its dealings with QFIs.

d. If the Authority considers that circumstances amounting to an emergency requires it do so, it may assume any Assessing Authorized Person's rights against a QFI upon sending written notice of such fact from the Authority to the relevant QFI and the Assessing Authorized Person.

29.7 PART 5: POWERS OF THE AUTHORITY IN RELATION TO QFIs

Article 20: Powers of the Authority in relation to QFIs

a. If the Authority considers that any of the events specified in paragraph (d) of this Article has occurred in relation to a QFI, or is likely to occur, the Authority may:

1) require the QFI to provide such information, documents and\or written explanation as the Authority requires in respect of the matters giving rise to its consideration;
2) require the QFI or its representative, to attend before the Authority to answer questions and explain any matter the Authority considers relevant;
3) carry out any enquiries that it considers appropriate;
4) take any steps to verify any information furnished by the QFI, including by communicating with overseas regulatory authorities;
5) suspend the QFI's qualification or prohibit the QFI;
6) cancel the QFI's qualification,;
7) exercise any of its other powers under the Capital Market Law.

b. Suspension or cancelation of qualification under sub-paragraphs (5), (6) of paragraph (a) of this Article shall be effective immediately upon sending a written notice of such fact from the Authority to the QFI or the relevant Assessing Authorized Person.

c. The Authority may publish the identity of any institution whose qualification has been suspended or revoked.

d. The events referred to in paragraph (a) of this Article include the following:

1) The QFI no longer meets the conditions, obligations or requirements stated in these Rules;
2) An insolvency event has occurred in relation to the QFI;
3) The QFI has breached any of its obligations under the Capital Market Law and its Implementing Regulations and/or any other laws of the Kingdom;
4) The QFI has obtained its qualification on the basis of incomplete, unclear, inaccurate or misleading information;
5) The QFI has been the subject of any material legal or regulatory sanction in any jurisdiction;
6) Any restructuring of the QFI; and

7) Any other event that the Authority believes necessitates its intervention in order to protect investors or safeguard the functioning of the capital market within the Kingdom.

e. Following revocation or suspension of qualification, the investor in question may not purchase any listed securities.

f. Following revocation or suspension of qualification, the investor in question may not dispose of securities held in its account with the Depositary Center without the prior consent of the Authority.

29.8 PART 6: CLOSING PROVISIONS

Article 21: Publication and Entry into Force These Rules shall become effective in accordance with their approval resolution.

30 Frequently Asked Questions on the Rules for Qualified Foreign Financial Institutions Investment in Listed Securities

Issued by the Capital Markets Authority

30.1 Introductory Questions

The Board of the Capital Market Authority issued its Resolution Number 3-42-2015 dated 15-7- 1436H (4-5-2015G) approving the Frequently Asked Questions on the Rules for Qualified Foreign Financial Institutions Investment in Listed Securities. The Board of the Capital Market Authority has also issued its Resolution Number 1-115-2016 dated 28-11-1437H (31-8-2016G) approving the updated version of the Frequently Asked Questions on the Rules for Qualified Foreign Financial Institutions Investment in Listed Securities

The Board of the Capital Market Authority has also issued a Resolution Number 1-63-2018 dated 19-9-1439H (4-6-2018G) approving the updated version of the Frequently Asked Questions on the Rules for Qualified Foreign Financial Institutions Investment in Listed Securities (the Rules).

The CMA has published this document to answer the questions that may be raised by foreign investors, Authorized Persons and other relevant parties in relation the Rules.

The content of this document shall not prejudice the provisions of the Capital Market Law and its Implementing Regulations and any other relevant laws.

30.2 PART A: Introductory Questions

1. What is the definition of a Qualified Foreign Investor (QFI)?

A QFI is a Qualified foreign investor to invest in securities listed in the Saudi Stock Exchange, in accordance with the Rules.

2. What are the securities that the Rules permit QFIs to invest in?

The Rules are governing the investment of foreign financial institutions in listed securities in the Saudi Stock Exchange, including equity, debt instruments, and listed funds.

3. Can a QFI invest in fund not managed by him and invest directly in the Saudi Exchange?

Yes, the QFI can invest directly in listed securities in the local market as well as invest in the following investment funds, according to the regulations set by the Authority:

- Foreign Investment Fund Qualified as QFI according to the Rules.
- Investment fund that invests in the Saudi Stock Exchange through the swap agreement.
- Approved local investment funds by the Authority.

4. How can non-resident foreign investors that do not qualify as QFIs be able to gain exposure to the Saudi listed securities?

Non-resident foreign investors that do not qualify as QFIs may enter the Saudi capital market through the Swap Agreements Framework or investment funds, in accordance with the procedures issued by the CMA in this regard.

5. How is investing through the QFI Framework different from investing through the Swap Agreements Framework?

The QFI Framework allows for legal ownership of Saudi listed securities under the name of the QFI, and participants in the Framework are able to exercise all rights as shareholders that are related to that securities including voting rights, appointing a representative to the board of directors of listed companies in accordance with the Companies Law, as well as trading rights during rights issues in accordance with CMA regulations. In contrast, the Swap Agreements Framework does not allow for legal ownership of the underlying securities. The investor only receives economic benefits from the securities under the Swap Agreements Framework.

6. Are QFIs subject to the Saudi Income Tax Law?

As per the Saudi Income Tax Law, QFIs are subject to a 5% withholding tax from the total dividends distributed by the listed company. Capital gains are not subject to tax. The Saudi Income Tax Law and its Implementing Regulations may be viewed through the following link: https://www.gazt.gov.sa/

7. Who is responsible for deducting the withholding tax on dividends distributed to QFIs?

Listed companies are responsible for deducting the withholding tax from dividends that they distribute to QFIs.

8. Can QFIs participate in Initial Public Offerings (IPOs)?

Yes, in accordance with the relevant IPO prospectus.

9. Can QFIs vote in general assembly meetings?

Yes, in accordance with the Companies Law.

10. Are QFIs able to vote by proxy in relation to the shares they own?

Yes, in accordance with the Companies Law.

11. Are QFIs able to vote electronically in respect of the shares owned by them?

Yes, in accordance with the Tadawul system.

12. Can QFIs nominate representatives for the board of directors of listed companies?

Yes, in accordance with the Companies Law.

13. Can GCC citizens and foreign residents invest in listed securities through the QFI Framework?

No, GCC citizens and foreign residents are prohibited from investing in listed securities through the QFI Framework. Both GCC citizens and foreign residents, by virtue of the rights already offered to them, can invest directly in Saudi listed securities in accordance with regulations set by the Authority.

14. How do the Rules define GCC citizens?

The Rules define GCC citizens as citizen meeting either of the following conditions:

A natural person holding the citizenship of one of the Cooperation Council for the Arab States of the Gulf countries.

A legal person that (i) capital of which is majority owned by citizens or governments of the Cooperation Council for the Arab States of the Gulf, and (ii) holding the citizenship of one of the Cooperation Council for the Arab States of the Gulf countries.

15. Can a legal person that capital of which is majority owned by citizens or governments of the Cooperation Council for the Arab States of the Gulf (GCC) and holding the citizenship of foreign nationality, submit an application to be as a QFI?

Yes, the legal person that capital of which is majority owned by citizens or governments of the Cooperation Council for the Arab States of the Gulf (GCC) and holding the citizenship of non- GCC nationality can submit the application for qualification as QFI if it satisfies the conditions prescribed by the Rules, because in this case, the definition of GCC citizens as referred to in paragraph (c) of Article 2 of the Rules, does not apply to the applicant. As described in the answer of question (14) of this document; the applicant must be a person that capital of which is majority owned by citizens or governments of the GCC and holding the citizenship of one of the GCC countries.

16. What is the process to submit a waiver from any of the provisions of the Rules in whole or in part?

In accordance with Article 3 of the Rules, an applicant, a QFI, or an AP can apply for a waiver from any of the Rules provisions in whole or in part by sending a request for a waiver along with justifications to CMA's Chairman. The CMA will study the request to reach a decision to whether accept or reject it. The decision will be sent to the applicant of the waiver with explanation of rejection or the process to be followed if the request is approved.

30.3 PART B: Qualification Conditions for QFIs

17. What are the QFI qualification conditions set out in the Rules?

a.The applicant must be a financial institutions that has a legal personality which falls within one of the following types:

1. Banks
2. Brokerage and securities firms
3. Insurance companies
4. Government and government related entities
5. Investment funds
6. Any other financial institution considered eligible by the Authority

b.With the exception of government and government related entities, the applicant must have assets under management or custody of SAR 1,875,000,000 one billion eight hundred and seventy five million Saudi Riyals (or an equivalent amount) or more.

c.The financial institutions in sub-paragraphs (1), (2), (3) of paragraph (a) of this answer must be licensed or otherwise subject to regulatory oversight by a regulatory authority in a jurisdiction that applies regulatory and monitoring standards equivalent to those of the CMA or acceptable to it.

d. The financial institutions in sub-paragraphs (4), (5) of paragraph (a) must be incorporated in a jurisdiction that applies regulatory and monitoring standards equivalent to those of the Authority or acceptable to it.

e.The affiliates of a QFI or a foreign portfolio manager who meets the requirements stated in paragraph (b) of Article 6 of the rules, and the managed funds by them, shall be considered as a qualified foreign investor without applying for a separate application conditioned by meeting paragraph (a) of Article 6 of the rules.

18. Is it required for Investment Funds to be licensed by a regulatory authority in a jurisdiction that applies regulatory and monitoring standards equivalent to those of the CMA or acceptable to it to fulfill the conditions of qualification?

No, investment funds need only to be incorporated in a jurisdiction that applies regulatory and monitoring standards equivalent to those of the CMA or acceptable to it.

19. What are the jurisdictions that apply regulatory and monitoring standards equivalent to those of the CMA or acceptable to it?

The CMA provided Authorized Persons (APs) who have a dealing or custody licenses with the standards to determine jurisdictions that apply regulatory and monitoring standards equivalent to those of the CMA or acceptable to it, by pursuance what Financial Action Task Force (FATF) issues In regard to non-compliant or non-cooperative countries without contradicting with the related laws, regulations in force In the kingdom, and The Permanent Committee for Anti-Money Laundering.

20. Can newly established Financial institutions submit an application to qualify as a QFI?

Yes, conditioned by the fulfillment of the qualification requirements specified in the Rules, given that the minimum asset under management requirement apply on the assets of the applicant or the group. If the applicant is an investment fund, this include also the assets of the foreign portfolio manager or its group.

21. Are affiliates and managed funds of a QFI or foreign fund manager will be qualified to invest in listed securities as a separate QFI?

Yes, after qualifying affiliates and managed funds of a QFI or foreign fund manager who fulfilled the requirements of paragraph (b) of Article 6 of the Rules, the affiliates and managed funds will be considered as an independent QFI and continuous obligation requirements in section 3 in the Rules will apply on them.

22. Does the cancellation of qualification of the QFI will cancel the qualification of the affiliates and managed funds as well?

No, this will not cancel affiliates and managed funds qualification as they will be considered as an independent QFI.

23. Is it required to qualify the foreign financial institution before qualifying its affiliates and managed funds?

No, the foreign financial institution can be qualified with its affiliates and managed funds in one application.

24. Is it required for foreign fund manager to be qualified to be able to qualify affiliates and managed funds?

No, if the foreign fund manager fulfilled paragraph (b) of Article 6, then they are able to qualify their affiliates and managed funds by only providing a list of them accompanied by a proof of fulfilling paragraph (a) of Article 6 of the Rules.

25. What is the requirement for qualifying affiliates and managed funds of a QFI or foreign fund managers in one application?

The affiliates and managed funds of a QFI or foreign fund managers are required to fulfill paragraph (a) of article (6) of the Rules.

26. What is the procedures for directly qualifying an affiliates and managed funds of a QFI or foreign fund managers?

The assessing Authorized Person and the QFI or foreign fund manager can determine the appropriate procedure.

27.Does the CMA require the assessing Authorized Person to use a specific form for determination letter?

No, the CMA does not require the Assessing Authorized Person to use a specific form for determination letter given that the minimum requirements stated in paragraph (b) of Article 9 of the Rules are met.

28. Does the CMA require the Assessing Authorized Person to use a specific form for assessment agreement?

No, the CMA does not require the Assessing Authorized Person to use a specific form for assessment agreement given that the minimum requirement stated in paragraph (b) of Article 10 of the Rules are met.

29. What do assets under management or under custody include?

Assets under management include:

Assets owned by the applicant or its group for the purpose of investment. And in relation to investment funds, including assets owned by the foreign portfolio manager or its group for the investment purposes; and

Assets under custody by the applicant or its group for the account of another person or persons.

Assets managed by the applicant or its group for the account of another person or persons. And in relation to investment funds, including assets owned by the foreign portfolio manager or its group for the account of another person or persons.

The term "group" is defined in the in the Glossary of Defined Terms Used in the Regulations and Rules of the CMA as: "in relation to a person, means that person and each affiliate of it". It defines the term "affiliate" as: "a person who controls another person or is controlled by that other person, or who is under common control with that person by a third person. In any of the preceding, control could be direct or indirect". The Glossary of Defined Terms Used in the Regulations and Rules of the CMA also defines the term "control" as: "the ability to influence the actions or decisions of another person through, whether directly or indirectly, alone or with a relative or affiliate (a) holding 30% or more of the voting rights in a company, or (b) having the right to appoint 30% or more of the members of the governing body;"controller" shall be construed accordingly".

30. How are investment fund assets will be calculated in the event of not fulfilling the minimum assets under management requirement and has appointed more than one foreign portfolio manager?

If the investment fund or its group does not fulfill the minimum assets under management requirement and has appointed more than one foreign portfolio manager, the investment fund or its group with one of the appointed portfolio managers or their group must have the assets under management of SAR (1,875,000,000) or more, and this condition is continuously met excluded from that any decline in the assets under management for market conditions or funds redemption reasons, and any decline for these reasons will not be considered a violation of the qualification conditions under Rules.

31. What are the government related entities?

The government related entities mean central banks and investment funds- including sovereign funds and funds that take the form of pension funds and endowments- that are fully owned directly or indirectly by a government entity.

32. Are there any conditions that must be met by the foreign portfolio manager?

Yes, the foreign portfolio manager must have a legal personality which manages the assets of clients and must be licensed or otherwise subject to regulatory oversight by a regulatory authority and incorporated in a jurisdiction that applies regulatory and monitoring standards equivalent to those of the Authority or acceptable to it and in which engages or intend to engage with the QFI or the applicant for the purpose of investing on its behalf in listed securities in the Saudi Stock Exchange.

33. is it required for the foreign portfolio manager to be a QFI?

The foreign portfolio manager is not required to be qualified, it is sufficient to provide a list of all the foreign portfolio managers to the AAP in which the QFI intends to deal with them and to be accompanied by the proofing information and documents in accordance with the Rules. Taking into account the required additional documents that must be submitted by the applicant who intends to deal with the foreign portfolio managers to invest in the Saudi market if they are not a QFI, as stipulated in the paragraph (b) of Annex 2.1 of the Rules.

34. Can QFI deal with a GCC portfolio manager?

Yes, the QFI can deal with a GCC portfolio manager for the management of its investments in the Saudi Stock Exchange.

35. Can a portfolio manager be an AP licensed by the Authority?

Yes, the QFI can deal with portfolio manager who is licensed by the CMA.

36. Can a QFI deal with more than one portfolio manager?

Yes, the QFI can deal with more than one portfolio manager at the same time, either if it was an AP authorized from the CMA or a foreign portfolio manager which includes a GCC portfolio manager, though, the QFI must notify the AAP when dealing with a new portfolio manager in accordance with Annex (3.1) of the Rules.

37. Is it possible for QFI to deal with another QFI to manage his investments in listed securities?

Yes, the QFI can deal with another QFI to manage his investments in listed securities and that does not prejudice the responsibility to abide by the law and its implementing regulations and market rules and its regulations, and other rules that are related.

38. Do assets under management include the assets of the funds managed by the applicant even if such funds did not satisfy the conditions required to be qualified as QFI?

Yes, assets under management include assets of the funds managed by the applicant even if such funds did not satisfy the conditions required to qualify as QFI.

30.4 PART C: Qualification Process

39. Who is an AAP? { *Assessing Authorized Person* }

An "AAP" is an Authorized Person "AP" {licensed} by the CMA to conduct custody or dealing activities, and has agreed with an applicant to assess its application for qualification. to invest in the Saudi Stock Exchange.

For the List of APs, please refer to the CMA website through the following link:

https://cma.org.sa/Market/AuthorizedPersons/Pages/default.aspx

40. What is the role of the AAP?

The AAP will assess the QFI's qualification request to ensure that the application complies with the requirements prescribed by the Rules. Then, the AAP will provide the determination regarding the application whether accepted or rejected.

41. When will the applicant become a QFI?

An applicant becomes a QFI from the date of the AAP accepting the applicant according to the Rules.

42. In the case that a request for Qualifying a foreign investor is rejected, can an applicant re- apply?

Yes, the applicant can re-apply and there is no specific time period which must lapse before the applicant can resubmit the application.

43. Can a QFI delegate the foreign portfolio manager to process the application for qualification and sign the assessment agreement with the AAP?

Yes, the QFI may delegate the foreign portfolio manager to process the application for qualification and sign the assessment agreement with the AAP, providing a proof of such delegation to the AAP when submitting the application.

44. Can an AAP rely on a third party to conduct Know Your Client "KYC" process?

Yes, the AAP can rely on a third party to conduct Know Your Client "KYC" process in accordance with the Anti-Money Laundering and Counter-Terrorist Financing Rules.

45. Is it required that the terms of business agreement to be signed between the Authorized Person and the qualified foreign investor?

In accordance with CMA Board's Resolution issued on 23/11/2017, paragraph (b) of Article (38) of Authorized Persons Regulations does not require that the terms of business with the clients be signed between the Authorized Person and the investor as a legal person or the qualified foreign investor directly. The agreement may be indirect, provided that the terms of business define the basis for conducting securities business with the client or for his account.

For example: a qualified foreign investor may delegate a third party to sign the terms of business agreement with the Authorized Person, or the Authorized Person may sign a master agreement with a third party covering the terms of business to the qualified foreign investor introduced by that party.

46. What is meant by the requirement of obtaining copies of the documentation and information of third party Costumer Due Diligence procedures as per sub-paragraph (5-a) of Article (14), of the Anti-Money Laundering and Counter-Terrorist Financing Rules?

The meaning of obtaining copies of the Customer Due Diligence documentation and information is to obtain copies of documents and information of the customer's due diligence procedures the third party undertakes to assess and assure the suitability of such procedures and their conformity with the local requirements stated in paragraph (6) of Article (14) as follows:

"Authorized Persons must conduct periodic reviews to ensure that a third party upon which it relies, continues to conform to the criteria set out above. This may involve review of the relevant policies and procedures and sample checks of the due diligence conducted."

In this case, copies of the documents mentioned in subparagraphs (a), (b) and (c) of paragraph(2) of Article (8) of the Anti-Money Laundering and Counter-Terrorist Financing Rules shall not be obtained, nevertheless appropriate steps shall be taken to ensure that the third party submits copies of documentation and data regarding the requirements of due diligence procedures towards the client upon request.

47. Is it permissible to rely on a third party to verify the documents required to open an investment account as per the Investment Accounts Instructions?

Yes, taking into consideration the provisions of reliance on third parties to conduct customer due diligence procedures as per the Anti-Money Laundering and Counter-Terrorist Financing Rules.

48. Is the AP when opening an investment account for a QFI, or relying on a third party for opening an investment account for a QFI, required to obtain copies of identifications of the QFI's owners, managers, authorized signatories and persons authorized to manage the account?

As per the CMA Board resolution issued in this regard, the Authorized Person (AP) when opening an investment account for a QFI is not required to obtain copies of the identification of the QFI's owners, managers, authorized signatories and persons authorized to manage the account, without prejudice to the AP's obligation to identify and verify their identity using reliable, independent source documents, data or information in accordance with the related laws, regulations and instructions.

This includes cases in which the AP rely on a third party for opening an investment account for a QFI, without prejudice to the AP's obligation to take adequate steps to ensure that copies of identification documents and other relevant documentation relating to the CDD requirements will be made available from the third party promptly upon request in accordance with the related laws, regulations and instructions.

49. Is the QFI required to obtain authorization by the CMA in relation to carrying on dealing as principal activity to invest in securities listed in the Saudi Stock Exchange?

The QFI is not required to obtain authorization by the CMA in relation to carrying on dealing as principal activity to invest in securities listed in the Saudi Stock Exchange.

50. Is the foreign portfolio manager required to obtain authorization by the CMA in relation to carrying on managing activity when managing listed securities belonging to a QFI in the Saudi Stock Exchange?

The foreign portfolio manager is not required to obtain authorization by the CMA in relation to carrying on managing activity when managing listed securities belonging to a QFI in the Saudi Stock Exchange.

51. Is the foreign custodian required to obtain authorization by the CMA in relation to carrying on custody activity when safeguarding listed securities belonging to a QFI?

The foreign custodian is not required to obtain authorization by the CMA in relation to carrying on custody activity when safeguarding listed securities belonging to a QFI without prejudice to appoint local custodian authorized by the CMA.

52. Is the foreign advisor required to obtain authorization by the CMA in relation to carrying on advising activity when providing advice to a QFI?

The foreign advisor is not required to obtain authorization by the CMA in relation to carrying on advising activity when providing advice to a QFI.

30.5 PART D: Trading

53. When can a QFI start trading listed securities?

A QFI may commence trading in any listed securities upon satisfying the following:

- Holding a client account.
- Holding an account with the Depositary Center.
- Any conditions as may be imposed by the CMA.

The term "client account" is defined in the Glossary of Defined Terms Used in the Regulations and Rules of the CMA as: "an account at a local bank which is in the name of an Authorized Person and fulfills the conditions required by the Client Money Rules".

54. How can the applicant satisfy the qualification requirements, the client account opening requirements and the requirements for opening an account with the Depository Center?

The CMA worked in coordination with the relevant authorities to facilitate the establishment of a unified platform [One-Stop-Shop] for the account opening requirements and the requirements for opening an account with the Depository Centre and bank account, to facilitate the fulfillment of such requirements, and the applicant will only need to provide the required information and documents in this regard to the AAP, provided that the concerned AAP takes the necessary actions in accordance with the procedures issued by the CMA in this regard.

55. What are the procedures to open a client account?

The concerned AP shall open a client account for the QFI pursuant to the applicable procedures set forth by the CMA and the Saudi Arabian Monetary Agency, which may be viewed through the following link: https://cma.org.sa/en/Market/QFI/Pages/default.aspx

56. What are the procedures to open an account with the Depositary Center?

The concerned AP shall open an account with the Depositary Center for the pursuant to the applicable procedures set forth by the CMA and the Saudi Stock Exchange, which may be viewed through the following link: https://cma.org.sa/en/Market/QFI/Pages/default.aspx

57. Is there a specific period to open an account with the Depositary Center after being qualified to invest in Saudi listed securities?

No, there is no specific period to open an account with depositary after being qualified to invest in Saudi Stock Exchange.

58. How can the QFI's investment account be linked to a bank account in the name of the QFI, and how could the Authorized Person ensure that the money transferred to the investment account is received from an account that belongs to the QFI?

The bank account is considered to be in the name of the QFI (belonging to the QFI) as indicated in the electronic record kept by the Authorized Person, that is based on the information provided by the QFI to the Authorized Person whether in the beginning of their contractual relationship or during such relationship. Such information may include the information obtained by the Authorized Person from an international bank (commercial or investment banks, brokerage and securities institutions including custodians) on behalf of the QFI, such as, a written statement to the Authorized Person confirming that the money transferred to the QFI investment account belongs to the same client.

Taking into consideration the Authorized Person's compliance with the client money rules in the Authorized Persons Regulations, and its obligation to take all necessary steps to ensure that the obtained information are true, according to Article (8) of the Anti-Money Laundering and Counter-Terrorist Financing Rules.

59. Should each QFI open a separate account in the Depositary Center?

Yes, every QFI shall open an independent account. After that, the QFI can open several investment portfolios that are linked to the account.

60. Who is the competent authority responsible for the resolution of disputes resulting from trading?

The Committee for the Resolution of Securities Disputes (CRSD) has the jurisdiction over the disputes falling under the provisions of the Capital Market Law, its Implementing Regulations, and the regulations, rules and instructions issued by the CMA and the Exchange, with respect to public and private actions, including any trading disputes that may arise among all parties subject to the Rules.

The CRSD's decision may be appealed before the Appeal Panel that is formed by a Council of Ministers' resolution. The Appeal Panel shall have the discretion to refuse to review the decisions of the CRSD, to affirm such decisions, to undertake a de novo review of the complaint or suit based on the record developed at the hearing before the Committee and to issue such decision as it deems appropriate in relation to the complaint or the suit. The decisions of the Appeal Panel shall be final.

The decisions issued by these committees are published in both Arabic and English on the Committees for the Resolution of Securities Disputes' website, and those decisions can be viewed through the following link: http://www.crsd.org.sa/

61. Can a QFI send trading orders through an international broker that is not qualified as a foreign investor?

If the international broker's role is limited to sending orders issued by the QFI to the AP, then the international broker is not required to qualify as a QFI, provided that the international broker must have the authority to send such orders.

62. Can a QFI establish a discretionary portfolio management (DPM)?

A QFI can establish a DPM with an AP in relation to its investments.

63. Are existing Swap Agreement's ultimate beneficiary allowed to invest as a QFI?

Yes, provided that the ultimate beneficiary satisfies the conditions prescribed in the Rules to be qualified as a QFI. In Addition, a foreign investor who wants to invest in the Saudi Stock Exchange as a QFI can retain a swap agreement account for not more than twelve months from the opening of the QFI account, afterward, all securities underlying the ultimate beneficiary swap account must be transferred to the QFI account.

The ultimate beneficiary is defined as "non-resident foreign investor that receives the economic benefits of the securities listed on the Saudi Stock Exchange through swap transactions executed under the Swap Agreements". 64. Can the foreign investor transfer owned securities from the ultimate beneficiary swap account to the QFI account within the twelve months period?

Yes, the foreign investor is allowed to transfer some of the securities from the ultimate beneficiary swap account to the QFI account and vice versa during the twelve months period.

65. What is the following procedure after the elapse of twelve months of opening a qualified foreign investor account while retaining ultimate beneficiary swap account?

After the elapse of twelve months of opening a QFI account, the Assessing Authorized Person (AAP) must ensure that the QFI closed one of the accounts and transferred all securities from the account which the foreign investor is intending to close to the account that foreign investor is intending to continue his investments through.

66. How securities are transferred from a Swap Agreement account to a QFI account?

The transfer operation is done according to the following:

1. QFI submits- through the AAP- a detailed transfer request of all securities underlying the Swap Agreement, where the ultimate beneficiary of such securities is the QFI, to his account with the Depositary Center, according to the form prepared by the Exchange for this purpose.

2. Submitting the transfer request, referred to in paragraph (1) above, must be done as soon as a request is submitted to open an account with the Depositary Center.

3. The Exchange takes the necessary procedures to execute the transfer operation from Swap Agreement account in relation to the QFI as stipulated in the circular issued in this regard.

4. The transfer operation shall be executed after ensuring that there are no obligations (such as: a pledge or a seizure of the securities) or outstanding buy and sell orders, regarding the securities requested to be transferred.

67. What are the costs of transferring securities from a Swap Agreement account to a QFI account?

The cost of transferring is 20 SAR for the securities of each listed company (not per security).

68. Does transferring securities from a Swap Agreement account to QFI account affect the market value of such securities?

Transferring securities from a Swap Agreement account to a QFI account does not affect the market value of the securities.

69. How long does it take to transfer securities from a Swap Agreement account to a QFI account?

The shares shall be transferred within 2 business days from the date on which all the requirements were completed.

70. Can a QFI be the Foreign Counterparty under a Swap Agreements Framework?

Yes, a QFI can be the Foreign Counterparty in Swap Agreements.

30.6 PART E: Investment Limit(s)

71. Does the ownership limit of 49% of the issued shares or convertible debt instrument of any listed company include the strategic foreign investors in such company?

Yes, all foreign investors (in all categories, whether residents or non-residents), including strategic foreign investors, cannot own more than 49% of the issued shares or convertible debt instrument for each listed company, including interests under the Swap Agreements Framework.

72. How can the information on ownership limits in listed companies stipulated in the Rules be obtained?

The Saudi Stock Exchange (Tadawul) shall publish on its website statistical information reflecting ownership percentage as per the paragraphs (a/2) of Article 14 of the Rules. In addition, according to the information received from listed companies, the Saudi Stock Exchange shall also publish on its website the limits stated in paragraphs (a/3) and (a/4) of Article 14 of the Rules.

73. What are the responsibilities of APs and QFIs with regard to the ownership limits in listed companies stipulated in the Rules?

APs must comply with the relevant rules set out in the Capital Market Law and its Implementing Regulations, in particular the Authorized Persons Regulations, Market Conduct Regulations and the Rules.

QFIs must comply with the ownership limits specified in subparagraphs (a/1), (a/3), and (a/4) of Article 14 of the Rules for investments in their account. It should be noted that the Saudi Stock Exchange (Tadawul) will automatically control the ownership limits specified in Article 14 of the Rules. An automatic control of a limit means that the Saudi Stock Exchange's (Tadawul) systems will reject orders that are not considered to be compliant with the ownership limits in listed companies stipulated in the Rules.

74. Who is responsible for complying with the investment limits and disclosure requirements when the QFI engages with foreign portfolio manager?

The QFI is responsible for complying with investment limits and disclosure requirements and abide by the Capital Market Law and its Implementing Regulations and the rules of the Exchange and other relevant laws.

75. What are the ownership limits in listed companies stipulated in the Rules that will be automatically controlled by the Saudi Stock Exchange (Tadawul)?

The following ownership limits will be automatically controlled by the Saudi Stock Exchange:

Each QFI may not own 10% or more of the shares of any issuer whose shares are listed or convertible debt instrument of the issuer.

The maximum proportion of the share of any issuer whose shares are listed or convertible debt instrument of the issuer that may be owned by all foreign investors (in all categories, whether residents or non-residents) in aggregate is 49%.

76. Can the foreign investor own a percentage that exceed 10% through his QFI account and his ultimate beneficiary swap account within the first twelve months after the opening of a QFI account while retaining an ultimate beneficiary swap account?

No, foreign investor ownership through the QFI account and the ultimate beneficiary swap account shall not exceed 10% of the shares of any issuer whose shares are listed or convertible debt instrument of the issuer for both accounts aggregated. Foreign investor must comply with the investment limitations provisions in the Capital Market Law and its Implementing Regulations, as well as the Rules and Regulations of the Exchange and other relevant laws.

77. What are the consequences for non-compliance of qualified foreign investor with the ownership limits in listed companies stipulated in the Rules?

In the case of non-compliance with the ownership limits, the foreign investor is considered in breach of the Rules, and the CMA can take the action it sees fit in accordance with Article (20) of the QFI Rules which includes the action stipulated in sub-paragraph (7/a) that enables the CMA to exercise any of its other powers under the Capital Market Law specifically the power stipulated under paragraph (a) of Article (59) of the Capital Market Law that states:

"If it appears to the Authority that any person has engaged, is engaging, or is about to engage in acts or practices constituting a violation of any provisions of this Law, or the regulations or rules issued by the Authority, or the regulations of the Exchange, the Authority shall have the right to bring a legal action before the Committee to seek an order for the appropriate sanction. The sanctions include the following: . . .(3) obliging the person concerned to take the necessary steps to avert the violation, or to take such necessary corrective steps to address the results of the violation".

30.7 PART F: Ongoing Obligations

78. Is the QFI required to provide the CMA with notifications?

Where a notifiable event, as set out in Annex 3.1 of the Rules, has occurred and the QFI reasonably believes that disclosure of the event to the AAP in accordance with paragraph (a) of Article 16 of the Rules would materially prejudice the operations and businesses of the QFI or a third party, the QFI may make a notification to the CMA in substitution for notifying the AAP.

79. What is the required period of time for the QFI to notify the AAP if any of the notifiable events occurs?

A QFI must within a reasonable period of time not exceeding 30 days notify the AAP engaged by it if any of the notifiable events occurs as set out in Annex 3.1.

80. Are the QFI required to provide the Exchange with notifications regarding their ownership in listed companies?

Yes, the QFI is required to notify the Exchange as per the events stipulated in article 68 of Rules on the Offer of Securities and Continuing Obligations which are as follows:

a) Any person must notify the Exchange if such person becomes the owner of, or is interested in, 5% or more of any class of voting shares or convertible debt instruments of the issuer at the end of the third trading day following the execution of the transaction or the occurrence of the event which results such ownership or interest; The person notification to the Authority shall also include a list of persons, in which those persons, have an interest in the shares or convertible debt instruments which they own or control".

b) The person referred to in paragraph (a) of this Article must notify the Exchange in the event of any change to the list of persons referred to in paragraph (a) of this Article including any event which requires the inclusion of a person to that list or the exclusion of any person who has been previously included in that list. Such notification must be made at the end of the third trading day following the occurrence of the relevant event.

c) For the purposes of this Article, in calculating the total number of shares or convertible debt instruments in which a person is interested, that person will be deemed to be interested in any shares or convertible debt instruments owned by or controlled by any of the following persons:

1) a relative of that person;
2) a company controlled by that person; or
3) any other persons with which that person has agreed to act in concert to acquire an interest in or exercise voting rights in the shares or in the convertible debt instruments of the issuer.

d) The notices referred to in this Article shall be in accordance with the form prepared for this regard. The notice referred to in paragraph (a) of this Article must contain at least the following information:

1) the names of the persons who own or have the right to dispose of the subject shares or convertible debt instruments;
2) details of the ownership process;
3) details of any loans or financial support for the ownership process that the person has received from any other persons.

81. What is meant by a person who is interested in shares or convertible debt instruments?

A person will be deemed interested in any shares or convertible debt instruments owned or controlled by any of the following persons:

a. A relative of that person;
b. A company controlled by that person;
c. Any other persons with which that person has agreed to act in concert to acquire interest in or exercise voting rights in the shares or in the convertible debt instruments of the issuer.

The term "person" is defined in the in the Glossary of Defined Terms Used in the Regulations and Rules of the CMA as: "any natural or legal person recognized as such under the laws of the Kingdom".

82. Is there a special notification form with regards to the ownership in listed companies?

Yes, the notification shall be in accordance with a form prepared by the Exchange, which may be viewed through the following link:

https://www.tadawul.com.sa/wps/portal/tadawul/knowledge-center/rules-%26-regulations/rules-forms

83. Can a QFI engage with more than one AAP at the same time?

Yes, a QFI may engage with more than one AAP at the same time.

84. Can a QFI become a client of another AP for the purpose of investing in listed securities?

Yes, a QFI can be a client of any other AP when investing in listed securities.

85. Can a QFI change its AAP?

Yes, the QFI can change its AAP at any time. In case the QFI is engaged only with one AAP, a QFI can find a replacement for AAP within 30 days after the lapse or termination of the QFI assessment agreement with the replaced AAP.

86. Can the QFI trade listed securities during the 30 day period after the lapse or termination of the QFI assessment agreement?

Yes, the QFI can trade listed securities during this period, provided that it adheres to its responsibilities to comply with the Rules.

87. When should an AAP notify the CMA when the QFI no longer meets the qualification conditions?

If an AAP finds at any time that a QFI by which it is engaged with no longer meets the applicable qualification conditions stated in the Rules or has breached any of its obligations under the Rules, the AAP must report such findings to the CMA in writing without delay.

88. Is the QFI required to notify the AAP in the event in which the QFI no longer engages with the foreign portfolio manager?

Yes, the QFI must notify the AAP in the event in which the QFI no longer engages with the foreign portfolio manager. Also, the AAP must notify the CMA in writing without delay in case that considered a breach of the qualification conditions as explained in Annex3.1.

89. Can the QFI apply for cancellation of QFI qualification?

Yes, The QFI may submit a cancellation request to an AAP.

90. Does a QFI need to be aware of other laws or regulations?

QFIs must be aware of the relevant provisions of the Capital Market Law and its Implementing Regulations, the rules and the regulations of the Saudi Stock Exchange and any other relevant laws. This includes the Rules of Offering Securities and Continuing Obligations, the Market Conduct Regulations, the Authorized Persons Regulations, the Merger and Acquisition Regulations, the Anti-Money Laundering and Counter-Terrorist Financing Rules.

30.8 PART G: Other Questions

91. What is the settlement cycle for securities listed in the Saudi Stock Exchange?

The settlement cycle for trading listed securities in the Saudi Stock Exchange is two business days after executing the transaction (T+2), and the prefunding condition is subject to the contractual arrangement with the concerned securities broker and is not a regulatory requirement.

92. What are the trading hours of the Saudi Stock Exchange?

Trading is open for one session from1 0:00 am – 3:00 pm, Sunday through Thursday. The Saudi Stock Exchange is closed during all official holidays.

93. Will the Depository Center allow APs who are licensed to conduct custody activities, but who do not have a dealing license, to be connected with the Depository and Settlement System, in order to enable them to offer independent custody services for investors in Saudi listed securities?

Yes, the Depository Center allows APs with custody licenses to be connected with the Depository and Settlement System, so that they can offer custody and all related services to the investors. Therefore, investors in Saudi listed securities are able to appoint an independent custodian different than the broker who executes their trades.

94. Can QFIs receive financing from local banks to fund their investments?

Yes, pursuant to the applicable procedures set forth by the CMA and the Saudi Arabian Monetary Agency, QFIs can receive financing from local banks to fund their investments.

95. What protection is available to minority shareholders in relation to Merger and Acquisition transactions?

The provisions of the Companies Law and Merger and Acquisition Regulations included a number of protection means for minority shareholders, such as:

First: The Companies Law Article 94:

- An extraordinary general assembly meeting shall not be valid only if attended by shareholders representing at representing at least one half of the company's capital, unless the company's bylaws provide for a higher proportion provided that such proportions shall not exceed the two-thirds .

- If this quorum has not been obtained at the first meeting in accordance with above paragraph, a notice shall be sent for a second meeting in the manner prescribed in Article (91) of the Companies Law. However, the second meeting may be held after an hour from the end of the period fixed for holding the first meeting. The notice sent for the first meeting must include an indication to the possibility of holding a second meeting. In all cases, such meeting shall be valid if attended by a number of shareholders representing at least one quarter of the company's capital.

- If this quorum has not been obtained at the second meeting, a notice shall be sent for a third meeting in the manner prescribed in Article (91) of the Companies Law, and such third meeting shall be valid regardless of the number of shares represented thereat, after the approval of the competent authority.

- Resolutions of an extraordinary general assembly shall be adopted by a two-thirds majority vote of the shares represented thereat. But if a resolution pertains to an increase or decrease in capital, or to extension of the term of the company, or to termination of the company prior to expiry of the term specified in its bylaws or to merger of the company into another company or firm, it shall be valid only if adopted by a three-fourths majority vote of the shares represented at the meeting.

- The Board of Directors must publish, in accordance with the provisions of Article (65) of the Companies Law, the resolutions adopted by an extraordinary general assembly meeting if such resolutions included an amendment of the company's bylaws.

Second: Merger and Acquisition Regulations

- Paragraph (c) of Article 3:In the case of an offer, All shareholders of the same class of an Offeree Company must be treated equally by an offeror.

- Paragraph (e) of Article 3: During the course of an Offer, or when an Offer is in contemplation by the Offeree Company, neither an Offeror, nor the Offeree Company, nor any of their respective advisors may furnish information to some shareholders which is not readily made available to all shareholders. This principle does not apply to the following: 1) the furnishing of information in confidence by the Offeree Company to a bona fide potential Offeror or vice versa in the context of an Offer; or 2) the furnishing of information in confidence by the selling shareholder and/or Offeree Company to an Offeror in the context of a Private Transaction.

• Paragraph (j) of Article 3: In case the board of the Offeree Company has reason to believe that a bona fide Offer might be imminent, the board of the Offeree Company may not take any action in relation to the affairs of the company, that may cause the rejection of the offer or preventing shareholders from making a decision on it, without the approval of the shareholders convened in a general assembly.

• Paragraph (o) of Article 3: A director shall not vote at a meeting of board or of its committees or a general assembly meeting on any resolution concerning an offer subject to these Regulations or any other relevant matter where the director, any relative or representative of his/her has a conflict of interest. In this context such a conflict of interest would arise if the director has, directly or indirectly, an interest related to the offer or the potential offer or the director is a shareholder in the Offeror and at the same time he/she is a director of the Offeree Company board, or vice versa. If the director is a director of the Offeror board and at the same time he/she is a board member of, or a manager in the Offeree Company, or vice versa.

• Paragraph (a) of Article 23: Where a person (or persons Acting in Concert with it) increase an aggregate interest in shares through a restricted purchase of shares or restricted offer for shares so that such person's ownership (individually or collectively with persons Acting in Concert with it) becomes 50% or more of a given class of shares listed on the Exchange carrying voting rights, the Board shall have the right to exercise its discretionary power in accordance with Article 54 of the Capital Market Law to order such person (and any person or persons Acting in Concert with it) to Offer to purchase the shares of the same class it does not own of the Offeree Company on the terms set out in this Article and in accordance with the other relevant provisions of these Regulations. When an obligation to make a general Offer is incurred under this Article, it is not necessary for the Offer to extend to treasury shares in the Offeree Company.

• Paragraph (a) of Article 24: Any person obtaining shares (or have control over them) by a deal or number of deals (in owned or controlled shares, or which is controlled by persons acting in concert with it) that represent 40% or more of a specific class of shares that carry voting rights, may not have control over its shares during the following 6 months of obtaining such percentage without the Authority's approval and in accordance with the conditions it specifies.

• Paragraph (a) of Article 35: Information about the Offer, including announcements, statements, presentations, circulars and information concerning companies involved in an Offer must be made equally available to all shareholders as nearly as possible at the same time and in the same manner, including publication on the website of the Offeror and Offeree Company, through the exchange or other Regulatory Information Service Providers (as applicable), no later than the end of the trading day.

• Sub-paragraph (2/b) of Article 36: Any break-up fee that is proposed must be of a minimal size (no more than 1% of the Offer value) and the Offeree Company board of directors and its Independent Financial Advisor must confirm to the Authority in writing that the fee is in the best interests of the Offeree Company's shareholders. Any break-up fee arrangement must be fully disclosed in the Offer Document and in the announcement made under paragraph (e) of Article 17.

31 Real Estate Investment Funds Regulations

Issued by the Board of the Capital Market Authority pursuant to its Resolution Number 1-193-2006 dated 19/6/1427 (15/7/2006)based on the Capital Market Law issued by Royal Decree No. M/30 dated 2/6/1424H as amended by Resolution of the Board of the Capital Market Authority Number 2-22-2021 dated 12/7/1442H (24/2/2021G)

Important Notice: The current version of these Regulations, as may be amended, can be found at the Authority's website: www.cma.org.sa

(According to the Authority's Board Resolution no. 2-22-2021 Dated 12/7/1442H. Corresponding to 24/2/2021G these Regulations shall become effective as of 19/09/1442H. corresponding to 01/05/2021G. Moreover, the Real Estate Investment Funds Regulations issued pursuant to the Authority's Board Resolution no. (1-193-2006) dated 19/06/1427H. corresponding to 15/07/2006G., which can be viewed via the following link:(https://cma.org.sa/RulesRegulations/Regulations/DocLib/REAL%20ESTATE%20INVE%20FUND%20REG__EN.pdf), shall remain effective until the effectivity date of these Regulations.)

Table of Contents

Part 1: General Provisions
Article 1: Preliminary
Article 2: Definitions
Article 3: Compliance with the Regulations
Article 4: Waivers
Article 5: Fees
Article 6: Right of Appeal
Part 2: Authorization
Article 7: Authorization Requirements
Article 8: Procedures and Powers of the Authority in Relation to an Application
Part 3: Regulating the Operation of Real Estate Investment Funds
Chapter One: Fund's Organizational Structure
Article 9: Legal Basis for Management of the Fund
Article 10: Types and Objectives of Real Estate Investment Funds
Article 11: Fund Board of Directors
Article 12: Responsibilities of The Fund's Board Members
Chapter 2: Fund Management
Article 13: Fund Management
Article 14: Books and Records Keeping
Article 15: Delegations by the Fund Manager
Article 16: Removal and Replacement of Fund Manager
Article 17: Investment Decisions
Article 18: Financial Statements
Article 19: Conflict of Interest and Discloser thereof
Article 20: Special Commission Arrangements
Article 21: Auditing Requirements
Article 22: Commissions, Services and Management Fees
Article 23: Unitholders Meeting
Chapter 3: Disclosure
Article 24: Disclosure
Article 25: Reporting to Unitholders
Chapter 4: Fundamental and Non-Fundamental Changes
Article 26: Approval of the Authority and Consent of Unitholders to Fundamental Changes
Article 27: Notification to the Authority and Unitholders of Any Non- Fundamental Changes
Chapter 5: Fund Assets Requirements, Custody of its Assets and Operational Rules
Article 28: Fund Assets Requirements
Article 29: Custody of Fund Assets and Related Documents
Article 30: Segregation of Fund Money
Article 31: Power of the Authority to Remove and Replace Custodian
Article 32: Removal of Custodian by the Fund Manager
Article 33: Property Management
Article 34: Appointment of Developer and Engineering Office
Article 35: Valuation
Article 36: Assessment of fund Asset and Calculation of Unit Price
Article 37: Register of Unitholders
Article 38: Subscription and Offering
Article 39: Units
Article 40: Restrictions on the Funds
Article 41: Trading
Article 42: Advertising
Article 43: Termination and Liquidation of the Fund
Part 4: Real Estate Investment Traded Fund
Article 44: Scope and Applications
Article 45: General Provisions
Article 46: Conditions of Offering the Real Estate Investment Traded Fund
Article 47: Offer Requirements for REITS
Article 48: REITs Buy-back and Sale of Its Units
Article 49: Discloser Requirements
Article 50: Merging Real Estate Investment Traded Funds
Part 5: Real Estate Investment Funds that Take the Form of a Special
Purposes Entities
Article 51: General Provisions
Article 52: Custodian
Article 53: Board of Directors of the Real Estate Investment Fund that Takes the Form of Special Purposes Entity.
Part 6: Publication and Entry into Force
Article 54: Publication and Entry into Force
Annexes
Annex 1: Requirements of the Terms and Conditions of Real Estate Investment
Public Fund
Annex 2: Requirements of the Terms and Conditions of Real Estate Investment
Traded Fund
Annex 3: Content of the Application for Offering Public Real Estate Investment
Fund Units
Annex 4: Content of Fund's Reports
Annex 5: Content of semi-Annual Statements
Annex 6: Content of the Quarterly Statements
Annex 7: Form of a Real Estate Investment Fund Manager's Letter
Annex 8: Form of a Real Estate Investment Traded Fund Manager's Letter
Annex 9: The Real Estate Investment Fund Manager's Dec-

larations
Annex 10: The Real Estate Investment traded Fund Manager's Declarations
Annex 11: Form of a Real Estate Investment Traded Fund's Legal Advisor's Letter
Annex 12: Approvals Requests and Notifications Submitted to the Authority
Annex 13: Fund Termination Report
Annex 14: Supplementary Annex for Real Estate Investment Fund

31.1 PART 1: GENERAL PROVISIONS

Article 1: Preliminary

a) These Regulations aim at regulating the real estate investment funds that the units of which are offered publicly in the Kingdom, with regards to offering, registration of its units, management and protection of its unitholders' rights.

b) These Regulations shall not have any prejudice to the provisions of the Capital Market Law or its Implementing Regulations, the Market Conduct Regulations, the Capital Market Institutions Regulations the Securities

Business Regulations and the Rules for Special Purposes Entities.

Article 2: Definitions

a) Any reference to the "Capital Market Law" in these Regulations shall mean the Capital Market Law issued by Royal Decree No. M/30 dated 2/6/1424H.

b) Expressions and terms in these regulations have the meaning which they bear in the Capital Market Law and the Glossary of Defined Terms Used in the Regulations and Rules of the Authority.

Article 3: Compliance with Regulations

a) A person who intends to offer units of a real estate investment fund publicly in the Kingdom must comply with these Regulations, and the provisions of the Rules for Special Purposes Entities (where applicable).

b) A fund manager, custodian, distributor and any member of the fund board of a real estate investment fund in the Kingdom shall comply with these Regulations, and the provisions of the Rules for Special Purposes Entities (where applicable).

Article 4: Waivers The Authority may waive a provision of these Regulations in whole or in part as it applies to a person either on an application from such person to whom the relevant provisions of this Article would otherwise apply or on the Authority's own initiative.

Article 5: Fees The Authority may impose a fee on the fund manager and the distributor as the Authority may prescribe.

Article 6: Right of Appeal Any person subject to these Regulations may appeal to the Committee in respect of any decision or action that the Authority takes under these Regulations.

31.2 PART] 2: AUTHORIZATION

Article 7: Authorization Requirements

a) The applicant, seeking the Authority's approval to offer units of a real estate investment fund must be a Capital Market Institution authorized by the Authority to conduct managing investments and operating funds activity.

b) Units of real estate investment fund shall not be offered by way of a public offer unless the Authority has first received and approved the information referred in the annex (3) of these regulations.

c) The applicant must provide any other requirement the Authority requests in accordance with the Capital Market Law and its Implementing Regulations.

(According to the Authority's Board Resolution no. 2-22-2021 Dated 12/7/1442H. Corresponding to 24/2/2021G., paragraph (a) of Article (7) of these Regulations shall become effective as of 28/05/1443H. corresponding to 01/01/2022G. Moreover, paragraph (a) of Article (3) of the Real Estate Investment Funds Regulations issued pursuant to the Authority's Board Resolution no. (1-193-2006) dated 19/06/1427H. corresponding to 15/07/2006G., which can be viewed via the following link:(https://cma.org.sa/RulesRegulations/), shall remain effective until the effectivity date of paragraph (a) of Article (7) of these Regulations.)

Article 8: Procedures and Powers of the Authority in Relation to an Application

a) In considering an application to offer units in a real estate investment fund, the Authority may:

1. Carry out any enquiries that it considers appropriate;
2. Require the applicant or its representative, to attend before the Authority to answer questions and explain any matter the Authority considers relevant to the application. An applicant becomes subject to these Regulations from the date of submission of an application;
3. Require the applicant to submit such additional information or verify the submitted information as the Authority considers appropriate within (30) days of the request; and
4. Verify any information provided by the applicant.

b) The Authority may refuse to consider the application where an applicant has failed to provide the required information, or has failed to provide them within the period specified in paragraph (a/3) of this Article. The Authority reserves the right to reject an application if it believes that the fund would not be in the best interests of investors or may not be suitable for the fund manager's capacity, or would result in a breach of the Capital Market Law and its Implementing Regulations.

c) The Authority shall, upon receipt of all information and documents required, notify the applicant in writing and shall take any of the following decisions within a maximum period of (30) days from the date of the notice:

1. Approve the application in whole or in part;
2. Approve the application subject to such conditions and limitations as it considers appropriate;
3. Reject the application, giving reasons.

d) The Authority will inform the applicant in writing with the decision it took regarding the application.

e) An applicant may not offer, market or advertise any units in the fund prior to receiving the Authority's approval decision.

31.3 PART 3: REGULATING THE OPERATION OF REAL ESTATE INVESTMENT FUNDS

31.3.1 Chapter 1: Fund's Organizational Structure

Article 9: Legal Basis for Management of the Fund A contractual relationship is established between the fund manager and the unitholders as after signing the terms and conditions of the fund licensed in accordance with these Regulations.

Article 10: Types and Objectives of Real Estate Investment Funds
a) Closed-ended real estate investment funds, which operate according to the following:

1. Initial Development then Selling: This is achieved by owning a piece of raw land, developing it, dividing it into residential or commercial plots, then selling it and terminating the fund.
2. Constructional Development then Selling: This is achieved by owning a piece of raw or developed land with the purpose of constructing residential or commercial units, then selling it and terminating the fund.
3. Initial or Constructional Development with the intention of leasing it for a certain period of time then selling it and terminating the fund.
4. Owning real states that are constructionally developed with the intention of leasing it for a certain period of time then selling it and terminating the fund.
5. investing in constructionally developed real estates, able to generate periodic and rental income

b) Funds with other types or purposes, other than those specified in paragraph (a) above, may be established, after fulfilling the conditions and requirements that the Authority deems necessary.

Article 11: Fund's Board of Directors
a) Each fund is supervised by a board appointed by the fund manager since establishment, the Authority's approval is required to be obtained (10) days prior to the appointment of the fund's board or any subsequent change in its composition.

b) The number of directors in the fund must not be less than three (3) directors. The number of independent fund directors of a fund board shall not be less than two, or one third of the total number of directors, whichever is greater.

c) If the quorum set forth in paragraph (b) of this Article is not fulfilled with regard to independent members, the fund manager shall appoint independent members, who satisfy the eligibility requirements set out in paragraph (i) of this Article.

d) The fund manager may not remove any independent board member, and the removal shall only be made by the unitholders in accordance with the provisions of Article (23) of these Regulations.

e) The fund manager must remove any member of the board of directors of the fund if a special fund resolution is issued by the fund's unitholders requesting the fund manager to remove that member.

f) When more than one real estate investment fund is managed by the same fund manager, those real estate investment funds may be supervised by a single fund board unless the number of the real estate investment funds is reasonably estimated by the fund manager to be too high to be supervised effectively by a single fund board. The fund board and the fund manager must review annually the number of the real estate investment funds supervised by that board and assess whether the number is such that effective supervision is compromised and a different board should be appointed for one or more of those real estate investment funds. The Authority reserves the right to require a fund manager to appoint another fund board if the Authority considers that the number of real estate investment funds the fund board supervises is too high.

g) The fund board shall conduct an annual assessment for each independent director to ensure that there are no relationships or circumstances that affect or may affect his/her independency.

h) A fund board director may vote on any resolution taken by the fund's board of directors to be taken on any matter in which such fund board director has any direct or indirect particular interest and shall disclose any such interest to the fund board

i) Any person appointed by the fund manager as a member of the fund board must fulfill the following eligibility requirements:

1) the person must not be bankrupt or subject to any bankruptcy or insolvency proceedings;
2) the person must not have committed an offense involving fraud or acted in breach of integrity and honesty; and
3) the person must possess the necessary experience and expertise.

j) If any If a member of the fund board ceases to meet the eligibility requirements set out in paragraph (i) of this Article, the fund manager must:

1) Notify the Authority immediately.

2) replace a member of the fund board with another person who fulfills the eligibility requirements within (45) days, in case the requirements set out in paragraph (b) of this Article are not met.

k) If any board director resigned or ceased to provide services, the fund manager must:

1) notify the Authority within (10) days
2) replace the member of the fund board with another person within (45) calendar days from the day the fund manager becomes aware of such resignation or cessation of services, in case the requirements set out in paragraph (b) of this Article are not met.

l) The fund manager must immediately disclose on its website and the Exchange's website or any other website available to the public according to the controls set out by the Authority (where applicable), any change in the membership of the fund's board of directors.

m) The fund manager must provide all necessary information about the public fund to all members of the fund's board in order to enable them to carry out their duties efficiently, the fund manager shall also provide any other information or documentation requested by the fund's board to enable it to perform its duties.

Article 12: The Fund's Board of Directors Responsibilities The Fund's Board of Directors responsibilities shall include the following:

1) approving material contracts, decisions and reports involving the fund, including, but not limited to, contracts for the provision of fund management services, contracts for the provision of custody services but excluding contracts entered into pursuant to investment decisions regarding underlying investments made or to be made by the fund.

2) Reviewing the report that includes assessment of the performance and quality of services provided by the parties involved in providing significant services to the fund referred to in sub-paragraph (6) of paragraph (c) of Article (13) of these Regulations, in order to ensure that the fund manager fulfills his responsibilities in the interest of unitholders in accordance with the terms and conditions of the fund and the provisions stipulated in these Regulations.

3) Adopt a written policy regarding voting rights related to the Fund's assets.

4) Supervision, and where appropriate, approval or ratification of any conflict of interest disclosed by the Fund Manager.

5) Meeting at least twice a year with the Fund Manager's compliance committee or with the compliance officer to review the fund manager's compliance with all applicable rules, laws and regulations, including (without limitation) the requirements stipulated in these Regulations.

6) Approve all changes stipulated in Articles (26) and (27) of these regulations prior to the fund manager obtaining the unitholders' and the Authority's approval, or prior to notifying them (where applicable).

7) Confirming the completeness and accuracy (complete, clear, accurate, and not misleading), and compliance with these Regulations, of the terms and conditions and any other document contractual or otherwise, that includes disclosures relating to the fund and/or the fund manager and its conduct of the fund. In addition to ensuring that the foregoing complies with the provisions of these regulations.

8) Ensuring that the fund manager carries out its obligations in the best interests of the unitholders, in accordance with these Regulations, the terms and conditions of the fund.

9) Assessing the mechanism of the fund manager's handling of the risks related to the fund's assets in accordance with the fund manager's policies and procedures that detect the fund's risks and how to treat such risks.

10) have a fiduciary duty to unitholders, including a duty to act in good faith, a duty to act in the best interests of the unitholders and a duty to exercise all reasonable care and skill; and

11) taking minutes of meetings that provide all deliberations and facts of the meetings and the decisions taken by the fund board.

12) Reviewing the report that includes all complaints and the measures taken to address them referred to in sub-paragraph (12) of paragraph (e) of Article (13) of these Regulations, in order to ensure that the fund manager fulfills its responsibilities in the interest of unitholders in accordance with the terms and conditions of the fund and the provisions stipulated in these Regulations.

31.3.2 Chapter 2: Fund Management

Article 13: Fund Management

a) The fund manager must act for the benefit of unitholders in accordance with these Regulations, the Capital Market Institutions Regulations and the terms and conditions of the fund.

b) The fund manager must comply with all principles and duties required under the Capital Market Institutions Regulations including the fiduciary duty towards unitholders which includes the duty to act in the best interests of the unitholders and duty to exercise all reasonable care and skill.

c) All disclosures by the fund manager must be complete, clear, accurate and not misleading.

d) The Fund will be managed by a portfolio manager working for the Fund Manager, and who must be a registered person with the Authority as per the provisions of the Capital Market Institutions Regulations.

e) Fund Manager's Duties:

1) set out decision making procedures that should be followed when executing technical and administrative issues of the Fund's businesses and projects.
2) comply with all laws and regulations valid in the Kingdom related to the Fund's business.
3) implementing a compliance monitoring program for every real estate fund under its manages, the fund manager must provide the Authority with the results of the implementation of the program upon its request.
4) developing policies and procedures that detect risks effecting the fund's investments and ensure treatment of these risks as soon as possible. These policies and procedures must include conducting risks assessment, at least, once a year.
5) cooperate with all persons concerned with the performance of tasks for the fund, including the custodian and the auditor. The fund manager must provide them with whatever necessary to perform their duties and tasks in accordance with these Regulations.
6) prepare an annual report that includes an assessment of the performance and quality of services provided by the parties involved in providing material services to the fund - including the custodian, developer and property manager as applicable - and the fund manager must submit the report referred to in this paragraph to the fund's board of directors.
7) to manage the Fund's assets in favor of the Unitholders benefit according to the Fund's Terms and Conditions.
8) ensuring the legality and validity of all contracts concluded for the benefit of the Fund.
9) The fund manager shall have the primary responsibility for compliance with these Regulations. Any delegation of the fund manager's responsibilities and duties to any other person pursuant to these Regulations shall not in any way limit, reduce or satisfy the fund manager's responsibilities under these Regulations and the Capital Market Institutions Regulations. The fund manager shall be responsible to unitholders for losses incurred by the investment fund which are caused by, fraud, negligence, misconduct or willful default of the fund manager.
10) The fund manager must comply with the provisions of Annex (12) of these Regulations when applying for an approval from or notifying the Authority requests.
11) The fund manager must comply with the fund's terms and conditions.

12) The fund manager must prepare an annual report that includes all complaints and the measures taken to address them, and it shall submit such report to the Fund's board.
13) The Fund Manager must comply with the Instructions for InvestmentFunds Announcements.

Article 14: Record Retention

a) The fund manager must maintain the books and records of all investment funds which the fund manager manages.

b) The fund manager must maintain, at all times, records of all units issued and cancelled, and must maintain at all times an up to date record of the balance of outstanding units for each real estate fund under its management.

c) Without prejudice to paragraph (b) of this Article, the fund manager must retain all books and records in accordance with these Regulations for a period of ten years, unless the Authority determines otherwise. The fund manager must retain copies of all books and records required pursuant to this Article for a period more than ten years in the event such books and records relate to any litigation or claim (including any litigation pending or threatened) or any on-going investigations, the fund manager must retain such books and records until the closure of that litigation, claim or on-going investigation.

Article 15: Delegation by the Fund Manager

a) A fund manager may, in respect to any investment fund which the Fund Manager manages, delegates one or more third parties or affiliates as a fund sub-manager. The remuneration of any fund sub-manager must be paid by the Fund Manager out of its own resources.

b) With the exception of the cases mentioned in paragraph (c) of this Article, the Fund Sub-Manager must be delegated in accordance with paragraph (a) of this Article as Capital Market Institution authorized to conduct investments management and funds operation activity3, and it must be delegated under a written contract.

c) A fund manager may appoint fund sub-manager operating in a jurisdiction outside the Kingdom to manage foreign investments of the investment fund, however the sub-manager shall be established, authorized and supervised in a jurisdiction that employs regulatory standards and requirements at least equivalent to those of the Authority, and must be appointed pursuant to a contract in writing.

d) The Authority shall have the discretion to assess whether the jurisdiction in which any fund sub-manager operates has regulatory standards and requirements at least equivalent to those of the Authority.

e) The fund manager may assign a third party or more, or any of his affiliate to work as a distributor to units of any real estate investment fund managed by the fund manager. The distributor's remuneration must be paid from the fund manager's own resources.

f) The distributor that has been assigned in the Kingdom pursuant to paragraph (e) of this Article, must be one of the following:

1. A Capital Market Institution licensed to carry out dealing activity.
2. A Capital Market Institution licensed to carry out advising activity.
3. A local bank.

g) The assignment referenced in paragraph (e) of this Article must be made pursuant to a contract in writing, and where the distributor is a local bank it must include the following controls at minimum:

1. The units of the publicly offered real estate investment funds shall be distributed through the distributor's websites only.
2. The website of the assigned distributor shall provide the ability to fill and sign the following documents including:
   a) The fund manager's investment account opening agreement.
   b) The "Know Your Customer" form provided in the Capital Market Institution Regulations.
   c) The Fund's subscription form, and the terms and conditions or the fund to be subscribed in.

h) Where the fund manager has assigned the distributor under paragraph (e) of this Article, the fund manager is responsible for complying with the Capital Market Law and its implementing regulations, and the Anti-Money Laundering Law, and its implementing regulations. The fund manager may rely on the assigned distributor to take due diligence measures towards the customer according to the relevant provisions contained in the Anti-Money Laundering Law and its implementing regulations.

i) The fund manager may assign a third party or more, to carry out the fund operations, including administrative services for the fund.

j) With exception for cases described in paragraph (k) of this Article, any third party assigned pursuant to paragraph (i) of this Article must be an Capital Market Institution authorized to carry out managing investments and operating funds activity4, and must be assigned pursuant to a written contract.

k) A fund manager may assign a third party operating in a jurisdiction outside the Kingdom to carry out the fund operations in relation to investment fund's foreign investments. The third party must be established, authorized and supervised in a jurisdiction that employs regulatory standards and requirements at least equivalent to those of the Authority, and must be assigned pursuant to a contract in writing.

l) The Authority shall have the discretion to assess whether the jurisdiction in which any third party operating has regulatory standards and requirements at least equivalent to those of the Authority.

(According to the Authority's Board Resolution no. no. 2-22-2021 Dated 12/7/1442H. Corresponding to 24/2/2021G, the requirement to obtain a license for managing investments and operating funds activity shall be effective as of 28/05/1443H., corresponding to 01/01/2022G., the requirement to obtain a license for management activity shall remain effective until the effectivity date of the requirement to obtain a license for managing investments and operating funds.)

Article 16: Removal and Replacement of Fund Manager

a) The Authority shall have the power to remove a Fund Manager in relation to a particular investment fund and to take any action it deems appropriate to appoint a replacement Fund Manager for that investment fund or to take any other measures it deems necessary in the event of:

1. the fund manager ceasing from carrying on management activities without notifying the Authority under the Capital Market Institutions Regulations;

2. the cancellation, withdrawal or suspension by the Authority of the Fund Manager's relevant Authorization(s) of carrying on management activities.
3. a request by the Fund Manager to the Authority to cancel its relevant Authorization of carrying on management activities;
4. the Authority believing that the Fund Manager has failed, in a manner which the Authority considers material, to comply with the Capital Market Law or its Implementing Regulations;
5. the death, incapacity or resignation of the portfolio manager who manages the assets of the relevant real estate investment fund, if no other registered person employed by the fund manager can manage the assets of the relevant real estate investment fund or the assets of the funds managed by the portfolio manager;
6. The Issuance of a special fund resolution by unitholders of a close ended fund requesting a removal of the Fund Manager; or
7. any other event determined by the Authority, on reasonable basis, to be of material importance.

b) Notice of any event described in sub-paragraph (5) of paragraph (a) of this Article must be provided by the fund manager to the Authority within (2) days of its occurrence.

c) Upon removal of the fund manager in accordance with the cases stipulated in subparagraphs (1), (2), (3), (4), (5) and (7) of paragraph (a) of this Article, the Authority shall directs the removed fund manager to call for a unitholders meeting within (15) days from the date of the Authority's removal decision, in order to appoint the custodian or other party, through an ordinary fund resolution, to find and negotiate with a replacement fund manager and specify the time limit for finding and negotiation.

d) Upon removal of the fund manager in accordance with the case stipulated in subparagraph (6) of paragraph (a) of this Article, the fund manager must issue an ordinary fund resolution at the same meeting in which unitholders voted on the request to remove the fund manager, in order to appoint the custodian or other party, to find and negotiate with a replacement fund manager and specify the time limit for finding and negotiation.

e) When any of the two cases stipulated in paragraphs (c) and (d) of this Article occurs, the Fund Manager must notify the Authority of the results of the unitholders meeting within two days of its convening.

f) The fund manager must cooperate and provide the custodian or the party assigned to find and negotiate any documents required by it for the purpose of appointing a replacement fund manager within (10) days from the date of the request, and both parties must maintain the confidentiality of the information.

g) The fund manager must, upon approval of the replacement fund manager to manage the fund and transfer of the fund management to it, send a written consent of the replacement fund manager to the Authority as soon as it is received.

h) If the Authority exercises its power pursuant to paragraph (a) of this Article, the relevant fund manager shall cooperate fully in order to help facilitate a smooth transfer of responsibilities to the replacement fund manager during the initial (60) day period after the appointment of the replacement fund manager. The Fund Manager must where necessary, appropriate and at the Authority its absolute discretion, transfer all of the contracts relating to the relevant real estate investment fund to the replacement fund manager.

i) Unitholders are entitled to request the liquidation of the fund by a special fund resolution in the event that a replacement fund manager has not been appointed within the period for search and negotiation stipulated in paragraphs (c) and (d) of this Article.

(According to the Authority's Board Resolution no. 2-22-2021 Dated 12/7/1442H. Corresponding to 24/2/2021G., the requirement to obtain a license for the managing investments and operating funds activity shall be effective as of 28/05/1443H., corresponding to 01/01/2022G.)

Article 17: Investment Decisions If a fund manager is removed pursuant to Article (16) of these Regulations, it shall cease to make any investment decisions in relation to the relevant fund as soon as the replacement fund manager is appointed or at any earlier time determined by the Authority.

Article 18: Financial Statements

a) The financial statements of the fund must be prepared in the Arabic language, at least semi-annually, and examined according to the accounting standards approved by the Saudi Organization for Certified Public Accountants. Additional copies may be prepared in other languages, and in case of any conflict between those copies, the Arabic text shall prevail.

b) The annual financial statements of the fund must be reviewed in accordance with the accounting standards approved by the Saudi Organization for Certified Public Accountants (SOCPA), and the auditor of the fund, through reviewing the financial statements and based on the information provided to it, must include in its report what may come to its attention of violations of the provisions of the Real Estate Investment Funds Regulations or the fund's terms and conditions.

(According to the Authority's Board Resolution no. 2-22-2021 Dated 12/7/1442H. Corresponding to 24/2/2021G., Article 43 of these Regulations shall be effective as of 28/07/1443H., corresponding to 01/03/2021G. Moreover, paragraph Article 18 of the Real Estate Investment Funds Regulations issued pursuant to the Authority's Board Resolution no. (1-193-2006) dated 19/06/1427H. corresponding to 15/07/2006G., which can be viewed via the following link:(https://cma.org.sa/RulesRegulations/Regulations/DocLib/REAL%20ESTATE%20INVE%20FUND%20REG__EN.pdf), shall remain effective until the effectivity date of Article 43 of these Regulations.)

Article 19: Conflict of Interests and Disclosure Thereof

a) A fund manager (or any of its affiliates) may not act as principal for its own account when dealing with investment funds managed by it.

b) Without prejudice to the provisions of paragraphs (a), (c), (d) and (e) of this Article, the Fund Manager must treat any conflicts of interest in accordance with the provisions the Capital Market Institutions Regulations.

c) If the Fund Manager (or the fund sub manager) does not carry out a prior (where possible) or immediate disclosure of the conflict of interest to the relevant fund board, and obtain the fund board's approval on that action, it must not engage in any action that involves:

1. A material conflict between the interests of the fund manager or fund sub manager and the interests of any investment fund it manages; or

2. A conflict between the interests of any investment fund it manages and another investment fund or another client account.

d) The fund manager (and fund sub manager), must ensure their affiliates do not engage in any action that involves any conflict of interest as described in paragraph (c) of this Article.

e) The fund manager shall disclose immediately, on its website and the Exchange's website or any other website available to the public according to the controls set out by the Authority (where applicable), and on the public fund's annual reports that has been prepared by the fund manager in accordance with Article (25) of these Regulations, any conflicts of interest that has been approved by the relevant fund board.

Article 20: Special Commission Arrangements

a) Any special commission arrangements entered into by the fund manager is subject to the Capital Market Institutions Regulations and must be disclosed in the terms and conditions of the fund.

b) Goods and services received by a fund manager under a special commission arrangement shall be restricted to those that are related to the execution of transactions on behalf of the real estate investment fund or comprise the provision of research for the benefit of relevant real estate investment fund.

c) The fund manager may not get sums of money under special commission or any other arrangements.

Article 21: Auditing Requirements

a) The Fund Manager must appoint an auditor prior to the establishment of the fund. The auditor of the public fund must be certified in the Kingdom in accordance with the rules for registering auditors of entities subject to the Authority's supervision, and must be independent from the fund manager according to the independence standard stated in the Certified Public Accountants Regulations and its Implementing Regulations.

b) Where a fund was established more than (9) months before such public fund's year-end, an audit must be conducted as of the end of its first fiscal year.

c) Where a fund was established (9) months or less before such fund's year-end, an audit may be conducted at the end of the second year end of the fund.

d) The approval of the Fund Board of Directors must be obtained to appoint or change any alternative auditor. The fund board must reject the appointment of an auditor, or instruct the fund manager to replace an auditor which has already been appointed in relation to the fund, if:

1. there are any outstanding and significant allegations of professional misconduct in relation to audit functions by the auditor;
2. If the auditor of the fund is no longer independent;
3. If the auditor of the fund is no longer registered with the Authority.
4. supervision the fund board determines that the auditor does not have sufficient qualifications and experience to perform a satisfactory auditing functions; or
5. The Authority, in its absolute discretion, instructs the fund manager to replace the auditor appointed in relation to the public fund.

e) The audit fees of the auditor shall be determined by the Fund Manager with the approval of the fund board.

Article 22: Commissions, Services and Management Fees

a) The Fund Manager must disclose in the Fund's Terms and Conditions any service commissions or fees charged by it or by any other parties.

b) The Fund's terms and conditions must specify all fees, charges and commissions whether they were charged on the Unitholders or on the Fund's assets.

c) The Authority may impose a cap for any of the service fees and commissions charged by the Fund Manager.

Article 23: Meeting of Unitholders

a) The fund manager may call for a meeting of unitholders on its own initiative. Provided that the subject of the invitation does not contradict with the responsibilities and duties of the Fund Manager in accordance with the provisions of these regulations.

b) The fund manager must call for a meeting of unitholders within (10) days of receiving a written request from the custodian.

c) The fund manager must call for a meeting of unitholders within (10) days of receiving a written request from a unitholder or more, holding individually or collectively at least (25%) in value of the units in the fund, and the fund manager must state it in the fund's terms and conditions.

d) The fund manager shall call for a meeting of unitholders by announcing it on its website and any other website available to the public according to the controls set out by the Authority, and by sending a notice in writing to all the unitholders and the custodian giving not less than (10) days' notice before the meeting and no more than (21) days' notice before the meeting. The announcement and notice must specify the date, place and time of the meeting and the proposed resolutions and its agenda. The fund manager must provide a copy of such notice to the Authority immediately without any delay.

e) When preparing the agenda for the unitholders' meeting, the fund manager must take into consideration the topics that the unitholders want to include, unitholders who own at least (10%) of the fund units' value are entitled to add one or more topics to the agenda of the unitholders' meeting. Provided that the proposed topic does not overlap with the responsibilities and duties of the Fund Manager in accordance with the provisions of these regulations.

f) The fund manager may amend the agenda of the unitholders meeting within the notice period referred to in paragraph (d) of this Article, provided that it announces that on its website and any other website available to the public according to the controls set out by the Authority, and by submitting a written notice to all unitholders and the custodian; 1) at least 10 days prior to the meeting; 2) within a maximum of 21 days prior to the meeting.

g) In case that the unitholders approve any of the decisions proposed at the unitholders' meeting, and this necessitates amending the fund's terms and conditions, the fund manager must amend the fund's terms and conditions according to the approved decision.

h) The quorum required to conduct a meeting of the unitholders shall be such number of unitholders owning together at least (25%) in value of the units in the fund or greater percentage as specified in the fund's terms and conditions.

i) If the quorum requirements set out in paragraph (h) of this Article are not met, the fund manager shall call for a second meeting by announcing it on its website and any other website available to the public according to the controls set out by the Authority and shall send a notice in writing to all the unitholders and the custodian giving not less than (5) days' notice prior to the second meeting. At the second meeting, any number of unitholder(s) holding any number of units present in person or represented by a proxy shall considered a valid quorum.

j) Every unitholder may entitle to appoint a proxy to represent such unitholder at the meeting of unitholders.

k) Every unitholder shall be entitled to exercise one vote at the meeting of the unitholders for each unit the unitholder holds as at the time of the meeting.

l) Substantial unitholders may not vote at the meeting of the unitholders on the decisions relating to the acquisition of real estate assets owned or utilized by them.

m) The unitholders meetings and its deliberations and voting on decisions may be conducted through modern technology in accordance with requirements set by the Authority.

n) The decision shall be effective upon the approval of unitholders holding more than (50%), or more than (75%) (where applicable), of the total units present in the meeting either by unitholders attending in person, appointed proxy or through contemporary technology.

o) The Treaded Fund is excluded from the requirement of sending a written notice to all unitholders mentioned in paragraphs (d), (f) and (i) of this Article, provided that such announcement is made on the fund manager's website and the Exchange's website.

31.3.3 Chapter 3: Disclosure

Article 24: Disclosure

a) The Fund Manager shall provide sufficient information with regards to the Fund's investment goals, risks and any other information that would enable Unitholders to make their investment decisions. The information materials about a Fund shall not contain any incorrect or misleading information.

b) The Fund Manager must disclose all expenses related to the offer of the real estate investment fund's units, if such expenses were incurred by the fund in fund's terms and conditions.

c) The fund manager must submit an updated version of the fund's terms and conditions to the Authority within (10) days from making any amendments to it, and also provide the custodian with the updated version immediately. The fund manager must also publish version copy of the fund's terms and conditions on its website and the Exchange's website or any other website available to the public according to the controls set out by the Authority (where applicable), and must announce the updated version of fund's terms and conditions on its website and the Exchange's website any other website available to the public according to the controls set out by the Authority (where applicable) within (10) days of making any changes to it, including the annual update of the fund's performance.

Article 25: Reporting to Unitholders

a) the real estate investment fund manager must publish a semi-annual statement of the fiscal year, and manager of the real estate investment traded fund must publish a quarterly statement of the fiscal year in accordance with the requirements of Annexes (5) and (6) of these Regulations (as applicable), within a period not exceeding (10) days from the end of the relevant half or quarter on its website and the Exchange's website or any other website available to the public according to the controls set out by the Authority (where applicable).

b) The fund manager must prepare and publish the annual reports on its website and the Exchange's website or any other website available to the public, according to the controls set out by the Authority (where applicable), in accordance with the requirements of Annex (4) of these Regulations.

c) the fund manager must make available to the public the interim financial statements, after reviewing it in accordance with the provisions of Article 18 of these Regulations, free of charge, within a period not exceeding (30) days after the end of the interim financial statements period, on websites and channels as specified in the Fund's terms and conditions, and on the fund manager's website and the Exchange's website or any other website available to the public according to the controls set out by the Authority (where applicable).

d) the Fund Manager must make the annual financial statements available to the public (including the annual financial statements reviewed in accordance with the provisions of Article 18 of these Regulations, free of charge, within a period not exceeding (3) months after the end of the reporting period, on websites and via channels as specified in the Fund's terms and conditions, and on the fund manager's website and the Exchange's website or any other website is available to the public according to the controls set out by the Authority (where applicable).

31.3.4 Chapter 4: Fundamental and Non-Fundamental Changes

Article 26: Approval of the Authority and Consent of Unitholders to Fundamental Changes

a) A fund manager must obtain the consent of the unitholders in the relevant fund to the proposed fundamental change by way of an ordinary fund resolution.

b) As an exception to paragraph (a) of this Article, the fund manager must obtain the consent of the unitholders in the relevant fund on the proposed fundamental change stipulated in sub-paragraph (9) of paragraph (d) of this Article by way of a special fund resolution.

c) A fund manager, after obtaining the consent of the unitholders specified in paragraphs (a) and (b) of this Article, must obtain the approval of the Authority in the proposed fundamental change to the fund.

d) The term "fundamental change" means:

1) a significant change in the fund's purposes, nature or class;
2) a change which may have a material adverse effect on the unitholders or their rights in relation to the closed-ended fund;
3) a change which alters the risk profile of the fund; or
4) the voluntary withdrawal of a Fund Manager from its position as the fund manager.
5) It usually causes unitholders to reconsider of their subscriptions in the closed-ended fund.
6) A change which results in any increased payments out of the assets of the closed-ended fund to a fund manager or any member of the fund board or an affiliate of either.
7) A change which introduces any new type of payment out of the assets of the closed-ended fund.
8) A change that materially increases other types of payment out of the assets of the closed-ended fund.

9) Change in the maturity date or termination of the closed-ended Fund.
10) Increase the total value of the ether fund assets by accepting cash or in-kind contributions, or both.
11) any other cases determined by the Authority from time to time and reported to the Fund Manager.

e) The fund manager must obtain the fund board's approval prior to any effecting fundamental change.

f) The fund manager must notify the unitholders and disclose details of fundamental changes on its website and any other website available to the public according to the controls set out by the Authority (10) days before of the date in which the change becomes effective.

g) Details of all fundamental changes shall be included in the next fund report prepared by the fund manager pursuant to Article (25) of these Regulations.

h) The unitholders of an open-ended fund have the right to redeem their units before any fundamental changes are effective; without incurring any redemption fees (if any).

i) A traded fund shall be exempted from the unitholders notification requirement set out in paragraph (f) of this Article, provided that the announcement of such is made on the fund manager's website and the Exchange's website.

Article 27: Notification to the Authority and Unitholders of Non-Fundamental Changes
a) The fund manager must notify the Authority and unitholders, and disclose on its website and any other website available to the public according to the controls set out by the Authority of any non-fundamental changes to the fund (10) days prior to the change becoming effective. Unitholders of an open- ended fund may redeem their units before the non-fundamental change becomes effective, and without incurring any redemption fees (if any).

b) The fund manager must obtain the fund board approval on any non- fundamental changes.

c) For the purposes of these Regulations, "non-fundamental change" means any change that does not fall within the provisions of paragraph (d) of Article (26) of these Regulations.

d) Details of all non-fundamental changes must be included in the next fund report prepared by the Fund Manager pursuant to Article (25) of these Regulations.

e) A traded fund shall be exempted from the unitholders notification requirement set out in paragraph (a) of this Article, provided that the announcement of such is made on the fund manager's website and the Exchange's website.

31.3.5 Chapter 5: Fund Assets Requirements, Custody of its Assets and Operation Rules

Article 28: Fund Assets Requirements The Fund Assets should include the following conditions:

a) All real estates of the Fund should be owned pursuant to valid title of deeds.

b) All real estates of the Fund that are the subject matter of the investment shall have been approved to be designed and constructed by an official document from the competent body, and for income generating real estate assets the fund manager must have a proof that it is ready for a legal use.

c) The fund manager must ensure the fairness and integrity of the lease agreements for income generating real estate assets.

d) All lease agreements must be legally documented to ensure the rights of all parties.

Article 29: Custody of Fund Assets and Related Documents
a) The custody of the fund assets shall be held by one or more custodians in the Kingdom pursuant to a written contract, who shall be a Capital Market Institution authorized to conduct custody activity.

b) A custodian may appoint one or more third parties or affiliates as a fund sub-custodian for any real estate investment fund, pursuant to a contract in writing, to take custody of the fund's assets. The remuneration of the fund sub-custodian shall be paid by the custodian out of its own resources and the fund sub-custodian must be a capital market institution authorized to conduct custody activity.

c) With exception of paragraph (b), a fund sub-custodian may be appointed from out of the Kingdom to conduct custody of the fund's foreign investments, and must be appointed pursuant to a contract in writing and shall be established, authorized and supervised in a jurisdiction that employs regulatory standards and requirements at least equivalent to those of the Authority.

d) The custodian appointed pursuant to paragraphs (a), (b) or (c) of this Article must not be a fund manager or a fund sub-manager to the relevant fund, or an affiliate of the fund manager or to the fund sub-manager.

e) The custodian must segregate each real estate investment fund's assets from its own assets and from the assets of its other clients, and must separately identify, by registration in the name of the custodian for the benefit of the relevant real estate investment fund the securities and other assets of such investment fund. The custodian must register the real estate assets of the fund and the ownerships in companies unlisted and not deposited at the depositary centre in the name of a fully owned company of the custodian.

f) With exception of paragraph (e) of this Article, in case the real estate investment fund takes the form of a special purposes entity, the custodian must segregate each real estate investment fund's assets from its own assets and from the assets of its other clients. Such assets must be specified independently by registering the securities and other assets in the name of the special purposes entity. The custodian must also maintain all necessary records and other documents that support the performance of its contractual obligations.

g) All related documents and records to the Fund must be maintained by the custodian, which includes, for example, the following documents:

a. Title of deed.
b. Investment decisions.
c. All material contracts related to the operation of the Fund.
d. Fund Board minutes of meeting.
e. Accredited Valuers' reports.

h) The custodian shall be fully responsible for its obligations in accordance with the provisions of these Regulations, weather the custodian carries out its duties on its own or assign it to a third party in accordance with the provisions of these Regulations or the Capital Market Institutions Regulations. The custodian shall be liable towards the fund manager and the unitholders for losses incurred by the investment fund, which are caused by fraud, negligence, misconduct or willful default of the custodian.

i) The custodian is responsible for maintaining and protecting the real estate investment fund assets for the benefit of unitholders, through a policy established by the fund manager in this regard.

j) The net assets of the Fund shall be owned collectively by the Unitholders in such fund. A fund manager, or custodian shall not have any interest in or claims against such assets, other than when the Fund Manager is a Unitholder, or for claims permitted under these regulations and disclosed in the Fund's Terms and Conditions.

k) With the exception of fund units owned by the Fund Manager, fund sub-manager, custodian, sub-custodian, investment advisor, or distributor, and within the limits of what is owned by the debtor, Creditors of such fund manager, fund sub-manager, custodian, sub-custodian, investment advisor, or distributor may not have any right to claim or entitlements to money or assets of the investment fund.

l) Real estate assets of the real estate investment fund can be mortgaged to a subsidiary of an entity licensed to provide loans, that extended a loan for the fund.

(According to the Authority's Board Resolution no. 2-22-2021 Dated 12/7/1442H. Corresponding to 24/2/2021G., paragraph (e) of Article 29 of these Regulations shall be effective as of 28/07/1443H., corresponding to 01/03/2022G. Moreover, paragraph (b) of Article (12) of the Real Estate Investment Funds Regulations issued pursuant to the Authority's Board Resolution no. (1-193-2006) dated 19/06/1427H. corresponding to 15/07/2006G., which can be viewed via the following link:(https://cma.org.sa/RulesRegulations/Regulations/), shall remain effective until the effectivity date of paragraph (e) of Article 29 of these Regulations.)

Article 30: Segregation of Fund Money

a) A custodian must open a separate local bank account in his name for each fund he is a custodian for, such account shall be in favor of the related real estate investment fund.

b) As an exception to the provisions of paragraph (a) of this Article, in the event of a real estate investment fund that takes the form of a special purposes entity, the custodian must open a separate account with a local bank in the name of such special purposes entity.

c) The custodian must deposit all cash belonging to the investment fund into the relevant bank account referred to in paragraphs (a) or (b) of this Article (as applicable), and must deduct from the relevant bank account the amounts used to finance the investments and the real estate investment fund management and operations expenses in accordance with the provisions of these Regulations, the fund's updated terms and conditions that it received from the Fund Manager, and the contract by which the custodian was appointed by the fund manager.

Article 31: Powers of the Authority to Remove and Replace Custodian

a. The Authority shall have the power to remove the custodian which was appointed by the fund manager or take any other measures it deems appropriate, in the event of:

1) The custodian ceasing to carry out custody activity without notification to the Authority under the Capital Market Institutions Regulations;
2) The cancellation or suspension by the Authority of the custodian's relevant Authorization to carry out custody activity under the Capital Market Institutions Regulations;
3) A request by the custodian to the Authority to cancel its Authorization to carry out custody activity;
4) The Authority believing that the custodian has failed, in a manner which the Authority considers material, to comply with the Capital Market Law or its Implementing Regulations;
5) Any other event determined by the Authority – based on reasonable grounds- to be of sufficient significance.

b. If the Authority exercises its power pursuant to paragraph (a) of this Article, the relevant fund manager must appoint a replacement custodian to that investment fund in accordance with the Authority's instructions, the fund manager as well as the removed custodian shall co-operate fully in order to facilitate a smooth transfer of responsibilities to the replacement custodian during the first (60) days of the appointing the replacement custodian. The custodian must transfer, where the Authority decides its necessary and applicable, all the contracts related to the relevant investment fund to the replacement custodian.

Article 32: Removal of Custodian by the Fund Manager

a. The custodian appointed by the fund manager of an investment fund shall be subject to removal by written notice by the fund manager of that investment fund upon the fund manager forming the reasonable opinion that the removal is for the interest of the unitholders, the fund manager shall notify the Authority and the unitholders in writing immediately.

b. Upon removal of the custodian under a written notice issued under paragraph (a) of this Article, the fund manager must appoint a replacement custodian within (30) days of such notice. The removed custodian must co-operate fully with the fund manager in order to facilitate a smooth transfer of responsibilities to the replacement custodian, and must transfer, where necessary and applicable, all contracts related to the relevant real estate investment fund to the replacement custodian

c. The fund manager must immediately disclose on its website and the Exchange's website or any other website available to the public according to the controls set out by the Authority (where applicable) the appointment of a replacement custodian for the real estate investment fund.

d. A traded fund shall be exempted from the requirement to notify unitholders in writing, stipulated in paragraph (a) of this Article, provided that the announcement of such is made on the fund manager's website and the Exchange's website.

Article 33: Property Management If any of the purposes of the fund was regarding investing in constructionally developed real estates, the fund manager must appoint one or more company(s) to carry out property management, after ensuring that it obtains the necessary approvals and licenses to conduct its business and activities from the relevant government bodies, to manage the real estate under investment, and that company must possess the necessary expertise in the field of real estate and its management, where applicable, the company shall be responsible for all services related to property management, including, but not limited to, property management and maintenance, leasing services and rent collection. The fund manager may agree with the lessee - under the leasing agreement - that such lessee be responsible for managing the property and carry out any maintenance during the leasing agreement period (where applicable).

Article 34: Appointing the Developer and Engineering Office In the event that one of the objectives of the fund includes the initial development or constructional development, the fund manager must appoint a developer and an engineering office independent6 from any of the related parties, after ensuring that they obtained the approvals and licenses required to carry out their business and activities from the relevant government entities. The engineering office shall - at minimum - oversee the implementation of the fund's business plan.

Article 35: Valuation

a) The real estate investment fund manager must, before purchasing or selling any of the Fund's assets, obtain a valuation from two accredited valuers known for their experience, integrity and knowledge of real estate activity and area under investment.

b) The real estate investment fund manager must ensure that any accredited valuer appointed pursuant to paragraph (a) of this Article meets the following conditions:

1) the accredited valuer must be independent from any related parties
2) the accredited valuer must have joined the Saudi Authority for Accredited Valuers.

c) The accredited valuers report must contain as a minimum the following:

1. The valuation method, mechanisms and assumptions on which such valuation is based.
2. An analysis of the variables related to the real estate market, such as the demand, supply and market trends.
3. Details and descriptions of the real estate.
4. The risks related to the real estate subject to valuation.

d) On purchasing or selling any of the fund's assets, the Fund Manager may not rely on any valuation report prepared before more than (3) months prior to purchasing or selling.

e) The Fund Manager must provide the accredited valuers, in a clear, accurate, and not misleading manners, with any information or documents concerning the assets of the real estate fund to be evaluated, which including but not limited to, related contracts, engineering reports, constructions costs and any information that would enable the accredited valuer preparing its report in accordance with regulatory provisions and accredited standards.

f) The fund manager must provide the valuation reports for the real estate prepared by (2) accredited valuers with the Saudi Authority for Accredited Valuers, and publish them during the offer period on its website and the Exchange's website or any other website available to the public according to the controls set out by the Authority (where applicable), provided that the valuation period did not exceed (3) months at the date of the commencement of the offering, in case of more than two accredited valuers were appointed, the fund manager must publish all the accredited valuers' reports.

g) The Fund Manager must submit a declaration from each accredited valuer confirming that he is complying with the Accredited Valuers Law and its Implementing Regulations and any other Regulations issued by the Saudi Authority for Accredited Valuers (TAQEEM),), and that the scope of the valuation reports is appropriate for the purpose of the fund manager's request and is valid for the public offering. The valuation reports shall include the rental market value of the relevant real estate, if they are different from the contractual rental value in the real estate leases (in case the real estates are income-generating).

h) The Fund Manager must replace the accredited valuers every (5) years at most. Any valuer who have served for such period of time may be re-appointed after a period of (1) year has elapsed from the date of last contract.

(According to the Authority's Board Resolution no. 2-22-2021 Dated 12/7/1442H. Corresponding to 24/2/2021G., the requirement for the independence of the developer from any of the related parties in relation to real estate investment traded funds shall become effective as of 28/07/1443H corresponding to 01/03/2022G.)

(According to the Authority's Board Resolution no. 2-22-2021 Dated 12/7/1442H. Corresponding to 24/2/2021G., subparagraph (2) of paragraph (b) of Article 35 shall become effective as of 08/06/1444H corresponding to 01/01/2023G.)

(According to the Authority's Board Resolution no. 2-22-2021 Dated 12/7/1442H. Corresponding to 24/2/2021G., the requirement to join the Saudi Authority for Accredited Valuers shall become effective as of 08/06/1444H corresponding to 01/01/2023G.)

Article 36: Valuation of Fund Asset and Calculation of Unit Price

a) The Fund Manager is responsible for performing fair valuation of the fund's assets.

b) The Fund Manager shall evaluate the Fund's assets at least once every (6) months based on a valuation prepared by two accredited valuers in accordance with the valuation policy set out in the fund's terms and conditions, and publish the accredited valuers' report on its website and the Exchange's website or any other website available to the public according to the controls set out by the Authority (where applicable) within a period not exceeding (15) days from issuing such report. The valuation reports shall include the rental market value of the relevant real estate (where applicable), and in case of more than two accredited valuers were appointed, the fund manager must publish all the accredited valuers' reports.

c) The net value of the unit shall be calculated by subtracting the Fund's total liabilities from its total assets, then dividing the result by the number of the fund's units, and this shall be considered as a benchmark price of the unit.

Article 37: Register of Unitholders

a) A Fund Manager shall establish and maintain a register of Unitholders.

b) A Fund Manager may engage a third party or parties pursuant to a contract in writing to establish and maintain a register of unitholders referred to in paragraph (a) above.

c) Notwithstanding the appointment of a third party, the Fund Manager shall remain responsible for the discharge of all its duties in relation to the register under these Regulations.

d) The register shall be conclusive evidence as to the persons entitled to units entered on the register.

e) The Fund Manager must maintain, at minimum, the following information in the register:

1) The name address and contact number of each Unitholder;
2) The national identification number, Iqama number, passport number or company registration number of the Unitholder;
3) The nationality of the Unitholder;
4) The number of units held by each unitholder; and
5) The date on which the Unitholder was registered in the register.

f) The register of unitholders must be made available for inspection by the Authority at its request. The fund manager must provide any unitholder, free of charge upon request, an extract that shows all the information relevant to the subject unitholder only.

g) The fund manager must update the register of unitholders immediately to reflect changes to information referred to in paragraph (e) of this Article.

h) The traded fund is excluded from the provisions of this Article.

Article 38: Subscription and Offering

a) Without prejudice to the Law of Real Estate Ownership and Investment by Non-Saudis, subscription in the Fund is open to any Saudi, GCC citizens, non- Saudi residents or foreigners non-residents in the Kingdom.

b) The applicant must commence the offer of the fund units within (6) months from the date of the Authority's decision referred to in sub-paragraphs (1) or (2) of paragraph (c) of Article (8) of these Regulations. If the applicant does not commence the offer of the fund's units during such period, the Authority's approval shall be deemed to be cancelled

c) The Fund's unit value must be fully paid during the fund's offering period in accordance with the Fund's Terms and Conditions.

d) the Fund Manager, who should ensure, before accepting any subscription, that the Unitholder obtains and signs a copy of the Fund's Terms and Conditions.

e) The Fund Manager shall issue a confirmation notice to the unitholder upon subscription in the units of the Fund.

f) The offering period of the Fund shall be specified, and in case the required minimum amount, which stipulated in the fund's terms and conditions that must be collected is not reached, the subscription amounts must be returned back to the unitholders, then the fund manager must cancel the offering and return the fund's unitholders without any deduction within a period not exceeding (5) days from the date of ending the offer.

g) The Real Estate Investment Fund offering period must not exceed a maximum period of (60) days.

h) The Fund Manager must submit to the Authority within (10) days of the end of the offering period, a statement of the offering results, and disclose it on its website, in accordance with the requirements of Annex (12) of these Regulations.

i) With the exception to the provisions of paragraph (e) of Article (45) of these Regulations, a unitholder who have subscribed in the fund with an in-kind contribution may reduce its ownership in the fund's units to a minimum of (50%) of the number of units issued corresponding to such right after one year from the date of subscription in the fund or the date of operation of the fund, whichever is further, unless the relevant fund's terms and conditions state a longer period.

j) The Fund Manager and its affiliates may subscribe for their own account in the fund units managed by the fund manager, provided that the fund manager discloses this in the fund's terms and conditions, provided that the following requirements are met:

1. the subscription condition of the fund manager and his affiliates in the units and related rights shall not have more privileges than the conditions and rights related to the units owned by the other unitholders of the same category.
2. That the Fund Manager and his affiliates shall not exercise voting rights related to the units they own.
3. The Fund Manager shall disclose the details of its investments in the fund units, by the end of each half for a real estate investment fund and each quarter for the real estate investment traded fund, on its website and the Exchange's website or any other website available to the public according to the controls set out by the Authority (where applicable), as well as in the reports prepared by the fund manager in accordance with Article (25) of these Regulations.

k) The total value of the fund's assets may be increased according to the following mechanism:

1. The fund manager must obtain the unitholders' approval to offer additional units to the fund by accepting in-kind contributions or by accepting cash contributions, or both in accordance with Article (26) of these Regulations.
2. The fund manager must obtain the Authority's approval to offer additional units to the fund by accepting in-kind contributions or by accepting cash contributions, or both.
3. The Fund Manager must commence offering the additional fund's units, within a period not exceeding (6) months from the date of the Authority's approval. If the applicant did not commence the offer of the fund's units during such period, the Authority's approval shall be deemed to be cancelled
4. In case that the total value of the fund's assets increased by accepting cash contributions or cash and in-kind contributions, the offering period of real estate fund shall be not exceeding, as a maximum, (60) days from the date of the Authority's approval.
5. In the event that the value of the units to be offered is collected, the offered units must be allocated to the registered fund's unitholders on the day of the unitholders meeting and then allocate the remaining units - if any - to the rest of the unitholders and return the surplus to all the unitholders in cash - if any - within a period that not exceeding (15) days from the end of the offering period set forth in the fund's terms and conditions. Provided that the ownership of the property to be acquired or its benefit is transferred to the interest of the fund within a period not exceeding (60) days from the end of the offering period.
6. In the event that the total value of the fund's assets is increased by accepting in-kind contributions, the additional units shall be allocated to the unitholders in the form of in-kind immediately, after obtaining the approval of the unitholders referred to in subparagraph (1) of paragraph (k)

of this Article. Provided that the ownership of the property to be acquired or its benefit shall be transferred to the fund's interest within a period not exceeding (60) days from the date of approval of the unitholders.
7. With regards to the provisions of subparagraph (3) of Paragraph (k) of this Article, and in the event that the minimum required to be collected and stipulated in the fund's terms and conditions is not collected, the Fund Manager must cancel the offering and return back the amounts to the fund's unitholders without any deduction within a period not exceeding (5) days from the date of ending the offering period.
8. The fund manager must submit to the Authority a supplementary annex to the fund's terms and conditions, for every increase in the net assets value of the fund by accepting in-kind contributions, cash contributions or both, in accordance with the requirements of Annex (14) of these Regulations.
9. The fund manager must publish the supplementary annex to the fund's terms and conditions referred to in subparagraph (8) of paragraph (k) of this Article, on its website and the Exchange's website or any other website available to the public according to the controls set out by the Authority (where applicable)

l) The traded fund is excluded from the provisions of paragraphs (d) of this Article.

Article 39: Units

a) The potential unitholder shall be the owner of the units to which it has subscribed for as soon as executing the subscription request in the next dealing day following the deadline for the submission of subscription and redemption requests.

b) The unitholder shall be entitled to exercise all rights in relation to the units (including, but not limited to, the right to vote at meetings of unitholders);

c) Other than losing his/her investment in the fund or part of it, the unitholder shall not be liable for the debts and obligations of the relevant fund.

d) A fund may issue more than one class of units, all unitholders from the same class shall have the same rights as each other and shall be treated equally by the fund manager. No class of unitholders shall have a deferent investment strategies and objectives from the investment strategies and objectives of another class in the same investment fund.

e) A class of a unitholders shall not benefit from the rights that prejudice the rights of unitholders of another class.

f) The traded fund is excluded from the provisions of paragraph (a) of this Article.

Article 40: Restrictions on the Fund

a) Using the Fund's Assets:

With regards to the provisions of sub-paragraph (3) of paragraph (b) of Article (46) of these Regulations, regarding a real estate investment traded fund, the Fund Manager must manage the available liquidity for the benefit of the Unitholders in low risk investment channels and without deducting any additional management fees to the invested amounts.

b) Borrowing:

The Fund -including a REIT fund on the Main Market- may not borrow more than (50%) of the fund's total assets value according to the last reviewed financial statements, however in the case of a REIT fund on the parallel market, the borrowing shall not exceed (100%) of the fund's total asset value, according to the last reviewed financial statements.

Article 41: Trading

a) After the end of the subscription period, a related party may not sell any fund unit during the fund's term.

b) As an exception to paragraph (a) of this Article, a unitholder who subscribed in the fund with cash contribution and whose ownership exceeds (5%) of the real estate investment fund's net assets value may sell his units in the fund, unless he is listed under one of the other categories stipulated in the definition of the term "Related Parties".

c) The Fund Manager and Custodian should take all necessary steps for facilitating unit's trading transfer and registering them.

d) The Fund Manager shall maintain a register for all purchasing orders requests and selling offers related to the Fund's units.

e) The Fund Manager shall inform investors, willing to purchase or sell, about the purchasing orders and selling offers register, the benchmark price of the unit and date thereof.

f) The traded fund is excluded from the provisions of this Article.

Article 42: Advertising

a) The Fund Manager shall, in any advertisements relating to the Fund, (as defined in the Capital Market Institutions Regulations) must satisfy the requirements of this Article and the applicable provisions of the Capital Market Institutions Regulations and the Securities Business Regulations and any relevant regulations.

b) The Capital Market Institution must submit any advertisement, brochure, marketing leaflet or any other methods used for the offering or selling of the fund units before it is used to the Authority.

c) The advertisement of the Fund should include the following details:

1) The manner for obtaining a copy of the Fund's Terms and Conditions, and its financial reports.
2) The Fund's purpose, the fund's total assets value, it's period, type and class.
3) Fund manager's license number and its authorized activities
4) A statement that the value of an investment in the Fund is variable and it may be subject to increase or decrease or loss of the full amounts.
5) A reference to the disclosure mentioned in the terms and conditions related to the major risks associated with investment in the Fund.

d) Any advertisements for the Fund shall not include any forecast of the future performance of the Fund.

Article 43: Termination and Liquidation of the Fund

a) The fund manager shall specify the termination provisions of a fund in the terms and conditions of the relevant fund.

b) The fund manager must complete the process of selling the fund's assets and distribute the unitholders' dues among them, prior to the end of the fund's term.

c) The fund manager may extend the fund's term to complete the sale process of the fund's assets or any other event, in accordance with the provisions of Article (26) of these Regulations.

d) For the purpose of terminating a fund, the fund manager must prepare a plan and procedures for the termination of the fund consistent with the unitholders interests, and must obtain the fund board of directors' approval on such plan prior to carrying out any action in this regard.

e) The fund manager must notify the unitholders and the Authority, in writing, of the details of the plan and procedures for the fund termination at least (21) days prior to the intended date for terminating the fund, without prejudice to the fund's terms and conditions.

f) The fund manager must comply with the plan and procedures for fund termination approved as per paragraph (d) of this Article.

g) The Authority and unitholders must be notified in writing of the fund termination within 10 days from the end of the fund's term in accordance with requirements in paragraph (d) of Annex (12) of these Regulations.

h) If the terms and conditions of the fund provide that the fund will be terminated upon the occurrence of specified events, the fund manager must terminate the fund immediately upon the occurrence of such event and notify the Authority and unitholders in writing within (5) days from the occurrence of such event that required the termination of the fund.

i) In the event of expiry of the fund's term and the fund manager has not completed the sale of the fund's assets before the expiry of its term, the fund manager must liquidate the fund's assets and distribute the unitholders' dues among them, within a maximum period of 6 months from the date of the expiry of the fund's term.

j) For the purpose of liquidating a fund, the fund manager must obtain the fund board of directors' approval on the plan and procedures for the liquidation of the fund, prior to carrying out any action in this regard.

k) The fund manager must comply with the plan and procedures for fund liquidation approved as per paragraph (j) of this Article.

l) The Authority and unitholders must be notified in writing of the end of the fund liquidation, within 10 days from the end of the fund liquidation in accordance with requirements in paragraph (d) of Annex (12) of these Regulations.

m) The fund manager must treat all unitholders equally during the fund termination or liquidation process.

n) The fund manager must immediately upon the end of fund's term or liquidation distribute the unitholders' dues among them, without delay and in a manner that does not conflict with the interest of unitholders and the fund's terms and conditions.

o) The fund manager must disclose on its website and the Exchange's website or any other website available to the public according to the controls set out by the Authority (where applicable), the end of the fund's term or its liquidation period.

p) The fund manager must provide the unitholders with the fund termination report in accordance with the requirements of Annex 13 of these Regulations within a period not exceeding (70) days from the date of completion of fund termination or liquidation, including the final audited financial statements of the fund for the period subsequent to the latest audited financial statements.

q) The Authority may remove the fund manager from the liquidation process in the event of a special fund resolution issued by the unitholders, provided that the replacement liquidator is appointed in the same meeting in which the unitholders voted to remove the fund manager.

r) If the fund manager was removed from the liquidation process, it must fully cooperate to transfer liquidation responsibilities to the appointed liquidator. It must also transfer to the appointed liquidator all the documents of the relevant real estate investment fund, that will enable it to complete the liquidation within (20) days from the issuance of the Authority's resolution to remove the fund manager and appoint a replacement liquidator.

s) The fund manager must notify the unitholders, in writing, in the event where the Authority issues a resolution of the removal of the fund manager and the appointment of a replacement liquidator under paragraph (q) of this Article.

t) In all cases, the fund manager must notify the unitholders and the Authority, in writing, immediately and without delay of any significant events occurring during the fund liquidation period.

u) The traded fund shall be exempted from the written notification requirement to all unitholders stipulated in paragraphs (e), (g), (h), (l), (s), and (t) of this Article, provided that the announcement for such is made on the fund manager's website and the Exchange's website.

(According to the Authority's Board Resolution no. 2-22-2021 Dated 12/7/1442H. Corresponding to 24/2/2021G., Article 43 of these Regulations shall be effective as of 28/07/1443H., corresponding to 01/03/2021G. Moreover, paragraph Article 18 of the Real Estate Investment Funds Regulations issued pursuant to the Authority's Board Resolution no. (1-193-2006) dated 19/06/1427H. corresponding to 15/07/2006G., which can be viewed via the following link:(https://cma.org.sa/RulesRegulations/Regulations), shall remain effective until the effectivity date of Article 43 of these Regulations.)

31.4 PART 4: REAL ESTATE INVESTMENT TRADED FUND

Article 44: Scope and Application The purpose of this Part is to regulate the offering, registration and management of REIT fund units and its operations and supervise its associated activities in the Kingdom.

Article 45: General Provisions

a) The offering, operations and management of the real estate investment traded funds in the Kingdom shall be in accordance with the provisions of this Part and these Regulations, and to the extent that such provisions do not contradict the nature of the fund.

b) In the event of offering a REIT fund units on the Parallel Market, the offer of such units shall be limited, under the provisions of this Part, to qualified investors.

c) The unitholder purchasing of REIT fund units from the Exchange is deemed to have read and accepted the funds terms and conditions.

d) As an exception to the provisions of paragraph (a) of Article 41 of these Regulations, any related party may buy or sell any unit of the fund after listing the units.

e) No person or group of persons having their names listed on the fund's terms and conditions, upon establishment, indicating their ownership of (5%) or more of the fund's units -through in-kind contribution- may dispose any of the units in which they subscribed during the first year of trading commencement of the relevant fund's units.

f) Without prejudice to paragraph (k) of Article (38) of these Regulations, it is not permissible to dispose the units allocated to subscribers by in-kind contributions of (5%) or more through the mechanism of increasing the fund's total assets value within the first year of its trading commencement.

g) The units of a REIT fund must be deposited with the Securities Depositary Center.

h) The fund manager must publish all the required information to be disclosed as per these Regulations on its website and the Exchange's website and such information must be complete, clear, accurate and not misleading.

i) Any fundamental changes to the terms and conditions of the fund during the offering period is prohibited.

j) The fund's terms and conditions shall allocate a percentage of the total offer for institutional investors.

k) The fund manager shall ensure when acquiring the assets of an existing real estate investment fund that is managed by the same fund manager, that such acquired assets have achieved rental net profit after deducting all expenses for the last (3) years for the constructionally developed and income generating real estates.

l) If any of the limitations set forth in these Regulations or in the fund's terms and conditions are breached due to a change of circumstances that is beyond the control of the fund manager and the breach has not been rectified within (5) days from the date of the occurrence of such breach, the fund manager must immediately notify the Authority of such event in writing, indicating the action taken and period of time required to rectify the matter. The Authority may at its absolute discretion vary the time limit for rectifying such breach.

m) Without prejudice to paragraph (h) of Article (38) of these Regulations, the fund manager must disclose to the Authority regarding the statement of the offering results on the Exchange's website.

n) To achieve the independence a member of the fund board of directors, the following must be complied with:

1. An independent fund director shall be able to perform his/her duties, express his/her opinions and vote on decisions objectively with no bias in order to help the board make sound decisions that contribute to achieve the interests of the fund.
2. With regards to the definition of "Independent fund director" stipulated in the Glossary of Defined Terms used in the Regulations and Rules of the Capital Market Authority, cases that negate the independence requirement for an independent director in the board of a REIT fund, include but are not limited to, the following:
   a) if he/she holds (5%) or more of the fund's units or the units of another fund under the management of the same fund manager; or is a first degree relative of someone who owns such percentage.
   b) if he/she is a representative of a legal person that holds (5%) or more of the fund's units or the units of another fund under the management of the same fund manager;
   c) if he/she is a representative of a legal person that holds (5%) or more of the shares of the fund manager, an affiliate of the fund manager, the custodian or an affiliate of the custodian;
   d) if he/she is a first degree relative of any member of the board of the fund or any other fund under the management of the same fund manager;
   e) if he/she is a first degree relative of any related party of the fund.
   f) if he/she is an employee or used to be an employee, during the preceding two years, of the fund manager or any party related to the fund, or if he/she, during the preceding two years, held a controlling interest in any of these parties.
   g) if he/she receives financial consideration from the fund in addition to the remuneration for his/her membership on the board.

o) A real estate investment traded fund may apply for listing on the Parallel Market after the issuance of a special fund resolution by the unitholders approving of such.

Article 46: Conditions for Offering REITs

a) The following conditions must be satisfied when applying:

1) The fund type: the REIT fund must be a closed-ended fund.
2) The minimum requirement for establishment: the fund's total assets value must be 500 million Saudi Riyals at least, upon establishment, to offer its units in the Main Market, and not less than (100) million Saudi riyals to offer its units in the Parallel Market.
3) The nominal value per unit: the nominal value per unit must be (10) Saudi Riyals.
4) Subscription fees: public unitholders may only subscribe by way of cash contributions.
5) Subscription limit: the minimum subscription must not exceed (1000)units per unitholder.

b) The fund manager must comply with the following at all times:

1) Investment policy: the fund's investments value in constructionally developed real estate, and qualified to generate periodic rental income must not be less than (75%) of the fund's total assets value according to the last audited financial statements.
2) Distributions: the distributed profits on unitholders must not be less than (90%) of the fund's net profits annually.
3) Asset restrictions:
   a) the fund manager may not invest in white lands. the fund manager is allowed to invest up to 25% of the fund's total assets value, according to the last audited financial statements, in any of the following:
      1. Real estate development, whether the real estate is owned by the fund manager or not.
      2. Renovation and re-development of real estate.
      3. Real estate re-purchase agreements.
      4. Cash and such, units of investment funds licensed by the Authority and real estate companies.
      5. In case of RIETs traded in the Main market, usufruct rights.
      6. Treasury units
      7. Debt instruments

b) The fund manager is prohibited from investing more than 25% of the fund's total assets value, according to the last audited financial statements in real estate outside the Kingdom.

c) A REIT may not own a percentage exceeding (20%) of the net assets value of the fund that its units were owned.

d) The investments of the REIT fund manager on the Parallel Market in usufruct rights shall not be subject to the restriction stipulated in sub-paragraph (a) of sub-paragraph (3) of paragraph (b) of this Article.

4) Fund's assets requirements: with regards to Articles (35) and (36) of these Regulations, the fund manager must ensure the provision of valuation reports for the real estate, prepared by two accredited valuers, with the Saudi Authority for Accredited Valuers, and publish them during the offer period on its website and the Exchange's website. The reports shall contain an assessment of market rents and the assessment period shall not exceed three months of the offering commencement date. Where more than two accredited valuers were appointed, the fund manager must publish all the accredited valuers' reports.

(According to the Authority's Board Resolution no. 2-22-2021 Dated 12/7/1442H. (24/2/2021G.), the requirement to join the Saudi Authority for Accredited Valuers shall become effective as of 08/06/1444H corresponding to 01/01/2023G.)

Article 47: Offering Requirements for REITs

a) A fund manager seeking to offer a REIT fund units on the Exchange must submit its application to the Authority, including the information required as per these Regulations. It shall, simultaneously, submit an application to the Exchange to list such units in accordance with the Listing Rules.

b) In addition to the requirements set forth in Article (7) of these Regulations, the fund's terms and conditions must include all necessary information to enable the potential unitholders to make an informed judgment based on sufficient information regarding the investment offered to them. This application shall contain the information provided in Annex (2) of these Regulations.

c) When submitting an application for offering, the fund manager must provide the Authority with a binding agreement to sell the real estate subject of investment or a binding agreement to transfer the real estate's interest, where the fund is investing in usufruct rights, as determined in the fund's terms and conditions, upon the completion of the fund units offering and before its listing.

d) When submitting an application for offering, the fund manager must provide the Authority with a memorandum of understanding between the fund manager and the company responsible for the property management or the lease contract, if agreed that the lessee is responsible for managing the property, as the case may be.

e) When submitting an application for offering, the fund manager must provide the Authority with the names of two receiving agents, at least.

f) When submitting an application for offering, the returns from any lessee must not exceed (25%) of the fund's total returns.

g) The fund manager may not offer units to the public without making prior arrangements for listing those units on the Exchange in accordance with the Listing Rules.

h) The approval of the application for offering will only be given by the Authority if:

1. the Authority has received a notification from the Exchange of the Exchange's conditional approval of the corresponding application for listing pursuant to the Listing Rules;
2. the conditional approval mentioned under sub-paragraph (1) of paragraph (h) of this part has not been withdrawn by the Exchange; and
3. the Authority is satisfied that the information contained in the terms and conditions is complete and fulfills the requirements of the Capital Market Law and its Implementing Regulations.

i) The fund manager must transfer the ownership of the real estate to be acquired or the right to its utility for the interest of the fund and to list the offered units on the Exchange within a period not more than (60) days from the end of the offering period.

Article 48: REITs Unit Buy-back and Sale

a) For the purpose of applying these regulations, The process of buying-back and selling a RIET fund of its units, in accordance with the provisions of these Regulations, is excluded from the acts and practices mentioned in paragraph (a) of Article (49) of the Capital Market Law.

b) a REIT fund may buy-back its units unless the fund's terms and conditions stipulate otherwise, in accordance with the following controls:

1. The buy-back of the fund's units is for the purpose of keeping them as treasury units or in order to cancel them.
2. With regards to the provisions of sub-paragraph (3) of paragraph (b) of Article (46) of these Regulations, the percentage of treasury units for the fund shall not exceed (10%) at any time.
3. Issuance of a special fund resolution by the unitholders approving the buy- back process, specifying the maximum number of units subject to the buy-back and its purposes, the sources of financing the buy-back process, and authorising the fund manager to complete the buy-back within a period not exceeding (12) months from the date of the issuance of the referenced special fund resolution. Moreover, unitholders may issue at any time issuing a special fund resolution to change the purposes of the buy-back.
4. Unless the purpose of buying-back the units of the fund is to cancel them, the units buy-backs must be made not exceeding (10%) of the quantity approved at the meeting of the unitholders for buy-back within one trading day, unless the approved quantity, or the remainder of the approved quantity that is not bought-back yet, is less than (10%) of the trading volume of the fund's units the day before the buy-back.
5. The buy-back price shall not exceed (5%) of the market closing price on the day preceding the day on which the buy-back is executed.
6. The buy-back does not result in a decrease in the ownership of public unitholders to less than the liquidity requirements stipulated in the Listing Rules (where applicable) for the units issued by the Fund.
7. The buy-back shall be made through the Exchange and not through a special transaction.
8. The treasury units bought-back by the fund shall have any no voting rights at the unitholders meeting and shall not have any right in fund distributions.

c) A REIT fund may not buy-back its units for use as treasury units except for the following purposes:

1. If the Fund's Board of Directors or whoever delegate believes that the price of the units in the Exchange is less than their fair value.
2. Swap operations in return for purchase of an asset.
3. Any other purpose approved by the Authority.

d) The REIT fund manager, regarding buy-back of the fund's units, must comply with the following:

1. Disclose on its website and the Exchange's website, the decision of the Fund's Board of Directors to approve the Fund's buy-back of its units, at least half an hour before the start of the trading period for the next day.
2. Call for a meeting of unitholders in accordance with the provisions of paragraph (d) of Article (23) of these Regulations.

e) In the event of a special fund resolution issued by the unitholders approving the buy-back process, The REIT fund manager must this on its website and the Exchange's website, at least half an hour before the start of the trading period for the next day.

f) The RIETS fund manager must immediately notify the Exchange according to the mechanism determined by the Exchange of the fund's buy-back of its units and the purpose of their buy-back, in order for the Exchange to publish that information in its periodic report on the funds buy-back of their units.

g) The REIT fund manager must include in the annual report of the fund details of the treasury units held by the fund, and details of disposal of these units.

h) A REIT fund may sell its treasury units if the terms and conditions of the fund stipulate that this is permissible, according to the following controls:

1. Executing the sale of treasury units shall not exceed 10% of the total amount of treasury units to be sold within one trading day, unless the approved quantity, or the remainder of the quantity to be sold is less than 10% of the trading volume of the fund's units the day before the buy-back.
2. The sale of the treasury units shall be through the Exchange and not through a special transaction. As an exception to this, the sale of these units is not required to be through the Exchange if the purpose of the treasury units is to be used as a compensation in the swaps in exchange for buying an asset in accordance with the terms and conditions of the fund.

Article 49: Disclosure Requirements

A) Disclosure of material developments:

1) the fund manager must disclose to the Authority and the unitholders without delay any material developments in its sphere of activity which are not public knowledge and which may affect the assets and liabilities, or financial position or the general course of business of the fund manager or any change affecting the status of the fund or leading to the voluntary withdrawal of the fund manager from its position as a fund manager and which may reasonably lead to movements in the price of the listed unit or significantly affect the fund's ability to meet its commitments in respect of the debt instruments.

2) In determining whether a development falls within the scope of this paragraph, the fund manager must assess whether a prudent investor would be likely to consider information about the development in making his investment decisions.

B) Disclosure of specific events:

The fund manager must disclose without any delay to the Authority and the unitholders any of the following developments (whether it is a material development as per paragraph (a) of this Article or not):

1) any transaction to purchase, sell, lease or mortgage an asset at a price equal to or greater than (10%) of the fund's net assets value according to the latest reviewed interim financial statements or audited annual financial statements, whichever is later;

2) any losses equal to or greater than (10%) of the fund's net assets; according to the latest reviewed interim financial statements or audited annual financial statements, whichever is later;

3) any dispute, including any litigation, arbitration or mediation where the value involved is equal to or greater than (5%) of the fund's net assets according to the latest reviewed interim financial statements or audited annual financial statements, whichever is later;

4) the increase or decrease of the fund's net assets equal to or greater than (10%) according to the latest reviewed interim financial statements or audited annual financial statements, whichever is later;

5) the increase or decrease of the fund's gross profit equal to or greater than (10%) according to the latest audited annual financial statements;

6) any transaction between the fund and a related party or any arrangement through which the fund and a related party invest in any project or asset or provide financing thereof if this transaction or arrangement is equal to or greater than (1%) of the fund's gross revenues according to the latest audited annual financial statements;

7) any interruption in the principal activities of the fund, in which has an effect equals to or greater than (5%) of the fund's gross revenues according to the latest audited annual financial statements;

8) the issuance of any judgment, decision, order or declaration by a court or judicial body, whether at first instance or on appeal, which may adversely affect the fund's utilization of any portion of its assets which in aggregate value represents a value exceeds (5%) of the fund's net assets according to the latest reviewed interim financial statements or audited annual financial statements, whichever is later; or

9) any proposed change to the fund's total assets value.

C) Complete, clear, accurate and not misleading disclosures:

1) All disclosures made by the fund manager must be complete, clear, accurate and not misleading and shall be published on the fund manager's website and the Exchange's website and as specified in the fund's terms and conditions.

2) Where, in the opinion of the fund manager, disclosure of any matter required by these Regulations, would be unduly detrimental to the fund and omission is not likely to mislead unitholders with regard to facts and circumstances, knowledge of which is essential for the assessment of the fund units in question, the fund manager may apply to postpone the relevant requirement or waive it. The fund manager must in that case provide the Authority on a strictly confidential basis with a statement of the

request together with the reasons why the fund manager believes that the information should not be disclosed at that time. The Authority may approve the application for postponing or waiving the relevant requirement or reject it. If the Authority approves the application, the Authority may at any time require the fund manager to disclose any information on the waiver or postponement of the disclosure.

3) All information and material developments set forth in this Article shall be deemed confidential until they are disclosed. Before disclosing such information, the fund manager shall be prohibited from communicating such information to parties not bound by a confidentiality obligation and an obligation to protect such information. A fund manager must also take all necessary steps to prevent the leakage of any information and material developments before disclosing them as per these Regulations.

D) The Fund Manager must determine the need to publish a disclosure to the public in response to rumors related to any material developments, and the Authority may require such publication to be made by the Fund Manager as it deems appropriate.

E) The Fund Manager must comply with the provisions of the Instructions for Investment Funds Announcements.

F) Disclosure relating to substantial unitholder dealings:

1. Any person must notify the Exchange if such person becomes the owner of, or is interested in, (5%) or more of the fund's units at the end of the third trading day the execution of the transaction or the occurrence of the event which results such ownership or interest; the person notification shall also include a list of persons, in which those persons, have an interest in the units that they own or control.

2. The person referred to in sub-paragraph (1) of paragraph (f) of this Article, must notify the Exchange the event of any change to the list of persons referred to in sub-paragraph (1) of paragraph (f) of this Article including any event which requires the inclusion of a person to that list or the exclusion of any person who has been previously included in that list. Such notification must be made, within a period not exceeding the end of the third trading day following the occurrence of the relevant event.

3. For the purposes of this paragraph, in calculating the total number of the fund's units in which any person has interest in, that person will be deemed to be interested in any units owned or controlled by any of the following persons:

a. a relative of that person;

b. a company controlled by that person; or

c. any other persons with which that person has agreed to act in concert to acquire an interest in the fund units.

4. the notification referred to in sub-paragraph (1) of paragraph (f) of this Article must contain at least the following information:

a. the names of the persons who own the units or who have the right to dispose of the subject units;

b. details of the ownership process; and

c. details of any loans or financial support for the ownership process that the person has received from any other persons.

G) In the event a real estate investment traded fund is investing in usufruct rights, the fund manager must disclose such rights 3 months prior to their end.

Article 50: Merging Real Estate Investment Traded Funds

a) Submitting an application to the Authority for merging REIT funds

1) after obtaining the approval of the unitholders of all the related funds by way of a special fund resolution, the fund manager may apply to the Authority for the approval to merge a number of REIT funds offered in accordance with these Regulations.
2) the merger shall be through combining one fund or more into an existing fund.
3) the unitholders must be notified about the merger details, which must be disclosed on the fund manager's website and on the Exchange's website, at least, (21) days prior to executing the merger.
4) The merger details must be incorporated in the fund's reports prepared by the Fund Manager pursuant to these Regulations, based on the type of offer.
5) the fund manager must disclose the resulted merger costs.

b) Additional information to be provided to unitholders

1) The fund manager must provide all the unitholders with complete information about the proposed merger that will enable them to reach a proper decision, as per the following:
   a) it is written in a way that is clear, accurate, and not misleading.
   b) it contains, in a detailed way, all the expected consequences of the proposed merger.
2) it contains a detailed comparison of the charges of all services, commissions and management fees that are imposed on the related funds.

31.5 PART 5: REAL ESTATE INVESTMENT FUNDS THAT TAKE THE FORM OF SPECIAL PURPOSE ENTITIES

Article 51: General Provisions

a) All the provisions mentioned in these Regulations and the Rules for The Special Purposes Entities shall apply to Real Estate Investment Fund that takes the form of a special purposes entity unless these Regulations indicate otherwise.

b) For establishing a Real Estate Investment Fund that takes the form of a special purposes entity, the fund manager must submit an application to establish a special purposes entity in accordance with the provisions contained in these Regulations and the provisions contained in the Rules for Special Purposes Entities as applicable.

c) For the purposes of this Part, any reference to the "fund" in these regulations, the Capital Market Law and its Implementing Regulations, applies to "Real Estate Investment Fund that takes the form of a special purposes entity".

Article 52: Custodian The custodian of the Real Estate Investment Fund that takes the form of a special purposes entity applies to the provisions contained in Chapter (3) of these Regulations, in accordance with the nature of such entity.

Article 53: The Board of Directors of the Real Estate Investment Fund that Takes the Form of a Special Purposes Entity The board of directors of Real Estate Investment Fund that takes the form of a special purposes entity shall be the special purposes entity's board of directors, and all the provisions related to the fund's board of directors stipulated in these Regulations shall apply to it.

31.6 PART 6: PUBLICATION AND ENTRY INTO FORCE

Article 54: Publication and Entry into Force These Regulations shall become effective in accordance with its approval resolution.

31.7 Annex 1: Requirements of the Terms and Conditions of Real Estate Investment Public Fund

The Fund Manager should present the fund's Terms and Conditions in the Arabic language, and in a way that is comprehensible and easy to understand by unitholders and potential unitholders. The fund's terms and conditions must include the following Information pursuant to the same sequence set out in this Annex:

I

Content of the Cover Page:

a. Name of the fund, indicating its class and type.
b. Name of the fund manager.
c. Name of the custodian.
d. Name of the developer (if any).
e. Must include explanatory statement and an acknowledgment of responsibility according to the following form:

"The Fund's terms and conditions has been reviewed and approved by the Fund's Board of Directors. The Fund Manager and the members of the Fund's Board of Directors collectively and individually bear full responsibility for the accuracy of the information presented herein. Having made all reasonable inquiries, the fund board of directors and the fund manager confirm the validity and completeness of the information in the terms and conditions, and further confirm that the information and data maintained in the terms and conditions are not misleading."

f. must contain a statement of disclaimer according to the following form: "The Capital Market Authority has approved the offer of units of the real estate investment fund. The Capital Market Authority does not, however, take any responsibility for the content of these terms and conditions, nor does it make any representation as to its accuracy or completeness. The Capital Market Authority does not make any recommendation as to the soundness or otherwise of investing in the investment fund, and that the approval of offering the units the fund does not mean the Authority recommends investment in the fund, and it emphasizes that the decision to invest in the fund is up to the investor or his representative."

g. For a Shariah-compliant real estate investment fund, the following statement must be added:

"[Name of fund] has been certified as a real estate investment fund that is Shariah compliant by the Shariah Board appointed for the investment fund."

h. Must add the following statement: (If the real estate investment fund is taking the form of a special purposes entity):

"[Name of fund] has been approved as a real estate investment fund that takes the form of a special purposes entity in accordance with the Real Estate Investment Funds Regulations and the Rules for Special Purposes Entities".

i. A statement that stresses the necessity to read the fund's terms and conditions and all other documentation of the real estate investment fund.

j. Issue date of the fund's terms and conditions and the latest update, if any.

k. The date of the Authority's approval to offer the units of the real estate investment fund.

l. In the event that the fund's total assets value is increased in accordance with paragraph (k) of Article 38 of these Regulations, the following statement must be added:

"the fund's total assets value was increased on (date) H. corresponding to (date) G., kindly refer to the supplementary annex no. (•) for more information."

II

Inside the Cover Page:

1) Name and Type of the fund.

2) Address of the head office of the Fund Manager and any website for obtaining any information about the fund or its Manager.

3) Fund term, and any extension periods (if any).

4) Fund objectives.

5) A description of the Fund's objectives and its investment objectives, with a statement of the fund's policy for dividends distribution among unitholders (if any).

6) A summary of the Fund's strategies to achieve its objective, which includes at least the Following:

a) A description of real estate type (or types) the Fund will invest in, provided it includes a statement of the information on the deed(s) of ownership of the subject real estate(s) (where applicable).
b) Any policy that may result in concentrating investment in a certain type of real estate assets or specific geographical region.
c) A table illustrating the fields of investments that the fund will be investing in, stating the minimum and maximum of the investment percentage.
d) A clear course of business plan for the projects approved by the developer (where applicable).
e) Borrowing rights for the Fund and the Fund Manager's policies in using those rights.
f) Methods and ways to invest the liquidity available in the fund.

7) Risks of investing in the Fund:

a) Setting out a description of the main risks related to investing in the Fund, which could affect the Fund's investments or any other circumstances that could affect the Fund's net assets value and its investment proceeds.
b) Notifying that investment in the Fund does not guarantee profits and does not protect from losses.
c) Establishing a risk classification for the fund.

8) Subscription:

a) Providing sufficient information on the subscription which includes subscription commencement and termination dates.
b) Stating the minimum limit of subscription.
c) Clarifying if the fund accepts subscriptions by in-kind contributions or not.
d) A statement that include an undertaking by the fund manager of its commitment to the Law of Real Estate Ownership and Investment by Non-Saudis.
e) A detailed statement of any minimum amount that the fund manager intends to raise, and the actions to be taken in case of not reaching that minimum.
f) Unitholders and the percentage of in-kind contributions in the fund out of the total value of the fund's assets.
g) Disclosure of the utilization details of the fund's offering proceeds.

9) Fees, charges and commissions

It must Include a disclosure of all fees and charges that will be incurred by the Fund's assets in details, so as to clarify the amounts of fees and charges and their percentage of the total assets of the Fund with the stated upper limit for all the charges and fees.

a) It must contain a table representing all fees and commissions and management fees, whether paid by the Unitholders or charged on the Fund's assets, and shall include:

1) Any fee paid by unitholders when purchasing or selling units in the fund.
2) Any management fees payable to the fund manager from the net assets of the fund.
3) Fees and expenses of the board of directors.
4) Any payment for custody charges, or other services provided by the Custodian.
5) Any fees paid to the auditor.
6) Any commission resulting from loans to the Fund.
7) Any charges related to registration of the Fund's units, or any other administrative service.
8) Fees paid to the developer and engineering office.
9) Fees paid to the property manager (if any).
10) Any early redemption fee collected from Unitholders (if any).
11) Any other amount paid by Unitholders, or any amount deducted from the Fund's assets.
12) Ratio of fund costs to the fund's total assets value.
13) All cases and situations where the Fund Manager has the right to waive or deduct any of the above mentioned fees should be stated.

b) Disclosure of the mechanism for calculating all fees.

c) A table containing the following:

1) Type of fee;
2) Imposed percentage, if any;
3) Imposed amount, if any;
4) Calculation method; and
5) Recurrence of the fee payment.

d) A default table showing the ratio of fund costs to the total value of the fund's assets, at the fund and the unitholders level, during the life of the fund and that includes the ratio of recurring and non-recurring costs.

e) A declaration from the fund manager stating that the fees mentioned in this paragraph include all fees imposed on the fund, and that it shall incur any other fees not stated herein.

10) Valuing the Fund's assets

Detailed description of the following must be stated:

a) Method of valuing the Fund's assets.
b) Number and timing of valuation.
c) Method for calculating the unit price.
d) 4) Manner of announcing unit price. (Sic)
e) Actions to be taken in case valuations or pricing where wrong or incorrect.

11) Trading of the Fund's units

a) Specifying the days of accepting order for subscription and redemption orders of the Fund's units.
b) Specifying the procedures for delivery of purchase or sale order of units.
c) Description of the provisions governing the transfer of units to other investors.
d) a statement that the register shall be the conclusive evidence as to the ownership of the units entered in it.
e) A statement that the fund manager will make a reasonable effort to facilitate the trading of units, and the transfer of ownership.

12) The Fund's Assets

a) A statement of registration mechanism of the fund's assets.

b) A statement that the assets of the investment fund are owned collectively by the unitholders. A fund manager, fund sub-manager custodian, sub-custodian, distributor or investment advisor shall not have any interest in or claims against such assets, other than when the fund manager, fund sub-manager, custodian, sub-custodian, distributor or investment advisor is a unitholder, to the extent of such person's ownership, and for claims permitted under these Regulations and disclosed in the terms and conditions of the fund.

13) Fund's Board of Directors

a) Stating the names and qualifications of the members of the Fund's Board of Directors, and disclosing the name of the Independent Director.
b) The total remuneration expected to be paid to the Board members during the period of the Fund.
c) A description of the nature of services provided by the Fund's Board.
d) Stating any other investment Fund supervised by any of the Board members.
e) A statement by the fund manager that all members of the fund board fulfill the following eligibility requirements:

1. the member is not bankrupt or subject to any bankruptcy or insolvency proceedings;
2. the member has never committed an offense involving fraud or acted in breach of integrity and honesty;
3. the member possess the necessary experience and expertise.

f) Declaration by the fund manager that the definition of an independent fund director in the Glossary of Defined Terms Used in the Regulations and Rules of the Capital Market Authority applies to the independent fund board members.
g) {Reserved}

14) Fund Manager

a) The name of the Fund Manager and its address.
b) A declaration that the Fund Manager is a Capital Market Institution according to the Capital Market Institutions Regulations, with its Authorization number and date.

c) A description of the services provided by all the Fund Manager's employees.
d) Functions, duties and responsibilities of the fund manager.
e) Provisions governing the removal/replacement of fund manager.
f) Any significant business activity or other interest for the Fund Manager's Board members or the Fund Manager, which could result in a conflict of interests with the fund's interest.
g) A description of any substantial conflict of interests that could affect the Fund Manager in performing his duties to the Fund.
h) Any functions or power related to the Fund's business delegated by the Fund Manager to a third party, with a detailed explanation of it.
i) A declaration whether the Fund Manager intends to invest in the Fund's units and the amount of such investment.
j) A letter from the fund manager regarding the due diligence report, as set forth in Annex (7) of these Regulations.

15) Custodian

a) Name and address of the Custodian, and the Authorization number granted by the Authority.
b) Functions, duties and responsibilities of the custodian.
c) Duties that the custodian has appointed to a sub-custodian in relation to the real estate investment fund.
d) Provisions governing the removal/replacement of custodian.

16) Developer

a) Name and address of Developer.
b) Functions, duties and responsibilities of the developer.
c) Disclosure of the criteria for choosing the developer.
d) Disclosure of whether the developer intends to invest in the units of the Fund and the value of these investments.

17) Engineering Office

a) Name and address of the engineering office.
b) Functions, duties and responsibilities of the engineering office.

18) The Auditor

a) Name and address of the fund Auditor.
b) Functions, duties and responsibilities of the Auditor.

19) Financial statements

A description of the financial statements in which will be provided to the unitholders, and provide a statement that the Fund's financial statements will be available to Unitholders without any charges, with a description of how to get them. The end of the Fund's fiscal year must also be specified.

20) Reporting to Unitholders

A description of the periodical reports provided to the Unitholders and the financial statements of the Fund, and how they will be provided to them.

21) Dividend Policy

This section must include an explanation of the policy regarding the distribution of sale or rent proceeds of the real estate investment fund to the unitholder.

22) Conflict of Interests

a) A statement of the transactions which include any conflicts of interest.

b) A statement that the policies and procedures to be applied in case of conflict of interest and any potential conflict of interest will be provided upon request, free of charge.

23) Meeting of Unitholders

a) Statement of the circumstances in which a meeting of unitholders is called

b) Statement of the processes and procedures for calling a meeting of unitholders, and the minimum attendance number required.

c) Statement that shows the manner in which unitholders would exercise their voting rights and a statement that shows the voting rights at meetings of the unitholders.

24) A List of Unitholders Rights

A list of unitholders rights.

25) Unitholders' Liability

A statement providing that other than losing his investment in the fund or part of it, the unitholder shall not be liable for the debts and obligations of the fund.

26) Fund Manager's Declarations

In addition to the declarations referred to in these Regulations and in Annex (9) of these Regulations, the fund manager must include all declarations related to the fund which may affect the decisions of investors for subscribing to the fund.

27) Other information

The inclusion of any significant information known (or supposed to be known) to the Fund Manager or Fund's Board at the time of issuing the Fund's Terms and Conditions.

28) Additional Information Requirements for Certain Types of Funds

In the case of a real estate investment fund that takes the form of a special purposes entity, must include the special purposes entity by-laws form.

29) Fund's Disclosures

Channels and websites through which the fund's disclosures will be published, which include the periodical reports and financial statements.

30) Shariah Board of the Fund

a) Names and qualifications of the Shariah committee members.
b) Description of the roles and responsibilities of Shariah Board.
c) Details on the remuneration of Shariah Board members.

31) Unit Characteristics

Provide a description of the various categories of units, if the fund has more than one category, including the names of all categories, and its details.

32) Amendments to the Fund's Terms and Conditions

A description of the procedures which will be followed for the notification of any amendments to the Fund's Terms and Conditions.

33) Termination and liquidation of the Fund

a) must state the Events that lead to Termination of the Fund.
b) State the expected period for liquidation.

c) state the possibility of accepting in-kind redemption, with the fund manager's compliance to the Law of Real Estate Ownership and Investment by Non-Saudis.
d) In case the term of the investment fund ends, the fund manager may not take any fees deducted from the fund's assets.

34) Governing Law

A statement that the Real Estate Investment Fund and the Fund's manager are subject to the Capital Market Law and its implementing regulations as well as other relevant laws and regulations applicable in the Kingdom of Saudi Arabia. and that the competent judicial body to consider any dispute arising as a result of investing in a real estate investment fund is the Committee for Resolution of Securities Disputes.

31.8 Annex 2: Requirements for the Terms and Conditions of a Real Estate Investment Traded Fund

The fund manager shall deliver the terms and conditions of the fund in Arabic, and in a manner that is easy to understand and comprehend for unitholders and potential unitholders. The terms and conditions shall include the following information in agreement with the sequence described in this Annex:

Content of the Cover Page:

1) The name of the fund, indicating its class and type.
2) Name of fund manager.
3) Name of custodian.
4) Fund size.
5) The number of offered units, their total value, and its percentage to the fund size.
6) The following disclaimer:

"The Capital Market Authority does not make any representation as to the accuracy or completeness of this document, and expressly disclaims any liability whatsoever for any loss arising from, or incurred in reliance upon, any part of this document. Prospective subscribers of the units offered hereby should conduct their own due diligence on the accuracy of the information relating to the units. If you do not understand the contents of this document, you should consult an authorized financial advisor."

7) For a Shariah-compliant real estate investment traded fund, the following statement must be added:

"[Name of fund] has been certified as a real estate investment traded fund that is Shariah compliant by the Shariah Board appointed for the real estate investment traded fund."

8) Must add the following statement: (If the real estate investment traded fund is taking the form of a special purposes entity):

"[Name of fund] has been approved as a real estate investment traded fund that takes the form of a special purposes entity in accordance with the Real Estate Investment Funds Regulations and the Rules for Special Purposes Entities".

9) A statement that the fund's terms and conditions shall be read in conjunction with the other documents of the real estate investment traded fund.

10) Date of issuance of the fund's terms and conditions, and the last update, if any.

11) Date of the Authority's approval on offering the units of the real estate investment traded fund.

12) In the event that the fund's total assets value is increased in accordance with paragraph (k) of Article 38 of these Regulations, the following statement must be added:

"the fund's total assets value was increased on (date) H. corresponding to (date) G., kindly refer to the supplementary annex no. (•) for more information."

Contents within the Cover Page:

1) Table of Contents.
2) Glossary of terms used in the terms and conditions
3) Fund Manual.
4) Summary of the offer
5) Name and type of the fund.
6) Address of the head office and the website of the fund manager.
7) Fund duration, indicating any extension period, if any.
8) A description of the fund's purpose and objectives, with a clarification of the dividends distribution policy to the unitholders.
9) A summary of the fund's strategies to achieve its objective, which includes at least the following:

a) A table illustrating the fields of investments that the fund will be investing in, stating the minimum and maximum of the investment percentage.

b) Description of the sector or sectors in which the fund will invest.

c) A detailed statement of the real estate assets to be owned.

d) A schedule of the following information for each real estate:

1. The name of the real estate;
2. The real estate owner(s) Information;
3. real estate type;
4. State / city;
5. Neighborhood / street;
6. Location (Croquis) map;
7. Land area;
8. Building area (according to the building permit);
9. Number of floors;
10. Types and numbers of units;
11. Occupancy rate of the real estate;
12. Completion date of building construction (according to the construction completion certificate);
13. Cost of purchasing the real estate;
14. Brief description of the current leases;
15. Revenues for the last (3) years of the real estate, if any; and
16. Any additional information.

e) Any policy that may result in concentrating investment in a certain type of real estate assets or specific geographical region, provided that it includes a provision that includes the information on the deed of ownership of the real estate(s) subject in the investment, where applicable.
f) Previous and targeted rental proceeds for each real estate/usufruct.

g) Borrowing rights for the fund and the fund manager policy in the exercise of these rights.
h) Methods and ways to invest the cash available in the fund.
i) Disclosure of the utilization details of the fund's offering proceeds.
j) Unitholders and the percentage of in-kind contributions in the fund to the fund's net asset value.

10) Risks of investing in the fund

a) Setting out a description of the main risks related to investing in the fund, which could affect the fund investments or any other circumstances that could affect the net assets of the fund and any investment proceeds; and

b) A statement that investment in the fund does not guarantee profits and does not protect against losses.

11) Subscription

a) Providing sufficient information on the subscription, including subscription and termination dates;
b) A detailed statement of real estate owners intending to subscribe in the fund with in-kind contributions and their ownership percentage, in addition to a table stating the ownership percentage of all subscribers;
c) A detailed statement of the fund manager's subscription amount in the fund during the offer period;
d) A statement that includes an undertaking by the fund manager of his commitment to to the Non-Saudis Real Estate Ownership and Investment Law;
e) A detailed statement of the minimum and maximum amount of subscription.
f) The means of applying for subscription;
g) A detailed explanation of the subscription method in the fund;
h) A detailed explanation of the subscription method of minors and dependents in the fund;
i) The mechanism that will be followed by the fund manager to allocate the units among subscribers;
j) The mechanism of increasing the fund's total assets value by accepting in-kind contributions or cash contributions, or both, if any; and
k) Set A timetable outlining the dates upon which is expected to start offering the units until the trading of such units.

12) Trading of the fund's units

a) A statement specifying the procedures of trading the REIT fund units on the Exchange.

b) The events that result in suspension of the fund and/or the cancelation of listing.

13) Dividend Policy

Without prejudice to sub-paragraph (2) of paragraph (b) of Article (46) of these Regulations, this section must include an explanation of the REIT fund's dividend policy regarding the distribution of its profits to the unitholders and maturity and distribution dates.

14) Termination and liquidation of the fund

a) Statement of any events, which will result in the termination of the fund.

b) Statement of information regarding the procedures followed to terminate and liquidate the fund, in addition to the liquidation timetable.

15) Fees, services charges, commissions and management expenses

a) It must Include a detailed disclosure of all fees and charges that will be incurred by the fund's assets, by clarifying the amounts of fees and charges and their percentage of the total assets of the fund with indicating the maximum limit for all the charges and fees. It should also contain a table showing all fees, charges, commissions and management expenses, whether paid by the unitholders or from the fund's assets, and shall include:

1. Fees and expenses of the board of directors.
2. Any charges imposed on the unitholders for subscription in the fund units.
3. Any charges paid to the fund manager from the fund's assets in for its management.
4. all custody services fees, or any other service provided by the custodian.
5. Fees paid to the auditor.
6. Any commission resulting from loans made to the fund.
7. Any fees related to the registration of fund's units, or any other administrative service.
8. Fees paid to the property manager.
9. Any other payment made by the unitholders, or any amount deducted from the investment fund assets.
10. Ratio of fund costs to the fund's total assets value.

All cases or circumstances in which the fund manager has the right to waive or deduct any of the aforementioned requirements must be stated.

b) A table containing the following:

1. Type of fee;
2. Imposed percentage, if any;
3. Imposed amount, if any;
4. Calculation method; and
5. Recurrence of the fee payment.

c) A table containing a default investment of the unitholder.

d) A declaration by the fund manager stating that the fees mentioned in this paragraph consist of all fees imposed on the fund, and he shall incur any other fees not stated herein.

16) Insurance

This section must include the assets that have been insured, the details of the insurance and the extent of its coverage.

17) The fund's assets

a) A statement of registration mechanism of the fund's assets.

b) A detailed statement of each:

1. Names of the accredited valuers to the fund's assets.
2. Method of valuation each asset owned by the fund
3. Cost of valuation for each asset to be invested in.
4. Number of valuation and their timing.

c) Announcing the net assets value for each unit.

d) A table indicating the following:

1. Real estate subject to acquisition.
2. Names of the accredited valuers.
3. Date of each valuation report.
4. Valuation cost for each real estate.
5. Average valuation costs.

6. Purchase price of each real estate.

18) Fund board

a) Names of the Board members of the Fund and a statement of their qualifications, and a disclosure of the independent members in the fund board of directors.
b) Details on the expected total remunerations to be paid to the fund board members during the period of the fund.
c) Description of the nature of the provided services by the fund board.
d) A statement of any other investment fund managed by any member of the fund's board.
e) A declaration by the fund manager that all board members of the fund fulfill the following eligibility requirements:

1) the member must not be bankrupt or subject to any bankruptcy or insolvency proceedings;

2) the member must not have committed an offense involving fraud or acted in breach of integrity and honesty; and

3) the member must possess the necessary experience and expertise.

f) Declaration by the fund manager that the definition of an independent fund director in the Glossary of Defined Terms Used in the Regulations and Rules of the Capital Market Authority applies to the independent fund director.

19) Fund manager

a) Name and address of the fund manager.
b) A statement that the fund manager is a Capital Market Institution in accordance with the Capital Market Institutions Regulations, and the number and date of the Authorization issued by the Authority.
c) A letter from the fund manager regarding the due diligence report, as set forth in Annex (8) of these Regulations.
d) Functions, duties and responsibilities of the fund manager.
e) Provisions governing the removal/replacement of fund manager.
f) Any other business activities or interests of the fund manager or its board members, that are of significance or could potentially conflict with those of the investment fund.
g) Description of any conflict of interest that could potentially affect the fund manager in performing its duties toward the fund.
h) Functions and powers that have been delegated to a third party by the fund manager related to the fund, with a detailed statement of such.
i) Disclosure if the fund manager intends to invest in the fund's units, and the value of such investments.
j) A summary on the fund manager, the fund manager's structure of assets management and the total assets value under its management. In addition to the number of public funds and their size and the number of the asset management employees.

20) Legal Advisor

A letter issued by the legal advisor, licensed to practice the profession in the Kingdom, regarding the legal due diligence report, as set forth in Annex (11) of these Regulations.

21) Custodian

a) Name of the custodian, address and the Authorization number granted to it by the Authority.
b) Functions, duties and responsibilities of the custodian.
c) Functions related to the real estate investment traded fund in which the custodian has appointed a sub-custodian.
d) Provisions governing the removal/replacement of custodian.

22) Property Management

a) The name of the company that carries out the property managements and its address.
b) Statement of the property management company's tasks, duties and responsibilities.
c) Disclosure of whether the company that carries out the property managements intends to invest in the fund's units, and the value of these investments.

23) Auditor

a) The name and address of the auditor of the fund.
b) A statement of the auditor's tasks, duties and responsibilities.

24) Financial Statements

A statement that indicates that the fund's financial statements will be available to unitholders free of charge and the means of obtaining them. Additionally, the fund's fiscal year-end date shall be indicated.

25) Conflict of Interest

Detailed disclosure of any conflict of interest in the fund, and including a statement indicating that the policies and procedures to be followed to resolve a case of actual and/or potential conflict of interest will be provided upon request free of charge.

26) Reporting to unitholders

Description of the periodic reports and financial statements that will be published and the means of publishing such reports and statements.

27) Meeting of unitholders

a) Statement of the circumstances in which a meeting of unitholders is called.
b) Statement of the procedures for calling a meeting of unitholders, and the minimum attendance number.
c) Statement clarifying the manner in which unitholders would vote and their voting rights at the unitholders meetings.

28) A list of unitholders rights

A list that contains the rights of unitholders.

29) Other information

The inclusion of any significant information known (or supposed to be known) to the Fund Manager or Fund's Board at the time of issuing the Fund's Terms and Conditions.

30) Additional Information Requirements for Certain Types of Funds

In the case of a real estate investment traded fund that takes the form of a special purposes entity, must include the special purposes entity by laws form.

31) Shariah Board of the fund:

a) Names and qualifications of the Shariah committee members.
b) Description of the roles and responsibilities of Shariah Board.
c) Details on the remuneration of Shariah Board members.

32) Unit Characteristics

Provide a description of the various categories of units, if the fund has more than one category, including the names of all categories, and its details.

33) Amending the fund's terms and conditions

A statement of the provisions governing changes of the fund's terms and conditions, and the specified approvals and notices under these Regulations.

34) The Fund Manager's Declarations

In addition to the declarations referred to in these Regulations and in Annex (10) of these Regulations, the fund manager must include all declarations related to the fund which may affect the decisions of investors for subscribing or trading in the fund.

35) Governing Laws

A statement that the real estate investment traded fund and the fund manager are subject to the Capital Market Law and its Implementing Regulations as well as other relevant laws and regulations applicable in the Kingdom of Saudi Arabia, and that the competent judicial body to consider any dispute arising as a result of investing in a real estate investment traded fund is the Committee for Resolution of Securities Disputes.

31.9 Annex 3: Content of the Application for Offering Public Real Estate investment Fund Units

This Annex clarifies the documents that are required to be included in an application file for submission to the Capital Market Authority.

The application must include the following:

a) Form (1) of this annex after it is being filed.

b) Type and purpose of the Fund, and proposed launch date.

c) Details regarding the Fund Manager's organizational structure, including a description of the investment decision making process by the fund manager, including the name and position of any registered persons involved in those decisions.

d) The name of the Compliance Officer or names of members of the Compliance Committee.

e) Review list of the documents submitted.

f) Providing a feasibility study of the Fund.

g) Nominating a Developer to attain the Fund's purposes.

h) Any contracts entered into by the Fund Manager for the benefit of the fund, including those made with affiliates or third parties in relation to the fund.

i) Draft of the fund's Terms and Conditions (with the fund's terms and conditions Checklist pursuant to Annex (1) or Annex (2) of these Regulations, whichever is applicable).

j) The Fund's Terms and Conditions signed by Fund Manager's CEO and the Compliance Officer. This should be prepared according to Annex (1) or annex (2) of these regulations, whichever is applicable.

k) Funds board member photo ID.

l) Subscription and Redemption Forms (where applicable).

m) A detailed description of risk management policies and procedures for the relevant fund.

n) A declaration from the fund manager regarding the existence of the administrative systems that will be adopted regarding the operational aspects related to the real estate investment funds, including the compliance monitoring program for the related real estate investment fund.

o) a declaration from each accredited valuer confirming that he is complying with the Accredited Valuers Law and its Implementing Regulations and any other Regulations issued by the Saudi Authority for Accredited Valuers (TAQEEM), The fund manager declares that it has confirmed to the accredited valuer that the scope of work on valuing report must be appropriate for the purpose of the Fund Manager's application to the Saudi Stock Exchange and is valid for use for public offering and including the market rental value of the relevant income-generating real estate if it is different from the contractual rental value in the property leases the fund's units.

p) Any other supporting documents.

q) Fees.

r) Electronic copies of all documents required under the above paragraphs.

s) Required approvals from relevant government entities (where applicable).

t) Submit any other requirement required by the Authority in accordance with the Capital Market Law and its implementing regulations.

u) Application form is available for public at the official Capital Market Authority's website: www.cma.org.sa

31.10 Form 1: Application to Offer a Public Real Estate Investment Fund

Instructions to fill out the form: the form can be filled digitally. Where there are supporting documents required under this form, please include them. Please tick ([*]) in the relevant boxes, where appropriate. If a question is not applicable, please state "N/A" in the space provided. If the space provided is insufficient for your requirements, please continue on a separate sheet of paper. Please indicate which question your additional information relates to. Please fill up one application form for each fund.

{Applicant} must keep a copy of any supporting documents submitted to the Capital Market Authority.

THE REAL ESTATE INVESTMENT FUND

Information about the Investment Fund that the units of which will be offered

1. Name of Fund
2. Fund's Type and Class
3. Investment Objectives
4. Investment Policies and practices
5. Proposed offering Date
6. Initial Offer Period
7. Duration of Investment Fund (if any)
8. Reasons for offering the units of public real estate investment fund.
9. The fund's marketing strategy (3-5 year plan)
10. Names of the proposed fund board members.

Note:

Please submit Due Diligence Report on the targeted fund and its' Fund Manager.

THE FUND MANAGER

Information on the Capital Market Institution managing the real estate investment fund

1. Name of the Capital Market Institution (the fund manager)
2. The Authorization Number granted by the Capital Market Authority
3. Organizational Structure (Whole Company and Asset Management Division) Please use a separate sheet of paper if space is insufficient.
4. Name(s) of the registered portfolio manager responsible for the fund (Including Contact Information)
5. Name(s) of Compliance Officer and/or Compliance Committee (Including Contact Information)
6.Will a fund sub-manager be appointed? Yes / No If yes, please submit a copy of the service contract.
7. If yes, name of fund sub-manager(s)
8. Name of portfolio manager responsible for the fund at the fund sub-manager
9. The Authorization number granted by the Capital Market Authority of the fund sub- manager (if applicable)
10. If the fund sub-manager is a foreign entity, please provide the following information:

   a) Place of Incorporation

   b) Regulatory Authority

   c) Address and contact details of fund sub-manager Address / Phone No / Email

   d) Is the fund sub-manager supervised in a jurisdiction that employs regulatory standards and requirements at least equivalent to those of the Authority? (If there are more than one fund sub-manager, please give the information required under para 6 – 10 above for each fund sub-manager.)

11. Will there be any other functions of the fund manager that are delegated to service providers? Yes / No If yes, please submit copies of the service contracts.
12. If yes, please list the functions that are delegated and give details of the service provider(s). Please use a separate sheet of paper if space is insufficient.

THE CUSTODIAN

Information on the Capital Market Institution licensed to carry out the custody activity

1. Name of the Capital Market Institution (the custodian)
2. The Authorization Number granted by the Capital Market Authority
3. Relationship with Fund Manager

Related Party Independent

Please submit a copy of the service contract / service level agreement.

4. Organizational Structure (Custody Division) Please use a separate sheet of paper if space is insufficient.
5. Will a sub-custodian be appointed? Yes / No If yes, please submit a copy of the service contract.
6. If yes, name of the sub-custodian
7. the Authorization number granted by the Capital Market Authority of the sub-custodian (if applicable)
8. If the sub-custodian is foreign, please provide the following information:

   a) Place of Incorporation

   b) Regulatory Authority

   c) Address and contact details of sub-custodian (Address/Phone No/Email)

   d) Is the sub-custodian supervised in a jurisdiction that employs regulatory standards and requirements at least equivalent to those of the Authority?

If there are more than one sub-custodian, please give the information required under ¶¶ 5 – 8 above for each sub-custodian. You may photocopy this page and complete for each sub-custodian.

9. Will there be any other functions of the custodian that are delegated to service providers? (Yes / No) If yes, please submit copies of the service contracts.
10. If yes, please list the functions that are delegated and give details of the service provider and the arrangements. Please use a separate sheet of paper if space is insufficient.

DECLARATION

Declaration of the Fund Manager and Custodian

For and on behalf of the Capital Market Institution (Fund Manager)

I hereby declare, to the best of my knowledge and belief and (after taken reasonable care to ensure that such) information given in this application form are complete, clear, accurate, and not misleading at the time of this application. I further declare that the proposed real estate investment fund and the contents of the Fund's Terms and Conditions do not conflict with the Capital Market Law and the Real Estate Investment Funds Regulations.

Name Position Signature Date
Name of person responsible for the application with the Fund Manager
Position
Phone number
Email

For and on behalf of the Capital Market Institution (Custodian)

I, the [name of Capital Market Institution], acting as a Custodian for the proposed real estate investment fund. I hereby declare and confirm that I will carry out my duties in accordance with the Real Estate Investment Funds Regulations, the fund's Terms and Conditions and the Capital Market Law.

Name Position Signature Date

Name of person responsible for the application with the custodian
Position
Phone number
Email
Offeror/Distributor
Information regarding the Capital Market Institution that offer/distribute investment fund units
Name and address of the Capital Market Institution or person delegated to offer/distribute investment fund units
Authorization number granted by the Capital Market Authority (where applicable)

31.11 Annex 4: Contents of Fund's Reports

Annual Reports must contain the following information:

1) Assets in which the fund is investing in.
2) Assets in which the fund is aiming to invest in, if any.
3) The percentage of the value of the leased real estates and the percentage of unleased real estates to the total value of the owned real estates, if any.
4) The percentage of rent amount for each asset in the total rent of the fund's assets.
5) For a REIT, the percentage of uncollected revenues from total revenues, and the ratio of non-cash expenditures from the fund's net profits.
6) Description of the fund's benchmark – where applicable – and the service provider's website (if any).
7) A comparative table covering the performance of the fund during the last (3) fiscal years (or since the establishment) including:

a. The fund net assets value at the end of each fiscal year.

b. The fund net assets value per unit at the end of each fiscal year.

c. Highest and lowest net asset value of the fund per unit for each fiscal year.

d. The number of units issued at the end of each fiscal year.

e. Income distribution per unit, if any.

f. the percentage of the fund's costs to the fund's total assets value

g. Results of comparing the fund's benchmark to the fund's performance.

h. Percentage of borrowed assets in the total asset value, their period for fulfillment and due date.

8) a performance record that covers the following:

a. The total revenue for (1), (3) and (5) years (or since establishment).

b. The annual total revenue for each of the last (10) fiscal years (or since establishment).

c. A table showing the fees, services and expenses incurred by the fund to third parties during the year. The total expenses percentage must also be clearly disclosed and if there are any circumstances, in which a Fund Manager may decide to waive or rebate any fees.

9) if there were fundamental or non-fundamental changes that occurred during the period and which affected the performance of the fund, these changes must be clearly disclosed.
10) the fund's annual report approved by the fund's board including, but not limited to, the topics discussed and issued resolutions, including the fund's performance and fund's achievement of its objectives.
11) a statement regarding any special commission received by the fund manager during the period, clearly identifying its nature and the manner in which they were utilized.
12) a risk assessment report.

31.12 Annex 5: Contents of the Semi-Annual Statement

The semi-annual statement for real estate funds must contain the following information, as a minimum:

1) the unit price at the end of the half in accordance with the last valuation.
2) A table illustrating the total expenses, fees and charges incurred by the fund and its percentage of the most recent value of the total assets of the fund, provided that it illustrates the cap limit of all expenses, by the end of the relevant half.
3) a list of names of all real estates consisting the fund's portfolio, and the percentage of the value of each property in the total assets, in addition to the occupancy percentage for each property as at the end of the relevant half.
4) the fund's total assets value.
5) the percentage of borrowing to the fund's total assets value, period for fulfillment and due date.
6) the fund units' net assets value.
7) the percentage of the fund's costs to the fund's total assets value.
8) any fundamental or non-fundamental changes that affects the fund's function during relevant half (where applicable).
9) a statement on the fund's dividends distributed to the unitholders, if any; by including the semi-annual statement with details as follows:

a) Total profits distributed in the relevant half.

b) The number of existing units for which distributions have been made during the relevant half.

c) The value of the profit distributed during the relevant half for each unit.

d) The percentage of distribution from the net asset value of the fund; and

e) Eligibility for cash dividends distributed during the relevant half.

In addition to the above mentioned, the fund manager must disclose the previous sale or rent proceeds distributions for the same half of the previous year. Such disclosure shall enable the unitholders to view the fund's distributions and their number and size.

31.13 Annex 6: Contents of the Quarterly Statement

The quarterly statement for REIT funds must contain the following information, as a minimum:

1) the unit price at the end of the quarter in accordance with the last valuation. Which is each of the unit's trading price in the Exchange (closing price), and the net asset value of the unit in the fund at the end of the relevant quarter, calculated by subtracting the total liabilities of the fund from its total assets and dividing the result by the number of fund units.
2) the rental income on the unit price, if any, it is the Fund's net income from its investment in income-generating real estate only during the relevant quarter to the market value of the units.
3) A table illustrating the total expenses, fees and charges incurred by the fund and its percentage of the most recent fund's total assets value, provided that it illustrates the cap limit of all expenses, by the end of the relevant quarter

4) The performance of the unit price in the Exchange (closing price) during the relevant quarter, in addition to the net asset value per unit in the fund for the same period.
5) a list of names of all real estates consisting the fund's portfolio, and the percentage of the value of each property in the total assets, in addition to the occupancy percentage for each property as at the end of the relevant quarter.
6) the fund's total assets value.
7) the percentage of borrowing to the fund's total assets value, period for fulfillment and due date.
8) the fund units' net assets value.
9) the ratio of the fund's costs to the fund's total assets value.
10) any fundamental or non-fundamental changes that affects the fund's function during relevant quarter (where applicable).
11) a statement on the fund's dividends distributed to the unitholders, if any; by including the quarterly statement with details as follows:

a) Total dividends distributed in the relevant quarter.

b) The number of existing units for which distributions have been made during the relevant quarter.

c) The value of the dividends distributed during the relevant quarter for each unit.

d) The percentage of distribution from the fund's net asset value;

e) Eligibility for cash dividends distributed during the relevant quarter.

In addition to the above mentioned, the fund manager must disclose the previous sale or rent proceeds distributions for the same quarter of the previous year. Such disclosure shall enable the unitholders to view the fund's distributions and their number and size.

31.14 Annex 7: Form of a Real Estate Investment Fund Manager's Letter

[To be provided on the Fund Manager's letterhead]

To: The Capital Market Authority

In our capacity acting as the fund manager of (name of the fund) in respect of offering a Real Estate Investment Fund under the name (name of the fund), and registering and listing its units in the Saudi Stock Exchange, we, (name of the fund manager) confirm, to the best of our knowledge, and through conducting due diligence and making enquiries of the fund, that the fund has satisfied all conditions required for registration and listing of its units and has satisfied all other matters required by the Capital Market Authority (the "Authority") as of the date of this letter. (name of the fund manager) further confirms that it has, to the best of its knowledge and within its capacity as fund manager, provided to the Authority any information or clarifications in such form and within such time limit as the Authority required for the purpose of verifying whether (name of the fund manager) and the fund have complied with the Capital Market Law and the Real Estate Investment Funds Regulations.

In particular, (name of the fund manager) confirms that:

It has provided all the relevant services required by the Real Estate Investment Funds Regulations; with due diligence and experience.

It has taken reasonable steps to ensure that the directors of the fund understand the nature and extent of their responsibilities under the Capital Market Law and its Implementing Regulations.

It has come to a reasonable opinion, based on due enquiries and professional experience, that:

The fund has satisfied all relevant requirements in the Real Estate Investment Funds Regulations (including provisions regarding the terms and conditions).

All nominated members of the fund's board of directors satisfy the eligibility requirements set out in the Authority's Rules and Regulations, and that the independent fund director satisfy the definition of the independent fund director as provided in Glossary of Defined Terms Used in the Regulations and Rules of the Capital Market Authority.

The real estate assets are free of any regulatory violations that prevent or may result in the non-utilization of the building, and or that may in turn cause costly repairs and major changes.

All matters known to (name of the fund manager) which must be taken into account by the Authority when considering the application for offering that have been disclosed to the Authority.

31.15 Annex 8: Form of a Real Estate Investment Traded Fund Manager's Letter

[To be provided on the Fund Manager's letterhead]

To: The Capital Market Authority

In our capacity acting as the fund manager of (name of the fund) in respect of offering a REIT Fund under the name (name of the fund), and registering and listing its units in the in the Saudi Stock Exchange (Tadawul), we, (name of the fund manager) confirm, to the best of our knowledge, and through conducting due diligence and making enquiries of the fund, that the fund has satisfied all conditions requir ed for registration and listing of its units and has satisfied all other matters required by the Capital Market Authority (the "Authority") as of the date of this letter. (name of the fund manager) further confirms that it has, to the best of its knowledge and within its capacity as fund manager, provided to the Authority any information or clarifications in such form and within such time limit as the Authority required for the purpose of verifying whether (name of the fund manager) and the fund have complied with the Capital Market Law, the Real Estate Investment Funds Regulations.

In particular, (name of the fund manager) confirms that:

It has provided all the relevant services required by the Real Estate Investment Funds Regulations, with due diligence and experience.

It has taken reasonable steps to ensure that the directors of the fund understand the nature and extent of their responsibilities under the Capital Market Law and its Implementing Regulations.

It has come to a reasonable opinion, based on due enquiries and professional experience, that:

The fund has satisfied all relevant requirements in the Real Estate Investment Funds Regulations (including provisions regarding the terms and conditions).

All nominated members of the fund's board of directors satisfy the eligibility requirements set out in the Authority's Rules and

Regulations, and that independent fund director satisfy the definition of the independent fund director as provided in Glossary of Defined Terms Used in the Regulations and Rules of the Capital Market Authority.

The real estate assets are free of any regulatory violations that prevent or may result in the non-utilization or operation of the building, and that the assets are technically intact and free of any major engineering faults or defects that may prevent or may result in the non-utilization or operation of the building, or that may in turn cause costly repairs and major changes.

The main activities of the main potential tenants of real estate assets are intact, and they are able to fulfill their obligations to the fund,

All matters known to (name of the fund manager) which must be taken into account by the Authority when considering the application for offering that have been disclosed to the Authority.

31.16 Annex 9: The Real Estate Fund Manager's Declaration

1- The Fund Manager declares that the terms and conditions of the "Fund Name" have been prepared in accordance with the Real Estate Investment Funds Regulations issued by the Capital Market Authority of Saudi Arabia.

2- The fund manager declares, after making all reasonable inquiries and to the best of its knowledge and belief, that there are no other facts that the non-inclusion of which in this document may result from any statement contained herein as misleading. The Capital Market Authority and the Saudi Stock Exchange Company shall not be liable for the content of the terms and conditions.

3- The fund manager declares that the property is free of any regulatory violations that prevent or may result in the non- utilization or operation of the building, and that the assets are technically intact and free of any major engineering faults or defects that may prevent or may result in the non-utilization or operation of the building, or that may in turn cause costly repairs and major changes.

4- The fund manager declares that there is no direct / indirect conflict of interests (other than what is disclosed) between any of the following:

- Fund manager.
- Manager(s) of properties associated with the fund.
- Owner(s) of properties associated with the fund.
- Tenant(s) of Real estate assets which their returns constitute 10% or more of the annual rental income of the fund.
- Accredited valuer.
- Developer.
- Engineering Office.

5- The fund manager declares that it took the necessary care to ensure that there is no direct / indirect conflict of interest between the property seller and the accredited valuers.

6- The fund manager declares that all members of the fund board of directors have not been subjected to any bankruptcy or insolvency claims or any bankruptcy or liquidation proceedings, nor have they committed any fraudulent, dishonest or deceitful acts. In addition to not having performed any violation involving fraud, deceit or dishonesty. The fund manager further declares that they have the necessary skills and experience to qualify as board members.

7- The fund manager declares that the definition of the independent director included in the Glossary of defined terms used in the Regulations and Rules of the Capital Market Authority apply to the independent fund directors, and that it will be applicable to any independent fund director appointed by the fund manager throughout the period of the fund.

8- The fund manager declares that no other significant business activities or other interests for the fund manager's board of directors, which is likely to conflict with the interests of the fund.

9- The fund manager declares that there is no conflict of interest that would affect the fund manager in the performance of its duties for the fund.

10- The fund manager declares that there are no fees other than those mentioned in the Fees and Expenses section mentioned in the terms and conditions.

11- The fund manager declares that no member of the board of directors may have a direct or indirect interest in the business and contracts made for the fund.

12- The fund manager declares that all contracts and agreements relating to the fund which may affect the investors' decisions to subscribe or trade in the fund have been disclosed in the terms and conditions, and that there are no contracts and agreements other than those mentioned in the terms and conditions.

13- The fund manager declares that unitholders are entitled to vote on matters raised at meetings of unitholders. In addition, the approval of a fundamental change to the fund shall be passed by obtaining the approval of the majority unitholders owning more than (50%) or more than (75%) (where applicable) of the total units holders of which are attending, in relation to carrying out any fundamental change to the fund, a fundamental change include the following:

- Significant change in the fund's objectives nature or class;
- A change that may have a material adverse effect on the unitholders or their rights with respect to the closed-ended fund;
- Change that may have an effect on the risk position of the fund;
- The voluntary withdrawal of a fund manager from its position as the fund manager.
- Any change that would reasonably cause the unitholders to reconsider their participation in the closed-ended fund;
- A change that materially increases the total of payment out of the assets of the closed-ended fund.
- A change in the eligibility date or the termination of the closed- ended fund.
- Any increase of the net assets value of the closed-ended fund as a result of accepting in-kind or cash contributions or both.
- Any other cases determined by the Authority from time to time and notifies the fund manager of them.

14- The fund manager declares that it will take all necessary steps in the benefit of the unitholders to the best of its knowledge and belief with due diligence and reasonable consideration. The fund manager, directors, officers, employees, agents, consultants, affiliates, custodian, Shariah advisor and board of directors shall exercise reasonable diligence and effort and act in good faith in order to meet the interests of the unitholders. If the fund, however, is subject to loss in any way, in the event of any unintentional action by any of the aforementioned parties in connection with the management of the fund, then such parties shall not be held liable for such loss provided that they have acted in good faith and in a manner serving the interest of the fund. Good faith shall be proved in the absence of any conduct, decision or correspondence indicating prior knowledge of the negative consequences of such conduct. Moreover, such act shall not involve gross negligence, fraud or deliberate misconduct.

15- The fund manager declares that it has confirmed to the accredited valuer that the scope of work on valuation report must be appropriate for the purpose of the Fund Manager's application to the Saudi Stock Exchange and is valid for use for public offering and including the market rental value if it is different from the contractual rental value in the property leases the fund's units.

31.17 Annex 10: The Real Estate Investment Traded Fund Manager's Declarations

1- The Fund Manager declares that the terms and conditions of the "Fund Name" have been prepared in accordance with the Real Estate Investment Funds Regulations issued by the Capital Market Authority of Saudi Arabia.

2- The fund manager declares, after making all reasonable inquiries and to the best of its knowledge and belief, that there are no other facts that the non-inclusion of which in this document may result from any statement contained herein as misleading. The Capital Market Authority and the Saudi Stock Exchange Company shall not be liable for the content of the terms and conditions.

3- The fund manager declares that the property is free of any regulatory violations that prevent or may result in the non- utilization or operation of the building, and that the assets are technically intact and free of any major engineering faults or defects that may prevent or may result in the non-utilization or operation of the building, or that may in turn cause costly repairs and major changes.

4- The fund manager declares that there is no direct / indirect conflict of interests (other than what is disclosed) between any of the following:

- Fund manager.
- Manager(s) of properties associated with the fund.
- Owner(s) of properties associated with the fund.
- Tenant(s) of Real estate assets which their returns constitute 10% or more of the annual rental income of the fund.
- Accredited valuer.

5- The fund manager declares that it took the necessary care to ensure that there is no direct / indirect conflict of interest between the property seller and the accredited valuers.

6- The fund manager declares that all members of the fund board of directors have not been subjected to any bankruptcy or insolvency claims or any bankruptcy or liquidation proceedings, nor have they committed any fraudulent, dishonest or deceitful acts. In addition to not having performed any violation involving fraud, deceit or dishonesty. The fund manager further declares that they have the necessary skills and experience to qualify as board members.

7- The fund manager declares that the definition of the term "Independent Board Director" included in the Glossary of Defined Terms Used in the Regulations and Rules of the Capital Market Authority apply to the independent fund director, and that it will be applicable to any independent fund director appointed by the fund manager throughout the period of the fund.

8- The fund manager declares that no other significant business activities or other interests for the fund manager's (Name of fund manager) board of directors, which is likely to conflict with the interests of the fund.

9- The fund manager declares that there is no conflict of interest that would affect the fund manager in the performance of its duties for the fund.

10- The fund manager declares that there are no fees other than those mentioned in the Fees and Expenses section mentioned in the terms and conditions.

11- The fund manager declares that the fund will only be listed upon the completion of the transfer of ownership of the real estate in favor of the fund or the transfer of its interest. If this is not completed after completion of the offer period specified in the terms and conditions, the full subscription amount will be returned to the investors.

12- The fund manager declares that no member of the board of directors may have a direct or indirect interest in the business and contracts made for the fund.

13- The fund manager declares that all contracts and agreements relating to the fund which may affect the investors' decisions to subscribe or trade in the fund have been disclosed in the terms and conditions, and that there are no contracts and agreements other than those mentioned in the terms and conditions.

14- The fund manager declares that unitholders are entitled to vote on matters raised at meetings of unitholders. In addition, the approval of a fundamental change to the fund shall be passed by obtaining the approval of the majority unitholders owning more than (50%) or more than (75%) (where applicable) of the total units) holders of which are attending, in relation to carrying out any fundamental change to the fund, a fundamental change include the following:

- Significant change in the fund's objectives, nature or class;
- A change that may have a material adverse effect on the unitholders or their rights with respect to the closed-ended fund;
- Change that may have an effect on the risk position of the fund;
- The voluntary withdrawal of a fund manager from its position as the fund manager.
- Any change that would reasonably cause the unitholders to reconsider their participation in the closed-ended fund;
- A change that materially increases the total of payment out of the assets of the closed-ended fund.
- A change in the eligibility date or the termination of the closed-ended fund.
- Any increase in the net assets value of the closed-ended fund as a result of accepting in-kind or cash contributions or both.
- Any other cases determined by the Authority from time to time and notifies the fund manager of them.

15- The fund manager declares that it will take all necessary steps in the benefit of the unitholders to the best of its knowledge and belief with due diligence and reasonable consideration. The fund manager, directors, officers, employees, agents, consultants, affiliates, custodian, Shariah advisor and board of directors shall exercise reasonable diligence and effort and act in good faith in order to meet the interests of the unitholders. If the fund, however, is subject to loss in any way, in the event of any unintentional action by any of the aforementioned parties in connection with the management of the fund, then such parties shall not be held liable for such loss provided that they have acted in good faith and in a manner serving the interest of the fund. Good faith shall be proved in the absence of any conduct, decision or correspondence indicating prior knowledge of the negative consequences of such conduct. Moreover, such act shall not involve gross negligence, fraud or deliberate misconduct.

16- The fund manager declares that it has confirmed to the accredited valuer that the scope of work on valuation report must be appropriate for the purpose of the Fund Manager's application to the Saudi Stock Exchange and is valid for use for public offering and including the market rental value if it is different from the contractual rental value in the property leases the fund's units.

31.18 Annex 11: Form of a Real Estate Investment Traded Fund's Legal Advisor's Letter

[To be provided on the legal advisor's letterhead]

To: The Capital Market Authority

We, acting as legal advisor to [*] [name of the fund manager] "Fund Manager" in respect of the fund manager's request to offer REIT funds units and list them in the in the Saudi Stock Exchange (details of the REIT fund). We further refer to the Terms And Conditions prepared in relation with the fund [details of the offer], and more specifically, in connection with the application submitted to the Capital Market Authority (the "Authority") for the offer of REIT fund's units and listing them in the Exchange, and in line with the requirements of the Capital Market Law, the Real Estate Investment Funds Regulations, we particularly advised the fund manager of the requirements that should be included in the legal sections of the terms and conditions, the fulfillment of the assets to all regulatory requirements and the soundness of the title deeds of such assets in possession. In this respect, we have carried out such further review and enquiries as we consider appropriate in the circumstances.

In this advisory capacity, we confirm that we are not aware of any material matter consisting a violation by the fund manager toward its compliance with the requirements of the Capital Market Law or any conditions required under Real Estate Investment Funds Regulations, in relation to the offering and listing of the units of a Real Estate Investment Traded Fund application, including the requirements of the content of the terms and conditions as is at the date of this letter.

31.19 Annex 12: Approvals and Notifications Submitted to the Authority

Approvals Requests and notifications must be submitted in the manner specified by the Authority, according to the following:

a. Approvals and notifications that require changes in the Fund's documents:

1) Fund's name.

2) The subject of the notice.

3) Detail the current version and the proposed amendment and detailed justifications for such change.

4) If the change requires the consent of parties other than the fund manager, their consent must be taken before sending the request, with referring to that in the request sent to the Authority.

5) Declaration of the fund manager that the proposed change does not conflict with the investment funds regulations and other regulations and any applicable Law in the Kingdom.

6) Any other documents in support of the request.

b. Approval and notifications that do not require changes in the Fund's documents:

1) name of the Fund.

2) the subject of the notice.

3) If the change requires the consent of parties other than the fund manager, their consent must be taken before sending the request, with referring to that in the request sent to the Authority.

c. Notices relating to the end of the offering:

1) the name of the Fund.

2) the subject of the notice.

3) the date of the end of the offering.

4) the amount collected (in SAR).

5) Date of fund operation.

d. Notification on the termination or liquidation of the Fund:

1) the name of the Fund.

2) the date of the distribution of investment amounts to unitholders.

3) the return on investment as a percentage (where applicable).

31.20 Annex 13: Fund Termination Report

The fund termination report is used to provide relevant information regarding the process of the real estate investment fund's termination or liquidation.

The fund termination and liquidation report must contain all the information required under this Annex.

Content of the fund reports:

a) Real estate investment fund information:

1. Name of the real estate investment fund.

2. Investments objectives and policies and practices

3. A statement that the fund's Reports are available upon request free of charge.

4. Number of the fund's units at establishment.

b) Fund performance (including liquidation period):

1. Net assets value of the fund at the end of each fiscal year.

2. Net assets value upon liquidation.

3. Net assets value of the fund per unit at the end of each fiscal year.

4. Net assets value of the fund for each unit upon liquidation.

5. Highest and lowest net asset value per unit for each fiscal year.

6. The number of units in issue at the end of each fiscal year.

7. Income distribution per unit (gross and net).

8. The total return for 1 year, 3 years and 5 years (or since inception).

9. The annual total return for each year of the last 10 fiscal years (or since inception).

10. Expenses percentage for each year.

11. a table showing actual fees and fund expenses paid by the investment fund during the year. The Total Expense Ratio should also be clearly disclosed. If there are any circumstances in which a fund manager may elect to waive or rebate any fees, this must also be disclosed.

c) Termination or liquidation process information:

1. Name and address of the fund manager.

2. Name and address of the fund sub-manager and/or investment advisor (if any).

3. Reasons for terminating or liquidating the fund.

4. Name of liquidator (if any).

5. Date of commencing the termination or liquidation.

6. Number of fund units.

7. Description of the termination or liquidation process and its latest updates.

8. Any material events occurring during the termination or liquidation period.

d) The custodian:

1. Name and address of the custodian.

2. Brief description of its duties and responsibilities

e) Fund board:

1. Names of the board of directors, stating the type of membership.

2. Summary of the board members' qualifications.

3. Description of the role and responsibilities of the fund board of directors.

4. Details of the board members' remunerations.

5. Statement of any current or potential conflict of interests between a board member's interest and the fund's interests.

6. Statement of all funds board of directors on which a board member of the relevant board is part thereof.

f) Name and address of the auditor. g) Financial statements:

The final audited financial statements of the real estate investment fund, for the period following the latest audited financial statements, must be prepared in accordance with the accounting standards approved by the Saudi Organization for Certified Public Accountants.

31.21 Annex 14: Supplementary Annex for Real Estate Investment Fund

Changes related to the increase of the total value of the fund assets:

a) Real estate assets to be owned during the process of increasing the total value of the fund assets:

1. A detailed statement of the real estate assets to be owned.

2. A schedule of the following information for each real estate:

a. The name of the real estate;

b. The real estate owner(s) Information;

c. real estate type;

d. State / city;

e. Neighborhood / street;

f. Location (Croquis) map;

g. Land area;

h. Building area (according to the building permit);

i. Number of floors;

j. Types and numbers of units;

k. Occupancy rate of the real estate;

l. Completion date of building construction (according to the construction completion certificate);

m. Cost of purchasing the real estate;

n. Brief description of the current leases;

o. Revenues for the last (3) years of the real estate, if any;

p. Any additional information.

3. Previous and targeted rental proceeds for each real estate/usufruct, and its percentage of the total rental income.

4. A table of the total and net targeted proceeds before and after increasing the fund's total assets value.

5. Valuation of the assets to be acquired: A table containing the following:

a. Real estate subject to acquisition.

b. Names of the accredited valuers.

c. Date of each valuation report.

d. Valuation price for each real estate.

e. Average valuation prices.

f. Purchase price of each real estate.

b) Private placement for the increase of the total assets value of the fund:

1. Total assets value of the fund before and after the increase.

2. Number of units before and after the increase of the total value of the fund assets.

3. Disclosure of the use of fund offering proceeds.

4. Detailed statement of the fund manager's subscription value in the fund during the offer period.

5. Detailed statement of the information of the real estate owners subscribing with in-kind contributions in the fund and their ownership percentages. In addition to a table illustrating the ownership percentages of all subscribers with in-kind contributions.

6. Detailed statement of the minimum and maximum limit for the sum of the increase of the fund's total assets value.

7. A timetable of the estimated periods from the commencement of the offer of units until the commencement of trading the units.

8. The mechanism to be followed by the fund manager to accept subscriptions and allocate units among unitholders.

9. Disclosure of the receiving agents.

c) Additional risks related to the increase of the total value of the fund assets:

d) Fees, services charges, commissions and management fees:

1. It must Include a detailed disclosure of all fees and charges that will be incurred by the Fund's assets in details, so as to clarify the amounts of fees and charges and their percentage of the total assets of the Fund with the stated upper limit for all the charges and fees. It must also contain a table representing all fees and commissions and management fees, whether paid by the Unitholders or charged on the Fund's assets, and shall include:

a) Fees and expenses of the board of directors.

b) Any fee paid by unitholders when purchasing units in the fund.

c) Any management fees payable to the fund manager from the net assets of the fund.

d) Any payment for custody charges, or other services provided by the Custodian.

e) Any fees paid to the auditor.

f) Any commission resulting from loans to the Fund.

g) Any charges related to registration of the Fund's units, or any other administrative service.

h) Fees paid to the property manager.

i) Any other amount paid by Unitholders, or any amount deducted from the Fund's assets.

j) Percentage of fund costs in the total assets value of the fund.

In addition to a statement of all cases and situations where the fund manager has the right to waive or deduct any of the above mentioned fees.

2. A table containing the following:

a) Type of fee;
b) Imposed percentage, if any;
c) Imposed amount, if any;
d) Calculation method;
e) Recurrence of the fee payment.

3. A table showing a default investment for the unitholder

4. A declaration from the fund manager stating that the fees mentioned in this paragraph include all fees imposed on the fund, and that it shall incur any other fees not stated herein.

e) Insurance:

This section must include the assets that have been insured, the details of the insurance and the extent of its coverage.

f) Other information:

The inclusion of any significant information known (or supposed to be known) to the Fund Manager or Fund's Board at the time of issuing the Fund's Terms and Conditions.

g) The company that carries out Property Managements

1. The name and address of the company that carries out property management.
2. Statement of the property management company's tasks, duties and responsibilities.
3. Disclosure of whether the company that carries out the property managements intends to invest in the fund's units, and the value of these investments.
4. Any fees paid to the property manager.

32 Rules for Registering Auditors of Entities Subject to the Authority's Supervision

Issued by the Board of the Capital Market Authority ursuant to its Resolution Number 1-135-2018 Dated 12/4/1440 H (19/12/2018 G) based on the Capital Market Law issued by Royal Decree No. M/30 dated 2/6/1424H

Important Notice: The current version of these Rules, as may be amended, can be found at the Authority website: www.cma.org.sa

Table of Contents

Part 1 : General Provisions
Article 1 : Preliminary
Article 2 : Definitions
Article 3 : Waivers
Article 4 : Right to Appeal
Part 2 : Registration
Article 5 : Mandating the Registration
Article 6 : Registration Procedures
Article 7 : Accounting Firm Registration Conditions
Article 8 : CPA Registration Conditions
Article 9 : Procedures and Powers of the Authority in Relation to an Application for Registration
Article 10 : Fees
Part 3 : Continuing Obligations
Article 11 : Conditions for Maintenance of Registration
Article 12 : Notification Requirements
Article 13 : Transparency Report
Article 14 : Periodic Information
Article 15 : Compliance with the Rules
Article 16 : Participation of the Registered CPA
Part 4: Issues Affecting Registration
Article 17 : Registration Cancelation and Suspension
Article 18 : Ceasing to Carry on Audit Engagements
Part 5: Final Provisions
Article 19 : Publication and Entry into Force
Annex (1) : Information Required in the Transparency Report

32.1 PART 1: GENERAL PROVISIONS

32.1.1 Article 1 : Preliminary

Purpose of Rules

(a) The purpose of these Rules is to set out the standards and conditions required for the auditors of the entities subject to the Authority's supervision, including the mandating of registration, its conditions, procedures and the continuing obligations on registered auditors.

b) These Rules shall have no prejudice to the provisions of the other related laws, and the obligations set out by the Saudi Organization for Certified Public Accountants under the Law of Certified Public Accountants.

32.1.2 Article 2 : Definitions

a) Any reference to the Capital Market Law in these Rules shall mean the Capital Market Law issued by the Royal Decree No. M/30 dated 2/6/1424H.

b) Without prejudice to paragraph (c) of this Article, expressions and terms in these Rules have the same meaning which they bear in the Capital Market Law and the Glossary of Defined Terms used in the Regulations and Rules of the Capital Market Authority, unless the context indicates otherwise.

c) For the purpose of implementing these Rules, the following expressions and terms shall have the meaning they bear as follows, unless the context indicates otherwise: - Law of Certified Public Accountants: the Law of Certified Public Accountants issued by Royal Decree no. (M/12) dated 13/05/1412 H. -

Entities Subject to the Authority's Supervision (ESAS): for the purposes of these Rules, shall mean the following:

1) The Exchange.
2) The Depositary Center.
3) Authorized Persons licensed to carry on securities business, except Authorized Persons licensed to carry on arranging or advising activities.
4) Investment Funds.
5) Listed Companies.

Audit Engagements: Audit of financial statements, prepared by an entity, in accordance with the auditing standards adopted by the Saudi Organization for Certified Public Accountants for the purpose of expressing an opinion as to whether such financial statements present fairly the financial position of the entity at a specific date, and the results of its operations for a specific financial period, or review of the interim financial statements, prepared by the entity, to determine if significant amendments are needed for the interim financial statements to be in agreement with the accounting standards adopted by the Saudi Organization for Certified Public Accountants.

Professional Standards: Accounting and auditing standards, the professional code of ethics and other standards and pronouncements adopted by the Saudi Organization for Certified Public Accountants.

Accounting Firm: The entity which carries on audit engagements in accordance with the provisions of the Law of Certified Public Accountants, whether it is an individual or professional firm.

Certified Public Accountant (CPA): The natural person who carries on and is responsible for audit engagements, its performance, and signing of audit reports issued by the accounting firm in accordance with the provisions of the Law of Certified Public Accountants.

Registration: Registration of the accounting firm or the CPA to carry on audit engagements for ESAS in accordance with the provisions of these Rules.

Inspection: Analyzing periodic data and information provided by the accounting firm and inspecting and assessing the quality control system and the degree of compliance with it.

Quality Control System: Policies and procedures approved by the accounting firm in order to reasonably verify the compliance of the firm's employees with the professional standards and related laws governing their performance in carrying on audit engagement, including the professional code of ethics approved by the Saudi Organization for Certified Public Accountants.

32.1.3 Article 3: Waivers

The Authority may waive a provision of these Rules in whole or in part as it applies to an applicant for registration, a registered accounting firm or a registered CPA, either upon a request from the applicant for registration, the registered accounting firm or the registered CPA or on its own initiative.

32.1.4 Article 4: Right to Appeal

Any person subject to these Rules may appeal to the Committee for the Resolution of Securities Disputes in respect of any decision or action that the Authority takes under these Rules.

32.2 PART 2: REGISTRATION

32.2.1 Article 5: Registration Required

a) No person may carry on audit engagements for ESAS unless it has been registered with the Authority.

b) The accounting firm and CPA must be registered with the Authority prior to being appointed to carry on audit engagements for ESAS.

(The Board of The Capital Market Authority has Issued its Resolution no. (1-135-2018) dated 12/4/1440H corresponding to 19/12/2018G for paragraph (a) of Article (5) of the Rules for Registering Auditors of Entities Subject to the Authority's Supervision to enter into force starting from 30/6/2019G 2 The Board of The Capital Market Authority has Issued its Resolution no. (1-135-2018) dated 12/4/1440H corresponding to 19/12/2018G for subparagraph (a) of paragraph (2) of Article (8) of the Rules for Registering Auditors of Entities Subject to the Authority's Supervision to be effective starting from 20/12/2021G.)

32.2.2 Article 6 : Registration Procedures

a) For the purpose of these Rules, the applicant for registration shall mean the accounting firm or the CPA who submits the application for registration to carry on audit engagements for ESAS. An applicant for registration becomes subject to these Rules from the date of submission of its application.

b) The accounting firm must submit its application for registration in accordance with the application form prescribed by the Authority.

c) The CPA must submit his application for registration through the accounting firm in accordance with the application form prescribed by the Authority.

d) The accounting firm must pay the fees for registration as prescribed by the Authority.

32.2.3 Article 7: Accounting Firm Registration Conditions

To register an accounting firm with the Authority, the following conditions must be satisfied:

1) It is licensed to practice the profession of account auditing in accordance with the Law of Certified Public Accountants.

2) It is fit and proper to carry on audit engagements for ESAS, including:

a. No judicial decision has been issued against it as a result of an offense involving fraud or any act involving a lack of integrity or dishonesty during the five years preceding the date of application for registration with the Authority.
b. It has adequate indemnity insurance for the risks of professional failures.

3) Any other conditions specified by the Authority.

32.2.4 Article 8: CPA Registration Conditions

To register a CPA with the Authority, the following conditions must be satisfied:

1) He is licensed to practice the profession of account auditing in accordance with the Law of Certified Public Accountants.

2) He is fit and proper to carry on audit engagements for ESAS, including:

a. To hold the Fellowship Certificate in accordance with the Law of Certified Public Accountants.
b. No judicial decision has been issued against him as a result of an offense involving fraud or any act involving a lack of integrity or dishonesty during the five years preceding the date of application for registration with the Authority.
c. He has not been sentenced to removal of his name from the Certified Public Accountant Register, imprisonment or fines under the Law of Certified Public Accountants within the five years preceding the date of application for registration with the Authority.
d. He has not been subjected to suspension under the Law of Certified Public Accountants, during the two years preceding the date of the application for registration with the Authority.
e. He has practiced the profession of account auditing after obtaining the license in accordance with the Law of Certified Public Accountants for a period not less than five years, including a period of not less than three years working in a supervisory level over the audit engagements for ESAS, the entities accepted by the Authority, or entities under the supervision of a foreign regulatory body that applies regulatory standards and requirements equivalent to those of the Authority or are accepted by it.

3) He is of integrity, and has sufficient skill, care and diligence.

4) Any other conditions specified by the Authority.

(The Board of The Capital Market Authority has Issued its Resolution no. (1-135-2018) dated 12/4/1440H corresponding to 19/12/2018G for paragraph (a) of Article (5) of the Rules for Registering Auditors of Entities Subject to the Authority's Supervision to enter into force starting from 30/6/2019G 2 The Board of The Capital Market Authority has Issued its Resolution no. (1-135-2018) dated 12/4/1440H corresponding to 19/12/2018G for subparagraph (a) of paragraph (2) of Article (8) of the Rules for Registering Auditors of Entities Subject to the Authority's Supervision to be effective starting from 20/12/2021G)

32.2.5 Article 9: Procedures and Powers of the Authority in relation to an Application for Registration

a) In considering an application for registration, the Authority may:

1) Carry out any enquiries that it considers appropriate;
2) Require the applicant for registration, or its representative, to attend before the Authority to answer any questions and explain any matter the Authority considers relevant to the application for registration;
3) Require to provide additional information; and
4) Verify the accuracy of any information furnished by the applicant for registration.

b) The Authority will aim to consider the application for registration within 30 days of receiving all information and documents that it considers pertinent.

c) The Authority may, after considering the application for registration, take any of the following actions:

1) Approve the application for registration;
2) Approve the application for registration subject to such conditions and limitations as it considers appropriate;
3) defer making a decision for such period as may be necessary to carry out further investigation or to allow for the provision of additional information; or
4) Reject the application for registration and give grounds for the rejection.

d) If the Authority resolves to approve the application for registration, it will add the name of the registered accounting firm or the registered CPA to the register that the Authority shall maintain for this purpose, and shall notify the applicant of such approval.

e) If the Authority resolves to reject the application for registration, it will notify the applicant in writing of the rejection and the grounds for the rejection.

32.2.6 Article 10: Fees

The registered accounting firm must pay such fees as the Authority may prescribe for the maintenance of the registration.

32.3 PART 3: CONTINUING OBLIGATIONS

32.3.1 Article 11: Conditions for Maintenance of Registration

As a condition of the maintenance of registration, the registered accounting firm and the registered CPA must comply at all times with the following:

1) The Law of Certified Public Accountants and its Regulations.
2) The Capital Market Law and Its Implementing Regulations.
3) The registration conditions.
4) Any Standards and Conditions specified by the Authority.
5) The Authority's instructions regarding the inspection and its results.
6) Providing the Authority immediately of all information and documents that the Authority may require for the purpose of implementing the provisions of Capital Market Law and Its Implementing Regulations.
7) Establishing the necessary arrangements to provide the technical consultation to the staff of the registered accounting firm, who conduct the audit engagements for ESAS, where such consultation is required.

32.3.2 Article 12: Notification Requirements

a) The registered accounting firm must notify the Authority in writing within 7 days of the date of any changes in the information provided to the Authority in the application form for registration of the accounting firm, in regards of the registered accounting firm's name, address, website, e-mail or partners names.

b) The registered accounting firm must immediately notify the Authority in writing upon a lawsuit being filed against the registered accounting firm or any of its partners, executive managers or audit managers, if the subject of the lawsuit relates to the firm's business or the practice of the profession of account auditing.

c) Upon receiving a notification in accordance with paragraphs (a) or (b) of this article, the Authority may:

1. Require the registered accounting firm to provide any additional information that the Authority deems necessary to properly assess the subject matter of such notification.
2. Impose any other conditions, restrictions or requirements that the Authority reasonably deems necessary to address the actual or potential effects of the subject matter of the notification.

32.3.3 Article 13: Transparency Report

The registered accounting firm must publish an annual transparency report on its website within a period not exceeding four months from the end of its financial year, which includes, at minimum, the information required in Annex 1 of these Rules.

32.3.4 Article 14: Periodic Information

The registered accounting firm shall submit periodic information to the Authority, in the form specified by the Authority, and within a period not exceeding four months from the end of its financial year.

32.3.5 Article 15: Compliance with the Rules

a) The registered accounting firm must ensure that its registered CPAs comply with the conditions of registration and the continuing obligations set out in these Rules.

b) The registered accounting firm must appoint a registered CPA to be in charge of communicating with the Authority and ensuring that the registered accounting firm and its registered CPAs comply with the conditions of registration and the continuing obligations set out in these Rules.

c) The registered accounting firm must immediately notify the Authority if it becomes aware that any of the registration conditions set out in these Rules are no longer fulfilled by it or by any of its registered CPAs.

32.3.6 Article 16: Participation of the Registered CPA

The registered CPA must participate for a sufficient amount of the working hours allocated for each audit engagement for an entity subject to the Authority's supervision which he issued a report in its regard, in order to ensure the quality of such engagement.

32.4 PART 4: ISSUES AFFECTING REGISTRATION

32.4.1 Article 17: Registration Cancelation and Suspension

The Authority may suspend or cancel the registration of any registered accounting firm or registered CPA if it has violated any of the provisions of the Capital Market Law or its Implementation Regulations.

32.4.2 Article 18: Ceasing to Carry on Audit Engagements

a) Upon the permanent or temporary ceasing of a registered accounting firm or any of its registered CPAs to carry on audit engagements for ESAS, the registered accounting firm must prepare a fair and appropriate plan for its clients of ESAS including, at minimum, the following:

1) Notifying the Authority in advance and in writing of the date on which the registered accounting firm or the registered CPA intends to cease to carrying on audit engagements, the period of its ceasing and the reasons thereof.
2) In case the registered accounting firm ceases to carry on audit engagements, it shall not contract with clients of ESAS to carry on audit engagements.
3) Notify its clients of ESAS within a reasonable period of its decision to cease carrying on audit engagements, the period of its ceasing and the reasons thereof.
4) Properly completing any remaining audit engagements with the registered accounting firm, or taking appropriate action to serve the interests of its clients of ESAS, without prejudice to other relevant laws.
5) Submission of a report to the Authority regarding the actions taken to implement this plan.

b) The registered accounting firm or the registered CPA shall not be exempted from the liability arising from any mistake, by any of them, that occurred prior to its ceasing to carry on audit engagements for ESAS.

32.5 PART 5: FINAL PROVISIONS

32.5.1 Article 19: Publication and Entry into Force

These Rules shall become effective in accordance with their approval resolution.

32.6 ANNEX 1: Information Required in the Transparency Report

The registered accounting firm must publish an annual transparency report which includes, at minimum, the following information:

1. A description of the registered accounting firm's legal structure, including the firms network that the registered accounting firm is a member of, or that are members of the registered accounting firm, and the relevant legal arrangements.

2. Statement on the governance of the registered accounting firm, including the following:

a. Description of the organizational structure including the name of the owner of the registered accounting firm or its partners, managers and senior executives, and a description of the committees formed in the registered accounting firm, including the name of the committee and its duties during the financial year (if any).
b. Name of the registered CPA, who works at the registered accounting firm, and who is a member of the board of directors of any of the ESAS, or in the committees of any of the ESAS, with the names of these entities.
c. The basis for determining the remunerations of partners.
d. A description of the independence policies applied by the registered accounting firm, and an acknowledgement that such policies have been properly prepared and implemented effectively.
e. A description of the quality control system applied by the registered accounting firm, and an acknowledgement that such system has been properly developed and implemented effectively.

3. The jobs nationalization percentage at the registered accounting firm.

4. Information on the latest internal inspection of the quality control system implemented within the registered accounting firm, including the date of conducting such inspection, how it was implemented, a description of its results and how such results were addressed.

5. Details of any punishment, penalty, precautionary measure or preventive restriction imposed on the registered accounting firm or its registered CPAs by the Authority or any other supervisory, regulatory or judiciary authority during the last financial year.

6. Details of any litigation or claim (including any litigation pending or threatened) or any ongoing investigations which may have a material effect on the registered accounting firm's business, during the last financial year.

7. A list of the clients of the registered accounting firm that are of the ESAS, and the registered CPA who carried on audit engagements for such clients during the last financial year.

8. Information on continuing professional education during the last financial year of the staff who conduct the audit engagements for ESAS.

9. The total number of working hours of audit engagements for the ESAS, and the percentage of those executed by the partners in the registered accounting firm, during the last financial year.

10. Financial information for the last financial year, including the following:

Financial Information of the Registered Accounting Firm (Amount in Saudi Riyals)

1. Total revenue
2. Total revenues from audit engagements for ESAS
3. Total revenues from other services for ESAS
4. Total revenues from other services for ESAS that are audited by the registered accounting firm
5. Total revenues from other services for ESAS that are not audited by the registered accounting firm
6. Total revenues from audit engagements for entities other than ESAS
7. Total revenues from other services for entities other than ESAS
8. Total revenue from other services for entities other than ESAS that are audited by the registered accounting firm
9. Total revenue from other services for entities other than ESAS that are not audited by the registered accounting firm

(Note: numbering was fixed in this #10)

33 Reporting Capital Market Law Violations

Regulation on the Reporting of Violations of the Capital Market Law, issued by the Board of the Capital Markets Authority, pursuant to Board Res. No. 2-135-2021, dated 9/5/1443H (13/12/2016G)

Table of Contents

Article One: Preamble
Article Two: Definitions
Article Three: Exemptions
Article Four: Right of Appeal
Article Five: Reporting Channels
Article Six: Requirements when Reporting
Article Seven: Conditions for Granting the Reward Article Eight: Determination of the Reward Amount Article Nine: Legal Support
Article Ten: Protection Policy for Reporting Individuals Article Eleven: Confidentiality
Article Twelve: Reporting by the Individual who Committed or Participated in Committing a Violation
Article Thirteen: Reporting an Untrue Incident Article Fourteen: Entry into Force

33.1 Article 1: Preamble

The purpose of this Regulation is to regulate the reporting of violations of the Capital Market Law and its implementing regulations, or violations of the regulations of the Exchange, the Depository Center, or the Clearing Center. This includes the determination of financial rewards for those who report such violations, the controls on granting such rewards, and the procedures that contribute to the protection of those who report violations.

Article 2: Definitions:

a) "Law" means the Capital Market Law issued by the Royal Decree No. M/30 dated 2/6/1424H.

b) Without prejudice to sub-section (c) of this Article, terms used in this Regulation shall have the same meaning provided in the Law and in the Glossary of Defined Terms used in the Rules and Regulations of the Capital Market Authority.

c) For the implementation of the provisions of this Regulation, and unless the context indicates otherwise, the following words and phrases shall have the meanings herein specified:

- "Reporting Individual" means a person who reports to the Authority any acts or practices that constitute a violation of any provisions of the Law or its implementing regulations, or of the regulations of the Exchange, the Depository Center, or the Clearing Center.

- "Reported Individual" means a person against whom a report to the Authority was made in relation to any acts or practices that constitute a violation of any provisions of the Law or its implementing regulations, or of the regulations of the Exchange, the Depository Center, or the Clearing Center.

- "Report" means information provided to the Authority – through channels to be determined by the Authority – in relation to any acts or practices that constitute a violation of any provisions of the Law or its implementing regulations, or of the regulations of the Exchange, the Depository Center, or the Clearing Center.

- "Information" means any statement or document – including audio recordings and digital or paper based data or documents – that indicates a violation or suspected violation of any provisions of the Law or its implementing regulations, or of the regulations of the Exchange, the Depository Center, or the Clearing Center.

- "Reward" means a monetary amount determined based on the amount of the fines and financial penalties collected as a result of the Report.

- "Relatives" includes the husband, wife, children and parents.

33.2 Article 3: Exemptions

The Authority may exempt any person from the application of any provisions of this Regulation in whole or in part, either through an application from that person or upon the Authority's own initiative.

33.3 Article 4: Right of Appeal

Any person that is subject to this Regulation may appeal to the Committee in relation to any decision or action taken by the Authority pursuant to the provisions of this Regulation.

33.4 Article 5: Reporting Channels

The Authority shall receive reports through the following channels:

a) The Authority's website.
b) Registered mail.
c) The Authority's headquarters.
d) The Authority's phone number.
e) The investor protection mobile application.
f) Any other means determined by the Authority.

33.5 Article 6: Requirements when Reporting

The Report must contain the information specified by the Authority, including the following:

1. The name of the Reported Individual and, if available, the Reported Individual's contact details.

2. A clear and comprehensive description of the incident that is the subject of the Report, as well as the evidence, information or documents pertaining to the acts or practices that constitute a violation of any provisions of the Law or its implementing regulations, or of the regulations of the Exchange, the Depository Center, or the Clearing Center.

Article 7: Conditions for Granting the Reward The Authority may grant the Reporting Individual a reward the value of which is determined by up to (20%) of the amount of the fines and financial penalties collected as a result of the reported violations, provided the following conditions are met:

1. The report includes the Reporting Individual's name and contact details, or those of his legal representative.
2. The Reporting Individual is a natural person and made the Report of his own volition.
3. That neither the Reporting Individual nor their Relatives is an employee of the Authority or of any similar supervisory body that has access to the Information that is the subject of the Report.
4. The Information contained in the report is not available to the Authority or has not been received beforehand by the Authority from others.
5. The Reporting Individual does not disclose to others any Information related to the Report.
6. The Report leads to the issuance of a final decision by the Authority or by the Committees for the Resolution of Securities Disputes imposing a fine or financial penalty.
7. That the Authority collects the imposed fines and financial penalties, and that the total amount of the fines and financial penalties collected as a result of the reported violations exceeds one million (1,000,000) Saudi riyals.

33.6 Article 8: Reward Amount Determination

When determining the Reward amount, and the apportioning of the Reward amount between more than one Reporting Individual if applicable, the following shall be taken into consideration:

1. The Reporting Individual's role in proving the violation.
2. The timing of the Report.
3. The weight, accuracy, completeness and reliability of the Information and evidence provided by the Reporting Individual.
4. The extent to which the Information provided by the Reporting Individual contributed to the finding of a violation and issuance of a final decision of the same.
5. Extent of the Reporting Individual's cooperation.
6. The extent of the Reporting Individual's contribution in persuading other parties to cooperate in relation to the Report.
7. The extent of the Reporting Individual's contribution in limiting the damages that would have resulted from the violation had it not been reported.
8. The degree of risk the Reporting Individual faced because of the Report.
9. That the information in the Report was not available to the public; this includes information deduced by the Reporting Individual based on the Reporting Individual's independent analysis of information available to the public.

33.7 Article 9: Legal Support

The Authority may provide legal support and assistance to an individual the Authority believes was harmed as a result of a Report made by such individual.

33.8 Article Ten: Protection Policy for Reporting Individuals

The Exchange, the Clearing Center, the Depository Center, Capital Market Institutions, and listed companies must set an internal policy, to be adopted by their boards of directors or their equivalent, for the protection of Reporting Individuals that are employed by them. Such policy must include, at minimum, a prohibition on taking disciplinary actions against Reporting Individuals employed by them or infringing upon their rights or employment benefits because of Reports submitted by them to the Authority.

(In accordance with the Board of the Authority Resolution no. (2-135-2021) Dated 9/5/1443H corresponding to 13/12/2021G, Article 10 of this Regulation shall become effective as of 9/8/1444H corresponding to 1/3/2023G.)

33.9 Article 11: Confidentiality

The information of the Reporting Individual or any information obtained by the Authority under the provisions of this Regulation is considered confidential.

33.10 Article 12: Violator Reporting

The Authority may take into consideration when determining its decision on the reported violation whether the individual who committed or participated in committing the violation has, as an initiative by such individual, submitted a Report on the violation before the Authority is aware of such violation.

33.11 Article 13: False Reporting

The Authority has the right to take whatever measures it deems appropriate against those who knowingly and in bad faith reported an untrue incident.

33.12 Article 14: Entry into Force

This Regulation shall enter into force upon its publication.

34 Securities Borrowing and Lending Regulations

Approved by the Board of the Capital Market Authority pursuant to its Resolution Number 1-28-2017 dated 16/6/1438H (15/3/2017G) as amended pursuant to Board Resolution Number 21-1-2021 dated 10/7/1442H (22/2/2021G)

TABLE OF CONTENTS

Part 1 Preliminary Provisions
Article 1 Preliminary
Article 2 Definitions
Part 2 Securities Borrowing and Lending Transactions
Article 3 SBL transactions
Article 4 Eligible participants
Article 5 Eligible listed securities
Article 6 Minimum collateral
Article 7 SBL agreement
Article 8 Return of borrowed securities and collateral
Part 3 Lending Agent and Borrowing Agent
Article 9 Lending agent
Part 4 Powers of the Authority and the Depository Centre
Article 10 Powers of the Authority and the Depository Centre
Part 5 Reporting and Record Keeping Requirements
Article 11 Copy of the SBL agreement
Article 12 Reporting of SBL transactions
Article 13 Public disclosure of information with regard to SBL transactions
Article 14 Record keeping
Part 6 General Provisions
Article 15 Limit of liability
Article 16 Waivers
Article 17 Publication and entry into force
Part 7 Annex
Annex 1 Matters to be included in SBL Agreements

34.1 PART 1 PRELIMINARY PROVISIONS

34.1.1 Article 1: Preliminary

The purpose of these Regulations is to set out the framework for securities borrowing and lending activities in respect of listed securities in the Kingdom.

34.1.2 Article 2: Definitions

a. Any reference to the "Capital Market Law" in these Regulations shall mean the Capital Market Law issued by Royal Decree No. M/30 dated 2/6/1424H.

b. Expressions and terms in these Regulations have the meaning which they bear in the Capital Market Law and in the Glossary of Defined Terms used in the Exchange Rules, unless the contrary intention appears.

34.1.3 Article 3: SBL Transactions

a. An SBL transaction is a privately negotiated trade settled in Depository Centre accounts, under the terms of which:

1) a lender temporarily transfers ownership of listed securities to a borrower; and
2) the borrower commits to return equivalent listed securities as specified by the Depository Centre.

b. An SBL transaction must not be entered into unless all of the following conditions are met:

1) the SBL transaction is entered into between eligible participants as specified in Article 4 of these Regulations;
2) the SBL transaction is entered into in respect of eligible listed securities as specified in Article 5 of these Regulations;
3) in relation to the borrower, the SBL transaction is entered into for one of the following purposes:
   i. executing a short selling transactions pursuant to the Short Selling Regulations;
   ii. relending Securities to the clients of the Broker, Custody Member, or the Qualified Foreign Investor;
   iii. the resolution of securities settlement failures;
   iv. return of borrowed securities;
   v. the creation of units of exchange traded fund; or
   vi. other purposes determined by the Depository Centre from time to time;
4) the SBL transaction complies with the minimum collateral requirement as specified in Article 6 of these Regulations;
5) the parties of the SBL transaction have in place a binding written SBL agreement in compliance with the requirements of Article 7 of these Regulations;
6) The borrower and the lender or its agent, if any, have suitable arrangements for custody and to execute the SBL transaction, either by being a Custody Member or appointing a Custody Member; and
7) the Custody Members referred to in subparagraph (6) of paragraph (b) of this Article and the lending agent, if any, must ensure that securities lending and borrowing by the investors that are not Qualified Investors is according to paragraph (b) of Article 4 of these Regulations.

c. The requirements set out in Article 43 except subparagraphs (1), and (2) of paragraph (j) of the Capital Market Institutions Regulations applies to the SBL transactions.

34.1.4 Article 4: Eligible Participants

a. Entering into an SBL transaction is limited to the Qualified Investors.

b. Notwithstanding paragraph (a) of this Article, investors who are not Qualified Investors may enter into an SBL transaction as a lender or a borrower (where applicable) after satisfying the following:

1) in case of entering the transaction as a lending party, it must appoint a Lending Agent in accordance with Article (9) of these Regulations.
2) in case of entering the transaction as a borrowing party, it must borrow the securities as a client from its Custody Member or Broker.

34.1.5 Article 5: Eligible Listed Securities

An SBL transaction may only be entered into in respect of listed securities which the Depository Centre specifies, after notifying the Authority.

34.1.6 Article 6: Minimum Collateral

a. A borrower entering into an SBL transaction shall provide and maintain financial collateral as specified in the SBL agreement.

b. The value of collateral provided by the borrower shall at all times be not less than 100% of the current market value of the borrowed securities.

34.1.7 Article 7: SBL Agreement

a. The parties of an SBL transaction must enter into a binding written SBL agreement which, as a minimum, contains terms which govern the matters specified in Annex 1 of these Regulations.

b. The Depository Centre may prohibit any potential party to an SBL transaction, whether as agent or principal (where applicable), from entering into an SBL transaction where in its view the terms of the SBL agreement do not meet the requirements set out in these Regulations.

c. The Depository Centre is not obligated to review the relevant SBL agreement or verify its contents.

34.1.8 Article 8: Return of Borrowed Securities and Collateral

a. A lender of borrowed securities or its agent shall accept every return of equivalent securities from the borrower as specified in the SBL agreement, and re-deliver collateral corresponding to such return to the borrower as agreed in the SBL agreement.

b. Where there has been a failure to return the borrowed securities or the collateral in accordance with the terms of the SBL agreement, the Custody Member entered into the SBL transaction shall notify the Depository Centre, and the Depository Centre will terminate the SBL transaction in accordance with the mechanism and controls prescribed by the Depository Centre from time to time.

34.2 PART 3 LENDING AGENT

34.2.1 Article 9: Lending Agent

a. A person may enter into an SBL transaction as lending agent if it is a Custody Member or a Broker.

b. Each person who acts as a lending agent for a client who is a lender must ensure, before entering into SBL transactions on behalf of such client, that:

1) a binding written SBL agreement with the relevant counterpart which complies with the requirements of these Regulations is in place;
2) the terms on which the lending agent will act on behalf of the client are documented in writing; and
3) the terms on which the Custody Member will act on behalf of the Broker referred to in paragraph (a) of this article are documented in writing, where applicable.

c. The lending agent may assign a third party to carry out any of its functions as specified in the SBL agreement.

34.2.2 Article 10: Powers of the Authority and the Depository Centre

a. The Authority, or the Depository Centre having obtained the approval of the Authority, may suspend or prohibit SBL transactions in respect of an eligible listed security, or may suspend or prohibit all SBL transactions in the Kingdom, at any time and as they deem fit, including but not limited to the following circumstances:

1) there are adverse events or developments which constitute a serious threat to financial stability or to market confidence;
2) for the protection of investors;
3) for the maintenance of an orderly market; or
4) trading in a listed security is suspended.

b. The Exchange will publish on its website any action taken by the Authority or the Depository Centre pursuant to their powers under paragraph (a) of this Article.

34.3 PART 5: REPORTING AND RECORD KEEPING REQUIREMENTS

34.3.1 Article 11: Copy of the SBL Agreement

The Depository Centre may at any time require some or all Custody Members who entered into an SBL transaction, to submit a copy of the SBL agreement with the relevant counterpart to the Depository Centre in accordance with the mechanism and the controls prescribed by the Depository Centre from time to time.

34.3.2 Article 12: Reporting of SBL Transactions

A Custody Member who has entered into an SBL transaction must report complete and accurate details of such transactions to the Depository Centre in accordance with the mechanism and the controls prescribed by the Depository Centre.

34.3.3 Article 13: Public Disclosure of Information

The Depository Centre may disclose any information with regard to SBL transactions as it deems fit.

34.3.4 Article 14: Record Keeping

a. A Custody Member who has entered into an SBL transaction must ensure recording and retaining sufficient information about its securities borrowing and lending activities to demonstrate compliance with the Capital Market Law, its Implementing Regulations, the Exchange Rules in general and these Regulations in particular.

b. A Custody Member must ensure the records required to be maintained by these Regulations are retained for a period of at least ten years from the date of the SBL transaction unless the Depository Centre specifies otherwise. In the event such records relate to any litigation or claim (including any potential litigation) or any on-going investigations, the Custody Member must ensure such records are retained until the conclusion of that litigation, claim or on-going investigation.

c. In addition to its powers under the Capital Market Law, the Depository Centre may request to inspect the records directly or through a person it appoints for that purpose upon giving reasonable prior notice in the context of the request to the Custody Member.

d. Records may be recorded in any form, but the Custody Member must be capable of reproduction in hard printed form. If the Depository Centre requires records to be produced in a particular electronic or other format, it shall give the Custody Member a reasonable period of time in the context to meet that request.

34.4 PART 6: GENERAL PROVISIONS

34.4.1 Article 15: Limit of Liability

a. Without prejudice to the provisions of the Capital Market Law, its Implementing Regulations and the Exchange Rules, the Exchange or the Depository Centre shall not be held liable for any losses or damages incurred by any participant referred to in Article 4 of these Regulations, their clients or any other person who deals with the Depository and Settlement System which may arise directly or indirectly as a result of:

1) any procedures, orders or transactions that are subject to these Regulations;
2) the use of the Depository and Settlement System for SBL activities;
3) the partial or complete suspension or prohibition of SBL transactions, or the interruption of activities and services provided by the Exchange or the Depository Centre;
4) the exercise by the Exchange or the Depository Centre of any of their relevant powers under these Regulations, the Capital Market Law, its Implementing Regulations and the Exchange Rules; or
5) any service failure attributable to the Exchange or the Depository Centre by reason of an event outside of its control.

b. Without prejudice to the provisions of the Capital Market Law, the Exchange and the Depository Centre shall have no liability in respect of the accuracy, timeliness or completeness of SBL transaction reports or any other information published on its website from time to time.

34.4.2 Article 16: Waivers

The Depository Centre may, after obtaining the Authority's approval, waive any requirement in these Regulations either based on a request from the relevant person or on its own initiative.

34.4.3 Article 17: Publication and Entry into Force

These Regulations shall become effective upon their publication.

34.5 ANNEX 1: MATTERS TO BE INCLUDED IN SBL AGREEMENTS

1. Parties

The names of all relevant parties of the SBL transaction including the borrower and the lender or any lending agent, as specified in paragraph (10) of this annex.

2. Duration

The SBL agreement period.

3. Return of borrowed securities

The provisions of the return of borrowed securities, including any related notice periods.

4. Securities

Unless the parties agree otherwise, the securities to be borrowed and any securities provided as collateral must be delivered to the other party free of any encumbrances or restrictions.

5. Acceptable collateral

Arrangements for the delivery of collateral, the maintenance of margin and the substitution of collateral.

6. Voting rights, distributions and corporate actions

Determining the rights of the parties in respect of voting rights, distributions, and corporate actions relating to the borrowed securities and any securities provided as collateral.

7. Recall right

The terms on which the lender has the right to recall the borrowed securities, if any, before the loan period end date.

8. Events of default

The rights and powers of either party in the event of a default by the other party, including with regard to collateral.

9. Notices

The methods of sending notices between the parties.

10. SBL agreement annex (in case of appointing lending agent)

a. lending Agent name.

b. all lending agent client's names in the SBL agreement.

Note: the SBL agreement and any other relevant agreements shall be in line with and not contradicting these Regulations and any Procedures issued by the Depository Centre from time to time.

35 THE RESOLUTION OF SECURITIES DISPUTES PROCEEDINGS REGULATIONS

Issued by the Board of Capital Market Authority pursuant to its Resolution No.1-4-2011 dated 19/2/1432H (23/1/2011G) based on the Capital Market Law issued by Royal Decree No. M/30 dated 2/6/1424H amended by Resolution of the Board of the Capital Market Authority No. 1-104-2017 dated 2/3/1439H Corresponding to 20/11/2017G.

The current version of these Regulations, as may be amended, can be found at the CMA website: www.cma.org.sa

TABLE OF CONTENTS

PART 1: PRELIMINARY PROVISIONS
Article 1: Definitions
PART 2: FILING THE SUIT AND PLACING IT IN THE COMMITTEE'S DOCKET
Article 2: Filing the Suit with the Committee
Article 3: Statement of Claim
Article 4: Submission of the Statement of Claim
Article 5: Placing the Suit in the Committee's Docket
Article 6: Means of Placing the Suit in the Committee's Docket
Article 7: Consideration of the Suit
PART 3: NOTICES AND SERVICE OF PROCESS
Article 8: Means of Notice and Service of Process
Article 9: Notice and Service of Process in Exceptional Cases
PART 4: COMMITTEE HEARINGS
Article 10: Hearings' Quorum
Article 11: Managing the Hearing
Article 12: Public Hearing
Article 13: Hearing's Minutes
PART 5: APPEARANCE AND ABSENCE OF SUIT'S PARTIES
Article 14: Plaintiff's Appearance and Absence
Article 15: Defendant's Appearance and Absence
Article 16: Charged person's Appearance in a Penal Suit
Article 17: Attendance Time
PART 6: EVIDENCE
Article 18: Forms of Evidence
PART 7: SEEKING EXPERTISE
Article 19: Seeking Expertise to Assist the Suit's Parties
Article 20: Failure to Pay the Expertise Fees
Article 21: Assigning of Expert
Article 22: Inspection and Taking Testimony
Article 23: Expenses of Deputation and Expertise
PART 8: CONSIDERATION PROCEDURES AND ISSUANCE OF DECISIONS
Article 24: Considering of Claims Against Decisions and Actions Taken by the Authority or the Exchange
Article 25: Filing the Claim with the Committee
Article 26: Suspending the Execution of the Challenged Decision or Action
Article 27: Statute of Limitations
Article 28: Examining the Suit's Documents
Article 29: Abandonment of a Suit
Article 30: Suspension of the Suit Upon the parties' Agreement
Article 31: Suspension of the Suit by a Committee Order
Article 32: Decision Issuance
Article 33: Pronouncement of the Decision
Article 34: Contents of the Decision
Article 35: Service of Decision
Article 36: Correcting and Interpreting the Errors
Article 37: Temporary Decision in Penal Suits
Article 38: Protective Attachment Lifting
PART 9: APPEAL
Article 39: Right to Appeal and its Time
Article 40: Appealing Default Decisions
Article 41: Appeal Date Documentation
Article 42: The Appeal Memorandum
Article 43: Joinder at the Appeal Stage
Article 44: Reconsideration of the Suit
PART 10: FINALITY OF DECISIONS AND ENFORCEMENT
Article 45: Final Decisions
Article 46: Enforcement of the Decision
Article 47: Execution on Properties
PART 11: Class Action Suit
Article 48: Scope and Application
Article 49: Submitting a Request of Registering a Class Action Suit
Article 50: The Committee's Decision on the Request of Registering the Class Action Suit
Article 51: Registering the Class Action Suit
Article 52: Decision of Approving the Class Action Suit
Article 53: Suspending Existing and New Suits and Their Joining to the Class Action Suit
Article 54: Withdrawal from the Class Action Suit
Article 55: The Defendant's Objection
Article 56: Parties of the Class Action Suit
Article 57: Announcements in the Class Action Suit Docket
Article 58: Announcing the Dates of the Hearings for the Members of the Group of Plaintiffs
Article 59: Information and Documents Related to the Class Action Suit
Article 60: The Effect of Withdrawing from the Class Action Suits on the Proceedings
Article 61: Participation of The Members of the Group of Plaintiffs
Article 62: Managing the Class Action Suit
Article 63: Issuing the Decision
Article 64: Settlement Proposal
Article 65: Approving the Settlement
Article 66: Announcing the Settlement and the Right to Withdraw
Article 67: Consequences of the Settlement of the Class Action Suit
Article 68: Appeal in the Class Action Suit
Article 69: Lead Appellant in a Class Action Suit
Article 70: Consequences of the Committee's Decisions on the Class Action Suit
Article 71: The Decision on the Costs of the Class Action Suit
Article 72: The Procedures of the Class Action Suit Followed when there are no Provisions Provided herein
PART 12: GENERAL PROVISIONS
Article 73: Procedures Followed when there are no Provi-

sions Provided herein
Article 74: Official Language
Article 75: Publication and Entry into Force

35.1 PART 1: PRELIMINARY PROVISIONS

Article 1: Definitions
(A) The following expressions and terms shall have the meaning they bear whenever they are stated in these Regulations as follows, unless the contrary intention appears:

1) Law: The Capital Markets Law issued by Royal Decree No.(M/30) dated 2/6/1424H

2) Authority: the Capital Market Authority.

3) Board: the board of the Capital Market Authority.

4) Exchange: the Saudi Stock Exchange.

5) Appeal Panel: the appeal panel formed pursuant to paragraph (g) of Article 25 of the Law.

6) Committee: the Committee for the Resolution of Securities Disputes established pursuant to paragraph (a) of Article 25 of the Law.

7) Secretariat: the secretariat of the Committees for the resolution of securities disputes.

8) Secretary: the secretary of the Committees for the resolution of securities disputes.

9) Charged person: a person who is charged with violation of any provision related to the public right of the provisions of the Law, its implementing regulations, and the regulations, rules and instructions issued by the Authority and the Exchange.

10) Member: a member of the Committee appointed by its establishment resolution and any member added to the Committee or appointed as a substitute of a former member. This term includes the Committee's chairman unless the contrary intention appears.

11) Complaint and the suit: without prejudice to these term's meanings in the Law, each term shall, in relation to the application of these Regulations, bear the following meaning: Complaint: filing a claim (against decisions and actions taken by the Authority or the Exchange), a right's request or defending a right with the Authority.

Suit: the complaint filed with the Committee starting from submitting it in a written statement of claim according to these regulations until the suit is closed by a final decision.

12) Day: the calendar day including official vacation days for the country. In relation to the dates mentioned in these regulations, if the last day is an official vacation then the date will be extended to the first business day thereafter.

13) Class Action Suit: a suit filed by a group of plaintiffs against one or more defendants, where the group of plaintiffs' suit share the same legal bases, merits and the subject matter of the requests. Any decision made on the case shall affect all of its parties.

14) Lead Plaintiff: A person who represents Members of the Group of Plaintiffs in the proceedings before the Committees for the resolution of securities disputes in connection with the Class Action Suit, and is appointed in accordance with the provisions of paragraph (b) of Article 56 of these Regulations.

15) Members of the Group of Plaintiffs: A group of persons who participate in filing a Class Action Suit.

16) Class Action Suits Docket: A docket created by the Committee for Class Action Suit.

(B) The other expressions and terms in these Regulations shall have the meaning which they bear in the Law and in the Glossary of Defined Terms used in the Regulations and Rules of the Capital Market Authority, unless the contrary intention appears.

35.2 PART 2: FILING THE SUIT AND PLACING IT IN THE COMMITTEE'S DOCKET

Article 2: Filing the Suit with the Committee To file a suit with the Committee, a proof shall be served that the compliant has been first filed with the Authority and a 90 day period has passed from the filing date or a notification shall be served that the Authority permits such filing prior to the expiration of this period. The merits of the suit shall not differ from the complaint filed with the Authority.

Article 3: Statement of Claim A plaintiff shall file the suit by submitting a statement of claim to the Committee in original and as many copies as there are defendants. The statement of claim shall contain the following:

1) The plaintiff's full name, address, means of communication, national ID number)or the equivalent for non-Saudi nationals, the full name of his/her representative ,if any, and address.

2) The defendant's full name and address.

3) The date of filing the statement of claim.

4) The merits of the suit, the plaintiff's requests and their supports.

Article 4: Submission of the Statement of Claim The statement of claim shall be submitted to the secretariat, and the plaintiff shall receive a dated receipt.

Article 5: Placing the Suit in the Committee's Docket Within a period not more than three days from the date the secretariat receives the statements of claims, the secretary shall present them to the Committee's chairman and they shall be placed in the Committee's docket as per the chairman's order or whoever he delegates after verifying that they fulfill the conditions stated by law.

Article 6: Means of Placing the Suit in the Committee's Docket The secretary shall place the statement of claim with a serial number on a docket prepared specifically for this purpose. The secretary is responsible of organizing the suits records, numbering and saving them as well as signing on all the pages.

Article 7: Consideration of the Suit The Committee shall start considering the suit within a period not to exceed 14 days from the date of filing the suit with the Committee by serving the statement of claim to the defendant and requesting a reply.

PART 3: NOTICES AND SERVICE OF PROCESS

Article 8: Means of Notice and Service of Process The notice and/or the service of process shall be done by the secretariat's designated personnel, by registered mail, fax, email, recorded phone call, or by any other means the Committee deems appropriate and sufficient to achieve the purpose of the notice and/or the service of process.

Article 9: Notice and Service of Process in Exceptional Cases Where the place of residence or the address of the person to be served or noticed is unknown or the service or notice could not be delivered, the Committee's chairman may decide the means that he deems appropriate and sufficient to achieve the purpose of the notice and/or the service of process including through the governmental authorities or a published announcement in the official gazette or any local newspaper.

35.3 PART 4: COMMITTEE HEARINGS

Article 10: Hearings' Quorum The Committee hearings shall be held to consider the filed suits by three members unless the Committee's chairman determines otherwise.

Article 11: Managing the Hearing The head of the hearing (the presiding member) is responsible of monitoring, managing and maintaining order during the hearing. In pursuance of this he may expel from the hearing room anyone who disturbs order, order the deletion of any immoral or offending phrases to public morality from any document or memorandum submitted by the parties in question, and he may order initiating a report on any violation or crime occurs during the hearing.

Article 12: Public Hearing The Committee hearings shall be public unless the Committee determines making it closed.

Article 13: Hearing's Minutes The Committee's clerk shall take minutes of the Committee's hearings under the supervision of the chairman in a special docket set for this purpose. The minutes shall include the date and the time of every hearing's opening and ending, the place of the hearing, the names of the Committee members who considered the suit and the suit's parties. The minutes shall also state all the actions and events that take place during the hearing, the testimonies heard in the hearing, statements of the parties, their requests and defenses. The members who considered the suit, the Committee's clerk, the parties and whoever made a statement that was entered into the minutes shall sign on the minutes. If any person refuses to sign such refusal shall be stated in the minutes.

35.4 PART 5: APPEARENCE AND ABSENCE OF SUIT'S PARTIES

Article 14: Plaintiff's Appearance and Absence The parties, or their representatives, shall appear at the hearing scheduled time. Where the plaintiff is absent from a Committee hearing without an excuse acceptable to the Committee, the Committee may adjudicate the suit, if suitable, or it may strike off the suit. If the suit is stricken off, the plaintiff may, within 60 days of date the suit was stricken off, request continued consideration of the suit, in which case the Committee shall continue consideration of the suit with a new serial number in the docket. If the continued consideration requires a hearing and the plaintiff is absent without an excuse acceptable to the Committee, the suit shall be stricken off and shall not be heard again.

Article 15: Defendant's Appearance and Absence Where the defendant is absent from the hearing, consideration of the suit may be postponed by the Committee to a subsequent hearing of which the defendant shall be served. Where the defendant is absent from this hearing without an excuse acceptable to the Committee, the Committee shall adjudicate the suit and its decision shall be considered a default decision with respect to the defendant, unless the defendant was served personally or through a representative or a legal representative, or submitted a reply, or attended any of the hearings or the defendant's absence was after the proceeding closure , in which cases the decision shall be considered in his appearance.

Article 16: Charged Person's Appearance in a Penal Suit The charged person shall appear in the hearings personally or through a representative in a penal suit. The Committee may order the charged person to be present personally. If the charged person or his representative is absent, he shall be requested again to appear for another hearing. If he is again absent or the Committee could not serve him, the Committee may request the executive authorities to force the charged person to appear at scheduled times. After that, if he or his representative does not appear, the Committee shall publish an announcement in the official gazette requesting his appearance and it may issue a decision as it deems appropriate including banning the charged person from traveling or from trading (buying) in the exchange or placing attachment on his investment and bank accounts or any of his properties. If the charged person does not appear before the Committee at the specified times after taking the pervious measures, the Committee may reserve the suit until he or his representative appears unless the Committee decides to issue a default decision with respect to the charged person. Such decision shall be considered in his presence if the charged person or his representative has appeared in one of the hearings or has submitted a defense memorandum.

Article 17: Attendance Time For the purposes of implementing the provisions of this part, failing to appear within 30 minutes of the hearing scheduled time shall be considered an absence unless the Committee decides to extend such period.

35.5 PART 6: EVIDENCE

Article 18: Forms of Evidence Evidence before the Committee may be admissible in all forms including electronic or computer data, telephone recordings, fax messages and electronic mail.

35.6 PART 7: EXPERTS

Article 19: Seeking Expertise to Assist the Suit's Parties Where the Committee determines, during the proceedings, the necessity of seeking expertise, it may decide to assign one or more experts. It shall specify in such decision the task of the expert, the time for filing his report and the time for the hearing based on the report, and shall also specify, when necessary, the advance payment to the account of the expert's expenses and fees and the party who shall deposit that payment and the time by which he shall make the deposit. It may also appoint an expert to give his opinion orally in a hearing, in which case the opinion shall be entered into the hearing's minutes.

Article 20: Failure to Pay the Expert Fees Where the assigned party does not deposit the payment he is required to deposit within the time limit set by the Committee, the other party may make that deposit without prejudice to his right to have recourse to his adversary if a decision is made in his favor. If neither party deposits the payment and resolving the suit is dependent on determination by experts, the Committee may suspend the suit until the payment is deposited.

Article 21: Assigning of Expert Where the parties agree on a particular expert, the Committee may accept their agreement; otherwise, it may select an expert itself.

Article 22: Inspection and Taking Testimony Where the Committee deems, during the proceedings, the necessity of conducting an inspecting action or a supplementary investigation, it shall do it itself or deputize someone to do it. It may delegate anyone of its choice to take a testimony as it deems important.

Article 23: Expenses of Deputation and Expertise The Committee may request the Authority, where it deems appropriate, to incur the necessary expenses to deputize an expert or whose testimony is deemed necessary to be taken or to incur the expenses of any other procedure necessary to consider the suit. The Committee shall specify in its decision who is obliged to pay the expenses incurred by the Authority.

PART 8: PROCEDURE

Article 24: Procedure for Appeals of Agency Action Prior to filing appeals of decisions and actions taken by the Authority or the Exchange with the Committee, the claims shall be filed first with the Authority within 60 days from the date the related decision or action has been known. The decisions and the actions shall be considered to be known if they are served to related person or published on the Authority's or the exchange's websites.

Article 25: Filing the Claim with the Committee Where the Authority serves a notice refusing a claim, or the elapse of 90 day period set forth in article 2 of these regulations without a resolution taken, a claim may be filed with the Committee within 90 days from becoming aware of such decision or from the elapse of 90 days set forth in article 2 of these regulations without a resolution taken.

Article 26: Stay of the Challenged Decision or Action Filing a claim with the Committee does not suspend the execution of the challenged decisions or actions taken by the Authority or the exchange.

Article 27: Statute of Limitations A suit under Articles 55, 56 and 57 of the Law shall not be heard if the complaint is filed with the Authority after the elapse of one year from the date when the claimant should have been aware of facts causing him to believe he had been the victim of a violation, and in no case may such suit be heard by the Committee after 5 years from the occurrence of the violation subject of the claim.

Article 28: Exchange of Evidence Reliance on a party's documents or memorandums shall not be without allowing the other party to examine them. Any of the parties or their representatives shall have the right to examine the suit's documents.

Article 29: Abandonment of Suit The Committee may consider that the plaintiff has abandoned his suit if the plaintiff fails to comply with the Committee's request to take an action related to the suit within the specified time period or within the period of 90 days of the request date, whichever is longer, or if the Committee could not serve him at the address specified in the statement of claim. The plaintiff has the right to request re-filing the suit by submitting a request to the Committee with a new serial number in the docket.

Article 30: Suspension of the Suit Upon the Parties' Agreement The suit may be suspended on the basis of an agreement by the parties not to proceed with it for a maximum of 180 days from the date the Committee approves the agreement. If the parties do not resume the suit proceedings within ten days that follow the end of the specified period, the plaintiff shall be deemed to have abandoned the suit.

Article 31: Suspension of the Suit by Committee Order If the Committee determines that its decision on the merits of a suit should be contingent on ruling on another issue on which the decision depends, it may order suspension of the suit and the parties may request proceeding with the suit when the cause of suspension lapses.

Article 32: Decisions The Committee's decisions shall be issued by at least three members including the Committee's chairman or whom he delegates. The decision shall be made unanimously or by the majority opinion. If opinions diverge into equal sides, the decision shall be the opinion supported by the Committee's chairman. Where the decision is issued by the majority, it shall be stated in it. The dissenting member shall submit a written opinion with the reasoning and it shall be attached to the suit's documents.

Article 33: Announcements of Decisions Pronouncement of the decision shall be made in a public hearing, except the decisions taken regarding temporary measures, precautionary actions and formality defenses. The Committee, at its discretion, may only serve the parties with the decision. The Committee shall explain to the parties that they have the right to appeal the decision within 30 days from the date the parties are served and that the decision is final and enforceable after the expiration of this period unless a party files an appeal during that period.

Article 34: Contents of the Decision The Committee's decisions shall be in writing and must contain, specifically, the decision number, date, place of issuance and a summarized presentation of the parties' statements, their names, their documents, the names of members who made the decision, their titles, their presence and absence, their signatures and the decision's grounds and text.

Article 35: Service of Decision Without prejudice to paragraph (b) of Article 63 of these Regulations, a copy of the decision shall be delivered to every related person. The copy must be stamped by the Committee's stamp. It must also be stamped to state that the decision is not enforceable unless it is otherwise as per the situations stated in Article 45 of these regulations. The service is delivered by means of serving a copy of the decision within 10 days of the pronouncement date.

Article 36: Correcting Errors The Committee shall, on its own initiative or upon a request from any related person, correct the purely tangible written or calculation errors in the decision. Where there is any ambiguity or uncertainty in the decision, any related party may request an interpretation from the Committee.

Article 37: Interim Measures in Criminal Cases The Committee may, upon the Authority's request, issue a preliminary judgment against the charged person banning him from traveling, placing a protective attachment on his properties including bank and investment accounts or banning him from trading (buying) in the exchange in accordance to the following procedures:

1) The Authority's request shall be attached with the legal documents and supporting proofs that justify its request.
2) If the request of the temporary decision was before charging the person, the Committee may issue its decision of protective attachment, a travel ban, or trading ban (buying) in the exchange for a period not more than 30 days. The Committee may extend this period or cancel it upon the Authority's request after giving the charged person a chance to present his defenses.
3) The person subject to the Committee's temporary decision may challenge such decision by filing a memorandum with the Committee stating the defenses and the elements that support the cancelation of the decision. The Committee shall issue a decision on such memorandum within a period not more than 7 days of its filing date.

Article 38: Release of Protective Attachment The Committee, at its discretion, may issue a decision lifting the protective attachment stated in article (37) of these regulations based on a petition from the person who is subject to the protective attachment. The Committee may instead request a submission of any guarantees it may accept.

35.7 PART 9: APPEAL

Article 39: Right and Time to Appeal The parties may appeal the decisions issued by the Committee before the appeal panel within 30 days from the date the decision has been served.

Article 40: Appeal of Default Decisions In case of a default decision, the party against whom the decision is rendered may appeal it within 30 days from the date the decision has been served. Where service could not be delivered within 30 days of the decision issuance date, the decision shall be published in the official gazette with a notification to the party against whom the decision is rendered that he may appeal in 30 days. If the party does not appeal, the decision shall be effective. If the absent convict appears later, he may petition the Committee to suspend the execution of the decision, and the Committee shall then issue a decision to suspend the execution for a period of time it deems sufficient for him to prepare his defense and statements. If he submits his defense and statements during the given period, the Committee shall look into what he submitted and where it deems the importance of reconsideration, it shall reconsider or it shall issue a decision to execute its previous decision.

Article 41: Appeal Date Documentation The appeal memorandum shall be submitted to the secretariat and the submission date must be written on it and a notation on the suit's file regarding this shall be made.

Article 42: Appeal Memorandum The appeal memorandum shall include the appealed decision, its number, date, grounds of the appeal and the appellant's requests.

Article 43: Joinder at the Appellate Stage Unless the person is a party in the suit, no person shall join the suit at the appeal stage.

Article 44: Reconsideration of the Suit The Committee shall reconsider its decision in the following two cases:

1) When constructive information in the suit is submitted and the Committee determines that there are serious reasons that prevented submitting it during the hearing and it is submitted after the hearings closure or after the issuance of the decision but before the expiration of the specified appeal period stated in Article (39) of these regulations.

2) When constructive information in the suit is submitted before the appeal panel and it could not be submitted during the Committee's hearings, or the appeal panel deems that the actions or information in the suit file are not sufficient and the appeal panel decides to send back the suit to the Committee, then the Committee will consider that. If the Committee deems what requires an amendment to its decision, it shall issue a decision regarding that and the decision shall be served to the parties. If the Committee finds what requires reopening the proceedings again, such decision shall be served to the parties. If the Committee does not deem what requires an amendment to its decision or reopening the proceedings, it shall issue a reasoned decision regarding that and refer it to the appeal panel.

35.8 PART 10: FINALITY AND ENFORCEMENT OF DECISIONS

Article 45: Final Decisions A decision is final in the following cases:

1) The expiration of the specified period to appeal the Committee's decision without appealing.

2) All parties express their conviction of the Committee's decision whether during pronouncement of the decision or after and before the appeal's deadline.

3) A decision by the appeal panel is issued affirming the Committee's decision.

4) A decision by the appeal panel is issued refusing the review of the Committee's decision.

5) A decision by the appeal panel is issued after reconsidering the suit.

Article 46: Enforcement of Decisions Where the decision is final, copies of such decision shall be served to the parties. The decision shall be enforced as per the Law or any other related laws.

Article 47: Execution on Property The Committee may issue an order to execute on the convicted parties' properties in a final decision upon the Authority's request.

35.9 PART 11: Class Action Suits

Article 48: Scope and Application The provisions of this part shall be applicable on civil suits related to securities disputes.

Article 49: Submitting a Request of Registering a Class Action Suit Any person may submit a request to register a class action suit as per the provisions stated in this Part by submitting a request for registering the class action suit to the Committee containing the requirements of the Statement of Claim that are set forth in Article (3) of these Regulations, in addition to the following terms:

1. The request shall contain all facts, information and circumstances that justify the establishment of the Class Action Suit, which represent that the suit of the applicant is identical to other suits in terms of the legal bases, merits and the subject matter of the requests.

2. The request shall contain what represents that the Committee's decision on the suit might have an effect on other existing or probable similar suits.

Article 50: The Committee's Decision on the Request of Registering the Class Action Suit
a) Accepting the request of registering the Class Action Suit is subject to the Committee's discretionary power; its approval is issued by a final decision upon the fulfillment of conditions related to the request that are set forth in Article (49) of these Regulations, in addition to one of the following:

1. Filing individual suits by Members of the Group of Plaintiffs will likely result in the issuance of conflicted or contradicted decisions by the Committees for the resolution of securities disputes; or may lead to unfair treatment of the same group members.
2. The Committee is convinced that legal matters and common facts of the suit is greater than legal matters and facts of each individual of the group, that the Class Action Suit will practically be more effective and productive than other means of filing a suit, and guarantees compensating more persons affected by the violations of the defendant.

b) The Committee announces the decision of accepting the request of registering the Class Action suit in the Class Action Suits Docket containing sufficient information related to the suit.

c) In case the Committee refuses a request of registering a Class Action Suit, this does not prejudice the rights of the applicant in filing the suit individually.

d) The Committee makes its decision on the request of registering a Class Action Suit within a period not exceeding 30 days of the date of submitting the request.

Article 51: Registering the Class Action Suit
a) Requests of registering Class Action Suit which are identical in term of the legal bases, merits and the subject matter of the requests shall be registered in the Class Action Suits Docket according to the date of accepting the request of registering the Class Action suit announcement.

b) The Class Action Suit Docket shall be made available to the public.

Article 52: Decision Approving the Class Action Suit
a) The Committee issues its decision approving the Class Action Suit when the number of requests, which share legal bases, merits and the subject matter of the requests, reaches at least ten requests within the 90 days following the announcement of the first request, provided that all these requests fulfill the requirements of the request of registering the Class Action Suit that are set forth in this Part.

b) The Committee announces its decision approving class action suits in the Class Action Suits Docket. The decision shall contain the legal bases, merits and the subject matter of the requests upon which the Committee approved the suit as a class action suit, in addition to the suit's summary.

c) A request for joining a class action suit may be submitted within the period mentioned in paragraph (a) of this Article. That is unless the Committee issues a resolution of extending such period as it deems appropriate, according to the datum provided to it. In any situation, the period shall not be more than 180 days from the date of announcing the first request.

d) In case the period specified in paragraph (c) of this Article has elapsed following announcing the acceptance of class action suit registration, and without fulfilling the conditions set forth in paragraph (a) of this Article, the Committee deems the request rejected and the plaintiff completes the suit proceedings individually as per the provisions of these Regulations.

Article 53: Suspension of Pending Litigation, Consolidation
a) Without prejudice to the provisions of paragraph (b) of this Article, following the announcement of accepting the class action suit registration request and having it registered in the Class Action Suits Docket, the Committee shall take initiative to issue a resolution to suspend all suits being considered if these suits are identical to the class action suit in terms of the legal bases, merits and the subject matter of the requests, for the purpose of joining these suits to the class action suit.

b) Within 30 days of announcing the suspension decision mentioned in paragraph (a) of this Article, the plaintiff may withdraw from the class action suit without the defendant's approval, even if the class action suit proceeding has already started.

c) Where the Committee determines that the legal bases, grounds or sough interests of the members of the group of plaintiffs might not be covered in one class action suit, it may order dividing the class action suit into several class action suits as it deems fit.

d) The Committee may, at its discretion, exclude any person or group of persons from the Members of the Group of Plaintiffs due to incompatibility in legal bases or grounds of the class action suit in any stage of the suit prior to the issuance of the Committee's decision thereon.

Withdrawal from the Class Action Suit The Lead Plaintiff and any member of the Members of the Group of Plaintiffs may request to withdraw from the class action suit by sending a written notification to the Committee within a period not exceeding (30) days of the date of announcing the decision of approving the class action suit without prejudice to his/her right to continue litigating his/her suit individually. The Lead Plaintiff and any member of the Members of the Group of Plaintiffs may not request to withdraw from the class action suit after the defendant had presented its defense without the defendant's acceptance.

Article 55: Objection by Defendant A defendant in a class action suit may object before the Committee to its decision of approving the class action suit within a period of 30 days of notification. The Committee's decision regarding the defendant's objection shall be final.

Article 56: Parties to the Class Action Suits
a) A class action suit has the following parties:

1. The Lead Plaintiff.
2. The defendant in the class action suit.
3. Members of the Group of Plaintiffs

b) The Members of the Group of Plaintiffs shall appoint the Lead Plaintiff from among them in a written agreement presented to the Committee, taking into account the following:

1. The Lead Plaintiff is fit to take the actions of the class action suit protecting the interests of Members of the Group of Plaintiffs by being capable in qualification and practice of protecting the interests of Members of the Group of Plaintiffs, and to assume these duties at all stages of the suit.
2. He/she shall adequately understand his/her duties towards the Members of the Group of Plaintiffs.
3. He/she shall be fully informed of the suit's details and related facts.
4. Without any prejudice to the provisions of this Part, in the agreement referred to in paragraph (b) of this Article, it shall be taken into consideration specifying all relative aspects that define the Lead Plaintiff's obligations toward the class action suit and the members of the group of plaintiffs. This shall include whether the Lead Plaintiff has the Authority to appoint a lawyer to proceed with the class action, in addition to determining the Lead Plaintiff or the lawyer's compensations (if any), and any other conditions, restrictions or obligations that the members of the group of plaintiffs deem appropriate.

c) The Lead Plaintiff shall commit to represent the interests of all Members of the Group of Plaintiffs with fairness and competency.

d) Plaintiffs who have not been selected as a Lead Plaintiff are considered Members of the Group of Plaintiffs.

e) The Committee, upon the request of a member of the Group pf Plaintiffs, may replace the Lead Plaintiff by appointing another Lead Plaintiff in accordance with criteria mentioned in paragraph (b) of this Article, in case the appointed Lead Plaintiff has not taken adequate action to litigate the class action suit, or where the Lead Plaintiff is no longer capable of litigating.

f) The Committee, upon objection of 30% or more, of the Members of the Group of Plaintiffs to the appointment of the Lead Plaintiff, shall replace the Lead Plaintiff by appointing another Lead Plaintiff in accordance with criteria mentioned in paragraph (b) of this Article.

Article 57: Announcements in the Class Action Suits Docket After the appointment of the Lead Plaintiff, the Committee announces the following in the Class Action Suits Docket:

1. Name of the Lead Plaintiff.

2. Name of the defendant in the class action suit.

3. The class action suit's number.

Article 58: Announcing the Dates of the Hearings for the Members of the Group of Plaintiffs Dates of the hearings are announced to the Members of the Group of Plaintiffs in the Class Action Suits Docket, without the need for stating their names in the services of process or summonses to the hearings.

Article 59: Information and Documents Related to the Class Action Suit The Committee may request the Members of the Group of Plaintiffs to submit information in addition to what was submitted by the Lead Plaintiff, within the time period specified by the Committee.

Article 60: The Effect of Withdrawing from the Class Action Suits on the Proceedings
a) In the event The Lead Plaintiff's withdrawal from the class action suit, the Members of the Group of Plaintiffs shall appoint a replacement Lead Plaintiff from among them in accordance with paragraph (b) of Article (56) of these Regulations.

b) The withdrawal of a Member of the Group of Plaintiffs from the class action suit does not affect the suit proceedings.

Article 61: Participation of The Members of the Group of Plaintiffs Any member of the Group of Plaintiffs may present defenses or supports, or to submit any objection to any action taken or proposed at any stage of the suit without prejudice to the Lead Plaintiff's role.

Article 62: Managing the Class Action Suits The Committees have full powers in managing the class action suit and issue any order or decision therein to ensure fairness of these suits and quick decisions thereon.

Article 63: Issuing the Decision
a) The Committee issues its decisions on the class action suit as per the provisions of Articles (32) and (33) of these Regulations.

b) All parties of the class action suit shall be informed of the Committee's decision. The Committee, as it deems fit, may announce the decision in the Class Action Suits Docket rather than inform the suit's parties, provided that the service of decision or the announcement of such is within (10) days of the Pronouncement of the Decision.

Article 64: Settlement Proposal
a) The Lead Plaintiff and the defendant in the class action suit may enter into settlement agreement by submitting a written settlement proposal to the Committee for the purpose of ending the class action suit, or by accepting a settlement proposal prepared by the Committee. At all cases, the settlement agreement shall not be deemed accepted unless approved by the Committee as per the provisions of Article (65) of these Regulations.

b) The settlement proposal approved by the Committee is effective unless %30 or more of the Members of the Group of Plaintiffs (whose amount of claims represents 30% or more of the total amount of claims) announce their withdrawal from the settlement proposal as per the provisions of Article (66) of these Regulations.

c) The Settlement proposal must contain provisions regulating the following as minimum:

1. Agreed obligations among the parties.
2. A sufficient proof of the parties' competency to fulfill their obligations as stated in the settlement.
3. Due date of the obligations.
4. Dividing the costs of the class action suit among the parties.

Article 65: Approving the Settlement Without prejudice to the provisions of paragraph (b) of Article (64) of these Regulations, the Committee approves the settlement by a decision if it deems the settlement fair for the Members of the Group of Plaintiffs, taking into consideration the status of the dispute in the class action suit and the Members of the Group of Plaintiffs' opinion on the settlement.

Article 66: Announcing the Settlement and the Right to Withdraw
a) The Members of the Group of Plaintiffs shall be notified of the settlement acceptance decision once it is issued, provided that such notification includes notifying the Members of the Group of plaintiffs of their right to withdraw from the settlement and the period granted for such withdrawal, in addition to the consequences of the accepted settlement.

b) Each Member of the Group of Plaintiffs may announce his/her withdrawal from the accepted settlement within 30 days of the notification mentioned in paragraph (a) of this Article, provided that he/she submits the withdrawal in writing to the Committee.

c) The withdrawal of a Member of the Group of Plaintiffs from the settlement, shall not prejudice his/her right to continue litigating his/her suit individually.

Article 67: Consequences of the Settlement of the Class Action Suit
a) The Committee approves the settlement, and issues its decision of the settlement's entry into effect. By announcing this decision, the settlement becomes effective for and against those parties who have not declared their withdrawal therefrom.

b) The settlement's entry into force results in ending the class action suit.

Article 68: Class Action Suit Appeals a) Except for the Committee's final decisions stated in this Part, any party of the class action suit may appeal decisions issued by the Committee before the Appeal Committee, according to the provisions of Article (39) of these Regulations.

b) The Appeal Committee announces in the class action suits Docket its decision of accepting the appeal request where the appeal request has been submitted in compliance with the statutory provisions and periods.

c) Any party of the class action suit may join appeal proceedings within 30 days of the announcement mentioned in paragraph (b) of this Article by submitting a written request to the Appeal Committee.

d) The Appeal Committee announces in the Class Action Suits Docket its decision issued on the appeal.

Article 69: Lead Appellant in a Class Action Suit
a) Where the Lead Plaintiff submits a request to appeal the decision issued by the Committee in connection with the class action suit, he/she continues taking the actions of the class action suits before the Appeal Committee as the Lead Appellant in the class action suit.

b) Where a Members of the Group of Plaintiffs, other than the Lead Plaintiff, submits a request to appeal decision issued by the Committee in connection with the class action suit, the plaintiffs joining the appeal request, pursuant to paragraph (c) of Article (68) of these Regulations, shall appoint a Lead Appellant from among them in accordance with criteria of appointing the Lead Plaintiff mentioned in paragraph (b) of Article (56) of these Regulations.

c) The provisions of Article (56) and Article (60) of these Regulations related to the Lead Plaintiff shall apply to the Lead Appellant (as applicable).

d) The provisions of Article (60) of these Regulations related to the withdrawal of any of the Members of the Group of Plaintiffs shall apply to the withdrawal of any of the plaintiffs joining the appeal request.

Article 70: Consequences of the Committee's Decisions in the Class Action Suit The Committee's decisions on the class action suit is effective as to and against all parties to the class action suit.

Article 71: The Decision on the Costs of the Class Action Suit The Committee has the discretionary power concerning the determination of the costs of the class action suit in a way that justice is achieved for all parties, and that the agreement referred to in sub-paragraph (4) of paragraph (b) of Article (56) of these Regulations is taken into consideration.

Article 72: Class Action Suit Procedure in Absence of Rules Provisions of these Regulations shall apply to the procedures of the class action suit concerning what no text has been provided in its regard in this Part.

Article 73: Procedures to be Followed in the Absence of Rules Specified Herein The Committee shall, in suits proceedings, comply with the Law and these regulations or any other rules or regulations issued by the Authority. The Committee may be guided by the Law of Criminal Procedure, Law of Civil Procedure and general rules applicable in the Kingdom when there are no provisions provided herein in a manner that is consistent with the nature of suits filed with the Committee.

Article 74: Official Language The Arabic language is the official language in suits proceedings. Any statements before the Committee in a language other than Arabic are unproved. Foreign language speakers shall accompany a translator who will sign the hearing's minutes. Any party who wants to submit documents written in a foreign language shall provide an official Arabic translation of those documents.

Article 75: Publication and Entry into Force These regulations shall become effective upon their publication.

36 Short Selling Regulations

Approved by the Board of the Capital Market Authority pursuant to its Resolution No. 1-28-2017 dated 16/6/1438H (15/3/2017G) and amended pursuant to Resolution No.21-1-2021 dated 10/7/1442H (22/2/2021G)

TABLE OF CONTENTS

Part 1: Preliminary Provisions
Article 1: Preliminary
Article 2: Definitions
Part 2: Short Selling
Article 3: Short Selling Transactions
Article 4: Eligible participants
Article 5: Eligible listed securities
Part 3: Powers of the Authority
Article 6: Powers of the Authority
Part 4: Reporting and Record Keeping Requirements
Article 7: Reporting
Article 8: Public Disclosure
Article 9: Record-Keeping
Part 5: General Provisions
Article 10: Limit of Liability
Article 11: Waivers
Article 12: Publication and entry into force

36.1 PART 1: PRELIMINARY PROVISIONS

Article 1: Preliminary The purpose of these Regulations is to set out the framework for short selling activities in respect of listed securities in the Kingdom.

Article 2: Definitions
a. Any reference to the "Capital Market Law" in these Regulations shall mean the Capital Market Law issued by Royal Decree No. M/30 dated 2/6/1424H.

b. Expressions and terms in these Regulations have the meaning which they bear in the Capital Market Law and in the Glossary of Defined Terms Used in the Exchange Rules, unless the contrary intention appears.

36.1.1 PART 2: SHORT SELLING

Article 3: Short Selling Transactions
a. A short selling transaction means any sale of a borrowed listed security in accordance with the SBL Regulations.

b. A person must not enter into as seller, and an Exchange Member must not execute as an agent or principal, a short selling transaction in respect of a listed security unless all of the following conditions are met:

1) the seller is an eligible participant as specified in Article 4 of these Regulations;
2) the short selling transaction is entered into in respect of eligible listed securities as specified in Article 5 of these Regulations;
3) before the execution of the sale, the relevant security has been transferred to the seller's short selling account opened in accordance with the Depository Centre Rules; and
4) the price of selling the security, underlying the transaction, is higher than the price of the best bid of that security.

c. The following trades do not constitute short selling transactions for the purposes of paragraph (a) of this Article:

1) a sale of a listed security where the seller has entered into a corresponding purchase transaction in respect of those securities that settles on or before the settlement date of the sale; or
2) a securities borrowing and lending transaction in a listed security which is entered into in accordance with the SBL Regulations.

Article 4: Eligible Participants Any persons permitted to invest in the Market may enter into a short selling transactions as a seller in accordance with the relevant Implementing Regulations and the Exchange Rules.

Article 5: Eligible Listed securities
a. Unless the Exchange specifies otherwise, a short selling transaction may be entered into in respect of all listed securities in accordance with the following limits:

1) The short ratio to Average Daily Traded Volume of the relevant security (total net short positions / Average Daily Traded Volume of the last 60 days) must not exceed 10 days; and
2) The total net short positions must not exceed 10% of the free floated securities of the relevant security.

b. The Exchange will publish a daily report for total net short positions after the Trading Day including limits specified in paragraph (a) of this Article.

c. Listed securities breaching the limits specified in paragraph (a) of this Article are not permitted for short selling in the next trading day, Exchange Member is responsible for the verification of not selling the securities where any limit specified in paragraph (a) of this article is breached.

36.2 PART 3: POWERS OF THE AUTHORITY

Article 6: Powers of the Authority
a. The Authority may prohibit or suspend short selling transactions in respect of a specific security, or may prohibit or suspend all short selling transactions in the Kingdom, at any time and as it deems fit, including but not limited to the following circumstances:

1) there are adverse events or developments which constitute a serious threat to financial stability or to market confidence;
2) for the protection of investors;
3) for the maintenance of an orderly market; or

4) where the aggregate sum of short positions in an eligible listed security across the market has reached a level where the Authority considers it necessary to exercise such powers.

b. The Exchange will publish on its website any action taken by the Authority pursuant to its powers under paragraph (a) of this Article.

36.3 PART 4: REPORTING AND RECORD KEEPING REQUIREMENTS

Article 7: Reporting An Exchange Member who entered into a short selling transaction, either as an agent or principal must report complete and accurate details of such transactions to the Exchange in accordance with the mechanism and the controls prescribed by the Exchange from time to time.

Article 8: Public Disclosure The Exchange may disclose any information in respect of short selling transactions and the related positions as it deems fit.

Article 9: Record-Keeping
a. An Exchange Member who has entered into a short selling transaction, either as an agent or principal, must record and retain sufficient information about its short selling activities to demonstrate compliance with the Capital Market Law, its Implementing Regulations, the Exchange Rules in general and these Regulations in particular.

b. Records required to be maintained by these Regulations must be retained for a period of at least ten years from the date of the short selling transaction unless the Exchange specifies otherwise. In the event such records relate to any litigation or claim (including any potential litigation) or any on-going investigations, the Exchange Member must retain such records until the conclusion of that litigation, claim or on-going investigation.

c. In addition to its powers under the Capital Market Law, the Exchange may request to inspect the records of an Exchange Member directly or through a person it appoints for that purpose upon giving reasonable prior notice in the context of the request to the Exchange Member.

d. Records made by an Exchange Member may be recorded in any form, but must be capable of reproduction in hard printed form. If the Exchange requires records to be produced in a particular electronic or other format, it shall give the Exchange Member a reasonable period of time in the context to meet that request.

36.4 PART 5: GENERAL PROVISIONS

Article 10: Limit of Liability
a. Without prejudice to the provisions of the Capital Market Law, its Implementing Regulations and the Exchange Rules, the Exchange and the Depository Centre shall not be held liable for any losses or damages incurred by any participant referred to in Article 4 of these Regulations, their clients or any other person that deals with the Depository and Settlement System which may arise directly or indirectly as a result of:

1) any procedures, orders or transactions that are subject to these Regulations;

2) the use of the Depository and Settlement System for short selling activities;
3) the partial or complete suspension or prohibition of short selling transactions, or the interruption of activities and services provided by Exchange or the Depository Centre;
4) the exercise by the Exchange or the Depository Centre of any of their relevant powers under these Regulations, the Capital Market Law, its Implementing Regulations and the Exchange Rules; or
5) any service failure attributable to the Exchange or the Depository Centre by reason of an event outside of their control.

b. Without prejudice to the provisions of the Capital Market Law, the Exchange and the Depository Centre shall have no liability in respect of the accuracy or completeness of short selling transaction reports or any other information published on its website from time to time.

Article 11: Waivers The Exchange may, after obtaining the Authority's approval, waive any requirement in these Regulations either based on a request from the relevant person or on its own initiative.

Article 12: Publication and Entry into Force These Regulations shall become effective upon their publication.

37 SECURITIES CENTRAL COUNTERPARTIES REGULATIONS

Issued by the Board of the Capital Market Authority pursuant to its Resolution Number 3-127-2019 Dated 21/3/1441H (18/11/2019G) based on the Capital Market Law issued by Royal Decree No. M/30 dated 2/6/1424H.

Important Notice: The current version of these Regulations, as may be amended, can be found at the CMA website: www.cma.org.sa

TABLE OF CONTENTS

Part 1: General Provisions
Article 1 – Preliminary
Article 2 – Definitions
Article 3 – Compliance with the Regulations and Rules
Article 4 – Compliance with the Principles for Financial Market Infrastructures
Article 5 – Waivers
Part 2: Authorization
Article 6 – General Provisions
Article 7 – Requirements for Authorization of a CCP Established in the Kingdom
Article 8 – Ownership Structure of a CCP Established in the Kingdom
Article 9 – Procedure and Powers of the Authority in relation to an Application for Authorization of a CCP Established in the Kingdom
Article 10: Requirements for Authorization of a CCP Established out of the Kingdom
Article 11: Maintenance of Authorization
Article 12 – Variation or Amendment to Authorization
Article 13 – Right of Appeal
Article 14 – Fees
Article 15 – Governance
Article 16 – Withdrawal of Clearing Services or Cancellation of Authorization
Part 3: Clearing
Article 17 – Effecting Clearing
Article 18 – Designated Securities
Part 4: Capital Base
Article 19 – General Business Risk Management
Article 20 – Capital Base
Part 5: Clearing Members
Article 21 – Categories of Clearing Members
Article 22 – Minimum Requirements
Article 23 – Clearing Membership
Article 24 – Monitoring the Compliance of Clearing Members
Article 25 – Exchange Members with no Clearing Memberships
Part 6: Collateral
Article 26 – Method of Delivering Collateral
Article 27 – Acceptable Collateral
Article 28 – Collateral Guaranteed by the Clearing Member or its Group
Article 29 – Haircuts and Valuation Practices
Article 30 – Avoiding Concentration of Collateral
Article 31 – Management of Collateral
Article 32 – Reuse of Collateral
Part 7: Custody and Investment Risks
Article 33 – Use of Custodians
Article 34 – Investment Policy
Part 8: Margin
Article 35 – Margin Requirement
Article 36 – Initial Margin Methodology
Article 37 – Variation Margin Methodology
Article 38 – Margin Calls
Article 39 – Testing Margin Coverage
Part 9: Credit Risk
Article 40 – Measuring, Monitoring and Mitigating Credit Risk
Article 41 – Default Fund
Article 42 – Dedicated own Resources Allocated from CCP's own Capital
Article 43 – Testing the Sufficiency of the CCP's Total Financial Resources
Part 10: Liquidity Risk
Article 44 – Measuring and Monitoring Liquidity Risk
Article 45 – Stress Testing Liquidity Needs and Resources
Part 11: Settlement Finality
Article 46 – Settlement Finality
Article 47 – Money Settlements
Article 48 – Physical Deliveries
Article 49 – Exchange-of-value Settlement System
Part 12: Segregation and Portability
Article 50 – Account Types
Article 51 – Framework for the Porting of Positions
Article 52 – Requirement to Disclose
Part 13: Clearing Member Default Management
Article 53 – Designation of Clearing Member as Defaulting
Article 54 – Default Rules and Procedures
Article 55 – Periodic Testing and Review of Default Procedures
Part 14: CCP Recovery
Article 56 – CCP Recovery Plan
Article 57 – Approving the CCP Recovery Plan
Part 15: Other CCP Obligations
Article 58 – Communication Procedures and Standards
Article 59 – Control Systems
Article 60 – Record Keeping
Article 61 – Disclosure of CCP Rules and Material Costs to Clearing Members
Part 16: Operational Risk
Article 62 – Identifying Sources of Operational Risk
Article 63 – Operational Risk Management
Article 64 – Business Continuity Management
Part 17: Links between CCPs
Article 65 – Interoperability Arrangements
Article 66 – Risk Management of Interoperability Arrangements
Article 67 – Provision of Margin among CCPs
Part 18: Qualifying Central Counterparty
Article 68 – Recognition of Qualifying Central Counterparty Status
Part 19: Publication and Entry Into Force
Article 69 – Publication and Entry Into Force

37.1 PART 1: GENERAL PROVISIONS

Article 1: Preliminary

a) The purpose of these Regulations is to regulate Securities Clearing activities in the Kingdom and specify the procedures and conditions for obtaining an Authorization to carry out such activities.

b) The provisions of these Regulations shall apply to each CCP authorized in accordance with the Capital Market Law and these Regulations and to any applicant applying for Authorization in accordance with the provisions of these Regulations.

c) The provisions of these Regulations shall not apply to the clearing services provided by SAMA to Local Banks.

d) The memorandum of cooperation between the Authority and SAMA shall specify the cooperation mechanism in the implementation of regulatory powers over the CCPs and Clearing Members that are Local Banks subject to SAMA oversight and supervision

Article 2: Definitions

a) Any reference to the "Capital Market Law" in these Regulations shall mean the Capital Market Law issued by the Royal Decree No. M/30 dated 2/6/1424H.

b) Subject to paragraph (c) of this Article, expressions and terms in these Regulations have the meaning which they bear in the Capital Market Law and the Glossary of Defined Terms Used in the Regulations and Rules of the Capital Market Authority, unless the context indicates otherwise.

c) For the purpose of implementing these Regulations, the following expressions and terms shall have the meaning they bear as follows, unless the context indicates otherwise:

Novation: a process whereby the original contract between one party and another party is discharged and replaced with two new contracts, one between the CCP and the first party and the other between the CCP and the second party.

Designated Securities: Securities in respect of which the CCP has issued a notice designating such Securities as not benefitting from the Clearing service.

Backtesting: an ex-post comparison of observed outcomes with expected outcomes derived from the use of margin models.

Interoperability Arrangement: an arrangement between two or more CCPs that involves a cross system execution of transactions.

Procyclical: the changes in risk-management requirements or practices that are positively correlated with business or credit cycle fluctuations and that may cause or exacerbate financial instability.

Pass Through Service: a service offered by the CCP in respect of Designated Securities to facilitate their settlement without providing Clearing services.

Liquid Net Assets: assets funded by equity (common stock, disclosed reserves or other retained earnings) which are not otherwise encumbered and freely available to cover General Business Risk.

Open Offer: a process whereby the CCP extends an open offer to act as a counterparty to market participants and is immediately interposed as counterparty in a transaction where the two parties agree on the terms when the pre-agreed conditions of the CCP are satisfied.

Independent Member: a non-executive member of the board who enjoys complete independence in his position and decisions, including having no business, family or other relationship that raises a conflict of interests regarding the CCP, its management or its Clearing Members, and who has had no such relationship during the five years preceding his membership of the board.

Clearing Member: a Direct Clearing Member or a General Clearing Member.

General Clearing Member: has the meaning specified in paragraph (a) of Article 21 of these Regulations.

Direct Clearing Member: has the meaning specified in paragraph (a) of Article 21 of these Regulations.

Convertible Currency: a currency that can be bought or sold without restrictions imposed by any governmental Authority in the Kingdom or in the jurisdiction which has issued the currency.

Client: a natural or legal person which:

1) is not a Clearing Member; and

2) has a contractual relationship with a Clearing Member which enables that person to clear its transactions with the CCP.

Appropriate Close-out Period: the time period to close all open positions of the defaulting Clearing Member which starts from the last collateral provided by the defaulted clearing member until the closing of his positions.

Principles for Financial Market Infrastructures: the international standards for financial market infrastructures issued by the Committee on Payment and Market Infrastructures (CPMI) and the Technical Committee of the International Organization of Securities Commissions (IOSCO).

General Business Risk: the risks and potential losses arising from the CCP's operation as a business, but excluding risks and losses related to a Clearing Member default. General Business Risk includes any potential impairment of the CCP's financial position as a consequence of a decline in its revenues or an increase in its expenses.

Wrong-Way Risk: the risk arising from exposure to a counterparty when the collateral provided by that counterparty is highly correlated with the credit quality of that counterparty.

Qualifying Central Counterparty: a CCP that has demonstrated that it is established and operating consistently with the Principles for Financial Market Infrastructures.

Clearing: the process of establishing each party's rights and obligations arising from Securities trading, including the calculation of net obligations, and ensuring that financial instruments or cash are available to secure the exposures arising from such obligations.

Margin: a Variation Margin or an Initial Margin.

Variation Margin: margin that is collected to cover the current exposure resulting from actual changes in market prices which affects the value of the Clearing Member's position.

Initial Margin: margin that is collected to cover the potential future exposure resulting from potential changes in the value of the Clearing Member's position over the appropriate close-out period in the event that Clearing Member defaults.

Article 3: Compliance with the Regulations and Rules
a) The CCP must comply with the Capital Market Law, these Regulations and the other relevant regulations and rules. The CCP must provide to the Authority without delay any information, records or documents that the Authority may require for the purpose of implementing the Capital Market Law and its Implementing Regulations.

b) The Governing Body and employees of the CCP must comply with any request issued by the Authority to appear to explain any matter or to assist in any enquiry relating to implementing the Capital Market Law and its Implementing Regulations.

Article 4: Compliance with Principles for Financial Market Infrastructures The CCP authorized in accordance with these Regulations shall be designated as a systematically important financial institution in the Kingdom. In this regard, the CCP is required to adhere to the Principles for Financial Market Infrastructures on an ongoing basis, including any related supplemental guidance issued from time to time by the Committee on Payment and Market Infrastructures and the International Organization of Securities Commissions.

Article 5: Waivers

a) The Authority may waive a provision of these Regulations in whole or in part as it applies to an applicant or a CCP either on an application from the applicant or the CCP or on its own initiative.

b) The Authority will make an announcement of the waiver of any provisions where it believes that:

1) the waiver of the provision may be of application to more than one CCP; and
2) the publication of the waiver will not materially prejudice the CCPs.

37.2 PART 2: AUTHORIZATION

Article 6: General Provisions
a) The CCP must have rules, procedures and contracts that are clear, understandable and consistent with the provisions of the Capital Market Law and these Regulations.

b) The CCP, upon obtaining an Authorization from the Authority in accordance with the Capital Market Law and these Regulations, shall be considered an exempt person in accordance with the provisions of the Securities Business Regulations.

c) The CCP shall submit an annual report to the Authority to ensure its compliance with all provisions of these Regulations.

Article 7: Requirements for Authorization of a CCP Established in the Kingdom
a) For the purposes of this Article, an applicant for Authorization means the person that is applying for Authorization to provide Securities Clearing services in the Kingdom. An applicant for Authorization becomes subject to these Regulations from the date of submission of its application.

b) An applicant for Authorization as a CCP Established in the Kingdom must demonstrate to the Authority that:

1) it has Liquid Net Assets greater than the higher of:
   a. SAR 100,000,000;
   b. six months anticipated operating expenses, excluding depreciation and amortization expenses; or
   c. such other amount as determined by the Authority in its absolute discretion;
2)it is fit and proper and has adequate expertise and resources to carry out Securities Clearing services in the Kingdom;
3) it has managerial expertise, financial systems, risk management policies and systems, technological resources, policies, procedures, and operational systems that are sufficient to fulfill its business and regulatory obligations;
4) its Governing Body and employees who will be involved in its Clearing services have the necessary qualifications, skills, experience and integrity;
5) the identities of the shareholders that have direct or indirect holdings of 5% or more of the capital and the amounts of those holdings, whether they are natural or legal persons;
6) it will, upon Authorization, be in compliance with the Principles for Financial Market Infrastructures including, without limitation, the disclosure framework and assessment methodology;
7) the time span for the CCP recovery in accordance with the provisions of Article 20 of these Regulations; and
8) it will be in compliance with such requirements as may be determined by the Authority, in its discretion, from time to time.

c) In addition to the Authorization requirements set out above, the Authority may stipulate additional Authorization requirements to be met by, or specific conditions or limitations to be applied to either all applicants for Authorization, or particular applicants or categories of applicants, as it considers appropriate.

d) An application for Authorization may be submitted by the founders or controlling shareholders of an applicant if the applicant is not yet established. The founders or controlling shareholders become subject to the provisions that apply to an applicant from the date of submission of the application.

e) The form and contents of the application and all information and documents filed with it must be as prescribed by the Authority.

f) An applicant for Authorization must notify the Authority immediately of any material changes to the information provided to the Authority for the purposes of application for Authorization.

g) As a condition for Authorization as a CCP Established in the Kingdom, the applicant must be a joint stock company established in the Kingdom.

h) If the applicant has close links with another natural or legal person, the Authority must be satisfied with the integrity, regulatory status, business record and financial soundness of any such natural or legal person, and that such close links will not impair the effective supervision of the applicant, or its operations and compliance with these Regulations.

Article 8: Ownership Structure of a CCP Established in the Kingdom
a) The Authority may refuse an application where it is not satisfied as to the suitability of the substantial shareholders of the applicant.

b) The CCP established in the Kingdom shall be required to obtain prior approval from the Authority for any change that exceeds 5% in its ownership structure.

c) The CCP established in the Kingdom must notify the Authority, in such form as the Authority may prescribe, that a person is intending to establish close links with the CCP at least 30 days in advance of the proposed effective date, or if such advance notice is not possible, immediately on the CCP becoming aware of any change in close links. The notice must include such information as the Authority requires to satisfy itself of the identity of the person with whom the CCP proposes to establish close links, its integrity, regulatory status, business record and financial soundness.

d) The CCP established in the Kingdom must not establish close links with another person unless the Authority has approved the close links in writing.

e) Before approving any close links, the Authority must be satisfied that such links will not impair the effective supervision of the CCP established in the Kingdom or its operations and compliance with the Capital Market Law and its Implementing Regulations.

f) Clearing Members, and Clients of Clearing Members, shall have no recourse to the equity of the CCP established in the Kingdom, save as provided in these Regulations and in the relevant CCP Rules. The liability of such CCP to its Clearing Members and their Clients is limited as set out in these Regulations and in the relevant CCP Rules.

Article 9: Procedure and Powers of the Authority in relation to an Application for Authorization of a CCP Established in the Kingdom

a) In considering an application, the Authority may:

1) carry out any enquiries that it considers appropriate;
2) require the applicant, or its representative, to attend before the Authority to answer questions and explain any matter the Authority considers relevant to the application;
3) require the applicant to provide such additional information as the Authority considers appropriate within 30 days of the request; and
4) verify any information furnished by the applicant.

b) The Authority may refuse to consider an application for Authorization where an applicant has failed to provide information requested from it, or has failed to provide information requested from it within the time requested.

c) The Authority shall, upon receipt of all information and documents required, notify the applicant in writing of the same, and shall take any of the following decisions within a maximum period of 30 days from the date of the notice:

1) approve the application in whole or in part; or
2) approve the application subject to such conditions and limitations as it considers appropriate; or
3) refuse the application, giving reasons.

d) The Authority may extend the period for assessment of an application for Authorization referred to in paragraph (c) of this Article if the applicant for Authorization intends to outsource any of its functions in accordance with paragraph (j) of Article 15 of these Regulations.

e) If the Authority resolves to authorize the applicant, it will inform the applicant of this in writing and of any conditions and limitations that the Authority may consider appropriate.

f) If the Authority resolves to refuse the application, it will notify the applicant in writing.

g) An applicant must not provide, or hold itself out as providing, Securities Clearing services in the Kingdom prior to receiving the Authority's decision referred to in paragraph (e) of this Article.

Article 10: Requirements for Authorization of a CCP Established out of the Kingdom

a) For the purposes of this Article, an applicant for Authorization means a legal person incorporated as a joint stock company out of the Kingdom that is applying for Authorization to provide Securities Clearing services in the Kingdom. An applicant for Authorization becomes subject to these Regulations from the date of submission of its application.

b) An applicant for Authorization as a CCP established out of the Kingdom must demonstrate to the Authority that:

1) it is authorized or otherwise subject to regulatory oversight by a regulatory authority and incorporated in a jurisdiction that applies regulatory and monitoring standards equivalent to those of the Authority or acceptable to it. For the purpose of this paragraph, the Authority may, at its absolute discretion, determine whether the regulatory and monitoring standards are equivalent to those of the Authority or acceptable to it;
2) it has given notice to its foreign regulator of its intention to provide Clearing services in the Kingdom;
3) by providing Clearing services in the Kingdom it will not violate any laws or regulations to which it is subject or any relevant requirements imposed by its foreign regulator;
4) its foreign regulator is either willing, or has already, put in place cooperation arrangements which provide for the exchange of information between the foreign regulator and the Authority regarding the applicant; and
5) it complies with all relevant requirements set out in the Principles for Financial Market Infrastructures.

c) Based on the application submitted in accordance with paragraph (b) of this Article and any additional documents requested by the Authority, the Authority shall have the discretion to determine whether to approve the application. The Authority may stipulate additional Authorization requirements to be met by, or specific conditions or limitations to be applied to either all applicants for Authorization as a CCP established out of the Kingdom, or particular applicants or categories of applicants, as it considers appropriate.

Article 11: Maintenance of Authorization

a) As a condition for the maintenance of Authorization, the CCP must continue to be fit and proper to carry out Securities Clearing services in the Kingdom.

b) The skills, experience, competence and integrity of a CCP's or applicant's employees and officers is an important factor in assessing whether it is fit and proper. The skills, experience, competence and integrity of the employees and officers will be assessed against the following criteria:

1) they must possess adequate qualifications and professional experience to carry out their responsibilities, including appropriate technical knowledge and skills;

2) they must have probity and soundness of judgement commensurate with their positions;
3) they must fulfill their responsibilities with diligence and to protect the interests of Clearing Members and Clients in accordance with these Regulations and the Implementing Regulations;
4) they must not have committed an offense involving fraud or dishonesty; and
5) they have not been insolvent.

c) Each CCP shall develop a code of conduct which will define acceptable and unacceptable behaviors and, at a minimum, should:

1) make clear that employees are expected to conduct themselves ethically and perform their job with skill, due care and diligence in addition to complying with all the relevant laws, regulations and policies;
2) require the CCP Board to oversee the investigation in suspicion of violation of the code of conduct, and approve by whom it shall be investigated and how it will be addressed.

d) The Authority may require, as it considers appropriate, the CCP to maintain a minimum rating from an internationally recognized rating agency as a condition to maintaining Authorization.

Article 12: Variation or Amendment to Authorization
a) The CCP must apply to the Authority for approval of any proposed variation or amendment to its Authorization.

b) The Authority has all the powers set out in this Part to consider a proposed variation or amendment, and may also require some or all of the information or documents referred in this Part to be updated.

c) The Authority will aim to process an application to vary or amend an Authorization within 30 days from receiving all information that it considers necessary.

d) After considering an application to vary or amend an Authorization, the Authority may:

1) approve the application for variation or amendment in whole or in part;
2) approve the application subject to such conditions and limitations as it considers appropriate;
3) defer making a decision for such period as it may consider necessary to carry out further study or examination or to allow for the provision of additional information; or
4) refuse the application, giving reasons.

e) If the Authority resolves to approve an application for an amendment in Authorization, it will inform the CCP of this in writing and provide it with the new Authorization, including any conditions and limitations that the Authority may consider appropriate.

f) The CCP must not provide (or hold itself out as providing) the amended Clearing services before receiving the Authority's notification under paragraph (e) of this Article.

g) If the Authority resolves to refuse the application for variation or amendment, it will notify the CCP in writing.

Article 13: Right of Appeal An applicant for Authorization or the CCP may appeal to the Committee in respect of any decision or action that the Authority takes under these Regulations.

Article 14: Fees
a) The applicant for Authorization must pay such fees as may be prescribed by the Authority.

b) The CCP must pay all such fees as the Authority may prescribe for the maintenance of the CCP's Authorization.

c) The CCP must obtain prior approval from the Authority for all fees for Clearing services provided by the CCP.

Article 15: Governance a) The CCP shall have documented governance arrangements which clearly and directly define the structure of the CCP Board, how management operates, division of responsibilities and reporting lines. The Authority will consider the CCP's governance arrangements as part of the Authorization process. In addition, the CCP shall disclose such arrangements to Clearing Members and the public.

b) As a minimum, the CCP's written governance arrangements shall include:

1) the composition of the CCP Board and its Committees and their responsibilities;
2) the Senior Executives structure;
3) reporting lines between Senior Executives and the CCP Board;
4) the ownership structure;
5) internal governance policy;
6) the policies and systems of risk management and internal controls;
7) procedures for the appointment of board members and Senior Executives; and
8) procedures for ensuring performance accountability.

c) Governance arrangements should ensure sufficient independence for key functions such as risk management and internal audit.

d) The number of Independent Members in the CCP Board shall not be less than two members or one-third of the CCP Board members, whichever is greater. The CCP Board members should have a clear understanding of their roles in corporate governance, be able to devote sufficient time to their roles, ensure to continuously develop their skills, and have appropriate incentives to fulfill their roles.

e) The CCP shall establish an audit Committee in accordance with the Capital Market Law and the Companies Law and their Implementing Regulations. In addition, the CCP Board shall establish the Committees referred to in paragraph (f) of this Article at a minimum, which shall be composed of suitable members that have the appropriate skills, experience, and knowledge of the CCP activities. Such committees may include the CCP Board members where needed.

f) The CCP Board shall establish, as a minimum, the following committees:

1) an information technology technical committee;
2) a nomination and remuneration committee;
3) a regulatory compliance committee; and
4)a risk committee.

All such committees, and any other committees the CCP Board considers appropriate, shall have clearly assigned responsibilities and procedures and shall document all decisions reached and any supporting rationale for such decisions.

g) The CCP Board policies and procedures shall include procedures to identify, address, and manage potential conflicts of interest of the CCP Board members.

h) The CCP Board shall establish a clear, documented risk-management framework that includes the CCP's risk-tolerance policy, assigns responsibilities and accountability for risk related decisions, and addresses decision making in crises and emergencies. The CCP Board shall regularly monitor the CCP's risk profile to ensure that it is consistent with the CCP's business strategy and risk-tolerance policy.

i) The CCP Board shall ensure that there is adequate governance surrounding the adoption and use of technical models, such as for the models of the credit, collateral, margining, and liquidity risk-management systems. The CCP shall validate, on an ongoing basis, the technical models and their methodologies used to quantify, aggregate, and manage its risks. The validation process should be independent of the development, implementation, and operation of the technical models and their methodologies, and the validation process should be subjected to an independent review of its adequacy and effectiveness.

j) The CCP may outsource specific functions to an external party provided that:

1) the appropriate safeguards are in place, which shall include a requirement that the external party implements equivalent business continuity requirements as are imposed on the CCP and undertakes to cooperate with the Authority in connection with the outsourced function;
2) the Authority approval is obtained prior to the outsourcing of any material CCP functions, and
3) none of its risk management functions are outsourced to an external party.

The CCP Board should ensure that outsourced functions meet the same requirements they would need to meet if they were provided internally by the CCP. The CCP shall have robust arrangements for the selection, close monitoring of the performance and substitution of such external parties and shall provide all information necessary to enable the Authority to assess the compliance of the performance of any outsourced functions with these Regulations.

k) The outsourcing of any function by the CCP will not derogate from the CCP's regulatory obligations.

l) The CCP Board shall take into consideration the interests of all relevant stakeholders, including those of Clearing Members and the Clients of Clearing Members, in making major decisions, including those relating to the CCP's design, rules, and overall business strategy.

Article 16: Withdrawal of Clearing Services and Cancellation of Authorization

a) The CCP that proposes to cease providing Securities Clearing services in the Kingdom must notify the Authority in writing of the date on which it intends to cease providing such Clearing services and the reasons for the decision:

1) at least 45 days in advance of that date; or
2) immediately on making such decision if such advance notice is not possible because cessation is caused by an external event of which the CCP was not aware.

b) Where the CCP decides to cease providing certain Clearing services, it must ensure that any such Clearing business that is outstanding is properly completed or, after obtaining the Authority prior approval, is transferred to an appropriate service provider. The CCP shall provide reasonable notice to its Clearing Members of the cessation of Clearing services.

c) The CCP may request the cancellation of its Authorization, and must in this case submit a written request to the Authority not less than three months prior to the proposed date of the cancellation.

d) A request to cancel an Authorization must include sufficient information concerning the circumstances of the cancellation to enable the Authority to determine whether to accept the cancellation, to postpone the date of the cancellation, or to require other measures that it considers necessary for the protection of Clearing Members of the CCP.

e) The Authority may refuse a request to cancel an Authorization if it considers that the maintenance of the Authorization is necessary to investigate any matter affecting the CCP, to protect the interests of a CCP's Clearing Members, or to impose a prohibition or requirements on such CCP under the Capital Market Law or its Implementing Regulations.

f) The Authority may suspend the CCP's Authorization on its own initiative if the CCP does not offer Securities Clearing services in the Kingdom for a period of 12 months, or 6 months following the date on which the CCP has ceased to offer any such Securities Clearing services after notification to the Authority in accordance with paragraph (a) of this Article.

g) The CCP continues to be subject to the jurisdiction of the Authority in respect of any act or omission that occurred before the cancellation of its Authorization and for two years thereafter. If at any time during this period the Authority commences any enforcement investigation or proceedings, the CCP shall continue to be subject to the jurisdiction of the Authority until the end of the enforcement investigation or proceedings.

37.3 PART 3: CLEARING

Article 17: Effecting Clearing

a) The CCP shall provide the services required to clear Securities transactions entered into on an Exchange or over-the-counter basis in accordance with the provisions of these Regulations. The CCP, after obtaining the Authority's approval, may provide any other services to Clearing Members.

b) The CCP shall prescribe the process through which it effects Clearing. Such processes may include:

1) Open Offer; or
2) Novation.

c) The CCP may employ in its CCP Rules different processes to effect Clearing depending on the type of Securities or type of transactions it is Clearing.

Article 18: Designated Securities
a) The CCP may determine that certain Securities are not appropriate to clear, including where Securities are unlisted or illiquid. Where the CCP makes such a determination, it must notify the Authority of its intention not to clear such Securities, and it shall issue a notice on its website specifying such Securities as Designated Securities which shall not benefit from its Clearing service but shall be capable of benefiting from a Pass Through Service.

b) The CCP shall not be permitted to become a counterparty to trades referencing Designated Securities, whether by way of Open Offer, Novation or otherwise. The CCP shall ensure Designated Securities will be excluded from the determination of a Clearing Member's default fund contribution.

c) The CCP may determine the appropriate margin requirements for Designated Securities that benefit from the Pass Through Service, with any Pass Through Service being outside of the remit of the margining provisions set out in Part 8 of these Regulations.

37.4 PART 4: CAPITAL BASE

Article 19: General Business Risk Management
a) The CCP shall have robust management and control systems to identify, monitor and manage General Business Risk. Such management and control systems shall include the following:

1) identifying the sources of General Business Risk and their potential impact on the CCP's operations and services, taking into account past loss events and financial projections where possible; and
2) considering a combination of tools, such as risk management and internal control assessments, scenario analysis and sensitivity analysis to manage General Business Risk.

b) The CCP shall notify the Authority immediately of any material changes to its General Business Risk management policy.

Article 20: Capital Base
a) As part of its management of General Business Risks, the CCP shall hold Liquid Net Assets so that enable it to continue operations as a going concern if it incurs general business losses.

b) When determining the amount of Liquid Net Assets to be held by the CCP, the CCP must take into consideration the time span required to achieve a recovery of the CCP's critical operations and services.

c) In order to determine the time span referred to in paragraph (b) o this Article, the CCP shall submit to the Authority its estimate of the appropriate time span for recovering its activities as a condition of its Authorization. The estimated time span shall be sufficient to ensure restructuring of its activities or reorganizing its operations. The CCP shall update its estimate of the appropriate time span for recovery whenever there is a material change in the assumptions underlying the estimation and submit this updated estimate to the Authority for approval.

d) In order to estimate the amount of Liquid Net Assets required, the CCP shall regularly analyze and understand how its revenue and operating expenses may change under a variety of adverse business scenarios as well as how it might be affected by extraordinary losses.

e) At a minimum, the CCP must hold Liquid Net Assets greater than the higher of:

1) SAR 100,000,000;
2) expected operating expenses of the time span required to achieve a recovery of the CCP's critical operations and services for, at a minimum, six months, excluding depreciation and amortization expenses; or
3) such other amount as required by the Authority in its absolute discretion.

f) If at any time the amount of Liquid Net Assets held by the CCP is lower than the amount required pursuant to paragraph (e) of this Article, the CCP shall immediately notify the Authority and provide a periodic update at least weekly or as the Authority may otherwise specify, until the amount of Liquid Net Assets held by such CCP returns above the approved amount.

g) Assets held by the CCP to cover General Business Risk should be of high quality and sufficiently liquid and include cash denominated in SAR, Convertible Currencies and liquid securities. When calculating Liquid Net Assets available to cover General Business Risk, the CCP shall not include any assets held to cover risks or losses relating to:

1) the default of a Clearing Member; or
2) the default of a third party, such as a settlement bank, payment system or other intermediary entity.

37.5 PART 5: CLEARING MEMBERS

Article 21: Categories of Clearing Members
a) The CCP shall establish, at a minimum, two categories of Clearing Members consisting of:

1) Direct Clearing Member: a Clearing Member who is authorized to clear Securities which it has traded in its capacity as a member of an Exchange, including Securities it has traded on its own account or on behalf of its Client(s). A Direct Clearing Member shall not be permitted to clear for Exchange members with no clearing memberships; and
2) General Clearing Member: a Clearing Member who is authorized to clear Securities on behalf of its Client(s), including Exchange members with no clearing memberships. A General Clearing Member, to the extent that it is a member of an Exchange, shall be permitted to clear Securities which it has traded in its capacity as a member of an Exchange, including Securities it has traded on its own account or on behalf of its Client(s).

b) The CCP Rules may introduce classes of Direct Clearing Members and General Clearing Members per type of Securities or transactions cleared.

Article 22: Minimum Requirements
a) The CCP Rules shall establish requirements applicable to Direct Clearing Members and General Clearing Members, which at a minimum must satisfy the following requirements:

1) a Direct Clearing Member must be, at all times, a member of the Exchange in respect of which it clear Securities;
2) a General Clearing Member shall have the necessary additional financial resources and operational capacity to perform the activity of Clearing Securities on behalf of Exchange members with no clearing memberships (in addition to Clearing Securities it has traded on its own account); and
3) Requiring for the Clearing Member to enter into a contract with the CCP summarising the key terms of their relationship, and to agree to be bound by such CCP Rules as such may be amended from time to time.

b) In establishing the minimum requirements set out in paragraph (a) of this Article, the CCP shall consider risk-related considerations to ensure the relevant Clearing Member meets appropriate legal, operational and functional requirements to allow it to fulfill its obligations to such CCP on a timely basis and so as to ensure fair and open access to services of the CCP.

c) The CCP Rules may impose specific additional obligations on Clearing Members, such as the requirement to participate in auctions of a defaulting Clearing Member's position. Such additional obligations shall be proportional to the risk brought by the relevant Clearing Member and shall not restrict participation to certain categories of Clearing Members.

Article 23: Clearing Membership In addition to the requirements set out in Article 22 of these Regulations, Direct Clearing Members and General Clearing Members must satisfy one of the following requirements:

1) be an Authorized Person authorized by the Authority to carry on dealing activity;
2) be an exempt person in accordance with the Securities Business Regulations; or
3) be a Local Bank which has received non-objection letters from both the Authority and SAMA to act as a Clearing Member. Upon becoming a Clearing Member, such Local Bank will be exempted from the Authorization requirement to carry on securities business in relation to its Securities clearing activities.

Article 24: Monitoring the Compliance of Clearing Members
a) The CCP shall ensure the application of the requirements referred to in Article 22 of these Regulations is satisfied on an on-going basis, and shall ensure its CCP Rules require delivery of timely and accurate information from Clearing Members. In addition, the CCP shall require the Clearing Members to deliver to the CCP information regarding the arrangements they adopt to allow their Clients access to services of the CCP, including in the case of General Clearing Members the arrangements they adopt to allow Exchange members with no clearing memberships access to services of the CCP. Responsibility for ensuring that Clients comply with their obligations shall remain with the relevant Clearing Member.

b) The CCP shall conduct, at least once a year, a comprehensive review of compliance with the CCP Rules (including the requirements referred to in Article 22 of these Regulations) by its Clearing Members. The CCP shall have objective and transparent procedures for the suspension and orderly exit of Clearing Members that no longer meet the requirements set out in their CCP Rules, in addition to the procedures implemented for the voluntary termination by a Clearing Member of its membership.

Article 25: Exchange Members with no Clearing Memberships
a) The CCP shall not permit the Exchange member with no clearing membership to clear Securities it has traded in its capacity as a member of an Exchange except through a General Clearing Member.

b) The CCP may require the Exchange member with no clearing membership to satisfy additional requirements, which may include without limitation:

1) entering into a direct contractual relationship with the CCP; and
2) providing additional information regarding its Clients on whose behalf it has traded transactions.

c) The CCP may permit the Exchange member with no clearing membership who has satisfied any additional requirement specified by such CCP in accordance with paragraph (b) of this Article to access certain services of the CCP including without limitation:

1) Opening, in its name, account(s) at the CCP detailing the positions of its Clients; and
2) Obtaining reports relating to the positions of its Clients.

d) At all times the Exchange member with no clearing membership shall be required to have a contractual relationship with a General Clearing Member, and such General Clearing Member shall remain liable to the CCP for all contracts cleared and attributable to such Exchange member. In this regard, such Exchange member shall not be required to:

1) contribute to the default fund in accordance with Article 41 of these Regulations; and
2) provide the CCP with margin in accordance with Part 8 of these Regulations, which shall each remain obligations of the such Exchange Member's General Clearing Member.

37.6 PART 6: COLLATERAL

Article 26: Method of Delivering Collateral The CCP shall require each Clearing Member to deliver collateral. Any method permitted for the delivery of collateral by a Clearing Member to the CCP as specified in the CCP Rules must ensure that:

1) any collateral delivered to the CCP shall be in accordance with these Regulations; and
2) the CCP's ability to liquidate collateral to cover the positions of a Clearing Member to which such collateral relates is not restricted.

Article 27: Acceptable Collateral
a) The CCP shall limit the assets it accepts as collateral to those with low market, liquidity and credit risks. It shall apply appropriate haircuts to such assets to reflect the risk that the collateral value may decline in the event of liquidation, particularly in stressed market conditions where the time taken to liquidate collateral may increase. The CCP shall take into consideration concentration risks when determining acceptable collateral and the haircuts to be applied to such collateral.

b) The CCP may accept the following assets as a collateral:

1) cash denominated in SAR, EUR and USD;
2) cash denominated in currencies other than those specified in paragraph (1) above, provided that it is a Convertible Currency and the CCP publishes procedures specifying how such currencies is accepted as collateral;
3) financial instruments issued or explicitly guaranteed by the government of the Kingdom;
4) financial instruments issued or explicitly guaranteed by a government or supranational organization recognized by the Kingdom, provided that the CCP can demonstrate they have a low market and credit risk based upon an internal assessment objectively carried out by the CCP and the CCP

publishes procedures specifying such additional financial instruments as acceptable collateral; and
5) financial instruments other than those specified in paragraphs (3) and (4) above, provided that the CCP can demonstrate they have low market and credit risk based upon an internal assessment objectively carried out by the CCP, such financial instruments are freely transferable without any regulatory or legal restrictions or third party claims that impair liquidation, such financial instruments have reliable price data published on a regular basis, and the CCP publishes procedures specifying such additional financial instruments as acceptable collateral.

Article 28: Collateral Guaranteed by the Clearing Member or its Group The CCP may not accept from a Clearing Member a collateral that is guaranteed by such Clearing Member or by the group to which the Clearing Member belongs.

Article 29: Haircuts and Valuation Practices
a) The CCP shall establish and implement prudent valuation policies and procedures, and develop haircuts that take into account stressed market conditions. The CCP's policies and procedures shall provide for marking the value of collateral to market at least on a daily basis.

b) The CCP shall monitor on a regular basis, and at a minimum annually and each time a material change occurs that affects the CCP's risk exposure, the adequacy of its valuation policies and procedures. Such monitoring should be carried out by persons independent to the persons who created and applied the valuation policies and procedures.

c) Haircuts shall reflect the potential for asset values and liquidity to decline over the interval between their last revaluation and the time by which the CCP can reasonably assume that the assets can be liquidated. The CCP will establish stable and conservative haircuts that are calibrated to include periods of stressed market conditions in order to reduce the need for Procyclical adjustments.

d) In determining the haircut to be applied to each collateral asset, the CCP shall produce a confidence level of at least 99% for cash and Securities traded in an Exchange and 99.5% for Securities traded over the counter, considering the following criteria:

1) the type of asset and level of credit risk associated with such asset based upon an internal assessment objectively carried out by the CCP;
2) the maturity of the asset;
3) the historical and hypothetical future price volatility of the asset in stressed market conditions. For this purpose, the CCP shall use 10 years of historical data if such data is available;
4) the liquidity of the underlying market. For this purpose, the CCP shall, at a minimum, assume a holding period of at least 2 days;
5) the foreign exchange risk, if any; and
6) any potential wrong-way risk associated with the collateral.

Article 30: Avoiding Concentration of Collateral
a) The CCP shall maintain policies and procedures regarding concentration limits to ensure collateral received remains sufficiently diversified to allow its liquidation quickly without significant market impacts. Such policies and procedures shall also detail the techniques to be employed by the CCP when concentration limits are breached.

b) The CCP shall monitor on a regular basis the adequacy of its concentration limit policies and procedures. The CCP shall review its concentration limit policy and procedure at least annually and whenever a material change occurs that affects the CCP's risk exposure.

c) The concentration limits will consist of:

1) minimum limit to be applied on the amount of SAR denominated cash to be provided as collateral; and
2) maximum limit to be applied on all other asset classes. With respect to financial instruments, such maximum limits shall be developed by the CCP on the basis of:
   a. individual issuer, taking into account the level of credit risk of the financial instrument issued by the issuer or the credit risk of the issuer itself, based upon an internal assessment objectively carried out by the CCP. In any event, no more than 10% of the total collateral received by the CCP may be guaranteed by a single issuer or by a legal person that is part of the same group as such issuer, save that such limitation shall not be applicable to financial instruments issued or guaranteed by the government of the Kingdom;
   b. issuers of the same type in terms of economic sector, activity, geographic region;
   c. the liquidity and the price volatility of the financial instruments;
   d. each Clearing Member; and
   e. all Clearing Members.

d)The CCP shall inform Clearing Members of the applicable concentration limits and of y amendment to these limits. If the CCP materially breaches a concentration limit set in its policies and procedures, it shall rectify the breach as soon as possible.

Article 31: Management of Collateral
a) The CCP shall establish and implement policies and procedures to continuously monitor the handling of collateral, including recording the reuse of collateral. Such policies and procedures will enhance the effectiveness, efficiency and flexibility of the systems operationally, which also allows to accommodate the timely deposit, withdrawal, substitution and liquidation of collateral.

b) The CCP shall review its policies and procedures regarding the management of collateral at least annually and each time a material change occurs that affects the CCP's risk exposure.

Article 32: Reuse of Collateral The CCP shall be permitted to use collateral provided to it by Clearing Members if:

1) the CCP Rules to which such Clearing Member is bound explicitly permit the use of such collateral by the CCP;

2) the CCP has clear rules and procedures regarding the reuse of collateral, which specify when such CCP may reuse collateral and the process of returning such collateral to Clearing Members; and

3) at all times the CCP is in adherence with its investment policy, in accordance with Article 34 of these Regulations.

37.7 PART 7: CUSTODY AND INVESTMENT RISKS

Article 33: Use of Custodians

a) The CCP shall establish rules and procedures to ensure that assets are held with authorized, supervised and regulated legal persons, and must undertake a risk assessment prior to holding assets with them, to ensure that the custodian has in place adequate arrangements to safeguard the assets, and is subject to appropriate standards of regulatory oversight. The CCP must conduct such assessment as frequently as necessary to ensure that the requirements stated in this paragraph are met on a continuing basis.

b) The CCP shall ensure that assets are held in a manner that assures the CCP of prompt access to such assets.

c) To mitigate the custody risk, the CCP must ensure that assets held in custody will be protected against claims of a custodian's creditors, provide for the segregation of assets.

d) Without prejudice to the requirements for custodians as set out in paragraph (a) of this Article, the CCP may only hold assets with:

1) Depositories Centres for assets held in the Kingdom, and central securities depositories and securities settlement systems for assets held out of the Kingdom that the CCP considers offer equivalent protections and safeguards as the Depositories Centres in the Kingdom;
2) banks or operators of payment systems where such assets are cash, either in the Kingdom and falling within the remit of SAMA or out of the Kingdom and in respect of which the CCP considers equivalent protections and safeguards are maintained, without prejudice to SAMA's authority in supervising and regulating payment systems in the Kingdom;
3) Authorized Persons authorized by the Authority to carry on custody business for assets held in the Kingdom, and persons authorized out of the Kingdom for assets held out of the Kingdom that the CCP considers offer equivalent protections and safeguards as the Authorized Persons in the Kingdom. Where assets are held with custodians, the CCP shall ensure that assets belonging to Clearing Members are segregated from the assets belonging to the CCP by means of differently titled accounts on the books of the custodian or any other equivalent measures that achieve the same level of protection; or
4) any other person approved by the Authority.

Article 34: Investment Policy

a) The CCP shall maintain policies and procedures to ensure that the financial instruments in which its financial resources are invested are at all times consistent with its overall risk management strategy, and disclose them to the Clearing Members.

b) The CCP shall invest its financial resources only in cash or in highly liquid financial instruments with minimal market and credit risk. The CCP's investments shall be capable of being liquidated rapidly with minimal adverse price effect.

c) The CCP shall determine concentration limits and monitor the concentration of its financial resources as they apply to investments at the level of:

1) individual financial instruments, taking into account the liquidity and the price volatility of such financial instruments;
2) individual issuer, taking into account the level of credit risk being taken on the issuer and the group to which such issuer belongs based upon an internal assessment objectively carried out by the CCP; and
3) issuers of the same type in terms of economic sector, activity and geographic region.

d) The CCP shall monitor on a regular basis the adequacy of its concentration limit policies and procedures as they apply to investments. The CCP shall review its concentration limit policy and procedure at least annually and whenever a material change occurs that affects its risk exposure.

e) The CCP shall inform Clearing Members of the applicable concentration limits and of any amendment to these limits. If the CCP materially breaches a concentration limit set out in its policies and procedures, it shall rectify the breach as soon as possible.

37.8 PART 8: MARGIN

Article 35: Margin Requirement

a) The CCP Rules shall specify margin requirements with clear models and parameters, and the CCP shall impose, call and collect margin to limit its credit exposure to its Clearing Members. The CCP's margin requirements shall establish margin levels commensurate with the risks and particular attributes of each product and market it serves and must reflect the availability of timely, high-quality pricing data.

b) The models and parameters adopted by the CCP must provide for Initial Margin and, where appropriate, Variation Margin and the CCP shall regularly monitor and, if necessary, revise its models and parameters to reflect current market conditions. Any such revisions shall take into account any potentially Procyclical effects. In addition, the CCP may provide, where a Clearing Member has breached limits set by the CCP, for the provision of additional margin as set out in the CCP Rules.

c) In calculating margin requirements, the CCP may allow offsets or reductions in required margin amounts between financial instruments that it clears if the risk of one product is significantly and reliably correlated with the risk of another product. The CCP shall base such offsets on a methodology that reflects the degree of price dependence between the products. Such methodology shall be documented and shall at least provide that the correlation, or an equivalent statistical parameter of dependence, between two or more products cleared is shown to be reliable over any specified lookback periods. Notwithstanding the foregoing, offsets or reductions in required margin amounts between financial instruments shall only be permitted to the extent such financial instruments are covered by the same default fund.

Article 36: Initial Margin Methodology

a) The CCP shall adopt a risk-based Initial Margin model that generates margin requirements that are sufficient to cover its potential future exposures to a Clearing Member in the interval between the last margin collection and the close out of positions following a Clearing Member default. Initial Margin should meet an established single- tailed confidence level of at least 99 percent with respect to the estimated distribution of future exposure.

b) As part of its risk-based Initial Margin model, the CCP shall:

1) select an appropriate close-out period for each product that it clears, which shall be no less than 2 days for transactions concluded on an Exchange and 5 days for transactions concluded over the counter, and document the close-out periods and related analysis for each product type. It shall base its determination upon historical price and liquidity data, as well as reasonably foreseeable events in a default scenario;
2) select an appropriate sample period to calculate required Initial Margin for each product that it clears and document the period and related analysis for each product type. Selection of the period should be carefully examined based on the theoretical properties of the model and empirical tests on these properties using historical data;
3) identify and mitigate any credit exposure that may give rise to specific wrong-way risk, where an exposure to a Clearing Member is highly likely to increase when the creditworthiness of that Clearing Member is deteriorating; and
4) address Procyclicality in its margin arrangements to limit the need and likelihood of large or unexpected margin calls in times of market stress.

c) Following the application of offsets and reductions in accordance with paragraph (c) of Article 35 of these Regulations and without prejudice to the provisions of this Article, the CCP needs to ensure that Initial Margin meets or exceeds the single-tailed confidence level of at least 99 percent with respect to the estimated distribution of the future exposure of the portfolio.

Article 37: Variation Margin Methodology

a) The CCP must:

1) ascertain its current exposure to each Clearing Member by marking each Clearing Member's outstanding positions to current market prices;
2) collect Variation Margin from Clearing Members whose positions have lost value; and
3) pay Variation Margin to Clearing Members whose positions have gained value.

b) The CCP has the right to settle any Variation Margin collected against gains and losses. Where the CCP intends to exercise such right, this must:

1) be provided for in the CCP Rules; and
2) shall also specify which Securities are subject to such right.

Article 38: Margin Calls

a) The CCP shall have the right and operational capacity to make both end of day and intraday margin calls, both scheduled and unscheduled, to Clearing Members. Such right shall be included in the CCP Rules.

b) Margin calls are transmitted to Clearing Members through an electronic system or other channels that are defined in CCP Rules. Clearing Members are obliged to meet each margin call within the stipulated deadlines determined by the CCP.

Article 39: Testing Margin Coverage

a) The CCP shall have a reliable source of timely price data as well as procedures and sound valuation models for addressing circumstances in which pricing data or third- party sources are not readily available or reliable. The valuation models used by the CCP shall be validated under a variety of market scenarios at least annually by a qualified and independent party to ensure that any such models accurately produce appropriate prices, and where necessary, the CCP should adjust its calculation of Initial Margin to reflect any identified model risk.

b) The CCP shall analyze and monitor its model performance and overall margin coverage by conducting rigorous daily backtesting and, on at least a monthly basis, sensitivity analysis. The CCP shall regularly conduct an assessment of the theoretical and empirical properties of its margin model in respect of all products it clears.

c) The CCP shall backtest its margin coverage using Clearing Members' positions from each day in order to evaluate whether there are any exceptions to its margin coverage. This assessment of margin coverage should be considered an integral part of the evaluation of the model's performance. In case backtesting indicates that the model did not identify the appropriate amount of Initial Margin necessary to achieve the intended coverage, the CCP should have clear procedures for recalibrating its margining system.

d) The CCP should test the sensitivity of its margin model coverage using a wide range of parameters and assumptions that reflect possible market conditions in order to understand how the level of margin coverage might be affected by highly stressed market conditions and should ensure that the range of parameters and assumptions captures a variety of historical and hypothetical conditions, including the most-volatile periods that have been experienced by the markets it serves and extreme changes in the correlations between prices.

e) The CCP shall report the results of its backtesting and sensitivity analysis to the Authority on a regular basis, and at a minimum quarterly.

37.9 PART 9: CREDIT RISK

Article 40: Measuring, Monitoring and Mitigating Credit Risk

a) The CCP shall identify sources of credit risk and effectively measure and monitor its credit exposures to Clearing Members and those arising from its payment, Clearing, and settlement processes. In particular, it shall regularly measure and monitor its credit risks throughout the day using timely information.

b) The CCP shall establish a robust framework to manage its credit exposures to Clearing Members and the credit risks arising from its payment, Clearing, and settlement processes. In order to estimate the potential future exposures that could result from Clearing Member defaults, the CCP should identify risk factors and monitor potential market developments and conditions that could affect the size and likelihood of its losses in the close out of a defaulting Clearing Member's positions.

c) The CCP shall mitigate its credit risks to the extent possible.

d) The CCP shall at all times maintain sufficient financial resources to cover its credit exposure to each Clearing Member fully with a high degree of confidence. In addition, the CCP shall maintain additional financial resources sufficient to cover a wide range of potential stress scenarios that should include, but not be limited to, the default of the two Clearing Members and their affiliates that would potentially cause the largest aggregate credit exposure to the CCP in extreme but plausible market conditions. The CCP shall document its rationale for determining its aggregate levels of total financial resources, and shall share this rationale with the Authority upon request.

e) The CCP is entitled to impose risk limits on each of its Clearing Members.

Article 41: Default Fund

a) To limit the CCP's credit exposure to its Clearing Members and reduce systemic risk in the market, the CCP shall maintain a pre-funded default fund to cover losses that exceed the losses covered by the margin requirements provided for in Part 8 of these Regulations.

b) The CCP may establish more than one default fund for the different classes of instrument that it clears. The level of the default fund shall be sufficient to enable the CCP to withstand the default of its largest Clearing Member or the default of its second and third largest Clearing Members (whichever is greater), each under extreme but plausible market conditions. The CCP shall develop scenarios of extreme but plausible market conditions, which shall include the most volatile periods that have been experienced by the markets for which the CCP provides its services and a range of potential future scenarios.

c) The determination of the size of the default fund in accordance with paragraph (b) of this Article shall be revalued on at least a monthly basis and each time a material change occurs that affects the CCP's risk exposure.

d) The CCP Rules shall establish the minimum size of contributions to the default fund and the criteria to calculate the contributions of each Clearing Member.

e) The contributions of each Clearing Member to the default fund shall be proportional to its risks.

f) All contributions provided by a Clearing Member to satisfy its default fund contribution must be provided from such Clearing Member's own balance sheet. The Clearing Member shall not be permitted to use any assets attributable to an Individual Client Account or an Omnibus Client Accounts, or otherwise legally or beneficially owned by a Client, to satisfy such Clearing Member's default fund contributions to the CCP.

g) The CCP shall open and operate separate accounts to maintain the default fund contributions of its Clearing Members.

Article 42: Dedicated own Resources Allocated from CCP's own Capital

a) The CCP shall maintain a certain level of financial resources to cover potential losses that exceed the losses covered by the margin requirements provided for in Part 8 of these Regulations and the default fund as provided for in Article 41 of these Regulations.

b) The CCP Board shall allocate the quantum of the additional financial resources referred to in paragraph (a) of this Article, but at a minimum shall be no less than 10% of the minimum capital requirement of the CCP as determined in accordance with Article 20 of these Regulations, and shall not be double counted as forming part of the capital base.

c) To the extent the CCP has more than one default fund, it shall allocate financial resources in accordance with this Article in proportion to the size of each such default fund.

d) The CCP Board shall review on an annual basis the amount of dedicated own resources.

In addition, it shall review on an annual basis, if applicable, the allocation to each default fund.

Article 43: Testing the Sufficiency of the CCP's Total Financial Resources

a) The CCP should regularly test the sufficiency of its total financial resources available in the event of a default or multiple defaults in extreme but plausible market conditions through rigorous stress testing. The CCP should have clear procedures to report the results of its stress tests to appropriate internal decision makers at the CCP and to use these results to evaluate the adequacy of and adjust its total financial resources.

b) The CCP shall conduct reverse stress tests, as appropriate, aimed at identifying the extreme default scenarios and extreme market conditions in which its total financial resources would be insufficient.

c) In conducting stress testing, the CCP shall consider the effect of a wide range of relevant stress scenarios in terms of both defaulters' positions and possible price changes in liquidation periods. Scenarios should include relevant peak historic price volatilities, shifts in other market factors such as price determinants and yield curves, multiple defaults over various time horizons, simultaneous pressures in funding and asset markets, and a spectrum of forward-looking stress scenarios in a variety of extreme but plausible market conditions.

d) Stress tests should be performed on a daily basis using standard and predetermined parameters and assumptions. The CCP, on a regular basis and at least monthly, shall perform a comprehensive and thorough analysis of stress-testing scenarios, models, and underlying parameters and assumptions used to ensure they are appropriate for determining the CCP's required level of default protection in light of current and evolving market conditions.

e) The CCP shall report the results of its stress test to SAMA and notify the Authority of it on a regular basis, and at a minimum quarterly.

37.10 PART 10: LIQUIDITY RISK

Article 44: Measuring and Monitoring Liquidity Risk

a) The CCP shall at all times have access to adequate liquidity and maintain sufficient liquid resources in all relevant currencies to settle its payment obligations on time with a high degree of confidence under a wide range of potential stress scenarios. Such scenarios should include, but not be limited to, the default of the Clearing Member and its affiliates that would generate the largest aggregate payment obligation to the CCP in extreme but plausible market conditions.

b) To measure its liquidity requirements, the CCP shall identify its sources of liquidity risk. Such sources shall include, but not to be limited to, the following:

1) potential defaults of Clearing Members;
2) the value and concentration of its daily settlement and funding flows through its settlement banks, payment systems, any bank at which currency is held (whether denominated in SAR or otherwise) and other intermediaries;
3) the risk that the CCP's investment activity does not generate the return expected;
4) payments to settle required margin and other payment obligations over multiple days to account for multiday hedging and close-out activities as directed by a CCP's default procedures;

5) the concentration of its liquidity risks, including its exposures to legal persons in the same group and interdependencies across different legal persons; and
6) foreign exchange risk, particularly where liquid resources and settlement obligations of the CCP are denominated in different currencies.

c) On the basis of the measure of liquidity carried out in paragraph (b) of this Article, the CCP shall assess its current and potential future liquidity needs on a daily basis and have in place effective operational and analytical tools to identify, measure, and monitor its settlement and funding flows on an ongoing and timely basis, including its use of intraday liquidity.

d) The CCP Rules of the CCP must explicitly enable it to effect same-day as well as, where appropriate, intraday and multiday settlement of payment obligations on time following any individual or combined default among Clearing Members. The CCP Rules should address unforeseen and potentially uncovered liquidity shortfalls.

e) The CCP shall carefully analyze its liquidity needs and shall maintain sufficient liquid resources in all relevant currencies to settle all payment obligations on time with a high degree of confidence under a wide range of potential stress scenarios. The CCP shall regularly assess the design and operation of their liquidity management framework, including considering the results of the stress tests carried out in accordance with Article 45 of these Regulations.

f) For the purposes of this Part, the following assets shall be considered liquid resources:

1) the CCP's cash deposited at SAMA;
2) the CCP's cash deposited at commercial banks;
3) committed lines of credit or equivalent arrangements, save that where such arrangement is with a defaulting Clearing Member it shall not longer be treated as a liquid resource;
4) highly marketable financial instruments held in custody and investments that are readily available and convertible into cash with prearranged and highly reliable funding arrangements, even in extreme but plausible market conditions;
5) other assets as described and provided for in the CCP Rules.

g) The CCP shall have detailed procedures, which shall be approved by its CCP Board, for using its liquid resources to complete settlement during a liquidity shortfall. Such procedures should clearly document the sequence for using each type of liquid resource.

Article 45: Stress Testing Liquidity Needs and Resources

a) To ensure that the CCP has sufficient liquid resources to effect settlement of payment obligations with a high degree of confidence under a wide range of potential stress scenarios, the CCP shall regularly test the sufficiency of its liquid resources through rigorous stress testing and shall have clear procedures to report the results of its stress tests to appropriate, internal, decision makers and to use these results to evaluate the adequacy of, and adjust its, liquidity risk management framework. In addition, the CCP should regularly test its procedures for accessing its liquid resources, including by drawing down test amounts from committed credit facilities.

b) In conducting stress testing, the CCP should consider a wide range of relevant scenarios. Such scenarios should include relevant peak historic price volatilities, shifts in other market factors such as price determinants and yield curves, multiple defaults over various time horizons, simultaneous pressures in funding and asset markets, and a spectrum of forward-looking stress scenarios in a variety of extreme but plausible market conditions.

c) The CCP shall conduct reverse stress tests aimed at identifying the extreme default scenarios and extreme market conditions for which its liquid resources would be insufficient.

d) Liquidity stress testing shall be performed on a daily basis using standard and predetermined parameters and assumptions. The CCP, on a regular basis and at least monthly, shall perform a comprehensive and thorough analysis of stress testing scenarios, models, and underlying parameters and assumptions used to ensure they are appropriate for achieving its identified liquidity needs and resources in light of current and evolving market conditions.

37.11 PART 11: SETTLEMENT FINALITY

Article 46: Settlement Finality

a) The CCP Rules shall clearly define the point at which settlement is final, including the irrevocable and unconditional transfer of an asset or financial instrument, or the discharge of an obligation by the CCP or its Clearing Members in accordance with the terms of the underlying contract.

b) The CCP shall complete final settlement no later than the end of the date defined in the CCP Rules on which the payment, transfer instruction or other obligation is due and the associated funds and securities are typically available to the receiving party, and preferably intraday or in real time, to reduce settlement risk. This means that any payment, transfer instruction, or other obligation that has been submitted to, and accepted by, the CCP in accordance with its risk management and other relevant acceptance criteria should be settled on the intended date specified in the CCP Rules.

c) The CCP Rules shall clearly define the point after which unsettled payments, transfer instructions, or other obligations may not be revoked by a participant and cut-off times and materiality rules for exceptions shall be clearly defined.

Article 47: Money Settlements

a) To avoid credit and liquidity risks, the CCP shall conduct its money settlements using money held with SAMA, where practical and available. The CCP may use money made available to it by SAMA subject to SAMA's policy, requirements, and conditions.

b) Where the CCP use of money held or made available at SAMA is not practical or available, it shall conduct its money settlements with little or no credit or liquidity risk. If this involves the CCP settling using money held or made available at a settlement bank, the CCP should monitor, manage, and limit its credit and liquidity risks arising from such settlement banks. In particular, the CCP, in its relation with settlement banks, shall establish and monitor adherence to strict criteria that take account of, without limitation, their regulation and supervision, creditworthiness, capitalization, access to liquidity and operational reliability.

c) In cash settlements referred to in paragraphs (a) and (b) of this Article, the timing of the finality of funds transfers should comply with Article 46 of these Regulations.

Article 48: Physical Deliveries The CCP Rules shall clearly state the CCP's obligations with respect to the physical deliveries. The obligations that the CCP may assume with respect to physical deliveries vary based on the types of assets the CCP settles. The CCP shall clearly state which asset classes it accepts for physical delivery and the procedures surrounding the delivery of each.

Article 49: Exchange-of-value Settlement System If the CCP is an exchange-of-value settlement system, it shall have in place an appropriate settlement mechanism to eliminate principal risk by ensuring that the final settlement of one obligation occurs if and only if the final settlement of the linked obligation also occurs, regardless of when finality occurs. The final settlement of two linked obligations can be achieved either on a gross basis or on a net basis.

37.12 PART 12: SEGREGATION AND PORTABILITY

Article 50: Account Types

a) The CCP shall ensure that it employs an account structure that enables it to readily identify positions of a Clearing Member's Client and to segregate related collateral.

b) The CCP shall provide for the benefit of each Clearing Member the following:

1) House Accounts: the CCP shall provide separate records and accounts that shall enable it, at any time and without delay, to distinguish in accounts with such CCP the assets and positions held for the account of one Clearing Member from the assets and positions held for the account of any other Clearing Member and from its own assets. Clearing Members shall not be permitted to assign to such House Accounts assets and positions held for the benefit of its Clients (which must be recorded in either an Omnibus Client Account or Individual Client Account);
2) Omnibus Client Accounts: the CCP shall provide separate records and accounts enabling such Clearing Member to distinguish in accounts with such CCP the assets and positions of that Clearing Member from those held for the accounts of its Clients. In the event of a shortfall attributable to an Omnibus Client Account, the CCP shall be permitted to apply any assets attributable to such account to cover any such shortfall, notwithstanding that the assets and positions may belong to different Clients held in the same Omnibus Client Account;
3) Individual Client Accounts: where the CCP provides for this type of account in the CCP Rules, the CCP shall provide separate records and accounts enabling such Clearing Member to distinguish in accounts with such CCP the assets and positions of a Client from those held for the accounts of its other Clients, its own assets and positions and those of the CCP. The CCP shall have no recourse to the assets and positions attributable to such Individual Client Account in the event of a shortfall in any other account of the Clearing Member (whether it be the House Account, an Omnibus Client Account or another Individual Client Account); and
4) other account types that are defined in the CCP Rules.

c) The CCP shall offer the Clearing Member, upon request, the possibility to open more accounts in their own name or for the account of their Clients.

d) Collateral that is maintained in an Individual Client Account or Omnibus Client Account shall, at all times, be attributed by the CCP to the Clients named in such accounts and shall only be used by the CCP to cover losses attributable to such account.

e) The Clearing Member shall keep separate records and accounts that enable it to distinguish both in accounts held with the CCP and in its own accounts its assets and positions from the assets and positions held for the account of its Clients at such CCP. Such records and accounts shall enable the Clearing Member to distinguish each Client's assets and positions from other Clients with respect to each Individual Client Account and Omnibus Client Account maintained at the CCP.

f) Where the CCP offers Individual Client Accounts, the Clearing Member shall offer its Clients the choice between Omnibus Client Accounts and Individual Client Accounts and inform them of the costs and level of protection associated with each option. The Client shall confirm its choice in writing.

g) The requirement to distinguish assets and positions with the CCP in accounts is satisfied where:

1) the assets and positions are recorded in separate accounts;
2) positions recorded on different accounts are prevented from being offset; and
3) the assets covering the positions recorded in an account are not exposed to losses connected to positions recorded in another account.

For the purposes of this Article, assets do not refer to default fund contributions.

Article 51: Framework for the Porting of Positions

a) The CCP shall ensure that its account structure is structured to facilitate the transfer of the positions and assets of a defaulting Clearing Member's Clients to a non-defaulting Clearing Member or, as the case may be, the orderly liquidation of the Clients' positions and the return of excess collateral to the Clients. Where the positions and assets are those of Exchange members with no clearing memberships, the account structure shall be structured to facilitate the transfer of the positions and assets from the defaulting General Clearing Member to a non-defaulting General Clearing Member.

b) The CCP shall not be required to guarantee that positions of a defaulting Clearing Member's Clients will be ported and shall not be liable for any failure to effect porting.

Article 52: Requirement to Disclose

a) The CCP shall disclose in its CCP Rules its segregation and portability arrangements in sufficient detail for Clients to understand:

1) the level of protection being provided, and in particular whether their positions and collateral held at or through the CCP are segregated from positions and collateral of their Clearing Member and such CCP;
2) how segregation is achieved, including who holds the segregated assets and whether such segregated assets are reflected on the books and records at the CCP or custodians that hold assets for the CCP;

3) under what circumstances Client collateral may be used by the CCP;
4) whether the CCP offers individual, as well as, omnibus Client segregation;
5) how portability is achieved; and
6) any risks or uncertainties associated with such Client segregation and portability arrangements.

b) The CCP Rules must mandate that each Clearing Member shall disclose to their Clients the costs associated with different levels of segregation they, and the CCP, provide and shall offer those services on reasonable commercial terms.

37.13 PART 13: CLEARING MEMBER DEFAULT MANAGEMENT

Article 53: Designation of Clearing Member as Defaulting

a) The CCP Rules shall clearly specify what circumstances constitute a Clearing Member default, and shall address both financial and operational defaults.

b) The CCP Rules shall specify whether a declaration of default is automatic or discretionary, and if discretionary, which person(s) exercise that discretion and shall set out the procedures to be followed if an event of default by a Clearing Member is not declared by the CCP.

c) The CCP shall review the CCP Rules annually and disclose the key aspects of the default rules and procedures to the public.

d) If the CCP designates a Clearing Member as defaulting, it shall immediately notify:

1) the Authority;
2) to the extent the defaulting Clearing Member is a Local Bank, SAMA;
3) the defaulting Clearing Member;
4) the relevant Exchange on which the cleared contracts of the defaulting Clearing Member related; and
5) the Depository Centre, to the extent the cleared contract relates to the Exchange.

e) Without prejudice to the obligation of the CCP to notify the parties specified in paragraph (d) of this Article, if the CCP designates a Clearing Member as defaulting, it shall also promptly publish a notice on its website to this effect. Such notice will be deemed to have informed participants in the market of the designation of the Clearing Member as defaulting.

Article 54: Default Rules and Procedures

a) Where the CCP considers that a Clearing Member is likely to default, including where it will not be able to meet its future obligations, the CCP shall promptly notify the Authority before the default procedure is declared. Such notification shall include a brief description of any measures taken or proposed to be taken by the CCP. Where such Clearing Member is a Local Bank, the CCP shall also promptly notify SAMA and consult and collaborate with it before the default procedure is declared.

b) The CCP's default rules and procedures shall enable the CCP to take prompt action to contain losses and liquidity pressures, before, at and after the point at which the Clearing Member has defaulted. In taking any action, the CCP shall ensure that the closing out of any positions of such Clearing Member does not impact its operations or expose non-defaulting Clearing Members to losses they cannot anticipate or control.

c) Without prejudice to paragraph (b) of this Article, the CCP Rules of the CCP may permit the CCP to:

1) require non-defaulting Clearing Members to agree in advance to bid on the defaulting Clearing Member's portfolio; and
2) should such auction fail, require the Clearing Member to accept an allocation of the portfolio.

d) Where used, such procedures should include consideration of the risk profile and portfolio of each Clearing Member before allocating positions so as to minimise additional risk for the non-defaulting Clearing Members.

e) In the default of a Clearing Member, the CCP shall use the resources in the following order:

1) proprietary assets provided by such defaulting Clearing Member, which shall include both collateral and the default fund contributions of that defaulting Clearing Member. The CCP shall not be entitled to use the assets of the Clients of such defaulting Clearing Member.
2) its dedicated own resources as provided for in Article 42 of these Regulations. Once these dedicated resources are exhausted, a party will have no recourse to any other asset of the CCP, as provided in paragraph (f) of Article 8 of these Regulations, unless otherwise provided in the CCP Rules;
3) default fund contributions of non-defaulting Clearing Members provided in accordance with Article 41 of these Regulations; and
4) additional default fund contributions from non-defaulting Clearing Members in accordance with the terms of the CCP Rules of such CCP.

f) Upon the default of a Clearing Member who has cleared positions on behalf of Clients (including Exchange members with no clearing memberships), the CCP shall be required to trigger the process of dealing with the assets and positions recorded in the accounts of Clients of such defaulting Clearing Member as follows:

1) where the account is an Omnibus Client Account, the CCP shall be permitted to apply any collateral attributed to the account to cover losses in such account notwithstanding that the collateral and losses may belong to different Clients held in the same Omnibus Client Account. To the extent another Clearing Member has agreed to accept the assets and positions attributable to such Omnibus Client Account, such assets and positions will be ported. If the transfer to another Clearing Member does not take place within the time specified in the CCP's default rules and procedures, the CCP may take all steps permitted by its rules to actively manage its risks in relation to such positions, including liquidating the assets and positions for the account of the Clients of such Omnibus Client Account;
2) where the account is an Individual Client Account, the CCP shall port the assets and positions in such Individual Client Account to the extent another Clearing Member has agreed to accept such assets and positions. If the transfer to another Clearing Member does not take place within the time specified in the CCP's default rules and procedures, the CCP may take all steps permitted by its rules to actively manage its risks in relation to the positions in such Individual Client Account, including liquidating the assets and positions for the account of the Client of such Individual Client Account;
3) without prejudice to the provisions of this Article, where the account is an account of an Exchange member with no clearing membership, the CCP may only permit porting

of such assets and positions to another General Clearing Member; and
4) to the extent there is any balance owed by the CCP after the completion of the defaulting Clearing Member's default management process, such balance shall be readily returned to those Clients when they are known to the CCP or, if they are not, to the Clearing Member for the account of its clients.

g) After the application of the proprietary assets of a defaulting Clearing Member, in accordance with paragraph (e) of this Article, the CCP shall use its default fund contributions, as provided for in Article 42 of these Regulations, before applying the default fund provided by non-defaulting Clearing Members.

Article 55: Periodic Testing and Review of Default Procedures The CCP shall test and review its default procedures to ensure that they are practical and effective. Such testing and review should be conducted at least annually or following material changes to the rules and procedures.

37.14 PART 14: CCP RECOVERY

Article 56: CCP Recovery Plan
a) The CCP shall have a comprehensive and effective recovery plan designed to permit it to continue to provide its critical services.

b) In determining its recovery plan, the CCP shall take into account the interests of all Clearing Members, Clients of Clearing Members and other stakeholders who are likely to be affected by the recovery plan and shall establish appropriate procedures to ensure consulting with them in the formulation of the recovery plan.

c) For the purposes of developing its recovery plan, the CCP shall identify:

1) The critical services it provides, which shall at a minimum include its clearing, settlement and recording functions;
2) scenarios that may prevent it from being able to provide its critical services, which shall at a minimum include credit losses or liquidity shortfalls created by a Clearing Member default, general business losses, liquidity shortfalls, the realization of investment losses and risks taken on third party providers, and on such basis identify:
a. the criteria that will trigger the implementation of part or all of the recovery plan;
b. the appropriate recovery tools, the necessary steps and time needed to implement them and the associated risks to the CCP, its Clearing Members, Clients of Clearing Members and the market more generally if such tools are employed.

d) The CCP should disclose, to those affected by the recovery plan, sufficient information about the recovery plan, including the degree of the CCP's discretion to exercise judgement.

e) The CCP shall be required to carry out periodic simulations and scenario exercises to test and review its recovery plan. Such testing must be carried out at least annually as well as following changes to the CCP Rules that would materially affect the recovery plan. The CCP shall update its recovery plan as needed after the completion of each test and review.

Article 57: Approving the CCP Recovery Plan
a) The CCP Board must approve the CCP recovery plan and obtain the Authority's and SAMA's approvals of such plan.

b) The CCP shall inform the Authority and SAMA immediately of any proposed changes to its recovery plan. Any proposed changes shall be subject to the Authority's and SAMA's approvals.

c) The CCP shall obtain SAMA's non-objection prior to the implementation of any part of the recovery plan, including the recovery tools to be employed as a result of such implementation, and shall also immediately notify the Authority.

37.15 PART 15: OTHER CCP OBLIGATIONS

Article 58: Communication Procedures and Standards
The CCP shall use internationally accepted communication procedures to facilitate effective communication between its information systems, and those of its Clearing Members, their Clients, and others that connect to the CCP such as service providers. It shall also use internationally accepted communication standards, such as standardized messaging formats and reference data standards for identifying financial instruments and Clearing Members.

Article 59: Control Systems
a) To establish a sound risk management framework, the CCP shall identify and regularly review the range of risks that arise within its system and the risks it directly bears from or poses to Clearing Members and Clients of Clearing Members. It shall identify those risks that could materially affect its ability to perform or to provide services as expected.

b) The CCP shall identify and regularly review the material risks it bears from and poses to other legal persons (such as payment systems, settlement banks, liquidity providers and service providers) as a result of interdependencies and develop appropriate risk management tools to address such risks.

c) The CCP Board and Senior Executives of a CCP are ultimately responsible for managing the CCP's risks. The board should determine an appropriate level of aggregate risk tolerance and capacity for the CCP and shall establish policies, procedures, and controls that are consistent with the CCP's risk tolerance and capacity. The CCP's policies, procedures, and controls should address all relevant risks, including legal, credit, liquidity, general business, and operational risks.

d) The CCP shall employ robust information and risk control systems to provide it with the capacity to obtain timely information necessary to apply risk management policies and procedures. In particular, these systems should allow for the accurate and timely measurement and aggregation of risk exposures across the CCP, the management of individual risk exposures and the interdependencies between them, and the assessment of the impact of various economic and financial shocks that could affect the CCP.

Article 60: Record-Keeping
a) The CCP shall retain the following for a period of ten years at a minimum (unless the Authority specifies otherwise):

1) all the records on the services and activity provided so as to enable the Authority to monitor the CCP's compliance with these Regulations; and
2) all information on all contracts it has processed following the termination of such contracts. That information shall at least enable the identification of the original terms of a transaction before Clearing by the CCP.

b) All records or information required to be kept by the CCP under these Regulations shall be provided to the Authority upon its request. The Authority may inspect the records directly or through a person it appoints for that purpose.

c) The CCP shall maintain records with respect to all transactions in all contracts cleared by the CCP and ensure that its records include all information necessary to conduct a comprehensive and accurate reconstruction of the Clearing process for each contract. Each record on each transaction shall be uniquely identifiable and searchable by all fields concerning the CCP, Clearing Member, Client of a Clearing Member, if known to the CCP, and financial instrument.

d) The CCP shall maintain records of positions held by each Clearing Member. Separate records shall be held for each account kept in accordance with Part 12 of these Regulations. The CCP shall ensure that its records include all information necessary to conduct a comprehensive and accurate reconstruction of the transactions that established the position. Each record shall be identifiable and searchable at least by all fields concerning the CCP, Clearing Member, Client of a Clearing Member, if known to the CCP, and financial instrument.

e) At the end of each business day, the CCP shall make a record in relation to each position including the following details, to the extent they are linked to the position in question:

1) the identification of the Clearing Member and Client of a Clearing Member, if known to the CCP;
2) the sign of the position; and
3) the daily calculation of the value of the position with records of the prices at which the contracts are valued, and of any other relevant information.

f) The CCP shall make, and keep updated, a record of the amounts of margins, default fund contributions and other financial resources called by the CCP and the corresponding amount actually provided by a Clearing Member at the end of day and changes to that amount that may occur intraday, with respect to each Clearing Member, Client of a Clearing Member, if known to the CCP.

g) The CCP shall maintain a register of all derivative contracts cleared by the CCP and the underlying Securities or instruments to which such transactions relate.

h) Records of the CCP may be recorded in any form, but must be capable of reproduction in hard printed form.

i) When a Clearing Member of the CCP or a former Clearing Member of the CCP requests any records kept during the regulatory record-keeping period, the CCP must make available, within a reasonable period, any of the following:

1) any written material or records which relate to that Clearing Member; and
2) copies of any correspondence received from or sent to that Clearing Member relating to Clearing services.

Article 61: Disclosure of CCP Rules and Material Costs to Clearing Members

a) The CCP shall adopt clear and comprehensive rules and procedures and fully disclose them to Clearing Members.

b) A CCP shall, at a minimum, publicly disclose free of charge the following:

1) information regarding its governance arrangements;
2) its CCP Rules;
3) its rights and obligations, as well as those of each Clearing Member;
4) key aspects of its default rules and procedures;
5) its fees at the level of individual services it offers as well as its policies on any available discounts; and
6) basic data on transaction volumes and values.

c) The CCP shall have a clear process for proposing and implementing changes to the CCP Rules.

d) The CCP shall make the information and data referred to in paragraph (b) of this Article available on its website in Arabic and any other language the Authority may require. The data should be accompanied by explanatory documentation that enables users to understand and interpret the data correctly.

37.16 PART 16: OPERATIONAL RISK

Article 62: Identifying Sources of Operational Risk

The CCP shall identify, monitor, and manage the various sources of operational risk and establish clear policies and procedures to address them. As part of this process, it should:

1) identify all potential single points of failure in its operations, which shall include internal processes (including, without limitation, deficiencies in its information systems, inadequate screening of its personnel and inadequate control of systems and processes) and external events (including, without limitation, the failure of critical service providers and the occurrence of natural disasters);

2) assess the evolving nature of the operational risk it faces on an ongoing basis, and

3) analyze its potential vulnerabilities and implement appropriate defence mechanisms.

Article 63: Operational Risk Management

a) The CCP Board, either directly or through a relevant committee, shall establish clear policies and procedures that mitigate and manage the CCP's sources of operational risk. In particular, such policies and procedures must explicitly define the roles and responsibilities for addressing operational risk and endorse the CCP's operational risk- management framework. The CCP's operational risk-management framework should include setting operational standards, measuring and reviewing performance, correcting deficiencies, formal change-management and project-management processes to mitigate operational risk arising from modifications to operations and policies. A key competent to a sound operational risk-management framework is the requirement for the CCP to employ sufficient, well qualified, personnel who should be able to operate the system safely and efficiently during both normal and abnormal circumstances.

b) The CCP shall test its arrangements with participants, including its operational policies and procedures, on a periodic basis. In order to minimise the effects of testing on operations, tests should be carried out in an environment which replicates, as far as possible, the environment under which such operations will need to adapt to abnormal circumstances and potential major incidents. This will include a periodic review to consider whether new technologies and business developments should be incorporated.

c) The CCP shall manage operation incidents carefully and have comprehensive and well- documented procedures in place to record, report, analyze, and resolve all such incidents. The CCP shall undertake a review after every significant disruption to identify the causes and any required improvement to the normal operations or business continuity arrangements.

Article 64: Business Continuity Management
a) The business continuity plan is a key component of the CCP's risk management framework. All aspects of the business continuity plan should be clearly and fully documented. The business continuity plan must:

1) identify and address events that pose a significant risk of disrupting operations, including events that could cause a wide-scale or major disruption;
2) focus on the impact on the operation of critical infrastructures and services if the identified events, including both internal and external threats, were to occur;
3) include clearly stated objectives which deal with both measures that prevent disruptions of critical operations and policies and procedures to mitigate the effect of such disruption events by allowing for the rapid recovery and timely resumption of the operations of the CCP following a disruption. In this regard, the CCP should be able to resume operations within two hours following disruption events and should be able to complete settlement by the end of the day even in extreme circumstances; and
4) include clearly defined procedures for crisis and event management.

b) To ensure that the CCP is able to meet its objectives, the CCP shall set up a secondary physical off-site with sufficient resources, capabilities, and functionalities and appropriate staffing arrangements that would not be affected by a wide-scale disruption and would allow the secondary physical off-site to take over operations if required. The secondary physical off-site should provide the level of critical services necessary to perform the functions consistent with the recovery time objective identified by the CCP, which at a minimum shall require that the information technology systems can resume operations within two hours following disruptive events.

c) The business continuity plan and associated arrangements of the CCP shall be subject to periodic review and testing. Tests should address various scenarios that simulate wide-scale disasters and inter-site switchovers. The CCP, after every test or significant disruption, shall undertake a review to identify the causes and any required improvement to its business continuity plan.

d) The CCP shall be required to communicate with the Authority in the case of a major disruption to its operations or any event of a wider market distress that affects the CCP. The CCP shall also promptly inform the Authority of any material amendments to its business continuity plan to the extent permitted. The Authority, in its discretion, may require the CCP to resubmit a copy of its amended business continuity plan.

37.17 PART 17: LINKS BETWEEN CCPS

Article 65: Interoperability Arrangements
a) The CCP may enter into an Interoperability Arrangement with other CCPs to enable its Clearing Members to clear transactions with participants in the other CCP and shall be permitted to do this where:

1) the requirements laid down in Article 66 and Article 67 of these Regulations are fulfilled; and
2) such CCP demonstrates its compliance with these requirements, as well as being able to demonstrate that the terms of the Interoperability Arrangement will provide for the smooth and orderly functioning of the market.

In addition, the Authority approval must be obtained prior to such Interoperability Arrangement becoming effective.

b) When establishing an interoperability arrangement with another CCP for the purpose of providing services to a particular trading venue, the trading venue must provide such CCP with the same level of access as afforded to other CCPs who satisfy the same operational and technical requirements mandated by the trading venue or its settlement systems.

Article 66: Risk Management of Interoperability Arrangements In order to enter into an Interoperability Arrangement, the CCP shall:

1) have in place policies, procedures and systems to identify, monitor and manage the risk arising from such Interoperability Arrangement, including the risk that a participant of the other CCP, or the other CCP itself, may default and how this would impact such CCP;

2) agree on each party's respective rights and obligations. Where the other CCP is established outside of the Kingdom, this agreement must also include the governing law which will govern the terms of such Interoperability Arrangement; and

3) to the extent the determination of exposure for transactions between the two CCP's differs, identify such differences, assess the risks that may arise from such differences and take appropriate measure to limit such risks on the CCP's operations.

Article 67: Provision of Margin Among CCPs
a) The CCP and each CCP with whom the CCP has an Interoperability Arrangement shall distinguish in accounts the assets and positions held for the account of the other CCP.

b) If the CCP with whom a CCP has an Interoperability Arrangement only provides initial margins to that other under a security financial collateral arrangement, the receiving CCP shall have no right of use over the margins provided by such CCP.

c) Collateral received in the form of financial instruments shall be deposited with operators of securities settlement systems.

d) The assets referred to in paragraphs (b) and (c) of this Article shall be available to the receiving CCP only in case of default of the CCP which has provided the collateral in the context of an Interoperability Arrangement.

e) In case of default of the CCP which has received the collateral in the context of an Interoperability Arrangement, the collateral referred to in paragraphs (b) and (c) of this Article shall be readily returned to the providing CCP.

37.18 PART 18: QUALIFYING CENTRAL COUNTERPARTY

Article 68: Recognition of Qualifying Central Counterparty Status
a) The CCP may apply to the Authority to be designated as a Qualifying Central Counterparty.

b) The Authority shall publish on its website the CCPs that it designates as Qualifying Central Counterparties.

c) To the extent the Principles for Financial Market Infrastructures are amended after the initial designation by the Authority, the Authority shall promptly review whether such changes impact a CCP's qualification as a Qualifying Central Counterparty. The CCP shall be required to promptly respond to any requests of the Authority for information or access in order for the Authority to make such a determination.

d) If the Authority revokes a CCP's designation as a Qualifying Central Counterparty, it shall publish a notice on its website confirming this and confirming the date on which such designation will be revoked, which will be no earlier than 6 months from the date of designation. Until such time as the Authority publishes such notice, participants including Clearing Members shall be entitled to rely on the existing designation being in full force and valid.

37.19 PART 19: PUBLICATION AND ENTRY INTO FORCE

Article 69: Publication and Entry into Force These Regulations shall become effective upon their publication.

38 SPECIAL PURPOSE ENTITIES RULES

Issued by the Board of the Capital Market Authority pursuant to its Resolution Number 4-123-2017 dated 9/4/1439 H. (27/12/2017 G.)based on the Capital Market Law issued by Royal Decree No M/30 dated 2/6/1424 H. amended by Resolution of the Board of the Capital Market Authority Number 1-7-2021 dated 1/6/1442 H. (14/1/2021 G.)

Important Notice: the current version of these Rules, as may be amended, can be found at the Authority website: www.cma.org.sa

TABLE OF CONTENTS

PART 1: GENERAL PROVISIONS
Article 1: Preamble
Article 2: Definitions
Article 3: Scope and Application
Article 4: Waivers
Article 5: Right of Appeal
PART 2: SPECIAL PURPOSES ENTITIES ISSUING OR INTEND TO ISSUE DEBT INSTRUMENTS
CHAPTER 1: GENERAL PROVISIONS
Article 6: Scope and Application
CHAPTER 2: AUTHORIZATION
Article 7: Licensing Requirements
Article 8: Licensing Conditions
CHAPTER 3: BY-LAWS
Article 9: By-Laws
CHAPTER 4: SPONSOR
Article 10: Requirement for Sponsor
Article 11: Statues of Sponsor
Article 12: Restrictions on Sponsor Rights Towards Special Purposes Entity
Article 13: Notifications and Record-Keeping Requirements and Powers of the Authority
Article 14: Changing Sponsor
CHAPTER 5: TRUSTEE OF A SPECIAL PURPOSES ENTITY
Article 15: Trustee of a Special Purposes Entity
Article 16: Responsibilities of the Trustee of a Special Purposes Entity
Article 17: Changing the Trustee of a Special Purposes Entity
CHAPTER 6: BOARD OF DIRECTORS
Article 18: Board Membership Requirements
Article 19: Residence
Article 20: Appointment, Removal and Remuneration of Directors
Article 21: Duties of Directors
Article 22: Decision-Making
Article 23: Powers and Authorities
Article 24: Delegation
Article 25: Responsibilities of The Directors
Article 26: Register of Directors
Article 27: Registration and the Powers and Procedures of the Authority
Article 28: Notification Requirements
Article 29: Suspension or Cancellation of Registration
CHAPTER 7: CUSTODIAN
Article 30: Appointment of a Custodian
Article 31: Custody of Real Estate Assets and Securities in Respect of Asset-Linked Recourse or Asset-Backed Transactions
Article 32: Custodian's Notifications, Record-Keeping Requirements and Powers of the Authority
Article 33: Powers of the Authority in Relation to Custodian
CHAPTER 8: ACCOUNTS AND AUDIT
Article 34: Appointment of an Auditor
Article 35: Reports Prepared by Directors
CHAPTER 9: RECORD-KEEPING
Article 36: Record-Keeping
CHAPTER 10: MERGER AND CONVERSION
Article 37: Prohibition on Merger or Conversion
PART 3: INVESTMENT FUNDS THAT TAKE THE FORM OF SPECIAL PURPOSES ENTITIES
CHAPTER 1: PRELIMINARY PROVISIONS
Article 38: Scope and Application
Article 39: Preliminary Provisions
CHAPTER 2: AUTHORIZATION
Article 40: Authorization Requirements and Conditions
CHAPTER 3: BY-LAWS
Article 41: By-Laws
CHAPTER 4: MONITORING PROCEDURES AND SYSTEMS
Article 42: Notifications and Record-Keeping Requirements and Powers of the Authority
PART 4: GENERAL PROVISIONS
CHAPTER 1: PROCEDURES AND POWERS OF THE AUTHORITY IN RELATION TO THE AUTHORIZATION APPLICATION
Article 43: Procedures and Powers of the Authority in Relation to the Authorization Application
Article 44: Effect of Authorization
CHAPTER 2: LIABILITY TOWARDS PRE-AUTHORIZATION CONTRACTS
Article 45: Pre-Authorization Contracts
CHAPTER 3: THIRD PARTY RELIANCE
Article 46: Third Party Reliance on Actions of the Special Purposes Entity
CHAPTER 4: SETTLEMENT AND INSOLVENCY PROCEEDINGS
Article 47: Compliance with the Bankruptcy Law
CHAPTER 5: FEES
Article 48: Fees
CHAPTER 6: AUTHORITY REGISTERS
Article 49: Register of Special Purposes Entities
Article 50: Register of Directors
Article 51: Access to Registers
Article 52: Forms
Article 53: Fees
CHAPTER 7: TERMINATION OF A SPECIAL PURPOSES ENTITY
Article 54: Termination of a Special Purposes Entity
PART 5: PUBLICATION AND ENTRY INTO FORCE
Article 55: Publication and Entry into Force
ANNEXES
Annex 1: Notification Requirements

38.1 PART 1: GENERAL PROVISIONS

Article 1: Preamble
(a) The purpose of these Rules is to regulate the special purposes entities including its establishment, licensing, registration, management and associated activities.

(b) These Rules shall have no prejudice to the provisions of the Capital Market Law and Its Implementing Regulations, including the provisions of the Capital Market Institutions Regulations, the Securities Business Regulations, the Investment Funds Regulations, the Real Estate Investment Funds Regulations and the Rules on the Offer of Securities and Continuing Obligations.

(c) Assets of the special purposes entity may not be transferred for any reason other than to issue debt instruments or investment units or for ancillary activities necessary to achieve its purposes.

Article 2: Definitions
(a) Any reference to the "Capital Market Law" in these Rules shall mean the Capital Market Law issued by Royal Decree No. M/30 dated 2/6/1424 H.

(b) Expressions and terms in these Rules shall have meanings, which they bear in the Capital Market Law and in the Glossary of Defined Terms Used in the Regulations and Rules of the Capital Market Authority unless the contrary intention appears.

Article 3: Scope and Application These Rules apply to any person referred to in them.

Article 4: Waivers The Authority may waive any provision of these Rules in whole or in part as it applies to any person either on an application from such person or on its own initiative.

Article 5: Right of Appeal Any person subject to these Rules may appeal to the Committee in respect of any decision or action that the Authority takes under these Rules.

38.2 PART 2: SPECIAL PURPOSES ENTITIES ISSUING OR INTEND TO ISSUE DEBT INSTRUMENTS

38.2.1 CHAPTER 1: GENERAL PROVISIONS

Article 6: Scope and Application
(a) The provisions of this Part shall apply to special purposes entities that are issuing or intend to issue debt instruments.

(b) If the special purposes entity is offering asset-linked recourse debt instruments or debt-based recourse debt instruments, through a public offer, the provisions of the Rules on the Offer of Securities and Continuing Obligations and the Listing Rules shall apply to such entity.

(c) If the special purposes entity is offering asset-backed debt instruments, asset-linked recourse debt instruments or debt-based recourse debt instruments, through a private placement, the provisions of the Rules on the Offer of Securities and Continuing Obligations shall apply to such entity.

CHAPTER 2: AUTHORIZATION

Article 7: Licensing Requirements
(a) A special purposes entity shall be licensed at all times in accordance with these Rules.

(b) A sponsor seeking the licensing of a special purposes entity shall submit an application to the Authority in the form prescribed by the Authority, and pay such application fees as the Authority prescribes under Article (48) of these Rules.

(c) A special purposes entity that is issuing or intends to issue debt instruments shall register its shares under the name of the trustee of a special purposes entity.

Article 8: Licensing Conditions A special purposes entity must fulfill the following conditions at all times:

1) the special purposes entity shall be established under, and comply with all applicable requirements of these Rules;

2) the special purposes entity shall not engage in any activity other than the following:

a. issuing of debt instruments.
b. issuing shares for establishment purposes, provided that the shares are in the name of the trustee of the special purposes entity.
c. ancillary activities necessary to achieve its purposes.

3) the special purposes entity shall have by-laws meeting the requirements of Chapter (3) of this Part.

38.2.2 CHAPTER 3: BY-LAWS

Article 9: By-Laws
(a) A special purposes entity must have by-laws that specify the following:

1) the name and registered office of the special purposes entity;
2) the name, registered office and business of the sponsor;
3) the name, registered office and business of the trustee of the special purposes entity;
4) the start and end dates of the special purposes entity's financial year;
5) the purposes, management, operation of the special purposes entity; and
6) the requirements set out in Paragraph (a) of Article 34 of these Rules, and any other provisions that must be specified in the by-laws in accordance with these Rules.

(b) The Authority may prescribe one or more standard forms of by-laws to be adopted by special purposes entities. Where the Authority has prescribed such standard form by-laws, no departure from that standard form is permissible without the prior written consent of the Authority, except for adding details required to be included in the standard forms prescribed by the Authority, or selections required to be made.

(c) A special purposes entity's by-laws shall be approved by the Authority. Upon approval by the Authority of the special purposes entity's by-laws, the by-laws shall be signed by the sponsor in the presence of a notary public or a notary certified in the Kingdom.

38.3 CHAPTER 4: SPONSOR

Article 10: Requirement for Sponsor A special purposes entity issued, or intends to issue debt instruments, and all of its financing transactions, shall be sponsored by a single sponsor.

Article 11: Statues of Sponsor
(a) A sponsor of a special purposes entity that issued debt instruments shall fulfill the following conditions at all times:

1) if a special purposes entity issues, or intends to issue, debt-based recourse debt instruments, asset-linked recourse debt instruments, the sponsor shall be a Saudi joint stock company, a capital market institution licensed to carry on securities business related to the business of special purposes entity, a local bank or a finance company;
2) if a special purposes entity issues, or intends to issue, asset-backed debt instruments, the sponsor shall be a Saudi joint stock or limited liability company, a Capital Market Institution licensed to carry on securities business related to the business of special purposes entity, a local bank or a finance company.
3) As an exception to the provisions of Sub-paragraph (1) of Paragraph (a) of this Article, if a special purposes entity issues, or intends to issue, debt-based recourse debt instruments, asset-linked recourse debt instruments through a private placement, the sponsor may be a Saudi limited liability company.

(b) A sponsor, that is not a Capital Market Institution, must submit to the Authority, at its request, a legal opinion that demonstrate that the business it carries on in relation to the special purposes entity does not require authorization under the Capital Market Law. The legal opinion referred to in this Paragraph must be issued by an independent lawyer/law firm licensed in the Kingdom.

Article 12: Restrictions on Sponsor Rights Towards Special Purposes Entity Neither a sponsor, nor any of its affiliates, may have any interest in, or claims against, the assets of the special purposes entity other than claims fully and fairly disclosed in the special purposes entity's documents.

Article 13: Notifications and Record-Keeping Requirements and Powers of the Authority
(a) A sponsor shall ensure that:

1) it complies with the notification requirements set out in Annex (1) of these Rules, which apply to it; and
2) all information it provides to the Authority in relation to its sponsorship is complete, clear, accurate and not misleading.

(b) Upon receiving a notification under Paragraph (a) of this Article, the Authority may require the sponsor to provide any information it considers necessary.

(c) A sponsor must record and retain sufficient information about its sponsorship to demonstrate compliance with these Rules, this includes records of all financial transactions with or relating to the special purposes entity. Such records must be maintained for a minimum of (10) years, in case of any litigation or claim (including any litigation pending or threatened) or any on- going investigations procedures relating to these information and records, the sponsor must retain such information and records until the closure of that litigation, claim or on-going investigation procedures.

(d) A sponsor must promptly provide the Authority with any information and documents that the Authority may require for the purpose of applying the provisions of the Capital Market Law and its Implementing Regulations.

(e) A sponsor must disclose its name and address in the debt instruments issuance prospectus.

Article 14: Changing Sponsor A sponsor of the special purposes entity that issues or intends to issue debt instruments may not be changed, except in the event of its bankruptcy and after obtaining the Authority's approval on such.

38.3.1 CHAPTER 5: TRUSTEE OF A SPECIAL PURPOSES ENTITY

Article 15: Trustee of a Special Purposes Entity
(a) The trustee of a special purposes entity shall not be deemed an owner of the special purposes entity, and it may not dispose of the shares of the special purposes entity registered under its name or carry out any structural changes in the special purposes entity unless the Authority's approval is obtained.

(b) Neither a trustee of the special purposes entity, nor any of its affiliates, may have any interest in, or claims against, the assets of the special purposes entity other than claims fully and fairly disclosed in the special purposes entity's documents.

(c) The sponsor may not be the trustee of the special purposes entity in the event that such sponsor is the beneficiary of the special purposes entity.

(d) In the event that the special purposes entity issues asset-backed debt instruments or asset-linked recourse debt instruments, the trustee of the special purposes entity must be a Capital Market Institution licensed to carry on custody business in the event that it takes custody of the assets of such entity in accordance to the provisions set out in Chapter (7) of this Part.

(e) The registered office of the special purposes entity may not be transferred to any other place except after obtaining a written consent of the trustee of the special purposes entity.

Article 16: Responsibilities of the Trustee of a Special Purposes Entity
(a) The trustee of the special purposes entity shall appoint the members of the board of directors, determine their remuneration, and ensure that they carry out all their duties and responsibilities towards the special purposes entity and the debt instruments holders.

(b) The trustee of the special purposes entity shall appoint a custodian to be responsible for taking custody of real estate assets and securities owned by the special purposes entity, and for taking all the administrative measures related to the custody of those real estate assets and securities in accordance with the provisions set out in Chapter (7) of this Part.

(c) The trustee of the special purposes entity is responsible for appointing an auditor for the special purposes entity.

Article 17: Changing the Trustee of the Special Purposes Entity Other than the cases in which the sponsor is the trustee of the special purposes entity, the sponsor may change the trustee of the special purposes entity in the event of its failure to carry out its responsibilities in accordance with the provisions of these Rules, or upon its failure to fulfill any of its obligations toward the sponsor or the special purposes entity.

38.3.2 CHAPTER 6: BOARD OF DIRECTORS

Article 18: Board Membership Requirements
(a) The directors of a special purposes entity must be registered with the Authority at all times in accordance with these Rules.

(b) A special purposes entity must have, at least, two board members, and all directors of a special purposes entity must fulfill the requirements of this Chapter.

Article 19: Residence At least one of the directors must be resident in the Kingdom.

Article 20: Appointment, Removal and Remuneration of Directors
(a) A special purposes entity's by-laws shall provide the procedures to appoint and remove directors and their remuneration.

(b) A person who is appointed as director shall comply with the special purposes entity's by-laws and all of its provisions.

Article 21: Duties of Directors
(a) A director of a special purposes entity owes the following duties towards the special purposes entity:

1) To act in accordance with the special purposes entity's by-laws.
2) To exercise its powers only for the purposes for which they are conferred.
3) To exercise its powers in a manner that does not conflict with the interests of the special purposes entity.
4) A director is responsible for ensuring that the special purposes entity carries on its businesses in accordance with these Rules.
5) The members of the board of directors must submit an annual report to the trustee of the special purposes entity that includes details of the businesses and decisions related to the issued debt instruments, and any relevant information or documents required by the trustee of the special purposes entity.

(b) A director must provide the Authority with all the information and documents required by the Authority.

(c) The provisions of this Article shall apply to any person who fulfills the role of a director of a special purposes entity, whether such person is registered or delegated in accordance with the provisions of Article (24) of these Rules.

(d) The Authority may carry out any necessary measures related to the role of a director of a special purposes entity.

Article 22: Decision-Making
(a) The special purposes entity's by-laws must specify the decision-making processes to be followed by directors.

(b) Minutes must be kept of every directors' meeting and of every resolution made by them.

Article 23: Powers and Authorities The directors of the special purposes entity must have all powers and authorities that do not interrelate with the powers and authorities of the sponsor or the trustee of the special purposes entity in accordance with the provisions of these Rules or the special purposes entity's by-laws. Such powers and authorities of the directors shall cease on and from the point at which the special purposes entity enters into the stage of liquidation.

Article 24: Delegation
(a) Subject to the provisions of Paragraph (b) of this Article, the directors may delegate any of their powers to any person, in writing, without prejudice to the responsibilities of the directors in regards to the exercise of any such delegated powers.

(b) A special purposes entity's board of directors must notify the Authority in writing of any arrangements relating to any director that delegating any of its powers to other person.

Article 25: Responsibilities of the Directors The directors shall be jointly responsible for compensating the special purposes entity or third parties for any damages sustained as a result of the directors violating the provisions of these Rules or the special purposes entity's by-laws, or any wrongful acts committed by them in the performance of their duties mentioned in Article (21) of these Rules. The liability of such shall be on all directors, if the wrongful act was due to their unanimous decision, as for the wrongful act caused by a decision that was not issued unanimously, the objecting director will not be liable as long as it explicitly reflects its objection on the minutes of meeting. Moreover, absenteeism from the meetings shall not consist a cause for pardoning a director from the liability, unless it became evident that the absent director was unaware of such resolution or could not object to it after becoming aware of such.

Article 26: Register of Directors A special purposes entity shall maintain a register of detailed information of each director, in accordance with the information stipulated in the by-laws of the special purposes entity.

Article 27: Registration and the Powers and Procedures of the Authority
a) The application for the registration of a director shall be made on the form prescribed by the Authority.

b) The Authority may carry out any necessary measures related to the registration application made by a director.

Article 28: Notification Requirements
(a) A director shall ensure that:

1) it complies with the notification requirements set out in Annex (1) of these Rules, where applicable; and

2) all information it provides to the Authority under these Rules is complete, clear, accurate and not misleading.

(b) Upon receiving a notification under Paragraph (a) of this Article, the Authority may require the director to provide any information it considers necessary.

Article 29: Suspension or Cancellation of Registration

(a) The Authority may suspend or cancel the registration of a director on notice to the trustee of the special purposes entity, if the director violates any provision of the Capital Market Law or its Implementing Regulations, commits any offense involving fraud, any act involving a lack of integrity and dishonesty or becomes insolvent.

(b) The trustee of the special purposes entity may terminate the services of a director upon its request or as otherwise provided by the provisions of these Rules or the by-laws of the special purposes entity.

(c) If a director's registration is suspended or cancelled, the trustee of the special purposes entity shall ensure that the person immediately ceases to act as a director of the special purposes entity.

(d) The trustee of the special purposes entity must notify the Authority in writing within (7) days of such director ceasing to be a director. Upon receipt of the notice by the Authority, the registration shall be deemed cancelled.

(e) In the event where the number of directors becomes less than the minimum required under Paragraph (b) of Article (18) of these Rules, or the resignation of the director residing in the Kingdom which will result in a violation of Article (19) of these Rules, the trustee of the special purposes entity must make the needed corrective measures to fulfill the requirements referred to, in a period no later than (30) calendar days from the date of the notice referred to in Paragraph (d) of this Article.

(f) A director continues to be subject to the jurisdiction of the Authority from the date of cancelling its registration in respect of any act or omission that occurred as a member of the board of directors, and for (2) years thereafter. And in case of any litigation or claim (including any litigation pending or threatened) or any investigation relating to its duty as a director of the special purposes entity, or the special purposes entity for which it acted as a director, the director with cancelled registration continues to be subject to the jurisdiction of the Authority until the closure of the investigation, litigation or related claim.

38.3.3 CHAPTER 7: CUSTODIAN

Article 30: Appointment of a Custodian

(a) In respect of the issuance of asset-linked recourse debt instruments and asset-backed debt instruments, the trustee of the special purposes entity must appoint a custodian to be responsible for taking custody of real estate assets and securities owned by the special purposes entity (if any) and for safeguarding and taking all administrative measures in relation to such real estate assets and securities in accordance with the provisions of Article (31) of these Rules;

(b) Other than the cases in which the trustee of the special purposes entity is the sponsor, the trustee of the special purposes entity may be the custodian, without prejudice to the obligations prescribed to the custodian as per the provisions of these Rules.

(c) The custodian must be a Capital Market Institution duly authorized to carry on the activity of custody.

(d) The appointment of the custodian must fulfill the following conditions:

1) the custodian must not be a sponsor of the special purposes entity, an affiliate of the sponsor or controlled by it;

2) the agreement under which the custodian is appointed shall:

   a. include a provision that enables the special purposes entity to report any information required under these Rules to the Authority;

   b. be consistent with the obligations of the custodian under this Part; and

   c. not include any encumbrance over the securities of the special purposes entity or right of set-off, or counterclaim with respect to any amounts deposited in an account of the special purposes entity unless clearly disclosed in the prospectus or the private placement offering document, as the case may be.

(e) Any fees, commissions or charges levied by the custodian shall be determined on fair basis.

(f) The special purposes entity must provide the custodian with all necessary data and information to perform its duties according to these Rules.

(g) The trustee of the special purposes entity may terminate the services of the custodian upon its request, or in accordance with the entity's by-laws. When the custodian receives a written notice of such, the custodian must not take any decision or action related to the special purposes entity after being notified of its removal decision, and must take all necessary actions to transfer businesses and all that in its possession related to the assets of special purposes entity.

Article 31: Custody of Real Estate Assets and Securities in Respect of Asset-Linked Recourse or Asset-Backed Transactions

(a) This Article applies in respect of real estate assets and securities owned by a special purposes entity.

(b) The custodian shall separately identify, by registration under the name of the relevant special purposes entity, the real estate assets and securities of the special purposes entity, and shall maintain all necessary documents and records to support the performance of its contractual responsibilities.

(c) A custodian may appoint one or more third parties or affiliates as a sub-custodian in relation to the real estate assets and securities of a special purposes entity. The fees of the sub-custodian shall be paid by the custodian out of its own resources unless otherwise disclosed in the prospectus or private placement offering document, as applicable.

(d) A sub-custodian operating in a jurisdiction outside the Kingdom may be appointed to hold custody of its real estate assets and securities located in other jurisdiction, and it shall be established, authorized and subject to the supervision of a regulator, that employs regulatory standards and requirements at least equivalent to those of the Authority.

(e) Any sub-custodian must be appointed pursuant to a contract in writing and must be a Capital Market Institution authorized to conduct the custody business, provided that the sub-custodian is not a sponsor of the special purposes entity or an affiliate of the sponsor or controlled by it.

(f) The Authority may, at its absolute discretion, assess whether the jurisdiction in which any sub- custodian operates outside the Kingdom has regulatory standards and requirements applicable to, at least equivalent, those applied by the Authority.

(g) The appointment by a custodian to one or more third parties or its affiliates as a sub-custodian does not constitute a prejudice to the custodian's responsibilities, toward its custody of the special purposes entity's real estate assets and securities pursuant to these Rules.

Article 32: Custodian's Notifications and Record-Keeping Requirements and Powers of the Authority

(a) A custodian shall ensure that:

1) it complies with the notification requirements set out in Annex (1) of these Rules, which apply to it; and
2) all information it provides to the Authority in relation to its functions are complete, clear, accurate and not misleading.

(b) Upon receiving a notification under Paragraph (a) of this Article, the Authority may require the custodian to provide any information it considers necessary.

(c) A custodian must record and retain sufficient information about its functions under these Rules, and maintain it in special records to demonstrate compliance with these Rules, this includes records of any financial transactions with or relating to the special purposes entity. Such records must be maintained for a minimum of (10) years, in case of any litigation or claim (including any litigation pending or threatened) or any on-going investigating procedures related to that information and records, the custodian must retain such information and records until the closure of that litigation, claim or on-going investigation procedures.

(d) A custodian must provide the Authority with any information and documents that the Authority may require for the purpose of implementing the Capital Market Law and its Implementing Regulations.

Article 33: Powers of the Authority in Relation to Custodian

(a) Without prejudice to the other relevant powers of the Authority, if the Authority deems that any of the events stipulated in Paragraph (d) of this Article has occurred or may occur, it may do the following:

1) require the custodian to submit any written clarification, information or documents it considers necessary to address any relevant matter.
2) request the custodian or its representative to appear before the Authority and to answer any question and explain any matter that the Authority considers relevant.
3) carry out any enquiries which it considers appropriate;
4) take any action to verify the information rendered by the custodian, including communicating with any relevant entity.
5) remove and replace the custodian.
6) take any other measures as it considers appropriate.

(b) The removal and replacement of the custodian under Subparagraph (5) of Paragraph (a) of this Article shall be effective immediately upon sending a written notice of such from the Authority to the removed custodian. The removed custodian must not take any decision or action related to the special purposes entity after being notified of its removal decision, and must take all necessary measures to transfer business and all that in its possession related to the special purposes entity from which it was removed from taking custody of its assets.

(c) The Authority may disclose the identity of any custodian removed under this Article.

(d) The events referenced in Paragraph (a) of this Article include any of the following:

1) The custodian does not continue to fulfill the conditions, obligations and requirements stipulated in these Rules.
2) The occurrence of any insolvency or bankruptcy case to the custodian.
3) The custodian's violation of any obligations stipulated in the Capital Market Law and its Implementing Regulations or any other relevant laws in the Kingdom.
4) the custodian ceasing to carry on its businesses;
5) the cancellation or suspension of the custodian's authorization;
6) a request by the custodian to cancel its authorizsation;
7) the Authority believing that the custodian has failed, in a manner which the Authority considers material, to comply with the Capital Market Law and its Implementing Regulations; or
8) any other event determined by the Authority to be of sufficient significance.

(e) If the Authority exercises its power pursuant to Paragraph (a) of this Article, the sponsor and special purposes entity shall cooperate fully with the Authority in order to appoint a replacement custodian.

(f) In the event where the trustee of the special purposes entity is the custodian of its assets, the trustee of the special purposes entity must immediately appoint another custodian upon the occurrence of any of the events stipulated in Paragraph (d) of this Article.

38.3.4 CHAPTER 8: ACCOUNTS AND AUDIT

Article 34: Appointment of an Auditor

(a) The special purposes entity's by-laws must provide provisions for the following:

1) the appointment of an auditor registered with the Authority in accordance with the Rules for Registering Auditors of Entities Subject to the Authority's Supervision;
2) the auditor's remuneration and term of office; and
3) procedures for removal of an auditor.

(b) The auditor shall be responsible for reviewing the financial statements stipulated under Paragraph (b) of Article (35) of these Rules, and must at any time have access to the special purposes entity's books, records and other documents. It must be provided with any information and clarifications as it may deem it necessary to obtain in order to verify the assets and liabilities of the special purposes entity.

Article 35: Reports Prepared by Directors

(a) The directors shall, within (1) month of the end of every financial year, prepare a report on the preceding financial year that includes the details referred to in Paragraph (a) of Article (9) of these Rules.

(b) The directors must within (3) months of the end of every financial year prepare the annual financial statements of the special purposes entity, in accordance with the accounting standards approved by the Saudi Organization for Certified Public Accountants, and audited by an auditor in accordance with the auditing standards approved by the Saudi Organization for Certified Public Accountants, and sign it by one of the directors. Provided it includes, among other items, details of all outstanding and issued debt instruments by the special purposes entity.

(c) The directors must immediately after signing the documents referred to in Paragraph (b) of this Article, send a copy of each of them to the Authority.

(d) Paragraphs (b) and (c) of this Article do not apply to a special purposes entity in which all of its debt instruments in issue are debt-based recourse debt instruments.

38.3.5 CHAPTER 9: RECORD KEEPING

Article 36: Record-Keeping
(a) A special purposes entity must keep complete and accurate books and records, which shall include at least the following:

1) the register of directors required by the provisions of Article (26) of these Rules;
2) minutes of all board meetings;
3) all board resolutions and trustee of the special purposes entity decisions where applicable;
4) the terms of all contracts and transactions entered into by the special purposes entity, including in relation to any issuance of debt instruments and any associated financing transactions;
5) details of the special purposes entity's income and expenditure;
6) details of the special purposes entity's assets and liabilities; and

(b) A special purposes entity must make its books and records available to the Authority immediately upon its request.

(c) The special purposes entity must maintain records and information referred to Paragraph (a) of this Article, for (10) years at least. Except if such information is related to a financing transaction, then it shall be kept for a period no less than (3) years from the date of the transaction entitlement or end, whichever is longer. Moreover, in case of any litigation or claim (including any litigation pending or threatened) or any on-going investigating procedures related to that information and records, the special purposes entity must retain such information and records until the closure of that litigation, claim or on-going investigation procedures.

38.3.6 CHAPTER 10: MERGER AND CONVERSION

Article 37: Prohibition on Merger or Conversion
(a) A special purposes entity may not merge with another special purposes entity or other legal person of any kind.

(b) A special purposes entity may not convert into a legal person in any other form.

38.4 PART 3: INVESTMENT FUNDS THAT TAKE THE FORM OF SPECIAL PURPOSES ENTITIES

38.4.1 Chapter 1: PRELIMINARY PROVISIONS

Article 38: Scope and Application
(a) The provisions of this Part shall be limited to investment funds that take the form of a special purposes entity.

(b) The provisions stipulated in the Investment Funds Regulations or the Real Estate Investment Funds Regulations – whichever applies – shall apply to investment funds that take the form of a special purposes entity.

Article 39: Preliminary Provisions
(a) All assets of the special purposes entity are jointly owned by unitholders, and shall be registered under the name of the special purposes entity.

(b) The manager of the investment fund that takes the form of a special purposes entity shall be responsible for managing the special purposes entity, in accordance with the provisions stipulated in the Investment Funds Regulations and the Real Estate Investment Funds Regulations (whichever applies).

(c) The capital of the special purposes entity shall be variable and based on the subscriptions of investors in the related fund.

38.4.2 Chapter 2: AUTHORIZATION

Article 40: Authorization Requirements and Conditions
(a) The manager of an investment fund that intends to issue investment units via a special purposes entity must fill out the part for the establishment of a special purposes entity in the fund establishment's form and shall attach the by-laws form for such entity.

(b) The following conditions must be met at all times:

1) That the investment fund that takes the form of special purposes entity shall be established in accordance with these Rules and the Investment Funds Regulations or the Real Estate Investment Funds Regulations (whichever applies), and complies with all relevant provisions.
2) The special purposes entity shall not engage in any activity other than the following:
   a. issuing investment units.
   b. ancillary activities necessary to achieve its purposes.
   c. The activities stipulated in both the terms and conditions of the fund that takes the form of a special purposes entity, and the by-laws of the special purposes entity.

38.4.3 CHAPTER 3: BY LAWS

Article 41: By-laws
(a) The Authority may prescribe one or more standard forms of by-laws to be adopted by the special purposes entity. Where the Authority has prescribed such standard forms by-laws, no departure from that standard form is permissible without the prior written consent of the Authority, except for adding details required to be included in the standard forms prescribed by the Authority or selections required to be made.

(b) The Authority's approval of the by-laws is required, and upon obtaining approval, the by-laws of the special purposes entity shall be signed by the manager of the investment fund that intends to issue investment units via a special purposes entity in the presence of a notary public or a notary certified in the Kingdom.

38.4.4 Chapter 4: MONITORING PROCEDURES AND SYSTEMS

Article 42: Notifications and Record-Keeping Requirements and Powers of the Authority
(a) A manager of an investment fund that takes the form of a special purposes entity must ensure that:

1) it complies with the notification requirements set out in Annex (1) of these Rules, where applicable; and
2) all information it provides to the Authority are complete, clear, accurate and not misleading.

(b) Upon receiving a notification under Paragraph (a) of this Article, the Authority may require the manager of an investment fund that takes the form of a special purposes entity (where applicable), to provide it with any additional information it considers necessary.

(c) A manager of an investment fund that takes the form of a special purposes entity, must record and retain sufficient information to demonstrate compliance with these Rules, this includes records of all financial transactions with or relating to the special purposes entity. Such records must be maintained for a minimum of (10) years, in case of any litigation or claim (including any litigation pending or threatened) or any on-going investigations procedures relating to these information and records, the fund manager of an investment fund that takes the form of a special purposes entity must retain such information and records until the closure of that litigation, claim or on-going investigation procedures.

(d) A manager of an investment fund that takes the form of special purposes entity must provide the Authority with any information and documents that the Authority may require for the purpose of implementing the Capital Market Law and its Implementing Regulations and relevant laws.

38.5 PART 4: GENERAL PROVISIONS

38.5.1 CHAPTER 1: PROCEDURES AND POWERS OF THE AUTHORITY IN RELATION TO THE AUTHORISATION APPLICATION

Article 43: Procedures and Powers of the Authority in Relation to the Authorization Application
(a) In considering an application made under the provisions of Paragraph (b) of Article (7) or the provisions of Paragraph (a) of Article (40) of these Rules, the Authority may carry out any enquiries that it considers appropriate;

(b) The Authority shall, upon receipt of all information and documents required, notify the sponsor or the manager of an investment fund that intends to issue investment units via a special purposes entity (whichever applies) in writing of the same, and shall make any of the following decisions within (5) days from the date of the notice:

1) to approve the application;
2) to approve the application subject to such conditions and limitations as it considers appropriate; or
3) to reject the application, and provide reasons.

(c) The Authority may reject an application if the Authority deems that the authorization of the special purposes entity may result in a breach of the Capital Market Law or its Implementing Regulations or any other relevant laws.

Article 44: Effect of Authorization Upon approval by the Authority of the application to license the special purposes entity, it shall be registered in the register referenced in Paragraph (a) of Article (49) of these Rules, with the effect that:

1) the special purposes entity shall have a legal personality and financial anatomy capable of exercising all of the functions of a special purposes entity;

2) the special purposes entity, its sponsor or the manager of an investment fund that takes the form of a special purposes entity (where applicable), its trustee (where applicable), and its directors must comply with all provisions of such entity's by-laws, to the effect that each of them understands all the provisions of the by-laws.

38.5.2 CHAPTER 2: LIABILITY TOWARDS PRE-AUTHORIZATION CONTRACTS

Article 45: Pre-Authorization Contracts Any person delegated to make a contract in the name of a special purposes entity before it obtains authorization is personally liable for the obligations arising from such contract unless the special purposes entity, after its establishment, adopts such obligations.

38.5.3 CHAPTER 3: THIRD PARTY RELIANCE

Article 46: Third Party Reliance on Actions of the Special Purposes Entity A person that deals with a special purposes entity is considered aware of the content and restrictions in these Rules and the special purposes entity's by-laws, but shall not be required to confirm the validity of the special purposes entity's internal proceedings.

38.5.4 CHAPTER 4: SETTLEMENT AND INSOLVENCY PROCEEDINGS

Article 47: Compliance with the Bankruptcy Law
(a) A special purposes entity must comply with the provisions of the Bankruptcy Law and its implementing regulations.

(b) A special purposes entity must notify the Authority in writing of the result of any action taken from the Bankruptcy Law procedures, within (14) days of the procedure's completion.

38.5.5 CHAPTER 5: FEES

Article 48: Fees The special purposes entity and the sponsor or the manager of an investment fund that takes the form of a special purposes entity (whichever applies), must pay such fees as the Authority may prescribe.

38.5.6 CHAPTER 6: AUTHORITY REGISTERS

Article 49: Register of Special Purposes Entities
(a) The Authority shall maintain a register of each special purposes entity that is established under these Rules in such form, as it deems appropriate.

(b) This register must record a copy of the special purposes entity's by-laws as at its incorporation, together with any subsequent amendments to the by-laws.

(c) A special purposes entity must notify the Authority immediately of any change to the information specified in Paragraph (b) of this Article.

Article 50: Register of Directors
(a) The Authority shall maintain a register of the directors of each special purposes entity that is established under these Rules in such form, as it deems appropriate.

(b) This register referred to in Paragraph (a) of this Article must record the following details:

1) The name of the special purposes entity and its commercial register;
2) names and addresses of the directors;
3) national identification number, residency identification (iqama) number or passport number of each director, as applicable;
4) nationality of each director;
5) business occupation of each director (if any);
6) date of appointment of each director; and
7) date of removal or resignation of each director (if applicable).

(c) A special purposes entity must promptly notify the Authority of any change to the information specified in Paragraph (b) of this Article.

Article 51: Access to Registers An extract of each of the registers referred to in Article (49) and Article (50) of these Rules shall be made available for public viewing in the manner prescribed by the Authority.

Article 52: Forms The Authority may publish forms to be used for the provision of the information that a special purposes entity is required to provide to the Authority under Articles (49) and (50) of these Rules.

Article 53: Fees The Authority may levy such fees as it deems appropriate in relation to the recording of, and the provision of access to, information required to be kept by it as set out in Articles (49) and (50) of these Rules.

38.5.7 CHAPTER 7: TERMINATION OF A SPECIAL PURPOSES ENTITY

Article 54: Termination of a Special Purposes Entity The special purposes entity shall cease to exist with the end of the purpose for which it was established for. The special purposes entity must notify the Authority in writing of such (14) days prior to the date of its termination.

38.6 PART 5: PUBLICATION AND ENTRY INTO FORCE

Article 55: Publication and Entry into Force These Rules shall become effective as per its approval resolution.

38.7 Annex 1: Notification Requirements

Notifications to be submitted at least (7) days before the relevant event

No.	Notification	Person required to notify	Required documents or information
A)	**Notifications to be submitted at least (7) days before the relevant event related to the establishment and licensing of the special purposes entity**		
1.	Any proposed amendments to the identity of any party responsible for managing the special purposes entity.	Directors of the special purposes entity that issued debt instruments or a manager of an investment fund that takes the form of a special purposes entity.	Details of the proposed amendments; copies of any documents or resolutions on which holders of debt instruments or investment unitholders (whichever applies). are approving the proposed amendments.

Immediate Notifications

No.	Notification	Person required to notify	Required documents or information
A)	**Immediate notifications to be promptly submitted in relevance to the establishment and licensing of the special purposes entity**		
1.	Any breach of the provisions of these Rules.	Sponsor or a manager of an investment fund that takes the form of a special purposes entity and directors of the special purposes entity that issued debt instruments and custodian.	Details of breach; assessment of impact on holders of debt instruments or investment unitholders, whichever applies, and proposed remediation plan.
2.	Any material breach of the terms of an agreement or document relating to the special purposes entity.	Sponsor or a manager of an investment fund that takes the form of a special purposes entity and directors of the special purposes entity that issued debt instruments and custodian.	Details of breach; assessment of impact on holders of debt instruments or investment unitholders, whichever applies, and the proposed remediation plan.
3.	The identification of irregularities in the accounting or other records of the special purposes entity.	Directors of the special purposes entity that issued debt instruments and the sponsor or a manager of an investment fund that takes the form of a special purposes entity and custodian.	Details of irregularities and the proposed remediation plan.
4.	any change to the identity of any person with responsibility for the management of the assets of the special purposes entity.	Directors of the special purposes entity that issued debt instruments or a manager of an investment fund that takes the form of a special purposes entity.	Details of the change.
5.	The insolvency of the sponsor.	Directors of the special purposes entity that issued debt instruments or a manager of an investment fund that takes the form of a special purposes entity.	Time and date of insolvency.
6.	The insolvency of the special purposes entity.	Directors of the special purposes entity that issued debt instruments or a manager of an investment fund that takes the form of a special purposes entity.	Time and date of insolvency.
7.	The insolvency of a registered director.	Directors of the special purposes entity that issued debt instruments or a manager of an investment fund that takes the form of a special purposes entity.	Time and date of insolvency.
8.	Any amendment made to the incomplete, or unclear, or inaccurate, and misleading information previously provided to the Authority, and an explanation of such.	Directors of the special purposes entity that issued debt instruments and custodian and sponsor or a manager of an investment fund that takes the form of a special purposes entity.	

Notifications to be submitted within (7) days

No.	Notification		Person required to notify	Required documents or information
A)	**Notifications to be submitted within seven (7) days related to the establishment and licensing of the special purposes entity**			
1.	Any change to the information submitted in the licensing application relating to the sponsor or the manager of an investment fund that takes the form of a special purposes entity, and shall not be considered among the required notifications under the section above related to immediate notifications.		Sponsor or a manager of an investment fund that takes the form of a special purposes entity.	Details of the change.
2.	Any change to:			
	(a)	the custodian; or	Directors of the special purposes entity that issued debt instruments or a manager of an investment fund that takes the form of a special purposes entity.	Details of the change.
	(b)	the bank which has the account of the special purposes entity.	Custodian.	Details of the change.
3.	The director ceasing to perform his functions.		Directors of the special purposes entity that issued debt instruments or a manager of an investment fund that takes the form of a special purposes entity.	Details of the cessation.

For the purpose of this Annex a person is considered "insolvent" in the event of any of the following occurring:

- becoming unable to pay its debts as they fall due;

- becoming insolvent, as defined under any insolvency laws applicable to it; and

- the commencement of a case or other procedures seeking or proposing liquidation, administration, restructuring its debts, performing settlement arrangements, the freeze or

- moratorium or other similar relief with respect to its debts under any bankruptcy, regulatory, supervisory laws, or seeking the appointment of a liquidator, or other similar officials of the sponsor or any part of the sponsor's assets in any jurisdiction.

39 Circular from the Capital Market Authority regarding its permission for Authorized Persons to enter into Swap Agreements

"**Greetings**,

Reference to the Capital Market Authority's (the "Authority") circular number (5/2132) dated 30/3/1431H corresponding to 16/3/2010G regarding its approval for Authorized Persons to enter into Swap Agreements, we would like to inform you that the Authority's Board of Commissioners has issued its resolution dated 00\00\0000 {stet} corresponding to 00\00\0000 {stet} which amends its resolution dated 20/3/1438H corresponding to 19/12/2016G regarding the approval for Authorized Persons to enter into Swap Agreements, to be as follows:

First: Authorized Persons are permitted to enter into Swap Agreements with foreign counterparties ("Foreign Counterparty") only for the benefit of non-resident foreign investors to transfer the economic benefits of securities listed on the Saudi Stock Exchange (Tadawul) to those investors ("Ultimate Beneficiary") through swap transactions executed under the Swap Agreements: in accordance with the following conditions and requirements:

1) The money and assets of the Ultimate Beneficiary shall be deemed client money and client assets as stated in the Authorized Persons Regulations including, the provisions therein which provide that client money and client assets must be segregated from the Authorized Person's own money and assets, and that the creditors of an Authorized Person do not have any claim or entitlement on the segregated money or assets of the clients.

2) The duration of any Swap Agreement shall not exceed (4) years from the date of its signature.

3) The Authorized Person may not enter into any Swap Agreement or execute any swap transaction where the ultimate beneficiary is any of the following parties:

a. A Qualified Foreign Investor, in accordance with the definition set out in the Rules for Qualified Foreign Financial Institutions Investment in Listed Securities.

b. Citizens of the Cooperation Council for the Arab States of the Gulf (The natural persons who hold the citizenship of one of the Cooperation Council for the Arab States of the Gulf countries, or legal persons that (i) capital of which is majority owned by citizens or governments of the Cooperation Council for the Arab States of the Gulf; and (ii) holding the citizenship of one of the Cooperation Council for the Arab States of the Gulf countries in accordance with the definition set out in the resolution of the Supreme Council of the Cooperation Council for the Arab States of the Gulf in its 15th session approved by the Council of Ministers Resolution number (16) dated 20/01 /1418H which states that:).

c. Foreign investors residing in the Kingdom.

d. A foreign person other than the ones mentioned in subparagraphs (a), (b) and (c) above, that owns securities of a company listed on Tadawul, in relation to swap transactions that involve the shares and convertible debt instruments of that listed company.

4) All orders to execute swap transactions must be sent to the Authorized Person by the foreign counterparty only or by a third party who is authorized by the foreign counterparty.

5) Any Swap Agreement an Authorized Person enters into shall include a clear clause that grants it all the voting rights attached to the shares underlying the swap transactions executed under the Swap Agreement, with no voting rights given to the foreign counterparty or the ultimate beneficiary.

6) An Authorized Person that enters into a Swap Agreement is prohibited from exercising any of the voting rights attached to the shares underlying the swap transactions executed under the Swap Agreements.

7) The Authorized Person that intends to enter into a Swap Agreement must be authorized by the Authority to conduct the securities business of dealing as principal.

8) The Authorized Person must notify the Authority ten working days prior to entering into a Swap Agreement through the automated system determined by the Authority for this purpose.

9) The Authorized Person has to ensure full compliance with the requirements of the Anti-Money Laundering Law and its implementing regulations and the rules issued by the Authority related to Anti-Money Laundering and Counter-Terrorist Financing, and any other related laws and regulations.

10) All Swap transactions must be fully covered during the whole period of the Swap Agreements through buying the underlying securities.

11) The Authorized Person must maintain systems and controls which are adequate enough to ensure the implementation of conditions and requirements of the Swap Agreements and ensure their validity.

12) The Authorized Person shall purchase and sell the securities underlying the swap transactions through an investment portfolio under its name with the Securities Depository Centre. Such investment portfolio shall include an indication that it is for the purpose of executing swap transactions under the Swap Agreement, and an indication of the Ultimate Beneficiary's name, nationality and identification information.

13) The investments of each Ultimate Beneficiary is subject to the following limitations:

a. The total securities underlying the swap transactions executed for each Ultimate Beneficiary must not reach 10% or more of the shares of any issuer whose shares are listed or convertible debt instrument of the issuer.

b. Other legislative limitations on foreign ownership in joint stock companies.

c. The limitations set forth in the articles of association or by-laws of companies listed on Tadawul or any instructions issued by the supervisory or regulatory authorities to which these companies are subject, in relation to foreign ownership.

14) The Authority may order, based on its absolute discretion, any Authorized Person to stop from entering into any Swap Agreements, or to impose any type of limitations, restrictions, or requirements in relation to the Swap Agreements entered by any Authorized Person, or to the foreign counterparty or to {the} ultimate beneficiary.

Second: With an exception of sub-paragraph (a) of paragraph (3) of the circular, the Authorized Person can continue to execute transactions under the swap agreement for the foreign investor who is accepted as qualified foreign investor (QFI) for a period not exceeding twelve months from the date of opening the QFI account. Provided that the total investments through swap transactions or through the QFI account or both must not reach 10% of the shares of any issuer whose shares are listed or convertible debt instrument of the issuer.

If you have any further clarification, please contact Investment Product Development Department via email QFI@cma.org.sa, or phone number 011-4906006."

www.ingramcontent.com/pod-product-compliance
Ingram Content Group UK Ltd.
Pitfield, Milton Keynes, MK11 3LW, UK
UKHW052301280926
15471UKWH00006B/1042

9 781945 979231